The Transnational Studies Reader

D0223448

Studying contemporary social life by comparing experiences within or across nations blinds us to many of the ways the world actually works. And the social scientists, from a variety of disciplines, who do study dynamics that cross borders tend to see themselves as part of different conversations. They look at transnational corporations, religions, the art world, or social movements in isolation and therefore fail to notice the many forms and patterns these domains have in common. But it turns out that transnational economic life displays many similarities with its transnational social, political and religious counterparts. What's more, these arrangements challenge deeply held notions about citizenship, democracy, and identity. Professors Sanjeev Khagram and Peggy Levitt believe that a new optic, which asks a different set of questions based on different assumptions, is called for.

This reader lays out the theoretical, methodological, and philosophical parameters of this new field, Transnational Studies, and highlights much of the scholarship that constitutes its intellectual foundations.

Sanjeev Khagram is Faculty Director of the Lindenberg Center and Associate Professor of Public Affairs and International Studies at the University of Washington. He is also Co-Director of the Transnational Studies Initiative and Co-Lead Steward of Global Action Networks-Net. He was previously Acting Dean of the Desmond Tutu Peace Centre and a faculty member at Harvard University's JFK School of Government. He published the book *Dams and Development* in 2004 and his co-authored book entitled *Transnational Architectures of Economic Life: Dynamics and Corporate Citizenship and Market Regulation* will also be available in 2008.

Peggy Levitt is Associate Professor and Chair of Sociology at Wellesley College and a Research Fellow at The Weatherhead Center and The Hauser Center at Harvard University where she co-directs the Transnational Studies Initiative. Her new book, *God Needs No Passport: Immigrants and the Changing American Religious Landscape*, was published in spring 2007.

ROUTLEDGE TITLES OF RELATED INTEREST

Australia: Nation, Belonging, and Globalization by Anthony Moran

Critical Globalization Studies, edited by Richard P. Applebaum and William I. Robinson

Deciphering the Global: Its Scales, Spaces and Subjects, edited by Saskia Sassen

Disposable Women and Other Myths of Global Capitalism by Melissa W. Wright

China and Globalization by Douglas Guthrie

Global Hong Kong by Gary McDonogh

Global Ireland: Same Difference by Tom Inglis

The Globalization of Israel: McWorld in Tel Aviv; Jihad in Jerusalem by Uri Ram

The Koreas by Charles Armstrong

Morocco: Globalization and its Consequences by Shana Cohen and Larabi Jaidi

The Netherlands: Globalization and National Identity by Frank J. Lechner

On Argentina and the Southern Cone by Alejandro Grimson and Gabriel Kessler

Surveillance and Security: Technological Politics and Power in Everyday Life
by Torin Monahan

Forthcoming

Globalizing Iberia by Gary McDonogh

Iran by Camron Amin

Turkey by Alev Cinar

The Transnational Studies Reader

Intersections and Innovations

Sanjeev Khagram and Peggy Levitt

EDITORS

Routledge
Taylor & Francis Group

NEW YORK AND LONDON

First published 2008
by Routledge
270 Madison Ave, New York, NY 10016

Simultaneously published in the UK
by Routledge
2 Park Square, Milton Park, Abingdon, Oxon OX14 4RN

Routledge is an imprint of the Taylor & Francis Group, an informa business

© 2008 Taylor and Francis

Typeset in Sabon by RefineCatch Limited, Bungay, Suffolk
Printed and bound in the United States of America on acid-free paper by
Edwards Brothers, Inc., Lillington, NC

Library of Congress Cataloging in Publication Data
The transnational studies reader : intersections and innovations / edited by Sanjeev Khagram and Peggy Levitt.
    p. cm.
  Includes bibliographical references.
  ISBN 978–0–415–95372–6 (cloth) – ISBN 978–0–415–95373–3 (pbk.) 1. Social movements. 2. International organization. 3. World politics. I. Khagram, Sanjeev. II. Levitt, Peggy, 1957–
  HM881.T77 2008
  303.48′409–dc22
  2007032643

ISBN10: 0–415–95372–3 (hbk)
ISBN10: 0–415–95373–1 (pbk)
ISBN10: 0–203–93591–8 (ebk)

ISBN13: 978–0–415–95372–6 (hbk)
ISBN13: 978–0–415–95373–3 (pbk)
ISBN13: 978–0–203–93591–0 (ebk)

CONTENTS

SECTION 2. METHODOLOGICAL PRACTICES

SECTION 3. HISTORICAL PERSPECTIVES

SECTION 4. QUESTIONS OF IDENTITY

SECTION 5. MIGRATING LIVES AND COMMUNITIES

SECTION 6. RELIGIOUS LIFE ACROSS BORDERS

SECTION 7. ARTS AND CULTURE

SECTION 8. THE DIFFUSION OF IDEAS, VALUES, AND CULTURE

SECTION 11. SECURITY, CRIME, AND VIOLENCE

PREFACE AND ACKNOWLEDGEMENTS

This jointly and equally conceived and co-edited volume began with a generative conversation between us in Cambridge several years ago. We had each been exploring and examining different sorts of phenomena and dynamics: migration and religion on the one hand; civil society and corporations on the other hand. Yet we realized that the ways we had begun to explore them were strikingly aligned. Our struggles to convey our insights to others were also similar.

The vision we excitedly generated was to help build an interdisciplinary field of transnational studies. We knew many scholars like ourselves who were also pushing the disciplinary boundaries of research on subjects ranging from the ones we had been working on to many others including culture, identities, ideas, crime, and violent conflict.

As we elaborate in the introductory chapter, what unites the field of transnational studies together is a critique of scholarship that takes nation-states and the nation-state system for granted, as well as other perspectives that do not take them seriously enough, like many of the conceptual perspectives on globalization. In contrast, transnational studies starts from the assumption that human interactions and social life have always involved the crossing and transforming of borders and boundaries from the trans-local to the transcontinental.

We have been very fortunate, while compiling this reader, to have received so much support from our colleagues, friends, and families. This project began when we were both affiliated with the Hauser Center for Nonprofit Organizations at Harvard University. We thank Mark Moore, Derek Bok, Shawn Bowen, Tiziana Dearing, L. David Brown, and Srilatha Batliawala for their vision and dedication.

Our work was also generously supported by the Kennedy School of Government and Weatherhead Center at Harvard University, Atlantic Philanthropies, the Ford Foundation, the Watson Institute at Brown University, Wellesley College, and the Stanford Institute for International Studies. This project would never have been completed without the financial and institutional contributions of the Lindenberg Center, Evans School, and Jackson School at the University of Washington.

We benefited greatly from our generative conversations along the way with Joseph Nye, Saskia Sassen, Alison Brysk, Gabrielle Bammer, Peter Dobkin Hall, Federico Besserer, Ludger Pries, Sally Merry, Nina Glick Schiller, Suzanne Shanahan, Peter Katzenstein, Lynn Eden, Taeku Lee, John Meyer, and so many others. The many colleagues who participated in the Transnational Studies Initiative's (www.transnational-studies.org) working groups and seminars over the past five years also contributed greatly to our thinking.

We thank David McBride, the editor who began with us on this project, and Steve Rutter and Ann Horowitz who saw it through to completion. Sarah Alvord, Wasim Rahman, Laura Ax, Kate Talbot-Minkin, Kate Skinner, Catrina Lucero, and several others made invaluable contributions along the way. We are particularly grateful to Karen Brooks without whom this book may never have seen the light of day. And, most of all, we thank our families – Raul, Ram, Regina, Urmila, and Ramesh for Sanjeev, and Robert, Dylan, and Wesley for Peggy. We dedicate this book to you.

NOTE ON TEXT EDITS

The chapters in this volume are mostly shortened versions of the original published pieces. Where cuts have been made, ellipses have been inserted in the text to indicate where these have occurred.

. . .   indicates omission of a few words in a sentence

[. . .]   within a paragraph indicates omission of at least a whole sentence

[. . .]   at the end of a paragraph or above the first paragraph in the piece indicates that at least a whole paragraph has been omitted

CHAPTER 1

Constructing Transnational Studies

Sanjeev Khagram and Peggy Levitt[1]

Social life crosses, transcends and sometimes transforms borders and boundaries in many different ways. Social movements mobilize constituencies around the globe on issues such as human rights, gender justice, and family values campaigns. Many adherents of pan-Muslim, Hindu, Christian, and other faith-based movements value their religious membership more than their national or ethnic allegiances. Economies are organized around transcontinental investment, manufacturing, and consumption chains. Associations set common standards for professionals working around the world. Hip-hop "heads" in Gugulettu and Rio draw inspiration from their Los Angeles counterparts; and tandoori chicken has become one of London's snack foods of choice.

The destruction of the World Trade Center, one of the most potent symbols of global capitalism, by members of the cross-border Al Qaeda terrorist network is a striking example of the "transnational" nature of the world.[2] While the U.S. government's response was to reassert the primacy of the nation-state, even a superficial analysis reveals that various transnational phenomena and dynamics—money laundering and criminal networks, trans-governmental police coalitions, dispersed but linked diasporic communities, humanitarian civil society nongovernmental organizations, and multinational business initiatives—were at work pre- and post-September 11th.

These ostensibly novel transnational phenomena have clear historical analogues. One need only think of colonialism and imperialism, missionary campaigns, anti-slavery and workers' movements, pirating networks, and jazz. Indeed, human social formations and processes have always been trans-border and trans-boundary to varying degrees. Even contemporary nation-states and the nation-state system have been transnationally constituted and shaped over time and space in powerful ways.

Studying contemporary social dynamics by comparing experiences within or across presumably bounded or closed societies or social units—whether they are localities, regions, nation-states, empires, or world systems—necessarily comes up short. Cross-border forms and processes are the focus of a burgeoning yet fragmented body of scholarship undertaken across the social sciences.[3] But the researchers working in these areas do not generally see themselves as part of the same conversation. They study transnational corporations, religions, or social movements in isolation from each other, without bringing to light the forms and patterns these domains share. Because, as it turns out, transnational economic forms and processes have a lot in common with their transnational political and religious counterparts, and these arrangements challenge deeply held notions about citizenship, democracy, and identity, we believe a new optic, which asks a different set of questions based on different epistemological assumptions, is called for. Not all of the scholars we include in Transnational Studies (TS) would identify with or agree with our intellectual agenda and, if they do, they are likely to disagree over its intellectual foundations. These differences, however, are as important to the vitality and prospects for transnational scholarship as are the areas of overlap and agreement.

Based on an ongoing, in-depth survey of scholarship to date, Transnational Studies includes at least five intellectual foundations:

1. **Empirical Transnationalism** *focuses on describing, mapping, classifying, and quantifying novel and/or potentially important transnational phenomena and dynamics.* These transnational processes are understood to be derivative of, or stand in contrast to, bounded and bordered units, actors, structures and processes that are generally associated with the local, regional, global, or the nation-state system. TS uses comparative–historical and ethnographic strategies to identify and explain similarities, differences, linkages, and interactions among different transnational phenomena. It looks at the social spaces in which these emerge, what flows within them, and the mechanisms of transmission. It also examines the differences between transnational and bounded forms and processes across space and over time.

2. **Methodological Transnationalism** involves, at a minimum, *reclassifying existing data, evidence, and historical and ethnographic accounts that are based on bounded or bordered units so that transnational forms and processes are revealed.* Even more so, it requires creating and implementing novel research designs and methodologies generating new types of data, evidence, and observations that more accurately and rigorously capture transnational realities. This often requires utilizing non-traditional or multiple units of inquiry, levels of analysis, and time frames. It means paying close attention to the interaction between the levels of social experience rather than giving greater analytical weight to one over the other.

3. **Theoretical Transnationalism** *formulates explanations and crafts interpretations that either parallel, complement, supplement, or are integrated into existing theoretical frameworks and accounts.* In some cases, theories generated by TS complement conventional theories by identifying and explaining previously obscured kinds of phenomena and dynamics. In others, transnational theories elucidate some aspects of these forms and processes better than traditional theories. Transnational theories may also compete with explanations of phenomena and dynamics previously theorized in local, national, international, or global terms. Finally, transnational accounts might be integrated with conventional explanations, which combined, produce more compelling theoretical accounts.

4. **Philosophical Transnationalism** *starts from the metaphysical assumption that social worlds and lives are inherently transnational.* In other words, transnational phenomena and dynamics are the rule rather than the exception, the underlying reality rather than a derivative by-product. Such a view *requires an epistemological lens or way of researching, theorizing, and understanding social relations that allows analysts to uncover and explain the transnational dynamics in which bounded and bordered entities are embedded and by which the latter are constituted.* Any explanation or interpretation that does not inquire about, identify, and explicate the proximate or deeper transnational forms and processes involved would be incomplete. This does not mean that TS does not enter into conversation with other philosophies of knowledge. Nor does it mean that every question evokes a transnational answer or that cross-border forces and factors are always at play. On the contrary, TS is purposefully framed to encourage encounters and exchanges with other perspectives from the positivist to the interpretivist to the constructivist. Its goal is to bring into sharp focus the interaction between different levels and sites of social experience.

5. **Public Transnationalism** creates space to imagine and legitimate options for social change and transformation that are normally obscured, by purposefully abandoning the expectation that most social processes are bounded and bordered. By letting go of this assumption, questions and problems can be reframed and innovative approaches may come to light that are obscured when we assume that the national is the primary organizing axis.

The first three pillars of TS are fairly common in the scholarly literature. The last two are less well represented because they challenge conventional paradigms and praxis more fundamentally, moving beyond dominant forms of scholarship, philosophical assumptions, and prescriptive orientations.

In the next section, we begin to differentiate transnational scholarship from existing perspectives and paradigms, distinctions we develop further throughout this article. We then lay out Transnational Studies' five intellectual foundations. We conclude by summarizing our central arguments and proposing ways to create a social science community that is itself transnational to achieve these intellectual goals.

DISTINGUISHING TRANSNATIONAL SCHOLARSHIP

Transnational scholarship is not entirely new nor does it argue for jettisoning completely related research paradigms and perspectives. But, as Hannerz (1996, p. 6) notes (see Chapter 20), it is a response to both strengths and weaknesses in contemporary scholarship:

> I am rather uncomfortable with the rather prodigious use of the term globalization to describe just about any process or relationship that somehow crosses state boundaries. In themselves, many such processes and relationships obviously do not at all extend across the world. The term "transnational" is in a way more humble, and often a more adequate label for phenomena which can be of quite variable scale and distribution, even when they do share the characteristic of not being contained within a state. It also makes the point that many of the linkages in question are not "international," in the strict sense of (only) involving nations—actually, states—as corporate actors. In the transnational arena, the actors may now be individuals, groups, movements, business enterprises, and in no small part it is this diversity of organization we need to consider. (At the same time, there is a certain irony in the tendency of the term transnational to draw attention to what it negates—that is, to the continued significance of the national.)

This view, which we associate largely with empirical transnationalism, and thus only a step in the direction we wish to pursue, nonetheless provides an entry point into the potential distinctiveness of transnational scholarship.

World systems and world society research, as well as more recent forays into globalization or global studies, have much to say about aspects of transnational forms and processes—particularly those that are transplanetary or at least transcontinental in scope. Few can deny the World System's Perspective's role in intellectually de-centering the nation-state as the predominant organizing principle of social experience. Building on this premise, World Society scholars have compellingly argued that nation-states are constituted and conditioned by worldwide cognitive and ideational scripts accounting for a range of formal institutions and organizations otherwise poorly explained.[4]

But this "worldist" scholarship tends to equate all trans-border and trans-boundary phenomena with planetary integration and worldwide isomorphism. Structures and processes that are really quite different are depicted as comparable in strength and character wherever they occur. Variations in scale and scope and the multidirectionality of flows and interactions are often overlooked. Even David Held who, with his colleagues, has developed some of the most nuanced theoretical ideas and empirical analysis in this field, conceptualizes globalization as "a process (or set of processes) which embodies a transformation in the spatial organization of social relations and transactions . . . generating transcontinental or interregional flows and networks of activity, interaction, and the exercise of power" (Held *et al.*, 1999, p. 1).[5]

Globalist scholarship, then, is often not fine-tuned enough to capture cross-border agents, structures, and interactions that are not all worldwide in scope. It often assumes a level of convergence and homogenization that does not occur. Furthermore, actors tend to be depicted as so heavily constrained that they cannot possibly react against these universalistic systemic forces. As Beverly Silver (2003) points out, for World Systems and World Society perspectives, "local attributes and behavior are seen as the product of a unit's location in the system. The larger system has a steamroller-like quality, transforming social relations at the local level along a theoretically expected path" (Silver, 2003, pp. 25–26, see Chapter 11, pp. 136–137 in this volume). Perhaps most importantly, much worldist and globalist scholarship takes for granted the very existence of bounded or bordered social units—particularly the "world" or the "nation-state"—and the structures and processes associated within them.[6]

Research focusing on the local, that equates micro-territorial units with micro-cultural communities, also contributes a great deal to the elucidation of transnational phenomena and dynamics. Especially in this period of globalization frenzy, this scholarship reminds us of the potential autonomy and enduring importance of other, personalized life-spaces. It drives home the importance of the socio-historical context and the danger of making universalistic generalizations that wash out critical shades of difference. It also demonstrates the continuing importance of individual agency, local knowledge, and cultural practices.[7]

But while these studies produce richly detailed accounts of local territorial and cultural spaces, they frequently overlook how broader social processes influence these localities. A great deal is learned about a particular site and a particular time but not enough about how the "local" is historically situated and connected to other levels and sites of social interaction. In contrast, a transnationally-oriented problematic answers the question so cogently framed by Arjun Appadurai, "What can locality mean in a world where spatial localization, quotidian interaction, and social scale are not always isomorphic?" (Appadurai, 1996, p. 167).[8] Moreover, a transnational lens opens up the possibility of conceptualizing the local or the micro in non-territorial terms such as an economic development project, the "cell" of a broader criminal network, the multi-sited patron saint day celebration, or a link in a larger commodity chain.

A transnational perspective does not assume away the importance of the global and local, or the nation-state system form.[9][10] It invites us to think about how these categories change when we don't assume that they are automatically linked to particular types of territory or space. It pushes us to confront how taken for granted categories, such as citizenship and identity, change when they are constituted across space.

Because the social sciences came of age in the nineteenth and twentieth centuries, during an intense period of "national-state" growth and legitimation, terms like "society," "government," "democracy," and "culture" carry with them embedded nationalist assumptions that impair our capacity to grasp transnational forms and processes.[11] Research on twentieth-century business development almost always uses comparative approaches that take the nation-state for granted instead of conceptualizing firms and markets as parts of cross-border networks of investment, production, distribution, and exchange.[12] Studies of religion and politics have been similarly hampered, despite abundant evidence that movements as diverse as evangelical Protestantism, Roman Catholicism, freemasonry, trade unionism, and political progressivism ignore national boundaries and create powerful transnational communities and identities.[13]

A number of scholars have called into question the widespread view that the social is automatically organized into neat, nation-state containers (Gupta and Ferguson, 1997a; Sparke, 2002; Braithwaite and Drahos, 2000). Such a view obscures the many processes, relations, and institutions that pre-date, cross, and transform borders and boundaries. It also gives too much credence to the historically recent, uneven, and incomplete articulation of the nation-state system.[14]

Transnational Studies goes even further by advancing the claim that the global, regional, national, and the local can be analyzed through transnational methodological, theoretical, and epistemological lenses; that is in contrast to traditional perspectives, which see transnational phenomena and dynamics as a subset of those occurring somewhere between the national and the global, TS includes another, in some cases, more productive option. What are assumed to be bounded and bordered social units are understood as transnationally constituted, embedded, and influenced social arenas that interact with one another.[15] From this perspective, the world consists of multiple sets of dynamically overlapping and interacting transnational social fields that create and shape seemingly bordered and bounded structures, actors, and processes.

Thus, the terms "transnational" or "transnationalism" or "transnationality" are partly misnomers, in that they imply that the only things we are interested in are dynamics across or beyond nations, states, or within the (nation-) state system. We also mean something else. By transnational, we propose an optic or gaze that begins with a world without borders, empirically examines the boundaries and borders that emerge at particular historical moments, and explores their relationship to unbounded arenas and processes. It does not take the existence of, or appropriateness of, the spatial unit of analysis for granted. A transnational perspective is also, therefore, a way of understanding the world, a shared set of questions and puzzles, and a different expectation about what constitutes an acceptable answer. In some cases, cross-border factors figure only peripherally in the dynamics we are trying to explain. A key component of a transnational approach, however, is to interrogate the territorial breadth and scope of any social phenomenon without prior assumptions.

At present, everyday and scholarly language does a poor job capturing transnational dynamics. Nevertheless, a heuristically powerful set of ideas and options is emerging that helps to clarify TS both conceptually and analytically. These intellectual foundations call into question fundamental assumptions about a range of sociological concerns. In the following section, we elaborate the components of a transnational perspective in greater detail.

EMPIRICAL TRANSNATIONALISM

A first foundation of TS **involves the identification, description, mapping, quantification, and categorization of transnational phenomena and dynamics.** Much of the scholarship on transnationalism to date addresses these tasks. Transnational economic processes and corporations, transnational social movements and nongovernmental organizations, and transnational migration and communities have received the bulk of attention.[16] There are also growing empirical literatures on transnational misconduct and governance but less work on subjects such as transnational religion, art and culture, and social stratification.[17]

Identification and description of a broad range of forms and processes, including ethnic communities, religions, professional associations, and terrorist groups, are two essential tasks of Empirical Transnationalism.[18] TS also encompasses discourses, material flows, cultural interactions, and artistic genres that are produced and exchanged across borders. It is concerned about what circulates, how it moves, and with explaining why certain ideas and practices take root while others are ignored. For example, according to Leslie Sklar, a novel transnational capitalist class has emerged that includes executives of multinational corporations, globalizing bureaucrats and politicians, professionals, merchants, and media that promote the globalization of capitalism and an associated consumer culture.[19] Mary Kaldor maps the transnational dynamics of "new wars" waged by a range of non-state actors and processes including ethnic militias, *hawala* financing, and U.N. peace-keepers.[20] Jackie Smith and colleagues identify transnational social movements while Margaret Keck and Kathryn Sikkink describe transnational advocacy networks as sets of activists across at least three countries linked by shared principled ideas and dense exchanges of information.[21] Peggy

Levitt and Sally Merry compare the translation of global ideas about women's rights in different local contexts.[22]

This descriptive work has generated useful generative classification systems. Consider the following typology of transnational collective actors categorized by their central motivation. Transnational corporations are organized around profit, social movements around moral values, epistemic communities around scientific ideas, professions around technical expertise and shared standards, and trans-governmental networks around common mandates.[23] These groups can then be sorted according to whether they employ physical violence. Like corporations, transnational criminal organizations are motivated by material gain, but unlike their profit-seeking counterparts they often use physical violence to achieve their goals.[24] Like cross-border social movements, transnational terrorists are likely to be motivated by powerful principled ideas, but unlike their social movement counterparts they often use violence to pursue them.

These analyses also point to the ways in which actors embedded in transnational social fields occupy similar positions and fulfill similar kinds of roles regardless of whether they are involved in economic, religious, or political activism. In social movement organizations, criminal networks, or firms, some people function as transporters and transmitters of new ideas and practices, while others act as translators or transformers.[25] They also bring to light patterns in organizational form. Migrant and religious networks share many structural features with the many money transfer networks that also operate across space. Bounded solidarity and enforceable trust are at work in these very different social groups.

METHODOLOGICAL TRANSNATIONALISM

To empirically map and categorize transnational phenomena and dynamics, as we have outlined, requires new kinds of observations and new kinds of methods for collecting them. A second intellectual foundation of TS—Methodological Transnationalism—**reformulates existing data and accounts, invents new kinds of information and evidence, applies existing investigative approaches in novel ways, and designs novel research tools and approaches with which to analyze, explain, and interpret transnational phenomena and dynamics.**

Most existing data sets, historiographies, and ethnographies make transnational analyses difficult if not impossible. They suffer from what is called "methodological nationalism" or the tendency to accept the nation-state form and even its contemporary borders as given. Many surveys are based on national-state units and are designed to make comparisons between countries. They were not designed to capture flows, linkages, or identities that cross or supersede other spatial units or the phenomena and dynamics within them. Understanding the regional identities generated in response to environmental crises, the trans-territorial underpinnings of organized crime, or the existence of transnational stratification systems is difficult because so few data lend themselves to these kinds of analyses. The researcher can only make inferences based on information from national (or other bounded) data sets that are unlikely to reveal transnational dynamics easily or cleanly.

Transnational scholarship requires that data be collected on multiple units, scales, and scopes of analysis.[26] Saskia Sassen's identification of the global city, Paul Gilroy's conceptualization of the Black Atlantic, and Arjun Appadurai's notion of scapes are all examples of this kind of research. While multi-sited and multi-level research is ideal for studying these interactions, transnational dynamics can also be investigated by asking interviewees about the cross-border aspects of their identities, beliefs, and activities, and those they are connected to, in a single setting.[27] TS thus reorients researchers away from traditional geographies of inquiry toward queries about the actual topography of social life.

Transnational scholarship also requires methods that can capture the complex temporalities in which particular dynamics or relations occur. Postmodern insights about time/space compression challenge expectations about the relationship between geography and history.[28] Transnational scholarship builds upon these by employing life-cycle, cross-generational, long duree, epiphenomenal, and cyclical types of temporal analyses.[29]

Transnational dynamics cannot be studied at one point in time because they involve multiple, interacting processes rather than single, bounded events. For example, because transnational migrants' practices ebb and flow over long periods, a one-time snapshot misses how people periodically engage with their home countries during election cycles, family or ritual events, or climatic catastrophes—their attention and energies shifting in response to a particular goal or challenge. Studying migrant practices longitudinally reveals that in moments of crisis or opportunity, even those who have never identified or participated transnationally, but who are embedded in transnational social fields, may be mobilized into action.[30]

Moreover, what makes the outsourcing of many high-tech service jobs to Bangalore and other "high-tech" cities possible today is that when people are asleep in Silicon Valley, it is the workday in South Asia and vice versa. The fact that, over the last 50 years, more and more South Asians have been educated and lead professional lives that cross borders has also contributed to these changing economic arrangements. Finally, even a brief foray into history drives home the necessity of taking the *long duree*. Most of the contemporary territorially demarcated states did not even exist at the turn of the nineteenth century.[31] In contrast to the current state of affairs in Iraq, for instance, Baghdad was the center of a transcontinental regional political-economic field that existed in the ninth century.

Beverly Silver's research strategy for her book, *Forces of Labor*, on workers' movements, provides an exciting example of transnational methodological innovation. She begins by engaging both the "encompassing comparison" utilized in world historical work and long-standing comparative-historical methods for cross-national research. But, Silver argues, these methods are inherently limited. They impede the analysis of relations between and among allegedly separate units, they obscure local agency, and they are based on assumptions about the type, if not characteristics, of the bounded units of analysis, even though how these units are constructed and transformed is a critical piece of the analysis. In response, Silver uses a combined "incorporating comparison" research methodology and modified "narrative mode" of causal analysis to capture how relational processes in space unfold in and through time.[32]

THEORETICAL TRANSNATIONALISM

Methodologically innovative research contributes to and is shaped by theory and theory building. A third intellectual foundation for the field of TS is to **construct and test explanations and craft interpretations that either parallel, complement, replace, or transform existing theoretical accounts.**

Many scholars recognize transnational phenomena and have proposed theoretical accounts to explain them. Transnational theories interact with conventional theories in several ways. In some cases, they are **parallel** exercises because they interpret or explain different phenomena and dynamics. In other **complementary** cases, they do a better job at explaining some aspects of the phenomena under study, while traditional theories are better at explaining others. Transnational theories also **compete** with accounts and models that are already well developed in local, national, international, or global terms. Finally, transnational scholarship is sometimes used in **combination** with conventional conceptual frameworks to generate hybrid theoretical accounts.

The academic enterprise is often about which theory wins. There is no question that competitive hypothesis testing plays a vital role in the development of knowledge. In the 1970s, Robert Keohane and Joseph Nye introduced a "transnational relations" framework for mapping world politics that highlighted the role of cross-border actors and interactions.[33] Theirs was not a theory of transnational relations but a pointing exercise that concluded that there were so many anomalies in the dominant state-centric realist paradigm that conceptual revisiting was required. They later elaborated a theoretical framework, in *Power and Interdependence*, that combined realist and transnational ideas to develop testable hypotheses.[34]

Certainly, scholarly debates about the rise and fall of nation-states and inter-state relations with other actors, structures, and processes across time and space will continue for the foreseeable future. Indeed, Arjun Appadurai, in *Modernity at Large*, argues that not only have nation-states weakened but also that the nation-state system itself is in crisis due to the influence of transnational phenomena and dynamics. Saskia Sassen writes of "denationaliza-tion" or the idea that power, authority, and identity formation will migrate away from the nation-state upwards towards inter-state and even supra-state institutions and agencies and downwards to "global cities" that are the geographical loci of dominant nodes of cross-border forms and processes.[35] But she also writes that the "global" is transnationally, albeit variably, reproduced ideationally and materially in the "national" and the "local," meaning that the nation-state is qualitatively transformed not just quantitatively weakened.

Thus, a transnational perspective involves multiple different types and forms of theorizing and processes of theory development. Its goal is not to arrive at a single paradigm or master narrative but to find ways to hold these different theoretical accounts and approaches in productive conversation with one another. The world is too broad, deep, and complex to be captured by just one theoretical apparatus. Instead, TS abandons that expectation, creating a broad enough tent to tolerate the productive tension between, possible co-existence of, and potential cross-fertilization among different theoretical frames.

PHILOSOPHICAL TRANSNATIONALISM

The fourth jumping-off point for the field of Transnational Studies is to adopt an alternative set of ontological and epistemological assumptions about the nature of the world and what knowledge consists of. Philosophical transnationalism is **based on the metaphysical view that social life is transnational to begin with—transnational phenomena and dynamics are the rule rather than the exception, the central tendency rather than the outlier.**

Philosophical transnationalism rejects the notion that social life is automatically or primarily organized within or between nations, states, or other types of bordered or bounded social system containers. Unlike traditional social science, with its dominant "unit-ism" or "system-ism," the ontological premise of TS is that social worlds are fundamentally cross-boundary and cross-border. A second premise is that social processes we assume to be bounded and bordered are, as a rule, embedded in and influenced by cross-border and cross-boundary phenomena and dynamics. Thus, scholarship should focus on the production of social difference and differentiation rather than investigating or comparing nations, societies, or cultures that are assumed to be whole.[36]

Philosophical transnationalism does not deny the importance of bounded or bordered social groups. Rather, one of the central meta-theoretical puzzles it attempts to solve is why certain boundaries arise to begin with and how are they reproduced and perpetuated. A transnational ontology assumes, for example, that the emergence of the nation-state system is historically idiosyncratic—a set of social facts that needs to be explained and interpreted.[37] It takes a similar approach to allegedly national religions and the transnational religious communities to which they belong. The local, regional, national, and global are not auto-matic, taken-for-granted social arenas but categories to be investigated as constructed and often-contested social facts. Rather than privileging one analytical layer over another, a central focus is to excavate the interaction between them.

Furthermore, a transnational ontology is based on the assumption that social phenomena and dynamics take place within (and across) transnational fields. Pierre Bourdieu used the concept of fields to call attention to the ways in which relations of power and meaning structure social interactions.[38] Sociological institutionalists theorize and examine organizational fields of various kinds.[39] Most recently, economic sociologists and social movement theorists have proposed the notion of "strategic action fields."[40] While this work does not rule out the possibility that these fields are transnational, it does not directly and systematically address that possibility either.

The Manchester School proposed a notion of social field similar to Bourdieu, which acknowledged that the migrants they studied belonged to tribal-rural localities and colonial-industrial cities at the same time. Migrant networks stretching between these two (or more) sites constituted a single social field created by a network of networks. By understanding social relations in this way, these researchers introduced levels of analysis underneath, across, and beyond the study of the individual, the community, the colony, and even the empire.[41]

Building on Bourdieu and the Manchester School, some transnational migration scholars define social fields as a set of multiple interlocking networks of social relationships through which ideas, practices, and resources are unequally exchanged, organized, and transformed. Social fields are multidimensional, encompassing interactions of differing forms, depth, and breadth, such as organizations, institutions, and movements. National boundaries are not necessarily contiguous with the boundaries of social fields. National social fields are those that stay within national boundaries while transnational social fields involve direct and indirect relations and dynamics across borders and boundaries that may or may not be national.[42]

A transnational ontology goes hand in hand with a transnational epistemology. **In order to describe, explain, interpret, theorize, and alter assumptions about the nature of social worlds, expectations about how social worlds can be known and understood must be rethought.** Philosophical transnational scholarship, building on ontological transnationalism, probes the extent to which cross-border dynamics are at work and attempts to explain variations in their strength and scope. Any analysis that does not take the possibility of transnational processes into account, while potentially useful and even illuminating, is likely to come up short. For example, Tamara Kay's work demonstrates that changes in transnational rather than national political systems and institutions stimulated alliances among workers in Canada, the United States, and Mexico.[43] Howard Winant's work on the dynamics of race relations over time highlights the analytical purchase gained by using a transnational lens, and William Julius Wilson explains the decline of African-American inner-city communities with an implicitly transnational explanation.[44]

PUBLIC TRANSNATIONALISM

A fifth entry point into Transnational Studies is a more open, ethical and prescriptive approach to scholarship. **Public transnationalism creates a space to imagine options for social transformation that are obscured when borders, boundaries, and the structures, processes, and actors within them are taken as given.** By calling into question borders and boundaries, and the assumption that the nation-state is the automatic container within which social life occurs, TS opens up a range of possibilities for political positions and praxis that might otherwise be obscured.

TS fits squarely within the social science's renewed commitment to forging stronger links between theory and praxis and between academics and practitioners because it tries to go beyond description, analysis, and understanding to practice.[45] It rejects the false neutrality characterizing much scholarship. Rather than ignoring the hard set of ethical and practical questions that research poses, it embraces them. At the same time, TS does not begin from a prescribed political position nor does it assume that transnational solutions are automatically best. Rather, an integral part of TS is to go beyond description, analysis, and explanation and specify the range of policy choices indicated by research findings. Ann Marie Slaughter's work on transgovernmental networks, which argues that a critical element in producing stability in world affairs is the links that bureaucratic agencies form across disaggregated and decentralized states, is an excellent example of this kind of scholarship.[46] Luis Guarnizo's work on the macro-economic impacts of migrants' micro-level transnational economic activities is another case in point.[47] Nikos Passas's work on the unintended negative consequences of nation-state and inter-state regulation of informal money transfer systems, like *Hawala*, is another example.[48]

Toward this end, TS is deeply concerned about the power dynamics underlying social relations. It pays careful attention to ways in which explicit ideological and methodological assumptions skew the questions that get asked, the answers that are proposed, and the practices that are pursued. It does not assume, for example, that everything originates and flows from the west and north but that the direction, intensity, and effects of global cultural flows are empirical questions. There are innumerable examples of various kinds of "brokers," "gatekeepers," "travelers," "bridgers," and "diffusers" contributing to the transnational spread and transformation of norms and practices, as well as promotion of greater cross-cultural understandings.[49] The resources, skills, and mobilization generated in one setting can be successfully applied to another. The often purposeful and targeted transnational diffusion of ideas and practices under the rubrics of good governance, accountability, and democracy are increasingly utilized tools. But these transfers are by no means one way. Ideas about micro-credit, participatory budgeting, or good water use can be, and have been, systematically spread from south to north and east to west. Thus, public transnationalism does not equate transnationality or transnationalization with global westernization or Americanization. It does not assume that everything originates and flows to the rest of the world from the west and north. Civil Rights activists like Martin Luther King and Ceasar Chavez in the United States, for example, were clearly inspired by the strategies Gandhi used in South Africa and India.

Rather than clinging to or trying to re-coup a world in which the nation prevails, TS wants to understand how citizenship, governance, human security, and cultural diversity, among others, change when we assume a world that is transnationally constituted. Moreover, transnational forces are clearly not a factor in every case. If we find, for example, that centralized states are better at alleviating human suffering and at promoting sustainable and equitable development, then scholarship and praxis should pursue that route. If research reveals, however, that novel, multi-stakeholder and cross-sectoral forms of transnational governance are more effective, then it is our responsibility to embrace that perspective.

TOWARDS A TRANSNATIONAL STUDIES PERSPECTIVE

Taken together, the five interacting components of TS offer an exciting set of intellectual foundations for this field. They provide grist for rethinking taken-for-granted categories like identity and membership. While not every scholar will work across all five, we believe they constitute a rich menu for research, theory, and action. We do not wish to imply there is a value hierarchy between these five elements. Rather, each can be understood as one point that, when connected, represent a pentagonal field of possibilities. Furthermore, we believe that productive research programs can be formulated within this intellectual space.

The task of Transnational Studies is to **uncover, analyze and conceptualize similarities, differences, and interactions among trans-societal and trans-organizational realities,** including the ways in which they shape bordered and bounded phenomena and dynamics across time and space.

This research can take several possible directions. We elucidate some exciting possibilities here. Ongoing research by Federico Besserer and Michael Kearney provides one excellent example. They began by studying indigenous migrant communities across different parts of Mexico and the United States. Their respondents are transnational because they live across various cultural and territorial borders and because they have always been at the interstices of symbolic and political boundaries (as subaltern citizens of Mexico, for example). They are neither global nor national nor local.

Besserer and Kearney soon realized that the discourses and practices they uncovered could not be understood without taking into account trans-regional economic dynamics and the political relations between local, state, and federal-level actors in all three countries. In addition, the human rights campaigns in the communities they studied borrowed heavily from the transnational nongovernmental advocacy networks these groups worked with. Moreover, their pre-Mexican indigenous governance systems had been extended across territories.[50]

Thus, a first type of inquiry arising from a transnational perspective involves analyzing a particular type of transnational form or process across space. There is already some evidence that we find similar types of transnational migrant community dynamics in Europe and the United States, but would we also find them in South Africa or Brazil? How do the transnationally-constituted experiences of people who migrate internally within a country and those who move across close or even contiguous borders within regions like Africa, eastern Europe or the Caribbean compare with those who move from "south" to "north"?[51] How do transnational religious practices vary across social contexts? Why is a much greater share of remittances from overseas Chinese directed towards business investment compared with that of non-resident South Asian Indian groups?

A second type of research examines a particular type of transnational form or process across time. How do contemporary human rights or environmental movements compare to the anti-slavery and labor movements of the past?[52] How do historical state responses to pirating networks compare to governmental attempts at controlling transnational terrorism?[53] Why do transnational infectious diseases and invasive species seem so prevalent in some historical eras and contexts but not in others? Scholarly exchange on the differences between transnational migration of the late nineteenth century with that of the late twentieth century is a particularly productive example of this type of scholarship.

A third type investigates different kinds of transnational activities. Transnational business, crime, professional, social movement, religious and migration networks all cross borders, but to what degree are their forms and activities like one another? Why do individuals join profit-making transnational corporations as opposed to violent transnational terrorist groups? What explains why different transnational groups interpret universal discourses, norms, and strategies cast in universalistic terms in distinct ways (Hall and Biersteker, 2002; Josselin and Wallace, 2001)? Are the factors that lead to "local" adoption of transnational fashion the same as that of transnational professional practices?

A fourth type examines interactions among transnationalisms. Some transnational forms and relations operate in isolation while others complement or subvert each other. Under what conditions do transnational epistemic communities alter the activities of transgovernmental networks? The social and financial organization of Al Qaeda provides another striking example. Its legitimacy and capacity depend, in part, on its social embeddedness in trans-national extended family, kinship, and religious communities. Its complex financial organization combines legal, philanthropic, and commercial concerns and illicit and criminal activities on a transcontinental scale.

A fifth type compares and contrasts transnational phenomena and dynamics with those that are ostensibly tightly bounded and bordered. How, for example, do the forms and consequences of internal migration from the Peruvian highlands to the capital, Lima, compare to those resulting from international migration from Lima to Barcelona, Spain? What difference does it make for people's everyday lives when they identify primarily with domestic unions rather than transnational labor federations? How does the way in which local small firms think about business responsibility compare to the ways in which multinational corporations approach these issues?[54]

A related and sixth type of analysis explores transnational phenomena and dynamics that allegedly compete with or supplant local, national, state, and global entities, with those that complement, interact with, or transform them. Transcontinentally organized economic activities often replace nationally organized production arrangements, while transnational civil society organizations are more likely to engage, influence, and be shaped by domestic social movement organizations. Commodity chains relegating aspects of the production process to the far corners of Southeast Asia replaced the factories that produced entire shoes in Lynn, Massachusetts. In contrast, Indonesian or Argentine human rights organizations often link up with transnational advocacy networks. Their domestic activities complement and are complemented by these cross-border partnerships. Similarly, some argue that the Mexican government's program to issue consular identity cards to Mexican migrants in the United States (so they can obtain driver's licenses and open bank accounts) is a transnationally organized political intervention that disrupts the sovereignty of the U.S. state. Others see this as a logical manifestation of the Mexican government's continuing responsibility for emigrants.

A seventh set of questions shifts the focus to the ideas, behaviors, symbols, and material culture that circulate through the networks and organizations embedded in transnational social fields. These researchers are concerned with what travels and how it changes throughout its journey, the mechanisms and actors involved in transmission, and the determinants of impact. How are transnational values and meanings articulated so that they make sense to local actors? What are the channels through which these cultural products flow? How do the ways in which issues are framed and the topographies through which they travel affect their portability and adoption? N. Rajaram and Vaishali Zararia found differences in how Indian women's groups translated the same global discourses. One used moral/ethical language, or what they called a Gandhian approach, because it resonated powerfully with the Gujarati context. The other stressed women's rights discourses' international roots and connections precisely because they provided resources and tools not available locally.[55] What is the comparative advantage of framing particular issues in particular ways?

A MAP OF THIS VOLUME

Transnational Studies is clearly driven by a different set of assumptions about the world and expectations about knowledge than most traditional scholarship. Since a central premise is that not all theories can do all things, and that more productive insights come from combining or contrasting different theoretical explanations and interpretations, its goal is to uncover the heuristic power of these theoretical interactions. One of its primary concerns, in fact, is to understand the intersection and collision of the many layers of relations, perspectives, and cosmologies.

A transnational perspective, therefore, allows for a creative interaction between different philosophies of knowledge—from positivism to postmodernism and from interpretivism to constructivism—in contrast to the all-too-common polarized and unproductive stalemates that arise when producing a single type of theoretical explanation is the goal. Those interested in formulating testable and potentially falsifiable hypotheses will find ample room within this optic; but there is also support and encouragement for postmodern critiques of "regimes of truth" that mask unequal power relations. Both this expectation about the nature of social worlds and of reality, and what we expect of scholarship that sheds light on it, reflect a set of beliefs about what academic interaction is capable of and responsible for doing. Instead of trying to artificially contain or clean up complexity and constructive conflict, a transnational perspective embraces, encourages, and facilitates it.

The success of this approach ultimately depends on the transnationalization of the social sciences. Clearly, there is already a good deal of scholarly exchange between and among scholars across borders and boundaries. But, in many ways, just as field building is constrained by rigid disciplinary boundaries, so U.S. and European scholarship is hindered because they build selective bridges to particular times and places. For one thing, a select group of primarily western scholars are usually the ones who participate. When people from the south or the east are included, they often do so as junior partners. Access to resources and opportunities among non-western scholars is limited and the legitimation process unequal because the English language predominates. The community of scholars within TS will be much more productive and successful to the extent that it becomes transnational itself. This requires casting a broader net and encouraging a wider range of collaborative partnerships structured on more equal terms. Indeed, we may learn how to do this through our studies of the transnational phenomena that concern us.

The goal of this book is to lay out the intellectual foundations for this optic, to start a conversation between scholars who have not always seen themselves as talking about the same things, and to begin bringing to light relationships and patterns that make us understand social life differently by bringing together all of these voices and topics. It is also to highlight an alternative set of ontological and epistemological expectations that drive our inquiry and guide our understanding of the relationship between research and praxis. Our selections are admittedly idiosyncratic. These are the pieces that influenced each of us independently to see the world in very similar ways, despite our very different positions as a migration and religion researcher and a scholar of politics and social movements. They are written by scholars from across the disciplines. They concern a wide range of topics. They employ all kinds of social science methods. And, taken together, they suggest a different way of seeing the world and of changing it.

NOTES

1. This is a co-authored paper, jointly conceived and written by both contributors. Support has been generously provided by the Hauser Center for Non-Profit Organizations, The John F. Kennedy School of Government, The Weatherhead Center for International Affairs, The Wellesley College Faculty Research Fund, Atlantic Philanthropies, The Ford Foundation, The Rockefeller Foundation, The National Science Foundation, The Stanford Institute of International Studies and the University of Washington's Evans School of Public Affairs and Jackson School of International Studies. Earlier versions were presented at the Hauser Center, University of California Davis Sociology Colloquium, Brown University Seminar on Anthropology and Demography, and the Princeton University Center for Migration and Development. We would like to thank the following people for their comments: John Meyer, Suzanne Shanahan, David Kyle, Joseph Nye, Jonathan Fox, Peter Dobkin Hall, Xavier Briggs, Viviana Selizer, Gabriele Bammer, Sally Merry, Nadya Jaworksky, and Josh DeWind. Correspondence should be sent to plevitt@wellesley.edu.

2. The hearings and conclusions of the 9–11 Independent Commission appointed by President George Bush have been particularly fascinating in this regard. One of the most revealing sentiments conveyed was that what happened on 9–11 was "completely beyond our imagination." Perhaps if those officials had a set of conceptual and analytical tools which brought transnational dynamics to light, these events would not have been so inconceivable.

3. See, among others: John Agnew and Stuart Corbridge, *Mastering Space, Territory and Political Economy* (New York: Routledge, 1995); Nina Glick Schiller, Linda Basch, and Christina Szanton-Blanc, eds., *Towards a Transnational Perspective on Migration: Race, Class, Ethnicity and Nationalism Reconsidered* (New York: New York Academy of Sciences, 1992); Michael Peter Smith and Luis Eduardo Guarnizo, eds., *Transnationalism from Below* (New Brunswick: Transaction, 1998); Peggy Levitt, *Transnational Villagers* (Berkeley: University of California Press, 2001); Peggy Levitt and Mary Waters, eds., *The Changing Face of Home* (New York: Russell Sage Publications, 2002); David Kyle, *Transnational Peasants: Migrations, Networks, and Ethnicity in Andean Ecuador* (Baltimore: Johns Hopkins University Press, 2000), Aiwa Ong, *Flexible*

Citizenship: The Cultural Logic of Transnationality (Durham: Duke University Press, 1999); Nadje Al-Ali and Khalid Moser, eds., *New Approaches to Migration: Transnational Communities and the Transformation of Home* (London: Routledge, 2001); Inderpal Grewal and Caren Kaplan, *Scattered Hegemonies: Postmodernity and Transnational Feminist Practices* (Minneapolis: University of Minnesota Press, 1994); Nancy Abelmann and John Lie, *Blue Dreams: Korean Americans and the Los Angeles Riots* (Cambridge: Harvard University Press, 1995); Ulf Hannerz, *Transnational Connections: Cultures, People, Places* (London: Routledge, 1996); Suzanne Hoeber Rudolph and James Piscatori, eds., *Transnational Religion and Fading States* (Boulder: Westview Press, 1997); Thomas Risse-Kappen, ed., *Bringing Transnational Relations Back in: Non-State Actors, Domestic Structures, and International Institutions* (Cambridge, UK: Cambridge University Press, 1995); Daphne Josselin and William Wallace, eds., *Non-State Actors in World Politics* (New York: Palgrave, 2001); Jackie Smith, Charles Chatfield, and Ron Pagnucco, eds., *Transnational Social Movements and Global Politics: Solidarity Beyond the State* (Syracuse, N.Y.: Syracuse University Press, 1997); Margaret Keck and Kathryn Sikkink, *Activists Beyond Borders* (Ithaca: Cornell University Press, 1999); Ann Florini, ed., *The Third Force: The Rise of Transnational Civil Society* (Washington, D.C.: Carnegie Endowment for International Peace, 2000); Sanjeev Khagram, James V. Rikker, and Kathryn Sikkink, eds., *Restructuring World Politics: Transnational Social Movements, Networks and Norms* (Minneapolis: University of Minnesota Press, 2002); Sanjeev Khagram, *Dams and Development: Transnational Struggles for Water and Power* (Ithaca: Cornell University Press, 2004); Leslie Sklair, *The Transnational Capitalist Class* (Oxford: Blackwell Publishers, 2001); various issues of the journal: *Transnational Organized Crime* (London: Frank Cass, 1995–); Nikos Passas, *Transnational Crime* (Brookfield: Ashgate, 1999); Ann Marie Slaughter, "The Real New World Order," *Foreign Affairs* 76, no. 5 (September/October 1997); Alejandro Portes, Luis Guarnizo, and Patricia Landolt, "Introduction: Pitfalls and Promise of an Emergent Research Field," *Ethnic and Racial Studies* 22 (1999): 463–478; Alejandro Portes, William J. Haller, and Luis Eduardo Guarnizo, "Transnational Entrepreneurs: An Alternative Form of Immigrant Economic Adaptation," *American Sociological Review* 67 (2002): 278–298; Luis Guarnizo, Alejandro Portes, and William J. Haller, "Assimilation and Transnationalism: Determinants of Transnational Political Action among Contemporary Migrants," *American Journal of Sociology* 108 (2003): 1211–1248; Christian Joppke and Ewa Morawska, eds., *Toward Assimilation and Citizenship: Immigrants in Liberal Nation-States* (Hampshire, UK: Palgrave Macmillan, 2003); Peggy Levitt, Josh DeWind, and Steven Vertovec, "Transnational Migration: International Perspectives," A Special Issue of *International Migration Review* 37, (2003): 566–575; Nina Glick Schiller and Georges Fouron, *Georges Woke Up Laughing* (Durham: Duke University Press, 2001); Kivisto, Peter, "Theorizing Transnational Migration: A Critical Review of Current Efforts," *Ethnic and Racial Studies* 24 (2001): 549–577; Brenda Yeoh, Katie Willis, and S.M. Abdul Khader Fakhri, "Introduction: Transnationalism and its edges," *Ethnic and Racial Studies* 26 (2003): 207–217; Roger Waldinger and David Fitzgerald, "Transnationalism in Question," *American Journal of Sociology* 109 (2004): 1177–1195; Paul T. Kennedy and Victor Roudometof, *Communities across Borders: New Immigrants and Transnational Cultures* (London & New York: Routledge, 2003); and Katharyne Mitchell, "Cultural Geographies of Transnationality," in *The Handbook of Cultural Geography,* eds. Kay Anderson, Mona Domosh, and Steven Pile (Thousand Oaks: Sage, 2003).

4. For world systems, a key source is Immanuel Wallerstein, *The Capitalist World Economy* (Cambridge, UK: Cambridge University Press, 1979) and the classic reference for world society studies is George M. Thomas, John W. Meyer, Francisco Ramirez, and John Boli, *Institutional Structure: Constituting State, Society and the Individual* (Newbury Park, UK: Sage, 1987). For an early volume that includes both approaches, see Albert Bergesson, ed., *Studies of the Modern World System* (New York: Academic Press, 1980). Of course, much more has been produced in these scholarly traditions over the last quarter-century. It is important to note that a great deal of the "dependency" scholarship of the 1970s departed from an overly rigid adoption of world unitism or systemism. We would consider much of the latter work to be firmly part of the field of TS and highly recommend Alain de Janvry's *The Agrarian Question and Reformism in Latin America* (Baltimore: Johns Hopkins University Press, 1981), chapters 1 and 2, for an excellent intellectual review of the world systems and dependency literatures.

5. Of the vast literature of variable quality on globalization, see also Frank J. Lechner and John Boli, *The Globalization Reader* (Malden, MA and Oxford, UK: Blackwell Publishers, 2000), as well as Federick Jameson and Masao Miyoshi, *The Cultures of Globalization* (Durham: Duke University Press, 1998).

6. It is revealing to note that a portion of the scholarship that uses the language of globalization, globality or globalism does in fact take cognizance of multi-directionality, cross-border/boundary phenomena and dynamics that are not necessarily transcontinental or planetary, as well as agency and variation across levels, scales, and scopes. Unfortunately, the language that is utilized tends to either obscure these factors and facets or inadequately theorizes them. For two of the better, albeit not fully successful, attempts at linking ideas of globalization and transnationality, see Arjun Appadurai, *Modernity at Large: Cultural Dimensions of Globalization* (Minneapolis: University of Minnesota Press, 1996) and Saskia Sassen, *Globalization and Its Discontents* (New York: The New Press, 1998).

7. The list of localist scholarship that includes village studies, community studies, neighborhood studies and so on is voluminous, making it virtually impossible to cite here.

8. Some "localist" scholars certainly do a better job at taking transnationalisms into account. In particular, see the selections in Akhil Gupta and James Ferguson, eds., *Culture, Power, Place: Explorations in Critical Anthropology* (Durham: Duke University Press, 1997), in particular. See also Sarah J. Mahler, *American Dreaming: Immigrant Life on the Margins* (Princeton: Princeton University Press, 1995); Luin Goldring, "The Mexican State and Transmigrant Organizations: Negotiating the Boundaries of Membership and Participation," *Latin American Research Review* 37, no. 3 (2002): 55–99; Raquel Parrenas, "Mothering from a Distance: Emotions, Gender, and Intergenerational Relations in Filipino Transnational Families," *Feminist Studies* 27, no. 2 (2001): 361–391.

9. By no means does this imply that other units such as regions are unimportant—indeed, the growing scholarship on various forms and kinds of regionalism is particularly useful in explicating transnational phenomena and dynamics.

10. In addition to the voluminous work on regional (especially European) integration in sociology and political science, see, for example, John Agnew and Stuart Corbridge, *Mastering Space, Territory and Political Economy*; Matthew Sparke, "Between Post-Colonialism and Cross-Border Regionalism," *Space and Polity*, 6(2), 2002, 203–213; and T. Courchene, "Globalization: The Regional/International Interface," *Canadian Journal of Regional Science*, XVIII, 1995, 1–20.

11. This linking of knowledge and institutional orders around the "national-state" has had a profound impact on scholarship. See James Scott, *Seeing like a State* (New Haven, CT: Yale University Press, 1998) and John Lie, *Modern Peoplehood* (Cambridge: Harvard University Press, 2004).

12. Virtually the entire sub-field of economic sociology has explicitly or implicitly taken the nation-state form and, even more so, contemporary countries for granted as the obvious units of analysis if not objects of study. See Harrison C. White, *Markets from Networks: Socioeconomic Models of Production* (Princeton: Princeton University Press, 2002); Neil Fligstein, *The Architecture of Markets: An Economic Sociology of Twenty-first-century Capitalist Societies* (Princeton: Princeton University Press, 2001); Mauro F. Guillén, *The New Economic Sociology: Developments in an Emerging Field* (New York: Russell Sage Foundation, 2002); and Mark S. Granovetter and Richard Swedberg, *The Sociology of Economic Life* (Boulder: Westview Press, 1992).

13. The key social movement texts, until recently, are all domestic or comparative-national in orientation, for example: Sidney F. Tarrow, *Power in Movement: Social Movements, Collective Action, and Politics* (Cambridge, UK: Cambridge University Press, 1994); Doug McAdam, Sidney G. Tarrow, and Charles Tilly, *Towards an Integrated Perspective on Social Movements and Revolution* (New York: Lazarsfeld Center at Columbia University, 1996); and Doug McAdam, John D. McCarthy, and Mayer N. Zald, *Comparative Perspectives on Social Movements: Political Opportunities, Mobilizing Structures, and Cultural Framings* (Cambridge, UK: Cambridge University Press, 1996). Although there is an ample body of work on religion and globalization (see, for example, Peter Beyer, *Religion and Globalization* [Thousand Oaks & London: Sage Publications, 1994] and Roland Robertson, *Globalization: Social Theory and Global Culture* [London: Sage, 1992]), scholars have only recently begun to formulate a transnational perspective on religion and there is little agreement about what that perspective actually entails. See, for example, Rudolph and Piscatori, *Transnational Religion*; Anna Lisa Peterson, Manuel A. Vásquez, and Phillip J. Williams, eds., *Christianity, Social Change and Globalization in the Americas* (New Brunswick: Rutgers University Press, 2001); Manuel A. Vasquez and Marie F. Marquardt, *Globalizing the Sacred: Religion across the Americas* (New Brunswick: Rutgers University Press, 2003); Peter Mandaville, *Transnational Muslim Politics: Reimagining the Umma* (London: Routledge, 2001); Steven Vertovec and Robin Cohen, *Migration, Diasporas, and Transnationalism* (Cheltenham, UK and Northampton, MA: Edward Elgar, 1999); Cecilia Menjivar, "Religious Institutions and Transnationalism: A Case Study of Catholic and Evangelical Salvadoran Immigrants," *International Journal of Politics, Culture, and Society* 12 (1999): 589–612; Pierrette Hondagneu-Sotelo, Genelle Gaudinez, Hector Lara and Billie Ortiz, " 'There's a Spirit that Transcends the Border': Faith, Ritual, and Post-national Protest at the U.S.–Mexico Border," *Sociological Perspectives* 47 (2004): 133–160; Jeremy Stolow, "Transnationalism and the New Religio-Politics: Reflections on a Jewish Orthodox Case," *Theory, Culture, and Society* 21, no. 2 (2004): 109–137; and Willfried Spohn, "Multiple Modernity, Nationalism, and Religion: A Global Perspective," *Current Sociology* 51, nos. 3/4 (2003): 265–286.

14. For perhaps the best work along these lines that could be considered transnational scholarship, see Charles Tilly, ed., *The Formation of National States in Western Europe* (Princeton: Princeton University Press, 1975), and his *Coercion, Capital, and European States, A.D. 990–1990* (Cambridge, UK: Basil Blackwell, 1990). See the growing literatures on sovereignty, for example, Thomas J. Biersteker and Cynthia Weber, *State Sovereignty as Social Construct* (Cambridge, UK: Cambridge University Press, 1996) and Stephen D. Krasner's *Problematic Sovereignty: Contested Rules and Political Possibilities* (New York: Columbia University Press, 2001) as well as *Sovereignty: Organized Hypocrisy* (Princeton: Princeton University Press, 1999).

15. There is thus an interesting set of overlaps between the Sociology of Transnationalism and Cultural Studies, particularly with regard to borderland and postcolonial studies. See, for example, Gloria Anzaldua and Mayfair Mei-hui Yang, "Goddess across the Taiwan Strait: Matrifocal Ritual Space, Nation-State, and Satellite

Television Footprints," *Public Culture* 16, no. 2 (2003): 209–238; Dilip Parameshwar Gaonkar, "Toward New Imaginaries: An Introduction," *Public Culture* 14, no. 1 (2002): 1–19; Inderpal Grewel, "Traveling Barbie: Indian Transnationality and New Consumer Subjects," *Positions* 7, no. 3 (Winter 1999): 799–826; Partha Chatterjee, "Beyond the Nation? Or Within?" *Social Text* 56 (Autumn 1998): 57–69; Hilary Cunningham and Josiah McC. Heyman, "Introduction: Mobilities and Enclosures at Borders," *Identities* 11 (2004): 289–302; and Edward Soja, *Postmetropolis: Critical Studies of Cities and Regions* (Malden: Blackwell, 2000).

16.   The literature on transnational corporations has a very long history indeed. For an important contribution, see George Modelski, ed., *Transnational Corporations and World Order: Readings in International Political Economy* (San Francisco: W.H. Freeman and Company, 1979). For two key books from the dependency tradition, see Fernando Henrique Cardoso and Enzo Faletto, *Dependency and Development in Latin America* (Berkeley: University of California Press, 1973) and Peter Evans, *Dependent Development: The Alliance of Multinational, State and Local Capital in Brazil* (Princeton: Princeton University Press, 1979). More recently, see Susan Strange, *The Retreat of the State: The Diffusion of Power in the World Economy* (Cambridge, UK: Cambridge University Press, 1996) and Leslie Sklair, *The Transnational Capitalist Class* (Oxford, UK: Blackwell 2001).

17.   For transnational popular cultural production, see Juan Flores, *From Bomba and Hip Hop: Puerto Rican Culture and Latino Identity* (New York: Columbia University Press, 2000); Doris Sommer, *Bilingual Aesthetics: A New Sentimental Education* (Durham, NC: Duke University Press, 2004); Deborah Pacini Hernández, Héctor D. Fernández-L'Hoeste and Eric Zolov, eds., *Rockin' Las Americas: The Global Politics of Rock in Latin/o America* (Pittsburgh: University of Pittsburgh Press, 2004); Helena Simonett, *Banda: Mexican Musical Life across Borders* (Middletown: Wesleyan University Press, 2001); Lisa Parks and Shanti Kumar, eds., *A Global Television Reader* (New York: New York University Press, 2002); Peter Hitchcock, *Imaginary States: Studies in Cultural Transnationalism* (Urbana and Chicago: University of Illinois Press, 2003); Ulf Hedetoft and Mette Hjort, eds., *The Postnational Self* (Minneapolis and London: University of Minnesota Press, 2002); Neil Lazarus, *Nationalism and Cultural Practice in the PostColonial World* (New York: Cambridge University Press, 1999); and Walter D. Mignolo, *Coloniality, Subaltern Knowledges, and Border Thinking* (Princeton: Princeton University Press, 2000).

18.   Some of the early transnational scholarship focused on social forms and processes that were initially seen as novel or particularly important in the contemporary period. Data were assembled to demonstrate the dramatic rise in transnational corporations, their expanding share of economic activity, and their growing capacity to shape social reality in various parts of the world. It was "discovered" that revolutionary and "ethnic" violent conflicts (most of which actually cross country borders or are "transnational" in other ways) far outnumbered inter-state wars between 1946 and 1999. Differences between transnational coalitions, networks, and social movements constituted largely by nongovernmental or social movement organizations were identified. Transnational migrants' identities and memberships were examined and documented. But as Roger Waldinger and David Fitzgerald (2004) rightfully note, transnational scholarship must be careful not to reproduce, "the familiar antinomies of social science, most notably that of a 'closed' past and 'open' present. . . ." Moreover, much of the work of empirical transnationalism has focused to date on phenomena that are, or are understood to be, by-products of the nation-state system, which unnecessarily limits Transnational Studies' potential analytical reach.

19.   Sklair, *Transnational Capitalist Class*, p. 22. Of course, work in the dependency tradition long ago posited the existence of transnational classes and class alliances.

20.   Mary Kaldor, *New & Old Wars: Organized Violence in a Global Era* (Stanford: Stanford University Press, 2001).

21.   Smith et al., *Transnational Social Movements*; Keck and Sikkink, *Activist Beyond Borders*.

22.   Peggy Levitt and Sally Merry, "Translating the Global into the Local: The Case of Women's Rights." Paper Presented at Wellesley College Conference, August 2006.

23.   See Sanjeev Khagram and Sarah Alvord, "Locating Contemporary Progressive Civic Transnational Advocacy," in L. David Brown and Srilatha Batliawala, eds., *Claiming Global Power: The Transnational Civil Society Reader*, Westport: Kumarian Press, forthcoming.

24.   Of course, many firms do use physical and other forms of violence so the difference between transnational corporate citizenship and corporate criminality is often a fine line.

25.   Peggy Levitt and B. Nadya Jaworsky, "Transnational Migration Studies: Past Developments and Future Trends," *Annual Review of Sociology* 33 (2007): 129–156.

26.   Systems thinking, when not rigidly applied, might be particularly usefully utilized.

27.   Peggy Levitt and Nina Glick Schiller, "Conceptualizing Simultaneity: Theorizing Society from a Transnational Social Field Perspective," *International Migration Review* 38 (2004): 1002–1039.

28.   See David Harvey, *The Condition of Postmodernity* (Oxford, UK: Blackwell Publishers, 1989).

29.   See Fernand Braudel, *On History* (New York: Harper and Row, 1980), as well as Susan Eckstein and L. Barberia, "Grounding Immigrant Generations in History: Cuban Americans and Their Transnational Ties," *International Migration Review* 36, no. 3 (2002): 799–838.

30.   Levitt and Glick Schiller, "Conceptualizing Simultaneity."

31. Enrique Dussel, "Globalization, Civilization Processes, and the Relocation of Languages and Cultures," in Jameson and Miyoshi, *Cultures of Globalization*.

32. Beverly Silver, *Forces of Labor: Workers' Movements and Globalization since 1870*. (Cambridge, UK & New York: Cambridge University Press, 2003), especially pp. 25–40.

33. See Robert O. Keohane and Joseph S. Nye Jr., eds., *Transnational Relations and World Politics* (Cambridge: Harvard University Press, 1971).

34. Robert O. Keohane and Joseph S. Nye Jr., *Power and Interdependence: World Politics in Transition* (Boston: Little, Brown, 1977).

35. This is very similar to Strange, *The Retreat of the State*, as well as numerous others.

36. Gupta and Ferguson, *Culture, Place, Power*.

37. Tilly, *The Formation of National States in Western Europe*.

38. See Pierre Bourdieu, *The Logic of Practice* (Stanford: Stanford University Press, 1980).

39. See Walter W. Powell and Paul J. DiMaggio, eds., *The New Institutionalism in Organizational Analysis* (Chicago: University of Chicago Press, 1991), and Richard W. Scott, *Institutions and Organizations* (Denver: Sage Publications, 2001).

40. See Neil Fligstein and Doug McAdam, "A Political and Cultural Approach to the Study of Strategic Action," paper presented at the Annual Meetings of the American Sociological Association, August 2003.

41. Ewa Morawska, "Immigrant Transnationalism and Assimilation: A Variety of Combinations and the Analytic Strategy It Suggests," in C. Joppke and E. Morawsk, eds, *Toward Assimilation and Citizenship: Immigrants in Liberal Nation-States* (Basingstoke, UK: Palgrave Macmillan, 2003) pp. 133–176.

42. See also Khagram, *Dams and Development* on transnational fields.

43. Tamara Kay, "Labor Transnationalism and Global Governance: The Impact of NAFTA on Transnational Labor Relationships in North America," *American Journal of Sociology*, forthcoming.

44. Howard Winant, *The World Is a Ghetto* (New York: Basic Books, 2001) and William Julius Wilson, *When Work Disappears: The World of the New Urban Poor* (New York: Vintage Books, 1997).

45. See, for example, Michael Burawoy, "Public Sociologies: Contradictions, Dilemmas, and Possibilities," *Social Forces* 82, no. 4 (2004): 1603–1618, and Craig Calhoun, "Word from the President: Toward a More Public Social Science," *Items and Issues 5* (Social Science Research Council Quarterly), nos. 1 & 2 (Spring/Summer 2004).

46. Ann Marie Slaughter, "The Real New World Order." See also Robert O. Keohane and Joseph S. Nye, Jr., "Transgovernmental Relations and International Organizations," *World Politics* 27: 39–62.

47. Luis Guarnizo, "The Economics of Transnational Living," *International Migration Review* 37, (2003): 666–700.

48. Nikos Passas, "Informal Value Transfer Systems and Criminal Organizations: A Study into So-called Underground Banking Networks," *Onderzoeksnotities*, The Hague, WODC, no. 1999/4.

49. See Joe Brandy and Jackie Smith, eds., *Coalitions Across Borders: Transnational Protest and the Neoliberal Order* (Lahman: Rowman & Littlefield, 2005), especially pp. 240–243.

50. Among their many individual and joint publications, see Federico Besserer and Michael Kearny, *Mixtepec: Ethnografía Multilocal de una Comunidad Transnacional Mixteca* (Mexico City: Universidad Autonoma Metropolitana, Iztapalapa, 2001).

51. See, for example, Mika Toyota, "Contested Chinese Identities among Ethnic Minorities in the China, Burma, and Thai Borderlands," *Ethnic and Racial Studies* 26, no. 2 (2003): 301–320.

52. See Keck and Sikkink, *Activists Beyond Borders*; Khagram et al., *Restructuring World Politics*; Silver, *Forces of Labor*; and Kay, *Labor Transnationalism*, among many others.

53. It is interesting to note that indigenous peoples and pirating networks of the eighteenth and nineteenth centuries were the only other non-state entities, besides contemporary transnational terrorists, against which federal governments declared war since U.S. independence in 1776. Of course, governments of many countries (such as the Tamil/Sinhalese conflicts in Sri Lanka) have been in long and protracted violent conflicts with transnational non-state groups (revolutionary, liberation, ethnic, etc.) of various kinds. For a more general perspective, see Thomas W. Gallant, "Brigandage, Piracy, Capitalism and State-Formation: Transnational Crime from a Historical World Systems Perspective," in Josiah McC. Heyman, ed., *States and Illegal Practices* (Oxford, UK: Berg, 1999), 25–61.

54. It has been argued that local businesses, because they are socially embedded in communities, are likely to act with greater responsibility and that transnational corporations that are comparatively disembedded are more likely to fit the ideal-typical profit-maximizing firm, in a Polyani-esque way.

55. Rajaram, N. and Vaishali Zararia, "Reducing Gender Injustice in a Globalizing World: Challenges in Translation of Women's Human Rights in Baroda, India," paper presented at Wellesley College conference, August 2006.

REFERENCES

Appadurai, A. (2003) *Modernity at Large: Cultural Dimensions of Globalization*. Minneapolis: University of Minnesota Press, p. 179.

Biersteker, T. J. and R. B. Hall (eds) (2002) *The Emergence of Private Authority in Global Governance*. Cambridge: Cambridge University Press.

Braithwaite, J. and Drahos, P. (2000) *Global Business Regulation*. Cambridge: Cambridge University Press.

Josselin, D. and Wallace, W. (eds.) (2001) *Non-State Actors in World Politics*. New York: Palgrave.

Sparke, M. (2002) "Between Post-Colonialism and Cross-Border Regionalism," *Space and Polity*, 6 (2): 203–213.

Waldinger, R. and D. Fitzgerald, "Transnationalism in Question", *American Journal of Sociology*, 109 (2004): 1177–1195.

SECTION 1

*T*he Broad Foundations

Introduction to Section 1

Territorial borders and cultural boundaries are once again contested, de-naturalized and hybridized at the dawn of the twenty-first century. The quest for theoretical frameworks that explain these complex phenomena and dynamics has also become more urgent and impassioned. The chapters in this section provide a range of compelling conceptual foundations for the emerging field of transnational studies. The authors draw on a variety of disciplinary, cultural, political, and geographical entry points yet still "speak to one another" and can be productively juxtaposed in manifold ways. Moreover, this diversity of perspectives endows Transnational Studies with a rich set of opportunities for generating intellectual dynamism for many years to come.

Joseph Nye and Robert Keohane's well-known work on "transnational relations" challenged the traditional state-centric international relations paradigm as an inadequate explanation of contemporary world politics. State-centric paradigms, most visible in mainstream debates between (neo-)realism and (neo-)liberalism, did not generally acknowledge the existence of transnational actors such as multinational corporations. Keohane and Nye introduced the building blocks of an alternative paradigm that said that looking only at state actions was not enough. They argued that transnational ("the movement of tangible or intangible items across state boundaries when at least one actor is not an agent of a government or intergovernmental organization"), transgovernmental (the relationships between governmental sub-units across national boundaries) and interstate interactions shape the dynamics of world politics in complex and often counterintuitive ways.

Whereas Nye and Keohane focus on the role of transnational relationships and actors from a largely northern liberal perspective, and are primarily in conversation with international relations colleagues, Fernando Cardoso and Henrique Faletto challenge reductionist world systems and dependency models in general from a global south and Latin American neo-marxist sense. Cardoso and Faletto reject the idea that internal or national socio-political processes in peripheral societies are simply and mechanically conditioned by a particular stage of global capitalist development. Yet they also argue that different configurations of internal–external dependency relationships powerfully structure paths of development. Their work thus probes the concrete, historically structured, transnational networks among the struggles of groups and classes, on the one hand, and political, economic structures of domination on the other. They also highlight that states are structurally embedded entities that can, from time to time, emerge under conditions of relative autonomy to actively alter transnational relations of domination and dependence.

Gloria Anzaldúa offers the most humanistic and literary interrogation of transnationality in this section. Anzaldúa introduced notions of transnationalized identities and cultures by intensively probing "borderlands." She does this, of course, with a specific focus on the Mexico–United States border, but the theoretical implications of borderlands—zones and spaces that have never fully become divided, and across which complex layers of material, cultural, and other flows are dynamically intertwined—are much farther-reaching. Powerfully deploying Spanish and English poetry, memoir, and historical analysis, she reminds her readers of the very fundamental human and personal ramifications of transnationality. Anzaldúa's contribution also highlights the historical dimension of transnationalism, the focus of the third section of this reader, and the methodological innovations required for their study, which we focus on in the section that follows.

The section then moves to Arjun Appadurai's *tour de force* anthropological exposition of transnationality, which in many ways provides the bridge between Anzaldúa and the two excerpts that came before her. Appadurai persuasively argues for the need to focus on the dynamics of cultural, political, and economic de-territorialization and re-territorialization, and provocatively probes the profound crises plaguing the nation-state system. He suggests that we view the world as consisting of complex, overlapping, and disjunctive ethnoscapes, mediascapes, technoscapes, financescapes, and ideoscapes. These various scapes are deeply perspectival constructs shaped by the interactions and inter-subjective understandings of the diversity of actors (nation-states, multinational corporations, diasporas, social movements, etc.) that constitute them. The configuration of these scapes is thus fundamentally fractal— that is, not possessing Euclidean boundaries and thus demanding polythetic rather than traditional nomothetic theoretical accounts.

Ann-Marie Slaughter offers a perspective grounded in international legal thought, examining two theories of world order—liberal internationalism and new medievalism. Yet, once again, she too finds both come up short for explaining today's world. To explain phenomena such as the cross-border, multi-layered legal communities created by international and national judges, she argues for the importance of transgovernmentalism (a notion identified earlier but less developed by Keohane and Nye). In her view, these transgovernmental networks of courts, national ministries, and other state bodies will increasingly be the basis of world order. Correspondingly, state sovereignty increasingly means membership in the international regimes created and sustained by transgovernmental networks.

Finally, Saskia Sassen proposes another account of transnationality, which she terms the new economic geography of centrality. New global cities have emerged that act as central financial and service production hubs connected to each other within a broader transnational grid. While these cities are highly interlinked, they often become disconnected from their resident countries and national governments. Sassen claims that while increasing transnationalization does not undermine the importance of the nation-state, it does change the role states play nationally and internationally. In many ways, writes Sassen, states have lagged behind in their capacity to construct new regulatory frameworks and to redefine the role they will play in a world that is both global and local. Moreover, Sassen suggests, new forms of transnationality emerge when the global is reproduced in the local (e.g. in global cities) and bypasses the national altogether.

CHAPTER 2

Transnational Relations and World Politics: An Introduction

Joseph S. Nye, Jr. and Robert O. Keohane

Students and practitioners of international politics have traditionally concentrated their attention on relationships between states. The state, regarded as an actor with purposes and power, is the basic unit of action; its main agents are the diplomat and soldier. The interplay of governmental policies yields the pattern of behavior that students of international politics attempt to understand and that practitioners attempt to adjust to or control. Since force, violence, and threats thereof are at the core of this interplay, the struggle for power, whether as end or necessary means, is the distinguishing mark of politics among nations.[1] Most political scientists and many diplomats seem to accept this view of reality, and a state-centric view of world affairs prevails.[2]

It is obvious, however, that the interactions of diplomats and soldiers do not take place in a vacuum. They are strongly affected by geography, the nature of domestic politics in the various states, and advances in science and technology. Few would question that the development of nuclear weapons has dramatically altered the nature of twentieth-century international politics or deny the importance of internal political structure for relations between states. From the state-centric perspective geography, technology, and domestic politics comprise aspects of the "environment" within which states interact. They provide inputs into the interstate system but for considerations of analytic convenience are considered to be outside the system.

The environment of interstate politics, however, does not include only these powerful and well-known forces. A good deal of intersocietal intercourse, with significant political importance, takes place without governmental control. For example, among the major Western countries this includes most trade, personal contact, and communication. Furthermore, states are by no means the only actors in world politics. Arnold Wolfers noted more than a decade ago that "the Vatican, the Arabian-American Oil Company, and a host of other nonstate entities are able on occasion to affect the course of international events. When this happens, these entities become actors in the international arena and competitors of the nation-state. Their ability to operate as international or transnational actors may be traced to the fact that men identify themselves and their interests with corporate bodies other than the nation-state."[3]

Although Wolfers and others have pointed out the importance of inter-societal interactions and "transnational actors" in international affairs, the impact of these phenomena on world politics has often been ignored both in policy-oriented writings and more theoretical works.[4] When they have been recognized, they have often been consigned with the factors mentioned above to the environment of interstate politics, and relatively little attention has been paid to them or to their connections with the interstate system. This volume, by contrast, focuses on these "transnational relations"—contacts, coalitions, and interactions across state boundaries that are not controlled by the central foreign policy organs of governments. It treats the reciprocal effects between transnational relations and the interstate system as centrally important to the understanding of contemporary world politics.

A glance at the table of contents will reveal that we are interested in a wide variety of transnational phenomena: multinational business enterprises and revolutionary movements; trade unions and scientific networks; international air transport cartels and communications activities in outer space. Yet, we do not explore transnational relations simply "because they are there"; on the contrary, we hope to use our analysis to cast light on a number of empirical and normative questions that are directly related to the contemporary concerns of statesmen and students of international affairs.

These questions can be grouped into five broad areas of inquiry: 1) What seems to be the net effect of transnational relations on the abilities of governments to deal with their environments? To what extent and how have governments suffered from a "loss of control" as a result of transnational relations? 2) What are the implications of transnational relations for the study of world politics? Is the state-centric view, which focuses on the interstate system, an adequate analytic framework for the investigation of contemporary reality? 3) What are the effects of transnational relations on the allocation of value and specifically on asymmetries or inequalities between states? Who benefits from transnational relations, who loses, who controls transnational networks, and how is this accomplished? 4) What are the implications of transnational relations for United States foreign policy? Insofar as the United States is indeed preponderant in transnational activity, what dangers as well as opportunities does this present to American policymakers? 5) What challenges do transnational relations raise for international organizations as conventionally defined? To what extent may new international organizations be needed, and to what extent may older organizations have to change in order to adapt creatively to transnational phenomena?

We elaborate these questions later in this introduction and return to them in the conclusion, drawing on evidence presented in the various essays to document our assertions, reinforce our speculations, and propose hypotheses for further research. We do not pretend to be definitive; we realize that we are just beginning to explore this field and that even our best-documented beliefs are only provisional. We hope to stimulate inquiry, not to codify knowledge.

Before considering these five broad questions in detail, however, it is necessary to define the two aspects of transnational relations on which we concentrate in this introduction—transnational interactions and organizations—and to analyze some of their effects on interstate politics. Definition and description therefore take priority at this point, although our broader and more speculative inquiries should not be forgotten. We return to them beginning with section III of this introduction.

I. TRANSNATONAL INTERACTIONS AND ORGANIZATIONS

In the most general sense one can speak of "global interactions" as movements of information, money, physical objects, people, or other tangible or intangible items across state boundaries. We can distinguish four major types of global interaction: 1) communication, the movement of information, including the transmission of beliefs, ideas, and doctrines; 2) transportation, the movement of physical objects, including war matériel and personal property as well as merchandise; 3) finance, the movement of money and instruments of credit; 4) travel, the movement of persons. Many international activities involve all four types of interaction simultaneously. Trade and warfare, for example, both require coordinated movements of information, physical objects, money, and persons; so does most personal participation by individuals in foreign societies—"transnational participation"—as discussed in Donald P. Warwick's essay.

Some global interactions are initiated and sustained entirely, or almost entirely, by governments of nation-states. This is true of most wars, a large amount of international communication, considerable trade, and some finance. These we consider "interstate" interactions along with conventional diplomatic activity. Other interactions, however, involve nongovernmental actors—individuals or organizations—and we consider these interactions "transnational." Thus, a transnational interaction may involve governments, but it may not involve only governments: Nongovernmental actors must also play a significant role. We speak of transnational communication, transportation, finance, and travel when we refer to nongovernmental or only partially governmental interactions across state boundaries. Thus, "transnational interactions" is our term to describe the movement of tangible or intangible items across state boundaries when at least one actor is not an agent of a government or an intergovernmental organization.[5]

Another way of looking at transnational interactions, and of distinguishing them from interstate interactions, is to refer to a diagram that we found useful in thinking about the subject. The classic paradigm of interstate politics, depicted in Figure 2.1, focuses on governments as the agencies through which societies deal politically with each other. Interstate politics is conceptually distinguished from, although linked indirectly to, domestic politics; transnational interactions are ignored or discounted. Governments may, however, interact through intergovernmental organizations; thus, this is included in the classic paradigm.

The additional lines drawn in Figure 2.2 indicate what we mean by transnational interactions. For each of the interactions rep-

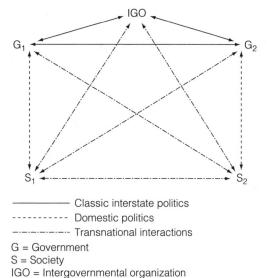

- Classic interstate politics
- Domestic politics
- Transnational interactions

G = Government
S = Society
IGO = Intergovernmental organization

Figure 2.2 Transnational interactions and interstate politics

resented by these lines at least one of the actors is neither a government nor an intergovernmental organization. The point can be made somewhat differently by referring to J. David Singer's distinction between two ways in which individuals and organizations in a given society can play roles in world politics: 1) They may participate as members of coalitions that control or affect their governments or 2) they may play direct roles vis-à-vis foreign governments or foreign societies and thus bypass their own governments.[6] Only the second type of behavior is transnational by our definition.

At the Center for International Affairs Conference on Transnational Relations the objection was raised that a definition such as ours concentrates exclusively on the position of an actor—whether within a government or outside it—and does not raise the question of whether governmental actors necessarily play governmentally defined roles. It was pointed out that even high officials may take actions that cannot be ascribed to their status as governmental actors. Military officers in the United States, for example, frequently share common interests with military men in allied countries and may sometimes act in concert with these foreign military officers against other elements of the American government to achieve common political goals.[7] Leon N. Lindberg and Stuart A. Scheingold

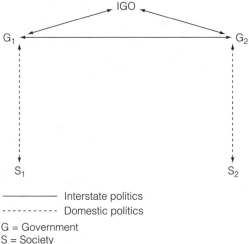

- Interstate politics
- Domestic politics

G = Government
S = Society
IGO = Intergovernmental organization

Figure 2.1 A state-centric interaction pattern

have noted the development of coalitions among agricultural officials from various countries of the European Economic Community (EEC): "The Ministers of Agriculture of the six and their aides and advisors, charged with primary negotiating responsibility along with the Commission, have come to share preoccupations and expertise. They are subject to similar constituency demands, engaged in annual budget battles against their respective Ministers of Finance, and they seek the same general goals of improving the conditions of farmers and of modernizing agriculture. Indeed, in the eyes of many of their colleagues in other governmental ministries, they have come to form 'an exclusive club, thoroughly defended by impenetrable technical complexities.' "[8]

The position of a governmental actor, however, is more visible and thus more easily known than his behavioral role. Furthermore, an actor's position is classifiable in one of three categories—governmental, intergovernmental, or nongovernmental—whereas his role may slide back and forth between the three. Even with perfect knowledge it would become extremely difficult and ultimately arbitrary to say exactly where a governmental agent stops playing a governmentally defined role and begins to act "on his own." Furthermore, since the essays in this volume focus primarily on nongovernmental activities and organizations, a definition that stresses the governmental/nongovernmental/intergovernmental distinction focuses attention on the relationships with which we are most concerned here. For a first approximation that can be easily applied in widely varying essays, therefore, we use the narrower and more precise definition, centering on the position of an actor, rather than a broader and vaguer definition in terms of role. In the conclusion, in which we contrast a world politics paradigm with the state-centric paradigm, we reintroduce the dimension of role and discuss the problems and prospects that it raises. The reader should be aware, therefore, that in this introduction we use the phrase "transnational relations" as shorthand for "transnational interactions and organizations," whereas in the conclusion we also consider relations between governmental

actors that are not controlled by the central foreign policy organs of their governments.

Many transnational interactions take place without the individuals involved leaving their localities or the organizations maintaining any branches outside their countries of origin. Domestic industries, trade unions, and farmers engage in international trade without necessarily changing their loci of activity; bankers can move vast sums of money without leaving their offices; student groups may broadcast their views via world television while remaining in Paris, Cambridge, or Tokyo; the *New York Times* would somehow be obtained in other world capitals even if it did not maintain sales offices abroad. Thus, purely domestic organizations, such as national trade unions, can participate in transnational interactions.

Yet, we are also concerned with the activities of nongovernmental organizations that do operate regularly in several states. Transnational relations by our definition therefore include the activities of transnational organizations, except within their home states, even when some of their activities may not directly involve movements across state boundaries and may not, therefore, be transnational interactions as defined above. Thus, the activities of IBM in Brazil or Unilever in the United States are within the context of transnational relations even though some of these activities may take place entirely within Brazil, on the one hand, or the United States on the other. It would seem extremely artificial, for example, to exclude an arrangement made between Standard Oil Company of New Jersey and the French government from the arena of transnational relations merely because all negotiations for the agreement may have taken place in Paris.[9]

Multinational business enterprises, international trade union secretariats, global religious organizations, and far-flung foundations are all transnational by our definition. This does not imply, however, that they are staffed by "citizens of the world" or that they are necessarily controlled by individuals from several states. In fact, most transnational organizations remain linked primarily to one particular national society. Multinational enterprises tend to be managed by citizens from the home state; thus, according to Sidney Rolfe, 21 percent of the employees, but only 1.5 percent of the managers, of 150 United States-based multinational enterprises in the 1960s were non-American.[10] In this volume J. Bowyer Bell points out that transnational revolutionary movements often aspire to become nationalist regimes, and Peter D. Bell shows that the Ford Foundation's international staff remains predominantly American. These organizations are transnational by our definition, but they are not "geocentric."[11] An organization becomes geocentric only when the composition of its leadership and its pattern of behavior indicate that it has lost all special ties to one or two particular states.

Intergovernmental organizations often devote considerable effort to assuring that they will be geocentric in fact as well as in name: One need only note the continuing attempts by less developed states in the United Nations to assure "equitable geographical distribution" of positions in the secretariat. Transnational organizations, by contrast, are rarely established as such but usually evolve gradually from national organizations. Furthermore, they frequently do not have autonomous constituent units—such as the states in intergovernmental organizations—to insist on geocentricity. Thus, transnational organizations tend to become geocentric gradually and quite frequently move in that direction only after pressure has been brought from outside, particularly by host governments.[12]

II. SOME EFFECTS OF TRANSNATIONAL RELATIONS ON INTERSTATE POLITICS

How do transnational interactions or organizations affect interstate politics? At the most general level our contention is that these transnational relations increase the sensitivity of societies to one another and thereby alter relationships between governments. This point is illustrated by two examples, one from the area of international trade and finance, the other from global mass communications.

Richard N. Cooper has convincingly argued the case for the economic arena: As the decision domains of business and banking transcend national jurisdictions, small changes in one state's policies may have large effects on the system.[13] The essay by Lawrence Krause in this volume makes a similar point. States may be able to reduce their sensitivity to outside influence but only at the high price of reducing the concomitant benefits which result from their intercourse.

As a result of global mass communications various groups in different societies, such as radical students, military officers, or racial minorities, can observe each other's behavior and copy it when it seems appropriate. Thus, student radicals may suddenly develop similar political demands and tactics without direct contact with one another. Their international "conspiracies" are carried on in public and transmitted with the assistance of attentive media. Precursors of this phenomenon can be found, but its scale, scope, and speed are largely products of global television. Although its immediate effects are on the sensitivity of one state's domestic politics to that of another, its secondary effects—or the effects of efforts to halt unwanted communication—may well have consequences for interstate politics.

We can become more specific by suggesting five major effects of transnational interactions and organizations, all with direct or indirect consequences for mutual sensitivity and thereby for interstate politics. Four of these may result from transnational interactions even without the presence of transnational organizations, although transnational organizations may produce them as well; the fifth effect necessarily depends on the presence of transnational organizations as autonomous or quasi-autonomous actors. We summarize these effects under the following headings: 1) attitude changes, 2) international pluralism, 3) increases in constraints on states through dependence and interdependence, 4) increases in the ability of certain governments to influence others, and 5) the emergence of autonomous actors with private foreign policies that may deliberately oppose or impinge on state policies. Our categorization does not pretend to be exhaustive or definitive but is rather designed systematically to suggest some effects of transnational relations on interstate politics.

Transnational interactions of all types may promote *attitude changes* which may have possible consequences for state policies. As Warwick's essay suggests, face-to-face interactions between citizens of different states may alter the opinions and perceptions of reality of elites and nonelites within national societies. Transnational communication at a distance, transmitted either electronically or through the printed word, may also promote attitude changes. Similar results may follow, although probably less directly, from transnational transportation, travel, and finance. World peace may not, as the IBM slogan has it, come through world trade, but buying a Toyota or a Fiat may very well influence one's attitudes toward Japanese or Italians.

New attitudes can also be fostered by transnational organizations as they create new myths, symbols, and norms to provide legitimacy for their activities or as they attempt to replicate Western beliefs, lifestyles, or social practices elsewhere in the world. Thus, James A. Field, Jr., traces the activity of missionaries and the "cultural package that accompanied the Protestant gospel" in the nineteenth century as well as the economic and evangelical activities of multinational business enterprises in the twentieth century. Peter B. Evans argues that advertising by these multinational enterprises affects popular attitudes in less developed societies to the detriment of their autonomy and economic development; Robert W. Cox refers to the multinational enterprise as the new hero of functionalist theory. Cox also gives examples of the justifications for transnational economic activity developed not only by corporations but also by certain union leaders. Examining the ideas of some trade unionists, Cox perceives an emerging "policy of symbiosis" between the trade union and the corporation in which both share power and through which unions would replace nation-states as the chief countervailing force to corporate dominance of the world economy.

It is clear to Cox and to other authors in this volume that the nation-state will not be as easily replaced as such visions might imply.

Indeed, many of the essays in this volume focus on the role of the state in transnational networks. Bowyer Bell observes that even transnational revolutionaries usually seek power within a state, although they may draw support from outside; Peter Bell and Ivan Vallier focus a good deal of their attention on relations between the Ford Foundation and the Roman Catholic church, on the one hand, and the nation-states within which they operate on the other. Whereas Krause and Raymond Vernon argue for new international agreements to accommodate increases in transnational exchanges, Robert Gilpin speculates that governments will be led to support regional intergovernmental organizations as defenses against global transnationalism. A welter of divergent trends, predictions, and proposals emerges from these essays. What is clear to anyone, however, is that the attitudes produced by transnational relations will not necessarily lead to either universal concord or to the continued growth of transnational relations themselves.

A second effect of transnational relations is the promotion of *international pluralism*, by which we mean the linking of national interest groups in transnational structures, usually involving transnational organizations for purposes of coordination. The essay by Kjell Skjelsbaek documents the rapid growth of international nongovernmental organizations which link national organizations having common interests. After their creation these transnational organizations may stimulate the creation of new national affiliates and thus contribute to the internationalization of domestic politics. But transnational organizations themselves are apparently the product of increasing specialization of societies combined with the phenomena of transnational communication, travel, and transportation which allow people to perceive the possibilities for transnational organizations and to implement their visions. The creation of organizational linkages, as the essay by Edward Miles indicates, may in turn affect attempts by national groups to influence governmental policy.

It is interesting to note that the first two suggested effects of transnational relations are similar to those that have been most frequently observed by students of European integration. The "cybernetic" school of theorists has stressed the effect of transactions on mass attitude changes, whereas the "neofunctionalist" approach emphasizes the roles of interest groups and elites, or international pluralism.[14] Theorists of both varieties attempt to specify certain effects of transnational relations that are likely to constrain governments and make their policies more cooperative.

A third effect of transnational relations, the creation of *dependence and interdependence*, is often associated with international transportation and finance. The essays by Krause and Edward L. Morse focus on this relationship, and the essays by Field, Gilpin, Robert L. Thornton, and Vernon also give it a good deal of attention. Yet, as we have suggested above, one may also become dependent on a transnational communication network or on transnational travel. Even totalitarian states, if their governments want to keep pace scientifically, may have to allow their scientists to read foreign journals and to participate in international conferences. States may also become dependent on transnational organizations, particularly if those organizations provide something—goods, services, information, managerial skills, religious legitimacy—that they need.

Dependence is translated into policy most directly when certain policies which a government might otherwise follow become prohibitively costly. Integration into a world monetary system may make it impossible for a state to follow an autonomous monetary policy without drastic changes in its economy; dependence on foreign companies for technology, capital, and managerial skill may deter less developed countries from following highly nationalistic and socialistic economic policies. Where transnational organizations become important within a host society, they may alter the patterns of domestic interests so that certain governmental policies become prohibitively costly politically even if they might be feasible economically. Furthermore, new actors, such as multinational enterprises, with new patterns of behavior may raise difficulties for bureaucratized governments that tend to follow standard operating procedures when reacting to change. Following an effective policy toward a new transnational actor may therefore be too costly on bureaucratic grounds.

Coping with dependence and interdependence raises special problems for large states. Small or weak states may well be able to make their decisions solely by considering the costs and benefits of various alternative policies to themselves, taking into account, of course, the probable reactions of other states. More powerful states, however, must also consider the effects of their own policies on the system of transnational relations. Insofar as the state benefits from a particular set of linked transnational arrangements, it will need to exercise care lest a reversion to autonomy in one area sets off retaliatory measures by other large states that could—quite apart from their direct effects on the first state—destroy the entire system. Yet, only if statesmen perceive both interdependence and system-fragility will they allow considerations such as these to constrain their actions. Perceptions of transnational relations by governmental elites are therefore a crucial link between dependence or interdependence, on the one hand, and state policies on the other.

We have just noted that transnational relations may make all states dependent on forces that none of them controls. But they may have a less evenhanded result as well by creating *new instruments for influence* for use by some governments over others. Among powers of roughly equal weight both sides may be able to take advantage of these instruments, as in the use of the Pugwash Conferences on Science and World Affairs by the United States and the Union of Soviet Socialist Republics to explore questions of arms control. But among unequal states transnational relations may merely put additional means of leverage into the hands of the more powerful states, located at the center of the transnational networks, to the disadvantage of those which are already weak.

Governments have often attempted to manipulate transnational interactions to achieve results that are explicitly political: The use of tourists as spies or the cultivation of sympathetic ethnic or religious groups in other states are examples of such "informal penetration."[15] Governments may also seek, however, to direct the flow of economic transactions to their own politico-economic ends. Through the use of tariff and quota policies powerful governments may attempt to affect the flow of international trade—for example, they can discourage manufacturing in less developed countries by levying higher tariffs on imports of processed and semiprocessed goods than on raw materials. Or, as the essay by Krause indicates, governments may try to produce changes in international monetary arrangements by unilateral or multilateral action. Insofar as states become dependent on one another, some states may acquire new means by which to influence others.

Transnational organizations are particularly serviceable as instruments of governmental foreign policy whether through control or willing alliance. This has been evident in the use of United States-based multinational business enterprises by the American government. Thus, in the mid-1960s the United States sought to retard the development of France's nuclear capability not by sending an ultimatum or launching a war but by forbidding IBM-France to sell certain types of computers to the French government. The United States has also used its influence over United States-based multinational enterprises as a means of internationalizing its embargoes against the People's Republic of China (Communist China) and Cuba.[16] Cox gives examples of British and American trade unions which, following private foreign policies similar to the public foreign policies of their governments, interfere in the domestic politics of other countries to combat real or imagined communism. Even when there is no explicit coordination, transnational organizations can be useful to states. The Ford Foundation has been one of few American links to many Arab states since 1967. Vallier argues that states which hold key positions in transnational resource systems are able, often with decisive advantage, to draw on, and to some degree mobilize, all the "funds" that the system encompasses.

The fifth effect of transnational relations on interstate politics depends on the presence of transnational organizations as *autonomous* or quasi-autonomous *actors* in world politics. Several essays in this volume discuss such organizations—revolutionary movements, trade unions, multinational business enterprises, and the Roman Catholic church among others—that maintain private foreign policies. In some cases these organizations possess enormous resources: In 1965 some 85 business enterprises each had annual sales larger than the gross national products of some 57 voting members of the United Nations.[17] As Krause points out, in the monetary field the resources in the hands of some twenty banks can, at least in the short run, render nugatory the efforts of national monetary authorities even in very powerful countries. Thus, autonomous transnational organizations are potential and sometimes actual opponents of governmental policy in a wide variety of areas—whether the policy is liberalizing divorce in Italy, living at peace with Israel in the Middle East, enforcing economic plans in France, or maintaining a strong balance-of-payments position in the United Kingdom. The conflict between government and transnational organizations may reflect the policies of a home government standing behind the transnational organization, but it may also result from differences between the policies of a host government and those of a transnational organization, without the home government, if any, becoming involved in the dispute.

Where home governments are involved, the presence of transnational organizations may exert a distinctive effect on the interstate relations that develop. Thus, it would be difficult to understand British-Iranian relations during 1951–1953 or American-Cuban relations between 1959 and 1961 without appreciating the role of certain international oil companies in both situations.[18] In these cases actions by the oil companies almost certainly aggravated existing interstate conflicts. It is possible, however, for a transnational organization also to facilitate good relations between states; certainly, these same oil companies have tried to foster cooperation between the United States and the Arab world. Their efforts have, in turn, been partially foiled by a very powerful transnational force—namely, Zionism—which has worked effectively for good American relations with Israel even at the expense of United States relations with Israel's adversaries. Not only may a struggle between transnational organizations, or between transnational organizations and states, lead to interstate conflict; interstate conflict, such as the Arab-Israeli conflict, may lead to struggles for influence among transnational organizations or movements. The interrelationships are complex and often reciprocal, but they can hardly be ignored.

III. TRANSNATIONAL RELATIONS AND "LOSS OF CONTROL" BY GOVERNMENTS

Our observations about changes in world politics do not deny that governments remain the most important players in the game. Although transnational organizations are immensely more plentiful and significant now than before 1914 or 1945, governments have attempted since World War I not only to maintain but also to extend their control over outside forces and events. Previously ignored areas of activity have been brought within the regulation and concern of governments. International monetary flows, for example, were of much less importance to governments before 1914 than they are now. In those years few governments consciously attempted to plan economic growth or to promote full employment at home. As Cooper has stressed, new tasks for governments "place greater burdens on the available instruments of policy" and make it more difficult to accept "the intrusions of international economic integration on national economic policy."[19] Thus, the sensitivity of governments to changes elsewhere increases as governments become more ambitious. Increased aspirations for control and increased interdependence go hand in hand.

It therefore becomes clear that to pose questions such as we did at the outset in terms of an alleged "loss of control" is to put the issue in a misleading way. Governments have generally not been able to control their environments successfully for long periods of time whenever those environments have changed rapidly as a result of large-scale social forces or advancing technology. Small and middle powers, and even great powers within a balance-of-power system, have had to accustom themselves to a very small degree of environmental control; they have had to adjust to changes rather than to shape the forces of history. It may be that United States policymakers have less control now than in the 1950s, but it was the 1950s that were exceptional, not the present.

As governments become more ambitious, however, the impact of transnational relations does create a "control gap" between the aspiration for control and the capability to achieve it. The essays by Morse, Krause, and Vernon discuss various facets of this problem. At the same time, as Vallier and Evans argue, transnational relations may redistribute control from one state to another and benefit those governments at the center of transnational networks to the disadvantage of those in the periphery.

It seems better, therefore, to raise the issue of governmental control as a question for investigation rather than to prejudge the issue at this point in terms of "loss of control." It is clear that governments are becoming more ambitious and that this forces them to react to, and often to adapt to, transnational interactions and organizations. The further governments seek to extend their reach, the more they involve themselves with the environment of interstate politics and particularly with transnational relations. Insofar as they are unwilling to pay the price for complete control, they must contend with relatively autonomous transnational forces. From the analyst's perspective, therefore, their behavior becomes more and more difficult to predict without a rather detailed knowledge of transnational relations. Our next question is therefore posed: Does the phenomenon of transnational relations make the state-centric paradigm inadequate for understanding contemporary world politics?

IV. TRANSNATIONAL RELATIONS AND THE STATE-CENTRIC PARADIGM

Sophisticated proponents of the state-centric view have observed transnational inter-actions, and they have certainly not been blind to the fact that actors other than states exist. Yet, they have deliberately excluded transnational relations from the interstate system on the grounds that their direct polit-ical importance is small and that their indirect effects enter, along with domestic factors, into the formation of national foreign pol-icies. Although this conclusion has partially relied on a definition of politics merely in terms of state behavior, it does contain a solid core of insight. States have been and remain the most important actors in world affairs, acting both directly and through intergovernmental organizations to which states, and only states, belong. States virtu-ally monopolize large-scale, organized force which remains the ultimate weapon and a potent bargaining resource. Thus, there would be no point in ignoring the nation-state. Instead, one might ask the following questions: Should more attention be paid to the effects of transnational relations on inter-state relations, and is the state-centric para-digm adequate if we wish to explore these effects? Evans has expressed this feeling pungently although in a somewhat "loaded" way: "It is not interesting to exclude tra-ditional state behavior and then study the residual only. What is interesting is the con-tamination of interstate relations by trans-national relations."[20]

If we depart from a state-centric, insti-tutional definition of politics, the need for a broader focus becomes evident immediately. The classic model as depicted in Figure 2.1 normally assumed as a definition of world politics the actions and interactions of states. Students of domestic politics, however, have moved away from such exclusive reliance on the state and have focused more broadly on the process by which societies make binding decisions.[21] The problems with definitions such as David Easton's are well known: Departing from a traditional, narrow view of politics seems to lead one to a definition without clear limits. Until we adopt a broader definition, however, we continue to view governments as more clearly unique than they are, and we are foreclosed from examin-ing the politics of trade unions, industrial corporations, or schools. Likewise, with international politics, a definition of politics in terms of state behavior alone may lead us to ignore important nongovernmental actors that allocate value and that use means similar to those used by governments to achieve their ends.

We therefore prefer a definition of politics that refers to relationships in which at least one actor consciously employs resources, both material and symbolic, including the threat or exercise of punishment, to induce other actors to behave differently than they would otherwise behave. Using this defin-ition of politics, we define world politics as all political interactions between significant actors in a world system in which a signifi-cant actor is any somewhat autonomous individual or organization that controls sub-stantial resources and participates in political relationships with other actors across state lines.[22] Such an actor need not be a state: At any point where a transnational organiza-tion employs techniques such as economic boycotts, airline hijackings, or religious excommunication to achieve the modifica-tion of other actors' behavior, it is behaving politically. International oil companies, for example, insofar as they act to maintain political stability in producing countries, are transnational political actors by this definition.[23]

If the effects of transnational relations were slight, variable, and perhaps transitory, consigning them to a vaguely specified and generally ignored environment would be acceptable as a parsimonious simplifying device. Yet, this entire volume testifies to the fact that the effects of transnational relations are much more important and pervasive than that. Knowing the policies and capabilities of a set of governments may not allow us accur-ately to predict outcomes or future character-istics of the system if significant transnational interactions or powerful transnational orga-nizations are involved. Even if states in some sense "win" confrontations with transnational forces, their anticipation of these forces, and of the actions of transnational organizations, may lead states to alter their policies in advance to avoid costly confrontations.

Transnational relations are not "new," although, as Skjelsbaek's essay indicates, the growth of transnational organization in the twentieth century has been spectacular. Yet, our contention is not only that the state-centric paradigm is inadequate for reasons indicated above but also that it is becoming progressively more inadequate as changes in transnational relations take place. As a partial view of international politics it was more useful in the past than in the present, and it is still more useful now than it is likely to be in the future. The essays shed some light on changes in transnational relations; the conclusion to this volume attempts to draw the evidence together in order to buttress the case that has been sketched above and to introduce our alternative "world politics paradigm" as a substitute for the state-centric analytic framework.

V. TRANSNATIONAL RELATIONS AND VALUES

Thus far in this essay we have been viewing transnational relations largely from an empirical perspective, but they can also be evaluated normatively. This immediately raises the question of who benefits from transnational relations. It could be argued that transnational relations enrich and strengthen the strong and the rich—in short, the most modernized, technologically adept segments of the world—because only these elements are able to take full advantage of its network of intersocietal linkages. The continuing debate on the effects of multinational business enterprises on welfare, for example, has raised numerous questions about the value of transnational relations for less developed countries in particular.[24] Many of the essays in this volume, particularly those in parts III and IV, raise questions of this kind. In producing a volume that emphasizes transnational interactions and organizations

we mean to point out their importance, not necessarily to celebrate their effects.

Some would regard transnational relations as a new name for the old phenomenon of imperialism. As one scholar has noted, however, the word "imperialism" is "entirely at the mercy of its user."[25] It is sometimes used to describe virtually any relationship across state boundaries between unequals that involves the exercise of influence. If this definition is used, "imperialism" includes most of world politics and thereby becomes virtually devoid of analytic value.

Imperialism may be used, however, in a more restricted although not very precise way to refer to cross-national relationships in which unequal power is used to achieve "unfair" allocations of value. Some actors, whether states or not, exploit others. Given an agreed concept of "fairness" (which is, of course, the chief difficulty) some transnational relations would presumably be "imperialistic" and others would not. Yet, the ambiguities present even in this use of "imperialism" are so great that we would rather ask directly about the effects of transnational relations than inquire whether a given set of transnational relations is "imperialistic" or not. Focusing on "asymmetries" or "inequalities" seems more useful to us than trying to employ older terms encrusted with many layers of ambiguous or contradictory meaning.

The reader should therefore bear in mind while reading these essays Harold Lasswell's definition of politics in terms of "who gets what." Do the activities of multinational business enterprises, trade unions, or the Ford Foundation redistribute economic resources? If so, in what direction does the flow go? Do these transnational organizations, or transnational interactions generally, differentially affect the welfare, security, or autonomy of various states or regions? To what extent are the effects unidirectional and to what extent are cross-currents more typical, with some benefits and some costs for each state or region? Once again, the conclusion attempts to draw together evidence from the essays in order to give at least a tentative answer to these questions.

NOTES

1. This is, of course, the orientation of Hans J. Morgenthau, but it also reflects the general point of view of eminent scholars like Raymond Aron and Kenneth N. Waltz. See Morgenthau, *Politics among Nations: The Struggle for Peace and Power* (4th rev. ed.; New York: Alfred A. Knopf, 1967); Aron, *Peace and War: A Theory of International Relations*, trans. Richard Howard and Annette Baker Fox (New York: Frederick A. Praeger, 1967); and Waltz, *Man, the State and War: A Theoretical Analysis* (Topical Studies in International Relations No. 2) (New York: Columbia University Press, 1959).

2. International lawyers and economists seem less prone to accept the state-centric paradigm as much of the literature in international economics and international law indicates. See, particularly, the works of Richard Cooper, Raymond Vernon, and Philip Jessup.

3. Arnold Wolfers, "The Actors in World Politics," in *Discord and Collaboration: Essays on International Politics*, ed. Arnold Wolfers (Baltimore, Md: Johns Hopkins Press, 1962), p. 23. This essay was first published in 1959 in William T. R. Fox, ed., *Theoretical Aspects of International Relations* (Notre Dame, Ind: University of Notre Dame Press, 1959). Other political scientists who have departed from the state-centric paradigm are John W. Burton, *Systems, States, Diplomacy and Rules* (Cambridge: Cambridge University Press, 1968); James N. Rosenau, ed., *Linkage Politics: Essays on the Convergence of National and International Systems* (New York: Free Press, 1969); Karl Kaiser, "Transnationale Politik: Zu einer Theorie der multinationalen Politik," *Politische Vierteljahresschrift*, 1969 (Special Issue, No. 1), pp. 80–109; and Horst Menderhausen, "Transnational Society vs. State Sovereignty," *Kyklos*, 1969 (Vol. 22, No. 2), pp. 251–275.

4. The most striking examples of neglect of transnational relations and complete concentration on state policies appear in the literature on the North Atlantic Treaty Organization (NATO). See, for example, Henry A. Kissinger, *The Troubled Partnership: A Re-Appraisal of the Atlantic Alliance* (New York: McGraw Hill Book Co. [for the Council on Foreign Relations], 1965). On the more theoretical side the editors of a recent volume of essays on international relations note that, despite ardent disagreement over methods, "each author clearly conceives the subject to consist of the individuals and groups who initiate and sustain the actions and interactions of nation-states." Klaus Knorr and James N. Rosenau, eds., *Contending Approaches to International Politics* (Princeton, N.J.: Princeton University Press, 1969), p. 4.

5. As our conclusion explains at greater length, "transnational interactions" constitute only one aspect of "transnational relations" by our definition. Yet, most of the essays that follow focus on transnational interactions and transnational organizations. Thus, in order to understand the essays, our definition of transnational interactions is crucial.

6. J. David Singer, "The Global System and Its Subsystems: A Developmental View," in Rosenau, p. 24.

7. Robert O. Keohane, "The Big Influence of Small Allies," *Foreign Policy*, Spring 1971 (Vol. 1, No. 2), pp. 161–182.

8. Leon N. Lindberg and Stuart A. Scheingold, *Europe's Would-Be Polity: Patterns of Change in the European Community* (Englewood Cliffs, N.J.: Prentice-Hall, 1970), p. 160. Their quotation is from "How Not to Rule the Roost: More Trouble in the Poultry Market," *Common Market*, July 1963 (Vol. 3, No. 7), p. 131.

9. It would seem equally absurd, on the other hand, to consider a grant by the Ford Foundation to Newark, New Jersey, or the sale of computers by IBM in Des Moines, Iowa, to be transnational activities. Thus, we exclude from transnational relations the activities of transnational organizations within their home states if the organizations retain such national identification.

10. Sidney Rolfe, *The International Corporation* (Paris: International Chamber of Commerce, 1969), p. 76.

11. For these terms see Howard V. Perlmutter, "The Tortuous Evolution of the Multinational Corporation," *Columbia Journal of World Business*, January-February 1969 (Vol. 4, No. 1), pp. 9–18.

12. To encompass transnational organizations as well as interactions Figure 2.2 would have to be three-dimensional. Transnational organizations would appear on the third dimension, linked to governments, national societies, and intergovernmental organizations by a variety of interactions. Since such a representation is beyond our artistic powers, the reader will have to be content with the reminder that transnational relations under our definition include these organizational activities as well as the interactions that Figure 2.2 depicts.

13. Richard N. Cooper, *The Economics of Interdependence: Economic Policy in the Atlantic Community* (Atlantic Policy Studies) (New York: McGraw-Hill Book Co. [for the Council on Foreign Relations], 1968), especially chapters 3, 4, and 6.

14. See Peter J. Katzenstein, "Hare and Tortoise: The Race toward Integration," *International Organization*, Spring 1971 (Vol. 25, No. 2), pp. 290–295.

15. See Andrew M. Scott, *The Revolution in Statecraft: Informal Penetration* (Random House Studies in Political Science, 551) (New York: Random House, 1965); and Richard W. Cottam, *Competitive Interference and Twentieth Century Diplomacy* (Pittsburgh, Pa.: Pittsburgh University Press, 1967).

16. For a discussion of some of the controls used by the United States for these purposes see Jack N. Behrman, *National Interests and the Multinational Enterprise: Tensions among the North*

Atlantic Countries (Englewood Cliffs, N.J.: Prentice-Hall, 1970), chapter 7, pp. 101–113.

17. G. Modelski, "The Corporation in World Society," *The Year Book of World Affairs, 1968* (London: Stevens & Sons [under the auspices of the London Institute of World Affairs], 1968), pp. 64–79.

18. For a discussion of these cases see Michael Tanzer, *The Political Economy of International Oil and the Underdeveloped Countries* (Boston: Beacon Press, 1969), chapter 24, pp. 319–348.

19. Cooper, p. 151.

20. This is a close paraphrase of a remark made by Evans at the Center for International Affairs Conference on Transnational Relations, Harvard University, June 4–5, 1970.

21. For a discussion of this trend see David Easton, "Political Science," *International Encyclopedia of the Social Sciences*, ed. David L. Sills (17 vols; n.p: Macmillan Co. and Free Press, 1968), Vol. 12, pp. 282–298.

22. These definitions borrow heavily and consciously, although with substantial modification, from an essay by Oran R. Young, "The Actors in World Politics," in *The Analysis of International Politics*, ed. James N. Rosenau, B. Vincent Davis and Maurice A. East (Glencoe, Ill: Free Press, forthcoming).

23. For an analysis of the activities of these corporations see Tanzer.

24. For some recent works on the subject see Charles P. Kindleberger, *American Business Abroad: Six Lectures on Direct Investment* (New Haven, Conn: Yale University Press, 1969); Harry Magdoff, *The Age of Imperialism: The Economics of U.S. Foreign Policy* (New York: Monthly Review Press, 1969); and Harry Johnson, "The Efficiency and Welfare Implications of the International Corporation," in *The International Corporation: A Symposium*, ed. Charles P. Kindleberger (Cambridge, Mass: M.I.T. Press, 1970), pp. 35–56.

25. Hans Daalder, "Imperialism," in the *International Encyclopedia of the Social Sciences*, Vol. 7, p. 108.

CHAPTER 3

"Conclusions" and "Post Scriptum" from *Dependency and Development in Latin America*[1]

Fernando Henrique Cardoso and Enzo Faletto

CONCLUSIONS

From a methodological standpoint, we attempt to reconsider the problems of economic development through an interpretation emphasizing the political character of the processes of economic transformation. At the same time, we try to demonstrate that the historical situation in which the economic transformations occur must be taken into account if these changes as well as their structural limitations are to be understood.

This formulation of the relation between economic process, structural conditions, and historical situations makes clear that theoretical schemes concerning the formation of capitalist society in present-day *developed* countries are of little use in understanding the situation in Latin American countries. Not only the historical moment but also the structural conditions of development and society are different. Recognizing these differences, we go on to criticize the concepts of underdevelopment and economic periphery and to stress both the economic aspects of underdevelopment and the political process by which some countries dominate others. We stress the specificity of installations of capitalist production in dependent societies.

We return to the tradition of political thought that there is no metaphysical relation of dependence between one nation and another, between one state and another. These relations are made possible through a network of interests and coercions that bind some social groups to others, some classes to others. This being the case, it is necessary to determine the way in which state, class, and production are related in each basic situation of dependence.

To characterize these relations, we show that Latin American class relations can be defined both in terms of the relationship between the production system and the international market and in terms of the form of control of production. Defining class relations in these ways reveals two basic historical situations. In one case, we point to the specificity of the enclave economies; in the other, to national control of the export system.

We go on to indicate how these historical transformations occur in particular social formations, and we avoid the two fallacies frequently found in similar interpretations: a belief that the internal or national sociopolitical situation is mechanically conditioned by external dominance; and the opposite idea that all is due to historical contingency. In fact, even the relation of dependence does not mean that national history in dependent nations will simply reflect changes in the external hegemonic center, although these changes are relevant to the possible autonomy of national history. There are structural limits to possible action, beginning with the available material base of production and the degree of development of the forces of production, and including the way in which these are combined with political and juridical relations within the country and its link with the hegemonic countries. Through the actions of groups, classes, organizations, and social movements in the dependent countries, these links are perpetuated, modified, or broken. Therefore, there is an internal dynamic that explains the course of events and thereby makes possible a political analysis.

We show how the different structural possibilities of an enclave situation and of a situation in which the export system is nationally controlled affect the social, political, and economic changes that take place in the countries under consideration.

In the final chapters we return to the general topic of the structural conditions of capitalist development in dependent countries. We characterize the contradictions between the pattern of dependent industrialization and the interests of the nation, as well as the conflicts in the relations among classes and social groups and between the latter and the state.

We also try to show the relative autonomy, the conflict, and the possibilities of convergence between the economic system and the political process. We point out that for an understanding of the present situation of the industrialized and dependent countries of Latin America, an analysis is required of the increasing control over the economic system of nations by large multinational corporations.

The originality of the hypothesis is not in its recognition of the existence of external domination—an obvious process. It is in its description of the form and the effects of this type of dependence on classes and state with reference to past situations. The present situation of dependent development goes beyond the traditional dichotomy between the terms "development" and "dependence," because it permits an increase in development while maintaining and redefining the links of dependency. The present situation is supported politically by a system of alliances that are different from those that previously assured external hegemony. It is no longer the exporting interests that subordinate the interests associated with the domestic market, nor rural interests that oppose urban ones as an expression of economic domination. The specificity of the present situation of dependence is in part that internal interests are rooted more and more in the sector producing for the domestic market and thus

that they are united in political alliances that are supported by urban populations. The formation of an industrial economy in the periphery of the capitalist system minimizes the effects of the typically colonial exploitation; this economy incorporates not only the dominant classes but also social groups tied to modern capitalist production, such as wage earners, technicians, entrepreneurs, and bureaucrats.

The great political movements that try to form and strengthen the domestic market and the national economy—populism and nationalism—lose meaning in the new situation of dependence.

We speculate how far dependence can be maintained within the transformation described, or whether it will have to be replaced by interdependence. In this connection, we analyze the specificity of the structural situation together with the political situation. It is shown that the power interests and the alliances to guarantee the hegemony of internal and external groups and class factions have to be considered if the situation of diversification of the economic system is to be explained.

The basic economic conditions of development are an open market, the exclusion of the dependent economies from the markets of the most developed countries, and the continuous transfer of new units of external capital in the form of advanced technology, which are more appropriate to the intrinsic needs of the mature economies than to those of the relatively backward economies. The combination of these conditions with the ideologies and legal relations among social groups makes possible "industrial economies in dependent societies." Whether the structural barriers to development remain or are overcome will be determined by how these economic conditions are used in the power game rather than by the particular economic conditions themselves. In this sense, we suggest that present or potential opposition may vitalize the industrialized and dependent countries of Latin America. There are structural possibilities for various types of social and political movements.

The course of history depends largely on the daring of those who propose to act in terms of historically viable goals. We do not try to place theoretical limits on the probable course of future events. These will depend, not on academic predictions, but on collective action guided by political wills that make work what is structurally barely possible.

"POST SCRIPTUM"

[. . .]

It was in the context we have briefly summarized above that multinational corporations expanded in Latin America and in the rest of the world. This expansion has contributed to speculation concerning the future of capitalist economy and the role which the state plays in it. In accord with a recently proposed characterization,[2] three fundamental ways of considering the relationship between the state and the multinationals may be mentioned:

—The liberal theory, followed by those who accept the "sovereignty at bay" model proposed by Raymond Vernon. This model sees in the multinationals the nucleus of future progress and the rationalizing principle of a new world market integrated under their control, and in which the state will play a marginal role.

—The "dependence" model, which denies the balancing effect of multinationals in the redistribution of wealth and benefits on a world scale. This model emphasizes that technical progress and financial control of the results of international expansion are concentrated in a few capitalist centers, which will go on exploiting and preserving the dependence and underdevelopment of the periphery. Despite the critical view of this model, the multinationals remain privileged actors in the world scene.[3]

—The mercantile model, which underlines the importance of the nation-state as a reorienting principle of world order, and which believes that the question of the future is not so much the disappearance of states and the preeminence of a kind of "world corporation" organized on the basis of the multinationals, but rather that it is precisely one of defining limits, conflicts, and compromises between states and multinationals, by means of the formation of regional blocks in the world market.

We believe that an approach combining the last two models offers a more adequate explanation of the role of multinational corporations in Latin America, both as to the countries where they have their headquarters and as to the host countries. We think that to consider the multinationals independently from these countries as if they were demiurges of history leads to a double reductionism: that is, it subordinates local reaction to the "logic of accumulation of multinational corporations" and therefore to "external factors," and it minimizes the importance of political factors in the development of contemporary capitalist economy, both internationally and in individual countries.

It should also be made clear that the type of linkage between industrial multinationals and national economies varies for economic reasons. The backward and forward effects that can be expected vary according to the type of goods produced (industrial, mineral, or agricultural) and according to the production techniques and the stage of consumption aimed at (industrial input, product parts for export, durable consumer goods, etc.).[4] In order to evaluate the effects of incorporating peripheral economies into world production, it is further necessary to distinguish at least four situations that can create a linkage between dependent economies and market internationalization:

—"Industrial platforms" for the exportation of industrial products may be established in countries where the multinational corporations primarily seek comparative advantages, such as the use of cheap labor, and where the final product is not consumed (as in the case of Singapore or Hong Kong).

—Former enclaves of colonial production may be transformed into enclaves controlled no longer by colonialist states, but rather by imperialist corporations, as in the case of mining in Africa and the production of tropical foods.

—Parts for complex industrial products may be produced which, although not necessarily consumed in the local market, presuppose more specialized labor and relatively advanced technology in the local economy.

—Consumer or capital industrial goods may be produced under the control of multinational corporations, but aimed primarily at local markets.

There have been cases of enclave economies in Latin America that have been redefined to the extent that the world economy has become "multinationalized," for example, bauxite production in Jamaica, oil drilling in Ecuador, or banana production in Guatemala. However, the last two forms of linkage are more significant because their effects are more complex and usually occur together. The region offers few relevant examples of "industrial export platforms" controlled by multinational corporations. Exportable industrial consumer goods, such as shoes and textiles, are controlled essentially by local companies, except in the special case of the cosmetics industry in Mexico. Consumer goods (automobiles, refrigerators, television sets, etc.) produced by multinationals may be exported, but in general this is due to pressures exerted by local governments wishing to solve incidental problems in their balance of payments. Even so, the bulk of durable consumer goods produced is destined for local markets.

This is why, particularly in the industrially more developed countries (Argentina, Brazil, Chile, Colombia, Peru, Venezuela, and Mexico), the issues of historical significance do not have to do with the relationship between a "consuming" bourgeoisie (such as is found in Asia or Africa) and the multinational corporations. Instead, they have to do with the relationships between local bourgeoisie, the state, and the multinationals, together with the various possible reactions to the alliances that these participants may define.

It is for this reason that in the case of the capitalistically more developed countries in the region, one must consider the form that dependence assumes when there is room for some kind of associated capitalistic develop-ment. Here the role of the state is fundamental, and it will be treated in a separate section. However, before we develop this theme, we should point out the immediate political effects brought about by the current way in which the internationalizing process of markets and production continues. It should be emphasized that if this line of analysis were followed, it would be too general (abstract) and therefore incorrect to insist solely on economic conditioning (that is, on the "logic of accumulation of multinationals") as if such conditioning (which is a point of departure for the explanation) did not depend on class struggle and, internationally, on conflicts between states. Let us consider, then, in decreasing order of abstraction, how the action of the states appears on the international stage. [. . .]

The contradiction between the state as the agent of capitalist enterprise, and the nation as something that is essentially popular, follows a movement that is not only different but *opposite*, in the recent history of Peru and Brazil. Though the Peruvian state may be bureaucratic-authoritarian, its policies are oriented toward the incorporation of the masses, or at least toward the partial consideration of peasant and popular interests. These objectives may have been frustrated and difficult to secure within a policy that stifled the spontaneity of popular reaction, congealed political parties, and harbored seeds of military-bureaucratism. However, its ideology and what it has done to reorganize the socio-economic order distinguish the Peruvian state from that of the bureaucratic-authoritarian state of Brazil.

Political regimes vary, as does the relation of bureaucratic-authoritarianism to the social bases of the state (viewed as a pact of domination). Nevertheless, the current form of dependency and the crucial role performed in it by multinational enterprises and by the state productive sector are no accident. It is necessary to draw a distinction between the state, as a basic part of domination (and not as the expression of a "social contract") which unites dominant classes in the exercise of domination over the rest of society, and the variable forms assumed by political *regimes*. The state expresses a situation of domination, reflects the interests of dominant classes, and expresses their capacity to impose themselves on subordinate classes. At the same time this discriminatory relationship (the domination of one part over the rest) must appear to the national consciousness to be the expression of a general interest. Consequently, the state constitutes a relationship of domination incorporating *an ideology* that masks that partiality. This process is not a simple distortion: it must also mirror, in some way, the generality it wishes to represent. Hence, even the most openly classist and repressive states use a language and propose policies (generally nonviable) that purport to reflect the "general interest."

So, the state expresses the imposition of one class or alliance of classes over others. But while it serves those interests on which it bases itself, the state proposes measures that lend verisimilitude to the "generality of interests" which it must assume to exist (people, equality, nation). In addition to expressing a relationship like this at this level, the state is also a bureaucratic-regulative organization and, in the case of modern states, becomes even a productive economic organization.

To summarize, any state, through bureaucratic and productive organizations, expresses a relationship of class domination (and consequently has social bases), assumes an ideology as if in the common interest, develops and implements policies that respond to the fundamental pact of domination, but also claims to attend to the aspirations of dominated groups. Officials of the state (notably in the judicial sector) have to adopt both an ideology of equality and generality ("all citizens are equal before the law") and a practice in which dominant interests impose themselves.

In the industrialized countries of Latin America which we are considering, the state embodies an alliance between the interests of the internationalized sector of the bourgeoisie and those of public and entrepreneurial bureaucracies. The local bourgeoisie links itself to these sectors. In part, the state in dependent capitalism generates its own social base, since its productive function is to assure capital accumulation, and since in performing this function, it creates a sector of public entrepreneurs. At times this stratum is called the "state bourgeoisie," to emphasize that these social agents are not simple bureaucrats nor do they simply implement the "public good." They function, sociologically, as the "officeholders of capital." For they support the accumulation of capital in the state enterprises. Both the accumulation of capital by public enterprises and the placing of all of the national wealth (mineral ore, impounded taxes, lands, roadways, etc.) at the disposal of private capital are fundamental requirements for the advancement of associated-dependent capitalism.

The state extends a bureaucracy and bases itself on a civil and military technocracy. The latter carries out the interests that are expressed by the state. Certainly, an inversion of this relationship can occur. The actors may occupy prominent positions on the political scene. The military bureaucracy may predominate in the control of the state. But in the end, long-term policies must be compatible with the social bases of the state. In the realization of policies of accumulation and development, though the bureaucratic framework may be in the hands of a technocratic-bureaucracy or a corporative military (together or separately), the nature of the dominant state relationship develops through the strengthening of the alliance between the local entrepreneurial sector, associated with the multinational foreign enterprises, and the state productive sector.

The same fundamental alliance which constitutes a dependent industrial capitalist state may organize itself institutionally within a context of authoritarianism, restricted democracy, or totalitarianism. There is little credibility in its structural compatibility with substantive forms of mass-democracy, populism, or even traditional caudillo (bossist) authoritarianism, since in these regimes the requisite policies leading to the expansion of industrial dependent capitalism become difficult to implement, because of the masses' interests in economic redistribution and political participation.

Not that Venezuela, Colombia, and Argentina will *necessarily* have to adapt themselves to the Brazilian or Peruvian military-bureaucratic-authoritarian model. These last two regimes are themselves quite different, both in the nature of their policies and in the nature of their respective social bases. The bureaucratic-authoritarian *form* of a regime like that of Brazil is not the *only* one capable of adapting to the "present stage" of capital accumulation. Economic reductionism in this case would fail to consider the changes that might occur from government to government (with, we repeat, the basic state pact maintained). There are many factors that function as sources of dynamism in history: (1) circumstantial factors such as explosions of collective protest (the 1974 Brazilian elections provide an example different from the Cordobazo, because the correlation of forces differs in the two countries); (2) struggles within dominant sectors; (3) the emergence of objective economic challenges (recessions, soaring inflation, a "new stage" of import substitution in the capital goods sector, for example); (4) the ability of the governing group to resolve problems and the opposition's ability to debate them, and so forth. Not all changes are always possible, to be sure, nor do political forces capable of taking advantage of opportunities for transformation always exist. But even in bureaucratic-authoritarian regimes, and even with the persistence of the alliance that underlies the state, there is room for regime-types to vary historically. What is at issue is not just a "mere change in form." The differences between a torturing autocratic regime and a "restricted democracy" arise out of the very possibilities for struggles among classes, and they in turn influence the historical opportunities of the dependent capitalist-industrial state.

A basic problem exists, posed by the present moment and by Latin American situations of dependency: the very penetration of multinationals requires a state that is capable of furnishing the multinationals with the resources for accumulation. So national wealth is necessary for foreign private accumulation. But this process is contradictory: for this to work, the state must fortify itself and expand its functions at both the administrative and the economic levels, in this way increasing its prospects for sovereignty.

Faced with the political challenges of dominated classes to radically reorder society, this entrepreneurial-regulative state militarizes itself, becoming even stronger and more autocratic. At this point the relative loosening of ties between the state and its *social base* may occur, which the economically ruling classes may perceive as a risk of "Bonapartization" of the state. The spectrum of this perceived risk ranges from the emergency of a new Perón to a "mythical Peruvianism" that would lead the armed forces to ally with the people. In the process of exercising sovereignty and equipping the state with entrepreneurial skills, which allow both international and local accumulation, the entrepreneurial-repressive state *dissociates* itself from the nation. *This* is the specific political contradiction in the current form of Latin American dependent development.

There may have been a redefinition of the "forms of dependency," in certain Latin American countries there may be "less dependency," and the state in these countries may be capable of exercising a greater degree of sovereignty. But for us, what is at issue is the nature of class conflicts and alliances which the dependency situation encompasses.

As we stated previously, the political struggle revolving around the state shows what is essential in this form of dependency: the style of development of the possibility of alternatives depends upon the resolution of this question of the state. In the Chilean Popular Unity, in Peru, and in the Popular Assembly of the Torres period in Bolivia, popular forces or forces with popular intentions momentarily assumed control of the state. We find, in these cases, ambiguity about what constitutes the "popular" and unanimity regarding *national* demands. The fundamental challenge of the present moment in Latin American social development consists in linking these two aspects of radical political movements, the popular and the national, and in getting to the bottom of the opposition between the popular and the proletarian. What is specific to the Latin American situation of dependency is the difficulty in conceiving of a political passage to socialism by a strictly proletarian route, given the structural conditions of industrial capitalism in the periphery. So, alliances between popular movements, national-popular demands, and properly working-class struggles are required to enforce new paths in society.

These questions, however, are not posed today as they were during the populist period. The advance of mass industrial society, urbanization, the revolution in communication, even the situations of dependent-*development* themselves, pose the political question of popular participation in such a way as to *exclude manipulative links with dominant classes through the state* as an option. Such links were the basis of populism's policy. The internationalization of production and of the market have advanced, and the state productive sector has expressed itself in capitalist form. For the ruling groups, the nation is embodied in the state as the stimulus for an enterprise economy. But, at the same time, for dominated classes, the paternalism of the traditional Latin American state (in both the oligarchical and populist versions) has been broken. Although politically frustrated, the guerrilla movements did serve the function of disrupting this paternalism and putting an end to manipulative types of alliance which once tied the people to the state in the name of the nation.

The practical issues that will permit development of an alternative type of state involve, first, knowing which course "substantive democratization" must take to affirm what is essential in the national and the popular and free from the rancidity of bureaucratization and authoritarianism, and second, knowing how to balance the need for organization and the vitality of spontaneous mass behavior. As in any case of social transformation, such questions go beyond analysis and anchor themselves in values: they are projected into the future to assist in the practical escape from a situation that reinforces the prevailing exploitative order. It is not within the boundaries of this book to pursue these questions. It is barely within those boundaries to point out, as we have, that social practice in Latin America has already begun to deal with these questions (even if in experiences that failed).

Researchers have directed their attention to ideology and corporativist forms in Latin America.[5] It appears to us that the fusion between enterprise and the state, both of them based on bureaucracies, and the role of armies in Latin American regimes, underscore the corporativist ties between the state and society.[6] During certain periods of political life, the relationship between civil society and the state seems to dispense with the mediation of parties: classes just appropriate segments of the state apparatus to defend their interests. Sometimes connections are formed through "bureaucratic rings," which are organized around high officials (cabinet ministers, generals, etc.) and which articulate the immediate interests of enterprises, government bureaus, the press, sometimes unions, repressive groups, and so forth around some specific policy or issue. In bureaucratic-authoritarian politics these semiformal structures substitute for an organization that is more stable and representative of class interests, namely parties. Particularly when regimes are centralized and positions at the top are decisive in the articulation of interests (Mexico, Chile, Brazil, Peru), bureaucratic rings seem to constitute the form of political linkage that establishes connections between civil society and the state. The linkage is not very stable, since the key official can be dismissed and the ring thereby broken.[7]

These formal aspects of the juncture between the state and civil society should not obscure the characteristics of the state in contemporary Latin America which we have already pointed out. The state is the expression of the dynamism of business enterprises and of the classes that control them as they operate in a context in which bureaucracies and the regulative and organizational capacities of the state are expanding. The basic ideology of the state is fundamentally "developmentalism." In view of the explicit ends of economic growth and national grandeur, the exploitation of workers, if not openly defended by the state, is justified by the argument that the tightening of belts is necessary "at the moment" so that "in the future" the results of this economy may be redistributed. We do not endorse studies of Latin American corporativism that see in it a "profound cultural trend," consonant with that society's patrimonialist structures. These structures were real in another and bygone situation, but in the current period of industrial-financial capitalist development, an insistence on the "necessity" of the corporative form in Latin American political relations seems to us an anachronistic and conservative point of view. When corporativist forms exist, and there are circumstances in which they do, they express the pact of dominion among classes trying to implant capitalist development, and the opposition which these attempts encounter in the political movements of subordinate classes.

Instead of insisting on the immutability of the "cultural dimension" and historical roots of corporativism, it seems to us that what is important is an understanding of the essence of contradiction between interests of people and current style of development, between the state and the nation. In these relationships of opposition, if any cultural dimension exists and carries significance, it is what Gramsci called a relationship of hegemony: the capacity to rule. The effective battle is not between corporativism and the democratic tradition. It is between technocratic elitism and a vision of the formative process of a mass industrial society which can offer what is popular as specifically national and which succeeds in transforming the demand for a more developed economy and for a democratic society into a state that expresses the vitality of truly popular forces, capable of seeking socialist forms for the social organization of the future.

NOTES

1. Translated by Victoria Garcia
2. See Gilpin, Robert, *U.S. Power and the Multinational Corporation: The Political Economy of Foreign Direct Investment* (New York: Basic Books, 1975).
3. It should be clear from reading this essay that the authors do not accept this formulation of the dependence thesis. Nevertheless, they recognize that this was the version generally disseminated in the United States.
4. On this point see Hirschman, Albert, "A Generalized Linkage Approach to Development with Special Reference to Staply" (Institute for Advanced Study, mimeo, 1976).
5. See Schmitter, Philip, "Still the Century of Corporativism?" in *World Politics*, 25 (January 1973), and his important book *Interest Conflict and Political Change in Brazil* (Stanford: Stanford University Press, 1971); also Stepan, Alfred, *The State and Society: Peru in Comparative Perspective*, forthcoming from Princeton University Press. See especially chapters 1 and 2.
6. See Stepan, Alfred, *op. cit.*, where corporativism is *not* inappropriately generalized to describe all authoritarian regimes. See also, in Schmitter's book, cited above, the specifications made in describing corporative relations between the state and civil society and among parts of the latter.
7. See especially, Cardoso, F. H., "A questão do Estado no Brasil," in *Autoritarismo e Democratização* (Rio de Janeiro, Paz e Terra, 1975).

CHAPTER 4

The Homeland, Aztlán / *El otro México*

Gloria Anzaldúa

[. . .]

"The *Aztecas del norte* . . . compose the largest single tribe or nation of Anishinabeg (Indians) found in the United States today. . . . Some call themselves Chicanos and see themselves as people whose true homeland is Aztlán [the U.S. Southwest]."[1]

Wind tugging at my sleeve
feet sinking into the sand
I stand at the edge where earth touches ocean
where the two overlap
a gentle coming together
at other times and places a violent clash.

  Across the border in Mexico
    stark silhouette of houses gutted by waves,
      cliffs crumbling into the sea,
        silver waves marbled with spume
          gashing a hole under the border fence.

        Miro el mar atacar
       la cerca en Border Field Park
      con sus buchones de agua,
an Easter Sunday resurrection
of the brown blood in my veins.

Oigo el llorido del mar, el respiro del aire,
  my heart surges to the beat of the sea.
    In the gray haze of the sun
      the gulls' shrill cry of hunger,
        the tangy smell of the sea seeping into me.

      I walk   through the hole in the fence
        to the other side.
  Under my fingers I feel the gritty wire
    rusted by 139 years
      of the salty breath of the sea.

Beneath the iron sky
Mexican children kick their soccer ball across,
run after it, entering the U.S.

      I press my hand to the steel curtain—
        chainlink fence crowned with rolled barbed
wire—

rippling from the sea where Tijuana touches San Diego
  unrolling over mountains
    and plains
        and deserts,
this "Tortilla Curtain" turning into *el río Grande*
  flowing down to the flatlands
    of the Magic Valley of South Texas
  its mouth emptying into the Gulf.

1,950 mile-long open wound
      dividing a *pueblo*, a culture,
      running down the length of my body,
       staking fence rods in my flesh,
       splits me   splits me
        me raja   me raja
    This is my home
    this thin edge of
      barbwire.

       But the skin of the earth is seamless.
       The sea cannot be fenced,
    el mar does not stop at borders.
To show the white man what she thought of his
         arrogance,
      Yemaya blew that wire fence down.

       This land was Mexican once,
        was Indian always
        and is.
        And   will be again.

    Yo soy un puente tendido
     del mundo gabacho al del mojado,
    lo pasado me estirá pa' 'trás
     y lo presente pa' 'delante.
    Que la Virgen de Guadalupe me cuide
    Ay ay ay, soy mexicana de este lado.

    The U.S.–Mexican border *es una herida abierta* where the Third World grates against the first and bleeds. And before a scab forms it hemorrhages again, the lifeblood of two worlds merging to form a third country—a border culture. Borders are set up to define the places that are safe and unsafe, to distinguish *us* from *them*. A border is a dividing line, a narrow strip along a steep edge. A borderland is a vague and undetermined place created by the emotional residue of an unnatural boundary. It is in a constant state of transition. The prohibited and forbidden are its inhabitants. *Los atravesados* live here: the squint-eyed, the perverse, the queer, the troublesome, the mongrel, the mulato, the half-breed, the half dead; in short, those who cross over, pass over, or go through the confines of the "normal." Gringos in the U.S. Southwest consider the inhabitants of the borderlands transgressors, aliens—whether they possess documents or not, whether they're Chicanos, Indians or Blacks. Do not enter, trespassers will be raped, maimed, strangled, gassed, shot. The only "legitimate" inhabitants are those in power, the whites and those who align themselves with whites. Tension grips the inhabitants of the borderlands like a virus. Ambivalence and unrest reside there and death is no stranger.

In the fields, *la migra*. My aunt saying, "*No corran*, don't run. They'll think you're *del otro lao*." In the confusion, Pedro ran, terrified of being caught. He couldn't speak English, couldn't tell them he was fifth generation American. *Sin papeles*—he did not carry his birth certificate to work in the fields. *La migra* took him away while we watched. *Se lo llevaron*. He tried to smile when he looked back at us, to raise his fist. But I saw the shame pushing his head down, I saw the terrible weight of shame hunch his shoulders. They deported him to Guadalajara by plane. The furthest he'd ever been to Mexico was Reynosa, a small border town opposite Hidalgo, Texas, not far from McAllen. Pedro walked all the way to the Valley. *Se lo llevaron sin un centavo al pobre. Se vino andando desde Guadalajara.*

During the original peopling of the Americas, the first inhabitants migrated across the Bering Straits and walked south across the continent. The oldest evidence of humankind in the U.S.—the Chicanos' ancient Indian ancestors—was found in Texas and has been dated to 35000 B.C.[2] In the Southwest United States archeologists have found 20,000-year-old campsites of the Indians who migrated through, or permanently occupied, the

Southwest, Aztlán—land of the herons, land of whiteness, the Edenic place of origin of the Azteca.

In 1000 B.C., descendants of the original Cochise people migrated into what is now Mexico and Central America and became the direct ancestors of many of the Mexican people. (The Cochise culture of the Southwest is the parent culture of the Aztecs. The Uto-Aztecan languages stemmed from the language of the Cochise people.)[3] The Aztecs (the Nahuatl word for people of Aztlán) left the Southwest in 1168 A.D.

> Now let us go.
> > *Tihueque, tihueque,*
> *Vámonos, vámonos.*
> > *Un pájaro cantó.*
> *Con sus ocho tribus salieron*
> > *de la "cueva del origen."*
> *los aztecas siguieron al dios*
> > *Huitzilopochtli.*

Huitzilopochtli, the God of War, guided them to the place (that later became Mexico City) where an eagle with a writhing serpent in its beak perched on a cactus. The eagle symbolizes the spirit (as the sun, the father); the serpent symbolizes the soul (as the earth, the mother). Together, they symbolize the struggle between the spiritual/celestial/male and the underworld/earth/feminine. The symbolic sacrifice of the serpent to the "higher" masculine powers indicates that the patriarchal order had already vanquished the feminine and matriarchal order in pre-Columbian America.

At the beginning of the 16th century, the Spaniards and Hernán Cortés invaded Mexico and, with the help of tribes that the Aztecs had subjugated, conquered it. Before the Conquest, there were twenty-five million Indian people in Mexico and the Yucatán. Immediately after the Conquest, the Indian population had been reduced to under seven million. By 1650, only one-and-a-half-million pure-blooded Indians remained. The *mestizos* who were genetically equipped to survive small pox, measles, and typhus (Old World diseases to which the natives had no immunity), founded a new hybrid race and inherited Central and South America.[4] *En 1521 nació una nueva raza, el mestizo, el mexicano* (people of mixed Indian and Spanish blood), a race that had never existed before. Chicanos, Mexican-Americans, are the off-spring of those first matings.

Our Spanish, Indian, and *mestizo* ancestors explored and settled parts of the U.S. Southwest as early as the sixteenth century. For every gold-hungry *conquistador* and soul-hungry missionary who came north from Mexico, ten to twenty Indians and *mestizos* went along as porters or in other capacities.[5] For the Indians, this constituted a return to the place of origin, Aztlán, thus making Chicanos originally and secondarily indigenous to the Southwest. Indians and *mestizos* from central Mexico intermarried with North American Indians. The continual intermarriage between Mexican and American Indians and Spaniards formed an even greater *mestizaje*. [. . .]

In the 1800s, Anglos migrated illegally into Texas, which was then part of Mexico, in greater and greater numbers and gradually drove the *tejanos* (native Texans of Mexican descent) from their lands, committing all manner of atrocities against them. Their illegal invasion forced Mexico to fight a war to keep its Texas territory. The Battle of the Alamo, in which the Mexican forces vanquished the whites, became, for the whites, the symbol for the cowardly and villainous character of the Mexicans. It became (and still is) a symbol that legitimized the white imperialist takeover. With the capture of Santa Anna later in 1836, Texas became a republic. *Tejanos* lost their land and, overnight, became the foreigners. [. . .]

In 1846, the U.S. incited Mexico to war. U.S. troops invaded and occupied Mexico, forcing her to give up almost half of her nation, what is now Texas, New Mexico, Arizona, Colorado and California.

With the victory of the U.S. forces over the Mexican in the U.S.-Mexican War, *los norteamericanos* pushed the Texas border down 100 miles, from *el río Nueces* to *el río Grande*. South Texas ceased to be part of the Mexican state of Tamaulipas. Separated from Mexico, the Native Mexican-Texan no longer looked toward Mexico as home; the

Southwest became our homeland once more. The border fence that divides the Mexican people was born on February 2, 1848 with the signing of the Treaty of Guadalupe-Hidalgo. It left 100,000 Mexican citizens on this side, annexed by conquest along with the land. The land established by the treaty as belonging to Mexicans was soon swindled away from its owners. The treaty was never honored and restitution, to this day, has never been made. [. . .]

The Gringo, locked into the fiction of white superiority, seized complete political power, stripping Indians and Mexicans of their land while their feet were still rooted in it. *Con el destierro y el exilo fuimos desuñados, destroncados, destripados*—we were jerked out by the roots, truncated, disemboweled, dispossessed, and separated from our identity and our history. Many, under the threat of Anglo terrorism, abandoned homes and ranches and went to Mexico. Some stayed and protested. But as the courts, law enforcement officials, and government officials not only ignored their pleas but penalized them for their efforts, *tejanos* had no other recourse but armed retaliation.

After Mexican-American resisters robbed a train in Brownsville, Texas on October 18, 1915, Anglo vigilante groups began lynching Chicanos. Texas Rangers would take them into the brush and shoot them. One hundred Chicanos were killed in a matter of months, whole families lynched. Seven thousand fled to Mexico, leaving their small ranches and farms. The Anglos, afraid that the *mexicanos*[6] would seek independence from the U.S., brought in 20,000 army troops to put an end to the social protest movement in South Texas. Race hatred had finally fomented into an all out war.[7]

My grandmother lost all her cattle,
they stole her land.

"Drought hit South Texas," my mother tells me. "*La tierra se puso bien seca y los animales comenzaron a morrirse de se'. Mi papá se murió de un* heart attack *dejando a mamá* pregnant *y con ocho huercos*, with eight kids and one on the way. *Yo fuí la mayor, tenía diez años.* The next year the drought continued *y el ganado* got hoof and mouth. *Se calleron* in droves *en las pastas y el* brushland, *pansas blancas* ballooning to the skies. *El siguiente año* still no rain. *Mi pobre madre viuda perdió* two-thirds of her *ganado*. A smart *gabacho* lawyer took the land away *mamá* hadn't paid taxes. *No hablaba inglés*, she didn't know how to ask for time to raise the money." My father's mother, Mama Locha, also lost her *terreno*. For a while we got $12.50 a year for the "mineral rights" of six acres of cemetery, all that was left of the ancestral lands. Mama Locha had asked that we bury her there beside her husband. *El cemeterio estaba cercado*. But there was a fence around the cemetery, chained and padlocked by the ranch owners of the surrounding land. We couldn't even get in to visit the graves, much less bury her there. Today, it is still padlocked. The sign reads: "Keep out. Trespassers will be shot."

In the 1930s, after Anglo agribusiness corporations cheated the small Chicano landowners of their land, the corporations hired gangs of *mexicanos* to pull out the brush, chaparral and cactus and to irrigate the desert. The land they toiled over had once belonged to many of them, or had been used communally by them. Later the Anglos brought in huge machines and root plows and had the Mexicans scrape the land clean of natural vegetation. In my childhood I saw the end of dryland farming. I witnessed the land cleared; saw the huge pipes connected to underwater sources sticking up in the air. As children, we'd go fishing in some of those canals when they were full and hunt for snakes in them when they were dry. In the 1950s I saw the land, cut up into thousands of neat rectangles and squares, constantly being irrigated. In the 340-day growth season, the seeds of any kind of fruit or vegetable had only to be stuck in the ground in order to grow. More big land corporations came in and bought up the remaining land.

To make a living my father became a sharecropper. Rio Farms Incorporated loaned him seed money and living expenses. At harvest time, my father repaid the loan and forked over 40% of the earnings. Sometimes we earned less than we owed, but always the corporations fared well. Some had major holdings in vegetable trucking, livestock auctions and cotton gins. Altogether we lived on three successive Rio farms; the second was adjacent to the King Ranch and included a dairy farm; the third was a chicken farm. I remember the white feathers of three thousand Leghorn chickens blanketing the land for acres around. My sister, mother and I cleaned, weighed and packaged eggs. (For years afterwards I couldn't stomach the sight of an egg.) I remember my mother attending some of the meetings sponsored by well-meaning whites from Rio Farms. They talked about good nutrition, health, and held huge barbeques. The only thing salvaged for my family from those years are modern techniques of food canning and a food-stained book they printed made up of recipes from Rio Farms' Mexican women. How proud my mother was to have her recipe for *enchiladas coloradas* in a book. [. . .]

La crisis. *Los gringos* had not stopped at the border. By the end of the nineteenth century, powerful landowners in Mexico, in partnership with U.S. colonizing companies, had dispossessed millions of Indians of their lands. Currently, Mexico and her eighty million citizens are almost completely dependent on the U.S. market. The Mexican government and wealthy growers are in partnership with such American conglomerates as American Motors, IT&T and Du Pont which own factories called *maquiladoras*. One-fourth of all Mexicans work at *maquiladoras*; most are young women. Next to oil, *maquiladoras* are Mexico's second greatest source of U.S. dollars. Working eight to twelve hours a day to wire in backup lights of U.S. autos or solder miniscule wires in TV sets is not the Mexican way. While the women are in the *maquiladoras*, the children are left on their own. Many roam the street, become part of *cholo* gangs. The infusion of the values of the white culture, coupled with the exploitation by that culture, is changing the Mexican way of life.

The devaluation of the *peso* and Mexico's dependency on the U.S. have brought on what the Mexicans call *la crisis*. *No hay trabajo*. Half of the Mexican people are unemployed. In the U.S. a man or woman can make eight times what they can in Mexico. By March, 1987, 1,088 pesos were worth one U.S. dollar. I remember when I was growing up in Texas how we'd cross the border at Reynosa or Progreso to buy sugar or medicines when the dollar was worth eight *pesos* and fifty *centavos*.

La travesía. For many *mexicanos del otro lado*, the choice is to stay in Mexico and starve or move north and live. *Dicen que cada mexicano siempre sueña de la conquista en los brazos de cuatro gringas rubias, la conquista del país poderoso del norte, los Estados Unidos. En cada Chicano y mexicano vive el mito del tesoro territorial perdido.* North Americans call this return to the homeland the silent invasion.

> "A la cueva volverán"
> —El Puma *en la cancion "Amalia"*

South of the border, called North America's rubbish dump by Chicanos, *mexicanos* congregate in the plazas to talk about the best way to cross. Smugglers, *coyotes, pasadores, enganchadores* approach these people or are sought out by them. "*¿Qué dicen muchachos a echársela de mojado?*" [. . .]

We have a tradition of migration, a tradition of long walks. Today we are witnessing *la migración de los pueblos mexicanos*, the return odyssey to the historical/mythological Aztlán. This time, the traffic is from south to north.

El retorno to the promised land first began with the Indians from the interior of Mexico and the *mestizos* that came with the *conquistadores* in the 1500s. Immigration continued in the next three centuries, and, in this century, it continued with the *braceros* who helped to build our railroads and who picked our fruit. Today thousands of Mexicans are crossing the border legally and illegally; ten million people without documents have returned to the Southwest.

Faceless, nameless, invisible, taunted with "Hey cucaracho" (cockroach). Trembling with fear, yet filled with courage, a courage born of desperation. Barefoot and uneducated, Mexicans with hands like boot soles gather at night by the river where two worlds merge creating what Reagan calls a frontline, a war zone. The convergence has created a shock culture, a border culture, a third country, a closed country.

Without benefit of bridges, the "*mojados*" (wetbacks) float on inflatable rafts across *el río Grande*, or wade or swim across naked, clutching their clothes over their heads. Holding onto the grass, they pull themselves along the banks with a prayer to *Virgen de Guadalupe* on their lips: *Ay virgencita morena, mi madrecita, dame tu bendición.*

The Border Patrol hides behind the local McDonald's on the outskirts of Brownsville, Texas or some other border town. They set traps around the river beds beneath the bridge.[8] Hunters in army-green uniforms stalk and track these economic refugees by the powerful nightvision of electronic sensing devices planted in the ground or mounted on Border Patrol vans. Cornered by flashlights, frisked while their arms stretch over their heads, *los mojados* are handcuffed, locked in jeeps, and then kicked back across the border.

One out of every three is caught. Some return to enact their rite of passage as many as three times a day. Some of those who make it across undetected fall prey to Mexican robbers such as those in Smugglers' Canyon on the American side of the border near Tijuana. As refugees in a homeland that does not want them, many find a welcome hand holding out only suffering, pain, and ignoble death.

Those who make it past the checking points of the Border Patrol find themselves in the midst of 150 years of racism in Chicano *barrios* in the Southwest and in big northern cities. Living in a no-man's-borderland, caught between being treated as criminals and being able to eat, between resistance and deportation, the illegal refugees are some of the poorest and the most exploited of any people in the U.S. It is illegal for Mexicans to work without green cards. But big farming combines, farm bosses and smugglers who bring them in make money off the "wetbacks" labor—they don't have to pay federal minimum wages, or ensure adequate housing or sanitary conditions.

The Mexican woman is especially at risk.

Often the *coyote* (smuggler) doesn't feed her for days or let her go to the bathroom. Often he rapes her or sells her into prostitution. She cannot call on county or state health or economic resources because she doesn't know English and she fears deportation. American employers are quick to take advantage of her helplessness. She can't go home. She's sold her house, her furniture, borrowed from friends in order to pay the *coyote* who charges her four or five thousand dollars to smuggle her to Chicago. She may work as a live-in maid for white, Chicano or Latino households for as little as $15 a week. Or work in the garment industry, do hotel work. Isolated and worried about her family back home, afraid of getting caught and deported, living with as many as fifteen people in one room, the *mexicana* suffers serious health problems. *Se enferma de los nervios, de alta presión.*[9]

La mojada, la mujer indocumentada, is doubly threatened in this country. Not only does she have to contend with sexual violence, but like all women, she is prey to a sense of physical helplessness. As a refugee, she leaves the familiar and safe homeground to venture into unknown and possibly dangerous terrain.

> This is her home
> this thin edge of
> barbwire.

NOTES

1. Jack D. Forbes, *Aztecas del Norte: The Chicanos of Aztlán.* (Greenwich, CT: Fawcett Publications, Premier Books, 1973), 13, 183; Eric R. Wolf, *Sons of Shaking Earth* (Chicago, IL: University of Chicago Press, Phoenix Books, 1959), 32.

2. John R. Chávez, *The Lost Land: The Chicano Images of the Southwest* (Albuquerque, NM: University of New Mexico Press, 1984), 9.

3. Chávez, 9. Besides the Aztecs, the Ute, Gabrillino of California, Pima of Arizona, some Pueblo of New Mexico, Comanche of Texas, Opata of Sonora, Tarahumara of Sinaloa and Durango, and the Huichol of Jalisco speak Uto-Aztecan languages and are descended from the Cochise people.

4. Reay Tannahill, *Sex In History* (Briarcliff Manor, NY: Stein and Day/Publishers/Scarborough House, 1980), 308.

5. Chávez, 21.

6. The Plan of San Diego, Texas, drawn up on January 6, 1915, called for the independence and segregation of the states bordering Mexico: Texas, New Mexico, Arizona, Colorado, and California. Indians would get their land back, Blacks would get six states from the south and form their own independent republic. Chávez, 79.

7. Jesús Mena, "Violence in the Rio Grande Valley," *Nuestro* (Jan/Feb. 1983), 41–42.

8. Grace Halsell, *Los ilegales*, trans. Mayo Antonio Sánchez (Editorial Diana Mexica, 1979).

9. Margarita B. Melville, "Mexican Women Adapt to Migration," *International Migration Review,* 1978.

CHAPTER 5

Global Ethnoscapes: Notes and Queries for a Transnational Anthropology

Arjun Appadurai

In my title, I use the term *ethnoscape*. This neologism has certain ambiguities deliberately built into it. It refers, first, to the dilemmas of perspective and representation that all ethnographers must confront, and it admits that (as with landscapes in visual art) traditions of perception and perspective, as well as variations in the situation of the observer, may affect the process and product of representation. But I also intend this term to indicate that there are some brute facts about the world of the twentieth century that any ethnography must confront. Central among these facts is the changing social, territorial, and cultural reproduction of group identity. As groups migrate, regroup in new locations, reconstruct their histories, and reconfigure their ethnic "projects," the *ethno* in ethnography takes on a slippery, nonlocalized quality, to which the descriptive practices of anthropology will have to respond. The landscapes of group identity—the ethnoscapes—around the world are no longer familiar anthropological objects, insofar as groups are no longer tightly territorialized, spatially bounded, historically unselfconscious, or culturally homogenous. We have fewer cultures in the world and more "internal cultural debates" (Parkin 1978).

By *ethnoscape*, I mean the landscape of persons who make up the shifting world in which we live: tourists, immigrants, refugees, exiles, guest-workers, and other moving groups and persons constitute an essential feature of the world and appear to affect the politics of and between nations to a hitherto unprecedented degree. This is not to say that nowhere are there relatively stable communities and networks of kinship, friendship, work, and leisure, as well as of birth, residence, and other filiative forms. But it is to say that the warp of these stabilities is everywhere shot through with the woof of human motion, as more persons and groups deal with the realities of having to move or the fantasies of wanting to move. What is more, both these realities and these fantasies now function on large scales, as men and women from villages in India think not just of moving to Poona or Madras, but of moving to Dubai and Houston; and refugees from Sri Lanka find themselves in South India as well as in Canada; and the Hmong are driven to London as well as Philadelphia. As the needs of international capital shift, as production and technology generate different consumer needs, as nation-states change their policies on refugee populations, these moving groups can never afford to let their imaginations rest too long, even if they wished to.[1]

In this paper, I seek, through a series of notes, queries, and vignettes, to reposition some of our disciplinary conventions, while trying to show that the ethnoscapes of today's world are profoundly interactive.

ALTERNATIVE MODERNITIES AND ETHNOGRAPHIC COSMOPOLITANISM

A central challenge for current anthropology is to study the cosmopolitan (Rabinow 1986) cultural forms of the contemporary world without logically or chronologically presupposing either the authority of the Western experience or the models derived from that experience. It seems impossible to fruitfully study these new cosmopolitanisms without analyzing the transnational cultural flows within which they thrive, compete, and feed off one another in ways that defeat and confound many verities of the human sciences today. One such verity concerns the link between space, stability, and cultural reproduction. There is an urgent need to focus on the cultural dynamics of what is now called *deterritorialization*. This term applies not only to obvious examples such as transnational corporations and money markets, but also to ethnic groups, sectarian movements, and political formations, which increasingly operate in ways that transcend specific territorial boundaries and identities. Deterritorialization (of which I offer some ethnographic profiles in another section of this paper) affects the loyalties of groups (especially in the context of complex diasporas), their transnational manipulation of currencies and other forms of wealth and investment, and the strategies of states. The loosening of the bonds between people, wealth, and territories fundamentally alters the basis of cultural reproduction.

Deterritorialization is one of the central forces of the modern world, since it brings laboring populations into the lower-class sectors of relatively wealthy societies, while sometimes creating exaggerated and intensified senses of criticism of, or attachment to, politics in the home state. Deterritorialization, whether of Hindus, Sikhs, Palestinians, or Ukranians, is now at the core of a variety of global fundamentalisms, including Islamic and Hindu fundamentalism. In the Hindu case, for example (Appadurai and Breckenridge: in press b), it is clear that the overseas movement of Indians has been exploited by a variety of interests both within and outside India to create a complicated network of finances and religious identifications in which the problem of cultural reproduction for Hindus abroad has become tied to the politics of Hindu fundamentalism at home.

At the same time, deterritorialization creates new markets for film companies, impressarios, and travel agencies, which thrive on the need of the relocated population for contact with its homeland. But the homeland is partly invented, existing only in the imagination of the deterritorialized groups, and it can sometimes become so fantastic and one-sided that it provides the fuel for new ethnic conflicts.

The idea of deterritorialization may also be applied to money and finance, as money managers seek the best markets for their investments, independent of national boundaries. In turn, these movements of monies are the basis of new kinds of conflict, as Los Angelenos worry about the Japanese buying up their city, and people in Bombay worry about the rich Arabs from the Gulf State, who have not only transformed the price of mangos in Bombay but have also substantially altered the profile of hotels, restaurants, and other services in the eyes of the local population—just as they have in London. Yet most residents of Bombay are ambivalent about the Arabs there, for the flip side of their presence is the absent friends and kinsmen earning big money in the Middle East and bringing back both money and luxury commodities to Bombay and other cities in India. Such commodities transform consumer taste in these cities. They often end up smuggled through air- and seaports and peddled in the "gray" markets of Bombay's streets. In these gray markets (a coinage which allows me to capture the quasi-legal characteristic of such settings), some members of Bombay's middle classes and of its lumpen proletariat can buy goods, ranging from cartons of Marlboro cigarettes to Old Spice shaving cream and tapes of Madonna. Similar gray routes, often subsidized by moonlighting sailors, diplomats, and airline stewardesses, who get to move in and out of the country regularly, keep the gray markets of Bombay, Madras, and Calcutta filled with goods not only from the West, but also from the Middle East, Hong Kong, and Singapore. It is also such professional transients who are increasingly implicated in the transnational spread of disease, not the least of which is AIDS.

It is this fertile ground of deterritorialization, in which money, commodities, and persons unendingly chase each other around the world, that the group imaginations of the modern world find their fractured and fragmented counterpart. For the ideas and images produced by mass media often are only partial guides to the goods and experiences that deterritorialized populations transfer to one another. In Mira Nair's brilliant film, *India Cabaret* (discussed in greater detail in another section), we see the multiple loops of this fractured deterritorialization as young women, barely competent in Bombay's metropolitan glitz, come to seek their fortunes there as cabaret dancers and prostitutes, entertaining men in clubs with dance formats derived wholly from the prurient dance sequences of Hindi films. These scenes cater to Indian ideas about Western and foreign women and their "looseness," while dancing provides tawdry career alibis for these girls. Some of these girls come from Kerala, where cabaret clubs and the pornographic film industry have blossomed, partly in response to the purses and tastes of Keralites returned from the Middle East, where their diasporic lives away from women distort their very sense of what the relations between men and women might be. These tragedies of displacement could certainly be replayed in an analysis of the relations between Japanese and German sex tours to Thailand and the tragedies of the sex trade in Bangkok, and in similar loops that tie together fantasies about the Other, the conveniences and seductions of travel, the economics of global trade, and the violent fantasies that dominate gender politics in many parts of Asia and the world at large.

The vision of transnational cultural studies suggested by the discussion so far appears at first sight to involve only modest adjustments of anthropologists' traditional approaches to culture. In my view, however, a genuinely cosmopolitan ethnographic practice requires an interpretation of the terrain of "cultural studies" in the United States today, and of the status of anthropology within such a terrain.[2]

CULTURAL STUDIES IN A GLOBAL TERRAIN

Since this volume concerns anthropologies of the present, it may be important to ask about the status of anthropology in the present and,

in particular, about its now-embattled monopoly over the study of "culture" (from now on, without quotation marks). The following discussion sets the stage for the critique of ethnography contained in subsequent sections.

As a topic, culture has many histories, some disciplinary, some that function outside the academy. Within the academy, there are certain differences between disciplines in the degree to which culture has been an explicit topic of investigation, and the degree to which it has been understood tacitly. In the social sciences, anthropology (especially in the United States; less so in England) has made culture its central concept, defining it as some sort of human substance—even though ideas about this substance have shifted, over the course of a century, roughly from Tylorean ideas about custom to Geertzian ideas about meaning. Some anthropologists have worried that the meanings given to culture have been far too diverse for a technical term; others have made a virtue of that diversity. At the same time, the other social sciences have not been unconcerned with culture: in sociology, Max Weber's sense of *verstehen* and Simmel's various ideas have mediated between the German neo-Kantian ideas of the late nineteenth century and sociology as a social science discipline. As in many other cases, culture is now a subfield within sociology, and the American Sociological Association has legitimized this segregation by creating a subunit in "the sociology of culture," where persons concerned with the production and distribution of culture, especially in Western settings, may freely associate with one another.

At the epicenter of current debates in and about culture, many diverse streams flow into a single, rather turbulent river: the many poststructuralisms (largely French) of Lacan, Derrida, Foucault, Bourdieu, and their many subschools. Some of these streams are self-conscious about language as their means and their model; others less so. The current multiplicity of uses that surrounds the three words *meaning, discourse,* and *text* should be sufficient to indicate that we are not only in an era of "blurred genres" (as Geertz [1980] said presciently a decade ago), but we are in a peculiar state that I would like to call "post-blurring," in which ecumenism has—happily in my opinion—given way to sharp debates about the word, the world, and the relationship between them.

In this post-blur blur, it is crucial to note that the high ground has been seized by English literature (as a discipline) in particular and by literary studies in general. This is the nexus where the word "theory," a rather prosaic term in many fields for many centuries, suddenly took on the sexy ring of a trend. For an anthropologist in the United States today, what is most striking about the last decade in the academy is the hijack of culture by literary studies—though we no longer have a one-sided Arnoldian gaze, but a many-sided hijack (where a hundred Blooms flower) with many internal debates about texts and antitexts, reference and structure, theory and practice. Social scientists look on with bewilderment as their colleagues in English and comparative literature talk (and fight) about matters which, until as recently as fifteen years ago, would have seemed about as relevant to English departments as, say, quantum mechanics.

The subject matter of cultural studies could roughly be taken as the relationship between the word and the world. I understand these two terms in their widest sense, so that *word* can encompass all forms of textualized expression, and *world* can mean anything from "the means of production" and the organization of life-worlds to the globalized relations of cultural reproduction discussed in this paper.

Cultural studies, conceived this way, could be the basis for a cosmopolitan (global? macro? translocal?) ethnography. To translate the tension between the word and the world into a productive ethnographic strategy requires a new understanding of the deterritorialized world that many persons inhabit and the possible lives that many persons are today able to envision. The terms of the negotiation between imagined lives and deterritorialized worlds are complex, and they surely cannot be captured by the localizing strategies of traditional ethnography alone. What a new style of ethnography can do is to capture the impact of deterritorialization on the imaginative resources of lived, local experiences. Put another way, the task of ethnography now becomes the unravelling of a conundrum: what is the nature of locality, as a lived experience, in a globalized, deterritorialized world? As I will suggest in the next section, the beginnings of an answer to this conundrum lie in a fresh approach to the role of the imagination in social life.

The master narratives that currently guide much ethnography all have Enlightenment roots, and all have been called into serious question. Foucault's searing critique of Western humanism and its hidden epistemologies has made it difficult to retain much faith in the idea of "progress" in its many old and new manifestations. The master narrative of "evolution," central to anthropology in the United States, suffers from a profound gap between its short-run, culturally oriented versions (as in the work of Marvin Harris) and its long-run, more appealing, but less anthropological versions such as the biogeological fables of Stephen Jay Gould. The "emergence of the individual" as a master narrative suffers not only from the counterexamples of our major twentieth-century totalitarian experiences, but also from the many deconstructions of the idea of self, person, and agency in philosophy, sociology, and anthropology (Parfit 1986; Giddens 1979; Carrithers, Collins, and Lukes 1985). Master narratives of the "iron cage" and the march of bureaucratic rationality are constantly refuted by the irrationalities, contradictions, and sheer brutality increasingly traceable to the pathologies of the modern nation-state (Nandy 1987). Finally, most versions of the Marxist master narrative find themselves embattled as contemporary capitalism takes on an increasingly "disorganized" and deterritorialized look (Lash and Urry 1987) and as cultural expressions refuse to bend to the requirements of even the least parochial Marxist approaches (see the debate between Frederic Jameson and Aijaz Ahmad in *Social Text* [Jameson 1986; Ahmad 1987]).

Cosmopolitan ethnography, or what might be called macroethnography, takes on a special urgency given the ailments of these many post-Enlightenment master narratives. It is difficult to be anything but exploratory about what such a macroethnography (and its ethnoscapes) might look like, but the following section seeks, by illustration, to point to its contours.

IMAGINATION AND ETHNOGRAPHY

We live in a world of many kinds of realism, some magical, some socialist, some capitalist, and some that are yet to be named. These generic realisms have their provinces of origin: magical realism in Latin American fiction in the last two decades; socialist realism in the Soviet Union of the 1930s; and capitalist realism, a term coined by Michael Schudson (1984), in the visual and verbal rhetoric of contemporary American advertising. In much aesthetic expression today, the boundaries between these various realisms have been blurred. The controversies over Salman Rushdie's *The Satanic Verses* (*Public Culture*, vol. 2, fall 1989: 2), over the Robert Mapplethorpe photographic exhibition in Cincinnati, and over many other works of art in other parts of the world remind us that artists are increasingly willing to place high stakes on their sense of the boundaries between their art and the politics of public opinion.

More consequential for our purposes is that the imagination has now acquired a singular new power in social life. The imagination—expressed in dreams, songs, fantasies, myths, and stories—has always been part of the repertoire, in some culturally organized way, of every society. But there is a peculiar new force to the imagination in social life today. More persons in more parts of the world consider a wider set of "possible" lives than they ever did before.[3] One important source of this change is the mass media, which present a rich, ever-changing store of possible lives, some of which enter the lived imaginations of ordinary people more successfully than others. Important also are contacts with, news of, and rumors about others in one's social neighborhood who have become inhabitants of these faraway worlds. The importance of media is not so much as direct sources of new images and scenarios for life possibilities, but as semiotic diacritics of great power, which also inflect social contact with the metropolitan world facilitated by other channels.

One of the principal shifts in the global cultural order, created by cinema, television, and VCR technology (and the ways in which they frame and energize other, older media), has to do with the role of the imagination in social life. Until recently, whatever the force of social change, a case could be made that social life was largely inertial, that traditions provided a relatively finite set of "possible" lives, and that fantasy and imagination were residual practices, confined to special persons or domains, restricted to special moments or places. In general, they were antidotes to the finitude of social experience. In the last two decades, as the deterritorialization of persons, images, and ideas has taken on new force, this weight has imperceptibly shifted. More persons throughout the world see their lives through the prisms of the possible lives offered by mass media in all their forms. That is, fantasy is now a social practice; it enters, in a host of ways, into the fabrication of social lives for many people in many societies. I should be quick to note that this is not a cheerful observation, intended to imply that the world is now a happier place with more "choices" (in the utilitarian sense) for more people, and with more mobility and more happy endings.

What is implied is that even the meanest and most hopeless of lives, the most brutal and dehumanizing of circumstances, the harshest of lived inequalities is now open to the play of the imagination. Prisoners of conscience, child laborers, women who toil in the fields and factories of the world, and others whose lot is harsh no longer see their lives as mere outcomes of the givenness of things, but often as the ironic compromise between what they could imagine and what social life will permit. The biographies of ordinary people, thus, are constructions (or fabrications) in which the imagination plays an important role. Nor is this role a simple matter of escape (holding steady the conventions that govern the rest of social life), for it is in the grinding of gears between unfolding lives and their imagined counterparts that a variety of "imagined communities" (Anderson 1983) is formed, communities that generate new kinds of politics, new kinds of collective expression, and new needs for social discipline and surveillance on the part of elites.

All this has many contexts and implications that cannot be pursued here. But what does it imply for ethnography? It implies that ethnographers can no longer simply be content with the "thickness" they bring to the local and the particular, nor can they assume that as they approach the local, they approach something more elementary, more contingent, and thus more "real" than life seen in larger-scale perspectives. For what is real about ordinary lives is now real in many ways that range from the sheer contingency of individual lives and the vagaries of competence and talent that distinguish persons in all societies to the "realisms" that individuals are exposed to and draw upon in their ordinary lives.

These complex, partly imagined lives must now form the bedrock of ethnography, at least of the sort of ethnography that wishes to retain a special voice in a transnational, deterritorialized world. For the new power of the imagination in the fabrication of social lives is inescapably tied up with images, ideas, and opportunities that come from elsewhere, often moved around by the vehicles of mass media. Thus, standard cultural reproduction (like standard English) is now an endangered activity that succeeds only by conscious design and political will, where it succeeds at all. Indeed, where insulation from the larger world seems to have been successful, and the role of the global imagination withheld from ordinary people—in places like Albania, North Korea, and Burma—what seems to appear instead is a bizarre state-sponsored realism, which always contains within it the possibility of the genocidal and totalizing lunacies of a Pol Pot or of long-repressed desires for critique or exit, as are emerging in Albania and Myanmar (Burma) as this paper is being written.

The issue, therefore, is not how ethnographic writing can draw on a wider range of literary models, models which too often elide the distinction between the life of fiction and the fictionalization of lives, but to figure out a way in which the role of the imagination in social life can be described in a new sort of ethnography that is not so resolutely localizing. There is, of course, much to be said for the local, the particular, and the contingent, which have always been the forte of ethnographic writing at its best. But where lives are being imagined partly in and through "realisms" that must be in one way or another official or large scale in their inspiration, then the ethnographer needs to find new ways to represent the links between the imagination and social life. This problem of representation is not quite the same as the familiar problem of micro and macro, small and large scale, though it has important connections to it. The connection between the problem of ethnographically representing imagined lives and of making the move from local realities to large-scale structures is implicit in Sherry Ortner's paper in this volume. Taken together, Ortner's argument and mine point to the importance of embedding large-scale realities in concrete life-worlds, but they also open up the possibility of divergent interpretations of what "locality" implies.

The link between the imagination and social life, I would suggest, is increasingly a global and deterritorialized one. Thus, those who represent "real" or "ordinary" lives must resist making claims to epistemic privilege in regard to the lived particularities of social life. Rather, ethnography must redefine itself as that practice of representation which illuminates the power of large-scale, imagined life possibilities over specific life trajectories. This is "thickness" with a difference, and the difference lies in a new alertness to the fact that ordinary lives today are increasingly powered not by the givenness of things but by the possibilities that the media (either directly or indirectly) suggest are available. Put another way, some of the force of Bourdieu's idea of the "habitus" can be retained (Bourdieu 1977), but the stress must be put on his idea of improvisation, for improvisation no longer occurs within a relatively bounded set of thinkable postures, but is always skidding and taking off, powered by the imagined vistas of mass-mediated

master narratives. There has been a general change in the global conditions of life-
worlds: put simply, where once improvisation
was snatched out of the glacial undertow of
habitus, habitus now has to be painstakingly
reinforced in the face of life-worlds that are
frequently in flux.

Three examples will suggest something of
what I have in mind. In January 1988, my
wife (who is a white American historian of
India) and I (a Tamil Brahman male, brought
up in Bombay and turned into *Homo aca-
demicus* in the United States), along with our
son, six members of my eldest brother's family, and an entourage of his colleagues and
employees, decided to visit the Meenaksi
Temple in Madurai, one of the great pilgrimage centers of South India. My wife has done
research there, off and on, for the last two
decades.

Our purposes in going were various. My
brother and his wife were worried about the
marriage of their eldest daughter and were
concerned to have the good wishes of as
many powerful deities as possible in their
search for a good marriage alliance. For my
brother, Madurai was a special place, since
he spent most of his first twenty years there
with my mother's extended family. He thus
had old friends and memories in all the
streets around the temple. Now he had
come to Madurai as a senior railway official,
with business to conduct with several private
businessmen who wished to persuade him of
the quality of their bids. Indeed, one of these
potential clients had arranged for us to be
accommodated in a garish "modern" hotel in
Madurai, a stone's throw from the temple,
and drove him around in a Mercedes, while
the rest of us took in our own Madurai.

Our eleven-year-old son, fresh from Philadelphia, knew he was in the presence of the
practices of heritage and dove to the ground
manfully, in the Hindu practice of prostra-
tion before elders and deities, whenever he
was asked. He put up graciously with the
incredible noise, crowding, and sensory rush
that a major Hindu temple involves. For
myself, I was there to embellish my brother's
entourage, to add some vague moral force to
their wishes for a happy marriage for their
daughter, to reabsorb the city in which my

mother grew up (I had been there several
times before), to share in my wife's excitement about returning to a city and a temple
that are possibly the most important parts of
her imagination, and to fish for cosmopolitanism in the raw.

So we entered the fourteen-acre temple
compound, an important entourage, though
one among many, and were soon approached
by one of the several priests who officiate
there. This one recognized my wife, who
asked him where Thangam Bhattar was.
Thangam Bhattar was the priest she had been
closest to and with whom she had worked
most closely. The answer was "Thangam
Bhattar is in Houston." This punch line took
us all a while to absorb, and then it all came
together in a flash. The Indian community in
Houston, like many communities of Asian
Indians in the United States, had built a
Hindu temple, this one devoted to Meenaksi,
the ruling deity in Madurai. Thangam Bhattar had been persuaded to go there, leaving
his family behind. He leads a lonely life in
Houston, assisting in the complex cultural
politics of reproduction in an overseas Indian
community, presumably earning some dollars, while his wife and children stay on in
their small home near the temple. The next
morning, my wife and niece visited Thangam
Bhattar's home, where they were told of his
travails in Houston, and they told the family
what had gone on with us in the intervening
years. There is a transnational irony here, of
course: Carol Breckenridge, American historian, arrives in Madurai waiting with bated
breath to see her closest informant and friend,
a priest, and discovers that he is in faraway
Houston, which is far away even from faraway Philadelphia.

But this transnational irony has many
threads that unwind backward and forward
in time to large and fluid structures of meaning and of communication. Among these
threads are my brother's hopes for his daughter, who subsequently married a Ph.D. candidate in physical chemistry in an upstate
New York university and recently came to
Syracuse herself; my wife's recontextualizing
of her Madurai experiences in a world that,
at least for some of its central actors, now
includes Houston; and my own realization

that Madurai's historical cosmopolitanism has acquired a new global dimension, and that some key lives that constitute the heart of the temple's ritual practices now have Houston in their imagined biographies. Each of these threads could and should be unwound. They lead to an understanding of the globalization of Hinduism, the transformation of "natives" into cosmopolites of their own sort, and the fact that the temple is now not only a magnet for persons from all over the world but also itself reaches out. The goddess Meenaksi has a living presence in Houston.

Our son, meanwhile, has in his repertoire of experiences a journey of the "roots" variety. He may remember this, as he fabricates his own life as an American of partly Indian descent. But he may remember more vividly his sudden need to go to the bathroom while we were going from sanctum to sanctum in a visit to another major temple in January 1989, and the bathroom at the guesthouse of a charitable foundation in which he found blissful release. But here too is an unfinished story, which involves the dynamics of family, of memory, and of tourism, for an eleven-year-old hyphenated American who has to go periodically to India, whether he likes it or not, and encounter the many webs of shifting biography that he encounters there. This account, like the ones that follow, needs not only to be thickened but to be stirred, but it must serve for now as one glimpse of an ethnography that focuses on the unyoking of imagination from place.

My second vignette comes from a collection of pieces of one kind of magical realism, a book by Julio Cortázar called *A Certain Lucas* (1984). Since there has been much borrowing of literary models and metaphors in recent anthropology, but relatively little anthropology of literature, a word about this choice of example seems appropriate. Fiction, like myth, is part of the conceptual repertoire of contemporary societies. Readers of novels and poems can be moved to intense action (as with *The Satanic Verses* of Salman Rushdie), and their authors often contribute to the construction of social and moral maps for their readers. Even more relevant for my purposes, prose fiction is the exemplary

province of the post-Renaissance imagination, and in this regard it is central to a more general ethnography of the imagination. Even small fragments of fantasy, such as Cortázar constructs in this brief story, show the contemporary imagination at work.

Magical realism is interesting not only as a literary genre but also as a representation of how the world appears to some people who live in it (for an interesting commentary on one aspect of this approach to literary narrative, see Felman 1989). Cortázar is doubtless a unique person, and not everyone imagines the world his way, but his vision is surely part of the evidence that the globe has begun to spin in new ways. Like the myths of small-scale society, as rendered in the anthropological classics of the past, contemporary literary fantasies tell us something about displacement, disorientation, and agency in the contemporary world (for an excellent recent example of this approach, in the context of cultural studies, see Rosaldo 1989: chapter 7).

Since we have now learned a great deal about the writing of ethnography (Clifford and Marcus 1986; Marcus and Fischer 1986; Geertz 1988), we are in a strong position to move to an anthropology of representation that would profit immensely from our recent discoveries about the politics and poetics of "writing culture." In this view, we can restore to the recent critiques of ethnographic practice the lessons of earlier critiques of anthropology as a field of practices operating within a larger world of institutional policies and power (viz., Hymes 1969).

The Cortázar story in question, which is both more light-handed and more heavy-hitting than some other, larger chunks of magical realism, is called "Swimming in a Pool of Gray Grits." It concerns the discovery in 1964, by a certain Professor José Migueletes, of a swimming pool in which, instead of water, there are gray grits. This discovery is quickly taken note of in the world of sports, and, at the Ecological Games in Baghdad, the Japanese champion, Akiro Tashuma, breaks the world record by "swimming five meters in one minute and four seconds" (Cortázar 1984: 80). Corázar's piece goes on to speak of how Tashuma solved the technical problem of breathing in this semisolid medium. The press then enters the picture, and here is the rest of the vignette (pp. 82–83), in Cortázar's own irreducibly spare words:

> Asked about the reasons why many international athletes show an ever-growing proclivity for swimming in grits, Tashuma would only answer that after several millenia it has finally been proven that there is a certain monotony in the act of jumping into the water and coming out all wet without anything having changed very much in the sport. He let it be understood that the imagination is slowly coming into power and that it's time now to apply revolutionary forms to old sports whose only incentive is to lower records by fractions of a second, when that can be done, which is quite rare. He modestly declared himself unable to suggest equivalent discoveries for soccer and tennis, but he did make an oblique reference to a new development in sports, mentioning a glass ball that may have been used in a basketball game in Naga, and whose accidental but always possible breakage brought on the act of hara-kiri by the whole team whose fault it was. Everything can be expected of Nipponese culture, especially if it sets out to imitate the Mexican. But to limit ourselves to the West and to grits, this last item has begun to demand higher prices, to the particular delight of countries that produce it, all of them in the Third World. The death by asphyxiation of seven Australian children who tried to practice fancy dives in the new pool in Canberra demonstrates, however, the limitations of this interesting product, the use of which should not be carried too far when amateurs are involved.

Now this is a very funny parable, and it could be read at many levels, from many points of view. For my purposes, I note first that it is written by an Argentine, born in Brussels, who lived in Paris from 1952 until his death in 1984. The link between magical realism and the self-imposed exile in Paris of many of its finest voices deserves further exploration—but what else does this vignette have to offer for the study of the new ethnoscapes of the contemporary world? The story is partly about a crazy invention that captures the faraway imagination of Tashuma, a person who believes that "the imagination is slowly coming into power." It is also

about the transnational journey of ideas that may begin as playful meditations and end up as bizarre technical realities that can result in death. Here one is forced to think about the trajectory of *The Satanic Verses*, which began as a satiric meditation on good, evil, and Islam, and ended up a weapon in group violence in many parts of the world.[4]

The vignette is also about the internationalization of sport, and about the spiritual exhaustion that comes from technical obsession with small differences in performance. Different actors can bring their "imaginations" to bear on the problem of sport in different ways. The Olympic Games of the past are full of incidents that reveal complex ways in which individuals situated within specific national and cultural trajectories imposed their imaginations on global audiences. In Seoul in 1988, the defeated Korean boxer who sat in the ring for several hours to publically proclaim his shame as a Korean, and the Korean officials who swarmed into the ring to assault a New Zealand referee for what they thought was a biased decision, were bringing their imagined lives to bear on the official Olympic narratives of fair play, good sportsmanship, and clean competition. The whole question of steroids, including the case of Ben Johnson, the Canadian runner (see MacAloon 1990), is also not far from the technical absurdities of Cortázar's story, in which the body is manipulated to yield new results in a world of competitive and commoditized spectacle. The vision of seven Australian children diving into a pool of grits and dying also deserves to be drawn out into the many stories of individual abnegation and physical abuse that sometimes power the spectacles of global sport.

Cortázar is also meditating on the problems of imitation and cultural transfer, suggesting that they can lead to violent and culturally peculiar innovations. The adjective "cultural" appears gratuitous here, and needs some justification. That Tokyo and Canberra, Baghdad and Mexico City are all involved in the story does not mean that they have become fungible pieces of an arbitrarily shifting, delocalized world. Each of these places does have complex local realities, such that death in a swimming pool has one kind of meaning in Canberra, as do hosting large spectacles in Iraq and making bizarre technical innovations in Japan. Whatever Cortázar's idea about these differences, they remain cultural, but no longer in the inertial mode that the word previously implied. Culture does imply difference, but the differences now are no longer, if you wish, taxonomical; they are interactive and refractive, so that competing for a swimming championship takes on the peculiar power that it does in Canberra partly because of the way some transnational forces have come to be configured in the imagination of its residents. Culture thus shifts from being some sort of inert, local substance to being a rather more volatile form of difference. This is an important part of the reason for writing *against* culture, as Lila Abu-Lughod suggests in her paper in this volume.

There are surely other macronarratives that spin out of this small piece of magical realism, but all of them remind us that lives today are as much acts of projection and imagination as they are enactments of known scripts or predictable outcomes. In this sense, all lives have something in common with international athletic spectacle, as guestworkers strive to meet standards of efficiency in new national settings, and brides who marry into households at large distances from home strive to meet the criteria of hypercompetence which these new contexts often demand. The deterritorialized world in which many people now live—some moving in it actively, others living with their absences or sudden returns—is, like Cortázar's pool of grits, ever thirsty for new technical competences and often harsh with the unprepared. Cortázar's vignette is itself a compressed ethnographic parable, and in teasing out the possible histories of its protagonists and their possible futures, our own ethnographies of literature can become exercises in the interpretation of the new role of the imagination in social life. There is in such efforts a built-in reflexive vertigo, as we contemplate Cortázar inventing Tashuma, but such reflexivity leads not only into reflections on our own representational practices, as writers, but also into the complex nesting of

imaginative appropriations that are involved in the construction of agency in a deterritorialized world.

But not all deterritorialization is global in its scope, and not all imagined lives span vast international panoramas. The world on the move affects even small geographical and cultural spaces. In several different ways, contemporary cinema represents these small worlds of displacement. Mira Nair's films capture the texture of these small displacements, whose reverberations can nevertheless be large. One of them, *India Cabaret*, is what I have called an ethnodrama.[5] Made in 1984, it tells about a small group of women who have left towns and villages, generally in the southern part of India, to come to Bombay and work as cabaret dancers in a seedy suburban bar-nightclub called the Meghraj.

The film contains (in the style of the early Godard) extended conversations between the filmmaker and a few of these women, who are presented facing the camera, as if they are talking to the viewer of the film. These interview segments, which are richly narrative, are intercut with dance sequences from the cabaret and with extended treatments of the sleazy paradoxes of the lives of some of the men who are regulars there. The film also follows one of the women back to her natal village, where we are shown the pain of her ostracism, since her occupation in Bombay is known to everyone. It is rumored that this scene was staged (replayed) for the benefit of the filmmaker, but if anything this replay adds to the awkwardness and pain of the sequence. The film is not about happy endings, and it leaves us with possibilities of various sorts in the lives of these women, all of whom are simultaneously proud and ashamed, dignified and defiant, de facto prostitutes who have fabricated identities as artists.

For the present purposes, what is most important about this film is the way in which it shows that the cabaret club is not simply a marketplace for desire but also a place where imagined lives are negotiated: the dancers act out their precarious sense of themselves as dancers; the second-rate band tries to work up its musical passions, which are fed by the aspiration of the Catholic community in Goa (western India) to play European and American instrumental music well. The men who come as customers clearly see themselves as participants in something larger than life, and they behave exactly like the customers in cabaret scenes in many Hindi commercial films. In fact, the scenario that provides the meeting ground for all these characters is provided by the cabaret sequences from Hindi commercial cinema.

In many such stock scenes, a tawdry nightclub quartet plays an oppressively sensuous melody, combining Western and Indian instruments and tonalities, while the villain and his cronies consume obviously nasty alcoholic drinks and watch a painfully explicit dance routine by a vampstar. The hero is usually insinuated into the action in some way that simultaneously emphasizes his virility and his moral superiority over the tawdry environment. These scenes are usually filled with extras from the film studio, who struggle to maintain the sophisticated visage of persons habituated to the high life. All in all, these scenes are stereotypically vicarious in their approach to drink, dance, and sound, and are somehow depressing. The clients, the dancers, and the band at the Meghraj seem to play out a slightly out-of-step, somnambulistic version of such classic Hindi film sequences.

Life in the Meghraj is surely driven by commercial cinematic images, but their force is inadequate to cover the anxieties, the self-abasement, and the agonized drama of leisure in which the characters are all engaged. Yet the characters in this ethnodrama have images and ideas of themselves that are not simply contingent outcomes of their "ordinary" lives (or simple escapes from them), but are fabrications based on a subtle complicity with the discursive and representational conventions of the Hindi cinema.

Thus, though this film is a documentary in conventional terms, it is also an ethnodrama, in the sense that it shows us the dramatic structure and the characters that animate a particular strand of Bombay's ways of life. These "actors" are also "characters," not so much because they have obvious idiosyncrasies attached to them but because they are fabrications negotiated in the encounter between the efforts of cinema to represent cabaret and of "real" cabarets to capture the excitement of cinema. It is this negotiation, not only the negotiation of bodies, that is the real order of business at the Meghraj. The women who work in the cabaret are deterritorialized and mobile: if you wish, they are guestworkers in Bombay. It is hard to see in them the discourse of resistance (though they are cynical about men, as prostitutes everywhere are), although their very bodily postures, their linguistic aggressiveness, their bawdy, quasi-lesbian play with each other does imply a kind of raunchy and self-conscious counterculture. What we have is a sense that they are putting lives together, fabricating their own characters, using cinematic and social materials at their disposal.

There are individuals here, to be sure, and agency as well, but what drives these individuals and their agency are the complex realisms that animate them: a crude realism about men and their motives; a sort of capitalist realism that animates their discourse about wealth and money; a curious socialist realism that underlies their own categorizations of themselves as dignified workers in the flesh trade, not very different from the housewives of Bombay. They constitute a striking ethnographic example for this essay because the very displacement that is the root of their problems (though their original departures turn out usually to be responses to even worse domestic horrors) is also the engine of their dreams of wealth, of respectability, of autonomy.

Thus, pasts in these constructed lives are as important as futures, and the more we unravel these pasts, the closer we approach worlds that are less and less cosmopolitan, more and more local. Yet even the most localized of these worlds, at least in societies like India, has become inflected, even afflicted, by cosmopolitan scripts that drive the politics of families, the frustrations of laborers, the dreams of local headmen. Once again, we need to be careful not to suppose that as we work backward in these imagined lives, we will hit some local, cultural bedrock, constituted of a closed set of reproductive practices, untouched by rumors of the world at large (for a different, but complementary, angle on these facts, see Hannerz 1989). Mira Nair's *India Cabaret* is a brilliant model of how ethnography in a deterritorialized world might handle the problems of "character" and "actor," for it shows how self-fabrication actually proceeds in a world of types and typification. It retains the tension between global and local that drives cultural reproduction today.

The vignettes I have used in this section have two purposes. One is to suggest the sorts of situations in which the workings of the imagination in a deterritorialized world can be detected. The second is to suggest that many lives are now inextricably linked with representations, and thus we need to incorporate the complexities of expressive representation (film, novels, travel accounts) into our ethnographies, not only as technical adjuncts but as primary material with which to construct and interrogate our own representations.

CONCLUSION: INVITATIONS AND EXHORTATIONS

Although the emergent cosmopolitanisms of the world have complex local histories, and their translocal dialogue has a complex history as well (Islamic pilgrimage is just one example), it seems advisable to treat the present as a historical moment and use our understanding of it to illuminate and guide the formulation of historical problems. This is not perverse Whiggishness; it is rather a response to a practical problem: in many cases it is simply not clear at present how or where one would locate a chronological baseline for the phenomena we wish to study. The strategy of "beginning at the beginning" becomes even more self-defeating when one wishes to illuminate the lived relationships between imagined lives and the webs of cosmopolitanism within which they unfold. Thus, not to put too fine a point on it, we need an ethnography that is sensitive to the historical nature of what we see today (which also involves careful comparison, as every good historian knows), but I suggest that we

cut into the problem through the historical present.

While much has been written about the relationship between history and anthropology (by practitioners of both disciplines) in the last decade, few have given careful thought to what it means to construct genealogies of the present. Especially in regard to the many alternative cosmopolitanisms that characterize the world today, and the complex, transnational cultural flows that link them, there is no easy way to "begin at the beginning." Today's cosmopolitanisms combine experiences of various media with various forms of experience—cinema, video, restaurants, spectator sports, and tourism, to name just a few—that have different national and transnational genealogies. Some of these forms may start out as extremely global and end up as very local—radio would be an example—while others, such as cinema, might have the obverse trajectory. In any particular ethnoscape (a term we might wish to substitute for earlier "wholes" such as villages, communities, and localities), the genealogies of cosmopolitanism are not likely to be the same as its histories: while the genealogies reveal the cultural spaces within which new forms can become indigenized (viz., tourism comes to inhabit the space of pilgrimage in India), the histories of these forms may lead outward to transnational sources and structures. Thus, the most appropriate ethnoscapes for today's world, with its alternative, interactive modernities, should confront genealogy and history with each other, thus leaving the terrain open for interpretations of the ways in which local historical trajectories flow into complicated transnational structures. Of course, this dialogue of histories and genealogies itself has a history, but for this latter history, we surely do not yet possess a master narrative. For those of us who might wish to move toward this new master narrative, whatever its form, new global ethnoscapes must be the critical building blocks. Michel-Rolph Trouillot, suggests that the historical role of anthropology was to fill the "savage slot" in an internal Western dialogue about utopia. A recuperated anthropology must recognize that the genie is now out of the bottle, and that speculations about utopia are everyone's prerogative. Anthropology can surely contribute its special purchase on lived experience to a wider, transdisciplinary study of global cultural processes. But to do this, anthropology must first come in from the cold and face the challenge of making a contribution to cultural studies without the benefit of its previous principal source of leverage—sightings of the savage.

NOTES

An earlier version of this paper was presented at the advanced seminar on "Representing Anthropology" at the School of American Research. This considerably revised version is a response, partly indirect, to the many important issues raised there, to critical readings of a subsequent draft by Carol Breckenridge and Sherry Ortner, and to several suggestive observations by Richard Fox.

1. These ideas about the cultural economy of a world in motion, as well as the logic of terms such as "ethnoscape," are more fully developed in Appadurai (1990).
2. This is not the place for an extended review of the emergent field of cultural studies. Its British lineages are carefully explored in Hall (1986) and Johnson (1986). But it is clear that this British tradition, associated largely with the now-diasporic Birmingham school, is taking new forms in the United States, as it comes into contact with American cultural anthropology, the new historicism, and language and media studies in the American tradition.
3. This theme, as well as a series of related ideas, is more fully developed in a book in progress, *Imploding Worlds: Imagination and Disjuncture in the Global Cultural Economy*, which I am writing with Carol Breckenridge.
4. The Rushdie controversy is well on its way to becoming an industry. Some of the issues in this controversy are touched on in *Public Culture*, vol. 1, no. 2, and are followed up in a special section devoted to the Rushdie debate in *Public Culture*, vol. 2, no. 1, fall 1989).
5. The following discussion draws heavily on Appadurai and Breckenridge (in press).

REFERENCES

Ahmad, Aijaz (1987) Jamesons's rhetoric of otherness and the "National Allegory." *Social Text* 17: 3–25.

Anderson, Benedict (1983) *Imagined Communities: Reflections on the Origin and Spread of Nationalism.* London: Verso.

Appadurai, Arjun (1990) Disjuncture and difference in the global cultural economy. *Public Culture* 2(2): 1–24.

Appadurai, Arjun, and Carol Breckenridge (in press a). Marriage, migration and money: Mira Nair's cinema of displacement. *Visual Anthropology.*

Appadurai, Arjun, and Carol Breckenridge (in press b). *A Transnational Culture in the Making: The Asian-Indian Diaspora in the United States.* London: Berg Press.

Bourdieu, Pierre (1977) *Outline of a Theory of Practice.* Trans. R. Nice. Cambridge: Cambridge University Press.

Carrithers, M., S. Collins, and S. Lukes, eds. (1985) *The Category of the Person.* Cambridge: Cambridge University Press.

Clifford, James, and George E. Marcus, eds. (1986) *Writing Culture: The Poetics and Politics of Ethnography.* Berkeley: University of California Press.

Cortázar, Julio (1984) *A Certain Lucas.* G. Rabassa, trans. New York: Knopf.

Felman, S. (1989) Narrative as testimony: Camus's "The Plague." In *Reading Narrative: Form, Ethics, Ideology.* J. Phelan, ed., pp. 250–71. Columbus: Ohio State University Press.

Geertz, Clifford (1980) Blurred genres: the refiguration of social thought. *American Scholar* 49: 125–59.

Geertz, Clifford (1988) *Works and Lives: The Anthropologist as Author.* Stanford: Stanford University Press.

Giddens, Anthony (1979) *Central Problems in Social Theory: Action, Structure and Contradiction in Social Analysis.* Berkeley: University of California Press.

Hall, S. (1986) Cultural studies: two paradigms. In *Media, Culture, and Society: A Critical Reader.* R. Collins, et al., eds., pp. 33–48. London: Sage Publications.

Hannerz, Ulf (1989) Notes on the global ecumene. *Public Culture* 1(2): 66–75.

Hymes, Dell (1969) *Reinventing Anthropology.* New York: Pantheon.

Jameson, Fredric (1986) Third World literature in the age of multinational capitalism. *Social Text* 15: 53–92.

Johnson, R. (1986) What is cultural studies anyway? *Social Text* 16: 38–80.

Lash, S., and J. Urry (1987) *The End of Organized Capitalism.* Madison: University of Wisconsin Press.

MacAloon, J. (1990) Steroids and the state: Dubin, melodrama and the accomplishment of innocence. *Public Culture* 2(2): 41–64.

Marcus, George, and Michael M. J. Fischer (1986) *Anthropology as Cultural Critique: An Experimental Moment in the Human Sciences.* Chicago: University of Chicago Press.

Nandy, Ashis (1987) *Traditions, Tyranny and Utopias.* Delhi: Oxford University Press.

Parfit, Derek (1986) *Reasons and Persons.* Oxford: Clarendon Press.

Parkin, David (1982) *Semantic Anthropology.* London: Academic Press.

Rabinow, Paul (1986) Representations are social facts:

modernity and post-modernity in anthropology. In *Writing Culture: The Poetics and Politics of Ethnography*. J. Clifford and G. Marcus, eds., pp. 234–61. Berkeley: University of California Press.

Rosaldo, Renato (1989) *Culture and Truth: The Remaking of Social Analysis*. Boston: Beacon Press.

Schudson, M. (1984) *Advertising, The Uneasy Persuasion*. New York: Basic Books.

CHAPTER 6

The Real New World Order

Anne-Marie Slaughter

THE STATE STRIKES BACK

Many thought that the new world order proclaimed by George Bush was the promise of 1945 fulfilled, a world in which international institutions, led by the United Nations, guaranteed international peace and security with the active support of the world's major powers. That world order is a chimera. Even as a liberal internationalist ideal, it is infeasible at best and dangerous at worst. It requires a centralized rule-making authority, a hierarchy of institutions, and universal membership. Equally to the point, efforts to create such an order have failed. The United Nations cannot function effectively independent of the major powers that compose it, nor will those nations cede their power and sovereignty to an international institution. Efforts to expand supranational authority, whether by the U.N. secretary-general's office, the European Commission, or the World Trade Organization (WTO), have consistently produced a backlash among member states.

The leading alternative to liberal internationalism is "the new medievalism," a back-to-the-future model of the 21st century. Where liberal internationalists see a need for international rules and institutions to solve states' problems, the new medievalists proclaim the end of the nation-state. Less hyperbolically, in her article, "Power Shift," in the January/February 1997 *Foreign Affairs*, Jessica T. Mathews describes a shift away from the state—up, down, and sideways—to supra-state, sub-state, and, above all, nonstate actors. These new players have multiple allegiances and global reach.

Mathews attributes this power shift to a change in the structure of organizations: from hierarchies to networks, from centralized compulsion to voluntary association. The engine of this transformation is the information technology revolution, a radically expanded communications capacity that empowers individuals and groups while diminishing traditional authority. The result is not world government, but global governance. If government denotes the formal exercise of power by established institutions, governance denotes cooperative problem-solving by a changing and often uncertain cast. The result is a world order in which global governance networks link Microsoft, the Roman Catholic Church, and Amnesty International to the European Union, the United Nations, and Catalonia.

The new medievalists miss two central points. First, private power is still no substitute for state power. Consumer boycotts of transnational corporations destroying rain forests or exploiting child labor may have an impact on the margin, but most environmentalists or labor activists would prefer national legislation mandating control of foreign subsidiaries. Second, the power shift is not a zero-sum game. A gain in power by nonstate actors does not necessarily translate into a loss of power for the state. On the contrary, many of these nongovernmental organizations (NGOs) network with their foreign counterparts to apply additional pressure on the traditional levers of domestic politics.

A new world order is emerging, with less fanfare but more substance than either the liberal internationalist or new medievalist visions. The state is not disappearing, it is disaggregating into its separate, functionally distinct parts. These parts—courts, regulatory agencies, executives, and even legislatures—are networking with their counterparts abroad, creating a dense web of relations that constitutes a new, transgovernmental order. Today's international problems—terrorism, organized crime, environmental degradation, money laundering, bank failure, and securities fraud—created and sustain these relations. Government institutions have formed networks of their own, ranging from the Basle Committee of Central Bankers to informal ties between law enforcement agencies to legal networks that make foreign judicial decisions more and more familiar. While political scientists Robert Keohane and Joseph Nye first observed its emergence in the 1970s, today transgovernmentalism is rapidly becoming the most widespread and effective mode of international governance.

Compared to the lofty ideals of liberal internationalism and the exuberant possibilities of the new medievalism, transgovernmentalism seems mundane. Meetings between securities regulators, antitrust or environmental officials, judges, or legislators lack the drama of high politics. But for the internationalists of the 1990s—bankers, lawyers, businesspeople, public-interest activists, and criminals—transnational government networks are a reality. Wall Street looks to the Basle Committee rather than the World Bank. Human rights lawyers are more likely to develop transnational litigation strategies for domestic courts than to petition the U.N. Committee on Human Rights.

Moreover, transgovernmentalism has many virtues. It is a key element of a bipartisan foreign policy, simultaneously assuaging conservative fears of a loss of sovereignty to international institutions and liberal fears of a loss of regulatory power in a globalized economy. While presidential candidate Pat Buchanan and Senator Jesse Helms (R-N.C.) demonize the U.N. and the wto as supranational bureaucracies that seek to dictate to national governments, Senators Ted Kennedy (D-Mass.) and Paul Wellstone (D-Mich.) inveigh against international capital mobility as the catalyst of a global

"race to the bottom" in regulatory standards. Networks of bureaucrats responding to international crises and planning to prevent future problems are more flexible than international institutions and expand the regulatory reach of all participating nations. This combination of flexibility and effectiveness offers something for both sides of the aisle.

Transgovernmentalism also offers promising new mechanisms for the Clinton administration's "enlargement" policy, aiming to expand the community of liberal democracies. Contrary to Samuel Huntington's gloomy predictions in *The Clash of Civilizations and the New World Order* (1996), existing government networks span civilizations, drawing in courts from Argentina to Zimbabwe and financial regulators from Japan to Saudi Arabia. The dominant institutions in these networks remain concentrated in North America and Western Europe, but their impact can be felt in every corner of the globe. Moreover, disaggregating the state makes it possible to assess the quality of specific judicial, administrative, and legislative institutions, whether or not the governments are liberal democracies. Regular interaction with foreign colleagues offers new channels for spreading democratic accountability, governmental integrity, and the rule of law.

An offspring of an increasingly borderless world, transgovernmentalism is a world order ideal in its own right, one that is more effective and potentially more accountable than either of the current alternatives. Liberal internationalism poses the prospect of a supranational bureaucracy answerable to no one. The new medievalist vision appeals equally to states' rights enthusiasts and supranationalists, but could easily reflect the worst of both worlds. Transgovernmentalism, by contrast, leaves the control of government institutions in the hands of national citizens, who must hold their governments as accountable for their transnational activities as for their domestic duties.

JUDICIAL FOREIGN POLICY

Judges are building a global community of law. They share values and interests based on their belief in the law as distinct but not divorced from politics and their view of themselves as professionals who must be insulated from direct political influence. At its best, this global community reminds each participant that his or her professional performance is being monitored and supported by a larger audience.

National and international judges are networking, becoming increasingly aware of one another and of their stake in a common enterprise. The most informal level of transnational judicial contact is knowledge of foreign and international judicial decisions and a corresponding willingness to cite them. The Israeli Supreme Court and the German and Canadian constitutional courts have long researched U.S. Supreme Court precedents in reaching their own conclusions on questions like freedom of speech, privacy rights, and due process. Fledgling constitutional courts in Central and Eastern Europe and in Russia are eagerly following suit. In 1995, the South African Supreme Court, finding the death penalty unconstitutional under the national constitution, referred to decisions from national and supranational courts around the world, including ones in Hungary, India, Tanzania, Canada, and Germany and the European Court of Human Rights. The U.S. Supreme Court has typically been more of a giver than a receiver in this exchange, but Justice Sandra Day O'Connor recently chided American lawyers and judges for their insularity in ignoring foreign law and predicted that she and her fellow justices would find themselves "looking more frequently to the decisions of other constitutional courts."

Why should a court in Israel or South Africa cite a decision by the U.S. Supreme Court in reaching its own conclusion? Decisions rendered by outside courts can have no authoritative value. They carry weight only because of their intrinsic logical power or because the court invoking them seeks to gain legitimacy by linking itself to a larger community of courts considering similar issues. National courts have become increasingly aware that they and their foreign counterparts are often engaged in a common effort to delimit the boundaries of individual rights in the face of an apparently overriding public interest. Thus, the British House of Lords recently rebuked the U.S. Supreme Court for its decision to uphold the kidnapping of a Mexican doctor by U.S. officials determined to bring him to trial in the United States.

Judges also cooperate in resolving transnational or international disputes. In cases involving citizens of two different states, courts have long been willing to acknowledge each other's potential interest and to defer to one another when such deference is not too costly. U.S. courts now recognize that they may become involved in a sustained dialogue with a foreign court. For instance, Judge Guido Calabresi of the Second Circuit recently allowed a French litigant to invoke U.S. discovery provisions without exhausting discovery options in France, reasoning that it was up to the French courts to identify and protest any infringements of French sovereignty. U.S. courts would then respond to such protests.

Judicial communication is not always harmonious, as in a recent squabble between a U.S. judge and a Hong Kong judge over an insider trading case. The U.S. judge refused to decline jurisdiction in favor of the Hong Kong court on grounds that "in Hong Kong they practically give you a medal for doing this sort of thing [insider trading]." In response, the Hong Kong judge stiffly defended the adequacy of Hong Kong law and asserted his willingness to apply it. He also chided his American counterpart, pointing out that any conflict "should be approached in the spirit of judicial comity rather than judicial competitiveness." Such conflict is to be expected among diplomats, but what is striking here is the two courts' view of themselves as quasi-autonomous foreign policy actors doing battle against international securities fraud.

The most advanced form of judicial cooperation is a partnership between national courts and a supranational tribunal. In the European Union (EU), the European Court of Justice works with national courts when questions of European law overlap national law. National courts refer cases up to the European Court, which issues an opinion and sends the case back to national courts;

the supranational recommendation guides the national court's decision. This cooperation marshals the power of domestic courts behind the judgment of a supranational tribunal. While the Treaty of Rome provides for this reference procedure, it is the courts that have transformed it into a judicial partnership.

Finally, judges are talking face to face. The judges of the supreme courts of Western Europe began meeting every three years in 1978. Since then they have become more aware of one another's decisions, particularly with regard to each other's willingness to accept the decisions handed down by the European Court of Justice. Meetings between U.S. Supreme Court justices and their counterparts on the European Court have been sponsored by private groups, as have meetings of U.S. judges with judges from the supreme courts of Central and Eastern Europe and Russia.

The most formal initiative aimed at bringing judges together is the recently inaugurated Organization of the Supreme Courts of the Americas. Twenty-five supreme court justices or their designees met in Washington in October 1995 and drafted the OCSA charter, dedicating the organization to "promot[ing] and strengthen[ing] judicial independence and the rule of law among the members, as well as the proper constitutional treatment of the judiciary as a fundamental branch of the state." The charter calls for triennial meetings and envisages a permanent secretariat. It required ratification by 15 supreme courts, achieved in spring 1996. An initiative by judges, for judges, it is not a stretch to say that OCSA is the product of judicial foreign policy.

Champions of a global rule of law have most frequently envisioned one rule for all, a unified legal system topped by a world court. The global community of law emerging from judicial networks will more likely encompass many rules of law, each established in a specific state or region. No high court would hand down definitive global rules. National courts would interact with one another and with supranational tribunals in ways that would accommodate differences but acknowledge and reinforce common values.

THE REGULATORY WEB

The densest area of transgovernmental activity is among national regulators. Bureaucrats charged with the administration of antitrust policy, securities regulation, environmental policy, criminal law enforcement, banking and insurance supervision—in short, all the agents of the modern regulatory state—regularly collaborate with their foreign counterparts.

National regulators track their quarry through cooperation. While frequently ad hoc, such cooperation is increasingly cemented by bilateral and multilateral agreements. The most formal of these are mutual legal assistance treaties, whereby two states lay out a protocol governing cooperation between their law enforcement agencies and courts. However, the preferred instrument of cooperation is the memorandum of understanding, in which two or more regulatory agencies set forth and initial terms for an ongoing relationship. Such memorandums are not treaties; they do not engage the executive or the legislature in negotiations, deliberation, or signature. Rather, they are good-faith agreements, affirming ties between regulatory agencies based on their like-minded commitment to getting results.

"Positive comity," a concept developed by the U.S. Department of Justice, epitomizes the changing nature of transgovernmental relations. Comity of nations, an archaic and notoriously vague term beloved by diplomats and international lawyers, has traditionally signified the deference one nation grants another in recognition of their mutual sovereignty. For instance, a state will recognize another state's laws or judicial judgments based on comity. Positive comity requires more active cooperation. As worked out by the Antitrust Division of the U.S. Department of Justice and the EU's European Commission, the regulatory authorities of both states alert one another to violations within their jurisdiction, with the understanding that the responsible authority will take action. Positive comity is a principle of enduring cooperation between government agencies.

In 1988 the central bankers of the world's major financial powers adopted capital adequacy requirements for all banks under their supervision—a significant reform of the international banking system. It was not the World Bank, the International Monetary Fund, or even the Group of Seven that took this step. Rather, the forum was the Basle Committee on Banking Supervision, an organization composed of 12 central bank governors. The Basle Committee was created by a simple agreement among the governors themselves. Its members meet four times a year and follow their own rules. Decisions are made by consensus and are not formally binding; however, members do implement these decisions within their own systems. The Basle Committee's authority is often cited as an argument for taking domestic action.

National securities commissioners and insurance regulators have followed the Basle Committee's example. Incorporated by a private bill of the Quebec National Assembly, the International Organization of Securities Commissioners has no formal charter or founding treaty. Its primary purpose is to solve problems affecting international securities markets by creating a consensus for enactment of national legislation. Its members have also entered into information-sharing agreements on their own initiative. The International Association of Insurance Supervisors follows a similar model, as does the newly created Tripartite Group, an international coalition of banking, insurance, and securities regulators the Basle Committee created to improve the supervision of financial conglomerates.

Pat Buchanan would have had a field day with the Tripartite Group, denouncing it as a prime example of bureaucrats taking power out of the hands of American voters. In fact, unlike the international bogeymen of demagogic fantasy, transnational regulatory organizations do not aspire to exercise power in the international system independent of their members. Indeed, their main purpose is to help regulators apprehend those who would harm the interests of American voters. Transgovernmental networks often promulgate their own rules, but the purpose of those rules is to enhance the enforcement of national law.

Traditional international law requires states to implement the international obligations they incur through their own law. Thus, if states agree to a 12-mile territorial sea, they must change their domestic legislation concerning the interdiction of vessels in territorial waters accordingly. But this legislation is unlikely to overlap with domestic law, as national legislatures do not usually seek to regulate global commons issues and interstate relations.

Transgovernmental regulation, by contrast, produces rules concerning issues that each nation already regulates within its borders: crime, securities fraud, pollution, tax evasion. The advances in technology and transportation that have fueled globalization have made it more difficult to enforce national law. Regulators benefit from coordinating their enforcement efforts with those of their foreign counterparts and from ensuring that other nations adopt similar approaches.

The result is the nationalization of international law. Regulatory agreements between states are pledges of good faith that are self-enforcing, in the sense that each nation will be better able to enforce its national law by implementing the agreement if other nations do likewise. Laws are binding or coercive only at the national level. Uniformity of result and diversity of means go hand in hand, and the makers and enforcers of rules are national leaders who are accountable to the people.

BIPARTISAN GLOBALIZATION

Secretary of State Madeleine Albright seeks to revive the bipartisan foreign policy consensus of the late 1940s. Deputy Secretary of State Strobe Talbott argues that promoting democracy worldwide satisfies the American need for idealpolitik as well as realpolitik. President Clinton, in his second inaugural address, called for a "new government for a new century," abroad as well as at home. But bipartisanship is threatened by divergent responses to globalization, democratization is a tricky business, and Vice President Al Gore's efforts to "reinvent government" have focused on domestic rather than international institutions. Transgovernmentalism can address all these problems.

Globalization implies the erosion of national boundaries. Consequently, regulators' power to implement national regulations within those boundaries declines both because people can easily flee their jurisdiction and because the flows of capital, pollution, pathogens, and weapons are too great and sudden for any one regulator to control. The liberal internationalist response to these assaults on state regulatory power is to build a larger international apparatus. Globalization thus leads to internationalization, or the transfer of regulatory authority from the national level to an international institution. The best example is not the WTO itself, but rather the stream of proposals to expand the WTO's jurisdiction to global competition policy, intellectual property regulation, and other trade-related issues. Liberals are likely to support expanding the power of international institutions to guard against the global dismantling of the regulatory state.

Here's the rub. Conservatives are more likely to favor the expansion of globalized markets without the internationalization that goes with it, since internationalization, from their perspective, equals a loss of sovereignty. According to Buchanan, the U.S. foreign policy establishment "want[s] to move America into a New World Order where the World Court decides quarrels between nations; the WTO writes the rules for trade and settles all disputes; the IMF and World Bank order wealth transfers from continent to continent and country to country; the Law of the Sea Treaty tells us what we may and may not do on the high seas and ocean floor, and the United Nations decides where U.S. military forces may and may not intervene." The rhetoric is deliberately inflammatory, but echoes resound across the Republican spectrum.

Transgovernmental initiatives are a compromise that could command bipartisan support. Regulatory loopholes caused by global forces require a coordinated response beyond the reach of any one country. But this coordination need not come from building more international institutions. It can be achieved through transgovernmental

cooperation, involving the same officials who make and implement policy at the national level. The transgovernmental alternative is fast, flexible, and effective.

A leading example of transgovernmentalism in action that demonstrates its bipartisan appeal is a State Department initiative christened the New Transatlantic Agenda. Launched in 1991 under the Bush administration and reinvigorated by Secretary of State Warren Christopher in 1995, the initiative structures the relationship between the United States and the EU, fostering cooperation in areas ranging from opening markets to fighting terrorism, drug trafficking, and infectious disease. It is an umbrella for ongoing projects between U.S. officials and their European counterparts. It reaches ordinary citizens, embracing efforts like the Transatlantic Business Dialogue and engaging individuals through people-to-people exchanges and expanded communication through the Internet.

DEMOCRATIZATION, STEP BY STEP

Transgovernmental networks are concentrated among liberal democracies but are not limited to them. Some nondemocratic states have institutions capable of cooperating with their foreign counterparts, such as committed and effective regulatory agencies or relatively independent judiciaries. Transgovernmental ties can strengthen institutions in ways that will help them resist political domination, corruption, and incompetence and build democratic institutions in their countries, step by step. The Organization of Supreme Courts of the Americas, for instance, actively seeks to strengthen norms of judicial independence among its members, many of whom must fend off powerful political forces.

Individuals and groups in nondemocratic countries may also "borrow" government institutions of democratic states to achieve a measure of justice they cannot obtain in their own countries. The court or regulatory agency of one state may be able to perform judicial or regulatory functions for the people of another. Victims of human rights violations, for example, in countries such as Argentina, Ethiopia, Haiti, and the Philippines have sued for redress in the courts of the United States. U.S. courts accepted these cases, often over the objections of the executive branch, using a broad interpretation of a moribund statute dating back to 1789. Under this interpretation, aliens may sue in U.S. courts to seek damages from foreign government officials accused of torture, even if the torture allegedly took place in the foreign country. More generally, a nongovernmental organization seeking to prevent human rights violations can often circumvent their own government's corrupt legislature and politicized court by publicizing the plight of victims abroad and mobilizing a foreign court, legislature, or executive to take action.

Responding to calls for a coherent U.S. foreign policy and seeking to strengthen the community of democratic nations, President Clinton substituted the concept of "enlargement" for the Cold War principle of "containment." Expanding transgovernmental outreach to include institutions from nondemocratic states would help expand the circle of democracies one institution at a time.

A NEW WORLD ORDER IDEAL

Transgovernmentalism offers its own world order ideal, less dramatic but more compelling than either liberal internationalism or the new medievalism. It harnesses the state's power to find and implement solutions to global problems. International institutions have a lackluster record on such problem-solving; indeed, NGOs exist largely to compensate for their inadequacies. Doing away with the state, however, is hardly the answer. The new medievalist mantra of global governance is "governance without government." But governance without government is governance without power, and government without power rarely works. Many pressing international and domestic problems result from states' insufficient power to establish order, build infrastructure, and provide minimum social services. Private actors

may take up some slack, but there is no substitute for the state.

Transgovernmental networks allow governments to benefit from the flexibility and decentralization of nonstate actors. Jessica T. Mathews argues that "businesses, citizens' organizations, ethnic groups, and crime cartels have all readily adopted the network model," while governments "are quintessential hierarchies, wedded to an organizational form incompatible with all that the new technologies make possible." Not so. Disaggregating the state into its functional components makes it possible to create networks of institutions engaged in a common enterprise even as they represent distinct national interests. Moreover, they can work with their subnational and supranational counterparts, creating a genuinely new world order in which networked institutions perform the functions of a world government—legislation, administration, and adjudication—without the form.

These globe-spanning networks will strengthen the state as the primary player in the international system. The state's defining attribute has traditionally been sovereignty, conceived as absolute power in domestic affairs and autonomy in relations with other states. But as Abram and Antonia Chayes observe in *The New Sovereignty* (1995), sovereignty is actually "status—the vindication of the state's existence in the international system." More importantly, they demonstrate that in contemporary international relations, sovereignty has been redefined to mean "membership . . . in the regimes that make up the substance of international life." Disaggregating the state permits the disaggregation of sovereignty as well, ensuring that specific state institutions derive strength and status from participation in a transgovernmental order.

Transgovernmental networks will increasingly provide an important anchor for international organizations and nonstate actors alike. U.N. officials have already learned a lesson about the limits of supranational authority; mandated cuts in the international bureaucracy will further tip the balance of power toward national regulators. The next generation of international institutions is also likely to look more like the Basle Committee, or, more formally, the Organization of Economic Cooperation and Development, dedicated to providing a forum for transnational problem-solving and the harmonization of national law. The disaggregation of the state creates opportunities for domestic institutions, particularly courts, to make common cause with their supranational counterparts against their fellow branches of government. Nonstate actors will lobby and litigate wherever they think they will have the most effect. Many already realize that corporate self-regulation and states' promises to comply with vague international agreements are no substitute for national law.

The spread of transgovernmental networks will depend more on political and professional convergence than on civilizational boundaries. Trust and awareness of a common enterprise are more vulnerable to differing political ideologies and corruption than to cultural differences. Government networks transcend the traditional divide between high and low politics. National militaries, for instance, network as extensively as central bankers with their counterparts in friendly states. Judicial and regulatory networks can help achieve gradual political convergence, but are unlikely to be of much help in the face of a serious economic or military threat. If the coming conflict with China is indeed coming, transgovernmentalism will not stop it.

The strength of transgovernmental networks and of transgovernmentalism as a world order ideal will ultimately depend on their accountability to the world's peoples.

To many, the prospect of transnational government by judges and bureaucrats looks more like technocracy than democracy. Critics contend that government institutions engaged in policy coordination with their foreign counterparts will be barely visible, much less accountable, to voters still largely tied to national territory.

Citizens of liberal democracies will not accept any form of international regulation they cannot control. But checking unelected officials is a familiar problem in domestic politics. As national legislators become increasingly aware of transgovernmental networks, they will expand their oversight capacities and develop networks of their own. Transnational NGO networks will develop a similar monitoring capacity. It will be harder to monitor themselves.

Transgovernmentalism offers answers to the most important challenges facing advanced industrial countries: loss of regulatory power with economic globalization, perceptions of a "democratic deficit" as international institutions step in to fill the regulatory gap, and the difficulties of engaging nondemocratic states. Moreover, it provides a powerful alternative to a liberal internationalism that has reached its limits and to a new medievalism that, like the old Marxism, sees the state slowly fading away. The new medievalists are right to emphasize the dawn of a new era, in which information technology will transform the globe. But government networks are government for the information age. They offer the world a blueprint for the international architecture of the 21st century.

CHAPTER 7

"Introduction" and "The State and the Global City" from *Globalization and Its Discontents*

Saskia Sassen

INTRODUCTION

[. . .]

A NEW GEOGRAPHY OF CENTRALITY AND MARGINALITY

The global economy materializes in a world-wide grid of strategic places, from export-processing zones to major international business and financial centers. We can think of this global grid as constituting a new economic geography of centrality, one that cuts across national boundaries and across the old North–South divide. It signals the emergence of a parallel political geography of power, a transnational space for the formation of new claims by global capital (See Sassen 1996, Chap. 2). This new economic geography of centrality partly reproduces existing in-equalities but also is the outcome of a dynamic specific to current types of economic growth. It assumes many forms and operates in many terrains, from the distri-bution of telecommunications facilities to the structure of the economy and of employment.

The most powerful of these new geogra-phies of centrality at the interurban level binds the major international financial and business centers: New York, London, Tokyo, Paris, Frankfurt, Zurich, Amsterdam, Los Angeles, Sydney, Hong Kong, among others. But this geography now also includes cities such as São Paulo, Buenos Aires, Bangkok, Taipei, Bombay, and Mexico City. The inten-sity of transactions among these cities, par-ticularly through the financial markets, trade in services, and investment, has increased sharply, and so have the orders of magnitude involved. At the same time, there has been a sharpening inequality in the concentration of strategic resources and activities between each of these cities and others in the same country. Global cities are sites for immense concentrations of economic power and com-mand centers in a global economy, while traditional manufacturing centers have suf-fered inordinate declines.

One might have expected that the growing number of financial centers now integrated into the global markets would have reduced the extent of concentration of financial activ-ity in the top centers. But it has not.[1] One would also expect this given the immense increases in the global volume of transac-tions.[2] Yet the levels of concentration remain unchanged in the face of massive trans-formations in the financial industry and in the technological infrastructure this industry depends on.[3]

The growth of global markets for finance and specialized services, the need for trans-national servicing networks because of sharp increases in international investment, the reduced role of the government in the regula-tion of international economic activity and the corresponding ascendance of other insti-tutional arenas, notably global markets and corporate headquarters—all these point to the existence of a series of economic pro-cesses, each characterized by locations in more than one country and in this regard transnational. We can see here the formation, at least incipient, of a transnational urban system (Sassen 1991, chap. 7; 1994, chap. 3; Knox and Taylor 1995).

The pronounced orientation to the world markets evident in such cities raises questions about the articulation with their nation-states, their regions, and the larger economic and social structure in such cities. Cities have typically been deeply embedded in the economies of their region, indeed often reflecting the characteristics of the latter; and generally they still do. But cities that are strategic sites in the global economy tend, in part, to become disconnected from their region and even nation. This conflicts with a key proposition in conventional scholarship about urban systems, namely, that these systems promote the territorial integration of regional and national economies.

Alongside these new global and regional hierarchies of cities and high-tech industrial districts lies a vast territory that has become increasingly peripheral, increasingly excluded from the major economic processes that fuel economic growth in the new global economy. A multiplicity of formerly important manufacturing centers and port cities have lost functions and are in decline, not only in the less developed countries but also in the most advanced economies. This is yet another meaning of economic globalization.

But also inside global cities we see a new geography of centrality and marginality. The downtowns of global cities and metropolitan business centers receive massive investments in real estate and telecommunications while low-income city areas are starved for resources. Highly educated workers employed in leading sectors see their incomes rise to unusually high levels while low- or medium-skilled workers in those same sectors see theirs sink. Financial services produce superprofits while industrial services barely survive. These trends are evident, with different levels of intensity, in a growing number of major cities in the developed world and increasingly in major cities of some of the developing countries that have been integrated into the global economy.

THE RIGHTS OF CAPITAL IN THE NEW GLOBAL GRID

A basic proposition in discussions about the global economy concerns the declining sovereignty of states over their economies.

Economic globalization does indeed extend the economy beyond the boundaries of the nation-state. This is particularly evident in the leading economic sectors. Existing systems of governance and accountability for transnational activities and actors leave much ungoverned when it comes to these industries. Global markets in finance and advanced services partly operate through a "regulatory" umbrella that is not state centered but market centered. More generally, the new geography of centrality is transnational and operates in good part in electronic spaces that override all jurisdiction.

Yet, this proposition fails to underline a key component in the transformation of the last fifteen years: the formation of new claims on national states to guarantee the domestic and global rights of capital. What matters for our purposes here is that global capital made these claims and that national states responded through the production of new forms of legality. The new geography of centrality had to be produced, both in terms of the practices of corporate actors and in terms of the work of the state in producing new legal regimes. Representations that characterize the national state as simply losing significance fail to capture this very important dimension, and reduce what is happening to a function of the global/national duality— what one wins, the other loses.

There are two distinct issues here. One is the ascendance of this new legal regime that negotiates between national sovereignty and the transnational practices of corporate economic actors. The second issue concerns the particular content of this new regime, which strengthens the advantages of certain types of economic actors and weakens those of others. The hegemony of neoliberal concepts of economic relations with its strong emphasis on markets, deregulation, and free international trade has influenced policy in the 1980s in the United States and Great Britain and now increasingly also in continental Europe. This has contributed to the formation of transnational legal regimes that are centered in Western economic concepts of contract and property rights.[4] Through the International Monetary Fund (IMF) and the International Bank for Reconstruction and

Development (IBRD), as well as the General Agreement on Tariffs and Trade (GATT) (the World Trade Organization since January 1995), this regime has spread to the developing world (Mittelman 1996). It is a regime associated with increased levels of concentrated wealth, poverty, and inequality worldwide. This occurs under specific modalities in the case of global cities, as discussed earlier.

Deregulation has been a crucial mechanism to negotiate the juxtaposition of the global and the national. Rather than simply seeing it as freeing up markets and reducing the sovereignty of the state, we might underline a much less noted aspect of deregulation: it has had the effect, particularly in the case of the leading economic sectors, of partly denationalizing national territory (see Sassen 1996). In other words, it is not simply a matter of a space economy extending beyond a national realm. It is also that globalization—as illustrated by the space economy of advanced information industries—denationalizes national territory. This denationalization, which to a large extent materializes in global cities, has become legitimate for capital and has indeed been imbued with positive value by many government elites and their economic advisers. It is the opposite when it comes to people, as is perhaps most sharply illustrated in the rise of anti-immigrant feeling and the renationalizing of politics.

The emphasis on the transnational and hypermobile character of capital has contributed to a sense of powerlessness among local actors, a sense of the futility of resistance. But the analysis in the preceding sections, with its emphasis on place, suggests that the new global grid of strategic sites is a terrain for politics and engagement. Further, the state, both national and local, can be engaged. Although certain agencies within the state have contributed to the formation and strengthening of global capital, the state is far from being a unitary institution. The state itself has been transformed by its role in implementing the global economic system, a transformation captured in the ascendance of agencies linked to the domestic and international financial markets in most governments of highly developed countries and

many governments of developing countries, and the loss of power and prestige of agencies associated with issues of domestic equity. These different agencies are now at times in open conflict.

The focus on place helps us elaborate and specify the meaning of key concepts in the discourse about globalization, notably the loss of sovereignty. It brings to the fore that important components of globalization are embedded in particular institutional locations within national territories. A strategic subnational unit such as the global city is emblematic of these conditions—conditions not well captured in the more conventional duality of national/global.

A focus on the leading industries in global cities introduces into the discussion of governance the possibility of capacities for local governmental regulation derived from the concentration of significant resources in strategic places. These resources include fixed capital and are essential for participation in the global economy. The considerable place-boundedness of many of these resources contrasts with the hypermobility of the outputs of many of these same industries, particularly finance. The regulatory capacity of the state stands in a different relation to hypermobile outputs than to the infrastructure of facilities, from office buildings equipped with fiber optic cables to specialized workforces.

The specific issues raised by focusing on the placeboundedness of key components of economic globalization are quite distinct from those typically raised in the context of the national/global duality. A focus on this duality leads to rather straightforward propositions about the declining significance of the state vis-à-vis global economic actors. The overarching tendency in economic analyses of globalization and of the leading information industries has been to emphasize certain aspects: industry outputs rather than the production process involved; the capacity for instantaneous transmission around the world rather than the infrastructure necessary for this capacity; the impossibility for the state to regulate those outputs and that capacity insofar as they extend beyond the nation-state. And the emphasis is by itself quite correct; but it is a partial account about the implications of globalization for governance.

The transformation in the composition of the world economy, especially the rise of finance and advanced services as leading industries, is contributing to a new international economic order, one dominated by financial centers, global markets, and transnational firms. Cities that function as international business and financial centers are sites for direct transactions with world markets that take place without government inspection, as for instance the euro-markets or New York City's international financial zone (i.e., International Banking Facilities). These cities and the globally oriented markets and firms they contain mediate in the relation of the world economy to nation-states and in the relations among nation-states. Correspondingly, we may see a growing significance of sub- and supranational political categories and actors.

UNMOORING IDENTITIES AND A NEW TRANSNATIONAL POLITICS

The preceding section argues that the production of new forms of legality and of a new transnational legal regime privilege the reconstitution of capital as a global actor and the denationalized spaces necessary for its operation. At the same time there is a lack of new legal forms and regimes to encompass another crucial element of this transnationalization, one that some, including myself, see as the counterpart to that of capital: the transnationalization of labor. However, we are still using the language of immigration to describe the process.[5] Nor are there new forms and regimes to encompass the transnationalization in the formation of identities and loyalties among various population segments which do not regard the nation as the sole or principal source of identification, and the associated new solidarities and notions of membership. Major cities have emerged as a strategic site not only for global capital but also for the transnationalization of labor and the formation of transnational identities. In this regard they are a site for new types of political operations.

Cities are the terrain where people from many different countries are most likely to meet and a multiplicity of cultures come together. The international character of major cities lies not only in their telecommunication infrastructure and international firms, but also in the many different cultural environments they contain. One can no longer think of centers for international business and finance simply in terms of the corporate towers and corporate culture at their center. Today's global cities are in part the spaces of postcolonialism and indeed contain conditions for the formation of a postcolonialist discourse (Hall 1991; King 1996).

The large Western city of today concentrates diversity. Its spaces are inscribed with the dominant corporate culture but also with a multiplicity of other cultures and identities. The slippage is evident: the dominant culture can encompass only part of the city.[6] And while corporate power inscribes these cultures and identifies them with "otherness" thereby devaluing them, they are present everywhere. For instance, through immigration a proliferation of originally highly localized cultures now have become presences in many large cities, cities whose elites think of themselves as cosmopolitan, as transcending any locality. Members of these "localized" cultures can in fact come from places with great cultural diversity and be as cosmopolitan as elites. An immense array of cultures from around the world, each rooted in a particular country, town, or village, now is reterritorialized in a few single places, places such as New York, Los Angeles, Paris, London, and most recently Tokyo.[7]

I think that there are representations of globality which have not been recognized as such or are contested representations. Such representations include immigration and its associated cultural environments, often subsumed under the notion of ethnicity. What we still narrate in the language of immigration and ethnicity, I would argue, is actually a series of processes having to do with the globalization of economic activity, of cultural activity, of identity formation. Too often immigration and ethnicity are constituted as otherness. Understanding them as a set of processes whereby global elements are localized, international labor markets are constituted, and cultures from all over the world are de- and reterritorialized, puts them right there at the center along with the internationalization of capital as a fundamental aspect of globalization.[8] This way of narrating the large migrations of the post-war era captures the ongoing weight of colonialism and postcolonial forms of empire on major processes of globalization today, and specifically those processes binding countries of emigration and immigration.[9] Although the specific genesis and contents of their responsibility will vary from case to case and period to period, major immigration countries are not passive bystanders in their immigration histories.

MAKING CLAIMS ON THE CITY

These processes signal that there has been a change in the linkages that bind people and places and in the corresponding formation of claims on the city. It is true that throughout history people have moved and through these movements constituted places. But today the articulation of territory and people is being constituted in a radically different way at least in one regard, and that is the speed with which that articulation can change. Martinotti (1993) notes that one consequence of this speed is the expansion of the space within which actual and possible linkages can occur. The shrinking of distance and the speed of movement that characterize the current era find one of its most extreme forms in electronically based communities of individuals or organizations from all around the globe interacting in real time and simultaneously, as is possible through the Internet and kindred electronic networks.

I would argue that another radical form assumed today by the linkage of people to territory is the unmooring of identities from what have been traditional sources of identity, such as the nation or the village. This unmooring in the process of identity formation engenders new notions of community, of membership, and of entitlement.

The space constituted by the global grid of cities, a space with new economic and political potentialities, is perhaps one of the most strategic spaces for the formation of transnational identities and communities. This is a space that is both place centered in that it is embedded in particular and strategic locations; and it is transterritorial because it connects sites that are not geographically proximate yet are intensely connected to each other. As I argued earlier, it is not only the transmigration of capital that takes place in this global grid, but also that of people, both rich (i.e., the new transnational professional workforce) and poor (i.e., most migrant workers) and it is a space for the transmigration of cultural forms, for the reterritorialization of "local" subcultures. An important question is whether it is also a space for a new politics, one going beyond the politics of culture and identity, though at least partly likely to be embedded in it.

Yet another way of thinking about the political implications of this strategic transnational space anchored in cities is the formation of new claims on that space. As was discussed earlier, there are indeed new major actors making claims on these cities over the last decade, notably foreign firms that have been increasingly entitled through the deregulation of national economies, and the increasing number of international businesspeople. These are among the new "city users." They have profoundly marked the urban landscape. Their claim to the city is not contested, even though the costs and benefits to cities have barely been examined.

The new city users have made an often immense claim on the city and have reconstituted strategic spaces of the city in their image: their claim is rarely examined or challenged. They contribute to changing the social morphology of the city and to constituting what Martinotti (1993) calls the metropolis of second generation, the city of late modernism. The new city of these city users is a fragile one, whose survival and successes are centered on an economy of high productivity, advanced technologies, and intensified exchanges.

On the one hand, this raises a question of what the city is for international businesspeople: it is a city whose space consists of airports, top-level business districts, top of the line hotels and restaurants—a sort of urban glamour zone, the new hyperspace of international business. On the other hand, there is the difficult task of establishing whether a city that functions as an international business center does in fact recover the costs for being such a center: the costs involved in maintaining a state-of-the-art business district, and all it requires, from advanced communications facilities to top-level security and "world-class culture."

Perhaps at the other extreme of legitimacy are those who use urban political violence to make their claims on the city, claims that lack the de facto legitimacy enjoyed by the new business city users. These are claims made by actors struggling for recognition and entitlement, claiming their rights to the city (Body-Gendrot 1993).[10] These claims have, of course, a long history; every new epoch brings specific conditions to the manner in which the claims are made. The growing weight of "delinquency," for example, smashing cars and shop windows, robbing and burning stores, in some of these uprisings during the last decade in major cities of the developed world, is perhaps an indication of the sharpened inequality. The disparities, as seen and as lived, between the urban glamour zone and the urban war zone have become enormous. The extreme visibility of the difference is likely to contribute to further brutalization of the conflict: the indifference and greed of the new elites versus the hopelessness and rage of the poor. [. . .]

The State and the Global City

THE GLOBAL GRID OF STRATEGIC SITES

The global integration of financial markets depends on and contributes to the implementation of a variety of linkages among the financial centers involved.[11] Prime examples of such linkages are the multinational networks of affiliates and subsidiaries typical of major firms in manufacturing and specialized services. Corporate service firms have developed vast multinational networks containing special geographic and institutional linkages that make it possible for client firms—transnational firms and banks—to use a growing array of service offerings from the same supplier (Marshall et al., 1986; Noyelle and Dutka 1988; Daniels and Moulaert 1991; Fainstein et al. 1993, chap. 2).[12] There is also a growing number of less directly economic linkages, notable among which are a variety of initiatives launched by urban governments which amount to a type of foreign policy by and for cities. For example, New York State has opened business offices in several major cities overseas.

Whether these linkages have engendered transnational urban systems is less clear. It is partly a question of theory and conceptualization. So much of social science is profoundly rooted in the nation-state as the ultimate unit for analysis, that conceptualizing processes and systems as transnational is bound to engender much controversy. Even much of the literature on world or global cities does not necessarily posit the existence of a transnational urban system: in its narrowest form it posits that global cities perform central place functions at a transnational level. But that leaves open the question as to the nature of the articulation among global cities. If one posits that they merely compete with each other for global business, then they do not constitute a transnational system; in this case, studying several global cities becomes an instance of traditional comparative analyses.

If one posits that besides competing they are also the sites for transnational processes with multiple locations, then one can begin to posit the possibility of a systemic dynamic binding these cities. Elsewhere (1991, chapters 1 and 7) I have argued that in addition to the central place functions performed by these cities at the global level, as posited by Hall (1966), Friedmann and Wolff (1982) and Sassen (1982), these cities relate to one another in distinct systemic ways. For example, the interaction among New York, London, and Tokyo, particularly in terms of finance and investment, consists partly of a series of processes that can be thought of as the chain of production in finance. Thus, in the mid-1980s Tokyo was the main exporter of the raw material we call money while New York was the leading processing center in the world. It was in New York that many of the new financial instruments were invented, and where money either in its raw form or in the form of debt was transformed into instruments that aimed at maximizing the returns on that money. London, on the other hand, was a major entrepôt which had the network to centralize and concentrate small amounts of capital available in a large number of smaller financial markets around the world, partly a function of its older network for the administration of the British empire. This is just one example suggesting that these cities do not simply compete with each other for the same business. There is, it seems to me, an economic system that rests on the three distinct types of locations these cities represent.[13] In my view, there is no such thing as a single global city, unlike what was the case with earlier imperial capitals—a single world city at the top of a system. The global city is a function of the global grid of transactions, one site for processes which are global because they have multiple locations in multiple countries (see also Abu-Lughod 1995; Smith and Timberlake 1995).

If finance and the advanced corporate services are in fact embedded in such transnational systems then this might be a rather significant factor in examinations of the possibilities on deregulation and globalization but also on a complex and dense grid of linkages and sites. The hypermobility of these industries and the associated difficulties for regulation are only part of the picture, albeit the most intensely studied and debated one; the global grid of linkages and sites within which this hypermobility is embedded and through which it flows is potentially another part of the picture, and one that will require more research to elucidate.

CONCLUSION: REGULATING THE GLOBAL GRID OF PLACES

Including cities in the analysis of economic globalization and the ascendance of information industries adds three important dimensions to the study of economic globalization. First, it decomposes the nation-state into a variety of components that may be significant in understanding international economic activity and regulatory capacities. Second, it displaces the focus from the power of large corporations over governments and economies to the range of activities and organizational arrangements necessary for the implementation and maintenance of a global network of factories, service operations, and markets; these are all processes only partly encompassed by the activities of transnational corporations and banks. Third, it contributes to a focus on place and on the strategic concentrations of infrastructure and production complexes necessary for global economic activity. Processes of economic globalization are thereby reconstituted as concrete production complexes situated in specific places containing a multiplicity of activities. Focusing on cities allows us to specify a global geography of strategic places as well as the microgeographies and politics unfolding within these places.

The transformation in the composition of the world economy, especially the rise of finance and advanced services as leading industries, is contributing to a new international economic order, one dominated by financial centers, global markets, and transnational firms. Correspondingly, we may see a growing significance of other political categories both sub- and supranational. Cities that function as international business and financial centers are sites for direct transactions with world markets.

These cities and the globally oriented markets and firms they contain mediate in the relation of the world economy to nation-states and in the relations among nation-states. Transnational economic processes inevitably interact with systems for the governance of national economies. Further, the material conditions necessary for many global economic processes—from the infrastructure for telematics to the producer services production complex—need to be incorporated in examinations of questions of governance and accountability in the global economy. They signal the possibility of novel forms of regulation and conditions for accountability.

In sum, an analysis focused on place and production has the effect of decoding globalization; the latter is conceptually reconstituted in terms of a transnational geography of centrality consisting of multiple linkages and strategic concentrations of material infrastructure. Globalization can then be seen as embedded and dependent on these linkages and material infrastructure. To a considerable extent, global processes are this grid of sites and linkages.

The existence of such a transnational grid of places and linkages that constitute the infrastructure for the globalization of finance and other specialized services points to regulatory possibilities. Precisely because of its strategic character and because of the density of resources and linkages it concentrates, this new geography of centrality could in turn be a space for concentrated regulatory activity. But the type of regulatory frameworks and operations it would entail need to be discovered and invented, as does the meaning of accountability and democratization of the new global information economy.

NOTES

1. Furthermore, this unchanged level of concentration has happened at a time when financial services are more mobile than ever before: globalization, deregulation (an essential ingredient for globalization), and securitization have been the key to this mobility—in the context of massive advances in telecommunications and electronic networks. (Securitization is the transformation of hitherto "unliquid capital" into tradeable instruments, a process that took off dramatically in the 1980s.) One result is growing competition among centers for hypermobile financial activity. In my view there has been an overemphasis on competition in general and in specialized accounts on this subject. As I have argued elsewhere (Sassen 1991, chap. 7), there is also a functional division of labor

among various major financial centers. In this sense we can think of a transnational system with multiple locations.

2. For example, international bank lending grew from US$1.89 trillion in 1980 to US$6.24 trillion in 1991—a fivefold increase in a mere ten years. Three cities (New York, London, and Tokyo) account for forty-two percent of all such international lending in 1980 and for forty-one percent in 1991 according to data from the Bank of International Settlements, the leading institution worldwide in charge of overseeing banking activity. There were compositional changes: Japan's share rose from 7.2 percent to 15.1 percent and Britain's fell from 26.2 percent to 16.3 percent; the U.S. share remained constant. All increased in absolute terms. Beyond these three, Switzerland, France, Germany, and Luxembourg bring the total share of the top centers to sixty-four percent in 1991, which is just about the same share these countries had in 1980. One city, Chicago, dominates the world's trading in futures, accounting for 60 percent of worldwide contracts in options and futures in 1991.

3. In this context it is worth noting that the discussion around the formation of a single European market and financial system has raised the possibility, and even the need if it is to be competitive, of centralizing financial functions and capital in a limited number of cities rather than maintaining the current structure in which each country has a city that aspires to become a major international financial center.

4. An issue that is emerging as significant in view of the spread of Western legal concepts is the critical examination of the philosophical premises about authorship and property that define the legal arena in the West. See Coombe 1993.

5. This language is increasingly constructing immigration as a devalued process insofar as it describes the entry of people from generally poorer, disadvantaged countries, in search of the better lives that the receiving country can offer; it contains an implicit valorization of the receiving country and a devalorization of the sending country. And it lacks some of the positive connotations historically associated with immigrants.

6. There are many different forms such contestation and "slippage" can assume. See King 1996; Dunn 1994; *Social Justice* 1993. Global mass culture homogenizes and is capable of absorbing an immense variety of local cultural elements. But this process is never complete. I have found the opposite dynamic in the manufacturing of electronic components which shows that employment in lead sectors no longer inevitably absorbs workers into a labor aristocracy. Thus, Third World women working in export processing zones are not empowered: capitalism can work through difference. Yet another case is that of illegal immigrants; here we see that national boundaries have the effect of creating and criminalizing differences.

These kinds of differentiations are central to the formation of a world economic system (Wallerstein 1990).

7. Tokyo now has several, mostly working-class concentrations of legal and unauthorized immigrants coming from China, Bangladesh, Pakistan, and the Philippines, among others. This is quite remarkable in view of Japan's legal and cultural closure to immigrants. Is this simply a function of poverty in those countries? By itself is not enough of an explanation, because they have long had poverty. I posit that the internationalization of the Japanese economy, including specific forms of investment in those countries, and Japan's growing cultural influence there, have created bridges between those countries and Japan that have reduced the subjective distance with Japan. See Sassen 1991, 307–415; Shank 1994.

8. There has been growing recognition of the formation of an international professional class of workers and of highly internationalized environments due to the presence of foreign firms and personnel, the formation of global markets in the arts, and the international circulation of high culture. What has not been recognized is the possibility that we are seeing an international labor market for low-wage manual and service workers. This process continues to be couched in terms of the "immigration story," a narrative rooted in an earlier historical period, and, probably, in a distinct cultural narrative.

9. The specific forms of the internationalization of capital over the last twenty years have contributed to mobilizing people into migration streams. They have done so principally through the implantation of Western development strategies, from the replacement of small-holder agriculture with export-oriented commercial agriculture and export manufacturing, to the Westernization of education systems. At the same time the administrative, commercial, and development networks of the former European empires and the newer forms these networks assumed under the Pax Americana (international direct foreign investment, export-processing zones, wars for "democracy") have not only created bridges for the flow of capital, information, and high-level personnel from the center to the periphery but, I argue, also for the flow of migrants from the periphery to the center.

10. Body-Gendrot (1993) shows how the city remains a terrain for contest, characterized by the emergence of new actors, often younger and younger. It is a terrain where the constraints placed upon, and the institutional limitations of governments to address the demands of equity, engender social disorders. She argues that urban political violence should not be interpreted as a coherent ideology but rather as an element of temporary political tactics, which permits vulnerable actors to enter in interaction with the holders of power on terms that will be somewhat more favorable to the weak.

11. There is a rapidly growing and highly specialized literature focused on different types of economic linkages that bind cities across national borders (Castells 1989; Noyelle and Dutka 1988; Daniels and Moulaert 1991; Leyshon, Daniels and Thrift 1987; Sassen 1991).

12. There is good evidence that the development of multinational corporate service firms was associated with the needs of transnational firms. The multinational advertising firm can offer global advertising to a specific segment of potential customers worldwide. Further, global integration of affiliates and markets requires making use of advanced information and telecommunications technology which can come to account for a significant share of costs—not only operational costs but also, and perhaps most important, research and development costs for new products or advances on existing products. The need for scale economies on all these fronts contributes to explain the recent increase in mergers and acquisitions, which has consolidated the position of a few very large firms in many of these industries, and further strengthened cross-border linkages among the key locations which concentrate the needed telecommunications facilities. They have emerged as firms that can control a significant share of national and international markets. The rapid increase in direct foreign investments in services is strongly linked with the growing tendency among leading service firms to operate transnationally. Subcontracting by larger firms and the multiplicity of specialized markets has meant that small independent firms can also thrive in major centers (Sassen 1991; Noyelle and Dutka 1988; Leyshon, Daniels and Thrift 1987).

13. The possibility of such a transnational urban system raises a question as to the articulation of such cities with their national urban systems. It is quite possible that the strengthening of cross-national ties among the leading financial and business centers is likely to be accomplished by a weakening of the linkages between each of these cities and their hinterlands and national urban system (Sassen 1991). Cities such as Detroit, Liverpool, Manchester, Marseille, the cities of the Ruhr, and now increasingly Nagoya and Osaka, have been affected by the territorial decentralization of many of their key manufacturing industries at the domestic and international level. This process of decentralization has contributed to the growth of service industries that produce the specialized inputs to run spatially dispersed processes and global markets for inputs and outputs. These specialized inputs—international legal and accounting services, management consulting, financial services—are heavily concentrated in business and financial centers rather than in these manufacturing cities themselves.

BIBLIOGRAPHY

Abu-Lughod, Janet Lippman (1995) "Comparing Chicago, New York and Los Angeles: Testing Some World Cities Hypotheses," in *World Cities in a World-System*, eds. Paul L. Knox and Peter J. Taylor. Cambridge, U.K.: Cambridge University Press, 171–91.

Body-Gendrot, Sophie (1993) *Ville et violence: L'irruption de nouveaux acteurs*. Paris: PUF (Presses Universitaires de France).

Castells, Manuel (1989) *The Informational City*. London: Blackwell.

Coombe, Rosemary J. (1993) "The Properties of Culture and the Politics of Possessing Identity: Native Claims in the Cultural Appropriation Controversy." *The Canadian Journal of Law and Jurisprudence*, vol. 6, no. 2, (July): 249–85.

Daniels, Peter W. and Frank Moulaert, eds. (1991) *The Changing Geography of Advanced Producer Services*. London and New York: Belhaven Press.

Dunn, Seamus, ed. (1994) *Managing Divided Cities*. Keele, U.K.: Keele University Press.

Fainstein, S. I. Gordon and M. Harloe (1993) *Divided Cities: Economic Restructuring and Social Change in London and New York*. Cambridge, Mass.: Blackwell.

Friedmann J. and Wolff G. (1982) "World City Formation: An Agenda for Research and Action." *International Journal of Urban and Regional Research*, vol. 3: 309–344.

Hall, P. (1966) *The World Cities*. London: Weidenfeld and Nicolson.

Hall, S. (1991) "The Local and the Global: Globalization and Ethnicity," in Anthony D. King, ed., *Culture, Globalization and the World-System: Contemporary Conditions for the Representation of Identity. Current Debates in Art History 3*. Department of Art and Art History, State University of New York at Binghamton.

King, Anthony, ed. (1996) *Representing the City: Ethnicity, Capital and Culture in the 21st Century*. London: Macmillan.

Knox, Paul and Peter J. Taylor, eds. (1995) *World Cities in a World-System*. Cambridge, U.K.: Cambridge University Press.

Leyshon, Andrew, Peter Daniels and Nigel Thrift (1987) "Large Accountancy Firms in the UK: Spatial Development." Working paper, St. David's University College, Lampter, UK and University of Liverpool.

Marshall, J.N., P. Damesick and P. Wood (1986) *Uneven Development in the Service Economy: Understanding the Location of Producer Services*. Report of the Producer Services Working Party, Institute of British Geographers and the ESRC, August.

Martinotti, Guido (1993) *Metropoli: La nuova morfologia sociale della città*. Bologna: II Mulino.

Mittelman, James, ed. (1996) *Globalization: Critical Reflections. International Political Economy Yearbook*, vol. 9. Boulder, Colo.: Lynne Reinner.

Noyelle, T., and A. B. Dutka (1988) *International Trade in Business Services: Accounting, Advertising, Law, and Management Consulting*. Cambridge, Mass.: Ballinger Publishing.

Sassen, Saskia (1982) "Recomposition and Peripheralization at the Core," in *Immigration and Changes in the New International Division of Labor*. San Francisco: Synthesis Publications, 88–100.

Sassen, Saskia (1991) *The Global City: New York, London, Tokyo*. Princeton: Princeton University Press.

Sassen, Saskia (1994) *Cities in a World Economy*. Thousand Oaks, Calif.: Pine Forge/Sage Press.

Sassen, Saskia (1996) *Losing Control? Sovereignty in an Age of Globalization*. New York: Columbia University Press.

Shank, G., ed. (1994) Japan Enters the 21st Century: A Special Issue of *Social Justice*, vol. 21, no. 2 (summer).

Smith, David A. and Michael Timberlake (1995) "Cities in Global Matrices: Toward Mapping the World System's City System," in *World Cities in a World-System*, eds. Paul L. Knox and Peter J. Taylor. Cambridge, U.K.: Cambridge University Press.

Social Justice (1993) "Global Crisis, Local Struggles." Special Issue, vol. 20, nos. 3–4 (fall—winter).

Wallerstein, Immanuel (1990) "Culture as the Ideological Battleground of the Modern World-System," in *Global Culture: Nationalism, Globalization and Modernity*, ed. Mike Featherstone. London: Sage.

SECTION 2

Methodological Practices

Introduction to Section 2

Most existing data sets, historical archives, and other scholarly resources are organized around national-state or other bounded units. They are designed to facilitate comparisons within or between specific spatial units instead of addressing the flows, linkages, or identities that cross or transform boundaries. This section includes works by scholars who challenge these methodological assumptions. They offer diverse and often innovative ideas, tactics, and models that facilitate creative transnational scholarship.

Akil Gupta and James Ferguson's request that scholars revisit the notion of "field" and "fieldwork" has important methodological and epistemological implications. The discipline of anthropology, they argue, is still strongly rooted in the highly localized and compartmentalized world of the past. To challenge this spatially bound world is to challenge traditional notions of fieldwork. Nothing less is at stake than how to do research and the conclusions we expect to be able to make about our findings. Indeed, scholars must confront the term "field" in order to rethink the boundaries and contents of anthropology and other disciplines. Gupta and Ferguson ask whether the clear boundaries once drawn between field and home, self and other, different and local, or in and out still hold, or if they were ever really useful. They suggest that current fieldworkers decenter the field as the privileged site of anthropological knowledge, instead incorporating it as one element in a multistranded methodology that examines relationships between multiple social-political sites.

Andreas Wimmer and Nina Glick-Schiller confront similarly ingrained conventions that challenge the emergence of Transnational Studies. From their perspective, the social sciences take for granted a state-centric, bounded container set of ontological and epistemological assumptions. They suffer from what Wimmer and Glick Schiller call "methodological nationalism" or the tendency to accept the nation-state form and contemporary nation-state borders as given. They examine how methodological nationalism became historically entwined with the development of general social science and migration studies in particular. When we take for granted that the nation is the natural scholarly unit, transnational phenomena and dynamics become the outliers and the exception. Describing immigrants as social others, political security risks, and as the exception rather than the rule exemplifies this methodological nationalist approach. Although transnationalism is not a new phenomenon, we continue to think of it in national terms. What is needed is the development of a rigorous "methodological transnationalism" that does not discount the enduring potency of the nation.

Luis Eduardo Guarnizo, Alejandro Portes, and William Haller's work demonstrates how innovatively collected and assembled quantitative and qualitative data contribute to a transnational approach. Their first research phase consisted of 350 in-depth interviews with members of three immigrant communities living in the United States and their homelands. A second phase surveyed a probability sample in four cities with high levels of immigrant concentration. Guarnizo, Portes, and Haller studied migrant involvement in electoral and non-electoral activities. They conclude that a significant minority engages in transnational political action, though their activities tend to be located in specific territorial jurisdictions and to reproduce power asymmetries rather than transform them.

In *Forces of Labor*, Beverly Silver models methodological innovations that are equal to the task of asking questions across borders. In her study of labor movements in global *and* comparative historical perspective, she asks what, if anything, is truly novel about contemporary labor mobilization. She begins by engaging the "encompassing comparison" utilized in world-historical work and long-standing comparative-historical methods for cross-national research. But, Silver argues, while such methods are useful and necessary, they are also inherently limited. They impede the analysis of relations between and among allegedly separate units (different forms and locations of labor movements), obscure local agency, and are based on assumptions about the type, if not characteristics, of particular bounded units of analysis, even though how these units are constructed and transformed should be a critical piece of the analysis. In response, Silver uses a combined "incorporating comparison" methodology and modified "narrative mode" of causal analysis to capture how relational processes across spatial units unfold in and through time.

Sanjeev Khagram deploys a "constructivist transnational" framework to highlight the comparative transformation of development dynamics during the twentieth century (and particularly since the 1950s) across the third world. He argues that the unanticipated growth of transnationally allied nongovernmental organizations interacting with the global spread and deepening of norms about indigenous peoples, human rights, and environmental sustainability, were critical cross-temporal shifts in the development field. The most dramatic changes in development, however, occurred when these developments were linked to democratic political opportunity structures and to strong and sustained grassroots mobilization. Khagram challenges competing accounts with his multi-layered and multi-sited analysis of the rise and fall of large dam projects, which are understood as both instruments and symbols of development. He bases his claims on quantitative and qualitative data collected at scores of large dam sites in numerous countries; public, private, and non-profit organizations; and actors operating at the grassroots to the global. Process-tracing, structure-focused comparison, counter-factual thought experiments, and analytic ethnography and historiography are just some of the methods he uses to propose an alternative transnational political economy of dams and development.

CHAPTER 8

Discipline and Practice: "The Field" as Site, Method, and Location in Anthropology

Akhil Gupta and James Ferguson

[. . .]

AREAS AND SITES

Anthropology, more than perhaps any other discipline, is a body of knowledge constructed on regional specialization, and it is within regionally circumscribed epistemic communities that many of the discipline's key concepts and debates have been developed (Fardon 1990; Appadurai 1988b). More than comparativists in other fields—political science, sociology, literature, history, law, religion, and business—anthropologists combine language learning and regional scholarship with long-term residence in "the field." Regional expertise is thus built into the anthropological project, constituting the other face of a discipline (at least implicitly) predicated on cultural comparison (Marcus and Fischer 1986). As we have argued elsewhere (Gupta and Ferguson 1992, 1997), it is precisely the naturalization of cultural difference as inhering in different geographical locales that makes anthropology such a regional science. From this, too, there follows the built-in necessity of travel; one can only encounter difference by going elsewhere, by going to "the field."

It is possible to situate "the field" more precisely as a site constructed through the shifting entanglements of anthropological notions of "culture areas," the institutional politics of "area studies," and the global order of nation-states. The notion of culture areas, supplemented by ideas such as peoplehood and ethnicity (e.g., "the Kurds"), religion (e.g., "the Islamic world"), language

(e.g., "Bantu-speaking Africa"), and race (e.g., "Melanesia" [see Thomas 1989a] or "Black Africa") attempted to relate a set of societies with common traits to each other. Thus the Mediterranean with its honor-and-shame complex constituted one culture area (Herzfeld 1987; while South Asia with the institution of caste hierarchy formed another (Appadurai 1988b), and Polynesia with its centralized chiefdoms constituted a third (Thomas 1989a). Although we anthropologists devote far less attention today to mapping "culture regions" than we used to (e.g., Wissler 1923; Murdock 1967; but cf. Burton et al. 1996), the culture area remains a central disciplinary concept that implicitly structures the way in which we make connections between the particular groups of people we study and the groups that other ethnographers study (cf. Fardon 1990; Thomas 1989a).[1]

However, and this is where issues become more complicated, ideas about culture areas in the anthropological literature are refracted, altered, and sometimes undermined by the institutional mechanisms that provide the intellectual legitimacy and financial support for doing fieldwork. To take but one example, the setting up of area studies centers in American universities has long been underwritten by the U.S. government. The definition of areas, the emphasis placed on various activities, and the importance of particular topics as research priorities have mostly been thinly disguised (if that) projections of the state's strategic and geopolitical priorities. As the state's interests shift, so do funding priorities and the definition of areas themselves. A few years ago, for instance, there was an effort to carve out a new area, "Inner

Asia," which would be distinct from Eastern Europe and Soviet studies on the one hand, and the Middle East and China on the other. The timing of this development remains mysterious unless one understands the concern with the war in Afghanistan and the fear of the possible ascendance of "Islamic republics" in the regions adjacent to what was then the Soviet Union.

As the institutional mechanisms that define areas, fund research, and support scholarship change, they intersect in complicated ways with changing ideas about "culture areas" to produce "fields" that are available for research. Thus, no major funding agency supports research on "the Mediterranean" or "the Caribbean." Some parts of the Mediterranean culture area are funded by European area studies and the others by Middle Eastern area studies. The more culturally exotic and geostrategically embattled parts thus become proper "anthropological" field sites, whereas Western Europe (which, besides having "less culture" [cf. Rosaldo 1988], is part of NATO) is a less appropriate "field," as the many Europeanists who struggle to find jobs in anthropology departments can attest.[2]

Similarly, anthropological ideas about culture areas and geographical specializations have been transformed by their encounter with the rude realities of decolonization. For instance, anthropologists working in Africa today normally construct their regional specializations in national terms that would have made no sense prior to the 1960s. Thus Victor Turner was not, as he would be styled today, a "Zambianist" but an "Africanist"; his *Schism and Continuity in an African Society* was "A Study of Ndembu Village Life," and the reader would have to comb the text with some care to find out that the study was in fact conducted in what was then northern Rhodesia. Evans-Pritchard's research freely crossed between the Belgian Congo (Azande), the Anglo-Egyptian Sudan (Nuer), and British East Africa (Luo); his regional specialization was not defined by such political territorializations. Yet just as Evans-Pritchard's work was enabled by the brute fact of colonial conquest,[3] so, too, the field sites in which contemporary anthropologists

work are shaped by the geopolitics of the postcolonial, imperial world. Decolonization has transformed field sites not merely by making it difficult, if not impossible, to move across national borders, but by affecting a whole host of mechanisms, from the location of archives to the granting of visas and research clearance. The institutions that organized knowledge along colonial lines have yielded to ones that organize it along national ones.[4]

A "good" field site is made, however, not only by considerations of funding and clearance, but by its suitability for addressing issues and debates that matter to the discipline. As Jane Collier shows, the idea of substantive "subfields" such as "legal anthropology," "economic anthropology," "psychological anthropology," and so on was until recently a key device through which such issues and debates were constituted. The problematics and conventions of such subfields helped to shape not only the topic of investigation, but also the conception of the field site itself, in a number of ways. First, as we have noted, culture areas have long been linked to subject areas; thus India, with its ideologies of caste and purity, was long taken to be an especially good site for an anthropologist of religion (Appadurai 1988b), and Africa (with its segmentary lineages) was thought ideal for the political anthropologist, just as Melanesia (with its elaborate systems of exchange) invited economic anthropologists (cf. Fardon 1990). But subfields have also carried more specific assumptions about fieldwork and methodology. The "fieldwork" of a legal anthropologist, for instance, might be expected to include the examination of written court records, while that of a psychological anthropologist working in the same area likely would not; in this manner, different subfields could construct the site to be studied in different ways. As Collier shows, however, the very idea of coherent "subfields" has broken down in recent years. The growing willingness to question received ideas of "field" and "fieldwork" may well be related to the recent decline of the well-defined subfields that once helped to define and bound field sites.

Field sites thus end up being defined by the crosshatched intersection of visa and clearance procedures,[5] the interests of funding agencies, and intellectual debates within the discipline and its subfields. Once defined in this way, field sites appear simply as a natural array of choices facing graduate students preparing for professional careers. The question becomes one of choosing an appropriate site, that is, choosing a place where intellectual interests, personal predilections, and career outcomes can most happily intersect. This is to be expected. What is more surprising is the recurrence of anecdotes in which experienced fieldworkers relate how they "stumbled" on to their field sites entirely "by chance."[6] Just as the culturally sanctioned discourse of "hard work" and "enterprise" enables the structurally patterned outcomes of career choice in competitive capitalism to disappear from view, so do the repeated narratives of discovering field sites "by chance" prevent any systematic inquiry into how those field sites came to be good places for doing fieldwork in the first instance. The very significant premises and assumptions built into the anthropological idea of "the field" are in this way protected from critical scrutiny, even as they are smuggled into the discipline's most central practices of induction, socialization, and professional reproduction.

IMPLICATIONS OF AN ARCHETYPE

As Stocking has pointed out (1992: 59), the classical Malinowskian image of fieldwork (the lone, white, male fieldworker living for a year or more among the native villagers) functions as an *archetype* for normal anthropological practice.[7] Because an archetype is never a concrete and specific set of rules, this ideal of fieldwork need not carry with it any specific set of prescriptions; its link to practice is looser than this, and more complex. Since the archetypal image is today often invoked ironically and parodically, it can easily be made to appear an anachronism—a caricature that everyone knows, but nobody really takes seriously anymore. Yet such easy dismissals may be premature. After all, archetypes function not by claiming to be accurate, literal descriptions of things as they are, but by offering a compelling glimpse of things as they should be, at their purest and most essential. In the contemporary United States, for instance, the image of the so-called "all-American" look (healthy, wholesome, and white) has the power of an archetype. Americans know, of course, that most Americans do not look like this. If asked, most would surely say that dark-skinned Americans are every bit as "American" as light-skinned ones. Yet at a more fundamental and spontaneous level, when people think of "an American"—a *real* American—it is the "all-American" image that is likely to come to mind. Such archetypes operate ideologically in a way that is peculiarly hard to pin down; their effects are simultaneously ineffable and pervasive. Yet it is impossible to understand the full implications of the anthropological concept of "the field" without taking account of the deep-seated images of the "real fieldworker," the "real anthropologist," that constitute a significant part of the "common sense" (in the Gramscian usage of the term) of the discipline.

In sketching some of the key consequences of the construction of the field of anthropology through the practice of fieldwork, we focus on three themes in particular: first, the radical separation of "the field" from "home," and the related creation of a hierarchy of purity of field sites; second, the valorization of certain kinds of knowledge to the exclusion of other kinds; and third, the construction of a normative anthropological subject, an anthropological "self" against which anthropology sets its "Others." We emphasize, again, that these are not simply historical associations, but archetypal ones that subtly but powerfully construct the very idea of what anthropology is. We will argue that even *ideas* about "the field" that are explicitly disavowed by contemporary anthropologists in intellectual terms continue to be deeply embedded in our professional *practices*.

"Field" and "Home"

The distinction between "the field" and "home" rests on their spatial separation.[8]

This separation is manifested in two central anthropological contrasts. The first differentiates the site where data are collected from the place where analysis is conducted and the ethnography is "written up." To do ethnographic work is thus to do two distinct types of writing. One kind is done "in the field." These "fieldnotes" are close to experience, textually fragmentary, consisting of detailed "raw" documentation of interviews and observations as well as spontaneous subjective reactions (Sanjek 1990). The other sort, done "at home," is reflective, polished, theoretical, intertextual, a textual whole—this is the writing of ethnographic papers and monographs. The former is done in isolation, sometimes on primitive equipment, in difficult conditions, with people talking or peering over one's shoulder; writing at "home" is done in the academy, in libraries or studies, surrounded by other texts, in the midst of theoretical conversation with others of one's kind. Moreover, the two forms of activity are not only distinct, but sequential: one commonly "writes up" after coming back from "the field." Temporal succession therefore traces the natural sequence of sites that completes a spatial journey into Otherness.

The second place the sharp contrast between "field" and "home" is expressed is in the standard anthropological tropes of entry into and exit from "the field." Stories of entry and exit usually appear on the margins of texts, providing the narrative with uncertainty and expectation at the beginning and closure at the end. According to Mary Louise Pratt (1986), the function of narratives of entry and exit is to authenticate and authorize the material that follows, most of which used to be written from the standpoint of an objective, distanced, observer.[9] Such stories also form a key piece of the informal lore of fieldwork that is so much a part of socialization into the discipline. Colonial-style heroic tales of adventurers battling the fierce tropics are, of course, out of favor nowadays, and the usual cliches of anthropological arrival are perhaps more often invoked today in a self-consciously ironic mode. But what needs to be emphasized is that *all* tropes of entry and exit, however playful, parodic, or self-conscious, may still function to construct the difference between "the field" and "home." The image of arriving in "another world" whose difference is enacted in the descriptions that follow, tends to minimize, if not make invisible, the multiple ways in which colonialism, imperialism, missionization, multinational capital, global cultural flows, and travel bind these spaces together. Again, most anthropologists today recognize this, but even as we reject ideas of isolated peoples living in separate worlds, the tropes of entry and exit and the idea of a separation of "fieldwork" from "writing up" continue to structure most contemporary ethnography.[10]

The very distinction between "field" and "home" leads directly to what we call a *hierarchy of purity* of field sites. After all, if "the field" is most appropriately a place that is "not home," then some places will necessarily be *more* "not home" than others, and hence more appropriate, more "fieldlike." All ethnographic research is thus done "in the field," but some "fields" are more equal than others—specifically, those that are understood to be distant, exotic, and strange. Here the parallel is striking with the older conception of anthropology as a field science, in which some sites offered better approximations of "the natural state" than others and were therefore preferred. Although anthropologists no longer think in terms of natural or undisturbed states, it remains evident that what many would deny in theory continues to be true in practice: some places are much more "anthropological" than others (e.g., Africa more than Europe, southern Europe more than northern Europe, villages more than cities) according to the degree of Otherness from an archetypal anthropological "home."

Largely because the idea of "the field" remains uninterrogated, such hierarchies of field sites live on in our professional practices. Among anthropologists who have done fieldwork, for instance, some are still understood to have done what is knowingly referred to as "real fieldwork"—that is, worked for a long time in an isolated area, with people who speak a non-European language, lived in "a community," preferably small, in authentic, "local" dwellings—while others have less pure field sites and thus are less fully anthropological. Anyone who doubts that such thinking continues to operate in the discipline should take a close look at anthropological job searches, where the question of who has or has not done "real fieldwork" (presumably in the "real field") is often decisive. Indeed, it is worth noting that the geographical categories by which such searches usually proteed[11] rule out from the start many outstanding job candidates who do not work, say, "in Africa" or "in Mesoamerica," but on such things as whiteness in the U.S. (Frankenberg 1993) or on the practices of transnational "development" agencies (Escobar 1994). That anthropology's archetypal "home" (the dominant, majority culture of the contemporary United States) is still considered only a poor approximation of "the field" is shown perhaps most clearly by the fact that when job advertisements offer a position for a "North Americanist," what is called for is nearly always a specialist on ethnic and racial minorities, most often on those who occupy a special place in white North American "imperialist nostalgia" (Rosaldo 1989b), namely Native Americans.[12]

A very large number of anthropologists, of course, do work in the United States, and by no means all of them focus on Native Americans or minorities. Yet working in the United States has long had a low status in the field, and even a certain stigma attached to it. Exotic fieldwork, Kuklick points out, has been a "gatekeeper" in Anglo-American anthropology. Since it requires external funding, not everyone can do it, and those who can are therefore marked as a select group. Indeed, one of us was actually told in graduate school that fieldwork in the United States was "for people who don't get grants." Such prejudices may have diminished in recent years, but they have hardly disappeared. The fact that today more high-status American anthropologists (the ones who *do* get the grants) are working "at home" is significant, but it should also be noted that they are mostly anthropologists whose careers are already established and who take on second field sites closer to home (a pattern often remarked to fit well with considerations both of tenure and of child rearing). It remains

extremely difficult for students who do their dissertation fieldwork entirely within the United States to get jobs at top departments. A quick survey of ten top American departments of anthropology reveals only 8 anthropologists (out of a total of 189) who claim a primary specialization in the nonnative United States. Only 1 of these 8 had received a Ph.D. within the last fifteen years.[13]

In pointing out the existence of such a hierarchy of field sites, we do not mean to suggest that anthropologists ought to give up working "abroad," or that the only fieldwork worth doing is "at home." On the contrary, many of the reasons that have led anthropologists to leave their homes for faraway field sites seem to us excellent ones. If nothing else, the anthropological insistence that "out of the way places" matter (Tsing 1993, 1994) has done much to counter the Eurocentric and parochial understandings of culture and society that dominate most Western universities. What we object to is not the leaving of "home," but the uncritical mapping of "difference" onto exotic sites (as if "home," however defined, were not also a site of difference, cf. Greenhouse 1985) as well as the implicit presumption that "Otherness" means difference from an unmarked, white Western "self" (which has the effect of constructing the anthropologist as a very particular sort of subject, as we discuss below). The issue, then, is not whether anthropologists should work "abroad" or "at home," but precisely the radical separation between the two that is taken for granted as much by those who would insist that anthropology remain "at home" as by those who would restrict its mission to fieldwork "abroad."

Fieldwork-Based Knowledge

A second consequence of anthropology's emphasis on "the field" is that it enables certain forms of knowledge, but blocks off others. With the idea that knowledge derived from experience in "the field" is privileged comes a foregrounding of face-to-face relations of community, while other, less localized relations disappear from view (see Thomas 1991). Ethnographic knowledge is heavily dependent on the presence and experience of the fieldworker. More than any other discipline, the truths of anthropology are grounded in the experience of the participant observer. This experience yields much that is valuable, but also severely circumscribes the knowledge obtained. Why, for instance, has there been so little anthropological work on the translocal aspects of transnational corporations and multilateral institutions (cf. Nash 1979; Ghosh 1994)? Why are there so few ethnographic treatments of the mass media?[14] More generally, why do translocal phenomena of various kinds evade classical methods of participant observation?

Though anthropologists often picture themselves as specialists in "the local," we suggest that the idea of locality in anthropology is not well thought out. Clearly geographical contiguity and boundedness are insufficient to define a "local community"; otherwise, high-rise buildings in urban metropolises would automatically qualify, and office-dwellers crammed together for large parts of the day would constitute ideal subjects for fieldwork. That we don't readily think of these "localities" as field sites should give us pause. Is the idea of the local a way of smuggling back in assumptions about small-scale societies and face-to-face communities that we thought we had left behind? Why is it that, for example, local politics is so anthropological, whereas national or international politics is not ("natives" as political actors are rarely described in terms that would situate them within a political world we share—"left-wing," "rightist," or "Social Democrat")?[15] Similarly, the household economy has long been considered eminently anthropological, but the study of labor unions or international finance much less so. One can, of course, use a "local" site to study a "nonlocal" phenomenon. But what makes a site "local" in the first place? In an oft-cited passage, Geertz has pointed out that "Anthropologists don't study villages (tribes, towns, neighborhoods . . .); they study *in* villages" (1973a: 22). But what remains unasked, conspicuously, is *why* we study "in villages" in the first place.[16]

As with field sites, then, there is clearly also a hierarchy of topics or objects of study,

ranked according to their anthropological-ness. Things that are unfamiliar, "different," and "local" (read: not like at home) become defined as suitable anthropological objects, whereas phenomena and objects that are similar to "home" or already in some way familiar are deemed to be less worthy of ethnographic scrutiny. Thus an account of an indigenous ritual, especially if it is strange, exotic, and colorful, is almost automatically "anthropological," and eminently suited to publication in a leading anthropological journal; television viewing, meanwhile, has remained until recently largely terra incognita for anthropology.[17] Even if one were to accept the problematic idea that anthropology's mission is that of "cultural critique," the topics that are deemed suitably "anthropological" already circumscribe the form and scope of that critique.

The Fieldworker as Anthropological Subject

We now turn to the third of our themes, the construction of an archetypal fieldworker and the consequent ordering of the identities of ethnographers. Anthropologists often speak, sometimes half-jokingly, of fieldwork as a "rite of passage," a ritual of initiation into a mature professional identity. We suggest that it would be useful to take this formulation seriously, instead of allowing it to pass as a joke, by asking precisely what kind of a social being such a ritual of initiation produces. If a heroized journey into Otherness is indeed a rite of passage, what sort of subject might we expect to be formed by such a rite?

We have seen that ideas about Otherness remain remarkably central to the fieldwork ritual. But any conception of an Other, of course, has implications for the identity of the self. We will argue that even in an era when significant numbers of women, minorities, and Third World scholars have entered the discipline, the self that is implied in the central anthropological ritual of encountering "the Other" in the field remains that of a Euro-American, white, middle-class male. We will demonstrate how this unmarked category is constructed through an examination of disciplinary practices that endow certain kinds of research questions, methods, and textual production with "excellence."

The rhetoric of meritocracy, with its powerful roots in capitalist ideology and the competitive conditions of academic production, and its seeming objectivity, appears to be socially neutral in the sense that it does not automatically privilege certain groups of people. Who wouldn't agree with the goal of hiring the best scholars, rewarding the best researchers, and training students so that they become the best anthropologists? The problem is, of course, that there is no neutral grid through which such judgments can be made.[18] The hierarchy of field sites noted above assigns positions based on degrees of Otherness. But Otherness from whom? Is Africa more Other than Europe for a Third World anthropologist? For an African American? For whom are minority populations in the United States more worthy anthropological objects? The hierarchy of field sites privileges those places most Other for Euro-Americans and those that stand most clearly opposed to a middle-class self. Similarly, the notion of going to "the field" from which one returns "home" becomes problematic for those minorities, post-colonials, and "halfies"[19] for whom the anthropological project is *not* an exploration of Otherness. Such people often find themselves in a double bind: some anthropologists regard them with suspicion, as people who lack the distance necessary to conduct good fieldwork; on the other hand, well-intentioned colleagues thrust on them the responsibility of speaking their identity, thus inadvertently forcing them into the prison-house of essentialism.

Amory shows how ideas about Otherness, and the taking for granted of an unmarked, white subject, have helped to shape the field of African studies in the United States, and to produce a durable division between it and Afro-American studies. She shows that African American scholars were discouraged from working in Africa, on the grounds that they were "too close" and would not manage to be "objective," while white scholars were judged to have the appropriate distance from the black "Other." This helps to explain the fact that the contemporary field of African studies (like the field of anthropology itself) contains remarkably few black American scholars.[20] Unexamined assumptions about Otherness that came along with the idea of "a good field site" thus turned out to be racially exclusionary.

Likewise, the implicit standard against which "good fieldwork" often continues to be judged is highly gendered. The archetypal ideal of the lone, manly anthropologist out in the bush, far away from the creature comforts of First World life, derives, as Kuklick notes, from Romantic notions of (implicitly masculine) personal growth through travel to unfamiliar places and endurance of physical hardship. To be sure, women as well as men have over the years credentialed themselves—and even become powerful figures in the discipline—through the fieldwork rite of passage, and anthropology has historically been less closed to women than many other disciplines. Indeed, a certain romantic image of the female anthropologist seems to have a fairly prominent place in the American public imagination (probably due largely to the celebrity of primatologists such as Jane Goodall and Diane Fossey—though it is worth remembering that Margaret Mead was also a highly visible and influential public figure in her time). But it is no slight to the achievements of such women to say that they established themselves as "real anthropologists" only by beating the boys at their own (fieldwork) game. Many other women were not so lucky; historically, a very high proportion of women trained in anthropology have failed to secure institutional positions appropriate to their training (Behar and Gordon 1995).

Passaro suggests that the image of field research as heroic adventure or quest remains with us today in the widespread, if often implicit, expectation that authentic fieldwork ought to involve physical hardship and even danger. Such expectations are far from neutral in gender terms.[21] For example, young women are discouraged from attempting "difficult" rural fieldwork in some areas of North India, because of the ever-present threat of rape and sexual violence; later, in the Western academy, their failure to spend long periods in rural areas where the "real" India lives is construed to show the absence of "good fieldwork"—a question of merit, not gender discrimination.

Similarly, the notion that field sites should be selected solely for disinterested scholarly reasons continues to be highly influential. Although it is widely recognized that this is not how most of us choose our field sites, the vocabulary of justification employed in grant proposals, books, and research reports requires that such choices be cast in terms of the theoretical problems that the research site was especially suited to think about. Such a view privileges those who have no compelling reason to work in particular localities or with particular communities other than intellectual interest. For those interested in working with their "own" communities, engaged in activist organizing, or responsible for supporting financially strapped, extended families, exoticism has no inherent value. Leaving their commitments and responsibilities for the sake of untethered "research interests" is for many anthropologists a Faustian bargain, a betrayal of those people whose lives and livelihoods are inextricably linked to their own. Once again, what pass for universal, meritocratic norms end up supporting a particular structural and ideological location, one occupied most often by white, middle-class men.[22] In this context, we might understand the recent figures showing that, as of the 1992–1993 academic year, fully 90 percent of all full-time anthropology faculty in the United States were white, and 70 percent were male (American Anthropological Association 1994: 288, 291).

We do not want to be misunderstood as suggesting that an academic discipline can or should attempt to do without standards of excellence. Our point is only that the social and political implications that any such standards must contain ought to be made explicit and open to debate and negotiation. The alternative to evaluating anthropologists according to prevailing norms of fieldwork is not to forgo all evaluation (which would be neither possible nor desirable), but to develop different and better-justified criteria of evaluation, based on a different conception of what should count as "good work" in anthropology. Where might such a conception come from, and how might it be legitimated? It is with such questions in mind that we briefly survey some alternative traditions of "field" and "fieldwork" on which it might be possible to draw. [. . .]

REINVENTING "THE FIELD": METHODOLOGY AND LOCATION

It is clear that anthropologists have in recent years been more and more inclined to depart from the conventions of archetypal fieldwork as they have taken on research projects not easily approached via the traditional model of immersion within a community. Reflecting on their experiences of testing and even transgressing the disciplinary boundaries set by the expectations of "real fieldwork," several of the contributors to this book help point the way toward developing of new practices and conventions for the field. In this section, we will first briefly discuss how Weston, Passaro, Malkki, Des Chene, and Martin have contributed to a rethinking of field and fieldwork. We will then offer a general reformulation of the fieldwork tradition that we believe can preserve what is most vital and valuable in it, while not only leaving room for but properly valuing and legitimating the diverse and innovative new practices of the field that are evident in the contributions to this book and elsewhere.

Toward New Practices of the Field: Problems and Strategies

One of the most profound issues raised by recent work in anthropology is the question of the spatialization of difference. The unspoken premise that "home" is a place of cultural sameness and that difference is to be found "abroad" has long been part of the common sense of anthropology. Yet some of our contributors, drawing on recent work on gender and sexuality, begin their "fieldwork" with the opposite premise—that "home" is from the start a place of difference.

Kath Weston points out that studying such "difference at home" as gay and lesbian communities in the United States profoundly unsettles anthropological sensibilities. Who is the native and who is the ethnographer when "queers study queers"? Trying to speak as a professionally qualified ethnographer of gays and lesbians, Weston finds that she is heard as a "native"—speaking for "her own people," maybe even "an advocate" (cf. Narayan 1993). As a "Native Ethnographer," she must alternate between "I, Native" and "I, Ethnographer," losing "the nuance of the two as they are bound up together," the hybridity of the Native Ethnographer positioning. The reason, of course, is that the position "Native Ethnographer" itself blurs the subject/object distinction on which ethnography is conventionally founded. Speaking from such a position, at least within the discipline as currently constituted, implies not simply exclusion, but something more complicated that Weston calls "virtuality": a condition in which one is an anthropologist, but not "a real anthropologist," in which one has done fieldwork, but not "real fieldwork." The virtual anthropologist, Weston argues, must always be the one who lacks an authentic Other—unless she speaks *as* an authentic Other, in which case she ceases to be an authentic *anthropologist*. Yet, significantly, Weston suggests that the very studies that are most suspect in these terms are the ones that "could complicate [the] dichotomy between Us and Them in useful ways"; the virtual anthropologist may be the one who can contribute most to "the thoroughgoing reevaluation of the anthropological project that an understanding of hybridity entails."

Joanne Passaro's research among the homeless in New York City raises some related issues. Like Weston, she reports encountering skepticism that researching the lives of homeless, transient people in her "own" society could constitute "real fieldwork." Well-meaning advisors pressed her to adopt a nativizing community-study model ("That family shelter sounds fascinating. Why not stay there and do an ethnography of it?"), imagining a stable territorial community even for people defined in the first place by their mobility, marginality, and lack of any stable "home." Tellingly, Passaro reports, "I often felt that my various disciplinary interrogators would be happiest if I discovered some sort of secret communica-

tion system among homeless people like the codes of hoboes earlier in the century," in which case a suitable "subculture" would have been found in which one could immerse oneself! Yet Passaro resisted the temptation to construct "a homeless village," and developed instead an innovative, hybrid methodology that involved a number of "sites that would afford . . . positionalities at varying points along a participant-observer continuum." Combining different sites and styles of "fieldwork" with various kinds of volunteer and advocacy work provided a successful, if unorthodox, methodological strategy for an ethnographic study that ended up yielding powerful and surprising insights into the predicaments of homeless people (cf. Passaro 1996).

Liisa Malkki discusses a different way in which the methodological demands of one's research may require a reconfiguring of "the field." Her research among Hutu refugees in Tanzania led her to question one aspect of the fieldwork tradition that is commonly celebrated as a great virtue—its emphasis on the ordinary, the everyday, and the routine. As she points out, such an emphasis tends to direct attention away from those things that the refugees she worked with cared about most—the extraordinary and exceptional events that had made refugees of them, and the atypical and transitory circumstances of their lives in a refugee camp. She observes that a division of labor between anthropology and journalism has made all big, extraordinary happenings into "stories" to be covered by journalists, while the durable, ordinary, everyday occurrences are to be found in "sites" suitable for long-term anthropological fieldwork. What would it mean, she asks, to direct an anthropological gaze on singular, exceptional, and extraordinary events? What sorts of fieldwork would be appropriate to studying the "communities of memory" formed in the aftermath of such events? A different sort of engagement than that of the usual "anthropological investigation" of a geographical "field site" might, she suggests, be warranted.

For Mary Des Chene the issue is the relation between fieldwork and history, and the way knowledge gained through archival research is received and valued within anthropology. As she points out, historical material is widely valued in anthropology as a supplement to "real fieldwork," but considerable anxiety is provoked if it begins to take center stage. Des Chene asks how different the two modes of acquiring knowledge really are, skillfully distinguishing the real differences from the mythology that valorizes fieldwork-based knowledge as necessarily truer or less mediated than other types. She also confronts the question of how ethnographic methods can be adapted for studying spatially dispersed phenomena, raising the issue of multisite ethnography (cf. Marcus 1995; Hastrup and Olwig 1996).

Finally, Emily Martin also takes up the question of social and cultural processes that are not well localized spatially. She points out that even many ethnographers of science have retained an idea of a "scientific community" as spatially bounded, to be examined through the traditional methods of the community study. The reaction of one such traditionalist to Martin's own multisite methods ("Don't you know how to stay put?") tells us that the localizing conventions of "the field" remain strong even in an area such as the ethnography of science, which one might expect to have traveled far from the Malinowskian archetype. But Martin insists that key developments in science are also occurring simultaneously elsewhere in society and that we need different models and metaphors than those provided by "the field" to grasp such changes. She proposes several new metaphors and shows how she used them in her own research, laying out a "tool kit" for exploring processes that occur neither in a single field site nor in some unlocated global space, but in many different spaces that are discontinuous from each other.

Retheorizing Fieldwork: From Spatial Sites to Political Locations

We begin our own efforts to rethink "the field" by building on recent critical reflections about how place has figured in anthropological conceptions of culture (cf. Gupta and Ferguson, eds., 1992, 1997; Appadurai

1988a). We have argued that the passage in and out of "the field" rests on the idea that different cultures inhere in discrete and separate places. Therefore, to go into "the field" is to travel to another place with its own distinctive culture, to live there is to enter another world, and to come back from "the field" is to leave that world and arrive in this one—the one in which the academy is located.[23] To challenge this picture of the world, one made up of discrete, originally separate cultures, is also to challenge the image of fieldwork as involving the movement in and out of "the field." "Where is the field?" D'Amico-Samuels (1991: 69) asks, when one studies gender, color, and class in Jamaica, writes about those experiences in New York, and participates in a seminar in Trinidad. "Which if any of these three experiences was fieldwork? Does fieldwork still carry the connotation of colonial geography—so that only activities in a Third World setting apply? . . . Do we think still of fieldwork in the archetype of the white-faced ethnographer in a sea of black or brown faces?" (1991: 72). Perhaps we should say that, in an interconnected world, we are never really "out of the field." Yet, if this is true, then what does change when anthropologists go from (usually) First World universities to various destinations around the world?

Ethnography's great strength has always been its explicit and well-developed sense of location, of being set here-and-not-elsewhere. This strength becomes a liability when notions of "here" and "elsewhere" are assumed to be features of geography, rather than sites constructed in fields of unequal power relations. But it is precisely this sense of location that is missing in a great deal of universalizing and positivist social science. Ethnography has always contained at least some recognition that knowledge is inevitably both "about somewhere" and "from somewhere," and that the knower's location and life experience are somehow central to the kind of knowledge produced. Yet, through the anthropological notion of "the field," this sense of location has too often been elided with locality, and a shift of location has been reduced to the idea of going "elsewhere" to look at "another society."

Taking as a point of departure the idea of "location" that has been developed in recent feminist scholarship,[24] we believe that it is possible to rethink the anthropological fieldwork tradition in quite a fundamental way, while preserving what we think are its real virtues. We wish to be clear that, however significant the problems with "the field" are, there remain many aspects of the fieldwork tradition that we continue to value—aspects that have allowed ethnographically oriented work in sociocultural anthropology (with all its faults) to serve as an extraordinarily useful corrective to the Eurocentrism and positivism that so often afflict the social sciences. We believe a well-developed attentiveness to location would preserve and build upon these aspects of the fieldwork tradition, which we will now discuss individually.

1. The fieldwork tradition counters Western ethnocentrism and values detailed and intimate knowledge of economically and politically marginalized places, peoples, histories, and social locations. Such marginalized locations enable critiques and resistances that would otherwise never be articulated (hooks 1990; Spivak 1988). Since anthropology departments continue to be among the few places in the Western academy not devoted exclusively or largely to the study of the lives and policies of elites, they constitute potentially important nodes for politically engaged intervention in many forms of symbolic and epistemic domination. We emphasize once again that our analysis of anthropology's "hierarchy of purity" of field sites is *not* meant to suggest that anthropologists should no longer work in far-flung and peripheral places—only that it is necessary to question the way that dominant conceptions and practices of "the field" have constructed such places. As Anna Tsing (1993) has recently demonstrated, by bringing marginality itself under the anthropological lens, instead of simply taking it for granted, it is possible to write about "out-of-the-way places" without distancing, romanticizing, or exoticizing them.

2. Fieldwork's stress on taken-for-granted social routines, informal knowledge, and embodied practices can yield understanding that cannot be obtained either through standardized social science research methods (e.g., surveys) or through decontextualized readings of cultural products (e.g., text-based criticism). One does not need to mystify or fetishize knowledge gained through long-term immersion in a social milieu to recognize its importance and value. Nor does one need to grant an unwarranted epistemological privilege to face-to-face interaction in order to appreciate the virtues of a research tradition that requires its practitioners to *listen* to those they would study, and to take seriously what they have to say.

3. Fieldwork reveals that a self-conscious shifting of social and geographical location can be an extraordinarily valuable methodology for understanding social and cultural life, both through the discovery of phenomena that would otherwise remain invisible and through the acquisition of new perspectives on things we thought we already understood. Fieldwork, in this light, may be understood as a form of motivated and stylized dislocation. Rather than a set of labels that pins down one's identity and perspective, location becomes visible here as an ongoing project. As in coalition politics a location is not just something one ascriptively *has* (white middle-class male, Asian American woman, etc.) —it is something one strategically *works* at. We would emphasize, however, that (as in coalition politics) shifting location for its own sake has no special virtue. Instead, the question of what might be called location work must be connected to the logic of one's larger project and ultimately to one's political practice. Why do we *want* to shift locations? *Who* wants to shift? Why? (D. Gordon 1993; Visweswaran 1994: 95–113; Enslin 1994).

What emerges, then, is a set of possibilities for rethought and revitalized forms of fieldwork. We are not advocating the abandonment of the practice of fieldwork, but rather its reconstruction—decentering "the field" as the one, privileged site of anthropological knowledge, then recovering it as one element in a multistranded methodology for the construction of what Donna Haraway (1988) has called "situated knowledges." We might emerge from such a move with less of a sense of "the field" (in the "among the so-and-so" sense) and more of a sense of a mode of study that cares about, and pays attention to, the interlocking of multiple social-political sites and locations.

Such a reconstruction of the fieldwork tradition is, as we have emphasized, already well under way in anthropological practice. Participant observation continues to be a major part of positioned anthropological methodologies, but it is ceasing to be fetishized; talking to and living with the members of a community are increasingly taking their place alongside reading newspapers, analyzing government documents, observing the activities of governing elites, and tracking the internal logic of transnational development agencies and corporations. Instead of a royal road to holistic knowledge of "another society," ethnography is beginning to become recognizable as a flexible and opportunistic strategy for diversifying and making more complex our understanding of various places, people, and predicaments through an attentiveness to the different forms of knowledge available from different social and political locations. Although more and more ethnography today is proceeding along these lines, however, the institutionalized disciplinary framework of reception and evaluation too often continues to see experiential, "field-based" knowledge as the privileged core of an ethnographic work that is then "fleshed out" with supplementary materials.

Any serious decentering of "the field" has the effect, of course, of further softening the division between ethnographic knowledge and other forms of representation flowing out of archival research, the analysis of public discourse, interviewing, journalism, fiction, or statistical representations of collectivities. Genres seem destined to continue to blur. Yet instead of assuming that truly anthropological truths are only revealed in "the field," and attempting to seal off the borders of anthropology from the incursions of cultural studies and other disciplines, it might be a far healthier response to rethink "the field" of anthropology by reconsidering what our commitment to fieldwork entails.

Such a rethinking of the idea of "the field," coupled with an explicit attentiveness to location, might open the way for both a different kind of anthropological knowledge and a different kind of anthropological subject. We have attempted to demonstrate that the uncritical loyalty to "the field" in anthropology has long authorized a certain positionality, a particular location from which to speak about Others. Without an explicit consideration of the kind of subject and the kind of knowledge that ethnographic work produces—by what method? for whom? about whom? by whom? to what end?—we anthropologists will continue to valorize, in the universalizing language of meritocracy, a very particular social, racial, gendered, and sexual location. Practicing decolonized anthropology in a deterritorialized world means as a first step doing away with the distancing and exoticization of the conventional anthropological "field," and foregrounding the ways in which we anthropologists are historically and socially (not just biographically) linked with the areas we study (E. Gordon 1991). In other words, we have to move beyond well-intentioned place-marking devices such as "Western, white anthropologist," which too often substitute a gesture of expiation for a more historical and structural understanding of location. It also means taking away lingering evolutionist and colonialist ideas of "natives in their natural state," and denying the anthropological hierarchy of field sites that devalues work in so many intellectually and politically crucial areas (homelessness, AIDS, sexuality, the media) that are often deemed insufficiently "anthropological." But a heightened sense of location means most of all a recognition that the topics we study and the methods we employ are inextricably bound up with political practice (Bourgois 1991).

The traditional commitment to "the field" has entailed, we have argued, its own form of political engagement, in terms of both the knowledge it has produced and the kind of disciplinary subject it has created. Our focus on *shifting locations* rather than *bounded fields* is linked to a different political vision, one that sees anthropological knowledge as a form of situated intervention. Rather than viewing ethnographic intervention as a disinterested search for truth in the service of universal humanistic knowledge, we see it as a way of pursuing specific political aims while simultaneously seeking lines of common political purpose with allies who stand elsewhere—a mode of building what Haraway (1988) has termed "web-like interconnections" between different social and cultural locations. Applied anthropology and especially activist anthropology have long had the virtue of linking ethnographic practice to a specific and explicit political project. Partly for this reason, they have been consistently devalued in the domain of academic anthropology (cf. Ferguson forthcoming). Yet we would emphasize that associating one's research with a political position does not by itself call into question the location of the activist-anthropologist in the way that we have suggested is necessary, since even the most politically engaged "experts" may still conceive of themselves as occupying an external and epistemologically privileged position. Rather than viewing anthropologists as possessing unique knowledge and insights that they can then share with or put to work for various "ordinary people," our approach insists that anthropological knowledge coexists with other forms of knowledge. We see the political task not as "sharing" knowledge with those who lack it, but as forging links between *different* knowledges that are possible from different locations and tracing lines of possible alliance and common purpose between them. In this sense, we view a research area less as a "field" for the collection of data than as a site for strategic intervention.

The idea that anthropology's distinctive trademark might be found not in its commitment to "the local" but in its attentiveness to epistemological and political issues of location surely takes us far from the classical natural history model of fieldwork as "the detailed study of a limited area." It may be objected, in fact, that it takes us *too* far—that such a reformulation of the fieldwork tradition leaves too little that is recognizable of the old Malinowskian archetype on which the discipline has for so long relied for its self-image and legitimation. At a time of rapid and contentious disciplinary change, it might be argued, such a reworking of one of the few apparently solid points of common reference can only exacerbate the confusion. But what such worries ignore is the fact that the classical idea of "the field" is *already* being challenged, undermined, and reworked in countless ways in ethnographic practice, as several of the chapters in this book, along with other works discussed in this chapter (and in chapter 10) illustrate. An unyielding commitment to the virtues of an unreconstructed Malinowskian "field" cannot reverse this transformation, though it can do much to misunderstand it. Indeed, if, as we have suggested, much of the best new work in the discipline challenges existing conventions of "field" and "fieldwork," the refusal to interrogate those conventions seems less likely to prevent disciplinary confusion and discord than to generate it. Like any tradition valued by a community, anthropology's fieldwork tradition will manage to secure its continuity only if it is able to change to accommodate new circumstances. For that to happen, as Malinowski himself pointed out, such a tradition must be aggressively and imaginatively reinterpreted to meet the needs of the present.

NOTES

1. As Thomas notes, the fact that "there is virtually no discussion now of what regions are, [and] of what status they are supposed to have as entities in anthropological talk" (1989: 27) shows not that anthropology no longer relies on culture areas, but that it relies on unacknowledged, untheorized, and taken-for-granted territorializations of cultural difference. The uncritical use of such mappings, Thomas shows, may unwittingly perpetuate evolutionist and racist assumptions inherited from the colonial past. For an attempt to locate an empirical basis for the division of the world into culture areas, see Burton et al. (1996).

2. It seems to be the case that doing fieldwork in Europe is much more acceptable in anthropology when it is a second field site developed later in the

career, rather than a dissertation site (see the discussion of fieldwork in the United States, below). It is also true that southern and eastern Europe seem to be distinctly more "anthropological" than northern and western Europe. Herzfeld (1987) shows that the "anthropological-ness" of Greece, like its "European-ness," is historically variable and subject to contestation and debate.

3. It does not follow from this that Evans-Pritchard therefore worked in the service of colonial rule—that is a different proposition requiring independent demonstration.

4. We realize that these categories are not as neatly opposed as this formulation might seem to imply. Much of the creation of knowledge about Third World nation-states continues to occur in, and through, former colonial centers.

5. We use the term *visa procedures* here as shorthand for the whole complex of mechanisms used to regulate the production of knowledge within and about nation-states.

6. We are reminded of Bellah et al.'s analysis (1985) of the systematic patterns by which people fall in love, each supposing their love to be entirely unique.

7. We borrow the term *archetype* from Stocking, but it should be noted that we develop it in ways that probably depart from his intended meaning.

8. Visweswaran (1994: 95–130) has discussed this constrast.

9. "Even in the absence of a separate autobiographical volume, personal narrative is a conventional component of ethnographies. It turns up almost invariably in introductions or first chapters, where opening narratives commonly recount the writer's arrival at the field site, for instance, the initial reception by the inhabitants, the slow, agonizing process of learning the language and overcoming rejection, the anguish and loss of leaving. Though they exist only on the margins of the formal ethnographic description, these conventional opening narratives are not trivial. They play the crucial role of anchoring that description in the intense and authority-giving personal experience of fieldwork. . . . Always they are responsible for setting up the initial positionings of the subjects of the ethnographic text: the ethnographer, the native, and the reader" (Pratt 1986: 31–32). See the thoughtful discussion of anthropological arrivals in Tsing (1993).

10. The phrase "writing up" is itself suggestive of a hierarchy of texts mapping itself onto a hierarchy of spaces. One "writes up" the disjointed, fragmented, immanent text found in fieldnotes into something more complete and polished. One also "writes up" in a space that is superior, more conducive to reflection and the higher arts of theoretical and mental work.

11. A survey of job ads for sociocultural anthropologists that appeared in the *Anthropology Newsletter* between September 1994 and April 1996 showed that most advertised positions (100 out of 178) specified preferred geographical areas (25 Asia, 37 Latin America, 37 North America, 15 Sub-Saharan Africa, 10 Caribbean, 3 Middle East, 3 Oceania, 2 Europe), while another 11 specified a geographical area negatively (e.g., "non-West" or "non-U.S."). (Note that the figures for the different areas add up to more than the total number of area-based positions, because some jobs mention more than one area.) Of the positions, 65 did not refer to area, and 2 referred to specific diasporic groups.

12. In the survey discussed in note 11, we found that of the 37 ads that included a call for a North America area focus (sometimes as one of several possible areas), 16 specifically called for a specialization on Native Americans. Another 10 requested African American specialists, along with 2 for Asian American specialists, and 1 for Asian American/Chicano. Of the 8 remaining positions, 4 were described in regional terms (e.g., "Southeastern U.S.," "U.S. Southwest"), leaving only 4 jobs that were unqualified by ethnic or regional descriptors. These results are generally consistent with those of another, slightly different employment survey carried out by Judith Goode of the Society for the Anthropology of North America (SANA 1996), which found that out of 730 job listings (all subfields) sampled between 1986 and 1994, 64 were specifically designated as North Americanist positions, of which 45 required specialization on a specific U.S. ethnic group (SANA 1996: 31).

By pointing out such hiring patterns, we do not mean to imply that anthropologists should not focus on Native Americans or minority groups, but only to insist that the casting of the anthropological net to include sites ranging from "Samoa to South Central" (as a recent anthropological video catalogue from Filmmakers Library put it) does not displace the old conventions that locate the subject matter of anthropology in terms of white, Western, middle-class alterity. (The no-doubt-unintended primitivizing effects of such disciplinary definitions are made particularly clear when we open the Filmmakers Library brochure and find the "South Central" film located just opposite the "Primate Social Behavior" section.)

13. The "top ten" departments were taken from the recent National Research Council study of U.S. doctorate programs (Goldberger, Maher, and Flattau 1995: 475) and included: Michigan, Chicago, Berkeley, Harvard, Arizona, Pennsylvania, Stanford, Yale, UCLA, and UCSD. For each department, we counted all social-cultural anthropologists (including linguistic anthropologists) listed in the *AAA Guide to Departments of Anthropology* as "Full-time Faculty"—including joint appointment faculty, but not "Anthropologists in Other Departments" or courtesy (secondary) appointments. We found a total of 189 social-cultural anthropologists, of which 184 stated area specializations. We found that 23 of these anthropologists listed North America or the United States as

their primary area (i.e., listed it first, in cases of more than one area focus), of which 15 could be determined to be specialists on Native Americans, leaving 8 primary specialists in nonnative North America. We found an additional 26 anthropologists who listed North America or the United States as a secondary area interest (i.e., listed it, but did not put it first).

14. Some who have ventured to examine the mass media ethnographically are: Heide 1995; Ang 1985 (1982); Morley 1980, 1986; Powdermaker 1950; Seiter et al. 1989; Abu-Lughod 1993; Mankekar 1993a, 1993b; Dickey 1993; Spitulnik 1994. See Spitulnik 1993 for a full review and discussion.

15. The reason for this historical tendency, we suggest, cannot simply be that such supralocal political identifications have developed only recently. For instance, during Robert Redfield's classic 1927 fieldwork (to take only one of many possible examples), the ethnographer witnessed "Bolsheviks" fighting in the streets of Tepoztlan as part of a Zapatista uprising, and he described the local people he knew as "very Zapatista in sentiment." But we know this from his personal papers and his wife's diary; his ethnography painted a very different picture of peaceful villagers living local lives with little interest in national or international politics (Vincent 1990: 206–207).

16. In posing this question, we do not mean to imply that there are not often excellent reasons for choosing to work in villages. Indeed, we have each carried out village-level fieldwork in our own studies and appreciate fully the methodological opportunities and advantages often provided by such settings. Our point is only to question the conventional mapping of "field site" onto exotic "local community" that is so economically expressed in the archetypal anthropological image of "the village."

17. Indeed, even much older communications technologies such as telephones remain strikingly under-researched in anthropology, as Orvar Löfgren has pointed out recently (Löfgren 1995).

18. This does not mean, of course, that judgments of excellence cannot or should not be made, but only that (1) such judgments must always be made in terms of standards and principles that are never the only ones possible, and (2) every choice of a set of standards and principles for judgment will have social and political implications; the "grid" will not in this sense be "neutral."

19. The term is Kirin Narayan's (cited in Abu-Lughod 1991).

20. It is also interesting to note how few Africans are involved in the anthropological study of Africa. Jane Guyer (1996: 30) has recently surveyed the percentage of dissertations on Africa written by African-surnamed authors, and found that of eighteen surveyed disciplines, anthropology had by far the lowest percentage of African authors (only 18 percent of anthropology dissertations on Africa were written by authors with African surnames, compared with, e.g., 54 percent in political science, 70 percent in sociology, and 33 percent in history). See also her thoughtful remarks on the fieldwork tradition and its future in African studies (1996: 78–80).

21. Bell, Caplan, and Karim (1993) explore the myriad ways in which supposedly gender-neutral norms of fieldwork clash with highly gendered actual experiences of fieldwork.

22. In our discussion so far, we have not even touched on those micropractices of the academy that screen candidates in the name of "collegiality" and "suitability" for class, race, and sex (see Rabinow 1991).

23. Deborah D'Amico-Samuels (1991: 75) has put it very well: "The real distancing effects of the field are masked in the term 'back from the field.' These words perpetuate the notion that ethnographers and those who provide their data live in worlds that are different and separate, rather than different and unequal in ways which tie the subordination of one to the power of the other."

24. On the politics of location, see Rich (1986), Anzaldúa (1987), Spivak (1988), Pratt (1984), Martin and Mohanty (1986), Reagon (1983), Wallace (1989), Haraway (1988), Lorde (1984), Kaplan (forthcoming), Nicholson (1990).

REFERENCES

Abu-Lughod, Lila (1991) Writing against Culture. In Recapturing Anthropology: Working in the Present. Richard G. Fox, ed. Pp. 137–162. Santa Fe, N.Mex.: School of American Research Press.

Abu-Lughod, Lila, ed. (1993) Screening Politics in a World of Nations. Public Culture 5 (spring): 465–604.

American Anthropological Association (1994) AAA Guide to Departments of Anthropology, 1994–1995. Arlington, Va.: American Anthropological Association.

Ang, Ien (1985[1982]) Watching Dallas: Soap Opera and the Melodramatic Imagination. Della Couling, trans. New York: Routledge.

Anzaldúa, Gloria (1987) Borderlands/La Frontera: The New Mestiza. San Francisco: Spinsters/Aunt Lute.

Appadurai, Arjun (1988a) Introduction: Place and Voice in Anthropological Theory. Cultural Anthropology 3(1): 1, 16–20.

Appadurai, Arjun (1988b) Putting Hierarchy in Its Place. Cultural Anthropology 3(1): 36–49.

Behar, Ruth, and Deborah A. Gordon, eds. (1995) Women Writing Culture. Berkeley: University of California Press.

Bell, Diane, Pat Caplan, and Wazir Jahan Karim, eds. (1993) Gendered Fields: Women, Men, and Ethnography. New York: Routledge.

Bellah, Robert, Richard Madsen, William M. Sullivan, Ann Swidler, and Steven M. Tipton, eds. (1985) Habits of the Heart: Individualism and Commitment in American Life. New York: Harper and Row.

Bourgois, Philippe (1991) Confronting the Ethics of Ethnography: Lessons from Fieldwork in Central America. In Decolonizing Anthropology: Moving Further Toward an Anthropology for Liberation. Faye V. Harrison, ed. Pp. 110–126. Washington, D.C.: Association of Black Anthropologists, American Anthropological Association.

Burton, Michael L., Carmella C. Moore, John W. M. Whiting, and A. Kimball Romney (1996) Regions Based on Social Structure. Current Anthropology 37(1): 87–123.

D'Amico-Samuels, Deborah (1991) Undoing Fieldwork: Personal, Political, Theoretical and Methodological Implications. In Decolonizing Anthropology: Moving Further toward an Anthropology for Liberation. Faye V. Harrison, ed. Pp. 68–85. Washington, D.C.: Association of Black Anthropologists, American Anthropological Association.

Dickey, Sara (1993) Cinema and the Urban Poor in South India. Cambridge, England: Cambridge University Press.

Enslin, Elizabeth (1994) Beyond Writing: Feminist Practice and the Limitations of Ethnography. Cultural Anthropology 9(4): 537–568.

Escobar, Arturo (1994) Encountering Development: The Making and Unmaking of the Third World. Princeton: Princeton University Press.

Fardon, Richard, ed. (1990) Localizing Strategies: The Regionalization of Ethnographic Accounts. Washington, D.C.: Smithsonian Institution Press.

Ferguson, James (Forthcoming) Anthropology and Its Evil Twin: "Development" in the Constitution of a Discipline. In Development Knowledge and the Social Sciences. Frederick Cooper and Randall Packard, eds. Berkeley: University of California Press.

Frankenberg, Ruth (1993) White Women, Race Matters: The Social Construction of Whiteness. Minneapolis: University of Minnesota Press.

Geertz, Clifford (1973a) The Interpretation of Cultures: Selected Essays. New York: Basic Books.

Geertz, Clifford (1973b) Thick Description: Toward an Interpretive Theory of Culture. In The Interpretation of Cultures: Selected Essays. Pp. 3–30. New York: Basic Books.

Ghosh, Amitav (1994) The Global Reservation: Notes toward an Ethnography of International Peacekeeping. Cultural Anthropology 9(3): 412–422.

Goldberger, Marvin L., Brendan A. Maher, and Pamela Ebert Flattau, eds. (1995) Research Doctorate Programs in the United States: Continuity and Change. Washington, D.C.: National Academy Press.

Gordon, Deborah A. (1993) Worlds of Consequence: Feminist Ethnography as Social Action. Critique of Anthropology 13(4): 429–443. Special issue on Women Writing Culture. Ruth Behar, ed.

Gordon, Edmund T. (1991) Anthropology and Liberation. In Decolonizing Anthropology: Moving Further toward an Anthropology for Liberation. Faye V. Harrison, ed. Pp. 149–167. Washington, D.C.: Association of Black Anthropologists, American Anthropological Association.

Greenhouse, Carol J. (1985) Anthropology at Home: Whose Home? Human Organization 44(3): 261–264.

Gupta, Akhil, and James Ferguson (1992) Beyond "Culture": Space, Identity, and the Politics of Difference. Cultural Anthropology 7(1): 6–23.

Gupta, Akhil, and James Ferguson (1997) Culture, Power, Place: Ethnography at the End of an Era. In Culture, Power, Place: Explorations in Critical Anthropology. Akhil Gupta and James Ferguson, eds. Durham, N.C.: Duke University Press.

Gupta, Akhil, and James Ferguson, eds. (1997) Culture, Power, Place: Explorations in Critical Anthropology. Durham, N.C.: Duke University Press.

Guyer, Jane I. (1996) African Studies in the United States: A Perspective. Atlanta, Ga.: African Association Studies Press.

Haraway, Donna (1988) Situated Knowledges: The Science Question in Feminism and the Privilege of Partial Perspective. Feminist Studies 14(4): 575–599.

Hastrup, Kirsten, and Karen Fog Olwig, eds. (1996) Siting Culture. London: Routledge.

Heide, Margaret J. (1995) Television Culture and Women's Lives: Thirtysomething and the Contradictions of Gender. Philadelphia: University of Pennsylvania Press.

Herzfeld, Michael (1987) Anthropology through the Looking Glass: Critical Ethnography in the Margins of Europe. Cambridge, England: Cambridge University Press.

hooks, bell (1990) Choosing the Margin as a Space of Radical Openness. In Yearning: Race, Gender, and Cultural Politics. Pp. 145–153. Boston: South End Press.

Löfgren, Orvar (1995) The Nation as Home or Motel? On the Ethnography of Belonging. Presidential address to the Society for the Anthropology of Europe at the annual meeting of the American Anthropological Association, Washington, D.C. November.

Lorde, Audre (1984) Sister Outsider: Essays and Speeches. Freedom, Calif.: Crossing Press.

Mankekar, Purnima (1993a) National Texts and Gendered Lives: An Ethnography of Television Viewers in a North Indian City. American Ethnologist 20(3): 543–563.

Mankekar, Purnima (1993b) Television Tales and a Woman's Rage: A Nationalist Recasting of Draupadi's "Disrobing." Public Culture 5: 469–492.

Marcus, George E. (1995) Ethnography in/of the World System: The Emergence of Multi-sited Ethnography. Annual Review of Anthropology 24: 95–117.

Marcus, George E., and Michael M. J. Fischer (1986) Anthropology as Cultural Critique: An Experimental Moment in the Human Sciences. Chicago: University of Chicago Press.

Martin, Biddy, and Chandra Talpady Mohanty (1986) Feminist Politics: What's Home Got to Do with It? In Feminist Studies/Critical Studies. Teresa de Lauretis, ed. Pp. 191–212. Bloomington: Indiana University Press.

Morley, David (1980) The "Nationwide" Audience. London: British Film Institute.

Morley, David (1986) Family Television. London: Comedia/Routledge.

Murdock, George P. (1967) The Ethnographic Atlas: A Summary. Pittsburgh: University of Pittsburgh Press.

Narayan, Kirin (1993) How Native is the "Native" Anthropologist? American Anthropologist 95(3): 19–34.

Nash, June (1979) Anthropology of the Multinational Corporation. In The Politics of Anthropology: From Colonialism and Sexism: Toward a View from Below. Gerrit Huizer and Bruce Mannheim, eds. Pp. 421–446. The Hague: Mouton Publishers.

Nicholson, Linda J., ed. (1990) Feminism/Postmodernism. New York: Routledge.

Passaro, Joanne (1996) The Unequal Homeless: Men on the Streets, Women in their Place. New York: Routledge.

Powdermaker, Hortense (1956) Hollywood, the Dream Factory. New York: Grosset and Dunlap.

Pratt, Mary Louise (1986) Fieldwork in Common Places. In Writing Culture: The Poetics and Politics of Ethnography. James Clifford and George Marcus, eds. Pp. 27–50. Berkeley: University of California Press.

Pratt, Minnie Bruce (1984) Identity: Skin, Blood, Heart. In Yours in Struggle: Three Feminist Perspectives on Anti-Semitism and Racism. Elly Burkin, Minnie Bruce Pratt, and Barbara Smith, eds. Pp. 11–63. Brooklyn: Long Haul Press.

Rabinow, Paul (1991) For Hire: Resolutely Late Modern. In Recapturing Anthropology: Working in the Present. Richard G. Fox, ed. Pp. 59–72. Santa Fe, N.Mex.: School of American Research Press.

Reagon, Bernice Johnson (1983) Coalition Politics: Turning the Century. In Home Girls: A Black Feminist Anthology. Barbara Smith, ed. Pp. 356–368. New York: Kitchen Table Press.

Rich, Adrienne (1986) Notes toward a Politics of Location. In Blood, Bread, and Poetry: Selected Prose, 1979–1985. New York: Norton.

Rosaldo, Renato (1988) Ideology, Place, and People Without Culture. Cultural Anthropology 3(1): 77–87.

Rosaldo, Renato (1989) Imperialist Nostalgia. In Culture and Truth: The Remaking of Social Analysis. Pp. 68–87. Boston: Beacon Press.

Sanjek, Roger, ed. (1990) Fieldnotes: The Makings of Anthropology. Ithaca, N.Y.: Cornell University Press.

Seiter, Ellen, Hans Borchers, Gabriele Kreutzner, and Eva-Maria Warth, eds. (1989) Remote Control: Television, Audiences, and Cultural Power. New York: Routledge.

Society for the Anthropology of North America (SANA) (1996) Anthropology Newsletter 37(3): 31–32.

Spitulnik, Debra (1993) Anthropology and Mass Media. Annual Review of Anthropology 22: 293–315.

Spitulnik, Debra (1994) Radio Culture in Zambia: Audiences, Public Words, and the Nation-State. Ph.D. diss. University of Chicago.

Spivak, Gayatri Chakravorty (1988) Can the Subaltern Speak? In Marxism and the Interpretation of Culture. Cary Nelson and Lawrence Grossberg, eds. Pp. 271–313. Urbana: University of Illinois Press.

Stocking, George W., Jr. (1992) The Ethnographer's Magic and Other Essays in the History of Anthropology. Madison: University of Wisconsin Press.

Thomas, Nicholas (1989) The Force of Ethnology: Origins and Significance of the Melanasia/Polynesia Division. Current Anthropology 30(1): 27–41.

Thomas, Nicholas (1991) Against Ethnography. Cultural Anthropology 6(3): 306–322.

Tsing, Anna Lowenhaupt (1993) In the Realm of the Diamond Queen: Marginality in an Out-of-the-way Place. Princeton: Princeton University Press.

Tsing, Anna Lowenhaupt (1994) From the Margins. Cultural Anthropology 9(3): 279–297.

Vincent, Joan (1990) Anthropology and Politics: Visions, Traditions, and Trends. Tucson: University of Arizona Press.

Visweswaran, Kamala (1994) Fictions of Feminist Ethnography. Minneapolis: University of Minnesota Press.

Wallace, Michelle (1989) The Politics of Location. Framework 36: 42–55.

Wissler, Clark (1923) Man and Culture. New York: Thomas Y. Crowell.

CHAPTER 9

Methodological Nationalism, the Social Sciences, and the Study of Migration: An Essay in Historical Epistemology

Andreas Wimmer and Nina Glick Schiller

[. . .]

Methodological nationalism is the naturalization of the nation-state by the social sciences. Scholars who share this intellectual orientation assume that countries are the natural units for comparative studies, equate society with the nation-state, and conflate national interests with the purposes of social science. Methodological nationalism reflects and reinforces the identification that many scholars maintain with their own nation-states.[1] We begin by reviewing the deep-seated nature of methodological nationalism in the social sciences. We then examine the way in which postwar migration studies were shaped by methodological nationalism. We add a historical dimension by outlining how processes of nation-state formation, the creation of and response to migration flows by these states, and the social science description of these phenomena were interlinked in producing this mainstream post-war approach. In the last section we examine the conditions under which a transnational framework for the study of migration arose against this mainstream and show how far it supersedes and how far it merely refurbishes methodological nationalism in new ways.

Our argument focuses on what we perceive as the major, dominant trends in social science thinking of the past century that have shaped migration studies. We do not discuss coterminous currents that contradicted the hegemonic strands. Especially in times of intensified global interconnections, theories reflecting these developments appeared and provided tools for analysis not colored by methodological nationalism. The most obvious of these currents was political economy in the Marxian tradition, always devoting attention to capitalism as a global system rather than to its specific national manifestations, and especially the studies of imperialism by Rosa Luxemburg and others before World War I, when transnational movements of commodities, capital and labor first reached a peak. Wallerstein's world-system theory belongs to a second wave of theorizing that developed in the 1970s, when transnational connections again were intensifying and multiplying. A second and equally important line of development not included in our discussion is methodological individualism in its various forms where the analysis does not rely on explicit reference to larger social entities (such as the school of marginal utility and rational choice in economics and political science or interactionism in sociology).

These views remained heterodox, however, and did not shape the social science program in the same way as the currents discussed in this article. Rather, the epistemic structures and programs of mainstream social sciences have been closely attached to and shaped by the experience of modern nation-state formation. The global forces of transnational capitalism and colonialism that reached their apogee precisely in the period when social sciences formed as independent disciplines left few traces in the basic paradigmatic assumptions of these disciplines and were hardly systematically reflected upon.

THE THREE VARIANTS OF METHODOLOGICAL NATIONALISM WITHIN THE SOCIAL SCIENCES

We have identified three variants of methodological nationalism: 1) ignoring or disregarding the fundamental importance of nationalism for modern societies; this is often combined with 2) naturalization, *i.e.*, taking for granted that the boundaries of the nation-state delimit and define the unit of analysis; 3) territorial limitation which confines the study of social processes to the political and geographic boundaries of a particular nation-state. The three variants may intersect and mutually reinforce each other, forming a coherent epistemic structure, a self-reinforcing way of looking at and describing the social world. The three variants are more or less prominent in different fields of inquiry. Ignoring is the dominant modus of methodological nationalism in grand theory; naturalization of "normal" empirical social science; territorial limitation of the study of nationalism and state building.

In the first variant of methodological nationalism, ignoring, the power of nationalism and the prevalence of the nation-state model as the universal form of political organization are neither problematized nor made objects of study in their own right. This variant has marked especially the sociological tradition of social theory. As a host of scholars have argued repeatedly, the classic theory of modernity has a blind spot when it comes to understanding the rise of nation-states as well as of nationalism and ethnicity (A. Smith, 1983; Esser, 1988; Guiberneau, 1997; Imhof, 1997; Thompson and Fevre, 2001). In the eyes of Marx, Durkheim, Weber and Parsons, the growing differentiation, rationalization and modernization of society gradually reduced the importance of ethnic and national sentiments. Most classic grand theory was constructed as a series of sociostructural types (from feudalism through capitalism to communism, from Gemeinschaft to Gesellschaft, organic to mechanic solidarity, traditional to modern society, etc.). Nationalism was attributed to middle stages in the continuum of social evolution, a transitory phenomenon on the way to the fully modern, rationalized and individualized class society based on achievement (*see* A. Smith, 1983; Guiberneau, 1997; Weber, 1895).

The failure of social theory until the 1980s to address the significance and sources of nationalism in the modern world in part can be attributed to the disciplinary division of labor that was established at the beginning of the twentieth century (Wimmer, 1999). The study of the rise of nationalism and the nation-state, of ethnonational wars of nineteenth- and early-twentieth-century Europe was relegated to history.[2] Anthropology, and, later, modernization and development theory in political science took on the study of communal identities and nation building processes outside of Europe and the United States. Sociology focused its attention to the study of modern industrial nations and defined the limits of society as coterminous with the nation-state, rarely questioning the nationalist ideology embedded in such a founding assumption.

Thus, even the most sophisticated theorizing about the modern condition accepted as a given that nationalist forms of inclusion and exclusion bind modern societies together (Berlin, 1998). Nation-state principles were so routinely structured into the foundational assumptions of theory that they vanished from sight. Whether Parsons and Merton or Bourdieu, Habermas and Luhmann: none of these authors discusses in any systematic fashion the national framing of states and societies in the modern age. Interestingly enough, such nation-blind theories of modernity were formulated in an environment of rapidly nationalizing societies and states—sometimes, as was the case with Max Weber and Emile Durkheim, on the eve or in the aftermath of nationalist wars that profoundly structured the course that the modern project has taken in the West.

Empirically oriented social science has displayed what can be understood as a second variant of methodological nationalism, naturalization. They have systematically taken for granted nationally bounded societies as the natural unit of analysis. Naturalization produced the container model of society that encompasses a culture, a polity, an economy and a bounded social group (*cf.* Taylor, 1996). To cast this in an image borrowed from Giddens (1995), the web of social life was spun within the container of the national society, and everything extending over its borders was cut off analytically. Assuming that processes within nation-state boundaries were different from those outside, the social sciences left no room for transnational and global processes that connected national territories.

Naturalization owes its force to the compartmentalization of the social science project into different "national" academic fields, a process strongly influenced not only by nationalist thinking itself, but also by the institutions of the nation-state organizing and channeling social science thinking in universities, research institutions and government think tanks. The major research programs of funding bodies address the solution of national problems in economics, politics, and social services. In most states, universities are linked to national ministries of education that favor research and teaching on issues of "national relevance." Add to this the fact that almost all statistics and other systematic information are produced by government departments of nation-states and thus take the national population, economy and polity as their given entity of observation (*cf.* Smith 1983:26; Favell, forthcoming a), and we understand why naturalizing the nation-state has become part of the everyday routine of postwar social sciences, in international relations as much as in economics, history or anthropology.

International relations assumed that nation-states are the adequate entities for studying the world. While the anarchical nature of this interstate system and the changing dynamics of hegemony and polycentrism have been discussed at length, it was only very late that a counter-trend calling for the study of connections forged by nonstate institutions emerged (Nye) or that scholars began to wonder why the global political system emerged as an international one (Mayall, 1990). Similarly, post World War II scholarship on the newly independent states approached nation building as a necessary,

although somewhat messy aspect of the decolonization process (*see, e.g.,* Wallerstein, 1961). Nation building and state formation made natural bedfellows in the works of modernization theorists such as Lerner or Rostow, since the nation-state model represented the only thinkable way of organizing politics.

Economics followed a similar trajectory in studying the economy of nationally bounded entities or their relations to each other through trade, capital flows and the like. Since the publication of Adam Smith's "An Inquiry into the Nature and Causes of the Wealth of Nations" (1983 [1789]) and Friedrich List's masterpiece, "Das nationale System der politischen Ökonomie" (List, 1974 [1856]), the distinction between internal economy and external relations has become a guiding principle for the evolution of the discipline. Maynard Keynes and other major political economists of the twentieth century remained faithful to this perspective and took the distinction between national, domestic economy and international, external economy for granted.

Historians also reflect the methodological assumption that it is a particular nation that provides the constant unit of observation through all historical transformations, the "thing" whose change history was supposed to describe (Bender, 2001; Rodgers, 1998). Modern mainstream history was largely written as a history of particular nation-states or of their relations to each other. When in the 1990s the newly reconstituted states of Eastern Europe began to organize their historiography, art history and archaeology, most accounts continued this form of historical narrative.

When anthropology abandoned diffusionism as an explanatory paradigm, it also began to be shaped by variants of methodological nationalism. The anthropology of ethnic groups within modernizing or industrial nation-states focused on cultural difference from the "majority" population—thus mirroring the nation-state project to define all those populations not thought to represent the "national culture" as racially and culturally different, producing an alterity which contributed to efforts to build unity and identity (Williams, 1989; Glick Schiller, 1999a; b; c; Wimmer, 2002).

Most interestingly, methodological nationalism, often in the form of territorial limitation, also shaped the social science analysis of the nation-state building process itself. Historically, the concepts of the modern state and of a national population have developed within transborder rather than territorially limited national spaces. In many cases, these transborder spaces were delimited by the practice and ideology of colonial and imperial domination, and ideas of popular sovereignty and republican independence were formed within transborder networks of literate circles. We have to think outside of the box of dominant national discourses to see such transborder foundations of particular nation-state building projects, to see the dynamics between English domination of Ireland and English national identity or the linkage between French ideas about citizenship and civilization and the French colonial project (Lebovics, 1992). Accepting the prevailing paradigm that divides a state's affairs into internal, national matters and international affairs that have to do with state-to-state relations, the history of such transborder and transnational nation-state building becomes invisible. The writing of national histories compounds this invisibility by confining the narrative within state borders.

This tendency of territorial limitation has restricted our understanding of the rise of the modern nation-state in several ways. First, most current theories and histories of democracy have looked at the inner dynamics of the evolving democratic polities and lost sight of the nationalist principles that historically defined its boundaries.[3] As an effect of this segregation, nationalism appears as a force foreign to the history of Western state building. It is the ideology of nondemocratic, non-Western others, projected onto the ethnic violence of Balkan leaders or African tribesmen turned nationalists. Western state building was re-imagined as a non-national, civil, republican and liberal experience, especially in the writings of political philosophers such as Rawls (*cf.* Sen, 1999). However, what we nowadays call ethnic cleansing or

ethnocide, and observe with disgust in the "ever troublesome Balkans" or in "tribalistic Africa," have been constants of the Western European history of nation building and state formation, from the expulsion of Gypsies under Henry VIII and the Muslims and Jews under Fernando and Isabella. Many of these histories have disappeared from popular consciousness—and maybe have to be forgotten if nation building is to be successful, as Ernest Renan (1947 [1882]) suggested some hundred years ago.

State formation and nation building thus have become two separate objects of inquiry. Most scholars of nationalism discussed the nation as a domain of identity—far removed from the power politics of modern state formation. The nation is understood to be a people who share common origins and history as indicated by their shared culture, language and identity (*cf.* Calhoun, 1997; McCrone, 1998; A. Smith, 1998). In contrast, the "state" is conceived as a sovereign system of government within a particular territory (*see* Abrams, 1988; Corrigan and Sayer, 1985; Joseph and Nugent, 1994 for alternative approaches to nation and state). In political science, this has allowed a mainstream theory to emerge, which sees the state as a neutral playing ground for different interest groups—thus excluding from the picture the fact that the modern state itself has entered into a symbiotic relationship with the nationalist political project. [. . .]

PHASES OF NATION BUILDING AND DISCOURSES ON IMMIGRATION

So far our argument has largely been conceptual and abstract, proceeding through analogies between the ideologies of nation-state building and the conceptual schemes of the social sciences and of postwar migration studies. We should now like to historically situate this relationship and sketch a broad picture of how different phases of nation-state formation have influenced both the state's attitude towards migrations and the way that these have been conceptualized by the social science. We will see that the postwar situation, with nationalist closure paralleling container reasoning in the social sciences, is the result of a long history of interaction between nation-state building, migratory flows and social science discourse.

The scenario for telling this story is a world expanding and contracting in phases of globalization and nationalization, but still remaining—as a perspective not limited by methodological nationalism allows us to see—an interconnected realm of cross-border relationships. From such a perspective, we may have a better view on how nation-state building, migration and the social science project are related to each other. We identify four periods, painting the changes that are of interest in broad strokes so as to gain an overview of the landscape and using dates as only approximate markers of global historical transformations: 1870–1918, 1919–1945, 1946–1989, 1990–present, the last phase being discussed in a section of its own.

Phase I: The Prewar Era

Our historical portrait begins in a period that stems from the 1870s to World War I. The period was marked by two trends that were related to each other in complex ways that are rarely explored. This was a time that was simultaneously one of nation-state building and intensive globalization. While industries developed within the confines of these nationalizing states, protected by tariffs from competing capitalist interests, commercial competition tied to concepts of national interest launched a new period of colonialism. This was the epoch in which European states "scrambled" for Africa, as well as a time of heightened competition between European states and the United States for the control of raw materials produced in the Caribbean, Latin America and Asia. It was also a period in which, as part of this effort to monopolize sources of raw materials and obtain labor for their production, imperialism was practiced and theorized.

In response to these various and interactive developments, labor migration was widespread, spanning the globe. Free workers selling their labor force on a newly established world market for labor made up a section of this migration. Another section was composed of indentured laborers replacing slaves on the plantations or constructing railroads and other major infrastructure projects all around the world, especially in the colonies (Potts, 1990). Poles and Italians migrated to northern France, Switzerland welcomed diverse populations, England saw influxes from the continent, and German industrial development fueled migrations from the east and south. Brazil welcomed migrants from Europe, the Middle East and Japan. Indians and Chinese laborers went to the Caribbean and southern and eastern Africa. Mexicans, Turks, Syrians and populations from southern and Eastern Europe migrated to the United States.

The United States, now portrayed as historically a land of immigrants, unlike European states, was actually the first and for a time the only state to erect any significant barriers, when it passed the Chinese exclusion act in 1882. For a certain period, Germany, which contained within its borders land that had been part of an earlier Polish state, tightly controlled and supervised the movement of Polish speakers, but not of Italians and other immigrants. In general, however, this was a period when not even passports and entry documents were required. Most European countries abolished the passport and visa systems they had installed in the first half of the nineteenth century after France took the lead in eliminating such barriers to the free movement of labor in 1861 (Torpey, 2000). Some states tried to keep workers from leaving, fearing labor shortages, but these efforts were relatively ineffective. Switzerland, France, England, Germany, the United States, Brazil and Argentina built industrialized economies with the help of billions of labor migrants who worked in factories, fields, mills and mines.

Workers migrated into regions in which there was industrial development and returned home or went elsewhere when times were bad. Many maintained their home ties, sent money home to buy land, and supported home areas with remittances. At the same time, at the beginning of this period it was still easy for migrants to gain citizenship even in Germany. This easy access to citizenship reflected the fact that the term "the people" was still basically defined in terms of shared citizenship rights—the people as nation and as a group of mutual solidarity were important only in the coming period of nation-state building. Mirroring the lack of barriers to migration and the open citizenship regimes, E. G. Ravenstein (1889), in the first systematic analysis of migration, did not differentiate analytically between internal and international migration. Instead, Ravenstein treated all movements of people across the terrain as part of a single phenomenon, largely determined by the distribution of economic opportunities over physical space. He found that international migration followed the same "laws" as internal migration, maintaining that in all cases migration consisted of movements from country to town and from poorer to richer areas (Ravenstein, 1889:286)

Yet the nation-state building that emerged within this period of globalization eventually fostered conceptualizations of "the people" that would dramatically affect migration and alter the way in which social scientists thought about migration. An "ethnic" and/or "racial" concept began to replace the "civic" approach to peoplehood, initially articulated by Enlightenment philosophers and concretized in the course of the U.S., French and Haitian revolutions. "The people" began to mean a nation united by common ancestry and a shared homeland, no matter where its members might have wandered. This concept of people gave each nation its own national character, its peculiar nature and homeland, and a claim to a place in the sun. This nationalized view of the people developed within a growing competition for political pre-eminence in Europe. National chauvinisms and racisms legitimated both the colonial empire building of the period and the culmination of this competition in World War I. It was in the context of this competition and of the salience of ideas about nation and race that nation-state builders, including elites, political leaders, state officials and intellectuals, initiated systematic efforts to erase, deny or homogenize the internal cultural and national diversity that existed within all of the industrializing states of Europe and the Americas.

In this paper we are particularly concerned with the role of the social sciences in this reconceptualization. The social sciences emerged as distinct intellectual enterprises during this period and were both shaped by and contributed to the transformation of concepts of nation and immigrant. In the transition from civic to nationalized concepts of the people, folklore studies in Europe and anthropology in both Europe and the United States played a crucial role. Increasingly, nations were seen as organic wholes, nourished by the pure lore, tradition or rural virtue of the peasant, yeoman or farmers. Ideas about nation as races based on blood were popularized globally, entering into the nation-state building projects and imperial ideologies used to legitimate colonial expansion (Dikötter, 1997). Meanwhile, sociology developed those grand schemes of progress—from tradition to modernity, community to society—that made the national framing of these epochal transformations invisible.

Distinctions drawn between natives and colonizers or between immigrants and natives served to homogenize and valorize the national culture of the colonizing country and popularize the notion that it was a unitary and bounded society, distinguishable from the subordinated peoples by a racial divide (Hall, McClelland and Rendall, 2000; Gilroy, 1991; Glick Schiller, 1999a, b; Lebovics, 1992; Rafael, 1995; Stoler, 1989). Nation-state building in France, England and even the United States (as it took on colonies and began to police the Caribbean) was shaped by distinctions popularized from social science. As nationalist concepts of people and society took hold, the conception of immigrants began to change. By the turn of the century, while the flow of migration generally remained unrestricted, migrants began to be conceptualized as continuing to have memberships in their ancestral homelands. Many actors contributed to popularizing this idea, and it was in many ways only the other side of the conceptualization of the world as divided up into peoples, each made up of a national citizenry and sovereign.

The presence of non-national citizens thus became a major risk for national sovereignty and security.

On the other hand, and again conforming to the newly nationalized notion of people-hood, emigrant-sending states, including Italy and Austro-Hungary, started to see their emigrants as still members of their home countries and expected them to return (Cinel, 1982; Harrington, 1982; Wyman, 1993). Remittances from abroad were understood to be a significant part of the economies of many regions. Emigrant-sending states established institutions to protect emigrants as well as police them. Areas of Europe in which nationalist struggles percolated dispersed political exiles, who continued to wage their struggles transnationally. In exile these leaders saw the dispersed workers of their region as compatriots and sought to engender within them nationalist identities and emotions through meetings, newspapers, and religious and fraternal organizations. Emigrant workers who moved back and forth between home regions and countries of immigration both within Europe and across the Atlantic to the Americas began to become engaged in these nation-state building projects in their homelands. Both European and Asian immigrants began to believe that the degree of respect they would be accorded abroad would be increased if the power and prestige of their motherland increased, and many became fervent nationalists (Cinel, 1982; Kwong, 1987).

All these transnational political activities and engagements seemed to justify the fears of nationalizing states that immigrants undermined the stability and territorial boundedness of the nation. By the end of this first period, immigrants had come to be seen as politically dangerous and nationally or racially fundamentally different others whose presence endangered the isomorphism between citizenry, sovereign and state. Meanwhile, in Europe, political leaders who faced the political repercussions of intensive industrialization, the vast disparities between rich and poor exacerbated by processes of globalization, and internationalist revolutionary workers movements fanned the wave of distrust and hatred to non-nationals that exploded with the outbreak of the Great War.

Phase II: From World War I to the Cold War

The Great War ended the period of the free movement of labor and other aspects of intensive globalization. The disruption of economies, first by war and the reconstitution of many regions into newly independent states along national lines, contributed to the continuing closure of borders instituted as part of national defenses of these newly nationalizing states. At the same time, the warlike process of nation-state formation, with all its ethnic cleansings and the mass denaturalizations it entailed, was (and still is) the major force producing refugees who seek to cross borders in search of security and peace (Zolberg, 1983; Sassen, 1999)—a paradox that constituted a major preoccupation of Hanna Arendt's *The Origins of Totalitarianism* (1951).

The mass slaughtering in the name of national honor and independence had given the idea of a national community of destiny an unprecedented plausibility, making national affiliations a question of life and death not only in the trenches but in the larger society as well. Distinguishing between friend and foe on the basis of national background had become commonsense practice and ideology. The success of the Russian Revolution fanned the surveillance of migrants as potential threats to national security and reinforced the differentiation between national and foreign ideas and ideologies. The political turbulence of the times, in which the Great Depression was countered by revolutionary politics with armed insurrection in Germany and the rise of Republican Spain, contributed to the efforts by nationalist states to police borders and limit the movements of political and labor activists.

Previous efforts at developing a system of migration control were revised and developed into historically novel forms of border policing. It now became necessary for a person to have a permit to enter a country and reside there, creating both the differentiation between nationals—who did not need such permits—and foreigners, as well as between legal and illegal residents of states. The power to issue permits became concentrated in the central government. In the United States, this power strengthened the position of the federal government and its role in the delineation of the nation from its enemies. In Europe, the new regime of visas began to link the right to reside in a country with a work permit, virtually defining a foreigner as a temporary worker. In short, an entire central state apparatus of overseeing, limiting and controlling immigration was institutionalized between the wars. Immigrants, by the logic of border control and rising security concerns, were now natural enemies of the nation.

Meanwhile, the devastation of the war in Europe had disrupted the transnational ties of family members abroad by impeding the sending of letters, money and packages. As refugees fled from war zones in Europe and borders changed, many transmigrants living in the United States lost track of their families, some permanently. The massive unemployment and poverty of the Depression also made it difficult to send remittances. People thrown out of work in the Americas returned to the homes they had been building in their regions of origin. At the same time, limits on immigration in the United States effectively halted the back and forth travel that had been a mainstay of immigrant families, communities and nationalists before the war. Similar developments occurred for migrants within Europe.

The brief period between World War I and World War II was a turning point in the growth of methodological nationalism, and it is in this period that the mainstream concept of immigration—as discussed in the previous section—developed. The social sciences began to play an important role in this conceptualization. The Chicago School of sociology elaborated the first systematic approach to migration. Their models carried with them a series of national values and norms about the way in which immigration was to be understood. They established a view of each territorially based state as having its own, stable population, contrasting them to migrants who were portrayed as

marginal men living in a liminal state, uprooted in one society and transplanted into another. They advocated assimilation, not by formulating plans for societal intervention but by proposing a "race-relations cycle" in which the process of acculturation and assimilation of immigrants occurred normally and naturally in the course of several generations (Park, 1950). Their casual use of the word race accepted the conflation of race and nation and placed together southern and eastern European immigrants, Jewish immigrants, and African Americans as all racially different from mainstream America, although with different degrees of distance that would affect their rates of assimilation. The movement of immigrants was counter-posed to the immigrant receiving state, whose society seemed fixed within a homogenous national culture. The placing of African Americans with immigrants within the race-relations cycle, portrayed them as outside of the nation, although they had been part of the Americas since the period of conquest. This discursive move marked the nation as white and normalized the color line (Williams, 1989; Lieberson, 1980).

Immigrants were now seen not only as a security risk, but also as destroying the isomorphism between nation and people and thus a major challenge to the ongoing nation building project, constantly forcing the machinery of assimilation to absorb new waves of cultural heterogeneity. The fact that nation-state building was an ongoing process and that the state contained within its borders significant differences between classes, cultures, genders and regions became more difficult to perceive. National integration and cultural homogeneity of the national society were taken as givens. While seemingly ahistorical, these concepts were very much a product of the collapse of the globalized world during World War I and the Great Depression of the 1930s. In fact, it seems to us that it was the reduced degree of global economic integration during this period that prompted and facilitated the qualitative leap in nation-state building and the emergence of the container model in the social sciences that the Chicago School helped to propagate. Social order contained within the nation-state became the taken-for-granted premise of the new social science as well as of migration studies. Even the fact that there had been a period of free labor migration within previous periods of globalization was soon forgotten. As the new image of migration as threatening social order became dominant, the social movements that had so readily crossed borders and fueled political and intellectual life also faded first from view and then from memory, including the internationalism of labor, the first women's movement, pan-Africanism, and various forms of "long distance nationalism" (Gabaccia, 2000; Gilroy, 1993; Lemelle and Kelley, 1994; Rodgers, 1998). In point of fact, the actual data produced by the Chicago School and those influenced by this school demonstrated ongoing and significant transnational familial, religious, economic and political ties of most migrant populations. However, because their vision was limited by the container model of society, all evidence of transnational connections was defined as a transitory phenomenon that would disappear in the wake of a natural process of assimilation.

Phase III: The Cold War

During the period known as the Cold War, the blind spot became a blindness, an almost complete erasure of the historical memories of transnational and global processes within which nation-states were formed and the role of migration within that formation. Modernization theory made it look as if Western Europe and United States had developed national identities and modern states within their own territorial confines rather than in relationship to a global economy and flows of ideas. The growth of the United Nations and the granting of formal independence to most former colonies popularized a vision of the world as divided into a host of nation-states of equal significance and sovereignty. The European postwar terrain of displaced persons and refugees was rapidly reordered by the insistence that everyone must belong somewhere. In the United States, school-children read morality tales about the "man without a country" and sang patriotic songs

that celebrated their "native land." Throughout the world, civic education had become equated with lessons in patriotism. People were envisioned as each having only one nation-state, and belonging to humanity was thought to require a national identity. The social sciences neither investigated nor problematized this assumption.

By recalling just briefly the Cold War context in which the social sciences grew to maturity, we can gain some additional insights into the way methodological nationalism of migration studies was shaped by this environment. In Europe, the competition with the Soviet Union spurred the development of social democratic ideologies and a form of social welfare capitalism. The people now comprised not only a nation, citizenry and a sovereign, but a group of solidarity as well. With the establishment of national welfare states, the nationalist project reached its culmination and fulfillment. Membership in this group of solidarity was a privilege, and state boundaries marked the limitation of access to these privileges (*cf.* Wimmer, 1998).

In addition, Cold War tensions and suspicions called for an ever tighter policing of borders and a careful investigation of the motives of all those seeking to cross national borders. Immigration became ever more problematic. To cross the Iron Curtain, one had to be a political refugee. In the West, only those who fled communism were allocated the right to move and resettle permanently. Otherwise, the consensus held that national borders should limit the flow of populations and serve as vessels within which national cultures were contained and cultivated. Yet as industrial structures became reconstituted in the wake of war, and after depression and war had depopulated the old continent, new demands for labor arose in Western Europe and the United States.

In this conjuncture, England, France and the Netherlands turned to their own colonial populations, populations who had been educated to see the colonial power as the motherland, and shared language and a system of education with those motherlands. Germany sought to restrict and control influxes of workers by the use of labor contracts that recruited guestworkers. The United States used a bit of both strategies, utilizing its colonial Puerto Rican populations and developing the *Bracero* Program of Mexican contract labor. While seeming very different, both strategies provided for the needs of industry while minimizing the challenge to the concept if not the practice of national closure, naturalized and normalized by social science.

In the United States, despite massive efforts at assimilation, the previous waves of immigrants settled in urban areas maintained their national identities, even if their cultural practices were increasingly similar to their working class neighbors (Gans, 1982). These groups were designated "nationalities" in popular parlance, reflecting ideologies about national belonging of the prewar period. Politicans campaigning in immigrant neighborhoods during this period recognized these connections, promising to develop or support American foreign policies to help the homelands of whatever nationality group they were addressing—Irish, Italian, Polish, Serbian or Greek (Glick Schiller, 1999a, b; Redding, 1958; Weed, 1973). But due to the limitations that the container model of society imposed on the social sciences, much of this history has yet to be recovered. In the United States, until Glazer and Moynihan's (1963) seminal statement to move "beyond the melting pot," the social sciences ignored these persisting identities and the ways in which U.S. urban political life was organized to give salience to competing ethnic groups, rather than respond to class-based discourse (*cf.* Steinberg, 1989). Instead, immigrants were portrayed as uprooted from their homelands, and much time and resources were invested in measuring rates and degrees of assimilation.

Much of this rhetoric changed abruptly in the 1960s in the United States, and the effects of these changes on the rhetoric of nation-state building and on social science resonated around the world, especially after the end of the Cold War. The catalyst for the changes was the U.S. civil rights movement that exposed the unstated but institutionalized equation of American identity with whiteness. As black activists strove to develop for themselves a differentiated and contestational political identity, they reached back to the pre-war pan-African movement and rekindled an African-American cultural politic (Ture and Hamilton, 1992 [1967]). In the wake of the Black Power movement, other populations, which had been excluded from the U.S. racialized nation building project with its normative whiteness, began to elaborate ideologies of cultural pluralism (Glick Schiller Barnett, 1975; Glick Schiller, 1977; Steinberg, 1989; Glazer and Moynihan, 1963). In this context, which included the Cold War implications of the exposure of U.S. racism, the racially construed national quotas embedded in the U.S. immigration law were finally eliminated in 1965. [. . .]

OUTLOOK: SAILING BETWEEN SCYLLA AND CHARYBDIS

Going beyond methodological nationalism requires analytical tools and concepts not colored by the self-evidence of a world ordered into nation-states. Increasingly, observers of the social sciences see this as one of the major tasks that confront us. We certainly are not able to offer such a set of analytical tools here. Instead, our objective has been to clarify the nature of the barriers which have stood in the path leading to a revised social theory. Confronting the manner in which our perceptions of migration, including some of the recent work on transnational migration, have been shaped by the hegemony of the nation-state building project is an important step. It may prevent us from running, enthusiastically searching for newness, along the most promising-looking road, without knowing exactly how we got to the crossroads where we actually find ourselves. Looking back may help us to identify the paths that will bring us right back to where we now stand. We described three modes of methodological nationalism that have shaped the social science program— ignoring, naturalization and territorial limitation—and we have identified the ways in which these have influenced mainstream migration studies. Describing immigrants as political security risks, as culturally others, as socially marginal, and as an exception to the rule of territorial confinement, migration studies have faithfully mirrored the nationalist image of normal life.

Our second aim was to sketch out, in admittedly rather audacious and broad strokes, a history of the past century that would help us to understand how this binding of the scientific eye to the body of the nation came about and how this relationship has evolved through different phases of nation building. For all these different phases, we have described how the process of nation-state building has generated, as one of its aspects, different stances towards cross-border migration and immigrant integration that were mirrored, if not sometimes sustained or even produced, by the basic concepts of migration research. We have taken the point of view of an observer of second order, observing what professional observers observe and what they do not.

Such a historical approach does not provide the well developed conceptual tools that would allow us to elaborate this perspective more systematically. This remains a task for the future. However, a word of caution is in order here. It would certainly be naïve to think that we will ever develop a theoretical language not profoundly influenced by the social and political forces around us. Most of us have come to understand that any observation is shaped by the positionality of the observer—including the ones unmasking methodological nationalism. While we are still striving for an adequate terminology not colored by methodological nationalism, we can already predict that emerging concepts will necessarily again limit and shape our perspective, again force us to overlook some developments and emphasize others. Every clear conceptual structure necessarily limits the range of possible interpretations, as well as the empirical domains that can be meaningfully interpreted. The task is to determine what reductions of complexity will make best sense of the contemporary world and which ones are leaving out too many tones and voices, transforming them into what model builders call 'noise.'

We note that many who have attempted

to escape the Charybdis of methodological nationalism are drifting towards the Scylla of methodological fluidism. It makes just as little sense to portray the immigrant as the marginal exception than it does to celebrate the transnational life of migrants as the prototype of human condition (Urry, 2000; Papastergiadis, 2000). Moreover, while it is important to push aside the blinders of methodological nationalism, it is just as important to remember the continued potency of nationalism. Framing the world as a global marketplace cannot begin to explain why under specific circumstances not only political entrepreneurs, but also the poor and disempowered, including immigrants, continue to frame their demands for social justice and equality within a nationalist rhetoric (Glick Schiller and Fouron, 2001 a, b). Nor can we blithely take up the perspective of cosmopolitanism, either as a description of the post-national stage of identity or as a political goal to be reached (*cf.* Beck, 2000). Such a stance may be helpful for a deconstruction of nationalism, taking a very different tack than previous discussions of the invention or imagination of community. But it does not acknowledge that nationalism is a powerful signifier that continues to make sense for different actors with different purposes and political implications. Having hinted at the Scylla of fluidism and of the rhetorics of cosmopolitanism, the challenge remains to develop a set of concepts that opens up new horizons for our understanding of past and contemporary migration.

NOTES

1. We owe the term to Herminio Martins (1974: 276), who mentioned it *en passant* in an article on social theory. *See also* Smith (1983:26).

2. There are a few exceptions, such as a small essay by Durkheim written immediately after World War I. French and German social scientists have pointed to the blind spot in their respective literatures (*see* Hondrich, 1992; Radtke, 1996; Taguieff, 1991:46). In the Anglo-Saxon world, the early works on nationalism of historical sociologists such as Deutsch, Kedouri, Gellner and Smith had little impact until recently on mainstream social theory.

3. Thus, with few exceptions, such as Snyder's

(2000) recent book or an essay by the Georgian philosopher Ghia Nodia (1992), it is only during the last decade that the blinders of methodological nationalism have been overcome by going beyond the dichotomy between state and nation without falling into the trap of naturalizing the nation-state (Mann, 1993; Breuilly, 1993; Wimmer, 1996, 2002).

REFERENCES

Abrams, P. (1988) "Notes on the Difficulty of Studying the State," *Journal of Historical* [1977] *Sociology*, 1(1):58–89.

Arendt, H. (1951) *The Origins of Totalitarianism*. New York: Harcourt Brace.

Beck, U. (2000) "The Cosmopolitan Perspective: Sociology of the Second Age of Modernity," *British Journal of Sociology*, 51(1):79–105.

Bender, T. (2001) "Writing National History in a Global Age," *Correspondence. An International Review of Culture and Society*, 7:13f.

Berlin, I. (1998) "Nationalism: Past Neglect, Present Power." In *The Proper Study of Mankind. An Anthology of Essays*. Ed. H. Hardy and R. Hausheer. London: Pimlico.

Breuilly, J. (1993) *Nationalism and the State*. Manchester: Manchester University Press.

Calhoun, C. (1997) *Nationalism*. Minneapolis: University of Minnesota Press.

Cinel, D. (1982) *From Italy to San Francisco: The Immigrant Experience*. Stanford, CA: Stanford University Press.

Corrigan, P. and D. Sayer (1985) *The Great Arch: English State Formation as Cultural Revolution*. Oxford: Basil Blackwell.

Dikötter, F. (1997) "Racial Discourse in China: Continuities and Permutations." In *The Construction of Racial Identities in China and Japan: Historical and Contemporary Perspectives*. Ed. F. Dikötter. Honolulu: University of Hawaii Press. Pp. 12–33.

Esser, H. (1988) "Ethnische Differenzierung und Moderne Gesellschaft," *Zeitschrift für Soziologie*, 17(4):235–248.

Favell, A. (2003) "Integration Nations: The Nation-state and Research on Immigrants in Western Europe," *Comparative Social Research*, Yearbook vol. 22, Nov, pp.13–42. (Reprinted in *International Migration Research: Constructions, Omissions and the Promise of Interdisciplinarity* (2005). Ed. Michael Bommes and Ewa Morawska. London: Ashgate, pp.41–67). http://www.sscnet.ucla.edu/soc/faculty/favell/grete.pdf.

Gabaccia, D. R. (2000) *Italy's Many Diasporas: Elites, Exiles and Workers of the World*. Seattle: University of Washington Press.

Gans, H. (1982) *The Urban Villagers: Group and Class in the Life of Italian-Americans*. New York: Free Press.

Giddens, A. (1995) *National State and Violence*. Los Angeles: University of California Press.

Gilroy, P. (1993) *The Black Atlantic: Modernity and Double Consciousness*. Cambridge: Harvard University Presss.

Gilroy, P. (1991) *There Ain't No Black in the Union Jack: The Cultural Policies of Race and Nation*. Chicago: University of Chicago Press.

Glazer, N. and D. P. Moynihan (1963) *Beyond the Melting Pot: The Negroes, Puerto Ricans, Jews, Italians, and Irish of New York City*. Cambridge, MA: M.I.T. Press.

Glick Schiller Barnett, N. (1975) "The formation of a Haitian Ethnic Group." Ph.D. dissertation. Department of Anthropology, Columbia University.

Glick Schiller, N. (1999a) "Transmigrants and Nation-States: Something Old and Something New in U.S. Immigrant Experience." In *Handbook of International Migration: The American Experience*. Ed. C. Hirschman, J. DeWind and P. Kasinitz. New York: Russell Sage.

Glick Schiller, N. (1999b) " 'Who Are These Guys?': A Transnational Perspective on National Identities." In *Identities on the Move. Transnational Processes in North America and the Caribbean Basin*. Ed. L. Goldin. Houston: University of Texas Press.

Glick Schiller, N. (1999c) "Transnational Nation-States and Their Citizens: The Asian Experience." In *Globalisation and the Asia Pacific: Contested Territories*. Ed. K. Olds *et al*. London: Routledge.

Glick Schiller, N. (1977) "Ethnic Groups are Made Not Born." In *Ethnic Encounters: Identities and Contexts*. Ed. G. L. Hicks and P. E. Leis. North Scituate, MA: Duxbury Press. Pp. 23–35.

Glick Schiller, N. and G. Fouron (2001a) *Georges Woke Up Laughing: Long Distance Nationalism and the Search for Home*. Durham, NC: Duke University Press.

Glick Schiller, N. and G. Fouron (2001b) "I Am Not a Problem without a Solution: Poverty, Transnational Migration, and Struggle." In *New Poverty Studies: The Ethnography of Politics, Policy and Impoverished People in the U.S.* Ed. J. M. Good and J. Good. New York: New York University Press.

Guiberneau, M. (1997) "Marx and Durkheim on Nationalism." In *Rethinking Nationalism and Ethnicity. The Struggle for Meaning and Order in Europe*. Ed. H-R. Wicker. Oxford: Berg.

Hall, C., K. McClelland and J. Rendall (2000) *Defining the Victorian Nation: Class, Race, Gender and the British Reform Act of 1867*. Cambridge: Cambridge University Press.

Harrington, M. (1982) "Loyalties: Dual and Divided." In *The Politics of Ethnicity*. Ed. S. Thernstrom. Cambridge, MA: Belknap Press. Pp. 104–109.

Hondrich, K. O. (1992) "Wovon wir Nichts wissen Wollten," *Die Zeit vom* 25. September.

Imhof, K. (1997) "Nationalism and the Theory of Society." In *Rethinking Nationalism and Ethnicity. The Struggle for Meaning and Order in Europe*. Ed. H-R. Wicker. Oxford: Berg.

Joseph, G. M. and D. Nugent (1994) "Popular Culture and State Formation in Revolutionary Mexico." In *Everyday Forms of State Formation: Revolution and The Negotiation of Rule in Modern Mexico*. Ed. G.

M. Joseph and D. Nugent. Durham, NC: Duke University Press, Pp. 3–23.

Kwong, P. (1987) *The New Chinatown*. New York: Hill and Wong.

Lebovics, H. (1992) *True France: The Wars over Cultural Identity, 1900–1945*. Ithaca, NY: Cornell University Press.

Lemelle, S. and R. Kelley (1994) *Imagining Home: Class, Culture, and Nationalism in the African Diaspora*. London: Verso.

Lieberson, S. (1980) *A Piece of the Pie. Black and White Immigrants since 1880*. Berkeley: University of California Press.

List, F. (1974) [1856] *National System of Political Economy*. New York: Garland.

Mann, M. (1993) *The Sources of Social Power, Volume II: The Rise of Classes and Nation-States, 1760–1914*. Cambridge: Cambridge University Press.

Martins, H. (1974) "Time and Theory in Sociology." In *Approaches to Sociology. An Introduction to Major Trends in British Sociology*. Ed. J. Rex. London and Boston: Routledge & Kegan Paul. Pp. 246–294.

Mayall, J. (1990) *Nationalism and International Society*. Cambridge: Cambridge University Press.

McCrone, D. (1998) *The Sociology of Nationalism*. London: Routledge.

Nodia, G. (1992) "Nationalism and Democracy," *Journal of Democracy*, 3(4):3–22.

Papastergiadis, N. (2000) *The Turbulence of Migration: Globalization, Deterritorialization and Hybridity*. Cambridge: Polity Press.

Park, R. E. (1950) *Race and Culture*. Glencoe, IL: Free Press.

Potts, L. (1990) *The World Labour Market: A History of Migration*. London: Zed.

Radtke, F. (1996) "Fremde und Allzufremde. Zur Ausbreitung des ethnologischen Blicks in der Einwanderungsgesellschaft." In *Das Fremde in der Gesellschaft. Migration, Ethnizität und Staat*. Ed. H-R. Wicker *et al.* Zurich: Seismos.

Rafael, V. (1995) *Discrepant Histories: Translocal Essays on Filipino Cultures*. Philadelphia: Temple University Press.

Ravenstein, E. G. (1889) "The Laws of Migration. Second Paper," *Journal of Royal Statistical Society*, 52(2):241–305.

Redding, J. (1958) *Inside the Democratic Party*. Indianapolis: Bobbs-Merrill.

Renan, E. (1947) "Que'est-ce qu' une Nation?" *Oeuvres complètes*, vol. 1. Paris: Calmann-[1882] Levy.

Rodgers, D. (1998) *Atlantic Crossings: Social Politics in a Progressive Age*. Cambridge, MA: Belknap Press of Harvard.

Sassen, S. (1999) *Guests and Aliens*. New York: New Press.

Sen, A. (1999) *Reason before Identity*. Oxford: Oxford University Press.

Smith, A. (1983) *An Inquiry into the Nature and Causes of the Wealth of Nations*. Oxford: [1789] Oxford University Press.

Smith, A. D. (1998) *Nationalism and Modernism: A Critical Survey of Recent Theories of Nations and Nationalism*. London: Routledge.

Smith, A. D. (1983) "Nationalism and Social Theory," *British Journal of Sociology*, 34(1):19–38.

Snyder, J. (2000) *From Voting to Violence. Democratization and Nationalist Violence*. New York: Norton.

Steinberg, S. (1989) *The Ethnic Myth: Race, Ethnicity, and Class in America*, Boston: Beacon Press.

Stoler, A. (1989) "Making Empire Respectable: The Politics of Race and Sexual Morality in 20th Century Colonial Cultures," *American Ethnologist*, 16(4):634–660.

Taguieff, P. (1991) "Le 'Nationalisme des Nationalistes.' Un Problème pour l'Histoire des Idées Politiques en France." In *Theories du Nationalisme*. Ed. G. Delannoi and P-A. Taguieff. Paris: Éditions Kimé.

Taylor, P. J. (1996) "Embedded Statism and the Social Sciences: Opening up to New Spaces," *Environment and Planning*, 28:1917–1928.

Thompson, A. and R. Fevre (2001) "The National Question: Sociological Reflections on Nation and Nationalism," *Nations and Nationalism*, 7(3):297–315.

Torpey, J. (2000) *The Invention of the Passport. Surveillance, Citizenship and the State*. Cambridge: Cambridge University Press.

Ture, K. and C. Hamilton (1992) *Black Power: The Politics of Liberation in America*. New York: Vintage [1967] Books.

Urry, J. (2000) *The Turbulence of Migration: Globalization, Deterritorialization and Hybridity*. London: Routledge.

Wallerstein, I. (1961) *Africa: The Politics of Independence*. New York: Vintage.

Weber, M. (1895) *Der Nationalstaat und die Volkswirtschaftspolitik. Akademische Antrittsrede*. Freiburg: Mohr.

Weed, P. (1973) *The White Ethnic Movement and Ethnic Politics*. New York: Praeger.

Williams, B. F. (1989) "A Class Act: Anthropology and the Race to Nation across Ethnic Terrain," *Annual Review of Anthropology*, 18:401–444.

Wimmer, A. (2002) *Nationalist Exclusion and Ethnic Conflict. Shadows of Modernity*. Cambridge: Cambridge University Press.

Wimmer, A. (1999) "Verwischte Grenzen. Zum Verhältnis zwischen Soziologie, Ethnologie und Volkskunde." In *Borderlines. Soziologie, Kulturanthropologie und Ethnologie*. Ed. C. Giordano. Annali di Sociologia – Soziologisches Jahrbuch 12.

Wimmer, A. (1998) "Binnenintegration und Aussenabschliessung. Zur Beziehung Zwischen Wohlfahrtsstaat und Migrationssteuerung in der Schweiz des 20. Jahrhunderts." In *Migration in Nationalen Wohlfuhrtsstaaten. Theoretische und Vergleichende Untersuchungen*. Ed. M. Bommes and J. Halfmann. Osnabrück: IMIS.

Wimmer, A. (1996) "L'État-Nation – Une Forme de Fermeture Sociale," *Archives Européennes de Sociologie*, 37(1):163–179.

Wyman, M. (1993) *Round-Trip to America: The Immigrants Return to Europe 1880–1930*. Ithaca, NY: Cornell University Press.

Zolberg, A. (1983) "The Formation of New States as a Refugee-generating Process." In *The Global Refugee Problem: U.S. and World Response*. Ed. G. Loescher and J. Scanlan. *The Annals of American Academy of Political and Social Science*, 467.

CHAPTER 10

Assimilation and Transnationalism: Determinants of Transnational Political Action among Contemporary Migrants

Luis Eduardo Guarnizo, Alejandro Portes, and William Haller

[. . .]

Grassroots symbolic and material relations connecting societies across national borders expanded to historic levels during the last third of the 20th century. These transnational connections simultaneously affect more than one nation-state and are often generated from below by human migration (Glick Schiller, Basch, and Szanton Blanc 1992; Basch, Glick Schiller, and Szanton Blanc 1994; Portes 1996; Smith and Guarnizo 1998), social movements (Smith, Chatfield, and Pagnucco 1997; Tarrow 1998), and nongovernmental organizations (Keck and Sikkink 1998; Boli and Thomas 1999). The proliferation of grassroots transnational ties worldwide is a phenomenon of great significance but one that, so far, has received little attention in the sociological literature. Our goal in this article is to investigate one particular form of transnational engagement, namely the political activities conducted by contemporary immigrants across national borders, affecting communities, parties, and official institutions in the sending nations. From this analysis, we hope to draw general lessons modifying conventional expectations of what an immigrant is and what the process of adaptation to the host society is about.

Our main concern is to probe the extent, implications, and social determinants of cross-border political relationships initiated and maintained by contemporary migrants to the United States. Our analysis focuses specifically on the transnational political activities of three major Latin American immigrant groups residing in four major U.S. metropolitan areas. We seek to establish what types, scale, and intensity of political engagement prevail among these immigrants and to determine the individual and social factors that shape such participation.

In the past few years, the term "transnational" has become commonly and conspicuously displayed in the titles of conferences and discussion panels at scholarly meetings in the United States and Europe. This surge in interest has been accompanied, however, by mounting theoretical ambiguity and analytical confusion in the use of the term. Thus, while some scholars have started to embrace and deploy the concept in their work, others have responded with intense skepticism. Seeking to clarify the meaning of the term, several scholars have provided explicit definitions of "transnational migration" and "transnational fields." For Glick Schiller and Fouron (1999, p. 344), for example, "transnational migration is a pattern of migration in which persons, although they move across international borders, settle, and establish relations in a new state, maintain ongoing social connections with the polity from which they originated. In transnational migration people literally live their lives across international borders. Such persons are best identified as 'transmigrants.' "

The problem with this definition is that it does not establish explicit criteria for differentiating those who participate in these activities from those who do not. If the simple act of sending remittances to families or traveling home occasionally qualifies a person as a "transmigrant," the entire field is subject to the charge of banality since it is well known that international migrants have always engaged in these activities (Foner 1997).

The main difficulty with the field of transnationalism, as developed so far, is that its empirical base relies almost exclusively on case studies.[1] While useful, these studies invariably sample on the dependent variables, focusing on those who take part in the activities of interest, to the exclusion of those who do not participate. The unintended result is to exaggerate the scope of the phenomenon by giving the impression that everyone in the studied communities is involved. While the occasional trip home or a sporadic financial contribution to a home country political party certainly helps to strengthen the transnational field, these intermittent activities do not justify by themselves the coining of a new term. It is the rise of a new class of immigrants, economic entrepreneurs or political activists who conduct cross-border activities on a *regular* basis, that lies at the core of the phenomenon that this field seeks to highlight and investigate.[2] These are, to use Glick Schiller and Fouron's (1999) term, the true "transmigrants."

In this article, we focus on the phenomenon of political transnationalism as it manifests itself among immigrant groups in the United States. We have assembled data that allow us to answer or explore three fundamental questions: (1) Is there such a thing as a class of political transmigrants—immigrants who become involved in their home country polities on a regular basis? (2) If so, who are they and what are the main determinants of their participation in this form of activism? (3) If so, are there patterned differences across immigrant nationalities in the incidence and forms adopted by this phenomenon? [. . .]

GROUPS STUDIED

Salvadoran, Dominican, and Colombian immigrants form part of the newest wave of mass immigration in the United States. These groups make up approximately 15% of the Latin American immigrant population (Farley 2001). Despite common cultural origins, these communities represent very different migratory experiences, shaped by the combined effects of global forces and national realities. We expect these national variations to affect, in predictable ways, the course of immigrant adaptation. For this reason, a brief introduction to the history of each group is in order.

Immigrants from Colombia (which has a population of 43 million) first started to arrive in significant numbers in New York and Los Angeles in the wake of the Second World War. The first wave of Colombians was formed mostly by upper-middle-class and professional people. After the 1965 immigration reform, the social composition of the inflow included mostly middle- and working-class immigrants in search of economic improvement (Chaney 1976; Cruz and Castaño 1976; Cardona et al. 1980). Since the mid-1980s, a deepening political and economic crisis in Colombia and growth of the drug trade have resulted in a significant expansion of migration, primarily from urban areas (Urrea-Giraldo 1982).

Recent research points to high levels of mutual distrust among Colombian immigrants stemming from insecurity at home and the shadow of the drug trade (Guarnizo and Diaz 1999): Colombians seldom cluster in tightly knit communities and become dispersed instead in large metropolitan areas. The major destination is New York City, where two-fifths of a U.S. Colombian population estimated at 750,000 resides. Even in New York, these immigrants remain relatively invisible, except in certain sections of Queens, such as Jackson Heights (Guarnizo, Sánchez, and Roach 1999; U.S. Census Bureau 1993c). Because of this spatial dispersion and their relatively high educational levels, Colombians have not been targets of extensive discrimination in the United States—notwithstanding the stigma of drug trafficking attached to Colombia. These circumstances, in addition to their alienation from traditional electoral politics and the convulsed sociopolitical situation of their country, lead us to predict limited involvement in political transnationalism. We suggest that this holds true despite the political rights, including voting rights from abroad and congressional representation, granted to them by the Colombian state. Relative to other groups, Colombians should tend to avoid continuous political engagement with their home nation.

Emigration from the Dominican Republic was severely constrained during the 30-year Trujillo dictatorship, but it suddenly increased after the dictator's assassination in 1961 (Hendricks 1974; Grasmuck and Pessar 1991). At the time, a substantial number of opposition leaders were forcefully expatriated by a provisional government seeking to alleviate domestic pressures. The U.S. government expeditiously issued visas to these deportees and, later, "cooperated at the provisional government's request, by refusing to permit the deportees to leave the United States" (Martin 1966, p. 347). This politically driven out-migration, concentrated in New York City, established the beachhead for subsequent waves of economic immigrants to the same area. By the end of the 1990s, approximately 10% of the Dominican population was residing in the United States (U.S. Census Bureau 1999, p. 12). Areas with a high concentration of Dominicans in New York City, such as Washington Heights, and in some smaller northeast cities such as Providence, Rhode Island, have become sites for intense Dominician economic, cultural, and political activity (Itzigsohn et al. 1999).

Given the political roots of Dominican emigration and the active presence of national parties in this expatriate community, we expect political transnationalism to be relatively more common than among other migrants. The Dominican Republic is at peace and democracy has taken hold, so that active competition for office takes place regularly among the three largest national parties (Lozano 1997). Voting rights for Dominicans living abroad have been approved, and the consul general in New York has been selected in recent years from among leaders of that community (Itzigsohn et al. 1999; Levitt 2001a, 2001b). Such gestures contribute to reinforcing the web of transnational political ties between the sending nation and its emigrants.

Salvadorans come from a small (6.4 million) and densely populated Central American country that has been highly dependent on U.S. economic and geopolitical interests. During the early 1960s, Salvadoran immigration to the United States increased and was dominated by professionals, technocrats, and investors. These well-to-do immigrants opened channels for labor migration by importing Salvadoran domestic workers (Repak 1995; Mahler 1995). The civil war between 1980 and 1992 set off a massive exodus to the United States, mostly from rural areas (Aguayo and Fagen 1988; Montes Mozo and Garcia Vasquez 1988; Zolberg, Suhrke, and Aguayo 1989; Córdoba 1995; Lungo 1997). By 1999, about half of the total Salvadoran immigrant population in the United States, estimated at over 800,000, resided in the Los Angeles metropolitan area (U.S. Census Bureau 1999; Waldinger and Bozorgmehr 1996; Chinchilla, Hamilton, and Loucky 1993). The Washington, D.C., metropolitan area hosts the second largest concentration of Salvadorans, with an estimated population of close to 250,000 (Landolt, Autler, and Baires 1999, p. 293).

Although the majority of Salvadorans left their country because of political violence, their claims to asylum were routinely denied by U.S. authorities, who classified them as illegal immigrants (Lopez, Popkin, and Tellez 1996). Despite their precarious legal and economic status, Salvadoran migrants managed to maintain close ties with their communities and families of origin and to support them economically. Their remittances have consistently surpassed $1 billion per year during the last decade and constitute the country's single most important source of foreign exchange today (Banco Central de El Salvador 1996; Landolt 2000).

Most Salvadoran immigrants come from small towns and rural areas severely affected by the country's civil war. The strong bonds forged during that war were sustained and expanded after the country returned to peace. A still incipient democracy and frail political parties have failed to create many opportunities for migrant participation in Salvadoran electoral politics. Instead, expatriates and their organizations have concentrated their efforts at the local level, seeking to aid and improve their communities of origin (Landolt 2000; Menjivar 2000). Salvadoran transnationalism can thus be expected to follow a distinct course, defined by the historical context under which the original migration took place: unlike Colombians, Salvadorans are expected to sustain strong ties with their country of origin; unlike Dominicans they do not channel such ties through national political parties but link directly with the towns and regions of origin.

As previously noted, all three sending nations have implemented policies designed to sustain the loyalty of their expatriates and to encourage a continuing flow of remittances and investments (Guarnizo et al. 1999; Landolt 2000; Levitt 2001b). Despite these common policies, we expect the three groups to differ systematically even after controlling for individual variables. These differences reflect their distinct histories of departure and resettlement, as just seen. Table 10.1 presents a profile of the countries of origin and characteristics of each immigration according to the latest official figures.

DATA AND METHOD

Data for this study come from the Comparative Immigrant Enterprise Project (CIEP), a collaborative effort focused on entrepreneurship and institutional development among the three groups described.[3] The project included both qualitative and quantitative data gathered between fall 1996 and winter 1998. The first phase of the study consisted of in-depth interviews with 353 key informants in six areas of immigrant concentration in the United States (two for each nationality) and two cities, including the capital, of each country of origin. The second phase was

Table 10.1 Immigrants' country of origin and U.S. profile

	Colombians	Dominicans	Salvadorans
Country of origin:			
2001 population (in millions)	43.0	8.5	6.4
2001 GDP per capita ($)	1,916	2,494	2,141
1997 income share of poorest quintile (%)*	3.0	5.1	3.7
1997 income share of richest quintile (%)*	60.9	53.3	55.3
1997 Gini index of income inequality*	.57	.47	.51
2000 average years of education*	8.9	9.3	8.3
1999 open unemployment (%)*	14.7	15.9	7.0
1999 informal employment (%)*	46.3	44.0	35.0
1990 households below poverty line (%)	41.0	32.0	40.0
Capital city	Bogotá	Santo Domingo	San Salvador
U.S. immigrant population:			
Size (in thousands), 1999	435	692	765
Rank in recorded immigration	16	14	8
Arrived in 1990s (%)	41.3	42.3	39.6
Naturalized by 1999 (%)	38.6	33.8	19.7
Most common destination	New York City	New York City	Los Angeles
Median age, 1990	34.4	32.5	28.7
High school graduates (%)†	66.8	41.9	32.5
College graduates†	15.7	7.8	4.7
Professional occupations (%)†	17.0	10.8	5.8
Median household income‡	29.1	19.9	23.5

Note:—Data are drawn from International Labour Organization (2000, 2003), ECLAC (2003), U.S. Census Bureau (1993a), Camarota (2001), Farley (2001), and the World Bank (2003a, 2003b).
* Statistics reflect conditions in urban areas. For Colombians, "2000 average years of education" (8.9) is drawn from 1999 data and "1999 informal unemployment" (46.3) is drawn from 2001 data.
† Education completion is measured in persons 25 years old and older; professional occupations is measured among employed persons 16 years and older.
‡ In thousands of 1989 dollars.

a probability survey of immigrant communities in four cities corresponding to the principal areas of concentration of the target nationalities. Dominicans were contacted and interviewed in the Washington Heights area of Manhattan and in Providence, Rhode Island; the Colombian survey took place in New York City, mainly in the borough of Queens; and the Salvadoran survey was conducted simultaneously in central and selected suburban areas of Los Angeles and Washington, D.C. The CIEP survey was completed in 1998, gathering data on a total of 1,202 adult family heads.[4]

The survey can be considered representative of each immigrant nationality in its principal areas of concentration, especially because nonresponse rates were uniformly low. However, sampling fractions—the ratio of the sample to the eligible population in each area—varied significantly among surveyed communities. To adjust for this problem we developed a set of weights based on the estimated sampling fraction in each area. Sampling fractions were computed by dividing the final sample by 1990 Census figures of the adult population of the target nationality in each area. Weights are the reverse of these sampling fractions (Kish 1967; Frankel 1983). The adjusted figures allow us to compare national samples and avoid unequal probability bias in the estimation of coefficients based on the full sample. [. . .]

Conventionally, political participation is measured by electorally related indicators. However, immigrants also seek to be represented and participate in decision making through political means other than elections. Thus, under the concept of transnational political participation, we include both electoral and nonelectoral activities aimed at influencing conditions in the home country. Each type of political participation is measured by a count of the number of activities in which respondents are involved on a regular basis. Transnational electoral participation includes membership in a political party in the country of origin, monetary contributions to these parties, and active involvement in political campaigns in the polity of origin. Transnational nonelectoral politics includes membership in a hometown civic association, monetary contributions to civic projects in the community of origin, and regular membership in charity organizations sponsoring projects in the home country.

Nonelectoral activities of this type are political because they influence local and regional governments by determining which public projects receive migrants' financial support. By so doing, they compel authorities to take immigrant wishes and priorities into account. As Levitt (1997a, 1997b) and Landolt (2000) have noted, helping finance local development projects or contributing to philanthropic works represent effective mechanisms to uphold high status and political influence in the localities of origin.[5]

Questionnaire items measuring involvement in each of these six types of political activities provided three response categories: "never," "occasionally/once in a while," and "regularly." In keeping with the previous theoretical discussion concerning reasons for operationally restricting the meaning of transnationalism, our primary focus in the following analysis is on activities in which respondents were involved on a regular basis. This definition identifies the class of migrants who have become most committed to transnational political action. As noted previously, however, the transnational field is also nurtured by the more occasional activities of other immigrants, and we also pay attention to these activities.

Among independent variables, age, sex, marital status, and years of U.S. residence are self-measured by individual questionnaire items. National origin corresponds to the original survey screening question used to determine sampling eligibility. Education is measured as years completed, coded into three ordered achievement categories. U.S. citizenship acquisition is coded "1" if the respondent had naturalized American and "0" otherwise. Corresponding to the remaining hypotheses, urban/rural places of origin are coded into three mutually exclusive size categories (large city, small city, and rural); SEDs of migration is a dummy variable coded "1" if the respondent's family expected the journey abroad to be temporary and "0" otherwise; downward mobility is the ratio of the occupational status of the last regular job in the country of origin to the first in the United States. Higher values of this variable, coded along a five-point status scale, indicate greater downward mobility.

Network size is measured by the absolute number of persons in the respondent's social networks, and network spatial scope by the ratio of out-of-town contacts, including those living abroad, to those in the city of residence. Both measures are drawn from a name-generator module in the CIEP questionnaire, designed to elicit first names and characteristics of individuals on whom respondents could rely for both occupational and personal needs (Burt and Minor 1983; Scott 1991; N. Lin 1998). The CIEP data set provides the first quantitative estimates of the phenomenon of transnationalism, allowing us to examine effects of both network size and spatial scope on each dependent variable.[. . .]

RESULTS

General Characteristics of the Sample

Table 10.2 presents a general profile of the sample. It shows that respondents are, on average, middle-aged and married; they arrived in the United States at a prime productive age, mainly from urban metropolitan areas, and have resided here for some 15 years. Close to one-third had become U.S. citizens by the time of the survey, but one-fourth still have children living in the country of origin and almost one-fifth travels there on a regular basis. Average group characteristics of the CIEP sample correspond in order of magnitude to figures from the 1990 census (see Table 10.1). Both indicate that Colombians are on average older, have higher levels of educational attainment and personal incomes, and the highest rate of naturalization (44%) of the three groups. Dominicans are mostly at the opposite end regarding educational attainment and income, while Salvadorans exhibit the lowest naturalization rate.[6]

Table 10.3 presents frequency distributions of transnational political activism based on the strict definition adopted previously and on a more inclusive approach that includes both regular and occasional partici-

pation in these activities. The latter results show that the transnational field engages, in one form or another, up to a third of each immigrant group. Core transnational activists, on the other hand, are much less numerous, representing less than one-sixth of the sample. This figure contrasts markedly with past ethnographic descriptions of transnationalism as a form of political action adopted by entire immigrant communities. Around these averages, however, there are statistically significant variations by nationality: Dominican immigrants are most likely to engage in electoral party politics and Salvadorans most likely to focus on hometown civic committees and community projects; close to one-fifth of the Salvadoran sample takes part in these kinds of activities on a regular basis. Differences by nationality correspond to our predictions based on the known contexts of exit and reception of each group. To separate these group effects from those of individual-level factors, we incorporate all predictors in models of political transnationalism, defined strictly and loosely.

Predictive Models

Our dependent variable, the number of transnational political activities in which immigrants become involved, is a count variable with a range of 0–6. Following the preceding definition, regular participation or involvement is coded "1" and occasional or no participation "0." The use of linear regression for this dependent variable can result in inconsistent, inefficient, or biased estimates. The distribution of such variables is commonly modeled as a Poisson process. Deviations of the univariate distribution from Poisson are usually accounted for by heterogeneity in the average rate and are modeled accordingly (Long 1997, p. 221).

Poisson regression models rarely fit the data, however, because of the assumption of equidispersion in the conditional distribution, $\mu_i = \delta = \exp(x_i\beta)$. In practice, the variance frequently exceeds the mean. Preliminary analysis shows that this condition, known as overdispersion, is present in our data. Negative binomial regression models (NBRM) obviate this constraint by replacing

Table 10.2 Characteristics of the CIEP sample (%)

Variable	Colombians	Dominicans	Salvadorans	All
Personal characteristics:				
Sex (male)...	52.1	41.8	63.3	53.2***
Average age (years)...	43.3	42.1	39.6	41.1***
Married..	54.7	55.4	51.8	53.6**
High school graduate	82.0	49.3	50.9	54.9***
Monthly income:				
$2,000—$4,000...	31.0	9.3	14.4	15.2***
Over $4,000...	11.9	3.9	9.7	8.0***
Characteristics of migration:				
Place of origin:				
Rural..	17.0	9.9	31.5	20.9***
Small/medium city...	22.5	10.9	34.5	23.4***
Large city..	60.5	79.2	34.2	55.8***
Place of current residence[a]:...............................				
Los Angeles			80.3	36.8
New York...	100.0	96.7		52.9
Providence		3.3		1.3
Washington, D.C..			19.7	9.0
Age at immigration (in years)	26.2	26.8	25.3	26.0***
Years in U.S.	17.0	15.2	14.3	15.1***
U.S. citizen..	43.6	35.4	24.8	31.8***
Home country ties:				
Children in country of origin...............................	22.3	22.0	31.2	26.3***
Invests in country of origin................................	6.5	5.4	5.3	5.4
Travels annually to country of origin.....................	17.0	20.5	18.6	19.1*
N (unweighted)	311	418	473	1,202

Note:—P values are from F-test of significance of between-group differences. Definitions and measurements of variables appear in app. table B1.
[a] Weighted samples are used for residence in U.S. cities.
* P <.003.
** P <.001.
*** P <0001.

the conditional mean μ_i by a random variable μ_i where $\mu_i = \exp(x_i\beta + \varepsilon_i)$ and ε_i is random error uncorrelated with x_i The conditional mean of the negative binomial distribution is the same as the Poisson distribution, but the variance differs (Long 1997, p. 233). The extent of overdispersion is estimated by the NBREG routine of Stata, which also provides a likelihood ratio test of significance.

Predictor variables in our models follow the preceding theoretical discussion and include gender, education, size of community of origin, years in the United States, SEDs of migration, downward mobility, and national origin. As control variables, we add the linear and quadratic forms of age and marital status. The CIEP survey contains several different measures of respondents' social networks. Following the preceding discussion, we include network size (absolute number of respondent's social ties) and scope (the ratio of long-distance to local ties in the city of residence). The assumption is that larger and more geographically dispersed networks will be more conducive to transnational activism.

NBR coefficients can be transformed into percentages indicating the net increase/decrease in the relative probabilities of the dependent variable associated with a unit increase in each predictor. For clarity of presentation, we present these figures for all NBR coefficients that are statistically significant. The percentage change associated with significant coefficients has the advantage of not depending on the value of other predictors, unlike NBR coefficients that predict the actual count of transnational activities contingent on other variables. We use robust variance estimators to correct for the two-stage cluster sample design in different cities.

Table 10.3 Transnational political practices

	Regular Engagement (%)				At Least Occasional Engagement (%)			
	Colombian	Dominican	Salvadoran	All	Colombian	Dominican	Salvadoran	All
Electoral politics:								
Membership in home country political party	10.0	12.6	7.6	9.9	18.7	22.8	14.3	18.3
Gives money to home country political party	2.3	10.8	5.6	7.2	5.1	15.8	9.8	11.5
Takes part in home country electoral campaigns and rallies	3.2	12.4	5.2	7.7	10.6	18.8	10.7	13.8
Nonelectoral politics:								
Membership in a civic hometown association	7.1	9.6	19.3	13.7	18.0	19.9	37.5	27.7
Gives money for community projects in home country	6.1	8.5	12.8	10.1	18.7	18.4	33.6	25.4
Membership in charity organization active in home country	13.2	6.4	21.5	14.3	29.9	21.6	40.3	31.4

Note:—Data are drawn from CIEP (1998). All between-group differences are significant at the .001 level.

The corrected variances do not affect the actual coefficients, but they adjust for understimation of errors that can lead to inflated Z-scores. Robust standard errors provide a much more demanding criterion for statistical significance than ordinary ones so that regression coefficients that meet this criterion can be confidently tagged as reliable.

Table 10.4 presents our results in two sets of columns. The first regresses political transnationalism, defined according to the strict criterion given above. These results provide the main source for our conclusions. The second column redefines the dependent variable based on a broader definition of transnationalism that codes as "I" both regular and occasional involvement in each of the activities counted as part of the index. These results allow us to examine to what extent determinants of political transnationalism vary according to the empirical definition of the concept.

The first column of the table highlights the nonlinear effect of age, as indicated by a significant negative quadratic coefficient. This means that engagement in transnational politics increases substantially during adulthood but declines in old age. The gender and marital status coefficients show that transnational activists are overwhelmingly married males. The column presenting the percentage change associated with each significant coefficient indicates that the gender effect is very strong, with males being over twice more likely to be involved in these activities. The tendency increases by an additional 13% for those married.

Both high school and college graduations lead to significant increases in the probability of political transnationalism. The high school effect is the strongest, exceeding 10 times its standard error and increasing regular engagement in these activities by 173% relative to nongraduates. These results supports predictions based on conventional theories of political participation rather than on those

Table 10.4 Negative binomial regressions of immigrant political transnationalism on selected predictors, 1998

	Transnationalism, Strict Definition			Transnationalism, Broad Definition		
	Coefficient	Z	% Change	Coefficient	Z	% Change
Demographic:						
Age................................	.101	3.10**	10.6	.032	2.08*	3.3
Age²	−.001	−2.90**	−.1	−.000	−1.50	. . .
Gender (male)	1.209	2.27*	235.3	.710	2.22*	103.4
Marital status (married)	.118	4.41***	12.6	−.056	−1.39	. . .
Place of origin:						
Large city	.185	.51	. . .	−.135	−1.03	. . .
Small city or town	.099	.27	. . .	−.132	−.78	. . .
Human capital:						
High school graduate	1.003	10.00***	172.7	.646	5.74***	90.8
College graduate	.324	3.00**	38.3	.320	3.44**	37.3
Assimilation;						
Years in United States.............	.034	7.25***	3.5	.010	1.08	. . .
U.S. citizen	−.041	−.30	. . .	.189	1.66	. . .
Downward mobility[a]	−.058	−.43	. . .	−0.007	−0.25	. . .
Temporary SEDs	.440	4.36***	55.3	.218	2.76**	24.4
Social networks:						
Network size	.095	5.42***	10.0	.078	3.49***	8.2
Network scope[b]	−.84	−1.25	. . .	−0.031	−.79	. . .
Nationality:						
Colombian..........................	−1.212	−19.85***	−70.2	−1.077	−15.84***	−65.9
Salvadoran	−.018	−.31	. . .	−.021	−.50	. . .
Constant	−5.813		. . .	−2.148		
α[c]	2.037	3.66***		.837	2.44*	
LR (2)		2331.25***			2731.87***	
Pseudo-R^2		.104			.078	

Note:—Data for predictors is a weighted sample. For description of the variables, see app. table B1. The reference category for "place of origin" is "rural"; for "human capital," It is "less than high school education", for "nationality," it is "Dominican." The significance levels and z-scores are computed with robust estimates of SEs.
[a] Ratio of last home country occupation to first occupation in the United States.
[b] Radio of nonlocal to local ties in respondent's city of residence.
[c] Test of equidispersion of conditional variance. Higher values indicate departures from the assumption that $\mu = \sigma = \exp(x, \beta)$ and, hence, the inappropriateness of Poisson regression models for these data.
* $P < .05$.
** $P < .01$.
*** $P < .001$.

derived from assimilation theory. Other hypotheses derived from the same perspective are also unsupported by the data: U.S. citizenship acquisition has no effect on the dependent variables, and length of U.S. residence actually increases the probability of political transnationalism.

These findings suggest that it is not the least educated, more marginal, or more recent arrivals who are most prone to retain ties with their home country politics. While running contrary to conventional expectations concerning immigrant assimilation, a moment's reflection suffices to make sense of these results. Educated immigrants are more capable of following events in their home

countries and seeking a role in them; the passage of time and acquisition of U.S. citizenship do not necessarily reduce this interest since their assimilative potential is balanced by the greater security and stability that they produce. A U.S. passport enables former migrants to travel back and forth without restrictions; greater time in the United States is usually associated with economic stability and more resources to invest in favored political causes.

The hypothesis concerning significant effects of urban versus rural origins is not supported by the data, nor is that predicting greater transnational activism among the downwardly mobile. We interpret these results as supportive of the previous findings, indicating that transnationalism is not a compensatory mechanism for migrants most affected by the traumas of adaptation to urban life or those suffering from status loss. We further interacted downward mobility with gender to test Jones-Correa's (1998) notion that the proclivity of males to engage in home country politics is a consequence of status loss. The resulting coefficient (not shown) is statistically insignificant and does not alter the pattern of effects presented in Table 10.4. Once again, it appears that transnationalism is not a refuge for the marginal and downtrodden, but a practice associated with greater stability and greater resources brought from the home country.

The hypothesis of socially expected duration is, however, strongly supported. Immigrants whose families expect them to return at some point (temporary SEDs) are significantly more likely to retain political ties with their countries than those never expected to return. The increase in the count of regular transnational activities brought about by the temporary SEDs is 55%. Along the same lines, respondents with larger social networks are much more likely to participate. We find that it is the size of the networks rather than their physical location that makes the difference. Each additional tie, regardless of whether it is local or not, increases the count of transnational activities by 10%.[7] Taken together, these findings indicate that political transnationalism is associated with well-connected migrants who remain normatively attached to their home communities by kin and friendship ties.

With Dominicans as the reference category, results show that Colombian immigrants are the least likely to take part in home country politics, while Salvadorans and Dominicans are about equally likely to do so. The Colombian negative coefficient is very strong, exceeding 19 times its standard error. This finding is important for two reasons: first, it confirms the influence of national origin and the associated contexts of exit and reception for each immigrant group; second, it fits well the history of each nationality and its particular resettlement experiences. Colombians want little to do with their coun-

try's politics, having escaped a situation of profound instability, official corruption, and widespread violence. The return to social peace in El Salvador and the relative political stability in the Dominican Republic facilitate regular cross-border ties by their expatriates, though, as we will see, their form and determinants also vary.

A look at the second sets of columns of Table 10.4 shows that "broad" political transnationalism follows a parallel course, but that effects are generally weaker. For example, the gender effect is more than halved, while that of high school graduation drops 82 percentage points. Importantly, neither marital status nor length of U.S. residence have significant effects in this alternative definition of the dependent variable. This suggests that the greater stability associated with marriage and permanent settlement in the United States increases the probability of regular, core transnational engagement but has no bearing on occasional participation. Broad political transnationalism emerges from this analysis as a diluted version of the strict version. It is affected by the same set of determinants, only less so. A probable reason is that occasional transnationalism is conjunctural and, hence, less dependent on the social and educational resources and political traditions that sustain regular involvement.

Table 10.5 summarizes our results to this point, indicating how each hypothesis has fared in the analysis as predictor of both versions of the dependent variable and the resulting evaluation of the underlying theories. Classic assimilation predictions are consistently rejected while those stemming from gender differences and contexts of exit and reception are supported. Political transnationalism is, in this analysis, strongly associated with national origin and a product of greater human capital, greater stability and experience in the receiving society, plus strong social connections and enduring moral ties with sending communities.

Interaction Effects

The resilient effects of national origin on both dependent variables suggests that different contexts of exit and reception may not only

Table 10.5 Theoretical results of analysis of determinants of political transnationalism

	Observed Effects		
Theory and Hypothesis	Strict	Broad	Conclusion
Classic assimilation:			
Years of U.S. residence (+)	+	0	Reject
U.S. citizenship (−)	0	0	Reject
Education (−)	+	+	Reject
Conventional political participation:			
Education (+)	+	+	Support
Gender differences:			
Males (+)	+	+	Support
Contextual embeddedness of immigration:			
Rural origin (+)	0	0	Reject
Temporary SEDs (+)	+	+	Support
Downward mobility (+)	0	0	Support
National origins:			
Colombians (−)	−	−	Support
Dominicans (+)	+	+	Support
Salvadorans (community politics +)	+	+	Support
Social networks:			
Size (+)	+	+	Support
Scope(+)	0	0	Reject

Note:—A negative sign represents the prediction or finding of an inverse relationship between each individual predictor and the dependent variable; a positive sign indicates the opposite; a zero indicates no relationship. Signs in parentheses indicate the predictions associated with each theory.

affect political transnationalism additively, but also interact with other predictors. We examine this possibility by running separate regressions for each immigrant nationality of political transnationalism on the same set of predictors considered previously. Because determinants of broad transnationalism continue to have parallel, albeit weaker effects than those bearing on a strict definition of the concept, we omit them from this analysis. Table 10.6 presents these results, which reveal several major differences among the three groups. The last column of the table presents formal tests of significance of these differences.[8] The overall trend is for Colombian transnationalism to be not only exceptional but also more weakly determined. This is shown by the corresponding R^2 and the few predictors that achieve statistical significance in this case.

For Colombians, only place of origin and a college education affect the dependent variable. The original hypothesis concerning the positive effect of rural origins on the perpetuation of home country ties is supported in this instance. In addition, college graduation also increases participation in these

activities. Hence, it appears that whatever transnational political activism exists among Colombian immigrants, it follows a bimodal pattern involving highly educated individuals and those coming from traditional rural areas. As seen before, most Colombians show little inclination to engage in home country politics of any kind. Since migrants from that country come increasingly from urban areas and experience a dominant political culture of disengagement (Guarnizo and Diaz 1999), our results suggest that this pattern of disinterest in transnational activities may become even stronger in the future.

Dominicans and Salvadorans are much more vigorously involved in the politics of their home countries. The corresponding regressions introduce controls for city of residence, since both national samples were drawn from more than one city. No statistically significant differences between areas of residence were found in either case. In both cases, however, network size increases transnationalism significantly: each additional tie raises the net count of Dominican transnational activities by 16% and the count for Salvadorans by 9%. The effect of education

Table 10.6 Negative binomial regressions of political transnationalism by immigrant nationality, 1998

Transnationalism (Strict Definition)

Predictors	Colombians Coefficient	Z	% change	Dominicans Coefficient	Z	% change	Salvadorans Coefficient	Z	% change	P^a
Demographic:										
Age	.052	.71	...	.163	2.36*	17.7	.103	1.60	...	NS
Age²	.000	−.43	...	−.002	−2.28*	−.2	−.001	−1.61	...	NS
Gender	−.137	−.47	...	2.316	6.21***	913.7	.701	3.15**	101.6	.001
Marital status	.396	1.35	...	−.025	−.08	...	.104	.52	...	NS
Place of origin:										
Large city	−1.082	−3.34***	−66.1	.574	1.04	...	.382	1.57	...	.001
Small city or town	−1.184	−3.14**	−69.4	.603	.94	...	.240	.96	...	.01
City of residence:										
Providence, R.I.	...	...	...	.073	.14	...	...	...	...	...
Washington, D.C.	...	...	...	...	...	...	−.136	−.70	...	...
Human capital:										
High school graduate	.553	1.26	...	1.005	3.25***	173.6	1.156	4.81***	217.7	NS
College graduate	.811	2.69**	125.1	−.022	−.05	...	.416	1.84	...	NS
Assimilation:										
Years in U.S.	.023	1.31	...	.026	1.34	...	.023	1.18	...	NS
U.S. citizen	.461	1.29	...	.034	−.10	...	.066	−.26	...	NS
Downward mobility	−.057	−.42	...	−.538	−2.33*	−41.6	.081	.98	...	.05
Temporary SEDs	.171	.53	...	.562	1.85	...	.423	2.17*	52.7	NS
Social networks:										
Network size	.038	1.89	...	.150	3.42**	16.2	.084	4.02***	8.8	.05
Network scope	.159	.84	...	−2.53	−.95	...	−.073	−.33	...	NS
Constant	−4.102			−8.003			−5.427			
α	2.458	3.78***		1.927	3.52***		1.232	4.38***	129.07***	
Wald χ²		53.72***			163.52***					
Pseudo R^2		.08			.19				.11	
National origin effect on transnationalism:										
Electoral	−1.372	−9.02***	−74.6	...	...	...	−1.112	−7.29***	−67.1	.05
Community	−.981	−37.18***	−62.5	...	...	...	.491	5.96***	63.5	NS

Note.—Description of variables can be found in app. table B1. Significance levels and z-scores computed with robust estimates of SE. For "place of origin," "rural" in the reference category; for "city of residence," "New York is the omitted category for Dominicans and Los Angeles" is the reference category; in "assimilation," "downward mobility" is the ratio of the last home country occupation to the first occupation in the United States; for Salvadorans; for "human capital," "less than high school" is the reference category; in "social networks," "network scope" is the ratio of nonlocal-to-local ties in the respondents city of residence. In "national origin effect on transnationalism," we control for all other predictors included in table 10.4 above; no results are reported for Dominicans, as they are the reference category in this predictor. NS = nonsignificant interaction effect.

^{a} This column reports the significance of interaction effect between each predictor and national origins. * $P < .05$. ** $P < .01$. *** $P < .001$.

is also similar for both groups. Since so few Salvadoran or Dominican immigrants are college educated, the key human capital effect is that of high school graduation and it is quite strong in both cases. Differences between Salvadorans and Dominicans, on the one hand, and Colombians, on the other, in the effects of social networks are significant, as shown in Table 10.6. Differences in the interaction effects between education and nationality approach, but fail to achieve, statistical significance.

The same pattern is evident with gender effects. Unlike Colombians, among whom gender is an insignificant predictor, Dominican and Salvadoran males are much more likely to participate in transnational politics. The effect is especially strong among Dominicans, where it exceeds six times its standard error. Temporary SEDs of migration have positive effects among Dominicans and Salvadorans, but only the latter effect is significant, increasing the count of transnational activities by 53%. By contrast, the effect of downward occupational mobility proves to be significant among Dominican immigrants only. In this instance, the direction of the effect runs contrary to the original hypothesis: instead of increasing the tendency to engage in transnational activity, downward mobility actually decreases it. The interaction between nationality and this variable is significant, as shown in the last column.

Where Dominican and Salvadoran immigrants differ most is in the *orientation* of their respective political activities. This was observed in Table 10.3 and is further illustrated by the net effect of nationality on each sub-type of transnationalism, controlling for other variables. These are presented in the bottom rows of Table 10.6. With Dominicans as the reference category, the Salvadoran effect on party politics is significant and negative and that on civic community activism is significant and positive. As expected, Colombian effects are uniformly negative. These results support the conclusion that Dominican immigrants are more likely to concentrate on party politics, while Salvadorans bypass it to focus on the affairs of their local hometowns and regions.

Thus, the meaning and scope of political transnationalism is not uniform. Although there are common forces bearing on all immigrants, the particular circumstances of each community also affect the extent and character of these activities. For some immigrants, transnational politics is a means to maintain an active presence in their country's centers of power; for others, it is a means to avoid such centers in order to provide direct assistance to their native regions; and for still others, it is a practice to be avoided in order to leave a violent and unsettling past behind. [. . .]

NOTES

1. Studies of various transnational activities have been conducted among a number of immigrant groups in the past. These include Brazilians (Margolis 1994); Central Americans (Hamilton and Chinchilla 1991; Mahler 1995, 1998, 1999); Dominicans (Georges 1990; Grasmuck and Pessar 1991; Portes and Guarnizo 1991; Levitt 2001*b*; Graham 1997; Guarnizo 1998; Sorensen 1998); Ecuadorans (Kyle 2000); Mexicans (Massey et al. 1987; Rouse 1992; Massey et al. 1994; Massey and Parrado 1994; R. Smith 1994, 1998; Goldring 1998); Haitians (Glick Schiller et al. 1995; Glick Schiller and Fouron 1999, 2001); Filipinos (Basch et al. 1994; Wolf 1997); Chinese (Zhou 1992; Mitchell 1997; Smart and Smart 1998; J. Lin 1998; Ong 1999); and Indians (Lessinger 1992). With the exception of the studies by Massey and his collaborators and Kyle's work on Ecuadorans, most of this literature is nonquantitative and based on ethnographic evidence.

2. Transnational engagement is not limited solely to public sphere activities, though. Transnational actors also include members of families or households residing in more than one country who maintain steady relations with each other (i.e., providing economic, social, and emotional support and keeping family relations, loyalties, and obligations alive) across borders (see Kyle 2000, pp. 102–12; Glick Schiller and Fouron 2001, chap. 4; Gardner and Ralph Grillo 2002).

3. The project involved an initial collaborative agreement between Johns Hopkins University, the University of California at Davis, and Brown University. It is currently headquartered at the Center for Migration and Development, Princeton University.

4. The CIEP sample was gathered through a two-pronged sampling design that aimed at providing representative data on the respective immigrant communities while including a sufficient number of economic and political entrepreneurs for subsequent analysis. The core survey was a two-stage random sample of households in areas of

immigrant concentration. Within target census tracts, city blocks were designated as primary sampling units (PSUs) and selected through random sampling. In selected PSUs, a systematic canvassing of each fourth or fifth household was conducted to determine eligibility. If a target household proved ineligible because of different nationality or other characteristics, it was replaced. This sampling fraction preserved sample representativeness by keeping the number of interviews in each PSU (city block) proportional to the size of its eligible population (Kish 1967). This design was supplemented by a purposive sample of entrepreneurs identified through informant leads gathered during the first phase of the project. The number and diversity of informants insured multiple entry points to entrepreneurial activities, giving the sample broad coverage of such activities in each community and avoiding the familiar limitations of single snowball chains (Singleton and Straits 1999, pp. 156–63).

5. A recent study in El Salvador based on the first phase of this project concluded that "life conditions in municipalities that receive grassroots transnational aid confirm the relevance of this collective remittance strategy. Towns with a hometown association have paved roads, electricity, and freshly painted public buildings. The quality of life in transnational towns is simply better" (Portes and Landolt 2000, p. 543).

6. Figures in Tables 10.1 and 10.2 do not coincide because of the differences in dates of data collection and target universes. Census figures are for the entire population of each nationality in 1990; the CIEP survey data are limited to adult heads of the three nationalities in these respective areas of concentration.

7. We recognize that social networks can also be strengthened by transnational activities and, hence, that the relationship between both variables may involve a causal loop. However, commonsense scholarship and our own in-depth interviews during the first phase of CIEP indicate that socially isolated immigrants are unlikely to take the first steps toward transnational political participation. It is well-connected immigrants, both locally and abroad, who are most motivated and able to take part in these activities. Their networks can be increased as a result, but the primary causal linkage runs in the direction of social contacts leading to transnational involvement.

8. This is a Wald test of significance of the interaction effects between nationality and each individual predictor. It is computed by comparing the NBR coefficients associated with each X_jN_i predictor in a pooled regression where X_j equals the predictor variable and N_i equals each specific nationality (see Judge et al. 1985, pp. 20–28; McDowell 2001; StataCorp 1999).

References

Aguayo, Sergio, and Patricia Weiss Fagen. 1988. *Central Americans in Mexico and the United States*. Washington, D.C.: Hemispheric Migration Project, Center for Immigration Policy and Refugee Assistance, Georgetown University.

Banco Central de El Salvador. 1996. Personal interviews. October 17.

Basch, Linda, Nina Glick Schiller, and Cristina Szanton Blanc. 1994. *Nations Unbound: Transnational Projects, Postcolonial Predicaments and the Deterritorialized Nation-State*. New York: Gordon & Breach.

Boli, John, and George M. Thomas, eds. 1999. *Constructing World Culture: International Nongovernmental Organizations since 1875*. Stanford, Calif.: Stanford University Press.

Burt, Ronald, and M. Minor. 1983. *Applied Network Analysis*. Newbury Park, Calif.: Sage Publications.

Camarota, Steven A. 2001. "Immigrants in the United States 2000. A Snapshot of America's Foreign-Born Population." Report. Center for Immigration Studies, Washington, D.C., January.

Cardona, Ramiro, Carmen Inés Cruz, Juanita Castaño, Elsa M. Chaney, Mary G. Powers, and John J. Macisco Jr. 1980. *El éxodo de colombianos: Un estudio de la corriente migratoria a los Estados Unidos y un intento para propiciar el retorno*. Bogotá: Ediciones Tercer Mundo.

Chaney, Elsa M. 1976. "Colombian Migration to the United States (Part 2)." Pp. 87–141 in *The Dynamics of Migration: International Migration*. Interdisciplinary Communications Program, Occasional Monograph Series 5.2. Washington, D.C.: Smithsonian Institution.

Chinchilla, Norma, Nora Hamilton, and James Loucky. 1993. "Central Americans in Los Angeles: An Immigrant Community in Transition." Pp. 51–78 in *In the Barrios: Latinos and the Underclass Debate*, edited by Joan Moore and Raquel Pinderhughes. New York: Russell Sage Foundation.

Córdoba, Carlos. 1995. "Central American Migration to San Francisco: One Hundred Years of Building a Community." Working paper in Central Americans in California: Transnational Communities, Economies and Cultures series. University of Southern California, Center for Multiethnic and Transnational Studies.

Cruz, Carmen Inés, and Juanita Castaño. 1976. "Colombian Migration to the United States (Part 1)." Pp. 41–86 in *The Dynamics of Migration: International Migration* Interdisciplinary Communications Program, Occasional Monograph Series 5.2. Washington, D.C.: Smithsonian Institution.

ECLAC (Economic Commission for Latin America and the Caribbean). 2003. *Indicadores de desarrollo social*. http://www.eclac.cl/publicaciones/Desarrollo-Social/ 3/LCG2183Pl/Anexos_2002

Farley, Reynolds. 2001. "Immigrants and Their Children: Evidence from the Census Bureau's Recent

Survey." Paper presented at the meetings of the American Sociological Association, Anaheim, Calif.

Foner, Nancy. 1997. "What's New about Transnationalism? New York Immigrants Today and at the Turn of the Century." Paper presented at the Transnational Communities and the Political Economy of New York in the 1990s Conference, New School for Social Research, February.

Frankel, Martin. 1983. "Sampling Theory." Pp. 21–67 in *Handbook of Survey Research*, edited by P.H. Rossi, J. D. Wright, and A. B. Anderson. New York: Academic Press.

Gardner, Katy, and Ralph Grillo, eds. 2002. Special issue: "Transnational Households and Ritual." *Global Networks: A Journal of Transnational Affairs* 2(3).

Georges, Eugenia. 1990. *The Making of a Transnational Community: Migration, Development, and Cultural Change in the Dominican Republic*. New York: Columbia University Press.

Glick Schiller, Nina, Linda Basch, and Cristina Szanton Blanc, eds. 1992. *Toward a Transnational Perspective on Migration: Race, Class, Ethnicity and Nationalism Reconsidered*. New York: Annals of the New York Academy of Sciences.

——. 1995. "From Immigrant to Transmigrant: Theorizing Transnational Migration." *Anthropological Quarterly*, 68 (1): 48–63.

Glick Schiller, Nina, and George E. Fouron. 1999. "Terrains of Blood and Nation: Haitian Transnational Social Fields." *Ethnic and Racial Studies* 22 (2): 340–66.

——. 2001. *Georges Woke Up Laughing: Long Distance Nationalism and the Search for Home*. Durham, N.C.: Duke University Press.

Goldring, Luin. 1998. "The Power of Status in Transnational Social Fields." Special issue, "Comparative Urban and Community Research. *Transnationalism from Below* 6:165–95.

Graham, Pamela M. 1997. "Reimagining the Nation and Defining the District: Dominican Migration and Transnational Politics." Pp. 91–126 in *Caribbean Circuits: New Directions in the Study of Caribbean Migration*, edited by Patricia Pessar. New York: Center for Migration Studies.

Grasmuck, Sherri, and Patricia Pessar. 1991. *Between Two Islands: Dominican International Migration*. Berkeley and Los Angeles; University of California Press.

Guarnizo, Luis Eduardo. 1998. "The Rise of Transnational Social Formations: Mexican and Dominican State Responses to Transnational Migration." *Political Power and Social Theory* 12: 45–94.

Guarnizo, Luis Eduardo, and Luz M. Diaz. 1999. "Transnational Migration: A View from Colombia." *Ethnic and Racial Studies* 22 (March): 397–421.

Guarnizo, Luis Eduardo, Arturo Ignacio Sánchez, and Elizabeth M. Roach. 1999. "Mistrust, Fragmented Solidarity, and Transnational Migration: Colombians in New York City and Los Angeles." *Ethnic and Racial Studies* 22 (2): 367–96.

Hamilton, Nora, and Norma Stolz Chinchilla. 1991. "Central American Migration: A Framework for

Analysis." *Latin American Research Review* 26 (1): 75–110.

Hendricks, Glenn L. 1974. *The Dominican Diaspora: From the Dominican Republic to New York City—Villagers in Transition*. New York: Teachers College Press.

International Labour Organization. 2000. "Panorama laboral: La estructura del empleo urbano en el periodo 1990–1998." Report of the ILO Regional Office. http:// www.ilolim.org.pc/panorama/1999.

——. 2003. *General Labor Statistics*. http://laborstat.ilo.org/cgi-bin/brokerv8.exe

Itzigsohn, Jose, Carlos Dore, Esther Hernandez, and Obed Vazques. 1999. "Mapping Dominican Transnationalism: Narrow and Broad Transnational Practices." *Ethnic and Racial Studies* 22 (2): 316–39.

Jones-Correa, Michael. 1998. "Different Paths: Gender, Immigration and Political Participation." *International Migration Review* 32 (2): 326–49.

Judge, G. G., W. E. Griffiths, R. C. Hill, H. Lütkepohl, and T. C. Lee. 1985. *The Theory and Practice of Econometrics*, 2d ed. New York: John Wiley & Sons.

Kearney, Michael. 1995. "The Local and the Global: The Anthropology of Globalization and Transnationalism." *Annual Review of Anthropology* 24:547–65.

Keck, Margaret E., and Kathryn Sikkink. 1998. *Activists beyond Borders: Advocacy Networks in International Politics*. Ithaca, N.Y.: Cornell University Press.

Kish, Leslie. 1967. *Survey Sampling*. New York: Wiley.

Kyle, David. 2000. *Transnational Peasants; Migrations, Networks, and Ethnicity in Andean Ecuador*. Baltimore: Johns Hopkins University Press.

Landolt, Patricia. 2000. "The Causes and Consequences of Transnational Migration: Salvadorans in Los Angeles and Washington, D.C." Ph.D. dissertation. Johns Hopkins University, Department of Sociology.

——. 2001. "Salvadoran Economic Transnationalism: Embedded Strategies for Household Maintenance and Immigrant Incorporation." *Global Networks* 1 (July): 217–41.

Landolt, Patricia, Lilian Autler, and Sonia Baires, 1999. "From Hermano Lejano to Hermano Mayor: The Dialectics of Salvadoran Transnationalism." *Ethnic and Racial Studies* 22 (2): 290–315.

Lessinger, Johanna. 1992. "Investing or Going Home? A Transnational Strategy among Indian Immigrants in the United States." Pp. 53–80 in *Towards a Transnational Perspective on Migration*, edited by Nina Glick Schiller, Linda Basch, and Cristina Blanc-Szanton. New York: Annals of the New York Academy of Sciences.

Levitt, Peggy. 1997a. "Transnationalizing Community Development: The Case of Migration between Boston and the Dominican Republic." *Nonprofit and Voluntary Sector Quarterly* 26 (4): 509–26.

——. 1997b. "Variations in Transnationalism: Lessons from Organizational Experiences in Boston and the Dominican Republic." Working draft. Department of Sociology, Harvard University.

——. 2001*a*. "Transnational Migration: Taking Stock and Future Directions." *Global Networks* 1 (July): 195–216.

——. 2001*b*. *The Transnational Villagers*. Berkeley and Los Angeles: University of California Press.

Lin, Jan. 1998. *Reconstructing Chinatown; Ethnic Enclave, Global Change*. Minneapolis: University of Minnesota Press.

Lin, Nan, 1998. "The Position Generator: A Measurement of Social Capital." Paper presented at the Conference on Social Networks and Social Capital, Duke University, October 30–31.

Long, Scott J. 1997. *Regression Models for Categorical and Limited Dependent Variables*. Thousand Oaks, Calif.: Sage.

Lopez, David, Eric Popkin, and Edward Tellez, 1996. "Central Americans: At the Bottom, Struggling to Get Ahead." Pp. 279–304 in *Ethnic Los Angeles*, edited by Roger Waldinger and Mehdi Bozorgmehr. New York: Russell Sage Foundation.

Lozano, Wilfredo. 1997. "Dominican Republic: Informal Economy, the State, and the Urban Poor." Pp. 153–89 in *The Urban Caribbean: Transition to the New Global Economy*, edited by A. Portes, C. Dore, and P. Landolt. Baltimore: Johns Hopkins University Press.

Lungo, Mario, ed. 1997. *Migración international y desarrollo*, vols. 1 and 2. San Salvador: Funde.

Mahler, Sara J. 1995. *American Dreaming: Immigrant Life on the Margins*. Princeton, N.J.: Princeton University Press.

——. 1998. "Theoretical and Empirical Contributions toward a Research Agenda for Transnationalism." Pp. 64–100 in *Transnationalism from Below*, vol. 6: *Comparative Urban and Community Research*, edited by Michael Peter Smith and Luis Eduardo Guarnizo. New Brunswick, N.J.: Transaction.

——. 1999. "Engendering Transnational Migration: A Case Study of Salvadorans." *American Behavioral Scientist* 42 (4): 690–719.

Margolis, Maxine L. 1994. *Little Brazil; An Ethnography of Brazilian Immigrants in New York City*. Princeton, N.J.: Princeton University Press.

Martin, John B. 1996. *Overtaken by Events: The Dominician Crisis—from the Fall of Trujillo to the Civil War*. Garden City, N.Y.: Doubleday.

Massey, Douglas S., Rafael Alarcón, Héctor González, and Jorge Durand. 1987. *Return to Aztlán: The Social Process of International Migration from Western Mexico*. Berkeley and Los Angeles: University of California Press.

Massey, Douglas S., Luin Goldring, and Jorge Durand. 1994. "Continuities in Transnational Migration: An Analysis of Nineteen Mexican Communities." *American Journal of Sociology* 99:1492–533.

Massey, Douglas S., and Emilio Parrado, 1994. "Migradollars: The Remittances and Savings of Mexican Migrants to the USA." *Population Research and Policy Review* 13:3–30.

McDowell, Allen. 2001. "Testing the Equality of Coefficients Across Independent Regressions." In Stata FAQs, available from http://www.stata.com/support/faqs/stat/testing/html. College Station, Tex.: Stata Corporation.

Menjívar, Cecilia. 2000. *Fragmented Ties: Salvadoran Immigrant Networks in America*. Berkeley and Los Angeles: University of California Press.

Mitchell, Katharyne. 1997. "Transnational Discourse: Bringing Geography Back In." *Antipode* 29:101–14.

Montes Mozo, Segundo, and Juan Jose Garcia Vasquez. 1988. *Salvadoran Migration to the United States: An Exploratory Study*. Georgetown University Hemispheric Migration Project, Center for Immigration Policy and Refugee Assistance, Washington, D.C.

Ong, Aihwa. 1999. *Flexible Citizenship*. Durham, N.C.: Duke University Press.

Portes, Alejandro. 1996. "Transnational Communities: Their Emergence and Significance in the Contemporary World System." Pp. 151–68 in *Latin America in the World Economy*, edited by Roberto Patricio Korzeniewicz and William C. Smith. Westport, Conn.: Greenwood Press.

Portes, Alejandro, and Luis E. Guarnizo. 1991. "Tropical Capitalists: U.S.-bound Immigration and Small Enterprise Development in the Dominican Republic." Pp. 37–59 in *Migration, Remittances, and Small Business Development*, edited by Sergio Díaz-Briquets and Sidney Weintraub. Boulder, Colo.: Westview.

Portes, Alejandro, and Patricia Landolt. 2000. "Social Capital: Promise and Pitfalls of Its Role in Development." *Journal of Latin American Studies* 32:529–47.

Repak, Terry A. 1995. *Waiting on Washington: Central American Workers in the Nation's Capital*. Philadelphia: University Press.

Rouse, Roger. 1992. "Making Sense of Settlement: Class Transformation, Cultural Struggle, and Transnationalism among Mexican Migrants in the United States." Pp. 25–52 in *Towards a Transnational Perspective on Migration: Race, Class, Ethnicity, and Nationalism Reconsidered*, edited by Nina Glick Schiller, Linda Basch, and Cristina Blanz-Szanton. New York: New York Academy of Science.

Scott, J. 1991. *Network Analysis: A Handbook*. Newbury Park, Calif.: Sage.

Singleton, Royce A., and Bruce C. Straits. 1999. *Approaches to Social Research*, 3d ed. New York: Oxford University Press.

Smart, Alan, and Josephine Smart. 1998. "Transnational Social Networks and Negotiated Identities in Interactions between Hong Kong and China." Pp. 103–29 in *Transnationalism from Below*, vol. 6: *Comparative Urban and Community Research*, edited by Michael Peter Smith and Luis Eduardo Guarnizo. New Brunswick, N.J.: Transaction.

Smith, Jackie, Charles Chatfield, and Ron Pagnucco, eds. 1997. *Transnational Social Movements and Global Politics: Solidarity beyond the State*. Syracuse, N.Y.: Syracuse University Press.

Smith, Michael P., and Luis Eduardo Guarnizo, eds. 1998. *Transnationalism from Below*, vol. 6: *Comparative Urban and Community Research*. New Brunswick, N.J.: Transaction.

Smith, Robert C. 1994. "Los Ausentes Siempre Presentes: The Imagining, Making and Politics of Transnational Communities between the U.S. and Mexico." Ph.D. dissertation. Columbia University, Department of Political Science.

Sørensen, Ninna Nyberg. 1998. "Narrating Identity across Dominican Worlds." Pp. 241–69 in *Transnationalism from Below*, vol. 6: *Comparative Urban and Community Research*, edited by Michael Peter Smith and Luis Eduardo Guarnizo. New Brunswick, N.J.: Transaction.

StataCorp. 1999. *Stata Users Guide*, vol. 4, ver. 6.0. College Station, Tex.: Stata.

Tarrow, Sidney. 1998. *Power in Movement: Social Movements and Contentious Politics*. 2d ed. Cambridge: Cambridge University Press.

Urrea-Giraldo, Fernando. 1982. "Life Strategies and the Labor Market: Colombians in New York City in the 1970s." Occasional Paper no. 34. New York University, Center for Latin American and Caribbean Studies.

U.S. Census Bureau. 1993a. *The Foreign-Born Population of the United States, 1990*. CPH-L-98. Washington, D.C.: Government Printing Office.

——. 1993c. *1990 Census of the Population—Social and Economic Characteristics—New York*. Sec. I, Washington, D.C.: Bureau of the Census.

——. 1999. *Profile of the Foreign-Born Population in the U.S.* Current Population Reports, Series P23–195. Washington, D.C.: Government Printing Office.

Waldinger, Roger, and Mehdi Bozorgmehr. 1996. "The Making of a Multicultural Metropolis." Pp. 3–37 in *Ethnic Los Angeles*, edited by Roger Waldinger and Mehdi Bozorgmehr. New York: Russell Sage Foundation.

Wolf, Diane L. 1997. "Family Secrets: Transnational Struggles among Children of Filipino Immigrants." *Sociological Perspectives* 40 (Fall): 455–82.

World Bank. 2003a. *World Development Indicators Database*. April. http://worldbank.org/data/countrydata.html

——. 2003b. *Health, Nutrition, and Population Statistics*. http://devdata.worldbank.org/hnpstats/files/tab2_8.xls

Zhou, Min. 1992. *Chinatown: The Socioeconomic Potential of an Urban Enclave*. Philadelphia: Temple University Press.

Zolberg, Aristide, Astri Suhrke, and Sergio Aguayo. 1989. *Escape from Violence: Conflict and the Refugee Crises in the Developing World*. New York: Oxford University Press.

CHAPTER 11

"Introduction" from *Forces of Labor: Workers' Movements and Globalization since 1870*

Beverly J. Silver

I. CRISIS OF LABOR MOVEMENTS AND LABOR STUDIES

During the last two decades of the twentieth century, there was an almost complete consensus in the social science literature that labor movements were in a general and severe crisis. Declining strike activity and other overt expressions of labor militancy (Screpanti 1987; Shalev 1992), falling union densities (Western 1995; Griffin, McCammon, and Botsko 1990) and shrinking real wages and growing job insecurity (Bluestone and Harrison 1982; Uchitelle and Kleinfeld 1996) were among the trends documented. The bulk of the empirical literature focused on trends in wealthy countries (especially North America and Western Europe), yet many saw the crisis as world-scale, adversely affecting labor and labor movements around the globe.

This sense that labor movements are facing a general and severe crisis contributed to a crisis in the once vibrant field of labor studies. As William Sewell (1993: 15) noted: "Because the organized working class seems less and less likely to perform the liberating role assigned to it in both revolutionary and reformist discourses about labor, the study of working class history has lost some of its urgency" (see also Berlanstein 1993: 5).

For many, this double crisis of labor studies and labor movements is long term and structural—intimately tied to the momentous transformations that have characterized the last decades of the twentieth century going under the general rubric of "globalization." For some, the crisis is not just severe, it is *terminal*. Aristide Zolberg, for one, argued

that late-twentieth-century transformations have brought about the virtual disappearance of "the distinctive social formation we term 'working class.' " With "post-industrial society," the "workers to whose struggles we owe the 'rights of labor' are rapidly disappearing and today constitute a residual endangered species" (1995: 28). Similarly, Manuel Castells argued that the dawn of the "Information Age" has transformed state sovereignty and the experience of work in ways that undermine the labor movement's ability to act as "a major source of social cohesion and workers' representation." It also has undermined any possibility that workers might become emancipatory "subjects" in the future—the source of a new "project identity" aimed at rebuilding the social institutions of civil society. Non-class-based identity movements, for Castells, are the only "potential subjects of the Information Age" (1997: 354, 360).

Nevertheless, beginning in the late 1990s, a growing number of observers were suggesting that labor movements were on the upsurge, most visible as a mounting popular backlash against the dislocations being provoked by contemporary globalization. Among the events indicating a backlash was the massive French general strike against austerity in 1995—what *Le Monde* rather Eurocentrically referred to as "the first revolt against globalization"[1] (quoted in Krishnan 1996: 4). By the time of the World Trade Organization meeting in Seattle in November 1999, the force of the backlash was sufficient to derail the launch of another round of trade liberalization and to be front-page news around the world. Commentators began to suggest that the Seattle demonstrations together with the new activist (organizing) stance of the AFL-CIO (American Federation of Labor and Congress of Industrial Organizations) were signs that a revitalized U.S. labor movement was "rising out of the ashes" of the old (Woods et al. 1998; more broadly, Panitch 2000). Inspired by the new activism, social scientists in the United States, where the obituary of labor movements and labor studies had been written most insistently, showed a resurgent interest in labor movements. New journals were founded that sought to actively engage academics with the labor movement (e.g., *Working USA*), large academic conferences on the new labor movement were organized, and a new section of the American Sociological Association on labor movements was founded in 2000.

For some, the new activism (while still scattered and weak) was potentially the first sign of an impending major earthquake of mass labor insurgency. For others, it was likely to remain too weak and scattered to affect the much more powerful, disorganizing forces of globalization.

Which of these divergent expectations about the future of labor movements is more plausible? This book starts from the premise that in order to answer this question adequately we need to recast labor studies in a longer historical and wider geographical frame of analysis than is normally done. Assessments about the future of labor movements are based—explicitly or implicitly—on a judgment about the historical novelty of the contemporary world. Those who see a terminal crisis of labor movements tend to see the contemporary era as one that is *fundamentally new and unprecedented*, in which global economic processes have completely reshaped the working class and the terrain on which labor movements must operate. In contrast, those who expect the reemergence of significant labor movements tend to perceive historical capitalism itself as being characterized by recurrent dynamics, including the continual re-creation of contradictions and conflict between labor and capital. This suggests that forecasts about the future of labor movements should be based on a comparison between contemporary dynamics

and analogous past periods. For only through such a comparison can we distinguish historically recurrent phenomena from phenomena that are truly new and unprecedented. [. . .]

IV. RESEARCH STRATEGIES

The Time and Space of Labor Unrest

As mentioned at the outset of this chapter, a central premise of this book is that a full understanding of the dynamics of contemporary labor movements requires that we cast our analysis in a longer historical and wider geographical frame than is normally done. Assessments about the future of labor movements are based—explicitly or implicitly—on a judgment about the historical novelty of the contemporary world. Those who see a terminal crisis of labor movements tend to see the contemporary era as one that is *fundamentally new and unprecedented*, in which global economic processes have completely reshaped the working class and/or the terrain on which labor movements must operate. In contrast, those who expect the reemergence of significant labor movements tend to perceive historical capitalism itself as being characterized by recurrent dynamics, including the continual creation of contradictions and conflict between labor and capital. To the extent that this latter perspective is plausible, it suggests that forecasts about the future of labor movements must be based on a comparison of contemporary dynamics with analogous dynamics of past historical periods. Thus, the book reaches back in time in search of patterns of recurrence and evolution, so as to be able to isolate what, if anything, is truly novel about the situation currently facing labor movements.

The justification for widening the geographical scope of the analysis beyond that which is typical in labor studies is, in part, related to the same issue of *newness*. It is by now fairly commonplace to assume that the fate of workers and labor movements in one locale can crucially affect the outcome of labor–capital conflict in another locale (especially as mediated through processes of trade and capital mobility). Nevertheless, this assumption is widely regarded as relevant only for the study of late-twentieth-century labor movements and beyond, not for earlier periods, because contemporary globalization is seen as a fundamental historical divide.

Yet, if globalization is taken to mean "an increase in the geographical range of locally consequential social interactions" (Tilly 1995), then, as many argue, the current period of globalization is not the first such period. Among those who see globalization as a recurrent phenomenon, there is some debate about how far back in history globalization processes can reasonably be identified.[2] Nevertheless, there is widespread agreement among these same individuals that strong analogies exist between the current phase of globalization and the late nineteenth century. Indeed, some argue that the interconnectedness of national economies and societies is no greater today than it was at the end of the nineteenth century—that is, the period widely taken to mark the birth of the modern labor movement.

One clear example of late-nineteenth-century interconnectedness (and one with a significant impact on labor and labor movements) is the massive global labor migration of that period.[3] This migration played a major role both in transmitting styles of labor unrest and in precipitating Polanyi-esque movements of "self-protection" (i.e., campaigns to restrict immigration). This example simultaneously demonstrates the strong interconnectedness of late-nineteenth-century economies and societies and the relevance of this interconnectedness for labor movement behavior and outcomes, while also suggesting that late-twentieth-century globalization (with its tighter restrictions on labor mobility) is not a simple repeat of the past.

In broad terms, then, a central methodological premise of the book is that workers and workers' movements located in different states/regions are linked to each other by the world-scale division of labor and global political processes. An understanding of *relational processes among "cases" on a world scale across both time and space* is fundamental to understanding the dynamics of labor movements since at least the late nineteenth century.

Throughout the book, special attention will be paid to both "direct" and "indirect" relational processes. In the case of direct relational processes, the actors are aware of and consciously promoting the links among the cases. These direct relational processes can take two different forms: diffusion and solidarity. In the case of diffusion, actors located in "cases" that are separated in time and space are influenced by the spread of information about the behavior of others and its consequences (Pitcher, Hamblin, and Miller 1978). "Social contagion" is a common image used in the methodological literature on diffusion. The contagion of a language of workers' rights "caught" by African trade unionists (discussed earlier) would be one example of diffusion. This type of diffusion can take place without active cooperation between the source site and recipient site of the "social disease" (e.g., cooperation between European and African trade unionists). In contrast, the second form of direct relational processes singled out earlier—that is, solidarity—involves personal contact and the development of social networks—transnational social networks in the case of labor internationalism (Tarrow 1998; McAdam and Rucht 1993: 69–71; Keck and Sikkink 1998).

In the case of indirect relational processes, the affected actors are often not fully conscious of the relational links. Rather, actors are linked behind their back by systemic processes including the unintended consequences of a series of actions and reactions to what we have been calling the system-level problem. If a strong labor movement leads capitalists to respond by relocating production to a new site (thus weakening labor in the de-industrializing site but strengthening labor in the industrializing site), then we can say that the fates of these two labor movements are linked by indirect relational processes. Indeed, the implicit argument underlying the "new international division of labor" literature is that industrialization in low-wage areas and de-industrialization in high-wage areas have been two sides of the same coin. (See, among others, Fröbel et al. 1980; Bluestone and Harrison 1982; Sassen 1988; MacEwan and Tabb 1989; Dicken 1998.)

In the example of late-nineteenth-century migration, we can detect both indirect and direct relational processes linking labor movements across time and space. The spread of labor movement ideologies and practices as workers moved across the globe (referred to earlier) is an example of diffusion. But, we can also detect critical indirect relational processes. The U.S. labor movement's success in having open immigration outlawed in the 1920s set the stage for the stabilization of the U.S. working class and contributed to the subsequent CIO (Congress of Industrial Organizations) victories in the 1930s. At the same time, however, this U.S. labor movement "success" shut off what had been an essential social safety valve for Europe in the nineteenth century. It thereby transformed the terrain on which workers' movements operated in Europe and, according to E. H. Carr (1945), helped set the stage for the defeat of European labor movements and the rise of fascism.

Lumping and Splitting the World Labor Movement

By making the relationship among cases across time and space a central part of the explanatory framework, this book departs in strategy from the comparative-historical approach to labor studies. The comparative-historical perspective, like the approach outlined here, criticizes the strategy of making generalizations from one or a limited number of cases, and thus calls for a widening of the geographical scope of the analysis. In particular, comparative-historical scholars have criticized the tendency in traditional labor studies to set up a single model of working-class formation (the so-called master narrative) as the standard against which all actual historical experiences are judged as "exceptional" or "deviant" (Katznelson and Zolberg 1986: 12, 401, 433). Instead, the approach involves a "variation finding" strategy that analyzes how the *same* experience of proletarianization has led to *different* outcomes. Put differently, much of the comparative-historical literature follows the strategy of "splitting" in search of distinctiveness, in contrast to the strategy of "lumping" cases in search of commonalties and generalizations (Hexter 1979: 241–3; Collier and Collier 1991: 13–15). These differences in outcome are then generally traced to preexisting and *independently produced* differences in the *internal* characteristics of the various cases.[4]

While some of the most interesting recent scholarship in labor studies comes out of the comparative historical approach, a total reliance on the comparative-historical strategy impedes full access to what we take to be a key explanatory variable of labor movement behavior and outcomes (i.e., the relationships among the cases themselves). As Charles Tilly (1984: 146) among others has pointed out, the results of a strict cross-national analysis may be misleading. A social unit's connection to the whole system of social relationships in which it is embedded "frequently produces effects [that] seem to be autonomous properties of the social unit itself." As a result, the patterned diversity among social units *appears* to be consistent with cross-national variation-finding explanations. This has been referred to as Galton's problem in the anthropology literature: that is, in a situation in which cases are *presumed* to be independent—but are actually linked relationally—the relations among the cases become a lurking (unexamined) variable. In the examples given earlier, and throughout the book, similarity/variation is not merely the outcome of the cases' similar/different independent and preexisting internal characteristics. Rather, relationships among the cases, and relationships between the cases and the totality, are key parts of the explanation of similar/different outcomes.[5]

In sum, the perspective adopted in this book requires an analytical strategy that is sensitive to the relational processes among key actors (labor, capital, states) in the system as a whole, as well as the systemic constraints affecting those actors. Needless to say, such an approach presents enormous problems of complexity, and a strategy for reducing complexity and making research feasible is needed.

The most well-known strategy for reducing the complexity of world-historical analysis is what Tilly (1984) labeled "encompassing comparison" and is best illustrated by Immanuel Wallerstein's approach to the study of the "modern world-system" and John Meyer's approach to the study of "world society" (see, e.g., Wallerstein 1974; Meyer et al. 1997). Encompassing comparisons reduce complexity by starting "with a mental map of the whole system and a theory of its operation." Similarities/differences in the attributes and behavior of the units are then traced to their similar/different position within the overarching totality (Tilly 1984: 124). Meyer's "mental map" of the system leads him to emphasize a growing convergence among national cases as a result of a world-scale process of "rationalization." Wallerstein's mental map, in contrast, leads him to emphasize a process of recurrent geographical differentiation among core and periphery resulting from the unequal distribution of rewards in a capitalist world economy. Yet for both, local attributes and behavior are seen as the product of a unit's location in the system. The larger system has a steamroller-like quality transforming social relations at the local level along a theoretically expected path.[6]

The strength of this perspective is that it emphasizes the very real constraints that the totality imposes on the range of possible action open to local actors. But its weakness is that it excludes a priori a situation in which local action (agency) significantly impacts local outcomes, much less a situation in which local agency impacts the operation of the system as a whole. Moreover, as should be clear from the preceding discussion of borders and boundary drawing, the units of the system cannot be part of an initial mental map because they themselves are constructed, and this process of construction is itself a critical part of the story of working-class formation.

Thus, while keeping in focus the real systemic constraints that the totality imposes on local actors, this study cannot adopt the "encompassing comparison" approach as a strategy for reducing complexity. Instead, the research strategy followed in this book most closely resembles what Phillip McMichael (1990) called "incorporating comparison"—a strategy in which the interactions among a multiplicity of subunits of the system are seen

as *creating* the system itself over time. The resultant conceptualization is one in which relational processes in space unfold in and through time.

The most appropriate type of causal analysis for the strategy adopted here—and the primary one used in this book—is a modified version of the narrative mode advocated by most comparative-historical sociologists. The narrative strategy, Larry Griffin (1992: 405) argued, allows us to understand social phenomena "as temporally ordered, sequential, unfolding, and open-ended 'stories' fraught with conjunctures and contingency." As a strategy for *explanation*, "descriptively accurate narratives, which depict a sequence of events in chronological order . . . do more than tell a story," according to Jill Quadagno and Stan Knapp (1992: 486, 502). Such narratives can "serve, among other purposes, to identify causal mechanisms" because "when things happen . . . affects how they happen."[7]

But while historical-sociologists have stressed the importance of treating *time* as dynamic, they have generally continued to treat *space* as static (e.g., conceptualizing national cases as fixed, independent units). This may be seen as a reasonable strategy for reducing the complexity of the analysis. However, as should be clear by now, it is not a strategy that can be followed here. In contrast, this book attempts to create a narrative of working-class formation in which events unfold in *dynamic time-space*.[8]

Having rejected the two most common strategies for reducing complexity in the study of macro-historical social change (i.e., encompassing comparison and cross-national comparative research), the problem of managing the complexity of the analysis remains. A first complexity-reduction strategy used here is to place limits on the number of levels at which the analysis simultaneously proceeds. In an attempt to unpack the class-in-itself/class-for-itself "master narrative," Katznelson and Zolberg (1986: 14–21) distinguish four levels at which the study of working-class formation should proceed. These are (1) the structure of capitalist economic development, (2) ways of life, (3) dispositions, and (4) collective action. This book is primarily an analysis of the interrelationship between the first and the fourth level (i.e., the interrelationship between the political-economic dynamics of world capitalist development and the world-historical patterning of labor unrest). Levels 2 and 3 are touched upon at various points, but no attempt is made to integrate these levels systematically into the analyses presented here.

In leaving aside Katznelson's second and third levels, we are also sidestepping a whole range of issues that have been the subject of ongoing trench warfare in labor studies.[9] In some cases, our intention *is* to abstain from the debate. For example, no particular assumption is being made here about the relationship between intense phases of labor militancy and the presence or absence of working-class consciousness (or the exact nature of that consciousness). As E. P. Thompson suggested, it is possible, even likely, that class consciousness emerges out of struggles; that is, "in the process of struggling" the protagonists "discover themselves as classes" (Thompson 1978: 149; see also Fantasia 1988; McAdam et al. 2001: 26). Or, it is possible that important transformations in cognition must take place before collective action can emerge.[10] It is also possible that major waves of labor militancy are neither preceded by, nor lead to the development of something we might meaningfully call working-class consciousness. While it would no doubt be important to uncover patterned relationship between collective action and consciousness, to do so for the macrohistorical sweep of cases included here, *in a way that is methodologically relational and dynamic*, is simply unfeasible in the context of this book.

Moreover, our choice of levels would seem to imply a favoring of structural processes over cultural processes in explaining global and historical patterns of labor militancy. This is not strictly the case. It is true that at various points the book makes a strong claim that the patterns of labor unrest being described *cannot* be attributed to cultural factors. Most notably, a central argument of Chapter 2 is that *strikingly similar* labor movements emerged among mass production autoworkers in *vastly different* cultural

and political settings over the course of the twentieth century. Moreover, the anomalous (and least conflict-prone) case in the chapter —Japan[11]—shares a cultural tradition of Confucianism with one of the most conflict-prone cases analyzed in the chapter (Korea). If, as in Chapter 2, we treat different national movements, not as independent fixed entities, but as interrelated parts of an unfolding systemic totality, then cultural explanations of cross-national *differences* often prove less than compelling.

All this is not to say that there are no differences between the kind of language and symbols that labor movements use to mobilize in, say, Brazil, South Africa, Japan, or South Korea. Moreover, it is not to say that these different symbols and rituals of mobilization are not attributable to distinct cultural heritages. Nevertheless, for a book such as this, whose main focus is on explaining the long-term, world-scale patterning of labor movements, such cultural *differences between* national labor movements are less relevant than the *relationships among* these movements.

It is also true that most of the relationships among workers and workers' movements emphasized in this book are classically "structural" in nature (e.g., the impact of the geographical location and relocation of productive capital on the world-scale distribution of employment and workers' bargaining power). Nevertheless, some are "cultural" in nature. Section III pointed to some ways in which labor movements are linked to each other through what we might call macrocultural relational processes—or the culture of world capitalism. For example, we have already referred to the transnational diffusion of a discourse about workers' and citizens' rights carried by migrating workers. This might be conceptualized as a form of transnational cultural diffusion *from below*. But we have also referred to the role of empires (e.g., the British and French empires in Africa) in spreading discourses about universal rights that were later picked up and transformed into a basis for legitimating claims made by local labor movements. This second type might be labelled a form of transnational cultural diffusion *from above*.

This type of diffusion plays a central role in the story told in Chapter 4, where a Gramscian concept of world hegemony is employed in the analysis of the post-Second World War period. U.S. world hegemony is seen, among other things, as a transnational cultural construct that attempted to formulate a response at the cultural level to the worldwide waves of labor unrest and revolutionary upheavals of the first half of the twentieth century. In so doing, it also inadvertently provided universal cultural elements for framing and legitimating challenges by workers' movements well beyond the borders of the United States.

A final note of clarification is needed with regard to our approach to Katznelson and Zolberg's fourth level—collective action. This book does not attempt to analyze all forms of workers' collective action.[12] Our focus is rather on periods of particularly intense labor unrest—what Piven and Cloward (1992: 301–5) labeled episodes of nonnormative conflict, or what McAdam et al. (2001: 7–8) call "transgressive action."[13] These major waves of labor unrest, rather than more institutionalized forms of protest, provoke capitalists/states to implement innovations and are thus the most relevant form of labor unrest for understanding periods of dramatic transformation in the world capitalist system (e.g., the contemporary phase of globalization). Put differently, by focusing on these major waves of labor unrest, we expect to be able to analyze both the Polanyi-esque pendulum swings and the Marxian stages conceptualized in Section III, and hence better understand the shifting grounds on which contemporary world labor movements unfold.[14]

This brings us to our final strategy for reducing the complexity of the analysis. This book would have been impossible to write without an empirical map of the time-space patterning of labor unrest. This map allows us to identify the times/places of major waves of labor unrest and thus has provided a way to navigate a path through the bewildering totality of potentially relevant episodes of labor unrest in the world over the past century. In other words, it allows us to identify patterns across time/space and thus make informed decisions about what (where/when)

to study more closely. The empirical map allows us to "lump" and "split" cases as a tactic for uncovering patterns; the latter will be explained through the construction of relational narratives. The empirical map, successively drawn in the following chapters, is based on a new data source on labor unrest that covers the world for the entire twentieth century—the World Labor Group (WLG) database—to which we now turn.

Mapping World-Scale Patterns of Labor Unrest: The World Labor Group Database

In order to pursue the research strategy set out here, we need a picture of the overall patterning of labor militancy. The picture must be of sufficient historical and geographical scope to allow for an examination of the potential feedbacks among local level actions as they unfold over time. Given our emphasis on the totality of relationships among local actions, we need this information for all the potentially related cases (i.e., for the social whole), in this case, for the world from the beginnings of the modern labor movement in the late nineteenth century to the present.

Until recently, information on labor unrest of such historical and geographical scope simply did not exist. Long-term time series of strike activity—the most commonly used indicator of labor unrest—exist only for a handful of core countries. For most countries, either there are no strike statistics at all, or they begin only after the Second World War. Furthermore, with the exception of the United Kingdom, all countries' series contain major gaps (e.g., during the period of fascism and world wars in Germany, France, and Italy and for a period in the early twentieth century when the U.S. government decided to discontinue strike data collection). Moreover, the strike statistics that do exist are often collected according to criteria that exclude what may be very relevant strikes from the point of view of measuring "labor unrest." For example, most countries at one time or another have excluded "political strikes" from the official count of strike activity. Yet, workers' demands directed at their states (e.g., through political strikes) rather than at their employers have been a critical dimension of world-scale labor unrest throughout the twentieth century.

Data collections covering nonstrike forms of labor unrest are even more rare, yet they are important to the overall construction of a map of labor unrest. The strike is not the only significant form in which labor unrest is expressed. Labor unrest frequently manifests itself in nonstrike forms of struggle ranging from slowdowns, absenteeism, and sabotage to demonstrations, riots, and factory occupations. Anonymous or hidden forms of struggle such as undeclared slowdowns, absenteeism, and sabotage are especially significant in situations where strikes are illegal and open confrontation difficult or impossible.

This book relies on a new database specifically designed to overcome the geographical (core-centric), temporal (short-term), and action-type (strike-oriented) limitations of previously existing data sources on labor unrest. The World Labor Group database was specifically designed for the kind of dynamic global analyses of labor unrest carried out in this book.[15] Building on a well-established tradition within the social sciences, the WLG constructed the database by using information from newspaper reports of labor unrest (strikes, demonstrations, factory occupations, food riots, etc.) throughout the world beginning in 1870. The result is a database with over 91,947 "mentions" of labor unrest for 168 "countries" covering the 1870–1996 period. The remainder of this section will provide a brief overview of issues related to the construction and use of the WLG database.

Tapping major newspapers as a source to construct indexes of social protest (including labor unrest) has become a fairly widespread and developed practice in the social sciences. Existing studies have used information gleaned from local/national newspapers to measure occurrences of local/national protest. The WLG's goal, however, was to construct reliable indicators of *world* labor unrest. Recording all reports of labor unrest from a major national newspaper for *each* country in the world over the past century would have been an unfeasible project. Moreover, even if the data collection effort were

feasible, intractable problems of comparability of data sources would arise in attempting to combine the information retrieved from different national sources into a single world indicator. The WLG's solution was to rely, at least initially, on the major newspapers of the world's two hegemonic powers—*The Times* (London) and the *New York Times*.

There were several reasons behind the choice of sources. First, *The Times* (London) and the *New York Times* have had world-level information-collecting capabilities throughout the twentieth century. As a result, geographical bias rooted in the technological limits of newspaper reporting is not a major problem (especially with respect to *The Times*). Second, as the major newspapers of the two world-hegemonic powers of the twentieth century, the two sources' coverage is more likely to be global than alternative sources. Third, while the reporting of both newspapers can be expected to be global, both are also likely to show regional biases in favor of areas that have been historically considered special spheres of influence or interest (e.g., South Asia and Australia for *The Times* [London] and Latin America for the *New York Times*). Combining the two sources into a single indicator of world labor unrest helps to counterbalance the regional biases of each source taken separately. (Because of the overwhelming bias of each source in favor of domestic events, we excluded reports of labor unrest in the United Kingdom from our search of *The Times* [London] and reports of labor unrest in the United States from the *New York Times*.)

Individual members of the research group read through the Indexes of *The Times* (London) and the *New York Times* from 1870 to 1996 and recorded each incident of labor unrest identified onto a standard data collection sheet. Working from a conceptualization of labor as a "fictitious commodity" (see discussion of Marx and Polanyi), the goal was to identify all reported acts of resistance by human beings to being treated as a commodity, either at the workplace or in the labor market. This would include all consciously intended open acts of resistance (but also "hidden" forms of resistance when these were widespread, collective practices). Labor unrest generally targets either the employer directly or the state as an intermediary or as an agent of capital. Nevertheless, given the importance of boundary drawing in workers' efforts to protect themselves from being treated as a commodity (see Section III), mobilization by one group of workers against competition from another group of workers was also conceptualized as labor unrest, and any reports of such actions were recorded.

It is necessary to emphasize that the data collection project was *not* designed to produce a count of *all or even most incidents* of labor unrest that have taken place in the world over the last century. Newspapers report on only a small fraction of the labor unrest that occurs. Instead, the procedure is intended to produce a measure that reliably indicates *the changing levels* of labor unrest—when the incidence of labor unrest is rising or falling, when it is high or low—*relative to* other points in time and locations in space. And given the underlying theoretical perspective emphasizing the role of major waves of labor unrest in provoking periods of transformation/restructuring, we were particularly interested in being able to identify major *waves* of labor unrest.

Extensive reliability studies of the database have been carried out in which the temporal profile of labor unrest derived from the WLG database was compared to that derived from other existing sources (the labor history literature and any existing statistical sources). Based on these reliability studies, we have concluded that the WLG database is an effective and reliable tool for identifying years of exceptionally high or intense levels of labor unrest within individual countries.[16] More specifically, we found that the central strength of the WLG database is its fairly consistent ability to identify those waves of labor unrest that represent turning points in the history of labor–capital relations.[17]

In sum, then, the WLG database provides a reliable map of the world-scale patterns of major waves of labor unrest over the century. We use this map to navigate our way through the story of world-scale labor unrest told in the central chapters of the book. Appendix A contains a significantly more in-depth

discussion of conceptualization, measurement, and data collection issues related to the construction and use of the WLG database than that which has been offered here. Appendix B reproduces the data collection instructions used by coders. Readers interested in a more detailed treatment of methodological issues related to the database may wish to consult these appendices before moving on to the next chapters of the book. [. . .]

NOTES

1. Indeed, for those whose field of vision extended beyond the wealthy countries of the North, an "unprecedented international wave of [mass] protests" against International Monetary Fund (IMF)-imposed austerity politics could already be seen throughout the developing world in the 1980s (Walton and Ragin 1990: 876–7, 888).
2. For a sample of the debate, see Tilly (1995), Wallerstein (1979), Gills and Frank (1992), Chase-Dunn (1989), and O'Rourke and Williamson (1999).
3. As David Held and his co-authors have shown, migration flows in the late nineteenth and early twentieth century, relative to world population, were more significant than migration flows in the late twentieth century (Held et al. 1999: Chapter 6; see also O'Rourke and Williamson 1999: Chapters 7–8).
4. Examples of this strategy abound. Richard Biernacki (1995: 1–3) argued that divergent shop-floor practices and labor movement strategies developed in German and British textile industries despite their technical uniformity (same kinds of machines, same markets) because of differing cultural conceptions of the meaning of buying and selling labor. As a result of these different cultural understandings, Germany and Britain took "opposite journeys among an array of developmental pathways to wage labor in western Europe." Likewise, among the conclusions that Katznelson and Zolberg (1986: 450) reached—on the basis of essays on France, Germany, and the United States in their edited volume—is the crucial role played by the nature of the state at the time of initial working-class formation. The "single most important determinant of the variation in the patterns of working class politics . . . is simply whether, at the time this class was being brought into being by the development of capitalism . . . it faced an absolutist state or liberal state." In other words, they trace the divergent outcome among labor movements in terms of the degree to which they were heavily involved in politics to preexisting and independent differences in the character of the individual cases (states).
5. On Galton's problem, see Naroll (1970) and

Hammel (1980). For a methodological critique of the comparative-national approach from a world-systems perspective, see Hopkins (1982b).

6. This approach has led to complaints from otherwise sympathetic scholars that "world-systems theory," in "assuming the systematicity and functionality of the capitalist world system," has produced a "mechanical picture of different labor forms in different parts of the world" (Cooper 2000: 62).

7. As will become evident, statistical elaboration abounds in this book. Its purpose is not "explanation" but the identification of patterns of labor unrest across time and space that then become the explicandum of a multidimensional causal "story" (see Hopkins 1982a: 32; Danto 1965: 237).

8. McAdam, Tarrow, and Tilly's (2001: 26) emphasis on "relational mechanisms" that operate at the level of "webs of interactions among social sites" moves in this direction. But their approach assigns priority to what they call "cognitive mechanisms" over "environmental mechanisms" (e.g., processes of capitalist development). As a result, to the extent that they trace relational processes beyond the local or national level, they tend to emphasize only what we have called direct relational processes. Their approach abstracts from crucial indirect relational processes that operate behind the backs, and independently of the cognitive awareness of affected groups and individuals (see previous subsection). Put differently, they do not operate with a conceptualization of capitalism as a historical social system. The approach adopted in this study, in contrast, concurs with Don Kalb's (2000: 38) point that "(t)o get at class . . . we need to recapture capitalism." Or as Frederick Cooper put it, in rejecting the "meta" (of meta-theory), it would be too bad if scholars shy away from the "mega," for "capitalism remains a megaquestion" (1996: 14; 2000: 67).

9. See for example, the articles collected under the title of "Scholarly Controversy: Farewell to the Working Class?" in the Spring 2000 issue of *International Labor and Working-Class History.*

10. Thus, Doug McAdam, John McCarthy, and Mayer Zald (1996: 6–8) argued that protest action presupposes "shared understandings of the world . . . that legitimate and motivate collective action."

11. It is anomalous in the sense that it is the one case where a rapid expansion of mass production in the automobile industry did not lead to a mass wave of labor unrest within a generation. As Chapter 2 points out, that expansion was *preceded* by a major wave of labor unrest.

12. For Katznelson and Zolberg (1986: 20), working-class "collective action" refers to "classes that are organized through movements and organizations to affect society and the position of the class within it."

13. McAdam et al. (2001: 7–8) distinguish between "contained contention" and "transgressive contention." Transgressive contention differs from contained contention in that "at least some of the parties to the conflict are newly self-identified political actors, and/or . . . at least some of the parties employ innovative collective action."

14. In terms of the protagonists of collective action, our focus is on the "proletariat" (i.e., those who must sell their labor power in order to survive). The proletarian condition encompasses a range of concrete situations, from those who possess scarce skills that are in demand (and hence have relatively strong marketplace bargaining power) to those who are unemployed. It includes those who are employed by private entrepreneurs and those who are employed by the state, for the latter are ultimately no more insulated from the pressures of being treated as a commodity than, say, workers in the internal labor market of a large firm. In both cases, when push comes to shove, the demands of profitability (and their links with tax receipts) can wipe away in short order whatever insulation from the labor market had existed.

15. The results of the first phase of the project were published in Silver, Arrighi, and Dubofsky (1995).

16. For extensive reliability studies on the World Labor Group database, see Silver et al. (1995).

17. This reliability in identifying turning-point waves of unrest is tied to the particular characteristics of newspapers as a source for sociohistorical data. That is, newspapers tend to be biased against reporting routine events (such as institutionalized strike activity) and biased in favor of reporting labor unrest that is not routine (episodes that either quantitatively or qualitatively depart from the norm). Given our focus on nonnormative or transgressive episodes of labor unrest (see earlier in this section), this bias is actually beneficial for this study.

REFERENCES

Berlanstein, Lenard R. 1993. "Introduction." In Lenard R. Berlanstein, ed., *Rethinking Labor History: Essays on Discourse and Class Analysis.* Urbana: University of Illinois Press.

Biernacki, Richard. 1995. *The Fabrication of Labor: Germany and Britain, 1640–1914.* Berkeley: University of California Press.

Bluestone, Barry, and Bennett Harrison. 1982. *The Deindustrialization of America: Plant Closings, Community Abandonment, and the Dismantling of Basic Industry.* New York: Basic.

Carr, Edward H. 1945. *Nationalism and After*, London: Macmillan.

Castells, Manuel. 1997. *The Information Age, vol. 2: The Power of Identity.* Oxford: Blackwell.

Chase-Dunn, Christopher. 1989. *Global Formation: Structures of the World-Economy.* Cambridge, MA: Basil Blackwell.

Collier, Ruth Berins and David Collier. 1991. *Shaping the Political Arena: Critical Junctures, the Labor Movement, and Regime Dynamics in Latin America.* Princeton, NJ: Princeton University Press.

Cooper, Frederick. 1996. *Decolonization and African Society: The Labor Question in French and British Africa*. Cambridge: Cambridge University Press.

—— 2000. "Farewell to the Category-Producing Class?" *International Labor and Working-Class History*, 57, Spring, 60–68.

Danto, Arthur C. 1965. *Analytical Philosophy of History*. Cambridge: Cambridge University Press.

Dicken, Peter. 1998. *Global Shift: Transforming the World Economy*. New York: Guilford Press.

Fantasia, Rick. 1988. *Cultures of Solidarity: Consciousness, Action and Contemporary American Workers*. Berkeley; CA: University of California Press.

Fröbel, Folker, Jürgen Heinrich, and Otto Kreye. 1980. *The New International Division of Labour: Structural Employment and Industrialization in Developing Countries*. Cambridge: Cambridge University Press.

Gills, Barry, and Andre G. Frank. 1992. "World System Cycles, Crises, and Hegemonic Shifts, 1700 BC to 1700 AD." *Review* (Fernand Braudel Center), 15 (4), 621–87.

Griffin, Larry. 1992. "Temporality, Events, and Explanation in Historical Sociology: An Introduction." *Sociological Methods and Research*, 20 (4), May, 403–27.

Griffin, Larry J., Holly J. McCammon, and Christopher Botsko. 1990. "The 'Unmaking' of a Movement? The Crisis of US Trade Unions in Comparative Perspective." In Maureen Hallinan, David Klein, and Jennifer Glass, eds., *Change in Societal Institutions*, pp. 169–94. New York: Plenum Press.

Hammel, E. A. 1980. "The Comparative Method in Anthropological Perspective." *Comparative Studies in Society and History*, 22 (2), April, 145–55.

Held, David, Anthony McGrew, David Goldblatt, and Jonathan Perraton. 1999. *Global Transformations. Politics, Economics and Culture*. Stanford, CA: Stanford University Press.

Hexter, J. H. 1979. *On Historians*. Cambridge, MA: Harvard University Press.

Hopkins, Terence K. 1982a. "World-Systems Analysis: Methodological Issues". In Terence K. Hopkins, Immanuel Wallerstein and Associates. *World Systems Analysis: Theory and Methodology*, pp. 145–58. Beverly Hills, CA: Sage.

—— 1982b. "The Study of the Capitalist World-Economy." In T. K. Hopkins, I. Wallerstein and Associates, *World-Systems Analysis: Theory and Methodology*, pp. 9–38. Beverly Hills: Sage.

Kalb, Don, 2000. "Class (in Place) Without Capitalism (in Space)?" *International Labor and Working-Class History*, 57, Spring, 31–9.

Katznelson, Ira, and Aristide Zolberg. 1986. *Working-Class Formation: Nineteenth-Century Patterns in Western Europe and the United States*. Princeton, NJ: Princeton University Press.

Keck, Margaret E., and Kathryn Sikkink. 1998. *Activists Beyond Borders: Advocacy Networks in International Politics*. Ithaca, NY: Cornell University Press.

Krishnan, R. 1996. "December 1995: The First Revolt Against Globalization." *Monthly Review*, 48 (1), May, 1–22.

MacEwan, Arthur, and William K. Tabb. eds. 1989.

Instability and Change in the World Economy. New York: Monthly Review Press.

McAdam, Doug and Dieter Rucht. 1993. "The Cross-National Diffusion of Movement Ideas." *The Annals of the American Academy of Political and Social Science*, 528, July, 56–74.

McAdam, Doug, John D. McCarthy, and Mayer N. Zald. 1996. "Introduction: Opportunities, Mobilizing Structures, and Framing Processes—Toward a Synthetic, Comparative Perspective on Social Movements." In D. McAdam, J. D. McCarthy, and M. N. Zald, eds., *Comparative Perspectives on Social Movements: Political Opportunities, Mobilizing Structures, and Cultural Framings*, pp. 1–20. Cambridge: Cambridge University Press.

McAdam, Doug, Sidney Tarrow, and Charles Tilly. 2001. *Dynamics of Contention*. Cambridge: Cambridge University Press.

McMichael, Philip. 1990. "Incorporating Comparison within a World-Historical Perspective: An Alternative Comparative Method." *American Sociological Review*, 55, 385–97.

Meyer, John W., John Boli, George M. Thomas, and Francisco Ramirez. 1997. "World Society and the Nation-State." *American Journal of Sociology*, 103 (1), July, 144–81.

Naroll, Raoul. 1970. "Galton's Problem." In Raoul Naroll and Ronald Cohen, eds., *A Handbook of Method in Cultural Anthropology*, Chapter 47, pp. 974–89. Garden City, NY: The Natural History Press.

O'Rourke, Kevin H., and Jeffrey G. Williamson. 1999. *Globalization and History: The Evolution of a Nineteenth Century Atlantic Economy*. Cambridge, MA: MIT Press.

Panitch, Leo. 2000. "Reflections on Strategy for Labour." In Leo Panitch and Colin Leys, eds., *Socialist Register 2001* (Working Classes, Global Realities), pp. 367–92. London: Merlin Press.

Pitcher, Brian L., Robert L. Hamblin, and Jerry L. L. Miller. 1978. "The Diffusion of Collective Violence." *American Sociological Review*, 43 (1), February, 23–35.

Piven, Frances Fox and Richard A. Cloward. 1992. "Normalizing Collective Protest." In Aldon D. Morris and Carol McClurg Mueller, eds., *Frontiers in Social Movement Theory*, pp. 301–25. New Haven, CT: Yale University Press.

Quadagno, Jill, and Stan J. Knapp. 1992. "Have Historical Sociologists Forsaken Theory: Thoughts on the History/Theory Relationship." *Sociological Methods and Research*, 20 (4), May, 481–507.

Sassen, Saskia. 1988. *The Mobility of Labor and Capital*. Cambridge: Cambridge University Press.

Screpanti, Ernesto. 1987. "Long Cycles of Strike Activity: An Empirical Investigation." *British Journal of Industrial Relations*, XXV (1), March, 99–124.

Sewell, Jr., William H. 1993. "Toward a Post-materialist Rhetoric for Labor History". In Lenard R. Berlanstein, ed., *Rethinking Labor History*, pp. 15–38. Urbana: University of Illinois Press.

Shalev, Michael. 1992. "The Resurgence of Labor

Quiescence." In Marino Regini, ed., *The Future of Labour Movements*, pp. 102–32. London: Sage.

Silver, Beverly J., Giovanni Arrighi, and Melvyn Dubofsky, eds., 1995. "Labor Unrest in the World Economy, 1870–1990." A special issue of *Review* (Fernand Braudel Center), 18 (1), Winter.

Tarrow, Sidney. 1998. "Fishnets, Internets and Catnets: Globalization and Social Movements." In Michael P. Hanagan, Leslie P. Moch, and Wayne te Brake, eds., *Challenging Authority*, pp. 228–44. Minneapolis: University of Minnesota Press.

Thompson, E. P. 1978. "Eighteenth-Century English Society: Class Struggle without Class?" *Social History*, 3/2, May, 146–64.

Tilly, Charles. 1984. *Big Structures, Large Processes, Huge Comparisons.* New York: Russell Sage Foundation.

—— 1995. "Globalization Threatens Labor's Rights." *International Labor and Working-Class History* 47, 1–23.

Uchitelle, Louis, and N. R. Kleinfeld. 1996. "The Downsizing of America: On the Battlefields of Business, Millions of Casualties," *The New York Times*, March 3, p. A1.

Wallerstein, Immanuel. 1974. *The Modern World System 1. Capitalist Agriculture and the Origins of the European World-Economy in the Sixteenth Century.* New York: Academic Press.

—— 1979. *The Capitalist World-Economy.* Cambridge: Cambridge University Press.

Walton, John and Ragin, Charles. 1990. "Global and National Sources of Political Protest: Third World Responses to the Debt Crisis." *American Sociological Review*, 55, December, 876–90.

Western, Bruce. 1995. "A Comparative Study of Working-Class Disorganization: Union Decline in Eighteen Advanced Capitalist Countries." *American Sociological Review*, 60 (2), April, 179–201.

Woods, Ellen Meiksens, Peter Meiksens, and Michael Yates, eds., 1998. *Rising front the Ashes? Labor in the Age of Global Capitalism.* New York: Monthly Review Press.

Zolberg, Aristide. 1995. "Response: Working-Class Dissolution." *International Labor and Working Class History*, 47, 28–38.

CHAPTER 12

"Transnational Struggles for Water and Power" and "Dams, Democracy, and Development in Transnational Perspective"

Sanjeev Khagram

TRANSNATIONAL STRUGGLES FOR WATER AND POWER

[. . .]

THE RISE AND DECLINE OF BIG DAMS GLOBALLY

The trajectory of big dam building over the last 100 years provides a striking illustration of a broader transformation in the transnational political economy of development. The rise and global spread of big dam building is clearly a 20th-century phenomenon. In 1900, there were approximately 600 big dams in existence, many of the oldest of which were built in Asia and Africa. The figure grew to nearly 5,000 big dams by 1950, of which 10 were major dams. By the year 2000, approximately 45,000 big dams, including approximately 300 major dams, had been constructed around the world (see Figure 12.1)! Thus, over 90 percent of big dams were built over the last forty years.[1]

Big dam building also spread or was transferred from a small number of river basins to all regions of the world during this period: these projects have now been erected in at least 140 different countries.[2] Great Britain had more than half of the world's big dams at the turn of the last century.[3] In 1902, British authorities constructed the low Aswan Dam on the Nile River, subsequently raising it twice to over 100 feet in height by 1933.[4] The Desprostoi on the Dnieper River in the Soviet Union was built a year earlier; it was the world's first major and most powerful hydropower dam at the time.[5] By the 1930s, the United States Bureau of Reclamation (BuRec) had built over 50 big dam projects and had commenced work on the mammoth Hoover Dam.[6] Completion of the Hoover Dam, and the establishment of the Tennessee Valley Authority (TVA), which built 38 large dams before 1945, followed by the construction of the even larger Shasta and Grand Coulee projects, heralded the big dam era in the United States.[7] Similar efforts were under way in other countries around the world, particularly in the former Soviet Union and in Western Europe.[8]

Transnationally allied proponents of big dam projects increasingly became more linked during these early years, contributing to the formation of an informal international big dam regime. In 1929, an array of engineers, builders, and bureaucrats established a transnational professional association called the International Commission on Large Dams (ICOLD) to collect information and coordinate the exchange of knowledge about big dam building around the world.[9] Beginning in the 1930s and 1940s, big dam-building bureaucracies, including national agencies such as BuRec or the former Soviet Union's Hydrological Planning Agency and river valley organizations like the TVA, proliferated around the world. The wave of decolonization and state-formation that began in South Asia in 1947 substantially contributed to the spread of these institutions across the third world. By 1955, BuRec Commissioner Michael Strauss claimed that "the American concept of comprehensive river basin development," involving the creation of these bureaucratic agencies and the

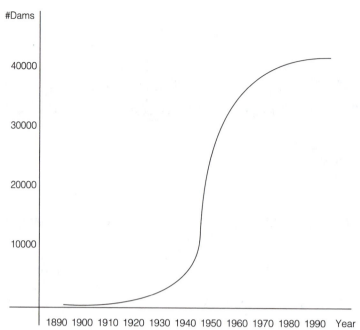

Figure 12.1 Cumulative number of big dams constructed worldwide

building of big dams, had "seized the world imagination."[10]

The World Bank, which soon emerged as the premier multilateral development agency, took the lead in supporting the construction of big dams across the third world. The first loan it ever awarded outside Europe underwrote three big dams in Chile, and its first loans to fourteen other developing countries were for similar projects. Promotion of comprehensive river basin planning was also taken up in earnest.[11] As noble-prize winning development economist Albert Hirschman later wrote, "any river valley scheme, whether it concerned the Sao Francisco in Brazil, the Papaloapan River in Mexico, the Cauca in Colombia, the Dez in Iran, or the Damodar in eastern India, was presented to a reassured public as a true copy of the Tennessee Valley Authority."[12] Since then, by one estimate, the Bank lent over $58 billion for more than 604 big dam projects in 93 countries. Of the 527 loans made by the Bank for big dams, more than 100 were the largest made to the borrowing country at the time of approval.[13]

The growth of a private dam industry and other development aid and credit agencies greatly augmented the power of big dam pro-

ponents, further contributing to the spread, growth, and legitimacy of big dam building across the third world. Prominent transnational corporations, such as Asea Brown Boveri, Siemens, GEC Alsthom, Kvaerner, Bechtel, Acres, and others, expanded rapidly during the 1950s and 1960s. Other multilateral organizations besides the World Bank, such as the specialized wings of the United Nations, especially the Food and Agriculture Organization and UN Development Program, and the Inter-American and Asian development banks, also increasingly played a major role in promoting big dams in developing countries. Bilateral aid and credit agencies like the British Overseas Development Administration (ODA) or the United States Export Import Bank increasingly became important funders of these projects, often in partnership with bureaucratic agencies in the third world, transnational corporations, and multilateral organizations.[14]

Despite the estimated more than US $2 trillion spent on big dam and major river valley projects over the last century, approximately one billion people currently do not have adequate supplies of water. By the year 2025, it is estimated that three billion people spanning fifty-two countries will be plagued by water stress or acute shortages of this precious life-sustaining resource.[15] Frictions between states over water resources are predicted by some to intensify, because nearly 40 percent of the world's river basins is shared by two or more countries.[16] Within and across countries, these conflicts are just as volatile, if not more so. As a result, water is now at the top of the global agenda.[17]

While conflicts over water have remerged as a central concern, those over power are just as intense. The share in world energy consumption held by developing countries is expected to continue to rise from the current 25 percent to over 40 percent by 2010.[18] In anticipation of this growth, third world governments have focused increased attention on the energy sector. Despite the heavy investments on power projects and increasing private sector involvement in the sector, however, there are still more than two billion people in the world without stable sources of electricity.[19] Such shortfalls, exacerbated by the decline in hydropower big dam building and increasing concerns about the contribution of fossil fuel energy generation to global warming, present increasingly potent transnational political challenges.

Given the powerful set of big dam interests and institutions, along with the tremendous need for water and power around the world, the rapid decline globally over the last quarter century in the rate of big dam building is especially puzzling (see Figure 12.2). The number of big dam projects completed per year had grown from approximately thirty in 1900 to nearly two hundred and fifty by mid-century. Thereafter, the rate exploded and peaked when, it was estimated, more than one thousand big dams were being finished annually by the mid-1960s. But even more dramatically, the number of these projects completed per year then fell precipitously to under two hundred by the turn of this century, representing a 75 percent drop in the construction rate of big dams in less than two decades (see Figure 12.2)! The number of major dams completed over time similarly declined: during the 1970s, ninety-three of these mega-projects were constructed, while approximately twenty-five were built in the 1990s.[20]

Four main types of arguments can be offered to explain this puzzling trend: technical, financial, economic, and political. The technical argument highlights the decreasing availability of sites for big dam building to account for the falling completion rate around the world. Yet, 95 percent of big dams are concentrated in twenty-five countries in which more than one hundred have been built, while less than 2 percent are spread over the more than one hundred fifty other countries of the world where sites are still readily available, if not plentiful.[21] Only slightly more than 10 percent of the world's technically available hydropower potential has been developed by energy industry estimates.[22] During the 1990s, the number of big dams under construction remained flat at between eleven and twelve hundred per year, as did big dam-starts averaging three hundred per year.[23] Thus, there has been a diverging trend over time between the number of sites still available, as well as the number of dams being started and under construction, compared to the number of big dams actually being completed every year.

Financial and economic factors, such as shortages in available funding and the increasing relative viability of "conventional" alternatives for the services provided by big dams, are two other possible explanations for the decline in big dam building.[24] The 1973 and 1979 oil crises, worldwide recession during the 1980s, growth in indebtedness by many third world states, donor fatigue among foreign lenders, and a strategy shift toward privatization all contributed to the decreasing availability of public and international financing for these projects.[25] The lower costs of other conventional forms of energy production from time to time, such as natural gas power plants, relative to the development of hydro-power, reduced the comparative economic feasibility of big dams.[26] The increasing time and cost overruns associated with big dam projects further detracted from expected financial and economic returns and improved the marginal utility of investing in other projects.[27]

These technical, financial and economic factors have clearly made big dams less attractive, but they do not tell the whole

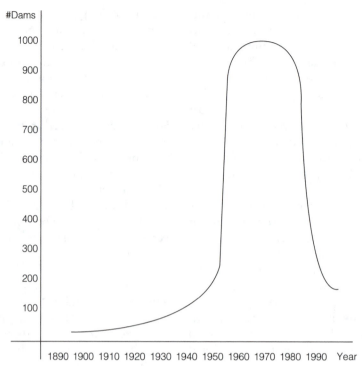

Figure 12.2 Average number of big dams completed worldwide.

story. Political-economic dynamics have increasingly contributed to the decreasing financial viability of and changing economic benefit-cost calculations regarding big dam building. Mounting public protests against big dams have caused time overruns and cost overruns.[28] Costs have also increased because big dam builders and authorities have been compelled to investigate and mitigate negative environmental and social effects, such as adequately compensating displaced peoples. When these environmental and social costs were internalized, benefit-cost or internal rate of return criteria for approving these projects were less likely to be satisfied. These requirements for the formulation, sanctioning, and implementation of big dams either did not exist or were not followed in the past.[29] Critics have additionally argued that many big dam projects are not financially or economically feasible and that less costly alternatives are available.

The technical argument of site depletion, moreover, has actually been as much a cause for the generation of political opposition to big dams as it has been a direct factor in the decline of big dam building. Beginning in

North America and Western Europe, the growing loss of free flowing rivers associated with the damming of more and more sites sparked much of the initial organization and mobilization of critical domestic conservation groups. Indeed, the success of early anti-dam campaigns contributed to the growth of national environmental movements in numerous countries in these regions during the 1950s and 1960s.[30] The declining opportunities for big dam building in the first world, increasing demand and support for them across the third world as well as among development aid and export credit agencies subsequently drove proponents such as transnational corporations to shift more of their activities to developing countries. As a result, approximately two-thirds of the big dams built in the 1980s and three-quarters under construction during the 1990s were in the third world.[31]

But since the 1970s, coalescing from a multitude of struggles and campaigns waged from the local to the international levels, transnationally allied critics and opponents of big dams have dramatically altered the dynamics of big dam building across the world. Environmental nongovernmental organizations from the industrialized countries, in addition to those promoting human rights, the protection of indigenous peoples and other issues, have increasingly focused their energies on halting the global spread of big dam building. At the same time, directly affected people, grassroots groups, social movements, and domestic nongovernmental organizations in the rest of the world have increasingly empowered themselves and become more organized to reform or block the completion of big dams in their own river basins and countries, often by forging direct linkages with these like-minded foreign supporters. As a result, in contrast to the past when domestic technical, financial-economic, and political factors contributed relatively equally and interacted to cause the decline in big dam building, the primary explanation for these changing dynamics over time is increasingly political-economic, having to do with the shifting transnational power relations and meanings associated with the construction of big dams.

THE CHANGING TRANSNATIONAL POLITICAL ECONOMY OF DEVELOPMENT

A novel form of transnational dynamics constituted primarily by grassroots groups, social movements, and nongovernmental organizations from all over the world—and covering a wide range of issues, including security, trade, democratization, human rights, indigenous peoples, gender justice, and the environment—has become a common feature of world politics.[32] This study argues that a similar set of transnationally allied actors have also altered the political economy of development. These actors have been empowered by, and have also contributed to, the global spread and international institutionalization of norms in areas such as the environment, indigenous peoples, and human rights. But, as we shall see in the examination of the changing dynamics of big dam building across the third world, this combination of novel and increasingly influential transnationally linked action and

globalizing norms has been most effective when undergirded by mass mobilization and multilevel advocacy in more democratic institutional contexts.

The tremendous proliferation of nongovernmental organizations around the world during the 20th century has been central to the new transnational political economy of development. Domestic nongovernmental organizations draw membership from, or are located in, only one country but can have either a domestic and/or an international focus, such as the United States-based Sierra Club or Cultural Survival.[33] In contrast, *transnational nongovernmental organizations*, such as Amnesty International or Greenpeace, draw membership from, and are active in, multiple countries and do not necessarily have allegiance to any particular state or society.[34] According to one estimate, the number of these transnational actors has exploded over the past century from 176 in 1909, to 832 in 1951, to 4518 in 1988. The ratio between transnational nongovernmental and international organizations, like the World Bank or the International Energy Agency, similarly rose during the period: from 5 to 1 in 1909, to about 8 to 1 by the 1950s, to more than 14 to 1 in 1988.[35]

The rapid growth in numbers of transnational nongovernmental organizations is especially visible with those groups publicly and nonviolently promoting social change in areas such as human rights, environment, and development (see Table 12.1).[36] For example, in 1953 there were 33 transnational nongovernmental organizations working on human rights. The number at least doubled each decade between 1973 and 1993, growing from 41 to 190. Similarly, in the areas of environment and development, the number of transnational non-governmental organizations grew gradually between 1953

Table 12.1 The growth of transnational nongovernmental advocacy organizations.

Issue area	1953	1963	1973	1983	1993
Human rights	33	38	41	79	190
Environment	2	5	10	26	123
Development	3	3	7	13	47

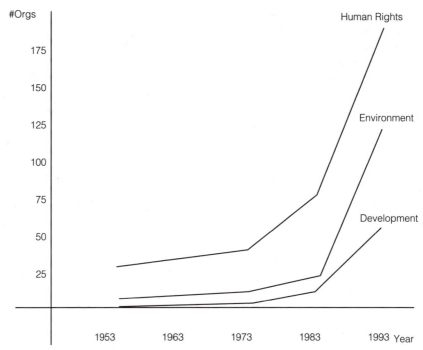

Figure 12.3 The growth of transnational nongovernmental advocacy organizations.

and 1973, but then dramatically increased after that. Over the last decade, similar groups promoting development grew by over 500 percent, while the number of transnational environmental organizations skyrocketed (see Figure 12.3)![37]

Not only have the numbers of transnational nongovernmental organizations grown, but transnational coalitions and networks linking nongovernmental organizations along with other allied actors, both domestic and transnational, have also increasingly been formed to promote social change in various issue areas.[38] *Transnational coalitions* are sets of actors linked across borders who publicly and nonviolently coordinate to formulate and implement a specific campaign, a shared strategy, or set of tactics.[39] *Transnational networks*, in contrast, are sets of actors linked across borders by some core shared normative concerns and dense exchanges of information and services.[40]

Transnational coalitions linking nongovernmental organizations, grassroots groups, and social movements across developed and developing countries are often formed for strategic purposes, in particular, to increase their potential to effect outcomes. In the third world, domestic actors are likely to construct transnational links with foreign or transnational counterparts to further their own goals, often when they face barriers in directly gaining access to, and leveraging, states, multilateral organizations, and transnational corporations. First world nongovernmental organizations engaged in issues that are international or transnational in nature often seek to build connections with third world allies to exchange information, increase their power, and gain legitimacy.[41] Although geographical distance, language and other cultural differences, varying organizational structures, and imbalances in resources pose substantial barriers to the effective functioning of these transnational coalitions, these types of interactions have nevertheless become more common.

Transnational coalitions, in contrast to transnational networks, can be formed when the strategic interests of different actors converge even if they are not bound together by deeply shared normative concerns. Thus, actors promoting women's rights and those working on environmental conservation may coordinate a campaign to increase funding for women's education because it contributes to gender justice and decreases population growth. A campaign, or more likely a series of campaigns, waged by the same or different transnational coalitions can lead to the formation and continuation of a transnational network by contributing to the development of shared norms and dense exchanges of information and services. Over time, the existence of transnational networks makes the formation of additional links to other actors much easier. The existence of transnational networks also facilitates the construction of transnational coalitions in order to wage specific campaigns. Transnational coalitions and networks are often spawned, sustained, or invoked by nongovernmental organizations.

Thus transnational nongovernmental organizations, coalitions, and networks interact over time and increasingly constitute broader fields or sectors—that is, relatively enduring structures of global dynamics.[42] For example, International Alliance of Indigenous Peoples (IAIP) is a formal transnational nongovernmental organization that is dedicated to protecting the rights of indigenous peoples globally. Transnational coalitions composed primarily of nongovernmental organizations and grassroots groups, often including IAIP, have been formed around specific campaigns such as promoting "Latin American Indian Rights." Over time, an identifiable transnational network, focused on furthering norms on indigenous peoples and cultural preservation, has emerged with IAIP as one of its core members.[43] These different forms of transnational collective action, interacting with other types of organizations, have resulted in a transnational field on indigenous peoples. Similar transnational organizational and social fields have evolved in other issue areas such as human rights, the environment, gender, and informal workers.

The changing dynamics around big dams, as we shall see, have especially been shaped by the emergence and interaction of various forms of transnational action in the fields of indigenous peoples, human rights, and the environment, among others. The early transnational anti-dam coalitions linked nongovernmental organizations, and often drew upon preexisting transnational networks, primarily from these three issue areas. Subsequently, nongovernmental organizations were specifically established to oppose big dams and promote the wise social and environmental use of rivers globally, such as the United States based International Rivers Network (IRN). In turn, IRN participates in transnational coalitions with like-minded or strategically allied human rights, indigenous peoples, and/or environmental actors in campaigns against specific big dam projects in different parts of the world. More recently, a transnational sustainable rivers network dedicated to reforming and halting big dam building around the world has emerged— co-led by IRN, along with such groups as the Brazilian Movement of Dam Affected Peoples and the Narmada Bachao Andolan based in India.

The continued transnationalization of communications, transportation, and economic exchange has clearly facilitated the emergence and perseverance of these forms of coordinated and collective action. But transnational advocacy efforts of grassroots groups, social movements, and nongovernmental organizations are most likely to be found in areas for which international and global arenas have opened up space and legitimated certain types of norms, institutions, and practices, such as the various United Nations conferences or world commissions. And to the extent that issues are already transnationalized, for example, when transnational corporations, international professional associations, multilateral organizations or multiple states are involved, when international laws or regimes exist, or when the issue area itself has been constructed as supranational in scope, links are not only more easily forged and maintained, they are also far more likely to be consequential.

RECONSTITUTING DEVELOPMENT: THE TRANSNATIONAL INSTITUTIONALIZATION OF EMERGENT NORMS

The proliferation of various forms of transnational advocacy and contentious action generated primarily by nongovernmental organizations, grassroots groups, and social movements by itself does not directly produce visible impacts in either the international or domestic arenas. The degree to which norms and principles in issue areas, such as the environment, human rights, and indigenous peoples, among others, spread globally and become institutionalized in the procedures and structures of states, multilateral agencies, and multinational corporations, among others, greatly increases the likelihood that transnationally allied action will be effective in altering development dynamics.[44] Although the formation and consolidation of these "international regimes" or, better, "transnational fields" of norms and principles do not constitute a sufficient condition to ensure the ultimate success of transnational advocacy efforts, they are generally critical for empowering historically weak and marginal actors in world politics.[45]

The global spread and institutionalization of norms and principles have increasingly contributed to the gradual but still partial structuring of a world society.[46] In the absence of a centralized world state, various types of transnational norms—constitutive, regulatory, practical, and evaluative—have generated appropriate and acceptable identities and behaviors of actors across the world.[47] The historical period since the end of World War II has involved the dramatic spread and increasing density of these norms. In particular, deeply embedded principles of sovereignty and self-determination have historically constituted the state as a privileged form of political organization endowed with authority and agency in world society.[48] Indeed, the external legitimation of the state, its proper organizational forms and goals, represents the core of this world society.

Although it involves highly asymmetric patterns of power and influence, this partially structured world society is ostensibly constituted by formally equal states and an inter-state system. The tendency in an increasingly dense and integrated world society of formally equal states is that of diffusion and imitation. Promoting development —generally defined as progress and operationalized as increasing wealth, as well as justice operationalized in terms of increasing equity—remains one of the central and appropriate orientations of contemporary states.[49] Rapid changes in state policies and institutions often, and increasingly, reflect processes of conformity to globally spreading transnational norms of development rather than the diversity of forms and more gradual shifts expected from variations in domestic structures, interactions and processes. Similarly, in areas ranging from military organization and security, to science and education policy, to human rights, ethnicity, and environment, a remarkable degree of institutional isomorphism in the procedures and structures of states, and for that matter in various types of organizations, is evident.[50]

The area of environmental issues is an excellent example of the rise and global spread of norms that has produced international and cross-national institutional isomorphism around the world. As one authoritative study noted:

> Widespread and mobilized world concern about the environment is heavily dependent on universalistic and scientific ideologies and principles. These have tended to arise and achieve codification in world discourse before, not after, they become local and national issues in most nation-states. And in fact, the rise of the world environmental domain clearly precedes and causes the formation of generalized national structures formalizing and managing the issues involved.[51]

The most striking evidence of the effects of this increasingly global framework is the historical process by which environmental institutions have been established by states. Prior to preparations for the United Nations Conference on Human Environment held in Stockholm in 1972, not a single state environmental bureaucracy existed. Subsequently, environmental agencies and ministries were formed at a rapid rate with approximately sixty being created by 1988, and dozens more being formed around the 1992 United Nations Conference on Environment and Development held in Rio de Janeiro, Brazil. By the late 1990s, virtually every state in the world had some type of environmental agency. Procedures such as environmental impact assessments have spread along with the formal establishment of these bureaucratic agencies, increasing the potential for development dynamics to be altered based on environmental evaluation and justification.[52]

At the international level, the United Nations Environment Program, the first environmental unit at the World Bank, which eventually became the Office of Environmental and Scientific Affairs (OESA), and even an environmental section of the International Commission on Large Dams (ICOLD), were all created after the 1972 UN Conference. The United Nations Commission on Sustainable Development, a Vice-Presidency for Environmentally Sustainable Development at the World Bank, and the Global Environmental Facility were formed as a result of the Brundtland Commission on Environment and Development and the 1992 Rio Conference that it recommended. Scores of other international organizations dedicated to various environmental issues have been established during this period. The global spread of novel environmental norms and their incorporation into the procedures and structures of states, international organizations, and multinational corporations provides strong evidence that an international environmental regime is becoming increasingly institutionalized.[53] This transnational environmental regime has been critical to the changing dynamics of big dam building, as well as broader transformation in the global political economy of development.[54]

Another clear example of the global rise and spread of norms that have contributed to altering and reconstituting the transnational political economy of development is that of human rights. Based on an analysis of the constitutions of 140 independent countries between 1870 and 1970, one study found a tremendous increase in the number of states formally ensuring a broad set of human rights. These rights were disaggregated into three categories: civil, among them, free speech and due process; political, most importantly, the vote; and social or economic, e.g., unemployment insurance and social security. In each area, there was a remarkable transformation in the number of constitutions that included these rights over this period, particularly after World War II. Civil rights expanded by 43 percent, political rights by 120 percent, while social and economic rights grew by a tremendous 340 percent.[55]

Moreover, social and economic rights appeared in virtually no constitutions before 1930, yet spread rapidly after that— especially after the United Nations Declaration of Human Rights. Although no study of newer or revised constitutions ratified since the wave of democratization that began in the 1970s is yet available, the expectation is that these documents are even more likely to include expanded lists of rights, with more on categories such as gender justice, indigenous peoples and other ethnic minorities, which have become more prominent over the past two decades.[56] By the end of the 1990s, the principle of a healthy environment was being promoted as a basic human right that should be ensured by states in their laws, procedures, and activities.[57]

At the international level, human rights norms and principles were the hallmark of the United Nations from its inception. The UN Charter—specifically the Universal Declaration of Human Rights—includes a wide-ranging set of human rights.[58] Moreover, while prior to 1948 not one international organization focusing on human rights existed, by 1990 approximately twenty-seven were significantly dedicated to this work.[59] These international organizations range from the UN Commission on Human Rights and Subcommission on the Protection of Minorities to the International Labor Organization. Numerous international conferences have been organized around human rights, and international human rights law is progressively well developed. It is thus evident that a broad international human rights regime grew extensively in the 20th century, particularly since the 1970s.[60]

The global diffusion of norms in different issue areas, however, is not a teleological or ubiquitous process marching around the world. The mechanisms by which such isomorphic institutions and change are produced should be more clearly delineated.[61] Moreover, the growing similarities in the procedures and structures of states, multilateral organizations, and multinational corporations tend to be formal and are often decoupled from actual practices.[62] In other words, institutional isomorphism does not imply complete equifinality; radical junctures between formal organization and observable practices are likely to persist.[63] This is particularly the case when the institutional incorporation of transnational norms is poorly matched or is at cross-purposes with extant and often deeply consolidated norms, principles, procedures, and structures—not to mention balances of power and interests in domestic or local contexts.[64]

Thus, theoretical and empirical analysis of the "transnational structuration" processes by which globalizing norms and principles are promoted, become institutionalized, and alter concrete practices is required.[65] The causal pathway proposed in this study involves the interaction between the global spread and institutionalization of norms interacting with the transnationally allied activities of nongovernmental organizations, peoples' groups, and social movements.[66] This latter type of transnational politics directly or indirectly contributes to the creation of novel sets of norms and principles. These norms and principles rise and spread via transnational campaigns, through world conferences and other global forums from the practices of members of professional and scientific associations, by being adopted by the most powerful states, multilateral organizations, or multinational corporations, and hence become further legitimated. For example, drafts initially formulated for the United Nations Charter barely mentioned human rights. A range of nongovernmental advocacy organizations and other actors introduced and intensively lobbied for the inclusion of human rights and were ultimately successful.[67] Subsequently, most states formally embraced the protection of these rights in

their constitutions; though considerably fewer actually met the standards set by the procedures and structures they had adopted.[68] During the 1990s, more and more multinational corporations began adopting codes of conduct including human rights principles.[69] At the same time, transnational human rights networks actively began promoting "rights-based" approaches to development to contend with neo-liberal, market "price-based" models of development.

International organizations, professional associations and epistemic communities, and, critically, transnational advocacy groups, in turn, are leading propagators of globalizing norms; they author, codify, validate, and lend authoritative status to these rules of appropriate behavior. The more linked states are to this partially structured world society or, in other words, the more they interact with transnational actors, the more likely they are to incorporate transnational norms into their own institutions.[70] These formal procedures and structures can empower nongovernmental organizations, peoples' groups, and social movements by giving them new and greater institutional spaces and opportunity structures in which to gain access to and pressure states, multilateral agencies, and multinational corporations. By pressuring the powerful to be accountable to their adopted procedures and structures, these and other subaltern actors can generate changes in practices and types of outcomes that otherwise would not have occurred and seem unexplainable.

As the evidence in this study will demonstrate, the transnational institutionalization of emergent norms on human rights, as well as on indigenous peoples and the environment, has also contributed to transforming the extant international big dam regime, the dynamics of dam building more broadly and, correspondingly, the transnational political economy of development. Again, the issue area of human rights is instructive. Transnationally allied nongovernmental organizations, peoples' groups, and social movements promoting human rights across countries have utilized the increasingly pervasive international human rights regime to alter repressive state practices over the last two decades. As a result, transnational human rights coalitions and networks have contributed to processes of democratization in some of the most authoritarian regimes in Latin America, Eastern Europe, and elsewhere.[71]

Thus, the proposed constructivist analysis emphasizes the consequences of transnational norms and institutions, in addition to international military and economic power relations, for world politics. Specifically, international regimes—which have conventionally been conceived of as "sets of implicit or explicit principles, norms, rules and decision-making procedures around which actors' expectations converge"— clearly matter in ways not adequately theorized in the existing literature.[72] They may not directly constrain but create enabling conditions that increase the likelihood that the practices of states, international organizations, multinational corporations, professional and scientific associations, and other powerful actors can be more readily altered by the transnationally allied activities of nongovernmental organizations, grassroots groups, and social movements.

But many governments, in particular, remain resistant to changing their concrete practices even after the norms and principles embodied in these international regimes are formally incorporated into state structures and procedures.[73] This is partly because state institutions and governmental practices are also conditioned by domestic actors, interactions, and processes: relations between dominant classes and class coalitions, self-interested actions of political elites, inter-ethnic relations, or waves of social mobilization by subaltern groups.[74] Indeed, while transnational contentious politics interacting with the global spread and institutionalization of norms are important conditions for altering the general dynamics of development, states and other powerful actors generally have to be pressured to follow these transnational norms and principles by the mobilizing, lobbying, and monitoring activities of newly or further empowered and organized domestic and transnational actors.

REDIRECTING DEVELOPMENT: DOMESTIC DEMOCRATIZATION AND SOCIAL MOBILIZATION

The growth of transnationally allied advocacy generated primarily by nongovernmental organizations, grassroots groups, and social movements interacting with the global spread and institutionalization of norms over time has not produced identical outcomes across the world. The domestic presence of organized and sustained social mobilization as well as the presence of democratic institutions or a significant degree of democratization are critical factors that condition the broader impacts of growing transnational contentious politics and spreading global norms on the political economy of development.

More specifically, democracies that have nongovernmental organizations, peoples' groups, and social movements with the capacity to organize and mobilize large numbers of people and conduct multilevel advocacy are most likely to exhibit changes in development dynamics. Development activities— such as the building of big dams—are least likely to be altered by this form of transnational political economy, however, in states with authoritarian regimes and domestic actors that have little or no capacity to generate grassroots resistance (see Figure 12.4). The latter cases are less conducive to the formation of transnational linkages among domestic and foreign actors or to the adoption of globalizing norms and principles.

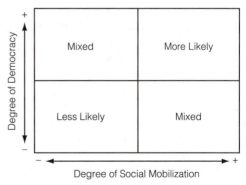

Figure 12.4 Impact of domestic democracy and social mobilization

Because they are by definition based on the rule of law, democracies, to the contrary, increase the potential impact of globalizing norms once they have been adopted domestically.[75]

Why the levels of domestic social mobilization and advocacy might be stronger or weaker across contexts and/or over time depends on a variety of factors. Social and political activism by historically (or recently) marginalized actors was previously thought to be conditioned by two interrelated factors: the increasing scarcity and unequal distribution of resources. Development processes and outcomes, like those associated with the construction of large-scale projects such as big dams that result in environmental and social dislocation and reallocations of resources, would thus spawn public mobilization and protest. These in turn would generate or exacerbate struggles between social groups and corrode extant or prevent the emergence of durable social institutions.[76]

But the organization and effectiveness of such collective political action often depend more on the mobilization of those resources that are available, the existence of facilitating social networks, and the conduciveness of the prevailing political opportunity structures.[77] These factors, moreover, are increasingly shaped by and shape the transnational linkages of domestic actors, as well as the global spread and institutionalization of norms on the environment, indigenous peoples, human rights, among others.

Significantly empowered and mobilized domestic nongovernmental organizations, grassroots groups, and social movements are crucial to the strength and viability of transnational political action "from below." These actors are critical sources of information, ideas, power, strategies, and legitimacy within transnational coalitions and networks.[78] Perhaps as importantly, they are the central actors that monitor and lobby state authorities and officials, as well as other non-state domestic and transnational actors, and hold them accountable to globalizing norms, international regimes, and domestic policies. When, due to the pressure of domestic nongovernmental organizations and peoples' groups, states incorporate the procedures and structures embodied in transnational norms, new points of access and leverage can also be opened up for these actors. Thus, for example, domestic nongovernmental organizations, grassroots groups, and social movements are greatly empowered to stop or reform big dam projects when state agencies on indigenous peoples or the environment are established.[79] [. . .]

DEVELOPMENT, DEMOCRACY, AND DAMS IN TRANSNATIONAL PERSPECTIVE

To summarize: in this book I argue that transnationally allied nongovernmental organizations, grassroots groups, and social movements have unexpectedly altered the political economy of development. This transformation in development has been conditioned by the global spread and international institutionalization of norms and principles in the issue-areas of environment, human rights, and indigenous peoples, among others. However, as the examination of big dam building demonstrates, these transnational structuration processes have been most successful in changing development outcomes and practices when linked to domestic actors with the ability to generate social mobilization in democratic contexts.

The two most likely competing explanations for the decline in big dam building—the decreasing availability of sites for big dams and the comparative financial and economic unviability of these projects—were addressed earlier and are further examined in the following chapters. Various implementation bottlenecks associated with ineffective decision-making structures could also have slowed down the execution of various big dam projects. Alternatively, political authorities could have reformed or stopped the building of big dams proactively, because they found more attractive forms of patronage and/or alternative means by which to satisfy the interests of powerful groups such as landed elites and industrialists. Finally, states, international organizations, and multinational or domestic companies might have independently decided that more viable options exist either for promoting development or making profits. But support for these competing hypotheses is not born out by empirical examination, given that they would require evidence that multilateral organizations, state and other non-state big-dam proponents primarily altered their big dam building policies and practices prior to, and/or separately from, the mechanisms and processes that have been posited in as central to this study.

Each of the hypotheses that as a group constitute the general theoretical argument of this book is also a potential alternative explanation. First, the lobbying of foreign and transnational nongovernmental organizations may have been the sole factor that changed the dynamics of big dam building in the third world. Second, the global spread of emergent norms on indigenous peoples, human rights, and the environment could have been so powerful that international organizations, state and non-state proponents altered their big dam building practices as a result of independently adopting and actually following these principles. Finally, it is possible that domestic advocacy and social mobilization, particularly in democracies, was sufficient by itself to stop or reform big dam projects. The diachronic and synchronic analysis that is presented in the following chapters provides support for the interactive and cumulative effects of these factors.

In order to examine the central theoretical argument of this study, as well as competing hypotheses, both cross-temporal and cross-sectional research and analytic methods have been used.[80] The cross-temporal analysis is critical for demonstrating the emergence and effects of the transnationally allied opposition to big dams as well as the global spread and international institutionalization of supportive human rights, indigenous peoples, and environmental norms over time. This specifically involves within "case," intensive process-tracing of the changing dynamics of big dam projects and big dam building in India as compared to historical trajectories in Brazil, Indonesia, China, and South Africa/Lesotho, as well as the evolution of transnationally allied anti-dam activities and their

impact on the international big dam regime.[81]

The cross-sectional comparisons highlight the crucial importance of domestic social mobilization and democracy in terms of explaining outcomes, even when transnational advocacy exists and globally spreading norms have become more institutionalized. This involves structured-focused examination of the changing dynamics of big dam building in the countries of India, Brazil, Indonesia, China, and South Africa/Lesotho, as well as at the international level with respect to the World Bank and other international organizations.[82] Following the proposed theoretical argument, these country cases have been selected in order to investigate and demonstrate variation produced by different levels of domestic social mobilization and democracy (see Figure 12.5).

Research for this study, which involved the gathering of both quantitative and qualitative data, is primarily based on original fieldwork conducted at numerous sites in India, Brazil, South Africa, Indonesia, China, Great Britain, the United States, and numerous other countries around the world. Statistics on big dam building, official and unofficial documents, technical reports, letters and e-mails from various government archives, international agencies, multinational corporations, and nongovernmental organizations were collected and analyzed. In addition, over three hundred interviews were conducted in English, Hindi, Gujarati, Portuguese, and Spanish with a wide range of participants, including indigenous people, peasants, landed elites, industrialists,

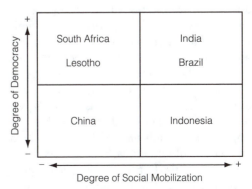

Figure 12.5 Comparative country case selection.

engineers, academic experts, bureaucrats, politicians, representatives of various international organizations, as well as nongovernmental activists working in both the domestic and international arenas.[83]

The transformation in the political economy of big dam building and development in India is examined in chapters 2 through 4. Big dam building in India is a theory generating case for this study. Big dam projects have played a prominent role in India's development since its Independence, and India was one of the leading big dam builders in the world over the second half of the 20th century. More important, India was one of the first tropical countries in which transnationally anti-dam opposition, as well as human rights, indigenous peoples, and environmental norms emerged. That country has also had the longest lasting democracy in the third world and a history of strong, domestic social mobilization. Big dam building in India is thus also a tough test of a most likely case, i.e., strong support for the theoretical argument should be found because all the variables posited as critical do operate at significant levels in this case.

In chapter 2, I examine the experience with a number of early big dam projects and the more general record of big dam building in India through the first two decades after Independence in 1947. I argue that an overwhelming state-society elite consensus undergirded support for the construction of big dams, and I show that when domestic criticism and opposition against these projects did occur, it was unsuccessful in reforming or halting them, even though a democratic political system existed in India. The striking absence of transnationally allied opposition against, and globalizing norms delegitimizing, big dams in this earlier period is empirically contrasted with the subsequent emergence of these factors in India during the 1970s. This transnationalization of contestation and newly emerging institutional context greatly strengthened domestic big dam opponents through the 1980s and 1990s, as an analysis of numerous struggles over these projects reveals. But the analysis also shows that sustained grassroots mobilization within a persistent democratic regime proved crit-

ical to the dramatically changing dynamics of big dam building and development in India over the subsequent twenty-five years.

Correspondingly, in chapters 3 and 4, I conduct an in-depth case study of the Narmada Dam Projects because of their centrality to the changing dynamics of development in India, at the international level and worldwide. Big dams were initially formulated for the Narmada River Valley by Indian authorities as far back as 1946, but construction did not begin in earnest until the early 1980s. The historical process by which the structure and functioning of India's democracy produced a three-decade delay in sanctioning the Narmada River Valley Dam Projects is depicted in chapter 3. I also show that domestic social mobilization against the proposed big dams did not exist during most of this period and, when it finally did emerge in the late 1970s, was ineffective in independently altering the course of projects proposed for the Narmada River. It was only after a transnational coalition of nongovernmental organizations and grassroots tribal peoples' groups was forged, conducting a five-year campaign to defend the human rights of tribal peoples to be displaced by the Sardar Sarovar major dam, that proponents, such as Indian and World Bank authorities, reformed their policies and practices on resettlement and rehabilitation.

In chapter 4, I continue my ethnographic and process-tracing examination of the trajectory of Narmada River Valley Dam Projects from the early 1980s on, focusing on the formation of a second transnational coalition dedicated to halting the Sardar Sarovar major dam altogether and thereby altering the course of the broader initiative. I demonstrate that the continuing and intensifying transnationalization of contestation and the changing institutional context for big dam building—particularly the rise, spread, and deepening of environmentalism, human rights principles, and norms on indigenous peoples globally and domestically in India— were critical to the eventual stalling of construction on these projects. Lobbying by foreign and/or transnational nongovernmental organizations would not have produced this outcome independently, however, had it not been linked to strong, domestic social mobilization. And once again, India's democratic regime strongly conditioned the effects of the transnationally allied opposition and domestically institutionalized global norms.

In order to further refine my general theoretical argument and compare it with alternatives, I conduct a comparative historical cross-country analysis in chapter 5. In particular, I examine the emergence and effectiveness of anti-dam activity in four prolific, big dam building, third world contexts: Brazil, Indonesia, South Africa/Lesotho, and China. All these cases had similar, relatively robust, records of big dam building to that of India from the 1950s through the 1970s.

As in the case of India, it is expected that the blocking and/or reform of these projects in Brazil noticeably increased because of the formation of transnationally allied opposition, the increasing domestic institutionalization of global norms on the environment, human rights, and indigenous peoples, the growth and increasing organization of domestic anti-dam mobilization as well as the democratization of the political regime since the late 1970s. The dynamics of big dam building in South Africa and Lesotho, however, demonstrate that the impact of primarily external transnational organizing, the existence of supportive globalizing norms, and even domestic democratization during the 1990s will be limited without the presence of strong, grassroots social mobilization and advocacy.

In Indonesia, likewise, big dam projects have by and large continued to be executed. Although the existence of lobbying by domestic nongovernmental organizations and grassroots anti-dam mobilization has resulted in some reforms, the authoritarian regime that persisted in that country until recently has generally given big dam proponents a relatively unchecked ability to repress opponents. Even with the adoption and internalization of environmental norms and principles into the Indonesian state, the subversion of human rights, judicial, and other democratic procedures has limited the possibilities for effective transnational links to be formed and for domestic opposition to be effective.

In the case of China, the absence of both domestic social mobilization and the persistence of a dominant authoritarian regime has resulted in even less change in the dynamics of big dam building than in Indonesia. For example, despite the fact that an emergent transnational anti-dam network has prevented foreign donors (e.g., the United States Export Import Bank) and multilateral development agencies (e.g., the World Bank) from supporting China in its endeavor to build the mammoth Three Gorges Project, construction has continued. But the case of the Three Gorges does highlight that even when transnationally allied anti-dam activity has encountered unfavorable domestic-level conditions, it has increasingly been able to have a noticeable and non-negligible effect on development processes and outcomes.

In the sixth and final chapter of this book, I correspondingly investigate the formation and institutionalization of a transnational anti-dam network and its effects on big dam building dynamics, particularly at the international level with respect to the policies and practices of the World Bank and other powerful prodam actors. I also examine two critical transnational gatherings that took place in the late 1990s. The first conference contributed to the building of a transnational anti-dam network by bringing together critics and dam-affected peoples from twenty different countries. Leading members of this emergent transnational network, along with representatives of multinational corporations, international agencies, professional associations, states, and others participated in a second and subsequent conference that established a novel global governance initiative to review the historical performance of these projects and establish new global big dam building norms and principles for the 21st century. Given these events, I propose that the "international big dam regime" or "transnational big dam field" was dramatically altered during the 20th century.

In closing, I reevaluate the theoretical explanation and the alternatives offered to account for this unexpected change in big dam building in light of the weight of evidence offered in the book. After some empirical and conceptual extensions, I suggest that a profound transformation in the transnational political economy of development has occurred, reflected by the dramatic fall and reforms in big dam building and shifts in the international big dam regime. I conclude with some reflections on broader empirical and theoretical implications of the study, as well as identify avenues for future research. These include a proposed constructivist transnationalism agenda for the social sciences as well as a linked scholarly agenda on development dynamics in a transnationalized world. [. . .]

DAMS, DEMOCRACY, AND DEVELOPMENT IN TRANSNATIONAL PERSPECTIVE

The dramatic and inter-linked changes in big dam building and the international big dam regime indicate that a broader transformation in the transnational political economy of development has occurred. This is because big dams are activities and symbols that reflect, are conditioned by, and shape larger dynamics of development, dynamics that are transnational in nature. Correspondingly the more general implications of this book contribute to theoretical and empirical advances as well as future research agendas in the scholarly fields of development and transnationalism.

This study offers important insights into the long-standing social scientific debates on the relationships between institutions and development. The evidence presented in this book supports the argument that democratic institutions increase the likelihood that transnational advocacy, certain types of globalizing norms, and domestic mobilization reduce and/or substantially reform big dam building. Many would argue that such changes around these projects contributed to sustainable development, if sustainable development is understood as longer-term progress toward greater public participation, political accountability, social equity, and environmental sustainability. Thus, it could be concluded that democratic institutions are more conducive to the promotion of (sustainable) development.

However, if more and not fewer big dam projects were considered necessary for development, then an authoritarian regime might be posited as more conducive. Suppose economic growth through increased agricultural production and industrialization is the prevailing vision of development, and electricity, irrigation, and other outputs of big dams are considered necessary to achieve that (economic) development. Then authoritarian regimes would increase the likelihood of development by minimizing the effects of transnational contestation, globalizing norms, and domestic mobilization that might have otherwise prevented these projects from being built.

This suggests that scholarly research investigating the effects on development of democratic versus authoritarian regimes—or a wider range of institutions including the rule of law or enforceable property rights or certain types of norms, or other factors such as "good governance," "social capital," levels of instability, savings, or investment more broadly—that operationalizes development in different ways would contribute to advances in knowledge. Scholars can no longer, if they ever could, assume that the conceptualization of development they adopt will be universally acceptable.[84]

In other words, a general theoretical implication of this study is that the causes of development depend on the meanings of development, at least in part. In other words, development is socially produced and reproduced as well as socially constructed and reconstructed. Moreover, in order to (causally) reform or transform development, the meanings of development may have to be contested and reconstituted.

In fact, opponents had to challenge the taken-for-granted equivalence between big dams and development partly by critiquing the vision of development that legitimated these projects (and offering alternative notions). Thus, explicating, interpreting, and understanding (the genealogies, structures, and effects of different socially constructed) meanings of development are in and of themselves important scholarly tasks.[85]

Constructivist scholarship based on such understandings offers a productive and dialogical option in relation to important but ultimately unsatisfactory positivist and interpretivist approaches to development studies. Indeed Frederick Cooper and Randall Packard suggest in their incisive sociological interrogation of knowledge on development in the social sciences that two more extreme versions of these alternative approaches increasingly polarized the study of development from the 1980s on. They write: "One set might be called ultramodernist. It consists of economic theorists who insist that the laws of economics have been proven valid," and scholarship that considers the basic assumptions and tools of economics as of predominant utility in research on development. In contrast, a "second set is postmodernist. This group sees development discourse as nothing more than an apparatus of control and surveillance ... a 'knowledge-power regime,' that scholars should critically excavate and unmask."[86] This book offers an example of how the insights of these contending scholarly approaches can be drawn on and complement other epistemological, ontological, theoretical, and methodological perspectives to illuminate and explain development dynamics in a constructive constructivist way.

Furthermore, development is not just an essentially contested concept for scholarly research in isolation; development is also an intensely conflict-ridden empirical phenomenon.[87] Big dams as development activities and symbols provide ample proof of this claim. Indeed, this book offers compelling evidence that suggests that struggles over development occur not just from inequalities in control or outcomes but also from contending understandings about the causes and meanings, goals and evaluations of development.[88]

Moreover, conflicts over development and development dynamics more generally are (perhaps increasingly but certainly always have been) transnationally constructed. The pervasiveness of transnational interactions among 'agents' and 'structures', causes and meanings, can be seen in any issue area that is linked to or involves development, from natural resources and mining to trade, debt, finance and investment, to humanitarian intervention and peace building. For example, complex sets of transnational structuration mechanisms contributed to the global rise and spread of both state-led import-substituting industrialization development models in the 1950s and '60s as well as the progressive shift towards market-led, neoliberal strategies from the 1980s on.

This book is therefore also part of a reemergent social scientific research agenda on transnationalism in addition to a contribution to scholarship on development. It contributes to this "new transnationalism" literature by elaborating different types of novel transnational actors and institutions, and by identifying key conditions and mechanisms through which these agents and structures (re-)shape dynamics of development across multiple contexts and levels.

The analysis herein further reveals how the identities of various actors involved in these novel forms of transnational action are themselves altered over time. Big dam critics from the West were primarily environmental conservationists, whereas those from developing countries were primarily focused on social justice issues. Through their interaction over time, these actors not only began to adopt the norms and discourses of their counterparts but novel reframings occurred such as an increasing explication of a "rights and sustainable livelihoods" perspective that was linked to struggles over big dams and debates over development more broadly.[89]

The novel form of transnational contestation around development as reflected by the struggles over big dams analyzed in this study is by no means unique; rather, these struggles have become pervasive aspects of world affairs. As discussed in several places in this book and examined elsewhere, similar sets of transnationally allied actors have been organizing and mobilizing advocacy in a variety of areas including nuclear weapons, women's rights, democratization, land mines, anticorruption, debt-relief, and others.[90]

Indeed, a range of these transnational actors has evolved from informal and short-term coalitions to more formal and institutionalized issue networks and organizations. As a result, they increasingly constitute structural parts of the broader transnational organizational sectors or social fields of security, governance, etc., that parallel and overlap with the transnational field of development. Investigation of the structuring of these transnational organizational sectors and social fields, their empirical implications for world affairs and theoretical implications for social science knowledge is a critical area for further research.

Compared with other scholarship like it, the interactions among such novel "transnationalisms from below" with extant and evolving "transnationalisms from above" with respect to big dam building were also explicated in this book.[91] The latter included the activities of various types of transnational actors such as multinational corporations, international professional associations, and multilateral agencies, among others. These agents interacted to generate and perpetuate the norms, principles, and procedures of what was called an international big dam regime. But these transnationalisms from above, imbricated with the international big dam regime, had also become relatively durable and structural parts of the transnational field of big dam building and thus development, even earlier than the novel phenomena and dynamics that contributed to the transformation of this field.

In sum, this study contributes to the building of a research program on "constructivist transnationalism" for the study of world affairs. The recent wave of scholarship on transnationalism in political science and sociology remains primarily liberal and actor-centric in orientation.[92] This study generates a strong case for a more explicit focus on different types of power (albeit with a much broader notion of power than the neo-realist tradition) as well as structures and structuration processes, in addition to the motivations and strategies of actors in order to explain and understand transnational phenomena and dynamics.

The book correspondingly links emerging propositions about transnational actors with conventional arguments about international regimes and more recent "constructivist" theorizing in international relations. The leading international relations work in the constructivist tradition has predominantly focused on states and the inter-state system, and has not by and large explicitly examined transnational non-state agents, structures, or dynamics.[93] Moreover, as Peter Katzenstein, Robert Keohane, and Stephen Krasner state: "There is a growing body of work in international relations and in security studies but, significantly, not yet in IPE (international political economy) that is self-conscious in conducting empirical research from a constructivist perspective."[94] This book is thus a conscious attempt to contribute an empirically grounded and conceptually rigorous study in the constructivist tradition linked to scholarship on transnational actors in the international political economy issue area.

It does so, however, by drawing and adopting insights from the world society, neoinstitutionalist and other traditions in sociology that have so forcefully explicated and documented the institutionalization of social and organizational fields. But the book also explicates processes and specific mechanisms of norm and field emergence, spread, adoption, and internalization that are generally not identified in this sociological research agenda. Moreover, world society and world system approaches in sociology largely investigate different types of global social structures, whether ideational and cognitive as in the case of the former or materialist and economic in the latter, identify states as the primary units embedded in and conditioned by these structures, and minimize the role of agency whether of state or non-state and transnational actors.[95]

The constructivist transnationalism scholarship promoted in this book offers a potentially productive option to these more institutionalized research programs in sociology and political science for the study of world affairs. This emergent paradigm is based on at least the following three conceptual moves: (1) from international-statist and world-statist to transnationalist (or multiple actors and structures that potentially cross borders and boundaries) theory; (2) from rationalist and structuralist to structurationist ontology; and (3) from positivist and interpretivist to constructivist epistemology. A constructivist transnationalism is exciting because it offers a research program that can inform the study of world affairs given the permeability of borders and boundaries and import of cross-border and cross-boundary factors to dynamics from the local to the global levels.[96]

Several avenues for future research in a constructivist transnationalism scholarly agenda would be well worth pursuing. The first is continued comparative investigation across issue areas and institutional contexts of transnational structuration "from below" to further improve understanding of the forms it takes and the conditions under which it can generate change. Correspondingly, comparative examination across issue areas and institutional contexts of the responses of transnationally allied dominant groups such as multinational corporations and business associations and/or various types of governments, among others, to these challenges from below would be of great utility in illuminating critical interactions in world affairs.

Research on the shifts occurring in extant international organizations and emergent transnational governance forms would also be extremely valuable.[97] Perhaps of greatest interest and importance for a research program on "constructivist transnationalism" would be to systematically examine and analyze over time and across space various transnational phenomena (agents and structures) and structuration dynamics (meanings and causes)—transnational terrorist and criminal networks, transnational religions and communities, transnational financial flows, transnational migration, transnational nongovernmental organizations and social movements, transgovernmental relations, transnational cultural models, etc.—and how these fields (re)shape identities, processes, and outcomes from the local to the global levels around the world. The potential significance of such a constructivist transnationalism research agenda is great given the knowledge it could generate for the complex and dynamic world of the 21st century. This book, with all its remaining flaws, will hopefully inspire more and better scholarship of this kind.

NOTES

1. Transnational Struggles for Water and Power

[. . .]

1. I include both "large" and the even more massive "major" dams in the category of "big dams." According to instructions of the International Commission on Large Dams, domestic dam agencies can report dams with heights over 15 meters, and those of 10–15 meters if they meet other technical requirements, as "large dams." "Major dams" meet one or more of the following requirements: height of over 150 meters, volume greater than 15 million cubic meters, reservoir storage of more than 25 cubic kilometers, and/or electricity generation of more than 1,000 megawatts. See ICOLD, *World Register of Large Dams* (Paris: ICOLD, 1988), and T.W. Mermel, "The World's Major Dams and Hydroplants," in *International Water Power and Dam Construction Handbook* (Sutton, U.K.: IWPDC, 1995)

2. Norman Smith, *A History of Dams* (London: Peter Davies, 1971).

3. See Nicholas Schnitter, *A History of Dams: The Useful Pyramids* (Rotterdam: Balkania, 1994), 158.

4. See John Waterbury, *Hydropolitics of the Nile Valley* (Syracuse, N.Y.: Syracuse University Press, 1979).

5. See A. D. Rassweiler, *The Generation of Power: The History of Dneprostroi* (Oxford: Oxford University Press, 1988).

6. See Donald Worster, "The Hoover Dam: A Study in Domination," in *The Social and Environmental Effects of Large Dams*, ed. Edward Goldsmith and Nicholas Hildyard, vol. 2 (Wadebridge: Wadebridge Ecological Centre, 1986), 21.

7. See Marc Reisner, *Cadillac Desert: The American West and Its Disappearing Water* (London: Seeker and Warburg, 1986), and W. Chandler, *The Myth of the TVA: Conservation and Development in the Tennessee Valley, 1933–1983* (Cambridge: Ballinger, 1984).

8. See Patrick McCully, *Silenced Rivers: The Ecology and Politics of Large Dams* (London: Zed Books, 1996).

9. A similar type of international professional, technical, voluntary, and nongovernmental association called the International Commission on Irrigation and Drainage (ICID) was established in 1950 with offices in India. ICID was initially founded by individuals from eleven countries. The

number of "member" countries rose to nearly one hundred, fifty years later. ICID's mission has predominantly focused on the transfer of water management technology for irrigated agriculture, making it a very active big dam proponent in the world.

10. Quoted in Worster, in Goldsmith and Hildyard, 21.

11. See Edward Mason and Robert Asher, *The World Bank Since Bretton Woods* (Washington, D.C.: Brookings Institution, 1973).

12. Albert O. Hirschman, *Development Projects Observed* (Washington, D.C.: Brookings Institution, 1967).

13. Leonard Sklar and Patrick McCully, "Damming the Rivers: The World Bank's Lending for Large Dams," in *International Rivers Network Working Paper Number 5* (Berkeley: International Rivers Network, November 1994).

14. See McCully.

15. See Ismail Serageldin, "Toward Sustainable Management of Water Resources," in *Directions in Development Working Papers* (Washington, D.C.: World Bank, 1996), 1–5.

16. See Thomas F. Homer-Dixon, *Environmental Scarcity and Global Security* (New York: Foreign Policy Association, 1993); Miriam R. Lowi, *Water and Power: The Politics of a Scarce Resource in the Jordan River Basin* (Cambridge: Cambridge University Press, 1995); and Ben Crow et al., *Sharing the Ganges: The Politics and Technology of River Development* (New Delhi: Sage Publications, 1995).

17. See Sandra Postel, "Forging a Sustainable Water Strategy," in *State of the World 1996*, ed. Lester R. Brown et al. (New York: W. W. Norton, 1996), 40–59. Several international initiatives were organized in this area during the 1990s, including the Global Water Partnership, World Water Commission, and World Commission on Dams.

18. International Energy Agency, *Energy in Developing Countries* (Paris: IEA, 1995), 3.

19. See World Bank, *Energy Strategies for Rural and Poor People in the Developing World* (Washington, D.C.: Industry and Energy Department, World Bank, 1995).

20. The numbers of big dams being completed decreased partially as a result of the larger and larger size of projects that were initiated over time. For example, 10 major dams were built before 1950, 35 during the 1950s, 64 during the 1960s, and 93 during the 1970s. Figures calculated from Mermel (1993–1996) and ICOLD, *World Register of Dams* (Paris: ICOLD, 1998).

21. ICOLD (1998).

22. See Jose Roberto Moreira and Alan Douglas Poole, "Hydropower and Its Constraints," in *Renewable Energy: Sources for Fuels and Electricity*, ed. Thomas B. Johansson et al. (Washington, D.C.: Earth Island Press, 1993).

23. See ICOLD, Circular Letter 1427, December 1995; Circular Letter Number 1388, 16 January 1995; and Circular Letter 1342, 4 October 1993, Paris: ICOLD, as well as ICOLD (1998). "Under construction" and "starts" can mean anything from receiving formal approval from authorities to actually being in the process of being built with a greater likelihood of completion.

24. This does not include nonconventional and renewable sources of energy generation, such as wind or solar power.

25. See World Bank, *World Development Report: The Challenge of Development* (Oxford: Oxford University Press, 1991) and World Bank, *Meeting the Infrastructure Challenge in Latin America and the Caribbean* (Washington, D.C.: World Bank, 1995a).

26. See World Bank, *World Development Report: Infrastructure* (Oxford: Oxford University Press, 1994).

27. See R. Repretto, *Skimming the Water: Rent-Seeking and the Performance of Public Irrigation Systems* (Washington, D.C.: World Resources Institute, 1986), and E. W. Morrow and P. F. Shagraw, *Understanding the Costs and Schedules of World Bank Supported Hydroelectric Projects* (Washington, D.C.: World Bank Industry and Energy Department, 1990).

28. See Ian Pope, "Solving the Project Funding Puzzle," *Hydro Review Worldwide* (April 1996): 30–32; Robert Goodland, "The Big Dam Controversy: Killing Hydro Promotes Coal and Nukes: Is that Better for Environmental Sustainability?" (paper presented at GTE Technology and Ethics Series, Michigan Technological University, May 1995); and Robert Goodland, "Large Dams: Learning From the Past, Looking to the Future" (paper presented to the IUCN—The World Conservation Union & The World Bank Group Joint Workshop, Gland, Switzerland, 10–11 April 1997).

29. The World Bank estimated that a one-year delay in completion will reduce the benefit-cost ratio by one-third and a two-year delay by over one-half and that costs associated with resettlement can increase project costs up to 30 percent. World Bank, *The Bankwide Review of Projects Involving Involuntary Resettlement* (Washington, D.C.: World Bank, 8 April 1996).

30. For the United States, see Tim Palmer, *Endangered Rivers and the Conservation Movement* (Berkeley: University of California Press, 1986), and R. Gottlieb, *Forcing the Spring: The Transformation of the American Environmental Movement* (Washington, D.C.: Earth Island Press, 1993).

31. See Lester Brown et al., *Vital Signs, 1995* (London: Worldwatch Institute/Earthscan, 1995); and Anthony Churchill, "Meeting Hydro's Financing, Development Challenges," *Hydro Review Worldwide* (Fall 1994). See also World Commission on Dams, *Dams and Development: A Framework for Decision-Making* (London: Earthscan, 2000).

32. See Sanjeev Khagram et al., eds., *Restructuring World Politics: Transnational Social Movements,*

Networks and Norms (Minneapolis: University of Minnesota Press, 2002); Ann Florini, ed., *The Third Force: The Rise of Transnational Civil Society* (Washington, D.C.: Carnegie Endowment for International Peace, 2000); John Boli and George M. Thomas, eds., *Constructing World Culture: International Nongovernmental Organizations since 1875* (Stanford: Stanford University Press, 1999); Jonathan A. Fox and L. David Brown, eds., *The Struggle for Accountability: The World Bank, NGOs and Grassroots Movements* (Cambridge: MIT Press, 1998); Jackie Smith et al., eds., *Transnational Social Movements and Global Politics: Solidarity Beyond the State* (Syracuse, N.Y.: Syracuse University Press, 1997); Thomas Risse-Kappen, ed., *Bringing Transnational Relations Back in: Non-State Actors, Domestic Structures, and International Institutions* (Cambridge: Cambridge University Press, 1995); Matthew Evangelista, "The Paradox of State Strength: Transnational Relations, Domestic Structures, and Security Policy in Russia and the Soviet Union," *International Organization* 49 (Winter 1995): 1–38; David Zweig, " 'Developmental Communities' in China's Coast: The Impact of Trade, Investment, and Transnational Alliances," *Comparative Politics* 27, no. 3 (April 1995): 253–274; Patricia Chilton, "Mechanics of Change: Social Movements, Transnational Coalitions, and Transformation Processes in Eastern Europe," *Democratization* 1, no. 1 (Spring 1994): 151–181; Kathryn Sikkink, "Human Rights, Principled Issue-Networks and Sovereignty in Latin America," *International Organization* 47, no. 3 (Summer 1993); Allison Brysk, "From Above and Below: Social Movements, the International System, and Human Rights in Argentina," *Comparative Political Studies* 26, no. 3 (October 1993): 259–285; and Thomas Princen and Matthias Finger, *Environmental NGOs in World Politics: Linking the Local and the Global* (London: Routledge, 1994).

A previous literature on transnationalism dates back to the 1970s. This research program generated a great deal of work and debate but was overshadowed by state-centric and world system approaches that subsequently became dominant in political science and sociology. For political science, see Robert O. Keohane and Joseph S. Nye Jr., eds., *Transnational Relations and World Politics* (Cambridge: Harvard University Press, 1971). The more sociological world systems and "dependency" research program that emerged in the 1960s and 1970s, and focused on the trends, patterns, and affects of transnational capitalist expansion contributed greatly along these lines as well. See generative work such as Fernando E. Cardoso, "Dependency and Development in Latin America," *New Left Review*, no. 74, 83–95; Andre Gundre Frank, *Capitalism and Underdevelopment in Latin America* (Cambridge: Cambridge University Press, 1969); Arghiri Emmanuel, *Unequal Exchange* (New York: Modern Reader, 1972);, Samir Amin, *Unequal Development* (New York: Monthly Review Press, 1976); Immanuel Wallerstein, *The Modern World System* (New York: Academic Press, 1974); Peter B. Evans, *Dependent Development: The Alliance of Multinational, State and Local Capital in Brazil* (Princeton: Princeton University Press, 1979); and others.

33. I provide data in this chapter solely on the increasing numbers of transnational non-governmental advocacy organizations. This classification is similar to the one offered in Khagram, Riker, and Sikkink, 2002.

34. See Robert O. Keohane and Joseph S. Nye Jr. (1971); Peter Willets, ed., *Pressure Groups in the Global System: The Transnational Relations of Issue-Oriented Non-Governmental Organizations* (New York: St. Martin's Press, 1982); Jamie Leatherman et al., "International Institutions and Transnational Social Movement Organizations: Challenging the State in a Three-Level Game of Global Transformation" (paper delivered at International Studies Association, Washington, D.C., 28 March to 1 April 1994); and Paul K. Wapner, *Environmental Activism and World Civic Politics* (Albany: State University of New York Press, 1996).

35. See Risse-Kappen, "Introduction" (1995). Another set of data shows that while only 37 of these groups existed before 1875, by 1973 over 6,000 from the International Red Cross to the World Wildlife Fund for Nature were on record as having been founded.

36. These groups should be contrasted with those transnational actors clandestinely and often violently seeking to advance principled ideas (such as terrorists) or seeking to gain materially (organized criminals). See various issues of the journal *Transnational Organized Crime* (London: Frank Cass), and Bruce Hoffman, *Inside Terrorism* (New York: Columbia University Press, 1998).

37. See Kathryn Sikkink and Jackie Smith, "Infrastructures for Change: Transnational Organizations 1953–1993," in Khagram et al. (2002).

38. In fact, the establishment of transnational non-governmental organizations often results from the activities of already existing transnational coalitions.

39. Identity groups and communities such as diasporas, migrant communities, and border groups which cross territorial boundaries in multiple ways are also transnational. However, these are not central to the analysis I offer in this study. See for example, Nina Glick Schiller, Linda Basch, and Christina Balnc-Szanton, eds., *Towards a Transnational Perspective on Migration: Race, Class, Ethnicity and Nationalism Reconsidered* (New York: New York Academy of Sciences, 1992), vol. 645; Arjun Appadurai, *Modernity at Large: Cultural Dimensions of Globalization* (Minneapolis: University of Minnesota Press, 1996); and Ulf Hannerz, *Transnational Connections:*

Cultures, People, Places (London: Routledge, 1996). I also do not include trans-governmental relations in this list, because they do not include nongovernmental organizations. See Ann Marie Slaughter, "The Real New World Order," *Foreign Affairs* 76, no. 5 (September/October 1997).

40. Keck and Sikkink also add a common discourse to their definition of networks. Transnational networks of nongovernmental organizations are said to be based on shared normative concerns, as opposed to the instrumental goals of transnational corporations, or the common causal ideas of epistemic communities. See Margaret E. Keck and Kathryn Sikkink, *Activists Beyond Borders: Advocacy Networks in International Politics* (Ithaca: Cornell University Press, 1998); Peter B. Evans et al., eds., *States versus Markets in the World System* (Beverly Hills: Sage Publications, 1985); and Peter Haas, "Knowledge, Power, and International Policy Coordination," *International Organization* 46 (Winter 1992): 1–39. This means that all these actors can and do act strategically, but that they are motivated for different purposes or interests.

41. See Paul J. Nelson, *The World Bank and Non-Governmental Organizations: The Limits of Apolitical Development* (New York: St. Martin's Press, 1995).

42. On organizational fields see Walter W. Powell and Paul J. Dimaggio, *The New Institutionalism in Organizational Analysis* (Chicago: University of Chicago Press, 1991). For social fields, see Pierre Bourdieu, *The Logic of Practice* (Stanford: Stanford University Press, 1990).

43. Allison Brysk, "The International Politics of Indians in Latin America," *Latin American Perspectives* 23, no. 2, (1996), 38–57.

44. I define norms broadly as shared expectations of appropriateness held by a community of actors. Norms are institutions, but depending on the context, the term institution in this study is often used to denote more formalized procedures and structures that guide behavior. Thus the notion that environmental factors must be included in the evaluation of development projects is a norm, while the more explicit requirement that environmental impact assessments must be completed before development projects can be implemented would be considered an institution. For discussions on norms and rules in social life from differing perspectives see, for example, Jon Elster, *Nuts and Bolts for the Social Sciences* (Cambridge: Cambridge University Press, 1989); Anthony Giddens, *The Constitution of Society* (Berkeley: University of California Press, 1984); John Searle, *Speech Acts: An Essay in the Philosophy of Language* (Cambridge: Cambridge University Press, 1969); and Fred R. Dallmayr and Thomas A. McCarthy, eds., *Understanding and Social Inquiry* (Notre Dame: University of Notre Dame Press, 1977). For discussions of norms in world affairs, see Martha Finnemore, *National Interests in*

International Society (Ithaca: Cornell University Press, 1996); Peter Katzenstein, *The Culture of National Security: Norms and Identity in World Politics* (New York: Columbia University Press, 1996); and Martha Finnemore and Kathryn Sikkink, "International Norm Dynamics and Political Change," *International Organization* 52, no. 4 (1998).

45. Scholars have debated and remain divided over the existence and efficacy of norms and institutions in world politics. See Stephen D. Krasner, *Structural Conflict: The Third World Against Global Liberalism* (Berkeley: University of California Press, 1985); Robert O. Keohane, "International Institutions: Two Approaches," *International Studies Quarterly* 32 (1988): 379–396; and Volker Rittberger, *Regime Theory and International Relations* (Oxford: Oxford University Press, 1993). The constructivist challenge in international relations has involved a strong claim that norms, identities, and culture not only influence the dynamics of world politics, but also that the core variables of states, power capabilities, and interests are reciprocally constituted and transformed by these broader sets of ideas and institutions. See Alexander Wendt and Raymond Duvall, "Institutions and Order in the International System," in *Global Changes and Theoretical Challenges*, ed. Ernst Otto Czempiel and James Rosenau (London: Lexington, 1989); Alexander Wendt, "The Agent-Structure Problem in International Relations Theory," *International Organization* 41 (1987): 335–370, and "Anarchy Is What States Make of It: The Social Construction of Power Politics," *International Organization* 46 (1992): 391–425; David Dessler, "What's at Stake in the Agent-Structure Debate?" *International Organization* 43, no. 3 (Summer 1989); Friedrich Kratochwil and John Ruggie, "International Organization: A State of the Art or an Art of the State," *International Organization* 40 (1986): 753; John G. Ruggie, "Transactors and Change: Embedded Liberalism in a Post-War Economic Order," in *International Regimes*, ed. Stephen D. Krasner (Ithaca: Cornell University Press, 1983); John G. Ruggie, *Multilateralism Matters: The Theory and Praxis of an Institutional Form* (New York: Columbia University Press, 1993); and Yosef Lapid and Friedrich Kratochwil, *The Return of Culture and Identity in IR Theory* (Boulder, Colo.: Lynne Rienner, 1996). For more empirically grounded accounts, see Ethan A. Nadleman, "Global Prohibition Regimes: The Evolution of Norms in International Society," *International Organization* 44 (1990): 479–526; Jutta Weldes, "Constructing National Interests: The Logic of U.S. National Security in the Postwar Era" (Ph.D. diss., University of Minnesota, 1992); Richard Price, "Genealogy of the Chemical Weapons Taboo," *International Organization* 49 (1995); Audie Klotz, *Norms in International Relations: The Struggle Against Apartheid* (Ithaca: Cornell

University Press, 1995); Finnemore (1996); and Katzenstein (1996).

46. See George M. Thomas et al., *Institutional Structure: Constituting State, Society, and the Individual* (Newbury Park: Sage, 1987); and John Meyer et al., "World Society and the Nation State," *American Journal of Sociology* 103 (1997): 144–181. For a similar but more interpretative research program along these lines, see Barry Buzan, "From International System to International Society: Structural Realism and Regime Theory Meet the English School," *International Organization*, 47, no. 3 (Summer 1993): 327–352. For a classic work from this perspective, see Hedley Bull and Adam Watson, eds., *The Expansion of International Society* (Oxford: Clarendon Press, 1984).

47. Regulatory norms define standards of appropriate behavior, constitutive norms define actor identities, practical norms focus on commonly accepted notions of best solutions, and evaluative norms stress questions of morality. See Katzenstein (1996).

48. The existence of norms that legitimate the state as the only natural form of political organization in the world system provides a powerful explanation for why completely dysfunctional states not only persist, but also why these entities continue to be propped up by other states and international organizations. But the same principles of sovereignty and self-determination can be used by groups to de-privilege states in their demands to secede. See Robert Jackson and Carl Rosberg, "Why Africa's Weak States Persist: Empirical and Juridical Statehood," *World Politics* 35 (1982): 1–24; John W. Meyer, "The World Polity and the Authority of the Nation-State," in Thomas et al. (1987); David Strang, "From Dependency to Sovereignty: An Event History Analysis of Decolonization," *American Sociological Review* 55 (1990): 846–860; and Cynthia Weber, *Simulating Sovereignty: Intervention, the State, and Symbolic Exchange* (Cambridge: Cambridge University Press, 1995).

49. National security has perhaps been the central role ascribed to all states and state leaders.

50. See Dana P. Eyre and Marc C. Suchman, "Military Procurement as Rational Myth: Notes on the Social Construction of Weapons Proliferation," *Sociological Forum* 7 (1992): 137–161; Gili Drori, "Global Discourse, State Policy, and National Governance: The Case of the Globalization of Science Policy," *MacArthur Foundation's Consortium—Research Series on International Peace and Cooperation*, Working Paper no. 7 (1997); Francisco O. Ramirez and Jane Wise, "The Political Incorporation of Women," in *National Development and the World System*, ed. John Meyer and Michael Hannan (Chicago: University of Chicago Press, 1979); and John Boli, "The Expansion of Nation-States," in Thomas et al. (1987).

51. John Meyer et al., "The Rise of an Environmental Sector in World Society" (paper presented at the Annual Meetings of the American Sociological Association, Los Angeles, 1994), 15.

52. See David John Frank et al., "The Nation-State and the Natural Environment over the Twentieth Century," *American Sociological Review* (2000): 96–116.

53. See Oran R. Young, "The Politics of International Regime Formation: Managing Natural Resources and the Environment," *International Organization* 43, no. 3 (Summer 1989): 349–375; and Oran R. Young, *The Effectiveness of International Environmental Regimes: Causal Connections and Behavioral Mechanisms* (Cambridge: MIT Press, 1999).

54. The report of the preparatory meeting for the UN Stockholm Conference on the Human Environment in September 1971 stated that while development was the cure for environmental problems—like those that arise from widespread poverty—in developing countries, development had produced environmental problems in industrialized countries. Correspondingly, the report stated that "as the process of development gets under way, the latter type of problem is likely to assume greater importance. The process of agricultural growth and transformation, for example, will involve the construction of reservoirs and irrigation systems, the clearing of forests, the use of fertilizers and pesticides, and the establishment of new communities. These processes will certainly have environmental implications. ..." Quote from Darryl D'Monte, *Temples or Tombs?, Industry Versus Environment: Three Controversies* (New Delhi: Centre for Science and Environment, 1985), 8.

55. See various chapters in Thomas et al. (1987).

56. See Samuel P. Huntington, *The Third Wave: Democratization in the Late Twentieth Century* (Norman: University of Oklahoma Press, 1991); Francisco O. Ramirez and John W. Meyer, *Citizenship Principles, Human Rights, and the National Incorporation of Women, 1870–1990*, proposal to U.S. National Science Foundation, 1996; Karen Brown Thompson, "Changing Global Norms Concerning Women's and Children's Rights and their Implications for State-Citizen Relations," in Riker, Khagram, and Sikkink (2002); and Connie McNeely, *Constructing the Nation-State: International Organization and Prescriptive Action* (Westport, Conn.: Greenwood Press, 1995).

57. See Human Rights Watch and Natural Resources Defense Council, *Defending the Earth, Abuses of Human Rights and the Environment* (New York: Human Rights Watch and Natural Resources Defense Council, 1992); and Aaron Sachs, "Human Rights and the Environment," in Brown et al. (1996). See also campaigns of Earthrights International.

58. See John P. Humphrey, *Human Rights and the United Nations: A Great Adventure* (Dobbs Ferry, N.Y.: Transnational, 1984).

59. As noted before, there is an interactive process by which transnational norms are reshaped by local dynamics. While the origins of many 20th-century globalizing norms have been western, and although many of these are still likely to arise in the West, the dynamics of constructing a world society have become much more multidirectional and interactive.

60. Similar arguments and evidence could be offered in the cases of indigenous peoples, gender justice, children's rights, peace, and a range of other areas. See David P. Forsythe, *Human Rights and World Politics*, 2d ed. (Lincoln: University of Nebraska Press, 1989); N. G. Onuf and V. Spike Peterson, "Human Rights from an International Regime Perspective," *Journal of International Affairs* 38 (Winter 1984): 329–342; Jack Donnelly, "International Human Rights: A Regime Analysis," *International Organization* 40, no. 3 (Summer 1986): 599–642; and Jack Donnelly, *Universal Human Rights in Theory and Practice* (Ithaca: Cornell University Press, 1989).

61. For a treatment of causal mechanisms in the social sciences, see Jon Elster (1989).

62. The tremendous number of human rights violations that have been and continue to be perpetrated is ample evidence of this reality.

63. See Finnemore (1996) and Stephen D. Krasner, *Sovereignty: Organized Hypocrisy* (Princeton: Princeton University Press, 1999).

64. The rapid formal embracing of neoliberal procedures and structures in the third world with uneven implementation in practice is an excellent example of this. For the importance of domestic structures in mediating the ultimate outcomes from an earlier global spread of economic discourse, see Peter A. Hall, ed., *The Political Power of Economic Ideas: Keynesianism across Nations* (Princeton: Princeton University Press, 1989).

65. See Peter L. Berger and Thomas Luckmann, *The Social Construction of Reality: A Treatise in the Sociology of Knowledge* (Garden City: Doubleday, 1966); Pierre Bourdieu, *The Logic of Practice* (Stanford: Stanford University Press, 1980); and Anthony Giddens, *The Constitution of Society: Outline of the Theory of Structuration* (Cambridge: Polity Press, 1984).

66. On causal pathways, see David Dessler, "The Architecture of Causal Analysis" (working paper, Center for International Affairs, Harvard University, April 1992).

67. See Humphrey (1984).

68. See Freedom House, *Freedom in the World*, various years.

69. See Ans Kolk et al., "International Codes of Conduct and Corporate Social Responsibility," *Transnational Corporations* 8, no. 1 (April 1999).

70. See Haas (1992), 1–39; McNeely (1995), and Martha Finnemore, "Norms, Culture and World Politics: Insights from Sociology's Institutionalism," *International Organization* 49, no. 3 (1995): 325–348.

71. See Terry Lynn Karl and Philippe C. Schmitter, "Democratization Around the Globe: Opportunities and Risks," in *World Security: Challenges for a New Century*, ed. Michael T. Klare and Daniel C. Thomas (New York: St Martins Press, 1992), 43–62; Kathryn Sikkink (1993); Allison Brysk (1993), 259–285; Chilton (1994), 151–181; and Jackie Smith et al., "Globalizing Human Rights: The Work of Transnational Human Rights NGOs in the 1990s," *Human Rights Quarterly* 20 (1998): 379–412.

72. Krasner (1983), 2.

73. Many international organizations and multinational corporations are also resistant to changing actual behavior, but the analysis of these actors is somewhat different from those of states.

74. See Barrington Moore Jr., *Social Origins of Dictatorship and Democracy* (Boston: Beacon Press, 1966); Samuel P. Huntington, *Political Order in Changing Societies* (New Haven: Yale University Press, 1968); and Robert H. Bates, *Markets and States in Tropical Africa: The Political Basis of Agricultural Policies* (Berkeley: University of California Press, 1981). The proposition that states are shaped by external factors does not preclude but complements domestic level accounts. See also Fernando Henrique Cardoso and Enzo Faletto, *Dependencia y Desarrollo en America Latina; Ensayo de Interpretacion Sociologica* (Mexico: Siglo Veintiuno Editores, 1969); Guillermo A. O'Donnell, *Modernization and Bureaucratic-authorities; Studies in South American Politics*, Politics of Modernization Series, no. 9 (Berkeley, Institute of International Studies, University of California, 1973); Peter B. Evans (1979); Robert D. Putnam, "Diplomacy and Domestic Politics: The Logic of Two-Level Games," *International Organization* (Summer 1988): 427–460; and Peter B. Evans et al., eds., *Double-edged Diplomacy: International Bargaining and Domestic Politics* (Berkeley: University of California Press, 1993).

75. Regime in the domestic arena denotes the set of political and administrative institutions that determine: (1) the forms and channels of access to principle state positions; (2) the characteristics of actors who are admitted to and excluded from such access; (3) the tactics that these actors can use to gain access, and (4) the procedures that are acceptable in the formulation and implementation of state decisions. Democracy, then, is a regime in which there exists at a minimum: (1) meaningful competition for all effective state positions through regular, free, and fair elections; (2) a highly inclusive level of political participation in which no social group is prevented from exercising the rights of citizenship; and (3) a level of civil and political liberties secured through equality under the rule of law. See Larry Diamond et al., chap. 1 in *Politics in Developing Countries: Comparing Experiences with Democracy* (Boulder: Lynne Rienner, 1995). For a more extensive definition of political democracy with which I am sympathetic,

see Philippe C. Schmitter and Terry Lynn Karl, "What Democracy Is . . . and Is Not," *Journal of Democracy* 2, no. 3 (Summer 1991): 75–88. For an excellent analysis of why the concepts of bureaucracy, regime, and government should be kept analytically distinct when examining state institutions, see Stephanie Lawson, "Conceptual Issues in the Comparative Study of Regime Change and Democratization," *Comparative Politics* (January 1993): 183–205.

76. See Ted Gurr, "On the Political Consequences of Scarcity and Economic Decline," *International Studies Quarterly* 29, no. 1 (March 1985): 51–75.

77. I do not elaborate in this section a major current of social movement theorizing that focuses less on external resource conflicts and macro-political opportunity structures and more on internal, micro-mobilizational strategies, discourses and identity dynamics. But the historical and ethnographic analysis presented in subsequent chapters offers a glimpse into these latter elements of collective organization and mobilization. For key texts from this "new social movement" approach see Clauss Offe, "New Social Movements: Changing Boundaries of the Political," *Social Research* 52 (1985): 817–868; Russell J. Dalton and Manfred Kuechler, eds., *Challenging the Political Order: New Social and Political Movements in Western Democracies* (New York: Oxford University Press, 1990); and Arturo Escobar and Sonia E. Alvarez, eds., *The Making of Social Movements in Latin America: Identity, Strategy and Democracy* (Boulder, Colo.: Westview, 1992). For a path-breaking attempt to "more successfully read, interpret, and understand the often fugitive political conduct of subordinate groups" see James Scott, *Domination and the Arts of Resistance* (New Haven: Yale University Press, 1990).

78. On the other hand, they are also strengthened by their transnational linkages to foreign and transnational nongovernmental organizations.

79. In the environmental issue area, see P.J. Sands, "The Role of Non-Governmental Organizations in Enforcing International Environmental Law," in *Control over Compliance With International Law*, ed. William E. Butler (The Hague, Netherlands: Martinus Nijhoff, 1991), 61–68; Oran Young, *International Cooperation: Building Regimes for Natural Resources and the Environment* (Ithaca: Cornell University Press, 1993); and Oran Young, *Global Environmental Change and International Governance* (Hanover, N.H.: Dartmouth Press, 1996).

[. . .]

80. See Adam Przeworski and Henry Teune, *The Logic of Comparative Social Inquiry* (Malabar: R. E. Krieger, 1982). In addition to these methods, a variant of multi-sited ethnography was conducted.

81. See Alexander George and Andrew Bennett, *Case Studies and Theory Development* (Cambridge: MIT Press, 2002).

82. See Henry E. Brady and David Collier, eds.,

Rethinking Social Inquiry: Diverse Tools, Shared Standards, New York: Rowman & Littlefield, 2002).

83. I also conducted participant observation in several settings, including as Senior Advisor for Policy and Institutional Analysis at the World Commission on Dams from 1998–2000. The broader research strategy was one of systematic triangulation of various units, research methods, types of data, and social science philosophies. See Todd Jick, "Mixing Qualitative and Quantitative Methods: Triangulation in Action," *Administrative Science Quarterly* 24, no. 4 (1999): 602–611; Ann Chih Lin, "Bridging Positivist And Interpretivist Approaches to Qualitative Methods," *Policy Studies Journal* 26, no. 1 (1998): 162–180; and James Mahoney, "Nominal, Ordinal, and Narrative Appraisal in Macro-Causal Analysis," *American Journal of Sociology* 104, no. 4 (1999): 1154–1196.

[. . .]

84. It is crucial to know, for example, whether particular postulated aspects of "good governance" such as human rights records are differently correlated with economic growth as opposed to advances in human capabilities such as longevity or literacy. For emergent conceptualizations and indicators of development, see the various annual Human Development Reports produced by the United Nations Development Program from 1990 on, or the extensive debate over the meaning of sustainable development that was sparked by the World Commission on Environment and Development's adoption of a particular understanding of that notion in its 1986 report.

85. See James Ferguson, *The Anti-Politics Machine: Development, Depoliticization, and Bureaucratic Power in the Third World* (Cambridge: Cambridge University Press, 1990), for a particularly compelling piece of scholarship along these lines.

86. Frederick Cooper and Randall Packard, eds., *International Development and the Social Sciences* (Berkeley: University of California Press, 1997), 2–3.

87. The intense debates during the World Commission on Dams process between 1998 and 2000 over what "development effectiveness" meant and how it could be operationalized to evaluate past experience with and to help formulate future norms for big dam projects is a stark example of this.

88. See Thomas Sowell, *A Conflict of Visions: Ideological Origins of Political Struggles* (New York: Basic Books, 1987).

89. See James G. March and Johan P. Olsen, "Institutional Dynamics of International Political Orders," in *Exploration and Contestation in the Study of World Politics*, ed. Peter Katzenstein, Robert Keohane, and Stephen Krasner (Cambridge: MIT Press, 1999).

90. See Smith et al. (1997); Fox and Brown (1998); Florini (2000); and Khagram, Riker, and Sikkink (2002).

91. For an example of work along these lines, see John Braithwaitte and Peter Drahos, *Global Business Regulation* (Cambridge: Cambridge University Press, 2000).

92. For a seminal predominantly liberal and actor-centric volume in this recent wave of scholarship, see Thomas Risse-Kappen, ed., *Bringing Transnational Relations Back In* (Cambridge: Cambridge University Press, 1995). This is less so the case for sociological work in the subfield of transnational migration.

93. For one of the premier books in this genre, see John Gerard Ruggie, *Constructing the World Polity: Essays on International Institutionalization* (London: Routledge, 1998).

94. Katzenstein, Keohane, and Krasner (1999), 35.

95. For a definitive article on the world society perspective, see John W. Meyer and John Boli, "World Society and the Nation-State," *American Journal of Sociology* 103, no. 1 (1997). For a recent and compelling book from the world systems approach, see Andre Gunder Frank, *Reorient: Global Economy in the Asian Age* (Berkeley: University of California Berkeley, 1998). For neo-institutionalist and field theory in sociology, see Walter W. Powell and Paul J. Dimaggio, eds., *The New Institutionalism in Organizational Analysis* (Chicago: University of Chicago Press, 1991), and Pierre Bourdieu, *Outline of a Theory of Practice* (Cambridge: Cambridge University Press, 1977).

96. A virtual landslide of writing on globalization emerged in the 1990s. Much of it focused on the economic aspects of supposed globalization. However, the scholarly literature on globalization ranges from work that is more about internationalization or international integration to that which is about worldwide de-territorialization to that which is about transnational phenomena and dynamics similar to the approach offered in this book. Some of the earlier and more prominent books from a range of theoretical and methodological approaches include Roland Robertson, *Globalisation: Social Theory and Global Culture* (London: Sage, 1992); Arjun Appadurai, *Modernity at Large: Cultural Dimensions of Globalization* (Minneapolis: University of Minnesota Press, 1996); Dani Rodrik, *Has Globalization Gone Too Far?* (Washington, D.C.: Institute for International Economics, 1997); Saskia Sassen, *Globalization and Its Discontents* (New York: New Press, 1998); and David Held et al., *Global Transformations: Politics, Economics, and Culture* (Stanford: Stanford University Press, 1999).

97. For example, research comparing and contrasting the emergence, process, and outcomes of the WCD with other experiments in "global governance" that emerged in the 1990s would be illuminating. Research on novel and emergent transnational institutional arrangements with respect to business-society relations and ethnicity-nation-state dynamics would also be of great theoretical, empirical, and practical value.

SECTION 3

*H*istorical Perspectives

Introduction to Section III

Grasping that people earn their livings, participate in election campaigns, or raise children across borders can be challenging. Most people take for granted that the world always has and always will be organized into sovereign nation-states. We are more likely to compare family life in different countries than to think of households as networks of people living in different locations who pool their income across space.[1] Most governments locate the causes and solutions to their problems inside their borders rather than thinking of health or educational status as produced by people living in several places at one time.

But such a view is short on history. Capitalism, imperial and colonial regimes, anti-slavery and workers' rights campaigns, illegal pirating networks, and religions have always crossed borders. The modern nation-state system did not even exist until after the Treaty of Westphalia in 1648. In the early 1900s, there were barely 130 sovereign states; the remaining 65 percent of the world's political entities were colonies and protectorates. Three-quarters (150) of the more than 200 countries recognized today came into existence in the last century.[2]

The selections in this section bring to light some of the ways in which the world has always been transnational. We chose them as much for their substantive content as for the ways in which they show the long historical trajectory of economic, biological, and ideational connection across the world regardless of its political organization.

In *Plagues and People*, historian William McNeill suggests that patterns of parasitism and human evolution have always been interrelated across time and space. For thousands of years, McNeill argues, cultural evolution has greatly affected, and been affected by, parasitic infection. What is of interest to us here are the multiple, interrelated things that travel across space and time. Disease spreads within populations of animals and humans, often with devastating consequences that get worse when civilizations come into contact through war and trade. But, ultimately, civilizations adapt, developing the capacity to withstand or become immune to specific disease strains, which allows them to stabilize and survive.

A 50,000-year perspective on history reveals constant, widespread interconnection that dramatically affected the rise and fall of civilization. As over-hunted large animals neared extinction, humans turned to oceans, lakes, and rivers for their survival. Agriculture grew in scope and warfare became more prevalent because people living within limited spaces competed over scarce resources. More sedentary populations were more vulnerable to parasitic infection. As animals became domesticated and a wider variety of plants were consumed, a "dense population of parasites," caused large numbers to become chronically ill. As the population exploded and European cities sprang up, "civilized disease", such as cholera, measles, and syphilis, also ran rampant and thinned out the population dramatically. New disease patterns emerged because peasants moving back and forth between rural and urban areas carried infections capable of wiping out entire villages. This "transportation of illness" was further exacerbated by two subsequent cultural developments: international trade and imperialism. New diseases carried by ship traversed the world. Ultimately, these transnational cultural evolutions resulted in such high levels of infection around the globe that large populations, as well as small villages, were eliminated.

Janet Abu-Lughod's contribution also drives home the long history of intercontinental connection and the relevance of these earlier world systems for understanding their current incarnations. Her book explores how international connections were forged, expanded, and strengthened during the thirteenth century and why, although the east and west were fairly equal partners, Europe achieved supremacy by the sixteenth century. Like today, regions had a great deal in common in the thirteenth century. Localities were more similar than different. In fact, at that time, many societies used money and credit, had mechanisms for pooling capital and distributing risk, and had a wealthy merchant class. Europe, Abu-Lughod argues, ultimately achieved superiority not because of its internal inventiveness or "unique" entrepreneurial spirit—other world powers also boasted sophisticated economic institutions and keen business acumen—rather, it was the geographic, political, and demographic context in which development occurred, not internal psychological or institutional factors, that ultimately explains why European hegemony triumphed.

The last two selections in this section provide a historical perspective on the sociopolitical consequences of idea flows that cross borders. Howard Winant's contribution shows how ideas about race were produced cross-regionally and what role they played in the emergence of the contemporary world-system. In his earlier work, Winant proposed the idea of racial formation as a national project. Here he takes this one step further, showing how race contributed to nation-building and empirical expansion. To create nations, leaders must make clear distinctions between themselves and others through rivalry and "othering." "Othering" is based on supranational distinctions, emphasizing regional distinctions between Europe and the rest, between "us," broadly defined, and the non-Christian, "uncivilized," non-white Other, who it is not only acceptable but imperative to subordinate on religious, philosophical, and political grounds. Race is at the heart of such collective identities. Imperial nations grew strong when their nationals (soldiers and settlers) enslaved and conquered the racialized Other. They did so not just as French or Portuguese but also as whites, masters, and Christians, drawing clear lines in the sand based on phenotype. This dichotomy, argues Winant, although later complicated by intermarriage and *mestizaje*, established the foundation for the national-political axes of the modern racial order and the modern world system. In place of empire, racially and nationally homogeneous entities (and identities) were created, and a new system of subordination developed.

Paul Gilroy is also concerned with how the powerful use race to build nations. His selection shows not only how transnational flows of ideas helped consolidate the idea of the "nation" as a monolithic and cultural whole, but also how African-Americans and blacks in the United Kingdom were excluded from that vision. In Europe, Gilroy argues, nations were defined as ethnically pure and their members as identifying in one way. But this fails to reflect that black, if not the English, experience. When culture travels, it doesn't do so in a way that respects the boundaries of what are understood to be essentially homogeneous nation-states. Black intellectual history, in fact, is crowded by scholars whose experiences criss-crossed the Atlantic, embedding them in several cultures at once. Their experiences challenge the dogmatic focus on national dynamics that characterizes so much of European thought. Taking the Atlantic as a single, complex unit of analysis, producing an explicitly transnational and intercultural analysis is a much needed corrective. How would such a lens help us to rewrite history? It would mean nothing less, Gilroy writes, than rethinking Garvey and Garveyism, pan-Africanism, and Black Power as hemispheric, if not global, phenomena.

NOTES

1.   For work on transnational families, see Bryceson and Vuorela (2000); Chamberlin (2002); Nyberg Sorenson, and Fog Olwig (2002); Parrenas, R. S. (2001); Pessar and Mahler (2003).
2.   In 1900, there were 43 generally recognized nation-states; by 1998, there were 193; today the number is over 200 (Martin 2003). The number doubled (90 to 180) from 1960 to the mid-1990s (Held et al. 1999).

REFERENCES

Bryceson, Deborah Fahy and Ulla Vuorela. 2002. *The Transnational Family: New European Frontiers and Global Networks*. Oxford/New York: Berg.

Chamberlain, M. 2002. "Small Worlds: Childhood and Empire." *Journal of Family History* 27:186–200.

Held, David, Anthony McGrew, David Goldblatt, and Jonathan Perraton. 1999. *Global Transformations: Politics, Economics and Culture*. Stanford, Calif.: Stanford University Press.

Martin, Philip. 2003. "Economic Integration and Migration: The U.S.-Mexico Case." World Institute for Development Economics Research, United Nations Univeristy, Helsinki.

Parreñas, Rhacel Salazar. 2001. *Servants of Globalization: Women, Migration and Domestic Work*. Stanford, CA: Stanford University Press.

Pessar, Patricia R. and Sarah J. Mahler. 2003. "Transnational Migration: Bringing Gender In." *International Migration Review* 37:812–846.

Sørensen, Ninna Nyberg and Karen Fog Olwig. 2002. *Work and Migration: Life and Livelihoods in a Globalizing World*. London and New York: Routledge.

CHAPTER 13

Breakthrough to History

William H. McNeill

[. . .]

The story is indeed dramatic. English settlers introduced rabbits to Australia in 1859. In the absence of natural predators, the new species spread rapidly throughout the continent becoming very numerous and, from the human point of view, a pest that ate grass that sheep might have otherwise consumed. The Australian wool pack was thereby reduced; so were the profits of innumerable ranchers. Human efforts to reduce the number of rabbits in Australia took a new turn in 1950 when the virus of myxomatosis (a distant relative of human smallpox) was successfully transferred to the rabbit population of that continent. The initial impact was explosive: in a single season an area as great as all of western Europe was infected. The death rate among rabbits that got the disease in the first year was 99.8 per cent. In the next year, however, the death rate went down to a mere 90 per cent; seven years later mortality among infected rabbits was only 25 per cent. Obviously, very rigorous and rapid selection had occurred among rabbits and among viral strains as well. Samples of the virus derived from wild rabbits became measurably milder in virulence with each successive year. Despite this fact, rabbit population has not recovered its former level in Australia and may not do so for a long time—perhaps never. In 1965 only about one fifth as many rabbits lived in Australia as had been there before myxomatosis struck.[1]

Before 1950 myxomatosis was a well-established disease among rabbits in Brazil. The virus provoked only mild symptoms among the wild-rabbit population of that country and exhibited a comparatively stable pattern of endemic incidence. It might be supposed, therefore, that the adaptation involved in transfer from Brazilian to Australian rabbits was less than the adaptation required for a parasite from some different host species to *Homo sapiens*. But this is not really the case, since despite their common name the rabbits of the Americas are of a different genus from those of Europe and Australia. Hence the shift to a new host that took place in 1950 under the eyes of experts resembled the presumed pattern whereby important human diseases once broke away from an animal host species and began to infect humankind.

Whether or not a new disease begins as lethally as myxomatosis did, the process of mutual accommodation between host and parasite is fundamentally the same. A stable new disease pattern can arise only when both parties manage to survive their initial encounter and, by suitable biological and cultural[2] adjustments, arrive at a mutually tolerable arrangement. In all such processes of adjustment, bacteria and viruses have the advantage of a much shorter time between generations. Genetic mutations that facilitate propagation of a disease organism safely from host to host are consequently able to establish themselves much more rapidly than any comparable alterations of human genetic endowment or bodily traits can occur. Indeed, as we shall see in a later chapter, historical experience of later ages suggests that something like 120 to 150 years are needed for human populations to stabilize their response to drastic new infections[3] [. . .]

The process of adaptation between host and parasite is so rapid and changeable that we must assume that patterns of infection prevailing now are only the current manifestations of diseases that have in fact altered their behavior in far-reaching ways during historic times. Yet in view of the figure of half a million needed to keep measles in circulation in modern urban communities, it is noteworthy that a recent estimate of the total population of the seat of the world's oldest civilization in ancient Sumeria comes out to exactly the same figure.[4] It seems safe to assume that the Sumerian cities were in close enough contact with one another to constitute a single disease pool; and if so, massed numbers, approaching half a million, surely constituted a population capable of sustaining infectious chains like those of modern childhood diseases. In subsequent centuries, as other parts of the world also became the seats of urban civilizations, ongoing infectious chains became possible elsewhere. First here, then there, one or another disease organism presumably invaded available human hosts and made good its lodgment in the niche increasing human density had opened for it.

Person to person, "civilized" types of infectious disease could not have established themselves much before 3000 B.C. When they did get going, however, different infections established themselves among different civilized communities in Eurasia. Proof of this fact is that when communications between previously isolated civilized communities became regular and organized, just before and after the Christian era, devastating infections soon spread from one civilization to another, with consequences for human life analogous to, though less drastic than, what happened to rabbits in Australia after 1950. [. . .]

Despite innumerable local setbacks, however, the areas subject to civilized patterns of organization did tend to increase across the centuries. Yet the number of discrete civilizations always remained modest, though whether one counts a total of half a dozen or two dozen depends on the criteria used to distinguish one style of civilized life from another. Such small numbers reflect the fact that civilizations do not characteristically expand by stimulating the elaboration of pre-existing local institutions, ideas, and skills to new heights of sophistication. Instead, civilizations regularly export key cultural elements from an already elaborated center onto new ground. Often, perhaps always, it was easier to borrow and imitate than to create anew. There was, however, another factor in the situation that goes far to explain the comparative ease with which civilized societies expanded into new territories, one that was a result not of conscious policies or of macroparasitic patterns, but of the dynamics of microparasitism. A moment's reflection will show what these were.

When civilized societies learned to live with the "childhood diseases" that can only persist among large human populations, they acquired a very potent biological weapon. It came into play whenever new contacts with previously isolated, smaller human groups occurred. Civilized diseases when let loose among a population that lacked any prior exposure to the germ in question quickly assumed drastic proportions, killing off old and young alike instead of remaining a perhaps serious, but still tolerable, disease affecting small children.[5]

The disruptive effect of such an epidemic is likely to be greater than the mere loss of life, severe as that may be. Often survivors are demoralized, and lose all faith in inherited custom and belief which had not prepared them for such a disaster. Sometimes new infections actually manifest their greatest virulence among young adults, owing, some doctors believe, to excessive vigor of this age-group's antibody reactions to the invading disease organism.[6] Population losses within the twenty-to-forty age bracket are obviously far more damaging to society at large than comparably numerous destruction of either the very young or the very old. Indeed, any community that loses a substantial percentage of its young adults in a single epidemic finds it hard to maintain itself materially and spiritually. When an initial exposure to one civilized infection is swiftly followed by similarly destructive exposure to others, the structural cohesion of the community is almost certain to collapse. In the early millennia of civilized history, the result was sporadically to create a fringe of half-empty land on the margins of civilized societies. Simple folk brought into contact with urban populations always risked demoralizing and destructive disease encounters. Survivors were often in no position to offer serious resistance to thoroughgoing incorporation into the civilized body politic.

To be sure, warfare characteristically mingled with and masked this epidemiological process. Trade, which was imperfectly distinct from warlike raiding, was another normal way for civilized folk to probe new lands. And since war and trade relations have often entered civilized records, whereas epidemics among illiterate and helpless border folk have not, historians have hitherto failed to take anything like adequate notice of the biological weapon urban conditions of life implanted in the bloodstreams of civilized peoples. Absence of documentation should not, however, deter us from recognizing the force of the epidemiological superiority civilized conditions of life created among those who had survived the local mix of childhood diseases. [. . .]

Observed from the civilized side of the frontier, an initial die-off and disruption of local social defenses opened the way for an overabundant civilized peasantry to move onto new ground and there find a fresh chance to thrive. For the most part this phenomenon remained sporadic and local. Suitable lands and surplus manpower were by no means always available. But it happened often enough across the centuries to allow recurrent bursts of expansion on the part of pre-existing civilized societies. In fact, it is fundamentally because of this phenomenon that civilized societies throughout history have so persistently tended to expand their geographical size.

Of course, collisions between expanding civilizations occurred too, beginning in relatively early times, when Mesopotamian and Egyptian imperial governments started to clash in Syria and Palestine after about 1300 B.C. Moreover, the epidemiological and cultural "digestion" of one society by another has sometimes dissolved civilized communities as well. This was the fate of Amerindian civilizations after 1500. It happened also to ancient Egypt and Mesopotamia in the course of their gradual incorporation into imperial structures stretching beyond their original borders—a process completed only after the Moslem conquests of the seventh century A.D.

Some readers will boggle at this series of assertions and *a priori* deductions, especially when applied to civilized societies *en bloc* and without taking account of local differences and alterations across time. Undoubtedly there were such differences. But surviving records are incapable of discerning them, since the few who could write were completely unaware of the biological process I have tried, even if clumsily, to anatomize. We must reconcile ourselves to the fact that until modern times, when the phenomenon assumed unparalleled proportions as a result of European oceanic explorations that broke through innumerable epidemiological barriers, surviving records simply do not take notice of what happened to the weak and unfortunate neighbors of civilized peoples.

Writers, naturally enough, tended to assume that the expansion of civilization (*their* own, of course) was only to be expected, since its charms and value were self-evident. Modern historians often unthinkingly assume the same thing. But given the normal attachment human beings feel for the ways of life to which they have been brought up, it is doubtful whether intact foreign communities ever opted for incorporation into an alien body social, even when the encroaching community possessed obvious and undeniable superiorities of skill, wealth and knowledge.

To be sure, barbarians often enough triumphed as conquerors only to be conquered in their turn by the seductions of civilized ways. Such invaders probably seldom foresaw what would happen to their inherited life style, and they often struggled against civilized corruption when they finally began to recognize what was happening. Moreover, as conquerors and rulers, they always had far more attractive prospects than any available to poor and humble folk on the borderlands, whose appointed role was to be assimilated into the most oppressed class of civilized society. Such peoples may therefore be presumed to have always resisted incorporation into civilized society insofar as it lay within their power.

If one tries to correct, therefore, for the built-in biases of available sources, the success civilizations so regularly demonstrated in incorporating border peoples into the fabric of metropolitan society needs explanation. Only if one gives appropriate weight to the epidemiological patterns described above does the expansion of civilized cultural frontiers become intelligible. Nothing else seems in the least adequate, or to accord with ordinary human behavior.

For my argument India offers a sort of test case. In that subcontinent, a civilized level of society arose initially in the semi-arid Northwest, where the Indus River runs through increasingly desert lands from the high Himalayas to the sea. Such a landscape was similar to that of ancient Mesopotamia and Egypt, and the irrigation agriculture that supported Indus civilization was probably very like that of the two ancient Middle Eastern civilizations. The basic pattern of Indian history was defined by massive barbarian (Aryan) invasions after 1500 B.C., followed by a slow reassertion of civilized patterns of life. This, too, closely conforms to the rhythms of ancient history as experienced in the other river valley civilizations.[7]

Divergence becomes unmistakable after about 800 B.C., however, when civilized social structures re-established themselves in northwestern India. These urban communities bordered to the south and east upon a landscape occupied by various "forest peoples" who lived, at least usually, in small, self-contained communities of a sort that in temperate zones were extremely vulnerable to epidemiological undoing by civilized diseases. There is no reason to think that civilized diseases were not just as disruptive in India as they were in more northerly parts of Eurasia. But the forest peoples in India did not crumple up and disintegrate as might have been expected. Instead, they had their own epidemiological riposte to the biological armament of civilization. Various tropical diseases and parasitic infestations that flourished in moist and warm climates protected them against the temperate zone pattern of

civilized encroachment. As was true later in Africa, death and debility lurked in too many forms to allow massive or rapid invasion of moist, warm regions by civilized personnel from India's drier North and West. A sort of epidemiological standoff ensued. Forest folk might be decimated by infections arising from contacts with civilized peoples, but civilized intruders were equally vulnerable to contacts with the tropical diseases and infestations familiar among the forest folk.

The upshot is well known. Instead of digesting the various primitive communities that had occupied southern and eastern Indian in the manner that was normal north of the Himalayas, Indian civilization expanded by incorporating ex-forest folk as castes, fitting them into the Hindu confederation of cultures as semi-autonomous, functioning entities. Local cultural and social traditions were therefore not destroyed before being fitted into Indian civilized social structures. Instead, a vast variety of primitive rites and practices survived for centuries. Every so often such elements surfaced within the Indian literate record, when orally transmitted ideas and rituals attracted the attention of literate individuals and were duly written down, elaborated or distorted so as to fit into the pullulating complexity of historic Hinduism.

Other elements and attitudes of course entered into the definition and maintenance of the caste principle in Indian society. Yet the taboos on personal contact across caste lines, and the elaborate rules for bodily purification in case of inadvertent infringement of such taboos, suggest the importance fear of disease probably had in defining a safe distance between the various social groups that became the castes of historic Indian society. Only after a prolonged process of epidemiological encounter, during which antibody immunities and tolerances of parasitic infestation were gradually equalized (or initial differences sharply reduced) did it become safe for Aryan-speaking intruders to live side by side with speakers of Tamil and other ancient tongues. Genetic blending (despite caste rules against intermarriage) no doubt accompanied this epidemiological exchange, and a fairly rigorous selective survival must have altered gene assortments among the forest peoples as well as among intrusive representatives of civilized styles of life.

Yet all such homogenizing processes fell short of the drastic "digestive" pattern characteristic of the other Old World civilizations. Consequently, the cultural uniformity and sociological cohesion of the Indian peoples has remained relatively weak in comparison to the more unitary structures characteristic of the northerly civilizations of Eurasia. One may, of course, attribute this peculiarity of the Indian style of civilization to chance or to conscious choices. Chance and choice may indeed have played a role in defining the caste principle; but the unique epidemiological situation confronting Indian civilization in its early phases of expansion must also have a great deal to do with making castes what they became, thereby defining the structure of Indian civilized society in a different way than prevailed elsewhere.

The situation in the Americas was different in another way. Civilized diseases of the kind that arose in the major Eurasian centers of urban life failed to establish themselves before 1500 in Mexico and Peru. Otherwise Montezuma would surely have had a more efficacious epidemiological revenge on the invading Spaniards than in fact manifested itself. It seems best, however, to reserve a more careful consideration of American disease patterns until a later chapter, when the epidemiological consequences of European arrival in America will become the subject of our consideration.

Here it remains to summarize the results of all these inferences and arguments based on modern notions of infectious disease. Despite the lack of conclusive literary or archaeological evidence, it seems sure that the major civilized regions of the Old World each developed its own peculiar mix of infectious, person-to-person diseases between the time when cities first arose and about 500 B.C. Water-borne, insect-borne, and skin-to-skin infections also had a much expanded scope within the crowded cities and adjacent regions of dense agricultural settlement. Such diseased and disease-resistant civilized populations were biologically dangerous to neighbors unaccustomed to so formidable an array of infections. This fact made territorial expansion for civilized populations much easier than would otherwise have been the case.

Exact boundaries between the different disease pools cannot be ascertained. No doubt the geographic range of any particular infection varied from year to year, depending on movement of people, fluctuations of virulence, and patterns of incidence within the civilized centers themselves. The result was acutely unstable. The novel biological balances—both micro- and macroparasitic—which civilized social structures had created were liable to further disturbance with every significant alteration of transport and communication, since none of the important new infections had reached geographical or other natural limits. Exploration of how these balances altered in the period from 500 B.C. to A.D. 1200 will be the theme of the next chapter.

NOTES

1. Frank Fenner and F. N. Ratcliffe, *Myxomatosis* (Cambridge, 1965), pp. 251, 286, and *passim*. Myxomatosis was also introduced into France and England in the 1950s with drastic and somewhat different results, owing largely to differences in the insect vectors that spread the infection.

2. Even here there are analogies. Careful observers reported that English rabbits reacted to the outbreak of myxomatosis by living more above ground, and spending less time in burrows. Fenner and Ratcliffe, op. cit., p. 346.

3. See below, p. 185.

4. Robert J. Braidwood and Charles A. Reed, "The Achievement and Early Consequences of Food Production: A Consideration of the Archaeological and Natural-Historical Evidence." *Cold Spring Harbor Symposium on Quantitative Biology*, 22 (1957), 28–29.

5. For modern examples of devastating disease encounters of this kind and an easily comprehensible outline of factors affecting immunity to infectious disease, see René Dubos, *Man Adapting* (New Haven and London, 1965), pp. 171–85.

6. Burnet and White, *Natural History of Infectious Disease*, pp. 79–81, 97–100. The influenza epidemic of 1918–19 was the most recent disease to manifest this surprising preference for killing off young adults.

7. Cf. William H. McNeill, *The Rise of the West* (Chicago, 1963), Chs. 4, 5.

CHAPTER 14

The World System in the Thirteenth Century: Dead-End or Precursor?

Janet Lippman Abu-Lughod

Most Western historians writing about the rise of the West have treated that development as if it were independent of the West's relations to other high cultures. At first, thinking about this, I attributed it to ethnocentrism, pure and simple. But then I was struck by something else: Virtually all Western scholars, and especially those who had taken a global perspective on the "modern" world, began their histories in about *A. D.* 1400—just when both East and West were at their low ebb and when the organizational system that had existed prior to this time had broken down. By selecting this particular point to start their narratives, they could not help but write a similar plot, one in which the West "rose," apparently out of nowhere.

What would happen to the narrative if one started a little earlier?[1] Even more important, what would happen to the theoretical assumption that the peculiar form of Western capitalism, as it developed in sixteenth-century western Europe, was a necessary and (almost) sufficient cause of Western hegemony? What if one looked at the system *before* European hegemony and if one looked at the organization of capital accumulation, "industrial" production, trade and distribution in comparative perspective? If one found wide variation among earlier economic organizations, all of which had yielded economic vitality and dynamism, then it might not be legitimate to attribute Europe's newly gained hegemony to "capitalism" in the unique form it took in Europe. It might be necessary, instead, to test an alternative hypothesis: that Europe's rise was substantially assisted by what it learned from other,

more advanced cultures—at least until Europe overtook and subdued them.

It was to explore such questions that I began to study the economic organization of the world in the thirteenth century. At the start, I had no intention of writing a book, but only of satisfying my curiosity over this puzzle. In the course of my five years of research, however, I found no single book, or even several books combined, that gave me a "global" picture of how international trade was organized at that time. Interestingly enough the separate histories I did find all hinted, usually in passing, at the manifold connections each place maintained with trading partners much farther afield. I became preoccupied with reconstructing those connections.[2]

The basic conclusion I reached[3] was that there had existed, prior to the West's rise to preeminence in the sixteenth century, a complex and prosperous predecessor—a system of world trade and even "cultural" exchange that, at its peak toward the end of the thirteenth century, was integrating (if only at high points of an archipelago of towns) a very large number of advanced societies stretching between the extremes of north-western Europe and China. Indeed, the century between A.D. 1250 and 1350 clearly seemed to constitute a crucial turning point in world history, a moment when the balance between East and West could have tipped in either direction. In terms of space, the Middle East heartland that linked the eastern Mediterranean with the Indian Ocean constituted a geographic fulcrum on which East and West were then roughly balanced.

Thus, at that time, one certainly could not

have predicted the outcome of any contest between East and West. There seemed no *historical necessity* that shifted the system in favor of the West, nor was there any historical necessity that would have prevented cultures in the eastern regions from becoming progenitors of a "modern" world system. This thesis seemed at least as compelling to me as its opposite.

True, the "modern" world system that *might* have developed, had the East remained dominant, would probably have had different institutions and organization than the historically specific version that developed under European hegemony. But there is no reason to believe that, had the West not "risen," the world under different leadership would have remained stagnant.

Therefore, it seemed crucial to gain an understanding of the years between A.D. 1250 and 1350.[4] During that period, an international trade economy climaxed in the regions between northwestern Europe and China, yielding prosperity and artistic achievements in many of the places that were newly integrated.

This trading economy involved merchants and producers in an extensive (worldwide) if narrow network of exchange. Primary products, including but not confined to specialty agricultural items, mostly spices, constituted a significant proportion of all items traded, but over shorter distances in particular, manufactured goods were surprisingly central to the system. In fact, trade probably could not have been sustained over long distances without including manufactured goods such as textiles and weapons. The production of primary and manufactured goods was not only sufficient to meet local needs but, beyond that, the needs of export as well.

Moreover, long-distance trade involved a wide variety of merchant communities at various points along the routes, because distances, as measured by time, were calculated in weeks and months at best, and it took years to traverse the entire circuit. The merchants who handled successive transactions did not necessarily speak the same languages, nor were their local currencies the same. Yet goods were transferred, prices set, exchange rates agreed on, contracts entered into, credit extended, partnerships formed, and, obviously, records kept and agreements honored.

The scale of these exchanges was not very large, and the proportion of population and even production involved in international exchange constituted only a very small fraction of the total productivity of the societies. Relatively speaking, however, the scale of the system in the later Middle Ages was not substantially below that in the "early modern age" (i.e., after 1600), nor was the technology of production inferior to that of the later period. No great technological breakthroughs distinguish the late medieval from the early modern period.

The book that resulted from my research, *Before European Hegemony*, describes the system of world trade circa A.D. 1300, demonstrating how and to what extent the world was linked into this common commercial network of production and exchange. Since such production and exchange were relatively unimportant to the subsistence economies of all participating regions, I did not have to defend an unrealistic vision of a tightly entailed international system of interdependence. Clearly, this was not the case. But it was also true in the sixteenth century. Thus, if it is possible to argue that a world system began in that later century, it is equally plausible to acknowledge that it existed three hundred years earlier.

It is important to recognize that *no system* is fully global in the sense that all parts articulate evenly with one another, regardless of whether the role they play is central or peripheral. Even today, the world, more globally integrated than ever before in history, is broken up into important subspheres or subsystems—such as the Middle Eastern and North African system, the North Atlantic system, the Pacific Basin or Rim system, the eastern European bloc (functionally persisting, even though its socialist orientation has crumbled), and China, which is still a system unto itself. And within each of these blocs, certain major cities play key nodal roles, dominating the regions around them and often having more intense interactions with nodal centers in other systems than with their own peripheries.

In the thirteenth century, also, there were subsystems (defined by language, religion and empire, and measurable by relative transactions) dominated by imperial or core cities, as well as mediated by essentially hinterland-less trading enclaves. Their interactions with one another, although hardly as intense as today's, defined the contours of the larger system. Instead of airlines, these cities were bound together by sealanes, rivers, and great overland caravan routes, some of which had been in use since antiquity. Ports and oases served the same functions as do air terminals today, bringing diverse goods and people together from long distances.

Given the primitive technologies of transport that existed during the early period, however, few nodes located at opposite ends of the system could do business directly with one another. Journeys were broken down into much smaller geographic segments, with central places between flanking trading circuits serving as "break-in-bulk" exchanges for goods destined for more distant markets. Nor was the world the "global village" of today, sharing common consumer goals and assembly-line work in a vast international division of labor. The subsystems of the thirteenth century were much more self-sufficient than those of today and therefore less vitally dependent on one another for common survival. Nevertheless, what is remarkable is that, despite the hardships and handicaps that long-distance trade then entailed, so much of it went on.

An analysis of the movements of such trade leads us to distinguish, for analytical purposes, three very large circuits. The first was a western European one that dominated the Atlantic coast and many parts of the Mediterranean. The second was a Middle Eastern one that dominated both the land bridge along the Central Asian steppes and the sea bridge, with a short intervening overland route, between the eastern Mediterranean and the Indian Ocean. And finally, the third was the Far Eastern circuit of trade that connected the Indian subcontinent with Southeast Asia and China beyond. At that time, the strongest centers and circuits were located in the Middle East and Asia. In contrast, the European circuit was an upstart

newcomer that for several early centuries was only tangentially and weakly linked to the core of the world system as it had developed between the eighth and eleventh centuries.

These three major circuits were, in turn, organized into some eight interlinked subsystems, within which smaller trading circuits and subcultural and political systems seemed to exist. . . . In the section that follows, we take up each of these circuits and subsystems in turn, but our emphasis is on how they connected with one another.
[. . .]

THE EUROPEAN CIRCUIT

By the middle of the thirteenth century, three European nodes were forming into a single circuit of exchange. The counties of Champagne and Brie in east-central France hosted the rotating fairs of Champagne, which took place sequentially in four towns: the trading and production centers of Troyes and Provins and the smaller market towns of Bar-sur-Aube and Lagny. A second nodal zone was the textile-producing region of Flanders; where the city of Bruges became the most important commercial and financial capital and nearby Ghent served as the chief industrial town. The third node was in Italy, with the two most international trading ports located on opposite sides of the peninsula: Genoa facing westward and Venice facing east.

The growth of this European circuit was causally linked to the Crusades, which, from the end of the eleventh century, had put western Europe into more intimate contact with the Middle East and which had stimulated the demand for goods available only in the East. Such stimulation in demand, in turn, generated heightened productivity on the European continent—to manufacture goods that could be exchanged for the spices and cotton and silk textiles from the East.

To reconstruct this process, it is important to establish a benchmark for growth. In the second century A.D. the Roman Empire covered a vast territory that included all regions abutting the Mediterranean Sea. The empire extended northward to encompass England and all of western Europe except Germany, eastward to encompass Greece, Anatolia, and the Fertile Crescent, and southward across the entire stretch of littoral North Africa. Rome's southern and eastern peripheral areas were in contact, via overland and sea routes, with sizable portions of the rest of the "Old World" as far away as India and, indirectly, even China. By that time, what might be called the first nascent world system had come into existence, although it did not survive the "fall of Rome."

Internal weakening of the overextended Roman Empire eventually made it possible for Germanic tribes occupying zones north and east of the Italian core—tribes that had formerly been blocked at the frontiers—to break through the Roman lines. The first waves of invasion occurred in the third century, but were soon spent; successive ones were not so easily repelled. Throughout the fifth century a series of more successful incursions culminated in the collapse of unified rule and the fragmentation of the western domains among the Gauls, Vandals, Visigoths, and, later, Lombards.

After the fall of the Roman Empire, much of western Europe underwent significant regression, initiating a period that in Western historiography is referred to as the Dark Ages.[5] Although it is true that much of the subcontinent's economic base retracted to highly localized subsistence activities, it is important to stress that in southern Europe this did not occur. Much of the Iberian Peninsula was under Muslim rule and its economy was thus inherently linked not to Europe's but to that of the thriving Islamic world. And at least parts of Italy, most particularly the port city-state of Venice, continued to prosper because it served as an outpost for the undefeated eastern Roman Empire, Venice's ally in Constantinople.

It is important to remember that the ninth century, when northwestern Europe was just beginning to emerge from its dark ages, was a civilizational highpoint both in the Middle East (under Abbasid rule) and in China (under the Tang Dynasty). These two central powers were establishing trade links with one another via the Persian Gulf–Indian Ocean route, a connection advantageous to both. (This is the time of Sindbad the Sailor).[6] The overthrown Umayyads had relocated to Iberia and were united there with powerful North African dynasties. The tenth and eleventh centuries in both Asia and the Middle East were periods of technological advance[7] and increasingly sophisticated business and credit practices.[8] Most of the "social" inventions that the Italians were to use so effectively, when they later provided the institutional "glue" that integrated the European subsystem, they learned from their Middle Eastern counterparts.

Western Europe was decisively drawn into the preexisting world system through the Crusades, the first of which took place at the end of the eleventh century. It was only after this first incursion that the fairs of Champagne began to expand as the central meeting place for Italian merchants, who imported Eastern goods via the Levant, and Flemish merchants, who marketed the woolen textiles that Europe exchanged for the silks and spices of the Orient.[9] Flemish textile production was greatly stimulated by the Orient's expanding demand for their high-quality cloth. With later Crusades, European colonies were established in the Levant, where merchants handled the import trade on the spot.

The fairs of Champagne had a relatively brief period of prominence as the middleman-exchange center between Flemish textile producers and Italian merchants. By the end of the thirteenth century, Genoese ships were exiting the Strait of Gibraltar and sailing up the Atlantic coast directly to Bruges; this resulted in relocating the "international" market from Champagne to that city. The Venetians were forced to follow suit, although they never became as prominent in Bruges as the Genoese or the Piedmont Italians. This bypassing of France's central massif, combined with the subsumption of the counties of Brie and Champagne under the French monarchy in 1285,[10] spelled the decline of the fairs. Bruges's prominence, however, was short-lived. Gradually, the city's harbors, despite their successive relocation outward, silted up until deep-draft vessels could no longer come directly into port. The Italians then moved their operations, and along with them the associated financial markets, to the better harbor at Antwerp.

During all this time, the Italians were increasing their control over the production and distribution of western European goods because it was their ships that came to control the shipping lanes in the Mediterranean. The Arabs withdrew from that sea, ceding to Pisan, Genoese, and eventually even more to Venetian galleys the task of ferrying goods back and forth between western Europe and the cores of the world system, still focused farther east.[11]

THE MIDDLE EASTERN CIRCUIT

European ships made three landfalls in the Middle East bridge to the Far East. The one on the north passed Constantinople through to the Black Sea. From ports toward the eastern end of the Black Sea, goods were transferred to the overland caravan route to China. The one at midpoint was on the coast of Palestine, from which caravans set out to Baghdad and thence to the head of the Persian Gulf for the long sea journey or joined the southern caravan route across Central Asia. The one on the south was at the Egyptian port of Alexandria, from which connections were then made via Cairo to the Red Sea and, from there, farther eastward through the Arabian Sea and Indian Ocean.

The Genoese and Venetians fought each other for dominance in the Mediterranean sealanes (their only rival, Pisa, was eliminated fairly early) and, by the thirteenth century, had reached some sort of modus vivendi in which Genoa gained hegemony over the northern route while Venice consolidated its virtually monopolistic relations with the Mamluks of Egypt and their Karimi merchants. Both lost out in the Levant when Saladin and later the Mamluk sultan Baybars drove them successively from the Crusader kingdoms Europeans had implanted in Palestine.

These landfalls were the anchors of the three Middle Eastern subsystems that connected the Levant with the Far East. The northern route crossed the Central Asian steppes and deserts that had been newly unified under Genghis Khan and his confederation of Mongol and Tatar tribes. This unification permitted the trading explorations of such notables as Marco Polo and his uncles in the latter part of the thirteenth century and the establishment of small colonies of Genoese and other Italian merchants in Beijing and other Chinese cities (by then under the Yuan, or Mongol, Dynasty). And it was the greater safety and stability of this area that facilitated the marked expansion of overland trade.

The routes through Arab lands were more protected from European incursions. At Palestine, European merchants met the caravans coming from Central Asia or from the Persian Gulf, but seldom followed them eastward on the long sea journey to India, the Malay Peninsula, or China. And at Egypt the European merchants were stopped entirely. They were not permitted to cross from the Nile to the Red Sea and thus had to exchange with local Karimi (wholesale) merchants, under government supervision, all the goods they brought from Europe or other parts of the Mediterranean for the spices, textiles, and other goods they sought to buy from the East. Toward the end of the period in question, the connection between Venice and Egypt strengthened until it virtually monopolized the exchange between the West and India and parts east.

THE ASIAN SYSTEM VIA THE INDIAN OCEAN

The Indian Ocean trade, which long predated Europe's interest and persisted well beyond the European explorers' "discovery" of the New World as an unintended by-product of their search for an alternative route to India, was itself subdivided into three circuits, only one of which over-lapped with the southern Middle East subsystems that connected the Red Sea and Persian Gulf with landfalls on the western coast of India. The ports at Gujarat (near current-day Bombay) and on the Malabar or pepper coast to the south contained merchant colonies of Muslims[12] from the Middle East who served as intermediaries and who also spread their religion and business practices wherever they went.

Muslim Arab and Persian merchants were considerably less visible in the second circuit of the Indian Ocean trade, which was anchored on the Coromandel coast on India's eastern side. There, indigenous Indian merchants intermediated much of the sea trade that moved eastward through the Straits of Malacca and Sunda (between the Malay Peninsula and present-day Sumatra and Java) to Chinese ports in the third circuit. Although Persian and Arab ships also participated in this circuit, at that time Europeans had no ships in either the Indian Ocean or the South China Sea. The few Europeans (including missionaries and a small number of traders) who ventured into these regions traveled on Asian ships. It was not until Vasco da Gama's successful circumnavigation of Africa in 1498 that European vessels entered the Indian Ocean arena, and it was not until after the Portuguese men-of-war had destroyed the small Egyptian and Indian fleet defending the Arabian Sea in 1516 that Europeans began to control, although not supplant, the large Asian merchant marine.

In that Asian circuit, the Strait of Malacca (and as a very secondary alternative, the Strait of Sunda between southern Sumatra and Java) was absolutely crucial. All ships traveling between India and China had to pass through the "gullet" of narrow sea that separated Sumatra from the Malay Peninsula. Tomé Pires, the astute Portuguese merchant and author who traveled in the area during the first half of the sixteenth century, acknowledged the undisputed strategic significance of Malacca to world trade, noting that "whoever is lord of Malacca has his hands on the throat of Venice" and that "if Cambay [the port of Gujarat] were cut off from trading with Malacca, it could not live."[13] His phrases were apt. Malacca, the chief entrepôt on the strait after the fall of Srivijaya,[14] served, like the fairs of Champagne, as the place where foreign merchants coming from different directions met to exchange goods, credit, and currencies.

But whereas the Champagne fairs owed their comparative advantage chiefly to political causes, the shifting ports on the strait (of which Singapore is simply the most recent manifestation) owed theirs to the weather. In the days of sailing ships, prevailing winds and monsoon seasons shaped the routes and timing of international trade. Because monsoon winds reversed at the Strait of Malacca, long layovers were required for boats traveling in both directions. Permanent colonies of merchants drawn from points throughout the Asian circuit coexisted in Malacca, giving to this port a cosmopolitan quality far beyond what local resources and institutions could have generated.

If the coasts of India were magnets because on them debouched the products of a rich and partially industrialized[15] subcontinent, and the Strait of Malacca was a magnet because sailors had no other options, China was a magnet par excellence in itself and for all. Through China, the overland subsystem that connected it to the Black Sea and the eastern sea subsystem that connected it to the Strait region and beyond were joined together in an all-important loop.

It is very significant that the entire world system of the thirteenth century functioned smoothly and to the benefit of all players when the connecting link through China operated well. It is perhaps of even greater significance that, as I later argue, the breaking up of the world system in the mid-fourteenth century was in large part due to the wedge driven between China and Central Asia by the Ming Rebellion (but more of this later).

China was by far the most developed civilization in the world and the world's leading technological and naval power until the late fifteenth century.[16] It did not merely sit complacently as (in its view) the "Middle Kingdom" of the universe, but actively conducted both "tribute" and "merchant" trade throughout its own waters and in the Indian Ocean and, periodically, up through the Persian Gulf. China had the world's largest and most seaworthy fleet,[17] capable of withstanding any attack and able to terrorize opponents into submission with flame-throwing weapons and gunpowder-driven missiles that were the equivalent of later European cannons.

Such naval power did not often have to be invoked, however, since over the centuries the trading nations of the Indian Ocean had evolved a remarkably tolerant system of coexistence, unlike the rivalries that plagued the Mediterranean in the post-Roman era. K. N. Chaudhuri has drawn a detailed and graphic image of that coexistence in his seminal books on the Indian Ocean.[18] Although piracy was not unknown in Eastern waters, it did not lead, as in the Mediterranean, to a war of all against all, nor was it suppressed by a single thalassocracy, a naval power capable of eliminating all resistance. Instead, it was contained within the interstices of a larger collaboration in which goods and merchants from many places were intermingled on each other's ships and where unwritten rules of reciprocity assured general compliance. This system was not decisively challenged until the sixteenth century, when Portuguese men-of-war violated all the rules of the game by burning or boarding ships, confiscating cargo, and imposing their system of passes[19] on the numerous indigenous but unarmed merchant fleets of the area.

The Fate of the Thirteenth-Century World System

Now that we have described the complex world system that existed before Europe's rise to hegemony, we are left with two basic puzzles. The first is why the thirteenth-century world system did not simply persist and continue to grow? The second is why the West "rose" when it did? Let us try to answer these questions.

Given the high level of sophistication reached and the widespread character of the contacts among the various participants in the thirteenth-century world system, it is natural to ask why it did not expand even farther and grow increasingly prosperous. After all, one of the laws of motion states that things in motion tend to remain in motion, if only because of the power of inertia, and this principle may also operate in history. (It is not until a trend is reversed that historians feel impelled to explain what happened!)

Yet we know that during the fifteenth century almost all parts of the then-known world experienced a deep recession. By then, the "state of the world" was at a much lower level than it had reached in the early fourteenth century. During the depression of the fifteenth century, the absolute level of intersocietal trade dropped, currencies were universally debased (a sure sign of decreased wealth and overall productivity), and the arts and crafts were degraded. It is natural to look in the fourteenth century for clues to this unexpected reversal of fortune.

Such clues are not hard to find. By the third and fourth decades of the fourteenth century, one finds evidence of problems in Europe: bank failures in Italy and the cessation of port expansions in both Genoa and Venice; scattered crop failures throughout northwestern Europe; labor unrest in Flanders that was not unrelated to the decline in the quality of Flemish cloth, once Spanish wool had to be substituted for the higher-quality English wool hitherto used in production; and local wars and increased costs of protection, as "law and order" began to break down. Signs of weakness were also to be seen at various points in the Middle Eastern and Asian systems.

Whether these were normal fluctuations that historians might have overlooked if the system had regained prosperity sooner, or whether they were symptoms of some larger endemic problems, cannot be determined from this distance in time. But certainly there were already weaknesses when catastrophe struck at midcentury.

Catastrophe came in the form of an epidemic so deadly and widespread that it has been singled out from all the regularly recurring epidemics of premodern times as the Black Death. It is obviously impossible to reconstruct the exact causes and course of this epidemic or even to tell whether plague outbreaks reported in the East had exactly the same medical descriptions as those in the West. But William McNeill, in his *Plagues and People*,[20] has attempted to reason backward from medical information today, and to combine this with known, but far from complete, "facts" from the earlier period.

He concludes that the bubonic plague

probably broke out first in the 1320s in a Mongol-patroled area near the Himalayas and that infectious fleas were probably carried in the saddlebags of fast-moving horsemen into south-central China. Certainly, he presents evidence, culled from Chinese yearly chronicles, that from about 1320 on, outbreaks of epidemics were reported in a series of Chinese provinces around the zone of initial infection. From China proper, McNeill contends, infected fleas were diffused to the northern steppes of Central Asia, where they attached themselves to new hosts, the burrowing rats of the plains. Since the populations exposed to the plague had little or no natural immunities to this new disease, mortalities were extremely high, especially, it would seem, among the mobile Mongol soldiers.

From that point on, the story becomes clearer, and we can actually track the spread of the disease along the well-established paths of trade by plotting the dates at which the plague was first reported in various places. The strengths of the system were, indeed, its undoing. Host rats infiltrated the Genoese port of Caffa on the Black Sea, probably from the Mongol forces that were besieging the Italians there. The rats then boarded ships that were returning to the Mediterranean, leaving plague-infected fleas at each of their ports of call. By midcentury, the major centers of trade had all experienced very heavy die-offs, almost proportional to their importance.[21]

Wherever it struck, the plague had long-lasting effects, since outbreaks recurred throughout the rest of the century. But the effects on, and of, depopulation were not at all uniform. The plague stirred the pot of social change, but not in the same way everywhere. First, places that were off the path of international trade suffered lower casualties than those that were central to the trade. England and Scandinavia, for example, had lower proportional mortalities than China, Egypt, or Italy. Second, the mortality rates were higher in cities than in the countryside. These differential mortalities to some extent altered the future "life chances" of various countries and the relative "bargaining power" of peasants versus city folk.

The disturbance to local power structures also permitted political changes that might not have occurred in the absence of the plague, although the effects were not uniform. In Europe, it is acknowledged that the ensuing labor shortage strengthened the hands of workers and yeomen and decisively ended the remnants of serfdom. In contrast, similar die-offs in Egypt had no such effect; there was a change in regimes at the top, but the new set of Mamluk rulers never reduced their pressures on the peasants. In China, however, the political effects were dramatic and had wide-reaching consequences.

The Ming Rebellion, accomplished by 1368, deposed the Yuan Dynasty that had been established after the time of Mongol conquest and replaced it by an indigenous Chinese dynasty. I suspect that the timing was not unrelated to the high plague casualties among the "foreign" military troops that enforced Yuan rule. While the results may have been favorable for Chinese "home rule" and autonomy, they were less advantageous to the world system, since the success of the rebellion once again split off China from Central Asia. Thomas Barfield argues that throughout history there was constant tension along the shifting frontier between the tribal groups of Central Asia and the settled population of China. Only once were the two regions unified politically, and that was in the thirteenth century and first half of the fourteenth century, when China was ruled by the Mongols.[22]

I am tempted to conclude that the thirteenth-century world system had benefited greatly from this union, since it facilitated the free flow of trade in a circuit completed by the Chinese "loop." When this connection broke down, as it did after the Ming Rebellion in the late fourteenth century, its lapse further undermined the viability of the world system as it had previously been organized.

The change in the Chinese regime had one other consequence of great significance: the collapse of the Chinese navy,[23] although that did not occur decisively until more than fifty years later. Chinese attitudes toward trade and the importance of maintaining naval strength were subjects of heated debate in the new dynasty. Some within the palace favored withdrawal from the world system to mend conditions internally. Others stressed the importance of maintaining an appearance of strength in the outside world. Among the latter was the admiral of the fleet, Cheng Ho, who from the early 1400s headed several expeditions of Chinese "treasure ships" (in convoys containing sixty or more vessels) that paraded through the Indian Ocean, stopping at all important ports.[24]

But these displays were eventually halted in the 1430s. After a few naval skirmishes had been lost, palace policy switched to Cheng Ho's opponents. Although the reasons for this reversal of policy remain shrouded in mystery and enigma, and scholars are far from agreeing on an explanation, the results were clear and disastrous for the prospects of continued Asian independence. The ships were ordered into port and deactivated. Within five years, according to Lo's careful research (cited earlier), the wooden ships had rotted and could not be easily repaired.

The significance of the Chinese withdrawal from the sea cannot be overestimated. The disappearance from the Indian Ocean and South China Sea of the only large and armed Asian navy left that vast expanse defenseless. When the Portuguese men-of-war, following the new pathway opened around the tip of Africa by Vasco da Gama's exploratory journey, finally breached the zone in the early decades of the sixteenth century and violated the "rules of the game" of mutual tolerance that had prevailed in that region for a thousand years, there was no one to stop them.

The rest is, as they say, history. The Portuguese proceeded to impose a harsh system of "passes" to extract protection fees from the unarmed Arab and Indian merchant ships that still carried the trade. Through their military arms, the Portuguese initiated the process of imposing a system of European hegemony over regions that had formerly been wealthy and vital. Successive European naval powers, the Dutch and then the British, followed along paths opened by the Portuguese to subjugate vast portions of the Indian Ocean arena and to establish their own plantations and factories to produce the spices and textiles they had long sought from the East.

It should come as no surprise that Holland and England eventually became the new cores of the "modern" world system. My argument, put simply, is that the "fall of the East" preceded the "rise of the West" and opened up a window of opportunity that would not have existed had matters gone differently.

The second question we must address is whether the later success of western Europe in a newly reorganizing world system was exclusively caused by the particular form of capitalism that developed there, or whether capitalism, under the protection of militarily powerful and more centralized nation-states, was able to take advantage of the windows of opportunity created not only by the collapse of the East but by the chance to exploit the "free resources" available in the New World? There is no way to resolve this controversy, and many historians and social thinkers, beginning with Karl Marx and Max Weber, have expended enormous effort in their attempts to add voices to the ongoing debate.

In what follows I present my own position and indicate in what ways my understanding of the thirteenth-century world system has contributed to that position. I do not believe that the Western invention of a particular variation of capitalism predetermined European hegemony from the sixteenth century on. The fact that a highly sophisticated world system—one that was equally as advanced both in economic and social "technologies"—predated the "modern" one casts doubt on the unique contributions of European capitalism. Because no uniformity prevailed with respect to culture, religion, or economic institutional arrangements in that earlier system, it is very difficult to accept a purely "cultural" explanation for Europe's later dominance. No particular culture seems to have had a monopoly over either technological or social inventiveness. Neither a unique syndrome of psychology nor a special economic form of organizing production and exchange (*pace* Marx) nor any particular set of religious beliefs or values (*pace* Weber) was needed to succeed in the thirteenth century. The fact that the West "won" in the sixteenth century, whereas the earlier system aborted, cannot be used to argue convincingly that *only* the institutions and culture of the West *could have succeeded.*

Indeed, what is noteworthy in the world system of the thirteenth century is that a wide variety of cultural systems coexisted and cooperated and that societies organized very differently from those in the West dominated the system. Christianity, Buddhism, Judaism, Confucianism, Islam, Zoroastrianism, and numerous other sects, often dismissed as pagan, all seem to have permitted and indeed facilitated lively commerce, production, exchange, risk taking, and the like. Similarly, a variety of economic systems coexisted in the thirteenth century—from "near" private capitalism, albeit supported by state power, to "near" state production, albeit assisted by private merchants. Moreover, these variations were not particularly congruent with either geographic region or religious domain. The organization of textile production in southeast India was not dissimilar from that in Flanders, whereas in China and Egypt larger-scale coordination was more typical. The state built boats for trade in both tiny Venice and vast China, whereas elsewhere (and even at different times in Genoa, China and Egypt) private vessels were commandeered when the state needed them.

Nor were the underlying bases for economic activities uniform. Participating in the world system of the thirteenth century were large agrarian societies such as India and China that covered subcontinents, in which industrial production was oriented mainly, although not exclusively, to processing agricultural raw materials. There were also small city-state ports such as Venice, Aden, Palembang, and Malacca, whose functions are best described as compradorial. In places as diverse as South India, Champagne, Samarkand, the Levant, and ports along the Persian Gulf, their importance was enhanced by their strategic location at points where flanking traders met. Other important places contained valued raw materials unavailable elsewhere (fine-quality wool in England, camphor in Sumatra, frankincense and myrrh on the Arabian peninsula, spices in the Indian archipelago, jewels in Ceylon, etc.) These resources did not account for the world system; they were products of it.

The economic vitality of these areas was the result, at least in part, of the system in which they participated. It is to be expected, then, that in the course of *any restructuring* of a world system, such as occurred in the sixteenth century, new places would rise to the fore. We have already suggested that part of that restructuring occurred in Asia and could be partially traced to a complex chain of consequences precipitated (but not "caused") by the Black Death. But, in the long run, the Europeans' ability to sail across the Atlantic must be judged even more important than their circumnavigation of Africa.

As we pass the five-hundredth anniversary of Columbus's voyage, it is important to recall its ultimate significance. It displaced the Mediterranean decisively from a core focus of trade, thus precipitating a long-term marginalization of the Middle East, reduced the relative indispensability of the Indian Ocean arena, and provided the nascent developing nations of western Europe with the gold and silver they needed, both to settle the long-standing balance-of-payments deficits with the East and to serve as the basis for a rapid accumulation of capital. This capital accumulation process, deriving "free resources" from conquered peripheries, eventually became the chief motor of European technological and social change.

While this story lies beyond the period covered in this essay, it is an appropriate point on which to conclude this section. Capitalism, in the form that took shape in Europe in the seventeenth and eighteenth centuries and, even more so, in the nineteenth, might not have "taken off" so dramatically had the shape of the world system not been transformed in the sixteenth century. That is why the study of the world system that preceded it is so important. It helps us to put the truly world-transforming developments of the sixteenth century in perspective and to give a more balanced account of the relationship between capitalism and the "rise of the West."[. . .]

NOTES

1. As every economist knows, in cyclical events it matters very much where one starts the data series and for how long one plots the data entries. Selecting the lowest point of a given "trend" as the initial entry cannot help but show "improvement," whereas on a longer trend this might appear as a small blip on an otherwise long-term downward secular trend. I began to suspect that there had been an unconscious bias that to some extent made the uniqueness of the miracle of the West an artifact, especially with respect to the past, albeit not with reference to the future.

2. In the course of my five years of research, I traveled to almost all the areas that were of central importance to what I came to define as the thirteenth-century world system in order to examine sites and explore local documentation. I also consulted a voluminous body of published primary and secondary sources. While, ideally, such a study should have taken a lifetime of scholarship, I saw my project as creating a synthesis of existing materials, albeit from a different perspective, in the hope that other scholars would not only fill lacunae in our knowledge but reevaluate their own findings in the context of the world system.

3. My conclusions were eventually incorporated into Janet Abu-Lughod, *Before European Hegemony: The World System A.D. 1250–1350* (New York: Oxford University Press, 1989). Several articles appeared somewhat before the book was completed: a preview of the thesis written in 1986, "The Shape of the World System in the Thirteenth Century," *Studies in Comparative International Development* 22 (Winter 1987–88): 1–25; as well as "Did the West Rise or Did the East Fall?" paper presented at the 1988 meetings of the American Sociological Association. The book was followed by "Restructuring the Premodern World-System," *Review* 13 (Spring 1990): 273–86, which critiques a mechanical application of world systems theory and tries to take it a bit further by making it a variable, rather than a constant. Four distinct "cycles" of world-system organization are set forth: a classical period one, between roughly 200 B.C. and A.D. 200; a medieval period, between roughly A.D. 1200 and A.D. 1450; a modern period, between roughly 1500 and 1914; and the "postindustrial" period in which we now find ourselves.

4. The following section of this essay depends heavily on portions of my larger and more detailed text, but it cannot substitute for the complete work. In this brief summary it is not possible to include the complex evidence presented in the complete version, to which the reader is referred.

5. For an excellent study of this period, see Perry Anderson, *Passages from Antiquity to Feudalism* (London: Verso, 1974; reprinted 1978).

6. See, for example, the work of George Hourani, *Arab Seafaring in the Indian Ocean in Ancient and Early Medieval Times* (Princeton: Princeton University Press, 1951).

7. The iron and steel production of the Sung Dynasty in the eleventh century exceeded that of England during the early industrial age. See Robert Hartwell, "A Revolution in the Chinese Iron and Coal Industries during the Northern Sung, 960–1126," *Journal of Asian Studies* 21 (1962): 153–62; and his "Markets, Technology, and the Structure of Enterprise in the Development of the Eleventh-Century Chinese Iron and Steel Industry," *Journal of Economic History* 26 (1966): 29–58.

8. An amazing account of the sophisticated business practices of Arab producers and traders (especially in Baghdad) can be found in Abraham Udovitch, *Partnership and Profit in Medieval Islam* (Princeton: Princeton University Press, 1970). It is clear from this document that many of the innovations in credit, corporate organization, risk equalization, and legal contracts that are usually invoked to compliment western ingenuity and the "genius" of the Italians were actually learned from their Arab trading partners after the Crusades had put the two in closer contact.

9. Europe traditionally ran a trade deficit with the more-developed economies of the Middle East and India, a deficit it met by exporting silver and even gold bullion. The deficit existed because Europe demanded more goods from the East than the Orient wanted from Europe.

10. One of the comparative advantages the fair towns had hitherto had was that they could offer "special" arrangements to traveling merchants; once they came under monarchy control, they lost this right to extend special privileges.

11. The finest study of this period is Frederic C. Lane's wonderful book, *Venice: A Maritime Republic* (Baltimore: Johns Hopkins University Press, 1973). The sources on Genoa are less rich, but see E. H. Byrne, *Genoese Shipping in the Twelfth and Thirteenth Centuries* (Cambridge, Mass.: Mediaeval Academy of America, 1930), for a fine account of Genoese skills in shipbuilding and financing.

12. Jewish trader families from Baghdad and Cairo had early on figured prominently in this trade, but by the thirteenth century, their Muslim compatriots had essentially displaced them. The work of S. N. Goitein is particularly relevant on this point. See, for example, his "From Aden to India: Specimens of the Correspondence of India Traders of the Twelfth Century," *Journal of the Economic and Social History of the Orient* 22 (1980): 43–66; as well as his "Letters and Documents on the India Trade in Medieval Times," *Islamic Culture* 37 (1963): 188–203.

13. Both quotations appear, along with their citations, in Abu-Lughod, *Before European Hegemony*, p. 291. The original source is *The Suma Oriental of Tomé Pires*, ed. A. Cortesão, 2 vols. (London: Hakluyt Society, 1944).

14. Srivijaya was a purported "kingdom" whose exact nature and location (probably on Sumatra) remain surprisingly opaque and mysterious. Without offering a coherent alternative description, most

scholars now discount what were earlier considered to be the definitive works by O. W. Wolters. See his *Early Indonesian Commerce: A Study of the Origins of Srivijaya* (Ithaca, N.Y.: Cornell University Press, 1967) and *The Fall of Srivijaya in Malay History* (Ithaca, N.Y.: Cornell University Press, 1970). Before the founding of Malacca in the fourteenth century by a putative "prince" from Palembang, the latter was Srivijaya's capital and presumably the most important port in the strait. Long-standing connections between India and both Srivijaya and Indonesia are obvious from the nomenclatures and are supported by epigraphic and archaeological evidence.

15. India's gossamer cotton textiles had been much sought after in classical Rome and continued to draw customers throughout the Middle Ages. Since, traditionally, others had wanted Indian products more than India had markets for their exported goods, the balance of payments was always in India's favor. Gold from elsewhere, therefore, tended to accumulate in India and remain there. The best sources on this eastward flow of bullion are Artur Attman, *The Bullion Flow between Europe and the East, 1000–1750* (Goteburg: Kungl. Vetemskaps-Och Vitterhessamhallet); and the more accessible John F. Richards, ed., *Precious Metals in the Later Medieval and Early Modern Worlds* (Durham, N.C.: Duke University Press, 1983). The rapid inflation in Europe during the early modern period has been attributed to this imbalance of payments in international trade.

16. See, for example, William McNeill, *The Pursuit of Power: Technology, Armed Force and Society since A.D. 1000* (Chicago: University of Chicago Press, 1982), which makes a stunning case for China's preeminence in the premodern world system.

17. The studies by Jung-Pang Lo prove this conclusively. See his "China as a Sea Power, 1127–1368," Ph.D. diss., University of California, Berkeley, 1957, as well as related articles that summarize his

thesis: "The Emergence of China as a Sea Power During the Late Sung and Early Yuan Periods," *Far Eastern Quarterly* 14 (1955): 489–503; and "Chinese Shipping and East-West Trade from the Tenth to the Fourteenth Century," in *Sociétés et compagnies de commerce en l'orient et dans l'Océan Indien* (Paris: S.E.V.P.E.N., 1970), pp. 167–74.

18. See K. N. Chaudhuri, *Trade and Civilisation in the Indian Ocean: An Economic History from the Rise of Islam to 1750* (Cambridge, England: Cambridge University Press, 1985), as well as its companion volume, *Asia before Europe: Economy and Civilisation in the Indian Ocean from the Rise of Islam to 1750* (Cambridge, England: Cambridge University Press, 1990), which, alas, appeared too late for me to use in preparing my 1989 book.

19. One can think of "passes" as written proof that protection money had already been paid to the Portuguese. A "pass" gave a ship presumed immunity from confiscation or destruction *by the Portuguese*, which sounds like extortion to me.

20. William McNeill, *Plagues and People* (Garden City, N.Y.: Anchor Books, 1976).

21. The only area for which I was unable to locate documentation about a particularly virulent epidemic at that time was India. Whether this is because scholars have not yet found the evidence or whether the Indian population already had gained some immunity from prior outbreaks cannot be determined.

22. Thomas Barfield, *The Perilous Frontier* (New York: Basil Blackwell, 1990).

23. See, inter alia, Jung-Pang Lo, "The Decline of the Early Ming Navy," *Extremus* 5 (1958): 149–68, for information on the early decline and eventual precipitous collapse of the Chinese fleet.

24. On Cheng Ho's expeditions, see Paul Pelliot, "Les grands voyages maritimes Chinois au début du XVe siècle," *T'oung Pao* 30 (1933): 235–455, a careful work based on primary sources.

CHAPTER 15

The Historical Sociology of Race

Howard Winant

Race has been a constitutive element, an organizational principle, a *praxis* and structure that has constructed and reconstructed world society since the emergence of modernity, the enormous historical shift represented by the rise of Europe, the founding of modern nation-states and empires, the *conquista*, the onset of African enslavement, and the subjugation of much of Asia. To explain how race came to play this part in the making of modernity, and to trace the general pathways through which the relationship between race and the modern world system have developed down to our own time, is the task of Part I of this book.

In this chapter I present the outline of a *historical sociological theory of race*. To do so presents a profound intellectual challenge. The vast literature on race generally treats it in a reductionist fashion: it is frequently considered a manifestation of some other, supposedly more profound or more "real" social relationship.[1] The task here is to rethink that logic, to resituate the development of the race-concept in a historically grounded framework. This enables an alternative view of race to emerge, one that sees it as a key causative factor in the creation of the modern world. Imperialism's creation of modern nation-states, capitalism's construction of an international economy, and the Enlightenment's articulation of a unified world culture, I argue, were all deeply racialized processes.[2]
[. . .]

How can we understand, how can we theorize, the multiple effects of race in shaping the transition to modernity? What Myrdal (no stranger to racial matters) called a logic of circular and cumulative causation was at work here (Myrdal 1963; see also Wallerstein 1991, 80–103). There is obviously no one "event" that marks the onset of modernity, no single chasm lying between the remote past and the start of the modern epoch in which we live. All the elements that were unevenly accumulated and accreted to create the modern world had their earlier incarnations; proto-capitalist systems for extraction of surpluses, for the organization and exploitation of labor; imperialisms with their states, their metropoles and hinterlands; and cultural logics of identity and meaning, can readily be found in the ancient and middle ages. Early forms of racial distinction can be identified throughout these precursive forms of sociohistorical organization.

Yet there is something different about the modern world system, as Wallerstein has argued extensively. This difference lies in its combination of global reach and lack of unified authoritative rule.[3] This system is a form of world-historical organization that came into being gradually, repeating organizational elements and social categories that had gone before, for example, slavery (here is Myrdal's "circularity"), yet combining and transforming these components in new ways, and achieving some sort of synergy (Myrdal's "cumulation") in the process.

Into the account of the origins and development of the modern world system—from which I have learned a great deal—I want to insert the theme of race. This account is not really a negation of other macro-historical sociologies; rather, it is an attempt to give race its due as *both* cause and effect in such accounts. I am especially opposed to relegation of race to an effect, an epiphenomenon, an outcome of, say, capitalist development, the emergence of the nation-state, the rise of Europe, or the onset of modernity.

Modernity, then, is a global *racial formation* project. In making this claim I draw not only on Myrdal and Wallerstein but on my earlier work with Michael Omi, which proposed that racial formation takes place in the national context through the clash of racial projects. In this approach, the key element in racial formation is the link between signification and structure, between what race means in a particular discursive practice and how, based upon such interpretations, social structures are racially organized. The link between meaning and structure, discourse and institution, signification and organization, is concretized in the notion of the racial project. To interpret the meaning of race in a particular way at a given time is at least implicitly, but more often explicitly, to propose or defend a certain racial policy, a specific racialized social structure, a racial order. By studying the range of racial projects in given historical contexts it becomes possible to study given racial formation processes in detail, giving particular attention to the ways in which projects intersect (Omi and Winant 1994, 55–61).

That argument was framed in a largely national and comparative context that overlaps with the present work. The task here is to develop the racial formation approach in a world-historical perspective:[4] global racial formation. Indeed, historical time could well be interpreted in terms of something like a racial *longue duree*. Does not the rise of Europe, the onset of African enslavement, the *conquista*, and the subjugation of much of Asia represent an epochal sociohistorical transformation, an immense planetary metamorphosis? I take the point of much poststructural scholarship on these matters to be quite precisely an effort to explain Western or colonial time as a huge project demarcating human "difference," or more globally (as Todorov, say, would argue) of framing partial collective identities in terms of externalized "others" (Todorov 1984). Just as, for example, the writers of the *Annales* school sought to locate the deep logic of historical time in the means by which material life was produced—diet, shoes, and the like[5]—so we

might usefully think of a racial *longue duree* in which the slow inscription of phenotypical signification took place upon the human body, in and through conquest and enslavement to be sure, but also as an enormous act of expression, of narration.[6]

The claim that race was one of the central ingredients in the circular and cumulative causation of modernity hinges on the presence of racial dynamics, key processes of racial formation, in all the main constitutive relationships that structured the origins and development of the modern world system. These crucial relationships involved the making of new forms of *empire and nation*; the organization of new systems of *capital and labor*; and the articulation of new concepts of *culture and identity*. Because these are circular and cumulative processes, they must be understood as thoroughly intertwined; there is no need or possibility of proposing one of these three as primary or causative. Nor is it desirable (or even possible) to offer any comprehensive theorization of these massive themes here. I simply indicate the presence of racial dimensions within each. Having suggested how in each area world-historical developmental and racial formation processes were intertwined, I trace the genealogy of the racial system of our own time. [. . .]

EMPIRE AND NATION

An important part of the transition to modernity was nation-building (Eisenstadt and Rokkan 1973; Bendix 1977[1964]), a process inextricable in Europe from conquest, exclusion, and the beginnings of empire. In becoming modern nations, in challenging their legacies of fragmentation and subordination to early empires, the countries on the Atlantic fringe of Europe both made themselves into racially/nationally homogeneous entities (with assorted tendentious and uncertain elements remaining, to be sure, but in much reduced and suppressed form) and sought new peoples to subordinate. They formed stronger, more centralized states (Tilly 1975); began the transition to capitalism, passing along various paths through plunder and mercantilism on the way; and sought adequate discursive representations of these undertakings in religious, philosophical, and political terms. All this was intertwined with the emergent racial projects of conquest and enslavement.

Only nation-states could tackle the immense efforts of restructuring the world economy (Polanyi 1980 [1944]). Yet nation-states themselves had to be created, both through internal unification and differentiation from peripheral "others"—whether local rivals, however recognizable, or distant and different peoples, however unknown and unrecognized.

Nation-building was a complex process. Within the local or regional context it involved expelling some of those viewed as "different" and incorporating others whose identities had to be amalgamated or subordinated in a greater, nascent, national whole. In the larger imperial sense, the transoceanic context, let us say, the process of nation-making entailed distinguishing the nation *en bloc* from other nations. There were two dimensions to this distinction: rivalry and "othering." Rivalry came from developing inter-imperial competition, which could be more or less ferocious and sanguinary. "Othering" came not from national, but from supranational distinctions, nascent regional distinctions between Europe and the rest of the world, between "us," broadly conceived, and the non-Christian, "uncivilized," and soon enough non-white "others,"[7] whose subordination and subjugation was justified on numerous grounds—religious and philosophical as much as political and economic.

Thus nascent states constructed their key instrumentalities, institutions, and capabilities for action, particularly their own political and military apparatuses. Thus they worked out the beliefs and collective identities that would allow imperial activities to be launched and organized. The emergence of early concepts of race was integral in these processes. With the initiation of transatlantic conquest and African slavery, race begins to appear as an important tool in the advancement and interpretation of these activities.

The suggestion that the modern nation has ethnic or racial origins is a familiar one (Smith 1987). Certainly the nations of imperial Europe only forged themselves into racially/ethnically homogeneous entities through prolonged processes combining both amalgation (Weber 1976) and exclusion (Hroch 1985; Hroch 1993; Gellner 1983). In part this process unified nation-states internally, while separating them more definitively from one another and indeed pitting them against each other. All this made the endeavors of conquest and enslavement more vital, thus helping to constitute the imperial mission. By evolving systems of enslavement and conquest that differentiated their "nationals" (soldiers, settlers)[8] from the proto-racial "others" who were the conquered and enslaved, imperial nations also consolidated themselves. They were not only the French, the Portuguese, the Dutch, the British; they were also the whites, the masters, the true Christians. A distinction crystallized between rulers and ruled that was readily "phenotypified," corporealized. This duality, complicated eventually by creolism, *mestizaje*, and the sometimes ambiguous status of workers, soldiers, and peasants (in both the mother-countries and the colonies), nevertheless laid out the national-political axes of the modern racial order and, as I have begun to suggest, of the modern world system.

Intermediate strata necessarily arose as colonization advanced and the slave system grew. Both class and status distinctions multiplied in colonies and metropoles, generated by burgeoning economic, political, and social contacts and conflicts among imperial enterprises: rivalries and competition, colloquy and debate, as well as outright warfare. As creole status-groups developed in the colonies, national rivalries with the colonial powers emerged (for example, *criollos* versus *peninsulares* throughout *Nueva España*). Often differentiated by a range of racial signifiers from the "true whites" of the mother-country, the creole (or planter, or settler, or *mestizo*) elites sought to establish their own national/political rights in various ways. Some wished only to administer their own slave systems, others to embark on a separate path of national independence, and still others to implement a new American version of the Declaration of the Rights of Man. Since such desires generally required armed revolt, it was often necessary to emancipate slaves, enfranchise *mestizos*, and redistribute land and wealth in order to raise a revolutionary army and thus win independence. So at later stages of what was a long process, nation-building took place through upheavals in racially determined social status.

There were, of course, many forms of upheaval, many types of resistance. Native peoples who were able to do so challenged their would-be conquerors and masters militarily, and took flight where possible. But confusion and division also characterized the subjugated. Amid the Africans and African-Americans of the New World, for example, many (intra-racial) divisions emerged from differences in national origin and the temporal/generational dimensions of exile from the African motherland.[9] That these particularities would have important consequences for the success of uprisings or patterns of escape and *marronage* is clear. Divisions between Afro-Creoles and native Africans are well recognized as crucial to the unfolding of the Haitian revolution, for example (Thornton 1991; Thornton 1993; Nicholls 1996).

Parallel complexities and social divisions emerged throughout the imperial world in respect to social class. These too had racial dimensions. In the earliest stages of American conquest there was not yet African enslavement. Native peoples were the first modern racial "others," and some Africans were among the *conquistadores*. African slavery only developed as a result of labor shortages of natives and indentured servants. Indigenous people were killed en masse, worked to death, fled, or occasionally went to war, none of which rendered them available for ongoing toil. Early imported labor (generally bonded and, although multiracial, largely poor and European) could not be had in sufficient quantity, nor degraded comprehensively enough, to produce profits from early mines or plantations (Morgan 1995; Rout 1976; Cope 1994; Russell-Wood 1998). Turning to Africa for exploitable labor meant creating a class of free persons, usually (although not always) white, usually (although not always) not slaveholders, and destined to be (or already perceiving themselves to be) competi-

tors with Africans, both enslaved and emancipated. Since this situation involved a range of potential political alignments (both labor versus planters and whites versus blacks were possible lines of conflict), nation-building meant steering away from class conflict and toward race conflict, or at least entrenched social hierarchy based on racial status (Breen and Innes 1980).

Thus, while we must note the tremendous variations within this process of national ontogeny, it is equally important to recognize the centrality of racial dynamics in forging both imperial nations and colonies, and ultimately in sundering those identities and bonds. [. . .]

THE STAKES TODAY

This is the situation that exists today, then. Colonialism is finished; apartheid, in both its South African and U.S. forms, has been discredited; the northern, post-industrial countries are all permanently polyracial; in the world's South, an ostensibly color-blind transnational capital seeks labor and markets without recourse to racialism, not to mention explicit white supremacy. Yet beneath the surface, below the commonsense understanding from which nefarious racism has been banished, a global racial order remains: transformed, but not transcended; revivified by decades of battle with (and yes, concessions to) the menial laborers and peasantries of the world, the darker peoples it formerly held in contempt.

At the same time those once-excluded peoples—ex-colonials, descendants of slaves, indigenes—confront the present from a greatly altered position. Many millions of them are long gone from the hinterlands, the *sertões*; they are to be found today in the metropolitan centers, of both the South and the North. They have achieved some measure of political inclusion and democratic rights that would have been inconceivable only a few years ago. Limited and uneven as their oppositional victories were over the past half century or so, the scope of their postwar challenge to white supremacy still dwarfs the accomplishments of any other movement of resistance to the world racial order that took center stage from about the fifteenth century on.

More yet: a variety of solidarities—let us call them southern or diasporic—has flowered in the last decades, both fulfilling and obviating earlier dreams of resistance. Pan-Africanism as a movement lost much of its rationale as the sun finally set on the British (and French, and Belgian, and Portuguese) empires, yet Afro-diasporic solidarity continues to flourish, impelled as in the past by cultural as well as political interchange, conscious as in the past of the necessity, as well as the perils, of black self-determination. Indigenous movements have probably reached new heights in the present, giving rise to hemispheric congresses of native peoples in the Americas and movements for reparations in such unexpected spots as New Zealand (Farnsworth 1997). Meanwhile, communities with origins in the sending regions of the world's South—such as Turkey, the Philippines, India, and China—are also experiencing new (if sometimes uncertain) diasporic impulses.

Undoubtedly one factor generating such transcontinental ties is simply the vastly reinforced presence of racialized minorities in the former imperial homelands; another is the relative freedom and ease of communication and travel, which in the past was the preserve largely of Europeans. But undoubtedly most important in the gestation of diasporae are the political achievements of the "others" since World War II's end. These gains—of voice, vote, and (sometimes) democratic inclusion; of the means of communication and cultural production; and here and there of the attainment of material well-being and the progressive redistribution of income and wealth—serve as models and resources across borders and beyond oceans.

Diasporic tendencies and movements call into question the nation-state. They are thus linked, as were their predecessors slavery and peonage, with capital's forms of accumulation and rule. Their presence, both within various national political scenarios and globally as circuits of labor, culture, and political influence, suggests that a new racial order is emerging. Without making predic-

tions, it is possible to identify the world racial dynamics that will shape the twenty-first century: in the near-term future the color-line will not be superseded, but will operate in a far more contradictory and contested way.

Hegemony works by incorporating opposition. Thus global racial dynamics will reflect the unstable equilibrium, the uneasy tension, between the centuries-long legacy of white supremacy and the post-World War II triumphs—ambiguous and partial but nevertheless real—of the movements of the colonized and racially excluded. The world racial system will therefore simultaneously incorporate and deny the rights, and in some cases the very existence, of the "others" whose recognition was only so recently and incompletely conceded. In short, we are witnessing the dawn of a new form of racial hegemony. In the twenty-first century, race will no longer be invoked to legitimate the crucial social structures of inequality, exploitation, and injustice. Appeals to white superiority will not serve, as they did in the bad old days. Law, political and human rights, as well as concepts of equality, fairness, and human difference will therefore increasingly be framed in "race-neutral" terms.

Yet the race-concept will continue to work at the interface of identity and inequality, social structure and cultural signification. The rearticulation of (in)equality in an ostensibly color-blind framework emphasizing individualism and meritocracy, it turns out, preserves the legacy of racial hierarchy far more effectively than its explicit defense (Crenshaw et al. 1995). Similarly, the reinterpretation of racialized differences as matters of culture and nationality, rather than as fundamental human attributes somehow linked to phenotype, turns out to justify exclusionary politics and policy far better than traditional white supremacist arguments can do (Taguieff 2001 [1988]).

These are merely some early indications of what the world racial system will look like in the twenty-first century, when it will have to operate under the contradictory (or dualistic) conditions that tend toward the development of a variety of "anti-racist racisms." Contemporary world racial dynamics are unique, most notably because they have had to adapt for the first time in half a millennium to a relatively comprehensive opposition to racial inequality and injustice. If the opposition that has developed since World War II has not achieved the elimination of racial injustice and inequality, it has at least succeeded to an unprecedented degree in legitimizing the struggle against these patterns. This alone is a great achievement, one that would not be intelligible without a comprehensive account of the evolution of the world racial order to the present day. Yet the reordering of world racial dynamics over the past decades does not suggest that we are in any way "beyond race," or that comprehensive patterns of racial inequality and injustice are no longer fundamental to the global social structure. It only means—and this is important enough— that world racial formation continues.

NOTES

1. This argument is presented in greater depth in Omi and Winant 1994.
2. There is a wide range of methodological limits to most social scientific approaches to race, limits that cannot be addressed in depth here. Schematically speaking, most social scientific approaches to race are *nomothetic* in terms of methodology: that is, they follow scientific norms assumed to operate universalistically. Thus they propose to investigate a clear cause-effect relationship between two or more sets of variables, some of which are known (dependent) and others of research interest (independent). The need for precise specification of each variable's dimensions, and for strict separation between cause and effect variables, is basic to such techniques.

    But if race is as constitutive of social order as I suggest it is, then assigning it to one or the other side of this equation is problematic. On the one hand, to treat racial phenomena as dependent variables—the effects of other, putatively more fundamental or "objective" social structures or relationships (such as social class, cultural identity, or nationality)—is prone to reductionism, as I have shown elsewhere (Omi and Winant 1994). On the other hand, to consider racial dynamics as independent variables—studying, say, the effects of race on family dynamics or employment patterns—tends to ignore the tremendous variability of the race-concept, which operates both as a social structure and a dimension of lived identity/ experience. The flexible and malleable character of race, which has evolved over an immense historical span, cannot be captured if it is merely treated as a fixed category. See Wallerstein 1991, 242–244.

3. No early empire could attain truly global scope. None could exist without a central administrative nucleus, a politico-military authority that extended and disciplined the imperial domain, directing the empire's accumulative flow toward the center by various means (tributary, coercive, etc.), and accepting no rivalry within the boundaries of the system.

4. Of course this is undertaken in light of many influences, among them "world-system" analysis and the pragmatic, progressive social science of Myrdal, as well as such other currents as Foucauldian post-structuralism and Gramscian theory.

5. For example, the magisterial work of Braudel 1975. See especially Braudel's treatment of slavery in vol. III.

6. In his story "In the Penal Colony" Franz Kafka depicts an infernal machine of punishment, designed to execute insubordinate natives in a prison colony located on an unnamed tropical island. The form of capital punishment is brutal and prolonged: tortuously, slowly, the rule which the condemned has violated (in the story, this rule is "HONOR THY SUPERIORS!") is written with needles on the condemned's body, embellished and elaborated until at last, bleeding from the very words it has defied, covered with the mark of its own shame, the body dies and is discarded (Kafka 1961).

7. Let this overly general assertion be qualified: early modern European relations with littoral African states and kingdoms, and indeed with native Americans (first in the Caribbean and then more widely), were not immediately and uniformly those of conquerors and subjects. There were wide variations in the early experiences of transcontinental contact. African fighters repelled European raids and efforts at pillage. In the fifteenth century, for example, there were naval battles between Portuguese vessels and large war canoes off the Senegambian and Kongolese coasts (Thornton 1998, 37–40). There were wars among Portuguese, Angolan, and Kongolese forces—often involving shifting patterns of alliance—as late as the end of the sixteenth century. Such experiences led to trading rather than raiding relationships (or complex combinations of the two), which often endured for long periods (Miller 1988, 551–552). In the early plantation experiments on the Atlantic islands, in early African slavery in the Americas (Rout 1976; Davidson 1961), and in the centuries-long process of subjugation of American native peoples, similar interweavings of depredation and coexistence can be discovered. Overall, of course, tendencies toward outright conquest and hierarchization, and the abundant testimonies of racialization, do predominate. But these patterns too are more circular and cumulative than abrupt, immediate, or unproblematic for the particular European power involved.

8. Such distinctions must always be seen as schematic,

for several reasons: early imperial missions of raiding or trading were staffed at all ranks by a variable and itinerant lot of seamen, soldiers, and freebooters of all types, many of whom were mercenaries, not "citizens." (Columbus himself is the most ready example.) Later imperial trading and shipping bred a seafaring working class whose national and indeed racial particularities tended to be homogenized by its conditions of labor (Rediker 1987).

9. Many of the slave revolts that took place throughout the hemisphere were organized along ethnic/linguistic lines (Thronton 1998).

BIBLIOGRAPHY

Bendix, Reinhard. *Nation-building and Citizenship: Studies of Our Changing Social Order.* 2nd ed. Berkeley: University of California Press, 1977[1964].

Braudel, Fernand. *Capitalism and Material Life, 1400–1800.* Translated by Miriam Kochan. New York: Harper Colophon, 1975.

Breen, T. H., and Stephen Innes. *"Myne Owne Ground": Race and Freedom on Virginia's Eastern Shore, 1640–1676.* New York: Oxford University Press, 1980.

Cope, Douglas. *The Limits of Racial Domination: Plebeian Society in Colonial Mexico City, 1660–1720.* Madison: University of Wisconsin Press, 1994.

Crenshaw, Kimberlé, et al., eds. *Critical Race Theory: The Key Writings That Formed the Movement.* New York: New Press, 1995.

Davidson, Basil. *Black Mother: The Years of the African Slave Trade.* Boston: Little, Brown, 1961.

Eisenstadt, Shmuel Noah, and Stein Rokkan. *Building States and Nations.* Beverly Hills, CA: Sage, 1973.

Farnsworth, Clyde H. "The Betrayed Maori Are Calling for a Reckoning." *New York Times,* March 20, 1997.

Gellner, Ernest. *Nations and Nationalism.* New York: Oxford University Press, 1983.

Hroch, Miroslav. "From National Movement to the Fully-Formed Nation: The Nation-Building Process in Europe." *New Left Review* 198 (March–April 1993).

Hroch, Miroslav. *Social Preconditions of National Revival in Europe: A Comparative Analysis of the Social Composition of the Patriotic Groups Among the Smaller European Nations.* Cambridge: Cambridge University Press, 1985.

Kafka, Franz. *In the Penal Colony.* Translated by W. E. Muir. New York, NY: Schocken Books, 1961.

Miller, Joseph C. *Way of Death: Merchant Capitalism and the Angolan Slave Trade, 1730–1830.* Madison: University of Wisconsin Press, 1988.

Morgan, Edmund S. *American Slavery, American Freedom: The Ordeal of Colonial Virginia.* 2nd ed. New York: Norton, 1995.

Myrdal, Gunnar. *Economic Theory and Under-Developed Regions.* London: Duckworth, 1963.

Nicholls, David. *From Dessalines to Duvalier: Race, Colour, and National Independence in Haiti.* Rev. ed. New Brunswick: Rutgers University Press, 1996.

Omi, Michael, and Howard Winant. *Racial Formation in the United States: From the 1960s to the 1990s.* Rev. ed. New York: Routledge, 1994.

Polanyi, Karl. *The Great Transformation.* Boston: Beacon, 1980 [1944].

Rediker, Marcus Buford. *Between the Devil and the Deep Blue Sea: Merchant Seamen, Pirates, and the Anglo-American Maritime World, 1700–1750.* Cambridge; New York: Cambridge University Press, 1987.

Rout, Leslie B., Jr. *The African Experience in Spanish America, 1502 to the Present Day.* New York: Cambridge University Press, 1976.

Russell-Wood, A. J. R. *The Portuguese Empire, 1415–1808: A World on the Move.* Baltimore: Johns Hopkins University Press, 1998.

Smith, Anthony D. *The Ethnic Origins of Nations.* New York: Blackwell, 1987.

Taguieff, Pierre-André. *The Force of Prejudice: On Racism and Its Doubles.* Translated by Hassan Melehy. Minneapolis: University of Minnesota Press, 2001; original French edition 1988.

Thornton, John. "African Soldiers in the Haitian Revolution." *Journal of Caribbean History* 25 (1991).

Thornton, John. "'I Am the Subject of the King of Kongo': African Political Ideology and the Haitian Revolution." *Journal of World History* 4, no. 2 (1993).

Thornton, John. *Africa and Africans in the Making of the Atlantic World, 1400–1680.* 2nd ed. New York: Cambridge University Press, 1998.

Tilly, Charles, ed. *The Formation of National States in Western Europe.* Princeton: Princeton University Press, 1975.

Todorov, Tsvetan. *The Conquest of America: The Question of the Other.* Translated by Richard Howard. New York: Harper & Row, 1984.

Wallerstein, Immanuel M. "The Myrdal Legacy: Racism and Underdevelopment as Dilemmas." In idem, *Unthinking Social Science: The Limits of Nineteenth-Century Paradigms.* Cambridge, UK: Polity, 1991.

Weber, Eugen Joseph. *Peasants into Frenchmen: The Modernization of Rural France, 1870–1914.* Stanford: Stanford University Press, 1976.

CHAPTER 16

The Black Atlantic as a Counterculture of Modernity

Paul Gilroy

[...]

Striving to be both European and black requires some specific forms of double consciousness. By saying this I do not mean to suggest that taking on either or both of these unfinished identities necessarily exhausts the subjective resources of any particular individual. However, where racist, nationalist, or ethnically absolutist discourses orchestrate political relationships so that these identities appear to be mutually exclusive, occupying the space between them or trying to demonstrate their continuity has been viewed as a provocative and even oppositional act of political insubordination.

The contemporary black English, like the Anglo-Africans of earlier generations and perhaps, like all blacks in the West, stand between (at least) two great cultural assemblages, both of which have mutated through the course of the modern world that formed them and assumed new configurations. At present, they remain locked symbiotically in an antagonistic relationship marked out by the symbolism of colours which adds to the conspicuous cultural power of their central Manichean dynamic—black and white. These colours support a special rhetoric that has grown to be associated with a language of nationality and national belonging as well as the languages of "race" and ethnic identity. [...]

Regardless of their affiliation to the right, left, or centre, groups have fallen back on the idea of cultural nationalism, on the overintegrated conceptions of culture which present immutable, ethnic differences as an absolute break in the histories and experiences of "black" and "white" people. Against this choice stands another, more difficult option: the theorisation of creolisation, métissage, mestizaje, and hybridity. From the viewpoint of ethnic absolutism, this would be a litany of pollution and impurity. These terms are rather unsatisfactory ways of naming the processes of cultural mutation and restless (dis)continuity that exceed racial discourse and avoid capture by its agents. [...]

Here the ideas of nation, nationality, national belonging, and nationalism are paramount. They are extensively supported by a clutch of rhetorical strategies that can be named "cultural insiderism."[1] The essential trademark of cultural insiderism which also supplies the key to its popularity is an absolute sense of ethnic difference. This is maximised so that it distinguishes people from one another and at the same time acquires an incontestable priority over all other dimensions of their social and historical experience, cultures, and identities. Characteristically, these claims are associated with the idea of national belonging or the aspiration to nationality and other more local but equivalent forms of cultural kinship. The range and complexity of these ideas in English cultural life defies simple summary or exposition. However, the forms of cultural insiderism they sanction typically construct the nation as an ethnically homogeneous object and invoke ethnicity a second time in the hermeneutic procedures deployed to make sense of its distinctive cultural content.

The intellectual seam in which English cultural studies has positioned itself—through innovative work in the fields of social history and literary criticism—can be indicated here. The statist modalities of

Marxist analysis that view modes of material production and political domination as exclusively *national* entities are only one source of this problem. Another factor, more evasive but nonetheless potent for its intangible ubiquity, is a quiet cultural nationalism which pervades the work of some radical thinkers. This crypto-nationalism means that they are often disinclined to consider the cross catalytic or transverse dynamics of racial politics as a significant element in the formation and reproduction of English national identities. These formations are treated as if they spring, fully formed, from their own special viscera. [. . .]

This chapter also proposes some new chronotopes[2] that might fit with a theory that was less intimidated by and respectful of the boundaries and integrity of modern nation states than either English or African-American cultural studies have so far been. I have settled on the image of ships in motion across the spaces between Europe, America, Africa, and the Caribbean as a central organising symbol for this enterprise and as my starting point. The image of the ship—a living, micro-cultural, micro-political system in motion—is especially important for historical and theoretical reasons that I hope will become clearer below. Ships immediately focus attention on the middle passage, on the various projects for redemptive return to an African homeland, on the circulation of ideas and activists as well as the movement of key cultural and political artefacts: tracts, books, gramophone records, and choirs. [. . .]

CULTURAL STUDIES IN BLACK AND WHITE

Any satisfaction to be experienced from the recent spectacular growth of cultural studies as an academic project should not obscure its conspicuous problems with ethnocentrism and nationalism. Understanding these difficulties might commence with a critical evaluation of the ways in which notions of ethnicity have been mobilised, often by default rather than design, as part of the distinctive hermeneutics of cultural studies or with the unthinking assumption that cultures always flow into patterns congruent with the borders of essentially homogeneous nation states. [. . .]

Histories of cultural studies seldom acknowledge how the politically radical and openly interventionist aspirations found in the best of its scholarship are already articulated to black cultural history and theory. These links are rarely seen or accorded any significance. In England, the work of figures like C. L. R. James and Stuart Hall offers a wealth of both symbols and concrete evidence for the practical links between these critical political projects. In the United States the work of interventionist scholars like bell hooks and Cornel West as well as that of more orthodox academics like Henry Louis Gates, Jr., Houston A. Baker, Jr., Anthony Appiah, and Hazel Carby, points to similar convergences. The position of these thinkers in the contested "contact zones"[3] between cultures and histories is not, however, as exceptional as it might appear at first. We shall see below that successive generations of black intellectuals (especially those whose lives, like James's, crisscrossed the Atlantic Ocean) noted this intercultural positionality and accorded it a special significance before launching their distinct modes of cultural and political critique. They were often urged on in their labour by the brutal absurdity of racial classification that derives from and also celebrates racially exclusive conceptions of national identity from which blacks were excluded as either non-humans or non-citizens. I shall try to show that their marginal endeavours point to some new analytic possibilities with a general significance far beyond the well-policed borders of black particularity. For example, this body of work offers intermediate concepts, lodged between the local and the global, which have a wider applicability in cultural history and politics precisely because they offer an alternative to the nationalist focus which dominates cultural criticism. These intermediate concepts, especially the undertheorised idea of diaspora examined in Chapter 6, are exemplary precisely because they break the dogmatic focus on discrete *national* dynamics which has characterised so much modern Euro-American cultural thought.

Getting beyond these national and nationalistic perspectives has become essential for two additional reasons. The first arises from the urgent obligation to reevaluate the significance of the modern nation state as a political, economic, and cultural unit. Neither political nor economic structures of domination are still simply co-extensive with national borders. This has a special significance in contemporary Europe, where new political and economic relations are being created seemingly day by day, but it is a worldwide phenomenon with significant consequences for the relationship between the politics of information and the practices of capital accumulation. Its effects underpin more recognisably political changes like the growing centrality of transnational ecological movements which, through their insistence on the association of sustainability and justice, do so much to shift the moral and scientific precepts on which the modern separation of politics and ethics was built. The second reason relates to the tragic popularity of ideas about the integrity and purity of cultures. In particular, it concerns the relationship between nationality and ethnicity. This too currently has a special force in Europe, but it is also reflected directly in the postcolonial histories and complex, transcultural, political trajectories of Britain's black settlers.

What might be called the peculiarity of the black English requires attention to the intermixture of a variety of distinct cultural forms. Previously separated political and intellectual traditions converged and, in their coming together, overdetermined the process of black Britain's social and historical formation. This blending is misunderstood if it is conceived in simple ethnic terms, but right and left, racist and anti-racist, black and white tacitly share a view of it as little more than a collision between fully formed and mutually exclusive cultural communities. This has become the dominant view where black history and culture are perceived, like black settlers themselves, as an illegitimate intrusion into a vision of authentic British national life that, prior to their arrival, was as stable and as peaceful as it was ethnically undifferentiated. [...]

Of this infamous trio, Wedderburn is perhaps the best known, thanks to the efforts of Peter Linebaugh and Iain McCalman.[4] The child of a slave dealer, James Wedderburn, and a slave woman, Robert was brought up by a Kingston conjure woman who acted as an agent for smugglers. He migrated to London at the age of seventeen in 1778. There, having published a number of disreputable ultra-radical tracts as part of his subversive political labours, he presented himself as a living embodiment of the horrors of slavery in a debating chapel in Hopkins Street near the Haymarket, where he preached a version of chiliastic anarchism based on the teachings of Thomas Spence and infused with deliberate blasphemy. In one of the debates held in his "ruinous hayloft with 200 persons of the lowest description," Wedderburn defended the inherent rights of the Caribbean slave to slay his master, promising to write home and "tell them to murder their masters as soon as they please." After this occasion he was tried and acquitted on a charge of blasphemy after persuading the jury that he had not been uttering sedition but merely practising the "true and infallible genius of prophetic skill."[5]

It is particularly significant for the direction of my overall argument that both Wedderburn and his sometime associate Davidson had been sailors, moving to and fro between nations, crossing borders in modern machines that were themselves micro-systems of linguistic and political hybridity. Their relationship to the sea may turn out to be especially important for both the early politics and poetics of the black Atlantic world that I wish to counterpose against the narrow nationalism of so much English historiography. Wedderburn served in the Royal Navy and as a privateer, while Davidson, who ran away to sea instead of studying law, was pressed into naval service on two subsequent occasions. Davidson inhabited the same ultra-radical subculture as Wedderburn and was an active participant in the Marylebone Reading Society, a radical body formed in 1819 after the Peterloo massacre. He is known to have acted as the custodian of their black flag, which significantly bore a skull and crossbones with the legend

"Let us die like men and not be sold as slaves," at an open air meeting in Smithfield later that year.[6] The precise details of how radical ideologies articulated the culture of the London poor before the institution of the factory system to the insubordinate maritime culture of pirates and other pre-industrial workers of the world will have to await the innovative labours of Peter Linebaugh and Marcus Rediker.[7] However, it has been estimated that at the end of the eighteenth century a quarter of the British navy was composed of Africans for whom the experience of slavery was a powerful orientation to the ideologies of liberty and justice. Looking for similar patterns on the other side of the Atlantic network we can locate Crispus Attucks at the head of his "motley rabble of saucy boys, negroes, mulattoes, Irish teagues and outlandish jack tars"[8] and can track Denmark Vesey sailing the Caribbean and picking up inspirational stories of the Haitian revolution (one of his co-conspirators testified that he had said they would "not spare one white skin alive for this was the plan they pursued in San Domingo").[9] There is also the shining example of Frederick Douglass, whose autobiographies reveal that he learnt of freedom in the North from Irish sailors while working as a ship's caulker in Baltimore. He had less to say about the embarrassing fact that the vessels he readied for the ocean—Baltimore Clippers—were slavers, the fastest ships in the world and the only craft capable of outrunning the British blockade. Douglass, who played a neglected role in English anti-slavery activity, escaped from bondage disguised as a sailor and put this success down to his ability to "talk sailor like an old salt."[10] These are only a few of the nineteenth-century examples. The involvement of Marcus Garvey, George Padmore, Claude McKay, and Langston Hughes with ships and sailors lends additional support to Linebaugh's prescient suggestion that "the ship remained perhaps the most important conduit of Pan-African communication before the appearance of the long-playing record."[11]

Ships and other maritime scenes have a special place in the work of J. M. W. Turner, an artist whose pictures represent, in the view of many contemporary critics, the pinnacle of achievement in the English school in painting. Any visitor to London will testify to the importance of the Clore Gallery as a national institution and of the place of Turner's art as an enduring expression of the very essence of English civilisation. Turner was secured on the summit of critical appreciation by John Ruskin, who, as we have seen, occupies a special place in Williams's constellation of great Englishmen. Turner's celebrated picture of a slave ship[12] throwing overboard its dead and dying as a storm comes on was exhibited at the Royal Academy to coincide with the world anti-slavery convention held in London in 1840. The picture, owned by Ruskin for some twenty-eight years, was rather more than an answer to the absentee Caribbean landlords who had commissioned its creator to record the tainted splendour of their country houses, which, as Patrick Wright has eloquently demonstrated, became an important signifier of the contemporary, ruralist distillate of national life.[13] It offered a powerful protest against the direction and moral tone of English politics. This was made explicit in an epigraph Turner took from his own poetry and which has itself retained a political inflection: "Hope, hope, fallacious hope where is thy market now?" Three years after his extensive involvement in the campaign to defend Governor Eyre,[14] Ruskin put the slave ship painting up for sale at Christie's. It is said that he had begun to find it too painful to live with. No buyer was found at that time, and he sold the picture to an American three years later. The painting has remained in the United States ever since. Its exile in Boston is yet another pointer towards the shape of the Atlantic as a system of cultural exchanges. It is more important, though, to draw attention to Ruskin's inability to discuss the picture except in terms of what it revealed about the aesthetics of painting water. He relegated the information that the vessel was a slave ship to a footnote in the first volume of *Modern Painters*.[15]

In spite of lapses like this, the New Left heirs to the aesthetic and cultural tradition in which Turner and Ruskin stand compounded and reproduced its nationalism and its ethnocentrism by denying imaginary, invented Englishness any external referents whatsoever. England ceaselessly gives birth to itself, seemingly from Britannia's head. The political affiliations and cultural preferences of this New Left group amplified these problems. They are most visible and most intense in the radical historiography that supplied a counterpart to Williams's subtle literary reflections. For all their enthusiasm for the work of C. L. R. James, the influential British Communist Party's historians' group[16] is culpable here. Their predilections for the image of the freeborn Englishman and the dream of socialism in one country that framed their work are both to be found wanting when it comes to nationalism. This uncomfortable pairing can be traced through the work of Edward Thompson and Eric Hobsbawm, visionary writers who contributed so much to the strong foundations of English cultural studies and who share a non-reductive Marxian approach to economic, social, and cultural history in which the nation—understood as a stable receptacle for counter-hegemonic class struggle—is the primary focus. These problems within English cultural studies form at its junction point with practical politics and instantiate wider difficulties with nationalism and with the discursive slippage or connotative resonance between "race," ethnicity, and nation.

Similar problems appear in rather different form in African-American letters where an equally volkish popular cultural nationalism is featured in the work of several generations of radical scholars and an equal number of not so radical ones. We will see below that absolutist conceptions of cultural difference allied to a culturalist understanding of "race" and ethnicity can be found in this location too.

In opposition to both of these nationalist or ethnically absolute approaches, I want to develop the suggestion that cultural historians could take the Atlantic as one single, complex unit of analysis in their discussions of the modern world and use it to produce an explicitly transnational and intercultural perspective.[17] Apart from the confrontation with English historiography and literary history this entails a challenge to the ways in which black American cultural and political histories have so far been conceived. I want to suggest that much of the precious intellectual legacy claimed by African-American intellectuals as the substance of their particularity is in fact only partly their absolute ethnic property. No less than in the case of the English New Left, the idea of the black Atlantic can be used to show that there are other claims to it which can be based on the structure of the African diaspora into the western hemisphere. A concern with the Atlantic as a cultural and political system has been forced on black historiography and intellectual history by the economic and historical matrix in which plantation slavery—"capitalism with its clothes off"—was one special moment. The fractal patterns of cultural and political exchange and transformation that we try and specify through manifestly inadequate theoretical terms like creolisation and syncretism indicate how both ethnicities and political cultures have been made anew in ways that are significant not simply for the peoples of the Caribbean but for Europe, for Africa, especially Liberia and Sierra Leone, and of course, for black America.

It bears repetition that Britain's black settler communities have forged a compound culture from disparate sources. Elements of political sensibility and cultural expression transmitted from black America over a long period of time have been reaccentuated in Britain. They are central, though no longer dominant, within the increasingly novel configurations that characterise another newer black vernacular culture. This is not content to be either dependent upon or simply imitative of the African diaspora cultures of America and the Caribbean. The rise and rise of Jazzie B and Soul II Soul at the turn of the last decade constituted one valuable sign of this new assertive mood. North London's Funki Dreds, whose name itself projects a newly hybridised identity, have projected the distinct culture and rhythm of life of black Britain outwards into the world. Their song "Keep On Moving" was notable for having been produced in England by the children of Caribbean settlers and then re-mixed in a (Jamaican) dub format in the United States by Teddy Riley, an African-American. It included segments or samples of music taken from American and Jamaican records by the JBs and Mikey Dread respectively. This formal unity of diverse cultural elements was more than just a powerful symbol. It encapsulated the playful diasporic intimacy that has been a marked feature of trans-national black Atlantic creativity. The record and its extraordinary popularity enacted the ties of affiliation and affect which articulated the discontinuous histories of black settlers in the new world. The fundamental injunction to "Keep On Moving" also expressed the restlessness of spirit which makes that diaspora culture vital. The contemporary black arts movement in film, visual arts, and theatre as well as music, which provided the background to this musical release, have created a new topography of loyalty and identity in which the structures and presuppositions of the nation state have been left behind because they are seen to be outmoded. It is important to remember that these recent black Atlantic phenomena may not be as novel as their digital encoding via the transnational force of north London's Soul II Soul suggests. Columbus's pilot, Pedro Nino, was also an African. The history of the black Atlantic since then, continually criss-crossed by the movements of black people—not only as commodities but engaged in various struggles towards emancipation, autonomy, and citizenship—provides a means to reexamine the problems of nationality, location, identity, and historical memory. They all emerge from it with special clarity if we contrast the national, nationalistic, and ethnically absolute paradigms of cultural criticism to be found in England and America with those hidden expressions, both residual and emergent, that attempt to be global or outer-national in nature. These traditions have supported countercultures of modernity that touched the workers' movement but are not reducible to it. They supplied important foundations on which it could build.

Turner's extraordinary painting of the slave ship remains a useful image not only for its self-conscious moral power and the striking way that it aims directly for the sublime in its invocation of racial terror, commerce, and England's ethico-political degeneration. It should be emphasised that ships were the living means by which the points within that Atlantic world were joined. They were mobile elements that stood for the shifting spaces in between the fixed places that they connected.[18] Accordingly they need to be thought of as cultural and political units rather than abstract embodiments of the triangular trade. They were something more—a means to conduct political dissent and possibly a distinct mode of cultural production. The ship provides a chance to explore the articulations between the discontinuous histories of England's ports, its interfaces with the wider world.[19] Ships also refer us back to the middle passage, to the half-remembered micro-politics of the slave trade and its relationship to both industrialisation and modernisation. As it were, getting on board promises a means to reconceptualise the orthodox relationship between modernity and what passes for its prehistory. It provides a different sense of where modernity might itself be thought to begin in the constitutive relationships with outsiders that both found and temper a self-conscious sense of western civilisation.[20] For all these reasons, the ship is the first of the novel chronotopes presupposed by my attempts to rethink modernity via the history of the black Atlantic and the African diaspora into the western hemisphere.

In the venturesome spirit proposed by James Clifford in his influential work on travelling culture,[21] I want to consider the impact that this outer-national, transcultural reconceptualisation might have on the political and cultural history of black Americans and that of blacks in Europe. In recent history, this will certainly mean reevaluating Garvey and Garveyism, pan-Africanism, and Black Power as hemispheric if not global phenomena. In periodising modern black politics it will require fresh thinking about the importance of Haiti and its revolution for the development of African-American political thought and movements of resistance. From the European side, it will no doubt be necessary to reconsider Frederick Douglass's relationship to English and Scottish radicalisms and to meditate on the significance of

William Wells Brown's five years in Europe as a fugitive slave, on Alexander Crummell's living and studying in Cambridge, and upon Martin Delany's experiences at the London congress of the International Statistical Congress in 1860.[22] It will require comprehension of such difficult and complex questions as W. E. B. Du Bois's childhood interest in Bismarck, his investment in modelling his dress and moustache on that of Kaiser Wilhelm II, his likely thoughts while sitting in Heinrich Von Treitschke's seminars,[23] and the use his tragic heroes make of European culture.

Notable black American travellers, from the poet Phyllis Wheatley onwards, went to Europe and had their perceptions of America and racial domination shifted as a result of their experiences there. This had important consequences for their understanding of racial identities. The radical journalist and political organiser Ida B. Wells is typical, describing her productive times in England as like "being born again in a new condition."[24] Lucy Parsons is a more problematic figure in the political history of black America,[25] but how might her encounters with William Morris, Annie Besant, and Peter Kropotkin impact upon a rewriting of the history of English radicalism? What of Nella Larsen's relationship to Denmark, where George Padmore was held in jail during the early 1930s and which was also the home base of his banned paper the *Negro Worker*, circulated across the world by its supporters in the Colonial Seamen's Association?[26] What of Sarah Parker Remond's work as a medical practitioner in Italy and the life of Edmonia Lewis,[27] the sculptor, who made her home in Rome? What effects did living in Paris have upon Anna Cooper, Jessie Fauset, Gwendolyn Bennett,[28] and Lois Maillou Jones?

It would appear that there are large questions raised about the direction and character of black culture and art if we take the powerful effects of even temporary experiences of exile, relocation, and displacement into account. How, for example, was the course of the black vernacular art of jazz changed by what happened to Quincy Jones in Sweden and Donald Byrd in Paris? This is especially interesting because both men played powerful roles in the remaking of jazz as a popular form in the early 1970s. Byrd describes his sense of Europe's appeal as something that grew out of the view of Canada he developed as a young man growing up in Detroit:

> That's why Europe was so important to me. Living across the river from Canada as a kid, I used to go down and sit and look at Windsor, Ontario. Windsor represented Europe to me. That was the rest of the world that was foreign to me. So I always had a feeling for the foreign, the European thing, because Canada was right there. We used to go to Canada. For black people, you see, Canada was a place that treated you better than America, the North. For my father Detroit was better than the South, to me born in the North, Canada was better. At least that was what I thought. Later on I found out otherwise, but anyway, Canada represented for me something foreign, exotic, that was not the United States.[29]

Richard Wright's life in exile, which has been written off as a betrayal of his authenticity and as a process of seduction by philosophical traditions supposedly outside his narrow ethnic compass,[30] will be explored below as an exemplary instance of how the politics of location and the politics of identity get inscribed in analyses of black culture. Many of the figures listed here will be dealt with in later chapters. They are all potential candidates for inclusion in the latest African-American cultural canon, a canon that is conditional on and possibly required by the academic packaging of black cultural studies.[31] Chapter 4 will discuss what version of the politics and philosophy of W. E. B. Du Bois will be constructed for that canon from the rich transnational textures of his long and nomadic life. Du Bois's travel experiences raise in the sharpest possible form a question common to the lives of almost all these figures who begin as African-Americans or Caribbean people and are then changed into something else which evades those specific labels and with them all fixed notions of nationality and national identity. Whether their experience of exile is enforced or chosen, temporary or permanent, these intellectuals and activists, writers, speakers, poets, and artists repeatedly articulate a desire to escape the restrictive bonds of ethnicity, national identification, and sometimes even "race" itself. Some speak, like Wells and Wright, in terms of the rebirth that Europe offered them. Whether they dissolved their African-American sensibility into an explicitly pan-Africanist discourse or political commitment, their relationship to the land of their birth and their ethnic political constituency was absolutely transformed. The specificity of the modern political and cultural formation I want to call the black Atlantic can be defined, on one level, through this desire to transcend both the structures of the nation state and the constraints of ethnicity and national particularity. These desires are relevant to understanding political organising and cultural criticism. They have always sat uneasily alongside the strategic choices forced on black movements and individuals embedded in national political cultures and nation states in America, the Caribbean, and Europe. [. . .]

NOTES

1. Werner Sollors, *Beyond Ethnicity* (New York and Oxford: Oxford University Press, 1986).

2. "A unit of analysis for studying texts according to the ratio and nature of the temporal and spatial categories represented . . . The chronotope is an optic for reading texts as x-rays of the forces at work in the culture system from which they spring." M. M. Bakhtin, *The Dialogic Imagination*, ed. and trans. Michael Holquist (Austin: University of Texas Press, 1981), p. 426.

3. Mary Louise Pratt, *Imperial Eyes* (London and New York: Routledge, 1992).

4. *The Horrors of Slavery and Other Writings by Robert Wedderburn*, ed. Iain McCalman (Edinburgh: Edinburgh University Press, 1992).

5. Iain McCalman, "Anti-slavery and Ultra Radicalism in Early Nineteenth-Century England: The Case of Robert Wedderburn," *Slavery and Abolition* 7 (1986).

6. Fryer, *Staying Power*, p. 216. Public Records Office, London: PRO Ho 44/5/202, PRO Ho 42/199.

7. Their article "The Many Headed Hydra," *Journal of Historical Sociology* 3, no. 3 (September 1990): 225–253, gives a foretaste of these arguments.

8. John Adams quoted by Linebaugh in "Atlantic Mountains," p. 112.

9. Alfred N. Hunt, *Haiti's Influence on Antebellum America* (Baton Rouge and London: Louisiana State University Press, 1988), p. 119.

10. Douglass's own account of this is best set out in Frederick Douglass, *Life and Times of Frederick Douglass* (New York: Macmillan, 1962), p. 199. See also Philip M. Hamer, "Great Britain, the United States and the Negro Seamen's Acts" and "British Consuls and the Negro Seamen's Acts, 1850–1860," *Journal of Southern History* 1 (1935): 3–28, 138–168. Introduced after Denmark Vesey's rebellion, these interesting pieces of legislation required free black sailors to be jailed while their ships were in dock as a way of minimising the political contagion their presence in the ports was bound to transmit.

11. Linebaugh, "Atlantic Mountains," p. 119.

12. Paul Gilroy, "Art of Darkness, Black Art and the Problem of Belonging to England," *Third Text* 10 (1990). A very different interpretation of Turner's painting is given in Albert Boime's *The Art of Exclusion: Representing Blacks in the Nineteenth Century* (London: Thames and Hudson, 1990).

13. Patrick Wright, *On Living in an Old Country* (London: Verso, 1985).

14. Bernard Semmel, *Jamaican Blood and the Victorian Conscience* (Westport, Conn.: Greenwood Press, 1976). See also Gillian Workman, "Thomas Carlyle and the Governor Eyre Controversy," *Victorian Studies* 18, no. 1 (1974): 77–102.

15. Vol. 1, sec. 5, ch. 3, sec. 39. W. E. B. Du Bois reprinted this commentary while he was editor of *The Crisis*; see vol. 15 (1918): 239.

16. Eric Hobsbawm, "The Historians' Group of the Communist Party," in M. Cornforth, ed., *Essays in Honour of A. L. Morton* (Atlantic Highlands, N.J.: Humanities Press, 1979).

17. Linebaugh, "Atlantic Mountains." This is also the strategy pursued by Marcus Rediker in his brilliant book *Between the Devil and the Deep Blue Sea* (Cambridge: Cambridge University Press, 1987).

18. "A space exists when one takes into consideration vectors of direction, velocities, and time variables. Thus space is composed of intersections of mobile elements. It is in a sense articulated by the ensemble of movements deployed within it." Michel de Certeau, *The Practice of Everyday Life* (Berkeley and London: University of California Press, 1984), p. 117.

19. See Michael Cohn and Michael K. Platzer, *Black Men of the Sea* (New York: Dodd, Mead, 1978). I have been heavily reliant on George Francis Dow's anthology *Slave Ships and Slaving*, publication no. 15 of the Marine Research Society (1927; rpt. Cambridge, Md.: Cornell Maritime Press, 1968), which includes extracts from valuable eighteenth- and nineteenth-century material. On England, I have found the anonymously published study *Liverpool and Slavery* (Liverpool: A. Bowker and Sons, 1884) to be very valuable. Memoirs produced by black sea captains also point to a number of new intercultural and transcultural research problems. Captain Harry Dean's *The Pedro Gorino: The Adventures of a Negro Sea Captain*

in Africa and on the Seven Seas in His attempts to Found an Ethiopian Empire (Boston and New York: Houghton Mifflin, 1929) contains interesting material on the practical politics of Pan-Africanism that go unrecorded elsewhere. Captain Hugh Mulzac's autobiography, *A Star to Steer By* (New York: International Publishers, 1963), includes valuable observations on the role of ships in the Garvey movement. Some pointers towards what a black Atlantic rereading of the history of Rastafari might involve are to be found in Robert A. Hill's important essay which accentuates complex post-slavery relations between Jamaica and Africa: "Dread History: Leonard P. Howell and Millenarian Visions in Early Rastafari Religions in Jamaica," *Epoché: Journal of the History of Religions at UCLA* 9 (1981): 30–71.

20. Stephen Greenblatt, *Marvellous Possessions* (Oxford: Oxford University Press, 1992). See also Pratt, *Imperial Eyes*.

21. James T. Clifford, "Travelling Cultures," in *Cultural Studies*, ed. Lawrence Grossberg et al. (New York and London: Routledge, 1992), and "Notes on Theory and Travel," *Inscriptions* 5 (1989).

22. *Manchester Weekly Advertiser*, July 21, 1860; *Punch*, July 28, 1860; *The Morning Star*, July 18, 1860; and F. A. Rollin, *Life and Public Services of Martin R. Delany* (Lee and Shepard: Boston, 1868), p. 102.

23. Peter Winzen, "Treitschke's Influence on the Rise of Imperialist and Anti-British Nationalism in Germany," in P. Kennedy and A. Nicholls, eds., *Nationalist and Racialist Movements in Britain and Germany before 1914* (Basingstoke: Macmillan, 1981).

24. Ida B. Wells quoted in Vron Ware, *Beyond the Pale: White Women, Racism, and History* (London and New York: Verso, 1992), p. 177.

25. Carolyn Ashbaugh, *Lucy Parsons: American Revolutionary* (Chicago: Charles H. Kerr, 1976). I must thank Tommy Lott for this reference.

26. Frank Hooker, *Black Revolutionary: George Padmore's Path from Communism to Pan-Africanism* (London: Pall Mall Library of African Affairs, 1967).

27. William S. McFeely, *Frederick Douglass* (New York: W.W. Norton, 1991), p. 329.

28. Michel Fabre, *Black American Writers in France, 1840–1980* (Urbana and Chicago: University of Illinois Press, 1991).

29. Ursula Broschke Davis, *Paris without Regret* (Iowa City: University of Iowa Press, 1986), p. 102.

30. I challenge this view in Chapter 5.

31. Some of the problems associated with this strategy have been discussed by Cornel West in "Minority Discourse and the Pitfalls of Canon Formation," *Yale Journal of Criticism* 1, no. 1 (Fall 1987): 193–201.

SECTION 4

Questions of Identity

Introduction to Section IV

Abandoning the expectation that nation-states naturally and automatically organize social experience challenges conventional understandings of identity and culture. Religion, capitalism, and democracy are no longer embedded in particular territories or legal regimes, nor are they encumbered by external political, cultural, or moral principles. Cultural referents, once bounded by ethnicity, language, and nation-state borders are disconnected or lifted out of national territories, rendering discussions of national identity and culture off the mark.

This section explores how identity and belonging changes when social life transcends national boundaries. We begin with a selection from W.E.B. Dubois because his is a classic statement of the kind of in-between identity we are trying to capture, be it caused by race, ethnicity, or nationality. He writes of the experience of being several things and not completely anything at once and how that causes the individual to understand him- or herself through the eyes of the "other." The Negro, he says, is "gifted with second-sight in this American world." He can only see himself by looking through the eyes of someone else. He always feels his "two-ness" as an American, a Negro—two warring ideals in one dark body. He wants to escape from the burden of that curse and be both, completely, at the same time.

This duality is key to the transnational experience and the authors who follow unpack, in their own ways, what happens to identity when we abandon that assumption that is unitary, static, and territorially based. Ulrich Beck challenges what he calls "the container theory of society." In this second stage of modernity, globalization changes not only the relations between and beyond national states and societies but also the inner quality of the social and political itself. We can no longer equate state with society. Distinctions between such things as developed and underdeveloped, tradition and modernity collapse. The critical question, he says, is how does people's cultural, political, and biological self-awareness change when they locate themselves in a world society rather than a nation-state? How should we re-image post-national political communities?

Such a condition makes identity particularly problematic. In a world of clearly bounded nation-states, a patriotic identity is the only true and legitimate option. But in this current post-national stage, people constantly reformulate, adapt, and abandon categorizations. Individuality is a result of overlaps and conflicts with other identities. Each individual is a creative achievement. In this way, the national project is replaced by a cosmopolitan project. Its participants constantly create and recreate combinations of overlapping, transnational identities and ways of life. The relationship between state, business, and society is redefined because mobility, migration, and transnational job-sharing reorder the post-national distribution of labor and wealth.

Kachig Tölölyan's piece, which introduced the journal *Diaspora*, offers one response to what belonging to a de-territorialized nation means. To people in Ireland, he begins, Irish emigrants in America will always belong to the Irish nation. Despite living in exile, individuals or communities continue to maintain faith with a national culture and community. They create and sustain real and imagined communities both in a land they call their own and in exile. They create diasporas, a term once used to describe Jewish, Greek, or Armenian dispersion, but that now captures, Tölölyan suggests, a larger semantic domain including the experiences of immigrants, expatriates, refugees, guest workers, and exile, overseas and ethnic communities. Diasporas can be ideological, financial, and political. They are the "emblems of transnationalism" because they "embody the question of borders, which is at the heart of any adequate definition of the Others and the nation-state."

Ulf Hannerz's focus is on how transnationality transforms culture. He prefers the term "transnational" to globalization, though both refer to processes and dynamics spanning territories. Most work on globalization, he says, automatically equates it with homogenization and greater openness. It depicts the global and the local as two discrete arenas of social experience, instead of recognizing and specifying the interaction between the two. In fact, what is happening is that culture is being globally reorganized across time and space and, in that process, new culture is invented that accentuates and flattens difference at the same time. The notion of "local cultures" no longer holds because while cultures are still tied to a particular place, imbuing them with some autonomy and integrity, the people in those places have experiences and relationships linking them to other countries and continents. Locales are permeated by things and ideas from far away. Moreover, the local is shaped by actors and processes at other levels of social experience including corporate and institutional actors, the state, and the marketplace. So while living in a transnational social field can expand people's "habits of meaning" by exposing them to distant places and people, they can also contract when people focus on what is near and familiar. The more modest and appropriate label "transnational" captures the variations in scale and scope and the activism of more than just nation-states.

Finally, Grewel and Kaplan ask how people who claim transnational identities act upon them. Their seminal article explores the creation of a strong, global feminist movement that takes into account and uses transnational factors to its advantage. Much of feminist theory, they say, misses the boat because it doesn't locate women's experiences within the context of transnational linkages and asymmetries. To do feminist work across cultural divides, we must understand the production and reception of different types of feminisms within a framework of transnational social, cultural, and economic movements. While transnational culture exists, it is not what we generally think. It is not just about a unified core or periphery but about all the connections that link them. The directions and circulations of cultural commodities—populations, influence, capital, technology, knowledge—are (at least) two-way, and successful movement activism has to be rooted in an understanding of these relationships. Without an analysis of transnational scattered hegemonies, or the fact that there are multiple core and peripheries, such as patriarchies, "authentic traditions," and religious fundamentalisms, each with their own power dynamics, feminist movements will remain isolated and just reproduce the "universalizing gestures of the dominant western cultures."

CHAPTER 17

Of Our Spiritual Strivings

W. E. B. Du Bois

Between me and the other world there is ever an unasked question: unasked by some through feelings of delicacy; by others through the difficulty of rightly framing it. All, nevertheless, flutter round it. They approach me in a half-hesitant sort of way, eye me curiously or compassionately, and then, instead of saying directly, How does it feel to be a problem? they say, I know an excellent colored man in my town; or, I fought at Mechanicsville[1]; or, Do not these Southern outrages make your blood boil? At these I smile, or am interested, or reduce the boiling to a simmer, as the occasion may require. To the real question, How does it feel to be a problem? I answer seldom a word.

And yet, being a problem is a strange experience,—peculiar even for one who has never been anything else, save perhaps in babyhood and in Europe. It is in the early days of rollicking boyhood that the revelation first bursts upon one, all in a day, as it were. I remember well when the shadow swept across me. I was a little thing, away up in the hills of New England, where the dark Housatonic[2] winds between Hoosac and Taghkanic to the sea. In a wee wooden schoolhouse, something put it into the boys' and girls' heads to buy gorgeous visiting-cards—ten cents a package—and exchange. The exchange was merry, till one girl, a tall newcomer, refused my card,—refused it peremptorily, with a glance. Then it dawned upon me with a certain suddenness that I was different from the others; or like, mayhap, in heart and life and longing, but shut out from their world by a vast veil. I had thereafter no desire to tear down that veil, to creep through; I held all beyond it in common con-tempt, and lived above it in a region of blue sky and great wandering shadows. That sky was bluest when I could beat my mates at examination-time, or beat them at a foot-race, or even beat their stringy heads. Alas, with the years all this fine contempt began to fade; for the worlds I longed for, and all their dazzling opportunities, were theirs, not mine. But they should not keep these prizes, I said; some, all, I would wrest from them. Just how I would do it I could never decide: by reading law, by healing the sick, by telling the wonderful tales that swam in my head,—some way. With other black boys the strife was not so fiercely sunny: their youth shrunk into tasteless sycophancy, or into silent hatred of the pale world about them and mocking distrust of everything white; or wasted itself in a bitter cry, Why did God make me an outcast and a stranger in mine own house? The shades of the prison-house closed round about us all: walls strait and stubborn to the whitest, but relentlessly narrow, tall, and unscalable to sons of night who must plod darkly on in resignation, or beat unavailing palms against the stone, or steadily, half hopelessly, watch the streak of blue above.

After the Egyptian and Indian, the Greek and Roman, the Teuton and Mongolian, the Negro is a sort of seventh son, born with a veil, and gifted with second-sight in this American world,—a world which yields him no true self-consciousness, but only lets him see himself through the revelation of the other world. It is a peculiar sensation, this double-consciousness, this sense of always looking at one's self through the eyes of others, of measuring one's soul by the tape of a world that looks on in amused contempt and pity. One ever feels his two-ness,—an American, a Negro; two souls, two thoughts, two unreconciled strivings; two warring ideals in one dark body, whose dogged strength alone keeps it from being torn asunder.

The history of the American Negro is the history of this strife—this longing to attain self-conscious manhood, to merge his double self into a better and truer self. In this merging he wishes neither of the older selves to be lost. He would not Africanize America, for America has too much to teach the world and Africa. He would not bleach his Negro soul in a flood of white Americanism, for he knows that Negro blood has a message for the world. He simply wishes to make it possible for a man to be both a Negro and an American, without being cursed and spit upon by his fellows, without having the doors of Opportunity closed roughly in his face.

This, then, is the end of his striving: to be a co-worker in the kingdom of culture, to escape both death and isolation, to husband and use his best powers and his latent genius. These powers of body and mind have in the past been strangely wasted, dispersed, or forgotten. The shadow of a mighty Negro past flits through the tale of Ethiopia the Shadowy and of Egypt the Sphinx. Throughout history, the powers of single black men flash here and there like falling stars, and die sometimes before the world has rightly gauged their brightness. Here in America, in the few days since Emancipation, the black man's turning hither and thither in hesitant and doubtful striving has often made his very strength to lose effectiveness, to seem like absence of power, like weakness. And yet it is not weakness,—it is the contradiction of double aims. The double-aimed struggle of the black artisan—on the one hand to escape white contempt for a nation of mere hewers of wood and drawers of water, and on the other hand to plough and nail and dig for a poverty-stricken horde—could only result in making him a poor craftsman, for he had but half a heart in either cause. By the poverty and ignorance of his people, the Negro minister or doctor was tempted toward quackery and demagogy; and by the criticism of the other world, toward ideals that made him ashamed of his lowly tasks. The would-be black *savant* was confronted by the paradox that the knowledge his people needed was a twice-told tale to his white neighbors, while the knowledge which would teach the white world was Greek to his own flesh and blood. The innate love of harmony and beauty that set the ruder souls of his people a-dancing and a-singing raised but confusion and doubt in the soul of the black artist; for the beauty revealed to him was the soul-beauty of a race which his larger audience despised, and he could not articulate the message of another people. This waste of double aims, this seeking to satisfy two unreconciled ideals, has wrought sad havoc with the courage and faith and deeds of ten thousand thousand people,—has sent them often wooing false gods and invoking false means of salvation, and at times has even seemed about to make them ashamed of themselves.

Away back in the days of bondage they thought to see in one divine event the end of all doubt and disappointment; few men ever worshipped Freedom with half such unquestioning faith as did the American Negro for two centuries. To him, so far as he thought and dreamed, slavery was indeed the sum of all villainies, the cause of all sorrow, the root of all prejudice; Emancipation was the key to a promised land of sweeter beauty than ever stretched before the eyes of wearied Israelites. In song and exhortation swelled one refrain—Liberty; in his tears and curses the God he implored had Freedom in his right hand. At last it came,—suddenly, fearfully, like a dream. With one wild carnival of blood and passion came the message in his own plaintive cadences:—

> "Shout, O children!
> Shout, you're free!
> For God has bought your liberty!"[3]

Years have passed away since then,—ten, twenty, forty; forty years of national life, forty years of renewal and development, and yet the swarthy spectre sits in its accustomed seat at the Nation's feast. In vain do we cry to this our vastest social problem:—

"Take any shape but that, and my firm nerves
Shall never tremble!"[4]

The Nation has not yet found peace from its sins; the freedman has not yet found in freedom his promised land. Whatever of good may have come in these years of change, the shadow of a deep disappointment rests upon the Negro people,—a disappointment all the more bitter because the unattained ideal was unbounded save by the simple ignorance of a lowly people.

The first decade was merely a prolongation of the vain search for freedom, the boon that seemed ever barely to elude their grasp,—like a tantalizing will-o'-the-wisp, maddening and misleading the headless host. The holocaust of war, the terrors of the Ku-Klux Klan, the lies of carpet-baggers, the disorganization of industry, and the contradictory advice of friends and foes, left the bewildered serf with no new watch-word beyond the old cry for freedom. As the time flew, however, he began to grasp a new idea. The ideal of liberty demanded for its attainment powerful means, and these the Fifteenth Amendment[5] gave him. The ballot, which before he had looked upon as a visible sign of freedom, he now regarded as the chief means of gaining and perfecting the liberty with which war had partially endowed him. And why not? Had not votes made war and emancipated millions? Had not votes enfranchised the freedmen? Was anything impossible to a power that had done all this? A million black men started with renewed zeal to vote themselves into the kingdom. So the decade flew away, the revolution of 1876 came, and left the half-free serf weary, wondering, but still inspired. Slowly but steadily, in the following years, a new vision began gradually to replace the dream of political power,—a powerful movement, the rise of another ideal to guide the unguided, another pillar of fire by night after a clouded day. It was the ideal of "book-learning"; the curiosity, born of compulsory ignorance, to know and test the power of the cabalistic letters of the white man, the longing to know. Here at last seemed to have been discovered the mountain path to Canaan; longer than the highway of Emancipation and law, steep and rugged, but straight, leading to heights high enough to overlook life.

Up the new path the advance guard toiled, slowly, heavily, doggedly; only those who have watched and guided the faltering feet, the misty minds, the dull understandings, of the dark pupils of these schools know how faithfully, how piteously, this people strove to learn. It was weary work. The cold statistician wrote down the inches of progress here and there, noted also where here and there a foot had slipped or some one had fallen. To the tired climbers, the horizon was ever dark, the mists were often cold, the Canaan was always dim and far away. If, however, the vistas disclosed as yet no goal, no resting-place, little but flattery and criticism, the journey at least gave leisure for reflection and self-examination; it changed the child of Emancipation to the youth with dawning self-consciousness, self-realization, self-respect. In those sombre forests of his striving his own soul rose before him, and he saw himself,—darkly as through a veil; and yet he saw in himself some faint revelation of his power, of his mission. He began to have a dim feeling that, to attain his place in the world, he must be himself, and not another. For the first time he sought to analyze the burden he bore upon his back, that dead-weight of social degradation partially masked behind a half-named Negro problem. He felt his poverty; without a cent, without a home, without land, tools, or savings, he had entered into competition with rich, landed, skilled neighbors. To be a poor man is hard, but to be a poor race in a land of dollars is the very bottom of hardships. He felt the weight of his ignorance,—not simply of letters, but of life, of business, of the humanities; the accumulated sloth and shirking and awkwardness of decades and centuries shackled his hands and feet. Nor was his burden all poverty and ignorance. The red stain of bastardy, which two centuries of systematic legal defilement of Negro women had stamped upon his race, meant not only the loss of ancient African chastity, but also the hereditary weight of a mass of corruption from white adulterers, threatening almost the obliteration of the Negro home.

A people thus handicapped ought not to be asked to race with the world, but rather allowed to give all its time and thought to its own social problems. But alas! while sociologists gleefully count his bastards and his prostitutes, the very soul of the toiling, sweating black man is darkened by the shadow of a vast despair. Men call the shadow prejudice, and learnedly explain it as the natural defence of culture against barbarism, learning against ignorance, purity against crime, the "higher" against the "lower" races. To which the Negro cries Amen! and swears that to so much of this strange prejudice as is founded on just homage to civilization, culture, righteousness, and progress, he humbly bows and meekly does obeisance. But before that nameless prejudice that leaps beyond all this he stands helpless, dismayed, and well-nigh speechless; before that personal disrespect and mockery, the ridicule and systematic humiliation, the distortion of fact and wanton license of fancy, the cynical ignoring of the better and the boisterous welcoming of the worse, the all-pervading desire to inculcate disdain for everything black, from Toussaint[6] to the devil, —before this there rises a sickening despair that would disarm and discourage any nation save that black host to whom "discouragement" is an unwritten word.

But the facing of so vast a prejudice could not but bring the inevitable self-questioning, self-disparagement, and lowering of ideals which ever accompany repression and breed in an atmosphere of contempt and hate. Whisperings and portents came borne upon the four winds: Lo! we are diseased and dying, cried the dark hosts; we cannot write, our voting is vain; what need of education, since we must always cook and serve? And the Nation echoed and enforced this self-criticism, saying: Be content to be servants, and nothing more; what need of higher culture for half-men? Away with the black man's ballot, by force or fraud,—and behold the suicide of a race! Nevertheless, out of the evil came something of good,—the more careful adjustment of education to real life, the clearer perception of the Negroes' social responsibilities, and the sobering realization of the meaning of progress.

So dawned the time of *Sturm und Drang:* storm and stress today rocks our little boat on the mad waters of the world-sea; there is within and without the sound of conflict, the burning of body and rending of soul; inspiration strives with doubt, and faith with vain questionings. The bright ideals of the past,— physical freedom, political power, the training of brains and the training of hands,—all these in turn have waxed and waned, until even the last grows dim and overcast. Are they all wrong,—all false? No, not that, but each alone was oversimple and incomplete,— the dreams of a credulous race-childhood, or the fond imaginings of the other world which does not know and does not want to know our power. To be really true, all these ideals must be melted and welded into one. The training of the schools we need to-day more than ever,—the training of deft hands, quick eyes and ears, and above all the broader, deeper, higher culture of gifted minds and pure hearts. The power of the ballot we need in sheer self-defence,—else what shall save us from a second slavery? Freedom, too, the long-sought, we still seek,—the freedom of life and limb, the freedom to work and think, the freedom to love and aspire. Work, culture, liberty,—all these we need, not singly but together, not successively but together, each growing and aiding each, and all striving toward that vaster ideal that swims before the Negro people, the ideal of human brotherhood, gained through the unifying ideal of Race; the ideal of fostering and developing the traits and talents of the Negro, not in opposition to or contempt for other races, but rather in large conformity to the greater ideals of the American Republic, in order that some day on American soil two world-races may give each to each those characteristics both so sadly lack. We the darker ones come even now not altogether empty-handed: there are to-day no truer exponents of the pure human spirit of the Declaration of Independence than the American Negroes; there is no true American music but the wild sweet melodies of the Negro slave; the American fairy tales and folklore are Indian and African; and, all in all, we black men seem the sole oasis of simple faith and reverence in a dusty desert of dollars and smartness. Will America be poorer if she replace her brutal dyspeptic blundering with light-hearted but determined Negro humility? or her coarse and cruel wit with loving jovial good-humor? or her vulgar music with the soul of the Sorrow Songs?

Merely a concrete test of the underlying principles of the great republic is the Negro Problem, and the spiritual striving of the freedmen's sons is the travail of souls whose burden is almost beyond the measure of their strength, but who bear it in the name of an historic race, in the name of this the land of their fathers' fathers, and in the name of human opportunity.

And now what I have briefly sketched in large outline let me on coming pages tell again in many ways, with loving emphasis and deeper detail, that men may listen to the striving in the souls of black folk.

NOTES

1. Mechanicsville] The battle of Mechnicsville (in Virginia), which took place on June 26, 1862; otherwise known as the battle of Beaver Dam Creek and part of the Seven Days' Battles. Lee's Confederate troops routed McClellan's Union troops, but ultimately the Confederacy sustained more losses.

2. Housatonic] New England river, flowing from the Berkshires (Massachusetts) to Long Island Sound.

3. "Shout . . . your liberty"] One of the many freedom spirituals.

4. "Take any shape . . . tremble"] From *Macbeth*, III, iv, 102–3.

5. Fifteenth Amendment] Ratified March 30, 1870; granted black suffrage (in theory) and enabled Congress to enforce this amendment.

6. Toussaint] Toussaint L'Ouverture, leader of the black forces in Haiti after the uprising against the white French government in August 1791. Napoleon, viewing Toussaint as an obstacle to French power in the New World, devised a scheme to trick him into going willingly to France in 1800, but even so, the French were unable to subdue the island.

CHAPTER 18

"The Cosmopolitan Perspective: Sociology of the Second Age of Modernity" [1]

Ulrich Beck

[. . .]

I.

The cosmopolitan gaze opens wide and focuses—stimulated by the post-modern mix of boundaries between cultures and identities, accelerated by the dynamics of capital and consumption, empowered by capitalism undermining national borders, excited by the global audience of transnational social movements, and guided and encouraged by the evidence of world-wide communication (often just another word for misunderstanding) on central themes such as science, law, art, fashion, entertainment, and, not least, politics. World-wide public perception and debate of global ecological danger or global risks of a technological and economic nature ('Frankenstein food') have laid open the cosmopolitan significance of fear. And if we needed any proof that even genocide and the horrors of war now have a cosmopolitan aspect, this was provided by the Kosovo War in spring 1999 when Nato bombed Serbia in order to enforce the implementation of human rights. [2]

In the face of this widening cosmopolitan perspective, the social sciences and Social Theory find themselves embracing contrary views and starting points. The nation-state society is the dominant societal paradigm. The mainstream considers that the concept of society is applicable only to the nation-state. Accordingly, the sociological perspective or gaze (the sociology of inequality, of the family, of politics and so on) is geared to and organized in terms of the nation-state.

On the whole, sociology observes, measures and comments on its phenomena, for example, poverty and unemployment within a national context rather than in the context of world society. Within this frame, the theme of globalization means that there are an increasing number of social processes that are indifferent to national boundaries. This is based on an understanding of globalization that decodes it as 'time–space compression' (Harvey 1989; Giddens 1996; Featherstone 1990; Appadurai 1990; Lash and Urry 1994; Albrow 1996; Adam 1998). Accordingly, for empirical purposes globalization is operationalized as interconnectedness (Held et al. 1999; Zürn 1997) between state societies. All three criteria—indifference to national boundaries, space–time compression and an increasing network-like interconnectedness between national societies—are exemplified primarily by economic globalization. But there are many more examples. As more processes show less regard for state boundaries—people shop internationally, work internationally, love internationally, marry internationally, research internationally, grow up and are educated internationally (that is, multi-lingually), live and think transnationally, that is, combine multiple loyalties and identities in their lives—the paradigm of societies organized within the framework of the nation-state inevitably loses contact with reality. These changing circumstances have prompted a never-ending debate on the condition of the nation-state: Does it still exist or is it already gone? Is the scope of its activity perhaps even growing as its autonomy—state sovereignty—is shrinking? Perhaps it has long since been converted into a Super-Supra-Inter-Post-Neo-Trans-Nation state? Or have politics and the state become zombies—dead long ago but still haunting people's minds? The heat generated by this debate derives in some degree from the premise that it is *only* in the framework of the nation-state that essential achievements of Western modernity including democracy, the legitimation of state action, the welfare state and the state of law (*Rechtsstaat*) are possible, real and thriving.

By contrast, within the paradigm of world society, globalization is considered normal and the perspective of the nation-state gives rise to continual bafflement: Why are the social sciences still dominated by a secret Hegelianism which sees society as derived from the state's claim to embody the principle of order? How is it that the theorists of the nation-state invariably identify society with a piece of land, 'like animals identifying with their territory or like the gangs of youths in Central Park who get ready to repel the intruder as soon as someone comes too close and trespasses on their territory?' Why are societies seen as 'somehow rooted in the land, as if they needed the soil'? (Kieserling 1998: 65; on this territorial bias of the social sciences—the container theory of society—see Beck 2000: 23).

In this article I will develop and discuss the opposing theories, real conflicts and transition between the cosmopolitan perspective and that of the nation-state within the framework of an epochal distinction between the familiar image of the first age of modernity and the indistinctness and ambivalence of a second age of modernity. The choice of words is in fact programmatic. Firstly, by distinguishing between a first and a second age of modernity, I distance myself from the theoretical schemes of postmodernism. While the followers of postmodernism emphasize destructuring and end of modernity, my concern is with what is beginning, with new institutions and the development of new social science categories. Secondly, the distinction between a first and a second age of modernity also challenges theories which suggest that the unfolding of modernity at the end of this millennium should be seen as a linear process of differentiation based on

'evolutionary universals' (Talcott Parsons) or modern 'basic institutions' (Wolfgang Zapf). Thirdly, the distinction between a first and a second age of modernity is intended to clarify misunderstandings which have emerged in the debate on 'reflexive modernization' (Beck, Giddens and Lash 1994). Reference to a second age of modernity is intended to make it clear that there is a structural and epochal break—a paradigm shift—and not merely a gradual increase in the significance of knowledge and reflection as is mistakenly suggested by the term 'reflexive modernization'.

Theory and sociology of the second age of modernity elaborate, therefore, the basic assumption that towards the end of the twentieth century the *conditio humana* opens up anew—with fundamentally ambivalent contingencies, complexities, uncertainties and risks which, conceptually and empirically, still have to be uncovered and understood. A new kind of capitalism, a new kind of economy, a new kind of global order, a new kind of politics and law, a new kind of society and personal life are in the making which both separately and in context are clearly distinct from earlier phases of social evolution. Consequently a paradigm shift in both the social sciences and in politics is required.[3] This article, however, can only investigate one aspect of this shift, namely which social science categories make the cosmopolitan perspective possible? [...]

IV.

In the cosmopolitan paradigm of the second age of modernity, therefore, new power strategies and rifts are emerging between the champions of the new democratic world order, that is, the original countries of the West, and the 'Global Underdogs', countries which do not or cannot satisfy these requirements. But this is only one side of the development. On the other side, in the transition from the first, nation-state, age of modernity to the second, cosmopolitan, age of modernity, the Western claim to a monopoly on modernity is broken and the history and situation of diverging modernities in all parts of the world come into view. In the paradigm of the first modernity, world society is thought in terms of the nation-state and nation-state society. Accordingly, globalization is seen as additive and not substitutive, in other words: globalization appears as a process coming from outside, which assumes as a given territorial principle of the social and the political. This view of globalization as a matter of increasing links 'between nations', 'between states' and 'between societies', does not call into question the distinctions between first and second world, tradition and modernity, but confirms them.

Within the paradigm of the second modernity, however, globalization not only alters the interconnectedness of nation-states and national societies but the internal quality of the social. Whatever constitutes 'society' and 'politics' becomes in itself questionable, because the principles of territoriality, collectivity and frontier are becoming questioned. More precisely: the assumed congruence of state and society is broken down and suspended: economic and social ways of acting, working and living no longer take place within the container of the state. The categories framing world society—the distinction between highly developed and underdeveloped countries, between tradition and modernity—are collapsing. In the cosmopolitan paradigm of second modernity the non-Western societies share the same time and space horizon with the West. Moreover, their position as 'provinces' of world society is derived from the same challenges posed by second modernity which are variously perceived, assessed and processed in a variety of cultural contexts and locations.

The epochal break results from the fact that the guiding ideas and with them the interdependent institutionalized core answers of the first age of modernity are no longer self-evident and persuasive: in the dimension of globalization this is the idea of territoriality, on the level of work society it is the idea of full employment, in the dimension of individualization the idea of a given, communal collectivity and hierarchy, in the dimension of gender relations the idea of the 'natural' division of labour between men and women, in the dimension of ecological crisis the idea

of the exploitation of nature as the basis of unlimited growth. This entails a significant consequence: the guiding ideas, the foundations and, ultimately, also the claim to a monopoly on modernity by an originally western European modernism are shattered.

In the first age of modernity the non-Western societies were defined by their foreignness and otherness, their 'traditional', 'extra-modern' or 'premodern' character. In the second age of modernity everyone has to locate himself in the same global space and is confronted with similar challenges, and now strangeness is replaced by the amazement at the similarities. This implies a degree of self-criticism of the Western project of modernity which can defend neither its role as spearhead of progress nor its claim to a monopoly on modernity. The extra-European world is defined on the basis of its own history and no longer regarded as the opposite or absence of modernity (even today, however, many social scientists believe that it is only necessary to study pre-modern Western societies in order to make useful statements on the situation and problems of non-Western societies!). In the second age of modernity, various cultures and regions of the world are proceeding along various routes to various ideas of modernity, and they may not achieve them for various reasons. Hence, the transition to the second age of modernity raises the problem of a comparison of cultures within the different, world-regional ('national') frames of reference in a radical way. It also makes necessary, on the basis of the recognition of multiple modernities, dialogue between them (Jameson and Miyoshi 1998). [. . .]

V.

The crucial question of the second age of modernity is, therefore: What happens to territorially bounded politics in world society? How do collective binding decisions become possible under post-national conditions? Will politics wither away? Or will it undergo a transformation? And if so, what will it be like? Will the transformation be evolutionary or will it be seen as a political process in itself? That is to say, it does not happen but is rather a function of the opening out of the cosmopolitan perspective. And if this transformation of the political can only be understood politically, will it, if at all, emerge from the world-wide conflict over the cosmopolitanization of nation-state societies? This is in fact the direction that is to be presented and sketched out—hypothetically—in this article. The cosmopolitan project contradicts and replaces the nation-state project.[4] An essential difference between the discourse of world society and of cosmopolitan society is first of all the fact that in the latter globality becomes reflexive and political, which is to say it is present in or even governs thinking and political action. In other words, the term world society is at once too big but also too unpolitical and undefined because it does not answer the key question: how do people's cultural, political and biographical self awareness change or how does it have to change if they no longer move and locate themselves in a space of exclusive nation-states but in the space of world society instead? So the question is: How to re-image post-national political communities? [. . .]

In the paradigm of the second age of modernity, however, the questions become acute and are addressed (Beck 2000: 26–113): what transformations do society and politics undergo in the course of the transition from national to cosmopolitan society and politics? Which political categories and theories, which actors, which political institutions and ideas, which concept of the state and of democracy corresponds to the epoch of world society? Who inhabits the transnational space—not only capital and knowledge elites but also Blacks, immigrants, the excluded? Is there only a class of cosmopolitans or a cosmopolitanization of classes? How do global problems and opportunities for the development of transnational associations effect individual consciousness and how can these associations become part of individuals' understanding of themselves? And which indicators and processes of the cosmopolitanization of national societies can be identified, analysed, commented on by the social sciences?

Old fashioned modernists believe (positively or negatively) that only an all-embracing national project, held together by language, military service and patriotism (with or without a constitution) makes possible the integration of modern society and guarantees it. Cosmopolitanization by contrast means that ethnic identities within a nation become plural and relate in a plural and loyal way to different nation-states. As, for example, Nathan Sznaider (1999) argues: Being an Israeli, for example, can mean that one reads Russian papers, watches Russian television, goes to a Russian theatre and listens to Russian rock music. But being an Israeli means equally that one takes one's Jewish-oriental identity seriously and, paradoxically, thanks to the influence of Western multiculturalism rejects everything Western. And, last but not least, being an Israeli also means that non-Jewish Israelis, Palestinians with an Israeli passport, claim multicultural autonomy for themselves.

For the inhabitants of the first, nation-state, age of modernity, who recognize patriotic identity as the only true and legitimate one, this 'ethnic' conflict is no more than a primitive tribal war which will be resolved by modernization in an all-embracing state. The inhabitants of the second, post-national, age of modernity, however, are constantly reformulating and abandoning new categorizations. The resulting mixture is not a sign of the failure of integration, it is rather precisely the specific individuality determining identity and integration in this global society (Beck-Gernsheim 1999).

Thus individuality is a result of overlaps and conflicts with other identities. For each individual this is a creative achievement. The national public sphere becomes a space in which divisions can be overcome through conflict and in which certain kinds of indifference and social distance make a positive contribution to social integration. Conflict is the driving force of integration. World society comes into being because it is divided. Tensions within national public spheres are immediately buffered by indifference and relativized by transnational identities and networks. The cosmopolitan project both *entails* the national project *and* extends it. From the perspective of transnational identities and ways of life this means that it will be easier to try out and rearrange various combinations. One chooses and weights different overlapping identities and lives on the strength of the combination (Bauman 1996). The effect is of central importance: the enclosed space of the nation-state is no longer extant in the cosmopolitan project. The various groups remain in touch beyond the boundaries of the state, not only for the benefit of business and the development of scholarship but also in order to contain and control national divisions and conflicts by embedding them in intersecting transnational loyalties.

The question remains as to what extent collectively binding decisions are possible under these conditions. It is no longer a matter of solidarity or obligation but of a conflict-laden coexistence side by side in a transnationally neutralized space.

VI.

In the first, nation-state, age of modernity, solidarity is always limited to one's own nation, it has degenerated to solidarity among equals. In the second age of modernity, therefore, the question to be asked is not how to revive solidarity, but how *solidarity with strangers*, among non-equals can be made possible. I will first explore the relationship between mobility and migration in this context and then develop the concept of transnational risk communities.

In the societal project of cosmopolitan modernity the significance of *mobility* and *migration* also changes. In the nation-state paradigm of the first age of modernity there is a very clear cut distinction between mobility and migrations in the sense that they are associated with diametrically opposite values. Movement within nation-states is called mobility and is highly desirable. Movement between nation-states is called migration and is extremely undesirable. At the borders of nation-states the virtue of flexibility mutates into the vice of potentially criminal immigration. The paradigm of cosmopolitan society can now be explained on the basis of the post-national distribution of labour and wealth (Elkins 1995)

(1) *Global population movements*: increasing inequalities on a world scale and the differences between the sparsely populated wealthy states of the North and the densely populated poor states of the South will, as many argue, lead to new mass migrations from the overpopulated areas of the world to the sparsely populated regions with their tempting standard of living.

(2) *Migration of labour*: not the people but the workplaces move. Jobs (combined with corresponding training opportunities) are exported to those places where the poor and the unemployed live, that is, to the overpopulated regions of the world.

(3) *Transnational job-sharing between rich and poor countries*: new ways of sharing work and wealth across borders and continents develop—without migration. In the long term this means that the elimination of distance—made possible by modes of production based on information technology—facilitates a cosmopolitan distribution of work and wealth. Rich countries would then export low skill jobs to poor countries, while jobs requiring greater skills would be located in sparsely populated but highly skilled countries.

Within the paradigm of the nation-state, the first scenario is regarded as a nightmare scenario. The metaphor of the boat which is allegedly full, fans the flames of xenophobia. The second scenario has been a reality for at least twenty years, but it meets with considerable resistance on the part of the states and trade unions of the 'job exporting' countries. The third scenario of international job-sharing deserves to be discussed as an alternative to mass emigration and Western protectionism. David J. Elkins argues that in cosmopolitan society two contrary questions are posed: assuming that transnational audiences and communities do in fact develop on the basis of a division of labour which implies a distribution of life chances will this lead to a decrease in the pressure leading to emigration? Does the cosmopolitan project contain a model to ease world tensions because the need to seek one's happiness on another continent, is diminished? To put the question differently: if territoriality and nationality no longer define one's identity and life chances why should one emigrate?

But one can also ask precisely the opposite question. If staying in one place becomes less and less important for social relations and context, why should migrants remain migrants and not be welcomed as mobile? If a pattern of social relations establishes itself in which transnational identities and networks dominate, that is, in which people also live and work across borders, why should they be prevented from emigrating to those places where they want to go?

The crucial question therefore is to what extent forms of the division of labour and distribution of wealth are linked to the cosmopolitan project. The protectionist double standard, distinguishing between undesired migration and desired mobility, will become meaningless if such a link is established. The idea of mobility—not only in the spatial sense but also culturally and intellectually—which was originally linked to modernity, is detached from the constraints of geographical labour mobility and the mobility of wealth. Consequently in a cosmopolitan society it will be possible to rediscover and explore the specific cultural meaning of 'mobility'. At the same time, it may become possible to reduce and overcome the tyranny of the spatial mobility of traffic.

What becomes evident in this context is that the cosmopolitan project also involves a new division of labour between business and politics. Business becomes, whether wittingly and willingly or not, the location and arm of transnational politics. Big companies determine the conditions and situations of people in society—usually unnoticed, often narrowmindedly and thus exclusively pursuing their own economic interests. In future much will depend on whether they—under state guidance—perceive and accept the politically formative role in world society which has become theirs. Since the companies determine the distribution of labour and income through their investment decisions, they create the basis for inequality, justice, freedom and democracy on a world-wide scale. Why

not, for example, privatize both profits and the costs of unemployment and ecological destruction so that businesses are held responsible for the social consequences of their decisions and have to anticipate those consequences in their own economic interest?

VII.

In the second age of modernity the relationship between state, business and a society of citizens must be redefined. The state-fixated perspective of nationally defined society seems to have particular difficulty in recognizing and exploring the benefit of the scenario of a society of citizens for the transnational revival and encouragement of politics and democracy. One thing, however, is certain. Without stronger citizen elements, solidarity with foreigners and a corresponding extension and restructuring of national institutions (trade unions, consumer movements) is impossible. Trade unions for instance would no longer be tied to plants and industries in a national frame but must adapt to fragile, risky labour conditions and operate along global chains of value creation.

This raises a key question. On what basis do transnational 'community ties', which are no longer supported by place (neighbourhood), origin (family) or nation (state organized solidarity of citizens), have their material basis and sense of obligation? How can decisions be made which are at once postnational and collectively binding, or, in other words, how is political activity possible in the age of globalization?

Whoever poses the question, how modern societies, having dissolved all givens and transformed them into decisions, handle the uncertainties of their own making, encounters a core invention of modern times: the socialization of shared risks or shared risk definitions (Beck 1992, 1996, 1999). Risks presuppose decisions, definitions and permit individualization. They relate to individual cases here and now. At the same time, however, they set an organizational pattern of formulae of community formations and bonds, which is separate from individual cases, and allows the establishment of mathematical calculable probabilities and scenarios, on the one hand, and negotiable standards of shared rights and duties, costs and compensation, on the other. In world risk society, the risk regime also implies a hidden, community building aspect and force (Elkins 1995). If, for example, the states around the North Sea regard themselves as a risk community in the face of the continuing threat to water, humans, animals, tourism, business, capital, political confidence and so on, then this means that an established and accepted definition of threat creates a shared space for values, responsibilities and actions that transcends all national boundaries and divisions. By analogy with the national space, this can create active solidarity among strangers and foreigners. This is the case, if the *accepted* definition of a threat leads to binding arrangements and responses. The accepted definition of a risk thus creates and binds—across national boundaries—cultural value frameworks with forms of more or less compensatory, responsible counter activities. It is a transnational answer to the key question of active solidarity. From whom can I expect help if and when necessary and to whom will I have to give help in an emergency? Risk communities, therefore, combine what is apparently mutually exclusive:

- They are based on culturally divergent values and perceptions.
- They can be chosen.
- They can be regulated informally or by contract.
- They conform to or create definitions of community.
- In culturally divided, socially constructed definitions of risk, they establish socially binding cross-frontier neighbourliness.
- They are not comprehensive but affectual, linked to certain themes and priorities.
- They create a moral space of mutual commitments across frontiers.
- This space is defined by answers to the question: From whom can I expect help? To whom will I have to give help if this or that happens? What kind of help can I expect or do I have to give?

The realities which are perceived and assessed as risks are secondary realities of civilization and not fate. The defining element of risk communities is, therefore, not a common destiny which has to be accepted but their covert political character, the fact that they are based on decisions and questions which can be made and answered differently. Who is responsible? What has to be done and changed on a small and on a large scale, locally, nationally and globally in order to avert risks?

VIII.

With that we once again come to the key question of this article: what does cosmopolitanization and/or cosmopolitan society mean? A further step towards answering this question is to specify and investigate empirical indicators of *cosmopolitanization* (without any claim to comprehensiveness and systematic exposition).

Cultural commodities: developments in the import and export of cultural commodities, transnationalization of the book trade, developments in the import and export of periodicals, in the number and proportion of local and foreign productions in the cinema, in the proportion of local and foreign productions in television, corresponding radio broadcasts and so on.

Dual citizenship: legal basis and official practice in dealing with migrants, asylum seekers; how are 'foreigners' defined statistically, in the media and in everyday (administrative) practice?

Political intensities: to what extent are various ethnic groups represented and present in the centres of national power—parties, parliaments, governments, trade unions?

Languages: who speaks how many languages? (Recently, for example, a news item was widely reported in the [German] media, according to which in a small town in Bavaria—Landshut—more than 20 different languages are spoken by children in one secondary modern school class).

Mobility: permanent immigration, development of immigration, development of labour migration; temporary immigration, development of refugee numbers, development in the number of foreign students;

Routes of communication: development of items sent by letter post, nationally and internationally; development of telephone conversations, nationally and internationally, of the corresponding data exchange through the electronic network and so on;

International travel: development of international passenger air travel, development of international tourism, the number and proportion of journeys abroad;

Activity in transnational initiatives and organizations: short or long-term involvement in campaigns by Greenpeace, Amnesty International, NGOs, etc, participation in international collections of signatures, consumer boycotts and so on;

Criminal activity: development of international (organized) criminality, development of politically motivated acts and/or acts of violence by transnational terrorism;

Transnational ways of life: diaspora communities and their cross-border private and public networks and decision-making structures, number and kind of transnational marriages, births of transnational children, new emerging 'hybrid' cultures, literatures, languages;

Transnational news coverage: for example of wars on television; to what extent is a change in perspectives taking place?

National identities: what is the relationship of the number and kind of national identities to citizenship identity? Does cosmopolitanism cancel national identity? Or is there something like a 'cosmopolitan nation' and what does that mean?

Ecological crisis: development in the (stratospheric) ozone layer, development of world climate, development of world-wide fish resources, development of cross-border air and water pollution, development of attitudes to local, national and global world crises, environmental legislation, environmental jurisdiction, environmental markets, environmental jobs. [. . .]

NOTES

1. Translated by Martin Chalmers.
2. This war is post-national (and therefore can no longer be grasped by the concept developed by von Clausewitz in his book 'On War') because it is neither waged in a national interest—'the continuation of politics by other means'—nor can it be seen in the context of older rivalries between more or less hostile nation-states. What makes the war in Kosovo post-national is in fact the opposite of this, namely the global weakening of the sovereign order of the nation-state, the debilitation, even barbarization of the state guilty of the expulsion and genocide of its own citizens and, at the same time, the belief in the morality of human rights as a source of civility (on this, see below).
3. See Beck and Bonß (1999) where the question of the change of paradigm between first and second age of modernity in many areas of the social sciences is formulated at the initiation of a research centre (funded by the *Deutsche Forschungsgemeinschaft* for an extended period).
4. This implies the prediction that in the global age the dominant polarization between political programmes and parties will be in behalf of the challenges of cosmopolitan movements and counter-movements and not (as it was in the first age of modernity) in the relation to the economy—capital vs. labour.

BIBLIOGRAPHY

Adam, B. 1998 *Timescapes of Modernity*, London and New York: Routledge.

Albrow, M. 1996 *The Global Age*, Cambridge: Polity Press.

Appadurai, A. 1990 'Disjuncture and Difference in the Global Cultural Economy', in M. Featherstone (ed.) *Global Culture*, London: Sage.

Bauman, G. 1996 *Contesting Culture—Discourses of Identity in Multi-ethnic London*, Cambridge University Press.

Beck, U. 1992 *Risk Society*, London: Sage.

—— 1996 *Ecological Politics in an Age of Risk*, Cambridge: Polity Press.

—— 1999 *World Risk Society*, Cambridge: Polity Press.

—— 2000 *What is Globalization?*, Cambridge: Polity Press.

Beck, U. and Bonß, W. (eds) 1999 *Reflexive Modernisierung*, Frankfurt/M.: Suhrkamp/

Beck, U., Giddens, A. and Lash, S. 1994 *Reflexive Modernization*, Cambridge: Polity Press.

Beck-Gernsheim, E. 1999 *Schwarze gibt es in allen Hautfarben*, Frankfurt/M.: Suhrkamp.

Elkins, D.J. 1995 *Beyond Sovereignty: Territory and Political Economy in the Twenty-first Century*, University of Toronto Press.

Featherstone, M. 1990 (ed.) *Global Culture*, London: Sage.

Giddens, A. 1996 *Beyond Left and Right*, Cambridge: Polity Press.

Harvey, D. 1989 *The Conditions of Post-modernity*, Oxford: Blackwell.

Held, D., McGrew, A., Goldblatt, D. and Perraton, J. 1999 *Global Transformations*, Cambridge: Polity Press.

Jameson, F. and Miyoshi, M. (eds) 1998 *The Cultures of Globalization*, Durham and London: Duke University Press.

Kieserling, A. 1998 *Massenmedien*, unpublished manuscript, München.

Lash, S. and Urry, J. 1994 *Economics of Sign and Space*, London: Sage.

Sznaider, Natan 1999 'Über nationale Identitäten und ob man sie konsumieren kann', unpublished manuscript, Munich.

Zürn, M. 1998 *Regieren jenseits des National-staats*, Frankfurt/M.: Suhrkamp.

CHAPTER 19

"The Nation-State and Its Others: In Lieu of a Preface"

Khachig Tölölyan

"*What ish my nation?*" asks the Scots officer Macmorris, speaking a foreign tongue, of his Welsh colleague Fluellen, who also serves in Henry the Fifth's polyglot "English" army in Shakespeare's *Henry V* (III.ii.121). The question focuses the spectrum of issues this journal will address as it considers the Nation and its Others. We find the query useful, as Shakespeare did when he set out in 1599 to instruct his audience about its fiction of "England" in 1415. He wrote from within a barely secure new nation about a time when English kings still viewed Normandy, Anjou, Aquitaine, and the inhabitants thereof as their land and their people, though not yet their nation(-state).

Writing *Ulysses* between 1914 and 1921, James Joyce has a Dublin citizen of 1904 ask the ambiguously Jewish Leopold Bloom: "*What is your nation[?]*" Bloom answers by indirection, defining "a nation [as] the same people living in the same place" (Joyce 331; emphasis added). This fails to satisfy the questioner, a nationalist who bristles at the rule of the British Empire and envisions liberation through a coming struggle in which a "greater Ireland" that includes the Irish diaspora will participate: "We'll put force against force. . . . We have our greater Ireland beyond the sea. They were driven out of house and home in the black [18]47. . . . Ay, they drove out the peasants in hordes. Twenty thousand of them died in the coffinships. But those that came to the land of the free remember the land of bondage" (Joyce 329–30). To the citizen, Irish emigrants in America are part of the Irish nation, and so Bloom's answer has unacceptable implications. Throughout *Ulysses*, written as the Irish fought Britain

and each other to make the Irish Free State between 1916 and 1921, Joyce uses the story of Odysseus's homeward journey to question the meanings of "home" and "nation," and of keeping faith with a national culture while living elsewhere, in individual or communal exile. *Ulysses* examines the idea of longed-for but exigent home that the nation-state would become.[1]

The conviction underpinning this manifesto disguised as a "Preface" is that *Diaspora* must pursue, in texts literary and visual, canonical and vernacular, indeed in all cultural productions and throughout history, the traces of struggles over and contradictions within ideas and practices of collective identity, of homeland and nation. *Diaspora* is concerned with the ways in which nations, real yet imagined communities (Anderson), are fabulated, brought into being, made and unmade, in culture and politics, both on land people call their own and in exile. Above all, this journal will focus on such processes as they shape and are shaped by the infranational and transnational Others of the nation-state.

Shakespeare's and Joyce's queries about nationhood bracket the centuries in which European nations forged themselves and their state apparatuses, even as they acquired colonies and empires. These projects were intertwined; both employed military, technological, political, and commercial strategies that extracted an extraordinary human toll, violently expelling some conquered populations while confining others to fractions of their land: the reservation "nations" of Native Americans and the ethnonational republics of the Soviet Union are among some of the products of such actions. Elsewhere, the most monstrous and sustained efforts of the western empires uprooted, killed, or transported millions into slavery, creating the African diasporas. Combinations of economic coercion and incentive encouraged the formation of overseas communities such as those of the Japanese, Indians, and Chinese, which, like the African-descended collectivities, now increasingly represent themselves to themselves and to others as diasporas (Pan).[2]

Some of the entities this history has shaped remain purely infranational: they endure within a particular state and resist the cohesion imposed by it (e.g., the Navajo, the Inuit, the Québecois, the Georgians of the USSR). Others are both infra- and transnational, living disadvantaged lives within reduced territory while reaching out to kindred people elsewhere (e.g., Moldavians, Armenians, Crimean Tatars, Palestinians, Iroquois, Magyars in Romania). Today, the processes of uprooting and dispersion continue, but already by 1916, the Irish subjects of Britain and the subjugated Arabs of the Ottoman Empire had launched uprisings that heralded the possibility of remaking old collectivities into new nations, while challenging the claims of existing states. What has emerged in the past two decades, under the impact of new transnational, global forces, is the view that nation-states may not always be the most effective or legitimate units of collective organization.

Of course, multicultural colonial empires —Hellenic and Roman, Persian and Ottoman —have existed since antiquity, and some of the phenomena characteristic of our transnational moment are as old as history: individual exile like Ovid's, collective dispersion like that of the Jews by the waters of Babylon. This journal will address that history. But the past five centuries have been a time of fragmentation, heterogeneity, and unparalleled mass dispersion; additionally, the past, five decades have been a time of cultural and political regrouping, of renewed confidence for ethnonations existing across the boundaries of established nation-states. In fact, migrations have led to a proliferation of diasporas and to a redefinition of their import-

ance and roles. Crucially, these dispersions, while not altogether new in form, acquired a different meaning by the nineteenth century, in the context of the triumphant nation-state, which as a polity claims special political and emotional legitimacy, representing a homogeneous people, speaking one language, in a united territory, under the rule of one law, and, until recently, constituting one market.

In naming this publication *Diaspora: A Journal of Transnational Studies*, we give equal emphasis to both sides of the colon. We use "diaspora" provisionally to indicate our belief that the term that once described Jewish, Greek, and Armenian dispersion now shares meanings with a larger semantic domain that includes words like immigrant, expatriate, refugee, guestworker, exile community, overseas community, ethnic community. This is the vocabulary of transnationalism, and any of its terms can usefully be considered under more than one of its rubrics. For example, Cubans outside Cuba are in certain ways a diaspora that stretches from Madrid to Miami and beyond, the result of both coerced and voluntary departure. The US media refer to them as an exile community, particularly when underscoring the ambitions of some leaders to overthrow Castro. And "Cuban" is of course an ethnic designation. Thus, Cubans are a transnational collectivity, broken apart by, and woven together across, the borders of their own and other nation-states, maintaining cultural and political institutions; the study of their specificity, their interpenetration and articulation with others is part of our enterprise.

To affirm that diasporas are the exemplary communities of the transnational moment is not to write the premature obituary of the nation-state, which remains a privileged form of polity. Conflicts like the Gulf War revive and reaffirm the nation-state's legitimacy even as new forms of economic and political interaction, communication, and migration combine to erode its sharply defined borders, increasingly turning even the mightiest and most ocean-buffered polities, like the United States, into "penetrated" (Brown)[3] and "plural" societies (Smith). Yet, as these incursions multiply and many nation-states confront the extent to which their boundaries are porous and their ostensible homogeneity a multi-cultural heterogeneity, other collectivities strive for nationhood through struggles conducted in both homeland and diaspora (e.g., Eritreans, Kurds, Palestinians, Sikhs, Tibetans, Armenians).

In such a context, transnational communities are sometimes the paradigmatic Other of the nation-state and at other times its ally, lobby, or even, as in the case of Israel, its precursor (Sheffer). Diasporas are sometimes the source of ideological, financial, and political support for national movements that aim at a renewal of the homeland (Sun Yat Sen, Yasser Arafat). In the cases of the now only nominally "Soviet" republics of Armenia and Lithuania, diasporan organizations operate across the boundaries of the multiethnic empire and bring to their kindred ethnonations new ideas, new money, even new languages. Elsewhere, it becomes impossible to comprehend the new shape of certain polities —Los Angeles, the European Community— without taking into account the effects of massive movements of Hispanic, North African, or Turkish migrations of "guest-workers"; similar claims apply to states as diverse as South Africa and Germany, Nigeria and Sweden. In these and other places, transnational forces are intervening in ways whose consequences are not yet clear.

Diaspora is concerned as well with all of the other forces and phenomena that constitute the transnational moment. These include massive and instantaneous movements of capital; the introduction of previously "alien" cultures through the practice of "media imperialism"; issues of the double allegiance of populations and the plural affiliations of transnational corporations. All these developments point to the need to interrogate the national context in which certain assumptions about collective identity once prevailed; they also raise questions about the global context.

Of the making and unmaking of nations and exile communities there is no end in sight. The recent Iraqi invasion of Kuwait was born of a tangle of motives, some less problematic than others, many comprehensible only from the transnational perspective. One was the impulse to enlarge the Iraqi "nation" of Kurds and Arabs; another was to make a united Iraq and Kuwait that would serve as a prototype of the Arab nation. The invader wanted to destroy the emerging territorial state of Kuwait, which was not quite a nation in August of 1990, though doubtless it will become one in the war's aftermath. The flood of refugees the invasion triggered (Indians and Pakistanis, Egyptians and Palestinians, Sri Lankans and Filipinos) reminds us that 60% of the population of Kuwait was not Kuwaiti, that in fact "before [Kuwait was] a nation, [it was] a business" (Kramer). In fact, many nations began as businesses, a fact concealed by mythologies of national origin but disclosed by the movements and histories of diasporas. It is not accidental that USA, like IBM, is an acronym for an establishment (as in Est. 1766) that was founded fairly abruptly, not in the intimate coevolution of a people and nation over centuries, like France and the French, say. The United States began, in part, as a set of commercial enterprises, as did British Canada: tracts for real-estate development and fur-trapping, units of the transatlantic economy. International commerce initiated the development of many nations; in some ways, it is now supplanting them, which is why "sovereignty," like "nation," is one of the concepts this journal will interrogate.

Diasporas are emblems of transnationalism because they embody the question of borders, which is at the heart of any adequate definition of the Others of the nation-state. The latter always imagines and represents itself as a land, a territory, a place that functions as the site of homogeneity, equilibrium, integration; this is the domestic tranquility that hegemony-seeking national elites always desire and sometimes achieve. In such a territory, differences are assimilated, destroyed, or assigned to ghettoes, to enclaves demarcated by boundaries so sharp that they enable the nation to acknowledge the apparently singular and clearly fenced-off differences *within* itself, while simultaneously reaffirming the privileged homogeneity of the rest, as well as the difference *between* itself and what lies over its frontiers.

In the past, diasporan communities confined in this way have remained self-protectively silent about their own view of themselves; their self-representations and assignments of meaning to their collective existence have been carefully policed. Stated too loudly and clearly, these representations would inevitably blur difference, even while pointing to an endemic doubleness, or multiplicity, of identities and loyalties, taboo topics both within and outside the diaspora community. Such silence long seemed necessary to the maintenance of the nation-state, whose frontiers were ideally absolute limits, crossed only in heavily regulated economic, cultural, and demographic interactions. This vision of a homogeneous nation is now being replaced by a vision of the world as a "space" continually reshaped by forces—cultural, political, technological, demographic, and above all economic—whose varying intersections in real estate constitute every "place" as a heterogeneous and disequilibriated site of production, appropriation, and consumption, of negotiated identity and affect.

Admittedly, this is an abstract description. On the one hand, it points to what we celebrate as the reinvigorated diversity of a plural society woven out of diasporas and ethnicities. But even the nation-states most receptive to this pluralism—Canada, the United States, Australia, as well as the somewhat more reluctant members of the European Community —must increasingly acknowledge the way in which few of the old "general" interests continue successfully to claim nationwide legitimacy and consent, except in the guise of hypocritical fictions of hegemony. Meanwhile, new and forcefully asserted concerns and claims, like those of transnational communities, perhaps anachronistically continue to be regarded as "special" interests. This changed state of affairs affects nearly every area of cultural, political, and scholarly endeavor; it is welcomed by some and detested by others. At any rate, the chain of analogies that once joined the image of the safely enveloped individual body (the site of unique personal identity) to the homogeneous territorial community (the site of national identity) is no longer plausible. The image of the ideal world as a League of (sovereign and united) Nations is under pressure, beset by what is seen as the threat or promise of what Roger Rouse calls, in his article in this issue, "an alternative cartography of social space." Such a cartography does not wager on the end of nationalism; in fact, it assumes that, precisely because the proliferation of infranational and transnational alternatives to the nation-state has led to a realignment of collective emotional investments, nationalism and other forms of loyalty will compete for a long time. *Diaspora* is a forum for debates about those concrete and theoretical remappings of global "order" that take both the nation-state and its transnational Others into account.

NOTES

1. Conversations with James Fairhall and Enda Duffy helped me to formulate my thoughts about *Ulysses*.

2. Most overseas Chinese do not yet think of their communities as diasporan, but this is beginning to change, as Pan's title suggests. Until the late 1960s, most African-Americans did not use the term either. It was first applied by a handful of intellectuals to the group for which they sought to speak; the term has now gained currency, both in the community and among scholars writing about it. In at least two communities, the Jewish and the Armenian, in North America and elsewhere, the vocabulary of "diaspora" and "galut" (*spurk* and *gaghut* in Armenian) is traditional and widespread, as it is in certain Greek communities.

3. I am deviating slightly from Brown's use of the term. He writes solely of Middle Eastern states and societies as "a penetrated subsystem of international relations" (4).

WORKS CITED

Anderson, Benedict. *Imagined Communities: Reflections on the Origin and Spread of Nationalism*. London: Verso, 1983.

Brown, Leo Carl. *International Politics and the Middle East*. Princeton, Princeton UP, 1984.

Joyce, James. *Ulysses*. 1922. New York: Random, 1961.

Kramer, Michael. "Towards a New Kuwait." *Time* 24 Dec. 1990: 28.

Pan, Lynn. *Sons of the Yellow Emperor: A History of the Chinese Diaspora*. Boston: Little, 1990.

Sheffer, Gabriel, ed. *Modern Diasporas in International Politics*. New York: St Martin's, 1986.

Smith, M. G. *The Plural Society in the British West Indies*. Berkeley: U of California P, 1965.

CHAPTER 20

"Nigerian Kung Fu, Manhattan *fatwa*" and "The Local and the Global: Continuity and Change"

Ulf Hannerz

NIGERIAN KUNG FU, MANHATTAN *FATWA*

The chapters in this book have grown in a certain biographical terrain. This will become apparent off and on, but let me sketch a few landmarks immediately: a modest hotel in one continent, a street scene in another, and a small village in a third.

Rosy Guest Inn, when I stayed there during several periods in the 1970s and 1980s, was a simple one-storey building, with bright yellow walls and blue shutters (and iron bars rather than glass in the windows), under a corrugated zinc roof. In the inside courtyard toward which rooms opened, there was a central water tap. The kitchen staff would slaughter a chicken or two under it in the morning, while otherwise it was available to the guests. Probably never more than half a dozen at any one time, these included ginger traders, itinerant magicians, and soldiers on a weekend spending spree.

I was in Kafanchan, the central Nigerian town where Rosy Guest Inn was located, to do anthropological field research, and became the only long-term guest in the establishment when I was confronted with a housing shortage in the town after a unit of the Nigerian army had based itself there, and the officers had spread themselves over much of whatever accommodation was available.[1] By staying at Rosy Guest Inn, I avoided the distractions of establishing a household of my own. (After a tiring day, I could come into the dining room and ask for a pot of tea, and the young woman in charge would bend over the table and ask, for clarification, "coffee or Tetley's?" As I had the only typewriter in the house, I could also help out retyping the menu.) But staying there also helped me gain a sense of both the physical and the mental mobility of contemporary Nigerian urban life, of the horizons of townspeople who came there for meals and boisterous arguments, and of the standards by which visitors judged Kafanchan. A trader from a bigger city found no local taxis plying Kafanchan's alternately muddy or dusty streets, and asked me what I would propose for local transportation. In jest I suggested he might check if one of the truck-pushers resting under the big tree in Danhaya Street would be willing to push him around. He looked at me in horror before he broke into laughter.

The proprietor of Rosy Guest Inn, a migrant from the south, did not live in Kafanchan, but he visited every week, coming in on his puffing motorcycle from the bigger city some distance away. There was another Rosy Guest Inn there, and a third in the university town a little further north; he also ran two book and stationery shops, one of them in Kafanchan, where I would go for newspapers. He preferred to staff his businesses with his relatives, although in Kafanchan an exception was made in the kitchen, where he preferred to have a man from Calabar, on the southeast coast of Nigeria. Since early colonial times, Calabar cooks have had a reputation as the best professional cooks in Nigeria (although perhaps the one in Kafanchan did not do much to uphold it).

I still have the studio photograph which Rosy Guest Inn's proprietor had taken of him and me on the eve of one of my departures, as well as his elegant name-card, in a sort of wooden finish, with his several business addresses, and the home address which he shared with wife and twelve children. At Rosy Guest Inn in Kafanchan I also first encountered Ben, a young electrician who was working there at the time when electricity was being introduced, in a period of Nigerian petroleum-based affluence, in Kafanchan as well as many other small towns.

Ben (whose father had been the first in his village to more or less give up tilling the soil and become a petty trader) turned out to be a person of many talents and interests, and so when the work of electrification was in large part done, he started working with me instead, in the varied roles of a field anthropologist's assistant—guide, advisor, interpreter, go-between. He would enjoy conversing and dancing the Kung Fu in Kafanchan's beer bars, would complain about having to kneel on the coarse cement floor in one of the small breakaway churches we visited, would sometimes ask leading local businessmen rather more pointed questions than I had dared do myself, and would also have endless questions for me about other cities, other countries. I was not surprised when he asked me if he could have my newspapers after I had read them, although perhaps a little disappointed when it turned out he would take them straight to the market place to sell them to traders who used them to wrap dried fish.

Again, this was in the 1970s. One of Ben's older brothers who was an army officer had named his first-born son Gagarin, after the Soviet cosmonaut. When Ben had his first son, he wanted to go one better, and named him Lenin. Some time later, when I was there, Ben discovered that the students at a teachers' college on the outskirts of Kafanchan (where he also did occasional electrical work) lacked a convenient shopping facility for soap, snacks, matches and other small items. So he thought of establishing a small shop there, which as a proud father he would operate in his young son's name—"Lenin's Supermarket." More than a decade before the demise of state socialism in the Soviet Union, this now seems remarkably foresightful.

A decade or so later, another urban scene: it is a winter morning in New York, and I stand in line on a lower Broadway sidewalk, hoping like a great many others to get into a public meeting where a number of leading American writers are to appear, to show their support for Salman Rushdie. *The Satanic Verses* has just appeared, and Ayatollah Khomeini has issued his *fatwa*.

Far too many people were out there under the umbrellas, so most of us (myself included) did not get into the small hall. Instead we witnessed, or took part in, the goings-on outside. On one side of Broadway, then, were the people who had wanted to get into the meeting, members of a well-educated American middle class, shouting "Free Speech! Free Speech!" or even "Hey hey, ho ho, Hizbollah has got to go." (One woman passed by and commented that this was like in '68.) On the sidewalk across the street was a gathering of Muslim immigrants, with their own speech choirs, and their own posters. One of the latter argued that "Islam promotes dialogue." And so there they were, east and west, or north and south if one so prefers, on opposing sides of lower Broadway, shouting at each other.

The third place is a village in southern Sweden, where I spend most summers. My great-grandfather bought a small house there after he realized that none of his sons was about to take over the family farm, a few miles away. My grandfather became a sea captain, and two of his brothers emigrated to America. Their two unmarried sisters remained in the house after the elderly parents had died, reporting in letters to their city relatives about seasonal changes in the garden, the habits of hedgehogs, and the arrivals and departures of birds of passage.

Over the years, the village has changed. Most of the villagers used to be artisans and farm people. Now many of them (or rather their successors) commute to nearby towns. The house next door belonged for a while to a famous former bank-robber who had started a new life; not so entirely easy, as people would still tend to remember the time when he was internationally televised, holding a frightened group of bank employees to ransom. Since he left, a retired farming couple live in that house. The wife, speaking the local dialect with an almost undetectable accent, grew up between the world wars as the daughter of a prosperous landowner in East Prussia, and entered adulthood in a new country just as the old way of life had been destroyed forever.

A few houses further away, a star ice hockey player resided fairly briefly, brought there by a wealthy local entrepreneur (not a village resident, however) who wanted to advance the fortunes of a team in a nearby town. But the hockey player was soon bought by a major Canadian team, in the National Hockey League in North America, and has not been seen since. Villagers still speak of his hot temper. The old village grocery has been turned into an art gallery, and the woman who runs it also teaches courses in intercultural communication at an adult education center in the town. Apart from the lady from East Prussia, only a few people originating in other countries have yet made their way, somehow, to this village. (In the nearest town, a fair number of Vietnamese appear to lead quiet lives.) Yet as elections are coming up, they and their neighbors find in their mailboxes a leaflet from a right-wing group in the city some twenty miles to the south, proclaiming that Sweden has been turning, in a few decades, from a welfare state and a *folkhem*, "home of the people," into a "multicultural inferno."

A GLOBAL ECUMENE

Distances, and boundaries, are not what they used to be. The local magnate who brought the ice hockey celebrity to our village also took some special interest in long-distance travel—he erected a small monument in the forest at the place where he had once on a summer evening encountered a spaceship and its crew, from another planet. Unfortunately, as one crew member had become ill and they all had to return to where they came from, nobody else saw them.

Mostly, we are not yet into interplanetary connections. But this is a time when transnational connections are becoming increasingly varied and pervasive, with large or small implications for human life and culture. People move about across national boundary lines, for different reasons: in the Swedish

village, because for someone an earlier way of life elsewhere has been destroyed, in a part of Germany no longer German, or because for someone else the pay in Canada is better. The technologies of mobility have changed, and a growing range of media reach across borders to make claims on our senses. Our imagination has no difficulty with what happens to be far away. On the contrary, it can often feed on distances, and on the many ways in which the distant can suddenly be close.

Anthropologists, it has been said, are "merchants of astonishment," dealing in the wonders of strange cultures (Geertz 1984: 275). No doubt there is a great deal to that description, although one might worry that the market for this kind of merchandise will shrink when some of the more remarkable customs in the global cultural inventory fade away, and when in any case more people have seen too much to be easily astonishable. At present, it seems that some of the goods consist of the astonishment of displacement and juxtaposition: Kafanchan Kung Fu, Manhattan *fatwa*. Yet the sheer surprise value of such goods may soon enough also decline, as we accumulate more and more anecdotal evidence of this type.

At least for as long as I have been in it, anthropology has been in the process of being "rethought," "reinvented," "recaptured." Some say this is because it is in a crisis, although it could just be a sign of vitality, and ongoing adaptation to changing circumstances (as well as of generational struggles, and the pressures of the academic marketplace). Anyhow, the desire to cultivate new understandings of how the world hangs together, of transnational connections, in the organization of meanings and actions—and move beyond mere astonishment over new mixtures and combinations—is clearly one increasingly important strand in changing anthropology now, as an intellectual enterprise and as a craft.

When I turned to anthropology in the early 1960s, this was the subject in the university which would allow you (or, perhaps more precisely, force you) to engage with exotic continents like Africa, and where the assumption indeed was that if you stayed on your course long enough, you would end up in a distant village in another continent, trying to make sense of a slice of local life. The world, to anthropologists at least, seemed to be made up of a myriad of such more or less local, bounded entities; a sort of global mosaic.

Then anthropology went through a period of critical scrutiny, from inside and outside, as colonialism's child. The idea of having a separate discipline for a study of "other cultures," for the West looking at the rest, appeared increasingly dubious, on moral and intellectual grounds. (Consequently there is no particular emphasis on "the rest" in this book, apart from the fact that I may show some predilection for things African.) More researchers began doing "anthropology at home," a rather stretchable notion. Yet even then, the assumption of the mosaic of small-scale, territorially anchored social and cultural units mostly remained in place.

By the time I came to Kafanchan, I expected to do a local study, an experiment in urban anthropology, a study of an internally complex and heterogeneous town as a whole. Surely this was already a step away from the traditions of anthropology. The people of the town, migrants from all over Nigeria, belonged to ethnic groups about which some of the discipline's classic monographs were once written—Ibo, Hausa, Yoruba, Tiv, Nupe. And ethnicity, "tribalism," was certainly one of the everyday principles of social organization in the life of the town. Yet it was not wholly uncontroversial. In the ledger at Rosy Guest Inn, where guests were requested to register their names, occupations, and addresses, and also their tribes, one guest wrote in an irritated paragraph of protest against the tribal column. This, he said, had no place in a united Nigeria. The practice was retrograde and should be abolished immediately. I suspect that the proprietor had really only copied the design from the guest ledger at the more prestigious state-run hotel on the outskirts of Kafanchan.

The tiff between the management and the enlightened guest at Rosy Guest Inn is a reminder that Nigeria is one of the many places where the national is understood to be threatened mostly from below, by sectional loyalties which are more local. All the same, the idea of the national was there, in a country which had not existed, either as an independent or as a dependent but coherent entity, at the last turn of a century. It was a conception imported from the outside, making Nigeria itself in significant part an organizational artifact of the integrative processes in the world.

As I was doing my urban study, I became increasingly preoccupied with the nature of contemporary Nigerian culture on this rather wider scale. How do you understand, and portray, a culture shaped by an intense, continuous, comprehensive interplay between the indigenous and the imported? What tools do we need to grasp the character of what may even be thought of as a new civilization? Beyond such questions, moreover, there was a larger one: in what kind of global interconnectedness does Kafanchan, a town built around a colonial-era railway junction, with inhabitants like Ben and his son Lenin, now have a place?

What follows is a series of partial attempts to approach an answer to that question; even as we will often seem far away from Kafanchan, for much the same question can accompany us to lower Broadway in Manhattan, or to the south Swedish village, or to any number of other settings.

In these introductory notes, I want to make some general points, and also say something about the organization of the chapters. First, a few comments on vocabulary may be in order. After a fashion, this is obviously a book on "globalization"—a key word of the present, and as such, a contested term. One almost expects any mention of globalization now to be accompanied by either booing or cheering. To business consultants and journalists, this is apparently often a word with a pleasant ring—newsworthy, promising of opportunities. In the sense of "cultural imperialism," on the other hand, it is understood to be bad, and listening to stories of "the global" versus "the local," we are expected to know where our sympathies should lie.

It would seem to me that contemporary interconnectedness in the world is really too complicated and diverse to be either condemned or applauded as a whole. Different aspects of it may quite justifiably draw different responses—detached analysis sometimes, a sense of wonder over its intricacies at other times, not always a rush to moral judgment. This book is not intended as a paean to globalization, nor as its opposite.

I am also somewhat uncomfortable with the rather prodigious use of the term globalization to describe just about any process or relationship that somehow crosses state boundaries. In themselves, many such processes and relationships obviously do not at all extend across the world. The term "transnational" is in a way more humble, and often a more adequate label for phenomena which can be of quite variable scale and distribution, even when they do share the characteristic of not being contained within a state.[2] It also makes the point that many of the linkages in question are not "international," in the strict sense of involving nations— actually, states—as corporate actors. In the transnational arena, the actors may now be individuals, groups, movements, business enterprises, and in no small part it is this diversity of organization that we need to consider.[3] (At the same time, there is a certain irony in the tendency of the term "transnational" to draw attention to what it negates— that is, to the continued significance of the national.)

Some things may be more truly global in themselves, however, and in their crisscrossing aggregate, transnational connections contribute to overall interconnectedness. By what term can we capture this quality of the entity as a whole? While the notion of the world as a mosaic now looks questionable—too much boundedness and stability—other metaphors may come to mind. In the mid-1960s, Marshall McLuhan (e.g. 1964: 93), provocatively rewriting world cultural history (past, present, future) in terms of communication media properties, suggested that there was now a "global village." The term has stuck in public consciousness, much more than most of McLuhan's far-reaching claims. (The Queen of England, for example, recently used it in a Christmas address to the British people. One can hardly imagine it coming from the mouth of one of her royal predecessors, during that period when the sun never set in the Empire, and much of the world map was colored pink.) Yet the "global village" is in some ways a misleading notion. It suggests not only interconnectedness but, probably to many of us, a sense of greater togetherness, of immediacy and reciprocity in relationships, a very large-scale idyll. The world is not much like that.

I prefer another term, drawn from anthropology's past. (Sometimes it is perhaps not so much "reinventing" that is needed, but—to begin with, at least—some mere "remembering," or "retrieving," in so far as previous generations have left certain unfinished, yet worthwhile business behind.) Around the mid-twentieth century, a handful of leading anthropologists, such as Alfred Kroeber and Robert Redfield, were engaged in different ways in shaping a sort of macroanthropology, dealing especially with conceptions of civilization. At a yet more encompassing level, in his 1945 Huxley Memorial Lecture to the Royal Anthropological Institute in London, Kroeber discussed the "ecumene" (*oikoumene*) of the ancient Greeks. That ecumene, the entire inhabited world as the Greeks then understood it, stretched from Gibraltar toward India and a China rather uncertainly perceived. In our time, the corresponding unit is both larger, in the sense of encompassing more, and smaller, in the more metaphorical senses of connectedness and reachability. Yet as Kroeber (1945: 9) had it, the ecumene "remains a convenient designation for an interwoven set of happenings and products which are significant equally for the culture historian and the theoretical anthropologist," and thus the global ecumene is the term I—and some others with me—choose to allude to the interconnectedness of the world, by way of interactions, exchanges and related developments, affecting not least the organization of culture.[4] It is in the global ecumene, then, that Ben in Kafanchan does the Kung Fu, that a *fatwa* pronounced in Teheran becomes a matter of a street shouting-match in Manhattan, and that someone in a south Swedish village turns out to be a teacher of intercultural communication.

CULTURE, PEOPLE, PLACES

The chapters of this book were written in different contexts, as papers for one conference or other (and in some cases thereafter published, in scattered places), and each is therefore a relatively independent piece. Yet they draw on a single, although evolving, perspective toward cultural processes in the contemporary world, and no doubt show some continuing preoccupations.[5] Quite literally, I believe, they are essays aiming at contributing to a conversation, partly public and partly perhaps taking place within the circles of the anthropological community, about the wider cultural interconnectedness and the ways we try to grasp it.[6] What are the recurrent motifs in the stories we tell each other about it, what scenarios do we have for its continued development? How well do our hidden assumptions, entrenched figures of thought, most favored metaphors, serve us as we try to orient ourselves in the emergent cultural order? And what are the strategic sites for observing it? Again, the continuous emphasis is on elaborating and exemplifying a point of view, a conceptualization, not on presenting new or more deeply researched facts. The ethnographic evidence will often be anecdotal (as it often is in arguments about globalization), a bit parachutist: Kafanchan now, lower Broadway next. And yet I hope it will contribute to a sense of the overall organization of diversity. Let me add that "organization," and the second word of the title, "connections," carry some weight here. In the tradition of social anthropology, I try to look at the coherence of the world in terms of interactions, relationships, and networks.

I have organized the chapters under three headings: culture, people, places. It is plain that these are not easily separable themes, and actually they tend to mingle throughout the book. Yet the differences in emphasis may be discernible.

Culture is really a continuous, overarching concern in the pages which follow. There are obviously many concepts of culture, and even that of anthropology is not entirely of one piece. I see at least three main emphases which it has tended to combine, and which have usually been assumed to coexist harmoniously.

One is that culture is learned, acquired in social life; in computer parlance, the software needed for programming the biologically given hardware. The second is that it is somehow integrated, neatly fitting together. The third is that it is something which comes in varying packages, distinctive to different human collectivities, and that as a rule these collectivities belong in territories.

The second of these assumptions, that a culture is highly integrated, and to be grasped as "a whole," has been deeply entrenched in anthropology for many years. It reached its high point with Ruth Benedict's *Patterns of Culture* (1934), probably still the discipline's all-time classic. In the 1960s and 1970s, however, some of the preeminent anthropological thinkers of the times—Fredrik Barth (1966: 12 ff.), Clifford Geertz (1973: 404 ff.), Victor Turner (1977)—began to express their doubts about it, along different lines. "Well, it is a matter of degree . . ."; "Too much integration may not be such a good thing . . ."; "In any case, it should be a matter for investigation." And the idea has hardly been quite the same since; surely not in times of postmodernism.[7] No doubt it has something to it, but as we look at lives including a quite noticeable share of contradictions, ambiguities, misunderstandings, and conflicts, we sense that making things go together is something that we at least have to work on.

The third characteristic, of cultures, in the plural, as packages of meanings and meaningful forms, distinctive to collectivities and territories, is the one most obviously affected by increasing interconnectedness in space. As people move with their meanings, and as meanings find ways of traveling even when people stay put, territories cannot really contain cultures. And even as one accepts that culture is socially acquired and organized, the assumption that it is homogeneously distributed within collectivities becomes problematic, when we see how their members' experiences and biographies differ.

Fundamentally, we seem to be left with the first of the three emphases, on culture as meanings and meaningful forms which we shape and acquire in social life. This seems to define the range of cultural analysis. With regard to the other two, I would suggest, the strategy now should be to reformulate them as core problematics in our thinking comparatively about culture, its variations and its historical shifts. How, and to what degree, do people arrange culture into coherent patterns as they go about their lives? How, as they involve themselves with the interconnectedness of the world, does culture sometimes, in some ways, become organized into the more or less tidy packages we have called "cultures," and under other circumstances take on other kinds of distribution?

In his 1945 address on the ecumene, Kroeber went on to argue that

> while any national or tribal culture may and must for certain purposes be viewed and analyzed by itself . . . any such culture is necessarily in some degree an artificial unit segregated off for expediency and that the ultimate natural unit for ethnologists is "the culture of all humanity at all periods and in all places". (Kroeber 1945: 9) [. . .]

THE LOCAL AND THE GLOBAL: CONTINUITY AND CHANGE

My wife and I were on vacation in Ireland, and stayed for a night in Carna, a fishing village in Connemara. Noticeably many young people were milling about on the village roads, but mostly, we found out, they were not locals. Carna is in one of those remote areas of western Ireland where Irish children come during the summer to live with Gaelic-speaking families, and thus improve their usually very limited knowledge of Gaelic. But the Gaelic language would probably soon be gone in Carna as well, the hostess of our bed-and-breakfast place told us. Hardly anybody now grew up to speak it fluently. As for herself, that morning she was on her way to Galway town, where her family would hold a reunion. She hoped, but was not sure, that a brother of hers, who had had a career of singing in music pubs in New York, would come flying home for the event. Her own adult life had mostly been in London, it turned out, and there were times when she missed the bright lights. Returning to rural Ireland, she said, "was a real culture shock, you know."

A very ordinary little tale, but it draws together a number of themes of contemporary life. It suggests that the greater time depth of cultures tends to be tied to particular places and regions, as Gaelic language and folk tradition are to villages like Carna, and it shows that people just about anywhere can turn out to have personal experiences and relationships linking them to places in other countries and on other continents. Moreover, it shows that this is something people are aware of and perhaps increasingly preoccupied with, and that the vocabulary for dealing with such matters is growing and spreading, so that a term like "culture shock," invented by an American anthropologist some half century ago, now comes readily to the lips of a boarding-house landlady in Connemara.

In the most general sense, globalization is a matter of increasing long-distance interconnectedness, at least across national boundaries, preferably between continents as well. That interconnectedness has a great many aspects. We have ways of meddling with other people's environments, from the destruction of rain forests and the intercontinental dumping of toxic wastes to global warming; and with their bodies, as in a growing transnational trade in human organs for transplants. The goods we buy may come from far away. This is a fact we sometimes ignore, but at other times the distant provenance has an aura of its own.[1] People whose ancestors lived thousands of miles from one another, and hardly knew of each other's kind, are now in each other's immediate presence, rubbing shoulders; but even when they are not, the proliferation of media technologies allows their ideas, and the tangible shapes which they give them, to circulate without much regard for distance.

These varied kinds of linkage, on the other hand, do not combine in the same way everywhere. Thus in the last half-century or so, the Second World, that of state socialism, for as long as it lasted mostly had its own globalization; the media could to some degree slip in from the outside, but mostly not the material goods, and people could seldom get either in or out.[2] This was also a world that hardly needed to import any environmental destruction. It has been the First World, industrial and capitalist, that has been most intensely involved, within itself, in all kinds of interconnectedness, and sharing some of it with the Third World on those unequal terms which have made globalization seem in large part synonymous with westernization. Meanwhile it has been the tragedy of the Fourth World of aboriginal peoples, during the same period, that it was mostly forced into retreating before that expansion of the First, Second and Third Worlds which again and again destroyed its environments.

As one of the key words of our times, "globalization" stands for a central challenge to intellectual traditions in the human sciences, and draws a variety of commentators of other kinds as well. But in that cacophony of what one commentator (J. Abu-Lughod 1991) has aptly called globalbabble, there is also some tendency to resort to hyperbole and excessive generalizations, to tell a story of dramatic shifts between "before" and "after." In fact, of course, interconnectedness across great distances is not altogether new—Kroeber's discussion of the ancient ecumene of the Greeks, referred to in Chapter 1, showed as much. That image of a cultural mosaic, where each culture would have been a territorial entity with clear, sharp, enduring edges, never really corresponded with realities. There were always interactions, and a diffusion of ideas, habits, and things, even if at times we have been habituated to theories of culture and society which have not emphasized such truths.

Moreover, if "globalization" literally refers to an increase in interconnectedness, we must realize that locally and regionally at least, there can be histories of deglobalization as well. The process is not irreversible. Countries—Myanmar (a.k.a. Burma), Hoxha's Albania—may pursue policies of cutting themselves off, delinking; a kind of active anti-globalization which is in a dialectical relationship with globalization itself. Or they, or parts of them, may deglobalize because

they can no longer afford to keep interconnectedness going, and the world does not need them any more. We may see something like this happening in some places in Africa. This might seem like parts of the Third World marching back into the Fourth, if it were not for the fact that so many traces of earlier globalization are still around.

Globalization, all this goes to say, is not brand new, it can move back and forth, it comes in many kinds, it is segmented, and it is notoriously uneven; different worlds, different globalizations. For an anthropologist, it is surely often tempting to take on the old responsibility of the slave, whispering in the ear of the grand theorist that "things are different in the south." To put it differently again, once in a while at least, globalization has to be brought down to earth.

In this chapter I will try to contribute a little to that with respect to some questions of culture. But these are fairly big questions, and so I think the best thing might be to move up and down, between grassroots view and overview, to try to catch what is going on. One is whether globalization leads to less culture, or more. Before we get to that, I would like us to have a look at the packaging of culture, the way we conceptualize units of meanings and meaningful forms in social space. Finally, I want to consider the nature of the local under conditions of globalization. We have now acquired the habit of contrasting the local and the global, and tend to take for granted that the local is to the global more or less as continuity is to change. The outside interferes with the reproductive processes of local culture, but meets with resistance of one kind or other. No doubt there is something to such assumptions, but there is apparently a certain risk of mystification here, and we might try to clarify what is going on in this encounter.

PACKAGING CULTURE

Two aspects of this encounter in particular seem to make the rules of the game for cultural organization rather different in the late twentieth century than they have been before: the mobility of human beings themselves, and the mobility of meanings and meaningful forms through the media.

Throughout human history, there have been people on the move; but usually not very far, or taking a long time to get anywhere. Large-scale air transportation, of jet-set business executives, academics, tourists, pilgrims, or labor migrants as well as refugees from political terror or ecological disasters, shifts people from one place to another more quickly over greater distances than ever before; for one thing, perhaps it did take that Irish-American bar performer from New York on an *Aer Lingus* flight to his family reunion in Galway. The media (in which I include all those communicative technologies, ranging from handwriting to television and electronic mail, that allow people to get messages across to one another without face-to-face co-presence) have not only become more effective in reaching across space. In their growing variety, they have also increased their capacity for handling different symbolic modes, one by one or in combination.

It is in large part due to these media and transport technologies that the world, or at least much of the world, is now self-consciously one single field of persistent interaction and exchange. Obviously, these technologies have not come into being in a vacuum, but in particular social matrices where major uses for them can be identified, and where resources for their development can be amassed. Let us beware of the simplest forms of technological determinism.[3] Yet the reason why I especially want to emphasize the importance of these tools for moving people and meanings is not only that they are so directly involved in globalization. It is also because once they have come into existence, their uses may multiply, their further development takes new turns, and their consequences for the organization of social life and culture in the world have hardly been altogether foreseeable.

People, meanings, and meaningful forms which travel fit badly with what have been conventional units of social and cultural thought. Social theorists now criticize again and again the established tendency to treat "societies" as autonomous universes, often only implicitly identified with the modern form of states—I will come back to the issue especially in Chapter 4. "Cultures," in the plural, have of course been almost the mirror image of "societies" here, perhaps a bit more emphatically suggesting the coexistence and diversity of the entities, but at the same time setting forth the idea of boundedness and distinctiveness even more explicitly. And one strong reason for this has been the historical affinity between mainstream cultural thought, in anthropology and elsewhere, and those ideas about nationhood which emerged in Europe mostly in the nineteenth century.[4]

The idea of an organic relationship between a population, a territory, a form as well as a unit of political organization, and one of those organized packages of meanings and meaningful forms which we refer to as cultures has for a long time been an enormously successful one, spreading throughout the world even to fairly unlikely places, at least as a guiding principle. Perhaps anthropologists, studying human lives even in places where states have not existed, should have been a bit more wary of the construct. But with the personal experience of citizenship surrounding them in their own lives, facing the classical conditions of local fieldwork, and under the influence of a natural history tradition in which cultures are seen more or less as taxonomically analogous with biological species, they have hardly been more inclined than anyone else to scrutinize the assumptions linking at least people, place, and culture.

Neither places nor nation-states may now be quite what they have been, however, and some indeed say that the noticeable increase in sophisticated interpretations of nationhood and nationalism recently is a sign of the decline of the nation-state; that is, with some distance, we see things more clearly now. [. . .]

HABITATS OF MEANING

It should not, however, be only the shifting relationship between culture and territory that bothers us. No less at issue is the assumption that the carrier of "a culture" is "a people"—that strongly sociocentric, collectivist understanding of culture, rooted at least in the anthropological tradition. The current parallels in social theory are obvious. There has been a resurgence of interest in agency, no doubt partly as a pendulum swing away from a previous strong emphasis on structure, system and social determinism; partly, I think, also because these ideas have been so firmly, if not always entirely visibly, set in the framework of the nation-state.[5] In anthropology, for some time now, the absence of any explicit notion of agency has been one of the points of criticism in arguments about the trouble with "culturalism," and in and out of that particular debate, there have now for some time been calls to bring human beings back in.[6]

In so doing, however, we must not lose sight of the diversity of actors and organizational contexts involved in managing contemporary complex culture. We cannot occupy ourselves only with the small-scale handling of meanings and symbols by individuals, or small groups, and assume that wider cultural entities come about simply through an aggregation of their activities. To grasp the nature of the culture we live with now, we must also take an interest in the management of meaning by corporate and institutional actors, not least by the state and in the market-place. As far as the state is concerned, this means that it is treated rather as one player among others, with its own interests and logic, rather than as the universe of analysis.

One of the recent writers on concepts of agency has been the Polish—English sociologist Zygmunt Bauman (1992: 190–191), generally one of the most insightful and interesting commentators on the relationship between theory and the emergent realities of contemporary life. Bauman suggests that a notion of agency should be combined, not with system, but with a flexible sense of habitat; a habitat in which agency operates and which it also produces, one where it finds its resources and goals as well as its limitations.

Adapting Bauman's point of view, I think a notion of "habitats of meaning" may serve us well in cultural analysis.[7] The relativist streak in cultural analysis has frequently led us to such turns of phrase as "worlds of meaning," but this again suggests too much autonomy and boundedness. Habitats can expand and contract. As they can overlap entirely, partially or just possibly not at all, they can be identified with either individuals or collectivities. But in the latter case, it is the analysis of cultural process in social relationships, rather than an axiomatic assertion, that has to convince us that a habitat of meaning is really shared. Much of the time, cultural process will be shaped rather by the way that fairly different habitats of meaning are made to intersect.

In the global ecumene, some people may indeed share much the same habitats of meaning, but these can also become quite idiosyncratic. The places we have been to and the people we have met in them, the books and newspapers we read, the television channels we can zap to, all these make a difference. My own daily habitat of meaning changed the day our apartment building installed cable TV, and I suddenly had access to British, French, German, Turkish, American, and Russian programming apart from the Swedish channels. Yet our habitats of meaning will of course depend not only on what in some physical sense we are exposed to, but also on the capabilities we have built up for coping with it knowledgeably: the languages we understand, write, or speak, our levels of literacy with respect to other symbolic forms, and so on.

What I have been saying so far is that the distribution of meanings and meaningful forms over people and social relationships in the world is now so complicated that any social units we work with in cultural studies must be more or less arbitrary, artifacts of particular analytical objectives. The idea of cultures in the plural is problematic; no doubt difficult to do away with for historical and ideological as well as scholarly reasons, but often little more than a tentative and limited intellectual organizing device. Yet at the same time, the idea of culture in the singular, encompassing the entire more or less organized diversity of ideas and expressions, may become more important than it has been, as we explore the way humanity inhabits the global ecumene. [. . .]

SENSES OF PLACE

In the meeting of the alien and the familiar, however, it seems that the familiar often wins out in the end. Having begun the chapter by drawing on a vacation experience in Ireland, let me turn to some other chance anecdotal evidence from a summer holiday.

The newspaper in the town next to that southern Swedish village where I spend summers is sometimes referred to facetiously as "the pig paper," since it is the newspaper of record for area farmers, for example when it comes to current pig prices. It is, like many small-town papers, quite intensely local, carrying foreign news from the major agencies in a rather routine, offhand way. But then at times, the outside world can itself be locally newsworthy, and so some years ago in mid-July there was a half-page spread under the headline "Adventures in the jungles of Borneo" (Siverson 1992).

A local man had won first prize in a photo contest, a three-week trip for two to Borneo. He and his wife went, and they had now returned, full of impressions: the heat, the hotel in Kuching which changed the towels three times a day, the upriver trip to the Iban tribe (ex-cannibals by reputation), the comfortable guest-house on high poles, the crocodile farm, the strange food and drink; indeed, a pig feast as well. They had seen just a few beggars and no drunkards in the entire trip. And not everything was unfamiliar. Danish beer was common, and taxis were cheap, although you had to settle the price with the driver before going. And in Kuching many people had wanted to talk about the ongoing European soccer championship, and had their particular favorite player on the Swedish team. Anyway, it had been nice to come home, and the first thing these two travelers did was to have a large glass of cold milk each. Now as photo enthusiasts they also brought back a collection of 700 slides, and looked forward to showing these to people at home, to community groups or wherever.

This, clearly, is a story about that encounter between "the global and the local"; the way one couple's habitat of meaning is dramatically enlarged, but also the way that among a multitude of first-time experiences,

they after all find some particular pleasure in reporting on what is familiar—the availability of Danish beer, the reputation of a Swedish soccer player. Moreover, what is not the same as at home can after all often be described in well-known categories—a frequent change of towels, how to take a taxi, drunkards or no drunkards, beggars or no beggars. And as a happy ending, two glasses of cold milk (nothing could be more Swedish).

For those who have some doubts that contemporary globalization changes everything, this is a beautiful story. It is of course a recurrent assertion on the part of various theorists that the local itself is not what it used to be. "In conditions of modernity," writes Anthony Giddens (1990: 18–19), for example, "place becomes increasingly *phantasmagoric*: that is to say, locales are thoroughly penetrated by and shaped in terms of social influences quite distant from them ... the 'visible form' of the locale conceals the distanciated relations which determine its nature." And Mark Poster asks:

> If I can speak directly or by electronic mail to a friend in Paris while sitting in California, if I can witness political and cultural events as they occur across the globe without leaving my home, if a database at a remote location contains my profile and informs government agencies which make decisions that affect my life without any knowledge on my part of these events, if I can shop in my home by using my TV or computer, then where am I and who am I? (Poster 1990: 74)

I have one sort of answer to that question in a moment. To get there, however, it may be useful to try and be clear about what it is that makes the local a likely source of continuity, and that safeguards the continuous importance of place.

A number of things tend to come together here.[8] One is that much of what goes on locally is what we describe as "everyday life." And if again we must try to be more specific about what this is, we might say that it tends to be very repetitive, redundant, an almost endless round of activities in enduring settings. Furthermore, everyday life is in large part practical. People participate actively, training their personal dexterities without necessarily reflecting much on the fact. There develops a trained capacity for handling things in one way, and—in Veblenesque terms—perhaps a trained incapacity for doing anything else.[9]

What is local also tends to be face-to-face, in large part in focused encounters and broadly inclusive long-term relationships. People can have each other under fairly close surveillance. Shared understandings can be worked out in detail in the back-and-forth flow of words and deeds. Deviations can be punished informally but effectively, changes may need to be negotiated. At the same time, obviously, these relationships can have a strong emotional content; they are often relationships to "significant others." This affects the meanings built up in them, and the commitment to these meanings.

Moreover, it is in the face-to-face, and what will turn out to be everyday, contexts that human beings usually have their first experiences. If we accept that they undergo a sort of continuous cultural construction work, whatever materials are put in place early will presumably have some influence on what can be assimilated later on. This may not be an argument that we want to push to the extreme, but most would probably agree that there is something to it.

To these fairly familiar points I would add that the local tends to be a special kind of sensual experience. People often make a distinction between a "real" experience and what they have only read about, or seen on television. So what is "unreal" about these latter kinds of experience? Of course, we can consider this only a figure of speech, but another way of looking at it is that people are in the local setting bodily, with all their senses, ready not only to look and listen but to touch, smell, and taste, without having their fields of attention restricted, prestructured for them. There is a feeling of immediacy, even of immersion, of being surrounded. What is experienced is also extensively contextualized. This is surely at least part of what the "real" is about. If there is now a growing celebration in social and cultural theory of the body as a symbolic site of self and continuity, and of the senses, a greater concern

with the body and the senses in their contexts might help us understand some of what "place" is about.[10] When Mark Poster, in the lines quoted above, asks rhetorically where he is, it seems he has already offered one not wholly trivial answer—at "home." Home is where that glass of cold milk is.

Taking these items together—the everyday, the face-to-face, the early and formative, the sensual and bodily experience—it would appear that a fairly strong case exists for the continued importance of the local. And this could be true as far as experienced reality is concerned even when much of what is in a place is shaped from the outside. We are just giving up the idea that the local is autonomous, that it has an integrity of its own. It would have its significance, rather, as the arena in which a variety of influences come together, acted out perhaps in a unique combination, under those special conditions. If I remember correctly one of the immortal sayings of J.R. Ewing of *Dallas*: "Once you throw integrity out of the window, the rest is a piece of cake."

Yet perhaps not quite. As an intellectual category, "the local" seems more protean than primordial. In identifying the typical components of localness, we may also come to realize more clearly that they are not all intrinsically local, linked to territoriality in general or only some one place in particular. That connection is really made rather by recurrent practicalities of life, and by habits of thought. And if somehow these characteristic features of local life become differently distributed in the social organization of space, so that for example everyday life is less confined, or those "real" experiences with a full range of senses are spread out more equally over some number of places which thus approach the qualities of "home," then the one and only local would appear to be a rather less privileged site of cultural process. I am not suggesting that it is really disappearing, losing all distinctiveness; only that by unpacking the category, we may entertain a more precise idea of the place of "place" in cultural organization.

Take the example of media. "Most students of contemporary culture agree on the unique role of the media as the principal vehicle of culture production and distribution," writes Zygmunt Bauman (1992: 31). In a way this seems to me an unfortunate formulation. The principal vehicles, I think, so far remain those which we largely take for granted as parts of local life, and which I have just tried to sketch. (The everyday and face-to-face may be small-scale; in the aggregate, it is massive.) But the cultural capacity of the media has not been constant, and perhaps in the terms I have suggested they can gradually acquire more of the qualities we have been used to thinking of as local. Mastering a wider range of symbolic modes, they can speak more broadly to the senses, make their contents seem more "real," than they could when only the printed word was at their command. Those media which are more interactive can begin to achieve some of the efficiency which face-to-face interaction has through rapid feedback. The local seems to be losing some of its superiority here.[11]

GUARDIANS OF CONTINUITY, AGENTS OF CHANGE

For all its real qualities, "the local" in cultural thought sometimes becomes a thing of romance and mystique. It reminds me a little of a certain animal in Viking mythology, the succulent boar *Särimner*, which the warrior heroes could eat every evening, only in order to find it alive and well, ready to be slaughtered again, the next day. In some comment on the global and the local, that is, local tradition seems to be just forever there, in limitless supply. The global is shallow, the local deep.

In a way, then, if as I said before, the global sometimes has to be brought down to earth, the local has to be brought up to the surface, to be demystified. The thing about cultural continuity is that there is no way for socially organized meanings to stay down there in the depths all the time, they must also come up and present themselves to the senses. And whenever they do so, they are also at risk: ready to be reinterpreted, reorganized, even rejected.[12]

No doubt the local is, for at least the reasons I suggested before, something special. In the end, however, it is an arena where various people's habitats of meaning intersect, and where the global, or what has been local somewhere else, also has some chance of making itself at home. At this intersection, things are forever working themselves out, so that this year's change is next year's continuity. We may wonder, then, both what the place does to people, and what people do to the place.

With regard to the former, let me just insert that one noteworthy thing may be that in the global ecumene, habitats of meaning seem to become increasingly malleable. In Zygmunt Bauman's terms again, there are more "diffuse offers and free choices" (yet again, more in the First World than in the others). The decision to migrate, or to stay, is less fateful than it has been when certain life styles are replicated in many places, together with the special markets to serve them, and when both media and jet flights allow you to shuttle between places.[13]

When it comes to people making places, we come back to the fact of uneven globalization, yet this time at the grassroots level. Locally, we may ask, who are the globalizers? To understand contemporary culture, this may be a key issue, but the answer is likely to be complicated.

In the past, in a great many places, it may have been common that transnational connections, or even any ties at all outside the local face-to-face community, were more or less an elite affair, a task in a community division of labour as well as an instrument of domination. Today it remains true that the high and mighty of politics, administration, and business are both frequent fliers and frequent faxers, and that the facilities of travel as well as media technology may be organized to serve their requirements especially. But that is not the entire story. In the First World, the working class is now in no small part from the Third World, and may increasingly become ex-Second World.

We should no doubt consider the matter in gender terms; in places where women are more sedentary, and less visible in public life, they may have a greater part in carrying local tradition into the present.[14] But this is hardly the case everywhere. In age terms, it would appear that some young people are now among those most at home in the global ecumene itself, footloose and uncommitted enough to spread their period of liminality over two or three continents, quickly cultivating the desirable literacies when media technologies change and new symbolic forms become available.[15] What happens to them as they get older? In a two-steps-forward, one-step-back fashion, they may become adults, too, but perhaps not quite the same kind of adults as their parents were.

And then there are old people. Certainly we will expect them to be the real guardians of continuity, as migrants from the past. Yet even this may need a closer look. Left to themselves, some of them turn out to become intensely involved with the media, rather than with the people next door. If they have not only time but other resources as well at their disposal, as many of them have recently had in more affluent parts of the world, they may choose to travel: go on trips, retire in a different climate. Squeezed between young ones and elders at leisure with wider horizons, working adults in their middle years may be the real locals.

Perhaps the main point in all this is that the arrangements of personal interconnectedness between the local and the global are getting increasingly opaque. So many kinds of kinship, friendship, collegiality, business, pursuits of pleasure, or struggles for security now engage people in transnational contacts that we can never be sure in which habitats of meaning these can turn up, and have a peripheral or a central part. I will return to this theme in later chapters.[16] Nor may it be either entirely predictable or entirely unpredictable who will turn out to set meanings acquired from afar in local circulation. The bed-and-breakfast landlady in Connemara may be an ex-Londoner and the sister of a New Yorker, and still keep a fairly low profile; I suspect that those Swedish amateur photographers with their 700 slides from Borneo most likely will not.

NOTES

Nigerian Kung Fu, Manhattan fatwa

1. I have discussed some aspects of the past and present of Kafanchan in other publications (Hannerz 1979, 1982, 1983, 1985, 1987, 1993).

2. One should realize, however, that the term is not entirely unambiguous; see Verdery (1994) for an illuminating discussion.

3. As I have put it elsewhere, "there is a cumulative microstructuring of . . . a fairly sizeable part of the new social landscape of the global ecumene" (Hannerz 1992a: 48). In political science, Rosenau (1990) has suggested the term "postinternational" in developing a related point of view.

4. Cf. Restivo (1991: 177 ff.), Hodgson (1993: 247 ff.), Wax (1993) and Patterson (1994). In the context of African cultural history, Kopytoff (1987: 10) has succinctly defined an ecumene as "a region of persistent cultural interaction and exchange," and this seems like a useful formulation on the global scale as well. I might perhaps add here that while I began thinking, speaking, and writing about this kind of issues in terms of the "world system," I found that term too definitively linked to theoretical assumptions made widely familiar through the work of Immanuel Wallerstein (e.g. 1974, 1991)—which, I should acknowledge, has obviously been immensely influential in stimulating my interest, like that of many others, in a global turn in the social sciences. There seemed also to be some risk that using that term, one could get trapped in rather unproductive debates over the "systemness" of the world. Once again, this may be a time when a sensitizing concept which carries less extra baggage serves us well as we try to get on with things.

5. That perspective is elaborated most fully in a previous book, *Cultural Complexity* (Hannerz 1992b).

6. For other contributions to that conversation see for example Appadurai (1990, 1991, 1993), Friedman (1994), and several articles in two thematic issues of the journal *Cultural Anthropology*, edited by Ferguson and Gupta (1992) and Harding and Myers (1994) respectively.

7. Archer (1988: 2 ff.) relates what she calls "the myth of cultural integration" to "the anthropological heritage," but does not seem very familiar with more recent anthropological trends.

The Local and the Global

1. The classic parody of our normal lack of awareness of the geographical origins of things is Linton's (1936: 326–327) "100% American."

2. For a macrosociological view of Second World globalization see Arnason (1995).

3. Raymond Williams (1975: 9 ff.) has a particularly lucid discussion of the historical relationship between technology and society.

4. See Handler's (1985) discussion of this point.

5. See e.g. Bauman (1992: 190).

6. See e.g. Ortner (1984: 144 ff.), Keesing (1987), and Obeyesekere (1990: 285 ff.).

7. This notion of habitats of meaning is related to my discussion of perspectives and horizons in *Cultural Complexity* (Hannerz 1992b: 64 ff.).

8. Heller's (1995) comments on conceptions of "home" are in some ways parallel to what follows.

9. Undoubtedly the characterization of everyday life here will be recognized to have an affinity with Bourdieu's (1977) conception of habitus.

10. For some relevant work see e.g. Bloch (1992), Howes (1991), Shilling (1993), Stoller (1989), and Synnott (1993).

11. For one extensive discussion of this theme see Meyrowitz (1985).

12. The formulation here is inspired by Sahlins (1985: ix).

13. Raban (1974) takes a similar view of contemporary urban life—I will refer to it in Chapter 14—and it may well be true that it is especially in cities that culture is increasingly a matter of choice. It may involve a class factor as well, but I do not think this type of relationship between agency and habitat is now entirely confined to more prosperous categories of people, at least in the First World.

14. See for example Rosander's (1991: 255 ff.) comments on the difference between Muslim men and women in Ceuta, the Spanish enclave on the coast of North Africa.

15. On various aspects of transnational tendencies in the culture of young people, see Jourdan (1995), Liechty (1995), Sansone (1995), Schade-Poulsen (1995), and Wulff (1992, 1995: 10 ff.)

16. I have also discussed the proliferation of transnational ties at the personal level elsewhere (Hannerz 1992a, 1992c).

REFERENCES

Abu-Lughod, J. (1991) "Going beyond global babble," in A.D. King (ed.) *Culture, Globalization and the World-System*, London: Macmillan.

Appadurai, A. (1990) "Disjuncture and difference in the global cultural economy," *Public Culture* 2, 2: 1–24.

—— (1991) "Global ethnoscapes: notes and queries for a transnational anthropology," in R.G. Fox (ed.) *Recapturing Anthropology*, Santa Fe, NM: School of American Research Press.

—— (1993) "Patriotism and its futures," *Public Culture* 5: 411–429.

Archer, M. (1988) *Culture and Agency*, Cambridge: Cambridge University Press.

Barth, F. (1966) *Models of Social Organization*, Occasional paper no. 23, London: Royal Anthropological Institute.

Bauman, Z. (1992) *Intimations of Postmodernity*, London: Routledge.

Benedict, R. (1934) *Patterns of Culture*, Boston: Houghton Mifflin.

Bloch, M. (1992) "What goes without saying: the conceptualization of Zafimaniry society," in A. Kuper (ed.) *Conceptualizing Society*, London: Routledge.

Bourdieu, P. (1977) *Outline of a Theory of Practice*, Cambridge: Cambridge University Press.

Ferguson, J., and Gupta, A. (eds)(1992) "Space, identity, and the politics of difference," *Cultural Anthropology* 7,1.

Friedman, J. (1994) *Cultural Identity and Global Process*, London: Sage.

Geertz, C. (1973) *The Interpretation of Cultures*, New York: Basic Books.

—— (1984) "Distinguished lecture: anti anti-relativism," *American Anthropologist* 86: 263–278.

Giddens, A. (1990) *The Consequences of Modernity*, Cambridge: Polity Press.

Handler, R. (1985) "On dialogue and destructive analysis: problems in narrating nationalism and ethnicity," *Journal of Anthropological Research* 41: 171–182.

Hannerz, U. (1979) "Town and country in Southern Zaria: a view from Kafanchan," in A. Southall (ed.) *Small Urban Centers in Rural Development in Africa*, Madison: African Studies Program, University of Wisconsin.

—— (1982) "Washington and Kafanchan: a view of urban anthropology," *L'Homme* 22,4: 25–36.

—— (1983) "Tools of identity and imagination," in A. Jacobson-Widding (ed.) *Identity: Personal and Socio-Cultural*, Stockholm: Almqvist & Wiksell International.

—— (1985) "Structures for strangers: ethnicity and institutions in a colonial Nigerian town," in A. Southall, P.J.M. Nas, and G. Ansari (eds) *City and Society*, Leiden: Institute of Cultural and Social Studies.

—— (1987) "The world in creolisation," *Africa* 57: 546–559.

—— (1992a) "The global ecumene as a network of networks," in A. Kuper (ed.) *Conceptualizing Society*, London: Routledge.

—— (1992b) *Cultural Complexity*, New York: Columbia University Press.

—— (1992c) "Networks of Americanization," in R. Lundén and E. Åsard (eds) *Networks of Americanization*, Stockholm: Almqvist & Wiksell International.

—— (1993) "Mediations in the global ecumene," in Gísli Pálsson (ed.) *Beyond Boundaries*, London: Berg.

Harding, S., and Myers, F. (eds)(1994) "Further inflections: toward ethnographies of the future," *Cultural Anthropology* 9,3.

Heller, A. (1995) "Where are we at home?," *Thesis Eleven* 41: 1–18.

Hodgson, M.G.S. (1993) *Rethinking World History*, Cambridge: Cambridge University Press.

Howes, D. (ed.)(1991) *The Varieties of Sensory Experience*, Toronto: University of Toronto Press.

Jourdan, C. (1995) "Masta Liu," in V. Amit-Talai and H. Wulff (eds) *Youth Cultures*, London: Routledge.

Keesing, R.M. (1987) "Anthropology as interpretive quest," *Current Anthropology* 28: 161–176.

Kopytoff, I. (1987) "The internal African frontier: the making of African political culture," in I. Kopytoff (ed.) *The African Frontier*, Bloomington: Indiana University Press.

Kroeber, A.L. (1945) "The ancient *Oikoumenê* as an historic culture aggregate," *Journal of the Royal Anthropological Institute* 75: 9–20.

Liechty, M. (1995) "Media, markets and modernization: youth identities and the experience of modernity in Kathmandu, Nepal," in V. Amit-Talai and H. Wulff (eds) *Youth Cultures*, London: Routledge.

Linton, R. (1936) *The Study of Man*, New York: Appleton-Century-Crofts.

McLuhan, M. (1964) *Understanding Media*, New York: McGraw-Hill.

Meyrowitz, J. (1985) *No Sense of Place*, New York: Oxford University Press.

Obeyesekere, G. (1990) *The Work of Culture*, Chicago: University of Chicago Press.

Ortner, S.B. (1984) "Theory in anthropology since the sixties," *Comparative Studies in Society and History* 26: 126–166.

Patterson, O. (1994) "Ecumenical America: global culture and the American cosmos," *World Policy Journal* 11,2: 103–117.

Poster, M. (1990) *The Mode of Information*, Cambridge: Polity.

Raban, J. (1974) *Soft City*, London: Hamish Hamilton.

Restivo, S. (1991) *The Sociological Worldview*, Cambridge, MA, and Oxford: Blackwell.

Rosander, E.E. (1991) *Women in a Borderland*, Stockholm Studies in Social Anthropology 26, Stockholm: Almqvist & Wiksell International.

Rosenau, J.N. (1990) *Turbulence in World Politics*, Princeton, NJ: Princeton University Press.

Sahlins, M. (1985) *Islands of History*, Chicago: University of Chicago Press.

Sansone, L. (1995) "The making of a black youth culture: lower-class young men of Surinamese origin in Amsterdam," in V. Amit-Talai and H. Wulff (eds) *Youth Cultures*, London: Routledge.

Schade-Poulsen, M. (1995) "The power of love: raï music and youth in Algeria," in V. Amit-Talai and H. Wulff (eds) *Youth Cultures*, London: Routledge.

Shilling, C. (1993) *The Body and Social Theory*, London: Sage.

Siverson, L. (1992) "Äventyr i Borneos djungel," *Nordvästra Skånes Tidningar*, July 12.

Stoller, P. (1989) *The Taste of Ethnographic Things*, Philadelphia: University of Pennsylvania Press.

Synnott, A. (1993) *The Body Social*, London: Routledge.

Turner, V. (1977) "Process, system and symbol: a new anthropological synthesis," *Daedalus* 106,3: 61–80.

Verdery, K. (1994) "Beyond the nation in Eastern Europe," *Social Text* 38: 1–19.

Wallerstein, I. (1974) *The Modern World-System*, New York: Academic Press.

—— (1991) *Unthinking Social Science*, Cambridge: Polity Press.

Wax, M.L. (1993) "How culture misdirects multiculturalism," *Anthropology and Education Quarterly* 24,2: 99–115.

Williams, R. (1975) *Television: Technology and Cultural Form*, New York: Schocken.

Wulff, H. (1992) "Young Swedes in New York: workplace and playground," in R. Lundén and E. Åsard (eds) *Networks of Americanization*, Stockholm: Almqvist & Wiksell International.

—— (1995) "Introducing youth culture in its own right: the state of the art and new possibilities," in V. Amit-Talai and H. Wulff (eds) *Youth Cultures*, London: Routledge.

CHAPTER 21

Introduction: Transnational Feminist Practices and Questions of Postmodernity

Inderpal Grewal and Caren Kaplan

[. . .]

In this collection of essays, we are interested in problematizing theory; more specifically, feminist theory. In many locations in the United States and Europe, theory often tends to be a homogenizing move by many First World women and men. That is, theory seems unable to deal with alterity at all or falls into a kind of relativism. Refusing either of those two moves, we would like to explore how we come to do feminist work across cultural divides. For we are committed to feminism and to seeing possibilities for political work within postmodern cultures that encompass, though very differently, contemporary global relations.

To begin, we want to explore how crucial key terms and concepts circulate. Given that we are not looking for terms that remain pure, authentic, or unmediated, we argue that the way terms get co-opted constitutes a form of practice, just as the way that they contain possibilities for critical use is also an oppositional practice. In particular, we critique the way that specific terms lose their political usefulness when they are disciplined by academia or liberal/conservative agendas.

In raising questions about the historical specificity of some of the primary terms in use in cultural criticism today, we are inquiring into the system of effects that structure postmodernity. Asking how postmodernisms and post-colonialisms are variously deployed by feminists and others in different locations provides us with an opportunity to trace the direction of flows of information and "theory" in transnational cultural production and reception. We see postmodernism as a critique of modernist agendas as they are manifested in various forms and locations around the world.[1] Our critiques of certain forms of feminism emerge from their willing participation in modernity with all its colonial discourses and hegemonic First World formations that wittingly or unwittingly lead to the oppression and exploitation of many women. In supporting the agendas of modernity, therefore, feminists misrecognize and fail to resist Western hegemonies. Thus we pursue two lines of questioning: (1) What kinds of feminist practices engender theories that resist or question modernity? (2) How do we understand the production and reception of diverse feminisms within a framework of transnational social/cultural/economic movements?

In response to these kinds of questions, the essays in this collection insert alternative, counterhegemonic feminist reading and writing practices from around the world. The essays also interrogate the discourse of postmodernism, which has been expressed in the West primarily as an aesthetic or cultural debate rather than a political one. Such debates ignore the radical changes in global economic structures that have occurred since the middle of this century. If the world is currently structured by transnational economic links and cultural asymmetries, locating feminist practices within these structures becomes imperative. Drawing on the languages and methods of contemporary cultural criticism, the essays in this collection develop a multinational and multilocational approach to questions of gender. [. . .]

We use the term "transnational" to problematize a purely locational politics of global-local or center-periphery in favor of what Mattelart sees as the lines cutting across them. As feminists who note the absence of gender issues in all of these world-system theories, we have no choice but to challenge what we see as inadequate and inaccurate binary divisions.[2] Transnational linkages influence every level of social existence. Thus the effects of configurations of practices at those levels are varied and historically specific. The theories of cultural homogenization that often accompany analyses of cultural flows cannot acknowledge these historicized effects and transformations at various levels. Arjun Appadurai takes into consideration movements of people, technologies, capital, and cultures in order to describe these forces as a "model of disjunctive flows" from which "something like a decent global analysis might flow."[3] Appadurai also warns against cultural homogenization theories, particularly those that simply equate homogenization with Americanization. His concern is that these same theories are used by nation-states to mask the fact that the threat of global commoditization is "more real than the threat of their own hegemonic strategies."[4]

A cultural flow such as CNN has an undeniably hegemonic effect, but it would be a mistake to see such flows as unidirectional or uniform. Instead of constructing monolithic, hegemonic effects, we should ask: What aspect of a commodity gets utilized in what way and where? Can we see these commodities as artifacts? How do we trace the cultural baggage of commodities from their point of origin (if this can be ascertained!)? For example, one scene that appeared on TV screens during the coup that ousted Ferdinand Marcos from the Philippines was that of the Marcos family at a party on their yacht, dancing and singing "We Are the World." We would not read this scene as the ludic play of postmodern syncretism. Rather, this scene signifies power and terror to a degree that insists that we examine the way in which the flows of cultural commodities are both linked and disjunctive. [. . .]

We mean to address precisely this construction of inert, ahistorical generalizations. The relationship between "transnational," "postcolonial," "center-periphery," and "diaspora" in contemporary usage can be found in the way modernity masks particularities in favor of the appearance of universal categories. In theorizing transnational feminist practices we are suggesting not only that communities are much more multiply organized than the conventional usages of these terms have implied, but that gender is crucially linked to the primary terms and concepts that structure and inform the economic and cultural theories of postmodernity.

POSTMODERNISM AND TRANSNATIONAL FEMINIST PRACTICES

If feminist political practices do not acknowledge transnational cultural flows, feminist movements will fail to understand the material conditions that structure women's lives in diverse locations. If feminist movements cannot understand the dynamics of these material conditions, they will be unable to construct an effective opposition to current economic and cultural hegemonies that are taking new global forms. Without an analysis of transnational scattered hegemonies that reveal themselves in gender relations, feminist movements will remain isolated and prone to reproducing the universalizing gestures of dominant Western cultures.

Notions such as "global feminism" have failed to respond to such needs and have increasingly been subject to critique.[5] Conventionally, "global feminism" has stood for a kind of Western cultural imperialism. The term "global feminism" has elided the diversity of women's agency in favor of a universalized Western model of women's liberation that celebrates individuality and modernity. Anti-imperialist movements have legitimately decried this form of "feminist" globalizing (albeit often for a continuation of their own agendas). Many women who participate in decolonizing efforts both within and outside the United States have rejected the term "feminism" in favor of "womanist" or have defined their feminism through class or race or other ethnic, religious, or regional struggles.

Yet we know that there is an imperative need to address the concerns of women around the world in the historicized particularity of their relationship to multiple patriarchies as well as to international economic hegemonies. We seek creative ways to move beyond constructed oppositions without ignoring the histories that have informed these conflicts or the valid concerns about power relations that have represented or structured the conflicts up to this point. We need to articulate the relationship of gender to scattered hegemonies such as global economic structures, patriarchal nationalisms, "authentic" forms of tradition, local structures of domination, and legal-juridical oppression on multiple levels.

Transnational feminist practices require this kind of comparative work rather than the relativistic linking of "differences" undertaken by proponents of "global feminism"; that is, to compare multiple, overlapping, and discrete oppressions rather than to construct a theory of hegemonic oppression under a unified category of gender. Kamala Visweswaran's essay in this volume undertakes such work; in examining the conjunction between nationalist discourse and ethnographic writing she raises the problematic of women's positionality as ethnographers and subjects of ethnographies. Both positions work within and against discourses controlled by the geopolitical context in which these particular women live and work. Visweswaran's critique of ethnographic practice enables her to explore the nuances of connection as well as the silences and betrayals in the acquisition of anthropological "information" in feminist contexts.

Feminists must continually question the narratives in which they are embedded, including but not limiting ourselves to the master narratives of mainstream feminism. As Kumkum Sangari and Sudesh Vaid assert:

If feminism is to be different, it must acknowledge the ideological and problematic significance of its own past. Instead of creating yet another grand tradition or a cumulative history of emancipation, neither of which can deal with our present problems, we need to be attentive to how the past enters differently into the consciousness of other historical periods and is further subdivided by a host of other factors including gender, caste, and class.[6] [...]

Part of any feminist self-examination necessitates a rigorous critique of emerging orthodoxies. In debates within the United States, for example, it is important to examine the ways in which race, class, and gender are fast becoming the holy trinity that every feminist feels compelled to address even as this trinity delimits the range of discussion around women's lives. What is often left out of these U.S. focused debates are other complex categories of identity and affiliation that apply to non-U.S. cultures and situations. U.S. feminists often have to be reminded that all peoples of the world are not solely constructed by the trinity of race-sex-class; for that matter, other categories also enter into the issues of subject formation both within and outside the borders of the United States, requiring more nuanced and complex theories of social relations. For example, emerging theories of homosexual formations in various locations demonstrate that the category of sexuality can be multiply constituted in the context of transnational cultures, pointing the way for detailed feminist studies of cultural production and reception.[7]

The question becomes how to link diverse feminisms without requiring either equivalence or a master theory. How to make these links without replicating cultural and economic hegemony? For white, Western feminists or elite women in other world locations, such questions demand an examination of the links between daily life and academic work and an acknowledgment that one's privileges in the world-system are always linked to another woman's oppression or exploitation. As Cynthia Enloe's recent work demonstrates, the old sisterhood model of missionary work, of intervention and salvation, is clearly tied to the older models of center-periphery relations.[8] As these models have become obsolete in the face of proliferating, multiple centers and peripheries, we need new analyses of how gender works in the dynamic of globalization and the countermeasures of new nationalisms, and ethnic and racial fundamentalisms. Feminists can begin to map these scattered hegemonies and link diverse local practices to formulate a transnational set of solidarities. For instance, we need to examine fundamentalisms around the world and seek to understand why Muslim fundamentalism appears in the media today as the primary progenitor of oppressive conditions for women when Christian, Jewish, Hindu, Confucian, and other forms of extreme fundamentalisms exert profound controls over women's lives.

What is the relationship between transnational economies and the intensification of religious fundamentalism? For example, when the United States gave billions to General Zia of Pakistan to fight the Soviets in Afghanistan, the United States propped up a regime that was inimical to women. U.S. feminists need to fight against this kind of aid on their home ground instead of abstractly condemning Islam as the center of patriarchal oppression. Simultaneously, we need to examine how the importance of Christian fundamentalism within the Republican party in the United States affects the lives of millions of women worldwide through funding and development practices that structure reproductive and other politics. Transnational feminist approaches link the impact of such policies on women on public assistance in the United States and women who have little agency in their dealing with U.S.-sponsored clinics and health centers that have been established in the so-called peripheries. The concept of multiple peripheries, therefore, can link directly the domestic politics of a world power such as the United States to its foreign policies. Transnational feminist alliances can work to change these policies only when such congruencies are accounted for and transformed into the basis for multiple, allied, solidarity projects.

In calling for transnational alliances, our purpose is to acknowledge the different forms that feminisms take and the different practices that can be seen as feminist movements. We do not wish to dictate exactly who can stand as a feminist, for as Norma Alarcón argues, such dicta posit a standpoint epistemology that requires the construction of gender differences as the primary categories of analysis to the extent of "working inherently against the interests of non-white women."[9] In arguing against a standpoint epistemology, we are not arguing that this is an era of postfeminism. We believe that many white, bourgeois feminists have announced a postfeminist era precisely because their particular definitions of feminism (which often require universalization) have not been able to withstand critiques from women of color as well as the deconstructions of poststructuralist or postmodern theory. The bases of these two critiques of white, bourgeois feminism are sometimes different and sometimes collaborative, but that is not the issue here. What concerns us is that some feminist responses to postmodern critiques of the subject, of the decentered Self, of Marxist notions of class as applied to gender as a class, have signaled regressive moves. [. . .]

NOTES

1. For critiques of modernity see Caren Kaplan, *Questions of Travels Postmodern Discourses of Displacement* (forthcoming. Duke University Press); Robert Young, *White Mythologist: Writing History and the West* (London: Routledge, 1990); Edward Said, *The World, the Text, and the Critic* (Cambridge: Harvard University Press, 1983); James Clifford, *The Predicament of Culture* (Cambridge: Harvard University Press, 1988); and see essays here by Lydia Liu, Tani Barlow, and Inderpal Grewal.

2. This point has emerged in discussions with Tani Barlow.

3. Arjun Appadurai, "Disjuncture and Difference in the Global Cultural Economy," *Public Culture* 2, no. 2 (Spring 1990): 21.

4. Ibid., 6.

5. See in particular Chandra Mohanty's critique of Robin Morgan's *Sisterhood Is Global: The First Anthology from the International Women's Movement* (Garden City, NY: Anchor Press/Doubleday, 1984), in "Feminist Encounters: Locating the Politics of Experience," *Copyright 1, 'Fin de Siecle 2000'* (1987): 30–44, especially 35–7.

6. Kumkum Sangari and Sudesh Vaid, in the introduction to their edited volume, *Recasting Women: Essays in Indian Colonial History* (New Brunswick, NJ: Rutgers University Press, 1990), 18.

7. See Katie King, "Lesbianism in Multi-National Reception. Global Gay Formations and Local Homosexualities." *Camera Obscura* 28 (1992): 79–99; Lourdes Arguelles and B. Ruby Rich, "Homosexuality, Homophobia, and Revolution: Notes toward an Understanding of the Cuban Lesbian and Gay Male Experience," Part I, *Signs 9*

(1984): 683–99, and Part II, *Signs* 11 (Autumn 1985): 120–36; Ana Maria Alonso and Maria Teresa Koreck, "Silences: 'Hispanics,' AIDS, and Sexual Practices," *differences* 1, no. 1 (Winter 1989): 101–24; and Lourdes Arguelles, *Homosexualities and Transnational Migration* (forthcoming).

8. Enloe, Cynthia *Bananas, Beaches, and Bases: Making Feminist Sense of International Politics* (Berkeley: University of California Press, 1989).

9. Norma Alarcón, "The Theoretical Subject(s) of *This Bridge Called My Back* and Anglo-American Feminism," in *Making Face, Making Soul/ Hariendo Caras: Creative and Critical Perspectives by Women of Color*, ed. Gloria Anzaldúa (San Francisco: Aunt Lute, 1990), 358.

SECTION 5

Migrating Lives and Communities

Introduction to Section V

The articles in this section represent nearly three decades of scholarly development in the study of transnational migration. The selection from Basch, Glick Schiller, and Szanton-Blanc's now classic book, *Nation's Unbound*, opens with three vignettes illustrating how migrants from Haiti, Grenada, and the Philippines who are firmly rooted in the United States, also remain actively involved in their homelands. Their stories also bring to light how political leaders, realizing that many of their citizens will settle permanently abroad, nevertheless grant them long-term membership without residence and engage them in new kinds of state-building processes.

Much scholarship has overlooked these dynamics, Basch and her colleagues argue, because migration is associated with permanent rupture and the assumption that migrants will abandon their homeland customs and lifestyles in exchange for something new. But today "immigrants develop networks, activities, patterns of living, and ideologies that span their home and host society" (p. 262). Transnationalism or "the processes by which migrants forge and sustain multi-stranded social relations that link together their societies of origin and settlement" (p. 263) is inextricably linked to global capitalism and has to be understood within the context of global flows of capital, labor, and power. Transmigrants live in two different cultures at the same time, creating social fields that cross national boundaries. They live in a specific geographic space yet occupy many social, religious, and political spaces simultaneously. They participate in the nation-building processes of two or more nation-states. Their identities and practices are shaped by hegemonic categories from the home and the host land that are integral to nation-building. Unity is achieved "in and through (not despite) differences" (Hall 1997 cited in Basch et al. p. 35).

Many social science concepts, however, obscure these dynamics by conflating physical location, culture, and identity. Transnational processes often go unnoticed and un-analyzed. Terms such as home, host, and visitor capture physical location but not cultural, political, and emotional affinities. We need new analytical tools that bring to light the relationship between culture and power, and the hegemonic discourses and values at play.

Michael Kearney's article also strongly influenced transnational migration studies. Like Basch and her colleagues, he too stresses the ways in which identity and experience are disconnected from space and transcend national boundaries. The excerpts from his article included here highlight the differences between globalization and transnationalism, which he sees as interconnected and overlapping, yet distinct. Whereas globalization is "decentered," and not attached to any particular state, transnationalism is "anchored in and transcends" nation-states. Unlike globalization, transnational processes, however far-reaching, are connected to "the cultural and political projects of nation-states . . .," while processes of globalization are "more abstract, less institutionalized, and less intentional." Both globalization and transnationalism are at odds with the jurisdiction and power of the nation-state and operate "trans-stately." Finally, transnationalism calls attention to the ways in which states, culturally and politically, compete for hegemony and national supremacy. Globalization, in contrast, implies more abstract, less institutionalized and less intentional processes that are outside the orbit of particular nation-states. In other words, globalization is universal and impersonal while the transnational is generally associated with a specific political and ideological project.

Kearney argues that while anthropology, his disciplinary base, has always been characterized by dichotomies—the beginning and end of time, the global and the local, the urban and the rural—capturing contemporary experience requires an analytical shift. To understand globalization we need to adopt a "multidimensional, global" view of space based on less boundary-defined, less nation-defined concepts and more on the idea of "discontinuous and interpenetrated sub-spaces." Such a global lens makes us recognize that production, consumption, communities, politics, and identities are now detached from local places. Transnational migrants move into and create some of these transnational spaces and, by doing so, Kearney hopes they can potentially liberate nationals from the totalizing hegemony exercised by strong states within their borders.

Portes, Guarnizo, and Landolt's contribution represents a second stage of scholarship on transnational migration. Their goal is to bring clarity to what they see as a "highly fragmented" field that has lacked a clear intellectual consensus. To redress this they lay out five guidelines intended to move the field onto firmer empirical ground. They also place transnational migration in historical perspective. Return migration and occasional visits to home communities have always existed. Participants in political diasporas, such as Russian Jews or Armenians, have always been active in homeland politics. But these cases were the exception rather than the rule. They were not driven, like today, by a cultural context in which migration is the norm or where regular, instant communication and ease of travel is so widespread. Thus, Portes et al. (p. 282) conclude, "contemporary transnationalism corresponds to a different period in the evolution of the world economy and to a different set of responses and strategies by people in a condition of disadvantage to its dominant logic."

Levitt and Glick Schiller's piece is part of a third wave of transnational migration scholarship. They propose a social field approach to the study of migration that calls into question neat divisions between the local, national, transnational, and global, and differentiates between *ways of being* and *ways of belonging*. Understanding migration in this way drives home that assimilation and enduring transnational ties are neither incompatible nor binary opposites, but that they are simultaneous processes that influence each other mutually. Rather than expecting newcomers to fully assimilate or to remain entirely focused on their homelands, they pivot back and forth between sending, receiving, and other orientations at different stages of their lives. The rest of this selection explores how our understandings of citizenship, political identity, and the nation-state-building process change when they are enacted in transnational arenas.

CHAPTER 22

"Transnational Projects: A New Perspective" and "Theoretical Premises"

Linda Basch, Nina Glick Schiller, and Christina Szanton Blanc

TRANSNATIONAL PROJECTS: A NEW PERSPECTIVE[1]

The Presidential Palace in Haiti, for decades under the Duvalier regime a location rumored to be the site of terrible tortures and beatings, was eagerly entered in January 1991 by over one hundred visitors from the Haitian diaspora. While many were U.S. citizens, most had been born in Haiti. Some had fled Haiti into exile and struggled to rebuild their lives, while others had grown up abroad and obtained educations, professional careers, and social standing in the United States and Canada. Both men and women, they were a prosperous group, well incorporated into their new societies. But their visit to Haiti was more than a sentimental journey. Their special invitation to the palace to witness and celebrate the inauguration of Father Aristide, Haitians' new and freely elected President, marked them as active participants in efforts to rebuild the Haitian nation-state. This became clear when the newly inaugurated President greeted them as members of *Dizyèm Depatman-an*, "the 10th Department," although the territory of the country of Haiti is divided into nine administrative districts, each called "*Depatman.*" In this pronouncement, which had no legal substance, Aristide was directly articulating what many Haitians had long maintained. No matter where they settle, or what passport they carry, people of Haitian ancestry remain an integral part of Haiti.

* * *

Approximately 200 well-dressed Grenadian immigrants, mostly from urban areas in Grenada and presently employed in white collar jobs in New York, gathered in 1984 in a Grenadian-owned catering hall in Brooklyn to hear the Grenadian Minister of Agriculture and Development. The Minister shared with Grenada's "constituency in New York" his plans for agricultural development in Grenada and encouraged the immigrants to become part of this effort. Addressing the immigrants as nationals of Grenada, even though many were U.S. citizens, the Minister asked the audience to encourage their relatives at home to become engaged in agricultural production, and to convince them that this generally demeaned activity was worthwhile and important. Further, treating the immigrants as national leaders and as people who could wield influence at home and even help develop an entire industry, the Minister implored the immigrants to assist in developing an exotic fruit industry for export. But in asking the immigrants to "do what they could" to introduce Grenadian agricultural goods to the U.S. market, including lobbying U.S. government agencies to obtain approval to import the fruits, the Minister was also addressing the immigrants as ethnics in the United States.

Several of the immigrants in the audience were in a position to provide some assistance with these tasks. Some of the immigrants had recently formed a Caribbean-American Chamber of Commerce, both to assist Caribbean immigrants in establishing businesses in the United States and to market West Indian goods. And some, including the organizers of this meeting, had been in the United States a minimum of ten years and were as involved in the local politics of New York City as they were in the political life of Grenada. Grenada's ambassador to the United Nations, for example, had been a leader in the New York West Indian community for over forty years and had spearheaded support groups to elect mayors of New York City.

* * *

In one of the offices of a company in New Jersey in 1988, an employee at a desk is helping a customer close the box of goods she is shipping "home" to her family in the Philippines and complete the listing of items it contains. A regular flow of such boxes leaves every day from seven to eight major Fillipino shipping companies. Anything—appliances, electronic equipment and the like—can be sent or carried back as long as these goods fit the weight, size and other prescriptions defining a *balikbayan* box; they can be admitted into the Philippines almost tax free.

President Marcos had first used the term "*balikbayan*" (Homecomers) during a major national speech in which he encouraged Filipino migrants overseas to visit their home country and announced new regulations to facilitate their return. Mrs. Aquino extended the *balikbayan* regulations and stated her concern for the numerous silent "heroes and heroines of the Philippines" working overseas. The Filipino returnees could purchase up to $1,000 in duty-free gifts upon entering the Philippines. The Filipino transnational social field, built on family networks and sustained through economic exchanges and gift-giving, has thus been further structured and officially sanctioned by the Philippine state.

* * *

Faced with the long-term and probably permanent settlement abroad of substantial sectors of their populations, the political leaderships of Grenada, St. Vincent, the Philippines, and Haiti, are engaged in a new form of nation-state building. Sometimes through specific public policies, as in the case of the *balikbayan* regulations, but often through the use of symbols, language, and political rituals, migrants and political leaders in the country of origin are engaged in constructing an ideology that envisions migrants as loyal citizens of their ancestral nation-state. This ideology recognizes and encourages the continuing and multiple ties that immigrants maintain with their society of origin. Ignored in this construction, however, is the ongoing incorporation of these immigrants into the society and polity of the country in which they have settled. Yet the significance of transmigrants to their country of origin in many ways rests on the extent of their incorporation into the national economy and political processes of their country of settlement.

Neither the representations nor the practices of these immigrants in relationship to their "home" nation-states are encompassed within the analytical paradigms that predominate in migration studies, focusing as they do on immigrant incorporation within the country of settlement. The time has come for all of us—social scientists and immigrants—to rethink our conceptions of the migration process, immigrant incorporation, and identity.

1. STATEMENT OF THE PROBLEM

The word "immigrant" evokes images of permanent rupture, of the abandonment of old patterns of life and the painful learning of a new culture and often a new language (Handlin 1973). The popular image of immigrant is one of people who have come to stay, having uprooted themselves from their old society in order to make for themselves a new home and adopt a new country to which they will pledge allegiance. Migrants, on the other hand, are conceived of as transients who have come only to work; their stay is temporary and eventually they will return home or move on. Yet it has become increasingly obvious that our present conceptions of "immigrant" and "migrant," anchored in the circumstances of earlier historic moments, no longer suffice. Today, immigrants develop networks, activities, patterns of living, and ideologies that span their home and the host society.

At first glance the problem seems to be a straightforward one of revamping our vocabulary to come to terms with this new kind of migrant flow. Consequently, increasing numbers of social scientists have begun calling the emergent migration process in which people live lives stretched across national borders "transnational" (Georges 1990; Kearney 1991; Sutton 1992), but the term is often used loosely and without specificity. Frequently the phenomenon of transnationalism is thought to be the outcome of transformations in the technology of communication and transportation, a product of accessible air travel and telecommunications (Wakeman 1988). Language is, however, part and parcel of the manner in which we understand and experience the world; the need to change or extend our language is driven by broader political and economic transformations (Asad 1986).

To come to terms adequately with the experience and consciousness of this new immigrant population, we believe that new conceptualizations and a new analytical framework are in order. The development of a transnational analytical framework is the task of this book. [. . .]

B. Definitions

We define "transnationalism" as the processes by which immigrants forge and sustain multi-stranded social relations that link together their societies of origin and settlement. We call these processes transnationalism to emphasize that many immigrants today build social fields that cross geographic, cultural, and political borders. Immigrants who develop and maintain multiple relationships—familial, economic, social, organizational, religious, and political—that span borders we call "transmigrants." An essential element of transnationalism is the multiplicity of involvements that transmigrants' sustain in both home and host societies. We are still groping for a language to describe these social locations. Transmigrants use the term "home" for their society of origin, even when they clearly have also made a home in their country of settlement. The migration literature describes the country of settlement as the "host," but such a term, though compact and convenient, carries the often unwarranted connotations that the immigrant is both "welcome" and a "visitor." Transmigrants take actions, make decisions, and develop subjectivities and identities embedded in networks of relationships that connect them simultaneously to two or more nation-states.

Our definition of transnationalism allows us to analyze the "lived" and fluid experiences of individuals who act in ways that challenge our previous conflation of geographic space and social identity. This definition also will enable us to see the ways transmigrants are transformed by their trans-national practices and how these practices affect the nation-states of the transmigrants' origin and settlement.

While we speak a great deal in this book about transnationalism as processes and of the construction of identities that reflect transnational experience, individuals, communities, or states rarely identify themselves as transnational. It is only in contemporary fiction (see Anzaldua 1987; Ghosh 1988; Marshall 1991; Rushdie 1988) that this state of "in-betweenness," has been fully voiced. Living in a world in which discourses about identity continue to be framed in terms of loyalty to nations and nation-states, most transmigrants have neither fully conceptualized nor articulated a form of transnational identity. Nation-states, as "hegemonic representations of . . . spatial identity," continue to be primary in "an increasingly postmodern world" (Gupta 1992:75).

Although the current period of capitalism is marked by new diasporas, identities of migrant populations continue to be rooted in nation-states. As part of this "reinscription of space" (Gupta 1992:63), both the political leaderships of sending nations and immigrants from these nations are coming to perceive these states as "deterritorialized." In contrast to the past, when nation-states were defined in terms of a people sharing a common culture within a bounded territory, this new conception of nation-state includes as citizens those who live physically dispersed within the boundaries of many other states, but who remain socially, politically, culturally, and often economically part of the nation-state of their ancestors. In the case of the Haitian "Tenth Department," the Grenadian "constituency" in New York, and the Filipino *balikbayan*, transnational ties are taken as evidence that migrants continue to be members of the state from which they originated.

Such reconstructions of nation-states and national loyalties are discrepant with the complexity of the lives of transmigrants. As transmigrants operate in the national arena of both their country of origin and country (or countries) of settlement, they develop new spheres of experience and new fields of social relations. In their daily activities transmigrants connect nation-states and then live in a world shaped by the interconnections that they themselves have forged. There is currently a gap between the daily practices of transmigrants and the ways both transmigrants and academics represent these practices. [. . .]

THEORETICAL PREMISES[1]

I. Our four premises:

1. Transnational migration is inextricably linked to the changing conditions of global capitalism and must be analyzed within the context of global relations between capital and labor.
2. Transnationalism is a process by which migrants, through their daily life activities and social, economic, and political relations, create social fields that cross national boundaries.
3. Bounded social science concepts that conflate physical location, culture, and identity can limit the ability of researchers first to perceive and then to analyze the phenomenon of transnationalism.
4. By living their lives across borders, transmigrants find themselves confronted with and engaged in the nation building processes of two or more nation-states. Their identities and practices are configured by hegemonic categories, such as race and ethnicity, that are deeply embedded in the nation building processes of these nation-states.

II. A FRAMEWORK FOR THE STUDY OF TRANSNATIONALISM

A. Premise One: Transnational Migration is Inextricably Linked to the Changing Conditions of Global Capitalism and Must be Analyzed Within the Context of Global Relations Between Capital and Labor

Transnational migration is actuated by the relationship between classes that is at the core of capitalism as a mode of production. We understand capitalism to be a historically constituted mode of production centered around the relationship between a capitalist class that possesses the means of production and a working class that produces surplus value or makes possible such production of value (Mohun 1983; Wolf 1982). Class is defined as a set of people whose positioning within the process of production is similar. Because class is about positioning, class is a description of social relationships. As a mode of production, capitalism also includes an array of other classes ranging from peasants, who own small bits of land, to professionals, who control some special knowledge or skill. While the capitalist class is increasingly global in the manner in which it incorporates all areas of the world into a single system of production, political processes that maintain the inequities between classes remain structured within separate states. The exercise of state power is normally central to the maintenance of class relations, since control of the productive forces is ultimately protected by force, and force is generally the province of the state. This summary statement is not meant to encompass the complexity of class relations and capitalist processes, but rather to serve as a grounding for our discussion of why the current historical conjuncture is a moment of widespread transnational migration. Inevitably issues of class will be interwoven into all of our analyses.

Some observers have pointed to advances in technology as a primary explanation for the fact that current immigrants seem to maintain much more intimate and enduring relations with their home countries than did earlier generations (Wakeman 1988). Jet planes, coupled with low cost fares, make it possible almost literally to have a foot in two countries, while telephones, fax machines, money transfer companies, and rapid freight shipments facilitate the movement of material goods and ideas. Today's electronic technology lends a sense of immediacy to the social relations of people who are geographically distant. According to this logic, the explanation for transnationalism is to be found within the elision of time and space made possible by modern technology.

The presence of technological innovations, however, explains neither why immigrants invest so much time, energy, and resources in maintaining home ties, nor why transportation and communication systems bridge distances between particular geographic locations and not others. Technological explanations for the emergence of more transnational patterns of migration prove to be incomplete when divorced from an analysis of the social relations of production.[2] Rather it is the current moment of capitalism as a global mode of production that has necessitated the maintenance of family ties and political allegiances among persons spread across the globe.

It is also possible to argue that transnationalism is not a new phenomenon and that although recent technological advances have facilitated communication, previous waves of migrants to countries such as the United States also maintained home ties. Certainly, a reading of immigrant history that argues that current transnational migration represents a continuity with past immigrant behavior would be resonant with recent efforts to build a global history. Wolf argues, for example, that the circulation of labor has been part of the entire expansion of capitalism (Wolf 1982). Both a barely remembered historiography and a recent reexamination of U.S. ethnic history provide evidence that the image of the "uprooted" may be as questionable a portrait of many earlier immigrant populations as it is of recent migrants (Takaki 1989). Many European immigrants of the 19th and early 20th century remained in communication with their home countries and participated in those countries' nationalist movements (Vassady 1982; Portes and Rumbaut 1990). Czech and Slovak immigrants in the United States provided propaganda and funds to wrest a Czechoslovakian state out of the Austro-Hungarian empire (Wittke 1940). Irish immigrants in the United States have been noted for their continuing

involvement with Ireland, but many other immigrants, including those from Italy, Germany, and central Europe have also maintained links to their countries of origin (Glazer 1954; di Leonardi 1984; Portes and Bach 1985).[3] Latin American immigrants also engaged in nation building movements from the shores of the United States. It was from the United States, for example that Cubans organized the struggle against Spain (Portes and Rumbaut 1990).

We believe, however, that current transnationalism marks a new type of migrant experience, reflecting an increased and more pervasive global penetration of capital. We also argue that only a global perspective of migration processes will enable social scientists to understand the similarities and differences between past and present migrations. [. . .]

B. Premise Two: Transnationalism is a Process by which Migrants, through Their Daily Life Activities and Social, Economic, and Political Relations, Create Social Fields that Cross National Boundaries [. . .]

If someone sends a barbecue grill home to Port-au-Prince, the grill does not stand in and of itself as an item of material culture reflecting and producing hybrid cultural constructions. The grill is a statement about social success in the United States and an effort to build and advance social position in Haiti. The grill will be used in a fashionable round of party going in which status is defined and redeemed in the context of consumption. When someone from a small town in St. Vincent, Grenada, or the Philippines who now lives in New York sends home a cassette player, how are we to interpret this flow? The player can be used along with imported cassettes to bring the latest musical forms and themes from around the world into these rural countrysides. But on this same cassette those sitting on a mountain side in Grenada, in a rural village in the Philippines, or on a family veranda in St. Vincent send messages, warnings, or information about kith and kin "at home" that shape and influence how people behave and what they think in New

York, Miami, or Los Angeles. Connections are continued, and a wider system of social relations is maintained and reinforced. [. . .]

To understand what "social relations" mean in the flow and fabric of daily life we must explore how linkages are maintained, renewed, and reconstituted in the context of families, of institutions, of political organizations, of political structures, and of economic investments, business, and finance. The case studies in the next section of the book will explore in four different settings the manner in which these connections have been forged, elaborated, and maintained over time. Each case study will also focus on the historical global context out of which these linkages arise as well as on the particular manifestations in that specific nation-state.

Our focus is on migrants as builders of social fields (see Basch, Wiltshire, Wiltshire, and Toney 1990) that provide the staging grounds for the construction and reappropriation of practices and identities. A handful of studies have examined transnational migration from this perspective. In 1975, in describing the migration of Barbadian immigrants, Sutton and Makiesky-Barrow (1992:114 [1975]) spoke of a "transnational sociocultural and political system." They linked such a system to "the bidirectional flow of ideas such that political events at home (e.g., independence) had an impact on the migrant communities abroad while migrant experiences were relayed in the opposite direction" (1992 [1975]:113). Rouse (1991:15) has used the term 'transnational migrant circuits' to describe dense social networks that link residents of a small town in Mexico with family and friends who have settled in Redwood City, California. "Through the continuous circulation of people, money, goods and information, the various settlements have become so closely woven together that, in an important sense they have come to constitute a single community spread across a variety of sites" (1991:15). Kearney notes that "transnational labor migration has now become a major structural feature of communities which have themselves become truly transnational" (1991:53).

Noting the constant penetration of bor-

ders, Kearney suggests that we have entered the age of transnationalism, a post-national age in which "members of transnational communities . . . escape the power of the nation-state to inform their sense of collective identity" (1991:59). In contrast, we think that the current period, in which the construct of the deterritorialized nation-state is being forcefully articulated, can best be conceived as the moment of a new nationalism. While transmigrants cannot be contained or restrained by national boundaries, the world is still very much divided politically into nation-states that are unequal in their power and that serve differentially as base areas of international capital.

C. Premise Three: Bounded Social Science Concepts such as 'Ethnic Group,' 'Race,' and 'Nation' Can Limit the Ability of Researchers First to Perceive and then to Analyze the Phenomenon of Transnationalism

Previous to the development of a concept of transnationalism, anthropologists had developed a rather large body of literature in anthropology to describe how people move between various social locations.[4] Descriptions of the movement of labor—often in rich detail—in which ties have been maintained in two settings can be found in the literature of both internal and international migration. This is not to say that there are no differences between internal and international migration. The use of political borders to categorize migrants as "guests," temporary or illegal, does shape migrant behavior and consciousness as well as influence the demand for such labor (Sassen-Koob 1981). However, in many ways these seemingly different movements of people can be seen as similar responses to worldwide deployments of capital and labor. What was lacking was a way to conceptualize and emphasize the interconnectedness that enabled migrants to remain actors in several disparate locations. [. . .]

Until recently, much of this literature has portrayed the maintenance of ongoing linkages and the following of social practices of both rural and urban settings as a temporary first phase of adjustment to industrialization or urbanization. "The continuing importance of kinship ties, customary ritual activities, 'peasant' modes of production in the city" (Roberts 1976:99) were seen as transitional, and therefore the implications of the continuing linkages between home and area of settlement were not fully explored. Even when long-term patterns of migration and continuing linkages with home societies were documented, the implications of these patterns for immigration dynamics and identity formation were not analyzed (Basch 1982). Caribbean migrants, for example, were described as belonging to "remittance societies" in which generations of migrants spent long periods away from home, supporting their families and often family landholdings or small enterprises with the money they sent home (Rubenstein 1983; Thomas-Hope 1985; Wood and McCoy 1985). The Caribbean experience was seen as a special case rather than as a growing global pattern that challenged our conceptualizations of migration and "the immigrant."

Yet studies of the "new immigrants" of the post-World War II era were replete with descriptions of the propensity of the newcomers to plant firm roots in their new world while maintaining vital ties to the old. In 1971 Fitzpatrick, noting the circulation of Puerto Ricans between their island and mainland homes, suggested that they are best understood as commuters rather than migrants (1971).[5] Richardson, writing about the seemingly circular movements of Caribbean migrants, pointed to the existence of this phenomenon elsewhere as well. He reported that "students of the movements of Pacific islanders have found human mobility there so routine that they now employ the term circulation rather than migration" (1983:176). Georges (1990) documented the vital economic links between Dominican migration and a small Dominican town. Pessar (1988) used the title *When Borders Don't Divide* for a volume of articles on labor migration and refugee movements in the Americas. And in his book *Double Passage*, Gmelch (1992) describes Barbadian immigrants in England and the United States who sustained ties with Barbados that led to their eventual return. [. . .]

The inability to conceptualize transnationalism fully reflects the limitations of the conceptual tool kit that all of us have been using. In the face of a crisis in conceptualization, some have reconfigured the entire ethnographic project (Tyler 1986), while others speak of a postmodern world in which the neat social fabric of bygone times has unraveled into the current *bricolage* of cultures and identities. Appadurai, for example, has argued that there is a need to reconceptualize the "landscapes of group identity," a need that flows from the current world conjuncture in which "groups are no longer tightly territorialized, spatially bounded, historically unselfconscious, or culturally homogeneous" (1991:191). Clifford reports that " 'cultural' difference is no longer a stable, exotic otherness; self-other relations are matters of power and rhetoric rather than of essence. A whole structure of expectations about authenticity in culture and art is thrown in doubt" (1988:14).

However, the epistemological problem is more fundamental. Bounded concepts of culture, whether signaled by the rubric of tribe, ethnic group, race, or nation, are social constructions. They are reflective not of the stable boundaries of cultural difference but of relations of culture and power. Moreover, while at any one time, culturally constructed boundaries—be they those of nations, ethnicities, or races—may seem fixed, timeless, or primordial, dynamic processes of reformulation underlie the apparent fixity. The current conflations of time and space brought about by global communications and transnational social relations only serve to highlight more deep-seated contradictions in the way in which we think about culture and society (Wolf 1988).

The people of the world have long been interconnected, populations often have been mobile, and their identities have long been fluid, multiple, and contextualized. It is possible to argue that since the beginning of state societies "the world of humankind constitutes a manifold, a totality of interconnected process" (Fried 1975:3), with identities of differentiation constructed by dominant powers or in resistance to them. Certainly since the expansion of Europe, the history of the people of the world has been tightly interwoven (Wolf 1982; Worsley 1984). [. . .]

A global perspective on history, as well as the contingencies of the current historical conjuncture, challenge us to move beyond bounded visions of culture and society. However, we are often confined by our analytical tool kit of concepts like nation, ethnic group, and tribe that divide the world into autonomous, geographically rooted, and culturally distinct units (Van Binsbergen 1981). These units have been treated as bounded entities, endowed with given, "natural," and "group-specific" properties.

To develop a perspective that emphasizes the constructed nature of bounded units is not to deny the significance of boundaries once they are constructed. Whether or not they share unspoken lifeways or distinctive and celebrated customs, once people find themselves conceptualized and come to conceptualize themselves as bound together with a common situation or identity, distinctiveness does indeed arise. Boundaries, whether legally created borders, as in the case of nation-states (Sahlins 1989), or socially forged created boundaries, as in instances of group ethnicities (Keesing 1989; Roosens 1989), once conceptualized, are given meaning and sentiment by those who reside within them. They acquire a life of their own. Conceived as culturally distinct, these social constructions persist and therefore shape and influence people's behavior and daily practices (Friedman 1992). They are also available to be reformulated and/or politicized according to specific politically and economically generated circumstances.

In order to problematize these categories that are "implicated in the texture of everyday life and . . . thoroughly presupposed in academic discourse on 'culture' and 'society' " (Gupta 1992:63), we need a global perspective and a sense of the processual and historical.

On the one side, we need to investigate processes of place making, of how feelings of belonging to an imagined community bind identity to spatial location such that differences between communities and places are cre-

ated. At the same time, we also need to situate those processes within a systematic development that reinscribes and reterritorializes space in the global political economy (Gupta 1992:62).

A major task of this book is to delineate the processes through which transmigrants, living lives stretched across borders, reterritorialize their practices as well as their identities. We also look for moments, locations, and cultural practices in which such reinscriptions become undone or fail to encapsulate experience.

D. Premise Four: By Living their Lives Across Borders, Transmigrants Find themselves Confronted with and Engaged in the Nation Building Processes of Two or More Nation-States. Their Identities and Practices Are Configured by Hegemonic Categories Such As Race and Ethnicity that are Deeply Embedded in the Nation Building Processes of these Nation-States

The paradox of the current world conjuncture is the increased production of cultural and political boundaries at the very time when the world has become tightly bound together in a single economic system with instantaneous communication between different sectors of the globe. In order to disentangle these contradictory trends, it is necessary to place the construction of cultural demarcations and political boundaries being erected between groupings of people within the context of contention for political power and control of productive resources, including labor power.

However, it has been difficult for social science to acknowledge that there is a relationship between the growth of capitalism, nation building processes, and the categories of race and ethnicity. The fact that discussions of race, ethnicity, and nation have been separate areas of social science discourse both reflects the lack of a critical perspective on the relationship between race, culture, and power and contributes to a failure to develop such a perspective. Part of the task of this book is to understand the manner in which the conceptual categories of race, ethnicity, and nation are hegemonic constructions and are all part of the historical exercise of state power and domination. With such a perspective, we can see the manner in which the emerging transnational populations are shaped by and participate in the shaping of such hegemonic constructions.

1. Nation Building and Constructions of Race and Ethnicity

Recent scholarship has made it clear that the legitimacy of political units defined as nation-states to exercise power over territory was established in the 18th and 19th century by invoking and inventing a historical past shared by a unified people (Anderson 1991; Gellner 1983; Herzfeld 1985; Kapferer 1988; Hobsbawm 1990). Classes and elite strata, striving to maintain or contend for state power constructed memories of a shared past and used this historical narrative to authenticate and validate a commonality of purpose and national interests. At first, the study of "nation" as a cultural construction sparked a debate over whether nations were built on primordial cultural roots (A. Smith 1981) or "invented traditions" (Hobsbawm and Ranger 1983). Increasingly we have come to understand that nation-states, whether they were "imagined" (Anderson 1991) in Western Europe, in postcolonial settings or as part of socialist projects, were not totally new visions. Rather they have been built out of historically grounded culture, including the religious and philosophical concepts that have been pervasive in particular regions (Herzfeld 1985; Kapferer 1988; Sahlins 1989; Verdery 1991).

While documenting the novelty and recent vintage of the concept of the nation-state and linking it to the rise of capitalism, the new scholarship has given us few insights into the manner in which nation building processes simultaneously include and exclude. Not adequately addressed by present approaches to nationalism are the multiple voices that contend and are differentially incorporated within the hegemonic processes of nation-states. Still to be explained are the processes by which national identity and nationalism spring up in opposition to state power. That

such explanations are overdue became obvious when the resurgence of nationalism in various sectors of the globe in the 1990s, including its dramatic and often violent manifestations in Eastern Europe and former Soviet Asia, took social scientists by surprise. [. . .]

In this book our focus of discussion will be on the way in which race is constructed within the nation building processes of the United States and the postcolonial states of St. Vincent, Grenada, Haiti, and the Philippines. Forged as they were out of a fabric of European conquest and movements of resistance and empowerment, postcolonial nation-states carry within them their own readings of race. Their nation building processes both reject and reinscribe the global meanings of race developed in the course of European conquest and colonialism. In the succeeding chapters, dominant classes within St. Vincent, Grenada, Haiti, and the Philippines will be shown to have shaped their hegemonic constructs of nation in response to and cognizant of the global racial constructions according to which their populations were defined as racially different and hence inferior and without history or culture.

Those who have written about the international division of labor tend to focus on the global economic and military dominance of core capitalist states (Wallerstein 1979; Portes 1978; Portes and Walton 1981; Sassen 1988). It is important to note that this dominance is accompanied by and legitimated by cultural influences that are ever more pervasive, as cinema, television, and other forms of media penetrate the post-colonial world. Within this cultural penetration, furthermore, racial categorizations continue to be used to differentiate and justify domination. Subordinated nation-states continue to be categorized in racial terms, so that civilization continues to be implicitly white. [. . .]

CONCLUSIONS

As this book will demonstrate, transmigrants of all classes live a complex existence that forces them to confront, draw upon, and rework different hegemonic constructions of identity developed in their home or new nation-state(s). Transmigrants simultaneously participate in nation building in their home country and in processes of nation building in the United States that are ordinarily subsumed under the rubric "ethnicity." At the same time, the racial structuring in the United States and in post-colonial countries and migrants' experiences of the linkage between race and nation in these various polities shape the nature of their participation in these nation-building processes. Faced with these processes of differentiation and subordination, Caribbean and Filipino immigrants have embraced the nation building processes of newly deterritorialized nation-states newly imagined by their political leadership.

Within the situations of political and economic domination and racial and cultural differentiation, building transnational social fields and imagining a deterritorialized nation-state can be seen as a form of resistance on the part of Caribbean and Filipino immigrants. However, the issue of resistance is a complex one that must be contextualized within the always partial and unfinished construction of identities shaped by the pressures of national hegemonies. Subordinated populations may internalize many of the meanings and representations that pervade their daily surroundings, but that internalization remains partial and incomplete. Meanings are often subverted and there is always, at the level of daily practice, some opening for innovation. Moreover, when hegemonic constructions are more fully internalized, that internalization provides the very basis for the reutilization of meanings in counter-hegemonic arguments against subordination.

In other words, there are many levels of resistance, beginning with the construction of individual identities and personal behaviors, but extending to group responses, organizational initiatives, and counter-hegemonic and revolutionary movements. In the following chapters we will make reference to many of these levels as we discuss transmigrant identities, practices, and struggles across national borders. In our conclusion we will then focus on two hegemonic constructs, race and deterritorialization, by which

transmigrants resist and reappropriate nation building processes even as they accommodate to situations of unequal power.

NOTES

Transnational Projects: A New Perspective

1. Portions of an earlier draft of this chapter appeared in Glick Schiller, Basch, and Blanc-Szanton (1992a, 1992b).

Theoretical Premises

1. Portions of the initial sections of this chapter appear in Glick-Schiller, Basch, and Blanc-Szanton (1992a, 1992b). Portions of the sections on race and nation were presented by Glick-Schiller (1992). The relationship of hegemonic categories and ethnic identities was discussed in Blanc Szanton (1982, 1985). The concept of transnational social field was set forth in Basch, Wiltshire, Wiltshire, and Toney (1990).

2. See Noble (1977) on technological reductionism.

3. Estimating that two-fifths of the immigrants were returning to Europe, the U.S. Immigration Commission Report of 1911 speculated that many among the returnees actually made multiple trips (cited in Portes and Bach 1985:31).

4. Appadurai has noted that since World War II, a concept of place has pervaded the construction of anthropological theory (1986).

5. Chaney suggests that "We must study the strategies involved in such migration variations as 'commuting,' 'trial,' migration, and 'visiting,' and what implications these apparently wide practices have for the receiving societies" (1979:210).

References

Anderson, Benedict (1991) Imagined Communities: Reflections on the Origins and Spread of Nationalism. Revised ed. London: Verso.

Anzaldua, Gloria (1987) Borderlands, La Frontera: The New Mestiza. San Francisco: Spinsters/Aunt Lute.

Appadurai, Arjun (1986) Theory in Anthropology: Center and Periphery. Comparative Studies in Society and History 28(1):356–361.

—— (1991) Global Ethnospaces: Notes and Queries for a Transnational Anthropology. In Recapturing Anthropology. R. Fox, ed., pp. 191–210. Santa Fe, NM: School of American Research Press.

Asad Talal (1986) The Concept of Cultural Translation in British Social Anthropology. In Writing Culture: The Poetics and Politics of Ethnography. James Clifford and George Marcus, eds., pp. 141–164. Berkeley: University of California Press.

Basch, Linda (1982) Population Movements Within the English-Speaking Caribbean: An Overview. New York: United Nations Institute for Training and Research.

Basch, Linda, Rosina Wiltshire, Winston Wiltshire, and Joyce Toney (1990) Caribbean Regional and International Migration: Transnational Dimensions. Ottawa, Canada: International Development Research Centre.

Blanc-Szanton, Cristina (1982) People in Movement: Mobility and Leadership in a Central Thai Town. PhD dissertation. Department of Anthropology, Columbia University.

—— (1985) Ethnic Identities and Aspects of Class in Contemporary Central Thailand. Paper presented at Symposium on Changing Identities of the Southeast Asian Chinese since World War II. Australia National University, Canberra.

Chaney, Elsa (1979) The World Economy and Contemporary Migration. International Migration Review 13:204–212.

Clifford, James (1988) The Predicament of Culture: Twentieth-Century Ethnography, Literature, and Art. Cambridge, MA: Harvard University Press.

di Leonardo, Michaela (1984) The Varieties of Ethnic Experience: Kinship, Class, and Gender among California Italian-Americans. Ithaca, NY: Cornell University Press.

Fitzpatrick, Joseph P. (1971) Puerto Rican Americans: The Meaning of Migration to the Mainland. 2nd ed. Englewood Cliffs, NJ: Prentice-Hall.

Fried, Morton (1975) The Notion of Tribe. Menlo Park, CA: Cummings Publications.

Friedman, Jonathan (1992) Myth, History, and Political Identity. Cultural Anthropology 7(2):194–210.

Gellner, Ernest (1983) Nations and Nationalism. Ithaca, NY: Cornell University Press.

Georges, Eugenia (1990) The Making of a Transnational Community: Migration, Development, and Cultural Change in the Dominican Republic. New York: Columbia University Press.

Ghosh, Amitav (1988) The Shadow Lines. New York: Viking Press.

Glazer, Nathan (1954) Ethnic Groups in America. In Freedom and Control in Modern Society. Morroe Berger, Theodore Abel, and Charles H. Page, eds., pp. 158–173. New York: Van Nostrand.

Glick Schiller, Nina (1992) The Implications of Haitian Transnationalism for U.S. Haitian Relations: Contradictions of the Deterritorialized Nation State. Paper delivered at the Meetings of the Haitian Studies Association, Boston.

Glick Schiller, Nina, Linda Basch, and Cristina Szanton Blanc (1992a) Towards a Definition of Transnationalism: Introductory Remarks and Research Questions. In Towards a Transnational Perspective on Migration: Race, Class, Ethnicity and Nationalism Reconsidered. N. Glick Schiller, L. Basch, and C. Szanton-Blanc, eds., pp. ix–xiv. New York: New York Academy of Sciences.

Glick Schiller, Nina, Linda Basch, and Cristina Szanton Blanc (1992b) Transnationalism: A New Analytic Framework for Understanding Migration. In Towards a Transnational Perspective on Migration: Race, Class, Ethnicity and Nationalism Reconsidered. N. Glick Schiller, L. Basch, and C. Szanton-Blanc,

eds., pp. 1–24. New York: New York Academy of Sciences.

Gmelch, George (1992) Double Passage: The Lives of Caribbean Immigrants Abroad and Back Home. Ann Arbor: University of Michigan Press.

Gupta, Akhil, and James Ferguson (1992) Beyond "Culture": Space, Identity, and the Politics of Difference. Cultural Anthropology 7(1):6–23.

Handlin, Oscar (1973) [1951] The Uprooted. 2nd ed. Boston: Little, Brown.

Herzfeld, Michael (1985) The Poetics of Manhood: Contest and Identity in a Cretan Mountain Village. Princeton: Princeton University Press.

Hobsbawm, Eric J. (1990) Nations and Nationalism since 1780: Programme, Myth and Reality. New York: Cambridge University Press.

Hobsbawm, Eric J., and Terence O. Ranger (1983) The Invention of Tradition. Cambridge, MA: Cambridge University Press.

Kapferer, Bruce (1988) Legends of People, Mythos of State: Violence, Intolerance, and Political Culture in Sri Lanka and Australia. Washington, DC: Smithsonian Institution Press.

Kearney, Michael (1991) Borders and Boundaries of the State and Self at the End of Empire. Journal of Historical Sociology 4(1):52–74.

Keesing, Roger (1989) Creating the Past: Custom and Identity in the Contemporary Pacific. Contemporary Pacific 1(1–2):19–42.

Marshall, Paule (1991) Daughters. New York: Atheneum.

Mohun, Simon (1983) Capital. In A Dictionary of Marxist Thought. Tom Bottomore, ed., pp. 60–67. Cambridge, MA: Basil Blackwell.

Noble, David (1977) America by Design: Science, Technology and the Rise of Corporate Capitalism. New York: Alfred A. Knopf.

Pessar, Patricia (Ed.) (1988) When Borders Don't Divide: Labor Migration and Refugee Movements in the Americas. Staten Island, NY: Center for Migration Studies.

Portes, Alejandro (1978) Migration and Underdevelopment. Politics and Society 8(1):1–48.

Portes, Alejandro, and Robert Bach (1985) Latin Journey: Cuban and Mexican Immigrants in the United States. Berkeley: University of California Press.

Portes, Alejandro, and Ruben Rumbaut (1990) Immigrant America, A Portrait. Berkeley: University of California Press.

Portes, Alejandro, and John Walton (1981) Labor, Class, and the International System. New York: Academic Press.

Richardson, Bonham (1983) Caribbean Migrants: Environment and Survival on St. Kitts and Nevis. Knoxville: University of Tennessee Press.

Roberts, Bryan (1976) The Provincial Urban System and the Process of Dependency. In Current Perspectives in Latin American Research. A. Portes and H. Browning, eds. pp. 99–131. Austin, Texas: Institute of Latin American Studies.

Roosens, Eugeen (1989) Creating Ethnicity: The Process

of Ethnogenesis. Newbury Park, CA: Sage Publications.

Rouse, Roger (1991) Mexican Migration and the Social Space of Postmodernism, Diaspora 1:8–23.

Rubenstein, Hymie (1983) Remittances and Rural Underdevelopment in the English Speaking Caribbean. Human Organization 42(4):306.

Rushdie, Salman (1988) The Satanic Verses. New York: Viking.

Sahlins, Peter (1989) Boundaries: The Making of France and Spain in the Pyrenees. Berkeley: University of California.

Sassen, Saskia (1988) The Mobility of Labor and Capital: A Study in International Investment and Labor Flow. New York: Cambridge University Press.

Sassen-Koob, Saskia (1981) Towards a Conceptualization of Immigrant Labor. Social Problems 29(1):-65–86.

Smith, Anthony (1981) The Ethnic Revival in the Modern World. Cambridge, MA: Cambridge University Press.

Sutton, Constance (1992) Introduction. *In* Caribbean Immigrants in New York, Revised ed. C. Sutton and E. Chaney, eds., pp. 15–29. New York: Center for Migration Studies.

Sutton, Constance, and Susan Makiesky-Barrow (1992) [1975] Migration and West Indian Racial and Ethnic Consciousness. *In* Caribbean Life in New York City: Sociocultural Dimensions New York, Revised ed. C. Sutton and E. Chaney, eds., pp. 86–107. New York: Center for Migration.

Takaki, Ronald (1989) Strangers from a Different Shore: A History of Asian Americans. New York: Penguin Books.

Thomas-Hope, Elizabeth M. (1985) Return Migration and Its Implications for Caribbean Development: The Unexplored Connection. *In* Migration and Development in the Caribbean: The Unexplored Connection. Robert Pastor, ed. Boulder, CO: Westview.

Tyler, Stephen (1986) Post Modern Ethnography: From Document of the Occult to Occult Document. *In* Writing Culture: The Poetics and Politics of Ethnography. J. Clifford and G. Marcus, eds., pp. 122–140. Berkeley: University of California Press.

Van Binsbergen, Wim (1981) The Unit of Study and the Interpretation of Ethnicity. Journal of South African Studies 8(1):51–81.

Vassady, Bella (1982) 'The Homeland Cause' as a Stimulant to Ethnic Unity: 'The Hungarian American Response to Karolyi's 1914 Tour. Journal of American Ethnic History 2(1):39–64.

Verdery, Katherine (1991) National Ideology under Socialism: Identities and Cultural Politics in Ceausescu's Romania. Berkeley: University of California Press.

Wakeman Jr., Frederic (1988) Transnational and Comparative Research. Items 42(4):85–88.

Wallerstein, Immanuel (1979) The Capitalist World Economy. Cambridge, MA: Cambridge University Press.

Wittke, Carl (1940) We Who Built America: The Saga of the Immigrant. New York: Prentice Hall.

Wolf, Eric (1982) Europe and the People Without History. Berkeley: University of California Press.

Wolf, Eric (1988) Inventing Society. American Ethnologist 15:752.

Wood, Charles, and Terrance McCoy (1985) Migration, Remittances and Development: A Study of Caribbean Cane Cutters in Florida. International Migration Review 19(9):251–277.

Worsley, Peter (1984) The Three Worlds. Chicago: University of Chicago Press.

CHAPTER 23

The Local and the Global: The Anthropology of Globalization and Transnationalism

Michael Kearney

[. . .]

The land surfaces of the earth are mostly divided into national territories. Globalization as used herein refers to social, economic, cultural, and demographic processes that take place within nations but also transcend them, such that attention limited to local processes, identities, and units of analysis yields incomplete understanding of the local (1:11–12). In other words, we are dealing with "the intensification of world-wide social relations which link distant localities in such a way that local happenings are shaped by events occurring many miles away and vice versa" (33:64). Furthermore, implicit in this idea is the assumption that globalization is deepening. Given cultural anthropology's commitment to study of local communities, globalization has implications for its theory and methods. Also, given the national character of anthropology, centered as it is in the so-called Western nations, globalization entails certain displacements of the production of anthropological knowledge from its historic national institutional and cultural contexts to other sites. One is tempted to say such displacement is from center to periphery, but as discussed below, globalization implies a decay of that distinction.

Transnationalism overlaps globalization but typically has a more limited purview. Whereas global processes are largely decentered from specific national territories and take place in a global space, transnational processes are anchored in and transcend one or more nation-states (1:5–10; 64). Thus transnational is the term of choice when referring, for example, to migration of nationals across the borders of one or of more nations (4–6, 10). Similarly, transnational corporations operate worldwide but are centered in one home nation.

The "nation" in transnational usually refers to the territorial, social, and cultural aspects of the nations concerned. Implicit in anthropological studies of transnational processes is the work of the "state," as for example the guardian of national borders, the arbiter of citizenship, and the entity responsible for foreign policy. Transnational and global phenomena conflict with the jurisdiction and power of states and are what might be called "trans-statal." This term has not gained common usage, but the conditions suggesting it are reflected in the works of those who write about globalization and transnationalism.

Transnational calls attention to the cultural and political projects of nation-states as they vie for hegemony in relations with other nation-states, with their citizens and "aliens." This cultural-political dimension of transnationalism is signaled by its resonance with nationalism as a cultural and political project, whereas globalization implies more abstract, less institutionalized, and less intentional processes occurring without reference to nations, e.g. technological developments in mass international communication and the impersonal dynamics of global popular and mass culture, global finance, and the world environment. This distinction between the universal and impersonal character of the former versus the political and ideological dimensions of the latter is indicated in the form of the terms as used herein, that is, use of the suffixes -*ization* versus -*ism*, respectively. [. . .]

GLOBAL THEORY

A proposition explored in this review is that movement is taking place in sociocultural anthropology from what might be called a modern constellation of general theory and problems to anthropological theory and problems appropriately called global. If such a shift is occurring, then the new perspective should be expressed as a reconfiguration of the images and assumptions of several basic world-view universals (9), namely space, time, and classification.

Globalization mediated by migration, commerce, communication technology, finance, tourism, etc entails a reorganization of the bipolar imagery of space and time of modern world view, which is also expressed in modern anthropological theory. It is a progressive bipolar time stretching between the beginning and the end of history. The spatial correlate of this time has metropolitan centers and peripheral sites stitched together by dendritic lines of communication that are replicated in hierarchical branching systems of classification and administration.

Globalization entails a shift from two-dimensional Euclidian space with its centers and peripheries and sharp boundaries, to a multidimensional global space with unbounded, often discontinuous and inter-penetrating sub-spaces. Movement in this direction has gone hand in glove with theory and research that refocused attention from communities bounded within nations and from nations themselves to spaces of which nations are components. [. . .]

DETERRITORIALIZATION

Running through the literature on globalization is a concern with how production, consumption, communities, politics, and identities become detached from local places. The term deterritorialization has several usages that speak to such processes. As noted above, Harvey discusses how capitalist enterprises control time and space by relocating oper-ations. As he puts it, "any struggle to reconstitute power relations is a struggle to reorganize their spatial bases," which is why capitalism constantly deterritorializes and reterritorializes (8:238).

Transnational migrants move into and indeed create transnational spaces that may have the potential to liberate nationals within them who are able to escape in part the total-izing hegemony that a strong state may have within its national borders (e.g. 2, 11, 12, 13). [. . .]

Literature Cited

1. Basch L, Glick Schiller N, Szanton-Blanc C. 1994. *Nations Unbound: Transnational Projects, Post-colonial Predicaments, and Deterritorialized Nation-States.* Langhorne, PA: Gordon & Breach

2. Chavez L. 1991. *Shadowed Lives: Undocumented Immigrants in American Society and Experiences of Incorporation.* New York: Harcourt Brace Jovanovich

3. Giddens A. 1990. *The Consequences of Modernity.* Stanford, CA: Stanford Univ. Press.

4. Glick Schiller N, Basch L, Blanc-Szanton C. 1992. Towards a definition of transnationalism: introductory remarks and research questions. See Ref. 6, pp. ix–xiv

5. Glick Schiller N, Basch L, Blanc-Szanton C. 1992. Transnationalism: a new analytic framework for understanding migration. See Ref. 6, pp. 1–24

6. Glick Schiller N, Basch L, Blanc-Szanton C, eds. 1992. *Towards a Transnational Perspective on Migration: Race, Class, Ethnicity, and Nationalism Reconsidered.* New York: NY Acad. Sci.

7. Hannerz U. 1989. Notes on the global Ecumene. *Public Cult.* 1(2):66–75

8. Harvey D. 1989. *The Condition of Postmodernity: An Inquiry into the Origins of Culture Change.* Cambridge: Blackwell

9. Kearney M. 1984. *World View.* Novato, CA: Chandler & Sharp

10. Kearney M. 1986. From the invisible hand to visible feel: anthropological studies of migration and development. *Annu. Rev. Anthropol.* 15:331–61.

11. Kearney M. 1991. Borders and boundaries of state and self at the end of empire. *J. Hist. Sociol.* 4:1:52–74

12. Rouse R. 1991. Mexican migration and the social space of postmodernism. *Diaspora* 1(1):8–23

13. Rouse R. 1992. Making sense of settlement: class transformation, cultural struggle, and transnationalism among Mexican migrants in the United States. See Ref. 6, pp. 25–52.

CHAPTER 24

The Study of Transnationalism: Pitfalls and Promise of an Emergent Research Field

Alejandro Portes, Luis Eduardo Guarnizo and Patricia Landolt

[. . .]

This issue of *Ethnic and Racial Studies* was conceived as a vehicle to bring to the attention of scholars and policy-makers a phenomenon that has only recently caught the eye of researchers in the field of immigration. Through this collection, we seek to provide evidence of the existence of this phenomenon and to advance theoretical notions to facilitate its interpretation. The events in question pertain to the creation of a transnational community linking immigrant groups in the advanced countries with their respective sending nations and hometowns. While back-and-forth movements by immigrants have always existed, they have not acquired until recently the critical mass and complexity necessary to speak of an emergent social field. This field is composed of a growing number of persons who live dual lives: speaking two languages, having homes in two countries, and making a living through continuous regular contact across national borders. Activities within the transnational field comprise a whole gamut of economic, political and social initiatives—ranging from informal import-export businesses, to the rise of a class of binational professionals, to the campaigns of home country politicians among their expatriates.

The growing number of ties linking persons across countries and the fluidity and diversity of these exchanges has given rise to many contradicting claims. In some writings, the phenomenon of transnationalism is portrayed as novel and emergent, whereas in others it is said to be as old as labour immigration itself. In some cases, transnational entrepreneurs are depicted as a new and still exceptional breed, whereas in others all immigrants are said to be participants in the transnational community. Finally, these activities are sometimes described as a reflection and natural accompaniment of the globalization of capital, whereas in others they are seen as a grass-roots reaction to this very process (Glick Schiller, Basch, and Blanc-Szanton 1992; Basch 1994; Guarnizo 1994; Smith 1995).

Transnational migration studies form a highly fragmented, emergent field which still lacks both a well-defined theoretical framework and analytical rigour. Narratives presented in existing studies, for example, often use disparate units of analysis (that is, individuals, groups, organizations, local states) and mix diverse levels of abstraction. This tendency threatens to frustrate the viability of an otherwise promising topic of research. In this issue, we present several diverse points of view, not all of which agree with our own, in the spirit of providing a representative overview of knowledge in this area. However, we also advance a set of conceptual guidelines, adhered to in our own empirical study of the topic, that seeks to turn the concept of transnationalism into a clearly defined and measurable object of research. We summarize these guidelines next as a way of fleshing out our present understanding of this concept and of facilitating its investigation. As will be evident shortly, these rules are of general applicability, but they are particularly important in a new and still fragile area of research.

STUDYING TRANSNATIONALISM: SOME PITFALLS

1. Establish the phenomenon

As Robert Merton (1987) admonished us, it is of no use attempting to explain a phenomenon whose existence has not been proved. Surprising, as it may seem, it is not so uncommon in the social sciences that elaborate explanations are advanced for processes whose reality remains problematic.[1] In the case of transnationalism, it is not enough to invoke anecdotes of some immigrants investing in businesses back home or some governments giving their expatriates the right to vote in national elections to justify a new field of study. To establish the phenomenon, at least three conditions are necessary:

a) the process involves a significant proportion of persons in the relevant universe (in this case, immigrants and their home country counterparts);

b) the activities of interest are not fleeting or exceptional, but possess certain stability and resilience over time;

c) the content of these activities is not captured by some pre-existing concept, making the invention of a new term redundant.

2. Delimit the phenomenon

The last condition above already suggests the following one. Once the reality of an event or process is established, it is important to delimit its scope to avoid redundancy with objects already studied under other concepts. Nothing is gained, for example, by calling immigrants 'transmigrants', when the earlier and more familiar term is perfectly adequate to describe the subjects in question. Delimiting the scope of predication of a term is also necessary to avoid its spurious extension to every aspect of reality, a common experience when a particular concept becomes popular.[2] For the case in hand, if all or most things that immigrants do are defined as 'transnationalism', then none is because the term becomes synonymous with the total set of experiences of this population. To be useful, a new term should designate a distinct class of activities or people different from those signified by more familiar concepts.

For purposes of establishing a novel area of investigation, it is preferable to delimit the concept of transnationalism to occupations and activities that require regular and sustained social contacts over time across national borders for their implementation. Thus defined, the concept encompasses, for example, the travels of a Salvadoran *viajero* delivering mail and supplies to immigrant kin on a monthly basis or those of a Dominican garment shop owner going to New York several times a year to sell her wares and acquire new fabrics and designs for her business. By the same token, it excludes the occasional gifts of money and kind sent by immigrants to their kin and friends (not an occupation) or the one-time purchase of a house or lot by an immigrant in his home country (not a regular activity).

Clearly, as Itzigsohn *et al.* (1999) point out, the occasional contacts, trips and activities across national borders of members of an expatriate community also contribute to strengthening the transnational field but, by themselves, these contacts are neither novel enough, nor sufficiently distinct, to justify a new area of investigation. What constitutes truly original phenomena and, hence, a justifiable new topic of investigation, are the high intensity of exchanges, the new modes of transacting, and the multiplication of activities that require cross-border travel and contacts on a sustained basis.

3. Define the Unit of Analysis

As in other areas of human activity, transnationalism involves individuals, their networks of social relations, their communities, and broader institutionalized structures such as local and national governments. The existing literature on the subject tends to mix these various levels, referring at times to the efforts and achievements of individual migrants, others to the transformation of local communities in receiving and sending countries, and still others to the initiatives of home governments seeking to co-opt the loyalty and resources of their expatriates. This mix contributes to growing confusion as to what the concept refers to and what its proper scope of predication is.

For methodological reasons, we deem it appropriate to define the individual and his/her support networks as the proper unit of analysis in this area. Other units, such as communities, economic enterprises, political parties, etc also come into play at subsequent and more complex stages of inquiry. Yet, the individual and his/her networks comprise the most viable point of departure in the investigation of this topic. This choice is not based on any *a priori* philosophical position, nor is it intended to deny the reality and importance of broader structures. On the contrary, we believe that a study that begins with the history and activities of individuals is the most efficient way of learning about the institutional underpinnings of transnationalism and its structural effects. From data collection based on individual interviews, it then becomes possible to delineate the networks that make transnational enterprises possible, identify the transnational entrepreneurs' counterparts in the home country, and garner information to establish the aggregate structural effects of these activities.

The choice of individuals as a point of departure for inquiry into this field is also motivated by its own origins. Grass-roots transnational activities were not initiated by actions or policies of governments, national or local. Nor were they the brainchild of large corporate managers. Instead, these activities commonly developed *in reaction* to governmental policies and to the condition of dependent capitalism fostered on weaker countries, as immigrants and their families sought to circumvent the permanent subordination to which these conditions condemned them (Portes and Guarnizo 1991; Roberts *et al.* 1999). State-sponsored transnationalism emerged, for the most part, subsequently as governments realized the importance of their expatriate communities and sought to circumvent or co-opt their initiatives (Smith 1996).

4. Distinguish Types

The heterogeneity of these activities suggests the logical next step. Not everything that falls within the scope of a given concept needs to be the same, either in terms of the form or purpose of the activities involved. A common mistake in the research literature inspired by certain theoretical ideas is to exclude a range of events or activities just because they are not identical to those that prompted the idea in the first place, even when they share many of the same characteristics.

Within the definition of transnationalism given previously, it is possible to accommodate a number of diverse activities. An initial working typology grounded on this concept would distinguish between the economic initiatives of transnational entrepreneurs who mobilize their contacts across borders in search of suppliers, capital and markets *versus* the political activities of party officials, government functionaries, or community leaders whose main goals are the achievement of political power and influence in the sending or receiving countries. A third and more diverse category comprises the manifold socio-cultural enterprises oriented towards the reinforcement of a national identity abroad or the collective enjoyment of cultural events and goods. This type of transnationalism includes the travels of musical folk groups to perform before immigrant audiences, the organization of games in the national sport between immigrant teams and those from the home country, the election of expatriate beauty queens to represent the immigrant community in national pageants, and the celebration of holidays abroad with participation of prominent political or artistic figures who travel to immigrant centres for that purpose.

This working typology of economic, political and socio-cultural transnationalism has undergirded our empirical study of the topic and has proved useful in organizing what otherwise would be a chaotic set of activities. Several of the ensuing articles make use of this typology to present and interpret their respective empirical material. A second useful distinction is between transnational activities initiated and conducted by powerful institutional actors, such as multinational corporations and states, and those that are the result of grass-roots initiatives by immigrants and their home country counterparts. These various enterprises have been respectively dubbed transnationalism 'from above' and 'from below' (Guarnizo 1997).

From an individual standpoint, both types fall appropriately within the definition of the concept. Thus, a diplomatic official or representative of a political party abroad is a transnational actor, as is the executive of a large corporation sent to work in a foreign country. These activities differ in organization, resources and scope from those of 'grass-roots' economic and political entrepreneurs. By bringing both types under the same conceptual umbrella, it becomes possible to highlight their similarities as well as to study systematically their distinct features. Table 24.1 presents a cross-tabulation of the two sets of types—by nature of activities and level of institutionalization—and illustrates them with examples from the existing literature.

At least some of the activities that fall within the label of transnationalism from above are well known and have been examined from alternative conceptual focuses, including economic globalization, international relations, or cultural diffusion (Sassen 1991; Meyer *et al.* 1997). For this reason, the emergent literature on transnationalism has focused, albeit not exclusively, on the less institutionalized initiatives of ordinary immigrants and their home country counterparts. They represent the more novel and distinct development in this area and, hence, the one that deserves greatest attention. Consular officials have been a common sight for centuries and multinational corporation managers have been well researched during the last decades; immigrant civic committees that literally take over public policy or public works in their hometowns have not. For this reason, most of the case-studies included in this issue concentrate on this grass-roots level.

5. Identify Necessary Conditions

Theorizing about the determinants and practical implications of present-day transnationalism must await the presentation and analysis of additional evidence. It is, however, possible at this point to take a first step in this direction by identifying the preconditions that make the phenomenon possible. This is because identification of these necessary conditions does not depend so much on new empirical evidence as on the logical contrast with earlier periods of immigration, when the same activities were not in evidence.

Transnational enterprises did not proliferate among earlier immigrants because the technological conditions of the time did not make communications across national borders rapid or easy. It was not possible for would-be transnational entrepreneurs to travel to Poland or Italy over the weekend and be back at their jobs in New York by Monday. Nor would it have been possible for leaders of an immigrant civic committee to keep in daily contact with the mayor of a Russian or Austrian town in order to learn how a public works project, financed with immigrant money, was progressing. Communications were slow and, thus, many of the transnational enterprises described in today's literature could not have developed.

The ready availability of air transport, long-distance telephone, facsimile communication, and electronic mail provides the technological basis for the emergence of transnationalism on a mass scale. While these technical innovations have enabled governments and major corporations to accelerate the process of transnationalism from above, their potential has not been lost on ordinary people who have availed themselves of the same facilities to implement their own brand of long-distance enterprises. The image of the immigrant businessman on his way to the airport to pick up a consignment of foreign goods shipped the previous day, while talking on his mobile telephone to a home country partner and sending a fax to another could not have materialized as early as two decades ago.

Identification of necessary conditions for the rise of a phenomenon is helpful as a guide for empirical research and also as a source of new hypotheses. With the case in hand, if technological innovations represent a necessary condition for the rise of grass-roots transnationalism, it follows that the greater

Table 24.1 Transnationalism and its types

		Sector		
		Economic	Political	Socio-cultural
Level of institutionalization	Low	– Informal cross-country traders – Small businesses created by returned immigrants in home country – Long-distance circular labour migration	– Home town civic committees created by immigrants – Alliances of immigrant committee with home country political associations – Fund raisers for home country electoral candidates	– Amateur cross-country sport matches – Folk music groups making presentations in immigrant centres – Priests from home town visit and organize their parishioners abroad
	High	– Multinational investments in Third World countries – Development for tourist market of locations abroad – Agencies of home country banks in immigrant centres	– Consular officials and representatives of national political parties abroad – Dual nationality granted by home country governments – Immigrants elected to home country legislatures	– International expositions of national arts – Home country major artists perform abroad – Regular cultural events organized by foreign embassies

the access of an immigrant group to space- and time-compressing technology, the greater the frequency and scope of this sort of activity. Immigrant communities with greater average economic resources and human capital (education and professional skills) should register higher levels of trans- nationalism because of their superior access to the infrastructure that makes these activities possible.

By the same token, if a second necessary condition for this phenomenon is the estab- lishment of networks across space, it follows that the more distant the nation of origin is the less dense the set of transnational enter- prises, other things being equal. This hypoth- esis is grounded on the higher cost and generally greater difficulty of regular contact imposed by longer distances, thus reducing the relative proportion of immigrants able to engage in transnational activities. On the contrary, those whose home countries are a short hop away and who are linked to them by a dense network of communications are in a generally better position to initiate cross-border ventures. Obviously, the space- compressing power of modern electronics allows persons who have command of these resources to engage in transnational activ- ities without the need for face-to-face con- tact. Hence, the barrier of distance gradually diminishes as communities become able to substitute traditional personal contact with new electronic means of communication.

Variants and exceptions to these hypoth- eses exist and to identify them, as well as the forces giving rise to each, there is no substi- tute for field research in sending and receiv- ing areas. This is the methodology on which case-studies and analyses reported in the art- icles included in this issue of ERS are based.

TRANSNATIONALISM IN HISTORICAL PERSPECTIVE

Though lacking the contemporary technolo- gies of communications and transportation, precursors of present immigrant transna- tionalism have existed for centuries. As noted previously, return migration and periodic visits to home communities have always taken place, at least among free labour migrants. Similarly, regular contacts have always existed among participants in polit- ical diasporas forced to resettle in a number of different countries (Cohen 1997). Russian Jews escaping the tsarist Pale of Settlement at the turn of the twentieth century represent a prominent example (Rischin 1962; Howe 1976). So do Armenians fleeing from Turkish oppression (Noiriel 1995), or the vast Span- ish diaspora following the fascist victory in that country (Weil 1991; Sole 1995).

While these activities of immigrants and refugees across national borders reinforced bonds between the respective communities, they lacked the elements of regularity, routine involvement, and critical mass characterizing contemporary examples of transnationalism. Few immigrants actually lived in two coun- tries in terms of their routine daily activities. While most dreamed of going back one day, this long-term goal was countermanded by the concerns and needs of their new lives and, for many, eventually faded away (Hand- lin 1973; Thomas and Znaniecki 1984).

There have, however, been some examples of economic and political transnationalism in history. They include what Curtin (1984) has labelled 'trade diasporas'; that is, com- munities composed of itinerant merchants who settled in foreign jurisdictions in order to engage in commerce. Those who simply settled abroad and became progressively integrated into local ways fit more appropri- ately the definition of immigrant entre- preneurs. Yet those who self-consciously pre- served their distinct identities as members of a trading diaspora, cultivating their net- works across space, and travelling back and forth in pursuit of their commercial ventures can legitimately be dubbed transnational entrepreneurs.

Thus, the foreign enclaves established by Venetian, Genoese and Hanse merchants throughout medieval Europe and identified by Pirenne (1970) with the revival of Euro- pean trade symbolize an early example of economic transnationalism under difficult political conditions. The international activ- ities of Genoese bankers under the protection of their Spanish Habsburg allies were so considerable as to have been identified, by at least one author, as initiators of the 'first wave' of modern capitalist accumulation (Arrighi 1994). Enclaves of commercial representatives engaged in various forms of transnational trade were established by the Portuguese, Dutch and English in successive stages of the European colonization of Africa and the Americas (Dobb 1963; Hardoy 1969; Arrighi 1994). In more recent times the overseas Chinese represent a typical example of a community of transnational traders (Freedman 1959; Lim 1983; Granovetter 1995).

Note the difference between these exceptional cases and the vast movement of European settlers into the newly-opened lands of Africa, the Americas and Oceania. Like subsequent labour immigrants, immigrant colonizers harboured dreams of riches and eventual return, but their daily activities confronted them with the realities of a new country and, in the process, many became permanently settled in the colonies (Wittke 1952; Tilly 1978; Portes and Walton 1981; Tinker 1995). By and large, early examples of economic transnationalism were of an élite type, involving merchants and commercial representatives of some means who maintained a firm affiliation with their home offices and communities, and who relied on long-distance networks for their own economic survival.

For examples of a more popular type of precursors to contemporary transnational activities, one must wait for the onset of induced circular labour migrations in the nineteenth century. The organization of circular movements of formally free foreign labourers across state borders does not materialize on a massive scale until that time. It corresponds to a period of relatively advanced industrial capitalism, where the expansion of industry and commercial agriculture ran up against the barrier of dwindling domestic labour supplies (Lebergott 1964). There is no question that the agents who engaged in organizing this traffic were transnational entrepreneurs. What made the venture transnational for the labourers themselves was their short tenure abroad, their dependence on home country networks for initiating the trip and investing its eventual profits, and the regularity with which

subsequent trips were made (Galarza 1977; Cohen 1988; Noiriel 1995).

The mass US-bound European labour migration at the turn of the twentieth century seldom took the form of a deliberately organized circular labour flow. However, other movements were. They include the mass recruitment of Poles for work in the heavy industries and mines of the Ruhr in Bismarck Germany (Weber 1906 [1958]), the engagement of Algerians and other North Africans by pre-World War II French industry (Weil 1991), and the mass labour migration of Mexicans to the American Southwest (Santibánez 1930; Barrera 1980). Indeed, the popularity of Mexican labour for American ranchers and railroad builders hinged on its temporary orientation and willingness to return when no longer needed. This feature became permanently institutionalized with the onset of the *Bracero* accord between Mexico and the United States (Samora 1971; Portes and Bach 1985).

Instances of early political transnationalism were even less common, but those that existed frequently had momentous consequences. They include the dedicated efforts of certain leaders and activists abroad to liberate their native lands from foreign control or to support a nascent national state. Examples were commonly found among immigrants coming from stateless nations in the nineteenth and early twentieth centuries. According to Glazer (1954, p. 161), the first paper in the Lithuanian language was published in the United States and the nation of Czechoslovakia was, in a sense, 'made in America', under the leadership of the sociologist Tomas Masaryk.

Labour immigrants seldom engaged in this kind of transnational politics full time, but they provided the money and moral support to keep the cause alive at home. Under the leadership of its honorary president, Paderewski, the Polish Relief Central Committee in the United States contributed hundreds of thousands of dollars to the cause of Polish national liberation in the early twentieth century (Glazer 1954; Rosenblum 1973). The Republic of Cuba was also, in a sense, founded in New York, first under the leadership of Jose Marti and his Cuban

Revolutionary Party, and then through the agitation of exiles that helped to bring about US intervention against Spain (Thomas 1971, pp. 291–309; Portell-Vila 1986, pp. 29–33).

These examples make clear that contemporary transnationalism had plenty of precedents in early migration history. Yet these examples were, for the most part, exceptional and lacked the novel features that have captured the attention of researchers and that justify the coining of a new concept. For all their significance, early transnational economic and political enterprises were not normative or even common among the vast majority of immigrants, nor were they undergirded by the thick web of regular instantaneous communication and easy personal travel that we encounter today. Contemporary transnationalism corresponds to a different period in the evolution of the world economy and to a different set of responses and strategies by people in a condition of disadvantage to its dominant logic. Herein lies the import of its emergence. [. . .]

NOTES

1. Examples are unfortunately numerous and range from treatises on hypothetical psychoanalytic concepts to more recent disquisitions on 'post-modernity', to name but a few. Extensive analyses have been devoted to such topics without a firm basis for establishing their existence or the range of empirical phenomena that they are supposed to encompass.

2. Once again, examples are not difficult to find. They include such terms as 'significant other', 'charisma', and, more recently, 'globalization', each of which has been applied in many disparate contexts. That proliferation of uses has led to contradictory interpretations and to the loss of the terms' heuristic value. As they devolved into journalistic clichés, they gradually ceased to be objects of serious scientific investigation. For the case of another imperilled concept, social capital, see Portes and Landolt (1996).

REFERENCES

ARRIGHI, GIOVANNI 1994 *The Long Twentieth Century: Money, Power, and the Origins of Our Times*, London: Verso Books

BARRERA, MARIO 1980 *Race and Class in the Southwest: A Theory of Racial Inequality*, Notre Dame, IN: Notre Dame University Press

BASCH, LINDA G. 1994 *Nations Unbound: Transnational Projects, Post-colonial Predicaments, and De-territorialized Nation-States*, Langhorne, PA: Gordon and Breach

COHEN, ROBIN 1988 *The New Helots, Migrants in the International Division of Labour*, Hants, England: Gower Publishing

—— 1997 *Global Diasporas: An Introduction*, London: UCL Press

CURTIN, PHILIP D. 1984 *Cross-cultural Trade in World History*, Cambridge: Cambridge University Press

DOBB, MAURICE 1963 *Studies in the Development of Capitalism*, New York: International Publishers

FREEDMAN, MAURICE 1959 'The handling of money: a note on the background to the economic sophistication of Overseas Chinese,' *Man*, vol. 59, pp. 64–65

GALARZA, ERNESTO 1977 *Farm Workers and Agri-business in California, 1947–1960*. Notre Dame, IN: Notre Dame University Press

GLAZER, NATHAN 1954 'Ethnic groups in America', in M. Berger, T. Abel and C. Page (eds), *Freedom and Control in Modern Society*, New York: Van Nostrand, pp. 158–73

GLICK SCHILLER, NINA, BASCH, LINDA and BLANC-SZANTON, CRISTINA 1992 'Towards a Transnationalization of Migration: Race, Class, Ethnicity, and Nationalism Reconsidered', *The Annals of the New York Academy of Sciences*, vol. 645: (24 pp)

GRANOVETTER, MARK 1995 'The economic sociology of firms and entrepreneurs', in A. Portes (ed), *The Economic Sociology of Immigration*, New York: Russell Sage Foundation, pp. 128–65

GUARNIZO, LUISE 1994 'Los "*dominican yorks*": the making of a binational society', *Annals of the American Academy of Political and Social Science*, vol. 533, pp. 70–86

—— 1997 'The emergence of a transnational social formation and the mirage of return migration among Dominican transmigrants', *Identities*, vol. 4, pp. 281–322

HANDLIN, OSCAR 1973 *The Uprooted. The Epic Story of the Great Migrations that Made the American People*, 2nd edn, Boston, MA: Little, Brown

HARDOY, JORGE E. 1969 'Two thousand years of Latin American urbanization', in J. E. Hardoy (ed.), *Urbanization in Latin America: Approaches and Issues*, Garden City: Anchor Books, pp. 3–55

HOWE, IRVING 1976 *World of Our Fathers*, New York: Harcourt Brace and Jovanovich

ITZIGSOHN, JOSE, CABRAL, CARLOS DORE, MEDINA, ESTHER HERNANDEZ and VAZQUEZ, OBED 1999 'Mapping Dominican transnationalism: narrow and broad transnational practices', *Ethnic and Racial Studies*, (this issue, pp. 316–39)

LEBERGOTT, STANLEY 1964 *Manpower in Economic Growth: The American Record Since 1800*, New York: McGraw-Hill

LIM, LINDA Y. C. 1983 'Chinese economic activity in Southeast Asia: an introductory review', in L. Y. C.

Lim and P. Gosling (eds), *The Chinese in Southeast Asia*, Vol. 1. Singapore: Maruzen

MERTON, ROBERT K. 1987 'Three fragments from a Sociologist's Notebook: establishing the phenomenon, specified ignorance, and strategic research materials', *Annual Review of Sociology*, vol. 13, pp. 1–28

MEYER, JOHN W., BOLI, JOHN, THOMAS, GEORGE M. and RAMIREZ, FRANCISCO 1997 'World society and the nation state', *American Journal of Sociology*, vol. 103, pp. 144–81

NOIRIEL, GERARD 1995 'Russians and Armenians in France', in R. Cohen (ed.), *The Cambridge Survey of World Migration*, Cambridge: Cambridge University Press, pp. 145–47

PIRENNE, HENRI 1970 *Medieval Cities: Their Origins and the Revival of Trade*, Princeton, NJ: Princeton University Press

PORTELL-VILA, HERMINIO 1986 *Nueva Historia de la República de Cuba*, Miami, FL: La Moderna Poesia

PORTES, ALEJANDRO and WALTON, JOHN 1981 *Labor, Class, and the International System*, New York: Academic Press

—— and BACH, ROBERT L. 1985 *Latin Journey: Cuban and Mexican Immigrants in the United States*. Berkeley, CA: University of California Press

—— and GUARNIZO, LUIS E. 1991 'Tropical capitalists: U.S.-bound immigration and small enterprise development in the Dominican Republic', in S. Díaz-Briquets and S. Weintraub (eds), *Migration, Remittances, and Small Business Development: Mexico and Caribbean Basin Countries*, Boulder, CO: Westview Press, pp. 101–31

—— and LANDOLT, PATRICIA 1996 'The downside of social capital', *The American Prospect*, vol. 26 (May–June), pp. 18–22

RISCHIN, MOSES 1962 *The Promised City: New York Jews 1870–1914*, Cambridge, MA: Harvard University Press

ROBERTS, BRYAN R., FRANK, REANNE and LOZANO-ASCENCIO, FERNANDO 1999 'Transnational migrant communities and Mexican migration to the US', (this issue, pp. 238–66)

ROSENBLUM, GERALD 1973 *Immigrant Workers: Their Impact on American Radicalism*, New York: Basic Books

SAMORA, JULIAN 1971 *Los Mojados: The Wetback Story*, Notre Dame, IN: Notre Dame University Press

SANTIBÁNEZ, ENRIQUE 1930 *Ensayo Acerca de la Inmigración Mexicana en los Estados Unidos*, San Antonio, TX: Clegg

SASSEN, SASKIA 1991 *The Global City*, Princeton, NJ: Princeton University Press

SMITH, ROBERT 1995 'Los Ausentes Siempre Presentes: The Imagining, Making and Politics of a Transnational Community Between Ticuani, Puebla, Mexico and New York City'. PhD dissertation, Department of Sociology, Columbia University, October

SMITH, ROBERT 1996 'Domestic Politics Abroad, Diasporic Politics at Home', paper presented at the session on Transnational Communities: Space, Race/Ethnicity, and Power, meetings of the American Sociological Association, New York City, August

SOLE, CARLOTA 1995 'Portugal and Spain: from exporters to importers of labour', in R. Cohen (ed.), *The Cambridge Survey of World Migration*, Cambridge: Cambridge University Press, pp. 316–20

THOMAS, HUGH 1971 *Cuba: The Pursuit of Freedom*, New York: Harper and Row

THOMAS, WILLIAM I. and ZNANIECKI, FLORLAN 1984 *The Polish Peasant in Europe and America*, 1918–1920, edited and abr. by Eli Zaretsky, Urbana, IL: University of Illinois Press.

TILLY, CHARLES 1978 'Migration in modern European history', in W. S. McNeill and R. Adams (eds), *Human Migration: Patterns and Policies*, Bloomington, IN: Bloomington University Press, pp. 48–72

TINKER, HUGH 1995 'The British colonies of settlement', in R. Cohen (ed.), *The Cambridge Survey of World Migration*, Cambridge: Cambridge University Press, pp. 14–20

WEBER, MAX 1906 [1958] 'Capitalism and rural society in Germany', in H. Gerth and C. Wright Mills (eds), *From Max Weber: Essays in Sociology*. New York: Oxford University Press, pp. 363–85. (Originally published as 'The Relations of the Rural Community to Other Branches of Social Science', Congress of Arts and Sciences, Universal Exposition, New York: Houghton-Mifflin, 1906)

WEIL, PATRICK 1991 *La France et ses Etrangères*, Paris: Gallimard

WITTKE, CARL 1952 *Refugees of Revolution: The German Forty-eighters in America*. Philadelphia, PA: University of Pennsylvania Press

Conceptualizing Simultaneity: A Transnational Social Field Perspective on Society[1]

Peggy Levitt and Nina Glick Schiller

[. . .]

Social scientists have long been interested in how immigrants are incorporated into new countries. In Germany and France, scholars' expectations that foreigners will assimilate is a central piece of public policy. In the United States, immigration scholars initially argued that to move up the socioeconomic ladder, immigrants would have to abandon their unique customs, language, values, and homeland ties and identities. Even when remaining ethnic became more acceptable, most researchers assumed that the importance of homeland ties would eventually fade. To be Italian American or Irish American would ultimately reflect ethnic pride within a multicultural United States rather than enduring relations to an ancestral land.

Now scholars increasingly recognize that some migrants and their descendants remain strongly influenced by their continuing ties to their home country or by social networks that stretch across national borders. They see migrants' crossborder ties as a variable and argue that to understand contemporary migration, the strength, influence, and impact of these ties must be empirically assessed. They call for a transnational perspective on migration (Basch, Glick Schiller and Szanton Blanc, 1994). The resulting analyses, in combination with other scholarship on transnational dynamics, are building toward a new paradigm that rejects the long-held notion that society and the nation-state are one and the same.

This article is not intended as a comprehensive review of the transnational migration scholarship. In fact, a special volume of this journal, published in Fall 2003, does just that. Instead, we explore the social theory and the consequent methodology that underpins studies of transnational migration. We argue that central to the project of transnational migration studies, and to scholarship on other transnational phenomena, is a reformulation of the concept of society. The lives of increasing numbers of individuals can no longer be understood by looking only at what goes on within national boundaries. Our analytical lens must necessarily broaden and deepen because migrants are often embedded in multi-layered, multi-sited transnational social fields, encompassing those who move and those who stay behind. As a result, basic assumptions about social institutions such as the family, citizenship, and nation-states need to be revisited.

Once we rethink the boundaries of social life, it becomes clear that the incorporation of individuals into nation-states and the maintenance of transnational connections are not contradictory social processes. Simultaneity, or living lives that incorporate daily activities, routines, and institutions located both in a destination country and transnationally, is a possibility that needs to be theorized and explored. Migrant incorporation into a new land and transnational connections to a homeland or to dispersed networks of family, compatriots, or persons who share a religious or ethnic identity can occur at the same time and reinforce one another.

Our goals in this study are fourfold. First, we propose a social field approach to the study of migration and distinguish between ways of being and ways of belonging in that field. Second, we argue that assimilation and enduring transnational ties are neither incompatible nor binary opposites. Instead, we suggest thinking of the transnational migration experience as a kind of gauge which, while anchored, pivots between host land and transnational connections. Third, we highlight social processes and institutions that are routinely obscured by traditional migration scholarship but that become clear when we use a transnational lens. Finally, we locate our approach to migration research within a larger intellectual project, undertaken by scholars of transnational processes in a variety of fields, to reformulate the concept of society such that it is no longer automatically equated with or confined by the boundaries of a single nation-state. [. . .]

BUILDING TO A TRANSNATIONAL SOCIAL FIELD THEORY OF SOCIETY

To further develop transnational migration studies, we revisit the concept of society as it has been generally deployed and put aside the methodological nationalism that has distorted many basic social science concepts (Martins, 1974; Smith, 1983). Methodological nationalism is the tendency to accept the nation-state and its boundaries as a given in social analysis. Wimmer and Glick Schiller (2003) identified three variants of methodological nationalism: 1) Ignoring or disregarding the fundamental importance of nationalism for modern societies. This tendency often goes hand and hand with 2) naturalization, or taking for granted that the boundaries of the nation-state delimit and define the unit of analysis. Finally, 3) territorial limitation confines the study of social processes to the political and geographic boundaries of a particular nation-state. According to Wimmer and Glick Schiller (2003: 578), the three variants may intersect and mutually reinforce each other, forming a coherent epistemic structure, a self-reinforcing way of looking at and describing the social world.

Because much of social science theory equates society with the boundaries of a particular nation-state, researchers often take rootedness and incorporation in the nation-

state as the norm and social identities and practices enacted across state boundaries as out of the ordinary. But if we remove the blinders of methodological nationalism, we see that while nation-states are still extremely important, social life is not confined by nation-state boundaries. Social and religious movements, criminal and professional networks, and governance regimes as well as flows of capital also operate across borders.

Recent developments in social theory have also challenged the nation-state container theory of society and provide insights into the nature of transnational flows that we build upon. Sassen, for example, reconfigured our understanding of the geography of cities by highlighting that some locations become global cities (Sassen, 1992). Discussing flexible capital accumulation, Harvey (1989) explored the time-space compressions that so revolutionize the objective qualities of space and time that we are forced to alter, sometimes in quite radical ways, how we represent the world to ourselves (p. 240). Other scholars have highlighted the interconnectedness of societies through flows of media, capital, and people (Held *et al.*, 1999). However, much of this work, according to Ulrich Beck (2000), continues to envision states as the primary unit and treats globalization as a process of interconnection between states. Such theories, Beck argues, continue "the container theory of society" on which most of the sociology of the first age of modernity is based. He calls for a new paradigm that changes not only the relations between and beyond national states and societies, but also the inner quality of the social and political itself which is indicated by reflexive cosmopolitization (p. 1).

Along with Beck, Faist (2000), Urry (2000) and a growing number of social theorists, we seek ways to move beyond the container theory of society. Many of these scholars, however, tend to underplay the concept of the social as they reconfigure the concept of society. Beck's formulation of reflexive cosmopolitization and much of the related literature on cosmopolitanism, for example, largely abandons an exploration of social relations and social context. In Beck's (2000) cosmopolitanism, as in Luhmann's world society, communication technologies become key. Global media flows and consumerism lead to a new form of consciousness. Social relations and social positioning fall out of the analysis; the individual and the global intersect. Without a concept of the social, the relations of power and privilege exercised by social actors based within structures and organizations cannot be studied or analyzed. In addition, by trying to move beyond methodological nationalism, much of this theory-building neglects the continuing power of the nation-state. Transnational migration studies, with their concrete tracing of the movement and connection of people, provide a useful corrective to these oversights by highlighting the concept of social field.

We propose a view of society and social membership based on a concept of social field that distinguishes between ways of being and ways of belonging. The notion of social field exists in social science literature in several different forms. We draw here on those proposed by Bourdieu and by the Manchester school of anthropology. Bourdieu used the concept of social field to call attention to the ways in which social relationships are structured by power. The boundaries of a field are fluid and the field itself is created by the participants who are joined in struggle for social position. Society for Bourdieu is the intersection of various fields within a structure of politics (Jenkins, 1992:86). According to Bourdieu, either individuals or institutions may occupy the networks that make up the field and link social positions. While his approach does not preclude the notion of transnational social fields, he does not directly discuss the implications of social fields that are not coterminous with state boundaries.

The Manchester School also informs our framework because these scholars recognized that the migrants they studied belonged to tribal-rural localities and colonial-industrial cities at the same time. Migrant networks stretching between these two sites were viewed as constituting a single social field created by a network of networks. By understanding society in this way, these researchers focused on a level of social analysis beyond the study of the individual.

Despite its importance, the term social field within transnational migration research has not been well defined. Building on Basch, Glick Schiller and Szanton Blanc (1994), we define social field as a set of multiple interlocking networks of social relationships through which ideas, practices, and resources are unequally exchanged, organized, and transformed (*see also* Glick Schiller and Fouron, 1999; Glick Schiller, 1999, 2003). Social fields are multidimensional, encompassing structured interactions of differing forms, depth, and breadth that are differentiated in social theory by the terms organization, institution, and social movement. National boundaries are not necessarily contiguous with the boundaries of social fields. National social fields are those that stay within national boundaries while transnational social fields connect actors through direct and indirect relations across borders. Neither domain is privileged in our analysis. Ascertaining the relative importance of nationally restricted and transnational social fields should be a question of empirical analysis.

The concept of social fields is a powerful tool for conceptualizing the potential array of social relations linking those who move and those who stay behind. It takes us beyond the direct experience of migration into domains of interaction where individuals who do not move themselves maintain social relations across borders through various forms of communication. Individuals who have such direct connections with migrants may connect with others who do not. We should not assume that those with stronger social ties will be more transnationally active than those with weaker connections nor that the actions and identities of those with more indirect ties are less influenced by the dynamics within the field than those with direct transnational ties. In any given study, the researcher must operationalize the parameters of the field they are studying and the scope of the networks embedded within it, then empirically analyze the strength and impact of direct and indirect transnational relations.

For example, there may be one central individual who maintains high levels of homeland contact and is the node through which information, resources, and identities flow. While other individuals may not identify with or take action based on those ties, the fact that they are part of the same transnational social field keeps them informed and connected so that they can act if events motivate them to do so. Recognizing that this individual is embedded in a transnational social field may be a better predictor of future transnational behavior than if we simply locate him or her solely within a nationally delimited set of relationships.

The concept of social field also calls into question neat divisions of connection into local, national, transnational, and global. In one sense, all are local in that near and distant connections penetrate the daily lives of individuals lived within a locale. But within this locale, a person may participate in personal networks or receive ideas and information that connect them to others in a nation-state, across the borders of a nation-state, or globally, without ever having migrated. By conceptualizing transnational social fields as transcending the boundaries of nation-states, we also note that individuals within these fields are, through their everyday activities and relationships, influenced by multiple sets of laws and institutions. Their daily rhythms and activities respond not only to more than one state simultaneously but also to social institutions, such as religious groups, that exist within many states and across their borders.

A social field perspective also reveals that there is a difference between ways of being in social fields as opposed to ways of belonging (Glick Schiller, 2003; 2004).[2] Ways of being refers to the actual social relations and practices that individuals engage in rather than to the identities associated with their actions. Social fields contain institutions, organizations, and experiences, within their various levels, that generate categories of identity that are ascribed to or chosen by individuals or groups. Individuals can be embedded in a social field but not identify with any label or cultural politics associated with that field. They have the potential to act or identify at a particular time because they live within the social field, but not all choose to do so.

In contrast, ways of belonging refers to practices that signal or enact an identity which demonstrates a conscious connection to a particular group. These actions are not symbolic but concrete, visible actions that mark belonging such as wearing a Christian cross or Jewish star, flying a flag, or choosing a particular cuisine. Ways of belonging combine action and an awareness of the kind of identity that action signifies.

Individuals within transnational social fields combine ways of being and ways of belonging differently in specific contexts. One person might have many social contacts with people in their country of origin but not identify at all as belonging to their homeland. They are engaged in transnational ways of being but not belonging. Similarly, a person may eat certain foods or worship certain saints or deities because that is what their family has always done. By doing so, they are not signaling any conscious identification with a particular ethnicity or with their ancestral homes. Here again, they are not expressing a transnational way of belonging.

On the other hand, there are people with few or no actual social relations with people in the sending country or transnationally but who behave in such a way as to assert their identification with a particular group. Because these individuals have some sort of connection to a way of belonging, through memory, nostalgia or imagination, they can enter the social field when and if they choose to do so. In fact, we would hypothesize that someone who had access to a transnational way of belonging would be likely to act on it at some point in his or her life.

If individuals engage in social relations and practices that cross borders as a regular feature of everyday life, then they exhibit a transnational way of being. When people explicitly recognize this and highlight the transnational elements of who they are, then they are also expressing a transnational way of belonging. Clearly, these two experiences do not always go hand in hand.

Finally, locating migrants within transnational social fields makes clear that incorporation in a new state and enduring transnational attachments are not binary opposites (Morawska, 2003; Levitt, 2003).

Instead, it is more useful to think of the migrant experience as a kind of gauge which, while anchored, pivots between a new land and a transnational incorporation. Movement and attachment is not linear or sequential but capable of rotating back and forth and changing direction over time. The median point on this gauge is not full incorporation but rather simultaneity of connection. Persons change and swing one way or the other depending on the context, thus moving our expectation away from either full assimilation or transnational connection but some combination of both. The challenge, then, is to explain the variation in the way that migrants manage that pivot and how host country incorporation and homeland or other transnational ties mutually influence each other. For example, Portes and his colleagues found that transnational entrepreneurs were more likely to be U.S. citizens, suggesting that by becoming full members of their new land, it became easier for them to run successful businesses involving their homeland. Similarly, some Latino communities use the same organizations to promote political integration in the United States that they use to mobilize around sending-country issues.

In this vein, Glick Schiller, Calgar and Karagiannis (2003) have proposed a useful distinction between mere connection and the kinds of connections that engage individuals institutionally in more than one nation-state. One can have friends, colleagues, or co-religionists with whom one communicates and exchanges information or objects across borders without ever coming into contact with the state or other institutions. But if one belongs to a church, receives a pension, or has investments in another land, one must necessarily negotiate his or her way through a set of public and private institutions that grounds those connections more firmly. His or her "pivot" is rooted in two or more legal and regulatory systems, encouraging a greater sense of embeddedness in the transnational social field and making the connections within it more likely to endure.

METHODOLOGY

Methodology and theory have an intimate relationship. To develop a transnational framework for the study of migration, we need a methodology that allows us to move beyond the binaries, such as homeland/new land, citizen/ noncitizen, migrant/nonmigrant, and acculturation/cultural persistence, that have typified migration research in the past. On the other hand, a framework that privileges transborder processes rather than incorporation-oriented activity may not capture the interrelationship between transnational connection and social relationships within a single nation-state.

Using a transnational framework implies several methodological shifts. First, we need to focus on the intersection between the networks of those who have migrated and those who have stayed in place, whether in the new land, homeland, or some other diasporic location. This focus allows for comparisons between the experiences of migrants and those who are only indirectly influenced by ideas, objects, and information flowing across borders. Although multi-sited research is ideal for studying these two different experiences, the impact of transnational relations can be observed by asking individuals about the transnational aspects of their lives, and those they are connected to, in a single setting.

Second, we need tools that capture migrants' simultaneous engagement in and orientation toward their home and host countries. And these dynamics cannot just be studied at one point in time. Transnational migration is a process rather than an event. Transnational practices ebb and flow in response to particular incidents or crises. A one-time snapshot misses the many ways in which migrants periodically engage with their home countries during election cycles, family or ritual events, or climatic catastrophes—their attention and energies shifting in response to a particular goal or challenge. Studying migrant practices longitudinally reveals that in moments of crisis or opportunity, even those who have never identified or participated transnationally, but who are embedded in transnational social fields, may become mobilized into action. Such a research strategy would help explain the transition from a way of belonging such as a diasporic identity—Armenian, Jewish, or Croatian—to direct engagement in transnational practices.

Each of the research methodologies used to study transnational migration has particular strengths. We believe that ethnography is particularly suited for studying the creation and durability of transnational social fields. Participant observation and ethnographic interviewing allow researchers to document how persons simultaneously maintain and shed cultural repertoires and identities, interact within a location and across its boundaries, and act in ways that are in concert with or contradict their values over time. The effects of strong and weak indirect ties within a transnational social field can be observed, and those connections, whether they take the form of institutional or individual actors, can be studied. Like surveys, ethnographic research can also begin with a random sample of persons who migrate and who have no intention of returning home.

POWER

When people belong to multiple settings, they come into contact with the regulatory powers and the hegemonic culture of more than one state. These states regulate economic interactions, political processes and performances, and also have discrete nation-state building projects. Individuals are, therefore, embedded in multiple legal and political institutions that determine access and action and organize and legitimate gender, race, and class status. Foucault (1980) wrote that the experience of power goes beyond mere contact with the law or the police. Rather, power pervades and permeates all social relations because what is legitimate, appropriate, and possible is strongly influenced by the state. People living in transnational social fields experience multiple loci and layers of power and are shaped by them, but they can also act back upon them.

Most migrants move from a place where the state has relatively little power within the global interstate system to a more powerful state. At the same time, many migrants gain more social power, in terms of leverage over people, property, and locality, with respect to their homeland than they did before migrating. It is this complex intersection between personal losses and gains that any analysis of power within transnational social fields must grapple with. Furthermore, migration often opens up the possibility for transnational migrants to contribute, both positively and negatively, to changes in the global economic and political system. For example, long distance nationalist movements have long influenced nation building and national transformation. Lithuania would not have become Lithuania without immigrants in the United States first imaging its emergence and then mobilizing to make it a reality (Glazer, 1954). Former Iraqi exiles are now playing a critical role in rebuilding the Iraqi state. Transnational migrants can also strengthen, alter, or thwart global religious movements like Islamic fundamentalism, Christian fundamentalism, or Hindu nationalism.

Not only can migrants potentially shift the position of states within the world economic order, they can also influence the internal functions of states as well. They may be forces for privatization because they want telephone systems that work and private schools and hospitals where their family members will be well attended. They may pressure states to institute conservative legislation that preserves traditional values. Acting within their transnational social fields, migrants may also fuel movements for rights, social justice, and anti-imperialist struggles.

Transnational migrants also shift power by redefining the functions of the host state. There are many instances, such as in the Cuban, Israeli, and Irish communities, in which migrants have successfully mobilized host country legislatures to support their homeland projects. The Mexican state and Mexican transnational migrants living in the United States have altered the ways in which some U.S. institutions categorize and process individuals. The Mexican state's issuing of the *matricula consular*, a consular ID card, to legal and unauthorized Mexican migrants in the United States has enabled migrants to pressure banks, motor vehicle bureaus, and car insurance companies to be more responsive to them.

Using a transnational social field perspective allows for a more systematic study of the social processes and institutions that have been routinely obscured by traditional migration scholarship and even by some studies of transnational migration. New perspectives emerge on a number of issues, including the effect of migration on gender hierarchies and racialized identities; family dynamics; the significance of nation-states, membership and citizenship; and the role of religion. In the following section, we discuss each in turn.

HOW CLASS, RACE, AND GENDER ARE MUTUALLY CONSTITUTED WITHIN TRANSNATIONAL SOCIAL FIELDS

Scholars have tended to study class, race, and gender as discrete realms of experience. Here we build on feminist theory by recognizing that since these social locations are mutually constituted, we must discuss them together. We approach all three as hierarchical positions that entail differential social power. Data on these varying statuses illustrate the analytical limits of methodological nationalism. Social scientists often use national income statistics to assess the socioeconomic status of migrants without considering the other statuses that they occupy. But when society differs from polity and is made up of sets of social relationships in intersecting and overlapping national and transnational social fields, individuals occupy different gender, racial, and class positions within different states at the same time. Recognizing that migrant behavior is the product of these simultaneous multiple statuses of race, class, and gender makes certain social processes more understandable.

For example, a transnational perspective can help explain contradictory data on the political attitudes and actions of immigrants. In some cases, immigrant women, who find themselves racialized in their new homes, appear to be quite conservative with respect to struggles for rights and recognition. Poor migrants of color in the United States, for example, often strive to differentiate themselves from African Americans rather than join efforts to advance minority group civil rights (Waters, 1999). They may re-enforce or even reinvent gender distinctions and hierarchies that are more rigid and traditional than those in their ancestral homes (Espiritu, 1997; Lessinger, 1995; Caglar, 1995). They accept low-status jobs in their new home, tolerate employment discrimination, and resist political projects or labor protests that would redress these wrongs. Ironically, this heightened gender stratification often occurs in households where immigrants women have entered the workforce and men have begun to share the responsibility for childrearing and housekeeping, thereby redefining other aspects of gender dynamics in more egalitarian terms.

Consideration of migrants' multiple positions within transnational social fields helps explain this seemingly conservative and contradictory behavior (Pessar and Mahler, 2003). When individuals elaborate markers of gender after they migrate, they may be preserving or creating status in other locations within the transnational social field. Conservative positions of women and men in relationship to struggles for rights or "family values" may be linked to the class position of migrants in the homeland. Migrants who are laborers, home health aides, or domestic workers in countries of immigration may also be educated and middle-class homeowners or business people in their homelands. Men who may have higher status than women at home are generally more interested in maintaining political homeland connections and identities (Grasmuck and Pessar, 1991). In contrast, women migrants may use income they earn abroad to improve their social standing at home. Transnational religious systems, such as Islam or Charismatic Christianity, also provide venues for asserting one's enhanced status and for acquiring social capital and resources (Peterson and Vásquez, 2001).

TRANSNATIONAL FAMILIES

Much work on globalization and transnational phenomena focuses on production. But reproduction also takes place across borders and is an important, if understudied, aspect of the migration experience. Just as transnational migration studies prompt us to rethink the terrain in which social processes take place, they also challenge our understanding of social reproduction.

Numerous studies illustrate the ways in which the boundaries of family life change over the life cycle. Members of the second and third generations in Europe and the United States continue to return to the Middle East and South Asia to find marriage partners (Hooghiemstra, 2001; Lesthaeghe, 2002; Levitt, 2002). Increasing numbers of women have joined the ranks of men who head transnational families (Parrenas, 2001; Hondagneu-Sotelo and Avila, 2003). Transnational family life entails renegotiating communication between spouses, the distribution of work tasks, and who will migrate and who will stay behind via long distance (Pessar and Mahler, 2001). Nonmigrants also imagine the gendered lives of their migrant peers and change their ideas about successful marriages and suitable marital partners. Levitt (2001) found that the young women in the Dominican village she studied only wanted to marry men who had migrated because they were considered the ideal breadwinner and life partner.

While adults make family decisions, children are the central axis of family migration and often a critical reason why families move back and forth and sustain transnational ties (Orellana *et al.*, 2001; Zhou, 1998). Adult-centered studies obscure the ways in which child raising actively shapes families' journeys, the spaces they move in, and their experiences within those social fields. This is particularly true as children mature into young adults. Kandel and Massey (2002), for example, found a culture of migration so deeply embedded in the Mexican communities they studied that transnational migration became the norm. Young men, in particular, came to see migration as an expected rite of passage and as the way to achieve economically what they could not attain in Mexico.

The studies we describe attest to the fact that in migrant households that are constituted transnationally and across generations, living transnationally often becomes the norm (Nyberg Sorenson and Fog Olwig, 2002). How must we rethink conventional wisdom about the family in response? First, using a transnational lens reveals the changing nature of the family as a socioeconomic strategic unit and how family ties are worked and reworked over time and space. Deborah Bryceson and Ulla Vuorela (2002) use the term relativizing to refer to the ways in which individuals establish, maintain, or curtail ties to specific family members. Within transnational social fields, individuals actively pursue or neglect blood ties and fictitious kinship. Based on their particular needs, individuals strategically choose which connections to emphasize and which to let slide. Second, in many cases, socialization and social reproduction occur transnationally in response to at least two social and cultural contexts. Even children who never return to their parent's ancestral homes are brought up in households where people, values, goods and claims from somewhere else are present on a daily basis. Similarly, the children of nonmigrants are raised in social networks and settings entirely permeated by people, resources, and what Levitt (1999) has called social remittances from the host country. For these individuals, the generational experience is not territorially bounded. It is based on actual and imagined experiences that are shared across borders regardless of where someone was born or now lives.

Locating migrants and their families squarely within transnational social fields requires rethinking the notion of generation and the term second generation (Glick Schiller and Fouron, 2002). Conceptualizing generation as a lineal process, involving clear boundaries between one experience and the other, does not accurately capture the experience of living in a transnational field because it implies a separation in migrants' and nonmigrants' socialization and social networks that may not exist. It also fails to take into account that generational experiences are shaped by common experiences during youth that create a shared worldview or frame of reference which influences subsequent social and political activism (Mannheim, 1952; Eckstein, 2002).

While many researchers now acknowledge the salience of transnational ties for the immigrant generation, many predict these ties will weaken among their children. In the United States, these researchers find that the transnational activities of the second generation are confined primarily to certain groups who are, by and large, physically and emotionally rooted in the United States and lack the language, cultural skills, or desire to live in their ancestral homes. Since these individuals are only occasional transnational activists, and their activities are confined to very specific arenas of social life, they are likely to have minimal long-term consequences (Rumbaut, 2002; Kasinitz *et al.*, 2002).

But whether or not individuals forge or maintain some kind of transnational connection may depend on the extent to which they are reared in a transnational space. Clearly, transnational activities will not be central to the lives of most of the second generation, and those who engage in them will not do so with the same frequency and intensity as their parents. But surveys concluding that transnational practices will be inconsequential may be short sighted. They may overlook the effect of the many periodic, selective transnational activities that some individuals engage in at different stages of their lives (Levitt, 2002; Glick Schiller and Fouron, 2002; Smith, 2002). They may also fail to differentiate between ways of being and possible ways of belonging—that the desire and ability to engage in transnational practices will ebb and flow at different phases of the lifecycle and in different contexts. At the point of marriage or child rearing, the same individuals who showed little regard for a parental homeland and culture may activate their connections within a transnational field in search of spouses or values to teach to their children (Espiritu and Tham, 2002). The children of Gujaratis who go back to India to find marriage partners, the second generation Pakistanis who begin to study Islam and Pakistani values when they have children, or the Chinese American business school students who specialize in Asian banking are doing just that. [...]

NOTES

1. This is a co-authored article, jointly conceived and written by both contributors.
2. Some analysts, such as Thomas Faist (2000), contrast social ties with "symbolic ties." By emphasizing ways of being, rather than social ties, we develop a concept that decouples social relationships from a notion of common interest or norms.

REFERENCES

Basch, L., N. Glick Schiller and C. Szanton Blanc, eds. (1994) *Nations Unbound: Transnational Projects, Postcolonial Predicaments, and Deterritorialized Nation-States*. Langhorne, PA: Gordon and Breach.

Beck, U. (2000) "The Cosmopolitan Perspective: Sociology in the Second Age of Modernity," *British Journal of Sociology*, 5(1): 79–107.

Bryceson, D. F. and U. Vuorela (2002) *The Transnational Family: New European Frontiers and Global Networks*. Oxford and New York: Berg.

Caglar, A. (1995) "German Turks in Berlin: Social Exclusion and Strategies for Social Mobility," *New Community*, 21(3):309–323.

Eckstein, S. (2002) "On Deconstructing and Reconstructing the Meaning of Immigrant Generations." In *The Changing Face of Home: The Transnational Lives of the Second Generation*. Ed. P. Levitt and M. Waters. New York: Russell Sage Publications. Pp. 367–399.

Espiritu, Y. (1997) *Asian Women and Men: Labor, Laws, and Love*, Thousand Oaks, CA: Sage.

Espiritu, Y. and T. Tran (2002) "Viet Nam, Nuoc Toi (Vietnam, My Country): Vietnamese Americans and Transnationalism." In *The Changing Face of Home: The Transnational Lives of the Second Generation*. Ed. P. Levitt and M. Waters. New York: Russell Sage Publication. Pp. 367–399.

Faist, T. (2000) *The Volume and Dynamics of International Migration*. New York: Oxford University Press.

Foucault, M. (1980) *Power/Knowledge: Selected Interviews and Other Writings, 1972–1977*. New York: Pantheon.

Glazer, N. (1954) "Ethnic Groups in America: From National Culture to Ideology." In *Freedom and Control in Modern Society*. Ed. M. Berger, T. Abel and C. Page. New York: Van Nostrand.

Glick Schiller, N. (2004) "Transnational Theory and Beyond." In *A Companion to the Anthropology of Politics*. Ed. D. Nugent and J. Vincent. Malden, MA: Blackwell.

—— (2003) "The Centrality of Ethnography in the Study of Transnational Migration: Seeing the Wetland

Instead of the Swamp." In *American Arrivals*. Ed. N. Foner. Santa Fe, NM: School of American Research.

—— (1999) "Transmigrants and Nation-States: Something Old and Something New in the U.S. Immigrant Experience." In *The Handbook of International Migration: The American Experience*. Ed. C. Hirschman, P. Kasinitz and J. DeWind. New York: Russell Sage. Pp. 94–119.

Glick Schiller, N., A. Calgar, and F. Karagiannis (2003) "Simultaneous Incorporation of Migrants." Paper delivered at the Max Planck Institute of Social Anthropology, Halle, Germany. July 17, 2003.

Glick Schiller, N. and G. Fouron (2002) "The Generation of Identity: Redefining the Second Generation within a Transnational Social Field." In *The Changing Face of Home: The Transnational Lives of the Second Generation*. Ed. P. Levitt and M. Waters. New York: Russell Sage Publications.

—— (1999) "Terrains of Blood and Nation: Haitian Transnational Social Fields," *Ethnic and Racial Studies*, 22(2):340–366.

Grasmuck, S. and P. Pessar (1991) *Between Two Islands: Dominican International Migration*, Berkeley: University of California Press.

Harvey, D. (1989) *The Condition of Postmodernity: An Enquiry into the Conditions of Cultural Change*. Oxford: Oxford University Press.

Held, D., A. McGrew, D. Goldblatt and J. Perraton (1999) *Global Transformations*. Cambridge: Polity.

Hondagneu-Sotelo, P. and E. Avila (2001) "I'm Here but I'm There: The Meaning of Latina Transnational Motherhood." In *Gender and U.S. Immigration*. Ed. P. Hondagneu-Sotelo. Berkeley: University of California Press.

Hooghiemstra, E. (2001) "Migrants, Partner Selection, and Integration: Crossing Borders?" *Journal of Comparative Family Studies*, 32(4):601–628.

Jenkins, R. (1992) *Pierre Bourdieu*. London: Routledge.

Kandel, W. and D. Massey (2002) "The Culture of Mexican Migration: A Theoretical and Empirical Analysis," *Social Forces*, 80(3):981–1004.

Kasinitz, P., M. C. Waters, J. H. Mollenkopf and M. Anil (2002) "Transnationalism and the Children of Immigrants in Contemporary New York." In *The Changing Face of Home: The Transnational Lives of the Second Generation*. Ed. P. Levitt and M. Waters. New York: Russell Sage Publication. Pp. 96–122.

Lesthaeghe, R. (2002) Turks and Moroccans in Belgium: A Comparison. Seminar presented at the Center for Population and Development Studies, Harvard University.

Lessinger, J. (1995) *From the Ganges to the Hudson*. New York: Allyn and Bacon.

Levitt, P. (2003) "Keeping Feet in Both Worlds: Transnational Practices and Immigrant Incorporation." In *Integrating Immigrants in Liberal Nation-States: From Post-Nationals to Transnational*. Ed. C. Joppke and E. Morawska. London: Macmillan-Palgrave.

—— (2002) "Why Should I Retire to Florida When I can Go To Lahore?: Defining and Explaining Variations in Transnational Migration." Paper presented at the Emerging Architectures of Transnational Governance Conference, Harvard University. December 2002.

—— (2001) *The Transnational Villagers*. Berkeley and Los Angeles: University of California Press.

—— (1999) "Social Remittances: A Local-Level, Migration-Driven Form of Cultural Diffusion," *International Migration Review*, 32(4):926–949.

Mannheim, K. (1952) "The Problem of Generations." In *Essays on the Sociology of Knowledge*. Ed. P. Kecksckemeti. New York: Oxford University Press.

Martins, H. (1974) "Time and Theory in Sociology." In *Approaches to Sociology: An Introduction to the Major Trends in Sociology*. Ed. J. Rex. London and Boston: Routledge and Kegan Paul. Pp. 246–294.

Morawska, E. (2003) "Immigrant Transnationalism and Assimilation: A Variety of Combinations and the Analytic Strategy It Suggests." In *Toward Assimilation and Citizenship: Immigrants in Liberal Nation-States*. Ed. C. Joppke and E. Morawska. Hampshire, UK: Palgrave Macmillan, Pp. 133–176.

Nyberg Sorenson, N. and K. Fog Olwig, eds. (2002) *Work and Migration. Life and Livelihoods in a Globalizing World (Transnationalism)*. London: Routledge.

Orellana, M. F., B. Thorne, A. Chee and W. S. E. Lam (2001) "Transnational Childhoods: The Participation of Children in Processes of Family Migration," *Social Problems*, 48(4):572–592.

Parrenas, R. S. (2001) "Mothering From a Distance: Emotions, Gender, and Intergenerational Relations in Filipino Transnational Families," *Feminist Studies*, 27(2):361–391.

Pessar, P. and S. Mahler (2003) "Transnational Migration: Bringing Gender In," *International Migration Review*, 37(3): 812–843.

Peterson, A. L. and M. Vásquez (2001) "Upwards: Never Down: The Catholic Charismatic Renewal in Transnational Perspective." In *Christianity, Social Change, and Globalization in the Americas*. Ed. A. Peterson, P. Williams and M. Vásquez. New Brunswick, NJ: Rutgers University Press.

Rumbaut, R. (2002) "Severed or Sustained Attachments? Language, Identity, and Imagined Communities in the Post-Immigrant Generation." In *The Changing Face of Home: The Transnational Lives of the Second Generation*, Ed. P. Levitt and M. Waters. New York: Russell Sage Publication. Pp. 43–95.

Sassen, S. (1992) *Global Cities*. Princeton, NJ: Princeton University Press.

Smith, A. D. (1983) "Nationalism and Social Theory," *British Journal of Sociology*, 34(1): 19–38.

Smith, R. C. (2002) "Life Course, Generation and Social Location as Factors Shaping Second-Generation Transnational Life." In *The Changing Face of Home: The Transnational Lives of the Second Generation*, Ed. P. Levitt and M. Waters. New York: Russell Sage Publication. Pp. 145–168.

Urry, J. (2000) "The Global Media and Cosmopolitanism." Paper presented at Transnational America Conference, Bavarian American Academy, Munich, June 2000, published by the Department of Sociology,

Lancaster University at <http://www.comp.lancs.ac.uk/ sociology/soc056ju.html>.

Waters, M. C. (1999) *Black Identities: West Indian Immigrant Dreams and American Realities.* New York and Cambridge, MA: Russell Sage Foundation.

Wimmer, A. and N. Glick Schiller (2003) "Methodological Nationalism, the Social Sciences and the Study of Migration: An Essay in Historical Epistemology," *International Migration Review,* 37(3):576–610.

Zhou, M. (1998) "Parachute Kids in Southern California: The Educational Experience of Chinese Children in Transnational Families," *Educational Policy,* 12(6):682–704.

SECTION 6

*R*eligious Life Across Borders

Introduction to Section 6

Social science predicted that religion would decline in importance as modernity increased. In fact, religion's salience seems to be increasing, if in different forms, in response to the rootlessness and cultural pressures associated with the modern and postmodern condition. Religion, the archetypical spatial and temporal boundary crosser, comes with built-in answers for people belonging to several communities in several places at once. It endows its followers with symbols, rituals, and narratives with which to imagine themselves in sacred landscapes. Sometimes these religious landscapes coexist easily with the actual physical and political geography. In others, the religious landscape takes precedence over the secular. The Catholic Church has the most highly developed, easily recognizable system of transnational governance. But Muslim, Hindu, and Evangelical Christian communities are also constructing transnational organizational architectures with a global reach.

This section explores the ways in which different aspects of religious experience change in response to globalization. Readers may be confused as to why we included these particular selections as Peter Beyer, Manuel Vásquez and Marie Marquardt are seemingly more interested in globalization than in transnationalism. We did so because theirs is some of the most influential writing about religious life across borders, and because these authors, while not sharing our entire vocabulary and conceptual apparatus, are concerned about religious experience and institutions that cross the boundaries of time and space. They also want to know about the interaction between the local, national, and global.

Peter Beyer examines how the institution of religion changes in the context of globalization. He wants to know what is needed for religion to remain salient and survive in a global world where secularization is overwhelmingly predicted to win out. Social theorists such as Parsons, Berger, and Luckmann see functional or institutional differentiation and pluralistic individual identities as basic features of modern society. What Luckmann calls "functionally differentiated societal subsystems" specialize around certain kinds of economic, political, or social activities. Secularization happens because the subsystems operate independently of each other. That is, economics and politics go on, without much influence from religious norms, values, and justifications. Furthermore, in this socio-structural context, religion not only retreats; it is also pressured to become compartmentalized and create an institutionally specialized subsystem of its own. "Privatization" is also spurred by the increasingly important role of experts in modern society, who become the principal public representatives of societal subsystems. Religious "privatization" occurs because decision-making about religious matters has become the individual's concern and because the public representatives of the religious system wield less influence. To overcome its subordinate position and remain viable, religious leaders and adherents have to convince the rest of us that religious norms and values are our collective obligation and that they are beyond the pale of individuals. Moreover, religion, unlike economics and politics, has something to offer everyone.

But what is it that religion can offer to ensure its continued viability? What would a shared moral solution consist of in a world where so many different groups make up global society?

In an interconnected world it is difficult to attribute evil to the outside "other," because who would that interloper be? The successful reincorporation of religion into the public sphere, Beyer argues, depends on its "function and form." The *function* refers to how it relates to society as a whole, and the *form* to how it relates to other social systems. Performance, Beyer predicts, will ultimately reestablish religion's influence. Its strength and relevance lie in its role as a cultural resource or its ability to solve the liberal and conservative problems that other social systems generate.

Susanne Rudolph is interested in the ways in which transnational religions transform international relations. More and more, she says, we see communities and processes that transcend national borders but we have not had the vocabulary to describe them. Yet this liminal space is increasingly occupied by various types of special interest, knowledge-based, value-laden communities organized less around their experience of shared territory and more around the interests, activities, and worldviews they have in common. These communities reshape the international system. World politics includes new ideas and actors including transnational civil society groups as well as sovereignty-sharing states. Rudolph's goal is to understand how religious groups and movements figure in these activities and, by doing so, the potential conflicts and cooperation that can occur.

Contemporary religious transnationalism, Rudolph tells us, shares some of the characteristics of its earlier Islamic and Christian variants but differs demographically and technologically. It grows out of the experience of ordinary individuals, rather than being superimposed from above. Because religious associations structure human relations and imbue them with meaning, they can facilitate action and encourage cooperation. At the same time, religions are often the source of the language, symbols, and motivations that cause conflicts within and between states. When can religion build bridges between groups and under what conditions will it divide them? asks Rudolph. If it can be an opiate that makes people resigned to social injustice, can it not also be a catalyst for collective action and transformation?

There is history we can draw upon to answer these questions. While today we generally assume that homogenization or assimilation are the sole paths to religious and ethnic civility, in many older civilizations, religious pluralism was the norm and foreigners from different places lived side by side. The ancient cities of Asia and Europe provide examples of thriving pluralistic multinational empires, and enduring poly-ethnic communities that can serve as contemporary models. But the contemporary political stage is not just occupied by state actors; transnational civil society, formed by non-state associations, discourses, and practices also plays a starring role. Religious communities, though well-represented contributors, are little understood. We need to explore, urges Rudolph, how variations in hierarchy and organization influence the way different transnational religious groups locate themselves between civil society and the state and their resulting political influence.

Finally, Manuel Vásquez and Marie Marquardt's contribution examines the theoretical insights gained by using a global framework to study religion. Religion, they say, is one of the principal forces behind the decoupling of culture from particular geographic and social spaces and "its re-attachment in new space–time configurations." Religion and globalization are linked in several ways. First, religions contribute to the emergence of an imagined world community and globally accepted ideas about human personhood. Religions provide maps for negotiating de-territorialization and re-territorialization and enable people to come up with alternative understandings of new spatio-temporal arrangements. Religion also contributes to globalization through the proliferation of faith-based organizational networks that channel the flow of economic, social, and cultural capital worldwide. These networks often do the work of "glocalization," or building bridges between the universal messages espoused by faith traditions and the everyday experience of ordinary individuals. These encounters, while sometimes leading to greater homogeneity, are more often a source of hybridity, heterogeneity, and change.

CHAPTER 26

Systemic Religion in Global Society

Peter Beyer

PRIVATIZATION AND PUBLIC INFLUENCE OF RELIGION

Since at least the 1960s, many sociologists have put forward the notion that religion, at least in the contemporary Western world, has become increasingly privatized. Most prominently, Talcott Parsons (1960; 1966: 134), Peter Berger (1967: 133f.), Thomas Luckmann (1967: 103), and Robert Bellah (1970a: 43) interpreted secularization in the modern world to mean that traditional religion was now primarily the concern of the individual and had therefore lost much of its 'public' relevance. People were voluntary adherents to a plurality of religions, none of which could claim practically to be binding on any but its own members.

Beyond this core idea, however, there are important variants of the privatization thesis. In particular, Parsons and Bellah relocate 'public' religion in *cultural* forms such as American civil religion or Marxism (see Bellah, 1970b; Parsons, 1974: 203ff). Here privatization characterizes only traditional, systemic religions. By contrast, Berger and Luckmann talk about private and public 'spheres', locating religion only in the former. They have a somewhat different idea of what counts as religion, favouring the systemic or institutionally specialized forms.

Aside from the question of variants, the privatization thesis is also part of the larger secularization debate. Privatization, as such, is not a central item for all participants in this debate. Yet, whether it is Roland Robertson's emphasis on individuation (Robertson, 1977), Bryan Wilson's focus on the loss of community (Wilson, 1976), or Rich-

ard Fenn's analysis of the lack of moral unity (Fenn, 1978), the critical core of the privatization thesis is implicitly present: traditional religious forms are no longer definitive for the society as a whole, but can still direct the lives of individuals or subgroups. Equally important, however, is the well-known disagreement among scholars about the meaning and validity of the secularization thesis itself. Does it mean a decline in the salience of religion as a human form of expression (see for example Wilson, 1982)? Does it mean only the compartmentalization or relocation of religion as the privatization thesis suggests? Or is it merely the expression of the cyclical decline of established religions followed by the rise of new or revitalized ones (see for example Stark and Bainbridge, 1985)? The first two positions imply that secularization is a result of the modernization of Western society and therefore unique to that historical process. The third view sees secularization as something that characterizes religion at all times and in all societies, and therefore has little to do with modernization as such.

Here is not the place to discuss these various options in any detail. I have introduced them because they point to ambiguity in the phenomenon, namely the place, importance, and form of religion in the contemporary social world. The privatization thesis has been one way of dealing with this ambiguity, and I believe an instructive one. In this chapter, I use it as the starting point for examining religion in the global context. How can the privatization thesis be used to understand better the role of religion in modern global society? As indicated in the previous chapter, my aim is to show that privatization is not the whole story but rather only a part of it. Specifically, the thesis that I explore here posits that the globalization of society, while structurally favouring privatization in religion, also provides fertile ground for the renewed public influence of religion. By public influence, I mean that one or more religions can become the source of collective obligation, such that deviation from specific religious norms will bring in its wake negative consequences for adherents and non-adherents alike; and collective action in the name of these norms becomes legitimate. In the light of the analyses of the previous chapter, the operative question is of course whether this is possible through functionally oriented, institutionally specialized, subsystemic communication; or whether religion will take the route of socio-cultural particularisms and become an important cultural resource for other types of system and other subsystems. [...]

The problem of public influence is then broken up into three interconnected arguments. First I argue that, if institutional religion is to be publicly influential, it is not enough that there be a high level of individual religiosity which adherents then translate into religiously inspired public action. It is also not enough that religious leaders and professionals form and concentrate that religiosity in organizations and movements which institutionalize religion. What is required for publicly influential religion is, at a minimum, that religious leaders have control over a service that is clearly indispensable in today's world as do, for instance, health professionals, political leaders, scientific or business experts. Second the structures of modern/global society greatly weaken most of the ways that religious leaders have accomplished this before. In this regard, the focal point in this chapter is that a global society has no outsiders who can serve as the social representatives of evil, danger, or chaos. Without these, the forces of order and good also become more difficult to identify *at the level of global society as a whole*, undermining or relativizing, for instance, deontological moral codes and the salience of other-worldly salvation. Third, therefore,

religion will have a comparatively difficult time in gaining public influence as a differentiated functional system, that is, at the level of global society as a whole; but such influence will be easier to attain if religious leaders apply traditional religious modalities for the purpose of subsocietal, especially political mobilization in response to the globalization of society. In terms of the question posed above, therefore, privatization applies to religion in global society if we look at it as a functional subsystem; public influence for religion is possible primarily when, like socio-cultural particularisms, it takes on the role of cultural resource for other systems. [...]

As I have argued, the autonomy of functionally specific rationalities runs counter to a priority of communal group boundaries. The resultant globalizing tendencies of society have radically altered the conditions under which the moralizing solution is still possible because the societal group now includes everyone. The situation of religion at the level of global society alters correspondingly.

To begin, the person who used to be the unequivocal outsider is now often literally my neighbour, whether I approve or not. This is what Rushdie called the metropolitan experience (see above, p.1). The outside/inside distinction readily at hand for reinforcing the internal moral codes of communal, and hence territorial, societies becomes at least difficult to maintain over the long run in a world of virtually instant global communication, itself a consequence of functional specialization. Not only, for example, does the leader of the 'evil empire' reveal himself to be less than totally evil when met face to face; more important, it is increasingly difficult not to meet with him, not for moral reasons, but for primarily political and economic ones. In the process, morality has lost its central structural position: the decadent and unjust West can be made to pay dearly for its oil, but economically, a sizeable portion of the petrodollars must be reinvested in the West.[1]

Translated into more theological language, the globalization of society does not lead to the death of God, as some Western theologians of the 1960s asserted. God is still in his heaven and his will still rules the world; but the visage of the devil is becoming increasingly indistinct. The result is that God can still be loved, but it is more difficult to fear him. He is still there, but does he make a difference? Is salvation still essential; or will it become the privatized proclivity of a minority, similar and not superior to other leisure pursuits? On the global level, the problem of specifying the transcendent and thus giving the central religious dichotomy meaningful definition and applicability must be addressed anew.

I do not wish to assert, with this analysis, that evil is disappearing from the face of the earth. Far from it. What is happening is that structural changes in, and the globalization of, modern society have made it more difficult than it used to be to personify this evil, to attach it to a self-evident social correlate. The morally other is less easily negated as the outsider or interloper. With this development the old solution to the problem of specifying the transcendent has been undermined, although, I stress again, only on the level of society as a whole. The conditions and implications of using the old solution have been altered. Religion, and, in the current context, religious professionals are therefore faced with a fundamental choice, even dilemma: whether to address the contemporary problem of religious influence without the old solution or by reasserting it.

Each of these two paths has its attendant problems. In what follows, I call them the conservative and liberal options. The first would correspond to the reassertion of the reality of the devil and the second to the acquiescence in his dissolution. Using the distinction as a point of departure, I want now to examine how contemporary developments in global religion reflect the structural tendencies outlined thus far. In the process, I again take up the various themes introduced above, but specifically the notion that, regardless of which option is taken, public influence for religion will be found in the direction of religious performance; while action concentrating on religious function will continue, with certain exceptions, to be the domain of privatized, highly pluralistic religiosity.

PRIVATIZED FUNCTION AND PUBLIC PERFORMANCE

The liberal option addresses the central problem of the determination of the transcendent only in a very abstract fashion; there is evil in the world, but it cannot be consistently and clearly localized or personified. It is a limitation in all of us, in all our social structures. It is especially not to be found in the fact of pluralism, including religious pluralism. If anything, the opposite is true: intolerance and particularistic ascription are a prime source of evil.[2] Religious professionals and adherents with this attitude tend to be ecumenical and tolerant. They see comparable possibilities for enlightenment and salvation in their tradition and in other religions. They are also polite. The central theological problem of this option, as critics (such as Berger, 1979; Kelley, 1972) point out, is that it makes few really *religious* demands: it conveys little specifically religious information that would make a difference in how people choose, or that people could not get from non-religious sources.

Professional responses to this dilemma under the liberal option reflect the difference between function and performance outlined above. In terms of function, the tendency is to orient the organization toward helping services, including the celebration of important life passages and, of course, the 'cure of souls' for those who feel the need (cf. Bibby, 1987 for excellent Canadian data). This response accommodates itself to what the private adherents evidently want. Function concentrates on private choices. God is preached as benevolent and not wrathful: his only real request is that people imitate his attitude in their relations with others. Evil exists but it is a negative deficiency to be filled and not a positive presence to be destroyed. Moreover, religious leaders with this ecumenical attitude have picked up the universalistic orientations of elitist strains in the major world religions: the possibility of enlightenment for all, the possibility of wisdom for all, the possibility of salvation for all. Now, however, as part of the globalization process, everyone is included, and not just upper strata virtuosi with the leisure for such functional specialization. The combination of pluralism and inclusion excludes very few from the virtually automatic benefits of the religious function.

Religious leaders and organizations that follow the liberal option therefore have difficulty in specifying both the benefits and the requirements of religion in functional or 'pure' form. This indeterminacy has led them to a reliance on performance relations to reestablish the importance of religion and hence the influence of the religious system. Here, often globally oriented issues ranging from gay liberation to political oppression are providing the opportunity to show that religion leads to benefits and demands that are far from insignificant.[3]

To repeat, the view of performance I am using sees it as the attempt by one system to solve problems that are generated elsewhere in the societal environmental but not solved there. As such, the problems addressed by religious performance are not religious problems at all, at least not directly. The solutions, therefore, while religiously inspired, will tend to take on the characteristics of the target system: economic solutions to economic problems, political solutions to political problems, and so forth.[4] The deliberate attempt to conform to this structurally encouraged pattern is characteristic of the liberal option inasmuch as it correlates with the basic structure of modern society. There is the conviction that educational problems are not going to be solved by adherence to the traditional faith; that health problems are not going to be solved by meditation, political problems not by the correct execution of rituals.

Instead, the liberal option returns to the communitarian past of religion to define its 'application' as that which is concerned for the community as a whole. In this modern case, however, humanity as a whole is the community and the religious task is to work for the fuller inclusion of all people in the benefits of this global community.[5] Hence religious leaders of this direction style the problems of global society in corresponding terms: conflict among various sectors of the world community is the result in large part of the marginalization of some (often the majority) from systemic benefits like 'adequate' income, political participation, health care, education, and so forth. Yet, the notion of a global community is very general and very vague, including as it does a vast variety of group cultures and individual lifestyles. The styling of the applied religion in terms of a global community in fact reflects the benign functional message of the liberal option. Combined with the respect for the independence of other systems, notably the political, this may work against such activity being recognized as specifically *religious* communication, as something that religion does for us. While this is a problem, it does not mean that such religious activity cannot be effective.

An example may help to illustrate this point. I treat the liberation theological movement in Latin America extensively in Chapter 6. Here I anticipate certain aspects of the arguments presented there.

Generally, liberation theologians (and their First World parallels) represent the liberal option.[6] They are concerned with justice and peace, values that point to the egalitarian inclusion of those marginalized from the benefits of modern institutions. This 'preferential option for the poor' rejects traditionally religious interpretations in favour of a contextual theology that uses present experience as the basis for finding the correct religious understanding. Liberation theologians do not present one particular group culture and its religion as being closer to the divine will than others. While the alleged opposition of the 'poor' and 'capitalism' sometimes comes close to being an opposition between good and evil, these religious leaders generally criticize the latter for its creation of vast, global inequalities and not for being an alien worldview destructive of the true and good order that their own group represents. Accordingly, they also do not discourage religious pluralism.

The critics of liberation theology accuse them of having lost the specifically religious (for example, Ratzinger) or of offering economic and political solutions that do not accord with economic and political realities (for example, Novak) (cf. Berryman, 1987; 179–200; McGovern, 1989). One attack is in terms of function, the other in terms of performance. In fact, liberation theology places primary emphasis on religious performance. While 'pure' religious belief and practice are important, they are so only to the extent that they contribute to the alleviation of social ills, leading to an emphasis on *praxis*. Essentially, liberation theologians respond to the privatization of religion by seeking a revitalization of the religious function in religious performances, particularly in the political realm. Sin becomes primarily social and the principal religious demand is for social justice (see G. Baum, 1975: 193ff.).

Seeking to establish religious influence by linking function and performance is, of course, not new or unusual. As discussed above, all religious traditions have historically done this. In modern circumstances, however, function and performance are more clearly distinguishable because we use function as a central way of dividing social action. Therefore, if working for social justice is going to be a recognized *religious* performance, then its necessary connection with religious *function* must be apparent, just as the necessary connection between Einstein's pure scientific endeavours and the building of the atomic bomb is apparent. The criticisms of liberation theology, that it is neither good religion nor good economics, indicate a problem here. And in fact, liberation theologians have relied heavily on non-religious interpretations like dependency theory and Marxist analysis to understand the problems, and prefer explicitly political courses of action.[7] The connection with the theology is clearly visible in the writings of its proponents; but it is anything but necessary. In this light, it should not be surprising that liberation theologians have sometimes been tempted to address the problem through an increasingly 'Manichaean' opposition of the poor and capitalism, with socialism, the group culture of the poor, as the vaguely defined, communitarian goal.

I do not want to suggest with this analysis that liberation theology is not legitimate theology. If anything, the opposite is true. The issue here is rather the position of religion in global society and how the problem of privatization reflects this position. Liberation

theologians are attempting to establish public influence for religion in the face of privatization. They are doing this through religious performances that concentrate on political involvement although they do not go so far as to advocate the legislation of religious norms. One can argue, as does Phillip Berryman (1984), that they have been somewhat successful in this endeavour (but see Mainwaring, 1989). Yet, whether this strategy can lead to a reestablishment of the public influence of religious communication in general in our society is still an open question.

While performance relations under the liberal option thus offer a possibility for religion to break out of its privatized functional ghetto and back onto the political stage especially, the possibilities are limited. In addition to problems just touched upon in the example of liberation theology, the pluralism permitted on the level of function implies an equal pluralism on the level of performance. Therefore, to the extent that religious leaders, such as those in North American liberal Protestant churches, can control their organizational levers and take a unified public stand on issues, to that extent they risk losing an appreciable portion of their adherents, regardless of the particular stand taken (cf. Bibby, 1987; Hadden, 1970). Mobilization becomes a serious and constant problem in this respect. In the absence of additional, non-religious measures (especially direct political involvement)[8], religious leaders are left with the kind of persuasion that in the Christian tradition is called evangelization: reliance on voluntaristic, privatized decision-making with its attendant fissiparous pluralism.

In spite of this difficulty on the part of the liberal option, its religious cosmos does correlate with the structural tendencies of a global society, as the above argument has outlined. To the degree that global society continues to become a more solid reality, the liberal option might be seen as the trend of the future. In the meantime and at least for the foreseeable future, however, it is not the only possible direction.

The conservative option (the reassertion of the tradition in spite of modernity), far from being merely a throwback correlating with bygone social structures, is in fact the one that is making religion most visible in today's world. It is a vital aspect of globalization and not a negation of it. Given the direction of the preceding analysis, this claim requires a bit of explanation. [. . .]

I want to make a similar argument with respect to the performance response under the conservative option: what seems to be running against globalization and modernity is actually better seen as reflective of it, albeit in a very different way when compared with the liberal option. To explain this requires a short digression.

Globalization, as I have tried to show in previous chapters, does not mean the inevitable, evolutionary progress toward a global spread of Western modernity. Such developmentalism in inadequate not only because the empirical facts negate the proposition, but also because, from the theoretical point of view, globalization should have as profound effects on the formerly territorial societies of the West as it is having on other formerly territorial civilizations around the world. Up until the middle of the twentieth century, the West may well have believed that its successful imperial expansion of the previous four centuries was essentially a one-way street. Today this illusion is rapidly revealing itself as what it is.

The resistance to, or perhaps better, digestion of globalization in various parts of the contemporary world has given rise to movements informed by the conservative religious option: above all political mobilization as the service (performance) of the religious faith. Whether the complaint is 'Westoxication' in the Middle East or the difficulty of 'making America great again', the problem is similar. In the West, former 'outsiders' (the Soviets, the Japanese, the Arabs et al.) are undermining the long-standing political, economic, and general cultural dominance of the West. The West can rely less and less on its economic, political (especially military), and scientific might to assure the continued hegemony of its culture. On the homefront, the functional differentiation that is such a key aspect of globalization continues to bring about rapid change in the old core structures:

the family, morality, and religion. In the non-West, in spite of increased political independence and/or economic power in many areas, Western cultural patterns still seem to be becoming increasingly dominant. What appears to some in the West as moral, economic, and political decline of their own culture, appears to many in the non-West simply as continued Western cultural, economic, and political imperialism. With its clear ties to communal group cultures, both in the past and still largely in the present, religion is an obvious candidate for structuring a response to both. [. . .]

When political and economic responses to these conflicts fail, religious performance may be able to fill the breach. Since the adherents to the various religions around the world are still by and large localized, leaders can often express regional conflicts and disparities in religious terms.[9] Here, the conservative option, grounded as it is in traditional, communally oriented societies, offers distinct advantages. Its solution to the problem of transcendence allows an approximate dichotomization of the world into the religiously pure and impure, into us and them. Such a clear religious message can, under the correct conditions, lead to successful mobilization of entire populations. Politicization on this religious basis then becomes a way for regions to assert themselves in the face of globalization and its consequences. Hitherto, the most visible examples of such conservative religious performance movements, in the Islamic Middle East and in the Sikh Punjab, have occurred after prolonged, unsuccessful political attempts to address problems attendant upon modernization and in the wake of significant increases in regional wealth (cf. Esposito, 1987; Keddie, 1980; Leaf, 1985; Telford, 1992; Wallace, 1986; 1988).

This combination of factors is probably not accidental. The modernization that correlates with globalization is not simply benevolent, let alone egalitarian. It destroys as well as creates. The attempt to gain some transcendent perspective on this historical process is understandable, especially when immanent techniques such as purely political nationalism, socialism, open-door capitalism, secularized education,[10] and even economic progress all seem to fail. If the necessary definition of the transcendent means applying the religious correlates of bygone social structures to the very different divisions of today, then this only indicates that contemporary structures do not offer a self-evident alternative.

Religious movements grounded in the conservative option contrast with their liberal counterparts in a number of ways. Critical among these is the conservative notion that the public influence of religion should be supported by law. Important religious norms should be enshrined in legislation; they should not have to rely on a 'demonstration effect' for their influence. The conservative religious leaders lay great stress on a particular group-cultural moral code as the manifestation of divine will. In a global social environment that is generally corrosive of group cultural boundaries and that therefore encourages religio-moral pluralism, there is little hope that one cultural outlook will prevail on the basis of its own unique merits.

The alternative is to gain control over a limited territory dominated by the particular culture and then control pluralism within it. This has certainly been the goal of the New Christian Right in the United States, Sikh extremists in Punjab, the politicized neo-orthodox camp in Israel, and Islamic fundamentalists in the Middle East. Given the problems of territorial boundaries, the coextension of legal and political systems, and the fact that the nation-state has already provided a locus of institutionalization for sociocultural particularisms under globalizing/modernizing conditions, it is not surprising that such efforts should so often be (ultra-)nationalist in ideology or effect. This difference between the liberal and conservative options in fact emphasizes the degree to which the latter uses and reinforces the segmentary and territorial differentiation within the modern global political system of states. It is another example of how the conservative direction within global religion is reflective of the structures of global society and not just a reaction against these.

Indeed, what I have been calling the conservative performance option for religion in the modern world does not at first glance seem to accord well with a primacy of instrumental, functional differentiation. One of the more explicit aims of many of the movements under scrutiny is to dedifferentiate many functional areas, mainly religion and politics, but also religion and the family, religion and education, religion and economy, among others. However, dedifferentiation in the absence of an alternative structural base, such as was provided by hierarchical status-group differentiation in older societies, is still a response to problems of globalization in terms of a primacy of function. Religious movements like the Iranian revolution want to solve overall societal problems by giving the religious system and its values first place among the various functional spheres. Like economic dominance in the nineteenth century West or political dominance in the People's Republic of China, a strategy which attempts to combat the effects of functional dominance under the banner of the religious system can perhaps best be seen as a critical accommodative response to a globalism in which function dominates.[11] It may stem the tide of modernization and some of the more disruptive consequences of globalization for quite some time in particular regions, perhaps even until the global system collapses under the weight of its own internally generated problems. But it does not negate the fundamental structure of global society. [. . .]

NOTES

1. With the result that moral differences are reduced, for instance, to the privatized stipulation that Saudi-backed racing-car drivers must toast their victories with orange juice instead of champagne!

2. A dramatic and graphic illustration of this option and its opposite appears in the 1986 Granada television documentary, *The Sword of Islam*. The film begins with Terry Waite asserting that 'true Islam' is tolerant and respectful of human rights, painting a picture of Islam that seems more consistent with liberal Protestantism than with the militant Islam of the film's subjects, al-Jihad in Egypt and Hizb Allah (Waite's apparent kidnappers) in Lebanon.

3. This point becomes especially important in religious environmentalism, for which see below, Chapter 9.

4. For examples, this time from Roman Catholic leaders in the United States and Canada, see the

documents in Baum and Cameron, 1984: 3–18; and in O'Brien and Shannon, 1977: 518–537.

5. See, for example, the concern for world community in more recent papal documents such as John XXIII's *Pacem in Terris*, and Paul VI's *Populorum Progressio* (both are reprinted in O'Brien and Shannon, 1977).

6. The liberation theology literature is quite large. A useful summary is Berryman, 1987. Representative samples from around the world are in Ferm, 1986.

7. The reliance on outside 'ideologies' and the direct political involvement are two of the central points on which the more conservative Roman Catholic hierarchy in Latin America opposes those who act on liberation theological principles. The fear on the part of these bishops is that the church will be compromised and lose its independence both from the point of view of its religious message and its ability to put that message into practice. For the clear manifestation of this conflict in Nicaragua, see Berryman, 1984: 226ff.; Bradstock, 1987.

8. Even here, the divergent selectivities of the religious and political systems may neutralize the religiously inspired efforts. Salient examples are the New Christian Right in the United States and Soka Gakkai in Japan. See, for example, Roof, 1986; Shupe, 1986; Chapter 5 below.

9. That the strategy breaks down and is even counterproductive when such correspondence between religion and territory does not obtain has been evidenced in, among other places, Lebanon. See Norton, 1987.

10. It cannot be without significance that both the typical member of al-Jihad in Egypt and the typical follower of Bhindranwale in the Punjab are and were comparatively well educated youths from the lower-middle and middle economic classes. See Nayar and Singh, 1984: 23; and Ibrahim, 1986: 355.

11. The strategy of giving priority to religious communication for the purpose of halting modernity was followed successfully in Quebec for almost a century. Eventually, however, in this instance, the religiously controlled structures set up to stem the tide provided some of the foundations for the rapid modernization of Quebec after World War II. See Beyer, 1989.

REFERENCES

Baum, Gregory (1975) *Religion and Alienation: A Theological Reading of Sociology*. New York: Paulist.

Baum, Gregory and Cameron, Duncan (1984) *Ethics and Economics: Canada's Catholic Bishops on the Economic Crisis*. Toronto: Lorimer.

Bellah, Robert N. (1970a) 'Religious Evolution', in *Beyond Belief: Essays on Religion in a Post-Traditional World*. New York: Harper & Row. pp. 20–50.

Bellah, Robert N. (1970b) 'Civil Religion in America', in *Beyond Belief: Essays on Religion in a Post-Traditional World*. New York: Harper & Row. pp. 168–189.

Berger, Peter L. (1967) *The Sacred Canopy: Elements of a Sociological Theory of Religion*. Garden City: Doubleday.

Berger, Peter L. (1979) *The Heretical Imperative: Contemporary Possibilities of Religious Affirmation*. Garden City: Doubleday.

Berryman, Phillip (1984) *The Religious Roots of Rebellion: Christians in Central American Revolutions*. Maryknoll, NY: Orbis.

Berryman, Phillip (1987) *Liberation Theology: The Essential Facts about the Revolutionary Movement in Latin America and Beyond*. New York: Pantheon.

Bibby, Reginald, W. (1987) *Fragmented Gods: The Poverty and Potential of Religion in Canada*. Toronto: Irwin.

Bradstock, Andrew (1987) *Saints and Sandinistas: The Catholic Church in Nicaragua and its Response to the Revolution*. London: Epworth.

Esposito, John L. (1987) *Islam and Politics*. Rev. 2nd ed. Syracuse: Syracuse University.

Fenn, Richard K. (1978) *Toward a Theory of Secularization*. Storrs, CT: Society for the Scientific Study of Religion.

Hadden, Jeffrey K. (1970) *The Gathering Storm in the Churches*. New York: Doubleday.

Ibrahim, Saad Eddin (1986) 'Egypt's Islamic Militancy Revisited', in Jeffrey K. Hadden and Anson Shupe (eds), *Prophetic Religions and Politics. Religion and the Political Order*, Volume 1. New York: Paragon. pp. 353–361.

Keddie, Nikki R. (1980) 'The Economic History of Iran 1800–1914 and Its Political Impact', in *Iran: Religion, Politics and Society. Collected Essays*. London: Frank Cass. pp. 119–136.

Kelley, Dean (1972) *Why Conservative Churches Are Growing*. New York: Harper & Row.

Leaf, Murray J. (1985) 'The Punjab Crisis', *Asian Survey*, 25: 475–498.

Luckmann, Thomas (1967) *The Invisible Religion: The Problem of Religion in Modern Society*. New York: Macmillan.

Mainwaring, Scott (1989) 'Grassroots Catholic Groups and Politics in Brazil', in Scott Mainwaring and Alexander Wilde (eds), *The Progressive Church in Latin America*. Notre Dame, IN: University of Notre Dame. pp. 151–192.

McGovern, Arthur F. (1989) *Liberation Theology and Its Critics: Toward an Assessment*. Maryknoll, NY: Orbis.

Nayar, Kuldip and Singh, Khushwant (1984) *Tragedy of Punjab: Operation Bluestar and After*. New Delhi: Vision Books.

Norton, Augustus Richard (1987) *Amal and the Shi'a: Struggle for the Soul of Lebanon*. Austin: University of Texas.

O'Brien, David J. and Shannon, Thomas A. (eds) (1977) *Renewing the Earth: Catholic Documents on Peace, Justice and Liberation*. New York: Doubleday Image.

Parsons, Talcott (1960) 'Some Comments on the Pattern of Religious Organization in the United States', in *Structure and Process in Modern Societies*. New York: Free Press.

Parsons, Talcott (1966) 'Religion in a Modern Pluralistic Society', *Review of Religious Research*, 7: 125–146.

Parsons, Talcott (1974) 'Religion in Postindustrial America: The Problem of Secularization', *Social Research*, 41: 193–225.

Robertson, Roland (1977) 'Individualism, Societalism, Worldliness, Universalism: Thematizing Theoretical Sociology of Religion', *Sociological Analysis*, 38: 281–308.

Roof, Wade Clark (1986) 'The New Fundamentalism: Rebirth of Political Religion in America', in Jeffrey K. Hadden and Anson Shupe (eds), *Prophetic Religions and Politics. Religion and the Political Order*, Volume 1. New York: Paragon. pp. 18–34.

Shupe, Anson (1986) 'Militancy and Accommodation in the Third Civilization: The Case of Japan's Soka Gakkai Movement', in Jeffrey K. Hadden and Anson Shupe (eds), *Prophetic Religions and Politics. Religion and the Political Order*, Volume 1. New York: Paragon. pp. 235–253.

Stark, Rodney and Bainbridge, William Sims (1985) *The Future of Religion: Secularization, Revival and Cult Formation*. Berkeley: University of California.

Telford, Hamish (1992) 'The Call for Khalistan: The Political Economy of Sikh Separatism'. MA thesis, McGill University, Department of Political Science, Montreal.

Wallace, Paul (1986) 'The Sikhs as a "Minority" in a Sikh Majority State in India', *Asia Survey*, 26: 363–377.

Wallace, Paul (1988) 'Sikh Minority Attitudes in India's Federal System', in Joseph T. O'Connell, et al. (eds), *Sikh History and Religion in the Twentieth Century*. Toronto: South Asian Studies, University of Toronto, pp. 256–273.

Wilson, Bryan R. (1976) 'Aspects of Secularization in the West', *Japanese Journal of Religious Studies*, 3: 259–76.

Wilson, Bryan R. (1982) *Religion in Sociological Perspective*. New York: Oxford Univeristy Press.

CHAPTER 27

Introduction: Religion, States, and Transnational Civil Society

Susanne Hoeber Rudolph

TRANSNATIONAL RELIGION IN LIMINAL SPACE: ITS DEMOGRAPHY

Religious communities are among the oldest of the transnationals: Sufi orders, Catholic missionaries, and Buddhist monks carried word and praxis across vast spaces before those places became nation-states or even states. Such religious peripatetics *were* versions of civil society.[1] In today's post-modern era, religious communities have become vigorous creators of an emergent transnational civil society.

Modern social science did not warn us that this would happen. Instead it asserted that religion would fade, then disappear, with the triumph of science and rationalism. But religion has expanded explosively, stimulated as much by secular global processes—migration, multinational capital, the media revolution—as by proselytizing activity. Contrary to expectations, its expansion has been an answer to and driven by modernity. In response to the deracination and threats of cultural extinction associated with modernization processes, religious experience seeks to restore meaning to life.[2]

Religious communities are helping to shape world politics. The language of international relations and security studies on the one hand and that of foreign policy and domestic politics on the other distinguish political life within states from the alleged imperatives of an imagined international system. This distinction and separation deploy a rich vocabulary for "inside" and "outside," to follow Rob Walker's language.[3] Until recently, there were no words and metaphors for designating and populating the liminal space that cuts across inside/outside, a space that is neither within the state nor an aspect of the international state system but animates both.

This liminal and cross-cutting arena is becoming more densely occupied by communities—environmentalists, development professionals, human rights activists, information specialists—whose commonality depends less on coresidence in "sovereign" territorial space and more on common worldviews, purposes, interests, and praxis.[4] Peter Haas has theorized them as epistemic communities.[5] Such communities, including religious communities and movements, have implications for the international system. Their existence has transformed how we understand and explain "international relations," that is, relations among sovereign states in anarchic space. It is possible to theorize these new transnational communities as constituting a world politics that encompasses both transnational civil society and sovereignty-sharing states. The object of this volume is to create a space for religious groups and movements in the consideration of such transnational solidarities.

The communities that populate transnational civil society do not affect the state "system" in the way some wish world governance might. They do not provide a statelike entity to impose order and perhaps justice "outside," in anarchic space, by monopolizing force and supplying universal arbitration and rule enforcement. They do not even supply what transnational regimes are meant to provide—predictable systems of rules that facilitate cooperation.[6] Instead, they create a pluralistic transnational polity. They shape perceptions and expectations that contribute to world public opinion and politics.

Their effects on transnational space are only beginning to be understood. Existential fright about "the coming anarchy" is probably premature.[7] But because a plurality of transnational spaces entails difference as well as commonality with respect to epistemes, identities, and expectations, transnational civil society can be the site of conflict as well as cooperation.

While the fluidity of religion across political boundaries is very old, recent migrations, communication links, and elite transformations joining East with West and North with South have generated unaccustomed flows: Hindus in Leicester, Muslims in Marseilles and Frankfurt, Pentecostals in Moscow and Singapore. Europeans found themselves in a minority at Vatican II, overwhelmed by 200 U.S. and 228 Asian and African bishops.[8] Since the mid-1960s American evangelism has helped to raise the proportion of Protestants to 12 percent of the population of Latin America, formerly a Catholic bastion.[9] In predominantly Chinese Singapore, the Christian population has doubled to one-fifth since 1985. In China proper, optimistic Christian estimates place the number of Christians at 80 million.[10]

It may surprise readers to learn that since the mid-1970s Oklahoma City has acquired five mosques, four Hindu temples, one Sikh *gurudwara*, and three Buddhist temples; that Denver has a similar configuration; that there may be as many as seventy mosques in the Chicago metropolitan area and fifty temples in the Midwest Buddhist Association; and that Muslims out-number Episcopalians in the United States two to one and are likely to out-number Jews in the near future.[11]

This explosion of religious formations seems to have been facilitated by the very forces that were supposed to dissolve them: increased print and electronic media, increased literacy—including the higher literacy of post-secondary education—and urbanization. Explaining the increase and intensification in religious discourse in Oman and its entry into everyday life and politics, Dale Eickelman writes:

The most profound change is associated with the spread of modern literacy and the new media through which ideas can be communicated. Mass literacy came late to Oman. . . . By the early 1980s Oman had a sufficient number of secondary school graduates, members of the armed services and civilian government with in-service training, and university students abroad . . . to engender a transformation in what constitutes authoritative religious discourse. The shift to a print and cassette-based religiosity and the exposure of large numbers of young Omanis to a written, formal, "modern standard" Arabic through schooling and the mass media have altered the style and content of authoritative religious discourse and the role this plays in shaping and constraining domestic and regional politics.[12]

These are the demographics of a new religious transnationalism. In an earlier transnationalism of Islam and Christianity, religion accompanied trade, conquest, and colonial domination. Versions of Christianity continue to flow outward from the West, but reverse flows are now conspicuous as well. Accustomed as we were to controlling the missionary terms of trade, we may be astonished to find "their" products flooding "our" market.

Much of this new transnationalism is carried by religion from below, by a popular religious upsurge of ordinary and quite often poor, oppressed, and culturally deprived people, rather than by religion introduced and directed from above. Well-known transnational structures—especially the hierarchical and bureaucratized Catholic Church, led by an evangelizing Pontiff with global aspirations—are an important component of the new transnational religion. But popular, populist, enthusiastic movements leavened by Pentecostals, Catholic charismatics, and "fundamentalist" Muslims have spread more by spontaneous diffusion. [. . .]

RELIGION: VEHICLE OF CONFLICT OR COOPERATION?

The essays in this volume problematize the role of religion with respect to conflict and cooperation. Under what circumstances does religion divide persons and groups? Under what conditions does it bring them together? Religion, as the term is used most of the time by our contributors, refers to practice more often than it does to belief. Although guided and sustained by the meaning systems of transcendent realms, religion as practiced is embedded in everyday life. In countries of the Western as well as of the non-Western world, the most significant form of social organization and source of worldviews for a growing number of people may be religious entities rather than trade unions, political parties, or interest groups. How are these entities related to conflict and cooperation?

"Much recent writing on transnational dimensions of religious change in Latin America has been concerned with overt political acts," writes Daniel Levine, "driven by fears about religion's possible links to revolution (especially in Central America), by false images of a repetition of the Iranian Revolution, or by hopes that religious change would somehow fuel a thoroughgoing cultural and social transformation."[13] The conflict-generating potential of religious mobilizations has received much more attention than their potential for cooperation.

We must remind ourselves that Enlightenment rationalism gave religion a bad name. Religion was false knowledge, the kind of knowledge that Voltaire, Condorcet, and Comte foresaw as disappearing from human consciousness. For Marx, the lingering effects of religions were actively negative, shoring up exploitation and oppression.[14] Modernist social scientists cannot imagine religion as a positive force, as practice and worldview that contributes to order, provides meaning, and promotes justice.

Now that modernity is on trial, in crisis or bankrupt, are there arguments for religion's having a positive role? It can be argued that how people understand their condition affects their sense of security as much as or more than do their objective conditions. If religion can be an opiate that reconciles humans to injustice, it can also provide the vision and energy that engender collective action and social transformation.

Daniel Levine and David Stoll, in this volume, tell of the earnest liberationists

and Pentecostal congregations of the Latin American poor empowered by religious self-teaching. It gives them "new orientations, social skills, and collective self-confidence," though less of all of these than the most optimistic liberationism anticipated. Writing earlier of Guatemala, Stoll stresses the role of the new Protestantism among uprooted populations and recent migrants to cities. They construct new institutions and practices to negotiate the shock of transfer, while those living under the surviving Hacienda regime, for whom the old-time Catholicism suffices, remain passive.[15] Ousmane Kane tells of mobile West African Sufis who spawn *zawiyas*, a familiar spiritual and social milieu, in new locations for the migrating faithful, that provide them with the security of identity, food, and education.[16]

Such accounts reveal how religious associations give structure and meaning to human relations, how they create communities and enable action. That the ritual and belief systems of religious communities have a "security" component, that they make possible both physical and cultural survival, is sometimes not visible until they are destroyed. Kane's account of the peaceable transnational trading and kinship networks of West African Sufis provides a benign contrast to the chaotic horrors of Rwanda and Somalia, where both states and civil society contributed to the problem rather than the solution. As Habermas remarks, "Sometimes it takes an earthquake to make us aware that we had regarded the ground on which we stand every day as unshakable."[17] States cannot, without the means of society, construct the ties that bind humans together in obligation.

If practice and belief of religious formations can, at various levels, orient and facilitate collective action and provide security, they can also generate conflict. Religions often provide not only the language and symbols but also the motives for cultural conflict between and within states: Shiite Iran, Orthodox Serbia, Jewish Israel and Muslim Palestine Liberation Organization (PLO), Buddhist Sinhalese and Hindu Tamils in Sri Lanka, Protestants and Catholics in Ireland, Muslims, Hindus, and Buddhists in Kashmir, Sikhs and Hindus in Punjab, Front Islamique du Salut (FIS) Islamists and Secular Socialists (is rationalism a religion?) in Algeria. Rather than reflecting disequilibria in the balance of power, state conflict has taken on the aura of the jihad and crusade. Holy war has joined self-help and ideology as a casus belli "outside," and the confessionally defined "other" has become the enemy within.

The notion that "war" is by definition an encounter between "states" has been shaken by a democracy of weapons that makes Weber's notion of states' monopolizing the use of force into a fairy tale of modernization. Increasingly wars present themselves as conflicts among civilian populations where more civilians than soldiers die. Civil wars like that in Kashmir, which by 1995 was engaging 600,000 Indian troops, more than the 1965 Indo-Pakistan war, and those in Algeria and Bosnia, are likely to be the main sources of violent conflict for the foreseeable future.

Religion is an important component of the identities that define inside conflicts. Low-level conflicts can arise when the practices of an immigrant religious group challenge the prevailing religious conventions and constitution of the host country. This has happened when Muslims in London demanded enforcement of blasphemy laws and those in Marseilles challenged compulsory dress codes in public education. More serious conflicts can arise when a religious minority lays claim to a separate political identity, as Sikhs did in Indian Punjab or Catholics have done in Northern Ireland. Such conflicts are exacerbated when transnational brethren of local religious minorities seeking political autonomy provide help—North American Sikhs in Punjab; Pakistani Muslims in Kashmir; Indian Tamils in Sri Lanka.

AVOIDING DOMESTIC CONFLICT: ASSIMILATION VERSUS DIFFERENCE

If modernization can no longer be counted on to erase religion from human consciousness and religion can be expected to trigger some conflicts, what are the possibilities for fewer rather than more domestic conflicts? Processes that foster domestic peace among religious groups have taken a number of forms. Homogenizing assimilation and multicultural pluralism represent contrasting cultural regimes. Neither has wholly succeeded, and neither has wholly failed. The stereotypical American story featured assimilating immigrants who "Americanized," that is, became more alike, more homogeneous. Newcomers were encouraged to emulate the mores of the dominant Anglo-Saxon Protestant cultural forms and to be different in private—for example, to speak Italian or Yiddish at home and not take religious differences into political arenas.

In recent decades multiculturalism has challenged the notion of Americanization and assimilationist homogeneity. Numerous movements recognize and celebrate religious as well as ethnic and racial identities and call for educational diversity. Threats of cultural extinction increasingly drive identity movements. Although threatened in both the United States and Europe by nativist fringe and mainstream backlash, political recognition of difference and pluralist settlements seem harder and harder to oppose or deny. The increase in migration to Europe and North America from non-Christian lands, or to the Middle East from non-Islamic ones, is enabled by the ease with which information technologies and jumbo jets allow immigrants to stay in touch with their home communities. We are likely to see "the indefinite survival of separate collective identities even among groups living in the same place and exchanging goods and services on a daily basis."[18]

In retrospect, the historical ubiquity of "ordered heterogeneity" makes the nation-state's insistence on homogeneity—"one culture fits all"—seem quixotic. The "high level of ethnic uniformity that modern European nations took for granted," writes William McNeill, "was very unusual. Religious pluralism, rather than homogeneity, was the starting point for older civilizations."[19] Mobile peoples moving from rural to urban areas or arriving from distant lands relied on their religious identities and practices to secure them against shocks of transition. Those who brought their religion with them were not perceived as disrupting the homogeneity of a host country. "The great cities of Asia and Eastern Europe adapted to this sort of permanent poly-ethnicity by allowing a series of religiously defined communities to exist side by side . . . Chinese and Indian cities also accorded extensive autonomy to enclaves of foreigners as a matter of course."[20] McNeill's accounts suggest that homogeneity is not the only mode that can govern how religious communities live with each other.

When and why does religious pluralism foster civility and order and when conflict and disorder? Consideration of the relationship between security and religion has to recognize both possibilities, that is, religious communities as conciliatory components of viable civil societies and as sources of mutual alienation, distrust, and conflict. The dominant path to religious and ethnic civility of most nineteenth-century nation-states was homogenization and assimilation. But this is not the only way to peaceable settlements. The pluralistic guarantees of multinational empires, and the permanent polyethnicity of the older cities in Asia and Eastern Europe represent an alternative cultural constitution. These approaches to conflict resolution are points on a continuum rather than opposites. Future negotiations about cultural security are likely to engage both alternatives. [. . .]

THINNING OUT MONOPOLY SOVEREIGNTY

Communities constituting transnational civil society may have authority and even power; they do not claim sovereignty. They have authority in that a formally organized religious transnational entity such as the Roman Catholic Church is in a position to license and de-license the activities of its organizational units in particular national sites, such as the National Councils of Bishops. An informally structured movement such as that of the West African Sufis is able to shape the transnational pilgrimages of its adherents across sacred territory; to satisfy, by negotiations with nation-states, its adherents' expectations and claims for free passage; and to regulate, via norms and conventional practice, the associated kinship transactions, market behaviors, and political demands.[21]

Religious networks and communities in domestic and transnational civil society render state claims to monopoly sovereignty problematic. This challenge is less familiar than the challenge from global markets in ideas as well as goods and services. It is now commonplace to show how markets, media, and telecommunications can create transnational arenas by forming networks and solidarities that circumvent the Westphalian state system with its emphasis on territoriality and sovereignty. Thousands of interveners in transnational space have the authority and power to provide an alternative to state activity, not replace it. The process being described here is not the collapse or demise of states but rather the thinning of their effect, function, and finality.

Transnational activity is guided by imaginary maps whose boundaries do not approximate the spaces depicted on political maps—for example, the (large) transnational realm of Catholic Christianity, or the (smaller) transnational realm of the Tijaniyya Sufis. Catholics and Sufis create arenas governed by considerations other than sovereignty. Such arenas do not replace or supersede political maps showing territorially defined states. We can imagine them as transparent plastic overlays, alternative meaning systems superimposed upon the meaning system of political maps. They do not replace state-defined space; they provide alternatives to it. In the nineteenth and twentieth centuries nation-states tried to make the overlays coincide. Ethnic cleansing in Bosnia and Rwanda are merely the pathological expressions of a more general impulse to coordinate linguistic community, religious community, and ethnic community. Such efforts seem increasingly atavistic.

I use the metaphor of plastic overlays as a counter to the zero-sum metaphors that often characterize the challenge that transnational forces offer the state. "The state is waning" suggests that it will vanish and be replaced by other forms of political organization. More likely is a progressive contraction of state activities and claims that would allow non-governmental phenomena to share functions and meaning now monopolized by states. What this suggests is less a waning of states than a more complex set of interrelations in which rival identities and structures jostle the state. New alliances and goals become possible as domestic civil society joins up with transnational civil society to challenge states and as states in concert employ elements in transnational civil society to limit particular states' sovereignty. [. . .]

NOTES

1. Churches may be the oldest creators of civil society in the West. One is reluctant to assert that they have universally had such a role because the very notion of civil society is often considered a product of liberal Western thought. Don Baker's essay in this volume, "World Religions and National States: Competing Claims in East Asia," suggests that the society-state dichotomy is not a "natural" or universal conceptualization. For a discussion of the uses of the concept of civil society, see my concluding essay.

2. "The new mass clientele for Protestant missionary activity . . . [arises from] the creation of converging trends in demography, social mobility, and the continuing appeal of religions that stress an intense spiritual life. Dramatic population shifts and accelerated urbanization have drawn Latin Americans to the cities while opening rural life to the outside world via expanded transport and communications." Daniel H. Levine, "The Latin American Experience of Transnational Religious Activism" (paper prepared for the SSRC Conference on Transnational Muslim Missionary Movements, University of Aberystwyth, Wales, October 1992), 8.

3. R. B. J. Walker, *Inside/Outside: International Relations as Political Theory* (Cambridge, England: Cambridge University Press, 1993).

4. This formulation does not make a distinction between ideas and practice but assumes that concept and praxis implicate each other.

5. See Peter Haas, "Introduction: Epistemic Communities and International Policy Coordination," special issue of *International Organization* 46 (1) (Winter 1992):1–35. The general omission of religious movements from the category of such epistemic communities is presumably a replication of the pervasive enlightenment conceit that draws boundaries between "rationalist" and "affective," between positive and imagined, between ascriptive and voluntaristic. For a theoretical critique of these distinctions, see my concluding essay.

6. Stephen D. Krasner, "Structural Causes and Regime Consequences: Regimes as Intervening Variables" in *International Regimes*, edited by Stephen D. Krasner (Ithaca: Cornell University Press, 1983); and Robert O. Keohane, *After Hegemony: Cooperation and Discord in the World Political Economy* (Princeton: Princeton University Press, 1984).

7. Robert D. Kaplan, "The Coming Anarchy," *Atlantic Monthly*, February 1994. The authors of this volume find the positive, motivating, and cooperative impact of religion as significant as it is negative, divisive, and conflictual. By contrast, Kaplan's undiscriminating view of ethnicity and religion, born especially of his perception of conflict in Africa, strikes a single note; all mobilizations are assigned to the negative column. Yet it is precisely the variable potential of religious and ethnic formations that needs to be investigated. For an account that is also pessimistic but more discriminating about Africa and does not assume that Africa is the world, see Aristide Zolberg, "The Specter of Anarchy: African States Verging on Dissolution," *Dissent*, Summer 1992.

8. Although Europeans no longer constituted a majority at the time of Vatican II, two-thirds of the college of Cardinals was still Italian. See José Casanova, "Globalizing Catholicism and the Return to a 'Universal' Church," in this volume.

9. For recent figures, see James Brooke, "Pragmatic Protestants Winning Converts in Brazil," *New York Times*, July 4, 1993. For accounts of this growth, see David Martin, *Tongues of Fire: The Explosion of Protestantism in Latin America* (London: Basil Blackwell, 1990); David Stoll, *Is Latin America Turning Protestant?* (Berkeley: University of California Press, 1992); and David Stoll and Virginia Burnett, eds., *Rethinking Protestantism in Latin America* (New York: Columbia University Press, 1993).

10. Nicholas Kristof, "Christianity Is Booming in China Despite Rifts," *New York Times*, February 7, 1993.

11. Diane L. Eck, "In the Name of Religions," *Wilson Quarterly* 17 (4) (Autumn 1993):99. These figures and estimates were gathered by the Pluralism Project of Harvard University's Committee on the Study of Religion. See also James Brooke, "Attacks on U.S. Muslims Surge, Even As Their Faith Takes Hold," *New York Times*, August 28, 1995. Philip Lewis provides an account for Britain in *Islamic Britain: Religion, Politics, and Identity Among British Muslims* (London: I. B. Tauris, 1994).

12. Dale F. Eickelman, "National Identity and Religious Discourse in Contemporary Oman," *International Journal of Islamic and Arabic Studies* 6(1) (1989):1–20.

13. Daniel Levine, "Transnational Religious Regimes in Latin America: Social Capital, Empowerment, Symbols, and Power" (working draft presented at the SSRC Working Group on Transnational Religious Regimes, New York, October 1993). This was an early draft of the chapter in this volume by Daniel Levine and David Stoll.

14. The Communist Party of India (Marxist) is debating whether its local cadres should be censured for

participating in, even organizing, the festival activities for Goddess Durga, which are a pervasive feature of the October festival season in Bengal, stronghold of the communists in India. The proponents of participation argue that not doing so is to lose a central means of communicating with the people. *Statesman* (New Delhi), October 9, 1995. For interesting neo-Marxian approaches that read religion as a language articulating the life-situation of believers, see writings by Indian historians in the "subaltern" tradition who attempt a new understanding of nineteenth- and twentieth-century "communalism": Gyan Pandey, *The Construction of Communalism in Colonial North India* (Oxford: Delhi, 1990), Shahid Amin, "Gandhi as Mahatma: Gorakhpur District, Eastern UP, 1921–2," in *Selected Subaltern Studies*, edited by Ranajit Guha and Gayatri Chakravorty Spivak (New York: Oxford University Press, 1988).

15. David Stoll, *Is Latin America Turning Protestant?*, 13. For an earlier account, see Emilio Willems, *Followers of the New Faith* (Nashville, TN: Vanderbilt University Press, 1967). The same religious orientations may be associated with a variety of practices, from quietism to activism. Today's Pentecostalism, speaking in tongues and recommending faith healing, may recommend tomorrow the cultivation of self-discipline and the will to seize one's fate. Nineteenth-century Evangelical fundamentalism in Great Britain underwent a shift toward "a social theology that made less of biblical doctrines of inherent personal sinfulness, guilt and divine punishment . . . whilst making more of practical service to others through the discipline of hard work as self-denial." Gerald Studdert-Kennedy, "The Imperial Elite," review of Clive Dewey, *Anglo-Indian Attitudes: The Mind of the Indian Civil Service* (London: Hambledon Press, 1993) in *Economic and Political Weekly*, July 9, 1994, 1722.

16. Ousmane Kane, "Muslim Missionaries and African States," in this volume.

17. Jürgen Habermas, *The Theory of Communicative Action*, vol. 2, *Lifeworld and System: A Critique of Functionalist Reason* (Boston: Beacon Press, 1984–1985), 400.

18. William McNeill, "Project Report: Fundamentalism and the World of the 1990s," *Bulletin of the American Academy of Arts and Sciences* 47 (3) (December 1993):29. For earlier discussions of assimilation in American life, see Milton M. Gordon, *Assimilation in American Life: The Role of Race, Religion, and National Origins* (New York: Oxford University Press, 1964); Nathan Glazer and Daniel Patrick Moynihan, *Beyond the Melting Pot: The Negroes, Puerto Ricans, Jews, Italians, and Irish of New York City* (Cambridge, MA: MIT Press, 1963); and Will Herberg, *Protestant, Catholic, Jew: An Essay in American Religious Sociology* (Chicago: University of Chicago Press, 1983). For a discussion of the role of cultural extinction in separatist movements, see Lloyd I. Rudolph, "India and the Punjab: A Fragile Peace," in The Asia Society, *Asian Issues 1985: Asian Agenda Report 3* (Lanham, MD: University Press of America, 1986).

19. Religious pluralism may have thrived in part because religion was too serious an aspect of life to be assigned to the private realm, a condition that homogenizing solutions encourage.

20. McNeill, "Project Report," 29–30. For an extended discussion of this type of pluralism, see Benjamin Braude and Bernard Lewis, eds., *Christians and Jews in the Ottoman Empire: The Functioning of a Plural Society*, 2 volumes (New York: Holmes and Meier, 1982), especially the introduction and the essay by Benjamin Braude. For a proposal to institutionalize a form of *millets*, or religious federalism, in India, see Partha Chatterjee, "Secularism and Toleration," *Economic and Political Weekly* 29 (28) (July 9, 1994): 1768–1778.

21. See Ousmane Kane, "Muslim Missionaries and African States," in this volume.

CHAPTER 28

Theorizing Globalization and Religion

Manuel A. Vásquez and Marie Friedmann Marquardt

Globalization, as Bauman (1998: 1) rightly complains, "is on everybody's lips; a fad word turning into a shibboleth, a magic incantation, a passkey meant to unlock the gates to all present and future mysteris." Indeed, a recent issue of *National Geographic* declares that "today we are in the throes of a worldwide reformation of culture, a tectonic shift of habits and dreams called, in the curious argot of social scientists, 'globalization' " (Zwingle 1999: 12). As we theorize globalization, we seek to avoid mystifications of this kind. We do not claim that a globalization framework can resolve all the conundrums of religion in the Americas and thus that we must reject wholesale the methods and insights of what we have called modernist approaches. Nevertheless, a globalization framework provides powerful tools to analyze changes in the religious field in the Americas that challenge some of the core assumptions of secularization theory and the New Paradigm.

This chapter explores the theoretical implications of a globalization framework for the study of religion in the Americas. Our aim is not to offer a new theory of globalization. Nor do we seek to provide an exhaustive review of the ever-expanding literature on globalization.[1] Rather, we concentrate on those global processes that are most entangled with changes in the religious field in the Americas. We believe that a focus on the interplay between religion and globalization not only provides novel ways of studying religious phenomena but also enriches our understanding of globalization in distinctive ways, foregrounding important dynamics hitherto ignored. We argue that

globalization scholars must take religion seriously, since religion in the Americas is deeply implicated in the dialectic of deterritorialization and reterritorialization that accompanies globalization. According to García Canclini (1995: 229), this dialectic entails "the loss of the 'natural' relation of culture to geographical and social territories and, at the same time, certain relative, partial territorial relocalizations of old and new symbolic productions." Religion, we believe, is one of the main protagonists in this unbinding of culture from its traditional referents and boundaries and in its reattachment in new space-time configurations. Through this Interplay of delocalization and relocalization, religion gives rise to hybrid individual and collective identities that fly in the face of the methodological purity and simplicity sought by modernist sociologies of religion. [. . .]

RELIGION AND GLOBALIZATION: SOME ANALYTICAL TOOLS

Having characterized the economic, political, and cultural processes at the heart of globalization, we now turn to religion's specific contributions. We are not the first to call attention to the interplay between religion and globalization. Roland Robertson (1992) argues that religion helps forge a shared consciousness of the world as a single place. On the one hand, because religions make universal claims about transcendence and the cosmos, they contribute to making the world "an imagined community" through "the global diffusion of a conception of a homogeneous, but gender-distinguished, humanity" (R. Robertson 1991: 283). Robertson calls this the emergence of "global humanization." On the other hand, dealing with personal conversion and salvation, religion also participates in a process of "global individualization: the global generalization of conceptions of the human person." In other words, religion universalizes as much as it particularizes, participating in the dialectical interplay between the global and the local. Along the same lines, Peter Beyer (1994: 3) contends that as the world becomes a single space, local cultures become relativized in the encounter among hitherto relatively segregated cultural units. This, in turn, leads to a reaffirmation of locality in the form of fundamentalist responses, which often use the tools of globalization to spread their particularistic claims beyond the local. In this "particularistic revitalization of a tradition in the face of relativization," religion plays a major role because, along with ethnicity and nationalism, it is key in the creation and maintenance of the intersubjective world where meaning, identity, and sense of place and belonging emerge (Beyer 1994: 10; R. Robertson 1992: 164–181).

There is much of value in Robertson's and Beyer's work, not least their efforts to demonstrate that religion continues "to be a determinative force in social structures and processes beyond the restricted sphere of voluntary and individual belief and practice" (Beyer 1994: 12). Robertson's and Beyer's focus on religion's role in mediating the tensions between the global and the local and between the universal and the particular is very helpful. Nevertheless, because both Robertson and Beyer work at a high level of abstraction and under the shadow of Parsonian and neo-Parsonian system models, their approaches fail to capture the multiple ways in which globalization and religion are intertwined in everyday life. As Marfleet (1998: 173) writes: "Consistent with its emphasis on larger issues, global theory strains to a higher level of generalization and 'empirical matters' are rarely a concern. The result is that global perspectives on religion strongly discourage contextual understanding. Indeed, global accounts in general evacuate beliefs, practices and institutions of their specific significance, leaving 'religion' as little more than a reference to 'the whole,' or to traditions of the supernatural, sacred, superempirical, or transcendent—whatever definition is in use."

The issue of abstraction is connected to the problem of idealism in global theories of religion. Tiryakian (1992: 309), for instance, observes that "Robertson has neglected technology and the hard aspects of social reality in favor of more non-material, idealistic factors, such as 'the idea of the national society,' and 'conceptions of individuals and of human kind' as 'reference points' for globalization." Among the "hard aspects" of social reality, Tiryakian includes the globalization of production and capital flows. More importantly, "the communicative structures of today's high technology (fax machines, e-mail, and interactive videos, in addition to television) render national boundaries extremely porous and make it possible for the whole world to be watching and witnessing, and on occasions sharing."

Elaborating on Tiryakian's point, we argue for the need to develop "thicker," empirically richer approaches to religion and globalization that specify concrete instances where global processes intersect with local lived experience. Religion's role in globalization is at once more widespread, concrete, and vital. What interacts with globalization is lived religion—specific religious practices, discourses, and institutions which constitute the fabric of local life for large segments of the population around the world. Thus, at stake is the formulation of a "cosmopolitan ethnography" (Appadurai 1996) of religion. This ethnography calls for a careful mapping of the mobile yet always situated ways in which religion links the daily micropolitics of individual and collective identity with a dense cluster of meso- and macrosocial processes, ranging from the urban and the national to the regional and global. To achieve its task, cosmopolitan ethnography must enter into conversation with political economy, critical geography, cultural and ethnic studies, and transnational migration. In what follows we offer the nuts and bolts of our anchored approach through an analysis of five specific ways in which religion interacts with globalization. These conceptual tools will inform in varying degrees our case studies.

Deterritorialization and Reterritorialization: Religion as Map

The core of globalization's time-space compression is interplay between deterritorialization and reterritorialization, understood as the "*breaking down and reconstitution of spatial scales*, from the most intimate spaces of the body, household, and home to the metropolitan region and the territorial nation-state" (Soja 2000: 200; emphasis in original). The relativization of taken-for-granted ways of organizing space and time means that culture, which was construed as organically bound with place and nation, gains autonomy and intensity and participates in the formation of new spatio-temporal arrangements that blend local, regional, and global dynamics. In the face of these changes, Jameson (1991) stresses the need to develop new "cognitive maps," "pedagogical and political cultural tools" that would allow us to have "some new heightened sense of . . . place in the global system." Our case studies show that religion is a key cultural component in the construction of both new spatio-temporal arrangements and emerging cognitive maps through which individuals and institutions try to locate themselves in the new landscapes generated by globalization.

Concern with space, place, and maps is fairly recent in the social sciences, for, as Soja (1989) argues, modern social science always privileged time over space. Here modern social science reproduces the Enlightenment prejudice that space is merely an inert reality in and against which historical subjects exercise agency. Space was something to be dominated and overcome in the name of progress. In contrast, space, and particularly the notion of territory, has always been central to the academic study of religion. In fact, Sam Gill (1998: 301) claims that "the academic study of religion began to emerge as a distinctive enterprise with the shift from theologically based to territorially based understandings

of religion." He sees this shift as part of the move away from "understanding religion as principally Christian or Western [toward] acknowledging religion as a distinct aspect of being human." Indeed, a long-standing tradition, running from Durkheim through Mircea Eliade to Jonathan Z. Smith, has focused on the ways in which religion maps and remaps space according to multiple tensions, such as those between the sacred and the profane, the this-worldly and the other-worldly, orthodoxy and heterodoxy, and elite/institutional and popular practices. Eliade, for example, argued that meaningful space and time are possible only through the appearance of foundational hierophanies, powerful expressions of the sacred in which order is created ex nihilo. "Revelation of a sacred space makes it possible to obtain a fixed point and hence to acquire orientation in the chaos of homogeneity, to 'found the world' and to live in a real sense. The profane experience, on the contrary, maintains the homogeneity and hence the relativity of space" (Eliade 1959: 23). The task of the history of religions approach, then, is to document cross-culturally hierophanies and the variety of ways in which humans seek to reenact these originative events through myth and ritual.

Clearly, in the current environment of anti-foundationalism and skepticism toward grand narratives, Eliade's ambitious comparative project of the history of religions is problematic.[2] Nevertheless, Jonathan Smith (1978, 1987), Sam Gill (1998), and others have reformulated understandings of space and time within the discipline of religion in ways that would greatly benefit globalization scholars as they seek to "map out" global processes and to study how people and institutions are involved in "place making" amid widespread dislocation and fragmentation. For, as Smith puts it (1978: 291), religion "is the quest, within the bounds of the human, historical condition, for the power to manipulate and negotiate one's 'situation' so as to have 'space' in which to meaningfully dwell. . . . What we study when we study religion is the variety of attempts to map, construct and inhabit such positions of power [i.e., over the natural and social environment] through the use of myths, rituals and experiences of transformation."

Analysis of religion's role in the creation of space has hitherto concentrated on "primitive" and "ancient" religions—exploring the links between sacred cosmology and architecture in Mesoamerican religions or the role of mythology and ritual in mapping landscapes among Australian aborigines. However, Orsi (1999: 47) observes that dwellers in modern American cities have drawn from religious resources to appropriate "public spaces for themselves and transformed them into venues for shaping, displaying, and celebrating their inherited and emergent ways of life and understandings of the world. They have remapped the city, superimposing their own coordinates of meaning on official cartographies." Religious cartographies "disclose coordinates of alternative worlds for practitioners, re-making the meaning of ordinary places and signaling the location of extraordinary ones, establishing connections between spaces of the city and other spaces, real and imaginary, between humans and invisible sacred companions of all sorts. American cities are composed of complex topographies of interleaved, sometimes incongruous domains of experience and possibility, knowledge of which is borne in the bodies and sense of city people who move through urban worlds in their everyday lives" (54).

"Religious mappings" are particularly important to transnational migrants faced with the dislocation produced by globalization, who must draw from their religious traditions "to delineate an alternative cartography of belonging. Religious icons and sacred shrines, rather than national flags, proclaim these religious spaces. The moral and physical geographies that result may fall within national boundaries, transcend but coexist with them, or create an additional place that supercedes national borders" (Levitt 2001: 19).

Religion also enters into a hermeneutics of movement whereby migrants transform their travels across national borders into moral journeys, rites of passage, theodicies of religious conversion, rebirth, and edification (Peterson and Vásquez 2001). Confronting

dislocation, liminality, and nostalgia for the homeland, many of these migrants narrativize their plight as a pilgrimage of the soul and body, producing "geographies of personal discovery" (Teather 1999). In constructing these narratives, migrants draw from religious themes like exile, diaspora and captivity, exodus and the search for the promised land, or Paul's conversion on the road to Damascus. Borrowing from cognitive psychology (Golledge 1999), we may say that religious narratives and tropes provide resources for "route learning" and "wayfinding," offering migrants moral and ritual landmarks to situate themselves amid dislocation.[3] These narratives, however, are not purely "mental" resources. They are inscribed in institutions and bodies, in local architecture, material culture, haircuts, and dress styles, as immigrants reconstruct and transpose abroad landscapes in their place of origin through the work of memory and imagination.[4] In addition, these narratives are not of one piece; they are contested and inflected by variables such as the migrant's gender, race, class, and conditions of arrival.

A focus on religion as a key variable and the use of analytical tools like religious territory and mapping can, thus, enrich our understanding of how globalization is both erasing and redrawing boundaries, and how people embedded in global processes negotiate multiple locations and identities.

Transnational Religious Networks

A genealogy of the category of religion shows that in the West religion has been tied primarily to inner mental and emotional states, to cognition and the production of meaning (Asad 1993: 40–54). Overcoming this "subjectivism," our case studies demonstrate that religion contributes to globalization not just by forming psycho-cognitive maps but also by establishing "material," organizational conduits for the flow of economic, social, and cultural capitals. As the rigid spatial centralization and temporal regulation associated with the Fordist-Keynesian regime is challenged by the geographical dispersion unleashed by flexible production, the hypermobility of capital, and new technologies of communication like the Internet, new forms of associational life emerge that are not predicated on a "metaphysics of presence and propinquity." Religious institutions, with their long experience in bridging universal claims and particularistic demands across various cultures, are well positioned to offer organizational resources for these new forms of associational life. Indeed the breakdown of "traditional" communities—built upon face-to-face encounters or on demographic concentration around now decaying Fordist factories—and the rise of gated communities, suburbs, and exurbs have been accompanied by the decline of mainline denominations and the rise of megachurches, small, adaptable, often interconnected storefront churches, and virtual congregations.

In other words, the new spatio-temporal arrangements generated by globalization dovetail with religious "morphologies of success," forms of religious organization and practice strategically equipped to deal with the existential predicaments generated by globalization at the level of everyday life. By changing our sense of time, space, and agency, globalization clearly affects the viability of religious congregations. The latter, however, are not mere passive subjects of more foundational economic forces. Religious congregations are also active in transmitting and shaping globalization. A case in point is Pentecostalism, which is experiencing remarkable growth in Latin America and among U.S. Latinos. On the one hand, part of Pentecostalism's success can be attributed to the fact that it offers believers resources to relocalize themselves, to renew broken selves and build tight affective communities in a world that has become increasingly baffling. On the other, Pentecostal churches can be unabashedly globalizing, combining skillfully the use of transnational webs of missionaries and storefront congregations with sophisticated global media to minister to highly mobile migrant populations. Building on Castells's work, Berryman (1999: 30) argues that, while the Catholic Church functions as a "vertical bureaucracy," Pentecostal churches appear to function under a network logic. "They are organizations built 'around process, not task; flat hierarchy;

team management; measuring performance by customer satisfaction; rewards based on team performance; maximization of contact with suppliers and customers; information, training and retraining of employees at all levels." Thus, Pentecostal churches are not mere premodern reactions to the disenchantment of the world, as secularization theory would have it. "The network style of Pentecostal churches may indicate that, at least in their organizational form, they may be surprisingly in tune with changes taking place at this end-of-millennium moment" (Berryman 1999: 34).

Pentecostalism is just one example of how religious organizations shape transnational networks. In her work on transnational migration, Levitt (2001) has identified at least three transnational religious organizational patterns. First, there are extended transnational religious organizations like the Catholic Church, where networks of local and national churches and pastoral initiatives are "connected and directed by a single authority but enjoy a good deal of autonomy at the local level." These networks "broaden, deepen, and customize a global religious system that is already legitimate, powerful, and well organized" (11–12). The second pattern is "negotiated transnational religious organizations" where the networks are "much less hierarchical, centralized . . . Instead, flexible ties, not subject to a set of pre-established rules must be constantly worked out" (14). In other words, "global connections are negotiated with respect to authority, organization and ritual." Many Pentecostal churches assume this pattern. Finally, there are "recreated transnational religious organizations," which "either function like franchises or chapters of their counterparts" in the sending societies. "Franchises are run primarily by migrants who periodically receive resources and guidance from sending-country leadership, while chapters are supported and supervised regularly by sending-country leaders" (16–17). Here, the example would be some Hindu and Muslim organizations in the United States.

Mahler (2001) has suggested that we expand our view beyond Levitt's patterns to include interfaith charity-based transnational ties, the activities of transnational entre-preneurial religious elites likes priests and ministers, and "religious tourism." While it is too early to provide a full account of the various facets of religious transnationalism, it is clear that religious networks serve as important conducts for transnational and global processes.

Glocalization

Transnational religious networks are particu-larly strong because they build bridges between universal messages of salvation and particular existential needs and between the overarching logics of translocal organizations and the discourses and practices of specific congregations. The concept of "glocaliza-tion" or "global localization" provides a helpful tool for understanding religion's cap-acity to build such bridges (R. Robertson 1995; Wilson and Dissanayake 1996; Swyn-gedouw 1997). The term originates from the Japanese practice of *dochakuka*, that is, adapting a global institution's practices to local conditions. *Dochakuka* has enabled Japanese corporations to remain globally competitive in the transition to flexible accumulation. Rather than producing for homogeneous markets under the Fordist-Keynesian economies of scale, many Japanese companies have decentralized production in ways that allow them to tailor their products to meet changing local markets. Product innovations that have been successful at the local level are fed back into the global system to augment its memory and repertoire. Under *dochakuka*, thus, global production and accumulation are not opposed to diversity and local specificity. Glocalization illustrates how globalization does not necessarily entail homogenization, the erasure of authoch-thonous cultures, languages, and religions, as some critics argue. Rather, glocalization sets up power-laden tensions between hetero-geneity and homogeneity and between trad-ition and modernity, which both global institutions and dispersed consumers must negotiate.

Transposing the concept of glocalization to the production of religious goods in the Americas, we can see that for Catholicism and evangelical Protestantism glocalization is nothing new. Christian organizations have always had to craft symbolic goods that ful-filled the interests of the clerical and secular elites in maintaining orthodoxy and hier-archy while being flexible enough to respond to local worldviews and needs. These churches have been able to produce and cir-culate their messages across national bound-aries through their dense organizational net-works. This, however, never guaranteed that the religious goods would be consumed in the ways the elite producers envisioned. Despite acting under structural and institutional con-straints, local actors appropriate the prod-ucts in unpredictable ways, leading often to unintended consequences—like syncre-tism and heresy—from the point of view of the elites.

The current round of globalization has made the age-old process of religious glocali-zation more complex, intense, and extensive. Religious goods now enter "a giddy pro-liferation of communication," in Vattimo's (1992) words. But it is not simply a matter of having faster and more far-reaching means of communication and transportation that bring cultures together instantaneously. At a deeper level, the autonomization of culture and the rise of postmodernism and virtuality have led to the deterritorialization of dis-courses and practices, opening them to mul-tiple appropriations and thus making them more resistant to orthodox readings. In this context, global religious institutions like the Catholic Church and evangelical Protestant churches are engaged in ever more precarious processes of glocalization. On the one hand, they have to reinforce their claims to uni-versal authority in a world that, as Robert-son argues, is increasingly felt as a single place but is also deeply skeptical of grand narratives. On the other hand, these organ-izations must respond to specific demands of individuals and communities who experience fragmentation and depthlessness as part of everyday life. In dealing with this tension, religious organizations often unintentionally produce more hybridity and fragmentation. Given the dynamics of the current episode of globalization, religious institutions become sources of heterogeneity and change, notwithstanding their best efforts to discipline chaos.

Hybridity and Nonexclusionary Identity

The hybridity produced by glocal or transnational religious institutions is just one aspect of the larger process of hybridization generated by the current round of globalization. This process entails the intermingling of previously territorialized cultures and the mixing or juxtaposition of temporalities, such as the premodern, modern, and postmodern (what García Canclini calls *tiempos mixtos*), in identities and cultural artifacts. In the present context, hybridization is fed by an explosion of popular culture, mass media, and electronic communications and by the subcultures of actors at the margins of society.

As in the case of glocalization, the mixing of cultures is nothing new. And here again, at least in the Americas, the discipline of religion offers conceptual elements important for understanding globalization. Terms like "syncretism," "bricolage," and "creolization" have long informed the study of religion and culture. The word "syncretism," for example, is derived from the ancient Greco-Roman world, where it was used to describe the meeting of people and cultures in the cosmopolitan cities of the Mediterranean (Stewart and Shaw 1994). In anthropology and folklore studies, Herskovits (1966) and Bastide (1978) used the term to explain the rise of mixed cultures and religions in the Americas as primarily an adaptation strategy to deal with the displacement and disorder produced by the destruction of native societies and by the slave trade. To move beyond the stress on adaptation and the functionalist view of religion and cultures as vehicles to reestablish homeostasis in the wake of social chaos, we have adopted the notion of hybridity, which has become a central concept in postcolonial studies. Homi Bhabha (1990, 1994), for instance, uses the notion of hybridity to show fractures in the sovereign, unified, and self-transparent Cartesian subject at the heart of the colonial enterprise. Empires sought to civilize those they encountered by transforming them into a homogenized and docile Other who

reflected, albeit imperfectly, the colonizer's values. Bhabha argues persuasively that this enterprise failed. Instead of producing coherent and disciplined colonial subjects, it generated destabilizing mixed identities in both colony and metropole.

Extending Bhabha's thought to the field of religion in the Americas, we find in hybridity a useful conceptual device to understand multiple, fluid, and often contradictory religious identities and practices that have proliferated with globalization. Hybridity points to "how newness enters the world," and specifically how cultures become the locus for multiple contestations, for creative resistance and appropriation. The term "hybridity" refers to the politics of culture and everyday life and highlights "the intricate and complex weave of any heterodox and heteroglossic community" (Kapchan and Strong 1999). It is cross disciplinary, in contrast to discipline-bound terms such as "syncretism" (in religious studies) and "bricolage" (in structuralist anthropology).

Despite these advantages, the notion of hybridity has its own problems. The term has strong eugenic connotations: the mixing of two purebreds leading to the birth of an impure, inferior species. Even when hybridity is stripped of its pejorative connotations, as when we speak of "hybrid vigor," the term still seems caught in a biological dichotomy between purity and impurity (Stross 1999). In his foreword to García Canclini's *Hybrid Cultures*, Rosaldo (1995: xv) takes the author to task for precisely this kind of dualism: "The term hybridity, as used by García Canclini, never resolves the tension between its conceptual polarities. On the one hand, hybridity can imply a space betwixt and between two zones of purity in a manner that follows biological usage. ... On the other hand, hybridity can be understood as the ongoing condition of all human cultures, which contain no zones of purity because they undergo continuous processes of transculturation (two-way borrowing and lending between cultures). Instead of hybridity versus purity, this view suggests that it is hybridity all the way down."

We use hybridity in the second sense suggested by Rosaldo. While hybridity has always existed, the time-space compression generated by the current episode of globalization has drastically intensified the mixing and remixing of cultural forms, placing hybridity at the center of our consciousness. Hybridity is no longer associated only with "impure," "lower" cultures at the margins struggling to adapt to modernity's inexorable homogenization and rationalization. The current round of globalization has carried hybridity to the "metropolitan" powers where the production of social scientific knowledge has been primarily located, forcing the West to come to terms with its own internal dynamics of hybridization. These dynamics, which have always simmered underneath modernity's drive to normalize difference under the straightjacket of binary oppositions, now emerge in full force (Spivak 1988; Said 1993; Bhabha 1994; Venn 1999). Hybridity is now recognized to be both local and global, part of both "traditional" and "modern" societies. Globalization makes Rosaldo's assertion that "it is hybridity all the way down" more plausible.

Recognition of the centrality of hybridity today has significant implications for the study of religion. As we saw in chapter 1, modernity and the social sciences, as products of the Enlightenment's quest for autonomy, set religion against reason in a teleological scheme. Religion would be increasingly displaced from the public arena, as each sphere of human action became self-legislating, developing its own rational rules and ground for legitimation. This was the core claim of the "old paradigm" of secularization. With the crisis of modernity and the production of *tiempos mixtos*, religion is released from modernity's teleological scheme and reenters the public sphere, becoming a key contributor to the process of hybridization. As globalization deterritorializes and reterritorializes culture, religion enters into recombination with multiple media, giving rise to hybrid cultural products that blur spatial, temporal, and conceptual distinctions at modernity's core, juxtaposing Aztec sacred buildings and liquid architecture, as in the movie *Blade Runner*, or Vedic rituals with pop music and videos, as in Madonna's "Ray of Hope."

Hybridity all the way down, however, not only challenges secularization's narrative of the decline or privatization of religion. It also aims at the heart of the New Paradigm, which presupposes that religious traditions are self-contained wholes competing against each other in a pluralistic market. As we saw in chapter 1, even the most sophisticated versions of the New Paradigm, like subcultural-identity theory, operate with an exclusionary notion of religious identity, positing a static relation between a unitary cultural or ethnic identity and a religious choice. The ever-presence of hybridity, as Bhabha argues, renders problematic binary oppositions and exclusionary difference because it constructs artifacts and identities that are "neither One nor the Other but something else beside, in between" (1994: 219). Hybridity challenges modern sociology of religion's stress on purity and full transparency, opening the way to understand phenomena such as multiple religious affiliation, cross-fertilization among religious traditions, and religious improvisation and innovation, which are at the heart of lived religion.

Lest we mistake the ever-presence of hybridity for total deterritorialization, the erasure of all distinctions or the "implosion of the social," as Baudrillard would have it, we must keep in mind that mixing also reterritorializes and reintroduces tension and power. Hybridity is not always emancipatory. The history of Latin America is full of examples of the use of notions of racial, cultural, and religious mixing to construct hegemonic ideas of nationhood (Beverley 1999). In Mexico, for example, *mestizaje* was championed by white, urban creole elites in the aftermath of the independence period as part of their nation-building projects. Such projects sought to domesticate heterogeneous populations and regions under a unified nation, which then became synonymous with the authoritarian state under the patriarchal figure of *el caudillo*. The caudillo and the new nation-state then appeared as the natural expression of the popular will, the embodiment of the (mestizo) consciousness of the masses. In Brazil the notion of *mulatez* became the key metaphor for the myth of racial democracy advanced by progressive scholars like Gilberto Freyre (1986) to attack European eugenics. This myth became part of a national discourse on race that, presenting the oversexualized body of the mulatta as the essence of Brazilianness, served the national elites to promote a romanticized image of Brazil for tourist consumption—Brazil as an exotic tropical paradise free of conflict. Further, the discourse of *mulatez* has obscured the continued exclusion and marginalization of dark-skinned Brazilians.

Friedman (1999) argues that hybridity serves as a self-justificatory construct for a "new global cultural elite." Hybridity is an ideology that satisfies the hunger for exoticism and authenticity among these cosmopolitan and "ecumenical collectors of culture." This hybridity, Friedman continues, "is quite opposed to the Balkanisation and tribalisation experienced at the bottom of the system," where poor people must form sharp defensive boundaries to protect themselves against the deleterious effects of globalization (Friedman 1997: 85). Along the same lines, Bauman (1998: 9) argues that the emphasis on mobility and deterritorialization applies only to a small cosmopolitan elite enjoying total freedom from all responsibility. In contrast, vast sectors of the population are "disempowered and disregarded residents of . . . 'fenced off,' pressed-back and relentlessly encroached-upon areas" (22). Thus, globalization "emancipates certain humans from territorial constraints and renders certain community-generating meanings extraterritorial—while denuding the territory, to which other people go on being confined, of its meaning and its identity-endowing capacity" (18).[5]

Processes of hybridization and deterritorialization are not exempt from power. We hope, however, to show that they are more widespread, more part of everyday life, than both Friedman and Bauman imagine. We agree with Neeverden Pieterse (1995) that hybridity can be deployed in multiple ways. Some deployments are hegemonic, serving to consolidate power asymmetries and advancing an integrationist agenda. Others are destabilizing, challenging exclusionary and normalizing practices and facilitating the formation of "alternative publics," to draw from Nancy Fraser (1997). But here again, we must be careful not to inscribe a new dichotomy between hegemonic and destabilizing hybridities, for as we shall see in our case studies, all hybrid expressions are ambiguous and polyvalent. In other words, no hybridity is "pure"; all carry both domination and resistance in varying degrees. To avoid romanticizing hybridity and to show that it entails both deterritorialization and reterritorialization, we hold hybridity in tension with border and borderlands. The notions of border and borderlands help us to "emplace" hybridity and locate it in global processes (Mitchell 1997). They foreground the domination and resistance involved in globalization's time-space compression.

Borders and Borderlands

In cultural studies, the notions of border and borderlands emerge from a reflection of the contradictions of life at the U.S.-Mexican *frontera*. The U.S.-Mexican border is unique because it is simultaneously a state-sponsored line of demarcation that produces naked difference and exclusion and a zone of contact and cultural creativity. On the one hand, the border is the epitome of environmental degradation, economic exploitation in *maquilas*, and sharp militarization by both the INS and global drug syndicates. (*Maquiladoras*, labor-intensive industrial operations normally supported by multinational corporations in cooperation with local capital or management, have been connected to labor and environmental abuses.) On the other, it is a liminal place, a landscape of transculturality, "one of the biggest laboratories of post-modernity," in García Canclini's words. The border is a place where Spanglish is the lingua franca and where age-old Catholic shrines stand side-by-side with *maquilas*, the monuments of neoliberal capitalism, where *el dia de los muertos* and mariachis meet the *electrónicas*. Chicana writer Gloria Anzaldúa expresses this ambivalence well: "The U.S.-Mexican border es una herida abierta where the Third World grates against the first and bleeds. And before the scab forms it hemorrhages again, the lifeblood of the two worlds merging to form a third country—a border culture" (1987: 3).

Cultural and Latino studies scholars like Rouse (1991), Kearney (1991), Gómez-Peña (1996), and Saldívar (1997) have used the ambivalence of border life to capture the dilemmas posed by the time-space compression associated with the present round of globalization. For example, without denying the specificity of the U.S.-Mexican border, Anzaldúa (1987: v) affirms that "psychological borderlands . . . sexual borderlands and . . . spiritual borderlands are not particular to the South-west. In fact, the borderlands are physically present wherever two or more cultures edge each other, where people of different races occupy the same territory, where under, lower, middle and upper classes touch, where the space between two individuals shrinks with intimacy." By deterritorializing culture and bringing together in ever new ways a plurality of lifeworlds, globalization and postmodernism have led to a proliferation of borderlands. Now, as Rosaldo (1989: 206) puts it, "our everyday lives are criss-crossed by border zones, pockets and eruptions of all kinds."

The notions of border and borderlands help us make sense of how religion operates in a global setting. Like borders and borderlands, religion marks both encounter and separation, both intermixing and alterity. On the one hand, religion generates hybridity, opening, in the same ways borderlands do, liminal spaces of transcultural creativity and innovation. For no matter how rigid they might be and how hard the nation-state and elites work to maintain them, borders are always permeable. On the other hand, religion, like borders, signals difference and even violent physical exclusion.

More than anything, the ambiguities within and between the notions of border and borderlands define religion's involvement in globalization. These ambiguities capture better than even the most sophisticated modernist approaches the complex and often contradictory roles religion plays in the Americas today. The New Paradigm has undoubtedly advanced the sociology of religion beyond the secularization paradigm by demonstrating that social differentiation

is not opposed to religious vitality. Religion is after all key to marking identity in an increasingly pluralistic world. Nevertheless, in focusing so narrowly on religious competition in unregulated markets, the NP can only tell us about the "border-making" aspects of religion without explaining the accompanying processes of "border crossing" and "border blurring." This is because the NP continues to operate with a static notion of border and a functionalist understanding of culture and religion, out of sync with deterritorializing aspects of globalization.

It is undeniable that religion marks antagonistic difference, perhaps even more so amid the turbulence created by globalization. Demerath (2001), for example, sees religion deeply involved in a "tribalistic culturalism," whereby ethnic and linguistic groups build claims to nationhood on the basis of invented myths of origin and traditions. Often this tribal culturalism is accompanied by violent and xenophobic attachment to homeland. Yet this militant affirmation of the "spaces of belonging" (Morley 2000) is also often supported by transnational networks and diasporic populations, as Kurien (1998, 2000) has shown in the case of Hindu fundamentalists outside India. These fundamentalists eagerly "take their place at the multicultural table" in the United States, while simultaneously supporting the BJP's politics of Hindu nationalism and religious purity in their country of origin. Such apparent contradiction illustrates that the production of territorialized, exclusionary difference does not exhaust the multiple roles religion plays in the Americas.

NOTES

1. For a good overview see Held et al. 1999 and Hardt and Negri 2000.

2. Eliade ontologized the sacred, turning it into a self-sustaining universal essence. Here we agree with Jonathan Smith (1987: 105) that "sacred and profane are transitive categories; they serve as maps and labels not substances; they are distinctions of office, indices of difference." For a discussion of Eliade and the future of the comparative study of religion, see Patton and Ray 2000.

3. McRoberts (2000: 96–126) uses Erving Goffman's concepts of framing and frame extension to show how migrants from Haiti, the West Indies, and the

U.S. South use the biblical notion of exile to make sense of their experience of "being culturally and/ or geographically out of place" in Boston. The Jewish exile in Babylon becomes an interpretive frame for the experiences of life at the margins in a bewildering city, for "the irony of faith in an apparently faithless world."

4. Simon Coleman (2000: 117–142) uses the term "narrative emplacement" to describe strategies of "scriptural incarnation" among evangelical Christians ("and the word became flesh and dwelt among us," John 1:14). Narrative emplacements like sermons and testimonies help articulate an "evangelical habitus in which the 'textualisation' of self is manifested in bodily dispositions and experiences." This habitus in turn is located in a global "landscape of evangelical action, ideals and characters."

5. Hardt and Negri (2000: xii, 143–146) argue that the new global order, which they call empire, "manages hybrid identities, flexible hierarchies, and plural exchanges through modulating networks of command." Thus, it is naive to assume that an attack on binary oppositions and a stress on hybridity will subvert the emerging power configuration. For us hybridity is purely a heuristic, conceptual tool to explore social complexity beyond the limitations imposed by modernist social science. We do not make a claim as to its universal emancipatory potential. "The politics of hybridity is conjunctural and cannot be deduced from theoretical principles. In most situations, what matters politically is who deploys nationality or transnationality, authenticity or hybridity, against whom, with what relative power and ability to sustain a hegemony" (Clifford 1997: 10).

REFERENCES

Anzaldúa, Gloria. 1987. *Borderlands/La Frontera: The New Mestiza*. San Francisco: Spinsters/Aunt Lute.

Appadurai, Arjun. 1996. *Modernity at Large: Cultural Dimensions of Globalization*. Minneapolis: University of Minnesota Press.

Asad, Talal. 1993. *Genealogies of Religion*. Baltimore: Johns Hopkins University Press.

Bastide, Roger. 1978. *The African Religions of Brazil*. Baltimore: Johns Hopkins University Press.

Bauman, Zygmunt. 1998. *Globalization: The Human Consequences*. New York: Columbia University Press.

Berryman, Phillip. 1999. "Churches as Winners and Losers in the Network Society." *Journal of Interamerican Studies and World Affairs* 41, 4:21–34.

Beverley, John. 1999. *Subalternity and Representation: Arguments in Cultural Theory*. Durham, N.C.: Duke University Press.

Beyer, Peter. 1994. *Religion and Globalization*. London: Sage.

Bhabha, Homi K. 1990. *Nation and Narration*. London: Routledge.

———. 1994. *The Location of Culture*. London: Routledge.

Clifford, James. 1997. *Routes: Travel and Translation in the Late Twentieth Century*. Cambridge: Harvard University Press.

Coleman, Simon. 2000. *Globalization of Charismatic Christianity*. Cambridge: Cambridge University Press.

Demerath, N. J. 2001. *Crossing the Gods: World Religions and Worldly Politics*. New Brunswick: Rutgers University Press.

Eliade, Mircea. 1959. *The Sacred and the Profane: The Nature of Religion*. New York: Harcourt Brace Jovanovich.

Fraser, Nancy. 1997. *Justice Interruptus: Critical Reflections on the 'Postsocialist' Condition*. New York: Routledge.

Freyre, Gilberto. 1986. *The Masters and the Slaves*. Berkeley: University of California Press.

Friedman, Jonathan. 1997. "Global Crisis, the Struggle for Cultural Identity, and Intellectual Porkbarrelling: Cosmopolitans versus Locals, Ethnics, and Nationals in an Era of De-homogenization." In *Debating Cultural Hybridity*, ed. Pnina Werbner and Tariq Modood. London: Zed Books.

———. 1999. "The Hybridization of Roots and the Abhorrence of the Bush." In *Spaces of Culture: City-Nation-World*, ed. Mike Featherstone and Scott Lash. London: Sage.

García Canclini, Néstor. 1995. *Hybrid Cultures: Strategies for Entering and Leaving Modernity*. Minneapolis: University of Minnesota Press.

Gill, Sam. 1998. "Territory." In *Critical Terms for Religious Studies*, ed. Mark C. Taylor. Chicago: University of Chicago Press.

Golledge, Reginald G. 1999. *Wayfinding Behavior: Cognitive Mapping and Other Spatial Processes*. Baltimore: Johns Hopkins University Press.

Gómez-Peña, Guillermo. 1996. *New World Border*, San Francisco: City Lights.

Hardt, Michael, and Antonio Negri. 2000. *Empire*, Cambridge: Harvard University Press.

Held, David, Anthony McGrew, David Goldblatt, and Jonathan Perraton. 1999. *Global Transformations: Politics, Economics, and Culture*. Stanford: Stanford University Press.

Herskovits, Melville. 1966. *The New World Negro*. Bloomington: Indiana University Press.

Jameson, Frederic. 1991. *Postmodernism: Or, the Cultural Logic of Late Capitalism*. Durham, N.C.: Duke University Press.

Kapchan, Deborah, and Pauline Turner Strong. 1999. "Theorizing the Hybrid." *Journal of American Folklore* 112, 4/5:239–253.

Kearney, Michael. 1991. "Borders and Boundaries of State and Self at the End of the Empire." *Journal of Historical Sociology* 4: 52–73.

Kurien, Prema. 1998. "Becoming American by Becoming Hindu: Indian Americans Take Their Place at the Multicultural Table." In *Gatherings in Diaspora: Religious Communities and the New Immigration*, ed. R. Stephen Warner and Judith Wittner. Philadelphia: Temple University Press.

——. 2000. The Emergence of American Hinduism: Genteel Multiculturalism and Militant Fundamentalism." Paper presented at the annual meeting of the Association for the Sociology of Religion, August 11–13, Washington, D.C.

Levitt, Peggy. 2001. "Between God, Ethnicity, and Country: An Approach to the Study of Transnational Religion." Paper presented at Social Science Research Council workshop, "Transnational Migration: Comparative Perspectives," June 29-July 1, Princeton.

Mahler, Sarah. 2001. "Bringing Religion to a Transnational Perspective: Clarifications and Initial Ideas on the Viability of the Framework." Paper presented at the University of Florida, April 2, Gainesville.

Marfleet, Phil. 1998. "Globalisation and Religious Activism." In Globalisation and the Third World, ed. Ray Kiely and Phil Marfleet. London: Routledge.

McRoberts, Omar. 2000. "Saving Four Corners: Religion and Revitalization in a Depressed Neighborhood." Ph.D. diss., Harvard University.

Mitchell, Katharyne. 1997. "Transnational Discourse: Bringing Geography Back in." Antipode 29, 2:101–114.

Morley, David. 2000. Home Territories: Media, Mobility, and Identity. London: Routledge.

Nederveen Pieterse, Jan. 1995. "Globalization as Hybridization." In Global Modernities, ed. Mike Featherstone, Scott Lash, and Roland Robertson. London: Sage.

Orsi, Robert, ed. 1999. Gods of the City: Religion and the American Urban Landscape. Bloomington: Indiana University Press.

Patton, Kimberley, and Benjamin Ray, eds. 2000. A Magic Still Dwells: Comparative Religion in the Postmodern Age. Berkeley: University of California Press.

Peterson, Anna, and Manuel Vásquez. 2001. " 'Upwards, Never Down': The Catholic Charismatic Renewal in Transnational Perspective." In Christianity, Social Change, and Globalization in the Americas, ed. Anna Peterson, Manuel Vásquez, and Phillip Williams. New Brunswick: Rutgers University Press.

Robertson, Roland. 1991. "Globalization, Modernization, and Postmodernization: The Ambiguous Position of Religion." In Religion and the Global Order, ed. Roland Robertson and William R. Garrett. New York: Paragon House.

——. 1992. Globalization: Social Theory and Global Culture. London: Sage.

——. 1995. "Glocalization: Time-Space and Homogeneity-Heterogeneity." In Global Modernities, ed. Mike Featherstone, Scott Lash, and Roland Robertson. London: Sage.

Rosaldo, Renato. 1989. Culture and Truth: The Remaking of Social Analysis. Boston: Beacon.

——. 1995. Foreword to Hybrid Cultures: Strategies for Entering and Leaving Modernity, by Nestor García Canclini. Minneapolis: University of Minnesota Press.

Rouse, Roger. 1991. "Mexican Migration and the Social Space of Postmodernism." Diaspora 1, 1: 8–23.

Said, Edward. 1993. Culture and Imperialism. London: Chatto and Windus.

Saldívar, José David. 1997. Border Matters: Remapping American Cultural Studies. Berkeley: University of California Press.

Smith, Jonathan Z. 1978. Map Is Not Territory: Studies in the History of Religion. Chicago: University of Chicago Press.

——. 1987. To Take Place: Toward a Theory in Ritual. Chicago: University of Chicago Press.

Soja, Edward. 1989. Postmodern Geographies: The Reassertion of Space in Critical Social Theory. London: Verso.

——. 2000. Postmetropolis: Critical Studies of Cities and Regions. Oxford: Blackwell.

Spickard, James, J. Shawn Landres, and Meredith McGuire, eds. 2002. Personal Knowledge and Beyond: Reshaping the Ethnography of Religion. New York: New York University Press.

Spivak, Gayatri. 1988. In Other Worlds: Essays in Cultural Politics. Edited by Donna Landry and Gerald MacLean. New York: Routledge.

Stewart, Charles, and Rosalind Shaw. 1994. Syncretism/Anti-Syncretism: The Politics of Religious Synthesis. New York: Routledge.

Stross, Brian. 1999. "The Hybrid Metaphor: From Biology to Culture." Journal of American Folklore 112, 445:254–267.

Swyngedouw, Erik. 1997. "Neither Global nor Local: 'Glocalization' and the Politics of Scale." In Spaces of Globalization, ed. Kevin Cox. New York: Guilford.

Teather, Elizabeth K. 1999. Introduction to Embodied Geographies: Spaces, Bodies, and Rites of Passage, ed. Elizabeth K. Teather. London: Routledge.

Tiryakian, Edward. 1992b. "From Modernization to Globalization." Journal for the Scientific Study of Religion 31:304–310.

Vattimo, Gianni. 1992. The Transparent Society. Cambridge: Polity.

Venn, Couze, 1999. "Narrating the Postcolonial." In Spaces of Culture: City-Nation-World, ed. Mike Featherstone and Scott Lash. London: Sage.

Wilson, Rob, and Wimal Dissanayake. 1996. Global/Local: Cultural Production and the Transnational Imaginary. Durham, N.C.: Duke University Press.

Zwingle, Erla. 1999. "Goods Move. People Move. Ideas Move. And Cultures Change." National Geographic, August, 12–33.

SECTION 7

*A*rts and Culture

Introduction to Section 7

The articles in this section explore the creation and management of the artistic and cultural products of transnationalism and their relationship to ethnic and homeland art. They compare the artistic expressions produced by different gazes, the relationship between them, and how they affect what is created and disseminated. What kinds of art do homeland, ethnic, and transnational locations produce and how do they interact with each other? What are the politics of representation? How does "immigrant" art speak to its home-country and native-born neighbors and what kinds of bridges and partnerships are made possible as a result?

Homi Bhabha wants to "locate culture" and to understand how strategies of representation and empowerment are formulated when the people they claim to represent have different ideas about what and where they should be. Groups gain legitimacy through traditions but they also need to challenge those traditions to become visible on their own terms. In the process of physical and social space-claiming, "in that interstitial passage between fixed identifications," fluid identities, not grounded in assumed or imposed hierarchies, become possible. What national culture means is redefined by marginalized groups and people who move. They live "in the beyond," which means, according to Bhabha, occupying an intervening space where it is still possible to intervene in the here and now. But to do so, requires *rasquachismo*, using available and culturally appropriate resources to produce delightful, and unexpectedly powerful, tools for living on both sides of the border and redefining it.

Elaine Kim locates Asian-American artists at the intersection between the Asian, American, and ethnic experience. Asian-American art, she says, is not the same as Asian art. Korean artists, for example, often use traditional forms and techniques to explore Korea's relation to the west. In contrast, Korean American identity "expresses tentative, multiple, and sometimes contradictory identities and allegiances" unconstrained by their direct lineage to a national self. Their full return to Korea is impossible because they are working two or three degrees of separation away from Korean artistic traditions. Korean-American artists are also engaged in a conversation with different partners and are judged by different standards than their Korean counterparts. They speak to their ethnic and native-born neighbors. Their work stands in relation to other "western" art and to other Asian-American expressive forms, as well as to Asian artistic practices. Asian-Americans tend to address different themes than their homeland counterparts. Homeland artists, for example, often dismiss ethnic Americans' focus on race as a self-indulgent "personal identity problem" that distracts them from more important topics like human rights, global capitalism, and art-historical concerns.

There is also a difference between the way homeland and ethnic art is received. Much of ethnic art in America grows out of the experience of race and racialization in the U.S.; art is the arena where race relations are explored and worked out. Moreover, art is often one of the ways race is talked about in the United States. African-American art, for example, is called "primitivist" while Asian-American art is approached with "orientalist expectations." Critics tend to expect minority artists to include elements of autobiography, to attest to their authenticity. But when they do, using craft or folk-artistic practices that are integral to their traditions, critics dismiss their work as popular art and, thus, less valuable than the "high" art category. Kim urges us not to understand Asian-American art as a copy of "American" art forms or as imperfect replicas of "real Asian art." Instead, it makes more sense to treat it as a combination of different visual languages, located in the untranslatable, incommensurate in-between, where creation, contradiction, and conflict result from "the continual collisions and transformations that comprise Asian-American cultural experiences." These artists challenge the expectation of an homogenous American culture. They also disappoint those who expect them to be exotic and foreign or to blend seamlessly into the American art scene. Because they are located at the intersection between Asia and America, black and white, aesthetics and politics, they view the world from several places at one time.

Néstor García Canclini is interested in how the global restructuring of economics and politics affects national elite and popular cultural forms. Two contradictory processes are at work. Public investment in education, science, and the arts has declined because of economic reforms. Both the elite and popular sectors consume less culture because of national and global factors. But not all art is in crisis. There is a growth of electronic cultures and museums, artisans and popular singers. Traditional cultural forms are not dying but are, rather, in transition, responding to modern processes. Certain groups recycle their knowledge and apply it to other areas. Neoartisans, for example, use skills like weaving and woodwork to make new, modern decorations. Hybrid transformations emerge, produced when several symbolic systems converge.

What García Canclini calls "reconversion" challenges the expectation that cultural identity is based on patrimony and that patrimony is based on belonging to a particular territory associated with a specific collection of works and monuments. Rather, urbanization and industrialization produce new cultural forms and shake up symbolic processes. There is a shift away from direct, micro-social interactions to consumption, via long distance, of serially produced goods. Those in charge of information networks control the power, rather than traditional opinion shapers like unions and community leaders. Local forms of opinion and taste, the last bastion of difference, are absorbed into national and transnational markets. As a result, many spaces once occupied by regional cultures now take their cue from trans-territorial systems of production and message circulation. Rather than homogenizing audiences, however, the mass media creates new social divisions. The distinction between high and popular culture persists alongside new differences based on age, gender, or socio-economic status. National differences are reconfigured through transnational interaction. Inequality is not just produced by mechanisms of exclusion and opposition on the ground, but also by processes shaping the experiences of those who occupy different social positions, are guided by different cognitive systems, or embrace different tastes.

Juan Flores also notes the emergence of new cultural forms that are not here nor there but combine both. From his perspective, the Latino experience in the United States has always been a kind of crossover, traversing geopolitical as well as cultural and social boundaries. Cultural crossovers are not just about entering the mainstream of American culture; they are about creating new cultural forms that move in both directions. Such convergence, as musician Rubén Blades calls it, does not require a visa because it does not stop at "being in America," but is about creating a new America as well.

Flores emphasizes the importance of language, in its many combinations, in enabling people to occupy many positions at once. Language captures people's multiple positions and subjectivities and allows them to challenge a culture that expects them to be one thing, in one place, at one time. To participate as equals with other groups, people have to be able to continue to speak in their ancestral tongues. The creative linguistic practices of Latinos are not another form of subalternity but a way of "prying open the larger culture" by calling its boundaries into question. Unbounded language, that mixes English and Spanish in combinations that creatively capture a particular moment, is the right response to an unbounded existence. These linguistic forms, as well as other forms of cultural blending, underlie a sea-change in thinking about ethnicity that redefines what is at the center and at the periphery, and instead sees the blended in-between as the frontier of cultural possibility.

CHAPTER 29

Locations of Culture

Homi K. Bhabha

> A boundary is not that at which something stops but, as the Greeks recognized, the boundary is that from which *something begins its presencing*.
>
> Martin Heidegger, 'Building, dwelling, thinking'

BORDER LIVES: THE ART OF THE PRESENT

It is the trope of our times to locate the question of culture in the realm of the *beyond*. At the century's edge, we are less exercised by annihilation—the death of the author—or epiphany—the birth of the 'subject'. Our existence today is marked by a tenebrous sense of survival, living on the borderlines of the 'present', for which there seems to be no proper name other than the current and controversial shiftiness of the prefix 'post': *postmodernism, postcolonialism, postfeminism*. . . .

The 'beyond' is neither a new horizon, nor a leaving behind of the past. . . . Beginnings and endings may be the sustaining myths of the middle years; but in the *fin de siècle*, we find ourselves in the moment of transit where space and time cross to produce complex figures of difference and identity, past and present, inside and outside, inclusion and exclusion. For there is a sense of disorientation, a disturbance of direction, in the 'beyond': an exploratory, restless movement caught so well in the French rendition of the words *au-delà*—here and there, on all sides, *fort/da*, hither and thither, back and forth.[1]

The move away from the singularities of 'class' or 'gender' as primary conceptual and organizational categories, has resulted in an awareness of the subject positions—of race, gender, generation, institutional location, geopolitical locale, sexual orientation—that inhabit any claim to identity in the modern world. What is theoretically innovative, and politically crucial, is the need to think beyond narratives of originary and initial subjectivities and to focus on those moments or processes that are produced in the articulation of cultural differences. These 'inbetween' spaces provide the terrain for elaborating strategies of selfhood—singular or communal—that initiate new signs of identity, and innovative sites of collaboration, and contestation, in the act of defining the idea of society itself.

It is in the emergence of the interstices—the overlap and displacement of domains of difference—that the intersubjective and collective experiences of *nationness*, community interest, or cultural value are negotiated. How are subjects formed 'in-between', or in excess of, the sum of the 'parts' of difference (usually intoned as race/class/gender, etc.)? How do strategies of representation or empowerment come to be formulated in the competing claims of communities where, despite shared histories of deprivation and discrimination, the exchange of values, meanings and priorities may not always be collaborative and dialogical, but may be profoundly antagonistic, conflictual and even incommensurable?

The force of these questions is borne out by the 'language' of recent social crises sparked off by histories of cultural difference. Conflicts in South Central Los Angeles between Koreans, Mexican-Americans and African-Americans focus on the concept of 'disrespect'—a term forged on the borderlines of ethnic deprivation that is, at once, the sign of racialized violence and the symptom of social victimage. In the aftermath of the *The Satanic Verses* affair in Great Britain, Black and Irish feminists, despite their different constituencies, have made common cause against the 'racialization of religion' as the dominant discourse through which the State represents their conflicts and struggles, however secular or even 'sexual' they may be.

Terms of cultural engagement, whether antagonistic or affiliative, are produced performatively. The representation of difference must not be hastily read as the reflection of *pre-given* ethnic or cultural traits set in the fixed tablet of tradition. The social articulation of difference, from the minority perspective, is a complex, on-going negotiation that seeks to authorize cultural hybridities that emerge in moments of historical transformation. The 'right' to signify from the periphery of authorized power and privilege does not depend on the persistence of tradition; it is resourced by the power of tradition to be reinscribed through the conditions of contingency and contradictoriness that attend upon the lives of those who are 'in the minority'. The recognition that tradition bestows is a partial form of identification. In restaging the past it introduces other, incommensurable cultural temporalities into the invention of tradition. This process estranges any immediate access to an originary identity or a 'received' tradition. The borderline engagements of cultural difference may as often be consensual as conflictual; they may confound our definitions of tradition and modernity; realign the customary boundaries between the private and the public, high and low; and challenge normative expectations of development and progress.

> I wanted to make shapes or set up situations that are kind of open. . . . My work has a lot to do with a kind of fluidity, a movement back and forth, not making a claim to any specific or essential way of being.[2]

Thus writes Renée Green, the African-American artist. She reflects on the need to understand cultural difference as the production of minority identities that 'split'—are estranged unto themselves—in the act of being articulated into a collective body:

> Multiculturalism doesn't reflect the complexity of the situation as I face it daily. . . . It requires a person to step outside of him/herself to actually see what he/she is doing. I don't want to condemn well-meaning people and say (like those T-shirts you can buy on the street) 'It's a black thing, you wouldn't understand.' To me that's essentialising blackness.[3]

Political empowerment, and the enlargement of the multiculturalist cause, come from posing questions of solidarity and community from the interstitial perspective. Social differences are not simply given to experience through an already authenticated cultural tradition; they are the signs of the emergence of community envisaged as a project—at once a vision and a construction—that takes you 'beyond' yourself in order to return, in a spirit of revision and reconstruction, to the political *conditions* of the present:

> Even then, it's still a struggle for power between various groups within ethnic groups about what's being said and who's saying what, who's representing who? What is a community anyway? What is a black community? What is a Latino community? I have trouble with thinking of all these things as monolithic fixed categories.[4]

If Renée Green's questions open up an interrogatory, interstitial space between the act of representation—who? what? where?—and the presence of community itself, then consider her own creative intervention within this in-between moment. Green's 'architectural' site-specific work, *Sites of Genealogy* (Out of Site, The Institute of Contemporary Art, Long Island City, New York), displays and displaces the binary logic through which identities of difference are often constructed —Black/White, Self/Other. Green makes a metaphor of the museum building itself, rather than simply using the gallery space:

> I used architecture literally as a reference, using the attic, the boiler room, and the stairwell to make associations between certain binary divisions such as higher and lower and heaven and

hell. The stairwell became a liminal space, a pathway between the upper and lower areas, each of which was annotated with plaques referring to blackness and whiteness.[5]

The stairwell as liminal space, in-between the designations of identity, becomes the process of symbolic interaction, the connective tissue that constructs the difference between upper and lower, black and white. The hither and thither of the stairwell, the temporal movement and passage that it allows, prevents identities at either end of it from settling into primordial polarities. This interstitial passage between fixed identifications opens up the possibility of a cultural hybridity that entertains difference without an assumed or imposed hierarchy:

I always went back and forth between racial designations and designations from physics or other symbolic designations. All these things blur in some way. . . . To develop a genealogy of the way colours and noncolours function is interesting to me.[6]

'Beyond' signifies spatial distance, marks progress, promises the future; but our intimations of exceeding the barrier or boundary—the very act of going *beyond*—are unknowable, unrepresentable, without a return to the 'present' which, in the process of repetition, becomes disjunct and displaced. The imaginary of spatial distance—to live somehow beyond the border of our times—throws into relief the temporal, social differences that interrupt our collusive sense of cultural contemporaneity. The present can no longer be simply envisaged as a break or a bonding with the past and the future, no longer a synchronic presence: our proximate self-presence, our public image, comes to be revealed for its discontinuities, its inequalities, its minorities. Unlike the dead hand of history that tells the beads of sequential time like a rosary, seeking to establish serial, causal connections, we are now confronted with what Walter Benjamin describes as the blasting of a monadic moment from the homogenous course of history, 'establishing a conception of the present as the "time of the now" '.[7]

If the jargon of our times—postmodernity, postcoloniality, postfeminism—has

any meaning at all, it does not lie in the popular use of the 'post' to indicate sequentiality—*after*-feminism; or polarity—*anti*-modernism. These terms that insistently gesture to the beyond, only embody its restless and revisionary energy if they transform the present into an expanded and ex-centric site of experience and empowerment. For instance, if the interest in postmodernism is limited to a celebration of the fragmentation of the 'grand narratives' of postenlightenment rationalism then, for all its intellectual excitement, it remains a profoundly parochial enterprise.

The wider significance of the postmodern condition lies in the awareness that the epistemological 'limits' of those ethnocentric ideas are also the enunciative boundaries of a range of other dissonant, even dissident histories and voices—women, the colonized, minority groups, the bearers of policed sexualities. For the demography of the new internationalism is the history of postcolonial migration, the narratives of cultural and political diaspora, the major social displacements of peasant and aboriginal communities, the poetics of exile, the grim prose of political and economic refugees. It is in this sense that the boundary becomes the place from which *something begins its presencing* in a movement not dissimilar to the ambulant, ambivalent articulation of the beyond that I have drawn out: 'Always and ever differently the bridge escorts the lingering and hastening ways of men to and fro, so that they may get to other banks. . . . The bridge *gathers* as a passage that crosses.'[8]

The very concepts of homogenous national cultures, the consensual or contiguous transmission of historical traditions, or 'organic' ethnic communities—*as the grounds of cultural comparativism*—are in a profound process of redefinition. The hideous extremity of Serbian nationalism proves that the very idea of a pure, 'ethnically cleansed' national identity can only be achieved through the death, literal and figurative, of the complex interweavings of history, and the culturally contingent borderlines of modern nationhood. This side of the psychosis of patriotic fervour, I like to think, there is overwhelming evidence of a more transnational and translational sense of the hybridity of imagined communities. Contemporary Sri Lankan theatre represents the deadly conflict between the Tamils and the Sinhalese through allegorical references to State brutality in South Africa and Latin America; the Anglo-Celtic canon of Australian literature and cinema is being rewritten from the perspective of Aboriginal political and cultural imperatives; the South African novels of Richard Rive, Bessie Head, Nadine Gordimer, John Coetzee, are documents of a society divided by the effects of apartheid that enjoin the international intellectual community to meditate on the unequal, asymmetrical worlds that exist elsewhere; Salman Rushdie writes the fabulist historiography of post-Independence India and Pakistan in *Midnight's Children* and *Shame*, only to remind us in *The Satanic Verses* that the truest eye may now belong to the migrant's double vision; Toni Morrison's *Beloved* revives the past of slavery and its murderous rituals of possession and self-possession, in order to project a contemporary fable of a woman's history that is at the same time the narrative of an affective, historic memory of an emergent public sphere of men and women alike.

What is striking about the 'new' internationalism is that the move from the specific to the general, from the material to the metaphoric, is not a smooth passage of transition and transcendence. The 'middle passage' of contemporary culture, as with slavery itself, is a process of displacement and disjunction that does not totalize experience. Increasingly, 'national' cultures are being produced from the perspective of disenfranchised minorities. The most significant effect of this process is not the proliferation of 'alternative histories of the excluded' producing, as some would have it, a pluralist anarchy. What my examples show is the changed basis for making international connections. The currency of critical comparativism, or aesthetic judgement, is no longer the sovereignty of the national culture conceived as Benedict Anderson proposes as an 'imagined community' rooted in a 'homogeneous empty time' of modernity and progress. The great connective narratives of capitalism and class drive the engines of social reproduction, but

do not, in themselves, provide a foundational frame for those modes of cultural identification and political affect that form around issues of sexuality, race, feminism, the lifeworld of refugees or migrants, or the deathly social destiny of AIDS.

The testimony of my examples represents a radical revision in the concept of human community itself. What this geopolitical space may be, as a local or transnational reality, is being both interrogated and reinitiated. Feminism, in the 1990s, finds its solidarity as much in liberatory narratives as in the painful ethical position of a slavewoman, Morrison's Sethe, in *Beloved*, who is pushed to infanticide. The body politic can no longer contemplate the nation's health as simply a civic virtue; it must rethink the question of rights for the entire national, and international, community, from the AIDS perspective. The Western metropole must confront its postcolonial history, told by its influx of postwar migrants and refugees, as an indigenous or native narrative *internal to its national identity*; and the reason for this is made clear in the stammering, drunken words of Mr 'Whisky' Sisodia from *The Satanic Verses*: 'The trouble with the Engenglish is that their hiss hiss history happened overseas, so they dodo don't know what it means.'[9]

Postcoloniality, for its part, is a salutary reminder of the persistent 'neo-colonial' relations within the 'new' world order and the multinational division of labour. Such a perspective enables the authentication of histories of exploitation and the evolution of strategies of resistance. Beyond this, however, postcolonial critique bears witness to those countries and communities—in the North and the South, urban and rural—constituted, if I may coin a phrase, 'otherwise than modernity'. Such cultures of a postcolonial *contramodernity* may be contingent to modernity, discontinuous or in contention with it, resistant to its oppressive, assimilationist technologies; but they also deploy the cultural hybridity of their borderline conditions to 'translate', and therefore reinscribe, the social imaginary of both metropolis and modernity. Listen to Guillermo Gomez-Peña, the performance artist who lives, amongst other times and places, on the Mexico/US border:

hello America
this is the voice of *Gran Vato Charollero*
broadcasting from the hot deserts of Nogales,
Arizona
zona de libre cogercio
2000 megaherz en todas direciones

you are celebrating Labor Day in Seattle
while the Klan demonstrates
against Mexicans in Georgia
ironia, 100% ironia[10]

Being in the 'beyond', then, is to inhabit an intervening space, as any dictionary will tell you. But to dwell 'in the beyond' is also, as I have shown, to be part of a revisionary time, a return to the present to redescribe our cultural contemporaneity; to reinscribe our human, historic commonality; *to touch the future on its hither side*. In that sense, then, the intervening space 'beyond', becomes a space of intervention in the here and now. To engage with such invention, and intervention, as Green and Gomez-Peña enact in their distinctive work, requires a sense of the new that resonates with the hybrid chicano aesthetic of '*rasquachismo*' as Tomas Ybarra-Frausto describes it:

the utilization of available resources for syncretism, juxtaposition, and integration. *Rasquachismo* is a sensibility attuned to mixtures and confluence . . . a delight in texture and sensuous surfaces . . . self-conscious manipulation of materials or iconography . . . the combination of found material and satiric wit . . . the manipulation of *rasquache* artifacts, code and sensibilities from both sides of the border.[11]

The borderline work of culture demands an encounter with 'newness' that is not part of the continuum of past and present. It creates a sense of the new as an insurgent act of cultural translation. Such art does not merely recall the past as social cause or aesthetic precedent; it renews the past, refiguring it as a contingent 'in-between' space, that innovates and interrupts the performance of the present. The 'past-present' becomes part of the necessity, not the nostalgia, of living.

Pepon Osorio's *objets trouvés* of the Nuyorican (New York/Puerto Rican) community —the statistics of infant mortality, or the silent (and silenced) spread of AIDS in the Hispanic community—are elaborated into baroque allegories of social alienation. But it is not the high drama of birth and death that captures Osorio's spectacular imagination. He is the great celebrant of the migrant act of survival, using his mixed-media works to make a hybrid cultural space that forms contingently, disjunctively, in the inscription of signs of cultural memory and sites of political agency. *La Cama* (*The Bed*) turns the highly decorated four-poster into the primal scene of lost-and-found childhood memories, the memorial to a dead nanny Juana, the *mise-en-scène* of the eroticism of the 'emigrant' everyday. Survival, for Osorio, is working in the interstices of a range of practices: the 'space' of installation, the spectacle of the social statistic, the transitive time of the body in performance.

Finally, it is the photographic art of Alan Sekula that takes the borderline condition of cultural translation to its global limit in *Fish Story*, his photographic project on harbours: 'the harbour is the site in which material goods appear in bulk, in the very flux of exchange.'[12] The harbour and the stock-market become the *paysage moralisé* of a containerized, computerized world of global trade. Yet, the non-synchronous time–space of transnational 'exchange', and exploitation, is embodied in a navigational allegory:

Things are more confused now. A scratchy recording of the Norwegian national anthem blares out from a loudspeaker at the Sailor's Home on the bluff above the channel. The container ship being greeted flies a Bahamian flag of convenience. It was built by Koreans working long hours in the giant shipyards of Ulsan. The underpaid and the understaffed crew could be Salvadorean or Filipino. Only the Captain hears a familiar melody.[13]

Norway's nationalist nostalgia cannot drown out the babel on the bluff. Transnational capitalism and the impoverishment of the Third World certainly create the chains of circumstance that incarcerate the Salvadorean or the Filipino/a. In their cultural passage, hither and thither, as migrant workers, part of the massive economic and political diaspora of the modern world, they embody the Benjaminian 'present': that moment blasted out of the continuum of history. Such conditions of cultural displacement and social discrimination—where political survivors become the best historical witnesses—are the grounds on which Frantz Fanon, the Martinican psychoanalyst and participant in the Algerian revolution, locates an agency of empowerment:

> As soon as I *desire* I am asking to be considered. I am not merely here-and-now, sealed into thingness. I am for somewhere else and for something else. I demand that notice be taken of my *negating activity* [my emphasis] insofar as I pursue something other than life; insofar as I do battle for the creation of a human world—that is a world of reciprocal recognitions.

> I should constantly remind myself that the real *leap* consists in introducing invention into existence.

> In the world in which I travel, I am endlessly creating myself. And it is by going beyond the historical, instrumental hypothesis that I will initiate my cycle of freedom.[14]

Once more it is the desire for recognition, 'for somewhere else and for something else' that takes the experience of history *beyond* the instrumental hypothesis. Once again, it is the space of intervention emerging in the cultural interstices that introduces creative invention into existence. And one last time, there is a return to the performance of identity as iteration, the re-creation of the self in the world of travel, the resettlement of the borderline community of migration. Fanon's desire for the recognition of cultural presence

as 'negating activity' resonates with my breaking of the time-barrier of a culturally collusive 'present'. [. . .]

NOTES

1. For an interesting discussion of gender boundaries in the *fin de siècle*, see E. Showalter, *Sexual Anarchy: Gender and Culture in the Fin de Siècle* (London: Bloomsbury, 1990), especially 'Borderlines', pp. 1–18.
2. Renée Green interviewed by Elizabeth Brown, from catalogue published by Allen Memorial Art Museum, Oberlin College, Ohio.
3. Interview conducted by Miwon Kwon for the exhibition 'Emerging New York Artists', Sala Mendonza, Caracas, Venezuela (xeroxed manuscript copy).
4. ibid., p. 6.
5. Renée Green in conversation with Donna Harkavy, Curator of Contemporary Art at the Worcester Museum.
6. ibid.
7. W. Benjamin, 'Theses on the philosophy of history', in his *Illuminations* (London: Jonathan Cape, 1970), p. 265.
8. M. Heidegger, 'Building, dwelling, thinking', in *Poetry, Language, Thought* (New York: Harper & Row, 1971), pp. 152–3.
9. S. Rushdie, *The Satanic Verses* (London: Viking, 1988), p. 343.
10. G. Gomez-Pena, *American Theatre*, vol. 8, no. 7, October 1991.
11. T. Ybarra-Frausto, 'Chicano movement/chicano art' in I. Karp and S.D. Lavine (eds) (Washington and London: Smithsonian Institution Press, 1991), pp. 133–4.
12. A. Sekula, *Fish Story*, manuscript, p. 2.
13. ibid., p. 3.
14. F. Fanon, *Black Skin, White Masks*, Introduction by H. K. Bhabha (London: Pluto, 1986), pp. 218, 229, 231.

CHAPTER 30

Interstitial Subjects: Asian American Visual Art as a Site for New Cultural Conversations

Elaine H. Kim

[. . .]

Asian American art is not synonymous with Asian art. There are striking contrasts between the Korean and Korean American art featured in the 1993 Queens Museum exhibit *Across the Pacific: Contemporary Korean and Korean American Art*. Korean curator Young Chul Lee sees a similarity between Korean American artists who are "rootlessly drifting along the margins of [U.S.] society" and the Korean artists who "are strongly influenced by the West but [who remain] on its periphery."[1] But while the Korean artists contest the Korean establishment, their work expresses a sense of Korean citizenship, of belonging to a Korean nation and its sociocultural life, and of continuity with something understood as "Korean tradition" and the "Korean experience of modernity." According to Lee, "They all focus on trying to understand Korea at the end of the [twentieth] century," many of them by reconstituting a "Korean self" separate from Western culture in an attempt to challenge the center-periphery hierarchy between the United States and Korea.[2] Their work is accomplished in conversation with traditional Korean art forms, such as eighteenth-century portrait art and nineteenth-century folk art that features panoramic two-dimensional scenes of everyday village life. The social commentary directly addresses such issues as the destruction of farming communities and the patriarchal subjugation of women in Korean society. By contrast, the Korean American art expresses tentative, multiple, and sometimes contradictory identities and allegiances not bounded by the sense of direct cultural lineage or links to national selfhood expressed in the Korean art. Jinme Yoon's *Screens*, for example, is an installation composed of text fragments that trace the irregular movements of a daughter away from her immigrant mother as she loses one language and gains another. Byron Kim's monochromatic green paintings titled *Koryo Celadon Ceramics* refer to the *pisaek* or secret glaze color used by twelfth-century Korean potters. The secret of the glaze has long been lost and can never be replicated, thus, there can be no return for the Korean American. [. . .]

The American roots of Asian American art are embedded in the story of race and racialization in U.S. life, including the little-discussed lateral relationships among racialized groups. Asian American art is imbricated in many other discourses, particularly cross-racial ones. It exists within the broader context of struggles for cultural definitions in other racialized American communities, such as the struggles against homogenization, decontextualization, curatorial eclecticism, and exoticization that Guillermo Gómez-Peña describes as occurring in Chicano cultural communities.[3] While African American art has been interpreted as "primitivist" and Asian American art has been subjected to orientalist expectations, Native American and Chicano art have been particularly susceptible to being thought of as ethnographic artifact. And the assumption that diversity and artistic quality are mutually exclusive has affected African American, Chicano, and Native American as well as Asian American art communities, which have at various times rejected purely formalist standards in light of the importance to so many artists of color of elements outside the artwork itself. As Lowery Sims has noted:

> There is no denying that the contributions of Black, Hispanic, Native American or Asian Americans have had an indelible influence on the flavor of American culture as a whole. But, if we continue to consume the products of these cultures while the populations within which they are engendered remain excluded, oppressed and exploited in the arenas of world and art politics, then as professionals and cultural consumers we can no longer maintain our smug self-images as social liberals, and must confront the inherent contradictions that permeate our chosen field of endeavor.[4] [. . .]

Instead of viewing Asian American art as either soullessly copying "American" art forms or imperfectly replicating "real Asian art," perhaps we can think of it—and of American art in general—as a mixture or partial fusion of different visual languages, and critical assessments can at last move away from the economy of the copy to the narrative of similarity. Located on the untranslatable, incommensurate in-between, in the interstice between mainstream and Asian American (as opposed to Asian) cultural traditions, perhaps Asian American art can be thought of as a site of creation, contradiction, and conflict emerging from the continual collisions and transformations that comprise Asian American cultural experiences.[5] Perhaps the question to ask is how Asian American art has expressed and continues to express a hybrid or even mutant culture that engages, extends, and transforms American art. [. . .]

Artists who identify themselves as Asian American challenge the notion of a homogenous "American" culture. Exploring subjectivity in all its complexities and contradictions is not necessarily a clichéd descent into identity politics. It could also constitute a critical contestation of the kinds of sameness global capitalism is creating as it transforms people and communities around the globe to suit the needs of transnational corporate interests. People create culture to express their thoughts and feelings in complex, mediated responses to diverse historical circumstances, which in turn are shaped as their

consciousness shifts in an ongoing mutual relationship between ideas and material conditions. Writing about fashion and theater, Dorinne Kondo has characterized the world of representation and aesthetics as "a site of struggle, where identities are created, where subjects are interpellated, where hegemonies can be challenged."[6]

Rethinking the importance of Asian American art as process, not exotic artifact or investment item, so that we can appreciate both the political identities it expresses and the aesthetic processes that are inseparable from these identities, inspires the creative expression of Asian Americans who have felt excluded by particular forms of racialization from conversations about American culture. It might also lead to a long overdue reevaluation of the impact of the artistic output of various racialized American groups on "American art." At the same time, it could help us all more clearly recognize our own potential to break the invisible bonds that hold us as unwitting slaves in our individual cells, apart from one another, devoting our work and creative potential to enabling the commodification of and sale to the highest bidder of whatever brilliance, beauty, and community we manage to create. [. . .]

Art is inspiring because it can offer us new visions of the world and of ourselves. That this is often said makes it no less true. While work by early Asian American artists might have been tolerated as harmlessly exotic, today's critics have at times tried to stifle and dismiss what they read as social protest or preoccupation with shallow identity issues and concerns in Asian American art by denigrating both medium and message. But the Asian American artists brought together here refuse to separate new aesthetic practices from expressions of alternative cultural and political values that emerge from the particular location of Asian Americans within U.S. and world cultures. Location on the interstices of Asia and America, of black and white, of cultural nationalism and feminism, of aesthetics and politics, makes it possible to view the world from several different vantage points at the same moment. This double and triple vision engenders in Asian American visual art *fresh* and *daring* expressions of great beauty and feeling as well as invaluable critiques of contents, forms, subjects, and regimes of representation.

NOTES

1. Young Chul Lee, "Culture in the Periphery and Identity in Korean Art," in *Across the Pacific: Contemporary Korean and Korean American Art* (Queens, N.Y.: Queens Museum of Art, 1993), 12.
2. Ibid., 10.
3. Guillermo Gómez-Peña, "From Art-mageddon to Gringostroika," *High Performance* (Fall 1991): 51.
4. Lowery Sims, "The New Exclusionism," *Atlanta Art Papers* (July–August 1988): 38.
5. According to Stuart Hall, the diaspora experience is defined "not by essence or purity, but by the recognition of a necessary heterogeneity, diversity; by a conception of 'identity' which lives with and through, not despite, difference. ... [Diaspora] identities [are] constantly producing and reproducing themselves anew, through transformation and difference" (Hall, "Identity and Representation," in Maybe B. Cham, ed., *Ex-iles: Essays on Caribbean Cinema: The New World Presence* [Trenten, N.J.: Africa World Press, 1992], 234).
6. Dorinne Kondo, *About Face: Performing Race in Fashion and Theater* (New York: Routledge, 1997), 4.

CHAPTER 31

Cultural Reconversion

Néstor García Canclini

Translated by Holly Staver

[. . .]

RECONVERSION

Economic reconversion and other neoconservative reforms have had powerful repercussions on cultural policies, and these are even greater in the countries of the periphery. These countries are in the process of decreasing state investment in education, science, and art: salaries have fallen and unemployment has increased, widening the scientific and cultural gap between the metropolis and dependent societies. But they have also aggravated a long-standing cultural crisis. For this reason the recent decrease in the production and consumption of the classical cultural of elites (film, theater, magazines) and of popular sectors (higher education, spectacles) should not be attributed only to the economic recession of the 1980s. The exhaustion of certain cultural resources and relationships becomes more intelligible when seen as part of a global restructuring of society and politics.

Not all traditions or all forms of modernization are in crisis. Old and new symbolic products still offer attractive investment opportunities. At the same time, there is the growth of electronic cultures and also of museums and their publics; artisans and popular singers prosper and expand their audience. Instead of the death of traditional cultural forms, we now discover that tradition is in transition, and articulated to modern processes. Reconversion prolongs their existence [. . .]

But cultural reconversions, in addition to being strategies for social mobility, or for following the movement from the traditional to the modern, are hybrid transformations generated by the horizontal co-existence of a number of symbolic systems. This is characteristic of any complex society. It enables the conservatory musician to use knowledge of classical or contemporary harmony to produce erudite experiments in rock, jazz, or salsa. It allows a painter to use what she or he has learned not just from the history of painting, but also from graphic design, cinema, and video clips. In Latin American countries, where numerous traditions coexist with varying degrees of modernity, and where sociocultural heterogeneity presents a multiplicity of simultaneous patrimonies, this process of interchange and reutilization is even more intense. High, popular, and mass art nourish each other reciprocally.

Reconversion thus challenges the assumption that cultural identity is based on a patrimony, and that this patrimony is constituted by the occupation of a territory and by collections of works and monuments. It further undermines the belief that the secularization of cultural spheres—their autonomy and autonomous development—contributes to the expansion, experimental innovation, and democratization of societies. It questions the notion that popular sectors achieve emancipation and are integrated into modernity by means of the socialization of hegemonic cultural assets through education and mass dissemination. Finally, reconversion casts into doubt the idea that localistic or nationalistic fundamentalisms can be overcome by new global technologies of communication that also encourage cultural creativity.

What is now happening, however, is entirely different. Urbanization and industrialization not only generate new cultural forms but contribute to the reorganization of all symbolic processes. The fact that 60 to 70 percent of the population is now concentrated in big cities and is connected to national and transnational networks means that the contents, practices, and rites of the past—including those of migrant *campesinos*—are reordered according to a different logic. Radio, TV, and video generate specific formats and messages, but above all they imply the passage from direct, microsocial interactions to the distant consumption of serially produced goods within a centralized system.

The basic processes, organization, and agents of cultural production and dissemination are changing. Simpler crafts and industry are being displaced by advanced technologies; the direct producers (artisans, artists, designers) are no longer the principal creators and administrators of the processes of social signification. The role of traditional promoters of cultural activity (states, the agricultural sector of the oligarchy, and social movements) has diminished, while that of organisms linked to the expanding modes of capitalist development (financial institutions, cultural foundations, and chains of art galleries related to finance capital or high-tech industries) is on the rise.

A corresponding modification is taking place in the constitution of political culture and the valuation of the aesthetic. Traditional opinion shapers (political, union, and community organization leaders) and those who determine artistic value (artisans, artists, critics, teachers) are relinquishing some of their functions to those who control the new structure of the symbolic market: information networks, *marchands*, entrepreneurial-minded galleries and publishing houses, radio and television producers, and video and record producers. Local forms of opinion and taste that preserve any differences are incorporated into the national and transnational market. Consequently, many spaces that have represented regional cultures (theaters, magazines, cultural centers) are becoming attuned to transterritorial systems for the production and circulation of messages.

Contemporary hybrid cultures respond to an oblique organization of power and social differentiation. Big business competes with state cultural administration, artistic movements, and traditional entrepreneurs and sponsoring organizations (such as schools, churches, and amateur associations). Instead of eliminating them, commercial culture tends to absorb these agents. Similar effects can be observed in habits of audience perception and reception. The mass media have been accused of homogenizing audiences, but, in fact, they encourage new techniques of segmentation by broadcasting diversified information and programs that appeal to varied consumers. The old distinction between high and popular coexists with other ways of dividing up the social spectrum: children, youth, adults; national differences reconfigured through transnational interaction; and newly legitimized sexual identities. To study inequalities and differences today is not simply to see mechanisms of exclusion and opposition; it is also necessary to identify the processes that unequally articulate social positions, cognitive systems, and the tastes of diverse sectors.

The dense web of cultural and economic decisions leads to asymmetries between producers and consumers and between diverse publics. But these inequalities are almost never imposed from the top down, as is assumed by those who establish Manichaean oppositions between dominating and dominated classes, or between central and peripheral countries. The survival of popular culture is often attributed to simple resistance based on tradition. A more nuanced understanding of the process by which popular culture negotiates its position leads to a more decentered and complex vision of how hegemony is allied to subalternity in the practices of power. [. . .]

DETERRITORIALIZATION

Migration today is not limited to writers, artists, and political exiles as in the past; it now includes people of all social strata and moves in many different directions. The new cultural flows set into motion by displacements of Latin Americans to the United States and Europe, from the less developed to the more prosperous countries of our own continent, and from poor regions to urban centers, can no longer be attributed to imperialist domination alone. According to the most conservative estimates, two million Argentines, Chileans, Brazilians, and Uruguayans emigrated for political or economic reasons during the 1970s.

It is fitting, then, that the most insightful reflections on deterritorialization should emerge from the busiest crossing point in the hemisphere: the border between Mexico and the United States. Although uprooted and unemployed peasants and Indians who left their lands seeking survival predominate, this area is also the scene of a new and powerful creativity. The 250 Spanish-language radio and television stations, the 1,500 periodicals in Spanish, and the great interest in Latin American literature and music in the United States are evidence of a vast "Hispanic" market of nearly thirty million (12 percent of the population; 38 percent in New Mexico, 25 percent in Texas, and 23 percent in California). Films like *Zoot Suit* and *La Bamba*, the music of Rubén Blades and Los Lobos, experimental theater like that of Luis Valdez, and visual artists who combine popular culture with modern and postmodern media all demonstrate an increasing integration into the North American "mainstream."[1]

Deterritorialization thus cuts across class lines, as Roger Rouse, for instance, has shown in his migration study of Aguililla, a small farming town in southwestern Michoacán that is connected to the rest of Mexico by a single dirt road. The main economic activities of this town are subsistence farming and cattle raising. However, emigration dating from the 1940s has provided another source of income: dollars from relatives in California, especially Redwood City, on the margins of an important center of microelectronics and postindustrial culture in Silicon Valley. The emigrants from Michoacán work there mainly in the service sector. Most spend brief periods in the United States; those who stay longer are in constant touch with their hometown. As a result, the two communities have become inextricably intertwined:

> By their constant back-and-forth migration and their increasing use of the telephone, Aguililllenses reinforce their cultural identity with people who live two thousand miles away as easily as with their next-door neighbors. The continual circulation of people, money, commodities, and information, as well as the intermingling of the two localities, leads us to understand them as a single community dispersed in several places.[2]

These "intertwined economies, intersecting social systems, and fragmented personalities" pose a challenge to two conventional categories of social theory. The first, the idea of community, refers to isolated peasant villages and also to the abstraction of a cohesive national state, both of which are defined by a circumscribed territory. The premise is that the community functions as the organizing dynamic because of struggles among its members. The second category, the opposition between center and periphery, is the "abstract expression of an idealized imperial system" in which power is distributed in concentrically organized hierarchies that are concentrated at the center and diminishing toward the margins. Neither of these models is adequate today. According to Rouse, social space is more accurately mapped in terms of "circuits" and "borders."

A similar dislocation holds in the United States, where national capital is increasingly being displaced by foreign capital and the population is increasingly of mixed origin. In downtown Los Angeles, for example, 75 percent of the real estate belongs to foreign capital and 40 percent of the population of the greater metropolitan area is composed of Asians and Latinos. By the year 2010, this percentage is expected to rise to 60 percent.[3] According to Renato Rosaldo, the "Third World is imploding into the First", and

> the idea of an authentic culture as an internally cohesive and autonomous space is untenable except, perhaps, as a useful fiction or a revealing distortion.[4]

The mix of groups in California—immigrants from Mexico, Colombia, Norway, Russia, Italy, and the East Coast of the United States—once led Michel de Certeau to observe that "life in the United States is a constant crossing of borders."[5]

During my two research trips (1985 and 1988) to study intercultural conflicts on the Mexican side of the border, it often occurred to me that, along with New York, Tijuana is one of the major laboratories of postmodernity.[6] In 1950 it had no more than sixty thousand inhabitants; today it tops one million, with emigrants from every region of Mexico, especially Oaxaca, Puebla, Michoacán, and Mexico City. Large numbers cross the border from Tijuana into the United States, some every day and migrant workers during planting and harvest seasons. Even many of those who remain in Tijuana are also involved in commercial transactions between the two countries; they work either in *maquiladoras* (assembly plants) set up by U.S. companies on Mexican soil or in the tourist industry, serving the three or four million U.S. citizens who visit Tijuana every year.

Historically, Tijuana was known primarily as a casino town. With new factories, modern hotels, cultural centers, and access to international networks of information, Tijuana has become a city of contradictions, with both cosmopolitan and strong regional characteristics. Border markers may be rigidly fixed in place or torn down. Buildings may be evoked in different sites than where they are or were. Every day the city reinvents itself and offers new spectacles.

The artists and writers of the border experiment with these hybrid phenomena. Guillermo Gómez-Peña, editor of the Tijuana–San Diego bilingual journal *La Línea Quebrada/ The Broken Line*, for example, emphasized the protean character of cultural identity in a recent radio interview:

REPORTER: If you love our country as much as you claim, why do you live in California?
GÓMEZ-PEÑA: I'm demexicanizing myself in order to mexiunderstand myself better.
REPORTER: And what do you consider yourself?
GÓMEZ-PEÑA: Post-Mexican, Pre-Chicano, Pan-Latino, Trans-Territorial, Art-American . . . It all depends on the day of the week or the project I'm working on.[7]

Many Tijuana journals have as their main project the redefinition of identity and culture based on the border experience. *La Línea Quebrada*, the most radical, is aimed at a generation who grew up "watching cowboy [*charro*] movies and science fiction flicks, listening to *cumbias* and the Moody Blues, building altars and making super-8 movies, reading *El Corno Emplumado* and *Artforum*." Falling into the "crack between two worlds," "not being what [they] might have been because [they] don't fit in, never going home because [they] don't know where it is," these border artists opt for all available identities. Gómez-Peña declares that

> when I'm asked about my nationality or ethnic identity, I can't give a one word answer, since my identity now has multiple repertoires: I'm Mexican, but also Chicano and Latin American. On the border they call me *chilango* or *mexiquillo*; in Mexico City I'm a *pocho* or *norteño*; and in Europe I'm a *sudaca*. Anglos call me "Hispanic" or "Latino," and Germans have at times taken me for a Turk or an Italian.

Expressing feelings equally valid for a migrant worker and a young rocker, Gómez-Peña says "the deepest emotion of our generation is the loss we feel on picking up and leaving." But, in exchange, the experience has gained them "a more experimental, that is, a more tolerant and multifocal culture."[8]

Other Tijuana artists and writers challenge the euphemistic treatment of the contradictions and uprooting that they discern in the work of *La Línea Quebrada*. They reject the celebration of migrations caused by poverty in the homeland and in the United States. Native Tijuanos or those who have resided there for fifteen years or longer are outraged by the insolence of these artists' unconcerned parodies: "These are people who have just arrived and immediately tell us who we are, they dictate how we should discover ourselves."[9]

Those who celebrate the city for its openness and cosmopolitan character are also quick to fix its rituals and marks of identity and to distinguish themselves from passing tourists and anthropologists.

The editors of the Tijuana journal *Esquina Baja* stressed the importance of "creating a reading public" and having "a local journal of high quality design, layout, and so on in order to counter the centralizing tendency that prevails in our country. There is a prejudice against what we do in the provinces; if it doesn't make it in Mexico City it's not worth much, so they say."[10]

"Missionary" cultural activities promoted by the central government meet with objections. Baja Californians, for example, counter programs of national affirmation with their own expressions of Mexicanness. Given their experience at the margin of U.S. culture they are not as susceptible to its glamour as Mexicans of the more distant capital. The contact between traditional symbolic systems and international information networks, cultural industries, and migrant populations does not diminish the importance of identity, national sovereignty, and the unequal access to knowledge and cultural capital. Conflict does not disappear, as postmodern neoconservatives would have it, but becomes less polarized and intransigent. This more flexible cultural affirmation is less subject to fundamentalist backlash.

NOTES

1. Two historians of Chicano art, Shifra M. Goldman and Tomás Ybarra Frausto, have documented this cultural production and offered highly original analyses. See the introductions to their book, *Arte Chicano: A Comprehensive Annotated Bibliography of Chicano Art, 1965–1981* (Berkeley: Chicano Studies Library Publications Unit—University of California, 1985). See also their articles in Ida Rodríguez Prampolini, ed., *A través de la frontera* (México: UNAM-CEESTEM, 1983).

2. Roger Rouse, "Mexicano, Chicano, Pocho: La migración mexicana y el espacio social del posmodernismo," *Página Uno* (literary supplement of *Unomasuno*), Dec. 31, 1988, 1–2.

3. Ibid., 2.

4. Renato Rosaldo, *Culture and Truth: The Remaking of Social Analysis* (Boston: Beacon Press, 1989), 217.

5. Michel de Certeau, "Californie, un théâtre de passants," *Autrement*, 31 (April 1981), 10–18. It goes without saying that Michel de Certeau's conception of life as a constant border-crossing is not wholly adequate in the case of "second-class" United States citizens, such as blacks, Puerto Ricans, and Chicanos.

6. For the research report, see Néstor García Canclini and Patricia Safa, *Tijuana: La casa de toda la gente* (México: ENAH-UAM-Programa Cultural de la Frontera, 1989). The authors were assisted by Jennifer Metcalfe, Federico Rosas, and Ernesto Bermejillo.

7. [Many of the same topics discussed in this interview are covered, almost verbatim, in Guillermo Gómez-Peña, "Documented/Undocumented," in *Multi-Cultural Literacy: Opening the American Mind*, ed. Rick Simonson and Scott Walker (St. Paul, Minn.: Graywolf Press, 1988), 127–34.—Trans.]

8. Guillermo Gómez-Peña, "Wacha ese border, son," *La Jornada Semanal*, 162 (Oct. 25, 1987), 3–5. [See also "Documented/Undocumented," 129—Trans.]

9. Personal testimony recorded in García Canclini and Safa, *Tijuana*.

10. Ibid.

CHAPTER 32

Living Borders / *Buscando América*: Languages of Latino Self-Formation

Juan Flores, with George Yúdice

[. . .]

Latino experience in the U.S. has been a continual crossover, not only across geo-political borders but across all kinds of cultural and political boundaries. Political organization, for example, is necessarily coalitional; in order to have an impact Latinos have formed alliances to elect officials who will represent their interests. Throughout the sixties and seventies, Latinos formed or reformed dozens of national lobbying organizations. Uppermost in their lobbying efforts are counterarguments against discriminatory practices in immigration, hiring and educational policies, opposition to government intervention in Latin America, especially Central America and, of course, promotion of language issues. It should be added that Latinos of all backgrounds (with only the partial exception of Cuban Americans) are assiduous supporters and participants in the solidarity and sanctuary movements. These forums are very important because they exert a progressive influence, especially as regards women's issues like abortion, on groups that have a conservative cultural heritage. Furthermore, the political and cultural crossover involved in these activities contributes to the creation of alternative public spheres in the United States.

Crossover does not mean that Latinos seek willy nilly to "make it" in the political and commercial spheres of the general culture. These spheres are vehicles which Latinos use to create new cultural forms that cross over in both directions. The music of Willie Colón, Rubén Blades, and other U.S.-based Latino and Latin American musicians is a new pan-Latino fusion of Latin-American forms (Cuban *guaguancós*, Puerto Rican *plenas*. Dominican *merengues*, Mexican *rancheras*, Argentine *tangos*, Colombian *cumbias*, barrio drumming) and U.S. pop, jazz, rock, even do-wop, around a salsa base of Caribbean rhythms, particularly Cuban *son*. Salsa cuts across all social classes and Latino groups who reside in New York, home ground of this fusion music. Originating in the barrios, it made its way to "downtown" clubs and across borders to the diverse audience of the Latin American subcontinent. The crossovers have resulted in a convergence phenomenon which does not represent anything other than its malleability and openness to incorporation.[1]

Salsa, perhaps better than any other cultural form, expresses the Latino ethos of multiculturalism and crossing borders. Willy Colón, for example, became a *salsero* precisely to forge a new "American" identity:

> Now look at my case; I'm Puerto Rican and I consider myself Puerto Rican. But when I go to the island I'm something else to them. And in New York, when I had to get documents, I was always asked: "Where are you from?" "I'm American." "Yeah, but from where?" They led me to believe that I wasn't from America, even though I have an American birth certificate and citizenship . . . I live between both worlds but I also had to find my roots and that's why I got into salsa.[2]

Finding one's "roots" in salsa means creating them more from the heterogeneous sounds that traverse the barrio than going back to some place that guarantees authenticity. Salsa is the *salsero*'s homeland and the means to self-validation.[3]

Despite its popularity and certain minor breakthroughs, salsa has not (yet?) "made it" in mainstream U.S. culture. Latino artists and entrepreneurs have had to form their own labels, an alternative recording industry. Only in recent years, especially with the impetus of Rubén Blades's thematization of "crossing over" in the film "*Crossover Dreams*," has the dominant recording industry not only taken on *salseros* on national labels (Blades's *Agua de Luna*, based on the stories of García Márquez, is on Elektra) but also marketed them nationally. Furthermore, the alternative public spheres of contemporary rock, such as "Rock Against Racism," have been opened up by the collaborations of such "mainstream" musicians as the Rolling Stones, David Byrne and Paul Simon with *salseros*, Chicano rockers such as Los Lobos and Latin American stars such as Milton Nascimento and Caetano Veloso.[4] Hip Hop has also brought together Afro-Americans, Latinos and Afro-Latin Americans.[5]

TRANS-CREATING A MULTICULTURAL AMERICA

Rubén Blades has insisted that a culturally effective crossover, which he prefers to call "convergence," is not about "abandonment or sneaking into someone else's territory. I propose, rather, convergence. Let's meet half way, and then we can walk either way together."[6] At the end of the interview he adds that he does "not need a visa" for the musical fusion which he seeks. He does not want "to be in America" but rather participate in the creation of a new America.

Latinos, then, do not aspire to enter an already given America but to participate in the construction of a new hegemony dependent upon their cultural practices and discourses. As argued above, the struggle over language signals this desire and the opposition to it by dominant groups. This view of language, and its strategic operationality in achieving a sense of self-worth, is the organizing focus of Gloria Anzaldúa's *Borderlands/ La Frontera. The New Mestiza.*[7] "Ethnic identity is twin skin to linguistic identity—I am my language. Until I take pride in my

language, I cannot take pride in myself."[8] Like Rondón's arguments about salsa,[9] the language of the new mestiza is the migratory homeland in which "continual creative motion [...] keeps breaking down the unitary aspect of each new paradigm."[10] Anzaldúa acknowledges that her projection of a "new mestiza consciousness" may seem cultureless from the perspective of "male-derived beliefs of Indo-Hispanics and Anglos;" for her, on the contrary, she is

> participating in the creation of yet another culture, a new story to explain the world and our participation in it, a new value system with images and symbols that connect us to each other and to the planet[11]

Another way of constructing Anzaldúa's mestiza poetics is as an articulation of the premise that all cultural groups need a sense of worth in order to survive. Self-determination, which in this case focuses on linguistic self-determination, is the category around which such a need should be adjudicated and/or legislated as a civil right. In order for this right to be effective, however, it would have to alter the nature (or, to be more exact, the social relations) of civil society.

Such a claim, constructed in this way, only makes sense in a social structure that has shifted the grounds for enfranchisement from one of rights discourse to the interpretations that underpin such discourse. What is the justification, however, for needs interpretation? Our claim is that group ethos, the very stuff (or the "ethical substance," in Foucault's terminology)[12] of self-formation, is what contingently grounds the interpretation of a need as legitimate so that it can be adjudicated or legislated as a right. Another claim is that group ethos is constituted by everyday aesthetic practices such as the creative linguistic practices of Latinos which in the current historical conjuncture do not amount to subalternity, but rather to a way of prying open the larger culture, by making its physical, institutional and metaphorical borders indeterminate, precisely what we have seen that the dominant culture fears.

Latino self-information as trans-creation—to "trans-create" the term beyond its strictly commercialist coinage—is more than a culture of resistance, or it is "resistance" in more than the sense of standing up against concerted hegemonic domination. It confronts the prevailing ethos by congregating an ethos of its own, not necessarily an outright adversarial but certainly an alternative ethos. The Latino border trans-creates the impinging dominant cultures by constituting the space for their free intermingling—free because it is dependent on neither, nor on the reaction of one to the other, for its own legitimacy. Dialogue and confrontation with the "monocultural other" persists, but on the basis of what Foucault has called "the idea of governmentality," "the totality of practices, by which one can constitute, define, organize, instrumentalize the strategies which individuals in their liberty can have in regard to each other."[13] [. . .]

In the post-modern context, the mnemonic "arts" of border expression are conducted in "inventive languages," a key phrase of Gómez-Peña signaling the characteristic expressive tactic of this process. Language itself, of course, is the most obvious site of Latino inventiveness. Whether the wildest extravagance of the bilingual poet or the most mundane comment of everyday life, Latino usage tends necessarily toward interlingual innovation. The interfacing of multiple codes serves to de-canonize all of them, at least in their presumed discrete authority, thus allowing ample space for spontaneous experimentation and punning. Even for the most monolingual of Latinos, the "other" language looms constantly as a potential resource, and the option to vary according to different speech contexts is used far more often than not. "Trans-creation," understood in this sense of intercultural variability and transferability, is the hallmark of border language practice.

The irreverence implicit in trans-creative expression need not be deliberately defiant in motive; it reflects rather a largely unspoken disregard for conventionally bounded usage insofar as such circumscription obstructs the need for optimal specificity of communicative and cultural context. The guiding impulse, articulated or not, is one of play, freedom and even empowerment in the sense

that access to individual and collective referentiality cannot ultimately be blocked. Inter-lingual puns, multi-directional mixing and switching, and the seemingly limitless stock of borrowings and adaptations attest to a delight not only in excluding and eluding the dominant and exclusionary, but in the very act of inclusion within a newly constituted expressive terrain. Rather than rejecting a language because of its association with a repressive other, or adopting it wholesale in order to facilitate passage, Latino expression typically "uses" official discourse by adapting it and thereby showing up its practical malleability.

Nuyorican vernacular includes the verb "gufear," from which has derived the noun "el gufeo." The colloquial American word "goof" is clearly visible and audible, and certainly the "Spanglish" usage has its closest equivalent in the phrase "goofing on" someone or something. But as a cultural practice, "el gufeo" clearly harkens to "el vacilón," that longstanding Puerto Rican tradition of funning and funning on, fun-making and making fun. Popular culture and everyday life among Puerto Ricans abound in the spirit of "el vacilón," that enjoyment in ribbing at someone's or one's own expense, for which a wider though overlapping term is "el relajo." We might even speak, in fact, of a Puerto Rican ethos of "el relajo" which, in its interplay with "el respeto," serves to mark off consensual guidelines for interpersonal behavior.[14] Setting limits of "respectability" and testing them, "relaxing" them, conditions the dynamic of Puerto Rican culture at the level of behavioral expression. The role of "el relajo," often practiced of course by the subaltern classes in their interaction with their masters, is not derivative of or conditioned by "el respeto"; rather, the delineation of individual and group dignity draws its power from the ability to "relax (on)" the prevalent codes of "respect." [. . .]

"El gufeo" takes the process even one step further: Latino "signifyin(g)" in the multicultural U.S. context adds to the fascination of its home-country or African-American counterparts because of its interlinguality. Double-talk in this case is sustained not merely by the interplay of "standard" and vernacular significations but by the crossing of entire language repertoires. Border vernacular in fact harbors a plurality of vernaculars comprised of their multiple interminglings and possible permutations. The result is not simply an extended range of choices and juxtapositions, the kind of "splitting of tongues" exemplified by border poet Gina Valdés at the end of her poem "Where You From?":

> soy de aquí
> y soy de allá
> I didn't build
>   this border
> that halts me
> the word fron
> tera splits
> on my tongue[15] [. . .]

Poetic and colloquial language use is of course only the most obvious and readily illustrated case of re-figuration in Latino cultural expression. Examples are multiplied when account is taken of the traditions of musical "signifyin(g)" in salsa, Latin jazz, *Tejano* and Latin rock, or the characteristic interplay of Caribbean or Mexican visual worlds with North American settings among Nuyorican and Chicano artists. One thinks of Jorge Soto and his "signifyin(g)" on that classical work of a Puerto Rican painting, Francisco Oller's "El Velorio" (1893). Soto reenacts and transfigures the *jíbaro* wake of the original by populating the scene with the trappings of New York tenement life. A particularly suggestive example from recent years is provided by the "casitas," the small wooden houses which have proliferated in the vacant lots of the South Bronx, El Barrio and other Puerto Rican neighborhoods. Though modeled after working class dwellings on the Island of the earlier decades, before the industrialization process overran the neighborhoods with concrete boxes, the "casitas" are typically decorated and furnished with objects pertinent to the immediate New York setting: billboards, shopping cans, plastic milk cartons and the like. The effect is a remarkable pastiche in which otherwise disparate visual and sculptural worlds cohabit and collapse into one another

in accordance with the inter-generational historical experience of the Puerto Rican migrant community. Perhaps most impressive cultural "signifyin(g)" occurs as the contrasting of urban spatial languages, as the tropical "casita" with its strong rural reminiscences in the form of open porches, truck gardens and domestic animals jars with and yet strangely complements the surrounding scene of strewn lots and gutted buildings. Nostalgia and immediacy parody each other in the "invention" of a tradition which captures, in striking and cogent ways, the texture of "multiculturalism" in contemporary "America."[16]

For, as Gómez-Peña suggests, in order for the "multicultural paradigm" to amount to more than still another warmed-over version of cultural pluralism, the entire culture and national project need to be conceived from a "multicentric perspective." It is at the border, where diversity is concentrated, that diversity as a fact of cultural life may be most readily and profoundly perceived and expressed. It is there, as Gloria Anzaldúa describes it in her work *Borderlands/La Frontera*, that the mestiza "learns to juggle cultures. She has a plural personality, she operates in a pluralistic mode . . . Not only does she sustain contradictions, she turns the ambivalence into something else."[17] Renato Rosaldo sees in Anzaldúa's Chicana lesbian vision a celebration of "the potential of borders in opening new forms of human understanding"; "She argues that because Chicanos have long practiced the art of cultural blending, 'we' now stand in a position to become leaders in developing new forms of polyglot cultural creativity. In her view, the rear guard will become the vanguard."[18]

Understood in this sense, multiculturalism signals a paradigmatic shift in ethnicity theory, a radically changed optic concerning center and margins of cultural possibility. The presumed "subcultural" tributaries feel emboldened to lay claim to the "mainstream," that tired metaphor now assuming a totally new interpretation. Tato Laviera once again is playing a pioneering role in this act of resignifying: in his new book, entitled *Mainstream Ethics*, Laviera demonstrates that it is the very concurrence of multiple and diverse voices, tones and linguistic resources that impels the flow of the whole culture of "America." The challenge is obviously aesthetic and political in intent, but it is also, as the title indicates, an eminently ethical one. "It is not our role," the book's introduction announces, "to follow the dictates of a shadowy norm, an illusive *main* stream, but to remain faithful to our collective and individual personalities. Our ethic is and shall always be current." Appropriately, the Spanish subtitle of the volume, "*ética corriente,*"[19] is more than a translation; it is a "transcreation" in the full sense, since "current" or "common," with its rootedness in the cultural ethos of everyday life, stands in blatant contrast to the fabricated, apologetic implications of "mainstream" in its conventional usage.

The Chicano poet Juan Felipe Herrera has an intriguing *gufeo* fantasy. "What if suddenly the continent turned upside-down?" he muses.

What if the U.S. was Mexico?
What if 200,000 Anglosaxicans
were to cross the border each month
to work as gardeners, waiters,
3rd chair musicians, movie extras,
bouncers, babysitters, chauffers,
syndicated cartoons, feather-weight
boxers, fruit-pickers & anonymous poets?
What if they were called waspanos?
waspitos, wasperos or wasbacks?
What if we were the top dogs?
What if literature was life, eh?[20]

The border houses the power of the outrageous, the imagination needed to turn the historical and cultural tables. The view from the border enables us to apprehend the ultimate arbitrariness of the border itself, of forced separations and inferiorizations. Latino expression forces the issue which tops the agenda of American culture, the issue of geography and nomenclature.

Let's get it straight: American is a continent not a country. Latin America encompasses more than half of America. Quechuas, Mixtecos and Iroquois are American (not U.S. citizens). Chicano, Nuyorrican, Cajun, Afro-Caribbean and Quebequois cultures are American as well.

Mexicans and Canadians are also North Americans. Newly arrived Vietnamese and Laotians will soon become Americans. U.S. Anglo-European culture is but a mere component of a much larger cultural complex in constant metamorphosis.[21]

For the search for "America," the inclusive, multicultural society of the continent has to do with nothing less than an imaginative ethos of re-mapping and renaming in the service not only of Latinos but all claimants.

NOTES

1. "[E]l barrio es el hilo conductor"; "[la salsa] representa plenamente la convergencia del barrio urbano de hoy [porque asume] la totalidad de ritmos que acuden a esa convergencia"; "La salsa no es un ritmo, y tampoco es un simple estilo para enfrentar un ritmo definido. La salsa es una forma abierta capaz de representar la totalidad de tendencias que se reúnen en la circunstancia del Caribe urbano [incluyendo Nueva York] de hoy; el barrio sigue siendo la única marca definitiva." Cf. César Miguel Rondón, *El libro de la salsa. Crónica de la música del caribe urbano* (Caracas: Editorial Arte, 1980), pp. 32–64 *et passim.* "We object to Philip Morris or any other companies who are advertising in languages other than English," said Stanley Diamond, head of the California chapter of U.S. English, an advocacy group. "What they are doing tends to separate out citizens and our people by language." "... This fall Diamond ... chapter launched a coupon mail-in protest against a Spanish-language Yellow Pages ..." "We certainly would feel that the corporations, the telephone company with the Spanish Yellow Pages should change ... We will do everything we can to put this advertising in English only ... and in no other language," said Diamond. In Florida, U.S. English spokeswoman Terry Robbins ... has written as a private citizen to McDonald's and Burger King protesting Spanish in fast-food menus. "Why does poor Juan or Maria have a problem ordering a Whopper?" she asked. "It isn't that they aren't able to, they don't want to."

2. Humberto Márquez, "Willie Colón inventa cosas para que la vida no duela," *El Diario de Caracas* (February 23, 1982): 14–15.

3. *Ibid.*

4. Cf. Jon Pareles, "Dancing Along with David Byrne," *The New York Times* (November 1, 1989): C 1. George Lipsitz makes a similar argument about Los Lobos' networking with other groups to create a new mass audience, a new public sphere: "For [drummer] Pérez, the world of rock-and-roll music is not a place that obliterates local cultures by rendering them invisible; rather it

is an arena where diverse groups find common ground while still acknowledging important differences. The prefigurative counter-hegemony fashioned by Los Lobos has indeed won the allegiance of musicians from other marginalized cultures. Their songs have been recorded by country and western star Waylon Jennings as well as by polka artist Frankie Yankovic. The Cajun accordion player and singer Jo-El Sonnier views Los Lobos as artists whose cultural struggles parallel his own." "Cruising Around the Historical Bloc—Post-modernism and Popular Music in East Los Angeles," *Cultural Critique*, 5 (Winter 1986–87), p. 175.

5. Cf. Juan Flores, "Rappin', Writin', and Breakin': Black and Puerto Rican Culture in New York," *Dissent* (Fall 1987): 580–84.

6. *Chicago Sunday Times* (January 26, 1987).

7. (San Francisco: Spinsters/Aunt Lute, 1987).

8. *Ibid.*, p. 59.

9. Letter from Gerda Bikales, Executive Director of U.S. English, to the Secretary of the Federal Communications Commission (September 29, 1985), quoted in *Califa*, pp. 319–20. Cf. also Associated Press, "Group Wants to Stops Ads in Spanish," *San Jose Mercury News* (December 23, 1985).

10. (San Francisco: Spinsters/Aunt Lute, 1987), p. 80.

11. *Ibid.*, p. 81.

12. The "ethical substance" is one of the four dimensions that comprise "ethics." It delimits what moral action will apply to: for example, the pleasures among the Greeks, the flesh among the early Christians, sexuality in Western modernity, and, we argue, group ethos—ethnic, feminist, gay, lesbian, etc.—in multi-cultural societies. Cf. Michel Foucault, *The Use of Pleasure* (New York: Vintage, 1986), pp. 26–28.

13. Michel Foucault, "The Ethic of Care for the Self as a Practice of Freedom," in *The Final Foucault*, eds. James Bernauer and David Rasmussen (Cambridge: MIT Press, 1988), p. 19.

14. Cf. Antonio Lauria, " 'Respeto,' 'Relajo' and Interpersonal Relations in Puerto Rico," *Anthropological Quarterly*, 37, 2 (1964): 53–67.

15. Gina Valdés, "Where You From?" *The Broken Line / La Línea Quebrada*, 1, 1 (May 1986).

16. For discussions of *casitas* see the planned volume sponsored by the Bronx Council on the Arts, especially Luis Aponte, "*Casitas* as Place and Metaphor" and Joseph Sciorra, " 'We're not just here to plant. We have culture': A Case Study of the South Bronx *Casita, Rincón Criollo*." Cf. the discussion of Sciorra's work in Dinita Smith, "Secret Lives of New York: Exploring the City's Unexamined Worlds," *New York* (December 11, 1989): 34–41.

17. Anzaldúa, p. 79.

18. Renato Rosaldo, *Truth in Culture: The Remaking of Social Analysis* (Boston: Beacon, 1989), p. 216.

19. Tato Laviera, *Mainstream Ethics* (Houston: Arte Público Press, 1988).

20. Juan Felipe Herrera, "Border Drunkie at 'Cabaret Babylon-Aztlán,' " *The Broken Line / La Línea Quebrada*.

21. Gómez-Peña, "The Multicultural Paradigm," p. 20.

SECTION 8

*T*he Diffusion of Ideas, Values, and Culture

Introduction to Section 8

Christmas of 2004 marked the first time that Italian Catholics could receive free video transmissions of Pope John Paul's Midnight Mass and his Christmas Day message on their cell phones. In fact, the Holy See stays in touch with its faithful by texting "The Papal Thought of the Day" to subscribers. The service, available in Italy, Ireland, Malta, Britain, and the United States, costs 30 cents per transmission. And Christians are not the only ones using technology to spread the Word. The British-based Islamic Prayer Alert Service, which sends out 70,000 messages each month, reminds its subscribers when it is time to pray and provides a daily quotation from the Koran. While this service costs more—25 pence per message, or about 550 GBP (1,100 US dollars) a year—65 percent of the profits are donated to charity.[1]

Just as computers and cell phones have transformed the way we make money and govern, so they are transforming the way culture is produced and spreads. But global cultural diffusion, though evident everywhere, is little understood. The articles in this section examine how different aspects of cultural diffusion work at different levels of transnational social fields.

The transnational perspective we propose in this volume is informed by World Society Theorists, such as John Meyer and his colleagues, but also differs from it. We are interested in similar questions, and our answers have something in common. A transnational perspective goes further, however, by paying much closer attention to the variations in direction, strength, and impact of ideational flows. It unpacks the different levels of global cultural creation and dissemination and tracks how they interact with each other. It also gives much more credence to cultural recipients' agency.

Meyer et al. ask why such economically and culturally distinct nation-states are organized in such similar ways? The answer, they argue, is that global processes shape national life. Highly influential templates define and legitimize agendas for local action and shape how national- to local-level actors act in every social domain. Nation-states, therefore, are not autonomous. Instead, they are constructed in response to these broad cultural models. As a result, they have three characteristics in common. First, nation-states generally function like rational actors, with territorial boundaries, delimited populations, sovereignty, self-determination, and clear goals like economic development, equality, and opportunity for all. Second, there is a disconnect or a decoupling between the values they articulate and the actions they engage in because the external factors they respond to are out of sync with local circumstances. Finally, the disjuncture between global culture and local circumstances leads to extensive structuration, or the creation and spread of explicit, rationalized, differentiated organizational forms among nations and organizations.

Martha Finnemore's review is an excellent companion to the Meyer piece. Like World Society Theorists, she agrees that those who see formal bureaucratic organizations as devoid of culture, because of their technical, rational nature, are mistaken. The context in which these organizations operate, she says, is inherently cultural. The social values it embodies support and legitimize some organizational activities and forms, while rejecting others. From her perspective, external cultural legitimation, rather than task demands or functional needs, explains the widespread similarities we see in organizational behavior. And while lots of research acknowledges that national and local culture are important, cultural environments also operate at other levels. The local is embedded in the national and the transnational.

The remainder of this excerpt discusses the origins and content of the global culture now at play. It is, Finnemore argues, western culture, with its roots in western Christendom and capitalism, which produced the bureaucratized, marketized, and individuated world we now live in. Nation-states and western-style bureaucracies proliferated in response to culture not function. Societies could get along without modern-day bureaucracies, but they still need to meet basic requirements to be able to participate in the international system. Like Meyer, she acknowledges that so much isomorphism can create conflict when global structures and local conditions don't mix.

Thus, Finnemore concludes with a critique. By emphasizing structure at the expense of agency, institutionalists get the social structural mechanisms that produce change wrong. They emphasize congruence and consensus at the expense of the power and coercive dynamics that are also at play.

While Meyer et al. and Finnemore want to explain the dissemination of institutional forms, the other authors in this section are concerned with flow and adaptation of particular behaviors and ideas. In his study of natural resource governance in the Mediterranean region, Peter Haas also stresses the role of culture in idea diffusion as well as the role of expert actors who translate ideas so that they are accessible to potential adopters. A shared culture about natural resource management, he argues, enabled a new transnational governance regime to emerge that altered the balance of power between Mediterranean states and relevant experts. These professionals played a key role in developing compatible state policies that, in turn, aided the regime. What Haas calls "learning" or idea diffusion occurred in two ways—persuasion, whereby marine scientists and members of the ecological epistemic community informed foreign ministry officials of the need to control certain pollutants; and also because members of the epistemic community took over responsibility for policy-making from bureaucrats.

Jason Kaufman and Orlando Patterson study the dissemination of cricket to draw larger lessons about global cultural spread. Why, they ask, did the game become so popular in some parts of the British Empire and not in others? Neither climatic differences, national values, nor social networks explain adequately these differences. Rather, they argue, cultural diffusion is influenced by social actors who have the position and power to shape the cultural meaning and institutional accessibility of what is being diffused. One key, they say, was the degree to which elites appropriated the game for themselves, prevented others from participating, or actively encouraged popular participation. A second important factor was the degree to which the game was promoted by cultural entrepreneurs who encouraged interest among athletes and spectators. Global cultural diffusion, they conclude, is not just about carrying things from place to place; it also depends on the ways in which social status affects equality of access, as well as on the extent to which groups can limit access to new cultural imports.

Finally, James Watson is interested in how cultural products change in response to the encounters precipitated by diffusion. Cultural dissemination, he argues, is not a one-way wholesale imposition of one cultural form onto another but an interactive exchange. The spread of McDonald's throughout East Asia has brought about small but influential changes in regional eating habits. But the locals also talk back, transforming their neighborhood McDonald's into local institutions of their own.

McDonald's is so successful, according to Watson, because people anywhere know what to expect anytime they walk through the door. This does not mean that McDonald's stubbornly refuses to adapt to local settings; changes in menu, setting, and use of space abound. So, Watson asks, are we witnessing 'McDonaldization' or localization? Watson concludes it is the former. In all five cases in his book, McDonald's was treated as a cultural import, a taste of America. Eating at McDonald's, unlike having a coke, is a total experience that is still strikingly different from other regional culinary experiences. Localization has hardly begun because what consumers are after is a cultural experience, not just fast food at a cheap price. "The process of localization correlates closely with the maturation of a generation of local people who grew up eating at the Golden Arches. By the time the children of these original consumers enter the scene, McDonald's is no longer perceived as a foreign enterprise" (p. 405).

NOTE

1.　Robin Curnow, "Wireless: Dial a Prayer, Updated," *The International Herald Tribune*, pp. 1–2, January 17, 2005.

CHAPTER 33

World Society and the Nation-State

John W. Meyer, John Boli, George M. Thomas, and Francisco O. Ramirez

[. . .]

This essay reviews arguments and evidence concerning the following proposition: *Many features of the contemporary nation-state derive from worldwide models constructed and propagated through global cultural and associational processes.* These models and the purposes they reflect (e.g., equality, socioeconomic progress, human development) are highly rationalized, articulated, and often surprisingly consensual. Worldwide models define and legitimate agendas for local action, shaping the structures and policies of nation-states and other national and local actors in virtually all of the domains of rationalized social life—business, politics, education, medicine, science, even the family and religion. The institutionalization of world models helps explain many puzzling features of contemporary national societies, such as structural isomorphism in the face of enormous differences in resources and traditions, ritualized and rather loosely coupled organizational efforts, and elaborate structuration to serve purposes that are largely of exogenous origins. World models have long been in operation as shapers of states and societies, but they have become especially important in the postwar era as the cultural and organizational development of world society has intensified at an unprecedented rate.

The operation of world society through peculiarly cultural and associational processes depends heavily on its statelessness. The almost feudal character of parcelized legal-rational sovereignty in the world (Meyer 1980) has the seemingly paradoxical result of diminishing the causal importance of the organized hierarchies of power and interests celebrated in most "realist" social scientific theories. The statelessness of world society also explains, in good measure, the lack of attention of the social sciences to the coherence and impact of world society's cultural and associational properties. Despite Tocqueville's ([1836] 1966) well-known analysis of the importance of cultural and associational life in the nearly stateless American society of the 1830s, the social sciences are more than a little reluctant to acknowledge patterns of influence and conformity that cannot be explained solely as matters of power relations or functional rationality. This reluctance is most acute with respect to global development. Our effort here represents, we hope, a partial corrective for it.

We are trying to account for a world whose societies, organized as nation-states, are structurally similar in many unexpected dimensions and change in unexpectedly similar ways. A hypothetical example may be useful to illustrate our arguments, and we shall carry the example throughout the essay. If an unknown society were "discovered" on a previously unknown island, it is clear that many changes would occur. A government would soon form, looking something like a modern state with a many of the usual ministries and agencies. Official recognition by other states and admission to the United Nations would ensure. The society would be analyzed as an economy, with standard types of data, organizations, and policies for domestic and international transactions. Its people would be formally reorganized as citizens with many familiar rights, while certain categories of citizens—children, the elderly, the poor—would be granted special protection. Standard forms of discrimination, especially ethnic and gender based, would be discovered and decried. The population would be counted and classified in ways specified by world census models. Modern educational, medical, scientific, and family law institutions would be developed. All this would happen more rapidly, and with greater penetration to the level of daily life, in the present day than at any earlier time because world models applicable to the island society are more highly codified and publicized than ever before. Moreover, world-society organizations devoted to educating and advising the islanders about the models' importance and utility are more numerous and active than ever.

What would be unlikely to happen is also clear. Theological disputes about whether the newly discovered *Indios* had souls or were part of the general human moral order would be rare. There would be little by way of an imperial rush to colonize the island. Few would argue that the natives needed only modest citizenship or human rights or that they would best be educated by but a few years of vocational training.

Thus, without knowing anything about the history, culture, practices, or traditions that obtained in this previously unknown society, we could forecast many changes that, upon "discovery," would descend on the island under the general rubric of "development." Our forecast would be imprecise because of the complexity of the interplay among various world models and local traditions, but the likely range of outcomes would be quite limited. We can identify the range of possibilities by using the institutionalist theoretical perspective underlying the analysis in this essay to interpret what has already happened to practically all of the societies of the world after their discovery and incorporation into world society. [. . .]

PROPERTIES OF THE CULTURALLY CONSTITUTED NATION-STATE

As we develop our argument, we want to keep in the forefront a number of empirical observations about contemporary nation-states.

First, nation-states exhibit a great deal of isomorphism in their structures and policies. Second, they make valiant efforts to live up to the model of rational actorhood. Third, and partly as a result of the second observation, they are marked by considerable, and sometimes extraordinary, decoupling between purposes and structure, intentions and results. Fourth, they undergo expansive structuration in largely standardized ways. The generality of these observations makes sense only if nation-states are understood as, in part, constructions of a common wider culture, rather than as self-directed actors responding rationally to internal and external contingencies. [. . .]

Rational Actorhood

As we discuss further below, in world culture the nation-state is defined as a fundamental and strongly legitimated unit of action. Because world culture is highly rationalized and universalistic, nation-states form as rationalized actors. Out of all the possible forms political entities might take, one—the model of the rational and responsible actor—is utterly dominant. This is how nation-states routinely present themselves, both internally (e.g., in their constitutions) and externally (e.g., in seeking admission to the United Nations and other intergovernmental bodies). They claim all the features of the rational state actor: territorial boundaries and a demarcated population; sovereign authority, self-determination, and responsibility; standardized purposes like collective development, social justice, and the protection of individual rights; authoritative, law-based control systems; clear possession of resources such as natural and mineral wealth and a labor force; and policy technologies for the rational means-ends accomplishment of goals.

Consider this last item—goals. Nation-states are remarkably uniform in defining their goals as the enhancement of collective progress (roughly, gross domestic product [GDP] per capita) and individual rights and development (roughly, citizen enhancement and equality). This occurs in constitutions, which typically emphasize goals of both national and equitable individual develop-ment (Boli 1987), in general statements on national education, which frequently follow suit (Fiala and Gordon-Lanford 1987), in depictions of the nation and the individual citizen in educational curricula (Wong 1991), and in vast amounts of formal economic policy (McNeely 1995). Goals outside the standard form (the nation in service to God, a dynasty, an ethnic or religious group, or imperial expansion), while still common enough, are usually suspect unless strongly linked to these basic goals of collective and individual progress.

Nations have traditions of piling up the skulls of their neighbors in war, but these are no longer announced as goals. War is no longer an acceptable "continuation of polit-ics by other means"; war departments have been relabeled departments of defense (Eyre and Suchman 1996). Nation-states present themselves as not simply rational actors but rather nice ones at that.

Thus our island society would likely adopt a purposive nation-state structure almost immediately, with the appropriate goals of economic development, equality, and enhancement of individual opportunity. A purposive nation-state actor would be con-structed to take formal responsibility for such matters, even under the most unlikely social and economic circumstances (Jackson and Rosberg 1982; Meyer 1980).

Decoupling

Both realist and microphenomenological arguments suggest, for different reasons, that nation-states should be tightly coupled struc-tures—due to functional requirements, the control structures imposed by external powers, or their own domestic cultures and interpretive schemes. This is notoriously not the case. For example, commitments to egali-tarian citizenship, which are ubiquitous in constitutions and public discourse, are fre-quently contradicted by policies that make formal distinctions between genders and among ethnic groups. At the same time, both the claims and the policies are frequently inconsistent with practice.

Decoupling is endemic because nation-states are modeled on an external culture that cannot simply be imported wholesale as a fully functioning system (Meyer and Rowan 1977; Riggs 1964). World culture contains a good many variants of the domin-ant models, which leads to the eclectic adoption of conflicting principles. Diffusion processes work at several levels and through a variety of linkages, yielding incoherence. Some external elements are easier to copy than others, and many external elements are inconsistent with local practices, require-ments, and cost structures. Even more prob-lematic, world cultural models are highly idealized and internally inconsistent, making them in principle impossible to actualize (Strang and Meyer 1993). [. . .]

Expansive Structuration

By structuration we mean the formation and spread of explicit, rationalized, differentiated organizational forms. Here we argue that the dependence of the modern nation-state on exogenous models, coupled with the fact that these models are organized as cultural prin-ciples and visions not strongly anchored in local circumstances, generates expansive structuration at the nation-state and organ-izational levels.

The structuration of the nation-state greatly exceeds any functional requirements of society, especially in peripheral countries. Impoverished countries routinely establish universities producing overqualified person-nel, national planning agencies writing unre-alistic five-year plans, national airlines that require heavy subsidization, and freeways leading nowhere—forms of "development" that are functionally quite irrational. This observation poses a problem for both realist and microphenomenological theories.

One common intellectual response to this decoupled structuration is neglect of its gen-erality. Typically, political and organiza-tional theorists try to explain the apparent irrationalities of specific structural changes as products of local constellations of power and interests—the delusions of a self-aggrandizing leader, perhaps, or the interests of dominant elites. But the process operates everywhere and in many different sectors of social life. Holding constant the functional pressures of size, resources, and complexity, in recent decades nation-states and other organizations have clearly expanded inordinately across many different social domains. This is precisely the period during which world society has been consolidated (Meyer et al. 1975; Strang 1990), making world models universally known and legitimated. Nation-states and organizations may have distinct and complex histories, but they all have expanded structurally in similar ways in the same historical period (Jepperson and Meyer 1991; Soysal 1994; Dobbin 1994; Guillen 1994).

Present-day universities and firms, for instance, have a multitude of offices that an organization of the same size and goals would not have had just a few decades ago: accounting, legal, personnel, safety, environment, and counseling offices, among others. After the fact, all of these seem functionally necessary, and the power coalitions that produced them can certainly be identified, but this sort of explanation simply does not account for the worldwide simultaneity of the process. So also with nation-states, which undergo structuration to manage the expanding externally defined requirements of rational actorhood. Common evolving world-societal models, not a hundred different national trajectories, have led states to establish ministries and other agencies purporting to manage social and economic planning, education (Ramirez and Ventresca 1992), population control (Barrett and Frank 1997), the environment (Frank et al. 1997), science policy (Finnemore 1996), health, gender equality (Berkovitch 1997), the welfare of the old and the young (Boli-Bennett and Meyer 1978), and much more. This worldwide process affects both core and peripheral countries, though with variable impact depending on local resources and organizational capacities.

The enormous expansion of nation-state structures, bureaucracies, agendas, revenues, and regulatory capacities since World War II indicates that something is very wrong with analyses asserting that globalization diminishes the "sovereignty" of the nation-state (Duchacek et al. 1988; Nordenstreng and Schiller 1979). Globalization certainly poses new problems for states, but it also strengthens the world-cultural principle that nation-states are the primary actors charged with identifying and managing those problems on behalf of their societies. Expansion of the authority and responsibilities of states creates unwieldy and fragmented structures, perhaps, but not weakness. The modern state may have less autonomy than earlier but it clearly has more to do than earlier as well, and most states are capable of doing more now than they ever have been before. [. . .]

In this section, we concentrate on the social structural frame that organizes, carries, and diffuses world cultural models, leaving the content of the models aside. The content is widely discussed in the literature under the heading of "modernization": well-known, highly abstract, and stylized theories of the "functional requirements" of the modern society, organization, and individual, and the linkages among them. In these theories, the legitimated goals of properly constructed actors center on collective socio-economic development and comprehensive individual self-development. Society and individuals are bound together by rationalized systems of (imperfectly) egalitarian justice and participatory representation, in the economy, polity, culture, and social interaction. These are global conceptions, not local, expressed as general principles to be applied everywhere (e.g., the World Congress of Comparative Education's [1996] sweeping affirmation of education's importance for justice and peace in all countries). Many other international professional associations, and nongovernmental organizations more generally, express similar goals (Chabbott 1997).

In world culture, almost every aspect of social life is discussed, rationalized, and organized, including rules of economic production and consumption, political structure, and education; science, technique, and medicine; family life, sexuality, and interpersonal relations; and religious doctrines and organization. In each arena, the range of legitimately defensible forms is fairly narrow. All the sectors are discussed as if they were functionally integrated and interdependent, and they are expected to conform to general principles of progress and justice. The culture of world society serves as a "sacred canopy" for the contemporary world (Berger 1967), a universalized and secularized project developed from older and somewhat parochial religious models. This section shows how this material is structured and rendered authoritative in world society.

Organizational Frame

The development and impact of global sociocultural structuration greatly intensified with the creation of a central world organizational frame at the end of World War II. In place of the League of Nations, which was a limited international security organization, the United Nations system and related bodies (the International Monetary Fund, World Bank, General Agreement on Tariffs and Trade [GATT]) established expanded agendas of concern for international society, including economic development, individual rights, and medical, scientific, and educational development (Jones 1992; Donnelly 1986). This framework of global organization and legitimation greatly facilitated the creation and assembly of expansive components of an active and influential world society, as we discuss below. A wide range of social domains became eligible for ideological discussion and global organization. The forces working to mobilize and standardize our island society thus gain strength through their linkage to and support by the United Nations system and the great panoply of nongovermental organizations clustered around it.

Diffusion among Nation-States

The organization of a Tocquevillian world, made up of formally equal nation-states having similar rationalized identities and purposes, has intensified diffusion processes among nation-states (Strang and Meyer 1993). In the West since at least the 17th century, nation-states have claimed legitimacy in terms of largely common models; this commonality led them to copy each other more freely than is usual in system of interdependent societies. The institutionalization of common world models similarly stimulates copying among all nation-states, in sharp contrast to traditional segmental societies in which entities jealously guard their secrets of success and regard copying as cultural treason.

Realist models expect this sort of copying only as a result of direct inter-dependence, especially domination, or in response to functional requirements imposed by competitive system. They therefore overlook the broad cultural thrust involved. Microphenomenological models, emphasizing local traditions and interpretive schema, overlook the extent to which the modern actor is a worldwide cultural construction whose identity and interpretations derive directly from exogenous meanings, which makes the local arena less determinative of actor structuration.

The contemporary world is rife with modeling. Obviously, much of this reflects the main dimensions of world stratification—the poor and weak and peripheral copy the rich and strong and central. The Japanese, on entering the system in the 19th century, self-consciously copied successful Western forms (Westney 1987). Aspiring to core status in the same period, the Germans and Americans paid careful attention to each other's educational successes (Goldschmidt 1992). In the 20th century, there has been a pronounced tendency to copy such American forms as the corporation (Takata 1995) and the liberal educational system. More recently, attention has shifted to Japanese work organization (Cole 1989) and education (Rohlen 1983). The emerging elites of our island society would undoubtedly turn first to American, Japanese, or European models for much of their social restructuring.

The world stratification system, however, is multidimensional; different countries parade distinctive virtues. For planning welfare programs, Sweden is the paragon of virtue. For promoting social equality, such "radical" countries as Maoist China and Cuba have been major models. On the other hand, even economically successful countries, if deemed opprobrious due to their failure to conform to important world principles, are unlikely models for imitation. South Africa is the best example.

Associations, Organizations, and Social Movements

As with any such polity, the decentralized world made up of actors claiming ultimate similarity in design and purpose is filled with associations. Both governmental and non-governmental voluntary organizations have expanded greatly, particularly since 1945 (Boli and Thomas 1997; Feld 1972). Hundreds of intergovernmental entities cover a broad range of rationalized activity, including science, education, the economy and economic development, human rights, and medicine. Thousands of nongovernmental organizations have even broader concerns, organizing almost every imaginable aspect of social life at the world level. They are concentrated, however, in science, medicine, technical fields, and economic activity—the main arenas of rationalized modernity and, thus, arenas where rationalized nation-states are seen as the principal responsible actors. Less often, they focus on more expressive solidarities, such as religion, ethnicity, one worldism, or regionalism (Boli and Thomas 1997). World organizations are, thus, primarily instruments of shared modernity.

Many of the international nongovernmental organizations have a "social movement" character. Active champions of central elements of world culture, they promote models of human rights (Smith 1995), consumer rights (Mei 1995), environmental regulation (Frank et al. 1997), social and economic development (Chabbott 1997), and human equality and justice (Berkovitch 1997). They often cast themselves as oppositional grass-roots movements, decrying gaps or failures in the implementation of world-cultural principles in particular locales and demanding corrective action by states and other actors. Agents of social problems, they generate further structuration of rationalized systems.

Clearly, our island society would quickly come under the scrutiny of all these international organizations. Its state and people would be expected to join international bodies, and they would find it advantageous to do so, gaining access to leading-edge technologies and ideas and enhancing their legitimacy as participants in the great human endeavor. The organizations themselves would also directly "aid" our island society in "developing." They would provide models for data, organization, and policy; training programs to help the island's elites learn the correct high forms of principle, policy, and structuration; consultants to provide hands-on assistance; and evaluation schemes to analyze the results. International organizations would collect data to assess the island's population, health care, education, economic structure (labor force, production, investment), and political status, all in fully rationalized terms redefining the society as a clear candidate for modernity.

Thus, the whole panoply of external organizations would set in motion efforts to increase social value and development on the island. Eventually, the locals would know how to push the process relatively autonomously, establishing such movements as a green party, women's organizations, and consumer rights' bodies to protect the new identities being constructed in the reorganizing society.

Sciences and Professions

Scientists and professionals have become central and prestigious participants in world society. Their authority derives not from their strength as actors—indeed, their legitimated postures are defined as disinterested rationalized others rather than actors—but from their authority to assimilate and develop the rationalized and universalistic knowledge that makes action and actorhood possible. This authority is exceptionally well organized in a plethora of international organizations, most of them nongovernmental. These organizations are usually devoted to specific bodies of knowledge and their dissemination, but their ultimate aims include the broad development of societies (Schofer 1997; Drori 1997).

Especially in the more rationalized and public arenas of social life, the sciences and professions are leading forces; the occupations involved are the most prestigious in stratification systems almost everywhere (Treiman 1977). Sustainable socioeconomic development calls for the knowledge of economists who can advise on production functions, natural scientists and engineers to create and manage technologies, and a variety of scientists to analyze environmental problems and costs. Individual development, rights, and equalities call for the expertise of social scientists, lawyers, psychologists, and medical professionals. These legitimated experts appeal to and further develop transnational accounts and models, yielding a self-reinforcing cycle in which rationalization further institutionalizes professional authority.

Scientific and professional authority is rooted in universal, rationalized ultimate principles of moral and natural law (on the rise of universities along these lines, see Riddle [1993]). Their rationalized knowledge structures constitute the religion of the modern world, replacing in good measure the older "religions" that have been spiritualized and reconstructed as more ordinary organizational actors, and they underlie the other mechanisms of world influence noted above. The models of national development or human rights carried by international associations have their roots in scientific and legal knowledge, such as theories and measures of national economic development or of individual social and economic equality. Similarly, diffusion among nation-states is heavily mediated by scientists and professionals who define virtuous instances, formulate models, and actively support their adoption. The current wave of Japanization in American economic and educational organization is defined and carried not directly by Japanese elites or American managers but by professors of business and education (Smith and O'Day 1990).

Organizations and consultants would flock around our island society, operating almost entirely in terms of scientific and professional (legal, medical, educational) models and methods. Very little would be presented to the island society as a matter of arbitrary cultural imposition; advice would be justified in terms of rational scientific authority. Scientists and professionals carry ultimate, rational, unified, universal truth, by and large shunning the image of self-interested power brokers. Science as authority is much more influential than scientists as an interest group (Meyer and Jepperson 1996).

Summary

The rapidly intensifying structuration of a world society made up of rationalized cultural elements and associational organizations rather than a centralized bureaucratic state is insufficiently appreciated in social research (Robertson 1992; Thomas et al. 1987). To show the coherence of what has happened, Boli and Thomas (1997) present correlations among longitudinal variables describing many dimensions of world-level development. The period covered is the last 80–100 years; variables are world totals, by year, for economic production, energy consumption, foundings of governmental and nongovernmental organizations, educational enrollments, urban population, trade, treaties in force, and so on. The point is not to sort out causal relations among these variables but to show the consistency of the trends involved. Almost all correlations are extremely high (.90 or above). The current period of intensive international organization (more treaties, nongovernmental organizations, intergovernmental bodies, trade, and international scientific and professional discourse) is also a period of intensive national organization and development and individual rationalization and modernization. World society is rationalizing in an extraordinarily comprehensive way. [. . .]

CONCLUSION

A considerable body of evidence supports our proposition that world-society models shape nation-state identities, structures, and behavior via worldwide cultural and associational processes. Carried by rationalized others whose scientific and professional authority often exceeds their power and resources, world culture celebrates, expands, and standardizes strong but culturally somewhat tamed national actors. The result is nation-states that are more isomorphic than most theories would predict and change more uniformly than is commonly recognized. As creatures of exogenous world culture, states are ritualized actors marked by extensive internal decoupling and a good deal more structuration than would occur if they were responsive only to local cultural, functional, or power processes.

As the Western world expanded in earlier centuries to dominate and incorporate societies in the larger world, the penetration of a universalized culture proceeded hesitantly. Westerners could imagine that the locals did not have souls, were members of a different species, and could reasonably be enslaved or exploited. Inhabiting a different moral and natural universe, non-Western societies were occasionally celebrated for their noble savagery but more often cast as inferior groups unsuited for true civilization. Westerners promoted religious conversion by somewhat parochial and inconsistent means, but broader incorporation was ruled out on all sorts of grounds. Education and literacy were sometimes prohibited, rarely encouraged, and never generally provided, for the natives were ineducable or prone to rebellion. Rationalized social, political, and economic development (e.g., the state, democracy, urban factory production, modern family law) was inappropriate, even unthinkable. Furthermore, the locals often strongly resisted incorporation by the West. Even Japan maintained strong boundaries against many aspects of modernity until the end of World War II, and Chinese policy continues a long pattern of resistance to external "aid."

The world, however, is greatly changed. Our island society would obviously become a candidate for full membership in the world community of nations and individuals. Human rights, state-protected citizen rights, and democratic forms would become natural entitlements. An economy would emerge, defined and measured in rationalized terms and oriented to growth under state regulation. A formal national polity would be essential, including a constitution, citizenship laws, educational structures, and open forms of participation and communication. The whole apparatus of rationalized modernity would be mobilized as necessary and applicable; internal and external resistance would

be stigmatized as reactionary unless it was couched in universalistic terms. Allowing the islanders to remain imprisoned in their society, under the authority of their old gods and chiefs and entrapped in primitive economic technologies, would be unfair and discriminatory, even though the passing of their traditional society would also occasion nostalgia and regret.

Prevailing social theories account poorly for these changes. Given a dynamic sociocultural system, realist models can account for a world of economic and political absorption, inequality, and domination. They do not well explain a world of formally equal, autonomous, and expansive nation-state actors. Microcultural or phenomenological lines of argument can account for diversity and resistance to homogenization, not a world in which national states, subject to only modest coercion or control, adopt standard identities and structural forms.

We argue for the utility of recognizing that rationalized modernity is a universalistic and inordinately successful form of the earlier Western religious and postreligious system. As a number of commentators have noted, in our time the religious elites of Western Christendom have given up on the belief that there is no salvation outside the church (Shils 1971; Illich 1970). That postulate has been replaced by the belief among almost all elites that salvation lies in rationalized structures grounded in scientific and technical knowledge—states, schools, firms, voluntary associations, and the like. The new religious elites are the professionals, researchers, scientists, and intellectuals who write secularized and unconditionally universalistic versions of the salvation story, along with the managers, legislators, and policymakers who believe the story fervently and pursue it relentlessly. This belief is worldwide and structures the organization of social life almost everywhere.

The colossal disaster of World War II may have been a key factor in the rise of global models of nationally organized progress and justice, and the Cold War may well have intensified the forces pushing human development to the global level. If the present configuration of lowered systemic (if not local) tensions persists, perhaps both the consensuality of the models and their impact on nation-states will decline. On the other hand, the models' rationalized definitions of progress and justice (across an ever broadening front) are rooted in universalistic scientific and professional definitions that have reached a level of deep global institutionalization. These definitions produce a great deal of conflict with regard to their content and application, but their authority is likely to prove quite durable.

Many observers anticipate a variety of failures of world society, citing instances of gross violations of world-cultural principles (e.g., in Bosnia), stagnant development (e.g., in Africa), and evasion of proper responsibility (in many places). In our view, the growing list of perceived "social problems" in the world indicates not the weakness of world-cultural institutions but their strength. Events like political torture, waste dumping, or corruption, which not so long ago were either overlooked entirely or considered routine, local, specific aberrations or tragedies, are now of world-societal significance. They violate strong expectations regarding global integration and propriety and can easily evoke world-societal reactions seeking to put things right. A world with so many widely discussed social problems is a world of Durkheimian and Simmelian integration, however much it may also seem driven by disintegrative tendencies.

REFERENCES

Barrett, Deborah, and David Frank. 1997. "Population Control for National Development: From World Discourse to National Policies." Pp. 198–221 in *World Polity Formation since 1875: World Culture and International Non-Governmental Organizations*, edited by John Boli and George M. Thomas, 1999. Stanford, Calif.: Stanford University Press.

Berger, Peter. 1967. *The Sacred Canopy*. Garden City, N.Y.: Doubleday.

Berkovitch, Nitza. 1997. "The International Women's Movement: Transformations of Citizenship." Pp. 100–126 in *World Polity Formation since 1875: World Culture and International Non-Governmental Organizations*, edited by John Boli and George M. Thomas, 1999. Stanford, Calif.: Stanford University Press.

Boli, John. 1987. "World Polity Sources of Expanding State Authority and Organizations, 1870–1970." Pp. 71–91 in *Institutional Structure*, by George M.

Thomas, John W. Meyer, Francisco O. Ramirez, and John Boli. Beverly Hills, Calif.: Sage.

Boli, John, and George M. Thomas. 1997 "World Culture in the World Polity: A Century of International Non-Governmental Organization." *American Sociological Review* 62:171–90.

Boli-Bennett, John, and John W. Meyer. 1978. "The Ideology of Childhood and the State." *American Sociological Review* 43 (6): 797–812.

Chabbott, Colette. 1997. "Defining Development: The Making of the International Development Field, 1945–1990." Pp. 222–248 in *World Polity Formation since 1875: World Culture and International Non-Governmental Organizations*, edited by John Boli and George M. Thomas, 1999. Stanford, Calif.: Stanford University Press.

Cole, Robert. 1989. *Strategies for Learning: Small-Group Activities in American, Japanese and Swedish Industry*. Berkeley and Los Angeles: University of California Press.

Dobbin, Frank. 1994. *Forging Industrial Policy: The United States, Britain, and France in the Railway Age*. New York: Cambridge University Press.

Donnelly, Jack. 1986. "International Human Rights: A Regime Analysis." *International Organization* 40:599–642.

Drori, Gili. 1997. "Science Education for Economic Development: Policy Discourse, Empirical Evidence, and Re-evaluation." Paper presented at the annual meetings of the American Sociological Association, Toronto.

Duchacek, Ivo D., Daniel Latouche, and Garth Stevenson, eds. 1988. *Perforated Sovereignties and International Relations: Trans-Sovereign Contacts of Subnational Governments*. New York: Greenwood.

Eyre, Dana, and Mark Suchman. 1996. "Status, Norms, and the Proliferation of Conventional Weapons." Pp. 79–113 in *Culture and Security*, edited by Peter Katzenstein. New York: Columbia University Press.

Feld, Werner. 1972. *Non-Governmental Forces and World Politics*. New York: Praeger.

Fiala, Robert, and Audri Gordon-Lanford. 1987. "Educational Ideology and the World Educational Revolution, 1950–1970." *Comparative Education Review* 31 (3): 315–32.

Finnemore, Martha. 1996. *National Interests in International Society*. Ithaca, N.Y.: Cornell University Press.

Frank, David, Ann Hironaka, John W. Meyer, Evan Schofer, and Nancy Tuma. 1997. "The Rationalization and Organization of Nature in World Culture." Pp. 81–99 in *World Polity Formation since 1875: World Culture and International Non-Governmental Organizations*, edited by John Boli and George M. Thomas, 1999. Stanford, Calif.: Stanford University Press.

Goldschmidt, Dietrich. 1992. "Historical Interaction between Higher Education in Germany and in the USA." Pp. 11–33 in *German and American Universities*. Kassel: Wissenschaftliches Zentrum für Berufs- und Hochschulforschung der Gesamthochschule.

Guillen, Mauro. 1994. *Models of Management: Work, Authority, and Organization in a Comparative Perspective*. Chicago: University of Chicago Press.

Illich, Ivan. 1970. *Deschooling Society*. New York: Harper & Row.

Jackson, Robert, and Carl Rosberg. 1982. "Why Africa's Weak States Persist: The Empirical and the Juridical in Statehood." *World Politics* 35 (1): 1–24.

Jepperson, Ronald, and John W. Meyer. 1991. "The Public Order and the Construction of Formal Organizations." Pp. 204–31 in *The New Institutionalism in Organizational Analysis*, edited by Walter W. Powell and Paul J. DiMaggio. Chicago: University of Chicago Press.

Jones, Philip W. 1992. *World Bank Financing of Education: Lending, Learning, and Development*. London: Routledge.

McNeely, Connie. 1995. *Constructing the Nation-State: International Organization and Prescriptive Action*. Westport, Conn.: Greenwood.

Mei, Yujun. 1995. "The Consumer Rights Sector in the World Polity: Its Rise and Diffusion." Master's thesis. Arizona State University, Department of Sociology.

Meyer, John W. 1980. "The World Polity and the Authority of the Nation-State." Pp. 109–37 in *Studies of the Modern World-System*, edited by Albert J. Bergesen. New York: Academic Press.

Meyer, John W., John Boli-Bennett, and Christopher Chase-Dunn. 1975. "Convergence and Divergence in Development." *Annual Review of Sociology* 1:223–46.

Meyer, John W., and Ronald Jepperson. 1996. "The Actor and the Other: Cultural Rationalization and the Ongoing Evolution of Modern Agency." Paper presented at the Institutional Analysis Conference, Tucson, Arizona, April.

Meyer, John W., and Brian Rowan. 1977. "Institutionalized Organizations: Formal Structure as Myth and Ceremony." *American Journal of Sociology* 83 (2): 340–63.

Nordenstreng, Kaarle, and Herbert I. Schiller, eds. 1979. *National Sovereignty and International Communication*. Norwood, N.J.: Ablex.

Ramirez, Francisco O., and Marc Ventresca. 1992. "Building the Institutions of Mass Schooling." Pp. 47–59 in *The Political Construction of Education*, edited by Bruce Fuller and Richard Rubinson. New York: Praeger.

Riddle, Phyllis. 1993. "Political Authority and University Formation in Europe, 1200–1800." *Sociological Perspectives* 36 (1): 45–62.

Riggs, Fred. 1964. *Administration in Developing Countries: The Theory of Prismatic Society*. Boston: Houghton Mifflin.

Robertson, Roland. 1992. *Globalization: Social Theory and Global Culture*. London: Sage.

Rohlen, Thomas. 1983. *Japan's High Schools*. Berkeley and Los Angeles: University of California Press.

Schofer, Evan. 1997. "Science Association in the International Sphere 1875–1990: The Rationalization of Science and the Scientization of Society." Pp. 249–266 in *World Polity Formation since 1875: World Culture and International Non-Governmental Organizations*, edited by John Boli and George M. Thomas. Stanford, Calif.: Stanford University Press, 1999.

Shils, Edward. 1971. "No Salvation outside Higher Education." *Minerva* 6 (July): 313–21.

Smith, Jackie. 1995. "Transnational Political Processes and the Human Rights Movement." *Research on Social Movements, Conflict and Change* 18:185–220.

Smith, Michael, and Jennifer O'Day. 1990. "Systemic School Reform." Pp. 233–67 in *The Politics of Curriculum and Testing*, edited by Susan Fuhrman and Betty Malen. Bristol, Penn.: Falmer Press.

Soysal, Yasemin. 1994. *Limits of Citizenship: Migrants and Postnational Membership in Europe*. Chicago: University of Chicago Press.

Strang, David. 1990. "From Dependency to Sovereignty: An Event History Analysis of Decolonization, 1870–1987." *American Sociological Review* 55: 846–60.

Strang, David, and John W. Meyer. 1993. "Institutional Conditions for Diffusion." *Theory and Society* 22: 487–511.

Takata, Azumi Ann. 1995. "From Merchant House to Corporation: The Development of the Modern Corporate Form and the Transformation of Business Organization in Japan, 1853–1912." Ph.D. dissertation. Stanford University, Department of Sociology.

Thomas, George M., John W. Meyer, Francisco O. Ramirez, and John Boli. 1987. *Institutional Structure: Constituting State, Society, and the Individual*. Beverly Hills, Calif.: Sage.

Tocqueville, Alexis de. (1836) 1966. *Democracy in America*. New York: Doubleday.

Treiman, Donald. 1977. *Occupational Prestige in Comparative Perspective*. New York: Academic Press.

Westney, Eleanor. 1987. *Imitation and Innovation: The Transfer of Western Organizational Patterns to Meiji Japan*. Cambridge, Mass.: Harvard University Press.

Wong, Suk-Ying. 1991. "The Evolution of Social Science Instruction, 1900–86." *Sociology of Education* 64 (1): 33–47.

World Congress of Comparative Education. 1996. "Call for Papers: Educating All for Peace and Justice." World Congress of Comparative Education, Sydney.

CHAPTER 34

Norms, Culture, and World Politics: Insights from Sociology's Institutionalism

Martha Finnemore

[. . .]

OVERVIEW OF SOCIOLOGY'S INSTITUTIONALISM

Culture and Organizations

Institutionalist arguments date from the mid-1970s when a group at Stanford University interested in cross-national analyses of political and economic change began to explore the relationship between formal organizational structures and culture.[1] Prevailing theories about bureaucracies and organizations held that, indeed, culture had little impact on those entities. In fact, formal bureaucratic organizations comprised the antithesis of culture; they were technical, rational, and therefore culture-neutral. They transcended culture.

The Stanford group challenged that view. Prevailing theories explained the rise, form, and spread of formal bureaucratic organizations in functional terms. Following Max Weber, the conventional wisdom held that rationalized bureaucratic structures were the most efficient and effective way to coordinate the complex relations involved in modern technical work. Expanding markets and technological changes create increasingly complex management tasks. Bureaucratic organizational forms must also then expand to coordinate these activities across more and more aspects of society. Bureaucratic organization was seen as the only way to divide labor, specify responsibilities, and institutionalize coordination and decision making in rational and efficient ways.

The problem with this view was that bureaucratic organizations have spread even more quickly than the markets and technology that were thought to have created the need for them. Cross-national analyses of political and economic change, especially in the developing world, made it abundantly clear that the world was being bureaucratized and organized much faster than it was being developed economically or technologically.[2] Further, the link between formal organizational structure—the blueprint for how the bureaucracy is supposed to function—and the organization's day-to-day activities was often very loose. Organization theorists had recognized this earlier, but cross-national analyses—especially those dealing with developing countries—underscored the point. If bureaucracies do not act according to their rationalized formal structures, then the efficiency of rational formal structure cannot be the reason for their proliferation.

The alternative explanation developed by Meyer and his colleagues emphasized the environment of these organizations. Formal bureaucratic structures did not spread as a result of their functional virtues as efficient coordinators of complex relationships (they may or may not be so) but because the wider environment supports and legitimizes rational bureaucracy as a social good. Organizations exist, proliferate, and have the form they do not because they are efficient but because they are externally legitimated.[3]

This is the entry point for culture. The content of this external environment is cultural. The social values that support and legitimate some organizational forms and not others, some social activities and not others, are cultural values. Culture had gotten a bad name in sociology for many of the same reasons it got a bad name in political science. Part of the institutionalists' self-described mission is to reclaim culture for macrosociology.[4] One way they do this is to make dominant Western culture the object of their study and thus to denaturalize features of social life that appear natural and inevitable to most of us because this is our own culture. We are so deeply embedded in it that it is hard to see beyond it. [. . .]

Institutionalists, by contrast, operate very much in the American social scientific tradition. Their theorizing and hypotheses are explicit, and their methods are positivistic and often quantitatively sophisticated, much more so than most IR research. This allows them to engage and challenge those who would dismiss arguments about culture based on more interpretive research methods. [. . .]

CONCLUSIONS

Institutionalist arguments emphasize structure at the expense of agency. Doing so has important intellectual benefits. It allows institutionalists to ask questions about features of social and political life that other perspectives take for granted—ubiquitous sovereign statehood and expanding claims by individuals, for example. Further, from an IR theory perspective, institutionalists' emphasis on structure allows for system-level explanations that compete with other dominant paradigms and so enrich the body of theory available to tackle puzzles in the field.

If the neglect of agency were only an omission, there would be little cause for concern. No theory explains everything. One can always explain a few more data points by adding a few more variables and increasing the complexity of the model. But the institutionalists' inattention to agency leads them into more serious errors. It leads them to misspecify both the mechanisms by which social structure produces change and the content of the social structure itself.

Cognitive processes may dominate organizational change in many empirical domains, but they compete with and often are eclipsed by coercion in many of the empirical domains that concern IR scholars. Educational curricula may change in peaceful ways driven by cognitive decision-making processes; state authority structures often do not. Violence is a fundamentally different mechanism of change than cognition. Both mechanisms may operate in a given situation. Often there are choices to be made even within the constraints imposed by force, but outcomes imposed externally through violence are not captured by a cognitive theoretical framework.

Institutionalists are not alone in this tendency to overlook power and coercion in explaining organizational outcomes. Much of organization theory shares this characteristic. Terry Moe has noted the failure of the new economics of organization to incorporate considerations of power, but even Moe, a political scientist, is not particularly concerned with issues of violence since these occur rarely in his own empirical domain—U.S. bureaucracy.[5]

Institutionalist models imply a world social structure made up of norms that are largely congruent. Their emphasis is on the mutually reinforcing and expansive nature of these norms. They stress the consensus that arises around various cultural models—of citizenship, of statehood, of education, of individual rights—to the point that these norms and institutions are taken for granted in contemporary life. The implication is that the spread of world culture is relatively peaceful. Institutionalists specify no sources of instability, conflict, or opposition to the progressive expansion of world culture. Yasemin Soysal's work is perhaps the most attuned to contradictions among the cultural elements of citizenship she studies. However, even in her work these contradictions result only in paradoxical arrangements with which people seem to live reasonably peacefully.[6]

The result of this specification is that all of politics becomes problematic in an institutionalist framework. If the world culture they specify is so powerful and congruent, the institutionalists have no grounds for explaining value conflicts or normative contestation—in other words, politics. A research design that attended to agency and the processes whereby isomorphic effects are produced would have prevented institutionalists from falling into this trap. Focusing more closely on process would draw attention to the contradictions among normative claims and force institutionalists to rethink both the specification of world culture and its likely effects.

These problematic features of institutionalist theory lie squarely on the turf of political scientists. Politics and process, coercion and violence, value conflict and normative contestation are our business. Institutionalism would benefit greatly from a dialogue with political scientists. Likewise, political scientists could learn a great deal from institutionalists. Thus far, IR scholars interested in norms have lacked a substantive systemic theory from which to hypothesize and carry out research. Institutionalism provides this. Taking its claims seriously may produce radical revisions to the existing sociologists' theories. It may also produce opposing theoretical arguments. Either outcome would advance research in both disciplines and enrich our understanding of world politics.

NOTES

1. For a good discussion of the intellectual roots of institutional analysis see DiMaggio and Powell 1991.

2. The studies in Meyer and Hannan 1979 point to this conclusion.

3. The seminal essay outlining this argument is Meyer and Rowan 1977. Early applications of the argument in cross-national contexts can be found in Meyer and Hannan 1979.

4. Thomas et al. 1987, 7.

5. Moe 1984.

6. Soysal 1995.

REFERENCES

Bull, Hedley, and Adam Watson, eds. 1984. *The expansion of international society.* Oxford: Clarendon Press.

DiMaggio, Paul J., and Walter W. Powell. 1991. Introduction. In *The new institutionalism in organizational analysis,* edited by Walter Powell and Paul DiMaggio. Chicago: University of Chicago Press.

Meyer, John W., and Michael T. Hannan, eds. 1979. *National development and the world system: Educational, economic, and political change, 1950–1970.* Chicago: University of Chicago Press.

Meyer, John W., and Brian Rowan. 1977. Institutionalized organizations: Formal structure as myth and ceremony. *American Journal of Sociology* 83:340–63.

Moe, Terry M. 1984. The new economics of organization. *American Journal of Political Science* 28: 739–77.

Soysal, Yasemin N. 1995. *Limits of citizenship: Migrants and postnational membership in Europe.* Chicago: University of Chicago Press.

Thomas, George M., John W. Meyer, Francisco O. Ramirez, and John Boli, eds. 1987. *Institutional structure: Constituting state, society and the individual.* Newbury Park, Calif.: Sage Publications.

CHAPTER 35

Do Regimes Matter? Epistemic Communities and Mediterranean Pollution Control

Peter M. Haas

An important and persistent question facing analysts of international regimes is, Do regimes matter?[1] Much attention has been paid to regime creation and regime maintenance, but few authors have studied the substantive nature of regimes or their direct effects on national behavior. Regimes are not simply static summaries of rules and norms; they may also serve as important vehicles for international learning that produce convergent state policies. This role for regimes has been seriously underestimated in the theoretical and empirical literature, which has tended to focus on two correlates of regimes—political order and economic growth—rather than on the transformative processes that regimes may initiate or foster. The literature has also paid little attention to the fact that some regimes stem from communities of shared knowledge and not simply from domestic or transnational interest groups.

Through the examination of the Mediterranean Action Plan (Med Plan), a regime for marine pollution control in the Mediterranean Sea, I seek to demonstrate that this regime played a key role in altering the balance of power within Mediterranean governments by empowering a group of experts, who then contributed to the development of convergent state policies in compliance with the regime. In turn, countries in which these new actors acquired channels to decision making became the strongest proponents of the regime.[2]

The Med Plan is widely hailed as a success. Commentators from a variety of viewpoints cite it as the crowning achievement of the United Nations Environment Pro-gramme's (UNEP's) Regional Seas Programme and an exemplary case of interstate cooperation.[3] Its success is distinctive because of the number of compelling factors militating against it. The extensive pollution of the Mediterranean is the result of intense coastal population pressures, combined with largely unregulated industrial, municipal, and agricultural emission practices. Constructing sufficient sewage treatment facilities region-wide to handle the wastes generated by up to 200 million summertime tourists and residents would require a regional investment of $10 to $15 billion over a ten-year period. Eighty-five percent of the pollution of the sea comes from land-based sources: agricultural run-offs, industrial wastes, direct emissions from cities lacking sufficient sewerage facilities, and other wastes transmitted by rivers. Eighty to ninety percent of the coastal municipal sewage is discharged into the sea completely untreated.[4] Thus, effective protection required the coordinated efforts of all the coastal states. Common pollution control standards had to be adopted for pollutants from tankers, offshore dumping, and a variety of land-based sources. Contending uses of the sea also had to be balanced: for instance, fishermen and tourists require much cleaner waters than do tanker and industrial interests.

Pollution of the Mediterranean Sea was widely regarded as a collective goods problem, since one country's pollutants could wash up on its neighbor's beaches. The Riviera, for example, is polluted by discharges from Spain, France, Italy, and Monaco. If France were the only country to build sewage treatment plants and to require coastal industries to reduce their emissions, the quality of the coast would only be partially improved, and French industry would be hampered by additional production costs that would not be met by Spanish and Italian competitors and would thus reduce the comparative advantage of French industries. Other Mediterranean basins, such as the Adriatic and Aegean Seas and the eastern basin, posed similar problems. Pollutants were not exchanged throughout the entire Mediterranean, but the entire Mediterranean region faced a number of smaller collective goods problems that impeded coordinated national action to control pollution. The political antipathies and economic disparities in the region militated against effective and equitable cooperation, and the global recessions of 1973–75 and 1980–84 made the expensive compliance with the regime even more problematic.

Negotiating the regime was difficult. Countries disagreed about which pollutants to control. Developed countries wanted to control all sources of pollution, whereas many of the less developed countries (LDCs) saw this as a thinly veiled attempt to control their industrialization practices and thus opted for the control of only municipal and tanker wastes. Algerian President Houari Boumediene, who initially was actively hostile toward environmental protection, announced in the early 1970s, "If improving the environment means less bread for the Algerians, then I am against it."[5] The Algerian delegate to the 1972 United Nations Conference on the Human Environment also firmly stated that Algeria "will not sacrifice development at the altar of the environment."[6] Later, Boumediene continued to "assure [the developed countries] that many of us would be very happy to help you solve your pollution problems by processing [raw materials] in our own countries."[7] Algeria blamed France for much of the Algerian coastal pollution but was loath to negotiate with the exploitative North. However, in 1983, Algeria ratified the very treaty against which such bombast had been directed.

Even though the Med Plan was successfully negotiated, its maintenance poses an anomaly in terms of conventional understanding of how regimes operate. The most intriguing puzzle regarding the Med Plan's effectiveness is why states comply, given the fact that so many were initially opposed to it. As Oran Young and Robert Keohane have noted, the most compelling argument for a regime's importance in promoting international order is the fact that compliance is achieved even when the regime's norms and principles run counter to the short-term interests of the participants (or the hegemon).[8] The highly technical dimension of the Med Plan makes it a "most expected case" for an explanation that emphasizes consensual scientific knowledge. However, the diversity of political interests in the region and the widespread political antipathy to international environmental protection initially inhibited the easy influence of scientists on their governments.

The Med Plan's successful creation was promoted by a community of ecologists and marine scientists. They served in UNEP's secretariat and were often granted formal decision-making authority in national administrations. In addition to their involvement in the policymaking process, they were given responsibility for enforcing and supervising pollution control measures. The members of this group became partisans for adopting the regime, complying with it, and strengthening it to deal with more pollutants from more sources. Following the involvement of these new actors, state interests came to increasingly reflect their environmental view, as seen in diplomats' statements and government policies, and state behavior came to reflect their interests as well, as was evident from state investment patterns and diplomatic actions. Compliance, as measured by the adoption of new policies which are consonant with the regime's norms and which ease its enforcement, has been strongest in countries in which the experts were able to consolidate their power most firmly.

As the case of the Med Plan shows, regimes may be transformative, leading to the empowerment of new groups of actors who can change state interests and practices. According to the explanation suggested here, if a group with a common perspective is able to acquire and sustain control over a substantive policy domain, the associated regime will become stronger and countries will comply with it. Such groups are most likely to be consulted after a crisis, especially when decision makers are uninformed about the technical dimensions of the problem at hand or are uncertain about the costs and benefits of international cooperation. New national policies, often in compliance with the regime, would then reflect the interests of the group consulted and empowered, and the duration of the new policies would depend upon the group's ability to consolidate and retain its bureaucratic power. The substantive nature of the regime would reflect the group's cause-and-effect beliefs. Because of the usual institutional rigidities and the overall administrative inertia at reviewing past decisions, such power would be likely to persist until a subsequent crisis incited other decision makers to consult with a new group or until the current group was weakened by internal disagreements or as a result of bureaucratic infighting with another group. It would follow logically, then, that the loss of consensus within the group or the loss of the group's access to high-level decision making would lead to a breakdown in compliance.

In the following sections, I describe the regime, analyze in greater detail the role of the new actors and the process by which national compliance occurred, and contrast this analysis with more conventional analyses of regimes and policy change. The data are derived from over ninety interviews with government officials and from United Nations archives, government publications, and more general secondary sources. [. . .]

CONCLUSION

The most notable aspect of the Med Plan is the domestic compliance with it. In the literature on international relations, few studies have focused on the reasons for which states actually comply with regimes. As argued above, coercion, public opinion, and anticipation of benefits do not fully explain the extent of compliance. The Med Plan's success was due to the regime's introduction of new actors who influenced national behavior and contributed to the development of coordinated and convergent policymaking in the Mediterranean states. In the face of uncertainty, a publicly recognized group with an unchallenged claim to understanding the technical nature of the regime's substantive issue-area was able to interpret for traditional decision makers facts or events in new ways and thereby lead to new forms of behavior.[9]

Common principles and norms gave rise to a common set of rules for pollution control. The principles also empowered new domestic groups of marine scientists, who led their governments to comply more strongly with the regime and to negotiate more constructively internationally. In turn, the regime's scope was broadened and stronger rules were negotiated—rules with which most states have complied.

As this analysis of the process of compliance with the Med Plan shows, regimes can play a transformative role in international affairs. Within the analytic framework explicitly or tacitly accepted by most proponents of international regime theory, regimes are valued as stable forms to order international behavior and mitigate conflict in an anarchic world. But this conventional approach does not go far enough. Regimes may also contribute to the empowerment of new groups. By relating shared norms and principles to the codified social conventions of a specific group, light is shed on the origins of a regime's substantive nature, often overlooked in most regime analyses. With the presence and durability of new groups, regimes may not be static arrangements. They may be evolving arrangements that contribute to greater understanding, recognition of common interests, and convergence on a new set of policies.

Epistemic communities may introduce new policy alternatives to their governments, and depending on the extent to which these communities are successful in obtaining and retaining bureaucratic power domestically, they can often lead their governments to pursue them. In the case of the Mediterranean, where the new policies were more integrative and reflected an acceptance of the interplay between a number of different environmental forces, the pursuit of these policies constituted governmental learning. Governments learned about the complexity of the pollution problem and accepted the need for more comprehensive and coordinated policies to accomplish state and regional goals. Thus, both power and knowledge can be viewed as explanatory variables for state behavior.

Is this process of regime creation and interest recalculation generalizable? Other contemporary environmental regimes suggest that it may well be. The 1987 Montreal ozone protocol to protect the stratospheric ozone layer was completed after a similar ecological epistemic community became influential in the UNEP secretariat and well-represented in the U.S. delegation to the Montreal meetings.[10] Collective policies for the control of European acid rain were adopted in the 1979 Economic Commission for Europe (ECE) Convention on Long-Range Transboundary Air Pollution after atmospheric scientists were consulted about the origins of regional acid deposition. The two principal sources of acid deposits, the Federal Republic of Germany and the United Kingdom, both became more supportive of multilateral controls and imposed domestic controls. Scientists' access to policymakers was facilitated in Germany by widespread dismay over the possible loss of the culturally valued Black Forest. In Britain, the influence of the scientists has been vitiated by the countering interests of public utilities and industries, and Britain has thus been less supportive of the overall initiative than have other countries.[11]

The failure to adopt a U.S.–Canada acid rain regime may well hinge on the failure of an epistemic community to gain access to high-level U.S. policymaking bodies.[12] In the case of the Med Plan, ozone protocol, and the European acid rain policies, new actors were consulted because of uncertainties about the environmental problems. In this case, however, it is already manifestly clear that the United States as a whole stands to gain by making Canada bear the externalities of U.S. energy generation, and the distribution of costs and benefits from possible

global climate change is sufficiently well estimated so as to inhibit the U.S. government from delegating authority to ecologically inclined atmospheric scientists.[13]

NOTES

1. See Oran Young, "International Regimes: Toward a New Theory of Institutions," *World Politics* 39 (October 1986), pp. 115–17; Robert O. Keohane, "The Study of International Regimes and the Classical Tradition in International Relations," paper presented at the 1986 annual meeting of the American Political Science Association, p. 14; and Stephan Haggard and Beth A. Simmons, "Theories of International Regimes," *International Organization* 41 (Summer 1987), pp. 491–517.

2. For a detailed analysis of the negotiation of the Med Plan, compliance with it, and a more thorough testing of alternative theoretical explanations of its success, see Peter M. Haas (1990) *Saving the Mediterranean: The Politics of International Environmental Cooperation* (New York: Columbia University Press, 1990). For other recent studies on environmental regimes, see Lynton Caldwell, *International Environmental Policy* (Durham, N.C.: Duke University Press, 1984); and Nigel Haigh, *EEC Environmental Policy and Britain* (London: Environmental Data Services, 1984). Although Haigh does not formally refer to regimes, he analyzes British compliance with the corpus of the European Economic Community (EEC) environmental directives that may reasonably be construed to constitute a regime. His conclusions about compliance, however, are equivocal.

3. See Peter Hulm, "The Regional Seas Programme: What Fate for UNEP's Crown Jewels?" *Ambio* 12 (January 1983); and George P. Smith II, "The U.N. and the Environment," in The Heritage Foundation, *A World Without a U.N.* (Washington, D.C.: The Heritage Foundation, 1984), pp. 44–45. The Med Plan serves as the model for ten other regional arrangements for controlling marine pollution.

4. UNEP/ECE/UNIDO/FAO/UNESCO/WHO/IAEA, *Pollutants from Land-Based Sources in the Mediterranean*, UNEP Regional Seas Reports and Studies, no. 32 (Geneva: UNEP, 1984).

5. NOVA, "Mediterranean Prospect," WGBH Transcripts, Boston, Mass., 1980, p. 13.

6. *El-Djeich* (Algiers), no. 107, April 1972, p. 28.

7. *Times of London*, 4 September 1974, p. A9.

8. See Young, "International Regimes"; and Keohane, "Study of International Regimes." Arthur Stein has suggested that compliance can be explained in terms of common aversions; however, the intensity with which many policymakers from LDCs expressed initial opposition to negotiating with the exploitative North during the early years of the New International Economic Order (NIEO)

negotiations far exceeded that of any common aversions to a polluted sea. See Arthur A. Stein, "Coordination and Collaboration: Regimes in an Anarchic World," in Stephen D. Krasner, ed., *International Regimes* (Ithaca, N.Y.: Cornell University Press, 1983), pp. 115–40.

9. Note that this proposition skirts an epistemological dispute regarding the relativity and accessibility of the natural world. Does the intermediation of different cognitive frameworks and cultures preclude the possibility of achieving a single acceptable image of the natural world? Does such incommensurability imply the lack of existence of a single accessible objective reality? For a good review of the various competing philosophical perspectives on these issues, see Martin Hollis and Steven Lukes, ed., *Rationality and Relativism* (Cambridge, Mass.: MIT Press, 1982).

10. In this case, the epistemic community had to actively defend itself from groups within the U.S. administration who opposed stringent controls on chlorofluorocarbons. The epistemic community only prevailed four months before the final adoption of the treaty, after four months of internal policy review by the domestic policy council. See David Doniger, "Politics of the Ozone Layer," *Issues in Science and Technology* 4 (Spring 1988),

pp. 86–92; and Peter M. Haas, "Ozone Alone, No Chlorofluorocarbons: Epistemic Communities and the Protection of Stratospheric Ozone," paper presented at the 1988 annual meeting of the American Political Science Association. The most recent measures introducing the Montreal ozone protocol into U.S. policy are discussed in *Federal Register* 53 (12 August 1988), pp. 30566–619.

11. See Peter H. Sand, "Air Pollution in Europe," *Environment* 29 (December 1987), pp. 16–29; Armin Rosencranz, "The Acid Rain Controversy in Europe and North America: A Political Analysis," *Ambio* 15 (January 1986), pp. 47–51; and Economic Commission for Europe, *National Strategies and Policies for Air Pollution Abatement* (New York: United Nations, 1987).

12. Ecologists lack access to decision-making channels in the U.S. government. Proposals for a bilateral treaty by Environmental Protection Agency Administrator William Ruckelshaus in 1983 were ignored by the White House. See Walter A. Rosenbaum, *Environmental Politics and Policy* (Washington, D.C.: CQ Press, 1985), pp. 307–8.

13. See Walter Orr Roberts and Edward J. Friedman, *Living with the Changed World Climate* (New York: Aspen Institute for Humanistic Studies, 1982).

CHAPTER 36

Cross-national Cultural Diffusion: The Global Spread of Cricket

Jason Kaufman and Orlando Patterson

Why do some foreign practices take root while others either arrive dead in the water or take hold only to wither and die? Modern diffusion studies have focused primarily on the structural aspects of diffusion, or the existence of tangible points of contact between adopters and adoptees, as well as the environmental contexts that modulate such interactions. But as Strang and Soule (1998:276) note, "[S]tructural opportunities for meaningful contact cannot tell us what sorts of practices are likely to diffuse," whereas an "analysis of the cultural bases of diffusion speaks more directly to what spreads, replacing a theory of connections with a theory of connecting." According to this more culturally minded approach, diffusing practices are most likely to be adopted when they are first made congruent with local cultural frames or understandings, and are thus "rendered salient, familiar and compelling" (Strang and Soule 1998:276; see also Gottdiener 1985; Rogers 1995). In other cases, however, more than just "congruence" is needed for successful adoption; institutional support, repeated exposure, and/or active instruction in the new practice are required for it to "take hold" in new settings. The original cultural profile of that practice is often transformed in the process (e.g., Appadurai 1996; Bhabha 1994; Guillén 2001; Watson 2002). Sometimes, moreover, it is the very difference in social, cultural, and political power between change agents and adopters that accounts for successful long-term diffusion.

One case that encompasses all of these factors is the cross-national diffusion of cricket. Cricket originated in England as an informal rural game, though it quickly emerged into a highly competitive sport. Over time, cricket evolved into an English national pastime, along with soccer, rugby, and horse racing (Allen 1990). Cricket began diffusing to other countries when British soldiers and settlers brought it with them to the various colonies of the empire, and today, most Commonwealth countries support active cricket cultures, though not all.

The case of Canada is particularly striking in this regard. Cricket was popular in Canada and the United States in the mid-nineteenth century—in fact, the first official international cricket match in the world took place between American and Canadian "elevens" in 1844 (Boller 1994:23). The game's popularity rivaled that of baseball until the late nineteenth century, after which interest declined sharply. The game languished in both countries until quite recently, when new immigrants from the Caribbean and South Asia began arriving in North America in significant numbers (Gunaratnam 1993; Steen 1999). This pattern of adoption-then-rejection poses important substantive and theoretical issues regarding the cross-national diffusion of cultural practices. Given Canada's—and to a lesser degree, America's—demographic, cultural, and sociopolitical connections to Britain, the game's unexpected demise there is puzzling, especially in contrast to its successful diffusion in far less "British" parts of the Commonwealth. At the same time, this disjuncture also seems at odds with several important perspectives in the sociological study of diffusion.

SITUATING CRICKET IN
DIFFUSION THEORY

There is widespread agreement that diffusion is the transmission, adoption, and eventual acculturation of an innovation by a recipient population (Coleman, Katz, and Menzel 1966; Rogers 1995; Wejnert 2002; cf. Palloni 2001). Most sociological studies of the diffusion process aim to identify the mechanisms by which an innovation spreads as well as the rate at which it does so in a given population. Although there is now a rich body of important findings about this process, several major problems and gaps still exist.

One major failing of the diffusion literature is the tendency to overlook cases where innovations are transmitted but eventually rejected, as well as cases where adoption might have been expected but did not occur. Palloni (2001: 73–75) highlights two aspects of this problem in his important recent review of the field. First, he notes the common failure to try and account for the persistence of diffused practices in their new surroundings—how and why, in other words, do diffused practices become part of the lived experience of those who have adopted them? Second, he notes the obverse: that after the initial adoption of an innovation, mechanisms might arise that undermine its retention. Palloni (2001:73) adds that, "Despite the fact that this is a key part of a diffusion process, it is rarely mentioned and almost never explicitly modeled or studied." The problem, we suspect, is that many diffusion studies track cultural practices that are not commonly rejected, such as the adoption of new, time-tested medical or agricultural practices. Strang and Soule (1998: 268) observe, for example, that there is "a strong selection bias in diffusion research, where investigators choose ultimately popular [i.e., widely diffused] practices as appropriate candidates for study." Issues such as the persistence and rejection of diffused practices are thus generally overlooked in the literature.

Another shortcoming of diffusion studies is highlighted by Wejnert (2002:299–302), who notes a tendency in the literature to ignore the role of characteristics unique to the practice or thing being diffused. Specific features of the innovation being adopted, such as its potential for replication and change, play an important but often overlooked role in the ultimate success or failure of diffusion. By confining their studies to simple physical objects or cultural routines that are diffused at the micro-social level, diffusion scholars have tended to create advanced formal models that overlook real-world obstacles to diffusion—those posed by the nature, complexity, continuity, and potential mutability of the innovations themselves. Wejnert (2002) also notes the often overlooked distinction between innovations that are diffused at the macro- and micro-social levels. Those involving large collective actors such as countries and industries likely have different consequences and diffusion mechanisms than those that involve mainly individuals or firms.

The dominant "relational" approach to diffusion research in sociology has improved our knowledge of the role of social networks in the transmission of information and ideas (e.g. Buskens and Yamaguchi 1999), but it tends to underspecify the role of social structural factors such as class, status, and power in the adoption or rejection of innovations. In this light, Burt (1987), Marsden and Podolny (1990), and Van den Bulte and Lilien (2001) have revised Coleman, Katz, and Menzel's (1966) classic study of the adoption of a new antibiotic drug among a community of Midwestern doctors, but diffusion research has otherwise largely neglected these topics. It is significant, note Mizruchi and Fein (1999), that sociologists have widely overlooked the role of power in DiMaggio and Powell's (1983) celebrated study of the diffusion of organizational forms. Inequality, in particular, seems to be a neglected subject in the diffusion literature. Rogers (1995:7) makes a distinction between homophilous and heterophilous diffusion processes—that is, those in which the change agents and adopters either share or do not share comparable social positions—but fails to explore the ramifications of the latter situation in detail. As we will see in the case of cricket, status differences and the attendant mechanisms of distancing and inclusion can be decisive variables in explaining the adoption of cross-nationally diffused cultural practices. It will be shown that a top-down, or vertically heterophilous, process of diffusion best explains diffusionary success in some cases.

Some sociologists who work within the institutional framework of diffusion studies have, happily, attempted to address these concerns (see, e.g., Clemens and Cook 1999; Cole 1989; Dobbin and Sutton 1998; Guillén 1994; Lillrank 1995; Meyer and Hannan 1979; Molotch, Freudenberg, and Paulsen 2000; Patterson 1994; Strang 1990; Strang and Meyer, 1993; Starr 1989). While we applaud the temporal and causal acuity of these studies, we think there are further insights to be gained from case studies that explore the cultural and structural complexities of the diffusion process in broad socio-historical terms.

The case study presented here will focus on a Western social practice that is, by any measure, an internally complex cultural entity with powerful symbolic and political consequences (Appadurai 1996; Beckles and Stoddart 1995; Bourdieu 1978; Maguire 1999; Malcolm 2001; Miller et al. 2001; Nandy 2000; Patterson 1995; Stoddart 1988). It involves cross-national diffusion among large collective entities engaging broad arrays of both practitioners and spectators. It illustrates both the successful diffusion of a politically potent national cultural practice and the potential for such diffusion to be discontinued midstream. Finally, the case of cricket highlights the roles of social structure and "cultural power" in the diffusion process.

We first dispense with several common explanations of the diffusion of cricket, each of which hinges on one or another argument about national culture. Instead, we demonstrate the need to consider four aspects of the adopting countries' social systems that appear to mitigate the potential diffusion of a cultural practice from a "dominant" power to its "subordinates": *social stratification, secondary education, entrepreneurship/ network-building,* and *indexical nationalism,* or the frame of reference in which citizens measure their own national accomplishments. Of the four, social stratification seems

to have had the most widespread (i.e., generalizable) impact on the global diffusion of cricket, though this occurred at least partially through indirect effects related to the other three. Before explaining any of this in more detail, however, we will enumerate our study population, evaluate evidence relating to the popularity of cricket and other sports in various countries, and outline the criteria by which we measure national sports cultures. [...]

TRADITIONAL EXPLANATIONS OF THE FAILURE OF CRICKET IN CANADA AND THE UNITED STATES

In trying to explain the virtual absence of popular interest in cricket in the US and Canada, we encountered several common arguments. The most obvious, having to do with climate, is tempting but ultimately unsatisfactory. True, Canadians are fanatical about ice hockey, a decidedly cold-weather sport; and true, most of the leading cricket-playing nations do not suffer particularly cold winters. On the other hand, Canadians enjoy a wide variety of warm-weather sports, including not only baseball but also field hockey, football, and lacrosse. Furthermore, England, where the game was invented, is hardly a "warm" country itself. Indeed, the game is played there only in the summer season, which is subject to more rain than many parts of Canada. Nor has cricket survived in the more temperate parts of the United States or Canada. Weather, obviously, is not the answer.

Some historians of cricket in the United States have suggested that the sport is not more popular among Americans because it is inconsistent with their cultural worldview (Adelman 1986; Kirsch 1989, 1991). Cricket is a long, slow, tightly regimented game, they argue, whereas Americans are always in a hurry and anxious for results. According to nineteenth-century sportswriter Henry Chadwick (1868:52, quoted in Kirsch 1991:12), for example, "We fast people of America, call cricket slow and tedious; while the leisurely, take-your-time-my-boy people of England think our game of baseball too

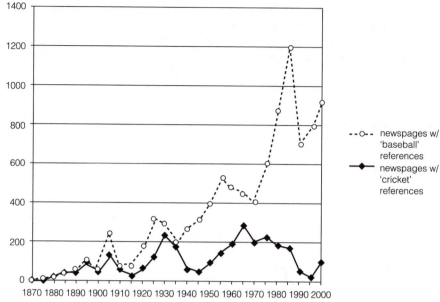

Figure 36.1 Canadian sports reporting: *The Globe and Mail*, 1870–2000.

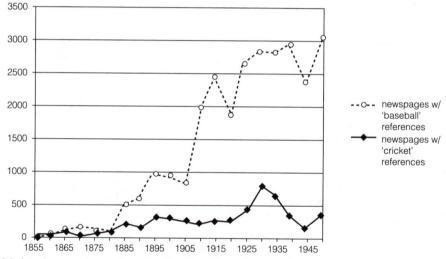

Figure 36.2 American sports reporting: *The New York Times*, 1850–1950.

fast. Each game, however, just suits the people of the two nations." True, cricket matches are generally longer than baseball games; nevertheless, time itself does not appear to be a sufficient explanation. While international test matches can last up to five days, many local matches are only one day in duration. In Australia, for example, an abbreviated "limited overs" version of cricket is popular with television audiences (Cashman 1998a). Anthropologist Arjun Appadurai (1996: 101) even argues that, "Cricket is perfectly suited for television, with its many pauses, its spatial concentration of action, and its extended format . . . It is the perfect television sport." Moreover, when played by amateurs, among whom wickets fall quickly, the game easily adapts to a spirited afternoon "knock" no longer than amateur soccer or base-ball games.

Note, too, that such perceptions are as much an effect of the differential status of sports as a cause thereof: Americans' pejorative descriptions of cricket are a product, as well as a cause of, the sport's wider failure to reach "hegemonic" status in the United States.

Similarly, cricket has been described by some as a sport that requires too much submission (i.e., orderly behavior) for Americans. Neither spitting nor swearing are officially condoned on the cricket field, for example, and disagreement with match officials is strictly forbidden.[1]

Nonetheless, while some might criticize Americans for their ungainly habits, this would hardly appear to constitute a satisfactory sociological explanation, particularly when Americans are so attracted to other sports that make similar demands of players, such as tennis and golf. And, even if this is true of Americans, it still leaves the question of Canadian habits unaccounted for. Given the frequency with which one hears Canadians described as modest, well-mannered, and community-minded people (e.g., Frye 1971; Lipset 1996), one would expect cricket to be wildly popular in the Dominion. In fact, a Canadian, James Naismith, invented basketball (in Massachusetts, USA) with these very characteristics in mind: "If men will not be gentlemanly in their play," he said in introducing the game to its first players (Wise 1989:124), "it is our place to encourage them to games that may be played by gentlemen in a manly way, and show them that science is superior to brute force with a disregard for the feelings of others." So why didn't Dr. Naismith merely foist cricket on these "ungentlemanly" young Americans? Such explanations echo, in homely terms, the "cultural understanding" argument of diffusion scholars. We discount such explanations as overly simplistic and, in some cases, patently biased.

This brings us to another popular explanation of "Americo-Canadian Exceptionalism"—Anglophobia. This perspective focuses on Canadians and Americans' (presumably negative) disposition toward England and the English. True, a significant minority of Canadians claim French, not English heritage, and a large percentage of Canada's Anglo-population also trace their heritage back to Scotland and Ireland—all possible reasons for Canadian antipathy toward a cultural practice as English as cricket. On the other hand, one can easily refute such arguments with reference to other cricket-playing countries: Australia was populated by many people of Scottish and Irish heritage, for example, and a large portion of its Anglo-population can actually blame the cruelties of the English penal system for sending their ancestors to Australia in the first place. The white population of South Africa, another cricketing nation, is also comprised of rival English and Dutch, as well as indigenous African, peoples. Why would Canadians be any more resistant to an English cultural practice like cricket than their counterparts in these other former colonies? Why, moreover, would Canadians be more hostile to English culture than the descendants of peoples cruelly subjugated by the English in places like Jamaica, Barbados, India, Bangladesh, Pakistan, and Sri Lanka? Finally, why would Americans be so enamored with tennis and golf, both sports with British origins, but not cricket?[2] While we will argue that nationalism did play a significant role in American and Canadian attitudes toward cricket, we do not accept so facile an explanation as their contempt for all things British. Cricket was widely perceived by American and Canadian audiences to be a British "affectation" for reasons particular to the game's history in their respective countries. Explaining how this came to be is a major part of this project.

One related thesis about the decline of American and Canadian interest focuses on changes in the rate of English immigration to both countries (e.g., Metcalfe 1987). It is true that many early adherents of the game were British immigrants, civil servants, and military personnel, particularly in Canada, where British troops were garrisoned until 1867. In the United States, moreover, some cricket clubs, such as the famous St. George Club of New York, were largely peopled by British residents. Such ethno-national social clubs were exceedingly popular in the United States in the late nineteenth century (Kaufman 2002). Nonetheless, there is clear evidence that many "native-born" Americans and Canadians participated in cricket alongside their British-born counterparts in the late nineteenth century. Consider, for example, the following observation made in the 1895 book, *Sixty Years of Canadian Cricket* (Patteson quoted in Hall and McCulloch 1895: 258): "The so-called American eleven in 1859 contained [only] one native-born American. . . . In 1860 the number of Americans had slightly increased. And now, in 1894, all are native Americans 'bar one.' " Furthermore, many of today's dominant cricketing countries have scarcely any population of direct British descent, and in the cases of Australia and New Zealand, one must still grapple with the question of how a British sport like cricket survived and flourished in the face of declining immigration flows and the declining influence of British culture and identity on their own national cultures. In other words, we must go beyond the question of cricket's *transmission* to the foregoing countries and ask how and why the sport was actually *adopted* by locals and reconstructed as a persistent national pastime (the final, *acculturation* phase of cultural diffusion).

One final "common" explanation of the failure of cricket in British North America is the rising popularity of baseball, an American sport with similar origins and style of play. There is some truth to this argument, at least to the extent that the rise of baseball and the decline of cricket do seem temporally related. Why this is so is hard to explain, however. Few Canadians would willingly admit that they prefer American to British culture. In fact, a large part of Canadian national identity is focused around their very distaste for Americans and American cultural hegemony (Frye 1971). Why would Canadians replace English cricket with a sport from a country to which they are so poorly disposed? We take seriously the need to explain the rise of baseball and decline of cricket in two countries with distinctive cultural ties to cricket's motherland, England. We turn first, however, to the initial invention and diffusion of cricket in the British Empire.

ANALYSIS—NETWORK-BUILDING AND CLASS COMPETITION IN THE GLOBAL DIFFUSION OF SPORT

The Invention of Cricket and its Original Transmission throughout the British Empire

Despite its stodgy reputation in America, cricket was not originally an aristocratic game. In its earliest incarnation cricket was, in fact, an agrarian pastime for modest farmers and craftsmen. Though historical precedents exist as far back as the twelfth century, English cricket is commonly thought to have come into its own in the seventeenth century (Allen 1990: 16–17; also Brookes 1978; James 1963:164). According to most historical accounts, it was gambling that truly inspired enthusiasm for cricket among England's upper classes (e.g., Allen 1990; James 1963; Sandiford 1994). Country gentlemen found that they could field highly competitive teams by hiring skilled "players" (i.e., professionals) to work on their estates, thus inaugurating a long tradition of collaboration between "gentlemen and players," in which elites and commoners played cricket side-by-side (Warner 1950).

At the same time, English elites encouraged their colonial subjects to play cricket because of the game's professed ability to discipline and civilize men, English and native alike.[3] The literature on colonial cricket is rather explicit in this regard. After touring India and Burma with an amateur team from Oxford University, author Cecil Headlam (1903:168–69) commented, "[C]ricket unites, as in India, the rulers and the ruled. It also provides a moral training, an education in pluck, and nerve, and self-restraint, far more valuable to the character of the ordinary native than the mere learning by heart of a play of Shakespeare." Interestingly, Indian cricket was originally supported by British and Indian elites alike. Britons like Lord Harris, governor of Bombay from 1890–95, sponsored tournaments between Indian and English teams. Similarly, cricket-playing was endorsed and encouraged by local elites as "an aristocratic game which upheld traditional notions of social hierarchy and patronage" (Cashman 1979: 197; also Bose

1990). Thus, it was a win-win situation for everyone concerned: cricket reaffirmed the authority of English and Indian elites over their respective constituencies while providing a forum for social interaction between them.

The same was true elsewhere in the colonies. Cricket was promoted as an English sport for both Englishmen and natives. In 1868, a famous all-Aborigine squad of Australian cricketers toured England. Parsi teams from India came in 1886 and 1888. Even in South Africa, non-whites were encouraged to play cricket, though on rigidly segregated terms (Merrett and Nauright 1998:55–57). The British colonies in the Caribbean are particularly well known for their legacy of interracial play (Beckles 1998a, 1998b; Beckles and Stoddart 1995; Cozier 1978; James 1963; Sandiford 1998c). "From as early as the 1860s the secondary schools and churches in Barbados deliberately began to use cricket as a socializing and civilizing agent," writes historian Keith Sandiford (1998c:1–2). "In those days the schools were dominated by headmasters who had come from Victorian Britain steeped in the public school ethos which then placed great store in team sports."

Indeed, the popularity of cricket in England itself owes much to its secondary education system. Cricket was regarded as an important right of passage for young British males, particularly those schooled in the elite "public schools" erected to train the future aristocrats of the empire (Mangan 1986; Penn 1999; Sandiford 1994; Stoddart and Sandiford 1998; Williams 2001).

> [British] educators encouraged cricket participation among their students in the profound conviction that it produced better citizens as well as scholars. . . . [They] argued that organized sports could bring order and discipline to aggressive groups of rich, spoilt and rebellious brats. . . . The public schools established the cricketing cult from about 1830 onwards. By 1860 it was an essential feature of their curriculum. (Sandiford 1998a:14)

So central did cricket become to British elite education that by the mid-nineteenth century, headmasters began hiring professional cricketers to coach their boys to victory over rival schools.

The creation of distinctly British secondary schools throughout the colonies of the British Empire also helped expose indigenous populations to the game. In Jamaica, for example, the educational system strongly promoted cricket in the secondary schools where, because of the merit principle in admissions, a substantial minority of darker lads of working-class background could be found. The same was true in the Asian Subcontinent, where promising young lads from low-status households were sometimes sent to English-style boarding schools and thus introduced to cricket. The importance of these schools in the cultivation of national cricket cultures is particularly evident in places where the educational system followed a different model. As Sandiford (1998b:4) points out, cricket languished in Anglo-African colonies like Kenya, Nigeria, and Uganda, where, in the nineteenth century, "European communities remained only minute fractions of the overall population and where the Victorian public school ethos never really took root." British-run secondary schools there were more committed to religious education than to competition and sport. This attitude was likely a result of the fact that British colonization began in these countries rather late, by which time the goals of imperialism had become somewhat more modest.[4] The virtual absence of a dedicated white settler population contributed to a garrison mentality in which the English sought to mollify, rather than civilize, their central African subjects. Similarly, the British did not encourage indigenous participation in cricket in the Far East (Stoddart 1998b:136–37).

Several unique features of the game itself appear to have facilitated its cross-national adoption and acculturation in many parts of the Commonwealth. That cricket requires no physical contact between players explains in part its diffusion to mixed-race and deeply class-divided colonies where "contact" sports like rugby and soccer/football were either ignored, practiced only among whites, or played along strictly segregated lines (meaning that white teams only played white teams, and so forth [Stoddart 1988]). Interracial play was permissible as long as it did not involve close contact, as with cricket. The formal attire of official cricket matches also helped smooth the way for integrated play—even in the searing heat of India and the Caribbean, players were expected to wear white or cream flannel trousers and long-sleeved white shirts. It is significant, too, that even the most minor of games required two umpires dressed in authoritative white overcoats and that a cardinal principle of the game was that the umpires' decisions were always final. (The umpires were also invariably members of the elite class in interclass games.) These arrangements effectively curtailed any rabble-rousing or arguments that would demean the "masters" or undermine the pervasive atmosphere of *noblesse oblige* in the colonial milieu. Thus, even in England, nonwhites were permitted to play on local cricket teams. In fact, one of the most famous batsmen in all of English cricket history is a man known by the name of Ranjitsinhji, a native of India who originally learned the game at Rajkumar College and later played at the University of Cambridge before going on to become an English sports celebrity (Williams 2001:22–32).

Another important feature of the game that facilitated interracial play was "stacking," or "positional segregation," within teams. From its earliest period in Britain, we find stacking along class lines in cricket: bowling and wicket-keeping were performed by low-status "players" while the roles of star batsmen and captain were mainly reserved for high-status "gentlemen." The practice of stacking thus allowed elite Englishmen to recruit nonwhite and lower-class players without compromising the social segregation prevalent in English society more generally. Gentlemen and players were allocated separate changing rooms and entrances to the field of play; and separate accommodations were arranged for team travel; team captains were exclusively drawn from

the amateur (i.e., high-status) ranks; and "professionals were expected, independently of relativities of age and skill, to call amateurs, 'Sir,' and, particularly when young, to perform menial duties around the ground" (Dunning and Sheard 1979:181). Stacking was even more important in multiracial British colonies, such as Jamaica, Barbados, and India, where "natives" were generally expected to specialize in bowling, thus leaving captaining, umpiring, and batting to their colonial overseers. Malcolm (2001) has shown that this pattern was not only transferred to the colonies but persists to this day in British cricket clubs where, as late as 1990, 70 percent of the bowlers were of West Indian and other colonial ancestry. Until fairly recently, even the most superlative nonwhite players were barred from captaining their clubs or national teams (Coakley 1998).

Nonetheless, enthusiasm for and participation in cricket became a national pastime in every former major colony of the British Empire *except* Canada and the United States. In the cricketing colonies, elite enthusiasm for the game was transferred to the population at large. In the United States and Canada, on the other hand, cricket remained largely a sport for country club members and elite boarding school students (Kirsch 1989, 1991; Lester 1951; Melville 1998; Metcalfe 1987; Redmond 1979). In other words, cricket culture had been transmitted to, and adopted by, some portion of the American and Canadian populations, but it failed to persist or develop as a popular pastime in both cases. Understanding variance in the global diffusion of cricket thus requires further investigation of the *acculturation* process, or the way the meaning and cultural significance of the game was transformed in the process of diffusion. As mentioned earlier, we do not find explanations based on "national values" or "cultural resonance" useful in this regard. Instead, we look carefully at the social systems of each country, as well as actual histories of the game (and related games) in them.

Adoption Followed by Failed Acculturation: Elite Versus Popular Sports in Canada and the United States

The most distinctive feature of the history of cricket in both the United States and Canada is its elevation to a pastime for elites only. In Canada, for example, cricket "gained a firm foothold among upper-class Canadians who were to perpetuate the game through the private schools. Cricket's longevity and persistence were directly related to its position within the highest levels of Canadian society" (Metcalfe 1987:8). Thus, one key to the rise and fall of Canadian cricket was the changing role of the game in Canada's elite universities and secondary schools. "Founded though they were by British public school alumni along British public school lines, the Canadian colleges refused to perpetuate the elitism of their prototypes or to preserve their outmoded curricula" (Sandiford 1994:148; also Dunae 1981). By the end of the nineteenth century, only the most elite boarding schools retained cricket, and even they began to encourage indigenous sports like hockey, lacrosse, and football in its stead (Mangan 1986:142–67). In the words of Donald King, Secretary to the Canadian Cricket Association (quoted in Sayen 1956:98), "[S]ome of our private schools play the game and feature it as part of their normal curriculum, but the private school here is in the minority and when the boys leave they often go and live in an area in which there is no cricket or perhaps the lure of golf or tennis proves stronger than enthusiasm for cricket when school days are over." Canadian boarding schools "kept alive the cult of athleticism," writes Sandiford (1994: 149), "but saw fit to promote a different brand of games. The behavior of the late-Victorian colleges in Canada differed markedly from that of their counterparts in [for example] India and the West Indies."

The Dismal Fate of Cricket in Canada

Translating these observations into sociological theory about diffusion failure requires some conjecture but is ultimately rather straightforward: As fewer Canadian elite schools devoted time to training young men in the finer points of cricket, the quantity and quality of play declined. Without fresh infusions of talent or widespread networks of league play, the game gradually took on the air of a marginal, old-fashioned pastime for antiquarians and Anglophiles. An 1895 account of Canadian cricket remarks, for example, that in Nova Scotia, "the same players were continually engaged in fighting out the same contests year after year, save only varied by the introducing of some fresh regiment or ship" (Wallace quoted in Hall and McCulloch 1895:124). "Cricket clubs of any size in Nova Scotia were few and far between," adds Wallace. "It needed, therefore, all the efforts of lovers of the game to keep up the necessary interest." Another 1895 commentator adds, "Only two or three comparatively small schools act as feeders to the ranks, always too rapidly depleted by the cares of life, by *anno domini*, and perchance, obesity" (Patteson quoted in Hall and McCulloch 1895:257–58). Sandiford (1994:148) concludes, "[D]uring the last quarter of the century, the game became associated more and more with an older and more old-fashioned Anglo-Saxon elite."

The central feature of the Canadian story is thus the isolation of cricket as a class-specific pastime. The clubby "Britishness" of Canadian elites may be one reason for this split, but the key causal factor remains the exclusivity of the sport, not its association with Britain per se. In looking at Canadian sports history of the late nineteenth and early twentieth centuries, one sees substantial evidence that cricket was an increasingly insular pastime, practiced only by those with the time and money to join exclusive clubs. Contributors to an 1895 volume, *Sixty Years of Canadian Cricket* (Hall and McCulloch, eds.), refer frequently to the gentlemanly, amateurish nature of the Canadian game, as compared to its quasi-professional English variant. In addition, Canadian sports historian Richard Gruneau (1983:108–9) notes that elite sports teams in Canada actually began avoiding competition with non-elite teams in the mid-to-late nineteenth century. Gruneau (1983:109) hypothesizes that "as the Canadian class structure began to elaborate, and as meritocratic liberal values began to develop widespread support, members of the dominant class apparently became unable to tolerate the possibility of defeat at the hands of those they considered to be their social inferiors. They also may have become progressively more alarmed at the prospect that commercialism in sport could very easily get out of hand under such conditions and vulgarize traditional upper-class views of 'the nobility of play.' " Cricket had become for them something precious, part of their heritage, an elite pastime more akin to ancestor worship than play. In England, by contrast, cricket remained something spirited and boisterous, as well as highly competitive, thus facilitating the incorporation of low-status "players" into the game.

Counterfactual: The Rise of Baseball in the United States

This last observation points to a second facet of cricket's ultimate rejection in North America: its failure to cultivate mass appeal through frequent matches in which large crowds, intense rivalries, and spirited fans might bring the sport to the attention of major portions of the population. The history of American baseball provides a telling comparison with that of cricket in both the United States and Canada. Though baseball and cricket both began as relatively informal leisure games in the United States, baseball was later blessed by a cadre of brilliant entrepreneurs determined to make it the "nation's pastime." One such person was A. G. Spalding, star player, manager, league organizer, and sports manufacturer. To call Spalding an impresario or a marketing genius would be a bit of an understatement. He engaged in every part of the game, from promoting star players and intercity rivalries to squelching nascent efforts at labor organization among players (Levine 1985).

In addition to cricket, baseball had other rivals for people's time and money in the United States—crew regattas were major business for some time, for example, as were bicycle races, track meets, and college football games (Smith 1988). Spalding helped secure baseball's place in American national culture through a two-part strategy: On the one hand, he promoted the highest possible level of play with the widest possible audience by creating and managing a system of professional league play throughout North America. On the other hand, he built a manufacturing and marketing empire devoted to selling youngsters the accoutrements of the game—the Spalding name still stands prominent in the world of sporting goods. In the late 1870s, after a successful career as player and manager, Spalding published an official rulebook for the game and also licensed official merchandise for play. Spalding also produced bats and balls of different sizes and shapes for players of various abilities and backgrounds. Noting that American educators were increasingly interested in finding healthy leisure pursuits for students, Spalding donated equipment and trophies to groups like the Public School Athletic League (Levine 1985:110–12).[5] Spalding is even credited with inventing the now widely discredited "Cooperstown myth," by which the origins of baseball were explained in a compelling story of its humble but ingenious small-town roots (see Spalding [1911] 1992).

Note too that A. G. Spalding worked hard to curry the interest of elites, as well as the masses, in baseball. Upon returning from an 1889 "world tour" in which Spalding traveled with a hand-picked squad of professionals to Australia, Sri Lanka [then Ceylon], Egypt, Italy, France, and the British Isles, Spalding had his team greeted by a grand parade in New York City and then hosted a 300-person banquet attended by "Teddy Roosevelt, Mark Twain, local politicians, baseball officials, Yale undergraduates, and 'popular members of the New York Stock Exchange,' " among others (Levine 1985: 107). Spalding's biographer, Peter Levine (1985:108) describes the tour's final, April 19th, stop in Chicago in terms worth repeating: "As the Chicago *Tribune* described it, 'the streets were thronged' with a crowd that 'represented all classes. Businessmen were in it, toughs and sports . . . also a great many ladies. And they went fairly crazy.' " The parade was concluded "over expensive cigars and fine brandy at a reception attended by Chicago's elite. . . ." Thus, Spalding made sure that the sport appealed to everyone, elites notwithstanding. He offered them a distinctive, exclusive niche from which to enjoy the game.

At the same time, Spalding contributed to the emerging American consensus that cricket was an effeminate game for men too precious to play baseball. In his best-selling 1911 book, *America's National Game*, Spalding boasts ([1911] 1992:7), "I have declared that Cricket is a genteel game. It is. Our British Cricketer, having finished his day's labor at noon, may don his negligee shirt, his white trousers, his gorgeous hosiery and his canvas shoes, and sally forth to the field of sport, with his sweetheart on one arm and his Cricket bat under the other, knowing that he may engage in his national pastime without soiling his linen or neglecting his lady.... Not so the American Ball Player. He may be a veritable Beau Brummel in social life. He may be the Swellest Swell of the Smart Set in Swelldom; but when he dons his Base Ball suit, he says good-bye to society, doffs his gentility, and becomes—just a Ball Player! He knows that his business now is to play ball, and that first of all he is expected to attend to business.... Cricket is a gentle pastime. Base Ball is War! Cricket is an Athletic Sociable [sic], played and applauded in a conventional, decorous and English manner. Base Ball is an Athletic Turmoil, played and applauded in an unconventional, enthusiastic and American manner."

Naturally, Spalding was mischaracterizing the nature of English cricket, and English society more generally. The English aristocracy had long prided itself on the rough and tumble sports practiced at its most elite boarding schools. The relevant point is that Spalding, and many like him, were contributing to the development of a specifically North American perception of cricket. Indeed, this stereotype of elite British society likely attracted some American and Canadian men to the game—Canadian cricketers increasingly focused on cultivating a gentlemanly ideal of elegant, amateur play. As for the United States, an 1875 description of life at Harvard College (Vaille and Clark 1875:421) says the following of the Harvard Cricket Club, founded in 1862: "Though

never very popular with the athletes of the College, it has always found supporters enough to keep it in a moderately vigorous existence." Thus, the emerging image of cricket as an ultra-elite pastime both repelled and attracted followers.

At the same time, however, many of the wealthy sons of American and Canadian society eschewed cricket for baseball, perhaps, in part, because of late-nineteenth-century rhetoric about the manliness of American culture. The 1875 *Harvard Book* does not include reference to a college baseball team, for example, but the *1887–88 Annual Report* (Harvard College 1889: 29) proudly reports a gift of $25,000 from Mr. Henry Reginald Astor Carey to build appropriate facilities for "the Baseball Nine." In fact, beginning in the 1860s and 70s, baseball became an intensely popular sport at the nation's most prestigious colleges. America's first recorded intercollegiate game took place in 1859 between Amherst and Williams. Bowdoin, Middlebury, Dartmouth, Brown, Trinity, Hamilton, Princeton, and Kenyon all had organized teams by 1862. "By the end of the 1870s, a group of eastern colleges, consisting of Amherst, Brown, Dartmouth, Harvard, Princeton, and Yale, were playing regular home and away series of games" (Smith 1988:59). College teams also regularly played professional teams, and play was extremely competitive; so much so that the colleges began offering "financial incentives" to especially talented players (Smith 1988:62–66).

The incipient professionalization of college athletics presented America's elite college presidents with something of a conundrum, another key to understanding the trajectories of cricket and baseball in the United States and Canada. Baseball's popularity grew through the result of excessive promotion, intense competition, and a do-anything-for-victory mentality among coaches and players. Aspiring athletes at America's elite colleges were clearly attracted by the glamour and notoriety of the game. (Posh summer jobs playing exhibition baseball at resort hotels and other financial "perks" for playing were probably also attractions.) At the same time, college masters and alumni objected strongly to this development; they preferred a sports ethic closer to Spalding's stereotype of English cricket—leisurely, good-natured, and safe. College presidents had previously tried to ban excessively violent sports to no avail—American-style tackle football was first developed at Harvard College, where it was repeatedly and unsuccessfully banned by the president. American college presidents responded to the emergence of pay-for-play with equal reproach. Even the notion of hiring professional, full-time coaches for college teams was originally considered anathema by college boards (Mrozek 1983; Smith 1988; Townsend 1996).

American college masters eventually managed to minimize financial incentives for student-athletes, but the wider "professionalization" of certain sports continued nonetheless. Crew, football, baseball, and track and field attracted enormous audiences, particularly when rival schools, such as Harvard and Yale, had their annual meetings. Winning teams often received valuable cash prizes. Competition became increasingly defined around key dates and rivalries. Thanksgiving Day became a focal point of the college football season, for example, and competitive schools could bring in tens of thousands of dollars at the gate. Major crew regattas and track meets could also bring in crowds of 10,000 or more (Smith 1988:30–34). By this time, therefore, any college athlete still devoted to cricket would had to have asked himself why he was willing to forego the glory and gammon of the era's more popular sports—especially baseball, which essentially requires the same skill-set as cricket.

Whereas football, crew, and track and field all remained more or less confined to the collegiate arena, baseball supported a number of professional leagues in addition to the college teams. An 1888 *New York Times* story ("The Game Was Stopped") reports a crowd of 40,000 spectators at a professional baseball game outside of Philadelphia; so many, in fact, that the game was "called" after a mob of unseated fans surged onto the field at the end of the first inning. Pro-am baseball games were also a common occurrence, which surely contributed to the sport's popularity on college campuses. American

baseball, in sum, increasingly resembled English cricket: a sport in which elites and commoners shared a passion for the game, one in which gambling, professionalism, and a willingness to do anything to win were fundamental.

Cricket in the United States
The place of cricket in late-nineteenth-century American society could hardly be more different: Though cricket was originally popularized in the United States by working-class immigrants from the British Isles, it later became a sport practiced by only a select few Americans (Melville 1998: 16–17, 25). Note, moreover, that while the increasing popularity of baseball did present a formidable challenge to American cricket, the two games existed comfortably side-by-side throughout the 1850s and 60s. It was not uncommon, in fact, for cricket and baseball teams to challenge one another to matches in their rival's sport (Melville 1998:67). In truth, it was American elites' exclusivist attitude toward cricket that led to the sport's decline among the population at large. As in Canada, American cricket players increasingly retreated to small, elite clubs, and competition with rival "elevens" was quickly restricted to a small coterie of suitable teams (Kirsch 1989:221–22).

Over time, the sport's snooty image took a toll on the popularity of cricket among Americans at large, an image that elites sought to cultivate. In contrast to the robust English tradition of "gentlemen and players," American cricket clubs strictly forbade professionals from play, even if it meant bitter defeat at the hands of traveling English and Australian teams. Melville (1998: 77; also 120–22) notes that, "As the old-line [American] competitive cricket clubs went into decline, their roles were assumed by cricket organizations dedicated to providing an environment of more socially selective participation upon strictly amateur lines." A 1907 *New York Times* story ("Cricket") quips, "Once more the game of cricket has been shown to be a languishing exotic in New York." It noted, "A visiting team of Englishmen have worked their will upon the local cricketers. . . . In the West, New York is supposed to be the seat and centre of Anglo-mania. But the West ought to be softened when it sees how very badly New York plays the Anglican national game. Cricketally [sic] speaking, Philadelphia is the Anglomaniacal town." Indeed, with the exception of a few New England college teams, cricket thrived only in Philadelphia by the end of the nineteenth century. As early as 1884, a *New York Times* story ("Philadelphia Cricketers") joked, "Residents of American cities where cricket is not played, except by a few home-sick Englishmen, assert that it is played in Philadelphia because cricket is the slowest of games and Philadelphia the slowest of cities."

Regardless of the Philadelphians' supposed motives, it is true that a handful of Philadelphia-based teams provided the bulk of American training and participation in the sport during the late nineteenth and early twentieth centuries. One finds little evidence, furthermore, that the Philadelphians were concerned about the overall decline of interest in American cricket; in fact, they appear to have encouraged it. They confined the game to prestigious country clubs like the Merion and Belmont Cricket Clubs, founded in 1865 and 1874 respectively. Sports historian George Kirsch (1991:15) sums up the Philadelphia scene, and the American milieu more generally, by saying,

> "The upper-class 'Proper Philadelphians' who patronized the sport after the Civil War did not wish to convert the masses. They preferred their leisurely game because they were amateur sportsmen who had plenty of time for recreation. They supported the English game until the early twentieth century, when tennis and golf became more popular amusements for the upper class. Elite Boston cricketers and working-class English immigrants also kept the game going into the 1900s. But by the eve of the First World War very few were still alive who could recall the days when cricket had a chance to become America's national pastime."

Approximately 120 cricket clubs are said to have existed in the Philadelphia area at one time or another, at least ten of which still exist today. One might hypothesize that cricket thrived there in part because of the nature of elite Philadelphian society in the late nineteenth century. Says E. Digby Baltzell, a sociologist who has studied the American elite in detail, "[T]he flowering of New England was the product of an aristocratic social structure led by men with deep roots in the governing class of the society, going back to the glacial age; Philadelphia's Golden Age, on the other hand, was the product of a heterogeneous and democratic social structure whose leadership elites came largely from elsewhere and from all classes within the city" (Baltzell [1979] 1996:54). By our thinking, then, social mobility in Philadelphia might have prompted its "old-money" elite to look for ways to segregate themselves from the city's nouveau riche and upwardly mobile populations. Boston Brahmins had no such cause for status anxiety, given their long-standing dominance of the city's cultural and urban affairs, though they did establish other forms of elite cultural institution in their midst (DiMaggio 1982). Nor were social mobility and status anxiety unique to Philadelphia at this time. Thus, we think that there is a more salient explanation of the Philadelphia-phenomenon in American cricket, one that mirrors the success of American baseball at the national level.

Cricket seems to have survived in Philadelphia primarily because there was a critical mass of clubs ready to field competitive teams. Thus, though comparable numbers of elite men in other cities may have been interested in cricket, they failed to build (elite) cricket leagues that would sustain (elite) interest in the game over time. Put in more formal terms, the Philadelphians created a network "dense" enough to sustain a local cricket culture; they stayed above the "threshold" at which interest in collective pursuits risks extinction (Granovetter and Soong 1983). Haverford College, the University of Pennsylvania, and Princeton University dominated the late-nineteenth-century game largely because of their proximity to the "cricket nurseries" of Philadelphia (Lester 1951), and the former remains a central hub of American cricket to this day—Haverford not only pays a professional cricketer to instruct its current "elevens" but also maintains a special library collection devoted to the history of the sport.[6] Elsewhere in the country (and in Canada), elite clubs failed to create viable leagues and thus faltered. The absence of a strong cricket culture in the notably stratified American South also makes sense in light of this explanation. The rural focus of late-nineteenth-century Southern elites seems to have predisposed them against team sports of any kind. Southern leisure activities were generally more grounded in agrarian pastimes like hunting, fishing, and riding. Only much later, following the rise of large state universities in the South, did team sports like football, basketball, and baseball become mainstays of sporting culture for Southern elites and non-elites alike.

Nonetheless, even with the exception of Philadelphia, it would appear that the popularity of cricket in both the United States and Canada suffered primarily from the exclusionism of its elite practitioners. North American cricket prevailed, though weakly, in places where status anxiety was high among wealthy families and where these families established and maintained multiple dense networks of rival cricket clubs. In both Canada and the United States, an egalitarian ethos encouraged economic elites to cultivate exclusive status-based activities with which to maintain their superior position in the social system. Cricket was not an inevitable response to this status anxiety, but it was one viable option.

At the same time, however, even elite tastes began changing in the early twentieth century. Increasingly, America's wealthiest families "placed maximum importance on the pleasuring of the individual sportsman taken as a consumer, albeit a wealthy one, and on gratification as a suitable goal in his life" (Mrozek 1983: 106). Country clubs, though still popular, increasingly built their reputations on the quality of their clubhouses, tennis tournaments, and golf courses. According to the sporting news of the day, even long-standing cricket clubs began hosting tennis and golf tournaments on their grounds. Cricket was languishing.

The obvious irony here is that elitism spelled the death of a once-popular pastime in two countries known for their exceptional egalitarianism. Thus we ask: Why would elites in other countries not have done the same? How did cricket become so popular in these societies? Answering these questions requires that we look back at the cases in which cricket was successfully adopted and espoused by wide segments of the population, places like Australia, New Zealand, India, South Africa, and the West Indies. Despite their vast social and political differences, what do all these countries have in common beside their British colonial roots?

Adoption and Successful Acculturation: Cricket Elsewhere in the Commonwealth

It would appear that, in part, it was the very lack of a rigid social system that encouraged elitist attitudes toward cricket in the United States and Canada. Cricket became a marker of high social status, and the game was thus not promoted among the population at large. Conversely, rigid social stratification systems in other British colonial societies appear to have nurtured segregated but inclusive cricket cultures. In India, for example, love for the game was spread through the organization of matches between rival ethno-religious groups, each of which welcomed talented players from within their communities regardless of rank (Bose 1990). C. L. R. James's autobiographical accounts of Trinidadian cricket culture support similar conclusions. In Trinidad, as in Jamaica and Barbados, blacks and whites sometimes played cricket together (though not as equals). Individual cricket clubs were established at each rung of the social hierarchy, from the lowest-caste blacks to lighter skinned "browns" and whites. "I haven't the slightest doubt that the clash of race, caste and class did not retard but stimulated West Indian cricket," writes James (1963:72). Thus we see that the specific criteria of social stratification are less important than the existence of a cohesive vertical hierarchy in the receiver nation. Racial, socioeconomic, and/or ethno-religious differences could provide the basis of stratification with the same result: elites' decision either to actively promote or at least passively to permit the acculturation of cricket among lower social strata.

There are three mechanisms underlying this process in the case of cricket: First, colonial elites, comfortable in their place atop the social hierarchy, had little reason to discourage those beneath them from playing a game that paid symbolic homage to British cultural and political hegemony; in fact, elites tended to regard cricket as a good means of "civilizing" natives in their own image. Given a rigid social system, furthermore, emulation of those at the top had benefits for those at the upper-middle and lower-middle rungs, particularly among nonwhites seeking "entry" into a white-dominant world. With opportunities for upward mobility so severely limited, moreover, cricket provided those of the lower castes some means of symbolic competence—that is, by competing against those of other castes, races, and classes, low-caste cricketers could assert themselves in ways not permitted in ordinary society (Malcolm 2001).

Thus cricket was attractive to all major strata in these colonial societies. Even in Australia and New Zealand, where class mobility was relatively more common, yearning for status in the eyes of England created opportunities for "liberation cricket." Having been settled largely by working-class British immigrants, many of them "transported" to Australia as criminals, the Antipodes have long had a sense of cultural inferiority to England. British culture thus had an elevated status for Australians and New Zealanders of all classes. Understanding the Australian and New Zealand cases nonetheless requires a bit of extra background information, to which we now turn.

Australia and New Zealand

Though contemporary Australia and New Zealand are egalitarian, socially mobile societies much like the United States and Canada, matters were significantly different in the nineteenth century, the key years in the global diffusion of cricket. Socioeconomically, early Australian society was stratified into three classes: an upper-crust of absentee (mostly English) landlords; a middle class of émigré soldiers, artisans, and professionals;

and a lower class of emancipated prisoners, their offspring, and the vast hordes of freemen tending sheep and sharecropping on other people's land (Clark 1995; Hughes 1986; Stone and Garden 1978). The key point about late-nineteenth-century Australia for our concerns is that its wealthiest citizens did not attempt to build strong institutional barriers between themselves and the rest of society. This may be the result of the elite's relative sense of security atop the Australian status hierarchy, though we suspect that it stems more directly from the fact that Australia was still a relatively new settlement at the time. Its richest citizens had yet to accumulate wealth or exclusive social networks comparable to those in the eastern United States and Canada. The separate classes desperately needed one another in the struggle to settle this vast, isolated continent. In the continent's burgeoning cities, for example, where Australian cricket truly thrived, the mercantile elite actively embraced the working classes, both socially and politically (Connell and Irving 1980). The presence of many British military men, moreover, coupled with the colony's distance from England, made English pastimes particularly valuable to Australians, particularly those activities that did not require fancy concert halls or awareness of the latest fads and fashions. Thus, Australia's various social strata cooperated in a nation-wide effort to cultivate British ideals and social practices, cricket foremost among them (Clark 1995; Hughes 1986). The Sydney *Gazette*, according to one account (Pollard 1987:10), stated in 1832 that "cricket was now the prevailing amusement of the colony and that no gentleman could expect to 'dangle at a lady's apron strings' unless he could boast of his cricket prowess."

Nonetheless, urban elites did establish some fairly exclusive cricket clubs in Australia—the Melbourne Cricket Club was founded in 1838 on such grounds, thus prompting the formation in 1839 of a rival middle-class club, the Melbourne Union Cricket Club (Pollard 1987: 40–42). In this way, Australian cricket resembled the stratified game in other British colonies, such as India and the Caribbean. The key to the widespread popularity of cricket in Australia was, again, the decision of its wealthiest citizens to "share" the game with those of lower strata. Competitiveness trumped exclusivity in the minds of Australia's socioeconomic elite, in other words, much as it had done in eighteenth-century England. Having issued a challenge of one thousand pounds to any team in Australia that could beat it, the prestigious Melbourne Cricket Club signed a contract with a professional English cricketer to bolster its competitiveness with rival clubs. The MCC also hired a groundskeeper to eject nonmembers from club grounds. Both practices resembled the English cricket tradition in full flower—assiduously maintaining status-group distinctions while facilitating whatever integration was necessary to maintain the highest possible level of play (Pollard 1987:46–47; Dunning and Sheard 1979:181). This competitiveness also helped cultivate large audiences for the game: Match organizers for the MCC insisted that "spectators would not attend cricket unless the best players were on view." (Pollard 1987:143). They were clearly interested in popularizing the game among the widest possible audience. In only a few instances, such as distant Tasmania (originally known as Van Dieman's Land), did anything like the American and Canadian elites-only attitude manifest itself. Pollard (1987: 37) refers, tellingly, to the fact that Tasmanian cricket did not thrive owing to "the strange reluctance of the strong, prestigious clubs in Hobart and Launceston to hire professional players to coach and strengthen their teams."

Over time, Australian cricket remained a national pastime despite the democratization of its social, political, and economic systems. In the late nineteenth century, teams were often stratified by class and ethnic background, while a spirit of inclusive competition prevailed nonetheless (Cashman 1984). The widespread role of publicans in promoting Australian cricket personifies its popular nature: "[P]ublicans quickly realised that the promotion of cricket stimulated their business," notes one historian (Pollard 1987:10). Creation of neighborhood and trade-based cricket clubs was, moreover, a source of

tremendous pride for urban boosters in cities like Sydney and Melbourne (Cashman 1998a; Pollard 1987). Sydney, in particular, struggled to distance itself from its origins as an English penal colony. Excellence at cricket appeared early on as a way for locals to make a statement about "the character of colonial society and the nature of the imperial relationship." "Thrashing the mother-land" was an indirect expression of "the love-hate relationship of a youthful colonial society attempting to define its identity and a greater sense of nationhood" (Cashman 1998a:36, 39; see also Mandle 1973:525–26). Hence, a long Australo-English rivalry began early on, and it is still a source of tremendous interest to Australian sports fans, particularly given their long-standing dominance over increasingly weak English teams. More important still is the fact that intra- and inter-provincial leagues were actively promoted early on in Australia, thus stimulating the creation of adequate playing grounds and competitive teams throughout the country.[7]

Cricket evolved along similar lines in New Zealand. Though New Zealand was never home to any English penal colonies, its wealthier citizens shared with those of Australia the sense that they needed to prove themselves in the eyes of the British. New Zealand cricket has its longest and strongest legacy of play in the province of Canterbury, "the most English of New Zealand provinces" and one founded upon economic principles designed to perpetuate the rigid social order of the English countryside (minus the truly poor). Here, class stratification and inclusive Anglophilia promoted cricket as a healthy pastime for all, excepting the native Maoris (Ryan 1998).[8] Christchurch was home to both exclusive and "open" clubs. Elite schools began early on to train young men in the game, and the hiring of professional coaches from England was also common beginning in the 1890s (Reese 1927:41, 49). A steady stream of English and Australian immigrants provided ready instruction and talent. Interprovincial play was also quite popular—when an annual match was first arranged between the neighboring provinces of Canterbury and Otago, "it was agreed that the teams should wear the great

English university colours," Canterbury in Oxford's dark blue, Otago in the light blue of Cambridge (Reese 1927:36). The creation of several annual prizes—the Plunket Shield for best "major" team (generally those from major cities) and the Hawke Cup for best "minor association," as well as the Heathcote Williams Shield for best secondary school team—helped create the kinds of well-anticipated sports rivalries vital to the creation of a "hegemonic sports culture."

Promotion of the game in minor population centers through the Hawke Cup competition was clearly important to the long-term survival of the game in New Zealand. Emphasis among New Zealand cricketers was not on the social status generated by membership in elite clubs but on the prestige gained by winning. This was so much the case that a visiting Australian star, Warwick Armstrong, reportedly advised that the "various [Kiwi] associations are too inclined to pick the coach who can help his province to win matches. What is really wanted is the coach who can impart knowledge and keenness to the boy" (quoted in Reese 1927:76). In sum, New Zealand, like Australia, followed a somewhat different path to "hegemonic" cricket than British colonies in which a minority white elite dominated a majority colored population. Cricket helped Antipodean elites cultivate their Englishness, but the size and isolation of their European settlements limited the extent to which they could be truly exclusive. Everyone involved in the game aspired to gentility but none was excluded on the grounds of wealth or social standing. "Proper conduct, rather more than heredity, was the mark of an amateur gentleman," comments one history of Australian cricket (Pollard 1987:65).

The Asian Subcontinent
Interestingly, it was not originally the intent of the British to popularize cricket in the subcontinent of Asia. British soldiers are said to have played the game in India as early as 1721, but it was not until the mid-nineteenth century that Indians actually began to play. Then, too, it was primarily the "middleman" Parsi population that first cultivated the game. The Parsis were an ancient immigrant community in India known for their wealth and success at business. "It was no accident that the first community [in India] to take up the game were the Parsis," comments one historian (Cashman 1979:190–91). They were "a wealthy entrepreneurial group who acted as cultural brokers between the British and Indian society. . . . In the tradition of colonial elites, the Parsis took up the game of cricket, along with other imperial customs, partly to demonstrate their fitness for the role of collaboration." Parsi success at the game also prompted India's elite Hindu and Muslim populations to take an active interest in it (Bose 1990:32).

From the start, indigenous participation in Indian cricket was centered around elites: Princes would build ornate cricket grounds and invite guests to watch them play. The princes would rarely even bowl or field the ball, relying on hired players to provide them easily hit balls. This provided valuable opportunities for Indians of lower social strata to get involved in the game. Audiences, too, were carefully segregated; Europeans from Indians, commoners from elite, men from women, and so on (Cashman 1998b: 126–67; Cashman 1980). "So cricket prospered," comments Bose (1990:36), "not because the different communities mixed but because they did not. Competition, not cooperation, was the spur." Thus, elite members of India's vastly segregated social system embraced the game as a way of distinguishing themselves vis-à-vis the British and one another. Important for our purposes is the fact that talented nonelites were encouraged to play the game. The relative security of elites within their own communities, as well as their competitiveness with elites in rival ethno-religious communities, allowed for this kind of segregated-integration.

"By the 1930s," writes Cashman (1998b: 123), "there were many cricketing princes, players and patrons, who lavished great sums of money and energy to secure the top prizes in cricket, control of the game and captaincy of the side. . . . Cricket prominence provided the princes with more clout in the Chamber of Princes and enhanced their status with the British." Rivalry between Indian and English sides developed from this, which subsequently helped cultivate further talent and interest among the public at large (Appadurai 1996; Bose 1990). The widespread incorporation of Indians into the British civil service system in India also exposed many indigenous men to the game. By 1947, when India became independent, cricket was a national passion, if not yet *the* national passion. Jawaharlal Nehru, first prime minister of India, further encouraged participation in the sport, himself having been educated at Harrow in England. In Bombay, where cricket has, perhaps, its longest history on the subcontinent, and where the Indian television and film industries are centered, star cricketers are given all the adulation and fame of their Bollywood counterparts (Cashman 1998b:130). Televised matches in indigenous languages have also helped build and maintain a wide fan base, as has the transference of regional political tensions onto the wicket—international test matches between India, Pakistan, Bangladesh, and Sri Lanka are, today, rabidly nationalistic events replete with hooliganism, jingoism, and sometimes outright violence (Appadurai 1996; Nandy 2000).

The West Indies

The historic status hierarchies that nurtured passion for cricket in Indian society have a close parallel in the West Indies, where the game is equally popular today. Though originally cultivated by and for white elites in the British Caribbean, high-status blacks and Indians were provided some training in the game early on, thus leading to the eventual formation of cricket clubs for nonwhites. Clubs were rigidly stratified on color and class lines. Nonetheless, the status hierarchy was sufficiently rigid that space could be created for interaction and competition among them—just so long as it remained on the field. Beating a team from an adjacent status position was a feat worthy of respect, and though it did not ultimately change the social order, it did at least provide an outlet for status emulation and achievement. The possibility of being recruited to play professionally in England was further incentive for talented athletes from poor families to devote time and energy to the game. Because

the symbolic stakes were high, moreover, large audiences would often turn out to watch and successful players would receive great acclaim. "Supporters of the respective sides had invested considerable amounts of emotional capital in the outcome," notes Stoddart (1998a:84), a development that later extended to international matches with sometimes violent consequences (Patterson 1995).

Thus we see another case where the relative stability of the status hierarchy within a society promoted a segregated but inclusive cricketing culture, one that gained valuable momentum from the muted tension of competition among status groups. Unique to the West Indies is the nature of their international "test" match status: rather than play as separate national teams, the "Windies" have traditionally comprised top players from throughout the Caribbean. The contemporary game in the Caribbean is thus less oriented around national pride than around racial and ethno-Caribbean solidarity (Beckles 1998b).

Southern Africa

The case of South African and Zimbabwean cricket is a bit more complicated and follows lines distinct from, though comparable to, those already described. The large presence of British military personnel provided a ready pool of talent for the game in southern Africa, but its diffusion to indigenous and Afrikaner populations was somewhat erratic. Some Afrikaners openly played cricket before the onset of the Boer War, and they gladly joined the British in a white unity movement during the Apartheid era, but the early twentieth century was a less active period for Afrikaner cricketers in the aftermath of the war. British whites, meanwhile, staked the very reputation of their settlements on the game. The small size of the Anglo-white population in South Africa meant that class distinctions among them were muted; cricket became a focal point of colonial life. Indeed, British South Africans and Rhodesians were in some ways more "British" than the British (Winch 1983). In colonial Rhodesia, for example, one memoirist noted, "Where previously one had to be a member of the la-di-da class to get a job in the Civil Service, now you had to beat the hide off a ball," meaning that prowess at cricket was sufficient means of attaining status and respect in the British community (G. H. Tanser quoted in Winch 1983).

Vitally important to the long-term success of cricket in southern Africa is the fact that the British allowed nonwhites to play the game there. Before the early 1900s, when government-sponsored race policies began their long descent toward apartheid, British settlers actually encouraged segregated play among middle-class blacks and Asians. "Because the ideology of respectability was crucial for the aspirations of middle-class blacks," they not only aspired to play the game well but also provided an example for less "respectable" blacks (Stoddart 1998b:56). Again, the relative stability of the status hierarchy in these societies allowed for the diffusion of the game from the top-down. Blacks were excluded from white cricket clubs, as well as the national teams, but they learned to play and to watch the game nonetheless. In the ensuing years, politics have been the greatest barrier to "hegemonic" cricket in South Africa and Zimbabwe. Opposition to apartheid limited South African participation in international test matches for a good part of the twentieth century, and the political turmoil in contemporary Zimbabwe may mean the permanent demise of cricket there.

Though the particulars motivating cricket adoption thus varied from one British colony to another, the development and perpetuation of a hegemonic cricket culture required in each case that members of high-status groups remained interested not only in cultivating their own cricket skills but also in sharing the game with those of lower orders. This did not occur in the United States or Canada.

DISCUSSION

Cricket and Sociological Models of Cultural Diffusion

Our analysis suggests an important extension of current diffusion theory. It is widely accepted among scholars in the field that diffusion is most likely to succeed where change agents and adoptees share the same culture and social category (especially the same socioeconomic status). Thus Rogers (1995:7) asserts as "an obvious principle of human communication that the transfer of ideas occurs most frequently between two individuals who are similar or homopholous," this being "the degree to which two or more individuals who interact are similar in certain attributes such as beliefs, education, social class, and the like. . . ." Rogers contrasts this with situations where relations are heterophilous (i.e., the social position of the change agent is different from that of the adopters) and notes that this can present a major obstacle to successful diffusion. The ideal situation in the initial adoption phase, he argues, is thus one in which change agents and potential adopters "would be homophilous on all other variables (education and social status, for example) even though they are heterophilous regarding the innovation" (Rogers 1995, 7; for similar views see Strang and Meyer 1993; Wejnert 2002).

We are inclined to agree that homophilous diffusion is indeed true in many, perhaps most, cases, especially those involving the intra-societal transfer of simple innovations among individuals. Our study, however, indicates that there is an important class of diffusion processes in which just the opposite might occur—i.e., cases in which a distinctly heterophilous relationship between change agents and would-be change-adopters promotes diffusion. In the case of cricket, it is precisely the stable status-inequality between those who brought the game from England and the lower-status colonial populations that adopted it that accounts for the successful diffusion of cricket. In such cases (i.e., top-down, or heterophilous, diffusion), it is the authority and high social status of change agents, combined with their willingness not simply to transmit but actively to participate in the promotion of the innovation, *and* their desire to continue their engagement with it even after it has begun to spread down and across the social hierarchy, that accounts for successful diffusion.

As shown in the case of cricket, all three elements are necessary for this kind of top-down diffusion to work: It is not enough for elites simply to introduce the innovation; they are required to promote it actively and to persist in lending it their prestige by continuing to practice it themselves. Where they do not, one of two outcomes, both fatal for the long-term acculturation of the innovation, is likely: One possibility is that the innovation becomes a fad, thereby enjoying a brief period of widespread popularity because of its upper-class origins, but later being abandoned by the elite transmitters because of this very popularity, thereby triggering a decline in overall popularity. The history of fashion is replete with examples of this (e.g., Crane 2000). Another possible "negative" outcome is that status-insecure first-adopters "capture" the innovation, thus preventing its diffusion into the population at large. Precisely this happened to cricket in Canada and the United States, as we have seen.

Naturally, the nature of social stratification in these Commonwealth countries is not sufficient to explain the success or failure of cricket in each country; nor does it fully explain the failed cases of Canada and the United States. Our earlier discussion of the rising popularity of baseball in the United States offers several keys to refining our explanation. Baseball was aggressively promoted throughout the United States by league-owners, sporting goods manufacturers, and "star" players. Inter-urban play helped promote widespread audiences. Youths were encouraged to play in and out of school, and the necessary equipment and playing grounds were made widely available. Similar efforts were made for football and basketball in the United States, and for cricket throughout much of the Commonwealth. Cross-class participation in such sports was supplemented, in other words, by intense efforts to recruit spectators, as well as new talent, to the games. At some point, such self-promotion seems to cross a threshold at which the game's popularity fuels itself: baseball was so popular and baseball rivalries so intense that even American elites flocked to it, thus leaving cricket virtually no following whatsoever. Absent celebrity play-ers and careful marketing, crew and track and field, in contrast, lost momentum and popularity among American audiences.

The lessons here are rather simple: On the supply side, would-be audiences must be offered a steady stream of well-publicized events between evenly matched, talented teams. Annual matches, such as Thanksgiving Day college football games or "The Ashes," a biennial cricket match between England and Australia, help solidify a sport's place in the public mind (cf. Schudson 1989). On the demand side, a surfeit of opportunities whereby talented athletes can find selective incentives to devote time and effort to one sport over another also appears to make a difference. Such factors, it should be noted, can also erode support for a sport even after it has been successfully adopted. The popularity of professional rugby in the Antipodes, for example, and the spread of basketball to the Caribbean, both potentially represent threats to their nations' hegemonic cricket cultures.

The evolution of the game in each country, then, is the result not only of the relative status position of interested parties but also such intangibles as the rise of sports entrepreneurs devoted to the promotion of a specific sport; the rise of competitive league play, which helps draw regular 'fans' from different strata of society; and the rise (or demise) of other seasonal sports competing for the same talent and audience base. Nonetheless, we feel that of these multiple factors, it is social stratification that lies most fundamentally at the heart of the matter. The extent to which an elite cultural practice like cricket was shared with or shielded from the general population was a direct result of elites' own sense of their place atop the social hierarchy. Had American elite cricketers felt less anxious about their social position, for example, they might have popularized the sport along the same lines as baseball (or golf and tennis).

CONCLUSION

What Might We Learn from the Global Diffusion of Cricket?

We began this project with both substantive and theoretical questions in mind.

Theoretically we questioned the propensity of diffusion models to emphasize solely structural or exclusively cultural factors in the adoption process. That is, we wondered what, besides cultural affinity or network ties, accounts for the successful diffusion of a cultural practice from one society to another. Furthermore, we wondered what sociological theories of diffusion might gain by considering examples where diffusion was initially successful and then failed. Substantively speaking, we wondered why Canadians were not more enthusiastic about cricket given their strong cultural and political connections to England. This case seemed especially compelling in light of all the recent attention put on globalization and the would-be homogenization of world culture. What might the global history of cricket tell us about other potentially diffusible phenomena, particularly those that bear with them such strong relations to their country of origin?

With regard to cricket, we have identified several factors that seem closely related to variance in the success or failure of the sport in countries connected to the former British Empire. Beyond merely being exposed to the sport, settler societies needed to dedicate time and resources to nurturing indigenous support for the game. In other words, some portion of the population needed to devote itself to playing cricket (*adoption*), and some larger portion needed to be persuaded to care about it (*acculturation*). We note, too, that in the final, acculturation phase, the game appears to take on cultural valence unique to its people; in other words, it becomes part of the national patrimony, as opposed to a simple cultural import. In some colonial societies, for example, cricket developed as a way for settlers to prove their "Britishness," whereas in others, excellence at the game offered an opportunity for natives literally to beat the British at their own game. In the unique case of Australia, moreover, both elements combined into a fiercely nationalist but ultimately anglophilic love of the game.

More specifically, cricket was elevated to a national sporting pastime in societies where players and audiences were recruited from an array of social class backgrounds. In the United States and Canada, elites literally took cricket from the public sphere and confined it to their own social circles. This contrasts sharply with the history of cricket in the other colonies of the British Empire, where racial inequality, selective access to secondary education, and quasifeudal land allocation systems limited socioeconomic mobility. Those at the top of the economic system felt comfortable sharing their pastimes with the masses. Elites actively promoted and stuck with the game even after it became a sport practiced by low-status members of society. Thus, cricket became a popular sport played and enjoyed by all.

The very nature of the game itself, we have argued, was also an important part of the diffusion process: Cricket's strong identification with English imperialism made it attractive to both those who cherished the "mother country" and those who wished for nothing more than symbolically to defeat it. The sport's absence of physical contact, its strictures on rowdiness, and its low costs when played informally—bats, balls, and stumps can all be handmade—also contributed to its diffusion throughout much of the British Commonwealth.

We argue, furthermore, that it was the relative social mobility of mid-nineteenth-century American and Canadian society that prompted elites there to protect their cultural patrimony from the masses. This reasoning is comparable to that offered in explanation of the development of other forms of exclusionary cultural practice. According to Elias ([1939] 2000), for example, economic elites in late medieval Europe responded to the status pressures of defeudalization by promoting specific repertoires of etiquette by which they might differentiate themselves from the masses. In a more modern context, social elites in late-nineteenth-century Boston responded to similar status pressure by cultivating tastes for European music, art, and theater, as well as creating exclusive social venues in which to partake of them (DiMaggio 1982; Levine 1988; see Dunae 1981 and Gruneau 1983 for comparable analyses of Canada). Seen from this perspective, equality of *economic* opportunity promoted elite efforts to limit equality of *cultural* opportunity.

In the big picture, the history of cricket highlights an important feature of global culture more generally. Global cultural diffusion relies not simply on the transmission of cultural "signals" from place to place, but also on: (1) The relationship among different categories of recipients in host societies, particularly with respect to the distribution of social status among them, as well as the equality of opportunity to gain such status; and (2) the ability of some groups of recipients to dominate or otherwise limit access to cultural imports, thereby "capturing" such imports for themselves. While limiting access to high-status goods might only make them more attractive to lower-status consumers, there is a point of diminishing returns at which popular interest will peak and subsequently subside. Thus, for example, ownership of raw commodities like diamonds and pearls may become more prevalent as their price increases; not so for cultural practices that are more easily "protected."

Access to cricket in the United States and Canada was "overprotected," so to speak, thus forestalling its acculturation as a "hegemonic sports culture." In point of fact, any cultural good or practice can be so protected if it requires: (a) *repeated points of contact*, as in the case of anything that must be learned, replenished, or maintained; (b) *extensive gatekeeping*, as with cultural practices that are sufficiently sophisticated, esoteric, or non-obvious as to require explanation, instruction, or prior evaluation by specialists; and/or (c) *wide-spread collaboration*, as with "social" goods such as musical performances or team sports that require interaction with groups of competitors and/or co-participants. While nearly anything can be had for the right price, some cultural commodities are simply too "social" to be assimilated without ready and consistent support. Thus, the global diffusion of cultural practices requires not only that those in "receiver" societies show interest in these practices, but that the resources necessary to adopt them are widely available. This access often hinges on indigenous elites' desire and ability to keep such resources to themselves.

We see here an important dimension of the cross-cultural diffusion process otherwise over-looked; something we have called, borrowing a term from Rogers (1995), *heterophilous*, or top-down, diffusion. While popular tastes and consumer agency play a large role in the reception and adoption of easily accessible foreign cultural goods and practices—so-called *homophilous* paths to successful diffusion—indigenous elites sometimes play an even more important role in casting imported cultural goods or practices as high- or low-brow items. Elites' ability to control access to such goods has significant ramifications for popular retention thereof. Presumably, cross-national variation in the diffusion of many such items can be explained in exactly this fashion. Thus, it may be that future studies of cross-national cultural diffusion should pay as much attention to elite as to popular tastes. So, too, should the institutionalization of such tastes across public and private venues be of increasing concern to those interested in the topic. Neither value nor venue are a priori features of cultural imports, we argue. Diffusion scholars must then strive for renewed sensitivity toward the culturally specific meanings of the items or practices being diffused, as well as toward the social strata associated with and/or in control of access to their use.

NOTES

1. We are told by an anonymous reviewer familiar with English cricket, however, that "country" cricket is rife with swearing and disputes with officials.

2. It should be noted, moreover, that the popular North American sports of baseball and football have direct ties to the English games of "rounders" and rugby respectively (Dunning and Sheard 1979: 7). In the nineteenth century, two other British "public school" sports, rowing and track and field, were directly incorporated into American collegiate life as well (Smith 1988).

3. Again, we regret the fact that women are not an especially relevant part of this case study. The question of English colonial attitudes toward the moral "improvement" of women is certainly a topic worth further consideration, though it is far beyond the purview of this particular study.

4 Note, however, that English colonial policy in places like India did not originally embrace the anglicization of their native populations either—this was an innovation of the mid-nineteenth century in India (Cashman 1998b:118).

5. PSAL was founded in New York City in 1900 with

the support of Andrew Carnegie, John D. Rock-efeller, and J. Pierpont Morgan. It soon spread to other cities around the United States (Levine 1985: 110–12).

6. The C. C. Morris Cricket Library at Haverford College is an especially useful repository of information about the past and present of American cricket. Online information, including a historical map of Philadelphia cricket clubs, can be found at http://www.haverford.edu/library/cricket.

7. Interestingly, rugby was first promoted in Australia as a way for local cricketers to keep in shape over the winter months (Hickie 1993).

8. It is not clear to us why white New Zealanders did not work to promote the game among Maoris in the same way that Australians did among the Aborigines. It may be related to the Maoris' fierce resistance to white settlement in the early years of the colony, but we were not able to confirm this.

REFERENCES

Adelman, Melvin L. 1986. *A Sporting Time: New York City and the Rise of Modern Athletics, 1820–1870.* Urbana, IL: University of Illinois Press.

Allen, David Rayvern. 1990. *Cricket: An Illustrated History.* Oxford, England: Phaidon Press.

Appadurai, Arjun. 1996. *Modernity at Large: Cultural Dimensions of Globalization.* Minneapolis, MN: University of Minnesota Press.

Baltzell, E. Digby. [1979] 1996. *Puritan Boston and Quaker Philadelphia.* New Brunswick, NJ: Transaction Publishers.

Beckles, Hilary McD. 1998a. *The Development of West Indies Cricket, vol. 1 The Age of Nationalism.* Barbados: Press of the University of the West Indies.

——, ed. 1998b. *A Spirit of Dominance: Cricket and Nationalism in the West Indies.* Barbados: Canoe Press.

Beckles, Hilary McD and Brian Stoddart, eds. 1995. *Liberation Cricket: West Indies Cricket Culture.* Manchester, England: Manchester University Press.

Bhabha, Homi. 1994. *The Location of Culture.* London, England: Routledge Press.

Boller, Kevin. 1994. "International Cricket: Launched by a Hoax." *The Canadian Cricketer* 22:23.

Bose, Mihir. 1990. *A History of Indian Cricket.* London, England: Deutsch.

Bourdieu, Pierre. 1978. "Sport and Social Class." *Social Science Information* 17:819–40.

Brookes, Christopher. 1978. *English Cricket: The Game and Its Players Throughout the Ages.* London, England: Weidenfeld and Nicholson.

Burt, Ronald. 1987. "Social Contagion and Innovation: Cohesion vs. Structural Equivalence." *American Journal of Sociology* 92:1287–335.

Buskens, Vincent and Kazuo Yamaguchi. 1999. "A New Model for Information Diffusion in Heterogeneous Social Networks." *Sociological Methodology* 29: 281–325.

Cashman, Richard. 1979. "The Phenomenon of Indian Cricket." Pp. 180–204 in *Sport in History: The Making of Modern Sporting History*, edited by Richard Cashman and Michael McKernan. Queensland, Australia: University of Queensland Press.

——. 1980. *Patrons, Players and the Crowd: The Phenomenon of Indian Cricket.* New Delhi, India: Orient Longman.

——. 1984. *'Ave a Go, Yer Mug! Australian Cricket Crowds from Larrikin to Ocker.* Sydney, Australia: Collins.

——. 1998a. "Australia." *The Imperial Game: Cricket, Culture and Society*, edited by Brian Stoddart and Keith A. P. Sandiford. Manchester, England: Manchester University Press.

——. 1998b. "The Subcontinent." *The Imperial Game: Cricket, Culture and Society*, edited by Brian Stoddart and Keith A. P. Sandiford. Manchester, England: Manchester University Press.

Chadwick, Henry. 1868. *American Chronicle of Sports and Pastimes* 1:52.

Clark, Manning. 1995. *A Short History of Australia.* 4th rev. ed. Victoria, Australia: Penguin Books.

Clemens, Elisabeth S. and James M. Cook. 1999. "Politics and Institutionalism: Explaining Durability and Change." *Annual Review of Sociology* 25:441–66.

Coakley, J.J. 1998. *Sport in Society.* St. Louis, MO: Mosby.

Cole, Robert E. 1989. *Strategies for Learning: Small-Group Activities in American, Japanese, and Swedish Industry.* Berkeley, CA: University of California Press.

Coleman, James S., Elihu Katz, and Herbert Menzel. 1966. *Medical Innovation: A Diffusion Study.* Indianapolis, IN: Bobbs-Merrill.

Connell, R. W. and T. H. Irving. 1980. *Class Structure in Australian History: Documents, Narrative and Argument.* Melbourne, Australia: Longman Cheshire.

Cozier, Tony. 1978. *The West Indies: Fifty Years of Test Cricket.* Brighton, England: Angus and Robertson.

Crane, Diana. 2000. *Fashion and Its Social Agendas: Class, Gender, and Identity in Clothing.* Chicago, IL: University of Chicago Press.

"Cricket." 1907. *New York Times*, Sept. 21.

DiMaggio, Paul J. 1982. "Cultural Entrepreneurship in Nineteenth-Century Boston." *Media, Culture, and Society* 4:33–50.

DiMaggio, Paul J. and Walter W. Powell. 1983. "The Iron Cage Revisited: Institutional Isomorphism and Collective Rationality in Organizational Fields." *American Sociological Review* 48:147–60.

Dobbin, Frank and John R. Sutton. 1998. "The Strength of a Weak State: The Rights Revolution and the Rise of Human Resources Management Divisions." *American Journal of Sociology* 104: 441–76.

Dunae, P.A. 1981. *Gentlemen Emigrants: From the British Public Schools to the Canadian Frontier.* Vancouver, Canada: Douglas and McIntyre.

Dunning, Eric and Kenneth Sheard. 1979. *Barbarians, Gentlemen and Players: A Sociological Study of the Development of Rugby Football.* New York: New York University Press.

Elias, Norbert. [1939] 2000. *The Civilizing Process.* Rev. ed. Oxford, England: Blackwell.

Frye, Northrop. 1971. *The Bush Garden: Essays on the Canadian Imagination*. Toronto, Canada: Anansi.

"The Game Was Stopped." 1888. New York Times, May 21.

Gottdiener, M. 1985. "Hegemony and Mass Culture: A Semiotic Approach." *American Journal of Sociology* 90:979–1001.

Granovetter, Mark and Roland Soong. 1983. "Threshold Models of Diffusion and Collective Behavior." *Journal of Mathematical Sociology* 9: 165–79.

Gruneau, Richard. 1983. *Class, Sports, and Social Development*. Amherst, MA: University of Massachusetts Press.

Guillén, Mauro F. 1994. *Models of Management: Work, Authority, and Organization in a Comparative Perspective*. Chicago, IL: University of Chicago Press.

——. 2001. *The Limits of Convergence: Globalization and Organizational Change in Argentina, South Korea, and Spain*. Princeton, NJ: Princeton University Press.

Gunaratnam, Visva. 1993. "I Have a Dream." *The Canadian Cricketer* 21: 11.

Hall, John E. and R. O. McCulloch. 1895. *Sixty Years of Canadian Cricket*. Toronto, Canada: Bryant.

Harvard College. 1889. *Annual Reports of the President and Treasurer of Harvard College, 1887–1888*. Cambridge, MA: Harvard College.

Headlam, Cecil. 1903. *Ten Thousand Miles Through India and Burma: An Account of the Oxford University Authentics' Cricket Tour with Mr. K. J. Key in the Year of the Durbar*. London, England: Dent.

Hickie, Thomas V. 1993. *They Ran with the Ball: How Rugby Football Began in Australia*. Melbourne, Australia: Longman Cheshire.

Hughes, Robert. 1986. *The Fatal Shore: The Epic of Australia's Founding*. New York: Vintage.

Humber, William. 1995. *Diamonds of the North: A Concise History of Baseball in Canada*. Toronto, Canada: Oxford University Press.

James, C.L.R. 1963. *Beyond a Boundary*. London, England: Hutchinson.

Kaufman, Jason. 2002. *For the Common Good? American Civic Life and the Golden Age of Fraternity*. New York: Oxford University Press.

Kirsch, George. 1991. "Massachusetts Baseball and Cricket, 1840–1870." Pp. 1–15 in *Sports in Massachusetts: Historical Essays*, edited by Ronald Story. Westfield, MA: Institute for Massachusetts Studies, Westfield State College.

Kirsch, George. 1989. *The Creation of American Team Sports: Baseball and Cricket, 1838–72*. Urbana, IL: University of Illinois Press.

Lester, John A., ed. 1951. *A Century of Philadelphia Cricket*. Philadelphia, PA: University of Pennsylvania Press.

Levine, Lawrence W. 1988. *Highbrow/Lowbrow: The Emergence of Cultural Hierarchy in America*. Cambridge, MA: Harvard University Press.

Levine, Peter. 1985. *A. G. Spalding and the Rise of Baseball: The Promise of American Sport*. New York: Oxford University Press.

Lillrank, Paul. 1995. "The Transfer of Management Innovations from Japan." *Organization Studies* 16: 971–89.

Lipset, Seymour Martin. 1996. *American Exceptionalism: A Double-Edged Sword*. New York: Norton.

Maguire, Joseph. 1999. *Global Sport: Identities, Societies, Civilizations*. Oxford, England: Polity Press.

Malcolm, Dominic. 2001. " 'It's Not Cricket': Colonial Legacies and Contemporary Inequalities." *Journal of Historical Sociology* 14: 253–75.

Mandle, W.F. 1973. "Games People Played: Cricket and Football in England and Victoria in the Late Nineteenth Century." *Historical Studies* 15(60): 511–535.

Mangan, J. A. 1986. *The Games Ethic and Imperialism: Aspects of the Diffusion of an Ideal*. London, England: Frank Cass.

Marsden, Peter and Joel Podolny. 1990. "Dynamic Analysis of Network Diffusion Processes." *Social Networks Through Time*, edited by J. Weesie and H. Flap. Utrecht, Netherlands: ISOR.

Melville, Tom. 1998. *The Tented Field: A History of Cricket in America*. Bowling Green, IN: Bowling Green State University Popular Press.

Merrett, Christopher and John Nauright. 1998. "South Africa." Pp. 55–78 in *The Imperial Game: Cricket, Culture and Society*, edited by Brian Stoddart and Keith A. P. Sandiford. Manchester, England: Manchester University Press.

Metcalfe, Alan. 1987. *Canada Learns to Play: The Emergence of Organized Sport, 1807–1914*. Toronto, Canada: McClelland and Stewart.

Meyer, John and Michael Hannan, eds. 1979. *National Development and the World System: Educational, Economic and Political Change, 1950–1970*. Chicago, IL: University of Chicago Press.

Miller, Toby, Geoffrey Lawrence, Jim McKay, and David Rowe. 2001. *Globalization and Sport*, London, England: Sage Publications.

Mizruchi, Mark S. and Lisa C. Fein. 1999. "The Social Construction of Organizational Knowledge: A Study of the Uses of Coercive, Mimetic, and Normative Isomorphism." *Administrative Science Quarterly* 44: 653–83.

Molotch, Harvey, William Freudenburg and Krista E. Paulsen. 2000. "History Repeats Itself, but How? City Character, Urban Tradition, and the Accomplishment of Place." *American Sociological Review* 65:791–823.

Mrozek, Donald J. 1983. *Sport and American Mentality, 1880–1910*. Knoxville, TN: University of Tennessee Press.

Nandy, Ashis. 2000. *The Tao of Cricket: On Games of Destiny and Destiny of Games*. New Delhi, India: Oxford University Press.

Palloni, Alberto. 2001. "Diffusion in Sociological Analysis." Pp. 67–114 in *Diffusion Processes and Fertility Transition: Selected Perspectives*, edited by John B. Casterline. Washington D.C.: National Academy Press.

Patterson, Orlando. 1994. "Ecumenical America: Global Culture and the American Cosmos." *World Policy Journal* 11: 103–17.

——. 1995. "The Ritual of Cricket." Pp. 141–47 in *Liberation Cricket*, edited by Hilary McD Beckles and Brian Stoddart. Kingston, Jamaica: Ian Randle Publishers.

Penn, Alan. 1999. *Targeting Schools: Drill, Militarism and Imperialism*. London, England: Woburn Press.

"The Philadelphia Cricketers." 1884. *New York Times*, July 15.

Pollard, Jack. 1987. *The Formative Years of Australian Cricket, 1803–1893*. North Ryde, Australia: Angus and Robertson.

Redmond, Gerald. 1979. "Some Aspects of Organized Sport and Leisure in Nineteenth-Century Canada." *Loisir et société/Society and Leisure* 2:73–100.

Reese, T. W. 1927. *New Zealand Cricket, 1814–1914*. Christchurch, New Zealand: Simpson and Williams.

Rogers, Everett M. 1995. *Diffusion of Innovations*. 4th ed. New York: Free Press.

Ryan, Greg. 1998. "New Zealand." Pp. 93–115 in *The Imperial Game: Cricket, Culture and Society*, edited by Brian Stoddart and Keith A. P. Sandiford. Manchester, England: Manchester University Press.

Sandiford, Keith A. P. 1994. *Cricket and the Victorians*. Aldershot, England: Scholar Press.

——. 1998a. "England." Pp. 9–33 in *The Imperial Game: Cricket, Culture and Society*, edited by Brian Stoddart and Keith A. P. Sandiford. Manchester, England: Manchester University Press.

——. 1998b. "Introduction." Pp. 1–8 in *The Imperial Game: Cricket, Culture and Society*, edited by Brian Stoddart and Keith A. P. Sandiford. Manchester, England: Manchester University Press.

——. 1998c. *Cricket Nurseries of Colonial Barbados: The Elite Schools, 1865–1966*. Barbados: Press of the University of the West Indies.

Sayen, Henry. 1956. *A Yankee Looks At Cricket*. London, England: Putnam.

Schudson, Michael. 1989. "How Culture Works: Perspectives from Media Studies on the Efficacy of Symbols." *Theory and Society* 18:153–80.

Smith, Ronald A. 1988. *Sports and Freedom: The Rise of Big-Time College Athletics*. New York: Oxford University Press.

Spalding, Albert G. [1911] 1992. *America's National Game*. Lincoln, NE: University of Nebraska Press.

Starr, Paul. 1989. "The Meaning of Privatization." Pp. 15–48 in *Privatization and the Welfare State*, edited by Sheila Kamerman and Alfred Kahn. Princeton, NJ: Princeton University Press.

Steen, Rob. 1999. *The Official Companion to the 1999 Cricket World Cup*. London: Boxtree.

Stoddart, Brian. 1988. "Sport, Cultural Imperialism, and Colonial Response in the British Empire." *Comparative Studies in Society and History* 30: 649–73.

——. 1998a. "West Indies." *The Imperial Game: Cricket, Culture and Society*, edited by Brian Stoddart and Keith A. P. Sandiford. Manchester, England: Manchester University Press.

——. 1998b. "Other Cultures." *The Imperial Game: Cricket, Culture and Society*, edited by Brian Stoddart and Keith A. P. Sandiford. Manchester

Stoddart, Brian and Keith A. P. Sandiford, eds. 1998. *The Imperial Game: Cricket, Culture and Society*. Manchester, England: Manchester University Press.

Stone, Derrick I. and Donald S. Garden. 1978. *Squatters and Settlers*. Sydney, Australia: Reed.

Strang, David. 1990. "From Dependency to Sovereignty: An Event History Analysis of Decolonization 1870–1987." *American Sociological Review* 55: 846–60.

Strang, David and John Meyer. 1993. "Institutional Conditions for Diffusion." *Theory and Society* 22:487–511.

Strang, David and Sarah Soule. 1998. "Diffusion in Organizations and Social Movements: From Hybrid Corn to Poison Pills." *Annual Review of Sociology* 24:265–90.

Townsend, Kim. 1996. *Manhood at Harvard: William James and Others*. Cambridge, MA: Harvard University Press.

Vaille, F. O. and H. A. Clark, eds. 1875. *The Harvard Book: A Series of Historical, Biographical, and Descriptive Sketches*. Cambridge: Welch, Bigelow.

Van den Bulte, Christophe and Gary L. Lilien. 2001. "Medical Innovation Revisited: Social Contagion versus Marketing Effort." *American Journal of Sociology* 106:1409–35.

Warner, Sir Pelham. 1950. *Gentlemen v. Players, 1806–1949*. London: George G. Harrap.

Watson, James L. 2002. "Transnationalism, Localization, and Fast Foods in East Asia." Pp. 222–32 *McDonaldization: The Reader*, edited by George Ritzer. Thousand Oaks, CA: Pine Forge Press.

Wejnert, Barbara. 2002. "Integrating Models of Diffusion of Innovations: A Conceptual Framework." *Annual Review of Sociology* 28:297–326.

Williams, Jack. 2001. *Cricket and Race*. Oxford, England: Berg.

Winch, Jonty. 1983. *Cricket's Rich Heritage: A History of Rhodesian and Zimbabwean Cricket, 1890–1982*. (Bulawayo, Zimbabwe: Books of Zimbabwe).

Wise, S. F. 1989. "Sport and Class Values in Old Ontario and Quebec." Pp. 107–129 in *Sports in Canada: Historical Readings*, edited by Morris Mott. Toronto, Canada: Copp, Clark, Pitman.

CHAPTER 37

Transnationalism, Localization, and Fast Foods in East Asia

James L. Watson

[. . .]

Chinese political leaders have expressed alarm at the growing influence of McDonald's, Kentucky Fried Chicken (KFC), Pizza Hut, and other foreign food firms. As Chinese state policy has begun to encourage an indigenous fast food industry, local media coverage has shifted accordingly.[1] Chinese leaders appear to be aligning themselves with European and American intellectuals who have long equated McDonald's and its rivals in the fast food industry as agents of *cultural imperialism*—a new form of exploitation that results from the export of popular culture from the United States, Japan, and Europe to other parts of the world.[2] "Culture" in this context is defined as popular music, television, film, video, pulp fiction, comics, advertising, fashion, home design, and mass-produced food. Corporations that are capable of manipulating personal "tastes" will thrive as state authorities lose control over the distribution and consumption of goods and services. Popular culture, in this view, generates a vision, a fantasy, of the good life, and if the Big Mac, Coke, and Disney cartoons are perceived as an integral part of that life, American companies cannot lose.[3]

Theorists who write about cultural imperialism argue that it is the domination of popular culture—rather than outright military or political control—that matters most in the postmodern, postsocialist, postindustrial world.[4] One of the clearest expressions of this view appeared recently on the Op-Ed page of the *New York Times*. The voice is Ronald Steel's: "It was never the Soviet Union, but the United States itself that is the true revolutionary power. . . . We purvey a culture based on mass entertainment and mass gratification. . . . The cultural message we transmit through Hollywood and McDonald's goes out across the world to capture, and also to undermine, other societies. . . . Unlike more traditional conquerors, we are not content merely to subdue others: We insist that they be like us."[5]

McDONALD'S AS A CORROSIVE FORCE?

Does the spread of fast food undermine the integrity of indigenous cuisines? Are food chains helping to create a homogenous, global culture better suited to the needs of a capitalist world order?

This book is specifically designed to address such questions. The authors of the following case studies have different perspectives on the cultural imperialism debate, reflecting circumstances in the societies studied. We do not celebrate McDonald's as a paragon of capitalist virtue, nor do we condemn the corporation as an evil empire. Our goal is to produce ethnographic accounts of McDonald's social, political, and economic impact on five local cultures. These are not small-scale cultures under imminent threat of extinction; we are dealing with economically resilient, technologically advanced societies noted for their haute cuisines. If McDonald's can make inroads in these societies, one might be tempted to conclude, it may indeed be an irresistible force for world culinary change. But isn't another scenario possible? Have people in East Asia conspired to change McDonald's, modifying this seemingly monolithic institution to fit local conditions?

The essays in this book demonstrate that the interaction process works both ways. McDonald's *has* effected small but influential changes in East Asian dietary patterns. Until the introduction of McDonald's, for example, Japanese consumers rarely, if ever, ate with their hands; as Emiko Ohnuki-Tierney shows in Chapter 5, this is now an acceptable mode of dining. In Hong Kong, McDonald's has replaced traditional tea-houses and street stalls as the most popular breakfast venue. And among Taiwanese youth, french fries have become a dietary staple, owing almost entirely to the influence of McDonald's.

At the same time, however, East Asian consumers have quietly, and in some cases stubbornly, transformed their neighborhood McDonald's into local institutions. In the United States fast food may indeed imply fast consumption, but this is certainly not the case everywhere. In Beijing, Seoul, and Taipei, for instance, McDonald's restaurants are treated as leisure centers, where people can retreat from the stresses of urban life. In Hong Kong, middle school students often sit in McDonald's for hours—studying, gossiping, and picking over snacks; for them, the restaurants are the equivalent of youth clubs. More will be said about the localization process in the following chapters. Suffice it to note here that McDonald's does not always call the shots. . . .

MODIFIED MENUS AND LOCAL SENSITIVITIES: McDONALD'S ADAPTS

The key to McDonald's worldwide success is that people everywhere know what to expect when they pass through the Golden Arches. This does not mean, however, that the corporation has resisted change or refused to adapt when local customs require flexibility. In Israel, after initial protests, Big Macs are now served without cheese in several outlets, thereby permitting the separation of meat and dairy products required of kosher restaurants.[6] McDonald's restaurants in India serve Vegetable McNuggets and a mutton-based Maharaja Mac, innovations that are necessary in a country where Hindus do not eat beef, Muslims do not eat pork, and Jains (among others) do not eat meat of any type.[7] In Malaysia and Singapore, McDonald's underwent rigorous inspections by Muslim clerics to ensure ritual cleanliness; the chain was rewarded with a *halal* ("clean," "acceptable") certificate, indicating the total absence of pork products.[8]

Variations on McDonald's original, American-style menu exist in many parts of the world: Chilled yogurt drinks (*ayran*) in Turkey, espresso and cold pasta in Italy, teriyaki burgers in Japan (also in Taiwan and Hong Kong), vegetarian burgers in the Netherlands, McSpagetti in the Philippines, McLaks (grilled salmon sandwich) in Norway, frankfurters and beer in Germany, McHuevo (poached egg hamburger) in Uruguay.[9]

Not all McDonald's menu innovations have been embraced by consumers: Witness the famous McLean Deluxe fiasco in the United States and a less publicized disaster called McPloughman's in Britain (a cheese-and-pickle sandwich).[10] The corporation has responded to constant criticism from nutritionists and natural food activists by introducing prepackaged salads, fresh celery and carrot sticks, fat-free bran muffins, and low-fat milk shakes.[11] These efforts may satisfy critics but they are unlikely to change McDonald's public image among consumers, few of whom stop at the Golden Arches for health food.

Irrespective of local variations (espresso, McLaks) and recent additions (carrot sticks), the structure of the McDonald's menu remains essentially uniform the world over: main course burger/sandwich, fries, and a drink—overwhelmingly Coca-Cola. The keystone of this winning combination is *not*, as most observers might assume, the Big Mac or even the generic hamburger. It is the fries. The main course may vary widely (fish sandwiches in Hong Kong, vegetable burgers in Amsterdam), but the signature innovation of McDonald's—thin, elongated fries cut from russet potatoes—is ever-present and consumed with great gusto by Muslims, Jews, Christians, Buddhists, Hindus, vegetarians (now that vegetable oil is used), communists, Tories, marathoners, and armchair athletes. It is understandable, therefore, why McDonald's has made such a fetish of its deep-fried potatoes and continues to work on improving the delivery of this industry winner. The Chairman of Burger King acknowledges that his company's fries are second-best in comparison to those of its archrival: "Our fries just don't hold up." A research program, code-named "stealth fries," is specifically designed to upgrade Burger King's offerings . . .[12]

CONCLUSION: McDONALDIZATION VERSUS LOCALIZATION

McDonald's has become such a powerful symbol of the standardization and routinization of modern life that it has inspired a new vocabulary: McThink, McMyth, McJobs, McSpirituality, and, of course, McDonaldization.[13] George Ritzer, author of a popular book entitled *The McDonaldization of Society*, uses the term to describe "the process by which the principles of the fast food restaurant are coming to dominate more and more sectors of . . . society."[14] Ritzer treats McDonald's as the "paradigm case" of social regimentation and argues that "McDonaldization has shown every sign of being an inexorable process as it sweeps through seemingly impervious institutions and parts of the world."[15]

Is McDonald's in fact the revolutionary, disruptive institution that theorists of cultural imperialism deem it to be? Evidence from this book could be marshaled in support of such a view, but only at the risk of ignoring historical process. There is indeed an initial, "intrusive" encounter when McDonald's enters a new market—especially in an environment where American-style fast food is largely unknown to the ordinary consumer. In all five cases surveyed in this book, McDonald's was treated as an exotic import—a taste of Americana—during its first few years of operation. Indeed, the company drew on this association to establish itself in foreign markets. But this initial euphoria cannot sustain a mature business.

Unlike Coca-Cola and Spam, for instance,

McDonald's standard fare (the burger-and-fries combo) could not be absorbed into the preexisting cuisines of East Asia. As Bak notes in Chapter 4, Spam quickly became an integral feature of Korean cooking in the aftermath of the Korean War; it was a recognizable form of meat that required no special preparation. Coca-Cola, too, was a relatively neutral import when first introduced to Chinese consumers. During the 1960s, villagers in rural Hong Kong treated Coke as a special beverage, reserved primarily for medicinal use. It was served most frequently as *bo ho la*, Cantonese for "boiled Cola," a tangy blend of fresh ginger and herbs served in piping hot Coke—an excellent remedy for colds. Only later was the beverage consumed by itself, first at banquets (mixed with brandy) and later for special events such as a visit by relatives. There was nothing particularly revolutionary about Coca-Cola or Spam; both products were quickly adapted to suit local needs and did not require any radical adjustments on the part of consumers.

McDonald's is something altogether different. Eating at the Golden Arches is a total experience, one that takes people out of their ordinary routines. One "goes to" McDonald's; it does not come to the consumer, nor is it taken home (in most parts of the world, that is). Unlike packaged products, McDonald's items are sold hot and ready-to-eat, thereby separating the buyer from the acts of cooking and preparation. One consumes a completed set of products, not the component parts of a home-cooked meal.

From this vantage point it would appear that McDonald's may indeed have been an intrusive force, undermining the integrity of East Asian cuisines. On closer inspection, however, it is clear that consumers are not the automatons many analysts would have us believe. The initial encounter soon begins to fade as McDonald's loses its exotic appeal and gradually gains acceptance (or rejection) as ordinary food for busy consumers. The hamburger-fries combo becomes simply another alternative among many types of ready-made food.

The process of localization is a two-way street: It implies changes in the local culture as well as modifications in the company's standard operating procedures. Key elements of McDonald's industrialized system— queuing, self-provisioning, self-seating— have been accepted by consumers throughout East Asia. Other aspects of the industrial model have been rejected, notably those relating to time and space. In many parts of East Asia, consumers have turned their local McDonald's into leisure centers and after-school clubs. The meaning of "fast" has been subverted in these settings: It refers to the *delivery* of food, not to its consumption. Resident managers have had little choice but to embrace these consumer trends and make virtues of them: "Students create a good atmosphere which is good for our business," one Hong Kong manager told me as he surveyed a sea of young people chatting, studying, and snacking in his restaurant.

The process of localization correlates closely with the maturation of a generation of local people who grew up eating at the Golden Arches. By the time the children of these original consumers enter the scene, McDonald's is no longer perceived as a foreign enterprise. Parents see it as a haven of cleanliness and predictability. For children McDonald's represents fun, familiarity, and a place where they can choose their own food—something that may not be permitted at home.

The case studies in this book also make it clear that localization is not a unilinear process that ends the same everywhere. McDonald's has become a routine, unremarkable feature of the urban landscape in Japan and Hong Kong. It is so "local" that many younger consumers do not know of the company's foreign origins. The process of localization has hardly begun in China, where McDonald's outlets are still treated as exotic outposts, selling a cultural experience rather than food. At this writing it is unclear what will happen to expansion efforts in Korea; the political environment there is such that many citizens will continue to treat the Golden Arches as a symbol of American imperialism. In Taiwan the confused, and exhilarating, pace of identity politics may well rebound on American corporations, in ways as yet unseen. Irrespective of these imponderables, McDonald's is no longer

dependent on the United States market for its future development. In 1994 McDonald's operating revenues from non-U.S. sales passed the 50 percent mark; market analysts predict that by the end of the 1990s this figure will rise to 60 percent.[16]

As McDonald's enters the twenty-first century, its multilocal strategy, like its famous double-arches logo, is being pirated by a vast array of corporations eager to emulate its success. In the end, however, McDonald's is likely to prove difficult to clone. The reason, of course, is that the Golden Arches have always represented something other than food. McDonald's symbolizes different things to different people at different times in their lives: Predictability, safety, convenience, fun, familiarity, sanctuary, cleanliness, modernity, culinary tourism, and "connectedness" to the world beyond. Few commodities can match this list of often contradictory attributes. One is tempted to conclude that, in McDonald's case, the primary product is the experience itself.

NOTES

1. See Lana Wong, "Noodles Take on Sesame Seed Buns," SCMP *International Weekly* (SCMPIW), July 13, 1996, p. B3. Ma Zhiping reports that the first "national development plan for fast food production . . . will soon be announced by the State Council" (*China Daily*, Mar. 14, 1996).

2. For a discussion of this theme, see John Tomlinson, *Cultural Imperialism: A Critical Introduction* (Baltimore: Johns Hopkins Univ. Press, 1991). Ester Reiter's book *Making Fast Food* (Montreal: McGill Queen's Univ. Press, 1991) focuses on Burger King's "invasion" of Canada; for another view, see Phil Lyon et al., "Is Big Mac the Big Threat?" *International Journal of Hospitality Management* 14(2): 119–22 (1995).

3. See John Huey, "America's Hottest Export: Pop Culture," *Fortune*, Dec. 31, 1990, pp. 50–60.

4. See, for example, Ariel Dorfman and Armand Mattelart, *How To Read Donald Duck: Imperialist Ideology in the Disney Comic* (New York: International General, 1975).

5. Ronald Steel, "When Worlds Collide," NYT, July 21, 1996.

6. Reuters, "First Kosher McDonald's Opens in Israel," Oct. 11, 1995. Clarinet.biz.industry-.food:3859. Earlier outlets in Israel were non-kosher and had sparked protests; see, e.g., Lisa Talesnick, "Rabbi Battles Golden Arches," *Boston Globe*, Mar. 23, 1995.

7. Jonathan Karp, "Food for Politics: McDonald's

Opens in India's Prickly Market," FEER, Oct. 24, 1996, p. 72; Dan Biers and Miriam Jordan, "McDonald's in India Decides the Big Mac Is Not a Sacred Cow," WSJ, Oct. 14, 1996, p. A11. Given KFC's recent problems with Hindu nationalists and radical vegetarians, other fast food chains (including McDonald's) appear to have shelved expansion plans for India; see Miriam Jordan, "U.S. Food Firms Head for Cover in India," WSJ, Nov. 21, 1995, p. A14. On January 30, 1996, demonstrators broke through a police cordon in Bangalore and ransacked a KFC outlet (NYT, Jan. 31, 1996). Earlier a KFC restaurant was closed by New Delhi health inspectors after they spotted two flies in the kitchen; the "discovery" caused great hilarity in the local press (NYT, Nov. 25, 1995, p. 4).

8. John Oleck, "When Worlds Collide," *Restaurant Business* 92 (10): 48–56 (July 1, 1993), p. 50.

9. Holly Chase, "The *Meyhane* or McDonald's?" p. 75; Silvia Sansoni, "Big Macs Al Dente?" BW, Nov. 28, 1994, p. 8 (Italy); Harlan Byrne, "Welcome to McWorld," *Barron's*, Aug. 29, 1994, p. 25 (Netherlands); *Welcome to McDonald's*, 1996, McDonald's Corp., McD 5–2940, p. 29 (Philippines, Norway, Germany, Uruguay); and personal observations in Japan, Taiwan, and Hong Kong.

10. Richard Gibson, "McDonald's Decides to Trim the Low Fat in Menu Shake-Up," WSJ, Feb. 5, 1996, p. B5; Simon Midgeley, "Big Mac Gets a Mouthful of Abuse," *The Independent*, Oct. 28, 1994.

11. James Scarpa, "McDonald's Menu Mission," *Restaurant Business*, July 1, 1991, p. 4.

12. Julie Vorman (Reuter), "Burger King to Dish Up 'Stealth' Fries," Mar. 20, 1996. Clarinet.biz.industry.food:4562; see also, "America's Fry-Meisters Go to War," BW, Sept. 16, 1996, p. 8.

13. Hamilton Beazley and John Lobuts, "Rational Teaching, Indentured Research, and the Loss of Reason," *Academe*, Jan.-Feb. 1996, p. 30 (McThink, McMyth); Douglas Coupland, *Generation X* (New York: St. Martin's, 1991) (McJobs); Eugene Kennedy, quoted in NYT, July 13, 1996 (McSpirituality).

14. George Ritzer, *The McDonaldization of Society* (Thousand Oaks, Calif.: Pine Forge Press, 1991), p. 1.

15. Ibid.

16. "All the World's a McStage," BW, May 8, 1995, p. 8. Meanwhile McDonald's has become the world's leading brand name, according to Interbrand, a consultancy that specializes in consumer recognition; McDonald's has surpassed Coca-Cola, which was the number one brand name in 1990. See *The Economist*, Nov. 16, 1996, p. 72.

SECTION 9

Corporations, Classes, and Capitalism

Introduction to Section 9

Studies of transnational capitalism, corporations, and classes are probably the best known and most numerous of the topics covered in this volume. Much of this literature examines cross-boundary dynamics that are transcontinental but not planetary in scope, or investigates the complicated linkages and layering of these phenomena across multiple scales and sites.

George Modelski's excerpt organizes the study of transnational enterprises around four interrelated questions: 1. how and where these transnational corporations operate; 2. what are the histories of the most important transnational entities; 3. how the fortunes of these transnational companies shift and the resulting changes in the broader transnational business sector over time; and 4. the world-historical orders (such as Pax Britannica) that shape the emergence and functioning of transnational enterprises. Modelski acknowledges that world-historical orders shaped by powerful states are critical to enabling or potentially disabling transnational corporations. But he also concludes that much more is at stake. Multiple types of research (comparative-historical, institutional, biographical, statistical, etc.) are needed to get at how transnational corporations actually behave and plan in various contexts.

Peter Evans continues the discussion by exploring the connections between imperialism, dependency, and dependent development. Although dependency theorists contribute to historical scholarship on imperialism, they focus less on the conditions giving rise to the global spread of capitalism from core countries and more on the linkages between changes in imperialism and capitalism and dynamics within peripheral countries. Evans reviews previous dependency scholars' notions of "transnational kernel," "transitional alliances," and "associated dependent development" to develop an argument about the "triple alliance"—a transnational coalition among locally dominant elites, international capital, and peripheral country states that allows some degree of industrialization in large countries, such as Brazil, to occur.

Gary Gereffi develops a commodity chains perspective that "highlights the need to look not only at the geographical spread of transnational production arrangements, but also their organizational scope." A commodity chain has three transnational dimensions: 1. an inter-linked input–output structure; 2. a "territoriality" or geographic dispersion of production; and 3. a governance structure that coordinates the production activities. Producer-driven governance structures are those in which transnational manufacturing corporations play the central controlling role. In contrast, buyer-driven governance structures are those where large retailers, brand-named merchandisers, and trading companies are the key decision-makers. From Gereffi's perspective, the latter is a relatively novel form of transnationally organized trade. It captures how large-volume buyers, located in developed countries, shape the production networks established in some newly industrialized exporting countries, which then develop subcontracting arrangements with producers in even more peripheral economies.

In the final excerpt in this section, Aihwa Ong critiques the analytic model of multiple modernities. She does not see globalization as capitalist economic rationality bereft of human agency and she does not place the local in cultural opposition to the global. She prefers to speak about transnationality not only because it suggests "new relations between nation-states and capital" but also because it "alludes to the *trans*versal, the *trans*actional, the *trans*gressive aspects of contemporary behavior and imagination." Ong interrogates these understandings of transnationality through an ethnography of "greater China" and the Asia-Pacific. Her focus on overseas Chinese yields new understandings of flexible citizenship, graduate sovereignty, and fraternal network capitalism.

CHAPTER 38

"Introduction" from *Transnational Corporations and World Order*

George Modelski

Knowledge of the world of business and of its impact on the world at large is to a substantial degree independent of knowledge of the theories that have been spun about business activities. The business world exists in large part irrespectively of the numerous concepts and theories that can be and have been applied to its understanding. Ultimately, and fundamentally, of course, such a clear-cut division between theory and reality cannot be maintained: what we perceive and what we know depend in turn on the validity of our theories and the strength of our concepts; but for practical purposes the division can be defended as a helpful expository device. This pool of empirical knowledge is in fact the common resource on which most observers of transnational business draw in their search for explanation and meaning.

A student of transnational enterprises, then, should acquire a store of basic information about:

1. How and where transnational enterprises operate.
2. The names and background of the most important of these corporations.
3. How changeable the world of business really is and how the fortunes of companies rise and fall.
4. The world order within which these enterprises function, and the historical circumstances from which they have emerged.

In 1972, the United Nations launched its own inquiry into the role and current situation of multinational corporations. According to the report of the Secretariat in New York which was used as a source of background information by the Group of Eminent Persons, whose recommendations we shall note in Part IV, multinationals are a global phenomenon. Even though the investment of United States firms is largest in volume, the firms of other countries are also active in this important field, and in some parts of the world, such as Africa and parts of Asia, they are more numerous and more important. The major part of all transnational business is located in the developed areas of North America, Western Europe, and Japan. Although only about one-third of all transnational corporate activity is conducted in the developing countries of the Third World, the political significance of that activity is greater than the proportion would suggest. Manufacturing accounts for about two-fifths of the total, all phases of the oil industry account for another third. Multinational banking, too, has grown spectacularly in recent years. International production, that is, the output of branches of transnational firms located outside the national base, is now a substantial proportion of the world product—possibly as high as one-fifth if the centrally planned economies are omitted from the calculation. Although these are global figures, an accurate picture of the situation must also include country-by-country variations; for instance, the extremely strong investment position of multinational firms (and in particular American firms) in Canada, and, by contrast, their rather weak position in Japan. There are also differences by industry; for example, multinationals invest heavily in petroleum refining and advanced technology, but not at all in public utilities or transportation, which were in earlier decades important fields for foreign investment. Finally, the role of multinationals in the centrally planned economies of the Soviet Union, Eastern Europe, and possibly even China, should not be ignored. But we should also bear in mind the necessity of keeping such a picture up to date, because the world, and international business conditions, are capable of rapid change.[1]

Students of transnational corporations will at some stage encounter the problem of definitions, and will find that a variety of terms are used to refer to what is basically one phenomenon. The United Nations study opens with a useful survey of definitions, which indicates that multinational activities require the physical presence of the corporation in a number of national jurisdictions, hence raising problems of supervision and control.

A classification scheme that has attracted considerable attention was described in an article by Howard V. Perlmutter of the Wharton School of Business at the University of Pennsylvania, which was published in 1968. Perlmutter proposes that firms be classified according to the attitudes and policies of their executives toward their international operations. He labels corporations either as "ethnocentric," "polycentric," or "geocentric," and these terms have proved useful in distinguishing among companies whose behavior might at first seem indistinguishable. Perlmutter himself is an enthusiast for geocentric enterprises; he sees them as a "new kind of institution" and views those building them as "the most important social architects of our time."

George Modelski, a specialist in international relations, demonstrates with the help of discriminant analysis that Perlmutter's notion that firms with large-scale international operations are likely to show greater viability over the long run was true for the world's fifty largest industrial firms in the period 1955–1975. He points out, too, that these large-scale international operations have yet to have a corresponding degree of international control (that is, non-national participation in decision-making). This article may also prove useful for the empirical

information it makes available about those very large companies. For large corporations are not unlike countries: they have a history and an identity of their own, and to be understood, each of them needs to be known on its own terms. The most important and the most interesting among them are the global firms, that is, those with high international content. Familiarity with these principal actors of world business is as necessary as knowledge of the major powers and the important states is to the student of world politics.

Robert Gilpin describes the historical background of transnational corporations and the conditions of world order within which all transnational corporations have to operate. After reviewing the various positions with regard to the interdependence of political and economic relations at the global level, he concludes that politics determine economic activity, and that therefore, transnational actors are influenced by peculiar patterns of international politics. In the nineteenth century, Britain provided the political context within which free traders, bankers, railroad builders, and other investors could successfully engage in a considerable degree of transnational activity. More recently, Gilpin argues, multinational corporations have flourished because it has been in the best interest of the United States that they should do so and within the power of the United States to ensure that they do. He clearly implies that a change in the interests or the power of the United States would have a severe effect on transnational enterprises.

Gilpin (who teaches political science at Princeton University), an exponent of what might be described as the "politics in command" thesis, sees multinational corporations principally as the product, or the resultant, of a pre-existing structure of world order. Although he acknowledges the power of the oil companies, for instance, he tends to underplay their influence on world politics. We should take note of this view, for we shall wish to return to it later for some additional and qualifying observations.

Mira Wilkins's *The Emergence of Multinational Enterprise*[2] is a study of the international involvement of American business in 1914, on the eve of World War I and prior to the assumption of a world role by the United States, and may be consulted as an alternative to Gilpin's broad generalizations. A business historian, she shows how remarkably active American business was transnationally even at the beginning of this century. She points out that, in proportion to gross national product, overseas investment probably was as great in 1914 as it was to become after 1945. For her, it would seem, American multinationals loom large today because the United States economy too has become larger and more productive; but relatively speaking, multinationals are no more important today than they were two or three generations ago. American firms flourished in 1914 because the United States economy was buoyant and because its innovative products (such as electrical equipment, cars, and petroleum) were sought the world over and the supplies needed to produce them were also sought all over the globe. Her model is one of "autodetermination" of transnational economic activity. Such processes unfold as an expression of the strength of particular economies and of their characteristics as areas of growth. Such "active zones" also give rise to strong transnational interpenetration.

But before the reader fully accepts such a position, he should look in some detail at the data. Transnational business cannot be so easily separated from world politics. In 1914 United States enterprises prospered generally in what was then still the British system of world order, even though that system had by that time already lost most of its vitality. The historical affinities between New York and London, and the growing convergence of United States and British diplomatic positions, also meant that American firms were particularly strong in the English-speaking parts of the world: in Britain itself (still the premier economy then), and in Canada, Australia, India, South Africa, and such important outposts as Hong Kong and Shanghai. In other words, American enterprise found congenial the conditions of the later phase of *Pax Britannica*, and could thus negotiate with some success the transition from the British to the American system of world order. Neither Gilpin nor Wilkins intends to

imply that the role of firms other than American should be ignored. The companies of Britain and other European countries flourished and competed in the years before 1914, but not all weathered well the period of the world wars.

The last step in attempting to understand how transnational corporations behave and decide in various contexts is to study a few individual corporations in some detail. To accomplish this objective we need accurate and interesting "biographical" studies of crucial firms, but considerations of space preclude the inclusion of selections on this subject. Histories commissioned by firms tend to concentrate on business problems at the expense of social and political insights. C. Wilson's *History of Unilever* [3] is a sober business history based upon company records, but as an account of the world's largest food and soap manufacturer it could have been written with more emphasis on the implications of such a role. Ida M. Tarbell's *History of the Standard Oil Company* (1904), on the other hand, remains to this day a classic radical critique of business enterprise and an example of the influence of pungent writing on the fortunes of business. No biographies of the transnational business leaders of the post-1945 era have so far been written, but the careers of such nineteenth-century pioneers of multinational enterprise as the Rothschilds, Vanderbilts, John D. Rockefeller, Friedrich Krupp, the Siemens brothers, the Nobels, and the McCormicks are worth remembering.

Among those readable and perceptive works that might be recommended as an introduction to the study of transnational corporations are popular books by Anthony Sampson. *The Sovereign State of ITT* (1973) is a fast-moving account of the history of one of the largest international corporations. In the early 1970s ITT attracted world-wide attention for its role in Chile and in the payoff scandals that led to Watergate. Sampson notes the symbiotic relationship between this communications company and the world of international politics, and the crucial role of ITT's chief executive officers in molding the company's personality. *The Seven Sisters* (1975) tells the story of the large international oil firms, from the discovery of oil in Pennsylvania in 1859 to the victory of the Organization of Petroleum Exporting Countries in 1973–1974. Brief descriptions of the great oil companies and their leading personalities alternate with occasionally scathing comments on oil company and government policies. This is an excellent introduction to the oil giants and the world they built. Sampson's most recent book, *The Arms Bazaar* (1977), is a timely report on the international trade in arms—"of all industries the most global." Much of it is devoted to a description of the Lockheed bribery scandals, which gave rise to world-wide investigations into the unethical practices of multinational business, and to a call for new rules to control unethical practices.

NOTES

1. An update of the 1973 survey was brought out by the United Nations in 1978 (*TNCs in World Development: A Re-examination*, Publication E/C 10/38). Among the findings of this new report are the following:

(1) The world stock of direct foreign investment grew by 80 percent between 1971 and 1976, at about the same rate as the GNPs of the developed market countries, hence somewhat slower than in the 1960s. Estimated at about $105 billion in 1967, it rose to 158 billion in 1971 and reached 287 billion by 1976.

(2) Between 1967 and 1976 the United States' share of the world stock of direct foreign investment fell from 54 to 48 percent and that of the United Kingdom from 17 to 11 percent; Japan's share rose from 1 to 7 percent.

(3) In the same period, foreign direct investment in the developing countries declined from about one-third to no more than about one-quarter of the total. This smaller share is now concentrated in a few of the larger countries, so that by 1975 Brazil, Mexico, India, Malaysia, and the OPEC countries accounted for just over one-half of all such investment.

(4) The service sector (such as banking and advertising) made up about one-quarter of all TNC assets.

2. Cambridge, Mass.: Harvard University Press, 1970. See in particular Chapter X: "The Status of American International Enterprise in 1914."

3. London: Cassell, 1954–68 (three vols.).

CHAPTER 39

Imperialism, Dependency, and Dependent Development

Peter Evans

[. . .]

IMPERIALISM AND DEPENDENCE

The founders of dependency theory included critical Latin American sociologists and historians such as Caio Prado, Jr., Sergio Bagu, and Florestan Fernandes (see Cardoso, 1977; Kahl, 1976), the work of Paul Baran (1968) as applied to the Latin American context by André Gundar Frank (1967), and the structuralist revisions of development economics that had been worked out by Raul Prebisch, Celso Furtado, and others (see Girvan, 1973). Drawing on this body of work, dependency theorists then aimed at discovering "those characteristics of national societies which express external relations" (Cardoso and Faletto, 1973:28).

More recently, the Latin American originators of dependency theory have been joined by others, such as Samir Amin, who work more directly with the theory of imperialism but who share dependency theory's focus on the consequences of imperialism for the internal evolution of peripheral countries.

The starting point is still relations with the external world. A dependent country is one whose development is "conditioned by the development and expansion of another economy" (Dos Santos, 1970:236). Dependent countries are classically those whose histories of involvement with the international market have led them to specialize in the export of a few primary products. While the income from these few products is absolutely central to the process of accumulation in the dependent country, for the center each product represents only a tiny fraction of total imports, and can usually be obtained from several different sources. The development of the dependent country, however, requires the continued acceptance of its products in the center. Therefore, economic fluctuations in the center may have severe negative consequences for the periphery, whereas an economic crisis in the periphery offers no real threat to accumulation in the center.

Complementing and often underlying dependence based on trade relations, is dependence based on foreign ownership of the productive apparatus of the dependent country. When the principal aspect of dependence is that key sectors of the local productive apparatus are integral parts of capital that is controlled elsewhere, then accumulation in the dependent country is externally conditioned more by the "development and expansion of center-based capital" rather than by the "development and expansion of another country." The asymmetry is there nonetheless.

Dependence is then defined most simply as a situation in which the rate and direction of accumulation are externally conditioned. Curiously, however, while external relations are the starting point for the analysis of dependence, most of the emphasis of dependency theorists is on the internal class relations of dependent countries. As Cardoso and Faletto (1973:140) say, ". . . there is no such thing as a metaphysical relation of dependency between one nation and another, one state and another. Such relations are made concrete possibilities through the existence of a network of interests and interactions which link certain social groups to other social groups, certain social classes to other classes."

Dependence includes a wide range of disparate situations. OPEC and the oil crisis provided a powerful reminder that exporting primary products does not universally entail having a weak position in international trade. Even more important, saying that a country is "dependent" does not indicate that its relation to the international economic system is immutably fixed. It means rather that the historic process of accumulation in that country exhibits certain distinctive features that are shared by other countries of the periphery and set it apart from the nations of the center.

Contemporary dependency theorists see the international division of labor as shifting substantially on the surface while continuing to have the same fundamental effect. Curiously, the most carefully elaborated theoretical underpinning for this view comes not from within the dependency tradition itself but rather from the latest version of the theory of comparative advantage, known as the "product life cycle model" (Vernon, 1966; Johnson, 1968; Wells, 1972). According to the product life cycle model, new products are likely to be first produced and sold in the center, later produced in the center and exported to the periphery, and finally produced in the periphery. Over time, more and more products will be manufactured in the periphery, but these products will continue to share certain characteristics.

Production moves to the periphery only after the technology involved has become routinized. At this point uncertainties are small and savings from cheap labor make a difference. Thus, the Schumpeterian "windfall profits" associated with new products always remain the prerogative of the center. In addition, the periphery is forced to rely on the low cost of its labor for its comparative advantage in the international market, making low living standards the basis of dependent development.[1]

The introduction of manufacturing on the periphery also lacks the traditional "multiplier effect" associated with manufacturing investments in the center. Peripheral economies are "disarticulated," that is, firms on the periphery are not connected to each other in the same way as firms in an autocentric economy. Firms in dependent countries buy their equipment and other capital goods from outside, so that the "multiplier effect" of new investments is transferred back to the center. Increases in the output of export sectors, dramatic as they may be, do not feed back into the peripheral economy in the same way that they would feed back into an autocentric economy. As Amin (1976:239) puts it: "When the iron ore of Lorraine is eventually worked out this may create a difficult reconversion problem for the region, but it will be able to overcome these difficulties, for an infrastructure has been formed on the basis of the mineral, which could be imported from elsewhere. But when the iron ore of Mauritania is worked out, that country will go back to the desert."

Disarticulation between technology and social structure reinforces the economy's lack of integration. Celso Furtado (1969:15) speaks of the importation of technology as contributing to a "structural deformation" of the peripheral economy. Productive technologies imported from the center are not designed to absorb the huge reserves of underemployed agricultural labor. Products developed in the center and assimilated by the periphery are luxury products in the context of the periphery. Their production uses scarce resources and results in a "distortion in the allocation of resources in favor of those products and to the detriment of mass consumption goods" (Amin, 1977b:9).

For the elite, disarticulation is an obstacle to self-sustained, autocentric accumulation, but for the mass its consequence is exclusion. Because accumulation depends primarily either on exports or on goods beyond their means, the mass of the population can be excluded as consumers. Capital intensive technologies in the modern sector make it possible to marginalize them as producers. Because they are effectively barred from economic participation, to allow them political participation would be disruptive. Social and cultural exclusion follow from political and economic exclusion.

Exclusion, like disarticulation, is a constant feature of dependency. The gross gap between elite and mass that characterized classic dependence was expected to diminish once a domestic manufacturing sector was established. But the record of the sixties shows increasing inequality (cf. Adelman and Morris, 1973; Chase-Dunn, 1975; Evans and Timberlake, 1977). On the political level, populism has not proved an enduring strategy. As O'Donnell's (1973) pessimistic but convincing comparative analysis of Latin American countries shows, the ruling groups in the more advanced peripheral societies have discovered that the kind of economic development they need to sustain their own lifestyles requires the increasing political exclusion of the mass of the population.

The internal disarticulation of the peripheral society is complemented and exacerbated by the integration of elites internationally. Contemporary elites do not send their shirts to Europe to be laundered as the traditional colonial rulers of Latin America supposedly did, but they are part of what Sunkel calls "the transnational kernel," that is, "a complex of activities, social groups and regions in different countries ... which are closely linked transnationally through many concrete interests as well as by similar styles, ways and levels of living and cultural affinities" (1973:146).

Arguing that certain features of dependent social structures will persist despite industrialization has been one main task of dependency theory, but mapping change and variation has been equally central. From the beginning, dependency theory has recognized that hand in hand with changes in the shape of imperialism have gone changes in peripheral social formations. In Latin America, where classic dependency occurred in the context of formal political independence, the great depression is usually seen as the "moment of the transition." The period of classic dependency in which primary products provided the basis of "externally oriented expansion" ran until the beginning of the thirties (Cardoso and Faletto, 1973:39–51). The crisis of the depression made survival on the old basis impossible and forced the transition to a focus on the dependent's internal market.

The "consolidation of the internal market," which is to say the growth of "easy" import-substituting industrialization, is followed in turn by the "internationalization" of the domestic market (Cardoso and Faletto, 1973:114–138) during which the penetration of the multinationals becomes more intense as import substitution moves from consumer nondurables to consumer durables, intermediary goods, and some capital goods. O'Donnell (1973:60–61) speaks of this as the transition from "horizontal" to "vertical" industrialization, and agrees with Cardoso and Faletto that its internal character, political as well as economic, is distinct from the earlier phase of import substitution.[2]

In Asia and Africa, the political crisis of World War II marked the beginning of the transition. In most of these countries consolidation of the internal market is still going on and "vertical industrialization" is a project for the future. Nonetheless, the relations between local industrial bourgeoisies and international capital have changed in ways that are quite similar to the evolution of the more advanced countries of Latin America.

Amin (1977a:35) talks of the local bourgeoisies as having "won victories that led to independence, agrarian reforms and industrial achievements" and suggests that their victories "led to the integration of these bourgeoisies into the imperialist alliance." Amin's description of the class alliances of the "second phase" of imperialism echoes themes common to Latin American descriptions of the recent history of dependency. Once the "internationalization of the domestic market" has occurred then the stage is set for an "internationalized bourgeoisie" (Cardoso and Faletto, 1973:134) or, in Sunkel's language, the dominance of the "transnational kernel." Alliance of local and international capital is the common element in all these descriptions.

Cardoso's model of "associated-dependent development" pushes the idea of alliance the furthest. Associated-dependent development involves, he says, "the simultaneous and differentiated expansion of three sectors of the economy: the private national, the foreign and the public" (Cardoso, 1974:57). Politically, associated-dependent development requires the "structuring of a system of relations among the social groups which control these economic sectors" (Cardoso and Faletto, 1973:130).

Dependency theory and the contributions of theorists like Amin lead away from the construction of models of stagnation and toward an analysis of dependent development. If we join Cardoso in defining development as "the accumulation of capital and its effect on the differentiation of the productive system" (1974:57), then dependent development implies both the accumulation of capital and some degree of industrialization on the periphery. Dependent development is a special instance of dependency, characterized by the association or alliance of international and local capital. The state also joins the alliance as an active partner, and the resulting triple alliance is a fundamental factor in the emergence of dependent development.

Dependent development was taking place even during the period of classic dependence and "export-oriented growth," at least in those countries which were later able to make the transition to the "consolidation of the internal market." If capital accumulation and some degree of industrialization had not been occurring in these countries, the transition to a more industrially oriented growth would have been impossible. But dependent development was the emerging antithesis rather than the main theme of classic dependency. Under classic dependence, the accumulation of industrial capital took place in spite of the interests of the dominant elite.

In countries characterized by the internationalization of the internal market (the "second phase" of imperialism, or "vertical industrialization"), however, dependent development is the dominant aspect of dependence. It is these instances of dependence to which the label "dependent development" applies in an unambiguous way. Throughout this study, "dependent development" will be used to refer to cases where capital accumulation and diversified industrialization of a more than superficial sort are not only occurring in a peripheral country, but are dominating the transformation of its economy and social structure.

Dependent development is *not*, it should be stressed, the negation of dependence. It is rather dependence combined with development. Amin (1976:287) even goes so far as to argue that "none of the features that define the structure of the periphery is weakened as economic growth proceeds: on the contrary these features are accentuated." Nor does dependent development eradicate contradictions between center and periphery. As Cardoso writes, "when one examines the relations between economies of 'dependent-associated development' and the central economies, it is not hard to perceive that the international division of labor persists, based on very unequal degrees of wealth, on unequal forms of appropriation of the international surplus and on monopolization of the dynamic capitalist sectors by the central countries" (1977:20).

Dependent development is not a phase that all peripheral countries will be able to reach. Only a few are chosen. International stratification is accentuated rather than leveled as those countries in which the local bourgeoisie and international capital can arrive at an alliance become increasingly differentiated from the majority of the third world. Wallerstein (1974b, 1974c) claims that the more advanced exemplars of dependent development occupy their own distinct position within the international system. They form the "semi-periphery."[3]

Those which "make it" into the semi-periphery have an ambiguous relation to those left behind. All are still disadvantaged vis-à-vis the center, but the semi-periphery is advantaged vis-à-vis its neighbors. The political and military resources of the semi-periphery may not be sufficient to generate "subimperialism" (cf. Marini, 1972), but it remains plausible that they "could advance faster on the path of the new dependence if they also had markets in the less developed countries and if they could have direct and cheap access to their supplies of raw materials and food" (Amin, 1977b:14–15).

The distinctive position of semi-periphery in the international economy makes the course of dependent development in these countries critical to the future of imperialism. The commitment of center country capital to the semi-periphery is sufficient for a crisis in these economies to have significant consequences not only for firms involved in raw materials production but for a broad range of multinationals. The poorest countries of the periphery can stagnate without their plight being reflected in any serious disturbances in the center, but crisis in the semi-periphery would rob the multinationals in several industries of an important alternate arena for accumulation. Should crisis in the semi-periphery result in the political disaffection of these states, the political stability of the overall system would be threatened as well. In Wallerstein's (1974c:3) view at least, "the creation of 'middle' sectors which tend to think of themselves as better off than the lower sector rather than as worse off than the upper sector" has been a major means of averting the political polarization of the international system.

The most recent phase of dependency entails a restructuring of external relations, but changes in this area depend upon the nature of capital accumulation within the countries of the semi-periphery; and this in turn is based on the triple alliance of the multinationals, the state, and the local bourgeoisie. The three partners and their interrelationships are the starting point for any analysis of the institutional basis of dependent development.

THE MULTINATIONALS[4]

Multinational corporations are the organizational embodiment of international capital. Their decisions reflect the dictates of imperialism. At the same time, these decisions are more than reflections of external exigencies; the organizational form itself has consequences. Just as imperialism is not simply capitalism, multinational corporations are not simply profit-making capitalist firms. Corporations remove control over production from those engaged in production; multinationals extend the alienation across political boundaries. Strategic decisions are made in the center. Even if a strategy is first conceived locally it must be validated in the center. Operational decisions may be made locally. Personnel who work in the periphery may influence strategy. The fact remains that long-term plans and the "larger picture" are put together in the center. For those who live in the periphery this realization is frustrating, perhaps even more for elites than for the mass of the population.

Many who analyze imperialism discount the question of who makes the decisions and where. Arrighi Emmanuel (1974:75) presents the case clearly:

I must confess that I have never understood what Canadian workers or the Canadian people would gain if the decision making centers of their industry were shifted from offices located in the skyscrapers of New York or Chicago to others located in the tower blocks of Montreal or Toronto and still less have I ever understood what the Indian masses, with their per capita income of $100 per annum, would stand to lose if the day came when capitalists with Indian passports handed over to capitalists with North American or Japanese ones.

Unfortunately, the behavior of capitalists is not as simple as Emmanuel suggests. To be sure, the structure of imperialism as a whole creates a common environment to which any firm, local or international must respond. But the logic of accumulation for individual firms depends on their specific relation to that environment.

Multinational have opportunities that local firms do not have. They will maximize their profits in terms of a global strategy, not a local one. In addition, the logic of profit is always ambiguous. What a corporation does depends on what opportunities it can see. Corporations, no matter how sophisticated, make decisions on the basis of incomplete, uncertain information (cf. Goodman, 1975). Choices about what products to produce, where to produce them, and how to produce them must be based on educated guesses and the direction of the guess depends on the environment in which it is made. Organization theorists describe the problem as "bounded rationality" (Simon, 1965; March and Simon, 1958; Cyert and March, 1963). By this they mean that a decision is rational only within the cognitive boundaries created by the information available to the decision maker. What information is available depends on who makes the decision and where it is made. A rational profit maximizer who grew up in Kansas City and works in

Chicago brings different information to a decision from one who grew up in São Paulo and works there.

Bounded rationality helps explain why foreign investors did not spontaneously start manufacturing operations in the periphery during the earlier phase of imperialism. From where they were sitting it did not look worth the risk. Sometimes they may have been right not to invest. The point is that if and when they were wrong, they were likely to be wrong in the direction of overestimating the riskiness of investment on the periphery. The classic entrepreneur is just the opposite. When he is wrong, it is likely to be because he underestimates risk. Bounded rationality makes the foreign investor a poor candidate for the entrepreneurial role, just as Baran argued.

The organizational logic of the multinational tends to slow down the implantation of industry on the periphery. It also helps to impose the kind of international division of labor implied by the product life cycle model and to reinforce the disarticulation of technology and social structure. Imperialism as a system of accumulation ensures that any profit-making firm will tend to gravitate toward technology designed for center country social conditions and focus on low return, routine kinds of production in peripheral locations, but the interests of multinationals powerfully increase these tendencies.

The ability to produce new products which other firms cannot replicate is one of the most important sources of multinationals' profits. Knowledge is hard to monopolize—harder if its production is not highly centralized. Multinationals have then every motivation to keep the innovative side of their businesses as close to home as possible. As long as they are free to make that choice, the industrialization of the periphery will remain partial. Facilities for the production of new knowledge will not be located there. New technology will continue to be generated by the center countries and later assimilated by the periphery.

A multinational also has every reason to try to persuade consumers on the periphery to imitate customers in the center. The further it can spread the products and ideas over which it has control the more profits it can make. The added cost of using technology in a new market is negligible compared to the cost of developing the technology in the first place. This applies, of course, to methods of production as well as to new products. The proprietary interests of the multinational lie in making the peripheral economy as permeable as possible to center technology. Reluctant to invest in innovative activities that might produce a more locally appropriate technology, the multinational is anxious to market existing ideas regardless of appropriateness.

New products will be sold in the third world as soon as the multinational can create a market for them, but unless political considerations intervene, their production will be moved there only after it becomes routine. As Barnet and Müller illustrate nicely in the case of television (1974:129–133), following the logic of the product cycle enables a multinational to prolong its returns on a given product over the longest possible period.

Finally, the products offered by the multinationals will, because of their rich country origins, find their market primarily among third world elites. Thus, multinationals have both an interest in keeping wages low so that they can make a profit on routine manufacturing operations and an interest in income concentration so that they will have a market for the kinds of products they are trying to sell. If they look after their own corporate interests, multinationals will exacerbate both the exclusionary tendencies of dependent development and the disarticulation of technology and social conditions.

The interests of the multinationals as firms contribute to other kinds of disarticulation as well. They provide natural channels for pulling their local managers and their other local allies into the "transnational kernel." They have connections with center country suppliers and servicing organizations, relationships that reinforce the tendency toward disconnection between the multinationals and other local firms. The efficiency of the ties that bind the corporate core of the multinational to its far-flung parts multiplies the "missing links" in the periphery (Amin,

1976:212). The phone circuits that connect downtown São Paulo with downtown New York are rapidly improved while those linking São Paulo to its own rural hinterland remain primitive and undependable.

Multinationals are more than the representatives of the international economic order. They are organizations whose internal structures both reflect and shape the international economy. The contradictions between the interests of the multinationals and development on the periphery were not just figments of Baran's imagination or transitional aberrations. They persist even after multinationals have begun to engage in manufacturing on the periphery, even in the context of the "internationalization of the internal market," "associated-dependent development," and the emergence of new partnerships with the national bourgeoisie.

LOCAL CAPITAL

The "national industrial bourgeoisie" is the stepchild of imperialism, never completely abandoned but never given a full opportunity to develop. The industrial bourgeoisie, insofar as it develops at all on the periphery, enters the scene under conditions severely disadvantageous to its own interests. Center country bourgeoisies have already "preempted" the world historic role of the "conquering bourgeoisie" (see Fernandes, 1975: 295). Furthermore, imperialism, as Baran (1968) pointed out, stimulates the growth of its more favored children—the export-oriented agrarian capitalists and a mercantile compradore class.

Even with the transformation of imperialism and the advent of industrialization in certain third world countries, hegemony was not the lot of the "national industrial bourgeoisie." One of the contributions of dependency theory has been to point out that industrialization was a project built on compromise and not on bourgeois domination. As Cardoso and Faletto (1973:93) put it, "This industrialization represented more a policy of accords, between diverse groups from agrarian to popular-urban, than the imposition of interests or will to power

of a 'conquering bourgeoisie.' " Traditional agrarian and export interests lost some ground but remained powerful, while the industrial bourgeoisie acquired new competitors.

Along with industrialization came the "presence of the masses" (Cardoso and Faletto, 1973:92), urban working class groups who, if organized in the context of a relatively open political system, could represent a substantial political force. At the same time the "new dependency," in the form of foreign investment in manufacturing, brought a new kind of competitive pressure on local industrialists. Dependent industrialization left the national industrial bourgeoisie with no opening for either political domination or economic hegemony. Its position and privileges were always contingent on its ability to make alliances with other elite groups.

Failure to attain a hegemonic position should not be confused with passivity or lack of entrepreneurship. At least in cases like the Brazilian one, economic historians (cf. Graham, 1968; Dean, 1969; Queiroz, 1972) uniformly emphasize the role of local industrialists in embarking on new activities and contributing to accumulation at the local level. But if the past role of local bourgeois entrepreneurs in fostering accumulation is more usually underestimated, predictions of the demise of the local industrial bourgeoisie occur with even greater regularity.

Predictions of the imminent disappearance of the national bourgeoisie are based on two premises. One is that any local capitalist who enters into an alliance with international capital is transformed into a subordinate whose behavior must reflect the interests of his new boss. The second is that independent local capital has no chance of survival. Thus, Fernandez and Ocampo (1974:58) divide the local bourgeoisie into the national bourgeoisie which "suffers intensely from imperialist domination" and the big bourgeoisie who "serve the interests of imperialist countries." But this Dr. Jekyl and Mr. Hyde version of the local bourgeoisie caricatures both segments.

The "internationalized" bourgeoisie which is allied with international capital retains an interest in local accumulation despite their ties to the center. This is undeniable in the case of partnerships based on joint ownership of industrial firms, and may even apply in a restricted way to those who merely service the multinationals. The local bourgeoisie cannot afford to relinquish nationalism even if international capital has become their principal ally. Fernandes catches the ambiguity of their position when he describes them as having a status "in part mediator and in part free" and suggests that the maintenance of this dual status is the "fulcrum of the real internal power of the bourgeoisie" (1975:326).

The desperation of local capital unable to form alliances, like the disloyalty of the new members of the "transnational kernel," is exaggerated. While independent local firms may be disappearing from certain industries, the overall destruction of locally owned industry is usually asserted rather than established empirically. The progress of concentration may eventually wipe out small capital (which is to say local capital) on the periphery as it may in the center, but, if the experience of advanced capitalist countries is any guide, that progress is likely to be glacial rather than cataclysmic. In fact, the local bourgeoisie may have a "comparative advantage" in certain industries, or at least there may be certain roles necessary to accumulation at the local level that multinationals or their indigenous employees cannot perform as well as members of the local owning class.

Fascination with the power of the multinationals has tended to distract attention from the power of local capital to either maintain a degree of bargaining leverage while entering into alliances or discover niches in the economy where the multinationals are less likely to penetrate. Dispassionate examination of the economic bases of the survival of the national industrial bourgeoisie is one of the most obvious requirements for any empirical analysis of dependent development.

The political position of the national industrial bourgeoisie is at least as ambiguous as its economic position. As a class that never achieved a hegemonic political position and never really had a "project" (cf. Cardoso, 1971:194), it is easy to relegate the dependent national bourgeoisie to the status of the nineteenth-century French bourgeoisie as described by Marx (cf. Evans, 1974), a class which was forced to admit that "in order to preserve its social power intact, its political power must be broken" (Marx, 1963:67). Some instances of dependent development may indeed follow a "bonapartist" political model, insofar as groups outside the bourgeoisie (such as the peasantry in France of 1852) have substantial political leverage. But, in cases where the political exclusion of subordinate classes is thoroughgoing, as in O'Donnell's (1973) description of Brazil and Argentina, post-Peron bonapartism is not an apt label.

Since the political power of local capital cannot flow from its dominant role in the process of accumulation, it must depend on the nature of its ties to the "technobureaucracy" that staffs the state apparatus. Estimates of this relation vary. Cardoso and Faletto (1973:136) come close to suggesting a bonapartist model when they argue that under conditions of dependent development (the internationalization of the market) the bourgeoisie does not have any political organizations at its disposal and consequently its control over the state is "purely 'structural.' " The technobureaucracy goes its own way unless its policies "conflict with the mechanisms of capitalist accumulation." This seems more reasonable as a description of the political strategy of the multinationals than of local capital.

Fernandes suggests a different interpretation of the political situation of the bourgeoisie. He argues (1975:308) that precisely because of the economic weakness of the national bourgeoisie, "state power emerges as the principal structure and real dynamo of bourgeois power" and that therefore dependent development involves the "modernization and rationalization of the articulation" between the dominant segments of the bourgeoisie and the state. Fernandes's model of "bourgeois autocracy" may underestimate the possibility of conflict between the "technobureaucracy" and private capital but, for most instances of dependent development, it is more plausible than a bonapartist model.

The bonapartist state executive mediating the interests of opposing classes is replaced under bourgeois autocracy by a state apparatus which brooks no opposition from subordinate groups when the interests of the bourgeoisie as a whole are in question. Yet still local capital is not hegemonic. The "national industrial bourgeoisie" must be seen as a class "fraction" or "segment"[5] whose ability to control the state becomes ambiguous when the interests of the multinationals are at stake or when the interests of entrepreneurial groups within the state apparatus itself are involved.

THE STATE

Regardless of ambiguities in its relation to the national bourgeoisie, the centrality of the state to accumulation on the periphery is incontrovertible. Imperialism as a process and the multinationals as organizations concentrate accumulation at the center of the international system. The local owning class has failed to achieve domination over local industry even in the most advanced peripheral countries. Unless the state can enforce a priority on local accumulation and push local industrialization effectively, there is no effective sponsor for peripheral industrialization.

The centrality of the entrepreneurial state to economic development is neither a novel phenomenon nor one peculiar to dependent capitalist development. From Gerschenkron's (1952) classic work on the role of the state in late European industrialization to Trimberger's (1972) analysis of entrepreneurial state bureaucrats in Japan and Turkey, comparative historical analysis has demonstrated the importance of "taking the state seriously as a macrostructure" (Skocpol, 1979). If Polanyi's (1944) questioning of the myth of the "laissez faire" state and Wallerstein's (1974a) emphasis on the strength of the early English state are correct, the state also played a central role in the original industrial revolution.

Even given the importance of the state in other instances of industrialization, the centrality of the state in dependent development is special. The disarticulated nature of the dependent social structure makes bureaucratic roles more independent of the dominant class. As Amin (1976:202) says, "The mutilated nature of the natural community in the periphery confers an apparent relative weight and special functions upon the local bureaucracy that are not the same as those of the bureaucratic groups at the center." At the same time, the penetration of the local economy by the multinationals means that the state's traditional role of dealing with the external environment has an internal economic dimension which demands as much attention as normal "state-craft."

The problem is to redirect the global rationality of the multinational when it conflicts with the necessities of local accumulation. The state must continually coerce or cajole the multinationals into undertaking roles that they would otherwise abdicate. The power and flexibility of the multinationals suggest that making the returns to desired local investments more attractive is the least problematic way of assuring a response, but this pure incentive method has other costs. It usually means shifting some of the local surplus to the multinationals at the expense of either the national bourgeoisie or the state itself. Relying too heavily on coercing multinationals is also costly. Not only are they likely to withdraw from entrepreneurial ventures, but they are also likely to try to mobilize political opposition both internally and externally. Achieving an effective blend of coercion and incentive is not likely to be easy.

The state apparatus must be willing to oppose the multinationals when questions of local accumulation are at stake. Supine compradore states are excluded from the game. Even the most militant state needs some chips to bargain with. A peripheral society that lacks valuable natural resources, an extensive local market, or an explitable labor force is hardly in a position to bargain. The capacity of the state apparatus is also important. States must have control over a sufficient segment of the surplus so that they can offer incentives as well as support their own activities. Finally, technical expertise and control over relevant information play a role.

Relations between states and multinationals have been the focus of some of the best recent empirical work in the dependency theory tradition. Moran's (1974) work on copper in Chile and Tugwell's (1975) study of oil in Venezuela have demonstrated the usefulness of examining the course of the bargaining over time. Their work indicates that at least in these industries there was a secular shift over the course of the last fifty years in the direction of an improved bargaining position for the state. This shift seems to be rooted both in the increasing political decentralization of imperialism and in a gradual process of learning within the state apparatus itself. In each case the state combined incentives and threats and ended up with a greater share of the returns.

While the same scenario may well apply to the evolution of state-multinational relations with respect to manufacturing industries, it is harder to document. Moran (1975) has suggested that the state stands the best chance of improving its position in industries involving extraction of raw materials, where technology is stable and fixed investment large; whereas in industries where intangible capital is more important and continual product innovation the rule, the multinationals have a stronger position. If he is correct, then any thoroughgoing analysis of state-multinational bargaining will have to take into account the spectrum of industries over which the bargaining is taking place as well as the overall capacities and resources of the state.

Simple bargaining is, of course, not the only alternative open to the state. In both Chile and Venezuela the end of the bargaining process was takeover of the industries in question by the state. State enterprise may also be the result of failure to convince the multinational to undertake a new venture, as in the case of the Brazilian steel industry. Whatever their origins, state enterprises add a new dimension to state-multinational bargaining. They can be used to provide extra incentives to the multinationals in the form of low cost inputs. Or, they may threaten the recalcitrant multinational with a new source of competition, vastly stronger than local private capital. The creation of state enterprises does more, however, than simply increase the capacity of the state to bargain. Just as the existence of multinationals

changes the effects of imperialism, the creation of state enterprises changes the institutional nature of the dependent capitalist state.

In Latin America, and to a lesser degree in the former colonies of Asia and Africa, state enterprises have existed for a long time. Traditional infrastructural activities or in a few cases production of raw materials have been their main activities and they have behaved more or less like other parts of the bureaucracy. New state firms, created on the model of modern private corporations and engaged in export and directly productive activities previously reserved for private capital, exhibit a more entrepreneurial approach. It has even been argued that they signify a "change from a classical administrative bureaucracy into a state bourgeoisie" (Amin, 1976:346; see also Cardoso, 1974).

Once the concept of the "state bourgeoisie" has been introduced, new possibilities emerge for describing the interaction of the state and the multinationals as well as the state and the national industrial bourgeoisie. If it exists, a state bourgeoisie would be the most natural agent of local capital accumulation. Hampered neither by the necessity of tending to international concerns that distracts the multinationals nor the resource limitations that constrain local private industrialists, a state bourgeoisie might take over the role of the "conquering bourgeoisie." But can there be a "state bourgeoisie"? A bourgeoisie by definition appropriates surplus to itself; yet as part of the state apparatus, managers of state enterprises are supposed to be directing the process of accumulation in the general interests of capital as a whole, and not in their own particular interests.

If a state bourgeoisie is directing accumulation, then the natural movement of the industrial structure should be in the direction of state capitalism. Yet, what is the political base of these state managers if not the support of the local private bourgeoisie? It seems unlikely that the managers of state enterprises should be so disconnected from the bourgeoisie as a whole that they would push "state capitalism" to the detriment of local private capital. Amin (1976:347) takes this view when he argues for the coexistence of state and private bourgeoisies, saying that "state bourgeoisies have never eliminated private bourgeoisies but have been satisfied with absorbing them or merging with them." Likewise, while the state enterprises may try to squeeze multinationals, they are more sensitive than other parts of the state apparatus to the importance of not losing the inputs that multinationals have to offer.

Rather than see the state bourgeoisie as a replacement for the national industrial bourgeoisie, we may consider it a sort of class "fraction" which participates in a common project with both the multinationals and local private capital. Each group may view the project as subject to different constraints and each may have particular interests that contradict those of the others, but they all have an interest in a high rate of accumulation at the local level.

The image of the dependent capitalist state cannot be based simply on its role as an agent of accumulation. It is also an agent of social control. As Skocpol (1979:33) says, "The state first and fundamentally extracts resources from society and deploys these to create and support coercive and administrative organizations." The extremely exclusionary nature of dependent capitalist development accentuates the coercive aspects of the state just as the necessity of coping with the multinationals accentuates the entrepreneurial side. In the context of European industrialization, it seemed even to Lenin that representative democracy was the "best possible political shell" for capitalist growth. In the context of dependent development, however, the association of bourgeois democracy and capitalist accumulation no longer holds. As Florestan Fernandes (1975:312, 316) puts it, the dependent bourgeoisie has been forced to "revise and redefine the ideologies and utopias assimilated from the bourgeois-democratic experience of Europe and North America." Instead they must "support the hardening of bourgeoisie domination and its transfiguration into a specifically authoritarian and totalitarian social force," that is, "bourgeois autocracy."

The tendency toward repression stems in part from the economic rationale of exclusion. Any rise in the wages of the work force threatens the attractiveness of a given peripheral country as a site for export-oriented routine manufacturing activities. At the same time, concentration of income enhances the market for luxury consumer goods, which is the most dynamic part of the domestic market. Because of the disarticulated nature of the local economy, "the existence of an objective relation between the rewarding of labor and the level of development of the productive forces is completely absent" (Amin, 1976:192).

Repression is especially necessary in those countries which have passed through the phase of "easy import substitution" and are trying to push the process of dependent industrialization further. Guillermo O'Donnell (1973:53) has illustrated this nicely by contrasting Argentina and Brazil in the late sixties with some less developed Latin American countries. In the more advanced areas of the periphery, the coercive apparatus must be "geared to exclude the *already activated* urban popular sector." The aim is to return the working class to the political position it held before it became urbanized and organized (albeit organized only partially and under the wing of the state). Repression is the only way to enforce such a step backward.

In the context of dependent development, the need for repression is great while the need for democracy is small. One of the functions of parliamentary regimes is to provide a forum for the resolution of differences among the bourgeoisie. During the original industrial revolution a degree of political consensus among the members of the owning classes was essential to carrying out their "class project" of capital accumulation. But when accumulation depends on the triple alliance of multinationals, state enterprises, and their local private allies, parliamentary means of achieving consensus are inappropriate. Neither the multinationals nor the state bourgeoisie are likely to be politically represented in proportion to their economic importance. For the local private bourgeoisie the disproportionate (relative to their economic position) representation of small capital could be a real problem. The lack of representative political bodies may make it harder for the local private bourgeoisie to forge an internal political consensus, but, since its role in accumulation is ancillary rather than dominant, an overall consensus is not crucial.

When repression of the urban working class, effective bargaining with the multinationals, and entrepreneurial initiative on the part of the state bourgeoisie are the critical components of capital accumulation, then imperative control, not consensus building within the bourgeoisie, is the response. There emerges, in Fernandes's words (1975:292), "a strong *rational* association between capitalist development and autocracy." To complement the state bourgeoisie in the economic sphere a professional bureaucratic group is required to staff the coercive apparatus, and the military are the obvious candidates.

Military rule is not only a good choice because the military are the immediate wards of the state's monopoly on violence; they are also an apt choice because the dependent capitalist state, despite its disavowal of popular mobilization, is likely to be nationalist. Like repression, nationalism is useful both in promoting accumulation and in maintaining order. Nationalism provides the ideological basis for giving priority to local accumulation and is therefore useful in arguments with the multinationals. It provides a legitimation for the activities of the state bourgeoisie in the eyes of private capital. It is also the only basis on which the state can claim common ground with the mass of the population, especially as "developmentalist" promises of future material rewards begin to lose their credence (cf. Portes, 1977).

NOTES

1. One stream of thinking which speaks to this point and has been left unexplored here is Arrighi Emmanuel's (1972) "theory of unequal exchange." In the absence of concrete work on Latin America which links the theory of unequal exchange to the dependency theory tradition, I decided to neglect Emmanuel's contribution, despite its important place in the development of the theory of imperialism. For a brief exposition of the theory of unequal exchange, see Amin (1976:138–154).

2. A number of parallel periodizations exist. Sunkel (1973), for example, emphasizes the rise of the multinational as a retreat from the rule of laissez-faire and so characterizes the contemporary period as the "age of neo-mercantilism." Pereira (1970) emphasizes the internal side of the transformation and speaks of "peripheral industrialization." Dos Santos (1970) simply uses the term "new dependence" for the post-World War II period.

3. Wallerstein is not a *dependentista*. His focus on the world system rather than on the internal social structures of peripheral nations gives his work a quite different theoretical orientation. He is included here both because of the obvious relevance of his concept of the "semi-periphery" to any discussion of dependent development and because, like Amin, he is a contributor to the theory of imperialism who has definitely drawn on and been influenced by dependency theory.

4. The term "multinationals" is obviously a misnomer in the fundamental sense that most multinationals are controlled by capital from a single center country. The newer term "transnational" is more accurate. I have continued to use "multinational" mainly because I feel that the language used in the analysis of dependent development contains more than its share of departures from common usage and that most readers have a reasonably clear idea of the empirical universe of corporations to which the term multinational refers.

5. The usefulness of the idea of "class segments" in the analysis of dependent development is nicely illustrated by the work of Zeitlin and his colleagues on the Chilean dominant class (Zeitlin, Ewen, and Ratcliff, 1974; Zeitlin and Ratcliff, 1975; Zeitlin, Neuman, and Ratcliff, 1976).

REFERENCES

Adelman, Irma and Cynthia Morris, 1973. *Economic Growth and Social Equity in Developing Countries.* Stanford: Stanford University Press.

Amin, Samir, 1976. *Unequal Development: An Essay on the Social Formations of Peripheral Capitalism.* New York: Monthly Review Press.

——, 1977a. "Capitalism, State Collectivism, and Socialism," *Monthly Review* (June), 29(2):25–41.

——, 1977b. "Self-Reliance and the New International Economic Order," *Monthly Review* (July–August), 29(3):1–21.

Baran, Paul, 1968. *The Political Economy of Growth.* New York: Monthly Review Press.

Barnet, Richard and Ronald Müller, 1974. *Global Reach: The Power of the Multinational Corporations.* New York: Simon and Schuster.

Cardoso, Fernando Henrique, 1971. *Política e Desenvolvimento em Sociedades Dependentes.* Rio de Janeiro: Editora Zahar.

——, 1974. "As Tradições de Desenvolvimento-Associado," *Estudos Cebrap*, 8:41–75.

——, 1977. "The Consumption of Dependency Theory in the United States," *Latin American Research Review*, 12(3):7–25.

Cardoso, Fernando Henrique and Enzo Faletto, 1973. *Dependendência e Desenvolvimento na America Latina: Ensaio de Interpretação Sociológica*. Rio de Janeiro: Editora Zahar.

Chase-Dunn, Christopher, 1975. "The Effects of International Economic Dependence on Development and Inequality," *American Sociological Review*, 40(6):720–739.

Cyert, Richard and James March, 1963. *A Behavioral Theory of the Firm*. Englewood Cliffs: Prentice-Hall.

Dean, Warren, 1969. *The Industrialization of Sao Paulo, 1880–1945*. Austin: University of Texas Press.

Dos Santos, Teotonio, 1970. "The Structure of Dependence," *American Economic Review*, 60(5):235–246.

Emmanuel, Arrighi, 1972. *Unequal Exchange*. New York: Monthly Review Press.

——, 1974. "Myths of Development versus Myths of Underdevelopment," *The New Left Review*, 85:61–82.

Evans, Peter, 1974. "The Military, the Multinationals, and the 'Miracle': The Political Economy of the 'Brazilian Model' of Development," *Studies in Comparative International Development*, 9(3):26–45.

—— and M. Timberlake, 1977. "Dependence and the Bloated Tertiary: A Quantitative Study of Inequality in Less Developed Countries." Presented at the annual meeting of the American Sociologic Association, Chicago.

Fernandes, Florestan, 1975. A *Revolução Burguesa no Brasil*. Rio de Janeiro: Zahar Editores.

Fernandez, Raul and José F. Ocampo, 1974. "The Latin American Revolution: A Theory of Imperialism, Not Dependence," *Latin American Perspectives*, 1(1):30–61.

Frank, André Gundar, 1967. *Capitalism and Underdevelopment in Latin America*. New York: Monthly Review Press.

Furtado, Celso, 1969. *Um Projeto para o Brasil*. Rio de Janeiro: Editora Saga S.A.

Gerschenkron, Alexander, 1952. "Economic Backwardness in Historical Perspective," in *The Progress of Underdeveloped Countries*. Bert Hoselitz, ed. Chicago: University of Chicago Press.

Girvan, Norman, 1973. "The Development of Dependency Economics in the Caribbean and Latin America: Review and Comparison," *Social and Economic Studies* (March), 22(1):1–33.

Goodman, Louis W., 1975. "The Social Organization of Decision Making in the Multinational Corporation," in *The Multinational Corporation and Social Change*, D. Apter and L. W. Goodman, eds. New York: Praeger.

Graham, Richard, 1968. *Britain and Modernization in Brazil: 1850–1914*. Cambridge: Cambridge University Press.

Johnson, Harry, 1968. *Comparative Cost and Commercial Policy Theory for a Developing World Economy*. Stockholm: Almquist and Wiksell.

Kahl, Joseph, 1976. *Modernization, Exploitation and Dependency*. New Brunswick, NJ: Transaction Press.

March, James and Herbert Simon, 1958. *Organizations*. New York: John Wiley and Sons.

Marini, Ruy Mauro, 1972. "Brazilian Subimperialism," *Monthly Review*, 23(9):14–24.

Marx, Karl, 1963 *The 18th Brumaire of Louis Bonaparte*. New York: International Publishers. (Originally published 1852).

Moran, T. H., 1974. *Multinational Corporations and the Politics of Dependence: Copper in Chile*. Princeton: Princeton University Press.

——, 1975. "Multinational Corporations and Dependency: A Dialogue for Dependentistas and Non-Dependentistas," Washington: Johns Hopkins School for Advanced International Studies (mimeo).

O'Donnell, Guillermo, 1973. *Modernization and Bureaucratic Authoritarianism*. Berkeley: University of California Press.

Pereira, L., 1970. *Ensaios de Sociologia do Desenvolvimento*. São Paulo: Livraria Pioneira Editora.

Polanyi, Karl, 1944. *The Great Transformation*. Boston: Beacon Press.

Portes, Alejandro, 1977. "Ideologies of Inequality and their Major Types and Evolution in Latin American History." Paper presented at the annual meeting of the American Sociological Association, Chicago.

Queiroz, Maurício Vinhas de, 1972. "Grupos Econômicos e o Modelo Brasileiro," Tese de Doutoramento, University of São Paulo.

Simon, Herbert, 1965. *Administrative Behavior*. New York: The Free Press.

Skocpol, T., 1979. *States and Social Revolutions in France, Russia and China*. Cambridge: Cambridge University Press.

Sunkel, Oswaldo, 1973. "Transnational Capitalism and National Disintegration in Latin America," *Social and Economic Studies*, 22:132–176.

Trimberger, Ellen Kay, 1972. "A Theory of Elite Revolutions," *Studies in Comparative International Development*, 7:191–207.

Tugwell, Franklin, 1975. *The Politics of Oil in Venezuela*. Stanford: Stanford University Press.

Vernon, Raymond, 1966. "International Investment and International Trade in the Product Cycle," *Quarterly Journal of Economics*, 80:190–207.

Wallerstein, Immanuel, 1974a. *The Modern World System: Capitalist Agriculture and the Origins of the European World-Economy in the Sixteenth Century*. New York: Academic Press.

——, 1974b. "The Rise and Future Demise of the World Capitalist System: Concepts for Comparative Analysis," *Comparative Studies in Society and History* (September), 15(4):387–415.

——, 1974c. "Dependence in an Interdependent World: The Limited Possibilities of Transformation within the Capitalist World-Economy," *African Studies Review*, 17(1):1–26.

Wells, Louis T., 1972. *Product Life Cycle and International Trade*. Boston: Harvard Graduate School of Business Administration, Harvard University.

Zeitlin, Maurice, L. A. Ewen, and R. Ratcliff, 1974. "New Princes for Old? The Large Corporation and the Capitalist Class in Chile," *American Journal of Sociology*, 80(1):87–123.

Zeitlin, Maurice and R. Ratcliff, 1975. "Research Methods for the Analysis of the Internal Structure of Dominant Classes: The Case of Landlords and Capitalists in Chile," *Latin American Research Review*, 10(3):5–61.

Zeitlin, Maurice, W. Lawrence Neuman and Richard Earl Ratcliff, 1976. "Class Segments: Agrarian Property and Political Leadership in the Capitalist Class of Chile," *American Sociological Review*, 41:1006–1029.

CHAPTER 40

The Organization of Buyer-driven Global Commodity Chains: How U.S. Retailers Shape Overseas Production Networks

Gary Gereffi

Global industrialization is the result of an integrated system of production and trade. Open international trade has encouraged nations to specialize in different branches of manufacturing and even in different stages of production within a specific industry. This process, fueled by the explosion of new products and new technologies since World War II, has led to the emergence of a global manufacturing system in which production capacity is dispersed to an unprecedented number of developing as well as industrialized countries (Harris, 1987; Gereffi, 1989b). The revolution in transportation and communications technology has permitted manufacturers and retailers alike to establish international production and trade networks that cover vast geographical distances. While considerable attention has been given to the involvement of industrial capital in international contracting, the key role played by commercial capital (i.e., large retailers and brand-named companies that buy but don't make the goods they sell) in the expansion of manufactured exports from developing countries has been relatively ignored.

This chapter will show how these "big buyers" have shaped the production networks established in the world's most dynamic exporting countries, especially the newly industrialized countries (NICs) of East Asia. The argument proceeds in several stages. First, a distinction is made between producer-driven and buyer-driven commodity chains, which represent alternative modes of organizing international industries. These commodity chains, though primarily controlled by private economic agents, also are influenced by state policies in both the producing (exporting) and consuming (importing) countries.

Second, the main organizational features of buyer-driven commodity chains are identified, using the apparel industry as a case study. The apparel commodity chain contains two very different segments. The companies that make and sell standardized clothing have production patterns and sourcing strategies that contrast with firms in the fashion segment of the industry, which has been the most actively committed to global sourcing. Recent changes within the retail sector of the United States are analyzed in this chapter to identify the emergence of new types of big buyers and to show why they have distinct strategies of global sourcing.

Third, the locational patterns of global sourcing in apparel are charted, with an emphasis on the production frontiers favoured by different kinds of U.S. buyers. Several of the primary mechanisms used by big buyers to source products from overseas are outlined in order to demonstrate how transnational production systems are sustained and altered by American retailers and branded apparel companies. Data sources include in-depth interviews with managers of overseas buying offices, trading companies, manufacturers, and retailers in East Asia and the United States, plus relevant secondary materials at the firm, industry, and country levels.[1]

PRODUCER-DRIVEN VERSUS
BUYER-DRIVEN COMMODITY CHAINS

Global commodity chains (GCCs) are rooted in production systems that give rise to particular patterns of coordinated trade. A "production system" links the economic activities of firms to technological and organizational networks that permit companies to develop, manufacture, and distribute specific commodities. In the transnational production systems that characterize global capitalism, economic activity is not only *international* in scope; it also is *global* in its organization (Ross and Trachte, 1990; Dicken, 1992). While "internationalization" refers simply to the geographical spread of economic activities across national boundaries, "globalization" implies a degree of functional integration between these internationally dispersed activities. The requisite administrative coordination is carried out by diverse corporate actors in centralized as well as decentralized economic structures.

Large firms in globalized production systems simultaneously participate in many different countries, not in an isolated or segmented fashion but as part of their global production and distribution strategies. The GCC perspective highlights the need to look not only at the geographical spread of transnational production arrangements, but also at their organizational scope (i.e., the linkages between various economic agents—raw material suppliers, factories, traders, and retailers) in order to understand their sources of stability and change (see Gereffi and Korzeniewicz, 1990).

Global commodity chains have three main dimensions: (1) an input-output structure (i.e., a set of products and services linked together in a sequence of value-adding economic activities); (2) a territoriality (i.e., spatial dispersion or concentration of production and distribution networks, comprised of enterprises of different sizes and types); and (3) a governance structure (i.e., authority and power relationships that determine how financial, material, and human resources are allocated and flow within a chain).

The governance structure of GCCs, which is essential to the coordination of trans-national production systems, has received relatively little attention in the literature (an exception is Storper and Harrison, 1991). Two distinct types of governance structures for GCCs have emerged in the past two decades, which for the sake of simplicity are called "producer-driven" and "buyer-driven" commodity chains (see Figure 40.1).

Producer-driven commodity chains refer to those industries in which transnational corporations (TNCs) or other large integrated industrial enterprises play the central role in controlling the production system (including its backward and forward linkages). This is most characteristic of capital- and technology-intensive industries like automobiles, computers, aircraft, and electrical machinery. The geographical spread of these industries is transnational, but the number of countries in the commodity chain and their levels of development are varied. International subcontracting of components is common, especially for the most labor-intensive production processes, as are strategic alliances between international rivals. What distinguishes "producer-driven" production systems is the control exercised by the administrative headquarters of the TNCs.

Hill (1989) analyzes a producer-driven commodity chain in his comparative study of how Japanese and U.S. car companies organize manufacturing in multilayered production systems that involve thousands of firms (including parents, subsidiaries, and subcontractors). Doner (1991) extended this framework to highlight the complex forces that drive Japanese automakers to create regional production schemes for the supply of auto parts in a half-dozen nations in East and Southeast Asia. Henderson (1989), in his study of the internationalization of the U.S. semiconductor industry, also supports the notion that producer-driven commodity chains have established an East Asian division of labor.

Buyer-driven commodity chains refer to those industries in which large retailers, brand-named merchandisers, and trading companies play the pivotal role in setting up decentralized production networks in a variety of exporting countries, typically located in the Third World. This pattern of trade-led

1) **Producer-driven Commodity Chains**
   (Industries such as automobiles, computers, aircraft, and electrical machinery)

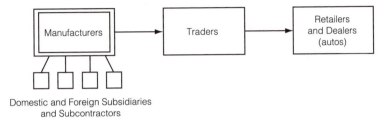

Domestic and Foreign Subsidiaries
and Subcontractors

2) **Buyer-driven Commodity Chains**
   (Industries such as garments, footwear, toys, and housewares)

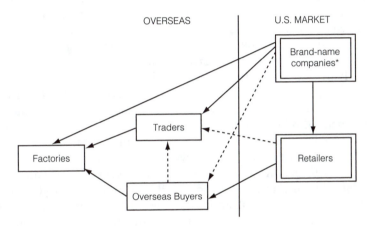

*These design-oriented, national brand companies, such as Nike, Reebok, Liz Claiborne,
and Mattel Toys, typically own no factories. Some, like The Gap and The Limited, have
their own retail outlets that only sell private label products.

Figure 40.1 The organization of producer-driven and buyer-driven global commodity chains.

Note: Solid arrows are primary relationships; dashed arrows are secondary relationships.

industrialization has become common in labor-intensive, consumer-goods industries such as garments, footwear, toys, consumer electronics, housewares, and a wide range of hand-crafted items (e.g., furniture, ornaments). International contract manufacturing again is prevalent, but production is generally carried out by independent Third World factories that make finished goods (rather than components or parts) under original equipment manufacturer (OEM) arrangements. The specifications are supplied by the buyers and branded companies that design the goods.

One of the main characteristics of firms that fit the buyer-driven model, including athletic footwear companies like Nike,

Reebok, and L.A. Gear (Donaghu and Barff, 1990) and fashion-oriented clothing companies like The Limited, The Gap, and Liz Claiborne (Lardner, 1988), is that frequently these businesses do not own any production facilities. They are not "manufacturers" because they have no factories.[2] Rather, these companies are "merchandisers" that design and/or market, but do not make, the branded products they sell. These firms rely on complex tiered networks of contractors that perform almost all their specialized tasks. Branded merchandisers may farm out part or all of their product development activities, manufacturing, packaging, shipping, and even accounts receivable to different agents around the world.

The main job of the core company in buyer-driven commodity chains is to manage these production and trade networks and make sure all the pieces of the business come together as an integrated whole. Profits in buyer-driven chains thus derive not from scale economies and technological advances as in producer-driven chains, but rather from unique combinations of high-value research, design, sales, marketing, and financial services that allow the buyers and branded merchandisers to act as strategic brokers in linking overseas factories and traders with evolving product niches in their main consumer markets (Reich, 1991).

The distinction between producer-driven and buyer-driven commodity chains bears on the debate concerning mass production and flexible specialization systems of industrial organization (Piore and Sabel, 1984). Mass production is clearly a producer-driven model (in our terms), while flexible specialization has been spawned, in part, by the growing importance of segmented demand and more discriminating buyers in developed country markets. One of the main differences between the GCC and flexible specialization perspectives is that Piore and Sabel deal primarily with the organization of production in *domestic* economies and local industrial districts, while the notion of producer-driven and buyer-driven commodity chains focuses on the organizational properties of *global* industries. Furthermore, a buyer-driven commodity chain approach would explain the emergence of flexibly specialized forms of production in terms of changes in the structure of retailing, which in turn reflect demographic shifts and new organizational imperatives. Finally, while some of the early discussions of flexible specialization implied that it is a "superior" manufacturing system that might eventually displace or subordinate mass production, buyer-driven and supplier-driven commodity chains are viewed as contrasting (but not mutually exclusive) poles in a spectrum of industrial organization possibilities.

Our analysis of buyer-driven commodity chains will focus on the main companies that coordinate these economic networks: large U.S. retailers. Whereas in producer-driven forms of capitalist industrialization, production patterns shape the character of demand, in buyer-driven commodity chains the organization of consumption is a major determinant of where and how global manufacturing takes place. The economic agents of supply and demand do not operate in a political vacuum, however. They, in turn, respond to political pressures from the state.

THE ROLE OF STATE POLICIES IN GLOBAL COMMODITY CHAINS

National development strategies play an important role in forging new production relationships in the global manufacturing system (Gereffi and Wyman, 1990). Conventional economic wisdom claims that Third World nations have followed one of two alternative development strategies: (1) the relatively large, resource-rich economies in Latin America (e.g., Brazil, Mexico, and Argentina), South Asia (e.g., India and Bangladesh), and Eastern Europe have pursued import-substituting industrialization (ISI) in which industrial production was geared to the needs of sizable domestic markets; and (2) the smaller, resource-poor nations like the East Asian NICs adopted the export-oriented industrialization (EOI) approach that depends on global markets to stimulate the rapid growth of manufactured exports. Although the historical analysis of these transitions tends to have been oversimplified, today it is abundantly clear that most economies have opted for an expansion of manufactured or nontraditional exports to earn needed foreign exchange and raise local standards of living. The East Asian NICs best exemplify the gains from this path of development.

An important affinity exists between the ISI and EOI strategies of national development and the structure of commodity chains. Import substitution occurs in the same kinds of capital- and technology-intensive industries represented by producer-driven commodity chains (e.g., steel, aluminum, petrochemicals, machinery, automobiles, and computers). In addition, the main economic agents in both cases are TNCs and state-owned enterprises. Export-oriented industrialization, on the other hand, is channeled through buyer-driven commodity chains where production in labor-intensive industries is concentrated in small to medium-sized, private domestic firms located mainly in the Third World. Historically, the export-oriented development strategy of the East Asian NICs and buyer-driven commodity chains emerged together in the early 1970s, suggesting a close connection between the success of EOI and the development of new forms of organizational integration in buyer-driven industrial networks.

State policy plays a major role in GCCs. In EOI, governments are primarily facilitators; they are condition-creating and tend not to become directly involved in production. Governments try to generate the infrastructural support needed to make export-oriented industries work: modern transportation facilities and communications networks; bonded areas, like export-processing zones (including China's Special Economic Zones); subsidies for raw materials; customs drawbacks for imported inputs that are used in export production; adaptive financial institutions and easy credit (e.g., to facilitate the obtaining of letters of credit by small firms); etc. In ISI, on the other hand, governments play a much more interventionist role. They use the full array of industrial policy instruments (such as local content requirements, joint ventures with domestic partners, and export-promotion schemes), while the state often gets involved in production activities, especially in upstream industries.

In short, the role of the state at the point of production tends to be facilitative in buyer-driven commodity chains and more interventionist in producer-driven chains. However, there is an important caveat for buyer-driven chains. Since these are export-oriented industries, state policies in the consuming or importing countries (like the United States) also are highly significant. This is where the impact of protectionist measures such as quotas, tariffs, and voluntary export restraints comes in to shape the location of production in buyer-driven chains. If one compares the global sourcing of apparel (where quotas are prevalent) and

footwear (no quotas),[3] one sees that far more countries are involved in the production and export networks for clothes than for shoes. This is basically a quota effect, whereby the array of Third World apparel export bases continually is being expanded to bypass the import ceilings mandated by quotas against previously successful apparel exporters. Therefore the globalization of export production has been fostered by two distinct sets of state policies: Third World efforts to promote EOI, coupled with protectionism in developed country markets.

THE APPAREL COMMODITY CHAIN

The textile and apparel industries are the first stage in the industrialization process of most countries. This fact, coupled with the prevalence of developed country protectionist policies in this sector, has led to the unparalleled diversity of garment exporters in the Third World. The apparel industry thus is an ideal case for exploring the organization and dynamics of buyer-driven commodity chains. The apparel commodity chain is bifurcated along two main dimensions: (1) textile versus garment manufacturers; and (2) standardized versus fashion-oriented segments in the industry (see Taplin, chapter 10 in this volume, for a diagram incorporating both of these dimensions). A complete analysis also must take account of how backward and forward linkages are utilized in the apparel commodity chain to protect the profitability of leading firms.

Textile Versus Garment Producers

Textile manufacturers and garment producers inhabit different economic worlds. Textile companies are frequently large, capital-intensive firms with integrated spinning and weaving facilities. The major textile manufacturers "finish" woven fabrics into a variety of end products, including sheets, towels, and pillowcases. While the U.S. fiber industry is composed of TNCs that make synthetic as well as natural fibers, fabric producers are more diverse in size, including numerous small businesses along with industrial giants like Burlington Mills.

The apparel industry, on the other hand, is the most fragmented part of the textile complex, characterized by many small, labor-intensive factories. Two primary determinants explain shifts in the geographical location and organization of manufacturing in the apparel sector: the search for low-wage labor and the pursuit of organizational flexibility. Although apparel manufacturing depends on low wages to remain competitive, this fact alone cannot account for dynamic trends in international competitiveness. Cheap labor is what Michael Porter calls a "lower-order" competitive advantage, since it is an inherently unstable basis on which to build a global strategy. More significant factors for the international competitiveness of firms are the "higher-order" advantages such as proprietary technology, product differentiation, brand reputation, customer relationships, and constant industrial upgrading (Porter, 1990: 49–51). These assets allow enterprises to exercise a greater degree of organizational flexibility and thus to create as well as respond to new opportunities in the global economy.

Standardized Versus Fashion Segments

A second major divide in the apparel commodity chain is between the producers of standardized and fashion-oriented garments. In the United States, the majority of the 35,000 firms in the textile/apparel complex are small clothing manufacturers (Mody and Wheeler, 1987). For standardized apparel (such as jeans, men's underwear, brassieres, and fleece outerwear), large firms using dedicated or single-purpose machines have emerged. Companies that make standardized clothing include the giants of the American apparel industry, like Levi Strauss and Sara Lee (both $4 billion companies), VF Corporation (a $2.6 billion company with popular brands such as Lee and Wrangler jeans and Jantzen sportswear), and Fruit of the Loom (a $1.6 billion firm that is the largest domestic producer of underwear for the U.S. market). These big firms tend to be closely linked with U.S. textile suppliers, and they manufacture many of their clothes within the United States or they ship U.S. made parts offshore for sewing.[4]

The fashion-oriented segment of the garment industry encompasses those products that change according to retail buying seasons. Many of today's leading apparel firms like Liz Claiborne have six or more different buying seasons every year (Lardner, 1988). These companies confront far greater demands for variation in styling and materials, and they tend to utilize numerous overseas factories because of their need for low wages and organizational flexibility in this labor-intensive and volatile segment of the apparel industry.

It is the fashion-oriented segment of the apparel commodity chain that is most actively involved in global sourcing. In 1990, imports-accounted for 51 percent of U.S. consumer expenditures on apparel. Of the $75 billion spent on U.S. apparel imports (in a total U.S. market of $148 billion), $25 billion corresponded to the foreign-port value of imported clothing, $14 billion to landing, distribution, and other costs, and $36 billion to the retailers' average markup of 48 percent on imported goods (AAMA, 1991: 3). The consumer's retail price thus amounts to three times the overseas factory cost for imported clothing. Meanwhile, the wholesale value of domestic apparel production totaling $73 billion in 1990 was $39 billion, with another $34 billion going to the retailers' net markup of 46 percent. In other words, the global sourcing of apparel by major retailers and brand-named companies is big business in the United States and it is growing bigger every year. This is why the organization of global sourcing merits close attention.

The Impact of Backward and Forward Linkages

The severe cost pressures endemic in the labor-intensive segments of the garment industry highlight the interdependence between different economic agents in buyer-driven commodity chains. Throughout the 1980s, U.S. garment companies were demanding lower prices and faster delivery from their overseas (principally Asian) suppliers, as well as their largely immigrant core and secondary contractors in New York City and Los Angeles, who in turn squeezed their workers for longer hours and lower wages (Rothstein, 1989). But the intensity of these pressures has varied over time. Why do the garment manufacturers pressure their contractors more at some times than at others? In a related vein, how can we explain differences in the level and location of profits in this industry over time?

The answers to these questions lie in an analysis of the apparel industry's backward and forward linkages. Garment manufacturers are being squeezed from both ends of the apparel commodity chain. Textile firms in the United States have become larger and more concentrated as they turned to highly automated production processes. This allowed them to place greater demands on the domestic garment manufacturers for large orders, high prices for inputs, and favorable payment schedules (Waldinger, 1986). One response has been for U.S. garment companies to find more competitive overseas suppliers of textiles and fabrics. Since this option is constrained by quotas that limit the extent of U.S. textile imports, many apparel makers had little choice but to accede to the demands of their main domestic textile suppliers.

At the other end of the apparel commodity chain, U.S. retailers went through a merger movement of their own (Bluestone et al., 1981). A number of prominent retail companies have gone into bankruptcy, been bought out, or face serious economic difficulties.[5] Those "big buyers" that remain are becoming larger, more tightly integrated organizationally and technologically, and frequently more specialized. This has put increasing pressure on merchandise manufacturers to lower their prices and improve their performance.[6] The result is that garment firms again are squeezed, with negative consequences (e.g., lower purchase prices, increased uncertainty) for their domestic and overseas contractors and the affiliated workers who actually make the clothes.

These illustrations show the importance of considering the full array of backward and forward linkages in the production process, as the GCC framework does, rather than limiting our notion of transnational production systems to manufacturing alone. Industrial organization economics tells us that profitability is greatest in the more concentrated segments of an industry characterized by high barriers to the entry of new firms. Producer-driven commodity chains are capital- and technology-intensive. Thus manufacturers making advanced products like aircraft, automobiles, and computer systems are the key economic agents in these chains not only in terms of their earnings, but also in their ability to exert control over backward linkages with raw material and component suppliers, as well as forward linkages into retailing.

Buyer-driven commodity chains, on the other hand, which characterize many of today's light consumer goods industries like garments, footwear, and toys, tend to be labor-intensive at the manufacturing stage. This leads to very competitive and globally decentralized factory systems. However, these same industries are also design- and marketing-intensive, which means that there are high barriers to entry at the level of brand-named companies and retailers that invest considerable sums in product development, advertising, and computerized store networks to create and sell these products. Therefore, whereas producer-driven commodity chains are controlled by core firms at the point of production, control over buyer-driven commodity chains is exercised at the point of consumption.

In summary, our GCC approach is *historical* since the relative strength of different economic agents in the commodity chain (raw material and component suppliers, manufacturers, traders, and retailers) changes over time; it also is *comparative* because the structural arrangements of commodity chains vary across industrial sectors as well as geographical areas. Finally, contemporary GCCs have two very different kinds of governance structures: one imposed by core manufacturers in producer-driven commodity chains, and the other provided by major retailers and brand-named companies in the buyer-driven production networks. These have distinct implications for national development strategies and the consequences of different modes of incorporation into the world-economy.

THE RETAIL REVOLUTION IN THE UNITED STATES

In order to gain a better understanding of the dynamics of the governance structure in buyer-driven commodity chains, we need to take a closer look at the U.S. retail sector, whose big buyers have fueled much of the growth in consumer goods exports in the world economy. Changes in America's consumption patterns are one of the main factors that have given rise to flexible specialization in global manufacturing.

For the past two decades, a "retail revolution" has been under way in the United States that is changing the face of the American marketplace. A comprehensive study of U.S. department stores showed that the structure of the industry became more oligopolistic during the 1960s and 1970s as giant department stores swallowed up many once-prominent independent retailers (Bluestone et al., 1981). The growth of large firms at the expense of small retail outlets was encouraged by several forces, including economies of scale, the advanced technology[7] and mass advertising available to retail giants, government regulation, and the financial backing of large corporate parent firms. Ironically, despite the department store industry's transformation into an oligopoly, the price competition between giant retailers became more intense, not less (Bluestone et al., 1981: 2).[8]

In the 1980s, the department store in turn came under siege. In their heyday, department stores were quintessential middle-class American institutions.[9] These retailers offered a broad selection of general merchandise for "family shopping," with "the mother as 'generalist' buying for other family members" (Legomsky, 1986: R62).[10] While this format typically met the needs of the suburban married couple with two children and one income, by 1990 less than 10 percent of American households fit that description. Today the generalist strategy no longer works. The one shopper of yesterday has become many different shoppers, with each member of the family constituting a separate buying unit (Sack, 1989).

The breakup of the American mass market into distinct, if overlapping, retail constituencies has created a competitive squeeze on the traditional department stores and mass merchandisers,[11] who are caught between a wide variety of specialty stores, on the one hand, and large-volume discount chains, on the other.[12] The former, who tailor themselves to the upscale shopper, offer customers an engaging ambience, strong fashion statements, and good service;[13] the latter, who aim for the lower income buyer, emphasize low prices, convenience, and no-frills merchandising.

Tables 40.1 and 40.2 show the varied performance levels of some of the major U.S. retail chains in the 1980s and 1990s. In 1990, both Wal-Mart and Kmart surpassed Sears as the largest U.S. retailers in terms of sales (see Table 40.1). Wal-Mart, Kmart, and Target (a division of Dayton Hudson) now control over 70 percent of the booming discount store business in the United States. Wal-Mart and the leading specialty stores also have far better earnings than the department stores and mass merchandise chains. The 10-year compounded growth rates in net income for Wal-Mart (34.5 percent) and the two leading specialty retailers in apparel, The Gap (34.6 percent) and The Limited (33.5 percent),[14] are the highest of any of the stores listed. In addition, the specialty stores tend to have the top rate of return on revenues of any U.S. retailers between 1987 and 1991 (see Table 40.2).

Wal-Mart appears to be in a much stronger position for future growth than its leading challenger, Kmart. In 1990 Wal-Mart cleared $2 billion before taxes compared to Kmart's $1 billion on basically the same volume of sales (Saporito, 1991: 54). The performance of companies like Kmart,[15] J.C. Penney, and Woolworth have been hindered by their major corporate restructurings over the past several years. Although the specialty stores are considerably smaller than other types of U.S. retailers, the former have the highest ratio of sales per retail square footage of any U.S. retail establishments and they

Table 40.1 Sales of leading U.S. retailers, 1987–1992 (billions of dollars).

	1987	1988	1989	1990	1991	1992
Discounters						
Wal-Mart	16.0	20.6	25.8	32.6	43.9	55.5
Kmart	25.6	27.3	29.5	32.1	34.6	37.7
Mass Merchandisers						
Sears	28.1	30.3	31.6	32.0	31.4	32.0
Dayton Hudson	10.7	12.2	13.6	14.7	16.1	17.9
Woolworth	7.1	8.1	8.8	9.8	9.9	10.0
Department Stores						
J.C. Penney	16.4	15.9	17.1	17.4	17.3	19.1
May Department Stores	10.3	8.4	9.4	10.1	10.6	11.2
Specialty Stores						
Melville	5.9	6.8	7.6	8.7	9.9	10.4
The Limited	3.5	4.1	4.6	5.3	6.1	6.9
The Gap	1.1	1.3	1.6	1.9	2.5	3.0
Toys "R" Us	3.3	4.0	4.8	5.5	6.1	7.2

Source: Standard and Poor's Industry Surveys, "Retailing: Current Analysis," April 20, 1989, p. R79; May 2, 1991, p. R80; May 13, 1993, p. R80; and company annual reports.

Table 40.2 Net income and return on revenues of leading U.S. retailers, 1987–1991.

Company	Net Income[a] (millions of dollars)					Compound Growth Rate (%)			Return on Revenues[b] (%)		
	1987	1988	1989	1990	1991	1-yr.	5-yr.	10-yr.	1987	1989	1991
Discounters											
Wal-Mart	628	837	1076	1291	1608	24.6	29.0	34.5	3.9	4.2	3.7
Kmart	692	803	323	756	859	13.6	8.5	14.6	2.7	1.1	2.5
Mass Merchandisers											
Sears	1649	1032	1446	829	1279	43.4	−1.1	7.0	3.4	2.7	2.2
Dayton Hudson[c]	228	287	410	410	301	−26.6	3.4	6.6	2.1	3.0	1.9
Woolworth	251	288	329	317	−53	NM	NM	NM	3.5	3.7	NM
Department Stores											
J.C. Penney	608	807	802	577	264	−54.2	−13.0	−3.8	3.8	4.7	1.5
May Dpt. Stores[d]	444	503	515	500	515	3.0	6.2	15.1	4.2	5.4	4.9
Specialty Stores											
Melville[e]	285	354	398	385	347	−10.0	7.8	9.8	4.8	5.3	3.5
The Limited[f]	235	245	347	398	403	1.2	12.1	33.5	6.7	7.3	6.4
The Gap[f]	70	74	98	144	230	59.1	27.5	34.6	6.6	6.2	9.1
Toys "R" Us[g]	204	268	321	326	340	4.2	17.4	21.4	6.5	6.7	5.5

Source: Standard and Poor's Industry Surveys, "Retailing: Comparative Company Analysis," May 13, 1993, pp. R104–R107.
a "Net income" refers to profits derived from all sources after deduction of expenses, taxes, and fixed charges, but before any discounted operations, extraordinary items, and dividend payments (preferred and common).
b Net income divided by operating revenues.
c Dayton Hudson stores include: Target, Mervyn's, Marshall Field's, and Hudson.
d May Department Stores Company includes: Lord and Taylor, Filene's, Hecht's, Foley's, Kaufmann's, Robinson-May, Famous-Barr, and Meier & Frank, among others. May also owns the discount footwear chain of Payless ShoeSource stores.
e Shoes
f Garments
g Toys
NM = not meaningful

have a reputation for more fashionable and higher quality merchandise.

Unlike the earlier "retail revolution" when department stores became oligopolies, the current surge of specialty and discount formats is less a function of the evolution of retail institutions than of overriding demographic and life style changes in American society. "The fragmentation of the American marketplace . . . reflects the expanding ranks of single-person households, the greater proportion of two-income families, and the sharp rise in the number of working women" (Legomsky, 1986: R62).[16] Furthermore, there has been a widening of the gap between the rich and the poor in the United States.[17] The retail sector has mirrored this dichotomy—stores have either gone upscale or low-price, with middle-income consumers pulled in both directions.

This segmentation of the American market creates numerous opportunities for specialized retail formats. Just as the era of mass production is giving way to flexible manufacturing in the productive sphere, the renowned American mass market is becoming more customized and personalized. This has paved the way for increased trans-Atlantic competition by European and other foreign-based retailers, such as Benetton in Italy and Laura Ashley in the United Kingdom. According to Lester Thurow, professor of economics and management at the Massachusetts Institute of Technology. "The American economy died about 10 years ago, and has been replaced by a world economy. . . . [American retailers] are going to face an international challenge" (Legomsky, 1986: R61).

Department stores and other mass merchandisers in the United States have tried to develop effective counterstrategies to these trends. Some retailers like J.C. Penney have sought to upgrade their status from mass merchandiser to department store by adding higher-priced apparel, and to increase profitability by emphasizing higher-margin merchandise that has a faster turn-around time (Sack, 1989: R80). Other firms have begun to diversify their appeal by establishing their own specialty retail outlets (like the Foot Locker stores, which are owned by Woolworth Corporation).[18] On the international

front, retailers and manufacturers alike are acquiring large importers to shore up their position in global sourcing networks,[19] while unique organizational forms such as member-owned retail buying groups are being used in overseas procurement.[20]

In summary, the transformation of the retail sector in the United States has remained fast-paced throughout the 1980s and 1990s. This reflects not only the changing demography and purchasing power of American society, but as we will see in the next sections, it also proves to be a significant determinant of production patterns within the global economy.

THE ECONOMIC AGENTS IN BUYER-DRIVEN COMMODITY CHAINS

Big buyers are embedded in GCCs through the export and distribution networks they establish with overseas factories and trading companies. In order to understand the structure and dynamics of this relationship, we must first identify the economic agents in buyer-driven commodity chains (retailers, traders, overseas buyers, and factories), and then look at the impact of the main coordinating group (large retailers) on global production patterns.

Retailers

The organization of consumption in the United States is stratified by retail chains that target distinct income groups in the population. There are several types of retailers: large-volume, low-priced discount stores; mass merchandisers; department stores; and "fashion" or upper-end specialized retailers that deal exclusively with national brand-named products. These stores vary in their mixes of nationally branded, store-branded, and unbranded products.[21] The different categories of retailers also establish distinctive relationships with importers and overseas manufacturers. As one moves down this list of retailers, the quality and price of the goods sold increase, and the requirements for their international contractors become more stringent.

Traders

Trading companies have evolved from the global juggernauts that spanned the British, Dutch, and Japanese empires in centuries past to the highly specialized organizations that exist today. As recently as twenty-five years ago, there were no direct buying offices set up by U.S. retailers in Asia.[22] Originally, American retailers bought from importers on a "landed" basis—that is, the importer cleared the goods through U.S. customs.[23] In the late 1970s, importing began to be done on a "first-cost" basis. The buyer opened a letter of credit directly to the factory and paid the importer (or buying agent) a commission to get the goods to the export port. The buyer handled the shipping and distribution in the United States.

Before retailers established direct buying offices overseas, importers were the key intermediaries between retailers and their foreign contractors. There still is a broad array of specialized importers that deal in particular industries[24] or even in specific product niches within an industry.[25] While the importers handle production logistics and often help to develop new product lines, the leading apparel companies control the marketing end of the apparel commodity chain through their exclusive designs and brand-named products.[26]

Overseas Buyers

There is a symbiotic relationship between the overseas buying offices of major retail chains and the role played by importers and exporters. The direct buying offices of major retailers purchase a wide assortment of products, typically grouped into "soft goods" (like garments and shoes) and "hard goods" (such as lighting fixtures, kitchenware, appliances, furniture, and toys). Obviously, it is difficult for these buyers to develop an intimate knowledge of the supplier networks and product characteristics of such a diverse array of items. As a result, retail chains depend heavily on the specialized importers and trading companies that continuously develop new product lines with the local manufacturers and that provide retailers with valuable information about the hot items and sales trends of their competitors.

In general, the U.S.-based buyers for American retailers tend to work with importers and trading companies in the fashion-oriented and new-product end of consumer-goods industries, while their overseas buying offices purchase the more standardized, popular, or large-volume items directly from the factories in order to eliminate the importer's commission. Large retailers usually have their own product development groups and buying offices in the United States for their most popular or distinctive items.

Factories

The factories that produce the consumer products that flow through buyer-driven commodity chains are involved in contract manufacturing relationships with the buyers who place the orders. Contract manufacturing (or specification contracting) refers to the production of finished consumer goods by local firms, where the output is distributed and marketed abroad by trading companies, branded merchandisers, retail chains, or their agents.[27] This is the major export niche filled by the East Asian NICs in the world economy.

In 1980, for example, Hong Kong, Taiwan, and South Korea accounted for 72 percent of all finished consumer goods exported by the Third World to OECD countries, other Asian nations supplied another 19 percent, while just 7 percent came from Latin America and the Caribbean. The United States was the leading market for these consumer products with 46 percent of the total (Keesing, 1983: 338–39). East Asian factories, which have handled the bulk of the specification contracting orders from U.S. retailers, tend to be locally owned and vary greatly in size—from the giant plants in South Korea to the myriad small family firms that account for a large proportion of the exports from Taiwan and Hong Kong.[28]

LOCATIONAL PATTERNS OF GLOBAL SOURCING

Big retailers and brand-named merchandisers have different strategies of global sourcing, which in large part are dictated by the client bases they serve (see Figure 40.2 and Table 40.3). Fashion-oriented retailers that cater to an exclusive clientele for "designer" products get their expensive, nationally branded goods from an inner ring of premium-quality, high-value-added exporting countries (e.g., Italy, France, Japan). Department stores and specialty chains that emphasize "private label" (or store brand) products as well as national brands source from the most established Third World exporters (such as the East Asian NICs, Brazil, Mexico, and India), while the mass merchandisers that sell lower-priced store brands buy from more remote tiers of medium- to low-cost, mid-quality exporters (low-end producers in the NICs, plus China and the Southeast Asian countries of Thailand, Malaysia, the Philippines, and Indonesia). Large-volume discount stores that sell the most inexpensive products import from the outer rings of low-cost suppliers of standardized goods (e.g., China, Indonesia, Bangladesh, Sri Lanka, Mauritius, the Dominican Republic, Guatemala). Finally, smaller importers serve as industry "scouts." They operate on the fringes of the international production frontier and help

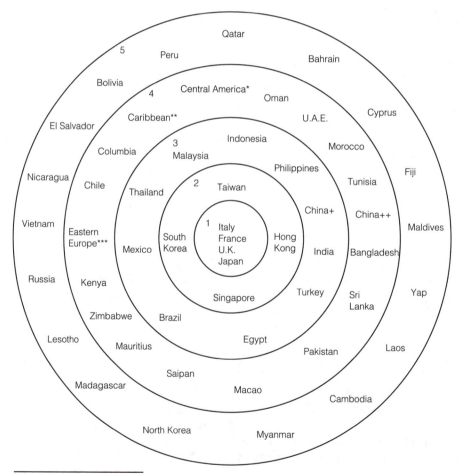

+ Southern China
++ Interior provinces of China
* Guatemala, Honduras, Costa Rica
** Dominican Republic, Jamaica, Haiti
*** Poland, Hungary, Czechoslovakia, Bulgaria

Figure 40.2 Production frontiers for global sourcing by U.S. retailers: the apparel industry.

Table 40.3 Types of retailers and main global sourcing areas.

Type of Retailer	Representative Firms	Main Global Sourcing Areas*	Characteristics of Buyer's Orders
Fashion-oriented Companies	Armani, Donna Karan, Polo/Ralph Lauren, Hugo Boss, Gucci	First and second rings	Expensive "designer" products requiring high levels of craftmanship; orders are in small lots
Department Stores, Specialty Stores, and Brand-named Companies	Bloomingdale's, Saks Fifth Avenue, Neiman-Marcus, Macy's, Nordstrom, The Gap, The Limited, Liz Claiborne, Calvin Klein	Second, third, and fourth rings	Top quality, high-priced goods sold under a variety of national brands and private labels (i.e., store brands); medium to large-sized orders, often coordinated by department store buying groups (such as May Department Stores Company and Federated Department Stores)
Mass Merchandisers	Sears Roebuck, Montgomery Ward, J.C. Penney, Woolworth	Second, third, and fourth rings	Good quality, medium-priced goods predominantly sold under private labels; large orders
Discount Chains	Wal-Mart, Kmart, Target	Third, fourth, and fifth rings	Low-priced, store-brand products; giant orders
Small Importers		Fourth and fifth rings	Pilot purchases and special items; sourcing done for retailers by small importers who act as "industry scouts" in searching out new sources of supply; orders are relatively small at first, but have the potential to grow rapidly if the suppliers are reliable

* For the countries in each of these rings, see Figure 40.2.

develop potential new sources of supply for global commodity chains (e.g., Vietnam, Myanmar, Saipan).

Several qualifications need to be mentioned concerning the schematic, purposefully oversimplified locational patterns identified in Figure 40.2 and Table 40.3. These production frontiers represent general trends that can vary by industry, by specific products, and by time period. More detailed analyses that trace the global sourcing of particular products over time are required to explore the factors that lead to shifts in these linkages. Two examples will illustrate the complexity of these arrangements.

The first example focuses on large volume discount stores such as Kmart and Wal-Mart. According to Table 40.3, they should source primarily from the three outer rings of the production frontiers, but our direct research indicates that these discounters also are prominent buyers in the second ring of East Asian NICs. Why? The reason is twofold. Apparel factories in relatively high-wage countries like Taiwan and South Korea work with anywhere from five to twenty clients (buyers) in a year. Although Kmart and Wal-Mart pay much less than department stores and specialty retailers like Macy's or Liz Claiborne, the factories use these discounters' large-volume orders to smooth out their production schedules so they don't have gaps or downtime. The other side of the equation is the discounter's vantage point. Kmart and Wal-Mart tend to source their most expensive, complicated items in the second-ring countries (e.g., infant's wear with a lot of embroidery). Thus they are using the more expensive and skilled workers in the NICs to produce relatively high-quality merchandise.

A second illustration deals with the upper-end retailers. Large apparel retailers like The Limited and The Gap, and brand-named companies like Phillips-Van Heusen and Levi Strauss, tend to source heavily in the second and third rings of Figure 40.2, but they also buy from countries located in the fourth and even the fifth rings. The reason they are positioned in the outer reaches of the production frontiers is that these companies engage in "price averaging" across their different manufacturing sites. A company like Phillips-Van Heusen, the number-one seller of men's dress shirts in the United States, is confident that its quality control procedures will allow it to produce identical dress shirts in its factories in the United States, Taiwan, Sri Lanka, or El Salvador. This also permits these companies to keep some of their production in, or close to, the United States for quick response to unexpectedly high demand for popular items as well as to gain the goodwill of the American consuming public.

Figure 40.2 highlights some methodological difficulties raised by the commodity chains perspective. Nation-states are not the ideal unit of analysis for establishing global sourcing patterns, since individual countries are tied to the world-economy through a variety of export roles (Gereffi, 1989a, 1992). Production actually takes place in specific regions or industrial districts *within countries* that have very different social and economic characteristics (Porter, 1990). Where commodity chains "touch down" in a country is an important determinant of the kind of production relationships that are established with retailers. Thus there can be several forms of international sourcing within a single nation.[29]

In the People's Republic of China, for example, Guangdong Province has very substantial investments from Hong Kong and Taiwan, while Fujian Province has a natural geographical and cultural affinity for Taiwanese investors. These two provinces in China are part of a Greater China Economic Region that includes Hong Kong and Taiwan. Thus China falls within both the third and the fourth rings of Figure 40.2: the quality and price of the products made in southern China (third ring) in affiliation with its East Asian NIC partners tend to be higher than for the goods produced in the interior provinces of China (fourth ring), where state enterprises are more prevalent.

Despite these qualifications, several generalizations can be made about the production frontiers identified in Figure 40.2. As one moves from the inner to the outer rings, the following changes are apparent: the cost of production decreases; manufacturing sophistication decreases; and the lead time needed for deliveries increases. Therefore there is a strong tendency for the high-quality, multiple-season "fashion" companies, as well as the more upscale department stores and specialty stores, to source their production from the three inner rings, while the price-conscious mass merchandisers and discount chains are willing to tolerate the lower quality and longer lead times that characterize production in the two outer rings. The "industry scout" role played by certain importers is particularly important for this latter set of buyers, since these importers are willing to take the time needed to bring the new, low-cost production sites located in the fourth and fifth rings into global sourcing networks. [. . .]

NOTES

The research for this paper was funded by grants from the Chiang Ching-Kuo Foundation for International Scholarly Exchange (United States), based in Taiwan, as well as the University Research Council at Duke University. I gratefully acknowledge these sources of support. I also appreciate the research assistance of Jeffrey Weiss at Duke, and the detailed comments provided by Phyllis Albertson, Bradford Barham, Miguel Korzeniewicz, Stephen Maire, and Karen J. Sack on earlier drafts of this paper.

1. The linkages between big buyers and their strategies of global sourcing were derived from numerous interviews carried out by the author in East Asia and the United States. A wide variety of trading companies, direct buying offices, and factories in Taiwan, Hong Kong, South Korea, and the People's Republic of China were visited in August-October 1991 and September-December 1992. Interviews also were conducted in the headquarters of major U.S. retailers and apparel firms in New York City and Los Angeles during the summers of 1991 and 1992.

2. The absence of factories also characterizes a growing number of U.S. semiconductor houses that

order customized as well as standard chips from outside contractors (Weber, 1991).

3. Orderly marketing agreements were imposed by the United States on footwear exporters in Taiwan and South Korea in 1977, but these were rescinded in 1981.

4. This used to be known as 807-production in the Caribbean and the Far East, and *maquiladora* assembly in Mexico. Now there is a new U.S. tariff classification system called the Harmonized Tariff Schedule that replaces the 807 section with a 9802 tariff code. The basic idea in this system is to allow a garment that has been assembled offshore using U.S.-made and -cut parts to be assessed a tariff only on the value added by offshore labor.

5. The much publicized bankruptcy of R. H. Macy & Company in 1992 is a recent example of the competitive problems that have affected the traditional department store (Strom, 1992).

6. Garment manufacturers have been required to add more buying seasons, offer a greater variety of clothes, agree to mandatory buy-back arrangements for unsold merchandise, provide retailer advertising allowances, and so on.

7. These new technologies include: electronic data interchange (EDI), which is a system for communicating to the retailer what is selling well and what needs to be replenished; computerized point-of-service inventory control; merchandising processing systems that monitor cash flows from order placement to shipping to billing and payment; and electronic mail hook-ups for every online store in worldwide networks of retail outlets.

8. Enhanced price competition is compatible with oligopoly because the economies of scale and scope of large-volume discount chains lead to high concentration levels in the retail sector, at the same time as the discounters stimulate considerable price competition because of their low-income customer base.

9. Many department stores carry familiar household names: Macy's, Bloomingdale's, Jordan Marsh, Mervyn's, Nordstrom, Dillard, Filene's, Kaufmann's, Saks Fifth Avenue. Numerous American retail chains today are owned by holding companies, such as the May Department Stores Company, Federated Department Stores, and Dayton Hudson. In Europe, where consumers were more inclined to shuttle from store to store for their individual apparel and accessory needs, the department store never developed into the prominent retailing institution that it has in the mass market of the United States.

10. General merchandise retailers provide a broad selection of "soft goods" (including apparel and home furnishings) and "hard goods" (appliances, hardware, auto, and garden supplies, etc.).

11. The best-known mass merchandising chains are Sears Roebuck & Co., Montgomery Ward, and Woolworth Corporation. These stores are a notch below the department stores in the quality of their merchandise and their prices, but they offer more service and brand-name variety than the large-volume discount retailers. In terms of their overall position in American retailing, though, department stores and mass merchandisers face similar competitive environments.

12. The three most prominent discount chains today are Wal-Mart, Kmart, and Target. Discount chains may focus on a specific product, such as shoes (Payless ShoeSource, Pic 'n Pay, and the 550-store Fayva Shoes retail chain owned by Morse Shoe). Historically, discount retail chains differed from department stores because the former carried broader assortments of hard goods (e.g., auto accessories, gardening equipment, housewares) and they relied heavily on self-service.

13. Department stores have tried to simulate a specialty-store ambience through the creation of "store-within-a-store" boutiques, each accommodating a particular company (like Liz Claiborne or Calvin Klein) or a distinct set of fashion tastes. Similarly, Woolworth Corporation has shed its mass merchandising image by incorporating dozens of specialty formats in its portfolio of 6,500 U.S. stores, including Foot Locker, Champs Sports, Afterthoughts accessories, and The San Francisco Music Box Co. Specialty stores now account for about half of Woolworth's annual revenue, up from 29 percent in 1983 (Miller, 1993).

14. The Gap, one of the most popular and profitable specialty clothing chains in American retailing today, only sells clothes under its own private label. In 1991 The Gap surpassed Liz Claiborne Inc. to become the second-largest clothes brand in the United States after Levi Strauss (Mitchell, 1992). The Limited is another major force in specialty apparel. It is regarded as the world's largest retailer of women's clothing. The Limited is composed of 17 divisions (such as Victoria's Secret, Lerner, Lane Bryant, and Structure), more than 4,100 stores, 75,000 employees, and 1991 sales of $6.3 billion.

15. Kmart's net income in 1990 recovered to $756 million, after its nosedive to $323 million in 1989. One of the areas where Kmart has been lagging, however, is its electronic data interchange (EDI) systems. In 1990 it embarked on a six-year store modernization program. Kmart management hopes that point-of-sale systems, a satellite network, and automated replenishment combined with just-in-time merchandise delivery will improve the performance of its 2,400 general merchandise stores. Kmart also has 2,000 specialty retail stores, including Waldenbooks, Pay Less Drug Stores, and PACE Membership Warehouse.

16. At the end of 1985, nearly 60 percent of mothers with children under eighteen were working, according to Labor Department figures, up nearly 5 percent from one year earlier.

17. Between 1977 and 1989, the richest 1 percent of American families reaped 60 percent of the growth in after-tax income of all families and an even

heftier three-forths of the gain in pretax income, while the pretax income of the bottom 40 percent of American families declined (Nasar, 1992). Similarly, a detailed study on family income prepared by the House Ways and Means Committee of the U.S. Congress found that from 1979 to 1987 the standard of living for the poorest fifth of the American population fell by 9 percent, while the living standard of the top fifth rose by 19 percent (Harrison and Bluestone, 1990: xi).

18. The eighteen-year-old Foot Locker chain, with 1,500 U.S. stores and $1.6 billion in annual sales, has generated an entire family of spin-offs, including Kids Foot Locker, Lady Foot Locker, and now World Foot Locker. Woolworth, which already garners 40 percent of its sales in foreign countries, plans to add 1,000 Foot Locker stores in Western Europe by the end of the decade (Miller, 1993).

19. For example, Payless ShoeSource International, the largest U.S. footwear importer, is owned by May Department Stores; and Meldisco, a division of Melville Corporation, handles the international purchasing of shoes for Kmart. Pagoda Trading Co., the second-biggest U.S. shoe importer, was acquired three years ago by Brown Shoe Co., the largest U.S. footwear manufacturer.

20. Associated Merchandising Corporation (AMC) is the world's largest retail buying group. It consolidates the overseas purchasing requirements of 40 member department stores, and it sources products from nearly 70 countries through its extensive network of buying offices in Asia, Europe, and Latin America.

21. Many brand-named companies like Liz Claiborne and Nike don't allow their products to be sold by discount stores or mass merchandisers, which has prompted the proliferation of "private label" merchandise (i.e., store brands).

22. Sears Roebuck, Montgomery Ward, and Macy's were the first U.S. companies to establish direct buying offices in Hong Kong in the 1960s. However, the really big direct orders came when Kmart and J.C. Penney set up their Hong Kong buying offices in 1970; within the next couple of years, these sprawling merchandisers had additional offices in Taiwan, South Korea, and Singapore. By the mid-1970s, many other retailers such as May Department Stores, Associated Merchandising Corporation, and Woolworth jumped on the direct buying bandwagon in the Far East.

23. The early importers with offices in the Far East were Japanese and American companies like Mitsubishi/CITC (a Japanese-U.S. joint venture), C. Itoh, Manow, and Mercury.

24. For example, Payless ShoeSource International, Pagoda, and E.S. Originals are large importers that deal exclusively in footwear.

25. There are different importers for women's shoes versus men's shoes, dress shoes versus casual footwear, women's dresses versus men's suits, adult versus children's clothes, and so on.

26. Nike, Reebok, and L.A. Gear are the major brand-named companies in athletic footwear, while Armani, Polo/Ralph Lauren, and Donna Karan are premium labels in clothes. However, all of these companies have diversified their presence in the apparel market and put their labels on a wide range of clothes, shoes, and accessories (handbags, hats, scarves, belts, wallets, etc.).

27. "Contract manufacturing" is more accurate than the commonly used terms "international subcontracting" or "commercial subcontracting" (Holmes, 1986) to describe what the East Asian NICs have excelled at. Contract manufacturing refers to the production of finished goods according to full specifications issued by the buyer, while "subcontracting" actually means the production of components or the carrying out of specific labor processes (e.g., stitching) for a factory that makes the finished item. Asian contract manufacturers (also known as contractors or vendors) have extended their production networks to encompass domestic as well as international subcontractors.

28. Taiwan and Hong Kong have multilayered domestic subcontracting networks, including large firms that produce key intermediate inputs (like plastics and textiles), medium-sized factories that do final product assembly, and many small factories and household enterprises that make a wide variety of components.

29. In Mexico, for instance, there is a vast difference between the *maquiladora* export plants along the Mexico-U.S. border that are engaged in labor-intensive garment and electronics assembly, and the new capital- and technology-intensive firms in the automobile and computer industries that are located further inland in Mexico's northern states. These latter factories use relatively advanced technologies to produce high-quality exports, including components and subassemblies like automotive engines. They pay better wages, hire larger percentages of skilled male workers, and use more domestic inputs than the traditional *maquiladora* plants that combine minimum wages with piecework and hire mostly unskilled women (Gereffi, 1991).

REFERENCES

American Apparel Manufacturers Association (AAMA). 1991. *FOCUS: 1991*. Washington, D.C.: AAMA.

Bluestone, Barry; Hanna, Patricia; Kuhn, Sarah; and Moore, Laura. 1981. *The Retail Revolution: Market Transformation, Investment, and Labor in the Modern Department Store*. Boston: Auburn House Publishing Company.

Dicken, Peter. 1992. *Global Shift: The Internationalization of Economic Activity*. 2d ed. New York: Guilford Publications.

Donaghu, Michael T., and Barff, Richard. 1990. "Nike Just Did It: International Subcontracting and Flexibility in Athletic Footwear Production." *Regional Studies* 24, 6: 537–52.

Doner, Richard F. 1991. *Driving a Bargain: Automobile Industrialization and Japanese Firms in Southeast Asia*. Berkeley: University of California Press.

Gereffi, Gary, 1989a. "Rethinking Development Theory: Insights from East Asia and Latin America." *Sociological Forum* 4, 4 (Fall): 505–33.

——. 1989b. "Development Strategies and the Global Factory." *Annals of the American Academy of Political and Social Science* 505 (Sept.): 92–104.

——, 1991. "The 'Old' and 'New' Maquiladora Industries in Mexico: What Is Their Contribution to National Development and North American Integration?" *Nuestra economía* 2, 8 (May–August): 39–63.

——. 1992. "New Realities of Industrial Development in East Asia and Latin America: Global, Regional, and National Trends." In *States and Development in the Asian Pacific Rim*, edited by Richard P. Appelbaum and Jeffrey Henderson, pp. 85–112. Newbury Park, CA: Sage Publications.

Gereffi, Gary, and Korzeniewicz, Miguel. 1990. "Commodity Chains and Footwear Exports in the Semiperiphery." In *Semiperipheral States in the World-Economy*, edited by William G. Martin, pp. 45–68. Westport, CT: Greenwood Press.

Gereffi, Gary, and Wyman, Donald, eds. 1990. *Manufacturing Miracles: Paths of Industrialization in Latin America and East Asia*. Princeton, NJ: Princeton University Press.

Harris, Nigel, 1987. *The End of the Third World*. New York: Penguin Books.

Harrison, Bennett, and Bluestone, Barry. 1990. *The Great U-Turn: Corporate Restructuring and the Polarizing of America*. New York: Basic Books.

Henderson, Jeffrey, 1989. *The Globalization of High Technology Production: Society, Space and Semiconductors in the Restructuring of the Modern World*. New York: Routledge.

Hill, Richard Child. 1989. "Comparing Transnational Production Systems: The Automobile Industry in the USA and Japan." *International Journal of Urban and Regional Research* 13, 3 (Sept.): 462–80.

Holmes, John, 1986. "The Organizational and Locational Structure of Production Subcontracting." In *Production, Work, and Territory: The Geographical Anatomy of Industrial Capitalism*, edited by Allen J. Scott and Michael Storper, pp. 80–106. Boston: Allen & Unwin.

Keesing, Donald B. 1983. "Linking Up to Distant Markets: South to North Exports of Manufactured Consumer Goods." *American Economic Review* 73: 338–42.

Lardner, James. 1988. "The Sweater Trade—I," *The New Yorker*, January 11, pp. 39–73.

Legomsky, Joanne. 1986. "The Europeanization of American Retailing." *Standard & Poor's Industry Surveys*, April 3, pp. R61–R65.

Miller, Annetta. 1993. "A Dinosaur No More: Woolworth Corp. Leaves Dime Stores Far Behind." *Newsweek*, January 4, pp. 54–55.

Mitchell, Russell. 1992. "The Gap: Can the Nation's Hottest Retailer Stay on Top?" *Business Week*, March 9, pp. 58–64.

Mody, Ashoka, and Wheeler, David. 1987. "Towards a Vanishing Middle: Competition in the World Garment Industry." *World Development* 15, 10/11: 1269–84.

Nasar, Sylvia. 1992. "The 1980's: A Very Good Time for the Very Rich." *New York Times*, March 5, p. 1A.

Piore, Michael J., and Sabel, Charles F. 1984. *The Second Industrial Divide*. New York: Basic Books.

Porter, Michael E. 1990. *The Competitive Advantage of Nations*. New York: Free Press.

Reich, Robert B. 1991. *The Work of Nations*. New York: Alfred A. Knopf.

Ross, Robert J. S., and Trachte, Kent C. 1990. *Global Capitalism: The New Leviathan*. Albany: State University of New York Press.

Rothstein, Richard. 1989. *Keeping Jobs in Fashion: Alternatives to the Euthanasia of the U.S. Apparel Industry*. Washington, D.C.: Economic Policy Institute.

Sack, Karen J. 1989. "Department Stores: Avoiding the Way of the Dinosaur." *Standard & Poor's Industry Surveys*, April 20, pp. R77–R82.

Saporito, Bill. 1991. "Is Wal-Mart Unstoppable?" *Fortune*, May 6, pp. 50–59.

Storper, Michael, and Harrison, Bennett, 1991. "Flexibility, Hierarchy and Regional Development. The Changing Structure of Industrial Production Systems and Their Forms of Governance in the 1990s." *Research Policy* 20, 5 (Oct.): 407–22.

Strom, Stephanie. 1992. "Department Stores' Fate: Bankruptcies Like Macy's Overshadowing Strong Consumer Loyalty, Experts Assert." *New York Times*, February 3, p. C1.

Waldinger, Roger. 1986. *Through the Eye of the Needle: Immigrants and Enterprise in New York's Garment Trades*. New York: New York University Press.

Weber, Samuel. 1991. "A New Endangered Species: Mulling a Fabless Future." *Electronics* 64, 7 (July): 36–38.

CHAPTER 41

"Flexible Citizenship: The Cultural Logics of Transnationality" and "Afterword: An Anthropology of Transnationality"

Aihwa Ong

FLEXIBLE CITIZENSHIP: THE CULTURAL LOGICS OF TRANSNATIONALITY

On the eve of the return of Hong Kong from British to mainland-Chinese rule, the city was abuzz with passport stories. A favorite one concerned mainland official Lu Ping, who presided over the transition. At a talk to Hong Kong business leaders (*taipans*), he fished a number of passports from his pockets to indicate he was fully aware that the Hong Kong elite has a weakness for foreign passports.[1] Indeed, more than half the members of the transition preparatory committee carried foreign passports. These politicians were no different from six hundred thousand other Hong Kongers (about ten percent of the total population) who held foreign passports as insurance against mainland-Chinese rule. Taipans who had been busy doing business with Beijing openly accumulated foreign passports, claiming they were merely "a matter of convenience," but in a Freudian slip, one let on that multiple passports were also "a matter of confidence" in uncertain political times.[2] The multiple-passport holder seems to display an élan for thriving in conditions of political insecurity, as well as in the turbulence of global trade. He is willing and eager to work with the Chinese-communist state while conjuring up ways of escape from potential dangers to his investment and family.

Another example of the flexible subject is provided by Raymond Chin, one of the founders of the Better Hong Kong Foundation, a pro-China business group. I heard a radio interview in which he was asked about his investment in China and the future of Hong Kong under communist rule. Here, I paraphrase him: "Freedom is a great thing, but I think it should be given to people who have earned it. We should take the long view and see the long-term returns on our investments in the mainland. Self-censorship and other kinds of responsible behavior may be necessary to get the kind of freedom we want."

This willingness to accommodate self-censorship reflects the displaced person's eagerness to hedge bets, even to the extent of risking property and life under different political conditions anywhere in the world. The Chinese in Hong Kong are of course a rather special kind of refugee, haunted by memento mori even when they seek global economic opportunities that include China. The novelist Paul Theroux notes that Hong Kong people are driven by the memory of previous Chinese disasters and shaped by their status as colonials without the normal colonial expectation of independence. They are people always in transit, who have become "world-class practitioners of self-sufficiency."[3] In this, they are not much different from overseas Chinese in Southeast Asia, who have largely flourished in postcolonial states and yet are considered politically alien, or alienable, when conditions take a turn for the worse. For over a century, overseas Chinese have been the forerunners of today's multiply displaced subjects, who are always on the move both mentally and physically.

The multiple-passport holder is an apt contemporary figure; he or she embodies the split between state-imposed identity and personal identity caused by political upheavals, migration, and changing global markets. In this world of high modernity, as one scholar notes, national and ethnic identities "become distinctly different entities, while at the same time, international frontiers become increasingly insignificant as such."[4] But are political borders becoming insignificant or is the state merely fashioning a new relationship to capital mobility and to manipulations by citizens and noncitizens alike?

Benedict Anderson suggests an answer when he argues that the goal of the classical nation-state project to align social habits, culture, attachment, and political participation is being unraveled by modern communications and nomadism. As a result, passports have become "less and less attestations of citizenship, let alone of loyalty to a protective nation-state, than of claims to participate in labor markets."[5] The truth claims of the state that are enshrined in the passport are gradually being replaced by its counterfeit use in response to the claims of global capitalism. Or is there another way of looking at the shifting relations between the nation-state and the global economy in late modernity, one that suggests more complex adjustments and accommodations? The realignment of political, ethnic, and personal identities is not necessarily a process of "win or lose," whereby political borders become "insignificant" and the nation-state "loses" to global trade in terms of its control over the affiliations and behavior of its subjects.[6]

If, as I intend to do, we pay attention instead to the *transnational practices and imaginings* of the nomadic subject and the social conditions that enable his flexibility, we obtain a different picture of how nation-states articulate with capitalism in late modernity. Indeed, our Hong Kong taipan is not simply a Chinese subject adroitly navigating the disjunctures between political landscapes and the shifting opportunities of global trade. His very flexibility in geographical and social positioning is itself an effect of novel articulations between the regimes of the family, the state, and capital, the kinds of practical-technical adjustments that have implications for our understanding of the late modern subject.

In this book, I intervene in the discussion of globalization, a subject heretofore dominated by the structuralist methods of sociologists and geographers. In *The Condition of Postmodernity*, David Harvey identifies flexibility as the modus operandi of late capitalism. He distinguishes contemporary systems of profit making, production, distribution, and consumption as a break from the earlier, Fordist model of centralized mass-assembly production in which the workers were also the mass consumers of their products. In the era of late capitalism, "the regime of flexible accumulation" reigns, whether in the realms of business philosophy and high finance or in production systems, labor markets, and consumption.[7] What is missing from Harvey's account is human agency and its production and negotiation of cultural meanings within the normative milieus of late capitalism. More recently, writers on "the information age" maintain that globalization—in which financial markets around the world are unified by information from the electronic-data stream—operates according to its own logic without a class of managers or capitalists in charge.[8]

These strategies—the decentralization of corporate activities across many sites, the location of "runaway" factories in global peripheries, and the reconfiguration of banking and investment relations—introduced new regimes in global production, finance, and marketing. These new modes of doing global business have been variously referred to as "globalization" by bankers and as "post-Fordism," "disorganized capitalism," and "flexible accumulation" by social theorists.[9] These terms are also significant in reflecting the new logic of capitalism whereby "nodes of capitalist development around the globe . . . [have] decentered capitalism . . . and abstracted capitalism for the first time from its Eurocentricism."[10]

Instead of embracing the totalizing view of globalization as economic rationality bereft of human agency, other social analysts have turned toward studying "the local." They are examining how particular articulations of the global and the local—often construed as the opposition between universalizing capitalist forces and local cultures—produce "multiple modernities" in different parts of the world.[11] Arjun Appadurai argues that such a "global production of locality" happens because transnational flows of people, goods, and knowledge become imaginative resources for creating communities and "virtual neighborhoods."[12] This view is informed by a top-down model whereby the global is macro–political economic and the local is situated, culturally creative, and resistant.[13]

But a model that analytically defines the global as political economic and the local as cultural does not quite capture the *horizontal* and *relational* nature of the contemporary economic, social, and cultural processes that stream across spaces. Nor does it express their *embeddedness* in differently configured regimes of power. For this reason, I prefer to use the term *transnationality*. *Trans* denotes both moving through space or across lines, as well as changing the nature of something. Besides suggesting new relations between nation-states and capital, transnationality also alludes to the *trans*versal, the *trans*actional, the *trans*lational, and the *trans*gressive aspects of contemporary behavior and imagination that are incited, enabled, and regulated by the changing logics of states and capitalism. In what follows, when I use the word *globalization*, I am referring to the narrow sense of new corporate strategies, but analytically, I am concerned with transnationality—or the condition of cultural interconnectedness and mobility across space—which has been intensified under late capitalism. I use *transnationalism* to refer to the cultural specificities of global processes, tracing the multiplicity of the uses and conceptions of "culture." The chapters that follow will discuss the transnationality induced by global capital circulating in the Asia Pacific region, the transnationalism associated with the practices and imagination of elite Chinese subjects, and the varied responses of Southeast Asian states to capital and mobility.[14]

This book places human practices and cultural logics at the center of discussions on globalization. Whereas globalization has been analyzed as consisting of flows of capital, information, and populations, my interest is in the cultural logics that inform and structure border crossings as well as state strategies. My goal is to tease out the rationalities (political, economic, cultural) that shape migration, relocation, business networks, state-capital relations, and all transnational processes that are apprehended through and directed by cultural meanings. In other words, I seek to bring into the same analytical framework the economic rationalities of globalization and the cultural dynamics that shape human and political responses. As a social scientist, I point to the economic rationality that encourages family emigration or the political rationality that invites foreign capital, but as an anthropologist, I am primarily concerned with the cultural logics that make these actions thinkable, practicable, and desirable, which are embedded in processes of capital accumulation.

First, the chapters that follow attempt an ethnography of transnational practices and linkages that seeks to embed the theory of practice within, not outside of or against, political-economic forces. For Sherry Ortner, "modern practice theory" is an approach that places human agency and everyday practices at the center of social analysis. Ortner notes that the little routines and scenarios of everyday life are embodiments and enactments of norms, values, and conceptual schemes about time, space, and the social order, so that everyday practices endorse and reproduce these norms. While she argues that social practice is shaped within relations of domination, *as well as* within relations of reciprocity and solidarity, Ortner does not provide an analytical linkage between the two. Indeed, her theory of practice, which is largely focused on the actors' intentions within the "system" of cultural meaning, is disembodied from the economic and political conditions of late capitalism. She seems to propose a view in which the anthropologist can determine the extent to which "Western capitalism," as an abstract system, does or does not affect the lives of "real people."[15] An approach that views political economy as separate from human agency cannot be corrected by a theory of practice that views political-economic forces as external to everyday meanings and action. Our challenge is to consider the reciprocal construction of practice, gender, ethnicity, race, class, and nation in processes of capital accumulation. I argue that an anthropology of the present should analyze people's everyday actions as a form of cultural politics embedded in specific power contexts. The *regulatory effects* of particular cultural institutions, projects, regimes, and markets that shape people's motivations, desires, and struggles and make them particular kinds of subjects in the world should be identified.

Second, I view transnationalism not in terms of unstructured flows but in terms of the tensions between movements and social orders. I relate transnational strategies to systems of governmentality—in the broad sense of techniques and codes for directing human behavior[16]—that condition and manage the movements of populations and capital. Michel Foucault's notion of governmentality maintains that regimes of truth and power produce disciplinary effects that condition our sense of self and our everyday practices.[17] In the following chapters, I trace the different regimes—state, family, economic enterprises—that shape and direct border crossings and transnational relations, at once conditioning their dynamism and scope but also giving structure to their patterning. These shifting patterns of travel, and realignments between state and capital, are invariably understood according to the logics of culture and regional hegemony. Given the history of diasporan trading groups such as the ethnic Chinese, who play a major role in many of the so-called Asian tiger economies, the Asia Pacific region is ideal for investigating these new modalities of translocal governmentality and the cultural logics of subject making.[18]

Third, I argue that in the era of globalization, individuals as well as governments develop a flexible notion of citizenship and sovereignty as strategies to accumulate capital and power. "Flexible citizenship" refers to the cultural logics of capitalist accumulation, travel, and displacement that induce subjects to respond fluidly and opportunistically to changing political-economic conditions.[19] In their quest to accumulate capital and social prestige in the global arena, subjects emphasize, and are regulated by, practices favoring flexibility, mobility, and repositioning in relation to markets, governments, and cultural regimes. These logics and practices are produced within particular structures of meaning about family, gender, nationality, class mobility, and social power.

Fourth, if mobile subjects plot and maneuver in relation to capital flows, governments also articulate with global capital and entities in complex ways. I want to problematize the popular view that globalization has weakened state power. While capital, population, and cultural flows have indeed made in-roads into state sovereignty, the art of government has been highly responsive to the challenges of transnationality. I introduce the concept of graduated sovereignty to denote a series of zones that are subjected to different kinds of governmentality and that vary in terms of the mix of disciplinary and civilizing regimes. These zones, which do not necessarily follow political borders, often contain ethnically marked class groupings, which in practice are subjected to regimes of rights and obligations that are different from those in other zones. Because anthropologists pay attention to the various normalizing powers of the state and capital on subject populations, we can provide a different take on globalization—one that goes beyond universalizing spatial orders.

Fifth, besides looking at globalization, the point of this book is to reorient the study of Chinese subjects. Global capitalism in Asia is linked to new cultural representations of "Chineseness" (rather than "Japaneseness") in relation to transnational Asian capitalism. As overseas Chinese and mainland Chinese become linked in circuits of production, trade, and finance, narratives produce concepts such as "fraternal network capitalism" and "Greater China," a term that refers to the economically integrated zone comprising China, Taiwan, and Hong Kong, but sometimes including the ethnic Chinese communities in Southeast Asia. This triumphant "Chinese capitalism" has induced long-assimilated Thai and Indonesian subjects to reclaim their "ethnic-Chinese" status as they participate in regional business networks. The changing status of diasporan Chinese is historically intertwined with the operations and globalization of capital, and their cultural experiences are the ethnographic ground from which my points about transnationality are drawn.

Sixth, I challenge the view that the pro-liferation of unofficial narratives associated with triumphant Chinese capitalism reflect insurmountable cultural differences. I argue that on the contrary, discourses such as "Asian values," "the new Islam," "saying no to the West," and "the clash of civiliza-tions" can occur in the context of funda-mentally playing (and competing) by the rules of the neoliberal orthodoxy. Despite the claims of some American scholars and policy makers that the emergence of the Pacific Rim powers heralds an irreducible cultural div-ision between East and West, these parallel narratives, I argue, disguise common civiliza-tional references in a world where the market is absolutely transcendental.

Through an anthropology of emigrating families, transnational publics, state strat-egies, and panreligious nationalist discourses, the following chapters will identify the cul-tural logics shaping individual, national, and regional relations of power and conflict. But before I turn to these themes, I will briefly review how anthropology and cultural stud-ies have approached the topics that can be loosely gathered under the rubrics of "dias-pora" and "transnationalism." [. . .]

AFTERWORD: AN ANTHROPOLOGY OF TRANSNATIONALITY

This book has considered the varied practices and policies—reworked, of course, in terms of local cultural meanings—that transform the meaning of citizenship in an era of global-ization. My focus on transnationality high-lights the processes whereby flexibility, whether in strategies of citizenship or in regimes of sovereignty, is a product and a condition of late capitalism. This work also represents an anthropological intervention into the study of changing relations between subjects, state, and capital, and it demon-strates why a keen grasp of cultural dynamics is essential to such an analysis. By tying eth-nography to the structural analysis of global change, we are able to disclose the ways in which culture gives meaning to action and how culture itself becomes transformed by capitalism and by the modern nation-state. An approach rooted in the ethnographic knowledge of a region also demonstrates that capitalism, which has been differently assimilated by different Asian countries, has become reconfigured and has taken on new cultural meanings and practices—whether at the level of the individual or the com-munity—that valorize flexibility, difference, and transnationality.

Anthropologists can grasp the history of the present in a way that universalizing arm-chair theorists, who persist in their view of the world as being divided into traditional and modern halves, cannot. Indeed, the modernity-tradition model assumes an intel-lectual division of labor between sociology and anthropology, and anthropologists are chastised for dealing with "traditional," "disappearing" cultures, when in fact, "non-Western" cultures are not disappearing but are adjusting in very complex ways to global processes and remaking their own modern-ities.[1] A further mistake in the rationalist and reductionist models of the world is the tendency to view non-Western cultures and human agency as passive or, at best, ineffec-tual. Let us briefly consider, for example, a dominant sociological framework for grasp-ing the dynamism of global relations and human interaction.

As formulated by Immanuel Wallerstein, the world-system theory views the world according to a tripartite scheme of core, per-iphery, and semiperiphery.[2] Wallerstein has been criticized for reducing capitalism to exchange relations (at the expense of produc-tion) and for his functionalist emphasis on the "needs" of core countries in shaping the global division of labor. At the same time, he downgrades the importance of politi-cal and military factors in processes of social change. Onto this system of (narrowly defined) transnational economic inter-dependencies Anthony Giddens has grafted a system of nation-states, seeking to emphasize the latter as a separate system of political power that counterbalances the economic power of global capital.[3] This separation of capitalism and state administrative power into disconnected entities reduces the usefulness of Giddens's approach for an understanding of globalization. Like Huntington's taxonomy of civilizations, such universalizing models based on systemic relations— economic, political, religious—all paper over the actual uneven spread of capitalism, the intertwining of capitalism and state power, the cultural forms of ruling, and the dynamism of cultural struggles in different parts of the world that do not fit their logical schemes.

More recently, totalizing discourses of globalization, which are drawn from business and management literature, represent the latest example to date of a unidirectional model that sees global forces transforming economies and societies into a single global order, which Castells calls "the network society."[4] Politics, culture, and human agency are viewed only as the effects of globalizing processes, such as trade, production, and communications, rather than as vital logics that play a role in shaping the distribution, directionality, and effects of global phenomena. In contrast, an approach that embeds global processes in a regional formation will yield a finer, more complex understanding of the reciprocal shaping of cultural logics and social and state relations in the course of uneven capitalist development.[5]

Anthropology is a field known for its distinctive methodology (regardless of the populations studied) in exploring the links between cultural and material processes in historically specific contexts and in using ethnographic understanding to explain the cultural logics that shape the relations between society, state, and capital. American anthropology has a long history of attending to local-global articulations and melding fine-grained ethnographic perspectives with an appreciation for the historical dynamics of capitalism and social change. Although earlier anthropologists were also influenced by the binarisms of modernity-tradition, core-periphery, and Europe-"people without history," their careful ethnographic study of the historical dynamics through which the multiple meanings and material practices of colonialism and capitalism are reworked point to the culturally specific ways societies have participated in global history.[6] A newer generation of anthropologists who are freeing themselves from the binarism of older models and deploying post-structuralist theories has refined the anthropological analysis of the complex interplay between capitalism, the nation-state, and power dynamics in particular times and places.[7]

But, in turning away from the overarching theories of social change, we may have rushed too quickly into the arms of cultural studies and postcolonial studies. In our post-cold war flirtations with the humanities, anthropologists have too often ceded ground to an anemic approach that takes as its object culture-as-text or that reduces cultural analysis to a North American angst-driven self-reflexivity or to an equally self-conscious, postcolonial, elite-driven discourse that ignores the structures of power in identity making and social change. A hermeneutic trend in anthropology involves witty texts that pose as a form of self-indulgent identity politics, literary works that build a stage for moral grandstanding, and studies of abstracted cultural globalization that are coupled with insubstantial claims. I am all for flirtations and skirmishes on the boundaries of knowledge and for serious interdisciplinary work, but what we want is not a resulting "lite" anthropology but rather an enlarged space for telling the stories of modernity in ways that capture the interplay between culture and the material forms of social life.[8]

The field must recapture its unique role in addressing the big questions of politics, culture, and society in ways that transcend the mechanical modernity-tradition, first world-third world, core-periphery models and the universalizing assumptions that underlie metropolitan theories of postcoloniality, modernity, and globalization. To the grounding of anthropology in political economy, cultural politics, and ethnographic knowledge, I have added a Foucauldian sensibility about power, thus offering a more complex view of the fluid relations between culture, politics, and capitalism. The different paths to modernity have depended upon political strategies that target, organize, and give meaning to bodies, populations, and the social forms of contemporary life. These biopolitical concerns have given a distinctiveness to particular cultural systems, and the kinds of capitalism they enable and produce.

Throughout, I treat culture as a contingent scheme of meanings tied to power dynamics, and I rigorously problematize even "natives'" claims about their "own" culture, since apprehension, ownership, and representation are practices embedded in strategies of positioning, control, and maneuver. I go beyond simple claims about the nonessentialized nature of culture, to show that culture-making involves not only processes of othering by dominant players but also processes of cultural self-theorizing and re-envisioning in relation to fluid power dynamics, whether at the level of interpersonal relations or at the level of national politics and geopolitical posturing. Second, this book shows that the cultural logics of family, religion, and nation are reworked in relation to capitalism, and that new practices of travel, subject making, and citizenship are interlinked with the reconfigured capitalisms we find in different parts of the world. Third, going beyond class or subaltern analysis, this book demonstrates that the varied regimes of regulation, and the strategies of multiple positioning that engage and evade these regimes, produce a more complex view of subject making. While global processes valorize mobility, flexibility, and accumulation, there are structural limits set by cultural norms, modes of ruling, and nationalist ideologies. Fourth, emerging transnational publics constitute fields of cultural normativity in intermingled spaces of Asian and Western capitalisms, thus setting the stage for the dynamic construction of new kinds of transnational ethnicized subjectivity. Fifth, in a critique of American orientalism that views Asian societies as inalienably different, I argue that Asian tigers in fact share "Western" liberal rationalities, but their liberalism uses culture as a legitimizing force—to regulate society, to attract global capital, and to engage in trade wars. Sixth, in contrast to arguments about the retreat of the state, I argue that postdevelopmental Asian states

respond positively to global capital, either by engaging in transnational linkages to capital and multilateral agencies or by experimenting with graduated sovereignty as a way to make their societies more attractive to global capital. Finally, by identifying the cultural forms that are shaped by globalization at the personal, state, and regional levels in the Asia Pacific region, this book seeks to document the existence of a vibrant center of globalization, which is now quite interpenetrated by the spaces and practices we used to associate exclusively with the West. This intermingling of spaces and practices of travel, production, discipline, consumption, and accumulation is a product of globalization, but its effects are apprehended, organized, and experienced in culturally distinctive ways. I hope the arguments presented above persuade anthropologists that they have something to say about the role of culture in constituting state and society under varying conditions of globalization, and thus a vital role in provincializing metropolitan theories of universal change. Surely, in an age when the state and capital are directly engaged in the production and the destruction of cultural values, we should cultivate a kind of nomadic thinking that allows us to stand outside a given modernity, and to retain a radical skepticism toward the cultural logics involved in making and remaking our worlds.

NOTES

Introduction: Flexible Citizenship: The Cultural Logics of Globalization

1. I thank Fred Chiu Yen Liang of the Hong Kong Baptist University for relating this story to me.
2. Edward A. Gargan, "A Year from Chinese Rule, Dread Grows in Hong Kong," *New York Times*, 1 July 1996, A1, 6.
3. Paul Theroux, "Memories That Drive Hong Kong," *New York Times*, 11 June 1997, A21.
4. Dieter Hoffmann-Axthelm, "Identity and Reality: The End of the Philosophical Immigration Officer," in *Modernity and Identity*, ed. Scott Lash and Jonathan Friedman (Oxford: Basil Blackwell, 1992), 199.
5. Benedict Anderson, "Exodus," *Cultural Inquiry* 20 (winter 1994): 323.
6. Alternatively, Bryan S. Turner argues that uncertainties associated with globalization may "produce strong political reactions asserting the

normative authority of the local and the national over the global and international." See Turner, "Outline of a Theory of Citizenship," *Sociology* 24 (May 1990): 2, 212.

7. See David Harvey, *The Condition of Postmodernity* (Oxford: Basil Blackwell, 1989), chaps. 10, 11.

8. See, for example, Martin Carnoy et al., *The New Global Economy in the Information Age* (University Park: Pennsylvania State University Press, 1993); and Manuel Castells, *The Information Age*, vol. 1., *The Rise of the Network Society* (Oxford: Basil Blackwell, 1996).

9. See Claus Offe, *Disorganized Capitalism* (Cambridge, Mass.: MIT Press, 1985); and Harvey, *Condition of Postmodernity*.

10. Arif Dirlik, *After the Revolution: Waking to Global Capitalism* (Hanover, N.H.: Wesleyan University Press, 1994), 62.

11. Alan Pred and Michael Watts, *Reworking Modernity: Capitalisms and Symbolic Discontent* (New Brunswick, N.J.: Rutgers University Press, 1992).

12. Arjun Appadurai, *Modernity at Large: Cultural Dimensions of Globalization* (Minneapolis: University of Minnesota Press, 1996), 178–99.

13. This point was also raised in Doreen Massey, "Power Geometry and a Progressive Sense of Place," in *Mapping the Futures: Local Cultures, Global Change*, ed. J. Bird et al. (London: Routledge, 1993).

14. The Asia Pacific region has been defined by Euroamerican imperialism and capitalisms and by the political struggles of peoples within the region over the past centuries. See Arif Dirlik, "Introducing the Pacific," in *What Is in a Rim? Critical Perspectives on the Pacific Region Idea*, ed. Arif Dirlik (Boulder, Colo.: Westview, 1992), 3–11.

15. See Sherry Ortner, "Theory in Anthropology since the Sixties," in *Culture/Power/History*, ed. Nicholas B. Dirks, Geoff Eley, and Sherry Ortner (Princeton, N.J.: Princeton University Press, 1994), 388–401. For a criticism of Ortner see Talal Asad, "Introduction," in *Genealogies of Religion* (Baltimore, Md.: Johns Hopkins University Press, 1993), 5–6.

16. See Michel Foucault, *Ethics: Subjectivity and Truth*, ed. Paul Rabinow, trans. Robert Hurley et al. (New York: New Press, 1997), 1:81.

17. See Michel Foucault, "Governmentality," in *The Foucault Effect: Studies in Governmentality*, ed. Graham Burchell, Colin Gordon, and Peter Miller (Chicago: University of Chicago Press, 1991).

18. See Aihwa Ong and Don Nonini, eds., *Ungrounded Empires: The Cultural Politics of Modern Chinese Transnationalism* (New York: Routledge, 1997). The term "Asian tiger economies" refers to the rapidly developing countries of South Korea, Taiwan, Hong Kong, Singapore, Malaysia, Thailand, and the "emerging tiger" economies of Indonesia and the Philippines. Busi-

ness enterprises and networks dominated by ethnic Chinese are prominent everywhere except in South Korea.

19. This concept was first articulated in Aihwa Ong, "On the Edge of Empires: Flexible Citizenship among Chinese in Diaspora," *positions* 1, no. 3 (winter 1993): 745–78.

Afterword: An Anthropology of Transnationality

1. This modern-traditional division of the world's societies is very evident in Anthony Giddens, *In Defense of Sociology* (London: Polity, 1996). Giddens maintains that because anthropology deals with "nonmodern" cultures, it is dealing with an "evaporating" subject (122).

2. Wallerstein, *Modern World System*.

3. Giddens, *Nation-State and Violence*.

4. Castells, *Rise of the Network Society*.

5. See Ashraf Ghani, "Space as an Arena of Represented Practices," in *Mapping the Futures: Local Cultures, Global Change*, ed. J. Bird et al. (London: Routledge, 1993).

6. See chapter 5. This tradition is associated with anthropological training at Columbia University, the University of Chicago, and Johns Hopkins University. For a summary see Vincent, *Anthropology and Politics*. A short list of leading works might suffice here: Steward, *People of Puerto Rico*; Eric Wolf, *Peasant Wars of the Twentieth Century* (New York: Harper and Row, 1969); Wolf, *Europe*; Marshall Sahlins, *Stone Age Economics* (Chicago: Aldine-Atherton, 1972); Sahlins, *Culture and Practical Reason* (Chicago: University of Chicago Press, 1976); Sydney Mintz, *Caribbean Transformations* (Chicago: Aldine, 1974); Mintz, *Sweetness and Power*; Scott, *Moral Economy*; Scott, *Weapons*; June Nash, *We Eat the Mines and the Mines Eat Us* (New York: Columbia University Press, 1979); and Vincent, *Teso in Transformation*. This important tradition is inexplicably ignored in Sherry Ortner's representation of political economy in Ortner, "Theory in Anthropology."

7. See Michael Taussig, *The Devil and Commodity Fetishism in South America* (Chapel Hill: University of North Carolina Press, 1980); Ann Stoler, *Capitalism and Confrontation in Sumatra's Plantation Belt, 1870–1979* (New Haven, Conn.: Yale University Press, 1985); Jean Comaroff, *Body of Power, Spirit of Resistance* (Chicago: University of Chicago Press, 1985); Scott, *Weapons*; Ong, *Spirits of Resistance*; Michael G. Peletz, *A Share of the Harvest* (Berkeley: University of California Press, 1988); William Roseberry, *Anthropologies and Histories* (New Brunswick: Rutgers University Press, 1989); James Ferguson, *The Anti-politics Machine: 'Development,' Depoliticization, and Bureaucratic State Power in Lesotho* (Cambridge: Cambridge University Press, 1990); Williams, *Stains on My Name*; John Comaroff and Jean

Comaroff, *Ethnography and the Historical Imagination* (Boulder, Colo.: Westview, 1992); Katherine Verdery, *What Was Socialism? What Comes After?* (Princeton, N.J.: Princeton University Press, 1995); and Gupta, *Postcolonial Developments*.

8. This is a point that Don Nonini and I raised in Nonini and Ong, "Introduction."

SECTION 10

Non-state Actors, NGOs, and Social Movements

Introduction to Section 10

The partly academic, partly popular categories used in the title of this section are entry points into a set of contentious theoretical, normative, and practical debates. Although there were struggles and campaigns across borders to abolish slavery, improve labor rights, or fight imperialism in the nineteenth century, these kinds of efforts have become much more visible once again since the end of the Cold War. Correspondingly, scholarship on transnational non-state actors, nongovernmental organizations (NGOs), and social movements has also burgeoned during the last two decades.

Thomas Risse-Kappen offers a framework that explains how and why transnational non-state actors can be critical shapers of domestic politics and the international relations of states and intergovernmental organizations. Actors are transnational if they link at least "two societies or sub-units of national governments (in the case of transgovernmental relations)." They include multinational corporations, international nongovernmental organizations (INGOs), epistemic communities, and coalitions of human rights groups, peace activists or central bankers that vary with respect to the degree of their level of institutionalization. Risse-Kappen's central claim is that differences in domestic structures within states and variations in international institutions mediate the policy impacts of transnational non-state actors.

John Boli and George Thomas then explore the historical emergence and structural similarities between international nongovernmental organizations (INGOs) since the 1850s. The INGOs they study include industry and professional associations; scientific and technical groups; humanitarian, human rights, and environmental organizations; and sports and leisure agencies. Boli and Thomas argue that the emergence of the INGO sector goes hand-in-hand with the emergence of a world polity that has existed for the last century. For these authors, the world consists of "a set of fundamental principles and models, mainly onto-logical and cognitive in character, defining the nature and purposes of social actors and action." INGOs represent, enact, improvise upon, and dramatize different and potentially conflicting world-cultural principles.

Louis Kriesberg examines a subset of Boli and Thomas's INGO sectors and Risse-Kappen's non-state actors, which he identifies as transnational social movement organiza-tions (TSMOs)—those transnational groups that are at least somewhat formally organized "to change rather than maintain the status quo." Political democratization; economic, social, and cultural integration; values diffusion and convergence; and the proliferation of inter-national organizations partially explain the rise of TSMOs, and affect the nature of their activities and impacts. According to Kriesberg, TSMOs have unique capabilities including the ability to work across multiple levels—from the international to the local—and the ability to complement one another. They affect policy and other forms of social change at different levels and across societies by: 1. building social infrastructures (such as trust) for collective action; 2. cultivating constituencies for intergovernmental organizations; 3. generating and distributing resources; 4. fostering new transnational identities; and 5. motivating groups contesting transnational sources of common problems.

Margaret Keck and Kathryn Sikkink explore the emergence, evolution, and effectiveness of what they call Transnational Advocacy Networks (TANs). They argue that such "voluntary, reciprocal" networks often develop around shared discourses and dense exchanges of information and services. These networks consist not only of domestic and international NGO activists but also like-minded individuals from other organizations including state and intergovernmental agencies. Information, leverage, accountability, and symbolic tactics are utilized, often in "boomerang models," whereby domestic parties (especially nongovernmental advocacy groups) influence their own unresponsive or repressive governments by linking up with external supporters to form TANs. The effectiveness of TANs depends on a host of characteristics ranging from high levels of network density, the nature of the issues they address, and the vulnerability of target actors to moral persuasion.

In the final excerpt in this section, Nancy Naples synthesizes recent scholarship on transnational feminist practice from a series of case studies on women's cross-border activism. She examines the continuing importance of location and localization in this arena, calling attention to "the limits of local struggles that fail to challenge the extra-local processes that shape them." However, transnational NGOs and advocacy networks, argues Naples, are also vulnerable to critique. One problem characterizing many of their activities is that NGOs and their leaders who are de-linked from citizens' groups and broader social movements are often called upon as experts to shape the programs of states and intergovernmental agencies. This critique, and others like it, Naples believes, is especially common in transnational feminist praxis, but is by no means unique to this field.

CHAPTER 42

Bringing Transnational Relations Back In: Introduction

Thomas Risse-Kappen

INTRODUCTION

Transnational relations, i.e., *regular inter-actions across national boundaries when at least one actor is a non-state agent or does not operate on behalf of a national government or an intergovernmental organization,*[1] permeate world politics in almost every issue-area. About 5,000 international non-governmental organizations (INGOs)—from Amnesty International and Greenpeace to the International Political Science Association—lobby international regimes and inter-state organizations for their purposes.[2] Some promote international cooperation, while others try to prevent regulatory regimes which would interfere with the activities of private citizens. Some of the approximately 7,000 multinational corporations (MNCs) with subsidiaries in other countries have gross sales larger than the gross national product (GNP) of even major countries and, thus, create adaptation problems for the foreign economic policies of many states. More loosely organized transnational alliances appear to be everywhere, too. Transnational dissident movements in Eastern Europe helped to topple the Communist regimes in 1989. Western social movements set the public agenda on peace and environmental questions in many countries during the 1980s. Transnational groups of scientists—"epistemic communities"[3]—contributed to a growing global awareness about various environmental issues. Trans*governmental* networks among state officials in sub-units of national governments, international organizations, and regimes frequently pursue their own agenda, independently from and sometimes even contrary to the declared policies of their national governments. Such knowledge-based or normative principle-based transnational and transgovernmental issue networks seem to have a major impact on the global diffusion of values, norms, and ideas in such diverse issue-areas as human rights, international security, or the global environment. But there is no reason to assume that transnational relations regularly promote "good" causes. Transnational terrorism poses a serious threat to internal stability in many countries, while some scholars have identified Islamic fundamentalism—another transnational social movement—as a major source of future inter-state conflicts.[4]

Almost nobody denies that transnational relations exist; their presence is well established. But despite more than twenty years of controversy about the subject, we still have a poor understanding of their impact on state policies and international relations. Transnational relations do not seem to have the same effects across cases. How is it to be explained, for example, that the spread of democratic values and human rights toward the end of this century, promoted by various INGOs and transnational alliances,[5] has affected some countries more than others—the former Soviet Union as compared to China, former Czechoslovakia as compared to Romania, and South Korea as compared to North Korea? Why have "epistemic communities" and INGOs been able to set the agenda on global warming in Japan and in many European Union (EU) countries, but apparently less so in the United States? How do we explain that the transnational peace movements of the early 1980s in Western

Europe and North America had a lasting impact on German security policy, made a significant short-term difference in the US, but had almost no influence on French foreign policy?[6]

This study suggests that the debate of the 1970s on transnational relations closed the book on the subject prematurely and that it is worthwhile to revive it. The earlier arguments set up the controversy in terms of a "state-centered" versus a "society-dominated" view of world politics. We claim instead that it is more fruitful to examine how the inter-state world interacts with the "society world" of transnational relations. If the conditions under which transnational actors matter are clearly specified, the claim that "the reciprocal effects between transnational relations and the interstate system" are "centrally important to the understanding of contemporary world politics"[7] can be made with greater confidence.

The main question to be asked in this volume is therefore: *under what domestic and international circumstances do transnational coalitions and actors who attempt to change policy outcomes in a specific issue-area succeed or fail to achieve their goals?*

Our question is *not* what difference transnational relations make in international politics in general. This would require one to vary empirical case studies with regard to the existence or non-existence of non-state actors. The methodological difficulties of such an approach seem to be almost insurmountable, since we do not know enough about the universe of cases to be able to specify whether our case selection constitutes a reasonably representative sample. Rather, we will take a more modest and feasible approach by comparing cases in which transnational coalitions and actors consciously sought to influence policies, mainly state behavior in the foreign policy arena. We take the existence of transnational coalitions and actors who aim to change policies in various issue-areas as the point of departure. The issue-areas investigated include the international economy . . . the environment . . . international security . . ., and human rights. . . . We look at the policy impact of transnational actors such as MNCs . . ., INGOs

. . ., transnational and transgovernmental actors within international institutions . . ., as well as loose alliances among societal groups. . . . We look at the differential impact of these actors on highly industrialized states . . ., on former Communist countries . . ., and on industrializing as well as less developed states. . . . Finally, the transnational relations investigated here vary with regard to their embeddedness in bilateral and/or multilateral institutions—from the EU . . . and the US–Japanese alliance . . . to the East–West détente of the Cold War, . . . and North–South relations. . . .

The volume builds upon and integrates two theoretical approaches which have been developed independently from each other and have rarely been brought together—the concepts of *domestic structures* and of *international institutions*. They both deal with structures of governance, they both have generated fruitful empirical research, and, thus, together enlighten this inquiry.

This book argues, in short, that the impact of transnational actors and coalitions on state policies is likely to vary according to:

1. differences in *domestic structures*, i.e., the normative and organizational arrangements which form the "state," structure society, and link the two in the polity; and

2. degrees of *international institutionalization*, i.e., the extent to which the specific issue-area is regulated by bilateral agreements, multilateral regimes, and/or international organizations.

Domestic structures are likely to determine both the availability of channels for transnational actors into the political systems and the requirements for "winning coalitions" to change policies. On the one hand, the more the state dominates the domestic structure, the more difficult it should be for transnational actors to penetrate the social and political systems of the "target" country. Once they overcome this hurdle in state-dominated systems, though, their policy impact might be profound, since coalition-building with rather small groups of governmental actors appears to be comparatively straightforward. On the other hand, the more fragmented the state and the better organized civil society, the easier should be the access for transnational actors. But the requirements for successful coalition-building are likely to be quite staggering in such systems.

Domestic structures and international institutionalization are likely to interact in determining the ability of transnational actors to bring about policy changes. The more the respective issue-area is regulated by international norms of cooperation, the more permeable should state boundaries become for transnational activities. Highly regulated and cooperative structures of international governance tend to legitimize transnational activities and to increase their access to the national polities as well as their ability to form "winning coalitions" for policy change. Transnational relations acting in a highly institutionalized international environment are, therefore, likely to overcome hurdles otherwise posed by state-dominated domestic structures more easily.

REFINING THE CONCEPT OF TRANSNATIONAL RELATIONS

An effort at renewing the debate about transnational relations has to overcome conceptual and empirical hurdles. The odds are against such an enterprise, since the earlier debate on the subject failed to clarify the concept which then did not generate much empirical research—except for the study of MNCs—and withered away.[8] The first debate essentially resulted in confirming the state-centered view of world politics. There are several reasons for this outcome.

The original concept of "transnational relations" was ill-defined. It encompassed everything in world politics except state-to-state relations. But transnational capital flows, international trade, foreign media broadcasts, the transnational diffusion of values, coalitions of peace movements, transgovernmental alliances of state bureaucrats, INGOs, and MNCs are quite different phenomena. To study the policy impact of transnational relations becomes virtually impossible if the concept is used in such a broad way.

This volume does not deal with transnational relations in an all-encompassing sense. It is not about *interdependence*, defined as patterns of interactions which are mutually costly to disrupt or break.[9] The volume also does not consider *transnational diffusion effects* of cultural values and norms or the impact of international communication networks on public attitudes and national societies. It is hard to develop propositions about these effects that can be measured empirically.[10]

This volume focuses on the policy impact of transnational relations maintained by clearly identifiable actors or groups of actors and linking at least two societies or sub-units of national governments (in the case of transgovernmental relations). Moreover, the transnational coalitions and actors considered are purposeful in the sense that they attempt to achieve specific political goals in the "target" state of their activities.

This sub-set of transnational relations still leaves a whole range of different actors. With regard to purpose, the volume concentrates on two types of actors—those motivated primarily by instrumental, mainly economic, gains and those promoting principled ideas as well as knowledge.[11] The former include multinational corporations . . ., while the latter range from INGOs . . ., transnational coalitions among human rights groups, peace movements, arms control experts, and central bankers . . . to transgovernmental networks among state officials. . . .

The notion of *transgovernmental coalitions*[12] raises additional conceptual problems. Transgovernmental relations could be regarded as the transnational equivalent of bureaucratic politics.[13] They are all-pervasive in world politics, since interactions among heads of states and governments only form a very small portion of inter-state relations. But conceptualized in this way, transgovernmental relations would become virtually indistinguishable from inter-state relations so that the notion loses any analytical strength. To put it differently, the parsimonious "government-as-unitary-actor" model should not be abandoned in the international realm too easily. Only those networks among governmental actors which cannot be captured in the framework of inter-state relations will be considered here. Sub-units of national governments have to act on their own in the absence of national decisions, not just on behalf of their heads of state implementing agreed-upon policies. Transgovernmental coalitions are then defined as networks of government officials which include at least one actor pursuing her own agenda independent of national decisions. The European Committee of Central Bank Governors monitoring the European Monetary System (EMS), for example, represents a transgovernmental institution given the independent status of some of its powerful members (e.g., the German Bundesbank; see Cameron's chapter). Transgovernmental coalitions among senior officials of various North Atlantic Treaty Organization (NATO) governments have been found to shape the transatlantic relationship significantly.[14] When Chancellor Kohl reaches an agreement with President Mitterrand on EU matters, however, such interaction can be conceptualized as inter-state relations and the concept of transgovernmental relations is unnecessary.

The transnational coalitions and actors investigated in this volume can be distinguished according to the degree of their institutionalization.[15] In order to qualify as a transnational *coalition*, the interaction has to occur with regularity over time. A merely "tacit alliance" across national boundaries would not be considered a transnational coalition.[16] Transnational alliances operate on the basis of both implicit and explicit rules based on informal understandings as well as formal agreements. Examples of informal networks include most transnational "epistemic communities" and transgovernmental coalitions. In this volume, two chapters examine the policy impact of rather loose transnational alliances formed across the East–West divide during the Cold War. . . .

The most highly institutionalized forms of transnational relations are INGOs and MNCs. They consist of bureaucratic structures with explicit rules and specific role assignments to individuals or groups working inside the organization.[. . .]

Two trends can be observed with regard to the institutionalization of transnational relations over time. First, the number of INGOs has exploded throughout this century, particularly during the 1970s and 1980s—from 176 in 1909 to 832 in 1951, 1,255 in 1960, 2,173 in 1972, and 4,518 in 1988.[17] This is particularly true for INGOs representing transnational social movements. Their number has increased from 1983 to 1993 by 73 per cent, from 319 to 533.[18] This trend helps to clarify the debate about whether or not transnational relations have increased over time. With the exceptions of capital mobility and of direct foreign investments, it is hard to sustain the thesis that transnational relations as such have multiplied. However, as others have noted before,[19] the data show that the institutionalization of transnational relations has definitely increased.

Second, this institutionalization took place in parallel to, but recently surpassed the creation of inter-state institutions. In 1909, there were on average less than 5 INGOs per International Governmental Organization (IO). From the 1950s to the early 1970s this ratio increased to about 7–9 INGOs per IO. From the late 1970s throughout the 1980s, the growth rate of INGOs surpassed the increase in interstate organizations. In 1988, the UN counted 4,518 INGOs and 309 IOs, i.e., a ratio of more than 14:1.[20]

Even if we can observe a trend toward the institutionalization of transnational relations, it is not clear that, therefore, they should affect state practices. Various examples suggest that neither institutionalization nor economic power alone are decisive for the policy impact of transnational actors:

In the *environmental issue-area*, "epistemic communities"—i.e., networks of professionals with an authoritative claim to policy-relevant knowledge[21]—and INGOs are often pitched against economically powerful MNCs. In the case of the ban against whaling, the epistemic community was initially unable to prevail over the whaling industry. When environmental INGOs adopted the cause, states moved to impose a ban on whaling. In the ozone-depletion case, an epistemic community set the international agenda on the issue and formed an alliance with INGOs against powerful

MNCs. When a major US MNC—DuPont—defected from the united front of chlorofluorocarbon (CFC) producers, the Montreal protocol to protect the ozone layer became possible.[22]

In the *international economic realm*, a recent example includes the European Community (EC)'s approach to the Uruguay Round of the General Agreement on Tariffs and Trade (GATT) negotiations. Economically almost irrelevant but politically powerful transnational farmers' associations were pitched against the entire European business community, which supported cutting agricultural subsidies in order to preserve the international free trade order. Nevertheless, the farmers' associations blocked an EC–US agreement for several years.[23]

In the *human rights area*, loose coalitions of anti-apartheid activists in various countries and human rights INGOs prevailed over MNCs in convincing powerful Western states to institute economic sanctions against South Africa which substantially contributed to bringing down the apartheid regime.[24] As Patricia Chilton argues in this volume, extremely fragile alliances among Western European peace and human rights activists, on the one hand, and dissident groups in Eastern Europe, on the other, nevertheless affected the evolution of civil societies in these countries in a crucial way.[25]

Examples concerning *international security* include the formulation of a joint European policy toward the nuclear non-proliferation regime. An epistemic community aligned with a transgovernmental coalition of foreign ministry officials against the European nuclear industry and economic ministries in various countries. In the end, the former coalition prevailed over the latter in convincing states to join the Nuclear Non-Proliferation Treaty (NPT) (France) or to strengthen its export controls (Germany).[26]

These examples do not suggest that epistemic communities, transnational coalitions, or INGOs always succeed over economically powerful MNCs. But they challenge the proposition that the degree to which transnational relations are institutionalized or the economic clout of transnational actors alone determine their political impact on state practices. The examples suggest that a more fruitful approach would be to analyze how transnational actors interact with the domestic and/or bureaucratic politics in the "target countries." Success or failure of transnational coalitions, INGOs, or MNCs to achieve their goals would then depend on their ability to persuade or line up with domestic and/or governmental actors. The above-mentioned examples also suggest that it might be fruitful to explore how international norms and institutions mediate the policy impact of transnational actors. [...]

The Concept of Domestic Structures

The notion of domestic structures refers to the political institutions of the state, to societal structures, and to the policy networks linking the two. Domestic structures encompass the organizational apparatus of political and societal institutions, their routines, the decision-making rules and procedures incorporated in law and custom, as well as the values and norms embedded in the political culture.

The concept, as used here, goes beyond earlier definitions in, for example, Katzenstein's *Between Power and Plenty*. These conceptualizations concentrated on organizational features of state and society, especially on the degree of their centralization. This led to the rather simplistic distinction between "weak" and "strong" states.[27] State strength was sometimes defined in terms of state capacity to extract resources from society or to achieve goals in the international environment. Such a conceptualization confuses structures and outcomes, leading to tautological propositions. The debate on the strength of the American state suffered from this confusion. It was argued that the US state is more autonomous from society in national security affairs than in economic questions, because government officials were able to overcome Congressional opposition in various defense-related questions.[28] But to infer institutional strength from individual policies obscures the problem that we need measurements of institutional strength independently of policy outcomes. The notion of "domestic structures" as used in this volume refers strictly to institutional features of the state, of society, and of state–society relations established separately from specific policies.

The second major difference from earlier conceptualizations of the domestic structure concept concerns the incorporation of political culture. Insights from the "new institutionalism" are included, in particular the emphasis on communicative action, duties, social obligations, and norms of appropriate behavior.[29] To incorporate values and norms and, thus, informal understandings and rules into a concept emphasizing "structure" only seems odd if one has a rather mechanical understanding of domestic structure. But political culture includes the collective self-understandings of actors in a given society that are stable over time. It defines their collective identity as a nation and, thus, provides them with a repertoire of interpretations of reality as well as of appropriate behavior.

As a result, the normative structure of state–society relations is not fully captured if one only focuses on organizational and legal characteristics of political and social institutions. For example, the Japanese decision-making norm of "reciprocal consent," the German understanding of "social partnership," and the American notion of "liberal pluralism" are only partly embodied in explicit regulations, but constitute nevertheless powerful cultural norms which define appropriateness with regard to the way decisions should be made in the political system.

Three tiers of domestic structures can be distinguished.[30] First, the structure of the *political institutions*—the state—can be analyzed in terms of its centralization or fragmentation. To what extent is executive power concentrated in the hands of small groups of decision-makers? To what degree is bureaucratic infighting considered as normal and expected behavior (US) or as inappropriate (Japan)? How do institutional features which regulate the relationship between the executive and the legislative constrain the national government's ability to control the parliamentary process (parliamentary democracies versus presidential systems)? How far does the domestic authority of the national government reach into the administration of regions and local communities (central or federal structures)? Does the political culture emphasize the state as a "benign" institution taking care of its citizens (France) or rather as a threat to individual liberties (US)? "Centralized states" would then be characterized by political institutions and cultures which concentrate executive power at the top of the political system, in which national governments enjoy considerable independence from legislatures (if they exist at all), and which emphasize the state as caretaker of the needs of the citizens.

Second, the *structure of demand-formation in civil society* can be examined with regard to the internal polarization in terms of ideological and/or class cleavages. Do political attitudes and beliefs about social and political life correlate with religious, ideological, or class cleavages, and how far are these beliefs apart from each other? To what extent can societal demands be mobilized for political causes, and how centralized is the structure of interest groups, societal coalitions, and social organizations? "Strong societies" are then characterized by a comparative lack of ideological and class cleavages, by rather "politicized" civil societies which can be easily mobilized for political causes, and by centralized social organizations such as business, labor, or churches.

Third, the institutions of the *policy networks* linking state and society and the norms regulating the coalition-building processes in these networks have to be investigated. To what degree do intermediate organizations such as political parties aggregate societal demands and channel them into the political process? Does the political culture emphasize consensual decision-making or rather distributive bargaining and dissent in the policy networks? Consensual polities would then be characterized by strong intermediate organizations operating in a compromise-oriented decision-making culture, while polarized polities would emphasize distributive bargaining, often leading to decision blockades.

These three components of domestic structures form a three-dimensional space with the axes defined as

1. the *state structure* (centralization versus fragmentation);

2. the *societal structure* (weak versus strong);
3. the *policy networks* (consensual versus polarized).

This framework should allow one to locate the domestic structures of specific countries. To reduce complexity, each of the three components of domestic structures can be dichotomized, as a result of which six distinct types of domestic structures emerge (see table 42.1).[31] These ideal types are then linked to specific propositions on the policy impact of transnational coalitions and actors (see below, pp. 466–8).

State-controlled domestic structures encompass highly centralized political institutions with strong executive governments and a rather weak level of societal organization. In the absence of strong intermediate organizations in the policy networks and/or a consensus-oriented political culture, civil society is too weak to balance the power of the state. Many of the former Communist systems with centrally planned economies and various authoritarian Third World states (less developed countries—LDCs) seem to fit the description. The countries represented in this volume which seem to match the state-controlled structure, are the former USSR, the former East Germany, and—as an extreme example—Communist Romania. . . .

State-dominated domestic structures can be distinguished from the state-controlled category because of the different nature of the policy networks. There are stronger intermediate organizations channeling societal demands into the political system and/or more consensus-oriented decision-making norms. The political culture of such systems often emphasizes the state as caretaker of the needs of its citizens. In other words, the political culture and/or intermediate organizations counterbalance the power of the state as compared to the state-controlled case. Countries in this volume which seem to approximate to this type are Singapore, South Korea, and Zimbabwe. . . .

"Stalemate" domestic structures are characterized by comparatively strong states facing strong social organizations in a highly polarized polity and a political culture emphasizing distributional bargaining. Social and political conflicts among the major players are unlikely to be resolved in this type of system; decision blockades are expected to occur frequently. Among the countries investigated in this volume, India and pre-1989 Hungary appear to resemble this domestic structure. . . .

Corporatist domestic structures are likely in cases in which powerful intermediate organizations such as political parties operate in a consensus-oriented political culture resulting in continuous bargaining processes geared toward political compromises.[32] The

Table 42.1 Types of domestic structures and countries investigated in this study.

		Society			
		Strong		Weak	
		Policy networks		Policy networks	
		Consensual	Polarized	Consensual	Polarized
Political institutions	Centralized	Corporatist (Japan)	Stalemate (India; pre-1989 Hungary)	State-dominated (Singapore; South Korea; Zimbabwe)	State-controlled (USSR; East Germany; Romania)
	Fragmented	Society-dominated (HongKong, Philippines, USA)		Fragile (Kenya; Russia)	

domestic structures of many of the smaller European states come close to this model. Among the countries investigated in this volume, Japan seems to fit the description to some degree. . . .

Society-dominated domestic structures are to be expected in countries with comparatively strong social interest pressure, but decentralized and fragmented political institutions. Among the countries investigated in this volume, the US and—to some degree—Hong Kong seem to represent this category. . . . The Philippines appear to represent a case of an even more fragmented state faced with strong social interest pressure in an extremely polarized political culture. . . .

Finally, *"fragile"* domestic structures combine fragmented state institutions, a low degree of societal mobilization, and weak social organizations. Many African states seem to resemble this type including Kenya. . . . The same appears to hold true for post-Soviet Russia. . . .

Transnational Relations and Domestic Structures

The main proposition investigated in this volume claims that, under similar international conditions, *differences in domestic structures determine the variation in the policy impact of transnational actors.* Domestic structures mediate, filter, and refract the efforts by transnational actors and alliances to influence policies in the various issue-areas. In order to affect policies, transnational actors have to overcome two hurdles. First, they have to gain access to the political system of their "target-state." Second, they must generate and/or contribute to "winning" policy coalitions in order to change decisions in the desired direction. Their ability to influence policy changes then depends on the domestic coalition-building processes in the policy networks and on the degree to which stable coalitions form sharing the transnational actors' causes. Domestic structures are likely to determine both the availability of access points into the political systems and the size of and requirements for "winning coalitions."

The extent to which transnational actors gain *access* to the political systems seems to be primarily a function of the state structure. National governments ultimately determine whether foreign societal actors are allowed to enter the country and to pursue their goals in conjunction with national actors. Governments have considerable leeway to enable or constrain transnational activities. . . . They distribute visas, issue export licenses, and guarantee property rights.[33] The capacity of governments to prohibit transnational activities is itself a function of the state structure. The assumption advanced here is rather straightforward. The more centralized the political system, the less access points should transnational actors have to penetrate the institutions of the "target state." In other words access should be most difficult in state-controlled domestic structures while it is expected to be easiest in countries with "weak" political institutions. In countries with state-controlled domestic structures governments should have the most leeway to restrict transnational access. Examples include the enormous difficulties which Western peace and human rights groups encountered in establishing contact with dissident movements in Communist Eastern Europe. . . . The more fragmented the state structure, however, the less capable should national governments be to prevent transnational activities. In the case of society-dominated domestic structures, transnational actors and coalitions should have no trouble in penetrating the societal and political systems, since they provide multiple channels to influence policies. In some extreme cases of Third World countries, even the issuing of visas seems to be irrelevant with regard to transnational activities.

But easy access does not guarantee policy impact. As stated above, the ultimate success of transnational actors to induce policy change depends on their ability to form "winning coalitions" in the target country the size of which is again a function of domestic structures. While the first hurdle—access—can only be influenced in a very limited way by conscious strategies of the transnational coalitions, the second hurdle—building "winning coalitions"—depends to a large degree on their ability to adjust to the domestic structure of the "target country."[34] "Clever" transnational actors adapt to the domestic structure to achieve their goals; a prime example . . . is the success of Japanese lobbying in the US (chapter by Katzenstein and Tsujinaka). Some transnational coalitions, however, adopt strategies which might be suitable in the domestic structures of their home countries without acknowledging the differences encountered in the "target state." A good example is the ivory trade ban promoted by "public opinion" INGOs which proved counterproductive in a country like Zimbabwe with a self-sustaining conservation policy to preserve the elephant. . . .

If we assume that transnational actors normally tend to adjust their policy strategies to the specific situation of the target country, some domestic structures should make their task easier than others. First, while *state-controlled or state-dominated domestic structures* (see table 42.1) make it difficult for transnational actors to overcome the initial hurdle of gaining access, their policy impact might be profound, once this barrier is mastered. If powerful state actors are predisposed toward their goals, they can directly influence policies. . . . Alternatively, transnational contacts might serve to empower and legitimize the demands of otherwise weak social groups. . . .

In domestic structures characterized by *stalemate*, access of transnational actors might be a little easier than in the state-dominated case. However, one would expect the policy impact to be rather limited, given the structural disfunctionality of the societal and political institutions to produce policy changes. If change occurs, it is to be expected to come primarily from within the domestic polity, altering the domestic structure during the process. . . .

This is very different from what is to be expected in consensus-oriented *corporatist structures*. If transnational actors succeed in penetrating the powerful societal and political organizations in such countries, their policy impact can be as significant as in the state-dominated case. Given the slow and compromise-oriented decision-making processes in such systems, one would expect that transnational actors achieve their goals in a more incremental way than in the case of state-dominated systems. Since corporatist structures tend to institutionalize social and political compromises, the policy impact of transnational actors could last for a long time. . . .

Concerning the cases represented in the bottom row of table 42.1, governments are likely to have less control over the access of transnational actors into the societal and political institutions. But it is less clear whether easy access guarantees policy impact. Given the fragmented nature of the political institutions, the requirements for putting together "winning coalitions" are likely to demand much greater efforts by the transnational actors. Particularly in countries with a high degree of political mobilization and strong social organizations, there is always the possibility that transnational activities provoke countervailing coalitions which have to be dealt with. Policy impact requires quite elaborate efforts by transnational actors in coalition-building and nurturing different players in the political system. Moreover, the effect on policies might not last very long, given the fragmented structure of the state which prevents the institutionalization of domestic consensus.[. . .]

Finally, in the case of *"fragile"* domestic structures, there is not much that transnational actors can do to achieve their goals, even though they should have no trouble in penetrating the political institutions. Coalition-building with societal actors is next to impossible and bound to fail given their organizational weakness. Aligning with governmental actors does not help, either, given the fragmented nature of the state. Even if transnational actors do achieve their goals in changing policies, the state is expected to be too weak to implement decisions. Thomas Princen looks at this proposition with regard to Kenya and the ivory ban, while Matthew Evangelista explores it concerning post-Soviet Russia.

Table 42.2 summarizes how the ideal-types of domestic structures are expected to mediate the policy impact of transnational coalitions and actors.

Table 42.2 Propositions about the policy impact of transnational actors as mediated by domestic structures.

Domestic structure	Access to domestic institutions	Policy impact in case of access
State-controlled	Most difficult	Profound if coalition with state actors predisposed toward TNA goals or empowerment of social actors
State-dominated	Difficult	Ditto
Stalemate	Less difficult	Impact unlikely
Corporatist	Less easy	Incremental but long-lasting if coalition with powerful societal and/or political organizations
Society-dominated	Easy	Difficult coalition-building with powerful societal organizations
Fragile	Easiest	Impact unlikely

International Institutions and Transnational Actors

So far, the argument has exclusively focused on domestic structures. But state autonomy and state control over outcomes is not just a function of domestic structures, but also of the state's position in the international distribution of power. It is obvious that transnational coalitions which manage to influence great powers in a major international policy area have accomplished more than those who successfully affect the policies of a small state. This point is straightforward and reconcilable with the theoretical framework sketched out above.

It could be argued, though, that foreign policy changes can be explained as state responses to the conditions and constraints of the international environment. If so, transnational actors become epiphenomenal. But the structure of the international system does not simply determine state policies. Not even hard-headed structural realists claim that the foreign policy of states is solely a function of the international distribution of power.[35] If governments do have choices to respond to international pressures and opportunities, there is no a priori reason for excluding transnational actors from the consideration of agents who might influence such decisions.

But international structures do not just consist of power hierarchies. International relations are regulated by institutions defined as "persistent and connected sets of rules (formal and informal) that prescribe behavioral roles, constrain activity, and shape expectations."[36] After more than ten years

of empirical research, regime analysis has established that international institutions have substantial effects on government practices, both on policies and definitions of interests and preferences. State autonomy and governmental control over policies are affected by the degree of the state's embeddedness in international structures of governance. While differences in domestic structures affect state autonomy "from below," variations in international institutions should equally influence state capacities "from above," since both represent structures of governance.

If we assume that domestic structures mediate the policy impact of transnational coalitions, we can equally suppose that international structures of governance should filter such policy influence in a similar fashion.[37] It should make a difference whether transnational coalitions act in a heavily institutionalized environment such as the EU (...) or in a milieu unregulated by international agreements. ... In the latter case, the variation in domestic structures should account for the difference in policy impact almost exclusively. In the former case, things should become more complicated.

The more regulated the inter-state relationship by cooperative international institutions in the particular issue-area, the more are transnational activities expected to flourish and the less should national governments be able to constrain them. Examples include, again, the EU . . ., the transatlantic relationship,[38] and the American–Japanese security relationship. . . . The relationship does not have to be governed by formal institutions such as regimes and organizations. In the case of the Anglo-American "special relationship," for example, informal norms and tacit rules enable transnational activities to an extent unsurpassed by almost any other bilateral relationship. In the case of hostile interstate relationships, however, which are less regulated by cooperative regimes and institutions, governments are expected to put strong controls on transnational activities (from visas to export controls).

The emergence of trans*governmental* coalitions seems to be almost entirely a function of highly cooperative and institutionalized interstate relationships. Transgovernmental network-building involves behavior of bureaucratic actors which could be regarded as disloyal by their home governments. In the framework of international regimes and institutions, however, such practices become more legitimized, since most regimes and international organizations include frequent meetings and intergovernmental forums which permit transgovernmental activities. Such informal networks can then generate the high-quality information which international institutions provide for the participants.[39]

International institutions are then expected to facilitate the *access* of transnational actors to the national policy-making processes. International regimes and organizations are likely to increase the availability of channels which transnational actors can use to target national governments in order to influence policies. INGOs and transgovernmental networks lobbying governments can do so more easily in the framework of international institutions. To a certain degree, international regimes and organizations are likely to reduce the differences in filtering effects of the various types of domestic structures. Even countries with state-dominated domestic structures such as France are probably unable to cut themselves off from demands of transnational actors when dealing with international institutions. International regimes and organizations would then provide channels into the national political systems which domestic structures might otherwise limit.

But access does not guarantee influence. How do international institutions affect the policy impact of transnational actors on state policies, particularly the requirements for "winning coalitions?" Unfortunately, the interaction between international norms and institutions, on the one hand, and domestic politics, on the other, is not yet fully understood; work in this area has just begun.[40] Harald Müller has shown in an analysis of security regimes how international regime norms change the parameters of the domestic discourses in the respective issue-area. Concerning nuclear non-proliferation, for example, there is no longer a serious debate about whether proliferation should be allowed or not. Rather, the discourse shifts to the question whether specific practices are in compliance with the regime forcing opponents to make their cause within the framework of the institutional rules. Regime norms tend to strengthen those domestic coalitions advocating compliance.

Following this line of reasoning, one can then assume that international institutions have two effects on the policy impact of transnational actors. First, the demands of transnational coalitions for changes in national policies may be legitimized and strengthened by the respective regime norms, in which case such alliances would work as "transnational moral entrepreneurs."[41] When the domestic discourse is framed by the norms of the international regime, it should be easier for compliance-promoting transnational actors to find domestic coalition partners. Transnational actors opposing the respective norms and rules, however, are expected to be at a disadvantage in their attempts to form "winning" domestic coalitions.

Second, as argued above, cooperative and highly institutionalized inter-state relations tend to lower state boundaries thereby allowing for flourishing transnational relations. At the same time, these institutions also legitimize transnational activities in the "target state"; actors are less and less treated as "foreigners," but as almost indistinguishable from other domestic players. The collective identity of a pluralistic security community such as the transatlantic alliance enables transnational actors to influence policy decisions directly.[42] Such effects should also lower the requirements for building domestic "winning coalitions."

In sum, the degree to which the inter-state relationship in the respective issue-area is regulated by cooperative international institutions should have two effects on the ability of transnational actors to influence policies. First, international institutions are likely to facilitate access to the national political processes and, in particular, to enable the emergence of transgovernmental networks. Second, international institutions in the respective issue-area are expected to reduce the coalition-building requirements for transnational coalitions, particularly those advocating norm compliance.

CONCLUSION

A renewed attempt at theorizing about transnational relations requires, first, to specify the concept more clearly than the earlier debate did, and, second, to differentiate the international and domestic conditions under which transnational coalitions and actors are able to influence state policies. The major proposition put forward in this volume is that variation in domestic structures accounts for differences in the policy impact of transnational coalitions and actors. Moreover, the more cooperative international institutions regulate the inter-state relationship in the particular issue-area, the more channels should transnational coalitions have available to penetrate the political systems and the more should they be able to use international norms to legitimate their demands. Structures of governance—both domestic and international—interact in determining the policy impact of transnational actors.

Reviving the subject of transnational relations and linking it systematically to the concepts of domestic structures and international institutions does not re-invent the wheel in international relations theory. This volume does not develop a new theoretical approach but tries to promote theoretical and empirical progress by integrating various theories which have been developed separately from

each other, and by evaluating the resulting propositions through a set of comparative case studies. The attempt to combine the literature on domestic structures with that on international institutions promises fresh insights with regard to the subject of transnational relations. As a result, it is likely to overcome the shortcomings of the earlier debate.

NOTES

1. This definition builds upon, but slightly modifies the original definition of transnational relations by encompassing both trans-societal and trans-governmental relations. I will later address the concept of transnational relations in more detail. For the original definitions see Karl Kaiser, "Transnationale Politik," in Ernst-Otto Czempiel, ed., *Die anachronistische Souveränität* (Cologne-Opladen: Westdeutscher Verlag, 1969), pp. 80–109; Robert O. Keohane and Joseph S. Nye, Jr., "Introduction," in Keohane and Nye, eds., *Transnational Relations and World Politics* (Cambridge, MA: Harvard University Press, 1971), pp. xii–xvi.

2. For a discussion see Young Kim, John Boli and George M. Thomas, "World Culture and International Nongovernmental Organizations," paper presented at the Annual Meetings of the American Sociological Association, Miami Beach, 1993. See also Jackie Smith, "The Globalization of Social Movements: The Transnational Social Movement Sector, 1983–1993," paper presented at the Annual Meetings of the American Sociological Association, Los Angeles, August 5–9, 1994.

3. See Peter Haas, ed., *Knowledge, Power, and International Policy Coordination*, special issue of *International Organization*, 46, 1 (Winter 1992).

4. See, for example, Beau Grosscup, "Global Terrorism in the Post-Iran-Contra Era: Debunking Myths and Facing Realities," *International Studies*, 29, 1 (1992), pp. 55–78; Samuel Huntington, "The Clash of Civilizations?," *Foreign Affairs*, 79 (1993), pp. 22–49.

5. On this aspect see Kathryn Sikkink, "Human Rights, Principled Issue-Networks, and Sovereignty in Latin America," *International Organization*, 47, 3 (Summer 1993), pp. 411–41.

6. See David Meyer, *A Winter of Discontent. The Freeze and American Politics* (New York: Praeger, 1990); Thomas Rochon, *Mobilizing for Peace: The Anti-Nuclear Movement in Western Europe* (Princeton, NJ: Princeton University Press, 1988).

7. Keohane and Nye, "Introduction," p. xi. For a discussion see also M.J. Peterson, "Transnational Activity, International Society, and World Politics," *Millennium*, 21, 3 (Winter 1992), pp. 371–88.

8. Among the most important works of the earlier debate are Walter Bühl, *Transnationale Politik* (Stuttgart: Klett-Cotta, 1978); Czempiel, *Die anachronistische Souveränität*; Annette Baker Fox, Alfred O. Hero Jr., and Joseph S. Nye, Jr., *et al.*, eds., *Canada and the United States: Transnational and Transgovernmental Relations* (New York: Columbia University Press, 1976); Harold Jacobson, *Networks of Interdependence. International Organizations and the Global Political System* (New York: Knopf, 1979); Keohane and Nye, eds., *Transnational Relations and World Politics*; Robert O. Keohane and JosephS. Nye, Jr., *Power and Interdependence* (Boston: Little, Brown, and Co., 1977); Werner Link, *Deutsche und ainerikanische Gewerkschaften und Geschäftsleute 1945–75: Eine Studie über transnationale Beziehungen* (Düsseldorf: Droste, 1978); Richard W. Mansbach, Yale H. Ferguson, and Donald E. Lampert, *The Web of World Politics. Non-State Actors in the Global System* (Englewood Cliffs, NJ: Prentice Hall, 1976); Edward L. Morse, *Modernization and the Transformation of International Relations* (New York: Free Press, 1976); James N. Rosenau, *Linkage Politics* (New York: Free Press, 1969); James N. Rosenau, *The Study of Global Interdependence. Essays on the Transnationalization of World Affairs* (London: Frances Pinter, 1980); Peter Willets, ed., *Pressure Groups in the Global System. The Transnational Relations of Issue-Oriented Non-Governmental Organizations* (New York: St. Martin's Press, 1982).

9. See Keohane and Nye, *Power and Interdependence*. For a review of the "interdependence" literature concluding that there was no "integrated theoretical model" and that the concept only generated, "impressionistic descriptions" rather than rigorous empirical research see Beate Kohler-Koch, "Interdependenz," in Volker Rittberger, ed., *Theorien der internationalen Beziehungen* (Opladen: Westdeutscher Verlag, 1990), pp. 110–29, 125. See, however, James Rosenau and Hylke Tromp, eds., *Interdependence and Conflict in World Politics* (Aldershot: Avebury, 1989); James Rosenau, *Turbulence in World Politics. A Theory of Change and Continuity* (Princeton, NJ: Princeton University Press, 1990); Ernest-Otto Czempiel, *Weltpolitik im Umbruch. Das internationale System nach dem Ende des Ost-West-Konflikts* (Munich: Beck, 1991).

10. For pioneering work in this direction see the studies on the "world polity" initiated by John W. Meyer and other sociologists, for example, George M. Thomas, John W. Meyer, Francisco O. Ramirez, and John Boli, ed., *Institutional Structure. Constituting State, Society, and the Individual* (Beverly Hills, CA: Sage, 1987); John Meyer, "The World Polity and the Authority of the Nation-State," *ibid.*, pp. 41–70; John Meyer and Brian Rowen, "Institutionalized Organizations: Formal Structures in Myth and Ceremony," in Paul J. DiMaggio and Walter Powell, eds., *The New Insti-tutionalism in Organizational Analysis* (Chicago: University of Chicago Press, 1991).

11. I owe these categories to suggestions by Kathryn Sikkink; see her "Human Rights, Principled Issue-networks, and Sovereignty." On knowledge-based networks see Peter Haas, *Knowledge, Power, and International Policy Coordination*; Peter Haas, *Saving the Mediterranean* (New York: Columbia University Press, 1990); Ernst Haas, *When Knowledge Is Power* (Berkeley, CA: University of California Press, 1990).

12. See Robert O. Keohane and Joseph S. Nye, Jr., "Transgovernmental Relations and International Organizations," *World Politics*, 27 (1974), pp. 39–62.

13. The classic studies are Graham Allison, *Essence of Decision. Explaining the Cuban Missile Crisis* (Boston: Little, Brown, and Co., 1972); Morton Halperin, *Bureaucratic Politics and Foreign Policy* (Washington, DC: The Brookings Institution, 1974). There is one important conceptual difference between Allison's original concept and the notion of transgovernmental relations as used in this volume. Allison's bureaucratic actors are primarily motivated by instrumental goals, i.e., they want to increase their turf, their budget, and the like. But bureaucratic and transgovernmental coalitions might as well be motivated by principled ideas.

14. See Thomas Risse-Kappen, *Cooperation among Democracies. The European Influence on US Foreign Policy* (Princeton, NJ: Princeton University Press, 1995); also Helga Haftendorn, *Kernwaffen und die Glaubwürdigkeit der Allianz* (Baden-Baden: Nomos, 1994).

15. I follow Keohane's definition of institutions as sets of rules which shape expectations, prescribe roles, and constrain activities. See Robert O. Keohane, *International Institutions and State Power* (Boulder, CO: Westview, 1989), pp. 3/4.

16. For example, "hawks" in both the US and the former USSR frequently played into each other's hands during the Cold War. Implicit transnational alliances can be analyzed in the framework of "two-level games" and are not part of this project. On "two-level games" see Robert Putnam, "Diplomacy and Domestic Politics: The Logic of Two-Level Games," *International Organization*, 42, 3 (Summer 1988), pp. 427–60; Peter B. Evans, Harold K. Jacobson, Robert D. Putnam, eds., *Double-Edged Diplomacy. An Interactive Approach to International Politics* (Berkeley, CA: University of California Press, 1993).

17. Data in Jaap de Wilde, *Saved from Oblivion: Interdependence Theory in the First Half of the 20th Century* (Aldershot: Dartmouth, 1991), p. 36; Rosenau, *Turbulence in World Politics*, p. 409. For a discussion of INGOs and transnational social movements before 1945 see Charles Chatfield, "Networks and Junctures: International Non-governmental Organizations and Transnational

Social Movements to 1945," paper presented to the Workshop on International Institutions and Transnational Social Movement Organizations, University of Notre Dame, April 21–23, 1994.

18. For details see Smith, "The Globalization of Social Movements."

19. See, for example, Samuel Huntington, "Transnational Organizations in World Politics," *World Politics*, 25 (April 1973), pp. 333–68; Joseph Nye, "Transnational Relations and Interstate Conflicts: An Empirical Analysis," in Fox *et al.*, *Canada and the United States*, pp. 367–402, 383/384. For a more recent analysis see Kim *et al.*, "World Culture and Nongovernmental Organizations." For arguments disputing the increase in transnational interactions see, for example, Janice E. Thomson and Stephen Krasner, "Global Transactions and the Consolidation of Sovereignty," in Ernst-Otto Czempiel and James N. Rosenau, eds., *Global Changes and Theoretical Challenges* (Lexington, MA: Lexington Books, 1989), pp. 195–219; Kenneth Waltz, *Theory of International Politics* (Reading, MA: Addison-Wesley, 1979).

20. Calculated from data in de Wilde, *Saved from Oblivion*, p. 36, and Rosenau, *Turbulence in World Politics*, p. 409.

21. See Peter Haas, *Knowledge, Power, and International Policy Coordination*.

22. On the whaling case see M.J. Peterson, "Whalers, Cetologists, Environmentalists, and the International Management of Whaling," in Peter Haas, *Knowledge, Power, and International Policy Coordination*, pp. 147–86. For the ozone depletion case see Peter Haas, "Banning Chlorofluorocarbons: Epistemic Community Efforts to Protect Stratospheric Ozone," ibid. pp. 187–224. For a discussion of transnational issue networks in the environment and human rights areas see Margaret Keck and Kathryn Sikkink, "International Issue Networks in the Environment and Human Rights," paper for the Workshop on International Institutions and Transnational Social Movement Organizations, University of Notre Dame, April 21–23, 1994. See also Thomas Princen and Matthias Finger, *Environmental NGOs in World Politics: Linking the Local and the Global* (London: Routledge, 1994).

23. On transnational interest groups in the EC see Beate Kohler-Koch, "Interessen und Integration. Die Rolle organisierter Interessen im westeuropäischen Integrationsprozeß," in Michael Kreile, ed., *Die Integration Europas* (Opladen: Westdeutscher Verlag, 1992), pp. 81–119; Beate Kohler-Koch, "The Evolution of Organized Interests in the EC: Driving Forces, Co-Evolution, or New Type of Governance," paper prepared for the XVIth World Congress of the International Political Science Association, August 21–25, 1994, Berlin. On the EC's role during the GATT negotiations see Stephen Woolcock, *Trading Partners or Trading Blows?* (New York: Council of Foreign Relations Press, 1992).

24. See Audie Klotz, *Protesting Prejudice: Apartheid and the Politics of Norms in International Relations* (Ithaca, NY: Cornell University Press, 1995).

25. On this case see also Daniel Thomas, "When Norms and Movements Matter: Helsinki, Human Rights, and Political Change in Eastern Europe, 1970–1990," PhD dissertation, Cornell University, 1994.

26. See Harald Müller, ed., *A European Non-Proliferation Policy* (Oxford: Clarendon Press, 1987); Harald Müller, ed., *How Western European Nuclear Policy is Made. Deciding on the Atom* (London: Macmillan, 1991).

27. See Katzenstein, "International Relations and Domestic Structures;" Krasner, *Defending the National Interest*; Mastundano *et al.*, "Toward a Realist Theory of State Action."

28. Cf. Ikenberry *et al.*, *State and American Foreign Economic Policy*, particularly the essay by Michael Mastundano, "Trade as a Strategic Weapon: American and Alliance Export Control Policy in the Early Postwar Period," ibid., pp. 121–50.

29. See, for example, DiMaggio and Powell, *The New Institutionalism in Organizational Analysis*; James G. March and Johan P. Olsen, *Rediscovering Institutions. The Organizational Basis of Politics* (New York: The Free Press, 1989); Ikenberry, "Conclusion: An Institutional Approach"; Friedrich Kratochwil, *Rules, Norms, and Decisions* (Cambridge: Cambridge University Press, 1989); Sven Steinmo, Kathleen Thelen, and Frank Longstreth, eds., *Structuring Politics. Historical Institutionalism in Comparative Analysis* (Cambridge: Cambridge University Press, 1992); Thomas *et al.*, *Institutional Structure*.

30. The following builds upon and modifies Risse-Kappen, "Public Opinion, Domestic Structures, and Foreign Policy," p. 486. See also Katzenstein, "Introduction" and "Conclusion," in *Between Power and Plenty*; Evangelista, "Domestic Structure and International Change"; Gourevitch, *Politics in Hard Times*; Ikenberry, "Conclusion: An Institutional Approach."

31. In the case of a fragmented state faced with either strong or weak societies, the nature of the policy network seems to matter less. I have, therefore, summarized these types into one category each. I am fully aware of the fact that the following is simplistic and that the empirical reality of specific countries is more complex than suggested.

32. This description is broader than the original concept of "corporatism." See, for example, Philippe Schmitter and Gerhard Lehmbruch, eds., *Trends Towards Corporatist Intermediation* (London: Sage, 1979); Peter Katzenstein, *Corporatism and Change* (Ithaca, NY: Cornell University Press, 1984).

33. The centrality of governments in allowing or prohibiting transnational interaction was one of the reasons why the "state-centered" paradigm prevailed in the earlier debate. Again, framing the issue in such a way misses the mark. First, the

capacity of governments to control transnational activities is itself a function of domestic structures. Second, even if governments are crucial in enabling transnational activities the effects of these activities can still be significant.

34. I owe this point to Robert Keohane. [...]

35. Cf. Kenneth Waltz, "Anarchic Orders and Balances of Power," in Robert O. Keohane ed., *Neorealism and Its Critics.* (New York: Columbia University Press, 1986), pp. 98–130, 122: "Balance-of-power theory is a theory about the results produced by the uncoordinated actions of states ... What it does explain are the constraints that confine all states. The clear perception of constraints provides many clues to the expected reactions, but by itself the theory cannot explain those reactions." For a discussion see Robert Keohane, "Theory of World Politics: Structural Realism and Beyond," ibid. pp. 158–203.

36. Keohane, *International Institutions and State Power*, p. 3. See also Ernst-Otto Czempiel and James N. Rosenau, eds., *Governance Without Government: Order and Change in World Politics* (Cambridge: Cambridge University Press, 1992); Krasner, *International Regimes*; Kratochwil, *Rules, Norms, and Decisions*; Harald Müller, *Die Chance der Kooperation* (Darmstadt: Wissenschaftliche Buchgesellschaft, 1993); Rittberger, *Regime Theory and International Relations*; Young, *International Cooperation*.

37. Note that this volume—except for Cameron's chapter—does not investigate how transnational actors affect international institution-building and/or state compliance with international regimes. This would be an entirely different project following the line of reasoning developed by Keohane and Nye (in *Power and Interdependence*) that states form international regimes to cope with the effects of transnational interdependence. This volume, however, treats international institutions as intervening variables between transnational activities and state policies in an analogous way as domestic structures. For studies investigating how specific transnational actors affect international regimes see, for example, Alison Brysk, "Social Movements, the International System, and Human Rights in Argentina," *Comparative Political Studies*, 26, 3 (1993), pp. 259–85; Brysk, "Lost in the Palace of Nations? Latin American Indian Rights Movements at the United Nations," paper presented to the Workshop on International Institutions and Transnational Social Movement Organizations, University of Notre Dame, April 21–23, 1994; Finnemore, "Restraining State Violence"; Peter Haas, *Knowledge, Power, and International Policy Coordination*; Klotz, *Protesting Prejudice*; Nadelmann, "Global Prohibition Regimes."

38. See Risse-Kappen, *Cooperation Among Democracies.*

39. See Robert Keohane, "The Demand for International Regimes," in Krasner, ed. *International Regimes*, pp. 141–71, 162–66.

40. See, for example, Zürn, "Bringing the Second Image (Back) In." For the following see Müller, "The Internalization of Principles, Norms, and Rules by Governments."

41. See Nadelmann, "Global Prohibition Regimes."

42. For details see Risse-Kappen, *Cooperation among Democracies*. On pluralistic security communities see Karl W. Deutsch, *et al.*, *Political Community and the North Atlantic Area* (Princeton, NJ: Princeton University Press, 1957). [...]

CHAPTER 43

World Culture in the World Polity: A Century of International Non-governmental Organization

John Boli and George M. Thomas

Much recent scholarship analyzes global structures and processes as a distinct level of social reality. The world is more than networks or systems of economic and political interaction; it has become a single "international society," or world polity (Meyer 1987; Watson 1992). We adopt a world-polity perspective to study the formation of global structures and culture by analyzing international non-governmental organizations (INGOs).[1]

World-polity perspectives run counter to more common approaches to global analysis. For classic realists in international relations (Morgenthau 1960), the world is anarchic—only states and economic organizations matter internationally. "Neo-realists" acknowledge that action is conditioned by transnational institutions, but they conceptualize these institutions as "networks of interdependence" (H. Jacobson 1979) controlled by their members (Keohane 1984, 1986; Krasner 1983, 1985). In both perspectives, stability and change are the result of unanalyzed actors pursuing primordial interests; the metatheory at work is reductionist rationalism. In sociology, state-competition (Giddens 1985; Skocpol 1979; Tilly 1992) and world-system theories (Chase-Dunn 1989; Smith 1980; Wallerstein 1974) follow suit, reducing transnational structures to military or economic processes dominated by major world powers.[2] We refer to all such reductionist rationalist theories as "global neo-realism."

Many scholars dispute the assumptions of global neo-realism but nevertheless hesitate to conceptualize a cultural frame larger than states or nations (Czempiel and Rosenau 1992; Wendt 1992). In contrast, a world-polity approach puts the institutional character of transnational development front and center. Culture is increasingly global (Featherstone 1990; Hannerz 1987; Lechner 1989; Robertson 1992); a transnational "legal world order" operates with considerable independence from states (Berman 1988; Falk, Kratochwil, and Mendlovitz 1985; Weiss 1989); world cultural principles and institutions shape the action of states, firms, individuals, and other subunits (Boli 1993; McNeely 1995; Meyer et al. 1997; Strang 1990; Thomas 1994). In numerous ways, the world polity is not reducible to states, transnational corporations (TNCs), or national forces and interest groups (Mann 1986; Nettl and Robertson 1968; Thomas et al. 1987).

World-polity analyses thus emphasize the importance of cultural or institutional frames. Actors are treated not as unanalyzed "givens" but as entities constructed and motivated by enveloping frames (Jepperson 1992). The nature, purposes, behavior, and meaning of actors, whether individuals, organizations, social movements, or states, are subject to redefinition and change as the frames themselves change.

Empirical studies from a world-polity perspective find striking structural homology across countries (in education, women's rights, social security programs, environmental policy, constitutional arrangements) and argue that this homology results from an overarching world culture (Abbott and DeViney 1992; Boli 1987; Meyer et al. 1992; Ramirez and Weiss 1979; Strang 1990; Thomas and Lauderdale 1988). However, this culture is only inferred; direct evidence about its structure and operations is rare.

Our research directly explores world culture through the analysis of INGOs. INGOs have proliferated from about 200 active organizations in 1900 to about 800 in 1930, over 2,000 in 1960, and nearly 4,000 in 1980, but little attention has been given to this domain of global organization. INGOs are more or less authoritative transnational bodies employing limited resources to make rules, set standards, propagate principles, and broadly represent "humanity" vis-à-vis states and other actors. Unlike states, INGOs can neither make nor enforce law. Unlike global corporations, they have few economic resources. We argue, however, that a culturally informed analysis of INGOs is necessary to understand global development.

For a century and more, the world has constituted a singular polity. By this we mean that the world has been conceptualized as a unitary social system, increasingly integrated by networks of exchange, competition, and cooperation, such that actors have found it "natural" to view the whole world as their arena of action and discourse. Such a conceptualization reifies the world polity implicitly in the often unconscious adoption of this cultural frame by politicians, businesspeople, travelers, and activists, and explicitly in the discourse of intellectuals, policy analysts, and academicians.

Like all polities, the world polity is constituted by a distinct culture—a set of fundamental principles and models, mainly ontological and cognitive in character, defining the nature and purposes of social actors and action. Like all cultures, world culture becomes embedded in social organization, especially in organizations operating at the global level. Because most of these organizations are INGOs, we can identify fundamental principles of world culture by studying structures, purposes, and operations of INGOs. By studying INGOs across social sectors, we can make inferences about the structure of world culture. By studying the promotion of world-cultural principles that INGOs are centrally involved in developing, we can see how INGOs shape the frames that orient other actors, including states.

THE CULTURE IN WORLDWIDE INSTITUTIONS

Culture lies at the heart of world development. Technical progress, bureaucratization, capitalist organization, states, and markets are embedded in cultural models of the "nature of things" and the "purposes of action." These cultural conceptions do more than orient action; they also constitute actors. People draw on worldwide cultural principles that define actors as individuals who have certain "natural" needs, affectations, and capacities. Worldwide constructs provide social identities, selves, and roles by which individuals pursue their interests. World-cultural conceptions also define collective identities and interests of entities, like firms, states, and nations, along with rational organizational forms that are to be adopted by them (Meyer, Boli, and Thomas 1987; Meyer et al. 1997).

Actors may enact these cultural conceptions mechanically, but innovative enactment is common because the shared identities and rules supplied by world culture define actors as having agency. In any case, the enactment of cultural models re-presents actors everywhere as similar in nature, pursuing similar purposes by similar means, even as action in specific contexts varies almost without limit (Jepperson 1992). Because cultural structures contain numerous contradictions and local situations are complex, enactment routinely results in much ambiguity, disarticulation, and conflict (Sewell 1992; Wuthnow 1989).

Cultural principles and models are shared primarily at the ontological or cognitive level. Moral evaluations typically are conflictual; ontological definitions of the nature of things normally are taken for granted. Regardless of one's attitude toward the large corporation, for example, one has difficulty denying the social reality of Mitsubishi. Cognitive ontology is rarely called into question because it forms the foundation for action.

When we speak of culture as global, we mean that definitions, principles, and purposes are cognitively constructed in similar ways throughout the world. The existence, general nature, and purposes of states, school systems, and transnational corporations are known everywhere. They are Durkheimian social facts, whether revered or reviled. Thus, even though many of the world-cultural principles we discuss are contested and generate considerable conflict, their reification is enhanced by this very contestation.

A second sense in which culture is global is that it is held to be applicable everywhere in the world. World-cultural models are presumed to be universally valid, usually by functional-imperative reasoning. The state is presumed necessary for order and coordination; therefore, France and Vanuatu must have states. Mass schooling is necessary for national development; therefore, Malaysia and Paraguay must have schools. Models that do not have general applicability are suspect unless they are conceptualized as special adaptations of general models. African development models may emphasize labor-intensive projects, but their ultimate goals are still economic growth and rational societal management.

In contemporary world culture, the dominant global actors are states, transnational corporations (TNCs), and intergovernmental organizations (IGOs). These entities are defined as actors capable of wielding military, economic, and political power, and they enact this conception rather well. Alongside the *realpolitik* networks formed by these actors and intensely entwined with them, INGOs are much less well-conceptualized actors whose primary concern is enacting, codifying, modifying, and propagating world-cultural structures.

In speaking of world-cultural models that shape social reality, we recognize that competing models differ in important respects. Yet the competing models and discourses that make global culture so dynamic share fundamental conceptions regarding actors, agency, nature, technique, societal purposes, and much more. We also recognize that universal cultural principles may themselves generate conflict. For example, uniform conceptions of human purposes imply that actors have identical goals and therefore are likely to compete for the same resources. Conflict intensifies when, for instance, per-

ipheral regions are reorganized as progress-oriented societies. Their new, uniformly defined states may nationalize foreign industries, clash over territorial boundaries, or engage in other forms of interstate competition.

Dialectical processes of world-polity development thus generate struggles that would not arise in a less integrated world (Boli 1993; Meyer et al. forthcoming). Although INGOs generally favor peace and harmony, they also foster conflict by helping to homogenize the world polity. Simmel's (1955) insight is apt: Conflict is a form of interaction, and actors within the same cultural frame are likely to find more bases for conflict (and cooperation) than actors from barely intersecting frames.

AN HISTORICAL OVERVIEW OF THE INGO POPULATION

Data

Since 1850 more than 25,000 private, not-for-profit organizations with an international focus have debuted on the world stage. They include the Pan American Association of Ophthalmology, International Exhibitions Bureau, Commission for the Geological Map of the World, International Catholic Child Bureau, International Tin Council, and Tug of War International Federation. Most are highly specialized, drawing members worldwide from a particular occupation, technical field, branch of knowledge, industry, hobby, or sport to promote and regulate their respective areas of concern. Only a few, such as the Scout Movement, International Olympic Committee, International Red Cross, and World Wildlife Fund, are widely known.

We analyze data on 5,983 organizations founded between 1875 and 1988. They constitute the entire population of INGOs classified as genuinely international bodies by the Union of International Associations (UIA) in its *Yearbook of International Organizations* (UIA 1985, 1988).[3] We coded founding and dissolution dates, primary and secondary aims, type of membership, number of members, and type of dissolution.[4]

Our population includes all nongovernmental organizations listed in the "Universal," "Intercontinental," and "Regional" sections of the 1988 *Yearbook*, along with those in the "Dissolved" section of the 1985 *Yearbook*. We omit the far more numerous NGOs of international orientation that are not international in both membership and structure.

Data Quality and Coding Issues

The UIA limits INGOs to not-for-profit, nongovernmental organizations (TNCs and IGOs are excluded). They vary in size from a few dozen members from only 3 countries to millions of members from close to 200 countries.[5] About half of the INGOs in our data base have members from at least 25 countries, 20 percent have members from 50 or more countries, and only 11 percent have members from fewer than 8 countries.

Several features of the UIA's datagathering process convince us that the data are adequate for meaningful analysis. First, the UIA has long had semi-official status as compiler of information on INGOs and IGOs through ties with the League of Nations and United Nations (UIA 1985: 1654). Considered the definitive source of INGO data, it maintains continuous contact with over 13,000 organizations, including most of the active international organizations in our data set. Second, the UIA incorporates more information each year. Organizations are asked to identify other INGOs that have recently come to their knowledge and the UIA staff searches newspapers, magazines, and journals to identify INGOs not present in the data base. Even organizations that come to the editors' notice after they have ceased operations are included as dissolved bodies. Nineteen organizations in our data base dissolved in the same year they were founded, 260 dissolved within three years of founding, and 502 dissolved within five years.

Third, the possibility that the quality of the data is better for recent years, so that rising INGO founding rates would be partly artifactual, does not seem to be a serious concern. On the one hand, the magnitude of growth is stupendous: Even if as many as half of the INGOs founded in the early period have not been identified, the growth curve would still rise sharply. On the other hand, the history of the data base suggests that only a small proportion of early INGOs have been omitted. The first INGO compilation in 1909 identified about 200 organizations, many of which were not international in scope. Our coding yielded 371 international organizations founded prior to 1909 (of 5,035 bodies with known founding dates). Of these 371, some 334 were founded after 1874. Hence, much more is now known about the early period of INGO formation than was known at the time.

Every *Yearbook* is incomplete for the years immediately preceding its publication. We evaluated the length of the datagathering pipeline by comparing the number of foundings identified in one edition of the *Yearbook* with those published in previous editions. Our analysis suggests that about 60 percent of all INGOs enter the *Yearbook* within five years of founding, while 80 percent to 90 percent enter within ten years and the remainder are identified within another five years. Proceeding conservatively, we have settled on 1973 as the last year for which the 1988 *Yearbook* provides complete data. None of our analyses looks any different if the end date is extended to 1980 or 1985, except that the founding rate drops because many newer INGOs are omitted.

Measuring dissolutions poses a problem because many organizations never formally disband. The UIA classifies an organization as dissolved if it no longer responds to requests for information and no activity has been reported for five years. Our dates of dissolution are often taken from such phrases as "last reported activity 1948." In other cases dates of dissolution are more precise, especially if they involve mergers or absorption by other bodies.[6]

To classify the INGO population into sectors, we constructed a set of mutually exclusive and exhaustive categories from the organization titles and descriptions of aims in the *Yearbook* entries. Primary and secondary aims were coded independently by at least two coders. Inter-coder agreement was relatively low for each aim separately (about 60 percent), but reliability for primary and secondary aims taken together was high (about 90 percent). Agreement was higher still when we collapsed our 42 specific categories into 13 major sectors.[7] Disagreements were resolved by group discussion, resulting in a set of formal criteria for establishing priority of aims.

Basic Historical Patterns

Figure 43.1 presents the number of INGOs founded and dissolved in each year between 1875 and 1973.[8] Not-for-profit international organizing grew rapidly in the latter part of the nineteenth century, with about 10 new organizations emerging each year during the 1890s. The population burgeoned after the turn of the century, reaching a peak of 51 foundings in 1910. The severe collapse after that point led to a low of four foundings in 1915. Swift recovery after World War I yielded a period of fairly steady growth followed by some decline during the 1930s that preceded another steep fall going into World War II.

Following the war, international organizing exploded. By 1947 over 90 organizations a year were being founded, a pace that was maintained and even surpassed through the 1960s. The pattern for dissolved INGOs is similar, indicating a generally steady proportion of INGOs that eventually dissolved, but revealing peaks of fragility among organizations founded just before each of the wars.

INGO foundings and dissolutions thus match the general "state of the world" rather well, rising in periods of expansion and declining rapidly in times of crisis, with the declines beginning shortly before the outbreaks of the world wars. This finding raises the issue of what these patterns tell us about the formation of the world polity. We approach this issue by examining (1) the relationship of INGO formation to other world-level variables and (2) the structure and operations of INGOs as world-cultural constructs.

WORLD DEVELOPMENT, INGOs, AND CAPITALIST AND INTERSTATE SYSTEMS

We compiled an array of longitudinal indicators, many of them normally accounted at the nation-state level, and summed them to produce world totals. Most of these variables are annual but a few are at 20-year intervals.[9] Some reach back into the nineteenth century, while others are confined to recent decades. Many are not available for the war years 1914–1918 and 1940–1945.

The longitudinal correlations among these world-level variables, logged to eliminate skewness, are strikingly high. For the variables shown in columns 1 to 9 of Table 43.1, most coefficients are above .97, while a few are at .86 to .88. For example, government revenues correlate .97 with world exports (103 years' coverage); primary educational enrollment correlates .99 with the number of treaties among states; world energy production correlates .99 with tertiary education enrollment.

This extraordinary level of covariation is extremely robust. When we use standardized measures, such as GNP per capita and energy production per capita, the coefficients diminish only slightly (.10 to .15 units). Using three periods demarcated by the world wars, the intercorrelations have the same high magnitude for each period as for the entire series. Using different segments of the world economy based on country shares of world trade (Boli 1987), the intercorrelations are above .90 within each stratum. When we divide the world into a more developed one-third and a less developed two-thirds, the same results obtain within each stratum.

As column 10 in Table 43.1 shows, the correlations between INGO foundings and measures of world development are also extremely high—most are at .90 or above. The development of the INGO population is part and parcel of this general development of the world polity.

The strong covariation in world-polity development is partly artifactual, but in a

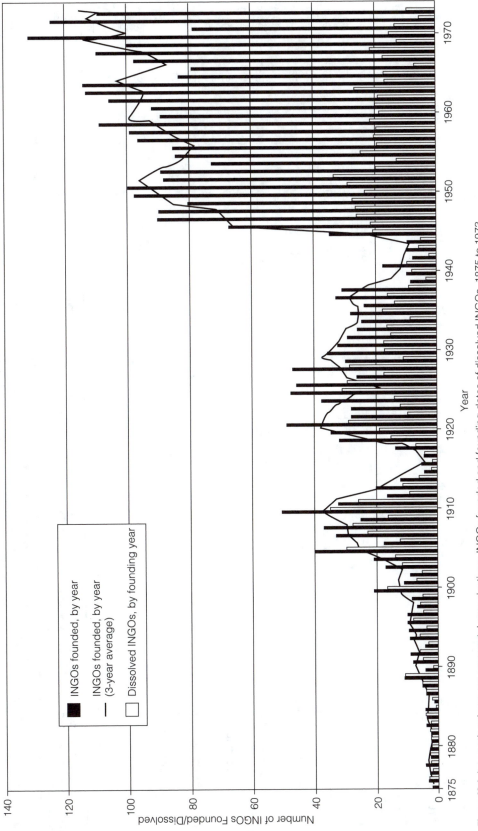

Figure 43.1 International non-governmental organizations: INGOs founded and founding dates of dissolved INGOs, 1875 to 1973

Source: Yearbook of International Organizations (UIA 1985, 1988).

Table 43.1 Correlations between measures of world development.

Variable	(1)	(2)	(3)	(4)	(5)	(6)	(7)	(8)	(9)	(10)	(11)
Government Revenue	.97*** (103)	.97*** (49)	.87*** (87)	.98*** (103)	.99*** (103)	.98*** (103)	.99*** (5)	.98*** (5)	.99*** (6)	.89*** (103)	.94*** (103)
(1) Exports	—	.97*** (49)	.86*** (87)	.98*** (103)	.99*** (103)	.97*** (103)	1.00*** (5)	.98*** (5)	.99*** (6)	.91*** (103)	.94*** (103)
(2) Energy production		—	.99*** (49)	.98*** (49)	.99*** (49)	.98*** (49)	— (5)	— (5)	1.00*** (3)	.87*** (49)	.90*** (49)
(3) Telephones			—	.89*** (87)	.91*** (87)	.92*** (87)	.93* (4)	.88* (4)	.88* (5)	.97*** (87)	.78*** (87)
(4) Primary educational enrollment				—	.99*** (103)	.99*** (103)	1.00*** (5)	.99*** (5)	.98*** (5)	.93*** (103)	.92*** (103)
(5) Tertiary educational enrollment					—	1.00*** (103)	1.00*** (5)	1.00*** (5)	.98*** (6)	.93*** (103)	.93*** (103)
(6) Urban population (cities ≥ 100,000)						—	1.00*** (5)	.98*** (5)	.97*** (6)	.93*** (114)	.91*** (103)
(7) Diplomatic representation							—	1.00*** (4)	.98*** (6)	.89* (5)	.96*** (5)
(8) Treaties among states								—	.99*** (5)	.93* (5)	.96*** (5)
(9) Citizen rights specified in constitutions									—	.81* (6)	.93*** (6)
(10) INGOs founded										—	.83*** (6)
(11) IGOs founded											— (119)

Notes: Variables are annual world totals; data is time series data from the nineteenth and twentieth centuries. Numbers in parentheses give the number of time points for which data are available. Some series use interpolated data for early years. Data for variables 7, 8, and 9 are taken at 20-year intervals. The endpoint for all series is 1973; most variables are missing for the world war years. All skewed variables are logged.

Variable definitions: Government revenue = total government revenue in $US; exports = total exports in $US; energy production = total energy produced in millions of tons of coal-equivalent; telephones = number of telephones; primary educational enrollment = students enrolled in primary schools; tertiary educational enrollment = students enrolled in post-secondary schools; urban population = people living in cities larger than 100,000; diplomatic representation = Singer and Small's (1966) index of diplomats received to 1930, Taylor and Hudson's (1970) indicator of diplomatic exchange thereafter (years divisible by 10 only); treaties = bilateral and multilateral treaties signed in each decade around the years divisible by 10 (e.g., the 1910 value is for the years 1906–1915); citizen rights = number of rights indicated in all constitutions in force in the years 1870, 1890, 1910, 1930, 1950, and 1970; INGOs founded = number of INGOs founded, including dissolved INGOs; IGOs = number of IGOs founded, including dissolved IGOs.

* *p* < .05   ** *p* < .01   *** *p* < .001 (one-tailed tests) highly revealing sense. Only dimensions of social life that are deemed relevant to societal rationalization, either as indicators of progress or measures of problems like poverty or crime, are quantified with enough uniformity to generate world-level indicators. As properties of the rationalizing world polity, they are likely to correlate highly with each other. Aspects of social life that are not quantified or are not standardized in the world accounting system might correlate less highly, but their marginality to the rationalizing project makes them unavailable.

These correlations would not be noteworthy in a world polity that was tightly managed by a world state; neither would they seem remarkable in a national society. In the absence of a world state, however, global neo-realism has trouble accounting for this degree of integration. It is not directly political, as state-competition theorists and neo-realists might suggest, because not even hegemons have had the power to control world development so comprehensively. Neither is it directly economic, as world-system theorists might claim, because they argue that rates of development in different segments of the world economy must vary substantially. Steep stratification certainly persists among nation-states, but the covariation between world strata taken as aggregates is also very high (e.g., government revenue in core states is correlated .91 with government revenue in peripheral states).

These high intercorrelations also are troubling to functionalist arguments depicting an anarchic world that is driven by technological imperatives and large-scale problems to create global organizations (Mitrany 1943). Like modernization theory, such arguments imply that high intercorrelations should also be found at the national level, but studies using nations as units report more moderate correlations (Meyer and Hannan 1979).[10] Like world-system theory, functionalism also implies that structural variation should abound because national conditions vary so much, but homology is the rule.

More fundamentally, the perception of problems as global rather than local is not simply a technical matter. For example,

pollution was almost certainly worse in the coal-burning nineteenth century than it is today, but a transnational environmental movement did not form at that time. What functionalists forget is that technique and the definition of problems as technical are themselves cultural processes (Ellul 1980).

World-polity development is more dialectical than global neo-realist perspectives would have it. Global organizing proceeds in mutually reinforcing tension with the expansion of the nation-state system (Boli 1993). INGOs began to proliferate during the heyday of nationalism and European imperialism; bringing the last "unclaimed" regions of the globe into the world economy and under the jurisdiction of states made the notions of "one world" and "one history" structurally compelling.

This dialectic is further evident in the effects of the world wars. The precipitous decline in INGO foundings after 1910 reflects the dominance of states for most of that decade, but the war also strengthened the conception of the world as a single polity and prompted expanded INGO (and IGO) efforts to organize the world polity. After a similar cycle in the 1930s and 1940s, a much broader discursive space for INGOs opened up as global technical and infrastructural resources increased exponentially. World-polity organizing jumped to a higher level than ever before, just as the independent nation-state form was adopted by or imposed on the rest of the world.

The dialectic between world-polity and national-level organization is also evident in the relationship between IGOs and INGOs. Many IGOs were founded as INGOs and later co-opted by states, including such major bodies as the World Meteorological Organization, the International Labor Organization. and the World Tourism Organization. Moreover, INGOs have often been instrumental in founding new IGOs and shaping IGO activities. Thousands of INGOs have consultative status with agencies of the United Nations (Wiseberg 1991)—over 900 with the Economic and Social Council alone—and most IGOs engage relevant INGOs as providers of information, expertise, and policy alternatives. IGO authority is not relinquished to INGOs, but IGO decisions are heavily influenced by INGO experts and lobbyists.

The process involved is one of mutual legitimation. INGOs gain prestige and influence by winning consultative status (Meyer 1994), while IGOs gain by the involvement of diverse INGOs that lend IGO policies a nonpartisan flavor as reflections of world public opinion or putative technical necessity. The high correlation (.83) between IGO and INGO foundings is therefore expected, as are the high correlations between IGO foundings and other measures (Table 43.1, column 11).

Hence, strong covariation between INGO foundings and world-development indicators is of far-reaching substantive significance. World-polity organizations emerged in tandem with the universalization of the state; INGOs grew with the incorporation of regions into the interstate system and world economy. Major wars have caused short-term declines but long-term intensification of world-polity discourse and organizing, as INGOs have expanded in the interstices of power networks.

INGOs AS ENACTORS AND CARRIERS OF WORLD CULTURE

Our findings to this point are consistent with nonreductionist sociological perspectives that focus on the cultural frames in which actors are embedded. INGOs are loci of transnational contextual knowledge. World-level conceptions constitute the locally situated individual as someone who can, may, and should act globally; they supply the purposes and meaning of action; they provide models for global organizing, forms of discourse and communication, and avenues for influencing states and other actors. The larger cultural reality is translated by individuals into specific forms and actions that reveal broad homologies.

The content of this cultural framework can, then, be inferred from the characteristics and operations of INGOS, even though the culture enacted by INGOs does not include all cultural elements that have worldwide character. How are INGOs constituted?

Almost all INGOs originate and persist via voluntary action by individual actors. INGOs have explicit, rationalized goals. They operate under strong norms of open membership and democratic decision-making. They seek, in a general sense, to spread "progress" throughout the world: to encourage safer and more efficient technical systems, more powerful knowledge structures, better care of the body, friendly competition and fair play. To achieve their goals they emphasize communication, knowledge, consensual values and decision-making, and individual commitment. Following are five basic world-cultural principles that underlie INGO ideologies and structures: universalism, individualism, rational voluntaristic authority, human purposes of rationalizing progress, and world citizenship.

Universalism

Humans everywhere have similar needs and desires, can act in accordance with common principles of authority and action, and share common goals. In short, human nature, agency, and purpose are universal, and this universality underlies the many variations in social forms. Most INGOs are explicit about this—any interested person can become an active member, and everyone everywhere is a potential beneficiary of INGO activity.

Universalism is evident also in the breadth of INGOs' claims about what they do. Physics and pharmacology are presumed to be valid everywhere. Techniques for playing better chess are not country-specific. Red Cross aid will alleviate suffering in Africa as well as Asia. Across every sector, the purposes and means of action promoted by INGOs are assumed to be useful and meaningful everywhere.

A world not characterized by universalism does not coalesce as a singular polity; rather, it develops distinct subworld polities (societies, civilizations, empires) across which joint mobilization is unlikely. At the opposite extreme, a world state would thoroughly incorporate and regulate individuals and organizations—universalism would prevail but it would be bureaucratically absorbed.

The present world polity lies between these two extremes. Neither segmental nor ad hoc, neither is it *etatisé*; legal-bureaucratic authority is partitioned among multiple states. The principle of universalism that INGOs embody remains culturally autonomous because INGOs operate in the interstices of this decentralized structure.[11]

Individualism

Most INGOs accept as members only individuals or associations of individuals; the main exceptions are trade and industry bodies, which often have firms as members. Individualism is also evident in their structures: INGOs use democratic, one-person–one-vote decision-making procedures, they assess fees on members individually, and they downplay national and other corporate identities in their conferences and publications. In the world-view embodied by INGOs, individuals are the only "real" actors; collectivities are essentially assemblages of individuals.

The combination of universalism and individualism may undermine traditional collectivities like the family or clan, but it also strengthens the one truly universalistic collectivity—humanity as a whole. INGOs habitually invoke the common good of humanity as a goal. The cultural dynamic at work parallels that characterizing national polities: As cultural constructs, the individual and the nation reinforce one another. In recent times, this centuries-old dynamic has shifted to the global level.

Rational Voluntaristic Authority

INGOs activate a particular cultural model when they organize globally, debate principles and models, and attempt to influence other actors. This model holds that responsible individuals acting collectively through rational procedures can determine cultural rules that are just, equitable, and efficient, and that no external authority is required for their legitimation (Thomas 1989). Such "self-authorization" runs counter to Weber's analysis of authority as forms of domination because INGOs cannot dominate in the conventional sense. INGOs have little sanc-

tioning power, yet they act as if they were authorized in the strongest possible terms. They make rules and expect them to be followed; they plead their views with states or transnational corporations and express moral condemnation when their pleas go unheeded.

INGO authority is thus informal—cultural, not organizational. It is the agency presumed to inhere in rational individuals organizing for purposive action. Its basis can only be the diffuse principles of world culture, for INGO authority does not flow from any legal-bureaucratic or supernatural source.

Rational voluntarism is encouraged by the decentralized character of formal authority; at the world level, it is practiced by states and transnational corporations as well. For example, because sovereignty implies that no state has authority over any other (Boli 1993), collective actions by states can occur only via rational voluntarism. This is why most IGOs, like INGOs, have resolutely democratic formal structures. It also helps explain why the legal-bureaucratic authority of states is brought into play to enforce INGO conceptions and rules.

Human Purposes: Dialectics of Rationalizing Progress

The rational character of INGOs is evident in their purposive orientation, formalized structures, and attention to procedures. INGOs in science, medicine, technical fields, and infrastructure activities are engaged in purely rationalized and rationalizing activity; almost all other INGOs rely on science, expertise, and professionalization in their operations and programs. What INGOs seek is, in essence, rational progress—not the crude nineteenth-century idea that steam engines and railroads would lead to heaven on earth, but the more diffuse and embedded concept of "development" that now prevails (Chabbott 1996). This concept includes not only economic growth but also individual self-actualization, collective security, and justice.

At all levels, progress is assumed to depend on rationalization. Rational social action is the route to equality, comfort, and the good life. Rational production and distribution achieve all sorts of collective purposes. The scientific method, technique, monetarization, logical analysis—these are the favored *modi operandi*. These instruments of progress may often be criticized, but they are built into worldwide institutions and the ideology of development.

Rationalization, however, has another face. A tension operates between the rational and the irrational that strengthens both (Thomas 1989). Disenchantment of the world via rationalization endows the agents of disenchantment with increasing substance and sacredness (Ellul 1975); the apparent failure of actors to behave entirely rationally leads to theorizing about actors' irrational selves or cultures. Rationalized actors are thus culturally constituted as having complex "nonrational" subjectivities that are more primordial than objectified rationality. À la Nietzsche, the irrational becomes the arena of authenticity. Moreover, this face of rationalization launches widespread movements claiming to be anti-science (Snow 1959), anti-Western, or postmodern: Western science, capitalism, and bureaucracy are imperialistic, dehumanizing forces against which authentic peoples must struggle to maintain their true, nonrational natures.

The rational/irrational tension thus generates conflict, but the irrational and subjective are continually channeled into rationalized activities and forms (e.g., revolution, UFO cults). Movements of self-exploration and expression, though rhetorically rejecting rationalism, also are rationalized (transcendental meditation becomes a test-improvement technique). Thus we find sports, leisure, spiritual, and psychological INGOs in abundance.

World Citizenship

The principles discussed so far come together in the construct of world citizenship. Everyone is an individual endowed with certain rights and subject to certain obligations; everyone is capable of voluntaristic actions that seek rational solutions to social problems; therefore, everyone is a citizen of the world polity. World citizenship rules infuse each individual with the authority to pursue particularistic interests, preferably in organizations, while also authorizing individuals to promote collective goods defined in largely standardized ways.[12]

World citizenship is strongly egalitarian. Individuals vary in their capacities, resources, and industry, but all have the same basic rights and duties. Correspondingly, only fully democratic governance structures are consistent with world citizenship. "Autocratic" tendencies are decried even within some INGOs (e.g., Greenpeace and the International Olympic Committee).

World citizenship is prominently codified in the Universal Declaration of Human Rights, which depicts a global citizen whose rights transcend national boundaries. The Declaration insists that states ensure the rights of their citizens and even that every human has the right to a national citizenship. In the absence of a world state, however, these obligations cannot be imposed on states. Acting as the primary carriers of world culture, INGOs translate the diffuse global identity and authority of world citizenship into specific rights, claims, and prescriptions for state behavior.

Here again we observe that states sometimes act as agents of informal world-polity authority. World citizens must turn to national states for protection of their rights, and INGOs back them up in the process. Increasingly, individuals need not be national citizens to make claims on the state (D. Jacobson 1996; Soysal 1994); noncitizen residents of many countries have extensive rights almost equivalent to those of citizens, simply because they are human.

The cultural principles *re*-presented by INGOs are also integral to the world economy and state system, but INGOs push them to extremes. Their discourse is often critical of economic and political structures, stigmatizing "ethnocentric" (nonuniversalistic) nationalism and "exploitative" (inegalitarian) capitalism. INGOs dramatize violations of world-cultural principles, such as state maltreatment of citizens and corporate disregard for the sacredness of nature. Such examples illustrate the contested nature of these principles (Meyer et al.

1997); they are widely known but by no means uncontroversial.

INGO SECTORS AND WORLD-CULTURAL STRUCTURATION

We now turn to a sectoral analysis of INGO activity as a means of studying the structure of world culture. INGOs cover a broad range of activities that we grouped into 13 sectors. Figure 43.2 charts the distribution across these sectors for all INGOs active in 1988.

We interpret Figure 43.2 as a sectoral description of world culture. The distribution suggests, first, that world culture is heavily "economic"—not-for-profit bodies concerned with business and economic development (industry and trade groups and tertiary economic organizations) account for about one-fourth of all active INGOs. But scientific knowledge and technique (medicine, the sciences, technical standards, infrastructure, and communications) are even more prominent, with just over one-third of the total. In all, nearly 60 percent of INGOs

concentrate on economic or technical rationalization.

This is the core of world culture: technical, functional, rationalizing, highly differentiated (some 2,400 organizations), and peculiarly invisible. These bodies bring together physicists, radiologists, electronic engineers, bridge designers, manufacturers. They set standards, discuss problems, disseminate information, argue points of law, and write codes of ethics—but few are seen as important world actors. The parallel with national organizations is plain: In most countries, only a handful of scientific, technical, or business associations are prominent in public discourse; most go quietly about their business of rationalizing and standardizing society, yet they are the most common type of association.

A second implication of Figure 43.2 emerges from the sports and leisure sector (more than 200 sports are organized at the world level). These INGOs sponsor the most visible rituals dramatizing the world polity, just as national and local sports dramatize lower-level polities. Their activities serve as a

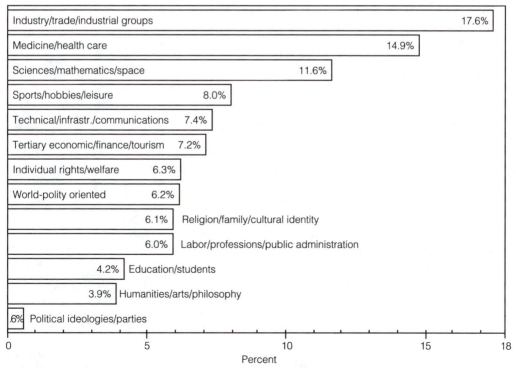

Figure 43.2 Percentage distribution of INGOs active in 1988 by sector.
Source: Yearbook of International Organizations (UIA 1988).

major source of identity and solidarity, offering avenues for personal fulfillment in contexts claimed to contribute to world harmony. Thus, sports-and-leisure INGOs express the subjective axis of world culture. Yet sports and leisure are highly rationalized. INGOs reflect this rationality and enhance it by centralizing and standardizing rules, training methods, and measurement procedures.

Of special interest are the "individual rights and welfare" INGOs and "world-polity oriented" INGOs. The individual rights and welfare sector includes organizations promoting universal, or sometimes particularistic, group rights (for minorities, women, indigenous peoples), and charity and relief organizations. Organizations in the world-polity sector promote world peace, international law, world federation, a world language (usually Esperanto), and environmental preservation. Each of these sectors accounts for about 6 percent of the INGO population.

These smaller sectors include many of the most prominent INGOs, especially environmental and human rights organizations, whose effectiveness depends on maintaining a high public profile. Amnesty International, for example, rallies world public opinion against states that violate universalistic human rights (Castermans et al. 1991). Greenpeace emphasizes duties: World citizens must protect the natural world, which has certain rights to inviolability. As these examples suggest, INGOs that openly conflict with states for not conforming to world-cultural principles are likely to be controversial, and hence are well-known (Willets 1982).

Finally, organizations promoting "primordial" social forms—religion, family, ethnic or cultural identity—account for about 6 percent of the INGO population. Most are religious bodies, often ecumenical.[13] Hence, neither the family nor ethnicity nor ethnic culture takes strong transnational form. Neither does politics, the smallest sector.

The small sectors in Figure 43.2 ("labor/ professions/public administration," "political ideologies/parties," and "religion/family/ cultural identity") are also sectors whose shares of the INGO population have declined, and their founding rates are less highly correlated with the world-level variables shown in Table 43.1 than are those of other sectors. Relative decline should occur in sectors that do not match evolving world-cultural principles, and this seems applicable here: The individualism of world culture works against collectivist forms of transnational organizing (labor, family, religion, distinctive cultural identity). The relative decline of these sectors indicates that individualism has become stronger since the early part of the twentieth century, when these sectors had their largest shares of the INGO population.

The decline in political INGOs reflects, we think, the worldwide expansion of state authority (Boli 1987). Coupled with a modest relative decline in educational INGOs, these trends suggest another hypothesis: Organizational dimensions tied directly to state-citizen relations are relatively unlikely to generate transnational structures. In future work we plan to evaluate these and other hypotheses regarding the dynamics of world-polity formation. [...]

NOTES

1   Often designated simply "non-governmental organizations." or NGOs, we emphasize the *international* focus of the organizations in our study by using the "INGO" acronym.

2   Western-originated world culture spread through colonization, economic expansion, and evangelization. Although Western countries are major contributors to world culture, world culture is not simply the latest phase of core domination. Tomlinson (1991) shows the weakness of cultural imperialism arguments; Krasner (1985) demonstrates that even intergovernmental organizations regularly develop anti-core agendas; many INGOs oppose core interests by, for example, promoting human rights ideology and critiquing world inequality. In addition, the assumption that core elites can shape world culture to their liking ignores the complexity and stubbornly decentralized character of the world polity.

3   The Union of International Associations traces its origins to the Central Office of International Associations, founded in Brussels in 1907. It was active in the founding of the League of Nations and the International Institute of Intellectual Cooperation, the predecessor of UNESCO, and in the 1920s it founded the first international university. Its official abbreviation is UAI, based on the French version of its name.

4 Earlier quantitative analyses of INGOs have used the same data source but have been largely descriptive and more limited in the range of data employed (Archer 1983; Feld 1971; Speeckaert 1957).

5. We treat all organizations as equivalent regardless of size. Too few organizations report membership numbers to make size a useful variable, although about three-fourths report the countries in which members reside. Analysis of 1994 country-of-residence data kindly provided by the UIA suggests that this measure of size (or scope) is rather uniformly distributed across organizational aims. The inferences we make here likely would apply if we were to select only large organizations.

6. In 83 percent of cases, dissolution means cessation of activities or formal disbanding; 15 percent have involved merger with or absorption by another INGO. Only 2 percent represent organizations shrinking to less than international scope.

7. Many of the following analyses were conducted using both primary and secondary aims, with similar results.

8. The *Yearbook* lists only 37 organizations founded before 1875, but the growth of INGOs does not mark the beginning of the contemporary world polity, which is rooted in Christendom and Western law (Collins 1986; Hall and Ikenberry 1989; Mann 1986), the Enlightenment (Watson 1992), and, at least through the nineteenth century, the Roman Church and its religious orders.

9. Sources include Banks (1975), International Bank for Reconstruction and Development (various years), UNESCO (1965–1990), United Nations (various years), and Boli[-Bennett] (1976). Some of the Banks data are interpolations between observations at irregular intervals, for the early part of the period.

10. Aggregation may account for some of the high covariation at the world level, but national-level correlations are so much lower (in the .6 to .7 range) that aggregation is likely not a major problem. In any case, several of these variables are not aggregates but measures of world properties.

11. The universalism promoted by INGOs is not without self-contradictory effects. Robertson's (1994) "universalization of particularism" implies that world-cultural principles and bodies also encourage national, ethnic, and other local identities (Meyer et al. 1997). Many INGOs promote this ironic form of universalism, but most stress the uniformity of human actors.

12. Recent work on world citizenship usually associates it with human rights and ecological movements (Turner 1993; van Steenbergen 1994). Falk's (1994) image of the "global management" citizen, more technical than political in orientation, is especially important in light of our findings on the sectoral distribution of INGOs.

13. Many religious orders are not classified as INGOs by the UIA. More work is needed to understand this particular category.

REFERENCES

Abbott, Andrew and Stanley DeViney. 1992. "The Welfare State as Transnational Event: Evidence from Sequences of Policy Adoption." *Social Science History* 16:245–74.

Archer, Clive. 1983. *International Organizations*. London, England: George Allen and Unwin.

Banks, Arthur S. 1975. *Cross-National Time Series Data Archive*. Binghamton, NY: Center of Comparative Political Research, State University of New York.

Berman, Harold J. 1988. "The Law of International Commercial Transactions." *Emory Journal of International Dispute Resolution* 2:235–310.

Boli[-Bennett], John. 1976. *The Expansion of Nation-States, 1870–1970*. Ph.D. dissertation, Department of Sociology, Stanford University, Stanford, CA.

Boli, John. 1987. "World-Polity Sources of Expanding State Authority and Organization, 1870–1970." Pp. 71–91 in *Institutional Structure: Constituting State, Society and the Individual*, edited by G. M. Thomas, J. W. Meyer, F. O. Ramirez, and J. Boli. Beverly Hills, CA: Sage.

———. 1993. "Sovereignty from a World-Polity Perspective." Paper presented at the annual meeting of the American Sociological Association, August 13–17. Miami Beach, FL.

Castermans, Alex Geert, Lydia Schut, Frank Steketee, and Luc Verhey, eds. 1991. *The Role of Non-Governmental Organizations in the Promotion and Protection of Human Rights*. Leiden, The Netherlands: Stichting NJCM-Boekerij.

Chabbott, Colette. 1996. *Constructing Educational Development: International Development Organizations and the World Conference on Education for All*. Ph.D. dissertation, School of Education, Stanford University, Stanford, CA.

Chase-Dunn, Christopher. 1989. *Global Formation: Structures of the World Economy*, Cambridge, MA: Basil Blackwell.

Collins, Randall. 1986. *Weberian Sociological Theory*. Cambridge, England: Cambridge University Press.

Czempiel, Ernst Otto and James Rosenau, eds. 1992. *Governance without Government: Order and Change in World Politics*. Cambridge, England: Cambridge University Press.

Ellul, Jacques. 1975. *The New Demons*. New York: Seabury.

———. 1980. *The Technological System*. New York: Continuum.

Falk, Richard A. 1994. "The Making of Global Citizenship." Chap. 10 in *The Condition of Citizenship*, edited by B. van Steenbergen. London, England: Sage.

Falk, Richard A., Friedrich Kratochwil, and Saul H. Mendlovitz, eds. 1985. *International Law: A Contemporary Perspective*. Boulder, CO: Westview.

Featherstone, Michael. 1990. *Global Culture: Nationalism, Globalization and Modernity* (A *Theory, Culture & Society* Special Issue). Newbury Park, CA: Sage.

Feld, Werner J. 1971. "Non-Governmental Entities and the International System: A Preliminary Quantitative Overview." *Orbis* 15:879–922.

Giddens, Anthony. 1985. *The Nation-State and Violence. A Contemporary Critique of Historical Materialism, Volume 2*. Cambridge, England: Polity.

Hall, John A. and G. John Ikenberry. 1989. *The State*. Minneapolis, MN: University of Minnesota Press.

Hannerz, Ulf. 1987. "The World in Creolisation." *Africa* 57(4):546–59.

International Bank for Reconstruction and Development (IBRD, World Bank). Various years. *World Tables*. Washington, DC: IBRD.

Jacobson, David. 1996. *Rights without Borders: Immigration and the Decline of Citizenship*. Baltimore, MD: Johns Hopkins University Press.

Jacobson, Harold K. 1979. *Networks of Interdependence: International Organizations and the Global Political System*. New York: Knopf.

Jepperson, Ronald L. 1992. *National Scripts: The Varying Construction of Individualism and Opinion Across the Modern Nation-States*. Ph.D. dissertation, Department of Sociology, Yale University, New Haven, CT.

Keohane, Robert O. 1984. *After Hegemony: Cooperation and Discord in the World Political Economy*. Princeton. NJ: Princeton University Press.

——, ed. 1986. *Neorealism and Its Critics*. New York: Columbia University Press.

Krasner, Stephen D., ed. 1983. *International Regimes*. Ithaca, NY: Cornell University Press.

——. 1985. *Structural Conflict: The Third World against Global Liberalism*. Berkeley, CA: University of California Press.

Lechner, Frank. 1989. "Cultural Aspects of the Modern World-System." Pp. 11–28 in *Religious Politics in Global and Contemporary Perspective*, edited by W. H. Swatos. New York: Greenwood Press.

Mann, Michael. 1986. *The Sources of Social Power*. Vol. 1, *A History of Power from the Beginning to A.D. 1760*. Cambridge, England: Cambridge University Press.

McNeely, Connie, 1995. *Constructing the Nation-State: International Organization and Prescriptive Action*. Westport, CT: Greenwood.

Meyer, John W. 1994. "Rationalized Environments." Pp. 28–54 in *Institutional Environments and Organizations*, edited by W. R. Scott and J. W. Meyer. Thousand Oaks, CA: Sage.

Meyer, John W., John Boli, and George M. Thomas. 1987. "Ontology and Rationalization in the Western Cultural Account." Pp. 12–37 in *Institutional Structure: Constituting State, Society and the Individual*, edited by G. M. Thomas, J. W. Meyer, F. O. Ramirez, and J. Boli. Beverly Hills, CA: Sage.

Meyer, John W., John Boli, George M. Thomas, and Francisco O. Ramirez. 1997. "World Society and the Nation-State." *American Journal of Sociology* 103:144–181.

Meyer, John W. and Michael T. Hannan. 1979. *National Development and the World System: Educational, Economic, and Political Change, 1950–1970*. Chicago, IL: University of Chicago Press.

Meyer, John W., David Kamens, Aaron Benavot, Yun-Kyung Cha, and Suk-Ying Wong. 1992. *School Knowledge for the Masses*. London, England: Falmer Press.

Mitrany, David. 1943. *A Working Peace System; An Argument for the Functional Development of International Organization*. London, England: Royal Institute of International Affairs.

Morgenthau, Hans. 1960. *Politics among Nations: the Struggle for Power and Peace*. New York: Knopf.

Nettl, J. P. and Roland Robertson. 1968. *International Systems and the Modernization of Societies; The Formation of National Goals and Attitudes*. London, England: Faber and Faber.

Ramirez, Francisco O. and Jane Weiss. 1979. "The Political Incorporation of Women." Pp. 238–52 in *National Development and the World System*, edited by J. W. Meyer and M. T. Hannan. Chicago, IL: University of Chicago Press.

Robertson, Roland. 1992. *Globalization: Social Theory and Global Culture*. London, England: Sage.

——. 1994. "Globalization or Glocalization." *Journal of International Communication* 1(1): 33–52.

Sewell, William H., Jr. 1992. "A Theory of Structure: Duality, Agency, and Transformation." *American Journal of Sociology* 98:1–29.

Simmel, Georg. 1955. *Conflict and the Web of Group-Affiliations*. New York: Free Press.

Singer, J. David and Melvin Small. 1966. "The Composition and Status Ordering of the International System: 1815–1940." *World Politics* 18 (January): 236–82.

Skocpol, Theda. 1979. *States and Social Revolutions: A Comparative Analysis of France, Russia, and China*. Cambridge, England: Cambridge University Press.

Smith, Anthony. 1980. *The Geopolitics of Information: How Western Culture Dominates the World*. London, England: Faber and Faber.

Snow, Charles Percy. 1959. *The Two Cultures*. Cambridge, England: Cambridge University Press.

Soysal, Yasemin Nuhoglu. 1994. *The Limits of Citizenship: Migrants and Postnational Membership in Europe*. Chicago, IL: University of Chicago Press.

Speeckaert, Georges Patrick. 1957. "The 1,978 International Organizations Founded Since the Congress of Vienna." *Documents for the Study of International Nongovernment Relations, no. 7*. Brussels, Belgium: Union of International Associations.

Strang, David. 1990. "From Dependence to Sovereignty: An Event History Analysis of Decolonization." *American Sociological Review* 55:846–60.

Taylor, Charles Lewis and Michael C. Hudson. 1970. *World Handbook of Political and Social Indicators II*. Ann Arbor, MI: University of Michigan Press.

Thomas, George M. 1989. *Revivalism and Cultural Change: Christianity, Nation-Building, and the Market in the Nineteenth-Century United States*. Chicago, IL: University of Chicago Press.

——. 1994. "U.S. Discourse and Strategies in the New World Order." Pp. 143–72 in *Old Nations, New World: Conceptions of World Order*, edited by D. Jacobson. Boulder, CO: Westview.

Thomas, George M. and Pat Lauderdale. 1988. "State Authority and National Welfare Programs in the

World System Context." *Sociological Forum* 3:383–99.

Thomas, George M., John W. Meyer, Francisco O. Ramirez, and John Boli. 1987. *Institutional Structure: Constituting State, Society and the Individual.* Beverly Hills, CA: Sage.

Tilly, Charles. 1992. *Coercion, Capital, and European States, A.D. 990–1992.* Rev. ed. Cambridge, MA: Blackwell.

Tomlinson, John. 1991. *Cultural Imperialism: A Critical Introduction.* London, England: Pinter.

Turner, Bryan S. 1993. "Outline of the Theory of Human Rights." Chap. 8 in *Citizenship and Social Theory,* edited by B. S. Turner. London, England: Sage.

Union of International Associations (UIA). 1985 and 1988. *Yearbook of International Organizations.* Vol. 21, *1984–85,* and Vol. 25, *1988–89.* Munich, Germany: K. G. Saur.

United Nations. Various years. *Statistical Yearbook.* New York: United Nations.

United Nations Educational, Scientific, and Cultural Organization (UNESCO). 1965–1990. *UNESCO Statistical Yearbook.* Louvain, Belgium: UNESCO.

van Steenbergen, Bart. 1994. "Towards a Global Ecological Citizen." Chap. 11 in *The Condition of Citizenship,* edited by B. van Steenbergen. London, England: Sage.

Wallerstein, Immanuel. 1974. *The Modern World-System: Capitalist Agriculture and the Origins of the European World Economy in the Sixteenth Century.* New York: Academic.

Watson, Adam. 1992. *The Evolution of International Society: A Comparative Historical Analysis.* London, England: Routledge.

Weiss, Edith Brown. 1989. "Legal Dimensions of Global Change: A Proposed Research Agenda." *International Social Science Journal* 121:399–412.

Wendt, Alexander, 1992. "Anarchy Is What States Make of It: The Social Construction of Power Politics." *International Organization* 46:395–421.

Willets, Peter, ed. 1982. *Pressure Groups in the Global System: The Transnational Relations of Issue-Orientated Non-Governmental Organizations.* London, England: Frances Pinter.

Wiseberg, Laurie S. 1991. "Human Rights NGO's." Pp. 23–44 in *The Role of Non-Governmental Organizations in the Promotion and Protection of Human Rights,* edited by A. G. Castermans, L. Schut, F. Steketee, and L. Verhey. Leiden, The Netherlands: Stichting NJCM-Boekerij.

Wuthnow, Robert. 1989. *Communities of Discourse.* Cambridge, MA: Harvard University Press.

CHAPTER 44

Social Movements and Global Transformation

Louis Kriesberg

The world is changing in ways that foster the growth of transnational social movement organizations (TSMOs) and increase their significance. TSMOs, in turn, contribute to these global changes by directly influencing particular policies and by affecting the context in which they are made. Those influences are mapped out in this chapter, and attention is given to global developments that constrain, as well as foster, the work of TSMOs.

TSMOs should be considered in the context of the more loosely bounded transnational social movements (TSMs) of which they are a part and in the context of the changing global system, because these form the environment in which TSMOs function. Furthermore, we are in a period of turbulence and transition, with old national and international structures being transformed (Rosenau 1990; Commission on Global Governance 1995). In such periods of flux, the little shifts in direction that TSMOs help bring about can have large, long-run effects.

Global changes involve powerful, large-scale social forces, and even shifts that appear abrupt are typically products of slowly evolving changes that develop largely undetected. Even efforts by powerful persons or organizations generally make only marginal—and rarely wholly intended—differences. For example, the end of the Cold War and the dissolution of the Soviet Union contributed in part to the recent surge in the establishment of TSMOs. The end of the Cold War and of the Soviet Union were triggered by actions initiated by Mikhail Gorbachev; but those actions and their unforseen effects can be explained only by profound global changes underway for many years. Furthermore, the activities of TSMOs in the areas of human rights and peace movements contributed to the transforming changes in Eastern Europe and the Soviet Union (Kriesberg and Segal 1992; Stokes 1993).

MAJOR TRENDS PROVIDING THE CONTEXT FOR TSMO ACTIVITIES

Four interactive trends shaping the contemporary world have profound implications for TSMOs: growing democratization, increasing global integration, converging and diffusing values, and proliferating transnational institutions. Each tends to support the formation and growth of nongovernmental organizations (NGOs), including TSMOs, and each also affects the nature of TSMO activities. The trends, however, do not all move steadily in the same direction; indeed, in some ways they contradict each other.

Growing Democratization

For more than two hundred years, the world has been undergoing fundamental democratization. More people are able to participate in the political process in more societies as suffrage has gradually been extended to men without property and to others who had been disenfranchised because of their race, ethnicity, sex, or social status.

Democratization is also manifested in the increasing freedom that individuals and collectivities have from control or interference by governments, as is evident in the growing legitimacy and protection of human and civil rights. Because it eroded the credibility and legitimacy of authoritarian rule, the dissolution of the Soviet Union provided a further boost for democratization in both the region controlled by the former Soviet Union and elsewhere in the world. Nevertheless, according to Freedom House estimates, in 1995 only 20 percent of the world's population lived in free countries; 40 percent lived in partly free countries, and 40 percent lived in closed or repressive countries. Compared to 1985 statistics, these trends represent progress, but they are reversals of gains made up to 1993. Thus, while there is reason for optimism about democratic expansion, threats of renewed authoritarianism remain.

The democratization trend is evident in social systems at the organizational, community, national, and global levels. Three of the developments from which it derives are particularly notable: extending supportive norms, improving means of communication, and increasing material surplus.

Extending supportive norms. Increased democratization results in part from changes in what people regard as moral and legitimate. Thus, the spread of ideas supporting individualism and the rights of every person to free expression also contributes to democratization, as may be seen in the growing acceptance of the norm, if not the reality, of universal human and civil rights.

Democratization is also supported by the legitimacy often accorded claims by ethnic or other communal groups to the right to use their language, practice their religion, and otherwise express their cultural traditions. This legitimacy may be seen in the decay and even active rejection of expressions of racism. At the same time, however, a rise in violent resistance against immigrants and other minorities threatens this democratic norm in some places.

Norms that uphold the value of an individual's participation in decisions affecting his or her life have spread within every society and across the world. One sign of this trend is the almost universal participation of people in elections, even if some elections allow little room for choice.

Indicators of normative support for these rights may be seen in the actions taken by the United Nations. The UN General Assembly approved the Universal Declaration of Human Rights in December 1948, and the international community built upon this Declaration and reinforced it with two legally binding International Covenants on Human Rights that entered into force in 1976. More recently, the UN has intervened (even militarily) to promote democratic elections within countries and to promote humanitarian objectives in internal conflicts.

The current widespread occurrence of ethnic and other communal conflicts, some of which have been genocidal, seem to belie the above observations. However, the ethno-nationalist claims for sovereignty and exclusiveness are assertions—admittedly extreme ones—of the collective rights that otherwise are seen as progressive and democratic. Furthermore, the international condemnation of large-scale human rights violations and the recent interventions to stop the violations reflect the existence of international norms against the suppression of one people's rights by the violent imposition of another people's. However, when perpetrators are strong, interests of possible defenders of the norm are not engaged, and when a high level of international consensus is not mobilized, the existence of norms is often insufficient to assure governments' compliance with them.

Improving means of communication. Rapidly improving technology and communication facilitates popular participation in collective decision making. Movies, telephones, television, audio and video tape cassettes, fax, and electronic mail provide multiple sources of information, and that information can be immediately transmitted. Until recently much of this information was sent from one person or organization to others who lacked the ability to respond. What is particularly striking about the recent innovations is that they make rapid exchanges and sustained social interaction possible.

Increases in people's ability to use these means of rapid communication also profoundly affect transnational mobilizing possibilities. One of these changes is the expansion in the numbers of people who have the skills to use both the old and the new means of communication; for example, the increase in literacy means that the printed means of communication are increasingly accessible. Another change is the increase in the ability of people to afford to use the improved technology. Because both the old and the new means of communication and transportation cost considerably less than they once did, more people are able to organize to advance their interests domestically and internationally.

Increasing material surplus. The material standard of living for most people has been improving over the last few centuries. The resources thus made available allow people in more countries of the world to use the newer technologies and be in communication with their counterparts elsewhere in the world. They also provide greater opportunities for people to form associations and participate in public life. Citizens are thus better able to mobilize themselves to express their dissatisfactions, and they sometimes obtain satisfaction.

This long-term increasing standard of living, however, is far from universal and is not steadily rising: for instance, the per capita Gross National Product (GNP) in 1994 was $37,500 in Switzerland, $25,510 in the United States, $730 in Egypt, and $150 in Chad (Sivard 1996). Some countries have had devastating collapses in the people's living standards, particularly those plagued by internal or cross-border wars. Even without such calamities, many countries suffer from economic recessions, and in the last few decades from stagnation and decline in wages.

Countering the potential for democratization are gross inequalities in technological and material growth. Many people undoubtedly have a higher standard of living than did previous generations, but many people in every society still live quite poorly and have little access to the resources needed to be active socially and politically. Large economic and social inequalities persist not only between different countries but also within countries.

Those inequalities limit democratization insofar as they give people different degrees of protection from control by others and different levels of participation in collective decision making. For example, within the United States electoral activity varies greatly among different income strata and ethnic groups; those of lower income and education levels vote and participate in politics much less than richer and more highly educated individuals. Moreover, there is increasing inequality in developed countries; this is most evident in countries formerly governed by the Communist parties, but it is also present within the United States.

Global inequalities in access to modern means of communication are immense. For example, in 1993 the number of television receivers per 1,000 people ranged from 16 in Ghana to 40 in India and 816 in the United States (American Almanac 1996–97, table 1342). Even more fundamental are literacy rates, which vary greatly among countries, and within countries by social differences such as gender. Thus, while in the United States literacy rates for both females and males are reported to be 99 percent, in Egypt it is 39 and 64 percent, respectively; and in India 38 and 66 percent (Sivard 1996; table 3).

The absence of social and economic conditions that support democracy inhibits its rapid expansion, perhaps even resulting in regressions from the most recent democratic advances.[1] As in the past waves of democratization, some regressions are likely. But for the reasons indicated, many will endure to secure one more incremental step toward greater global democracy.

Increasing Global Integration

Humans are believed to have originated in East Africa and migrated to all parts of the earth, living in relative isolation for many thousands of years. During the last few thousand years, however, human beings are becoming increasingly reintegrated. In recent decades that has been an exponential increase in social exchanges, and the human species increasingly recognizes that its members share a common fate, whatever that may be. Rapidly growing social integration is manifested in several developments, most notably, increasing economic interdependence, growing information exchange, and ever more challenging global problems.

Signs of increasing global economic interdependence abound in what we wear, eat, and see. The expansion of the global market and the attendant growth of international trade, foreign investments, and the transnational movement of labor reflect this interdependence. As a consequence of this economic integration, what happens in one economy greatly affects people in many others. Immigration flows, remittances, and investment transfers all occur transnationally, impacting locally on employment, wages, and the prices of commodities. Yet governments are increasingly limited in their ability to control these developments, which are shaped by decisions made by multinational corporations and intergovernmental organizations (IGOs).

The increasing diffusion and exchange of information and cultural products, important aspects of global integration, are most evident in the realm of popular culture. Music, film, and television from the United States or other first world countries are routinely transferred to many other countries. Less frequently, music or other elements of popular culture from countries in the third world become known around the globe.

Many problems are global or regional, unconstrained by state borders. For example, air and water pollution and resource exhaustion impact entire regions or even the whole world, as is evident in the effects on the ozone level and the warming of the earth.

In addition, population growth and the resulting increased demands on limited resources have impacts beyond a particular country or region, for example, by producing refugee flows. These problems require transnational responses and therefore stimulate the formation of TSMOs.

These multiple problems do not impact all peoples of the world with the same urgency, as witnessed by the varying priority given to environmental protection and economic development in the countries of the North and of the South. This derives in part from the immense economic and social inequalities in the world. Those inequalities also compound the difficulties associated with the increasing penetration of the global market. For these and other reasons, global inequalities constitute a major problem challenging all peoples.

Many problems that were formerly invisible or were considered local have become transnational as they have been made visible on television. Such has been the case with the plight of victims of famines and epidemics. Whether caused by natural disasters, by internal or international wars, or by various combinations of sources, these problems generate and sustain humanitarian and other TSMOs, which in turn help arouse popular attention.

Although global integration may encourage transnational cooperation, it may also bring more peoples into conflict with each other, for example, regarding migration and trade. Such conflicts may foster TSMOs, because new TSMOs often are formed to oppose or to differentiate themselves from those already established (cf. Zald and McCarthy 1980). Consequently, they may appear to negate each other's efforts, but such competition and conflict can provide better solutions than would have been found by any single actor.

These developments undermine state power. Many citizens are coming to believe that their national governments cannot solve their problems, that the forces operating are beyond the power of the state. Some people believe the solution is to strengthen state controls (on, for example, immigration); others suggest reducing state efforts and opening the economies further to free market forces. Increasingly, however, many citizens are beginning to see transnational efforts as necessary responses to the global developments that impact their lives. The vehicles for such efforts, however, are still in early experimental stages.

Converging and Diffusing Values

Increasingly, values and norms are widely shared. Some people see this tendency as the diffusion of Western and particularly U.S. ideas, a kind of hegemony. But the movement is not unidirectional. Challenges to the apparent Western cultural domination are evident in the growth of ethnic and religious particularism.

But long-term trends in the world move people toward shared values. The dissolution of the Soviet Union and the rejection of the Communist parties in the former Soviet bloc countries have discredited that alternative ideology. As a result, at least, for the present, we see greater international consensus on many values than had previously been evident.

As was discussed above, the recognition of basic human rights is another widely held value that helps underpin broad acceptance of the desirability of democracy and the value of tolerance of social and cultural differences. The promotion of and support for tolerance of diversity in particular has many of the qualities of an international social movement.

The convergence and diffusion of many values is widely (but not universally) discernible. Consumerism, the high priority many people give to having goods and services for consumption and enjoyment, has spread throughout the world. The current widespread faith in "free market forces" as the most effective way of producing consumer items exacerbates inequalities and conflicts about them.

The diffusion of some of these values helps create discrepancies between the expectations people have regarding what they should have and what they actually have. The gap between their actual conditions and their standards generates dissatisfaction. This dissatisfaction is a crucial element in the emergence of social movements to correct the unsatisfactory conditions.

Widespread elite and mass reactions against many modernizing trends must also be recognized. Particularistic claims are made in the name of an ethnic community, for example, as members of an ethnic community seek to advance the interests of their people relative to others. These particularistic claims may take the form of nationalist claims for political independence. Also, members of a particular religion or ethnicity or self-attributed social race may reject the value of tolerance and seek to give membership in their social category a privileged position in society.

Everywhere there are signs of diversity of values as well as commonalities. For example, many people express their concern about the importance of community solidarity over rampant individualism. Such views are expressed by persons of both the left and the right. Many people also react against consumerism and economic development, instead supporting environmental protection and policies that limit economic development.

Proliferating Transnational Institutions

The growing number and scope of transnational nongovernmental and governmental organizations has been remarkable. Governmental and nongovernmental organizations often oppose one another's policies, but some cooperate and interpenetrate each other. For example, certain NGOs at times have been substantially controlled by governments.

The United Nations and its specialized agencies have grown by expanding their membership and by increasing their functions and operations. This growth is important because the UN system is global and has many features that provide a basis for the formation and influence of INGOs, including TSMOs.

The UN gives citizen groups limited access to influence policymaking at the global level. Article 71 of the UN Charter provides that "The Economic and Social Council may make suitable arrangements for consultation with non-governmental organizations." The purpose of those consultations is to enable the Council "to secure expert information or advice from organizations having special competence . . . and, . . . to enable organizations which represent important elements of public opinion to express their views" (Lador-Lederer 1963, 71–72). For some groups, such as women's groups that are often excluded from political activities in their countries, Article 71 provides access not available at the national level.

The large ad hoc UN conferences, beginning with the UN Conference on the

Human Environment (UNCHE) in Stockholm in 1972, represent the major platform for TSMO access to UN decision making (Stephenson, 1995). Nongovernmental forums following the form established largely at UNCHE now parallel all major intergovernmental conferences.

Regional international governmental organizations are important forums within which international nongovernmental organizations (INGOs) function (Taylor 1984). This is especially true in Europe. Beginning with the establishment of the European Coal and Steel Community in 1952, numerous organizations were founded to address economic and other matters. These include, for instance, the European Economic Community and the European Atomic Energy Community, which were established in 1957. Despite setbacks in regional organization, such as the European Defense Community, the overall trend has been the expansion of the matters under European Community jurisdiction and the increase in membership beyond the original six countries.

The growth of regional IGOs, which can give citizens access to policymakers that they may not have in national arenas, fosters the formation of INGOs (Haas 1958; Kriesberg 1960). This tendency is evident in the rapid increase of international NGOs in Europe, paralleling the establishment of European intergovernmental institutions.

The evolution of the Conference on Security and Cooperation in Europe (CSCE) exemplifies the complex interaction between a major regional IGO and TSMs (Leatherman 1993). CSCE negotiations concluded in 1975 with the Helsinki Final Act, signed by thirty-five participating states. The CSCE's provisions for confidence-building measures and the protection of human rights was supported by peace and human rights national and transnational social movements, and those movements were, in turn, fostered and strengthened by the CSCE, (now the Organization for Security and Cooperation in Europe, or OSCE). Together, they contributed to the fundamental transformation in East-West relations (Thomas 1994).

International Nongovernmental Organizations (INGOs) include a wide variety of organizations with members from several countries.[2] Members are typically national associations but often also include individuals. They are generally organized to provide services and advance the interests of their members, for example, occupations and industries. The number of INGOs has been increasing and in 1993 totaled 4,830 (Union of International Associations 1993, 1698). The higher density of national nongovernmental organizations within the relatively well-to-do countries means that people from those countries are likely to have disproportionate influence on the work of INGOs. This impression is reinforced by the fact that most of the INGOs are headquartered in the United States or Western Europe.

Many INGOs reflect and reinforce the status quo. Sometimes, powerful and well-to-do persons and groups in various countries form transnational organizations to formulate policies that they believe will benefit their interests and values. The Trilateral Commission, founded in 1973 by North American, Western European, and Japanese business, labor, and political elites, reflects this tendency, developing policy prescriptions targeting common economic concerns (Sklar 1980).

TSMOs, in contrast, are INGOs, such as Greenpeace or Amnesty International, that seek to bring about a change in the status quo. TSMOs work for progressive change in the areas of the environment, human rights, and development as well as for conservative goals like opposition to family planning or immigration. Figure 44.1 illustrates the relationships between NGOs, INGOs, and TSMOs. The largest inclusive category consists of all NGOs, national and international, organized for religious, recreational, political, or functional purposes. SMOs are that subset of NGOs working to "[change] some elements of the social structure and/or reward distribution of society" (McCarthy and Zald 1977, 1212). INGOs are those NGOs whose memberships transcend national boundaries. At the intersection of SMOs and INGOs are transnational social movement organizations. In other words, TSMOs are INGOs that work specifically for

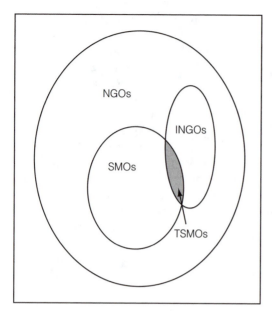

Figure not drawn to scale

Figure 44.1 Distinctions among nongovernmental organizations.

some social or political change and operate an international office or secretariat to serve a membership active in more than two states.

Because they facilitate international communication and cooperation and cultivate organizational skills, INGOs contribute to the development of TSMOs. Many INGOs, for instance, provide networks or social infrastructures that can process conflicts among different people and generate consensus about global problems and their solutions, thus facilitating the formation and growth of transnational social movements. In other words, some INGOs that have members from countries with diverse and even conflicting interests may indirectly provide channels for constructing options that help bridge antagonistic differences and contribute to peacebuilding (Kriesberg 1972).

Although INGOs often represent people who would otherwise be excluded from participation in transnational governance, many TSMOs and INGOs are not accountable to broad constituencies. Some are controlled by their managerial or charismatic leadership. Certainly multinational corporations are not controlled by the citizens at large, or even by their millions of shareholders; rather, their managers and major investors make policy.

In the past some INGOs were supported or assisted through covert government actions, such as those of the Central Intelligence Agency of the United States and the KGB or Communist Party of the Soviet Union. The involvement of the Soviet and Russian side has certainly decreased since the disintegration of the Soviet Union; and now there is an opportunity for a reduction from the United States side as well. However, other governments, such as those of Iran, Libya, and Syria have assisted TSMOs that help wage national liberation struggles, and they probably continue to assist them.

Developments such as the end of the Cold War and technological advances reinforce the conditions that make transnational social movement action possible. More people in more places in the world have the capability of communicating with each other and organizing. Second, they often provide incentives to form TSMOs, even making certain TSMOs essential. Particular environmental problems require transnational responses (Princen and Finger 1994). Finally, contentions among different actors in the world are vital for global democracy, giving expression to different perspectives, providing alternative solutions, and encouraging new syntheses. TSMOs often make the added contribution of reducing the dominance of the more powerful actors in a world characterized by immense inequalities.

TSMOs AS AGENTS AFFECTING THE TRENDS

As the cases in this volume demonstrate, TSMOs can be important agents of global change. The identities and organizations functioning in the subglobal domains may be barriers to forming broader global identities or organizations. TSMOs are fostered by the trends we have surveyed and, in turn, affect those trends. TSMOs tend to reinforce the trends by:

1. supporting networks of social relations

that are the social infrastructures for action

2. cultivating constituencies for intergovernmental organizations
3. providing reservoirs of resources and redistributing those resources
4. fostering new transnational identities and
5. stimulating one another to attack transnational sources of common problems.

TSMOs help transmit information by providing a network of relations for the diffusion of ideas and practices, thereby facilitating mobilization for movement goals. They also help diffuse norms and values about participation in policymaking and execution and serve as constituencies for other NGOs and for IGOs, thus fostering democratization.

TSMOs provide reservoirs of resources because members in one country or region may have great wealth that can be drawn upon by TSMOs and other INGOs in countries or regions with fewer resources. Moreover, as people work together to advance a particular goal, they strengthen their bonds and shared identity. That identity is likely to transcend identification with any single country. In the case of INGOs, that may mean a broader and stronger identity as a member of a particular profession. In the case of a TSMO, it may mean an identity as a human rights advocate.

The activities of some TSMOs foster the growth of other TSMOs because they sometimes arouse competition or even opposition. This phenomenon occurs at both the regional and global levels. For example, persons engaged in social movements to improve the position of women or to protect the environment differ in their analyses of the problem and in the strategies to be pursued to solve it. They are likely to form a variety of organizations reflecting those differences.

These activities tend to reinforce many aspects of the global trends previously described. Furthermore, they tend to do so in ways that foster continued growth of TSMOs. This does not mean that the world will become harmonious or that the TSMOs and the transnational social movements within which they function will work in harmony. Conflicts will continue to erupt, some of them pursued in destructive ways.

The multiplicity of TSMOs and INGOs is likely to mitigate conflicts insofar as the organizations cross-cut each other.[3] Conversely, when the organizations are based on coinciding lines of cleavage, interests, and identities, they make conflicts across those lines more intense and difficult to resolve. TSMOs and INGOs by definition cross-cut state borders; and they also are likely to cross-cut many other lines of cleavage, because they are based on many different interests, values, and identities.

EFFECTS OF TSMOs ON TRANSNATIONAL POLICIES

Global and regional activities are shaped by many kinds of intentional policies. These include declarations of principles, the establishment of intergovernmental institutions, placing different people in decision-making offices, and providing particular goods or services through the market place or through public or private nonprofit organizations.

TSMOs affect particular regional and global policies in several ways. A discussion of how they effectively influence global policies must also recognize some of the factors constraining them. First, it should be noted that operating internationally raises transaction costs and therefore sometimes inhibits action. Second, TSMOs sometimes block each other. Third, there are many difficulties in implementing international coordination.

Finally, TSMOs are only one of many global actors, and they are often relatively powerless when compared to other global actors such as governments, multinational corporations, and international banking institutions. Clearly, despite all these developments described above, states—particularly large, economically developed ones—remain very powerful global actors.

TSMOs nevertheless possess many capabilities that give them unique roles in global political processes and strengthen their influence on transnational policies. Those capabilities include operating at many levels and having complementary components. TSMOs help shape transnational policies in ways such as mobilizing support, broadening participation, sustaining activity, framing issues, and implementing policies.

TSMO Capabilities

As other chapters of this book reveal, TSMOs have many capabilities that give them particular advantages in bringing about changes in the status quo. Two in particular are related to the transnational character of TSMOs.

TSMOs Work at Many Levels. They can work by trying to influence IGOS and other INGOs by direct contacts. They often try to affect the views of the attentive public and of elites, at the regional or global level. In addition, they usually also work at the national level to influence officials, national organizations, and the public at large.

TSMOs Can Complement One Another. Members in different countries have varying kinds of resources, and therefore organizations in several countries can complement each other. For example, a TSMO can include people who speak out in one country even if members are silenced in another. The work of Amnesty International is based on that principle. Thus, although people in one country may be intimidated and endangered by protesting the wrongful imprisonment of individuals in their country, protests can be effectively mounted in other countries.

TSMOs provide safe havens and external bases in one country from which campaigns can be launched in another. There may also be a division of tasks, for example, having fighters in one country and fund raisers in another. This has often been the case for organizations waging national liberation struggles, during which members in exile or in the diaspora sustain the struggle by providing funds and a base for those engaged in resistance in the homeland. A division of labor also occurs in TSMOs with members from relatively more economically developed countries of the North complementing the efforts of persons from less developed countries of the South.

Methods of Shaping Global Policy

TSMOs affect global policies through a great variety of methods, which other chapters in this book document. Described below are five general ways various TSMOs attempt to alter the status quo.

TSMOs Help Mobilize Support for Particular Policies. Because many problems are difficult to solve within one country, transnational action is much more effective. For instance, the nineteenth-century campaign to end the slave trade was necessarily an international one. More recently, international campaigns on environmental issues reflect the growing realization of the need to develop transnational responses to global problems.

TSMOs Help Widen Public Participation in International Policy Processes. International policies are formed by agreements and actions of government representatives from several countries. Those representatives may consult with or otherwise take into account some of their constituents who may be affected by the policy change under consideration. The views of the constituents are filtered through their representatives, who have their own perceptions, values, and interests. In any case, these constituents tend to be from a narrow group with strong ties to government representatives.

TSMOs provide avenues for broader participation in policy-making. They offer a direct channel of communication between persons with similar concerns in different countries. Once established, they often develop offices for educating members and the public and for lobbying national representatives and IGOs.

TSMOs Help Sustain Attention on Critical Global Problems. Governments, particularly democratic ones, have short attention spans. Particular issues become salient and action seems necessary, but then attention wanes and another issue suddenly claims attention. TSMOs help keep the attention of the public and policymakers focused on the issues of concern to them. A TSMO therefore often provides continuity of action and develops expertise that can be utilized by persons in governments, international agencies, and the media when their attention turns (however briefly) to concerns of social movements.

TSMOs Help Frame Issues and Set the Policy Agenda. As international organizations, they are often in a better position to receive mass media attention than if they were an organization of only a single nation.

They can discuss and propose new options from a variety of national perspectives. For example, high-ranking physicists and others from the United States, the Soviet Union, and the United Kingdom, meeting in a group called Pugwash, discussed ways to monitor underground nuclear weapons testing and arrived at shared understandings that were used in official negotiations about limiting nuclear weapons testing (Pentz and Slovo 1981).

Some TSMOs and Other INGOs Carry Out Transnational Policies. This procedure is common in the human rights field, as TSMOs and other NGOs provide data on governments' compliance with or violations of human rights agreements. And in the early 1980s, a coalition of organizations initiated a global boycott of the Nestlé Corporation to bring about its compliance with new standards for the marketing of baby food (Sikkink 1986).

CONCLUSIONS

TSMOs contribute much to the shaping of policies at the global and regional level and will do more. They will continue to do so, however, within a system where their goals challenge or compete with the interests of powerful actors such as states and multinational corporations.

Many TSMOs seek to challenge the great inequalities in the world. The immense differences in wealth, power, and status within and among countries are oppressive for those people who have little. But the TSMOs can never be wholly outside or above those structured inequalities. Moreover, some TSMOs may pursue policies or reproduce leadership patterns that relatively disadvantaged persons view as supporting and reinforcing the inequalities.

A homogeneous, tightly ordered world is not to be expected or desired. Diversity is needed and, in any case, will always remain. TSMOs arise from that diversity and contribute to its flourishing. The multiplicity of TSMOs is a source of significant crosscutting ties that help mitigate destructive conflicts. As a totality, TSMOs help form global civil society. For a legitimate, egalitarian, and democratic international system to exist, underlying pluralistic social groupings must develop. Alexis de Tocqueville (1945), in celebrating American democracy, stressed the importance of the many public associations in America for the maintenance of freedom against tyrannies by the government or by the majority of the people. Perhaps in the future someone can celebrate a global democracy sustained by the proliferation of transnational associations.

NOTES

1. Karl and Schmitter (1994), for example, analyze the sources and duration of the wave of democratization starting in 1974, referring to it as the fourth wave of democratization. Huntington (1991) refers to the current wave as the third wave of democratization.

2. For discussions of international NGOs, see Lador-Lederer (1963), Kriesberg (1972), Feld (1972), and Taylor (1984).

3. The significance of cross-cutting ties for preventing the eruption of conflicts and for limiting their destructive pursuit has been posited and tested by research by many analysts. See, for example, Ross (1920), Dahrendorf (1959), and Kriesberg (1982).

REFERENCES

American Almanac, The. 1996. Austin, Tex.: Hoover's.

Commission on Global Governance. 1995. *Our Global Neighborhood.* New York: Oxford Univ. Press.

Dahrendorf, Ralf. 1959. *Class and Class Conflict in Industrial Society.* Stanford, Calif.: Stanford Univ. Press.

Feld, Werner. 1972. *Nongovernmental Forces and World Politics: A Study of Business, Labor, and Political Groups.* New York: Praeger.

Haas, Ernst B. 1958. *The Uniting of Europe: Political, Social, and Economic Forces 1950–1957.* Stanford, Calif.: Stanford Univ. Press.

Huntington, Samuel. 1991. *The Third Wave: Democratization in the Late Twentieth Century.* Norman and London: Univ. of Oklahoma Press.

Karl, Terry Lynn and Philippe C. Schmitter. 1994. "Democratization around the Globe: Opportunities and Risks." In *World Security Challenges for a New Century*, edited by M. T. Klare and D. C. Thomas, 43–62. New York: St. Martin's Press.

Kriesberg, Louis. 1960. "German Businessmen and Union Leaders and the Schuman Plan." *Social Science* 35 (Apr.): 114–21.

——. 1972. "International Nongovernmental Organizations and Transnational Integration." *International Associations* 24, no. 11: 520–25.

——. 1982. *Social Conflicts*. 2d ed. Englewood Cliffs, N.J.: Prentice-Hall.

Kriesberg, Louis, and David R. Segal, eds. 1992. *Social Movements, Conflicts and Change*, vol. 14, *The Transformation of European Communist Societies*. Greenwich, Conn: JAI Press.

Lador-Lederer, J. J. 1963. *International Non-Governmental Organizations*. Leyden: A. W. Sythoff.

Leatherman, Janie. 1993. "Conflict Transformation in the CSCE: Learning and Institutionalization." *Cooperation and Conflict* 28, no. 4: 403–31.

McCarthy, John D., and Mayer N. Zald. 1977. "Resource Mobilization in Social Movements: A Partial Theory." *American Journal of Sociology* 82: 1212–41.

Pentz, Michael J., and Gillian Slovo. 1981. "The Political Significance of Pugwash." In *Knowledge and Power in a Global Society*, edited by William M. Evan, 175–203. Beverly Hills/London/New Delhi: Sage.

Princen, Thomas, and Matthias Finger. 1994. *Environmental NGOs in World Politics*. London and New York: Routledge.

Rosenau, James N. 1990. *Turbulence in World Politics*. Princeton: Princeton Univ. Press.

Ross, Edward A. 1920. *The Principles of Sociology*. New York: Century.

Sikkink, Kathryn. 1986. "Codes of Conduct for Transnational Corporations: The Case of the WHO/UNICEF Code." *International Organization* 40: 815–40.

Sivard, Ruth Leger. 1996. *World Military and Social Expenditures*. Leesburg, Virginia: WMSE Publications.

Sklar, Holly, edited 1980. *Trilateralism*. Boston: South End Press.

Stephenson, Carolyn M. 1995. "Women's International Non-Governmental Organizations at the United Nations." In *Women, Politics and the United Nations*, edited by Ann Winslow. New York: Greenwood.

Stokes, Gale. 1993. *The Walls Came Tumbling Down: The Collapse of Communism in Eastern Europe*. New York: Oxford Univ. Press.

Taylor, Philip. 1984. *Nonstate Actors in International Politics*. Boulder, Colo., and London: Westview.

Thomas, Dan. 1994. "The Helsinki Movement: International Norms, Social Mobilization in Eastern Europe, and Policy Change in the United States." Paper presented at Workshop on International Institutions and Transnational Social Movement Organizations, Kroc Institute for International Peace Studies, Univ. of Notre Dame, 18–20 Apr.

Tocqueville, A. 1945. *Democracy in America*. New York: Vintage Books.

Union of International Associations. 1983, 1988, 1993, 1995. *Yearbook of International Organizations*. Brussels: UAI.

Zald, Mayer N., and John D. McCarthy. 1980. "Social Movement Industries: Competition and Cooperation Among Movement Organizations." In *Research in Social Movements, Conflict and Change*, edited by Louis Kriesberg, 1–20. Greenwich, Conn.: JAI.

CHAPTER 45

Conclusions: Advocacy Networks and International Society

Margaret E. Keck and Kathryn Sikkink

Scholars theorizing about transnational relations must grapple with the multiple interactions of domestic and international politics as sources of change in the international system.[1] The blurring of boundaries between international and domestic arenas has long been evident in international and comparative political economy, but its relevance for other forms of politics is less well theorized. Our work on transnational advocacy networks highlights a subset of international issues, characterized by the prominence of principled ideas and a central role for nongovernmental organizations. In this subset of issues, complex global networks carry and re-frame ideas, insert them in policy debates, pressure for regime formation, and enforce existing international norms and rules, at the same time that they try to influence particular domestic political issues. Throughout this book we have tried to achieve greater theoretical clarity in a number of areas. First, we specify how, why, among whom, and to what end transnational relations occur. Second, we discuss the characteristic content of such relations—what kinds of ideas and issues seem to require or be amenable to these linkages—and the strategies and tactics networks use. Finally, we consider the implications for world politics of forms of organization that are neither hierarchical nor reducible to market relations.

We suggest that scholars of international relations should pay more attention to network forms of organization—characterized by voluntary, reciprocal, and horizontal exchanges of information and services. Theorists have highlighted the role of networks in the domestic polity and economy. What is

distinctive about the networks we describe here is their transnational nature, and the way they are organized around shared values and discourses. Networks are difficult to organize transnationally, and have emerged around a particular set of issues with high value content and transcultural resonance. But the agility and fluidity of networked forms of organization make them particularly appropriate to historical periods characterized by rapid shifts in problem definition. Thus we expect the role of networks in international politics to grow.

Both technological and cultural change have contributed to the emergence of transnational advocacy networks. Faster, cheaper, and more reliable international information and transportation technologies have speeded their growth and helped to break government monopolies over information. New public receptivity arose partly from the cultural legacy of the 1960s and drew upon the shared normative basis provided by the international human rights instruments created after the Second World War. Transnational value-based advocacy networks are particularly useful where one state is relatively immune to direct local pressure and linked activists elsewhere have better access to their own governments or to international organizations. Linking local activists with media and activists abroad can then create a characteristic "boomerang" effect, which curves around local state indifference and repression to put foreign pressure on local policy elites. Activists may "shop" the entire global scene for the best venues to present their issues, and seek points of leverage at which to apply pressure. Thus international contacts amplify voices to which domestic governments are deaf, while the local work of target country activists legitimizes efforts of activists abroad.

Transnational networks have developed a range of increasingly sophisticated strategies and techniques. We highlight four: *information politics; symbolic politics; leverage politics*; and *accountability politics*. Networks stress gathering and reporting reliable information, but also dramatize facts by using testimonies of specific individuals to evoke commitment and broader understanding. Activists use important symbolic events and conferences to publicize issues and build networks. In addition to trying to persuade through information and symbolic politics, networks also try to pressure targets to change policies by making an implied or explicit threat of sanctions or leverage if the gap between norms and practices remains too large. Material leverage comes from linking the issue of concern to money, trade, or prestige, as more powerful institutions or governments are pushed to apply pressure. Moral leverage pushes actors to change their practices by holding their behavior up to international scrutiny, or by holding governments or institutions accountable to previous commitments and principles they have endorsed.

Issues involving core values—ideas about right and wrong—arouse strong feelings and stimulate network formation among activists, who see their task as meaningful. Activists capture attention where their issues resonate with existing ideas and ideologies. To motivate action, however, network activists must also innovate, by identifying particular social issues as problematic, attributing blame, proposing a solution, and providing a rationale for action, or by making new connections within accepted value frames.

We have claimed that network actors try to frame issues in ways that make them fit into particular institutional venues and that make them resonate with broader publics, use information and symbols to reinforce their claims, identify appropriate targets, seek leverage over more powerful actors to influence their targets, and try to make institutions accountable in their practices to the norms they claim to uphold. What can we say about what works and what doesn't?

EVALUATING NETWORK SUCCESS OR FAILURE

Networks influence politics at different levels because the actors in these networks are simultaneously helping to define an issue area, convince policymakers and publics that the problems thus defined are soluble, prescribe solutions, and monitor their implementation. We can think of networks being effective in various stages: (1) by framing debates and getting issues on the agenda; (2) by encouraging discursive commitments from states and other policy actors; (3) by causing procedural change at the international and domestic level; (4) by affecting policy; and (5) by influencing behavior changes in target actors.

The structure of domestic institutions is relevant here, some institutions being more open to leverage than others.[2] The closed political structure in societies where participatory channels are blocked or limited may lead citizens to seek international linkages to press their claims more effectively. The combination of closed domestic structure in one country with open structures in other countries and with international organizations is what activates the boomerang pattern characteristic of networks.

Still, domestic structures are only a starting point for understanding why and how actors form networks, rather than an explanation of the conditions under which networks can be effective. They cannot tell us why some transnational networks operating in the same context succeed and others do not. That similar institutional venues accommodate strikingly different outcomes owes more, we believe, to the nature of the issues and the networks than to domestic or international structures *per se*.

Institutional openness to leverage varies significantly across issue areas within a single institution or state structure. The environmental movement has leveraged the World Bank, getting stronger environmental conditions in loans, but has not always been able to get these conditions enforced. The human rights movement has tried to gain similar leverage in the bank and has failed. The human rights movement has had much greater success in convincing the United States and European countries to consider human rights in their military and economic aid policies. Much of the success of the human rights movement can be attributed to its ability to leverage state aid policies. The U.S. environmental movement has had much more difficulty in establishing a similarly routinized form of linkage; efforts to influence the NAFTA negotiations were only partially successful, and the discussion of trade linkages has exacerbated network divisions within the United States and internationally.

Our case studies suggested that understanding dynamic elements in domestic politics is at least as important to success as understanding domestic structures. Under some circumstances, political oppositions may mediate the influence of transnational actors as much as or more than institutional incumbents. The clearest cases of this in our research were the footbinding and female circumcision cases. The campaign against footbinding resonated within the modernizing discourse of an emergent reformist opposition; the campaign against female circumcision became a symbol for nationalists of colonialism's effort to destroy deeply held cultural values. For almost all transnational campaigns, how the issue of nationalism is engaged is crucial to achieving issue resonance.

Evaluating the influence of networks is similar to evaluating the influence of sanctions, about which there has been considerable study and much disagreement.[3] As in the sanctions literature, we must look at characteristics of the "target" and of the "sender" or "source," and at relations between the two. Because a network as a sender is not a single actor like a state, but a multiple actor, its influence is even more difficult to trace.

Issue Characteristics

Advocacy networks develop around issues where international relations theorists and theorists of collective action would not predict international cooperation. Except where repressive regimes (as in Haiti) caused serious refugee flows, policymakers could easily ignore human rights, and the doctrine of sovereignty and nonintervention instructed them to do so. The new social knowledge that democracies don't go to war with other democracies may change the stakes in the human rights game; if security (a collective good) is enhanced by the worldwide existence of democracy, then promoting democracy could become a self-interested policy, not just a principled one. Yet the transformation of human rights policies and regimes came well before the emergence of the new social knowledge. As with human rights, states have not traditionally seen women's or indigenous issues as posing collective goods problems. Some environmental issues do pose serious externalities, but these are not necessarily the issues around which advocacy networks form. The environmental networks discussed here, for example, bring pressure on issues that are recognized as posing problems of collective goods, but whose resolution is politically very costly; both sovereignty and property issues are on the table in tropical forest negotiations.

States have few incentives to cooperate on these issues, and because many of the network campaigns challenge traditional notions of state sovereignty, we might expect states to cooperate to block network activities. Active intervention by a committed actor is necessary to get these issues onto political agendas. Human rights violations must be deliberately brought to the foreign policy agenda of a third party or an international organization before influence can be brought to bear. Deforestation and misuse of infant formula became issues rather than mere problems when network activists gave them identifiable causes and proposed remedies.

Actors within government can also raise the salience of an issue, but for states to act, either the values in question must plausibly coincide with the "national interest" or the government acting must believe (correctly or not) that the action is not costly (or at least that it is less costly than not acting). Part of what networks do is to try to transform state understandings of their national interests, and alter their calculations of the costs or benefits of particular policies. Moreover, the activists promoting the issue must seek state actors who are either network members themselves (in terms of their willingness to take costly action to promote issues they care deeply about) or who have other incentives to act. Environmentalists in the multilateral bank campaign got crucial support from Wisconsin senator Robert Kasten, chair of the Foreign Operations Sub-committee of the Senate Appropriations Committee, more because of his general hostility to the multilateral banks than because of his principled support for their particular aims.

The second characteristic of network issues worth highlighting is that they are all *in their general form* issues around which sustained mass mobilization is unlikely. The problem is transforming diffuse agreement (protect the environment, defend human rights) into willingness to take action.[4] The difficulty of constituent mobilization is one explanation for the predominance of advocacy pressure tactics over mass mobilization campaigns in these issue areas. There are exceptions. Amnesty International's organizational model involves large numbers of people in regular activities; boycott strategies, such as those used in the infant formula campaign and the tropical timber campaign, have similar characteristics.

New ideas are more likely to be influential if they fit well with existing ideas and ideologies in a particular historical setting.[5] Since networks are carriers of new ideas, they must find ways to frame them to resonate or fit with the larger belief systems and real life contexts within which the debates occur.[6] The ability of transnational advocacy networks to frame issues successfully is especially problematic because, unlike domestic social movements, different parts of advocacy networks need to fit with belief systems, life experiences, and stories, myths, and folk tales in many different countries and cultures. We argue that the two types of issues most characteristic of these networks—issues involving bodily harm to vulnerable individuals, and legal equality of opportunity— speak to aspects of belief systems or life experiences that transcend a specific cultural or political context.

There are various explanations about why such issues appear most prominently in international campaigns. Although issues of bodily harm resonate with the ideological traditions in Western liberal countries like the United States and Western Europe, they also resonate with basic ideas of human dignity common to most cultures. Not all cultures have beliefs about human rights (as individualistic, universal, and indivisible), but most value human dignity.[7] Gross violations of human rights run contrary to these divergent conceptions of human dignity. Issues of bodily harm also lend themselves to dramatic portrayal and personal testimony that are such an important part of network tactics.

Another transcultural belief with wide resonance is the concern with protecting the most vulnerable parts of the population— especially infants and children. The contrast between the Nestlé boycott and other issues that did not lead to international boycotts may capture the importance of the ability to resonate transnationally. Although more deaths are attributed to tobacco use than to the misuse of infant formula, there has been no successful, sustained international consumer boycott of tobacco companies. The perceived harm to vulnerable infants and their mothers who believe they are using a quality product generates more concern than does harm to adults who choose to smoke. A campaign against "Joe Camel" cigarette advertisements is the exception that proves the rule: organizers achieved some success because they claimed that the ads attempted to market cigarettes to children.

The Nestlé boycott also illustrates the importance of framing issues to resonate with existing belief systems. Both the company and the boycott tried to capitalize on the transcultural desire to do the best thing for one's baby. The baby food companies tried to convince mothers that infant formula was a modern healthy way to feed their babies, but the baby food network mobilized information and testimony strategically to convert the bottle from a symbol of modernity and health into a potentially dangerous threat to infant health in the third world.

Campaigns involving legal equality of opportunity also appear to lend themselves to transnational campaigns. Why this issue should have transcultural resonance is not completely clear. Most of the societies where such campaigns are carried out have adopted liberal institutions of democracy and rule of law, yet exclude some significant part of the population from participation in these institutions. This disjuncture between the neutral discourse of equality implicit in liberalism and the unequal access to liberal institutions opens a space for symbolic political action and the accountability politics of networks. In other words, liberalism carries within it not the seeds of its destruction, but the seeds of its expansion, Liberalism, with all its historical shortcomings, contains a subversive element that plays into the hands of activists. We agree with the work of John Meyer and his colleagues that there is a global cultural process of expansion of liberal values; where we differ is how this leads to political transformation.[8] We argue that liberal discourse can provide opportunities for activists to expose the gap between discourse and practice, and that this has been an effective organizing tool. For example, the organizers of the first conference on women's rights at Seneca Falls in 1848 eloquently and effectively stated their grievances using the words of the U.S. Declaration of Independence but substituting the word "woman" for "man," and "men" for "King George."

Why would we expect concern about the gap between discourse and practice, especially in the authoritarian regimes that are often the target of network pressures? Scholars have long recognized that even repressive regimes depend on a combination of coercion and consent to stay in power. Network campaigns have been most successful in countries that have internalized the discourse of liberalism to such a degree that there exists a disjuncture to plumb and expose. Liberal discourse and institutions also place limits and constraints, which is another reason why issues involving equality of opportunity are easier to organize around than these involving equity of outcome.

Cross-cultural resonance of issues does not necessarily eliminate all of the tensions implicit in the encounter. This is particularly true of issues that address poverty and inequality within an intentionalist frame. Within all networks that involve activists from both developing and developed countries, awareness of vastly unequal access to resources underlies conversation about issue framing, and also about the relationships among network members.

Actor Characteristics: Networks and Targets

Not surprisingly, networks are more effective where they are strong and dense. Network strength and density involves the total number and size of organizations in the network, and the regularity of their exchanges.[9] Strong and dense networks also include many "nodes" within the target state of the campaign. Network campaigns against human rights violations were more successful in Argentina and Chile than in Guatemala in the mid- to late 1970s partly because well-organized domestic human rights organizations existed in those countries. Although rights violations in Guatemala were even more severe than in Argentina and Chile, no effective local human rights NGOs existed in Guatemala until the mid-1980s; the presence of such organizations as part of the network increased the success of human rights pressures on Guatemala in the early 1990s. Local network members contribute information and bestow increased legitimacy on the activities of the network as a whole.

The density and strength of networks comes both from their identity as defined by principles, goals, and targets, and from the structural relationships among the networked organizations and individuals. In other words, the network-as-actor derives a great deal of its effectiveness from the network-as-structure, within which ideas are formulated, reformulated, tested, and negotiated. However much an individual or representative of a particular organization may speak and act in the name of a network without necessarily consulting its other members regularly, the synergy of networking nonetheless transforms the timbre of his or her voice. The "voice" of the network is not the sum of the network component voices, but the product of an interaction of voices (and different from any single voice of a network member).

This is not to suggest that advocacy networks are egalitarian structures. We recognize the asymmetrical or lopsided nature of most network interactions. Power is exercised within networks, and power often follows from resources, of which a preponderance exists within northern network nodes. Stronger actors in the network do often drown out the weaker ones, but because of the nature of the network form of organization, many actors (including powerful northern ones) are transformed through their participation in the network. However amorphous or weak the structure, it is still true that the nature of the agency we are talking about derives from that structure—just as the structure is itself a creation of the singular agents embedded within it. Networks cannot be undermined simply by characterizing them (the structures) as "agents" of a particular actor or position. Undermining a dense network rather requires destructuring it—that is, eroding the relations of trust or mutual dependence that exist among networked actors. The Malaysian government attempted to do this in 1993, for example, by circulating a story claiming misuse of funds by NGOs doing fundraising in the Sarawak case, and accusing Randy Hayes of the Rainforest Action Network of fabricating a story about abuse of Penan tribesmen. Network communications were sufficiently strong to weather this set of accusations.

Crucial determinants of the effectiveness of international networks are the characteristics of the targets, especially their vulnerability to both material and moral leverage.[10] The target may be vulnerable to particular kinds of issue linkage, for example when external aid is dependent on human rights performance. Vulnerability may come from prior normative commitments, as when the World Bank, already committed in many statements to sound environmental performance, was criticized for loans that arguably worsened the environmental situation. Targets may experience greater vulnerability at particular junctures, as was the case with Mexico during the negotiations for the North American Free Trade Agreement; Mexico's need to safeguard its prestige in that context provided openings for both human rights and environmental networks to press claims. Finally, vulnerability may simply represent a desire to maintain good standing in valued international groupings.[11]

Large military and economic aid flows to Latin American countries in the 1970s and 1980s gave the human rights network leverage against repressive countries in the region. Pressuring a country like China or Burma was more difficult because neither was receiving large economic and military assistance from Western countries. The only available leverage was trade privileges—most favored nation status or the generalized system of preferences—the use of which is more controversial, as it hurts the exporters in Western countries. Ecological groups achieved influence in the bank campaign by providing information that convinced members of Congress and the Treasury Department to instruct U.S. executive directors of multilateral development banks to monitor closely the environmental impact of loans; similar processes took place in European countries.

Even if leverage is available, the target country must be sensitive to the pressures. As the failure of economic sanctions against Haiti in 1993–94 made clear, some governments can resist pressures successfully for long periods. Countries most sensitive to pressure are those that care about their international image. For issue linkage to work, the target country must value the carrot being extended (or good withheld) more than it values the policy being targeted. But as the cases of human rights in Haiti or tropical deforestation in Sarawak illustrate, linkage with money, trade, or prestige is not a sufficient condition for effectiveness. Haiti's military rulers chose to hang onto power in the face of universal moral censure and economic collapse. Only the threat of military invasion led to a last-minute agreement to relinquish power. In Sarawak, local politicians become immensely wealthy by granting logging concessions, and the state government depends on logging for a good part of its revenues. Although the Malaysian federal government was sensitive to attacks on its international status, it was even more vulnerable to threats by Sarawak's politicians to defect from the government coalition.

The Nestlé Corporation was vulnerable to the pressures of a consumer boycott because a large range of its consumer food items were identified by the company name (Nestlé Quik, Nestlé Crunch) and because it had invested heavily in a corporate image of quality goods ("Nestlé makes the very best") which could be easily undermined by the accusation that Nestlé goods led to infant deaths in the third world. Attempts to organize a similar boycott against other producers of infant formula in the United States have failed because they have targeted less familiar corporations—American Home Products, Abbott Laboratories—whose products rarely carry the company name.

IMPLICATIONS FOR INTERNATIONAL SOCIETY

Central to this project is an understanding of the international system not as anarchy but as international society. We share with Hedley Bull and the English school of international relations scholars the idea that we live in an international society when on the basis of common interest and values states "conceive themselves to be bound by a common set of rules in their relations with one another and share in the working of common institutions."[12] We disagree, however, with Bull's emphasis always on a society of *states*. Even in 1977 when he wrote his classic work, Bull recognized that international society was evolving, and that the human rights issue offered a particularly potent challenge to the logic of a society of sovereign states.

> Carried to its logical extreme, the doctrine of human rights and duties under international law is subversive of the whole principle that mankind should be organized as a society of sovereign states. For, if the rights of each man can be asserted on the world political stage over and against the claims of his state, and his duties proclaimed irrespective of his position

as a servant or a citizen of that state, then the position of the state as a body sovereign over its citizens, and entitled to command their obedience, has been subject to challenge, and the structure of the society of sovereign states has been placed in jeopardy. The way is left open for the subversion of the society of sovereign states on behalf of the alternative organizing principle of a cosmopolitan community.[13]

Our vision is closer to what Bull called "neo-medievalism," where nonstate actors begin to undermine state sovereignty. The term doesn't adequately portray the dynamism and novelty of the new global actors we discuss, but Bull's central insight of a new system with "overlapping authority and multiple loyalty" does capture part of the change we describe.[14] Bull issued two serious challenges, one empirical—the task of documenting the extent and nature of changes—and the other theoretical—to specify what kind of alternative vision of international politics might modify or supplant the centrality of interactions among sovereign states.

Recent empirical work in sociology has gone a long way toward demonstrating the extent of changes "above" and "below" the state. The "world polity" theory associated with John Meyer, John Boli, George Thomas, and their colleagues conceives of an international society in a radically different way. For these scholars, international society is the site of diffusion of world culture—a process that itself constitutes the characteristics of states. The vehicles for diffusion become global intergovernmental and nongovernmental organizations, but neither the sources of global cultural norms nor the processes through which those norms evolve are adequately specified.[15]

Proponents of world polity theory have documented the rise and diffusion of a wide range of cultural norms and practices and the related emergence of international nongovernmental organizations (INGOs) and intergovernmental organizations (IOs). These are presented as enactors of basic principles of the world culture: universalism, individualism, rational voluntaristic authority, human purposes, and world citizenship; there is thus no meaningful distinction between those transnational actors espousing norms that reinforce existing institutional power relationships and those that challenge them.[16]

We argue that different transnational actors have profoundly divergent purposes and goals. To understand how change occurs in the world polity we have to understand the quite different logic and process among the different categories of transnational actors. The logic of transnational advocacy networks, which are often in conflict with states over basic principles, is quite different from the logic of other transnational actors, such as the International Olympic Committee or, the International Electrotechnical Commission, who provide symbols or services or models for states. In essence, world polity theorists eliminate the struggles over power and meaning that for us are central to normative change. Martha Finnemore makes a similar point when she argues that despite its impressive achievements, world polity theory marginalizes politics, obscures power, and "omits conflicts, violence, and leadership." She challenges political scientists to engage in a dialogue with the world polity theorists because "political process, coercion and violence, value conflict and normative contestation are our business."[17]

Nevertheless, the world polity theorists have an important insight. At some point, they suggest, what was once unthinkable becomes obvious, and from then on change starts to occur much more rapidly. The early battles to gain the vote for women were fought tooth and nail country by country, and success came very slowly. This history does not look at all like the natural process of cultural change suggested by the polity theorists. But after a critical mass of countries adopted woman suffrage, it was naturalized as an essential attribute of the modern state, and many countries granted women the vote even without the pressure of domestic women's movements. Perhaps some understanding of "thresholds" might help integrate our work with that of world polity theorists. These sociologists have focused theoretically on the second part of the process of change, when norms acquire a "taken for granted quality" and states adopt them without any political pressures from domestic polities. Thus they privilege explanations for norma-

tive change that highlight the influence of world culture. We explore the earlier stages of norm emergence and adoption, characterized by intense domestic and international struggles over meaning and policy, and thus tend to privilege explanations that highlight human agency and indeterminancy. Rather than seeing these as opposing theoretical explanations for causes of normative change, an understanding of stages suggests that the process of creating and institutionalizing new norms may be quite different from the process of adhering to norms that have already been widely accepted.

World polity theories treat IOs and INGOs as conveyor belts carrying Western liberal norms elsewhere. Once again, our research suggests that much modern network activity does not conform to this pattern. Many networks have been sites of cultural and political negotiation rather than mere enactors of dominant Western norms. Western human rights norms have indeed been the defining framework for many networks, but how these norms are articulated is transformed in the process of network activity. For example, indigenous rights issues and cultural survival issues, at the forefront of modern network activity, run counter to the cultural model put forward by the world polity theorists.

In other words, as modern anthropologists realize, culture is not a totalizing influence, but a field that is constantly in transformation. Certain discourses such as that of human rights provide a language for negotiation. Within this language certain moves are privileged over others; without doubt, human rights is a very disciplining discourse. But it is also a permissive discourse. The success of the campaign in making the point that women's rights are human rights reveals the possibilities within the discourse of human rights. Because international human rights policies came simultaneously from universalist, individualist, and voluntarist ideas *and* from a profound critique of how Western institutions had organized their contacts with the developing world, they allowed broader scope for contradictory understandings than might be expected. These critiques led in a very undetermined fashion to the emergence of human rights policy; theorists in the late twentieth century should not assume that the trajectory was predetermined by homogenizing global cultural forces.

Reconceptualizing international society does not require abandoning a focus on actors and institutions to seek underlying forces that make states and other forms of association epiphenomenal. We do find, however, that enough evidence of change in the relationships among actors, institutions, norms, and ideas exists to make the world political system rather than an international society of states the appropriate level of analysis. We also believe that studying networks is extraordinarily valuable for tracking and ultimately theorizing about these evolving relationships.

In the world political system today, states remain the predominant actors. But even for theoretical purposes it is hard to imagine conceiving of the state as "a closed, impermeable, and sovereign unit, completely separated from all other states."[18] Although the notion of the unitary state remains a convenient convention for certain kinds of international interactions, central to most interstate relations (as well as relationships between states and other individuals or associations) is the recognition of internally differentiated states and societies.[19] But sovereignty is eroded only in clearly delimited circumstances. The doctrine of the exhaustion of domestic remedies that is embedded in human rights law, for example, captures the nature of the relationship between the society of states and the emerging cosmopolitan community: individuals who hope for recourse for the alleged violation of their rights must have exhausted domestic remedies or shown that attempts to do so are futile. Then, and only then, if they still believe that they have been unjustly treated, may they have recourse to the international arena. The cosmopolitan community can bring pressure to bear at stages of the domestic process, but the state is still in charge.

There are few theorists of international relations to whom we can turn for help in giving voice to this vision of the global potential and limitations of a cosmopolitan community of individuals. Anything that hinted

of idealism was so thoroughly discredited by the perceived failures of idealism in the interwar period that no self-respecting international relations theorist dared admit a role of individual human agency motivated by principles in transforming the global scene. Yet it was precisely the obvious failure of states to protect human dignity during the interwar period and the Second World War that for political philosophers, such as Hannah Arendt, made such agency necessary. Arendt, argues Jeffrey Isaac, was not a theorist of human rights, but a "theorist of the politics made necessary by a world that despoils human rights," a politics that "might encourage new forms of regional and international identity and moral responsibility."[20]

The international system we present is made up not only of states engaged in self-help or even rule-governed behavior, but of dense webs of interactions and interrelations among citizens of different states which both reflect and help sustain shared values, beliefs, and projects. We distinguish our view from what Sidney Tarrow has called the "strong globalization thesis" which sees structural forces inevitably pulling the world into even more tightly knit global process.[21] The globalization process we observe is not an inevitable steamroller but a specific set of interactions among purposeful individuals. Although in the aggregate these interactions may seem earthshaking, they can also be dissected and mapped in a way that reveals great indeterminacy at most points of the process. There is nothing inevitable about this story: it is the composite of thousands of decisions which could have been decided otherwise.

The problem with much of the theory in international relations is that it does not have a motor of change, or that the motor of change—such as state self-interest, or changing power capabilities—is impoverished, and cannot explain the sources or nature of the international change we study here. Classic realist theory in international relations has not been useful for explaining profound changes, such as the breakdown of the Soviet Union and the satellites states in Eastern Europe, the end of slavery, or the granting of women the right to vote throughout the world.

Liberal international relations theory has a more compelling explanation of change because it is based on the proposition that individuals and groups in domestic and transnational society are the primary actors, that these groups in turn determine the preferences of states, and that the nature and intensity of state preferences determine the outcomes in international politics. Liberalism places significant emphasis, then, on domestic regime type, because whether or not a state is democratic determines which groups and individuals it represents.[22] Regime type is also important because authoritarian governments can "stunt the growth of domestic and transnational civil society."[23] Structural liberalism also argues that there has been a "collapse of the foreign / domestic distinction," and that foreign policy is no longer insulated from domestic politics in the way that it was once perceived to be, an argument that finds substantial support in the cases discussed in this book.[24]

Our approach differs from liberalism in a number of important respects. Liberalism assumes self-interested and risk-averse actors, and therefore its theory of how individuals and groups change their preferences must be based on changes in context leading to changing calculations of interest or risk.[25] We study individuals and groups who are motivated primarily by principled ideas and who, if not always risk-takers, at least are not risk-averse. We share the liberal assumption that governments represent (imperfectly) a subset of domestic society, and that individuals influence governments through political institutions and social practices linking state and society. But liberalism, as currently formulated, lacks the tools to understand how individuals and groups, through their interactions, might constitute new actors and transform understandings of interests and identities. We argue that individuals and groups may influence not only the preferences of their own states via representation, but also the preferences of individuals and groups elsewhere, and even of states elsewhere, through a combination of persuasion, socialization, and pressure.

Network theory can thus provide a model for transnational change that is not just one of "diffusion" of liberal institutions and practices, but one through which the preferences and identities of actors engaged in transnational society are sometimes mutually transformed through their interactions with each other. Because networks are voluntary and horizontal, actors participate in them to the degree that they anticipate mutual learning, respect, and benefits. Modern networks are not conveyor belts of liberal ideals but vehicles for communicative and political exchange, with the potential for mutual transformation of participants.

In this sense, network theory links the constructivist belief that international identities are constructed to empirical research tracing the paths through which this process occurs, and identifying the material and ideological limits to such construction in particular historical and political settings.

The importance of this process of mutual constitution is particularly relevant for considering the issue of sovereignty, about which significant differences may exist among network members. For the most part, activists in the north tend to see the erosion of sovereignty as a positive thing. For human rights activists it gives individuals suffering abuse recourse against the actions of their own state; for environmental activists it allows ecological values to be placed above narrow definitions of national interest. Given the innumerable glaring violations of sovereignty perpetrated by states and economic actors, why should measures that protect individuals from harm raise such concern? Northerners within networks usually see third world leaders' claims about sovereignty as the self-serving positions of authoritarian or, in any case, elite actors. They consider that a weaker sovereignty might actually improve the political clout of the most marginalized people in developing countries.

In the south, however, many activists take quite a different view. Rather than seeing sovereignty as a stone wall blocking the spread of desired principles and norms, they recognize its fragility and worry about weakening it further. The doctrines of sovereignty and nonintervention remain the main line of defense against foreign efforts to limit domestic and international choices that third world states (and their citizens) can make. Self-determination, because it has so rarely been practiced in a satisfactory manner, remains a desired, if fading, utopia. Sovereignty over resources, a fundamental part of the discussions about a new international economic order, appears particularly to be threatened by international action on the environment. Even where third world activists may oppose the policies of their own governments, they have no reason to believe that international actors would do better, and considerable reason to suspect the contrary. In developing countries it is as much the idea of the state, as it is the state itself, that warrants loyalty.

For many third world activists involved in advocacy networks, the individuated and international model of action that networks imply—the focus on "rights talk"—begs the question of structural inequality. At conference after conference, this question has at some point moved to center stage. The issue of sovereignty, for third world activists, is deeply embedded in the issue of structural inequality.

It is over such issues that networks are valuable as a space for the negotiation of meanings. In the emergence of the focus on violence for the international women's networks, in the evolution of the multilateral bank campaign and the tropical timber campaigns, the political learning that took place within the networks involved not only strategies and tactics but normative shifts in understanding of shared identities and responsibilities. The tropical timber campaign's focus on consumers of tropical hardwoods as much as on producers is the result of such a shift. Because parts of states and international organizations also participate in these networks, this process of negotiation within the emergent cosmopolitan community is not "outside" the state. Instead it involves state actors in active reflection on state interests as well.

Recognizing this dual character of networks provides correction for the continuing inability of structuralist theory to motivate change in the international system.[26] If transnational advocacy networks involve patterned interaction among states and non-

state actors whose agency is expressed in the international system, then by derivation states are bringing more than their relations with other states into their systemic relations. They are bringing more even than the domestic political baggage implied by Putnam's two-level game formulation (which, nonetheless, has the virtue of bridging the domestic international divide in a mutually determining fashion).[27] State actors as network components bring to international relations identities and goals that are not purely derived from their structural position in a world of states—and that may even be constituted by relationships established with citizens of other states. These identities and goals, furthermore, may contain elements in profound contradiction to the usual systemic roles of these states. Resolving these contradictions may require shifts in interstate relations that are not driven either by national interest or by "self-help" as traditionally understood.

The conflicting identities and goals that states qua network components take into the international system are increasingly enmeshed in the structural interaction between state and nonstate actors that is the network. The agency of a network usually cannot be reduced to the agency even of its leading members. This is true even if the network's access to the international arena is dependent upon a state's representative role in relation to other states. However, if the network's agency cannot be reduced to that of its most powerful node, then the appearance of states to each other is described—and circumscribed—by the multiple relationships and identities they carry around always. From the negotiation of this multiplicity of agencies and structures in which states are embedded comes the possibility of change—not so much the negation of self-help as a richer rendering of the constitution of self, and of the substance of the helping.

The concept of a transnational advocacy network is an important element in conceptualizing the changing nature of the international polity and particularly in understanding the interaction between societies and states in the formulation of international policies. It suggests a view of multiple pathways into the international arena, a view that attributes to domestic actors a degree of agency that a more state-centric approach would not admit. States remain the major players internationally, but advocacy networks provide domestic actors with allies outside their own states. This approach suggests answers to some of the questions about how issues get on the international agenda, how they are framed as they are, and why certain kinds of international campaigns or pressures are effective in some cases but not in others. Our initial research has suggested that networks have considerable importance in bringing transformative and mobilizing ideas into the international system, and it offers promising new directions for further research.

NOTES

1. For example, see Robert Putnam, "Diplomacy and Domestic Politics: The Logic of Two-Level Games," *International Organization* 42 (Summer 1988): 427–60; David H. Lumsdaine, *Moral Vision in International Politics: The Foreign Aid Regime, 1949–1989* (Princeton: Princeton University Press, 1993); Peter Haas, ed., *Knowledge, Power, and International Policy Coordination* special issue, *International Organization* 46 (Winter 1992); James Rosenau, *Turbulence in World Politics: Non-State Actors, Domestic Structures, and International Institutions* (Cambridge; Cambridge University Press, 1995); Thomas Risse-Kappen, ed., *Bringing Transnational Relations Back In* (Princeton: Princeton University Press, 1990); Douglas Chalmers, "Internationalized Domestic Politics in Latin America," Studies, Princeton University, April 1993; Ronnie Lipschutz, "Reconstructing World Politics: The Emergence of Global Civil Society," *Millennium* 21:3 (1992): 389–420; and on transnational social movement organizations see Jackie G. Smith, Charles Chatfield, and Ron Pagnucco, *Transnational Social Movements and Global Politics: Solidarity beyond the State* (New York: Syracuse University Press, 1997).

2. On the influence of domestic structures on transnational relations, see Thomas Risse-Kappen, "Ideas Do Not Float Freely; Transnational Coalitions, Domestic Structures, and the End of the Cold War," *International Organization* 48 (Spring 1994): 185–214.

3. See David Baldwin, *Economic Statecraft* (Princeton: Princeton University Press, 1985); and Stefanie Ann Lenway, "Between War and Commerce: Economic Sanctions as a Tool of Statecraft," *International Organization* 42:2 (Spring 1988): 397–426.

4. This is similar to the problem of mobilization around consensus issues, discussed in social movement theories. For differing views, see Michael Schwartz and Shuva Paul, "Resource Mobilization versus the Mobilization of People: Why Consensus Movements Cannot Be Instruments of Social Change," pp. 205–23, and John D. McCarthy and Mark Wolfson, "Consensus Movements, Conflict Movements, and the Cooptation of Civic and State Infrastructures," pp. 273–300, in *Frontiers in Social Movement Theory*, ed. Aldon Morris and Carol McClurg Mueller (New Haven: Yale University Press, 1992).

5. Peter Hall, *The Political Power of Economic Ideas* (Princeton: Princeton University Press, 1989), pp. 383–84; Kathryn Sikkink, *Ideas and Institutions* (Ithaca: Cornell University Press, 1991), p. 26.

6. David Snow and Robert Benford suggest that four sets of factors account for successful framing: the "robustness, completeness, and thoroughness of the framing effort"; the internal structure of the larger belief system the framers want to affect; the relevance of the frame to the real world of the participants; and the relationship of the frame to the cycle of protest. Snow and Benford, "Ideology, Frame Resonance, and Participant Mobilization," in *Frontiers in Social Movement Theory*, p. 199.

7. See Jack Donnelly, *Human Rights in Theory and Practice* (Ithaca: Cornell University Press, 1989), pp. 49–50.

8. George M. Thomas, John W. Meyer, Francisco O. Ramirez, and John Boli, eds., *Institutional Structure: Constituting State, Society, and the Individual* (Newbury Park, Calif.: Sage, 1987).

9. Analysts of networks within cities or countries are able to measure network density, but the task is far more difficult for a far-flung transnational network.

10. Our notion of vulnerability includes but is not limited to the idea of "vulnerability interdependence" developed by Keohane and Nye. For them, when a country is faced with costs imposed by outside action, vulnerability rests on the "relative availability and costliness of alternatives." Robert Keohane and Joseph Nye, *Power and Interdependence*, 2d ed. (Glenview, Ill.: Scott, Foresman, 1989), p. 13.

11. Audie Klotz, *Norms in International Relations: The Struggle against Apartheid* (Ithaca: Cornell University Press, 1995).

12. Hedley Bull, *The Anarchical Society: A Study of Order in World Politics* (New York: Columbia University Press, 1977), p. 13.

13. Ibid., p. 146.

14. Ibid., p. 245.

15. See Martha Finnemore's excellent review essay on the world polity school, "Norms, Culture, and World Politics: Insights from Sociology's Institutionalism," *International Organization* 50:2 (Spring 1996): 339.

16. John Boli and George M. Thomas, "Introduction,"

in *World Polity Formation since 1875: World Culture and International Non-Governmental Organizations*, ed. Boli and Thomas (Stanford: Stanford University Press, 1999), p. 7 (manuscript).

17. Finnemore, "Norms, Culture, and World Politics," pp. 327, 339, 340, 344.

18. Arnold Wolfers, *Discord and Collaboration: Essays on International Politics* (Baltimore: Johns Hopkins University Press, 1962), p. 19.

19. Robert Putnam captures part of this reality with his two-level games metaphor. See "Diplomacy and Domestic Politics: The Logic of Two-Level Games," *International Organization* 42:3 (Summer 1988): 427–60.

20. Jeffrey C. Isaac, "A New Guarantee on Earth: Hannah Arendt on Human Dignity and the Politics of Human Rights," *American Political Science Review* 90:1 (March 1996): 67, 69.

21. Sidney Tarrow, *Power in Movement: Social Movements and Contentious Politics*, rev. ed. (Cambridge: Cambridge University Press, 1998), chapter 11.

22. This discussion of structural liberalism relies upon Andrew Moravcsik, "Liberalism and International Relations Theory," and Anne-Marie Slaughter, "International Law in a World of Liberal States," *European Journal of International Law* 6 (1995): 503–38.

23. Slaughter, "International Law," p. 509.

24. Ibid., p. 514.

25. Moravcsik, "Liberalism and International Relations Theory," p. 3.

26. But see also, for a different but similarly motivated argument, David Dessler, "What's at Stake in the Agent-Structure Debate?" *International Organization* 43:3 (Summer 1989): 441–73.

27. Putnam, "Diplomacy and Domestic Politics."

CHAPTER 46

The Challenges and Possibilities of Transnational Feminist Praxis

Nancy A. Naples

The complex processes of globalization and resistance highlighted in this book demonstrate the contradictory array of possibilities for our collective future. This *politics of possibilities* has two faces. One vision of this future foregrounds the oppressive consequences of global capitalism and military conflicts that constrain the achievement of economic justice and peace throughout the world. The other reflects the possibilities for resisting imperialism and for achieving equality and justice for people around the globe.[1] The case studies in this collection high-light this latter vision and focus attention on the challenges and possibilities of a transnational feminist praxis. The former vision is crystalized in the September 11, 2001 terrorist attacks and the subsequent bombing of Afghanistan. The events of September 11 have jolted people in the United States and around the world to contemplate possibilities of continued attacks from the global network of terrorists as well as to prepare for a global war against terrorism. These events give urgency to the call for a transnational feminist praxis informed by a rich understanding of grassroots feminist analyses of peace building and organizing across differences and across national borders.

Transnational feminist praxis foregrounds women's agency in the context of oppressive conditions that shape their lives. Although the primary justification for the U.S. retaliatory bombing of Afghanistan is to destroy al Qaeda, concern has been expressed about women's oppression under Taliban rule. For example, in an address to the nation on November 17, 2001, U.S. first lady Laura Bush highlighted women's loss of freedom in Taliban-controlled Afghanistan. However, missing from the dominant media and government discourse on women in Afghanistan is an acknowledgment of their role as political actors and political analysts. No mention is made, for example, of the Revolutionary Association of Women of Afghanistan (RAWA) that was established in 1977 to fight for human rights, adequate health care, education, and economic justice, and for democratic and secular rule in Afghanistan.

The case studies in our book highlight the role of women in helping to shape a future free of the oppressive features of globalization. The authors profile the challenges of resistance to the oppressive economic and political regimes as well as the possibilities for solidarity across class, culture, and national borders. In this concluding chapter I focus on the contradictory politics of location and neoliberalism as they constrain women's effectiveness as international political actors. I also outline how postliberalism can open up the possibilities for transnational feminist praxis.

GLOBALIZATION AND THE POLITICS OF LOCATION

The dominant discourse on *economic globalization* stresses the speed of communications and financial transactions that seem to render local economic activities and face-to-face transactions obsolete. However, as Saskia Sassen (1996) argues, "many of the resources necessary for global economic activities are not hypermobile and are, indeed, deeply embedded in place." In fact, she explains, "global processes are structured by local constraints, including the composition of the workforce, work cultures, and prevailing political cultures and processes" (631). Sassen, along with feminist geographers and Third-World feminist analysts, emphasizes the importance of place and locale in exploring the dynamics of globalization as well as articulating strategies of resistance. In fact, as Vandana Shiva (1997) notes, *localization* can provide "the countervailing citizens' agenda for protecting the environment and people's survival and people's livelihood" (43). In this section, I explore the "politics of location" in transnational feminist praxis and highlight some of the significant lessons derived from the case studies in the collection.[2]

Localization involves "subjecting the logic of globalization to the test of sustainability, democracy and justice" and "reclaiming the state to protect people's interest" (Shiva 1997, 43).[3] Local resistance strategies developed in response to oppressive forms of globalization may not necessarily offer effective counterhegemonic alternatives (see Kaplan 2002; Mackie 2001; Santos 2001; Sklar 1999; Tabb 2001).[4] Many scholars have written about the limits of locality-based struggles. For example, David Harvey (1999, 351) notes in his discussion of the environmental movement that "particularistic militances—fighting an incinerator here, a toxic waste dump there, a World Bank dam project somewhere else, and commercial logging in yet another place" do not provide the grounds from which to challenge the global processes that generate environmental degradation. He argues that a transnational movement must move beyond "narrow solidarities and particular affinities shaped in particular places ... and adopt a politics of abstraction capable of reaching out across space, across the multiple environmental and social conditions." In a related vein, Leslie Sklar points out that "[t]he knowledge that workers, citizens, churches, and other concerned groups all around the world are monitoring their activities clearly encourages some TNCs [transnational corporations] to act more responsibly than they otherwise might be doing" (299).[5]

Contributors to *Women's Activism and Globalization* recognize the limits of local struggles that fail to challenge the extralocal processes that shape them. Yet the authors also view the local as a site of *politicization* where activists collectively develop analyses of the complex economic, political, and social processes that contour locally experienced problems (see Naples 1998b). Authors depict locality and place as sites in which women generate the collective vision of an economically, politically, and socially just world. The *local* is also the site where activists work toward building the just world they envision by creating "more inclusive organizations and approaches that may help them confront capital more effectively in the future" (Dickinson and Schaeffer 2001, 220). For example, Betty Wells (in this volume) emphasizes the very "local" ways a small group of women built a network of activists, farmers, and consumers opposed to oppressive modes of capitalist production. As they worked together to organize Women, Food, and Agriculture Network (WFAN), they developed a vision that went beyond an exclusively economic one. Their political analysis also includes a political and social critique of the dominant processes of globalization. Their broad analysis provides a vehicle to link the issues of a variety of constituencies. For example, they define food security as a basic human right and see it as tied directly to sustainable agriculture and environmental health and safety, thus bringing together the interests of small farmers, consumers, and environmentalists.

These local sites are also highly contested places where members redefine their identities and strategies in the context of ever-changing community dynamics and international relations. Winifred Poster and Zakia Salime (in this volume) describe the process by which AMSSF (the Moroccan Association for Solidarity without Borders), was transformed from a small grassroots group that provided microcredit for poor entrepreneurs to a part of a hierarchical network of organizations that refocused the relationships between the leaders and clients in AMSSF. This ever-changing complex funding arrangement including relying on the Moroccan Association for Solidarity and Development

(AMSED) to access financial assistance from Catholic Relief Services working in Morrocco who in turn received funding from USAID. As a consequence, they lost the autonomy to manage their clients' loans. In addition to the externally imposed tensions they encountered, leaders and clients also experienced internal tensions based on their class differences. Despite these multiple tensions, Poster and Zakia remain optimistic about the potential for grassroots groups like AMSSF to use nongovernmental organization (NGO) linkages to create transnational feminist alliances.

Optimism about the significance of women's local activism in the context of economic globalization is reflected in Jennifer Bickham Mendez's analysis of the Central American Network of Women in Solidarity with Maquila Workers. The Network has raised the consciousness of local and state officials about the problems faced by women maquila workers. Network members have also experienced a deepening in their gender consciousness that led them to create autonomous women's groups and challenge male-dominated social movement organizations. As a consequence, women have gained greater visibility in local politics and legitimacy as political actors.

To further complicate our notion of the "local," it is important to point out that many of these sites for building alliances and political strategies may not be coterminous. Drawing inspiration from Benedict Anderson's (1983) notion of "imagined community," feminist scholars stress the myriad of ways that women who may never meet can draw strength from each other and organize across differences (see Mackie 2001; Mohanty 1991). Solidarity across "often conflictual locations and and histories" derives from "the political links we choose to make among and between struggles" (Mohanty 1991, 5). The Internet has facilitated the process of organizing across specific locales and further illustrates how the global lands in place. What may appear distant and remote is brought into view through a technology that also helps promote the very conditions against which people struggle. Yet how women activists use this technology must also be understood contextually as Ellen Kole (2001) demonstrates in her analysis of WomenAction in Africa. WomenAction was developed to facilitate the participation of nongovernmental organizations in evaluating the implementation of the Platform for Action developed during the United Nations Conference on Women Beijing in 1995.[6] Not surprisingly, Kole found that women's groups in Africa use the Internet in a manner that differs from the way women in the western world access and use the Internet. As importantly, diverse groups of African women use the Internet in ways that differ from each other.

As evident through the work of a number of authors in this collection, women have been able to create cross-class, cross-race, and cross-national coalitions that are enriched by the diversity of resources, political skill, and experiences. Sharon Navarro (in this volume) details how activists in La Mujer Obrera in El Paso work across the Mexican–United States border to achieve seven basic goals including access to stable employment, housing, education, nutrition, healthcare, peace, and political liberty. Clare Weber's chapter (in this volume) on the cross-national organizing between Nicaragua and organizations based in the United States demonstrates that knowledge and other resources can transfer from South to North as well as North to South when participating organizations remain self-conscious and actively work against power imbalances. In other cases, most clearly illustrated in Alexandra Hrycak's study . . . cross-class, cross-cultural, and cross-national alliances further reinforce inequalities across and within national contexts.

NEOLIBERALISM AND THE POLITICS OF ACCOUNTABILITY

Many of the cases reported in *Women's Activism and Globalization* emphasize the continued significance of the liberal claims for economic, social, and political rights. Many feminist scholars are concerned about the limits of the modernist, liberal framework for achieving political, social, and economic justice. The rhetoric of *liberalism* argues for a division between the so-called civic and political spheres, and between economics and politics (see Bayes, Hawkesworth and Kelly 2001, 3). University of Delhi law professor Upendra Baxi insightfully points out that "the neoliberal frame, even when cloaked in 'people-friendly' global governance, is about creating . . . 'market-friendly NGOs' that can cooperate with, and be co-opted by, but do not oppose CSOs [civil society organizations], states, and international organizations that support a neoliberal agenda" (quoted in Runyan 1999, 211).[7]

A key dimension of *neoliberalism* is the framing of social, political and economic issues in terms of "human rights." After years of organizing, feminists have achieved recognition for "women's rights as human rights." However, as Inderpal Grewal (1999) warns, by globalizing women's human rights discourse, the "notion of essential gender finds new impetus" (507).[8] As further evidence of the limits of neoliberal discourse, the recognition of poverty as a human rights issue has had much less success on the international political stage. The neoliberal human rights frame has been criticized most harshly by activists and scholars interested in native Indian and indigenous peoples' struggles for political sovereignty and for territorial rights. As Alexander and Mohanty (1997, xxxiv–xxxv) explain, "there is no language or conceptual framework to imagine territorial sovereignty as a feminist demand—or to theorize decolonization as a fundamental aspect of feminist struggle". However, a group rights claim as developed through the struggles of American Indians raises another issue of "who belongs or does not belong to the group and redefinitions and representations of traditions that define the group" (341; also see Grewal 1999; Howard 1992).[9]

Yet the discourse on human rights can be an effective tool for achieving progressive goals. Drawing on the Universal Declaration of Human Rights, United Nations Secretary General Kofi Annan invited corporations to follow the Global Compact, a voluntary effort to enlist transnational corporations in

efforts to improve the human rights of people around the world (Tabb 2001). Organizations such as NUDE have used international human rights agreements like the Universal Declaration of Human Rights to pressure their government to address the concerns of their constituency (see Karides in this volume). As Rachel Cichowski demonstrates (in this volume), women activists in Europe have successfully advocated for the Equal Pay Principal to be adopted by the European Union and have, in turn, drawn on this principal to press for similar policies in member states that had yet to pass such legislation. Susanna Wing (in this volume) documents how the women in the Sahelian State of Mali have used the international discourse on women's rights to increase women's activism on behalf of their constitutional rights and their political representation. Wing notes that after Mali began to pursue political liberalization in 1991, women succeeded in increasing their representation in the legislative seats from 2 percent to 13 percent in one electoral season.

Mary Meyer and Elisabeth Prügl (1999) stress that the significance of international documents is not that governments will quickly adopt them but that national and local groups can use such documents to hold their governments accountable. In effect, the groups can use these "universal standards" in different local contexts to further their own aims (also see Hoskyns 1999). Yet, it also remains to be seen how, and under what conditions, certain international statutes can be enforced at the level of the nation-state. For example, Meyer raises this question in the context of the terms of the Convention on Violence against Women established by the Inter-American Commission of Women, which also is known by its Spanish acronym, CIM (Comision Interamericana de Mujeres). As an autonomous commission of the Organization of American States (OAS), it cannot participate actively in the politics of enforcement.

The human rights frame was generated in the context of violence perpetrated by oppressive military and political regimes. More recently the frame has been used to highlight injustices in western countries like the United States. For example, the Permanent People's Tribunal held a special session in Spain on 1989 and determined that "the US government was denying the People of Puerto Rico their most fundamental human right: the right to self-determination" (Committee for Human Rights in Puerto Rico 2000, 143). When Amnesty International turned its attention to human rights violations in the United States and identified abuses in prisons and jails as well as in the treatment of asylum seekers and other immigrants, they generated a great stir among U.S. officials (Maran 2000, 49). The organization's campaign, Rights for ALL, added the United States to a list of countries that includes such well-known violators as Turkey, China, Sudan, Indonesia, and Colombia.

Amnesty International's report emphasized the problems that female prisoners face such as sexual abuse by male guards and being placed in leg irons or shackles, both of which, according to the report, are common practices. Radhika Coomaraswamy of Sri Lanka, special rapporteur on violence against women, charged that the United States "is criminalizing a large segment of its population, a segment overwhelmingly composed of poor persons of color and increasingly female"(61). When Coomaraswamy requested permission to visit three prisons in Michigan, the governor of the state refused her request. This response illustrates the extent to which the human rights frame has been used to maintain a hierarchical distinction between the "Western world" and non-Western nation-states. Viewing policies and practices in Western nation-states that increase economic, social, and political inequalities in the Western world through the human rights frame reveals the colonialist, ethnocentric, and racist assumptions underlying neoliberal policy.

NGOs AND INTERNATIONAL POLITICS

In response to global economic restructuring and international trade agreements as well as neoliberal policies, women are organizing through a variety of networks, transnational organizations, as well as through traditional vehicles like the International Ladies Garment Workers Union. In addition, they have put global restructuring on the agenda of national women organizations and are organizing across borders (Runyan 1996, 246). For example, Jennifer Bickham Mendez's chapter in this volume examines the efforts of the Network for Maquila Workers Rights in Central America. This network challenges the effects of global economic restructuring and neoliberal politics and policies in their effort to improve the situation of women maquila workers. Women workers in the network document their working conditions and gather detailed information about how fast they work, what they produce, for which TNCs, and their relationships with supervisors and others in managerial position. This information is used for local unionizing efforts and is communicated through network NGOs to enable groups in the North to undertake public consciousness-raising.

Marina Karides's chapter in this volume analyzes transnational activism and unionizing efforts of another major sector of the informal economy, namely domestic workers. She shows how Trinidad's National Union of Domestic Employees (NUDE) has worked for the rights of domestic workers, who are primarily women, by using the global rhetoric and international agreements signed by Trinidad to make the government accountable at home. When the government declined to address the grievances raised by NUDE, its activists wrote letters to various government ministers reminding them of their international commitment and undertook a public consciousness-raising campaign about the relationship between local and global injustices. Thus, through a form of public shaming they were able to make some changes, though to date they have not been successful in achieving all of their demands.

Many of the recent analyses on the role of NGOs and transnational networks highlight the limits as well as the possibilities of these organizations and advocacy networks for progressive social change (see Keck and Sikkink 1998). Sonia Alvarez (1999) raises a major concern in her discussion of what she calls "the Latin American feminist NGO boom" (181). She notes three troublesome trends:

> First, states and inter-governmental organizations (IGOs) increasingly have turned to feminist NGOs as *gender experts* rather than as citizens' groups advocating on behalf of women's rights. Second, neoliberal States and IGOs often view NGOs *as surrogates for civil society*, assuming they serve as "intermediaries" to larger social constituencies. And third, *States increasingly subcontract feminist NGOs* to advise on or execute government women's programs. (181, emphasis in the original)

NGO is a deceptively short acronym applying to a wide array of groups with more or less access to resources, to political influence, and to diverse membership. However, as a consequence of the processes Alvarez identifies, many feminist NGOs are transformed from advocates to professionals serving the needs of neoliberal states. Since the early 1980s, the contradictions inherent in the process of professionalization and institutionalization of feminist practice have become a focus of numerous scholarly accounts and a major concern among feminist activists.[10] For example, in the case of the battered women's movement, the development and expansion of battered women's shelters and rape crisis centers stand as a testament to the success of feminist political activism of the 1970s. On the one hand, battered women's shelters and rape crisis centers are now a site for organized public advocacy, community education, and crisis intervention on behalf of battered women as well as a place where incest survivors, rape victims and children, the elderly, and other abuse survivors find political allies and supportive services. On the other hand, the institutionalization of the activism against violence against women in shelter-based services and rape crisis centers has raised concerns for the continued vibrancy of the feminist antiviolence movement.[11] In this regard, Clare Weber . . . demonstrates the value of transnational feminist networks for rendering visible the limits of local and national organizing against violence against women. Nicaraguan women activists who met with U.S. antiviolence activists discussed their different organizing strategies and what they saw as the limits of the U.S. approach for ending violence against women.

As Weber and other authors in this book emphasize, to understand how local activists connect their organizing with transnational feminist movements, one must explore the institutional and network links among various actors at different sites. In the field of international relations, the term "civil society" is used to reference an extensive network of social interactions and institutions that mediate between individuals and the state (Warkentin 2001, 1). Global civil society is defined as a network that provides various "channels of opportunity for political involvement" (19; also see Wapner 1995). Networks associated with the so-called global civil society have more or less autonomy from local, national, and international institutions of the state.

In a special issue on gender and globalization of *Signs*, the coeditors note the frequency by which scholars of globalization distinguish between so-called spheres of civil society, state, and multinational corporations (Basu, Grewal, Kaplan, and Malkki 2001; also see Laclau 1994). Feminist analysts challenge the division of social, political, and economic life into these separate spheres. The role of the military in supporting multinational corporations provides the most powerful illustration of the intersection of civil society, the state and economic institutions (see Enloe 1983a, 1983b, 1990, 2000). Yoko Fukumura and Martha Matsuoka (in this volume) detail women's resistance to U.S. militarism in Okinawa and explain the complex role the U.S. military plays in supporting global trade, destroying the local environment, and placing residents of the Pacific region in jeopardy. The NGO, Okinawa Women Act against Military Violence (OWAAMV), has been effective in its struggle against the U.S. military present in Okinawa but OWAAMV activists are concerned that once the military sites become available for local development, another battle over control of the development process will ensue.

Nongovernmental organizations are one of the main mechanisms for participation in the so-called global civil society. Exclusive attention to NGOs renders invisible the multitudinous informal ways women organize on behalf of themselves and their communities (see Naples 1998a, 1998c). Furthermore, as political scientists Ann Marie Clark, Elisabeth Friedman, and Kathryn Hochstetler (1998, 2) point out, the fact that the number of NGOs with shared transnational goals has increased does not necessarily mean that a global civil society has been achieved. To begin with, these organizations are often founded and led by middle class, professional women, and have had little success incorporating poor women. For example, Meredith Weiss (1999), in her discussion of the role of NGOs in Singapore, describes the narrow class background of the Association of Women for Action and Research (AWARE), which she calls "the only avowedly feminist group in Singapore" (71). She reports that AWARE, founded in 1985 by 50 members grew to approximately seven hundred members by the late 1990s. Though the most active leadership comes from educated, middle-class women, the organization remains committed to working across class and other differences. Weiss reports that the leadership of AWARE appear "quite open to input from rank-and-file members; however, since such input is seldom forthcoming, this accessibility is rarely tested" (74).

Further complicating the politics of NGOs in the context of globalization are the relationships between Western and Northern NGOs and those in other parts of the globe. For example, constructions of feminism promoted by Western-based international feminist organizations and funding agencies often conflict with national women's movements in many locales, as Alexandra Hrycak details in her chapter in this volume. Differences in power and resources are also constructed in terms of a "North/South divide." However, in their analysis of NGO participation in United Nations World Conferences, Clark, Friedman, and Hochstetler (1998) conclude that the divide between the North and the South may not be the primary source of contestation. They explain that "this divide partially overlaps more persistent divisions

between the new generation of small grassroots organizations focused on local action and more professional, often larger and older, organizations with long-standing activists at the UN" (29). Rather than viewing these divisions as an expression of inequality among feminists in the North and those in the South, it is important to acknowledge the ways in which class and status differences frequently characterize relationships between women's groups within nation-states (see, e.g., Jad 1995). Anthropologist Deborah Mindry (2001) demonstrates this in her analysis of women's organizations in South Africa. She characterizes the role of the western imperialist and racist "politics of virtue . . . which constitutes some women as benevolent providers and others as worthy or deserving recipients of development and empowerment" (1189). Other scholars have also noted the significant alliances formed across the so-called First and Third Worlds by right wing religious groups and demoninations (see Kaplan, Alarcón, and Moallem 1999).

THE SIGNIFICANCE OF THE UNITED NATIONS FOR TRANSNATIONAL FEMINIST PRAXIS

Many of the authors in this collection, along with others writing on transnational feminist organizing, also stress the significance of international conferences, especially UN-sponsored events for expanding women's participation in the global political arena.[12] As Dianne Otto (1996) points out in her review of the changing relationship between NGOs and the UN, NGOs have had a somewhat antagonistic relationship with the UN and have only recently begun to fund openings for direct participation in UN conferences and other events. However, through parallel conferences and effective lobbying, NGOs have influenced official proceedings and gained more effective roles in UN deliberations. However, Otto wonders whether the UN, with its "state-centric world view," can "rise to the challenge of reorienting its focus to be inclusive of peoples as well as states" (128). Currently, representatives from

NGOs who are consultants to UN organizations like UNESCO (the United Nations Educational, Scientific and Cultural Organization) or UNICEF (the United Nations Children's Fund) may attend their meetings as observers and make proposals with permission from the presiding officer. However, these recommendations are merely advisory and may not be acted on by the specific UN groups.

Despite the limitations of the UN structure, women's groups have used UN conferences to build a transnational women's movement and bring their local concerns to the international political stage (see Seidman 2000). Eve Sandberg (1998) persuasively argues that the three United Nations world conferences on women (Mexico, 1975; Nairobi, 1985; Beijing, 1995) served as a catalyst for Zambian women's domestic organizing, legitimated their activism, and provided resources and strategies for successful mobilization though these benefits accure more to elite women than to less privileged Zambian women. Feminist scholars also note that a focus on preparation for UN conferences often has the effect of diverting attention from the issues of most direct concern to local activists (see Alvarez 1999).[13] In their discussion of the Alliance for Arab Women (AAW), Nawal Ammar and Leila Lababidy (1999, 15)—mother and daughter who are founding members of AAW—acknowledge the significance of the UN conferences for Egyptian women's domestic organizing but also point out that

> [s]ince the UN Third Conference on Women in Nairobi in 1985, some nongovernmental organizations concerned with women's issues in Egypt have changed their focus from welfare work to development of empowerment skills. Reasons for such changes are numerous, but most salient has been the priority of international funding sources. (15)

Elisabeth Friedman (1999, 357) concludes her analysis of the impact of UN conferences on the women's movement in Venezuela by stressing that "the stage of the national movement, its sources of funding, and the politics of particular national administrations all interact with conference preparation, with quite different outcomes at different junctures."

Manisha Desai addresses the contradictions of the United Nations for "transnational feminist solidarities" in her chapter in this volume (also see Wing in this volume). Her description of the four phases of UN policies on women demonstrate the effectiveness of transnational organizing for the incorporation of women into the design and implementation of UN programs. Despite inadequate funding for the implementation of UN programs designed to improve women's lives in different parts of the world and the failure to gain support from nations like the United States for the Convention on the Elimination of All Forms of Discrimination against Women (CEDAW), Desai argues that the establishment of programs like the International Research and Training Institute for the Advancement of Women and the United Nations Development Fund For Women, and the adoption of CEDAW by the UN, demonstrate the power of women's international organizing as well as help promote the expansion of transnational solidarities among women. The UN Conferences on Women provide further opportunities for women activists from around the world to share their experiences, learn from each other, and develop strategies to counter the intensification of religious fundamentalism, militarization, poverty and sexual abuse, and to expand women's political participation. Women's influence on the transnational political stage is further demonstrated by their leadership and broad-based participation in world conferences on the environment, human rights, population, social development.

POSTLIBERALISM AND THE POLITICS OF FEMINIST PRAXIS

In contrast to the liberal approach that is predominant in international organizing, Dianne Otto (1996) argues that a "postliberal perspective, which decenters states and stresses the importance of local participation in the international community, is allied with a postmodern understanding of power . . .

[as] conceptualized as dispersed throughout the global polity rather than . . . centralized in the state and the economy" (134). In shifting from a liberal to a postliberal frame, feminist scholars explore the possibilities for a transnational feminist politics that will work against global inequalities of region, gender, race, class, and sexuality and toward what Ernesto Laclau and Chantal Mouffe (1985) term "radical and plural democracy" within movement organizations and coalitions. The postliberal approach to women's movement politics recognizes that the feminist struggle is not based on "a definable empirical group with a common essence and identity—that is, women—but rather as a struggle against the multiple forms in which the category 'women' is constructed in subordination" (Mouffe 1993, 88l; also see Basu 1995; Grewal and Kaplan 1994).

The essays in *Women's Activism and Globalization* provide further evidence of the diversity of women's movements around the world as well as within different nation-states (see Basu 1995; Dickinson and Schaeffer 2001; Gluck et al. 1998). Like the authors in *The Challenge of Local Feminisms* (Basu 1995), we are interested in rendering visible "what actually existing women's movements have achieved and failed to achieve, of the challenges yet to be confronted together and separately" (4). In this collection, we define "women's movements" very broadly. Referring to women's movements in the plural as recommended by Gluck and colleagues (1998) reflects a deepening awareness of how the multitude forms of women's activism throughout the world all work to challenge patriarchal hierarchies. We also include forms of collective struggle that may not have achieved the level of a "movement." For example, Betty Wells's chapter in this volume analyzes the work of rural women who have been traditionally left out of women's movements. These women engage in local activism, offer insightful indigenous knowledge about daily survival strategies, and participate in national and transnational organizing.

Revisioning women's movements to include the diversity of women's political analyses and strategies also requires us to rethink the labels used to categorize feminisms more generally. Third World and post-colonial feminists have effectively criticized the imposition of the Western feminist world-view in women in different parts of the world (e.g., Hubbard and Solomon 1995). In the introduction to her edited collection, Basu (1995) discusses the widespread resistance to feminism, but she points out that many Third World critics "go on to identify indigenous alternatives to Western-style feminism" (18–19). Rather than pose indigenous and Western feminism as mutually distinctive alternatives, recent analyses demonstrate the inter-dependence of women's movements and feminist analysis in different parts of the world. As Gay Seidman (2000) illustrates in her case study of gendered politics in South Africa, "the international flow of ideas and resources has become a basic element in local debates involving gender equity" (123).

Victoria Bernal (1999) turns to the Tanzania Gender Network Programme (TGNP), a feminist group based in Dar es Salaam, to explore the relationship between the local and the global. She finds that the organization voices its concerns in language common to women's organizations worldwide, emphasizing that "Tanzanian NGOs such as TGNP speak an international language of democracy, human rights, and development" (1). When communicating in their national language, Kiswahili, the Tanzanian feminists sometimes simply adopt the English terms (as in the cases of "gender mainstreaming" and "patriarchy"), leading, Bernal writes, "to what some have called 'Kiswahenglish'" (1). However, Bernal concludes, "Neither the view of local organizations as somehow operating independent of their global context, nor the view of such organizations as mere puppets of external forces will allow us to explore the potentials and pitfalls in the globalized terrain of contemporary post-colonial political activism" (1).[14]

In the context of increased mobility and displacement, distinctions between home/abroad, insider/outsider, and Third World/First World, have become difficult to maintain. In her contribution to *Women's Activism and Globalization*, Bandana Purkayastha compares and contrasts her community activism during the latter part of twentieth century as an Indian-born woman in the United States with her mother's activism during the earlier part of the century in a rural Indian village. She argues that community activism facilitates the transmission of resistance strategies to counter the negative effects of global economic restructuring in local contexts.

Many of the lessons we have learned through more nationally defined feminist politics will continue to serve us as we expand the horizons of feminist organizing. These lessons include how to respond to problems that arise in organizing across class, race, ethnicity, sexualities, space, and religious and political perspectives; how to sustain feminist activist engagement over time; how to build and mobilize effective coalitions; how to create democratic structures at all levels of organization; and how to negotiate the politics of language, funding, representation, and social movement framing.

Along with the politics of naming, the politics of location, the politics of accountability, and the challenges of fighting against the scattered hegemonies of capitalism and patriarchy (see Naples in this volume), research on transnational feminist praxis reveals a number of contradictions that require careful consideration before we pass judgment on the limits or possibilities of different political strategies, organizational forms, or social movement frames. This collection of case studies deepens our understanding of the complexities, challenges, and possibilities of grounded struggles against oppressive forms of globalization associated with antidemocratic international politics and capitalist expansion.

NOTES

1. I would like to acknowledge Manisha Desai for her insightful comments on this chapter and for contributing the frame, "politics of possibilities." Her reflections on the events of September 11 form the basis for this opening discussion of the contradictory possibilities of globalization.

2. In her book *Questions of Travel*, Caren Kaplan (2000, 160) interrogates Rich's (1986) notion of "the politics of location" feminism. She observes that "[t]he local appears as the primary site of resistance to globalization through the construc-

tion of temporalized narratives of identity (new histories, rediscovered genealogies, imagined geographies, etc.), yet that very site prepares the ground for appropriation, nativism, and exclusion."

3. Resistance can take many forms. As economist William Tabb (2001) points out, "Resistance can have a strong element of moral witness (speaking truth to power), of rebellion (I'm mad and I won't take it any more), of reformist goals (our mutual ideals are violated, let us live up to our agreed-upon principles as in the adoption of the Universal Declaration of Human Rights), and of revolutionary transformation (the institutions of structured inequality and destructiveness are necessary to preserve their power; the system must be overthrown and a fundamentally different one put in its place)" (197).

4. Boaventura de Sousa Santos (2001) views "counter-hegemonic globalization" as "focused on the struggle against social exclusion, a struggle which in its broadest terms encompasses not only excluded populations but also nature" (20)

5. As sociologist Leslie Sklair (1999) notes, "[g]lobal production chains can be disrupted by strategically planned stoppages, but this generally acts more as an irritation than as a real weapon of labor against capital" (298). Sklair (1999) identifies several examples of anticonsumerist social movements that have the potential to pose such challenges. He describes the Seikatsu Club in Japan, which is "based on the idea of consumer self-sufficiency through cooperatives" (303) and Goss's suggestions for reclaiming the mall "for the people" by, among other strategies: "1. expose commodity fetishism, and force advertisers and retailers to become more honest;" and "2. resist the economic and spatial logic of malls by helping community groups struggle against redevelopment" (304–305).

6. Beijing 5+ was held at the United Nations in New York City five years after the Beijing Conference.

7. Transnational feminists are not blind to the limits of neoliberal framing For example, during the Vienna NGO Forum in 1994, Runyan (1999) reports, a coalition of groups—the Network Women in Development Europe based in Brussels, Alternative Women in Development, National Action Committee on the Status of Women in Toronto, and Canadian Research Institute for the Advancement of Women—produced a report entitled " 'Wealth of Nations—Poverty of Women' countering the optimistic rhetoric associated with globalization found in the ECE [Economic Commission for Europe] region draft platform" (215).

8. Grewal (1999) notes that the effort "to keep various kinds of difference alive in the womens' [sic] human rights arena is a difficult one, made even more difficult by the asymmetries of power within states, nations, and groups that both construct and fracture contemporary global conditions" (507; also see Charlesworth 1994).

9. In their study of *Activists Beyond Borders*, Margaret Keck and Kathryn Sikkink (1998) also point out the limits of the rights frame for stemming violence and other abuses in Guatemala during the 1970s and 1980s and in Colombia in the 1990s.

10. Myra Marx Ferree and Patricia Martin (1995) define "institutionalization" as "the development of regular and routinized relationships with other organizations" (6).

11. With the institutionalization of shelters, shelter work was frequently depoliticized and redirected toward an increasingly social service orientation. See Ferraro 1983; Loseke 1992; Matthews 1994; P. Morgan 1981; and Sullivan 1982.

12. According to Nawal and Labibady (1999), the most notable UN conferences for transnational feminist organizing include those held in Copenhagen in 1980, Nairobi in 1985, Cairo in August 1994, Copenhagen in March 1995, Beijing in August 1995, and Istanbul in August 1996 (154–155). Also see Pietilä and Vickers 1994.

13. Gayatri Spivak (1996) offers one of the most devastating critiques of the Beijing conference "as an example of 'Women' as 'global theater, stated to show participation between the North and the South, the latter constituted by Northern discursive mechanisms—a Platform for Action and certain power lines between the UN, the donor consortium, governments, and elite Non-Governmental Organizations." Spivak argues that "what is left out" of this performance piece "is the poorest women of the South as self-conscious critical agents, who might be able to speak through those very nongovernmental organizations of the South that are not favoured by these objective-constitution policies" (2).

14. Uma Narayan (1997) effectively argues, "Many Third-World feminist issues are hardly "foreign imports" or "Westernized agendas" imposed by feminists onto contexts where "culturally authentic" nonfeminist women would entirely fail to see what the feminist fuss was about." (12). Also see Seidman (2000).

REFERENCES

Alexander, M. Jacqui, and Chandra Talpade Mohanty, eds. 1997. *Feminist Genealogies, Colonial Legacies, Democratic Futures*. New York: Routledge.

Alvarez, Sonia E. 1999. "Advocating Feminism: The Latin American Feminist NGO 'Boom.'" *International Feminist Journal of Politics* 1(2): 181–209.

Ammar, Nawal H. Ammar, and Leila S. Lababidy. 1999. "Women's Grassroots Movements and Democratization in Egypt." Pp. 150–70 in *Democratization and Women's Grassroots Movements*, ed. Jill M. Bystydzienski and Joti Sekhon. Bloomington, IN: Indiana University Press.

Anderson, Benedict. 1983. "Imagined Communities: Reflections on the Origin and Spread of Nationalism." London: Verso.

Basu, Amrita, ed. 1995. *Women's Movements in Global Perspective*. Boulder, CO: Westview.

Basu, Amrita, Inderpal Grewal, Caren Kaplan, and Liisa Malkki. 2001. Editorial: Special Issue on Globalization and Gender. *Signs: Journal of Women in Culture and Society* 26(4):943–48.

Bernal, Victoria. 1999. "Gender Activism and the Globalization of Civil Society in Tanzania." Unpublished manuscript, University of California, Irvine.

Charlesworth, Hilary. 1994. "What Are 'Women's International Human Rights'?" Pp. 58–84 in *Human Rights of Women: National and International Perspectives*. Philadelphia: University of Pennsylvania Press.

Clark, Ann Marie, Elisabeth J. Friedman, and Kathryn Hochstetler. 1998. "The Sovereign Limits of Global Civil Society: A Comparison of NGO Participation in UN World Conferences on the Environment, Human Rights, and Women." *World Politics* 51(1):1–35.

Committee for Human Rights in Puerto Rico. 2000. "International Tribunal on Violation of Human Rights in Puerto Rico." *Social Justice* 27(4):143–51.

Dickenson, Torry D., and Robert K. Schaeffer. 2001. *Fast Forward: Work, Gender, and Protest in a Changing World*. Lanham, MD: Rowman & Littlefield.

Enloe, Cynthia. 1983a. *Does Khaki Become You? The Militarisation of Women's Lives*. Boston: South End.

———. 1983b. "Women Textile Workers in the Militarization of SE Asia." Pp. 407–25 in *Women, Men, and The International Division of Labor*, ed. June Nash and Maria Patricia Fernandez-Kelly. Albany: State: University of New York Press.

———. 1990. *Bananas, Beaches, and Bases: Making Feminist Sense of International Politics*. Berkeley: University of California Press.

———. 2000. *Maneuvers: The International Politics of Women's Lives*. Berkeley: University of California Press.

Ferraro, Kathleen. 1983. "Negotiating Trouble in a Battered Women's Shelter." *Urban Life* 12(3): 287–306.

Ferree, Myra Marx, and Patricia Yancey Martin, eds. 1995. *Feminist Organizations: Harvest of the New Women's Movement*. Philadelphia: Temple University Press, 1995.

Friedberg, Elisabeth J. 1999. "The Effects of 'Transnationalism Reversed' in Venezuela: Assessing the Impact of UN Global Conferences on the Women's Movement." *International Feminist Journal of Politics* 1(3):357–81.

Gluck, Sherna Berger, with Maylei Blackwell, Sharon Cotrell, and Karen Harper. 1998. "Whose Feminism, Whose History? Reflections on Excavating the History of (the) U.S. Women's Movement(s)." Pp. 31–56 in *Community Activism and Feminist Politics: Organizing across Race, Class, and Gender*, ed. Nancy A. Naples. New York: Routledge.

Grewal, Inderpal. 1999. "On the New Global Feminism and the Family of Nations: Dilemmas of Transnational Feminist Practice." Pp. 501–30 in *Talking Visions: Multicultural Feminism in a Transnational Age*, ed. Ella Shohat. Cambridge, MA: New Museum of Modern Art and MIT Press.

Grewal, Inderpal, and Caren Kaplan, eds. 1994. *Scattered Hegemonies: Postmodernity and Transnational Feminist Practices*. Minneapolis: University of Minneapolis Press.

Harvey, David 1999. "What's Green and Makes the Environment Go Round?" Pp. 327–55 in *The Cultures of Globalization*, ed. Fredric Jameson and Masao Miyoshi. Durham, NC: Duke University Press.

Hoskyns, Catharine. 1999. "Gender and Transnational Democracy: The Case of the European Union." Pp. 72–87 in *Gender Politics in Global Governance*, ed. Mary K. Meyer and Elisabeth Prügl. Lanham, MD: Rowman & Littlefield.

Howard, Rhoda E. 1992. "Dignity, Community, and Human Rights." Pp. 100–137 in *Human Rights in Cross-Cultural Perspectives*, ed. Abdullahi A. An-Na'im. Philadelphia: University of Pennsylvania Press.

Hubbard, Dianne, and Colette Solomon. 1995. "The Many Faces of Feminism in Namibia." Pp. 163–86 in *Women's Movements in Global Perspective*, ed. Amrita Basu. Boulder, CO: Westview.

Jad, Islah. 1995. "Claiming Feminism, Claiming Nationalism: Women's Activism in the Occupied Territories." Pp. 226–47 in *Women's Movements in Global Perspective*, ed. Amrita Basu. Boulder, CO: Westview.

Kaplan, Caren. 2000. *Questions of Travel: Postmodern Discourses of Displacement*. Durham, NC: Duke University Press.

Kaplan, Caren, Norma Alarcón, and Minoo Moallem, eds. 1999. *Between Woman and Nation: Nationalism, Transnational Feminisms, and the State*. Durham, NC: Duke University Press.

Keck, Margaret E., and Kathryn Sikkink. 1998. *Activists beyond Borders: Transnational Advocacy Networks in International Politics*. Ithaca, NY: Cornell University Press.

Kole, Ellen S. 2001. "Appropriate Theorizing about African Women and the Internet." *International Feminist Journal of Politics* 3(2):155–79.

Laclau, Ernesto. 1994. "Negotiating the Paradoxes of Contemporary Politics: An Interview." *Angelaki* 1(3): 1–3, 43–50.

Laclau, Ernesto, and Chantal Mouffe. 1985. *Hegemony and Socialist Strategy: Towards a Radical Democratic Politics*. London: Verso.

Loseke, Donileen. 1992. *The Battered Woman and Shelters: The Social Construction of Wife Abuse*. Albany: State University of New York Press.

Mackie, Vera. 2001. "The Language of Globalization, Transnationality and Feminism." *International Feminist Journal of Politics* 3(2):180–206.

Maran, Rita. 2000. "International Human Rights in the U.S.: A Critique." *Social Justice* 26(1):49–71.

Matthews, Nancy A. 1994. *Confronting Rape: The Feminist Anti-Rape Movement and the State*. London: Routledge.

Meyer, Mary K., and Elisabeth Prügl, eds. 1999. *Gender Politics in Global Governance*. Lanham, MD: Rowman & Littlefield.

Mindry, Deborah. 2001. "NGOs, 'Grassroots,' and the Politics of Virtue." *Signs* 26(4):1187–1211.

Mohanty, Chandra Talpade. 1991. "Under Western Eyes: Feminist Scholarship and Colonial Discourses." Pp.51–80 in *Third World Women and the Politics of Feminism*, ed. Chandra Talpade Mohanty. Bloomington: Indiana University Press.

Morgan, Patricia. 1981. "From Battered Wife to Program Client: The State's Shaping of Social Problems." *Kapitalistate* 9:17–39.

Mouffe, Chantal. 1993. *The Return of the Political*. London: Verso.

Naples, Nancy A., ed. 1998a. *Community Activism and Feminist Politics: Organizing across Race, Class and Gender*. New York: Routledge.

——. 1998b. "Conclusion: Women's Community Activism: Exploring the Dynamics of Politicization and Diversity." Pp. 327–49 in *Community Activism and Feminist Politics: Organizing across Gender, Race and Class*, ed. Nancy A. Naples. New York: Routledge.

——. 1998c. *Grassroots Warriors: Activist Mothering, Community Work, and the War on Poverty*. New York: Routledge.

Narayan, Uma. 1997. *Dislocating Cultures: Identities, Traditions, and Third World Feminism*. New York: Routledge.

Otto, Dianne. 1996. "Nongovernmental Organizations in the United Nations System: The Emerging Role of International Civil Society." *Human Rights Quarterly* 18(1):107–41.

Pietilä, Hilkka, and Jeanne Vickers. 1994. *Making Women Matter: The Role of the United Nations*. London: Zed.

Prügl, Elisabeth 1999. "What Is a Worker? Gender, Global Restructuring, and the ILO Convention on Homework." Pp. 197–209 in *Gender Politics in Global Governance*, ed. Mary K. Meyer and Elisabeth Prügl. Lanham, MD: Rowman & Littlefield.

Rich, Adrienne. 1986. *Blood, Bread, and Poetry: Selected Prose, 1979–1985*. New York: Norton.

Runyan, Anne Sisson. 1996. "The Places of Women in Trading Places: Gendered Global/Regional Regimes and Inter-nationalized Feminist Resistance." Pp. 238–52 in *Globalization: Theory and Practice*, ed. Eleanore Kofman and Gillian Youngs. New York: Pinter.

——. 1999. "Women in the Neoliberal 'Frame'." Pp. 210–20 in *Gender Politics in Global Governance*, ed. Mary K. Meyer and Elisabeth Prügl. Lanham, MD: Rowman & Little-field.

Sandberg, Eve. 1998. "Multilateral Women's Conferences: The Domestic Political Organization of Zambian Women." *Contemporary Politics* 4(3):271–83.

Santus, Boaventura de Sousa. 2001. "Can Law Be Emancipation?" Presented at the annual meetings of the Law and Society Association. July 4–6, Budapest, Hungary.

Sassen, Saskia. 1996. "Cities and Communities in the Global Economy." *American Behavioral Scientists* 39(5): 629–39.

Seidman, Gay. 2000. "Gendered Politics in Transition: South Africa's Democratic Transitions in the Context of Global Feminism," Pp. 121–44 in *Globalizing Institutions: Case Studies in Regulation and Innovation*, ed. Jane Jenson and Boaventura de Sousa Santos. Burlington, VT: Ashgate.

Shiva, Vandana. 1997. "Democracy in the Age of Globalization." Pp. 34–45 in *Women, Empowerment and Political Participation*, ed. Veena Poonacha. Bombay, India: Research Center for Women's Studies, S.N.D.T. Women's University.

Sklair, Leslie. 1999. "Social Movements and Global Capitalism." Pp. 291–311 in *The Cultures of Globalization*, ed. Fredric Jameson and Masao Miyoshi. Durham, NC: Duke University Press.

Spivak, Gayatri Chakravorty. 1996. " 'Women' as Theatre: United Nations Conference on Women, Beijing. 1995." *Radical Philosophy* 75:2–4.

Sullivan, Gail. 1982. "Cooptation of Alternative Services: The Battered Women's Movement as a Case Study." *Catalyst* 14:39–56.

Tabb, William K. 2001. *The Amoral Elephant: Globalization and the Struggle for Social Justice in the Twenty-First Century*. New York: Monthly Review Press.

Wapner, Paul. 1995. "Politics beyond the State: Environmental Activism and World Civic Politics." *World Politics* 47(3):311–40.

Warkentin, Craig. 2001. *Reshaping World Politics: NGOs, the Internet, and Global Civil Society*. New York: Rowman & Littlefield.

Weiss, Meredith L. 1999. "Democracy at the Margins: NGOs and Women's 'Unofficial' Political Participation in Singapore." Pp. 67–92 in *Democratization and Women's Grassroots Movements*, ed. Jill M. Bystydzienski and Joti Sekhon. Bloomington, Indiana: Indiana University Press.

SECTION 11

Security, Crime, and Violence

Introduction to Section 11

Crime and violence have never just been located within territorial borders or political boundaries. Numerous cross-border crimes, including slavery and piracy, have existed for centuries; and violence has also been transnational in one way or another. Indeed, one compelling and counterintuitive notion understands (nation-)state building generally, in Europe and perhaps elsewhere, as transnationally inflected organized crime. Clear linkages existed between groups (often between powerful states acting clandestinely) and independence or insurgency movements around the world during the colonial and Cold War periods. By the dawn of the twenty-first century, popular and scholarly interest in the cross-border and multi-level dynamics of crime, violence, and war had focused on transnational terrorisms. While there is a critical need for Transnational Studies to take up terrorist phenomena, we decided not to include a "foundational piece" on this topic in our volume due to the intensity of contemporary political and intellectual debates.

The selection by Ethan Nadelmann reminds us that many contemporary cross-border crimes and violent activities have always been legally sanctioned, the province of state actors, and morally supported by powerful social groups. Some of these, like human sacrifice or cannibalism, became illegal and virtually extinct because they lacked formal international legal support. Nadelmann, however, is primarily concerned about the evolution of global prohibition regimes that target criminal activities that transcend boundaries and that cannot be addressed by unilateral or bilateral governmental action. He attributes the emergence and effectiveness of these global prohibition regimes to the efforts of governments and non-governmental "transnational moral entrepreneurs" that promote and institutionalize norms based on moral and emotional concerns. He proposes a five-stage evolutionary pattern that these regimes share.

For Louise Shelley, transnational crime went from being a serious problem during the twentieth century to an acute one in the twenty-first century. The main reasons for this transformation are: 1. the complexities of transnational criminal organizations and activities that are too difficult to generalize; 2. their increasing transcontinental spread and proliferation in tandem with dramatic improvements in technology and increases in transnational business; and 3. their corrosive economic, political, and social impacts. Thus, Shelley claims that transnational crime is an "imminent threat" to nation-states as legitimate and authoritative entities. Although there is considerable diversity, similarities across groups include their "organizational flexibility, adaptability to new markets, and cross-group coordination." Only a similarly cross-border, cross-level, and cross-sectoral set of responses, she argues, will successfully address the challenges of transnational crime.

Mary Kaldor identifies transnationally complex forms of politicized violence emerging around the world in the 1980s and 1990s as "new wars." These new wars involve "a blurring of the distinctions between war . . . organized crime . . . and large-scale violations of human rights." They entail an array of cross-border and cross-level actors and relationships so that binary oppositions between internal and external, aggression and repression, public and private, formal and informal, or global and local no longer usefully characterize them. New wars are shaped by increasing interconnectedness, but these processes entail contradictions between "integration and fragmentation, homogenization and diversification, globalization and localization." They also occur in environments where there are significant declines in state autonomy and capacity. In new wars, goals are identity-based claims to power based on labels. They involve a complex method combining conventional warfare mixed with guerrilla and counterinsurgency tactics. The organizational forms and economic interactions that underlie them are disparate, decentralized, and networked. Kaldor argues that a transnationalized social and civic institutional reconstruction strategy is needed to bring these new wars to an end.

This section ends with a selection by David Kyle and John Dale who offer a nuanced analysis of human smuggling that critiques two contrasting conventional accounts as incomplete. Prior analyses, they argue, do not take into account that accelerated globalization has generated more powerful transnational criminal organizations. They also overlook the role of transnational "professional gangsters" who have the guile and greed to exploit weak and mostly innocent victim migrants. They argue that a more complete transnational explanation would integrate a range of additional actors as well as the enabling characteristics of diverse regional social structures. In this fuller account, sending country "regional elites," sending and receiving country government officials who are corrupt or who otherwise benefit, and employers at destination sites all play a crucial part in the transnational network of "crime that is organized," even if transnational "organized crime" does not play a key role. Kyle and Dale conclude, even more powerfully, that some of the individuals who benefit from these activities are often partially willing migrants. Those who consume the products and services produced by migrant-smuggling businesses are also part of a transnationally organized chain of responsibility.

CHAPTER 47

Global Prohibition Regimes: The Evolution of Norms in International Society

Ethan A. Nadelmann

The dynamics by which norms emerge, evolve, and expand in international society have been the subject of strikingly little study.[1] This article is concerned with a particular category of norms—those which prohibit, both in international law and in the domestic criminal laws of states, the involvement of state and nonstate actors in particular activities. Acts such as piracy, slavery, trafficking in slaves, counterfeiting of national currencies, hijacking of aircraft, trafficking in women and children for purposes of prostitution, and trafficking in controlled psychoactive substances are all prohibited by powerful global norms. Other acts, such as the killing of whales, elephants, and other endangered animal species, are becoming the subject of increasingly powerful norms. These norms strictly circumscribe the conditions under which states can participate in and authorize these activities and proscribe all involvement by nonstate actors. Those who refuse or fail to conform are labeled as deviants and condemned not just by states but by most communities and individuals as well. Both the substance of these norms and the processes by which they are enforced are institutionalized in global prohibition regimes.[2] This article analyzes how and why particular norms have evolved into global prohibition regimes and why they have proven more or less successful in suppressing deviant activities.

The global norms discussed here evolved and exist not only in the conventions and treatises of international law and the criminal laws of nation-states but also in the implicit rules and patterns that govern the behavior of state and nonstate actors as well as in the moral principles embraced by individuals. Laws are easily observed, patterns of behavior somewhat less so, but the thoughts and beliefs of individuals remain far more elusive. It is difficult and often impossible to determine whether those who conform to a particular norm do so because they believe the norm is just and should be followed, or because adherence to the norm coincides with their other principal interests, or because they fear the consequences that flow from defying the norm, or simply because conforming to the norm has become a matter of habit or custom. Much the same holds true for those who deviate from the norm. Our understanding of the impact of norms on state and nonstate behavior and of the processes by which norms evolve is thus limited by our inability to adequately penetrate the human consciousness.

It is true that international regimes tend to reflect the economic and political interests of the dominant members of international society. But it is also true—despite the inattentions of most international relations scholars—that moral and emotional factors related to neither political nor economic advantage but instead involving religious beliefs, humanitarian sentiments, faith in universalism, compassion, conscience, paternalism, fear, prejudice, and the compulsion to proselytize can and do play important roles in the creation and the evolution of international regimes.[3] This is particularly so of global prohibition regimes, which, like criminal laws, tend to involve moral and emotional considerations more so than most other laws and regimes. The evolution of global prohibition regimes, particularly those which involve intrasocietal interactions as well as interstate relations, thus entails highly complex processes in which not only economic and security interests but also moral interests play a prominent role, in which the actions of states must be understood as the culmination of both external pressures and domestic political struggles, in which national and transnational organizations and movements shape the actions of states as well as the actions and opinions of diverse societies, and in which the norms of dominant societies, notably those of Europe and the United States, are not only internationalized but also internalized by diverse societies throughout the world.

International prohibition regimes, like municipal criminal laws, emerge for a variety of reasons: to protect the interests of the state and other powerful members of society; to deter, suppress, and punish undesirable activities; to provide for order, security, and justice among members of a community; and to give force and symbolic representation to the moral values, beliefs, and prejudices of those who make the laws. They rely on force in the form of criminal justice and sometimes resort to military measures in part because the violators—be they pirates, slave traders, or elephant poachers—are themselves armed and reliant on violence to perform their illicit deeds; in part because efforts to prohibit anything that many people desire are bound to require some degree of coercion; and in part because criminal justice measures are the principal and typically the most punitive means of dealing with those who defy the norms of developed societies.

The criminal laws that evolve into international prohibition regimes are few in number, and those which attain global dimensions are even fewer. Human sacrifice and cannibalism are not only illegal but are virtually unknown in every nation today; neither practice, however, has been the subject of an international regime. Nor have rape and incest, both of which are criminalized in all states, been the targets of prohibition regimes. Only crimes that evidence a strong transnational dimension have become the subject of international prohibition regimes: larceny on the high seas, murder of diplomatic officials, cross-border commerce in slaves, ivory, counterfeit money, and psychoactive substances, and so on.

The most important inducement to the creation of international prohibition regimes is the inadequacy of unilateral and bilateral law enforcement measures in the face of criminal activities that transcend national borders. No government possesses sufficient resources to police effectively all of the high seas or to investigate and punish the array of illicit activites that are committed abroad and harm its interests or citizens. Nor is any government willing, except on rare occasions, to unilaterally pursue a criminal when doing so involves a blatant affront to another state's external sovereignty. International prohibition regimes are intended to minimize or eliminate the potential havens from which certain crimes can be committed and to which criminals can flee to escape prosecution and punishment. They provide an element of standardization to cooperation among governments that have few other law enforcement concerns in common. And they create an expection of cooperation that governments challenge only at the cost of some international embarrassment. In these respects, international prohibition regimes amount to more than the sum of the unilateral acts, bilateral relationships, and international conventions that constitute them.

Of almost equal importance in explaining why certain criminal laws evolve into international prohibition regimes is the role of moral proselytism. The compulsion to convert others to one's beliefs and to remake the world in one's own image has long played an important role in international politics—witness the proselytizing efforts of states on behalf of religious faiths or secular faiths such as communism, fascism, capitalism, and democracy. Similar compulsions underlie many criminal laws, notably those concerning slavery, abortion, prostitution, gambling, pornography, and the sale and use of alcohol and other psychoactive drugs. The existence of international prohibition regimes directed at the suppression of a number of these activities owes much to the proselytizing efforts of governments as well as the efforts of nongovernmental transnational organizations functioning as what might be called "transnational moral entrepreneurs."[4] These groups mobilize popular opinion and political support both within their host country and abroad; they stimulate and assist in the creation of like-minded organizations in other countries; and they play a significant role in elevating their objective beyond its identification with the national interests of their government. Indeed, their efforts are often directed toward persuading foreign audiences, especially foreign elites, that a particular prohibition regime reflects a widely shared or even universal moral sense, rather than the peculiar moral code of one society. Although the activities that they condemn do not always transcend national borders, those which do go beyond borders provide the proselytizers with the transnational hook typically required to provoke and justify international intervention in the internal affairs of other states.

Why do certain prohibition regimes reach global proportions? Certainly not all of them are destined or even intended to do so. Some reflect little more than the peculiar collective security concerns of a multinational region or an alliance of states confronting a common threat; current examples include the Counil of Europe's regional antiterrorism convention and CoCom, the regime established by members of the North Atlantic Treaty Organization (NATO) and Japan to restrict the flow of sophisticated technology to Warsaw Pact countries. Other regimes are concerned not with particular criminal activities but with the mechanisms of international cooperation against crime: extradition, mutual legal assistance, transfer of criminal proceedings, and transfer of prisoners.[5] These "procedural" regimes often prove essential to the effective functioning of the "substantive" prohibition regimes as well as to international cooperation against murder, rape, assault, white-collar crimes (such as tax fraud, money laundering, and insider trading), and other criminal activities that are not the subject of international regimes. Procedural regimes are limited in scope, however, by the fact that consensus on procedure in criminal justice matters often proves more elusive than consensus on sub-stance. Sufficient differences concerning the nature and process of the extradition obligation persist to preclude any active effort to construct a formal global extradition regime; nonetheless, all states today acknowledge the norm of extradition as well as the principles that underlie it.

Regimes that do attain global proportions typically share certain features. One powerful motivation is the need to minimize "regime leakage" by eliminating actual and potential havens and markets for transnational criminals, be they pirates, slave traders, airplane hijackers, or drug traffickers. Most of the other features, however, are in one way or another moral in nature. Global adherence to the norms of a particular prohibition regime typically gives the regime greater moral and symbolic force and helps qualify its norms as "international laws" that cannot be defied lightly.

Underlying the emergence of most global prohibition regimes and the emergence of much international cooperation in criminal matters has been the evolution of what British scholars have termed "a universal international society" grounded in the gradual homogenization and globalization of norms developed initially among the European states.[6] This development has manifested itself in a variety of ways: in the acceptance of norms and conventions that establish the ground rules of diplomatic interaction and protection; in the recognition of an identifiable corpus of international law embodying common principles regarding state behavior and obligations; and, most significantly, in the growing acknowledgment by states and societies that all individuals, regardless of their citizenship, race, religion, or other defining characteristics, are entitled to basic protections of life, property, and contract. Despite the current imperfections and hypocrisies of this "international society," even aside from its limited relevance to nations engaged in war, it now represents far more the rule than the exception in how states treat foreign citizens and the crimes of their own people against foreign citizens.

This is not to argue, I should stress, that "states" or governments hold moral views; rather, the capacity of particular moral arguments to influence government policies, particularly foreign policies, stems from the political influence of domestic and transnational moral entrepreneurs as well as that of powerful individual advocates within the government. In virtually every case, moreover, the relevant moral views are "cosmopolitan" in nature, concerned not with how states treat one another but, rather, with how states and individuals treat individual human beings. Therein lies their power, for whereas the "state" both politicizes and dehumanizes the outsider, as evidenced by its capacity to decriminalize violence against individuals during wartime, "cosmopolitan" moral views transcend the state, thereby de-politicizing the individual and emphasizing the existence of an international society of human beings sharing common moral bonds. The evolution of global prohibition regimes and of extradition and many bilateral law enforcement relations suggests that "cosmopolitan" notions of international morality have played an increasingly significant role in international relations over the past three centuries and particularly over the last century and a half. The following analysis thus lends support to the ideas of Charles Beitz and others who have favored the "cosmopolitan" view of morality in international politics, with its focus on persons, as opposed to the more conventional view, with its focus on the "morality of states."[7] And it responds to the concerns voiced by James Mayall, who has argued that "a central element in any international political theory must be an account of the moral bonds between men living in separate states."[8]

In the evolution of global society, the centrality of Western Europe initially and of the United States during this century cannot be overemphasized. Virtually all of the norms that are now identified as essential ingredients of international law and global society have their roots in the jurisprudence of European scholars of international law and in the notions and patterns of acceptable behavior established by the more powerful Western European states. This is particularly true of many of the norms reflected in global prohibition regimes. Their emergence within Europe reflected the needs and impositions of the most powerful states as well as the influence of the Enlightenment and contemporaneous religious and moral notions. The globalization of these norms, manifested by the emergence of global prohibition regimes, reflected the dominance of Europe over much of the world from approximately the seventeenth century to recent decades. To an extent virtually unprecedented in world history, a few European states and the United States proved successful in proselytizing to diverse societies, shaping the moral views of substantial sectors of elite opinion outside their borders, and imposing their norms on foreign regimes around the world.

Most global prohibition regimes, including those targeted against piracy, slavery, and drug trafficking, evidence a common evolutionary pattern consisting of four or five stages. During the first stage, most societies regard the targeted activity as entirely legitimate under certain conditions and with respect to certain groups of people; states often are the principal protagonists and abettors of the activity; and the central constraints on involvement in the activity have far more to do with political prudence and bilateral treaties than with moral notions or evolving international norms. During the second stage, the activity is redefined as a problem and as an evil—generally by international legal scholars, religious groups, and other moral entrepreneurs—and explicit government involvement in the activity is gradually delegitimized, although many individual governments continue to tolerate or even sponsor the involvement of private groups and individuals in the activity. During the third stage, regime proponents begin to agitate actively for the suppression and criminalization of the activity by all states and the formation of international conventions. The regime proponents include governments, typically those able to exert "hegemonic" influence in a particular issue-area, as well as transnational moral entrepreneurs. Their agitation takes many forms, ranging from the diplomatic pressures, economic inducements, military interventions, and propaganda campaigns of governments to the domestic and transnational lobbying, educational, organizational, and proselytizing efforts of individuals and non-governmental organizations.

If the efforts of the regime proponents prove successful, a fourth stage begins. During this stage, the activity becomes the subject of criminal laws and police action throughout much of the world, and international institutions and conventions emerge to play a coordinating role—that is, a global prohibition regime now comes into existence.[9] Although social pressures on all states to acknowledge and enforce the regime's norms are quite powerful,[10] the regime proponents must contend with the challenges of deviant states that refuse to conform to its mandate, weak states that formally accede to its mandate but are unable or unwilling to crack down on violators within their territory, and dissident individuals and criminal organizations that elude enforcement efforts and continue to engage in the proscribed activity.

In some cases, a fifth stage is attained, during which the incidence of the proscribed activity is greatly reduced, persisting only on a small scale and in obscure locations.[11] No international prohibition regime could attain this stage until the nineteenth century for the simple reason that states had not yet eliminated or neutralized the effective vacuums of sovereign authority, both on land and sea, on which regime dissenters depended for their freedom and sanctuary.[12] On the one hand, as the power of states vis-à-vis criminals both within and without their borders has grown over the past two centuries, so too has the potential of states to cooperate in suppressing undesirable activities. But on the other hand, the norms of external sovereignty and nonintervention have progressed more rapidly than the effective internal sovereignty of many states,[13] with the result that regime enforcers in this century are less able than their forebears to use coercive actions against dissident states and other regime violators.

Success in attaining the fifth stage of regime development has thus come to depend primarily on the nature of the criminal activity and its susceptibility to criminal justice measures, both of which can be strongly influenced over time by technological developments. Criminal laws and international prohibition regimes are particularly ineffective in suppressing those activities which require limited and readily available resources and no particular expertise to commit, those which are easily concealed, those which are unlikely to be reported to the authorities, and those for which the consumer demand is substantial, resilient, and not readily substituted for by alternative activities or products.[14] That is why, as I argue below, the global drug enforcement regime is destined never to achieve the success attained by regimes against piracy and slave trading or even those against currency counterfeiting and hijacking.

PIRACY AND PRIVATEERING

Prior to the seventeenth century, international norms proscribing banditry on the high seas were limited in scope and effect; indeed, piracy was widely sanctioned in much of the world.[15] The premises of medieval international law, Georg Schwarzenberger has written, were simple: "(1) In the absence of an agreed state of truce or peace, war was the basic state of international relations even between independent Christian communities. (2) Unless exceptions were made by means of individual safe conduct or treaty, rulers saw themselves entitled to treat foreigners at their absolute discretion. (3) The high seas were no-man's-land, where anyone might do as he pleased."[16]

Kings, princes, sultans, and other political magnates accordingly viewed piracy as a valued source of wealth and political power, useful both for increasing their own possessions and for undermining the strength of competitors. During the late Middle Ages, Schwarzenberger noted, "it was customary among the princes of Christendom to bind themselves by reciprocal treaties to prevent and punish piracy or the spoilage of shipwreck."[17] But with the broad expansion of European maritime commerce in the sixteenth century, the rewards and the incidence of piracy jumped dramatically. Much of it was officially or unofficially sponsored by European governments.[18] In wartime, the practice of privateering was in effect an officially sanctioned version of piracy directed toward a state's enemies and anyone engaged in trading with its enemies. In peacetime, the same private shippers were granted letters of reprisal by their governments. These authorized them to recoup any losses due to piracy by pirating from other ships bearing the same nationality as the pirates.[19] When professional privateers lost their official sanction as a consequence of a peace treaty between their sponsor and the enemy, they either sought employment by another monarch or became unsanctioned pirates. Even in the latter situation, it was often possible to find sponsors and protectors among high-ranking officials in the monarch's retinue, not excluding the monarch himself.

Early in the seventeenth century, Turkish corsairs began expanding their piratical activities from the Mediterranean to the Atlantic. "To the seventeenth-century [European] mind," C. M. Senior wrote, "the prospect of infidels carrying Christians into bestial captivity in North Africa gave efforts to eradicate piracy an urgency and crusading zeal which they had previously lacked. In a Europe strongly divided by political and religious differences, the one objective on which all Christian nations were agreed was the desirability of crushing the Turkish pirates."[20] Accordingly, French, Spanish, Dutch, and English fleets sailed against the pirate bases in North Africa between 1609 and 1620, transcending their own powerful disputes to unite against a more feared common enemy.

As the seventeenth century drew to a close, the rules and structures of Europe's international relations were beginning to change. There was a rapid increase in the volume of trade and diplomacy within Europe and between the European states and far-flung colonies and nations outside Christendom. The advantage to be derived from stealing from one another was giving way to the greater advantage of stable commercial relations. Governments wanted and needed to monopolize the forces of violence both within their borders and on the high seas. Accordingly, private fiefdoms and armies were coopted or eliminated, and pirates were warned to abandon their ways or risk the wrath of increasingly powerful navies. The dramatic expansion of the Royal Navy in the 1690s, which greatly improved England's power to police the high seas and its growing empire, gave particular force to the new injunction against pirating.[21] Pirates and their collaborators were hunted down, colonial administrators admonished to enforce the new antipiracy laws ardently, and foreign leaders warned to cease sponsoring pirate expeditions and to crack down on unauthorized pirates operating within and from their territories. Those who failed to comply often found British and other European naval forces crowding local harbors to lend force to their demands. "Piracy," observed Senior, "was in fact undergoing a transformation from being a national industry to becoming an international threat."[22] Wars may have been becoming fiercer; but in their absence, relations between governments were becoming more orderly. Where peacetime had previously been associated with anarchy, it increasingly promised a degree of security from both publicly and privately sponsored violence.

The civilizing of international society did not progress smoothly, of course, but in fits and starts. Even as the European states regularized their relations in and around the European continent, Adam Watson has noted, "both states and privateers continued to operate against one another in the Americas and Asia in ways that were no longer permissible in Europe between states not formally at war."[23] Nor did the European powers apply the same standards of behavior to their dealings with most nations beyond their continent as they did to one another. At the same time, non-European states and even some of the colonies regarded the European efforts against piracy and privateering as unwarranted and unwelcome infringements into local struggles over power and wealth.[24] In the American colonies, for instance, where imperial law and order were less easily enforced, business executives and public officials alike continued to provide havens and markets for pirate ships for decades after London ordered a halt to such activities; by the mid-eighteenth century, however, most had acceded to the ban on piracy. Elsewhere, government-sanctioned piracy persisted until well into the nineteenth century, when it was lagely eradicated by military force. The Barbary tradition of extracting tribute by piracy was stunned first by American naval intervention, then by a combined British and Dutch naval attack on Algiers, and finally ended with the French conquest of Algiers in 1830.[25] Pirate bases on Crete and Borneo were efficiently destroyed by British naval interventions in 1828 and 1849, respectively, after local rulers had failed to take satisfactory action.[26] In Oman and China, British forces combined with local forces to destroy pirate bases and fleets. And in the West Indies, piracy declined dramatically during the 1820s as a result of U.S. naval interventions, which succeeded in seizing dozens of pirate ships and destroying their bases.[27]

Privateering, or government-sanctioned piracy during wartime, was not effectively delegitimized until well into the nineteenth century. The U.S. government relied on privateers for most of its naval representation during both the Revolutionary War and the War of 1812.[28] The same was true of South American governments in their wars of independence with Spain.[29] Attacks on American maritime commerce by French privateers at the turn of the century almost brought the two nations to outright conflict. As long as governments legitimized the pirating of private vessels at sea during wartime, their efforts to delegitimize unsanctioned piracy were bound to meet with both skepticism and frustration.[30] Calls for the abolition of privateering began in earnest during the eighteenth century. Benjamin Franklin, who wrote of "this odious usage of privateers, ancient relic of piracy," was among the more influential and vocal of those involved in this effort.[31] In 1801, Lord Nelson echoed these sentiments: "Respecting privateers I own that I am decidedly of the opinion that with few exceptions they are a disgrace to our country; and it would be truly honourable never to permit them after this war. Such horrible robberies have been committed by those in all parts of the world, that it is really a disgrace to the country which tolerates

them."[32] In 1856, Great Britain, France, Russia, Prussia, Austria, Sardinia, and the Porte signed the Declaration of Paris, formally abolishing privateering; the United States, however, refused to accede, insisting that the small size of its navy required that it retain the option of privateering during wartime.[33] Only with the growth of the U.S. navy toward the end of the century and the growing sentiment that privateering no longer represented an acceptable mode of warfare did the U.S. government formally outlaw the practice.[34] By the end of the nineteenth century, a once customary form of waging war had been all but eliminated from the face of the earth.

The eventual globalization of the norms against piracy and privateering involved more, however, than merely the economic and security interests of the most powerful states in monopolizing the forces of violence on the high seas. As international society became more orderly and international relations more regularized, and as the high seas ceased to be perceived as a no-man's-land, larceny at sea became less justifiable. As with larceny on land, the fact that the victim was a stranger and a foreigner no longer excepted piracy from moral condemnation. Piracy increasingly was seen as an evil in its own right. The maxim that *pirata est hostice humani generis* (a pirate is an enemy of the human race) had seeped from the treatises on international law into the political psyches of governments. It reflected, in part, the passing of the ancient notion, affirmed even by Grotius, that the subjects of one's enemy were one's enemies as well. In his 1762 treatise, *On the Social Contract*, Rousseau articulated the shift in consensus: "War is not, therefore, a relation between man and man, but between State and State, in which private individuals are enemies only by accident, not as men, nor even as citizens, but as soldiers; not as members of the homeland but as its defenders."[35] Conversely, the norm of civilized behavior during peacetime extended not only to one's fellow citizens and allies but also to anyone other than an armed combatant. An international criminal law is most potent—indeed, some would say that it only exists—when it reflects not just self-interest but a broadly acknowledged moral obligation. The law against piracy was the first to attain such a consensus. And the international regime dedicated to the enforcement of this law was the first to attain global proportions.[36]

The delegitimation of government-sanctioned piracy was not, however, sufficient to ensure the virtual elimination of piratical activities from the high seas. Unlike privateering, piracy could subsist without the active support of governments. Yet pirates were finding even informal and discreet government sponsorship more elusive by the late 1700s. By the mid-1800s, island havens such as Madagascar and the Bahamas were no longer available as increasingly powerful states eliminated, one by one, the vacuums of de jure and de facto sovereignty on which unauthorized pirates had depended. Pirates also were acutely vulnerable to government action. The same sea vessels that allowed them access to the high seas also made them dependent on harbors and ports for rest and supplies. Their vessels could not be easily hidden; once captured, they afforded few opportunities for pirates to flee. Yet by all accounts, the fatal blow to piracy was delivered by the development of steam vessels. Pirates generally lacked the substantially greater resources needed to operate and build these vessels.[37] Legitimate steam cargo and passenger carriers thus became more elusive to the prey of pirates at the same time that naval steam vessels were increasingly available to pursue pirate ships. An early example of this occurred in 1837, "when a paddle wheeler, the *Diana*, of the East India Company, steamed toward six Malay pirate vessels against the wind and sank them all."[38] By the latter part of the nineteenth century, piracy had been all but eliminated from the high seas. That it persists on a small scale even today—notably in the Caribbean, off the West African coast, and, most extensively, in the seas of East Asia—reflects little more than the inevitably limited capabilities of governments to eliminate entirely anything that lies outside their total control.[39] [. . .]

NOTES

1. Robert Axelrod, "An Evolutionary Approach to Norms," *American Political Science Review* 80 (December 1986), p. 1101.

2. For a discussion of international regimes in general, see Stephen D. Krasner, ed., *International Regimes* (Ithaca, N.Y.: Cornell University Press, 1983); Oran R. Young, *International Cooperation: Building Regimes for Natural Resources and the Environment* (Ithaca, N.Y.: Cornell University Press, 1989); Stephan Haggard and Beth A. Simmons, "Theories of International Regimes," *International Organization* 41 (Summer 1987), pp. 493–95; and Robert O. Keohane, *After Hegemony: Cooperation and Discord in the World Political Economy* (Princeton, N.J.: Princeton University Press, 1984).

3. See Charles P. Kindleberger, "Hierarchy Versus Inertial Cooperation," *International Organization* 40 (Autumn 1986), p. 845, in which much of the regime literature is criticized for ignoring the role of "conscience, duty, obligation, or such old-fashioned notions as noblesse oblige."

4. The notion of "transnational moral entrepreneurs" conjoins Becker's concept of "moral entrepreneurs" and Huntington's notion of a "transnational organization." Becker indicates that moral entrepreneurs are those who "operate with an absolute ethic" in seeking to create new rules to do away with a perceived great evil. See Howard Becker, *Outsiders: Studies in the Sociology of Deviance* (New York: Free Press, 1963), p. 148. Huntington states that a transnational organization is "a relatively large, hierarchically organized, centrally directed bureaucracy . . . [that] performs a set of relatively limited, specialized, and in some sense, technical functions . . . across one or more international boundaries and, insofar as it is possible, in relative disregard of those boundaries." See Samuel Huntington, "Transnational Organizations in World Politics," *World Politics* 25 (April 1973), p. 333.

5. See M. Cherif Bassiouni, ed., *International Criminal Law* (Dobbs Ferry, N.Y.: Transnational Publishers, 1986).

6. See Martin Wight, "Western Values in International Relations," in Herbert Butterfield and Martin Wight, eds., *Diplomatic Investigations: Essays in the Theory of International Politics* (London: Allen & Unwin, 1966), pp. 89–131; Hedley Bull, "The Emergence of a Universal International Society," in Hedley Bull and Adam Watson, eds., *The Expansion of International Society* (London: Oxford University Press, 1984), pp. 117–26; and James Mayall, "International Society and International Theory," in Michael Donelan, ed., *The Reason of States: A Study in International Political Theory* (London: Allen & Unwin, 1978), pp. 122–41.

7. See Charles Beitz, "Bounded Morality: Justice and the State in World Politics," *International Organization* 33 (Summer 1979), pp. 405–24; and Keohane, *After Hegemony*, pp. 247–51.

8. James Mayall, "Introduction," in James Mayall, ed., *The Community of States: A Study in International Political Theory* (London: Allen & Unwin, 1982), p. 2.

9. The question of when a regime comes into existence, like the question of when a human being comes into existence, is a matter of debate. The answer is largely a function of how we define and make use of the term "regime."

10. Young, *International Cooperation*, pp. 76 and 203.

11. Global prohibition regimes that reach the fifth stage of development resemble other global regimes that have emerged since the mid-1800s to monitor, control, and prevent cholera, plague, yellow fever, smallpox, and other infectious diseases. For a fascinating analysis of how international cooperation against infectious diseases ultimately prevailed, see Richard N. Cooper, *International Cooperation in Public Health as a Prologue to Macroeconomic Cooperation* (Washington, D.C.: Brookings Institute, 1986).

12. See Janice E. Thomson, "Sovereignty in Historical Perspective: The Evolution of State Control over Extraterritorial Violence," in James A. Caparoso, ed., *The Elusive State* (Newbury Park, Calif.: Sage, 1989), pp. 227–54.

13. See Robert H. Jackson, "Quasi-States, Dual Regimes, and Neoclassical Theory: International Jurisprudence and the Third World," *International Organization* 41 (Autumn 1987), pp. 533–49.

14. States that are able and willing to employ totalitarian measures and states whose laws are bolstered by strong social sanctions are best able to suppress these types of criminal activities. International society, however, lacks both the potential to employ totalitarian methods and the cultural homogeneity that typically underlies powerful social sanctions.

15. For an overview of the subject, see Philip Gosse, *The History of Piracy* (New York: Longmans, Green, 1932).

16. Georg Schwarzenberger, "International Law," in *The New Encyclopedia Britannica*, 15th ed., vol. 21, p. 725.

17. Georg Schwarzenberger, "The Problem of an International Criminal Law," in Gerhard O. W. Mueller and Edward M. Wise, eds., *International Criminal Law* (South Hackensack, N.J.: Fred B. Rothman, 1965), p. 6.

18. See Fernand Braudel, *The Mediterranean and the Mediterranean World in the Age of Philip II*, vol. 2, trans. Sian Reynolds (New York: Harper Colophon Books, 1976), pp. 865–91.

19. Robert C. Ritchie, *Captain Kidd and the War Against the Pirates* (Cambridge, Mass.: Harvard University Press, 1986), p. 11.

20. C. M. Senior, *A Nation of Pirates: English Piracy in Its Heyday* (New York: Crane Russak, 1976), p. 149.

21. Ritchie, *Captain Kidd and the War Against the Pirates*, pp. 152–54.

22. Senior, *A Nation of Pirates*, p. 151.

23. Adam Watson, "European International Society and Its Expansion," in Bull and Watson, *The Expansion of International Society*, p. 25.

24. See, for example, Nicholas Tarding, *Piracy and Politics in the Malay World* (Melbourne: F. W. Cheshire, 1963).

25. See Ralph T. Ward, *Pirates in History* (Baltimore, Md.: York Press, 1974), pp. 112–27; and John B. Wolf, *The Barbary Coast* (New York: Norton, 1979), pp. 299–321.

26. Thomson, "Sovereignty in Historical Perspective," pp. 248–49.

27. Ward, *Pirates in History*, p. 158.

28. Francis R. Stark, "The Abolition of Privateering and the Declaration of Paris," dissertation, Columbia University, New York, 1897.

29. See, for example, Jane Lucas de Grummond, *Renato Beluche: Smuggler, Privateer, and Patriot, 1780–1860* (Baton Rouge: Louisiana State University Press, 1983).

30. Thomson, "Sovereignty in Historical Perspective."

31. Benjamin Franklin, cited in Edward Lucie-Smith, *Outcasts of the Sea* (New York: Paddington Press, 1978), p. 232.

32. Lord Nelson, cited in ibid.

33. Sir Francis Piggott, *The Declaration of Paris, 1856* (London: University of London Press, 1919), pp. 142–49.

34. "Privateer," in *The New Encyclopedia Britannica*, 15th ed., vol. 8, p. 713.

35. Jean-Jacques Rousseau, *On the Social Contract*, trans. Roger D. Masters and Judith R. Masters (New York: St. Martin's Press, 1978), p. 50.

36. That the regime was not codified in an international convention until the 1958 Convention on the High Seas may well be explained by the fact that global norms condemning piracy were so universally acknowledged by the middle of the nineteenth century that a convention would have been perceived as superfluous. Indeed, many states explicitly condemned other transnational activities, such as slave trading, by linking them with and even labeling them as piracy. See Barry H. Dubner, *The Law of International Sea Piracy* (The Hague: Martinus Nijhoff, 1980).

37. Ward, *Pirates in History*, pp. 158–59.

38. Ibid.

39. See G. O. W. Mueller and Freda Adler, *Outlaws of the Ocean* (New York: Hearst Marine Books, 1985), pp. 131–57; and Captain Roger Villar, *Piracy Today: Robbery and Violence at Sea Since 1980* (London: Conway Maritime Press, 1985).

CHAPTER 48

Transnational Organized Crime: An Imminent Threat to the Nation-State? (Transcending National Boundaries) [1]

Louise Shelley

Transnational organized crime has been a serious problem for most of the 20th century, but it has only recently been recognized as a threat to the world order. This criminality undermines the integrity of individual countries, but it is not yet a threat to the nation-state. Failure to develop viable, coordinated international policies in the face of ever-growing transnational criminality, however, may undermine the nation-state in the 21st century.

The "global mafia" has been sensationalized by an international press eager for exciting copy, and intelligence organizations are assessing the dimensions of international drug trafficking.[2] Furthermore, in November 1994 the United Nations sponsored an international conference to develop strategies to combat organized crime.[3] The European Union is also taking numerous initiatives in this area. Attention to such a serious international problem is long overdue.

The seriousness of the problem lies in the complexity of these organizations and their activities, their global penetration, and the threat they pose to democracy and legitimate economic development—these organizations clearly undermine the concept of the nation-state. For the purposes of this article transnational criminal organizations will be considered as organized crime groups that 1. are based in one state; 2. commit their crimes in one but usually several host countries, whose market conditions are favorable; and 3. conduct illicit activities affording low risk of apprehension.[4]

The complexity of transnational organized crime does not permit the construction of simple generalizations; there is no proto-typical crime cartel. Organized crime groups engage in such widely publicized activities as drugs and arms trafficking, smuggling of automobiles and people, and trafficking in stolen art. They also engage in such insidious activities as smuggling of embargoed commodities, industrial and technological espionage, financial market manipulation, and the corruption and control of groups within and outside the legal state system. Money laundering through multiple investments in banks, financial institutions, and businesses around the globe has become a central and transnational feature of these groups' activities, as they need to hide ever-larger revenues.[5]

Given this level of complexity and the political dynamics of the post-Second World War period, it is hardly surprising that no comprehensive international effort against organized crime has been initiated until recently. Transnational organized crime has been problematic for the last couple of decades, but it is only since the end of the Cold War that it has been addressed by so many countries and international bodies. The recently mounted attack on transnational organized crime is, indeed, partly a consequence of the need for security bodies (such as the CIA, KGB, and the Mossad) and international organizations (such as the U.N. and the Council of Europe) to develop new missions in the post-Cold War era. While the world focused on such highly visible problems as the superpower conflict or regional hostilities, the increasingly pernicious and pervasive transnational crime that now threatens the economic and political stability of many nations was ignored. Long-term neglect of this problem means that the world now faces highly developed criminal organizations that undermine the rule of law, international security, and the world economy, and which, if they are allowed to continue unimpeded, could threaten the concept of the nation-state.

FACTORS IN THE GROWTH OF TRANSNATIONAL ORGANIZED CRIME

The fundamental forces underlying the growth and increasingly international character of organized crime are the technological explosion and economic boom of the post-Second World War period as well as the current geopolitical situation, which has been rapidly evolving since the collapse of the socialist world. The 1960s represent the benchmark for many of the technological and economic changes affecting transnational crimes, whereas the political changes contributing to the spread of transnational crime emerged in subsequent decades.

The growth in transnational illegal activities is largely due to the increasingly international scope of legitimate business and the ease with which it is conducted. Significant technological advances affecting the growth of transnational crime include the rise of commercial airline travel, telecommunications (including telephone, fax, and computer networks), and the use of computers in business. For example, between 1960 and 1974, the passenger volume on international flights increased sixfold. By 1992, it had increased more than four times from 1974 levels. This rise has contributed to an increasingly mobile world population, a mobility equally enjoyed by carriers of illicit commodities and illegally obtained currencies. Concomitantly, between 1970 and 1990, global trade increased ten times.[6] Included in the increased flow of commodities are illicit commodities, as cargo is loaded and unloaded at numerous points around the globe to avoid detection. Advances in telecommunications and satellite technology, the development of fiber-optic cable and the miniaturization, and complexity of computers have resulted in a communications explosion of inter-

national telephone calls, fax transmissions, and wire transfers. Crime groups benefiting from the "global village" and its instant and anonymous telecommunications are able to operate without frontiers in unprecedented ways. With such a volume of travel and trade, criminals or traffickers are less easily distinguished from their fellow travellers or legitimate businesspersons.

This leads to another factor underlying the increase in international crime—the growth of international business. Organized crime groups follow the trends of international business. The increasing economic interdependence of the world requires both licit and illicit businesses to think internationally. Global markets have developed in both legitimate goods and illicit goods, the most notable of which is the international narcotics trade. Just as legitimate multinational corporations establish branches around the world to take advantage of attractive labor or raw-materials markets, so do illicit multinational businesses. Furthermore, international businesses, both legitimate and illicit, establish facilities worldwide for production, marketing, and distribution. These enterprises are able to expand geographically to take advantage of these new economic circumstances thanks to the aforementioned communications revolution.

The transnational character of organized crime means that these groups are now part of the global political agenda. As they develop from their domestic bases, their members establish links with fellow nationals living abroad. Tribal links among similar ethnic groups in different countries may facilitate international illicit activity, such as that seen across borders in Africa, the Golden Triangle, and along the southern frontier of the former Soviet Union (the Azerbaijani–Iran and Tadzhik–Afghan borders).[7]

The collapse of the socialist bloc in Eastern Europe and the dissolution of the USSR, along with the rise of the European Union (E.U.), have resulted in loosely controlled borders stretching from Europe to the Pacific Ocean and along a lengthy frontier with Asia. Not only do indigenous crime groups operate with near impunity in these areas, but also a lack of coordinated policy facilitates illicit commerce in goods and human beings as well as large-scale money laundering. The fall of communism has lessened the ability of the border police and the ministries of internal affairs of the successor states to strictly enforce former borders between the Asian successor states and their neighbors. With these porous borders, the geographical boundaries of individual countries are less important. For example, one goal of the E.U.—the free movement of peoples and goods among its member-states—has benefited these states but has also been exploited by European criminals as well as numerous crime groups from Asia, Africa, Latin America, and, most recently, eastern Europe.

Large-scale ideological confrontations have been replaced in recent decades by hundreds of smaller ethnic conflicts in many regions of the globe. These small-scale wars contribute to transnational organized crime by increasing the supply of narcotics and by feeding the trade in arms. Developing countries with poor economies that are dependent upon agricultural commodities are, with falling agricultural prices, often attracted to drug cultivation as a means of obtaining cash. This money can then be used to purchase arms for use in small-scale clashes. Weapons for such purposes are often bought on the illegal arms market, which is supplied by transnational organized crime groups.

However, despite the veritable explosion in illicit trade, the hegemony of global international crime is exaggerated. Increasing links exist among different international organized groups, but the idea advocated by Claire Sterling of a *pax mafiosa* is premature.[8] The cooperation among organized crime groups from different regions of the world enhances drug-trafficking capacities and permits the smuggling of nuclear materials as well as trafficking in human beings, but it does not yet present a consolidated threat to the established political order. An emerging *pax mafiosa* is precluded because many parts of the world are not under the domination of a particular organized crime group. The violence that exists in many western European cities, particularly Berlin, is evidence that there is strong competition among different organized crime groups for control.

PERNICIOUS CONSEQUENCES OF ORGANIZED CRIME

The costs of transnational organized crime are not exclusively monetary. Transnational organized crime undermines political structures, the world economy and the social order of the countries in which the international crime groups are based and operate. The resulting instability invites more crime, and may preclude the institutionalization of democratic institutions, the rule of law, and legitimate markets.

Transnational organized crime undermines civil society and human rights. Through intimidation and assassination of journalists in different countries, it limits freedom of the press and individual expression. Transnational organized crime also undermines the creation of civil society by dominating independent philanthropic organizations and by intimidating citizens in movements that challenge organized crime.[9] The infiltration of these groups into labor unions violates citizen labor rights. International trafficking in prostitution and pornography demeans both women and children, and the illegal smuggling of individuals to work in situations where they are often exploited raises serious human rights concerns.

TRANSNATIONAL CRIME, THE STATE, AND WORLD ORDER

The world political order becomes increasingly stable when more nations establish democratic forms of government based on respect for the rule of law and government through consensus. International organized crime is detrimental to existing democracies and to societies in transition to democracy. Transnational crime undermines the rule of law and the legitimacy of democratic government through its corruption of individuals and the judicial process. Organized crime groups often supplant the state in societies undergoing a transition to democracy, as their representatives assume key positions in the incipient legislatures, which are responsible for crafting the new legal framework for the society. Their presence within legitimate state institutions undermines political stability because their goals are to further their own criminal interests (illicit profits), not the interests of the populace at large.

Transnational organized crime groups in both developed and developing democracies seek to corrupt high-level government officials both on the groups' home turf and in the countries where they operate. But these groups are often more successful when their efforts are conducted in nation-states that are in political transition, because the controls over the legal process do not yet function as they do in a stable democracy.

Transnational organized crime groups also threaten states through their trafficking in nuclear materials. Now the world no longer worries about nuclear conflict between the world's superpowers. Instead, today the nuclear threat comes largely from the arms trafficking of organized crime, a new and highly pernicious form of illicit activity. The smuggling of nuclear materials may enable some country or crime group to produce a nuclear weapon independently, therefore raising the potential for nuclear blackmail.

Traditional scholarship applies the concept of the criminalized state to Nazi Germany. Yet it is equally valid to apply the term to a state apparatus used to further the goals of organized crime groups. This is evident in Italy where, for more than a century, a symbiotic relationship has existed between crime and politics.[10] The seven-time prime minister, Giulio Andreotti—the stalwart of the preeminent postwar Social Democratic Party—has twice been deprived of his parliamentary immunity for charges of collaboration with the mafia. Another former prime minister, Bettino Craxi of the Socialist Party, has been officially charged with corruption.[11] The consequences of the criminalization of the state in this way have deprived Italy of influence commensurate with its role as a major economic power and part of the G-7. As a noted mafia commentator has remarked, "Italy is distinguished in Europe today by

the penetration of organized crime into the state."[12]

In Colombia, the relationship between the government and the drug cartels is not as long-standing as in Italy, but its impact on the state and its democratic institutions has been devastating. The democratic process and the rule of law have been severely undermined in both the legislative process and the administration of justice. In the former Soviet Union, the infiltration of organized crime into the political process may lead to political clientelism and controlled markets, a variation on the old ways of Soviet government, only without the official state ideology. As political campaigns are financed by organized crime groups and their representatives or emissaries are elected to parliament, the possibilities of producing the legal structure needed to move a society from authoritarian to democratic rule are diminished.

Both Italy and Colombia have discovered that once organized crime penetrates the state, the latter will not be able to disassociate itself from the former—even with the investment of significant human and economic resources, the application of intense repression and the sacrifice of many well-meaning individuals. The states of the former Soviet Union that lack both the resources and the will to combat organized crime as well as a history of uncorrupted government will be even more susceptible to penetration than Italy or Colombia. While it is premature to classify any of the successor states to the Soviet Union as mafia-run governments, some regions of Russia as well as other newly independent states have already fallen under the influence of criminal organizations.[13] The consequences of penetration by organized crime into the state sector are devastating because the penetration effectively prohibits the state from combatting these groups in their home territories, thereby undermining legitimate democracy.

TRANSNATIONAL ORGANIZED CRIME AND THE WORLD ECONOMY

The impact of international organized crime groups on the world economic order is equally disturbing. Much has been written about the pernicious effects of multinational corporations that transfer operations outside their domestic base, often in order to elude domestic legal controls. A typical critique concludes that their "exploitative effects on rich and poor nations remain unchecked."[14] International law lacks the legal enforcement power necessary to control the behavior of such international corporations. The innate obstacles to regulating the abuses of multinationals (i.e. the diversity of laws among nations, the lack of extradition treaties and the desire of developing nations to attract foreign capital at any cost) are only amplified when replaced by illicit multinationals—transnational organized crime.

The practice by transnational criminal organizations of large-scale money laundering, of corrupting of key officials in economic and customs positions, and of utilizing banks, stock exchanges, venture capital opportunities, and commodities markets, all undermine the financial security of world markets. The pensions and savings of ordinary citizens are also jeopardized when banks and stock funds collapse because of illegal manipulation of the financial sectors by international organized crime groups. The BCCI affair may be the most notable of these scandals, as its fallout affected citizens in many different countries; but BCCI is unique only in its complexity, the scale of its losses, and the fact that it was uncovered, not in its occurrence.[15]

SOCIAL CONSEQUENCES OF TRANSNATIONAL CRIME

The social consequences of transnational organized crime are often understated. The most visible manifestations—violence, drug trafficking, gambling, prostitution, and the spread of AIDS—all have a very direct effect on quality of life. Not only do international crime groups run these illicit markets, but they coerce women and children into prostitution and develop drug dependencies among millions of individuals in order to create a market for their narcotics.

Furthermore, the control of illegal markets by international organized crime has a ripple effect throughout the economy, thereby affecting the quality of life of even those who do not participate in the market of illicit goods and services. Extortion activities and the monopoly of markets increase the costs of consumer goods. As a consequence, citizens pay more for food, housing, and medical services.[16]

Because organized crime groups are oriented toward immediate profits, their activities (cultivating drugs on unsuitable soil, harvesting and selling of protected species, and illegally overfishing sturgeon for the lucrative caviar trade) often lead to serious environmental damage.

THE COMPLEXITY OF ORGANIZED CRIME

Transnational organized crime groups thrive in different political environments, functioning with diverse internal structures and in various areas of activity.[17] They can be based in a collapsing superpower, the less-developed region of a developed democracy, and in a formerly stable democracy. These groups vary broadly in size as well as in their strategies for avoiding detection. International organized crime groups are based on every continent, and their activities, while probably most pronounced in the regions closest to their home country, are increasingly conducted across continents, often in conjunction with organized criminals from other parts of the world. Divergent legislative and enforcement policies among nations permit these transnational crime groups to more easily elude authorities by exploiting a particular environment. For example, the favorable banking laws and the lack of enforcement have made several Caribbean islands havens for money laundering.

The complexity and transnational nature of organized crime is probably most apparent in the area of drug trafficking. But this activity is not confined only to the distribution of narcotics, as these same networks can be (and have been) used to smuggle weapons and may be used to smuggle nuclear materials with equal facility.[18] Indeed, the trading and sale of drugs and weapons are often interrelated when, as indicated above, drugs become the most easily obtainable currency.[19]

The multinational character of the drug trade is revealed in major cases detected by law enforcement. For instance, one unmasked network involved criminals from Pakistan, Africa, Israel, eastern Europe, and Latin America.[20] The drugs (hashish) originated in Pakistan and were delivered to the port of Mombasa (Kenya), where they were added to a cargo of tea and re-shipped to Haifa (Israel) by way of Durban (South Africa). At Haifa, the cargo was put onto a ship of a company that ships to Constanza (Romania) every 15 days. From there it was to have been shipped by an Israeli–Romanian company to Italy, via Bratislava (Slovakia). The head of the network was a German citizen of Ugandan origin who worked for a Romanian company. This complex network was only disclosed because the perpetrators were apprehended in Constanza.[21]

In contrast, another large drug seizure of 517 kilos of cocaine at a Polish port linked Poles with Ecuadorians, members of the Cali cartel of Colombia, and members of Italian organized crime.[22] This drug network illustrates the collaboration of three of the most important transnational organized crime groups—the Colombian, Italian, and the recently emergent eastern and central European (unlike the previous case, which involved only a limited number of participants from these major crime groups).

Apart from these three major transnational organized crime groups, the Chinese Triads, Japanese Yakuza, and various Nigerian groups are also significant players in transnational organized crime.[23] Indeed, after the collapse of its oil boom, Nigeria became one of the largest drug-trafficking nations in the world, strategically placed as it is along ancient trade routes that link Asia and Europe as well as the Americas. At present there is not one region in the world without an indigenous transnational organized crime group or that is not plagued by the activities of an international organized crime group.[24]

Structural Analysis of Three Transnational Organized Crime Groups

In order to illustrate the diversity and complexity of transnational organized crime, three transnational organized crime groups —the Italian, Colombian, and post-Soviet mafias—are examined here according to similar key criteria. In fact, these three cases show that the emergence of such groups is not a natural stage in the political and economic transition from socialism to democracy, nor an inevitable stage in the development of a third world economy. These three cases from different parts of the world were chosen because they reveal the variety of political and economic conditions under which organized crime groups can operate.

Analysis of the three transnational crime groups is based on the following criteria:

1. longevity as an actor in organized and transnational crime;
2. stage in the country's development during which the group moved from domestic operations to the international scene;
3. political structure of the country in which the group is based;
4. economic structure of the host country;
5. form and strength of legal authority in the host country;
6. forms and variety of illicit activities;
7. organizational structure of the criminal group; and
8. investment of the proceeds from organized crime.

ITALIAN ORGANIZED CRIME

Italian organized crime groups are among the oldest in the world and some of the first to operate transnationality. They spread abroad more than half a century after they rose to prominence on their home territory. Long confined to the developing region of a developed country, they have corrupted the democratic process in their society. Engaging in a range of illicit activities, their strict hierarchies and codes of honor have helped them resist law-enforcement efforts. Only in the past 15 years has the Italian government acquired the political will and the legal capacity to combat this criminality—an attack that has been facilitated by the fact that much of organized crime's wealth has remained on Italian territory.

Italian organized crime consists of four major groups, but the Sicilian-based mafia (also known as the Cosa Nostra) is the most widely known and significant of these groups. The Sicilian mafia also assumes the most important role in the economic and political life of Italy.[25]

The origins of the Italian mafia at a particular moment in Italian state development are reflected in the present-day relationship between the Italian mafia and the government. In mid-19th-century Sicily there was a simultaneous collapse of feudalism and decline of the landed aristocracy, with the emergence of a new bourgeoisie and the unification of Italy under a centralized state. The period in which the mafia emerged (in the first half of the 19th century) was one of crisis in state authority.[26] The mafia provided the protection that the central state was incapable of giving to the emergent businesses and the new landholding class.[27] By the latter half of the 19th century the mafia in Sicily had usurped many of the functions of the state, resulting in a symbiotic relationship that has continually existed between the mafia and the government, first at the regional level and, since the end of the Second World War, at the national level.[28]

Italian organized crime developed and flourished because there were weakly developed legal institutions and little respect for legal norms among the citizenry in the four southern regions where organized crime was concentrated. The legal apparatus of the Italian state was not able to penetrate the closely structured organized crime groups, which are based on family ties.[29] The corruption of state authorities by organized crime groups has undermined efforts to combat such criminality.[30]

In the period before the Second World War, Italian organized crime groups began to expand their influence outside their regional base in southern Italy and to adapt to new markets. Italian organized crime, as a whole, was exporting members to the United States, Latin America, and north Africa.[31] There was another period of migration in the 1960s to the United States, Canada, Germany, and Australia to pursue economic opportunities and to escape repression in Italy. There is now also movement abroad in order to replace depleted cadres, reflecting the institutional flexibility of these groups.[32] The Cosa Nostra has benefited enormously from the collapse of the socialist bloc in eastern Europe, with its weak and easily penetrable markets, and from the unification of Europe, which has reduced border controls and has made movement of people (including criminals) and capital within Europe easier.[33]

Mafia activity began in the early and mid-nineteenth century with extortion and the provision of protection.[34] The Cosa Nostra accumulated great wealth by exploiting state contracts and by participating in traditional illicit activities such as prostitution and gambling. The mafia moved into large-scale international activities through cigarette smuggling in the 1960s, but soon moved into the much more lucrative heroin market. In the mid-1980s, the mafia (the Camorra and 'Ndrangheta groups together) entered the cocaine trade.[35]

Nevertheless, the Italian government has been engaged in a major effort since the 1980s to rid the state of the criminality that has penetrated to the core of its political process.[36] This recent attempt to fight the mafia has been a costly effort in terms of both human lives and economic resources. The state has made strides against organized crime through new anti-mafia legislation, the establishment of a national anti-mafia investigative board, laws against money laundering, and the implementation of a witness-protection program, which have led to the emergence of hundreds of pentiti (mafia turncoats) and the freezing of the illegal assets of these crime groups. By confronting these organizations through the legal process, its finances, and its "men of honor," the Italian state has crippled the mafia.

COLOMBIAN ORGANIZED CRIME

Colombian organized crime has developed in what was once a stable democracy. Its development into a major actor in international criminality in the past 20 years has been very rapid and has been facilitated by the corruption of domestic law enforcement. Its range of activities is limited and it has shown enormous flexibility in entering new markets, forging critical alliances with other crime groups and using sophisticated techniques to launder its money.

Colombian organized crime is quite different to the other organized crime groups because it operates as a cartel—its business is the monopolization of the illicit international narcotics trade. A cartel takes advantage of a monopoly position in the market to artificially control prices and access to particular commodities. Trafficking in illegal substances lends itself to monopoly control because there is no legitimate commerce in these goods. Thus, cartel organizers control not only the availability of the product, but also its price and quality.[37] Colombian organized crime—the Medellin and Cali cartels—emerged in the 1970s. The cartels were, almost from their inception, international organizations. Initially, drug traffickers from Colombia supplied cocaine to other criminal groups such as the Cosa Nostra and various Mexican and Cuban gangs. The profitability of cocaine led these traffickers to decide to run their own smuggling and distribution operations.[38] Their producers were the less-developed countries of Latin America and, in the initial stages, their primary market was the United States. In the 1980s, the Colombian drug traffickers expanded their market to include Europe, and they developed ties to the Italian mafia as well as such international criminal organizations as the Nigerian mafia and the Chinese Triads. More recently, links have been established with eastern European and post-Soviet organized crime groups.[39]

Before organized crime became such an integral part of the Colombian economy, Colombia was one of the most stable democracies in Latin America. Presently, the government and its legal institutions have been seriously undermined by corruption and violent threats against members of the judiciary. Colombia, like other countries in Latin America, has lost its political autonomy, as the United States has declared a "war on drugs" and intervened by sending personnel to train local troops in anti-drug operations.[40]

In Colombia, as in other countries in Latin America, the organized crime groups spend large sums on financing electoral campaigns at the local and national levels, and major drug figures in Colombia have campaigned for public office. Carlos Lehder, a major drug lord, even organized a political party named the Latin Nationalist Movement. This party's visible entrance into politics backfired because of its close association with the drug dealers and, for the last decade, the crime groups have participated more covertly than overtly.[41]

The criminal activity of the Cali and Medellin cartels is much more focused than that of other international crime groups because they have managed to achieve prominence in such a lucrative area. They trade in illicit drugs, but to accomplish their objectives—which involve so much cash—they must also engage in large-scale corruption and money laundering. The organizations are headed by family groups, but membership is not restricted to family members, thereby permitting them to acquire expertise as needed. The monopoly cartels are organized with strict internal hierarchies, much as one would find in a large multinational corporation. However, the two cartels are quite different in operating style. The Medellin cartel relies heavily on violence, while the Cali group has been more concerned with penetrating the legitimate sectors that allow its activities to be more sustainable.[42] The Cali cartel's strategy has been more successful and, therefore, it presently enjoys predominance.

Billions of dollars in profits from drug sales by the Colombian cartels have been returned to the country, thus raising prices of both rural and urban real estate. Approximately a third of the profit is also returned for the further development of narcotics production.[43] Yet the capital from organized crime activity has not led to industrial development nor to a developed and diversified economy. This is because a very significant share of the cartels' proceeds remains abroad, laundered into banks, foreign real estate, securities, and businesses throughout the world. Money laundering is most often carried out in the Caribbean and in such international banking centers as London, Switzerland, and Hong Kong.[44] By the late 1980s, the Medellin syndicate was reputed to have at least $10 billion worth of fixed and liquid assets in Europe, Asia, and North America.[45]

POST-SOVIET ORGANIZED CRIME

Post-Soviet organized crime, operating in a declining superpower, has emerged in the international arena with an intensity and diversity of activities that is unmatched by most other transnational crime groups. Its international development has been recent and rapid, but its roots date back at least 30 years. Emerging from a post-socialist economy where the resources of the state are being rapidly redistributed, particularly in Russia, these groups have the ability to capitalize on this redistribution of wealth. Unlike Italy or Colombia, where crime groups have reinvested significant resources in their countries, most of the wealth of post-soviet organized crime groups lies in foreign banks and is beginning to be invested in foreign economies. The law-enforcement structures and the military, as shown in the Chechnya conflict, are unable or unwilling to deal with this criminality.

While many crime groups specialize in a particular area such as drug trafficking, prostitution rings, gambling, or weapons smuggling, post-soviet organized crime is involved in a full range of illicit activities, including large-scale penetration into the newly privatizing (legitimate) economy.

Organized crime existed in the post-Stalinist period yet went unrecognized by the Soviet authorities until the final years of the Soviet state. In the 1960s and 1970s, individuals with access to socialist-state property embezzled raw materials and consumer goods from the state and resold it at a profit to satisfy the extensive consumer demand. These crimes linked them with corrupt state and Party functionaries and members of the law-enforcement community.[46] Just as the Cosa Nostra spread to the United States from Sicily through the emigration of its members, the emigration of hundreds of thousands of Soviet citizens in the 1970s and 1980s to Germany, the United States, and Israel (some of them with criminal records or ties to the underground economy) was the first stage in the internationalization of Soviet organized crime.

The collapse of the Soviet state also provided a tremendous impetus for the growth of these criminal organizations. With the opening of borders to Europe and Asia, as well as within the former USSR, criminals from Russia and the other successor states (in conjunction with organized crime groups in eastern Europe as well as in Asia) have, in the past five years, taken advantage of this new freedom of mobility to become major actors in transnational illicit activity.

In fact, privatization of the former Soviet economies invites participation by organized crime. Privatization presumes the need for a large influx of capital, transparent financial services and banking systems, and increased international trade. Because the capitalist infrastructure is not yet in place, however, a situation exists that can be exploited by domestic and foreign organized crime groups, which are more readily prepared to take capital risks than are legitimate investors. Organized crime groups exploit the privatization of the legitimate economy by investing illicit profits in new capital ventures, by establishing accounts in banks that have little regulation or do not question the source of badly needed capital, and by utilizing new (and ancient) trade routes for movement of illicit goods.[47]

Organized crime exploits the legitimate economy while simultaneously limiting the development of certain legitimate forms of investment and of open markets that benefit a cross-section of the population. Thus, the economy becomes dependent on illegitimate rather than legitimate economic activity, and illicit commodities become central to the state's participation in international markets.[48] This is probably the greatest threat to the post-Soviet economies—developing an economy such as those of southern Italy and Colombia, which are heavily dependent on their illicit commerce in drugs.[49] Russian organized criminals are trading valuable raw materials and military equipment, the supply of which is not unlimited, and reliance on this illegal commerce is already clear for many in the labor force. Furthermore, many of the successor states are dependent on the foreign currency acquired through this illicit trade.[50]

Despite the already active presence of Colombian and Italian organized crime in Europe, post-Soviet groups have been able to exploit their strategic ports in the Baltic, their long-standing links to eastern Europe, and the large number of military and organized crime contacts and personnel in Germany to develop bases of operation there. The links with foreign businesses, banks, and communications companies of members of the former Soviet security apparatus and the extensive foreign deposits of the Communist Party (which these personnel know how to access) have given post-Soviet organized crime groups the capital to initiate and run illicit businesses.[51]

Post-Soviet organized crime exploits the world market for illicit goods and services (prostitution, gambling, drugs, contract killing, supply of cheap illegal labor, stolen automobiles, etc.) and extorts legitimate businesses in the former USSR and émigré businesses abroad. These groups are also involved in such diverse activities as the illegal export of oil and valuable raw materials, the smuggling of conventional weapons, nuclear materials, and human beings as well as the aforementioned manipulation of the privatization process.

This unusual coalition of professional criminals, former members of the underground economy, and members of the Party elite and the security apparatus defies traditional conceptions of organized crime groups, even though much of its activity is conducted with the threat of violence. Yet, with the exception of the post-Soviet narcotics trade, there is no cartel operating within the former Soviet Union.[52] Different ethnic groups have formed loose associations within the former Soviet

Union and with compatriots abroad to market goods and launder money. They are particularly active along the old silk routes, where drugs are transported from the Golden Triangle, Pakistan, and India. There are approximately 4,000 to 5,000 organized crime groups in the former USSR, of which several hundred have international ties.

The penetration of the state by organized crime extends from the municipal level up to the federal level, as organized crime has financed the election of candidates to, and members of, the new Russian parliament as well as those of other countries of the Commonwealth of Independent States (CIS).[53] Russian organized crime groups have in many ways supplanted the state in providing protection, employment, and social services that are no longer available from the government due to the relinquishing of the socialist ideology and the state budgetary crisis.

The former Soviet Union has neither the legal infrastructure nor the law-enforcement apparatus capable of combatting organized crime; its centralized law-enforcement apparatus collapsed along with the USSR in 1991. The dissolution of the USSR into numerous separate countries resulted in a lack of border controls, no consistent legal norms and limited coordination among the justice systems of the successor states. Criminals who maintain their ties from the Soviet period benefit from the lack of legal regulations to launder their money both at home and abroad, as well as in providing services to foreign criminal groups to help them launder money in the former USSR.

The most lucrative element of post-Soviet transnational criminality lies in the area of large-scale fraud against government. In the United States, organized criminals from the former Soviet Union with links to Russia have perpetrated gasoline tax evasion in the New York–New Jersey area on a mass scale.[54] In Germany, they have exploited the subsidies the German state provides for Soviet military troops.[55] Their international prostitution rings, nuclear smuggling, counterfeiting rings, narcotics trafficking, and money laundering all make post-Soviet organized crime groups increasingly visible actors on the international crime scene.[56] The increased visibility of these groups, in particular, has triggered the beginning of a significant international response by law-enforcement groups, the banking community, legislative bodies, and international organizations, who have begun to share information and conduct joint operations.

CASE ANALYSIS: CONCLUSIONS

As this case analysis has shown, policy solutions cannot be simplistically homogenous, since transnational organized crime groups can develop under a variety of political and economic conditions. All benefit from weaknesses in law enforcement in their home countries, and each exploits conflicting criminal, banking, and investment laws among nations. There is no form of government that is immune to the development of a transnational criminal organization, no legal system that seems capable of fully controlling the growth of transnational organized crime, and no economic or financial system able to resist the temptation of profits at levels and ratios disproportionately higher than the licit system offers. The challenge is to use this knowledge to develop a new policy approach to combatting transnational organized crime.

As has been shown, transnational crime groups vary broadly as to their formation, development, and the stage of development at which they become international, as well as the means chosen for carrying out their activities and exercising their power. This diversity makes a policy response extremely difficult. Any policy must address the similarities among such groups— their organizational flexibility, adaptability to new markets, and cross-group coordination.

Why, indeed, attempt such an effort? The remainder of this article will explore the costs to our global society of transnational crime and argue that these costs are too high to be ignored. International cooperation in developing an effective policy to deal with transnational organized crime should be made a high priority for all nations.

COMBATTING TRANSNATIONAL ORGANIZED CRIME

The very nature of transnational organized crime precludes any one country from launching an effective campaign against transnational organized crime groups. The extensive penetration of such groups into the state sector has immunized most transnational groups from the law-enforcement controls of their home countries. These groups seek to corrupt the legal institutions in their host country or render them impotent through targeted attacks on judicial personnel.[57] A criminal organization that evolves into a transnational organized crime group has typically been successful in controlling local law-enforcement efforts against it. Once it does, indeed, become international, the likelihood of enforcement diminishes radically.

Transnational organized crime groups are now so multinational that no state can be fully responsible for their control. Moreover, even if one state cracks down on members of a particular group, these members can frequently find refuge in another country. The enforcement net, therefore, has too many holes. A successful policy must seek international harmonization in legislation combatting crimes in the areas of banking, securities law, customs, and extradition in order to reduce the opportunities for criminal activity and minimize the infiltration of transnational organized crime groups into legitimate business. Extradition treaties and mutual, legal assistance agreements among the broadest number of signatories would best protect against the ability of transnational criminals to elude detection. All nations must engage in a coordinated law-enforcement campaign to ensure that criminals do not exploit differentiated enforcement strategies.

International covenants established to address the human rights violations of individual countries should be attuned to the threats to human rights caused by international crime groups. Measures against transnational crime must be adopted at the national level as well as at the level of regional organizations and international organizations. Some such efforts to address this issue have already been made. For example, the adoption in 1988 of the United Nations Convention Against Illicit Traffic in Narcotics Drugs and Psychotropic Substances (referred to as the Vienna U.N. Drug Convention) requires mutual legal assistance for signatories to the convention. At the regional level, the Financial Action Task Force was created at the Economic Summit of Industrialized Countries in 1989 to help develop an international approach to combatting money laundering. Also, in late 1988 the Group of Ten countries formed the Basel Committee on Banking Regulations and Supervisory Practices, and the Council of Europe has a draft convention on money laundering.[58] In 1990, the European Community adopted the European Plan to Fight Drugs, which it expanded in 1992.[59] All of these efforts are important in combatting the proceeds of international crime, but more must be done to attack the illicit activities of organized crime.

Law-enforcement coordination must also include the sharing of intelligence concerning the activities of transnational organized groups. Law enforcers from over 100 countries met recently in Naples to share information gained by those working on transnational organized crime (or the activities of particular regional crime groups, such as those originating in the former Soviet Union). International protocols to further this type of intelligence sharing should be developed.

But limits to such efforts exist both at the national and international levels. The United States, for example, is currently vulnerable to the activities of transnational crime groups because federal law prohibits the CIA from sharing with the FBI intelligence that it collects abroad. Many legal protections of the American citizenry, particularly relating to rights of the accused, are exploited by the sophisticated transnational criminals.[60] Other gaps between intelligence gathering and law enforcement are similarly exploited by transnational groups throughout the world and need to be addressed by legal reforms.

In its policy proposals for the 1994 Ministerial Conference on Organized Transnational Crime, the United Nations suggested that the fight against these groups could be enhanced if more nations adopted legislation on the criminalization of participation in a criminal organization (which does not exist in many criminal codes), the criminalization of conspiracy, the prohibition of laundering of criminal profits, and the implementation of asset forfeiture laws.[61] The U.N. proposals also advocated the adoption of a convention specifically targeting transnational organized crime.[62] While an increasing number of countries is likely to participate in such international efforts, there will always be countries whose governments are too corrupted, or whose legal infrastructures are too primitive, to allow them to actively participate in such arrangements. Gaps will invariably remain in the international legislative framework and, consequently, in the enforcement capacities of different states.

CONCLUSION

Transnational crime is growing rapidly and represents a global phenomenon that is penetrating political institutions, undermining legitimate economic growth, threatening democracy and the rule of law and contributing to the post-Soviet problem of the eruption of small, regionally contained, ethnic violence. The disintegrative effect on the world political, economic, and social order transcends the enforcement ability of the nation-state. Indeed, the post-Soviet proliferation of nations, each with its own legal system, and the lack of adequate border controls in a vast geographical area (that now stretches from western Europe to the Pacific borders of the former Soviet Union) alter profoundly the previous world order, based on relatively stable, unified nation-states.

Another example of this geopolitical change is the European Union, which seeks the free movement of people and goods on a regional, transnational basis. In addition, the weakness of many states in Africa, parts of Latin America, and Asia that are unable to control their existing boundaries or establish proper internal legal institutions, creates vast areas in which boundaries are no longer delineated by walls—these borders have become webs of netting through whose holes passes the business of organized crime.

The threat to nation-states is not that of a single monolithic, international organized crime network; rather, the multiplicity of politically and economically powerful crime groups operating both regionally and globally is what truly threatens to undermine political and economic security as well as social well being. In many countries, the infiltration of organized crime into political structures has paralyzed law enforcement from within. Moreover, in many parts of the world where organized crime groups have supplanted the functions of the state, they impede economic development and the transition to democracy.

There is no economic incentive for transnational organized crime to diminish, and thus it will continue to threaten the world order in the 21st century. The international community must act now to abate the pernicious social, political, and economic consequences of transnational crime, but with the understanding that it will never be able to achieve fully consistent policies and enforcement that will eradicate transnational organized crime, though such efforts can constantly thwart it. Internationally coordinated legislative and law-enforcement efforts must be supported, because in their absence transnational crime threatens to penetrate to the core of democratic states. The corrupting influences of organized crime on the democratic governments of Colombia and Italy make this all too clear. Unless countries are willing to make a concerted effort against organized crime, they threaten their own institutions and the stability and longevity of their governments.

ACKNOWLEDGEMENT

The author wishes to thank Karen Telis for her perceptive comments on this manuscript and Ernesto U. Savona for many of the ideas on the enforcement policies needed to combat transnational crime.

NOTES

1. From *Journal of International Affairs*, 48, no. 2, (Winter 1995), pp. 463–89.

2. See, for example, the cover story by Michael Elliott et al., "The Global Mafia," *Newsweek*, 122, no. 24 (13 December 1993), 22(7); the related article by Russell Watson, "Death on the Spot: the end of a drug king," *Newsweek*, 122, no. 24 (December 1993), 18(4); and Claire Sterling, *Thieves' World* (New York: Simon and Schuster, 1994).

3. Giuletto Chiesa, "Piovra, tentacoli sul mondo," *La Stampa*, 20 November 1994, p. 12; Ottavio Lucarelli and Conchita Sannino, "Ecco l'internazionale anticrimine," *La Repubblica*, 21 November 1994, p. 9; Giovanni Bianconi, "A Napoli la Babele antimafia," *La Stampa*, 22 November 1994, p. 13; Alan Cowell, "Crime Money Troubles the U.N.," *New York Times*, 25 November 1994, p. A17.

4. Phil Williams, "Transnational Criminal Organizations and International Security," *Survival*, 36, no. 1 (Spring 1994), pp. 96–113. Examples of illicit activities with low risk of apprehension include smuggling, money laundering, and international drug trafficking.

5. Ernesto U. Savona and Michael Defeo, *Money Trails: International Money Laundering Trends and Prevention/Control Policies*, Helsinki Institute for Crime Prevention and Control (HEUNI) report prepared for the international conference on "Preventing and Controlling Money Laundering and the Use of Proceeds of Crime: A Global Approach" (Courmayeur, June 1994).

6. See Williams, "Transnational Criminal Organizations and International Security."

7. On Africa, see Tolani Asuni, "Drug Trafficking and Drug Abuse in Africa," in *Criminology in Africa*, ed. Tibamanya mwene Mushanga (Rome: United National Interregional Crime and Justice Research Institute, 1992), pp. 117–19. Alain Labrousse and Alain Wallon, eds., *La Planete des drogues: organisations criminelles, guerres et blanchiment* (Paris: Editions du Seuil, 1993) discusses the international trafficking in drugs. The Afghan–Tadzhik border also sees a very significant illegal arms trade.

8. See Sterling, *Thieves' World*.

9. In Sicily, organized crime has intimidated the heads of civic organizations that challenge the mafia, and in Russia, it is infiltrating the emergent charitable organizations.

10. Paolo Pezzino, *Una certa reciprocita difavori mafia e modernizzazione violenta nella Sicilia postunitaria* (Milano: Franco Angeli, 1990), p. 39.

11. Alan Cowell, "Italians Voting Today, with Mafia's Role a Top Issue," *New York Times*, 27 March 1993, p. 10.

12. Pino Arlacchi, "La grande criminalith in Italia," *La rivista dei libri* (April 1993), p. 38.

13. See, for example, "Authorities Deny Existence of Anti-Sobchak 'Center' in St. Petersburg," Foreign Broadcast Information Service (hereafter called FBIS), 17 June 1993, pp. 101–2.

14. William Greider, *Who Will Tell the People: The*

Betrayal of American Democracy (New York: Simon and Schuster/Touchstone, 1993), p. 377.

15. For more information on the 1992 Bank of Credit and Commerce International (BCCI) affair, see Nikos Passas, "I Cheat, Therefore I Exist: The BCCI Scandal in Context," in *International Perspectives on Business Ethics*, ed. W.M. Hoffman, et al. (New York: Quorum Books, 1993).

16. As a result of one medical fraud case perpetrated by international groups of criminals, the insurance premiums of each citizen in the state of California rose by 15 percent. In Russia, it is now estimated that prices are 20 to 30 percent higher because of organized crime control of consumer markets. Housing costs are also raised as organized crime groups acquire real estate in the capital and many other cities. See, for example, "Crime, Corruption Poses Political, Economic Threat," *Current Digest of the Soviet Press*, 46, no. 4 (23 February 1994), p. 14.

17. Robert J. Kelly, "Criminal Underworlds: Looking Down on Society," in *Organized Crime: A Global Perspective*, ed. Robert J. Kelly (Totowa, NJ: Rowman and Littlefield, 1986), p. 14. Some groups, such as the Cosa Nostra, are based on a pyramidal, hierarchical structure. Others are based on clan structures, such as some of the Caucasian groups, which are looser confederations. Some avoid detection by corrupting law-enforcement structures, while other groups hire sophisticated professionals to develop complex paper trails and money laundering strategies.

18. A Public Broadcasting Service (PBS) program is forthcoming that will document the alleged involvement of organized crime groups in the smuggling of nuclear weapons.

19. See Williams, "Transnational Criminal Organizations and International Security"; and Labrousse and Wallon, eds., *La Planete des drogues*.

20. Alain Labrousse and Alain Wallon, eds., *Etat des drogues, drogue des etats: observatoire geopolitique des drogues* (Paris: Hachette, 1994), p. 252.

21. Ibid.

22. Ibid., p. 258.

23. "Problems and Dangers Posed by Organized Transnational Crime in the Various Regions of the World," background document for World Ministerial Conference on Organized Transnational Crime (Naples, 21–23 November 1994).

24. At first the Nigerian government was tolerant of this activity. See Asuni, "Drug Trafficking and Drug Abuse in Africa," p. 120. Attention should also be paid to the American mafia, the Turkish, Pakistani, and Golden Triangle drug-trafficking organizations (Burma-Thailand-Laos). For a discussion of these groups see Labrousse and Wallon, *Etat des drogues*, pp. 139–62, 289–95. There are also smaller Australian groups that operate on a more regional basis. For a discussion of these, see Ian Dobinson, "The Chinese Connection: Heroin Trafficking between Australia and Southeast Asia," *Criminal Organizations*, 7, no. 2 (June 1992), pp. 1, 3–7; A. W. McCoy, *Drug Traffic: Narcotics and Organised Crime in Australia* (Sydney: Harper and Row, 1980).

25. The four major groups are: the mafia or Cosa Nostra in Sicily, the Neapolitan Camorra, the 'Ndragheta based in Calabria, and the lesser-known Sacra Corona in Apulia. Furthermore, the Cosa Nostra may have the greatest longevity of all these crime groups, although the origins of the Camorra can be traced to more than a century ago. For a discussion of these groups, see Adolfo Beria di Argentine, "The Mafias in Italy," in *Mafia Issues: Analyses and Proposals for Combatting the Mafia Today*, ed. Ernesto U. Savona (Milan: International Scientific Professional Advisory Council of the United Nations Crime Prevention and Criminal Justice Programme [ISPAC], 1993), pp. 22–3.

26. Anton Blok, *The Mafia of a Sicilian Village, 1860–1960: A Study of Violent Peasant Entrepreneurs* (New York: Harper & Row, 1975), p. 10.

27. For a fuller discussion of this, see Louise I. Shelley, "Mafia and the Italian State: The Historical Roots of the Current Crisis," *Sociological Forum*, 19, no. 4 (1994), pp. 661–72; Raimondo Catanzaro, *Men of Respect—A Social History of the Sicilian Mafia* (New York: Free Press, 1992); Diego Gambetta, *The Sicilian Mafia: The Business of Private Protection* (Cambridge: Harvard University Press, 1993).

28. Nicola Tranfaglia, *La mafia come metodo nell'Italia contemporanea* (Bari: Laterza, 1991); Nicola Tranfaglia, "L'onorevole e cosa nostra," *La Repubblica*, 13 May 1994, pp. 28–9.

29. The state also had difficulty penetrating the Cosa Nostra because it has strict initiation rights, a pyramidal structure, and organization tied to a specific territory.

30. Shelley, "Mafia and the Italian State: The Historical Roots of the Current Crisis."

31. Marie Anne Matard, "Presenza mafiosa in Tunisia?," presented at a conference entitled "Interpretazioni della mafia tra vecchi e nuovi paradigmi" (Palermo: 27–29 May 1993); Dennis J. Kenney and James O. Finckenauer, *Organized Crime in America* (Belmont, CA: Wadsworth, 1995), pp. 89–109, 230–55.

32. In Guido M. Rey and Ernesto U. Savona, "The Mafia: An International Enterprise?," in Ernesto U. Savona (ed.), *Mafia Issues* (Milan: ISPAC, 1993), p. 74, the authors discuss the fact that there was movement from Sicily to the U.S. in the 1960s and again more recently. The same is occurring in Germany.

33. Giovanni Falcone, "PM: Una carriera da cambiare," *MicroMega* (March 1993), p. 45.

34. See Gambetta, *The Sicilian Mafia*.

35. The wealth of the mafia is disbursed in four different ways. The smallest portion is used to buy drugs to further its transnational criminal activity. A second, more sizable part is deposited in foreign banks or is invested in Latin America, and more recently, in the eastern bloc because of the possibility of investing funds without detection. A third

portion is invested in the Sicilian economy in housing construction, agriculture, and tourism. The last portion lies in Sicilian banks. See Arlacchi, "La grande criminalita in Italia," pp. 209–10; and Rey and Savona, "The Mafia: An International Enterprise?," pp. 74–5, regarding development of the drug trade.

36. See Tranfaglia, *La mafia come metodo nell'Italia contemporanea.*

37. Labrousse and Wallon, *La planete des drogues,* p. 32.

38. See Kenney and Finckenauer, *Organized Crime in America*, p. 263.

39. This is the major theme of Sterling's *Thieves' World*, and she documents these links extensively throughout the book.

40. For a discussion of this, see several articles in the collection of Ana Josefina Alvarez Gomez, *Trafico y consumo de drogas: una vision alternativa* (Mexico City: Universidad Nacional de Mexico, Escuela Nacional de Estudios Profesionales Acatlan, 1991); Ethan A. Nadelmann, *Cops Across Borders* (University Park, PA: Pennsylvania State University Press, 1993); Alan A. Block, "Anti-Communism and the War on Drugs," in *Perspectives on Organizing Crime: Essays in Opposition* (Dordrecht: Kluwer Academic Publishers, 1991), pp. 209, 218–22; and Labrousse and Wallon, *Etat des drogues.*

41. See Rensselaer W. Lee III, *The White Labyrinth: Cocaine and Political Power* (New Brunswick, NJ: Transaction, 1990), pp. 130–9.

42. Ibid., p. 111.

43. Ibid., p. 3.

44. See Savona and Defeo, *Money Trails*, p. 65.

45. See Lee, *The White Labyrinth*, p. 3.

46. Vyacheslav Afanasyev, "Organized Crime and Society," *Demokratizatsiya*, 2, no. 3 (Summer 1994), p. 438.

47. Research by the Russian Academy of Sciences Analytical Center indicates that 55 percent of joint-stock companies, and 80 percent of voting shares, were acquired by criminal capital, according to Ninel Kuznetsova, "Crime in Russia: Causes and Prevention," *Demokratizatsiya*, 2, no. 3 (Summer 1994), p. 444.

48. For a fuller discussion of the economic consequences, see Louise I. Shelley, "Post-Soviet Organized Crime: Implications for Economic, Social and Political Development," *Demokratizatsiya*, 2, no. 3 (Summer 1994), pp. 344–50.

49. See Rensselaer Lee and Scott MacDonald, "Drugs in the East," *Foreign Policy*, no. 90 (Spring 1993), p. 96; Lee, *The White Labyrinth*; and Pino Arlacchi, *Mafia Business: The Mafia Ethnic and the Spirit of Capitalism* (London: Verso, 1986), pp. 187–210.

50. Seija Lainela and Pekka Sutela, "Escaping from the Ruble: Estonia and Latvia Compared," paper presented at the Third EACES workshop on "Integration and Disintegration in European Economies: Divergent or Convergent Processes?" (Trento, Italy: 4–5 March 1993).

51. For a discussion of the participation of some of the security apparatus in money laundering, see Vladimir Ivanidze, "Kto i kak otmyvaet 'griaznye' den'gi i chto izvestno g-nu Zhirinovskomu ob etoi 'stiral'noi mashine," *Liternaturnaia Gazeta*, 5 October 1994, p. 13.

52. "Increased Drug Trade Expected, Antidrug Campaign Urged," *FBIS Daily Report*, 29 May 1992, pp. 48–50.

53. "Duma Adopts Anticorruption Bills," *FBIS Daily Report*, 16 May 1994, p. 32; A. Uglanov, "Prestupnost' i vlast'," *Argumenty i Fakty*, no. 27 (July 1994), pp. 1–2.

54. Russian crime groups, in collaboration with Italian organized groups in the U.S., found ways of selling gasoline without paying the required federal taxes. "The Russian Con Men who Took California," *Newsweek* (13 December 1993), p. 28; State of New Jersey Commission of Investigation, *Motor Fuel Tax Evasion* (Trenton, NJ: State of New Jersey Commission of Investigation, 1992).

55. "Alarm, jetzt kommen die Russen," *Der Spiegel*, no. 25 (1993), pp. 100–11.

56. On narcotics trafficking, see Dimitri De Kochko and Alexandre Datskevitch, *L'Empire de la drogue: la Russie et ses marches* (Paris: Hachette, 1994). On money laundering, see Ivanidze, "Kto i kak otmyvaet 'griaznye' den'gi i chto izvestno g-nu Zhirinovskomu ob etoi 'stiral'noi machune," p. 13.

57. In Colombia and Italy, famous judges have been assassinated, and in Russia there are currently 1,000 vacancies in the judiciary, many of them unfilled due to intimidation of judges by members of organized crime groups.

58. See Savona and DeFeo, *Money Trails*, pp. 32–7.

59. Labrousse and Wallon, *La Planete des drogues*, p. 162.

60. For example, wire transfers made by money launderers cannot be easily followed up by law enforcers because of legal protections on bank accounts. Therefore, a transfer that goes through four different countries in four hours would take American law enforcement one year to trace.

61. "National Legislation and Its Adequacy to Deal with the Various Forms of Organized Transnational Crime: Appropriate Guidelines for Legislative and Other Measures to be Taken on the National Level," background document for the World Ministerial Conference on Organized Transnational Crime (Naples, 21–23 November 1994), p. 23.

62. "The Feasibility of Elaborating International Instruments, Including Conventions, Against Organized Transnational Crime," background document for the World Ministerial Conference on Organized Transnational Crime (Naples, 21–23 November 1994), pp. 7–12.

CHAPTER 49

"Introduction" from *New and Old Wars: Organized Violence in a Global Era*

Mary Kaldor

In the summer of 1992, I visited Nagorno-Karabakh in the Transcaucasian region in the midst of a war involving Azerbaijan and Armenia. It was then that I realized that what I had previously observed in the former Yugoslavia was not unique; it was not a throwback to the Balkan past but rather a contemporary predicament especially, or so I thought, to be found in the post-communist part of the world. The wild west atmosphere of Knin (then the capital of the self-proclaimed Serbian republic in Croatia) and Nagorno-Karabakh, peopled by young men in home-made uniforms, desperate refugees and thuggish, neophyte politicians, was quite distinctive. Later, I embarked on a research project on the character of the new type of wars and I discovered from my colleagues who had first-hand experience of Africa that what I had noted in Eastern Europe shared many common features with the wars taking place in Africa and perhaps also other places, for example South Asia. Indeed, the experience of wars in other places shed new light on my understanding of what was happening in the Balkans and the former Soviet Union.[1]

My central argument is that, during the 1980s and 1990s, a new type of organized violence has developed, especially in Africa and Eastern Europe, which is one aspect of the current globalized era. I describe this type of violence as 'new war'. I use the term 'new' to distinguish these wars from prevailing perceptions of war drawn from an earlier era. . . . I use the term 'war' to emphasize the political nature of this new type of violence, even though, as will become clear in the following pages, the new wars involve a blurring of the distinctions between war (usually defined as violence between states or organized political groups for political motives), organized crime (violence undertaken by privately organized groups for private purposes, usually financial gain) and large-scale violations of human rights (violence undertaken by states or politically organized groups against individuals).

In most of the literature, the new wars are described as internal or civil wars or else as 'low-intensity conflict'. Yet although most of these wars are localized, they involve a myriad of transnational connections so that the distinction between internal and external, between aggression (attacks from abroad) and repression (attacks from inside the country), or even between local and global, are difficult to sustain. The term 'low-intensity conflict' was coined during the Cold War period by the US military to describe guerrilla warfare or terrorism. Although it is possible to trace the evolution of the new wars from the so-called low-intensity conflicts of the Cold War period, they have distinctive characteristics which are masked by what is in effect a catch-all term. Some authors describe the new wars as privatized or informal wars,[2] yet, while the privatization of violence is an important element of these wars, in practice, the distinction between what is private and what is public, state and non-state, informal and formal, between what is done for economic or political motives, cannot easily be applied. A more appropriate term is perhaps the term 'post-modern',[3] which is used by several authors. Like 'new wars', it offers a way of distinguishing these wars from the wars which could be said to be characteristic of classical modernity.

However, the term is also used to refer to virtual wars and wars in cyberspace,[4] moreover, the new wars involve elements of premodernity and modernity as well. Finally, Martin Shaw uses the term 'degenerate warfare'. For him there is a continuity with the total wars of the twentieth century and their genocidal aspects; the term draws attention to the decay of the national frameworks, especially military forces.[5]

Among American strategic writers, there is a discussion about what is known as the Revolution in Military Affairs.[6] The argument is that the advent of information technology is as significant as was the advent of the tank and the aeroplane, or even as significant as the shift from horsepower to mechanical power, with profound implications for the future of warfare. However, the Revolution in Military Affairs is conceived by these writers within the inherited institutional structures of war and the military. They envisage wars on a traditional model in which the new techniques develop in a more or less linear extension from the past. Moreover, they are designed to sustain the imagined character of war which was typical of the Cold War era and utilized in such a way as to minimize own casualties. The preferred technique is spectacular aerial bombing which reproduces the appearance of classical war for public consumption and which has very little to do with reality on the ground. Hence Baudrillard's famous remark that the Gulf War did not take place.[7] These complex sophisticated techniques have been used not only in Iraq, but also in Bosnia–Herzegovina and Somalia with, I would argue, relatively little practical relevance even though they have caused many civilian casualties.

I share the view that there has been a revolution in military affairs, but it is a revolution in the social relations of warfare, not in technology, even though the changes in social relations are influenced by and make use of new technology. Beneath the spectacular displays are real wars, which, even in the case of the 1991 Iraq war in which hundreds and thousands of Kurds and Shiites died, are better explained in terms of my conception of new wars.

I argue that the new wars have to be understood in the context of the process known as globalization. By globalization, I mean the intensification of global interconnectedness—political, economic, military and cultural. Even though I accept the argument that globalization has its roots in modernity or even earlier, I consider that the globalization of the 1980s and 1990s is a qualitatively new phenomenon which can, at least in part, be explained as a consequence of the revolution in information technologies and dramatic improvements in communication and data-processing. This process of intensifying interconnectedness is a contradictory process involving both integration and fragmentation, homogenization and diversification, globalization and localization. It is often argued that the new wars are a consequence of the end of the Cold War; they reflect a power vacuum which is typical of transition periods in world affairs. It is undoubtedly true that the consequences of the end of the Cold War—the availability of surplus arms, the discrediting of socialist ideologies, the disintegration of totalitarian empires, the withdrawal of superpower support to client regimes—contributed in important ways to the new wars. But equally, the end of the Cold War could be viewed as the way in which the Eastern bloc succumbed to the inevitable encroachment of globalization—the crumbling of the last bastions of territorial autarchy, the moment when Eastern Europe was 'opened up' to the rest of the world.

The impact of globalization is visible in many of the new wars. The global presence in these wars can include international reporters, mercenary troops and military advisers, diaspora volunteers as well as a veritable 'army' of international agencies ranging from non-governmental organizations (NGOs) like Oxfam, Save the Children, Médecins Sans Frontières, Human Rights Watch and the International Red Cross to international institutions like the United Nations High Commissioner for Refugees (UNHCR), the European Union (EU), the United Nations Children's Fund (UNICEF), the Organization for Security and Co-operation in Europe (OSCE), the Organization for African Unity (OAU) and the United Nations (UN) itself, including peacekeeping troops. Indeed, the wars epitomize a new kind of global/local divide between those members of a global class who can speak English, have access to faxes, e-mail and satellite television, who use dollars or deutschmarks or credit cards, and who can travel freely, and those who are excluded from global processes, who live off what they can sell or barter or what they receive in humanitarian aid, whose movement is restricted by roadblocks, visas and the cost of travel, and who are prey to sieges, forced famines, landmines, etc.

In the literature on globalization, a central concern has to do with the implications of global interconnectedness for the future of the territorially based sovereignty—that is to say, for the future of the modern state.[8] The new wars arise in the context of the erosion of the autonomy of the state and in some extreme cases the disintegration of the state. In particular, they occur in the context of the erosion of the monopoly of legitimate organized violence. This monopoly is eroded from above and from below. It has been eroded from above by the transnationalization of military forces which began during the two world wars and was institutionalized by the bloc system during the Cold War and by innumerable transnational connections between armed forces that developed in the post-war period.[9] The capacity of states to use force unilaterally against other states has been greatly weakened. This is partly for practical reasons—the growing destructiveness of military technology and the increasing interconnectedness of states, especially in the military field. It is difficult to imagine nowadays a state or group of states risking a large-scale war which could be even more destructive than what was experienced during the first and second world wars. Moreover, military alliances, international arms production and trade, various forms of military cooperation and exchanges, arms control agreements, etc. have created a form of global military integration. It is also due to the evolution of international norms. The principle that unilateral aggression is illegitimate was first codified in the Kellogg–

Briand pact of 1928, and reinforced after World War II in the UN Charter and through the reasoning used in the war crimes trials in Nuremberg and Tokyo.

At the same time, the monopoly of organized violence is eroded from below by privatization. Indeed, it could be argued that the new wars are part of a process which is more or less a reversal of the processes through which modern states evolved. . . . The rise of the modern state was intimately connected to war. In order to fight wars, rulers needed to increase taxation and borrowing, to eliminate 'wastage' as a result of crime, corruption and inefficiency, to regularize armed forces and police and to eliminate private armies, and to mobilize popular support in order to raise money and men. As war became the exclusive province of the state, so the growing destructiveness of war against other states was paralleled by a process of growing security at home; hence the way in which the term 'civil' came to mean internal. The new wars occur in situations in which state revenues decline because of the decline of the economy as well as the spread of criminality, corruption and inefficiency, violence is increasingly privatized both as a result of growing organized crime and the emergence of paramilitary groups, and political legitimacy is disappearing. Thus the distinctions between external barbarity and domestic civility, between the combatant as the legitimate bearer of arms and the non-combatant, between the soldier or policeman and the criminal, are breaking down. The barbarity of war between states may have become a thing of the past. In its place is a new type of organized violence that is more pervasive, but also perhaps less extreme.

[. . .] I use the example of the war in Bosnia–Herzegovina to illustrate the main features of the new wars, mainly because it is the war with which I am most familiar. The war in Bosnia–Herzegovina shares many of the characteristics of wars in other places. But in one sense it is exceptional; it has become the focus of global attention. More resources—governmental and nongovernmental—have been concentrated there than in any other new war. On the one hand, this means that, as a case study, it has atypical features. On the other hand, it also means that it has become the paradigm case, from which different lessons are drawn, the example which is used to argue out different general positions, and, at the same time, a laboratory in which different ways of managing the new wars are experimented.

The new wars can be contrasted with earlier wars in terms of their goals, the methods of warfare and how they are financed. The goals of the new wars are about identity politics in contrast to the geo-political or ideological goals of earlier wars. [...] I argue that, in the context of globalization, ideological and/or territorial cleavages of an earlier era have increasingly been supplanted by an emerging political cleavage between what I call cosmopolitanism, based on inclusive, universalist, multicultural values, and the politics of particularist identities.[10] This cleavage can be explained in terms of the growing divide between those who are part of global processes and those who are excluded, but it should not be equated with this division. Among the global class are members of transnational networks based on exclusivist identity, while at the local level there are many courageous individuals who refuse the politics of particularism.

By identity politics, I mean the claim to power on the basis of a particular identity—be it national, clan, religious or linguistic. In one sense, all wars involve a clash of identities—British against French, communists against democrats. But my point is that these earlier identities were either linked to a notion of state interest or to some forward-looking project—ideas about how society should be organized. Nineteenth-century European nationalisms or post-colonial nationalisms, for example, presented themselves as emancipatory nation-building projects. The new identity politics is about the claim to power on the basis of labels—in so far as there are ideas about political or social change, they tend to relate to an idealized nostalgic representation of the past. It is often claimed that the new wave of identity politics is merely a throwback to the past, a resurgence of ancient hatreds kept under control by colonialism and/or the Cold War. While it is true that the narratives of

identity politics depend on memory and tradition, it is also the case that these are 'reinvented' in the context of the failure or the corrosion of other sources of political legitimacy—the discrediting of socialism or the nation-building rhetoric of the first generation of post-colonial leaders. These backward-looking political projects arise in the vacuum created by the absence of forward-looking projects. Unlike the politics of ideas which are open to all and therefore tend to be integrative, this type of identity politics is inherently exclusive and therefore tends to fragmentation.

There are two aspects of the new wave of identity politics which specifically relate to the process of globalization. First, the new wave of identity politics is both local and global, national as well as transnational. In many cases, there are significant diaspora communities whose influence is greatly enhanced by the ease of travel and improved communication. Alienated diaspora groups in advanced industrial or oil-rich countries provide ideas, funds and techniques, thereby imposing their own frustrations and fantasies on what is often a very different situation. Second, this politics makes use of the new technology. The speed of political mobilization is greatly increased by the use of the electronic media. The effect of television, radio or videos on what is often a non-reading public cannot be overestimated. The protagonists of the new politics often display the symbols of a global mass culture—Mercedes cars, Rolex watches, Rayban sunglasses—combined with the labels that signify their own brand of particularistic cultural identity.

The second characteristic of the new wars is the changed mode of warfare[11]—the means through which the new wars are fought. The strategies of the new warfare draw on the experience of both guerrilla warfare and counterinsurgency, yet they are quite distinctive. In conventional or regular war, the goal is the capture of territory by military means; battles are the decisive encounters of the war. Guerrilla warfare developed as a way of getting round the massive concentrations of military force which are characteristic of conventional war. In guerrilla warfare, territory is captured through political control of the population rather than through military advance, and battles are avoided as far as possible. The new warfare also tends to avoid battle and to control territory through political control of the population, but whereas guerrilla warfare, at least in theory as articulated by Mao Tse-tung or Che Guevara, aimed to capture 'hearts and minds', the new warfare borrows from counterinsurgency techniques of destabilization aimed at sowing 'fear and hatred'. The aim is to control the population by getting rid of everyone of a different identity (and indeed of a different opinion). Hence the strategic goal of these wars is population expulsion through various means such as mass killing, forcible resettlement, as well as a range of political, psychological and economic techniques of intimidation. This is why, in all these wars, there has been a dramatic increase in the number of refugees and displaced persons, and why most violence is directed against civilians. At the turn of the century, the ratio of military to civilian casualties in wars was 8:1. Today, this has been almost exactly reversed; in the wars of the 1990s, the ratio of military to civilian casualties is approximately 1:8. Behaviour that was proscribed according to the classical rules of warfare and codified in the laws of war in the late nineteenth century and early twentieth century, such as atrocities against non-combatants, sieges, destruction of historic monuments, etc., now constitutes an essential component of the strategies of the new mode of warfare.

In contrast to the vertically organized hierarchical units that were typical of 'old wars', the units that fight these wars include a disparate range of different types of groups such as paramilitary units, local warlords, criminal gangs, police forces, mercenary groups and also regular armies including breakaway units of regular armies. In organizational terms, they are highly decentralized and they operate through a mixture of confrontation and cooperation even when on opposing sides. They make use of advanced technology even if it is not what we tend to call 'high technology' (stealth bombers or cruise missiles, for example). In the last fifty years, there have been significant advances in lighter weapons—undetectable landmines, for example, or small arms which are light, accurate and easy to use so that they can even be operated by children. They also make use of modern communications—cellular phones or computer links—in order to coordinate, mediate and negotiate among the disparate fighting units.

The third way in which the new wars can be contrasted with earlier wars is what I call the new 'globalized' war economy. .... The new globalized war economy is almost exactly the opposite of the war economies of the two world wars. The latter were centralized, totalizing and autarchic. The new war economies are decentralized. Participation in the war is low and unemployment is extremely high. Moreover, these economies are heavily dependent on external resources. In these wars, domestic production declines dramatically because of global competition, physical destruction or interruptions to normal trade, as does tax revenue. In these circumstances, the fighting units finance themselves through plunder and the black market or through external assistance. The latter can take the following forms: remittances from the diaspora, 'taxation' of humanitarian assistance, support from neighbouring governments or illegal trade in arms, drugs or valuable commodities such as oil or diamonds. All of these sources can only be sustained through continued violence so that a war logic is built into the functioning of the economy. This retrograde set of social relationships, which is entrenched by war, has a tendency to spread across borders through refugees or organized crime or ethnic minorities. It is possible to identify clusters of war economies or near war economies in places like the Balkans, the Caucasus, Central Asia, the Horn of Africa, Central Africa or West Africa.

Because the various warring parties share the aim of sowing 'fear and hatred', they operate in a way that is mutually reinforcing, helping each other to create a climate of insecurity and suspicion—indeed, it is possible to find examples in both Eastern Europe and Africa of mutual cooperation for both military and economic purposes. Often, among the first civilians to be targeted are those who espouse a different politics, who try to maintain inclusive social relations and some sense of public morality. Thus though the new wars appear to be between different linguistic, religious or tribal groups, they can also be presented as wars in which those who represent particularistic identity politics cooperate in suppressing the values of civility and multiculturalism. In other words, they can be understood as wars between exclusivism and cosmopolitanism.

This analysis of new wars has implications for the management of conflicts. . . . There is no possible long-term solution within the framework of identity politics. And because these are conflicts with extensive social and economic ramifications, top-down approaches are likely to fail. In the early 1990s there was great optimism about the prospects for humanitarian intervention to protect civilians. However, the practice of humanitarian intervention has, I would argue, been shackled by a kind of myopia about the character of the new warfare. The persistence of inherited mandates, the tendency to interpret these wars in traditional terms, has been the main reason why humanitarian intervention has not only failed to prevent the wars but may have actually helped to sustain them in various ways, for example, through the provision of humanitarian aid, which is an important source of income for the warring parties, or through the legitimation of war criminals by inviting them to the negotiating table, or through the effort to find political compromises based on exclusivist assumptions.

The key to any long-term solution is the restoration of legitimacy, the reconstitution of the control of organized violence by public authorities, whether local, national or global. This is both a political process—the rebuilding of trust in and support for public authorities—and a legal process—the re-establishment of a rule of law within which public authorities operate. This cannot be done on the basis of particularistic politics. An alternative forward-looking cosmopolitan political project which would cross the global/local divide and reconstruct legitimacy around an inclusive, democratic set of values has to be counterposed against the politics of exclusivism. In all the new wars there are local people and places who struggle against the politics of exclusivism—the Hutus and Tutsis who called themselves Hutsis and tried to defend their localities against genocide, the non-nationalists in the cities of Bosnia-Herzegovina, particularly Sarajevo and Tuzla, who kept alive civic multicultural values, the elders in Northwest Somaliland who negotiated peace. What is needed is an alliance between local defenders of civility and transnational institutions which would guide a strategy aimed at controlling violence. Such a strategy would include political, military and economic components. It would operate within a framework of international law, based on that body of international law that comprises both the laws of warfare and human rights, which could perhaps be termed cosmopolitan law. In this context, peacekeeping could be reconceptualized as cosmopolitan law-enforcement. Since the new wars are, in a sense, a mixture of war, crime and human rights violations, so the agents of cosmopolitan law-enforcement have to be a mixture of soldiers and policemen. I also argue that a new strategy of reconstruction, which includes the reconstruction of social, civic and institutional relationships, should supplant the current dominant approaches of structural adjustment or humanitarianism.

[. . .] I discuss the implications of the argument for global order. Although the new wars are concentrated in Africa, Eastern Europe and Asia, they are a global phenomenon not just because of the presence of global networks, nor because they are reported globally. The characteristics of the new wars I have described are to be found in North America and Western Europe as well. The right-wing militia groups in the United States are not so very different from the paramilitary groups in Eastern Europe or Africa. Indeed, in the United States it is reported that private security officers outnumber police officers by 2:1. Nor is the salience of identity politics and the growing disillusionment with formal politics just a Southern and Eastern phenomenon. The violence in the inner cities of Western Europe and North America can, in some senses, be described as new wars. It is sometimes said that the advanced industrial world is integrating and the poorer parts of the world are fragmenting. I would argue that all parts of the world are characterized by a combination of integration and fragmentation even though the tendencies to integration are greater in the North and the tendencies to fragmentation may be greater in the South and East.

It is no longer possible to insulate parts of the world from other parts. Neither the idea that we can re-create some kind of bipolar or multipolar world order on the basis of identity—Christianity versus Islam, for example—nor the idea that the 'anarchy' in places like Africa and Eastern Europe can be contained is feasible if my analysis of the changing character of organized violence has some basis in reality. This is why the cosmopolitan project has to be a global project even if it is, as it must be, local or regional in application.

The book is based, first and foremost, on direct experience of the new wars, especially in the Balkans and the Transcaucasian region. As one of the Chairs of the Helsinki Citizens' Assembly (HCA), I have travelled extensively in these areas and learned much of what I know from the critical intellectuals and activists involved in local branches of the HCA. In particular, in Bosnia–Herzegovina, HCA was given the status of an implementing agency of UNHCR, which enabled me to move around the country during the war in support of local activists. I was also lucky enough to have access to the various institutions responsible for carrying out the policies of the international community; as chair of HCA, it was one of my tasks, along with others, to present the ideas and proposals of local branches to governments and international institutions such as the EU, NATO, the OSCE and the UN. As an academic, I was able to supplement and put into context this knowledge through reading, through exchanges with colleagues working in related fields and through research projects undertaken for the United Nations University (UNU) and the European Commission.[12] In particular, I was greatly helped by the news-letters, news digests, pleas for help and monitoring reports that now can be received daily on the internet.

[. . .] I have tried to provide information and to back my assertions with examples. [My] aim is to offer a different perspective, the perspective derived from the experiences of critically minded individuals on the ground, tempered by my own experience in various international fora. It is a contribution to the reconceptualization of patterns of violence and war that has to be undertaken if the tragedies that are encroaching in many parts of the world are to be halted. I am not an optimist, yet my practical suggestions may seem utopian. I offer them in hope, not in confidence, as the only alternative to a grim future.

NOTES

1. The research project was undertaken for the United Nations University's World Institute for Development Economics Research (UNU/WIDER). The results are published in Mary Kaldor and Basker Vashee (eds), *Restructuring the Global Military Sector: Volume I: New Wars* (Cassell/Pinter, London, 1997).

2. David Keen, 'When war itself is privatized', *Times Literary Supplement*, December 1995.

3. Mark Duffield, 'Post-modern conflict: warlords, post-adjustment states and private protection', *Journal of Civil Wars*, April 1998; Michael Ignatieff, *The Warrior's Honor: Ethnic War and the Modern Conscience* (Chatto and Windus, London, 1998).

4. Chris Hables Gray, *Post-Modern War: The New Politics of Conflicts* (Routledge, London and New York, 1997).

5. Martin Shaw, 'War and Globality: The Role and Character of War in the Global Transition,' in Ho-Won Jeong (ed.) *The New Agenda for Peace Research*, (UK: Aldershot, 1999) pp. 61–80.

6. See David Jablonsky, *The Owl of Minerva Flies at Night: Doctrinal Change and Continuity and the Revolution in Military Affairs* (US Army War College, Carlisle Barracks, PA, 1994); Elliott Cohen, 'A revolution in warfare', *Foreign Affairs* (March/April 1996); Robert J. Bunker, "Technology in a neo-Clausewitzean setting', in Gert de Nooy (ed.), *The Clausewitzean Dictum and the Future of Western Military Strategy* (Netherlands Institute of International Relations, 'Clingendael', Kluwer Law International, 1997).

7. Jean Baudrillard, *The Gulf War* (Power Publishers, London, 1995).

8. See Malcolm Waters, *Globalization* (Routledge, London, 1995); David Held, *Democracy and the*

Global Order: From the Modern State to Cosmopolitan Governance (Polity Press, Cambridge, 1995).

9. See Mary Kaldor, Ulrich Albrecht and Asbjörn Eide, *The International Military Order* (Macmillan, London, 1978).

10. Anthony Giddens makes a similar argument about the new political cleavage between cosmopolitanism and fundamentalism. See Anthony Giddens, *Beyond Left and Right: The Future of Radical Politics* (Stanford University Press, Stanford, CA, 1994).

11. On the concept of the mode of warfare, see Mary Kaldor, 'Warfare and capitalism', in E. P. Thompson *et al.*, *Exterminism and Cold War* (Verso, London, 1981).

12. In addition to the research project undertaken for UNU/WIDER, I and my colleagues at the Sussex European Institute undertook a research project in 1995 on Balkan reconstruction for the European Commission. See Vesna Bojičić, Mary Kaldor and Ivan Vejvoda, 'Post-war reconstruction in the Balkans', *SEI Working Paper* (Sussex European Institute, 1995). A shorter updated version is published in *European Foreign Affairs Review*, 2, 3 (Autumn 1997).

CHAPTER 50

Smuggling the State Back In: Agents of Human Smuggling Reconsidered

David Kyle and John Dale

Given the immediate policy and enforcement concerns of state agencies, it is unlikely that state representatives and others concerned with developing policies to combat human smuggling will reflect on either states' own role in creating and sustaining human smuggling or the nuances of its historical and sociological foundations. When a causal story is offered by state agencies or media, it usually takes the form of either of two conceptual extremes, one global and the other highly individualistic: first, globalization has created the conditions for greater transnational crime of all sorts, of which trafficking in humans is the most recent illicit global activity; or second, some very ruthless and greedy professional criminals (organized crime) are exploiting the weak and mostly innocent migrants who are either duped or coerced into a clandestine journey. Although there is an important element of truth to these statements regarding some smuggling operations, unfortunately they cover up more than they reveal, simplify more than they illuminate. We take issue with these two general axioms in this chapter through an examination of two very different cases of human smuggling: migrants contracting migration merchants in Ecuador to facilitate a journey to the United States, and young girls and women trafficked from northern Burma to Thailand and held in slavery. These two cases demonstrate the antithesis of the two axioms stated above; first, specific historical actions by politicians and other state actors in both sending and receiving states are largely responsible for the recent increase in global human smuggling, and, second, we need to recognize the extreme diversity of smuggling operations and activities, both among and within sending regions, and how they are integrated into wider regional social structures.

If reporting on human smuggling is rife with the two aforementioned axioms, there is also a well-recognized paradox that academic researchers have been quick to point out: state aggressiveness in combating human smuggling, in the form of tighter border controls and asylum policies, has prompted more people to seek smugglers and others to enter the migrant smuggling business, including ongoing transnational criminal enterprises attracted by the high profits and low risks of this activity. Of course, the rapid increase of United States' border enforcement activities in the mid-1990s . . . drives up the costs of illegal migration and increases the profits of human smuggling, thereby attracting the attention of criminal enterprises already engaged in other types of transnational smuggling, such as the drug trade. For would-be migrants, what used to be a relatively low-cost, informal affair of crossing the Rio Grande now requires greater risks and resources and is less likely to be attempted without some type of professional smuggler. . . . Of course, for those coming from more distant countries this has been the case for some time (Kyle, 2000).

What is telling about the positive correlation between the United States' enforcement actions along the border and the recent increase in the scope and profitability of professional smuggling is that U.S. government representatives, especially from the Immigration and Naturalization Service (INS), not only agree with this assessment but hint that this was the plan all along. However, unlike Andreas's detailed account ... of the unintended consequences of U.S. domestic politics leading to the militarization of the U.S.-Mexican border, which suggests a less than rational policy-making process, the specter of foreign terrorist threats is now consistently mentioned as a significant part of the border deterrence strategies of the 1990s. For example, a recent U.S. General Accounting Office report begins with these two sentences: "Alien smuggling is a significant and growing problem. Although it is likely that most smuggled aliens are brought into the United States to pursue employment opportunities, some are smuggled as part of a criminal or terrorist enterprise that can pose a serious threat to U.S. national security" (May 1, 2000:1). Hence, according to this interpretation, it wasn't the *Golden Venture* smuggling ship that ran aground in 1993 as much as the World Trade Center bombing a few months earlier that prompted U.S. government officials to reevaluate border security and strategy. In this scenario, it was desirable for the United States' security interests to diminish the chaos of small-scale mom-and-pop smuggling operations along the border in favor of larger, full-time criminal enterprises. Professional law enforcement techniques rely heavily on infiltration and disruption of stable and quite large criminal organizations rather than small-scale opportunists; in a nutshell, an ongoing professional criminal syndicate presents a much larger and weaker target than two cousins and an uncle moonlighting as migrant smugglers. Thus, by raising the physical and financial costs of clandestine crossing it was more likely that smaller operations would be driven out of business and migrants would be funneled through (monitored) criminal syndicates.

Interestingly, both of these alternative theories of the United States constructing institutional human smuggling along its border call into question the two axioms of human smuggling reportage, that unfettered globalization is the root cause and that those being smuggled are uniformly the victims of evil smugglers. In the first instance, the concept of technological globalization is much too nebulous and macrosociological to capture the specific actions and political and economic conditions in some regions that have led to increased human smuggling of the type we see today. In the U.S. case, given state complicity in driving would-be migrants into more onerous smuggling operations run by professional criminals who routinely use violent coercion, apportioning all the blame to the smuggler conveniently avoids the moral and political complexity that is a near universal trait of actual smuggling activities. When such complexities do emerge from actual human smuggling situations, such as the prominent case of Cuban boy Elián Gonzalez, depending on one's political agenda the story can be shoe-horned to fit within a preexisting morality story. In the Gonzalez case, it is striking that many who would otherwise be on the side of illegal migration control viewed the mother of Elián, who died in a smuggling operation, not as a victim but as someone who willingly risked her life in order to reach the United States and offer her son a better life. Thus, while the Mexican smuggler helping other Mexicans—many of whom come from indigenous minorities or rural backwaters persecuted by Mexican authorities—find a better economic and political environment in the United States is described as exploitative and cruel when a smuggling operation ends in a death, his Cuban counterparts risking choppy seas in little more than rafts are almost never so described. Once again, the many paradoxes one encounters in the uneven and unbalanced control of people across state borders need to be viewed within the larger political context of conflicting strategic policy goals, of which controlling undocumented labor is only one consideration.

AGENTS OF HUMAN SMUGGLING RECONSIDERED

In this section, we examine actors who are common to both of our cases as well as to other cases of migrant smuggling. First, however, in comparing these two differing cases of human smuggling from Ecuador and

Myanmar, what is most striking is what is largely missing: "transnational gangsters." Although many point to "transnational organized crime" as the driving social force behind the global increase in human smuggling (see, e.g., Godson and Olson, 1995), it plays only a supporting role, if at all, in these two cases. Given the nature of the human commodity being smuggled, it is predictable that some human smugglers are members of traditional crime organizations, though by some definitions even corrupt police could be segregated conceptually into the organized crime camp. There is much evidence that most smugglers of migrants around the world simply participate in what Finkenauer . . . calls "crime that is organized" but not "organized crime." An additional element to this crime that is organized recalls earlier forms of widespread smuggling; for many around the world participating in migrant exporting and even slave importing is not perceived, as a result of longstanding sociocultural norms, as a "real crime" in the region of origin.

Some migrant smugglers are more akin to the historical "free traders" of an earlier era when important commodities, in this case labor, were highly regulated and usuriously taxed. Migrant smugglers from the region of Azuay are not members of transnational organized crime in any traditional meaning of the term. Most are helping family and neighbors get to New York City. This is a case that illustrates that mass undocumented migration can rapidly increase without organized crime. In contrast, Myanmar presents a case of state-organized crime (Chambliss, 1989), entailing the smuggling of an illicit and, to be sure, morally bankrupt commodity. There is all too often a belief that a victim must somehow have deserved her or his fate. Especially on the migrant exporting end of the business, smugglers and moneylenders advertise in newspapers and do little to cover the nature of their business. Moreover, we have seen in the case of Myanmar that even states may subtly advertise to tourists the availability of commodities, the consumption of which are officially designated illicit, such as virgin prostitution. Similarly, it is the very parents of young girls who will some-times sell a daughter for a sum equal to one year's income.

Apart from problematizing the role of organized crime, our two cases implicate other, unusual suspects in the social organization of migrant smuggling: (a) states pursuing their official interests and corrupt state officials pursuing self-aggrandizement; (b) regional elites; and (c) employers at the destination.

Regional Elites

For many developing countries, local economic and political power is concentrated into relatively few regional elite families (Walton, 1977). This is especially striking in the case of Azuay, where such families are still referred to as "the nobles." Since the early 1960s, many elites have adopted the discourse, if not also the strategies, of successive waves of development experts from North America and Europe, especially as foreigners have brought financial and technological aid. Yet the results of the previous modernization period were mixed at best, in large part owing to the unwillingness of regional elites to give up real power and the ideologies of social stratification that legitimize privilege. Hence, we have a common local "development" situation in the 1990s in many parts of the world: great strides in isolated areas which raise expectations for a better life but which do not live up to their promise (Isbister, 1995).

Mass emigration may seem to be the ultimate measure of failure of a regional economy. However, mass transnational migration through an efficient, even rationalized, system of migration commodification and smuggling overcomes the two most important concerns for regional elites in the 1990s: migrant smuggling continues to profit from workers through remittances and curtails political upheaval associated with the broken promises of failed "development" projects.

Not only does the export of people have some of the advantages of other traditional exports, such as backward linkages (e.g., financial services) and forward linkages (e.g., construction), but it also does not have the most significant disadvantage—competition from other regions around the world; migrants represent a global export paradoxically contained within a locally controlled market. Hence, transnational undocumented migration is an unintended consequence of development through modernization—a sort of grassroots development project itself from which many regional elites continue to profit.

States and Corrupt State Officials

The commodification of migration affects sending and receiving states very differently, a fact that points to the real nature of human smuggling and undocumented migration vis-à-vis the saliency of the modern state system. State boundaries add to the value of any commodity needed across borders. Indeed, they are dependent on each other. In the case of human smuggling, sending states have generally viewed migration, whether legal or not, as a positive benefit. Remittances now rival many traditional sources of state revenue. Sending states have even reached out to include migrants abroad in domestic politics and have taken an active role in how undocumented co-nationals are treated in the United States and Europe. The Mexican ambassador Silva Herzog, speaking at the national convention of the League of United Latin American Citizens in Anaheim, California, observed, "It is particularly surprising that at a time of almost unprecedented success in the United States economy . . . the anti-immigration voices have once again taken the high ground. . . . Make no mistake about it, this is racism and xenophobia, and it has a negative impact on every person of Hispanic origin living in this country, regardless of their migratory status" (*Los Angeles Times*, June 26, 1997). Such aggressive campaigning for lessening immigration controls by a Mexican official in the United States is grounded not only in humanitarian concerns but also in the fear that the more than $4.5 billion remittances to families in Mexico every year will recede during a grave economic crisis at home.

Similarly, in Burma, the military government has cried foul because Thailand wants to repatriate Burmese nationals because of backlash against foreigners during a period of economic hardship. Illegal aliens from Myanmar working in Thailand manage to send substantial amounts of money home to their families (substantial, at least, to families living in a country where the annual per capita income is currently about U.S. $150). However, Myanmar's military tends to collect this remitted money through various forms of violence, bribery, and "taxation," which is paid either in cash, labor, or social capital.

Highly publicized in the international media have been the Myanmar military's violent campaigns and practices of coerced labor, extortion, "ethnic cleansing" (rape and murder), and crop burning against its rural ethnic minority communities living in the border regions of the state (see, e.g., http://www.soros.org/burma). We have also noted above how less publicized practices of bribery, or the payment of "tea money" to state employees, have become informally institutionalized.

However, the military also collects "taxes" from locals, which are typically imposed suddenly, as circumstances may dictate. Taxes may be imposed on particular villages for "beautification projects" (such as patching up ditches in the villages' dirt roads) purportedly designed to enhance tourism. Those who cannot pay the tax in cash pay the tax in labor, helping to patch up the roads. The state also collects taxes from local villages that do not produce the quota of rice required by the state—even when the state's military campaigns have destroyed the rice crops, making it impossible for the villagers to meet such quotas.

When a family within the village has no money to pay these taxes, the state requires that family to offer a male member of the household to serve either as a porter (without pay) in the military to fight in campaigns against rebel ethnic minority armies or in state construction projects. Few of these conscripts ever return to see their families. It is not uncommon to learn that they have been literally worked to death. If a poor family has neither the money nor a male member of the family to serve the military, it may be able to borrow the money from either a wealthier family in the village or from the state in order to hire a neighbor's son to serve in the military for it. In this sense, the state "taxes" the villagers' social capital.

In short, if the economically poor military state of Myanmar suspects that there are sources of wealth to be tapped within these villages, it can and does construct a justification for usurping that wealth. The state understands that a significant portion of that wealth is sustained through remittances from migrant members of the village working abroad. Thus it is not surprising that the proposal last year by Thailand's House Committee on Labor and Social Welfare met with protest from the state of Myanmar. In its effort to alleviate the burden of continuing to employ illegal workers from Myanmar, Thailand proposed to tax them all (including ethnic minorities) and remit the money directly to the state of Myanmar (Hutasingh, 1997). If Myanmar had accepted these conditions, then it would have meant that it had also accepted the status of its minority workers in Thailand—an acknowledgment Myanmar was unwilling to provide. After all, there was little to gain in doing so: Myanmar already receives at least as much in remittances by "taxing" local minorities who remain in Myanmar.

In regard to the receiving states, such as the United States, it would seem that the commodification of migration and the increasing use of smugglers would be uniformly negative. After all, some U.S. policymakers have been considered the elimination of birthright citizenship for "illegal aliens." Although employers benefit from falsely documented labor, such benefits cannot be collapsed into the interests of the state. In addition, the economic benefit of both documented and undocumented migration to the U.S. economy on the whole is an area of hot debate.

Unlike private employers, U.S. leaders and policymakers have a variety of pro-immigrant, anti-immigrant, and ethnic communities to contend with and placate (see Joppke, 1998; Freeman, 1994). Although immigration laws must be upheld by the state, and although anti-immigrant voices include some demographic and economic rationales that cannot simply be reduced to racism, there is also a political price for "bashing immigrants." High-profile state agencies can diminish the political fallout of migration controls through a diffusing strategy that relies on a variety of third-party actors such as airlines and privatized detention centers. In a similar manner, a more commodified migration process, also using third parties (i.e., smugglers), allows states to develop a discourse that emphasizes the criminality and evil of alien smuggling rings, which can then be contrasted with hardworking immigrants.

Employers and Slaveholders

North American employers of unskilled urban and farm labor directly benefit from an efficient underground source of labor. Were migrants dependent upon their own social networks to cross borders under conditions of heightened state monitoring, immigrant labor flow might subside. Thus, smugglers might be conceptualized as an extension of, and in some cases a replacement for, labor recruiters. In some undocumented smuggling streams, the migrant, and even the individual smuggler for that matter, becomes a sort of indentured servant working for the syndicate or a collaborator. In extreme cases, slavery has returned in the form of garment and sex workers held captive in Los Angeles and New York City. Contemporary slavery, as Bales (1999: 14) pointed out, is not about slave owning but "slave-holding," or complete control over people for economic profit. While this is a useful distinction between older and more contemporary forms of slavery, it is also one that is more disconcerting because the organization of work around the world under the globalization project has led to greater levels of labor control, practices that are increasingly legitimized as necessary for survival within a competitive global arena. Even when free to find employment on their own terms, illegal immigrants with large usurious debts make an especially docile and hardworking labor force—a point not overlooked by employers or states in receiving countries.

Thus, instead of conceptualizing contemporary slaves as "disposable people," the title of Bales' book, we might instead view them as an extreme, though not uncommon, example of the growing process by which labor is forced underground into invisibility as well as disposability. One could argue that the concept of "disposable people" per se is not particularly novel to the current globalization project but rather has been the lot of much of humanity historically. What is novel are the growing levels of work that is purposively hidden by employers and laborers from the global markets they are seeking to sell in or from the local clientele of "global cities" (Sassen, 1991). Tellingly, all the actors highlighted in this section—local elites, states, and employers—justify their less than honorable actions by invoking some form of the argument "globalization made me do it." Globalization *as an ideology* continues to blur the boundaries of what should be considered exploitative economic behavior first and foremost in the area of labor relations.

CONCLUSION

Existing studies of transnational human smuggling, its organization, and the actors that sustain this practice are typically shaped by a particularly ahistorical conception of "organized crime"—one that allows no conceptual space for analyzing the organizational sources of transnational human smuggling provided by, and thus implicating, regional elites, states, and employers (and, hence, consumers). Proceeding deductively from the common assumption that only large-scale transnational criminal organizations are driving increases in the levels of human smuggling fails to elucidate the central, proactive roles played by noncriminal migrants and criminal nonmigrants, including corrupt state representatives, in sustaining and transforming the practice of professional human smuggling. Other studies also suggest that even the premise of the deductive analysis of complex groups of transnational organized crime as necessary to the clandestine activities associated with human smuggling is faulty, especially in cases in which a previous legal activity has been converted to an illegal, heavily penalized one (see Reuter, 1985).

We have used a historical comparative approach in an attempt to understand the social organization, political benefits, and economic profitability of contemporary human smuggling as a diverse bundle of activities and participants. Our findings suggest that comparing processes of transnational migrant smuggling across different times and places reveals a wide range of social formations implicating a diverse configuration of actors. Yet we have conceptualized some significant differences between two fundamental types of smuggling enterprises: migrant exporting schemes and slave importing operations. Both can be just as deadly for the migrant and place him or her at great legal and physical risk, but we believe that effective policies need to distinguish among a range of smuggling operations, some which are aiding people to leave situations of political persecution and economic hopelessness and others that deliver them into precisely such circumstances. In broad terms, three themes emerge from this comparison of a migrant exporting scheme and a slave importing operation: global diversity, internal organizational complexity, and contradictory state involvement in human smuggling activities and human rights. Through empirical research, the following chapters help elucidate in diverse ways these three basic observations.

REFERENCES

Bales, Kevin, 1999. *Disposable People: New Slavery in the Global Economy*. Berkeley: University of California Press.

Chambllss, William J. 1989. "State-Organized Crime." *Criminology* 27 (2): 170–84.

Freeman, Gary. 1994. "Can Liberal States Control Unwanted Migration?" *Annals of the American Academy of Political and Social Science* 534:17–30.

Godson, Roy, and William J. Olson. 1995. "International Organized Crime." *Society* (January/February): 18–29.

Hutasingh, Onnucha. 1997. "Tough Fight against Illegal Alien Workers." *Bangkok Post*, December 15, p. 2, cols. 1–6.

Isbister, John. 1995. *Promises Not Kept: The Betrayal of Social Change in the Third World*. 3d ed. Hartford: Kumarian Press.

Joppke, Christian. 1998. "Why Liberal States Accept Unwanted Migration." *World Politics* 50 (2): 266–93.

Kyle, David. 2000. *Transnational Peasants: Migrations,*

Networks, and Ethnicity in Andean Ecuador. Baltimore: Johns Hopkins University Press.

Reuter, Peter. 1985. *The Organization of Illegal Markets: An Economic Analysis.* Research report, U.S. Department of Justice, National Institute of Justice. February.

Sassen, Saskia. 1991. *The Global City: New York, London, and Tokyo.* Princeton: Princeton University Press.

United States General Accounting Report to Congressional Committees. 2000. "Alien Smuggling: Management and Operational Improvements Needed to Address Growing Problem." May I. GAO/GGD-00-103.

Walton, John. 1977. *Elites and Economic Development: Comparative Studies on the Political Economy of Latin American Cities.* Austin, Tex.: Institute of Latin American Studies.

Rights and Permissions List

SECTION 1: THE BROAD FOUNDATIONS

2 Nye, Joseph and Robert Keohane. "Transnational Relations and World Politics: An Introduction." *International Organization* 25:329–346. Copyright © 1971, World Peace Foundation. Reprinted with the permission of Cambridge University Press.

3 Cardoso, Fernando Henrique and Enzo Faletto. "Conclusion" and "Post Scriptum," in *Dependency and Development in Latin America*. Copyright © 1979 by The Regents of the University of California. Reprinted with permission of University of California Press.

4 Anzaldúa, Gloria. "The Homeland, Aztlán / *El Otro México*." From *Borderlands/La Frontera: The New Mestiza*. Copyright © 1987, 1999 by Gloria Anzaldúa. Reprinted by permission of Aunt Lute Books.

5 Appadurai, Arjun. "Global Ethnoscapes: Notes and Queries for a Transnational Anthropology." Reprinted by permission from *Recapturing Anthropology: Working in the Present*, edited by Richard G. Fox. Copyright © 1991 by the School of American Research, Santa Fe. Reprinted by permission of the publisher.

6 Slaughter, Anne-Marie. "The Real New World Order." Reprinted by permission of *FOREIGN AFFAIRS*, 76(5) September/October 1997. Copyright © 1997 by the Council on Foreign Relations, Inc. Reprinted by permission of the publisher.

7 Sassen, Saskia. "Introduction" and "The State and the Global City," in *Globalization and Its Discontents*. Copyright © 1998 by Saskia Sassen. Reprinted with permission of The New Press.

SECTION 2: METHODOLOGICAL PRACTICES

8 Gupta, Akhil and James Ferguson. "Discipline and Practice: 'The Field' as Site, Method, and Location in Anthropology," in Gupta, Akil and James Ferguson, eds. *Anthropological Locations: Boundaries and Grounds of a Field Science*. Copyright © 1997 by The Regents of the University of California. Reprinted with permission of University of California Press.

9 Wimmer, Andreas and Nina Glick Schiller. "Methodological Nationalism, the Social Sciences, and the Study of Migration: An Essay in Historical Epistemology." *International Migration Review* 37 (2003). Originally published in *Global Networks: A*

SECTION 3: HISTORICAL PERSPECTIVES

SECTION 4: QUESTIONS OF IDENTITY

Press Incorporated. Reprinted by permission of University of Toronto Press Incorporated (www.utpjournals.com).

20 Hannerz, Ulf. "Nigerian Kung Fu, Manhattan *fatwa*" and "The Local and the Global: Continuity and Change," from *Transnational Connections: Culture, People, Places*, Ulf Hannerz, Copyright © 1996 Ulf Hannerz. Reproduced by permission of Taylor and Francis Books UK.

21 Grewal, Inderpal and Caren Kaplan. "Transnational Feminist Practices and Questions of Postmodernity," in *Scattered Hegemonies: Postmodernity and Transnational Feminist Practices*, edited by Inderpal Grewal and Caren Kaplan. Copyright © 1994 University of Minnesota Press. Reprinted with permission of University of Minnesota Press.

SECTION 5: MIGRATING LIVES AND COMMUNITIES

22 Basch, Linda, Nina Glick Schiller, and Cristina Szanton Blanc. "Chapter 1: Transnational Projects: A New Perspective" and "Chapter 2: Theoretical Premises," in *National Unbound: Transnational Projects, Postcolonial Predicaments, and Deterritorialized Nation-States*, by Linda Basch, Nina Glick Schiller, and Cristina Szanton Blanc. Copyright © 1994 by OPA (Overseas Publishers Association) Amsterdam B.V. Published under licence by Gordon and Breach Science Publishers SA. Reproduced by permission of Taylor & Francis Books UK.

23 Kearney, Michael. "The Local and the Global: Anthropology of Globalization and Transnationalism." *Annual Review of Anthropology* 24 (1995). Copyright © 1995 by Annual Reviews Inc. All rights reserved. Reprinted with permission of Annual Reviews Inc.

24 Portes, Alejandro, Luis Guarnizo and Patricia Landolt. "The Study of Transnationalism: Pitfalls and Promise of an Emergent Research Field." *Ethnic and Racial Studies* 2:(1999). Copyright © Routledge 1999. Reprinted by permission of the publisher, Taylor & Francis, Ltd, http//www.tandf.co.uk/journals.

25 Levitt, Peggy and Nina Glick Schiller. "Conceptualizing Simultaneity: A Transnational Social Field Perspective on Society". *International Migration Review* 38 (2004). Copyright © 2004 by the Center for Migration Studies of New York. All rights reserved. Reprinted by permission of the publisher, Blackwell Publishing.

SECTION 6: RELIGIOUS LIFE ACROSS BORDERS

26 Beyer, Peter. "Systemic Religion in Global Society," in *Religion and Globalization*. Copyright © Peter Beyer 1994. Reprinted by permission of SAGE Publications Ltd.

27 Rudolph, Susanne Hoeber. "Religion, States, and Transnational Civil Society," in *Transnational Religion and Fading States*, edited by Susanne Hoeber Rudolph and James Piscatori. Copyright © 1997 by Westview Press, A Member of The Perseus Books Group. Reprinted by permission of Westview Press, a member of Perseus Books, L.L.C.

28 Vásquez, Manuel A. and Marie Friedmann Marquardt. "Theorizing Globalization and Religion," in Manuel A. Vásquez and Marie Friedmann Marquardt, eds. *Globalizing the Sacred: Religion Across the Americas*. Copyright © 2003 by Manuel A. Vásquez and Marie Friedmann Marquardt. Reprinted by permission of Rutgers University Press.

39 Evans, Peter. "Imperialism, Dependency, and Dependent Development." *Dependent Development: The Alliance of Multinational, State and Local Capital in Brazil*. Copyright © 1979 Princeton University Press. Reprinted by permission of Princeton University Press.

40 Gereffi, Gary. "The Organization of Buyer-driven Global Commodity Chains: How U.S. Retailers Shape Overseas Production Networks," in *Commodity Chains and Global Capitalism*, edited by Gary Gereffi and Miguel Korzeniewicz. Copyright © 1994 by Gary Gereffi and Miguel Korzeniewicz. Reproduced with permission of Greenwood Publishing Group, Inc., Westport, CT.

41 Ong, Aihwa. "Introduction: Flexible Citizenship: The Cultural Logics of Transnationality" and "Afterword: An Anthropology of Transnationality," in *Flexible Citizenship: The Cultural Logistics of Transnationality*, pp. 1–8, 240–244. Copyright © 1999 Duke University Press. Used by permission of the publisher.

SECTION 10: NON-STATE ACTORS, NGOs, AND SOCIAL MOVEMENTS

42 Risse-Kappen, Thomas. "Bringing Transnational Relations Back In: Introduction," in *Bringing Transnational Relations Back In: Non-state Actors, Domestic Structures, and International Institutions*, edited by Thomas Risse-Kappen. Copyright © Cambridge University Press 1995. Reprinted with the permission of Cambridge University Press.

43 Boli, John and George M. Thomas. "World Culture in the World Polity: A Century of International Non-Governmental Organization." *American Sociological Review* 62 (April 1997). Copyright © 1997 by the American Sociological Association. Reprinted by permission of the American Sociological Association.

44 Kriesberg, Louis. "Social Movements and Global Transformation," in *Transnational Social Movements and Global Politics*, edited by Jackie Smith, Charles Chatfield, and Ron Pagnucco. Copyright © 1997 Syracuse University Press. Reprinted by permission of Syracuse University Press.

45 Keck, Margaret E. and Kathryn Sikkink. "Conclusions: Advocacy Networks and International Society." Reprinted from *Activists Beyond Borders: Advocacy Networks in International Politics*, by Margaret E. Keck and Kathryn Sikkink. Copyright © 1998 by Cornell University. Used by permission of the publisher, Cornell University Press.

46 Naples, Nancy A. "The Challenges and Possibilities of Transnational Feminist Praxis," in *Women's Activism and Globalization: Linking Local Struggles and Transnational Politics*, edited by Nancy A. Naples and Manisha Desai. Copyright © 2002 by Routledge. Reprinted with permission of Routledge, Taylor & Francis Group.

SECTION 11: SECURITY, CRIME, AND VIOLENCE

47 Nadelmann, Ethan. "Global Prohibition Regimes: The Evolution of Norms in International Society." *International Organization* 44 (Autumn, 1990). Copyright © 1990 by the World Peace Foundation and the Massachusetts Institute of Technology. Reprinted with the permission of Cambridge University Press.

48 Shelley, Louise. "Transnational Organized Crime: An Imminent Threat to the Nation-State? (Transcending National Boundaries)." *Journal of International Affairs* 48 (Winter 1995). Copyright © 1995 Columbia University School of International Public Affairs. Reprinted by permission of the publisher.

49 Kaldor, Mary. "Introduction," in *New and Old Wars: Organized Violence in a Global Era*. Copyright © 1999 Mary Kaldor. Reprinted by permission of Stanford University Press and Polity.

50 Kyle, David and John Dale. "Smuggling the State Back In: Agents of Human Smuggling Reconsidered," in *Global Human Smuggling: Comparative Perspectives*, edited by David Kyle and Rey Koslowski. Copyright © 2001 The Johns Hopkins University Press. Reprinted by permission of The Johns Hopkins University Press.